1 MONTH OF
FREE
READING

at

www.ForgottenBooks.com

By purchasing this book you are eligible for one month membership to ForgottenBooks.com, giving you unlimited access to our entire collection of over 1,000,000 titles via our web site and mobile apps.

To claim your free month visit:
www.forgottenbooks.com/free530367

ISBN 978-0-483-11310-7
PIBN 10530367

THOMAS GOODWIN, D.D.

THE

[H]ORY OF THE PURITANS,

OR

PROTESTANT NONCONFORMISTS;

FROM

[RE]FORMATION IN 1517, TO THE REVOLUTION IN 1688;

COMPRISING

An Account of their Principles;

[ATTEMPTS FOR A FARTHER REFORMATION IN THE CHURCH; THEIR SUFFERINGS;
AND THE LIVES AND CHARACTERS OF THEIR MOST CONSIDERABLE DIVINES.]

BY DANIEL NEAL, A.M.

REPRINTED

TEXT OF [D]R. TOULMIN'S EDITION: WITH HIS LIFE OF THE AUTHOR
AND ACCOUNT OF HIS WRITINGS.

[REV]ISED, CORRECTED, AND ENLARGED, WITH ADDITIONAL NOTES

BY JOHN O. CHOULES, A.M.

With nine Portraits on Steel.

THE

HISTORY OF THE PURITANS,

OR

PROTESTANT NONCONFORMISTS,

FROM

THE REFORMATION IN 1517, TO THE REVOLUTION IN 1688;.

COMPRISING

An Account of their Principles;

THEIR ATTEMPTS FOR A FARTHER REFORMATION IN THE CHURCH ; THEIR SUFFERINGS ;
AND THE LIVES AND CHARACTERS OF THEIR MOST CONSIDERABLE DIVINES.

BY DANIEL NEAL, A.M.

REPRINTED

FROM THE TEXT OF DR. TOULMIN'S EDITION : WITH HIS LIFE OF THE AUTHOR
AND ACCOUNT OF HIS WRITINGS.
REVISED, CORRECTED, AND ENLARGED, WITH ADDITIONAL NOTES,

BY JOHN O. CHOULES, A.M.

With nine Portraits on Steel.

IN TWO VOLUMES.

VOL. II.

NEW-YORK:

PUBLISHED BY HARPER & BROTHERS, 82 CLIFF-STREET.

1844.

HISTORY OF THE PURITANS.

PART III.—Continued.

CHAPTER VI.

THE PROGRESS OF THE WAR.—DEBATES IN THE ASSEMBLY ABOUT ORDINATION.—THE POWER OF THE KEYS.—THE DIVINE RIGHT OF PRESBYTERIAN GOVERNMENT.—COMMITTEES FOR COMPREHENSION AND TOLERATION OF THE INDEPENDENTS.

THE king's commissioners had been told at the treaty of Uxbridge that the fate of the English monarchy depended upon its success ; that if the treaty was broken off abruptly, there was a set of men in the House who would remove the Earl of Essex, and constitute such an army as might force the Parliament and king to consent to everything they demanded, or change the government into a commonwealth ; whereas, if the king would yield to the necessity of the times, they might preserve the general, and not only disappoint the designs of the enemies to monarchy, but soon be in circumstances to enable his majesty to recover all he should resign. However, the commissioners looked upon this as the language of despair, and made his majesty believe the divisions at Westminster would soon replace the sceptre in his own hands.*

The House of Commons had been dissatisfied with the conduct of the Earls of Essex and Manchester last summer, as tending to protract the war, lest one party should establish itself upon the ruins of the other ; but the warmer spirits in the House, seeing no period of their calamities this way, apprehended a decisive battle ought to be fought as soon as possible, for which purpose, after a solemn fast, it was moved that all the present officers should be discharged, and the army intrusted in such hands as they could confide in. December 9, it was resolved that no member of either House should execute any office, civil or military, during the present war ; accordingly, the ordinance, commonly called the Self-denying Ordinance, was brought in, and passed the Commons ten days after, but was laid aside by the Lords till after the treaty of Uxbridge, when it was revived and carried with some little opposition. The Earls of Essex, Manchester, Warwick, and Denbigh, the Lord Roberts, Willoughby, and others, were dismissed by this ordinance,† and all members of the House of Commons, except Lieutenant-general Cromwell, who, after a few months, was dispensed with, at the request of the new general.. All the regiments were disbanded, and such only listed under the new commanders as were determined to conquer or die. Sir Thomas Fairfax was appointed general,* and Oliver Cromwell, after some time, lieutenant-general ; the clause for preservation of the king's person was left out of Sir Thomas's commission ; nor did it run in the name of the king and Parliament, but of the Parliament only.. The army consisted of twenty-one thousand resolute soldiers, and was called in contempt by the Royalists, the new-modelled army ; but their courage quickly revenged the contempt.

Sir Thomas Fairfax was a gentleman of no quick parts or elocution ; but religious, faithful, valiant, and of a grave, sober, resolved disposition ; neither too great nor too cunning to be directed by the Parliament.† Oliver Cromwell was more bold and aspiring ; and being a soldier of undaunted courage and intrepidity, proved, at length, too powerful for his masters. The army was more at his disposal than at Fairfax's, and the wonders they wrought sprung chiefly from his counsels.

When the old regiments were broken, the chaplains, being discharged of course, returned to their cures ; and as new ones were formed, the officers applied to the Parliament and Assembly for a fresh recruit ; but the Presbyterian ministers being possessed of warm benefices, were unwilling to undergo the fatigues of another campaign, or, it may be, to serve with men of such desperate measures. This fatal accident proved the ruin of the cause in which the Parliament were engaged ; for the army being destitute of chaplains, who might have restrained the irregularities of their zeal, the officers set up for preachers in their several regiments, depending upon a kind of miraculous assistance of the Divine Spirit, without any study or preparation ; and when their imaginations were heated, they gave vent to the most crude and undigested absurdities ; nor did the evil rest there, for, from preaching at the head of their

---

* Clarendon, vol. ii., p. 595.

† " Thus almost all those men by whose interest, power, and authority the war with the king had been undertaken, and without whom no opposition, of any weight, could possibly have been raised, were in a short time deprived of their power and influence over their own army, and obliged, as we shall soon see, to truckle before them. So little can men see into futurity ! so different are the turns things take, from what men are apt to expect and depend on."—*Dr. Harris's Life of Oliver Cromwell*, p. 118.

* Sir Thomas Fairfax's power extended to the execution of martial law and the nomination of the officers under him. The army was put solely under the command of one man. " What was this (it has been properly asked) but to put it into his power to give law to the Parliament whenever he thought fit ?"—*Dr. Harris, ut supra.*—ED.

† Baxter's Life, p. 48.

regiments, they took possession of the country pulpits where they were quartered, till at length they spread the infection over the whole nation, and brought the regular ministry into contempt. Most of the common soldiers were religious and orderly, and when released from duty, spent their time in prayer and religious conferences, like men who carried their lives in their hands; but, for want of prudent and regular instruction, were swallowed up in the depths of enthusiasm. Mr. Baxter, therefore, observes very justly, "It was the ministers that lost all, by forsaking the army, and betaking themselves to an easier and quieter way of life. When the Earl of Essex's army went out, each regiment had an able chaplain, but after Edgehill fight most of them went home, and left the army to their own conduct." But, even after the decisive battle of Naseby, he admits, great numbers of the officers and soldiers were sober and orthodox; and from the little good which he did while among them, concludes, that if their ministers would have followed his measures, the king, the Parliament, and religion might have been saved.*

The new-modelled troops were kept under the severest discipline, commissioners being appointed to take care that the country was not oppressed; that no soldiers were quartered in any place but by appointment of the quartermaster; that ready money be paid for all provisions and ammunition; every soldier had sixpence a day for his diet, and every trooper eightpence. No inhabitants were compelled to furnish more provisions than they were able and willing to spare, under the severest penalties; whereas the royal army, having no regular pay, lived upon the plunder of those places that had the misfortune to receive them.

May 30, the king took the town of Leicester by storm, with a very great treasure, which the country people had brought thither for security, his soldiers dividing the spoil, and treating the inhabitants in a most cruel and unmerciful manner; after this conquest, his majesty wrote to the queen that his affairs were never in so hopeful a posture since the Rebellion.† The Parliament army were preparing to lay siege to the city of Oxford, but upon news of this disaster, had orders to follow the king and hazard a battle at all events; whereupon Sir Thomas Fairfax petitioned the two houses to dispense with their self-denying ordinance with respect to Lieutenant-general Cromwell, whose courage and counsels would be of great service in the present crisis: Cromwell was accordingly dispensed with during pleasure, and having joined the army with six hundred horse and dragoons, they overtook the king, and gave him battle June 14, at Naseby, about three miles from Harborough in Leicestershire.

The action began about ten in the morning, and ended about three or four in the afternoon, in an absolute defeat of the king's forces, which was owing, in a great measure, to the wise conduct and resolution of Lieutenant-general Cromwell on the one hand, and to the indiscreet fury and violence of Prince Rupert on the other. The armies were pretty equal in number, about twelve or fourteen thousand on a side, but the Parliament soldiers were better disciplined, and

fought with all the bravery and magnanimity that an enthusiastic zeal could inspire. General Fairfax, having his helmet beat off, rode up and down the field bareheaded; Major-general Skippon received a wound in the beginning of the engagement, upon which, being desired to go off, he answered, he would not stir as long as a man would stand. Ireton was run through the thigh with a pike, had his horse killed under him, and was made a prisoner, but found means to escape upon the turn of the battle. The king showed himself a courageous commander, but his soldiers were struck with such a panic, that, when they were once disordered, they would never rally; whereas, if their enemies were beaten from their ground, they presently returned, and kept their ranks till they received fresh instructions.* When Prince Rupert had routed Ireton's left wing, he lost his advantage, first, by following the chase almost three miles, and then by trying to become master of the train of artillery, before he knew the success of the main body; whereas, when Cromwell had broke the right wing of the enemy, he pursued them only a quarter of a mile, and leaving a small party of horse to prevent their rallying, returned immediately to the battle, and with his victorious troops charged the royal infantry in flank. The Parliament army took above five thousand prisoners; all the king's train of artillery, bag and baggage, with his cabinet of letters, some of which were afterward published to the world; not above six or seven hundred of his men being killed, with about one hundred and fifty officers. The king, with a party of horse, fled into Wales, and Prince Rupert to Bristol; but the Parliament forces pursued their victory with such eagerness, and marched with that rapidity over the whole west of England, to the very land's end, that in a few months all the royal forces were dispersed, and his majesty's garrisons surrendered almost before they were summoned.† The city of Bristol, into which Prince Rupert had thrown himself, capitulated before the besiegers approached the walls, which provoked the king to that degree that he commanded him by letter to depart the land, as did also the Prince of Wales, for the security of his person; so that, by the end of the campaign, the unhappy king was exposed to the mercy of his enemies, and shut up all winter, little better than a prisoner, in his garrison at Oxford.

To return to the affairs of the Church. When it is recollected what great numbers of clergymen had deserted to the king, or were otherwise dissatisfied with the new terms of conformity, we must conclude it very difficult to supply the vacant pulpits in the country with a learned and regular clergy: one of the universities was entirely useless, and the young students who adhered to the Parliament could not obtain ordination in a legal way, because all the bishops were in the opposition, and would ordain none but those of their own principles, which was another cause of the increase of unqualified preachers. To put some stop to the clamours of the Royalists, and to the mischiefs of lay preaching, which began to appear in the army, the Parliament ordained, April 26, "that no person shall be permitted to preach who is

---

* Baxter's Life, p. 51, 56.
† Whitelocke's Memoirs, p. 143, 144.

* Whitelocke, p. 145. Clarendon, vol. ii., p. 658.
† Rapin, vol. ii., p. 517, 518, folio.

not ordained a minister in this or some other Reformed church, except such as intend the ministry, who shall be allowed for the trial of their gifts, by those that shall be appointed thereunto by both houses of Parliament; and it is earnestly desired that Sir Thomas Fairfax take care that this ordinance be put in execution in the army. It is farther ordered to be sent to the lord-mayor, and committee of the militia in London; to the governors and commanders of all forts, garrisons, forces, cities, and towns, with the like injunction; and the mayor, sheriffs, and justices of the peace are to commit all offenders to safe custody, and give notice to the Parliament, who will take a speedy course for their punishment."

At the same time, the Lords sent to the Assembly† to prepare a new directory for the ordination of ministers of the Church in England, without the presence of a diocesan bishop. This took them up a great deal of time, by reason of the opposition it met with from the Erastians and Independents, but was at last accomplished, and passed into an ordinance, bearing date November 8, 1645, and was to continue in force, by way of trial, for twelve months; on the 28th of August following, it was prolonged for three years, at the expiration of which term it was made perpetual.

The ordinance sets forth, "That whereas the words presbyter and bishop do, in Scripture, signify the same function, though the title of bishop has been, by corrupt custom, appropriated to one who has assumed to himself, in the matter of ordination, that which was not meet; which ordination, notwithstanding being performed by him, we hold for substance to be valid, and not to be disclaimed by any that have received it; and whereas it is manifest that ordination, that is, an outward, solemn setting apart of persons for the office of the ministry in the Church by preaching presbyters, is an institution of Christ, it is therefore ordained by the Lords and Commons, with the advice of the Assembly of Divines at Westminster, that the several and respective classical presbyters, within their respective bounds, may examine, approve, and ordain presbyters according to the following Directory,"‡ which I have placed in

---

* Husband's Collections, p. 645.

† Everything touching this venerable council is interesting, and I would gladly add all that the light of history can furnish; but such has been the industry, research, and fidelity of Neal, that very little can be added. The Christian Review for December, 1843, while it speaks in commendation of Mr. Hetherington's History of the Assembly, adds, "In many respects, the account of the Assembly given by Neal in his 'History of the Puritans' is much more satisfactory than the work of Hetherington. The latter seems to have had access to few, if any, sources of information which were not known to the former. Neal, in his text and appendices, furnishes many items extremely valuable in themselves and necessary to a complete history of the Westminster Assembly, but which Hetherington wholly omits. Neal, being an Independent, gives all diligence that the Independents should have due honour. The Independents and Presbyterians, however, harmonized in so many points, both being Nonconformists, that justice to one is, in most cases, justice to both." In order to avoid any appearance of undue partiality, I have added few notes on this portion of the work.—C.

‡ Rushworth, part iv., vol. i., p. 212.

---

the Appendix,* and is in substance as follows:

First, "The person to be ordained must apply to the Presbytery, with a testimonial of his taking the Covenant, of his proficiency in his studies," &c.

Secondly, "He is then to pass under an examination as to his religion and learning, and call to the ministry."

Then follow rules for examination, as in the Appendix.

"After examination he shall receive a public testimonial from his examiners, which shall be read publicly before the people, and then fixed to the door of the church where he preaches for approbation, with liberty to any person or persons to make exceptions.

"Upon the day of ordination a solemn fast shall be kept by the congregation, when, after a sermon, the person to be ordained shall make a public confession of his faith,† and declare his resolutions to be diligent and constant in the discharge of his pastoral duty. After which he shall be separated or set apart to the pastoral office with a short prayer, and the laying on of the hands of the ministers present. After the ordination, there is to be an exhortation to minister and people, and the whole solemnity to conclude with a psalm and a prayer."

It is farther declared, "that all ordinations, according to the former usage of the Church of England, as well as those of Scotland and other Reformed churches, shall be esteemed valid.

"A register is to be kept by every presbytery of the names of the persons ordained by them, of the ministers concerned, and of the time and place where they were settled. No money or gift whatsoever shall be received from the person ordained, or from any on his behalf, for his ordination, or anything relating to it, except for the instruments or testimonials, which shall not exceed ten shillings."

Lastly, it is resolved, "that all persons ordained according to this Directory shall be forever reputed and taken, to all intents and purposes, for lawfully and sufficiently authorized ministers of the Church of England, and as capable of any ministerial employment in the Church, as any other presbyter already ordained, or hereafter to be ordained."

To give a short specimen of the debates upon this ordinance; when the passage in Timothy, of "laying on of the hands of the presbytery," was voted a full warrant for presbyters

---

* Appendix, No. 9.

† It deserves to be noticed here, that the advice and orders of the Westminister Assembly are, on this point, very general, namely: "That the person to be ordained be asked of his faith in Jesus Christ, of his persuasion of the truth of the Reformed religion according to the Scriptures, and of his zeal for the truth of the Gospel and unity of the Church, against error and schism." "This, I think, is an evident presumption," observes a late writer, "that the majority of the Assembly were against imposing human tests, and making subscription to their confession a necessary term of communion, either to ministers or other Christians."—"The Religious Establishment of Scotland Examined," &c., printed for Cadell, 1771, p. 105. This is the more remarkable, as, in other instances, this synod showed themselves dogmatical and intolerant.—ED.

ordaining without a bishop, Mr. Selden, Light-foot, and some others, entered their dissent, declaring that the imposition of hands there spoken of was only upon ordination of an elder; and though elders might ordain elders, it did not necessarily follow they might ordain bishops.

The Independents maintained the right of every particular congregation to ordain its own officers; this was debated ten days; and the arguments on both sides were afterward published by consent of the several parties, in a book entitled "The Grand Debate between Presbytery and Independency."* At length the question being put, that it is requisite no single congregation, that can conveniently associate with others, should assume to itself the sole right of ordination, it was carried in the affirmative, the following Independent ministers entering their dissent:

Tho. Goodwin,	Sidrach Simpson,
Phil. Nye,	William Bridge,
Jer. Burroughs,	Will. Greenhill.
William Carter,	

It was next debated whether ordination might precede election to a particular cure or charge; Dr. Temple, Mr. Herle, Vines, Palmer, Whitaker, and Calamy argued for the affirmative. 1. From the ordination of Timothy, Titus, and Apollos, without any particular charge. 2. Because it is a different thing to ordain to an office, and to appropriate the exercise of that office to any particular place. 3. If election must precede ordination, then there must be a new ordination upon every new election. 4. It would then follow that a minister was no minister out of his own church or congregation. And, 5. Then a minister could not gather or plant churches, or baptize new converts, because, according to the Independents, there must be a church before there can be a minister.†

Mr. Goodwin, Nye, Bridge, and the rest of the Independents, replied to the foregoing reasons, that Timothy and Titus were extraordinary officers; that it appeared to them absurd to ordain an officer without a province to exercise the office in; that they saw no great inconvenience in reordinations, though they did not admit the consequence that a person regularly ordained to one church must be reordained upon every removal; but they asserted that a pastor of one particular church might preserve his character in all places; and if there was extraordinary service to be done in planting new churches, or baptizing converts, the churches might send out their officers, or create new ones for that purpose. The grand difficulty with the Independents lay here, that ordination without election to a particular charge seemed to imply a conveyance of office-power, which, in their opinion, was attended with all the difficulties of a lineal succession. The debates upon this article continued several days, and issued, at last, in a compromise, in these words: "It is agreeable to the Word of God, and very expedient, that those who are to be ordained ministers, be designed to some particular church, or other ministerial charge." And with regard to the ceremony of imposition of hands, the Independents acquiesced in the practice, provided it was attended with an open declaration that it was not intended as a conveyance of office-power.

It may seem absurd to begin the reformation of the Church with an ordinance appointing classical presbyters to ordain ministers within their several districts, when there was not as yet one classical presbytery in all England; but the urgency of affairs required it; the scarcity of ministers would not suffer a delay till the whole fabric of Presbytery was erected;* therefore, to supply this defect for the present, the whole business was intrusted with the Assembly, who voted, December 24, 1645, that a committee for examination of ministers should sit every Tuesday and Thursday in the afternoon, at two o'clock, and the members of the Assembly should attend in their turns, as they shall be nominated and appointed by the scribe, according to the order of their names in the register-book, five at a time, and each to attend a week.

While the point of ordination was depending, committees were chosen to prepare materials for a new form of discipline and church government; a measure of the greater consequence, because the old form was dissolved, and no other as yet established in its room.† Here the Independents agreed with the Presbyterians, that there was a certain form of church government laid down in the New Testament, which was of Divine institution; but when they came to the question, What that government was? and whether it was binding in all ages of the Church? both the Erastians and Independents divided against them. The proposition was this, that the Scripture holds forth that many particular congregations may, and by Divine institution ought to be under one Presbyterial government. The debate lasted thirty days; the Erastians did not except against the Presbyterial government as a political institution, proper to be established by the civil magistrate, but they were against the claim of a Divine right. Upon this occasion, Bulstrode Whitelocke, Esq., one of the lay commissioners, stood up and made the following speech:‡

"Mr. Prolocutor,

"I might blush to speak in this reverend Assembly, upon the question now in debate before you, had I not, by the honour of being one of your members, seen your candour to others, and observed you to be most capable to give satisfaction to any scruple here, and to enable such as I am to satisfy objections abroad, where of I have met with some, your question not being under secrecy.

"By government all men understand the prudent and well-ordering of persons and affairs, that men may live well and happily; and by the government of the Church, the ordering and ruling of persons and matters having relation to the worship of God, in spiritual matters.

"The word presbyter was in great honour among the Jews, being given to the members of their great sanhedrin, and, therefore, is not now so properly to be attributed to the rulers of every small congregation. I am none of those, Mr. Prolocutor, who except against the Presbyterian government; I think it has a

---

*Grand Debate, p. 185.   † MS. *penes me.*

* Vide Appendix, No. 9.   † Ibid.

‡ Whitelocke's Memorials, p. 95.

good foundation, and has done much good in the Church of Christ.

" But, sir, whether this form of government be *jure divino* or not, may admit of some dispute; and whether it be now requisite for you to declare that it is so.

" If the meaning be that it is *jure divino ecclesiastico*, then the question will be raised of the magistrates imposing, forms upon men's consciences, for then they will be only the magistrates' imposition. But if the meaning be *jure divino absolulè*, it must then be the precept of God, and they are in a sad condition who are not under this government.

" But it is objected that no form of government is *jure divino*, but that, in general, all things must be done decently and in order. A government is certainly *jure divino*, but whether Presbytery, Episcopacy, Independency, or any other form of government be *jure divino* or not, that is, whether there be a prescript, rule, or command of Scripture for any of those forms, will not be admitted by many as a clear thing.

" It may, therefore, not be unworthy your consideration, whether it be not more prudent at this time to forbear to declare your judgments in this point; the truth will, nevertheless, continue the same.

" If this government be not *jure divino*, no opinion of any council can make it so; and if it be *jure divino*, it continues so still, though you do not declare it to be so.

" I therefore humbly submit it to your judgments, whether it be not better, at this time, to avoid giving, occasion to disputes of this nature, and only to present your judgment to the Parliament, that the government of the Church by Presbyteries is most agreeable to the Word of God, and most fit to be settled in this kingdom ; or in what other expressions you may think fit to clothe your question ; and I hope you may soon have a desired issue."

Mr. Selden and St. John were of this mind ; and the Rev. Mr. Colman was so zealous on this side that he declaimed against the Divine right, not only in the Assembly, but in the pulpit, apprehending Presbytery would prove as arbitrary and tyrannical as Prelacy if it came in on the foot of a Divine claim. He therefore proposed that the civil magistrate should have the sole power of the keys, by way of interim, till the nation was settled.

But the Independents opposed the proposition of the Divine right of Presbytery, by advancing a counter Divine right of their own scheme ; fifteen days they took the part of opponents, and fifteen days they were upon the defensive. To give a short specimen of their debates :

. The chief inquiries were concerning the constitution and form of the first Church of Jerusalem ; the subordination of synods and of lay-elders.* Upon the first question, the Independents maintained that the first church at Jerusalem was not larger than could meet in one place. In support of which allegation they produced several passages from the New Testament ; as, Acts i., 15, The whole number of disciples being about one hundred and twenty, met together with one accord. And Acts ii., 1, They were all with one accord in one place. When they were multiplied to three thousand, it is

still said, they met together with one accord, and in one place, Acts, ii., 46. When they were farther increased, multitudes being added to them, both men and women, they still met together with one accord, and in one place, Acts, v., 12, 14. When the number of disciples had received yet farther addition, so that it became necessary to choose deacons to take care of the poor, the whole multitude were called together, and chose out seven men from among themselves, and set them before the apostles, Acts, vi., 2, 5. And even after the general dispersion of the disciples mentioned Acts viii., it is recorded that those who remained met together in Acts, xv., 4, 22, " Then pleased it the apostles and elders, with the whole church, to send chosen men of their own company to Antioch." They allowed that there was a mention of a Presbytery in Scripture, but that it was no other than the Presbytery or elders of one particular church or congregation, it being nowhere expressed that God has set in the Church distinct sorts of Presbyteries, such as consistories, classes, provincial synods, and general assemblies, one above another. They objected, also, to the high powers claimed by the Presbyteries, as the right of admission and exclusion from the Christian Church, with pains and penalties, which, as they had no foundation in Scripture, were not very consistent with the powers of the civil magistrate.

By way of reply, the Presbyterians maintained that the Church of Jerusalem was made up of more congregations than one, as appeared from the multitude of disciples mentioned in divers places ; * from the many apostles and teachers in the Church of Jerusalem, who could not exercise their gifts in one assembly ; and from the diversity of languages mentioned, Acts, ii. and vi. Now, it being granted that the disciples were too numerous to assemble in one place, it must follow that they were under one Presbyterial government, because this being still called one church, Acts, viii., 1, the elders of which are often mentioned in the same history. The ablest critics in the Assembly were divided upon this head, as Dr. Temple, Lightfoot, Selden, Colman, Vines, and others, but it was carried for the Presbyterians.

It was alleged, in favour of the subordination, of synods, that the Scripture speaks of an appeal from one or two brethren to the whole church, Matt., xviii., 15, and of the appeal of the church at Antioch to the apostles and elders at Jerusalem, Acts, xv., 2.† But the Independents affirmed that a synod of Presbyters is nowhere called a church, and that the appeal of the Church of Antioch was only for advice, not for a judicial determination ; but that, supposing the assembly of the apostles at Jerusalem had been a synod, it could neither have been provincial nor national in respect of the church at Antioch, and, consequently, no proof of a subordination. The masters of Jewish antiquities displayed all their learning upon this subject, for the Jewish sanhedrin being proposed as the model of their Christian Presbytery, it was necessary to inquire what were the respective powers of the ecclesiastical and civil courts under the law.‡ Moses having appointed

---

* Grand Debate, p. 13, &c.

* Grand Debate, p. 41.   † Ibid., p. 115, 128, &c;
‡ Lightfoot's Remarks, p. 17.

that he that would not hearken to the priest or
the judge should die, Deut., xvii., 12, it was inferred, in favour of church power, that the priest
held one court and the civil magistrate another;
but Mr. Selden observed, that the Vulgar Latin,
till within these forty years, reads thus : " Qui
non obediveret sacerdoti ex decreto judicis
morietur" — " He that will not obey the priest
shall die by the sentence of the judge," and
Mr. Lightfoot added, that when the judges of
inferior courts went up to Jerusalem by way
of appeal, it was only for advice and consultation; but when the question was put, December 12, for a subordination of synods with
lay-elders, as so many courts of judicature,
with power to dispense church censures, it
was carried in the affirmative, and inserted in
their humble advice, with this addition, " So
Christ has furnished some in his Church, besides ministers of the Word, with gifts for government, and with commission to execute the
same when called thereunto, who are to join
with the minister in the government of the
Church, which officers the Reformed churches
generally call elders."*

Thus the main foundations of the Presbyterial government were voted of Divine appointment by a very great majority ; but the Independents entered their dissent in writing, and
complained to the world " of the unkind usage
they met with in the Assembly ; that the papers
they offered were not read ; that they were not
allowed to state their own questions, being told
they set themselves industriously to puzzle the
cause, and render the clearest propositions obscure, rather than argue the truth or falseness
of them ; that it was not worth the Assembly's
while to spend so much time in debating with
so inconsiderable a number of men ;† they also
declared that the Assembly refused to debate
their main proposition, viz., whether a Divine
right of church government did not remain with
every particular congregation." To all which
it was replied, that the Assembly were not conscious they had done them any injustice ; and
as for the rest, they were the proper judges of
their own methods of proceeding.

The Erastians, seeing how things were carried, reserved themselves for the House of Commons, where they were sure to be joined by all
the patrons of the Independents. The English
and Scots commissioners, being no less solicitous about the event, gave their friends notice to
be early in their places, hoping to carry the
question before the House should be full ; but
Mr. Glyn, perceiving their intention, spoke an
hour to the point of *jus divinum ;* and after him
Mr. Whitelocke stood up and enlarged upon the
same argument till the House was full, when
the question being put, it was carried in the
negative, and that the proposition of the Assembly should stand thus : " That it is lawful
and agreeable to the Word of God that the

Chuch be governed by congregational, classical,
and synodical assemblies "*

The disappointment of the Scots commissioners and their friends at the loss of this question
in the House is not to be expressed ; they
alarmed the citizens with the danger of the
Church, and prevailed with the common council to petition the Parliament [November 15]
that the Presbyterian discipline might be established as the discipline of Jesus Christ ; but the
Commons answered, with a frown, " that the
citizens must have been misinformed of the proceedings of the House, or else they would not
have precipitated the judgment of Parliament."
Not discouraged at this rebuke, they prevailed
with the city ministers to petition, who, when
they came to the House, were told by the speaker, " they need not wait for an answer, but go
home and look to the charges of their several
congregations," and immediately appointed a
committee to inquire into the rise of these petitions.

The Presbyterian ministers, despairing of
success with the Commons, instead of yielding
to the times, resolved to apply to the House of
Lords, who received them civilly, and promised
to take their request into consideration ; but no
advances being made in two months, they were
out of all patience, and determined to renew
their application ; and to give it the greater
weight, prevailed with the lord-mayor and court
of aldermen to join with them in presenting an
address, which they did January 16, " for a
speedy settlement of church government according to the Covenant, and that no toleration
might be given to popery, prelacy, superstition,
heresy, profaneness, or anything contrary to
sound doctrine, and that all private assemblies
might be restrained."† The Lords thanked
them for their zeal, and recommended it to the
city magistrates to suppress all such unlawful
assemblies ; but the houses were not to be
moved as yet by such disagreeable importunity ;
however, this laid the foundation of those jealousies and misunderstandings between the city
and Parliament which, in the end, proved the
ruin of the Presbyterian cause.

But the fiercest contention between the Assembly and Parliament arose upon the power
of the keys, which the former had voted to be
in the eldership or presbytery, in these words :
" The keys of the kingdom of heaven were committed to the officers of the Church, by virtue
whereof they have power respectively to retain
and remit sins, to shut the kingdom of heaven
against the impenitent both by the Word and
censures, and to open it to the penitent by absolution ; and to prevent the profanation of the
holy sacrament by notorious and obstinate offenders, the said officers are to proceed by admonition, suspension from the sacrament of the
Lord's Supper for a season, and by excommunication from the Church, according to the nature
of the crime and demerit of the person ;"‡ all
which power they claimed, not by the laws of the
land, but *jure divino,* or by Divine appointment.

The Independents claimed a like power for
the brotherhood of every particular congregation, but without any civil sanctions or penal-

---

* Vide Appendix, No. 9.
† This is a specimen of that insolence of spirit,
that pride and haughtiness in numbers, which a conviction of acting with the majority begets. These
men did not recollect that the Christians themselves,
at the beginning, were an inconsiderable number of
men, and the disciples of the true and faithful witness a "little flock." They had forgotten the gracious promise made to "two or three" only, gathered
together in the name of Christ.—ED.

* Whitelocke's Memoirs, p. 106.
† Vol. Pamp., No. xxxiv., p. 3.
‡ *Vide* Appendix, No. 9.

ties annexed; the Erastians were for laying the communion open, and referring all crimes to the civil magistrate. When the question, therefore, came under consideration in the House of Commons, the learned Mr. Selden delivered his opinion against all suspensions and excommunications, to this effect: "That for four thousand years there was no law to suspend persons from religious exercises. Strangers, indeed, were kept from the Passover, but they were pagans, and not of the Jewish religion. The question is not now for keeping away pagans in times of Christianity, but Protestants from Protestant worship. No divine can show that there is any such command as this to suspend from the sacrament. No man is kept from the sacrament, *eo nomine*, because he is guilty of any sin, by the constitution of the Reformed churches, or because he has not made satisfaction. Every man is a sinner; the difference is only, that one is in private and the other in public. *Die ecclesiæ* in St. Matthew were the courts of law which then sat at Jerusalem. No man can show any excommunication till the Popes Victor and Zephorinus, two hundred years after Christ, first began to use them upon private quarrels, whereby it appears that excommunication is a human invention taken from the heathens."*

Mr. Whitelocke spoke on the same side of the question, and said, "The Assembly of Divines have petitioned and advised this house, that in every presbytery, or Presbyterian congregation, the pastors and ruling elders may have the power of excommunication, and of suspending such as they shall judge ignorant or scandalous.† By pastors, I suppose, they mean themselves, and others who are or may be preachers, and would be bishops or overseers of their congregations. By ruling elders, they mean a select number of such in every congregation as shall be chosen for the execution of government and discipline therein. A pastor is one who is to feed his sheep; and if so, how improper must it be for such to desire to excommunicate any, or keep them from food; to forbid any to eat, or whomsoever they shall judge unworthy, when Christ has said, 'Take, eat, and drink ye all of it,' though Judas was one of them. But some have said it is the duty of a shepherd, when he sees a sheep feeding upon that which will do him hurt, to chase him away from that pasture; and they apply this to suspending those from the sacrament whom they fear, by eating and drinking unworthily, may eat and drink their own damnation. But it ought to be observed, that it is not receiving the sacrament, but the unworthiness of the receiver, that brings destruction; and this cannot be within the judgment of any but the person himself, who alone can examine his own heart; nor can any one produce a commission for another to be judge thereof. But it is said that ruling elders are to be joined with the pastors; now, in some country villages and congregations, perhaps, they may not be very learned, and yet the authority given them is very great: the word elders, among the Hebrews, signified men of the greatest power and dignity; so it was among the Romans, whose Senate was so called from *senes*,

elders. The highest title among the French, Spaniards, and Italians, *seigneur*, and *signiori*, is but a corruption of the Latin word *senior*, elder. The same may be observed in our English corporations, where the best and most substantial persons are called aldermen, or eldermen. Thus, the title of elders may be given to the chief men of every presbytery; but if the power of excommunication be given them, they may challenge the title of elders in the highest signification.

"Power is desired to be given to suspend from the sacrament two sorts of persons, the ignorant and scandalous; now it is possible, that they who are judged to be competent in one place, may be deemed ignorant in another; however, to keep them from the ordinances is no way to improve their knowledge. Scandalous persons are likewise to be suspended, and this is to be left to the discretion of the pastors and ruling elders; but where have they such a commission? Scandalous sinners should be admonished to forsake their evil ways, and amend their lives; and how can this be done better than by allowing them to hear good sermons, and partake of the holy ordinances? A man may be a good physician, though he never cuts off a member from his patient; and a church may be a good church, though no member of it has ever been cut off. I have heard many complaints of the jurisdiction of the prelates, who were but few; now in this ordinance there will be a great multiplication of spiritual men in government, but I am of opinion that where the temporal sword is sufficient for punishment of offences, there will be no need of this new discipline."

Though the Parliament did not deem it prudent wholly to reject the ordinance for excommunication, because it had been the popular complaint, in the late times, that pastors of churches had not power to keep unworthy communicants from the Lord's Table; yet the speeches of these learned gentlemen made such an impression, that they resolved to render it ineffectual to all the purposes of church tyranny; accordingly, they sent to the Assembly to specify in writing what degrees of knowledge in the Christian religion were necessary to qualify persons for the communion, and what sorts of scandal deserved suspension or excommunication; which, after much controversy, they presented to the houses, who inserted them in the body of their ordinance for suspension from the Lord's Supper, dated October 20, 1645, together with certain provisoes of their own.

The ordinance sets forth, that the several elderships, within their respective limits, shall have power to suspend from the sacrament of the Lord's Supper all ignorant and scandalous persons, within the rules and directions hereafter mentioned, and no others.*

Rules for Suspending from the Sacrament in case of Ignorance.

"All that do not know and believe the being of a God, and the Holy Trinity: They that are not acquainted with original sin, and the fall of man: They that do not believe Christ to be God and man, and our only Mediator and Redeemer; that Christ and his benefits are applied only by

---

* Rushworth, p. 203.
† Whitelocke, p. 163, 164.

* Rushworth, part iv., vol. i., p. 211.

faith, which faith is the gift of God, and implies a trusting in him, for the remission of sins, and life everlasting; the necessity of sincere repentance, and a holy life, in order to salvation; the nature and importance of the two sacraments, especially of the Lord's Supper; that the souls of the faithful do immediately live with Christ after death, and the souls of the wicked immediately go to hell; the resurrection of the body, and a final judgment."

Rules for Suspension in case of Scandal.

"The elderships shall have power to suspend from the sacrament all scandalous persons hereafter mentioned, and no others, being duly convicted by the oaths of two witnesses, or their own confession; that is to say,

"All blasphemers against God, his holy Word, or sacraments.

"Incestuous persons; adulterers; fornicators; drunkards; profane swearers and cursers; murderers.

"Worshippers of images, crosses, crucifixes, or relics.

"All that make images of the Trinity, or of any person thereof.

"All religious worshippers of saints, angels, or any mere creature.

"Such as declare themselves not to be in charity with their neighbours.

"Such as shall challenge others to a duel, or that shall accept such challenge.

"Such as knowingly shall carry a challenge, either by word, message, or writing.

"Such as profane the Lord's Day by dancing, playing at cards, or dice, or any other game; or that shall on the Lord's Day use masking, wakes, shooting, bowling, playing at football or stoolball, wrestling; or that shall resort to plays, interludes, fencing, bull-baiting, or bear-baiting; or shall use hawking, hunting, coursing, fishing, or fowling; or that shall publicly expose any wares to sale, otherwise than is provided by the ordinance of April 6, 1644; or that shall travel on the Lord's Day without reasonable cause.

"Such as keep known stews, or brothel-houses; or that shall solicit the chastity of any person for himself, or another.

"Such parents as give their consent to marry their children to papists; and such as do themselves marry a papist.

"Such as consult for advice, witches, wizards, or fortune-tellers.

"Such as assault their parents, or any magistrate, minister, or elder, in the execution of his office.

"Such as shall be legally attainted of barratry, forgery, extortion, or bribery.

"And the several elderships shall have power to suspend all ministers who shall be duly convicted of any of the crimes above mentioned, from giving or receiving the Lord's Supper.

"Persons suspended by one congregation shall not be admitted to the sacrament by another, without certificate from that congregation of which he was a member. But in all cases of suspension, if the party suspended shall manifest his repentance before the eldership by whom he was suspended, he shall be readmitted to the Lord's Supper, and the suspension taken off."

But then follow the provisoes, which stripped the Presbyteries of that power, of the keys which they were reaching at.

"Provided, always, that if any person find himself aggrieved with the proceedings of the presbytery to which he belongs, he may appeal to the classical eldership; from them to the Provincial Assembly; from them to the National; and from them to the Parliament."

It is farther provided, "that the cognizance and examination of all capital offences shall be reserved entire to the magistrate appointed by the laws of the kingdom, who, upon his committing the party to prison, shall make a certificate to the eldership of the congregation to which they belonged, who may thereupon suspend them from the sacrament.

"The presbytery or eldership shall not have cognizance of anything relating to contracts, payments, or demands; or of any matter of conveyance, title, interest, or property, in lands or goods.

"No use shall be made of any confession, or proof made before an eldership, at any trial at law of any person for any offence.

"And it is farther ordained, that those members of Parliament who are members of the Assembly of Divines, or any seven of them, shall be a standing committee, to consider of such other offences or scandals, not mentioned in this ordinance, which may be conceived to be a sufficient cause of suspension from the sacrament, and shall lay them before the Parliament."

By an ordinance of June 5, 1646, a discretionary power was lodged in a committee of Lords and Commons, not less than nine, to adjudge and determine scandalous offences not formerly enumerated, and report them to the two houses, that if they concurred with the committee, they might be added to the catalogue.

By these provisoes, it is evident the Parliament were determined not to part with the spiritual sword, or subject their civil properties to the power of the Church, which gave great offence to the Scots commissioners, and to most of the English Presbyterians, who declaimed against the ordinance, as built upon Erastian principles, and depriving the Church of that which it claimed by a Divine institution. They allowed of appeals from one spiritual court to another, but declared openly from the pulpit and press, that appeals to the Parliament or civil magistrate, as the dernier resort, were insufferable. The Parliament, observing their ambition of making the Church independent of the State, girt the laws closer about them, and subjected their determinations more immediately to the civil magistrate, by an ordinance dated March 14, 1645-6, which enacts, "that an appeal shall lie from the decisions of every classis to the commissioners chosen by Parliament out of every province, and from them to the Parliament itself. That if any person commit any scandalous offences not mentioned in the ordinance, the minister may forbear to administer the sacrament to him for that time; but then he shall, within eight days, certify the same to the commissioners, who shall send up the case, with their opinions, to the Parliament, by whose determination the eldership shall abide."

This ordinance of suspension from the sacrament was extorted from the two houses before the time, by the importunate solicitations of the city clergy; for as yet there were no classes or presbyteries in any part of England which ought to have been erected before they had determined their powers. The houses had voted that there should be a choice of lay-elders throughout England and Wales, and had laid down some rules for this purpose August 19, 1645; but it was on the 14th of March following before it passed into a law.

It was then ordained, 1. "That there be forthwith a choice of [ruling] elders throughout the kingdom of England and dominion of Wales.

2. "That public notice be given of such election in every parish, by the minister of the church, a fortnight before, and that on the Lord's Day on which the choice is to be made a sermon be preached suitable to the occasion.

3. "Elections shall be made by the congregation, or the major part of them then assembled, being heads of families, and such as have taken the Covenant.

4. "That certain persons be appointed triers in every classis, viz., six ministers and three laymen, whereof seven to be a quorum, to determine the validity of elections. All members of Parliament, and peers of the realm, to be triers in the parishes wherein they live.

5. "No man to be a ruling elder but for one congregation, and that in the parish where he lives.

6. "The qualifications of a ruling elder are, that he be of good understanding in religion, sound in the faith, prudent, discreet, grave, of unblameable conversation, willing to undergo the office, and in communion with the Church.

7. "All parishes, privileged places, exempt jurisdictions, and all other places whatsoever, shall be brought under the exercise of congregational, classical, provincial, and national assemblies, except chapels within any of the king's houses, or the House of Peers, which shall continue free for the exercise of religion, according to the Directory, but not otherwise.

8. "The province of London shall be divided into twelve classical elderships, each to contain about twelve parishes of the city and parts adjacent, and these to be the boundaries of the province of London.

9. "The several counties of England and Wales shall be divided into classical presbyteries by persons to be appointed by Parliament for this purpose, who shall settle the boundaries of each classis, and certify the same to the Parliament for their approbation.

10. "The presbytery or eldership of every parish shall meet once a week; the classical assemblies of each province once a month, by adjournment, in such places as may be most convenient; provincial assemblies shall meet twice a year; national assemblies as often as they shall be summoned by Parliament, and shall continue sitting as long as the Parliament shall direct and appoint, and not otherwise.

11. "Every congregational or parochial eldership shall send two elders, or more, not exceeding four, and one minister, to the classical assembly; every classical assembly within the province shall send two ministers, and four ruling elders at least, but not to exceed nine, to the provincial assembly. Every provincial assembly shall appoint two ministers, and four ruling elders, which shall constitute a national assembly, when such a one shall be summoned by Parliament."[*]

When this ordinance had passed the Commons, it stuck a considerable time with the Lords, insomuch that the Presbyterian clergy thought it necessary to quicken them by a petition, May 29, under the hands of three hundred ministers of Suffolk and Essex, lamenting the decay of religion, and the want of church discipline, and beseeching their lordships to put the finishing hand to the bill so long depending; which they did, accordingly, June 6, 1646.

Thus the Presbyterian form of church government became the national establishment, by way of probation, as far as an ordinance of Parliament could make it; for the preamble sets forth, "that if, upon trial, it was not found acceptable, it should be reversed or amended. It declares, farther, that the two houses found it very difficult to make their new settlement agree, with the laws and government of the kingdom; that therefore it could not be expected that a present rule in every particular should be settled at once, but that there will be need of supplements and additions, and perhaps alterations, as experience shall bring to light the necessity thereof."

The Parliament apprehended they had now established the plan of the Presbyterian discipline, though it proved not to the satisfaction of any one party of Christians; so hard is it to make a good settlement when men dig up all at once old foundations. The Presbyterian hierarchy was as narrow as the prelatical; and as it did not allow a liberty of conscience, claiming a civil as well as ecclesiastical authority over men's persons and properties, it was equally, if not more, insufferable. Bishop Kennet observes, that the settling Presbytery was supported by the fear and love of the Scots army, and that when they were gone home it was better managed by the English army, who were for Independency and a principle of toleration; but as things stood, nobody was pleased; the Episcopalians and Independents were excluded; and because the Parliament would not give the several presbyteries an absolute power over their communicants, but reserved the last appeal to themselves, neither the Scots nor English Presbyterians would accept it.

When the scheme was laid before the Scots Parliament and General Assembly, as a plan of uniformity between the two nations, they insisted upon the following amendments:

(1.) "That no godly minister be excluded from being a member of classical, provincial, or national assemblies.

(2.) "That the ordinary time for the meeting of the National Assembly may be fixed; with a reserve of power to the Parliament to convene them when they please, and liberty to the Church to meet oftener on necessary occasions.

(3.) "That the congregational eldership may have power to judge in cases of scandal not expressed. This, they conceive, cannot be construed lodging an arbitrary power in the Church; whereas, on the other hand, the appointing such provincial commissioners as are settled in the

---

ordinance, will occasion disputes, create a disconformity between this and other churches, and is a mixture in church government altogether without precedent. This business, therefore, they conceive may be better managed by assemblies of ministers and ruling elders.

(4.) "That the ordinance for ordination of ministers may be perpetual.

(5.) "The manner of subjecting church assemblies to the control and decision of Parliament, being very liable to mistakes; the exemption, likewise, of persons of distinction from ecclesiastical censures; and the administering the sacrament to some persons, against the conscience of the ministry and elderships; these, and some other particulars, being more than they can admit, they desire may be altered to general satisfaction.

(6.) "As to the articles relating to the perpetual officers of the Church, with their respective functions; the order and power of church assemblies; the directions for public repentance or penance; the rules for excommunication and absolution;"* all these they desire may be fixed and settled pursuant to the Covenant, and with the joint advice of the divines of both kingdoms [i. e., the Assembly at Westminster] long since offered to both houses.

After the delivery of these papers by the Scots commissioners, and before the houses had returned an answer, they were published with a preface by a private hand, which provoked the houses to such a degree, that, April 14, they voted it to be burned by the hands of the common hangman, which was done accordingly. April 17, the Commons published their answer to the commissioners' papers, in which they declare to the world, "that their real intentions are to settle religion according to the Covenant, and to maintain the ancient and fundamental government of this kingdom. They think it strange that any sober and modest men should imagine they are unwilling to settle any government in the Church, after they have declared so fully for the Presbyterian; have taken so much pains for the settling it; have passed most of the particulars brought to them by the Assembly of Divines, without any material alteration, save in the point of commissioners; and have published so many ordinances for putting the same in execution; only because they cannot consent to the granting an arbitrary and unlimited power and jurisdiction to near ten thousand judicatories to be erected within this kingdom, and this demanded in such a way as is not consistent with the fundamental laws and government of the same, and by necessary consequence excluding the Parliament of England from the exercise of all ecclesiastical jurisdiction. This, say they, has been the great cause that church government has not been long since settled; and we have the more reason not to part with this power out of the hands of the civil magistrate, since the experience of all ages will manifest that the reformation and purity of religion, and the preservation and protection of the people of God in this kingdom, have, under God, been owing to the Parliament's exercise of this power. If, then, the minds of any are disturbed for want of the present set-

tling of church government, let them apply to those [ministers] who, having sufficient power and direction from the houses on that behalf, have not as yet put the same in execution."

The English Presbyterians, having resolved to stand and fall with the Scots, refused peremptorily to comply with the ordinance, relying upon the assistance and support of that nation. Mr. Marshal stood up in the Assembly, March 20, and said, that since an ordinance of Parliament for church government was now published, and speedily to be put in execution; and since there were some things in that ordinance which lay very hard upon his conscience, and upon the consciences of many of his brethren (though he blessed God for the zeal of the two houses in settling the government of the Church thus far), yet, being much pressed in spirit with some things contained therein, he moved that a committee might be appointed to examine what things in the ordinance were contrary to their consciences, and to prepare a petition to present them to the two houses.*

A petition was accordingly drawn up, and presented March 23, by the whole Assembly, with Mr. Marshal at their head. In this petition they assert the Divine right of the Presbyterian government, and complain of a clause in the late ordinance, which establishes an appeal from the censures of the Church to a committee of Parliament. It was a sanguine and daring attempt of these divines, who were called together only for their advice, to examine and censure the ordinances of Parliament, and dispute in this manner with their superiors; the Commons, alarmed at this petition, appointed a committee to take into consideration the matter and manner of it, who, after some time, reported it as their opinion, that the Assembly of Divines, in their late petition, had broken the privileges of Parliament, and were guilty of a premunire; and whereas they insisted so peremptorily on the *jus divinum* of the Presbyterian government, the committee had drawn up certain queries, which they desired the Assembly might resolve for their satisfaction; the House agreed to the report of the committee, and on the 30th of April sent Sir John Evelin, Mr. Nathaniel Fiennes, and Mr. Browne, to the Assembly, to acquaint them with their resolutions. These gentlemen set before them their rash and imprudent conduct, and in several speeches showed wherein they had exceeded their province, which was to advise the houses in such points as they should lay before them, but not to dictate to those to whom they owed their being an assembly. Then they read the votes above mentioned, and delivered in the following questions, with the orders of the House thereupon:

Questions propounded to the Assembly of Divines by the House of Commons, touching the Point of Jus Divinum in the Matters of Church Government.

1. "Whether the Congregational and Presbyterial elderships appointed by ordinance of Parliament, or any other Congregational or Presbyterial elderships, are *jure divino*, and by the will and appointment of Jesus Christ? and whether

---

* Rushworth, p. 253.

* MS. penes me, sess. 609.

any particular church government be *jure divino*? and, what that government is?[*]

2. "Whether all the members of the said elderships, as members thereof, or which of them, are *jure divino*, and by the will and appointment of Jesus Christ?

3. "Whether the Classical, Provincial, and National Assemblies, all or any of them, and which of them, are *jure divino*, and by the will and appointment of Jesus Christ?

4. "Whether appeals from Congregational elderships to Classical, Provincial, and National Assemblies, or any of them, and to which of them, are *jure divino*, and by the will and appointment of Jesus Christ? and whether their powers upon such appeals are *jure divino*, and by the will and appointment of Jesus Christ?

5. "Whether Œcumenical Assemblies are *jure divino*? and whether there be appeals from any of the former assemblies to the said œcumenical *jure divino*, and by the will and appointment of Jesus Christ?

6. "Whether, by the Word of God, the power of judging and declaring what are such notorious and scandalous offences, for which persons guilty thereof are to be kept from the sacrament of the Lord's Supper, and of convening before them, trying, and actually suspending from the sacrament of the Lord's Supper such offenders, is either in the Congregational eldership, Presbytery, or in any other eldership, congregation, or persons? and whether such powers are in them only, or any of them, and in which of them, *jure divino*, and by the will and appointment of Jesus Christ?

7. "Whether there be any certain and particular rules expressed in the Word of God to direct the elderships or presbyteries, congregations, or persons, or any of them, in the exercise and execution of the powers aforesaid, and what are those rules?

8. "Is there anything contained in the Word of God that the supreme magistracy in a Christian state may not judge and determine what are the aforesaid notorious and scandalous offences, and the manner of suspension for the same; and in what particulars concerning the premises is the said supreme magistracy by the Word of God excluded.?

9. "Whether the provision of commissioners to judge of scandals not enumerated (as they are authorized by the ordinance of Parliament) be contrary to that way of government which Christ has appointed in his Church? and wherein are they so contrary?"

In the Assembly's answer to these propositions, the House of Commons ordered the proofs from Scripture to be set down, with the several texts at large, in the express words of the same; and that every minister of the Assembly, who should be present at the debate of any of these questions, should subscribe his respective name in the affirmative or negative, according as he gave his vote; and that those who dissented from the major part should set down their positive opinions, with the express texts of Scripture upon which their opinions are grounded.

It is easy to discover the masterly hands of Mr. Selden and Whitelocke in these questions; which were sent to the Assembly, not with any prospect of a satisfactory answer, but to employ,

and, it may be, to divide them, till they saw how they were like to settle with the king. The houses were afraid of being fettered with the Scot's discipline, and yet the Scots were not to be disgusted, because they had an army in the north, to whom the king had committed the custody of his person.

As soon as the Assembly had heard the resolutions of the House of Commons above mentioned, and the questions read, first by Sir J. Evelin, and then by their scribe, they adjourned in a very great fright till next morning, in order to consult their brethren in the city, and then appointed a day of fasting and humiliation for themselves, in reference to their present circumstances, and sent letters to all the members to give their attendance. The fast was observed within their own walls on Wednesday, May 6, from nine in the morning till four in the afternoon; and committees were appointed to consider of an answer to the questions, whose report we shall consider under the next year.

In the mean time, we must go back a little to take a view of the attempts which were making to comprehend the Independents, or dissenting brethren in the Assembly, within the new establishment, or, at least, to obtain a toleration for them;[*] the Parliament had ordered, September 13, 1644, that the "committee of Lords and Commons appointed to treat with the Scots commissioners, and the committee of divines, do take into consideration the differences of the opinions of the members of the Assembly in point of church government, and endeavour a union if possible; and if that cannot be accomplished, endeavour to find out some way how far tender consciences, who cannot in all things submit to the same rule, may be borne with, according to the Word of God, and consistent with the public peace." This was called the Grand Committee of Accommodation, which met the first time September 20, and chose a sub-committee of six divines of the Assembly, to consider the points of difference, and to prepare materials for the consideration of the grand committee: the names of these divines were, the Reverend Mr. Marshal, Mr. Herle, Mr. Vines, Dr. Temple, Mr. Goodwin, and Mr. Nye, who, after several consultations among themselves, delivered to the committee certain propositions [October 15, 1644], which were read by Mr. Vines, their chairman: the Independents would have stated the points in variance between the two parties, and endeavoured a compromise while the discipline of the Church was depending; but the Presbyterians insisted that the new form of government should first pass into a law as a standard, before the exceptions of the Independents be considered; upon which they were adjourned, by order of the House of Commons, till the affair should be determined in the Assembly, who agreed, April 4, 1645, that the brethren who had entered their dissent against the Presbyterian government should be a committee to bring in the whole frame of their government in a body, with their grounds and reasons.[†] The Independents desired liberty to bring in their objections by parts, as the Presbyterians had done their advices; but this not being admitted, they desired time to perfect their

_____
[*] Rushworth, p. 260.

_____
[*] Papers of Accommodation, p. 1.
[†] Remonstrance, p. 3.

plan before any other scheme passed into a law; but the Presbyterians, without any regard to the compromise, by the assistance of their Scots friends, pushed the affair to a conclusion in Parliament; upon which the Independents laid aside their own model, and published a remonstrance, complaining of the artful conduct of the Assembly, and that the discipline of the Church being fixed, it was too late to think any more of a comprehension. The House of Commons having seen their mistake, resumed this affair with their own hands, and by an order dated November 6, 1645, revived the Committee of Accommodation, which, besides the Scots commissioners, consisted of the following peers, viz.:

Earl of Northumberland, Lord Visc. Say and Seale,
Earl of Manchester,   Lord Wharton,
.   Lord Howard.

These were to be met by the following members of the Assembly; viz.:

Dr. Burgess,	Dr. Hoyle,	Dr. Temple,
Mr. Marshal,	Mr. White,	Mr. Palmer,
Mr. Herle,	Mr. Vines,	Mr. Tuckney,
Mr. Reynolds,	Mr. Hill,	Mr. Arrowsmith,
Dr. Smith,		Mr. Newcomen,
Mr. Seaman,		Mr. Young; -

with the dissenting brethren of the Assembly,

M. T. Goodwin, Mr. Nye, Mr. Bridge,
Mr. Simpson, Mr. Burroughs, Mr. Drury.

The committee met in the Jerusalem Chamber, November 17, and would have entered upon a scheme for comprehension, but the Independents moved only for an indulgence or toleration, observing that, as they had already moved, in the Assembly and elsewhere, that their scheme of government might be debated before the Presbyterian had passed into a law, and for this purpose had offered to prepare a complete model, if they might have been indulged a few days,* and that having been overruled, and another form of government settled, they apprehended themselves shut out from the establishment, and precluded from any farther attempts towards a union or comprehension; but still they were willing to enter upon the second part of the Parliament's order, which was to consider how far tender consciences, who cannot in all things submit to the established rule, may be indulged, consistent with the Word of God and the public peace. Accordingly, in their next meeting, December 4, they offered the following proposals:

Taking for granted that both sides shall agree in one confession of faith, they humbly crave,

1. That their congregations may have the power of ordination within themselves.

2. That they may not be brought under the power of classes, nor forced to communicate in those parish churches where they dwell, but that they may have liberty to join with such congregations as they prefer; and that such congregations may have power of all church censures within themselves, subject only to Parliament, and be as so many exempt or privileged places.

To the preamble the Presbyterians replied, that only such as agreed to their confession of faith and Directory should have the benefit of the forbearance to be agreed on, with which the committee concurred; but the Independents would admit only of the affirmative, that such

* Papers of Accommodation, p. 14, 24.

as agree with them should be tolerated; and would not consent to the negative, so as to set bounds or limits of forbearance to tender consciences, nor make such an agreement a necessary qualification for receiving the sacrament.*

To the request of the Independents, of being exempted from the jurisdiction of their classes, and having a liberty of erecting separate congregations, the Presbyterians replied,

1. That this implied a total separation from the established rule.

2. The lawfulness of gathering churches out of other true churches.

3. That the Parliament would then destroy what they had set up.

4. That the members of Independent churches would then have greater privilege than those of the establishment.

5. That this would countenance a perpetual schism. And,

6. Introduce all manner of confusion into families.†

They therefore proposed that such as, after conference with their parish minister, were not satisfied with the establishment, should not be compelled to communicate in the Lord's Supper; nor be liable to censures from classes or synods, provided they joined with the parish congregation where they lived, and were under the government of it in other respects.

The Independents replied, that they did not intend a total separation, but should agree with their brethren in the most essential points; as in worshipping according to the Directory, in choosing the same officers, pastors, teachers, ruling elders, with the same qualifications as in the rule. That they should require the same qualifications in their members as the Assembly had advised, that is, visible saints, professing faith in Christ, and obedience to the rules of faith and life taught by Christ and his apostles;‡ that they should practise the same church censures, being accountable for their conduct to their civil superiors. They would also hold occasional communion with the Presbyterian churches, in baptism and the Lord's Supper, communicating occasionally with them, and receiving their members to communion as occasion required. Their ministers should preach for each other, and, in cases of difficulty, they would call in their assistance and advice; and when an ordination falls out, they would desire the presence and approbation of their ministers with their own. Now surely, say they, this does not imply a total separation; but if in some things men cannot comply with the established rule without sin, we think such persons ought not to live without communicating in the Lord's Supper all their days, rather than gather into churches where they may enjoy all ordinances without offence to their consciences; nor ought such separation to be accounted schism, which is a name of reproach we desire not to be branded with, when we are willing to maintain Christian love and communion with our neighbours, as far as our consciences will permit.§ They add, farther, that if the state is pleased to grant them this liberty, they will refer themselves to the wisdom of the Legislature to consider of limit-

* Papers of Accommodation, p. 18, 19, 26, 27.
† Ibid., p. 20, 21.   ‡ Ibid., p. 29, 30.
§ Ibid., p. 35, 36.

ing their congregations to a certain number, to be as so many receptacles for pious persons of tender consciences.*

The Presbyterians, in their next reply, December 23, after having blamed the Independents for not going upon a comprehension, argue against the lawfulness of a separation after this manner : " That if a pretence of conscience be a sufficient ground of separation, men may gather impure and corrupt churches out of purer, because upon the dictates of an erring conscience they may disallow that which is pure, and set up that which is agreeable to their erring consciences ; and we very much doubt, say they, whether tenderness of conscience in doubtful points will justify a separation ; it may oblige men to forbear communion, but not to set up a contrary practice. If a church impose any-thing that is sinful, we must forbear to comply, yet without separation, as was the practice of the Puritans in the late times."† They then argue, from the concessions of the Independents, that because they agree with them in so many material points, therefore they should not separate. " If," say they, " you can commu-nicate with our church occasionally, once, or a second and third time, without sin, we know no reason why you may not do it constantly, and then separation will be needless : as for such a toleration as our brethren desire, we apprehend it will open a door to all sects ; and though the Independents now plead for it, their brethren in New-England do not allow it."‡

As to the charge of schism, they admit that difference in judgment in some particular points is not schism ; nor does an inconformity to some things enjoined deserve that name ; but our brethren desire, father, to set up separate communions, which is a manifest rupture of our societies into others, and is therefore a schism in the body.§ This is setting up altar against altar, allowing our churches (as the Independents do) to be true churches ; for St Austin says, " Schismaticos facit non diversa fides, sed com-munionis disrupta societas." And we conceive it is the cause of the separation that makes schism, and not the separation itself ; if, then, the cause of our brethren's separation be not sufficient, by what other name can it be called ? To all which they add, that this indulgence, if granted, will be the mother of all contentions, strifes, heresies, and confusions in the Church, and contrary to their Covenant, which obliges them to endeavour to their utmost a uniformity.

When the committee met the next time, February 2, 1645-6, the Independents replied chiefly to the point of uniformity, and argued that it was not necessary to the peace of the churches ; and ought not to extend beyond people's light and measure of understanding, according to the apostolical canon, " As far as we have attained, let us walk by the same rule," Phil., iii., 15.‖ As for a mere exemption from the censures of the classes, they declared frankly they could not acquiesce in it, because it would deprive them of the enjoyment of the Lord's Supper ; and that it was very hard to urge that, because they came so near the brethren, there-

fore they should be obliged to a total and con-stant conformity.

The committee met the last time, March 9, when the sub-committee of Presbyterian di-vines answered the last paper of the Independents, maintaining all their former positions, and concluding in this strange and wonderful man-ner : " That whereas their brethren say that uniformity ought to be urged no farther than is agreeable to all men's consciences, and to their edification ; it seems to them as if their breth-ren not only desire liberty of conscience for themselves, but for all men, and would have us think that we are bound by our Covenant to bring the churches in the three kingdoms to no near-er a conjunction and uniformity than is consist-ent with the liberty of all men's consciences ; which, whether it be the sense of the Covenant, we leave with the honourable committee."*

Hereupon the Reverend Mr. Jer. Burroughs, a divine of great candour and moderation, de-clared, in the name of the Independents, " that if their congregations might not be exempted from that coercive power of the classes ; if they might not have liberty to govern themselves in their own way, as long as they behaved peace-ably towards the civil magistrate, they were resolved to suffer, or go to some other place of the world, where they might enjoy their liberty. But while men think there is no way of peace but by forcing all to be of the same mind," says he ; " while they think the civil sword is an or-dinance of God to determine all controversies of divinity, and that it must needs be attended with fines and imprisonment to the disobedient ; while they apprehend there is no medium be-tween a strict uniformity and a general confu-sion of all things ; while these sentiments pre-vail, there must be a base subjection of men's consciences to slavery, a suppression of much truth, and great disturbances in the Christian world."

Thus ended the last committee of Lords and Commons, and Assembly of Divines, for ac-commodation, which adjourned to a certain day, but, being then diverted by other affairs, never met again. Little did the Presbyterian divines imagine that in less than twenty years all their artillery would be turned against themselves ; that they should be excluded the establishment by an act of prelatical uniformity ; that they should be reduced to the necessity of pleading for that indulgence which they now denied their brethren ; and esteem it their duty to gather churches for separate worship out of others, which they allowed to be true ones. If the leading Presbyterians in the Assembly and city had carried it with temper towards the Inde-pendents, on the foot of a limited toleration, they had, in all likelihood, prevented the dis-putes between the army and Parliament, which were the ruin of both ; they might then have saved the Constitution, and made their own terms with the king, who was now their prison-er ; but they were enamoured with the charms of Covenant uniformity and the Divine right of their Presbytery, which, after all, the Parliament would not admit in its full extent. Mr. Baxter, who was no friend of the Independents, says, " that the Presbyterian ministers were so little sensible of their own infirmities, that they would

* Papers of Accommodation, p. 40.
† Ibid., p. 51.   ‡ Ibid., p. 56.
§ Ibid., p. 65, 73, 74.   ‖ Ibid., p. 86.
Vol. II.—B

* Papers of Accommodation, p. 123.

not agree to tolerate those who were not only tolerable, but worthy instruments and members in the churches, prudent men, who were for union in things necessary, for liberty in things unnecessary, and for charity in all; but they could not be heard."*

Great was the resort of the city divines to Sion College at this time, where there was a kind of synod every Monday, to consult proper methods to propagate religion, and support the Assembly at Westminster in their opposition to the toleration of sectaries; for this purpose they wrote them a letter, dated January 15, 1645-6, in which they recite the arguments of the committee, and beseech them to oppose with all their might the great Diana of the Independents,† and not to suffer their new establishment to be strangled in the birth by a lawless toleration. The whole Scots nation was also commanded into the service; the Parliament of that kingdom wrote to the two houses at Westminster, February 3, telling them, that "it was expected the honourable houses would add the civil sanction to what the pious and learned Assembly have advised; and I am commanded by the Parliament of this kingdom," says the president, "to demand it, and I do in their names demand it. And the Parliament of this kingdom is persuaded that the piety and wisdom of the honourable houses will never admit toleration of any sects or schisms contrary to our solemn League and Covenant."‡ At the same time they appealed to the people, and published a declaration against toleration of sectaries and liberty of conscience; in which, after having taken notice of their great services, they observe, that there is a party in England who are endeavouring to supplant the true religion by pleading for liberty of conscience, which (say they) is the nourisher of all heresies and schisms. They then declare against all such notions as are inconsistent with the truth of religion, and against opening a door to licentiousness, which, to the

utmost of their power, they will endeavour to oppose; and as they have all entered into one Covenant, so to the last man in the kingdom they will go on in the preservation of it. And however the Parliament of England may determine in point of toleration and liberty of conscience, they are resolved not to make the least start, but to live and die, for the glory of God, in the entire preservation of the truth.

Most of the sermons before the House of Commons, at their monthly fasts, spoke the language of severity, and called upon the magistrate to draw his sword against the sectaries. The press teemed with pamphlets of the same nature; Mr. Prynne, against J. Goodwin, says, that if the Parliament and synod establish Presbytery, the Independents and all others are bound to submit, under pain of obstinacy. Another writes, that to let men serve God according to the persuasion of their own consciences, is to cast out one devil that seven more worse may enter.*

---

* Baxter's Life, p. 103.

† Their Diana was toleration, of which the ministers at Sion College expressed their detestation and abhorrence; and the design of their letter was to show the unreasonableness, the sin, and the mischievous consequences of it. "Not," said they, "that we can harbour the least jealousy of your zeal, fidelity, or industry, in the opposing and extirpating of such a root of gall and bitterness as toleration is and will be, both in present and future ages." Another instance of the same bitter spirit appeared in a piece published by the ministers and elders of London, met together in a provincial assembly, November 2, 1749, entitled "A Vindication of the Presbyterial Government and Ministry," in which they represent the doctrine of universal toleration as contrary to godliness, opening a door to libertinism and profaneness, and a tenet to be rejected as soul poison. The ministers of Lancashire published a paper in 1648, expressing their harmonious consent with their brethren in London, and remonstrate against toleration, as putting a cup of poison into the hand of a child, and a sword into that of a madman; as letting loose madmen with firebrands in their hands, and appointing a city of refuge in men's consciences, for the devil to fly to; and instead of providing for tender consciences, taking away all conscience. In the same year, another paper was published in Warwickshire, by forty-three ministers, breathing the same spirit, and expressing the like sentiments.—*Crosby's History of the English Baptists*, vol. i., p. 188, 192.—ED.

‡ Rushworth, p. 234.

* Prynne was foremost in this inglorious contest. Forgetful of his own sufferings, he transferred to the cause of intolerance the same zeal, intrepidity, and unwearied diligence, as had distinguished him in a better service. His publications were numerous, and all were directed to the one great end of his party, the suppression of sects and the triumph of Presbytery. "Up, therefore," said the fiery advocate of the Covenant, in one of his addresses to Parliament, "and be doing justice to some few chief offenders of this kind, for the present, to prevent execution upon many others, if not ruin on us all, for the future, and God himself, 'no doubt, will be with you; and not fear what flesh can do unto you, or secretaries speak or write against you."—*A Fresh Discovery of some Prodigious New Wandering, Blasting Stars, &c., Epistle dedicatory,* 1645.

The same course was enforced by the most celebrated Presbyterian divines in their discourses before Parliament. "If you do not labour," said Calamy, in a sermon preached before the Commons October 22, 1644, "according to your duty and power to suppress the errors thereby that are spread in the kingdom, all those errors are your errors, and those heresies are your heresies; they are sins, and God' calls for a parliamentary repentance from you for them this day. You are the Anabaptists, you are the Antinomians, and 'tis you that hold that all religions are to be tolerated."—See Crosby, vol. i., p. 176.

Baillie, speaking of the propositions of the Independents, in the Committee for Accommodation, says, "They plead-for an accommodation to other sects as well as to themselves; and with much ado could we get them to propose what we desired to themselves. In last they gave us a paper, requiring expressly a full toleration of congregation in their way everywhere, separate from ours. In our answer, we flatly denied such a vast liberty, and backed it with reasons, and, withal, we began to show what indulgence we could for peace' sake grant. Here Mr. Marshal, the chairman, has been their most diligent agent to draw too many of us to grant them much more than my heart can yield to, and which to my power I oppose. We have had many bickerings with the Independents about the indulgence for their separate congregations; for this point both they and we contend *tanquam pro oris et focis*."—*Letters,* vol. ii., p. 172, 174.

Dr. Price on this subject remarks, "Had they (the Assembly) yielded to the reasonable request of the Independents, the supremacy of the army might have been prevented, and the civil liberties of the nation have been established on an imperishable basis. But, by an opposite course, they threw the sectaries, as all dissenters from their policy were opprobriously styled, into the arms of the soldiery; and thus gave to the latter a *moral weight and influence* which enabled

But the cause of liberty was not destitute of advocates at this time; the Independents pleaded for a toleration so far as to include themselves and the sober Anabaptists, but did not put the controversy on the most generous foundation; they were for tolerating all who agreed in the fundamentals of Christianity, but when they came to enumerate fundamentals they were sadly embarrassed, as all must be who plead the cause of liberty, and yet do not place the religious and civil rights of mankind on a separate basis: a man may be an orthodox believer, and yet deserve death as a traitor to his king and country; and, on the other hand, a heretic or errant nonconformist to the established religion may be a loyal and dutiful subject, and deserve the highest preferment his prince can bestow.

The letter of the city divines to the Assembly received a quick reply from a writer of more generous principles, who complains, "that the Presbyterians, not content with their own freedom and liberty, nor with having their form of government made the national establishment, were grasping at as much power as the prelates before them had usurped; for this purpose they had obtained the privilege of licensing the press, that nothing might be written against them but what they should please to approve;* they were continually soliciting the Parliament to establish their church government, which they called the government of Christ, with a coercive power; they were always busy in framing petitions, and engaging the magistrates of the city to present them to the houses; and not content with this, they were now moving the Assembly of Divines, of whom themselves are a considerable part, to become the patrons of oppression." Our author maintains that "liberty of conscience is the natural right of every man, though, of all parties of men, those deserve least the countenance of the state who would persecute others, if it were in their power, because they are enemies of the society in which they live. He that will look back on past times, and examine into the true causes of the subversion and devastation of states and countries, will find it owing to the tyranny of princes and the persecution of priests. All governments, therefore, which understand their true interests, will endeavour to suppress in every sect, or division of men, whether Papist, Episcopal, Presbyterian, Independent, or Anabaptist, the spirit of dominion and persecution, which is the disturber of mankind and the offspring of the devil. But the ministers say, if we tolerate one sect we must tolerate all; which our author admits, and adds, that they have as good a right to the liberty of their consciences as to their clothes

them to crush the Parliament. The only alternative left to the assertors of civil liberty was to counterpoise the power of the Presbyterians by that of the army. The danger thus incurred has been proved by the event to be great; but it need not awaken surprise that men should have sought relief from a present and previous evil at the hazard of one that was distant and undefined. Nor must it be forgotten, in order to a correct appreciation of their conduct, that the army was yet submissive to the Parliament, and its officers free from those ambitious views by which their patriotism was ultimately eclipsed."—Vol. ii., p. 324.—C.

* Vol. Pamphlets, No. 52.

or estates; no opinions or sentiments of religion being cognizable by the magistrate, any farther than they are inconsistent with the peace of the civil government. The way to put an end to diversity of opinions is not by fines and imprisonments; can Bedlam, or the Fleet, open men's understandings, and reduce them from error? No, certainly, nothing but sound reason and argument can do it, which, it is to be feared, they are not furnished with, who have recourse to any other weapons. Schism and heresy are to be rooted out, not by oppression, but by reason and debate; by the sword of the Spirit, not of the flesh; by argument, not by blows, to which men have recourse when they are beat out of the other. Schism and heresy are words of terror thrown upon the adversary by all parties of men; and, perhaps, there may need an infallible judge to determine where the schism lies, before we venture upon extraordinary methods to extirpate it." He adds, "that persecution will breed more confusion and disturbance than toleration; and that their solemn League and Covenant ought to bind them no farther than it is consistent with the Word of God. Now that toleration, or liberty of conscience, is the doctrine of Scripture, is evident, 1. From the parable of the tares and wheat growing together till the harvest. 2. From the apostle's direction, 'Let every man be persuaded in his own mind.' 3. That 'of whatsoever is not faith, is sin.' 4. From our Saviour's golden rule, 'Whatsoever ye would that men should do to you, that do ye to them.'"

This pamphlet was answered by another, entitled "Anti-Toleration," in which the author endeavours to vindicate the most unbounded license of persecution; but neither the Assembly, nor the city divines, nor the whole Scots nation, could prevail with the Parliament to deliver the sword into their hands. The high behaviour of the Presbyterians lost them the affections of great numbers of people, who began to discover that the contention between them and the prelates was not for liberty, but power, and that all the spiritual advantage they were like to reap from the war was to shift hands, and instead of Episcopal government, to submit to the yoke of Presbyterial uniformity.

Lord Clarendon admits* that the king endeavoured to make his advantage of these divisions, by courting the Independents, and promising some of them very valuable compensations for any services they should do him; intimating that it was impossible for them to expect relief in their scruples from persons who pretended they were erecting the kingdom of Christ; but though the Independents were enemies to the Presbyterian discipline, they had no confidence in the king's promises. Mr. Whitelocke† agrees with the noble historian, that the king was watchful to take advantage of these divisions, and commanded one Ogle to write to Mr. Tho. Goodwin and Phil. Nye, two of the Independent ministers, and make them large overtures, if they would oppose the Presbyterian government intended to be imposed upon England by the Scots; but these two gentlemen very honestly acquainted their friends with the proposal, which put an end to the correspondence; all which might have convinced

* Vol. ii., p. 746.   † Ibid., p. 76.

the Presbyterians of the necessity of coming to some terms with the dissenters ; but the king's affairs were so low, that they were under no apprehensions of disturbance from that quarter at present.

The Assembly perfected nothing farther this year ; however, complaint being made of the obsolete version of the Psalms by Sternhold and Hopkins, the Parliament desired them to recommend some other to be used in churches ; accordingly, they read over Mr. Rouse's version, and after several amendments, sent it up to the House, November 14, 1645, with the following recommendation : " Whereas the honourable House of Commons, by an order bearing date November 20, 1643, have recommended the Psalms published by Mr. Rouse to the consideration of the Assembly of Divines, the Assembly has caused them to be carefully perused, and as they are now altered and amended do approve them, and humbly conceive they may be useful and profitable to the Church, if they be permitted to be publicly sung ;"* accordingly, they were authorized by the houses. Care was also taken to prevent the importation of incorrect Bibles printed in Holland.†

To return to the proceedings of Parliament. The committee for plundered ministers having reported to the House of Commons, January 28, 1645, certain blasphemies of Paul Best, who denied the Holy Trinity, the House ordered an ordinance to be brought in [March 28] to punish him with death ;‡ but several divines being appointed to confer with him, in order to convince him of his error, he confessed his belief of that doctrine in general terms before he was brought to his trial, and that he hoped to be saved thereby, but persisted in denying the personality, as a Jesuitical tenet; upon this confession his trial was put off, and he was at length discharged.

† The government of the Church being now changed into a Presbyterian form, and the war almost at an end, the Parliament resolved to apply the revenues of the cathedrals to other public uses; and accordingly, November 18, it was ordained, " That whereas the present Dean and Prebendaries of Westminster have deserted their charge, and were become delinquents to the Parliament, they did therefore ordain, that the Earl of Northumberland, with about ten other lords, and twenty-two commoners, should be a committee ; and that any person or more of them should have authority to order, direct, and dispose of the rents, issues, and profits belonging to the college, or collegiate church, and to do and execute all other acts that did any way concern either of them."§ They ordained, farther, " that the dean, prebendaries, and all other officers belonging either to the college or Church, who had absented themselves, and were become delinquents, or had not taken the Covenant, should be suspended from their several offices and palaces, and from all manner of benefit and profit arising from them, or from the arrears of them, Mr. Osbaldeston only excepted."

When the Cathedral of Hereford fell into the Parliament's hands, the dignitaries of that church were dispossessed, and their lands and revenues seized into the hands of the committee of that county. The dignitaries of the cathedral churches of Winchester and Carlisle were served in the same manner the latter end of this year, when the whole frame of the hierarchy was dissolved.

The Parliament, at the request of the Assembly of Divines, gave some marks of their favour to the University of Cambridge, which was reduced to such necessitous circumstances, by reason of the failure of their college-rents, that they could not support their students ; it was therefore ordained, April 11, 1645, "that nothing contained in any ordinance of Parliament concerning levying or paying of taxes should extend to the University of Cambridge, or any of the colleges or halls within the said university, nor to any of the rents or revenues belonging to the said university or colleges, or any of them, nor to charge any master, fellow, or scholar, or any of the said colleges, nor any reader, officer, or minister of the said universities or colleges, for any stipend, wages, or profit, arising or growing due to them, in respect of their places and employments in the said university."* They likewise confirmed all their ancient rights and privileges, and ordered the differences between the university and town to be determined according to law. On the same day, the ordinance for regulating the university, and removing scandalous ministers in the associated counties by the Earl of Manchester, mentioned in the beginning of the last year, was revived and continued.

On the 17th of April, this year, died Dr. Dan. Featly ; he was born at Charlton, in Oxfordshire, 1581, and educated at Corpus-Christi College, of which he was fellow ; upon his leaving the university he went chaplain to Sir Thomas Symmonds, the king's ambassador to the French court, where he gained reputation by his sermons and disputations with the papists.† When

* Husband's Collections, p. 636, 637.

† There was also a celebrated piece from his pen; levelled against the Baptists. It originated from a disputation which he held with four of that persuasion in Southwark, in the month of October, 1641. About two years afterward he published an account of this debate in a book entitled "The Dippers dipped ; or, the Anabaptists ducked, and plunged over head and ears, at a Disputation in Southwark." This title savoured of the taste and spirit of the times, and is no favourable omen of the strain of the work. In his dedication, he tells the reader, "that he could hardly dip his pen in anything but gall." The doctor wrote, indeed, under an irritation of spirits, from being deprived of two livings, which he enjoyed before the unhappy differences between the king and Parliament. He had the character, however, of an acute as well as vehement disputant. He had for his fellow-prisoner Mr. Henry Denne, educated at the University of Cambridge, and ordained, in 1630, by the Bishop of St. David, who signalized himself by his preaching, writing, disputing, and suffering for the baptistical opinion. As soon as he came into prison, Dr. Featly's book was laid before him in his apartment ; when he had read it, he offered to dispute with the author on the arguments of it. The challenge was accepted, and they debated on the first ten arguments, when the doctor declined proceeding, urging that it was not safe for them to dispute on the subject without license from government; but he bid Mr. Denne write, and said he would defend his own arguments. Mr. Denne, on this, drew up a learned and ingenious answer ; but it

* MS., sess. 535.   † Parl. Chr., p. 319.
‡ Whitelocke, p. 196.
§ Husband's Collections, p. 758.

he returned home he became domestic chaplain to Archbishop Abbot, and was presented by him to the Rectory of Lambeth, and in the year 1627, to that of Acton. In 1643 he was nominated of the Assembly of Divines, and sat among them till his correspondence with the court was discovered, by an intercepted letter to Archbishop Usher relating to their proceedings; upon which he was committed to Lord Peters's house as a spy, both his livings were sequestered, and himself expelled the Assembly.* The doctor was a thorough Calvinist, but very zealous for the hierarchy of the Church; so that when in prison he published the following challenge.:

"Whereas I am certainly informed that divers lecturers and preachers in London do in their pulpits, in a most insolent manner, demand where they are now that dare stand up in defence of the Church-hierarchy, or Book of Common Prayer, or any ways oppose or impugn the new-intended reformation, both in doctrine and discipline, of the Church of England; I do, and will maintain by disputation or writing, against any of them, these three conclusions:

1. "That the Articles of Religion agreed upon in the year 1562, by both houses of convocation, and ratified by Queen Elizabeth, need no alteration at all, but only an orthodox explication of some ambiguous phrases, and a vindication against false aspersions.

2. "That the discipline of the Church of England, established by many laws and acts of Parliament, that is, the government by bishops (removing all innovations and abuses in the execution thereof), is agreeable to God's Word, and a truly ancient and apostolical institution.

3. "That there ought to be a set form of public prayer; and that the Book of Common Prayer (the calendar being reformed in point of apocryphal saints and chapters, some rubrics explained, and some expressions revised, and the whole correctly printed with the Psalms, chapters, and allegations, out of the Old and New Testament, according to the last translation) is the most complete, perfect, and exact liturgy now extant in the Christian world."

The doctor was a little man, of warm passions, and exceedingly inflamed against the Parliament for his imprisonment, as appears by his last prayer a few hours before his death, which happened at Chelsea, whither he had been removed for the benefit of the air, in the sixty-fifth year of his age. His prayer had these words in it: "Lord, strike through the reins of them that rise against the Church and king, and let them be as chaff before the wind, and as stubble before the fire; let them be scattered as partridges on the mountains, and let the breath of the Lord consume them; but upon our gracious sovereign and his posterity let the crown flourish." A prayer not formed after the

model of St. Stephen's, or that of our blessed Saviour upon the cross.:

The writer of the life of Archbishop Usher says the doctor was both orthodox and loyal; but Lord Clarendon and Dr. Heylin cannot forgive his sitting in the Assembly, and being a witness against Archbishop Laud at his trial. "Whether he sat in the Assembly," says Heylin, "to show his parts, or to head a party, or out of his old love to Calvinism, may best be gathered from some speeches which he made and printed; but he was there in heart before, and therefore might afford them his body now, though, possibly, he might be excused from taking the Covenant, as others did."* ·

Soon after died famous old Mr. John Dod, whose pious and remarkable sayings are remembered to this day;† he was born at Shotlidge, in Cheshire, in the year 1550, and educated in Jesus College, Cambridge, of which he was fellow.‡ At thirty years of age he removed to Hanwell, in Oxfordshire, where he continued preaching twice on the Lord's-Day, and once on the week days, for above twenty years; at the end of which he was suspended for nonconformity by Dr. Bridges, bishop of the diocess. Being driven from Hanwell, he removed to Canons-Ashby, in Northamptonshire, and lived quietly several years, till, upon complaint made by Bishop Neal to King James, he commanded Archbishop Abbot to silence him. After the death of King James, Mr. Dod was allowed to preach publicly again, and settled at Faustly in the same county, where he remained till his death. He was a most humble, pious, and devout man, and universally beloved; an excellent Hebrician, a plain, practical, fervent preacher, a noted casuist, and charitable almost to a fault; his conversation was heavenly; but being a noted Puritan, though he never meddled with state affairs, he was severely used by the king's cavaliers, who plundered his house, and would have taken away his very sheets, if the good old man, hardly able to rise out of his chair, had not put them under him for a cushion; all which he endured patiently, calling to mind one of his own maxims,§ Sanctified afflic-

* Hist. Presb., p. 464.
† During the civil wars, when some of the soldiers came to his house and threatened to take away his life, this heavenly divine with holy confidence replied, "If you do, you will send me to heaven, where I long to be; but you can do nothing except God give you leave." His enemies called him "Faith and Repentance," because he was constantly recommending these two things. His last words were, "I desire to be dissolved, and to be with Christ."

Mr. Dod was utterly opposed to the war, and continued fixed in his allegiance to Charles. Archbishop Usher had the most exalted opinion of him, and said, "I desire that, when I die, my soul may rest with his." Nothing was ever objected to this meek and humble man but his being a Puritan! Fuller, Lloyd, Echard, and Bishop Wilkins, all praise him for holiness, learning, and great aptness to teach. He was the author of the well-known little sermon on the word "MALT." Mr. Dod is often styled the Decalogist, because he and Mr. Cleaver published "An Exposition of the Ten Commandments," 1635.—C.
‡ Clarke's Martyrol., p. 168 of the annexed lives.
§ His name has derived celebrity from his maxims, usually called Dod's Sayings: they having been printed in various forms, many of them on two sheets of paper, are still to be seen pasted on the walls of cottages. "An old woman in my neighbourhood told

does not appear that the doctor ever replied. He was esteemed one of the greatest ornaments of the Corpus-Christi College, and acquitted himself with great applause in a funeral oration on the death of its celebrated master, Dr. Rainolds, and in a public exercise with which he entertained the Archbishop of Spalato. Unwholesome air, bad diet, and worse treatment, hastened his death.—Crosby's History of the English Baptists, vol. i., p. 152 and 303; and Granger's History of England, vol. ii., p. 176, 177, 8vo.—ED. (Toulmin). 　　* See before, chap. ii.

tions are spiritual promotions.* He died of the strangury, in the ninety-six year of his age, and lies buried in his parish church at Faustly.

CHAPTER VII.

THE CONCLUSION OF THE FIRST CIVIL WAR, BY THE KING'S SURRENDERING HIS ROYAL PERSON TO THE SCOTS.—PETITIONS OF THE ASSEMBLY AND CITY DIVINES AGAINST TOLERATION, AND FOR THE DIVINE RIGHT OF THE PRESBYTERIAL GOVERNMENT, WHICH IS ERECTED IN LONDON.—DEBATES BETWEEN THE KING, MR. HENDERSON, AND THE SCOTS COMMISSIONERS.—HIS MAJESTY IS REMOVED FROM NEWCASTLE TO HOLMBY HOUSE.—FARTHER ACCOUNT OF THE SECTARIES.

THE king being returned to Oxford, November 6, 1646, after an unfortunate campaign, in which all his armies were beaten out of the field and dispersed, had no other remedy left but to make peace with his subjects, which his friends in London encouraged him to expect he might be able to accomplish by the help of some advantage from the growing divisions among the members, the majority of whom were inclined to an accommodation, provided the king would consent to abolish Episcopacy, and offer sufficient assurances to govern for the future according to law.† But though his majesty was willing to yield a little to the times, with regard to the security of the civil government, nothing could prevail with him to give up the Church. Besides, as the king's circumstances obliged him to recede, the Parliament, as conquerors, advanced in their demands. In the month of December, his majesty sent several messages to the Parliament, to obtain a personal treaty at London, upon the public faith, for himself and a certain number of his friends, residing there with safety and honour, forty days; but the Parliament would by no means trust their enemies within their own bowels, and therefore insisted peremptorily upon his signing the bills they were preparing to send him, as a preliminary to a well-grounded settlement.

The king made some concession on his part relating to the militia and liberty of conscience, but very far short of the demand of the two houses, who were so persuaded of his art and ability in the choice of ambiguous expressions, capable of a different sense from what appeared at first sight, that they durst not venture to make use of them as the basis of a treaty.‡ Thus the winter was wasted in fruitless messages between London and Oxford; while the unfortunate king spent his time musing over his papers in a most disconsolate manner, forsaken by some of his friends, and rudely treated by others. Mr. Locke says, the usage the king met with from his followers at Oxford made it a hard, but almost an even choice, to be the Parliament's prisoner, or their slave. In his majesty's letter to the queen he writes, "If thou knew what a

life I lead in point of conversation, I dare say thou would pity me." The chief officers quarrelled, and became insupportably insolent in the royal presence; nor was the king himself without blame; for, being deprived of his oracle the queen, he was like a ship in a storm without sails or rudder. Lord Clarendon,* therefore, draws a veil over his majesty's conduct in these words: "It is not possible to discourse of particulars with the clearness that is necessary to subject them to common understandings, without opening a door for such reflections upon the king himself as seem to call both his wisdom and steadiness in question: as if he wanted the one to apprehend and discover, and the other to prevent, the mischiefs that were evident and impending." And yet nothing could prevail with him to submit to the times, or deal frankly with those who alone were capable of retrieving his affairs.

The king having neither money nor forces, and the queen's resources from abroad failing, his majesty could not take the field in the spring, which gave the Parliament army an easy conquest over his remaining forts and garrisons. All the west was reduced before midsummer, by the victorious army of Sir Thos. Fairfax; the city of Exeter surrendered April 9, in which one of the king's daughters, Princess Henrietta, was made prisoner, but her governess, the Countess of Dalkeith, found means afterward to convey her privately into France. Dennington Castle surrendered April 1, Barnstaple the 12th, and Woodstock the 26th; upon which it was resolved to strike the finishing blow, by besieging the king in his headquarters at Oxford; upon the news of which, like a man in a fright, he left the city in the night, April 27, and travelled as a servant to Dr. Hudson and Mr. Ashburnham, with his hair cut round to his ears, and a cloke bag behind him, to the Scots army before Newark.† His majesty surrendered himself to General Leven, May 5, who received him with respect, but sent an express immediately to the two houses, who were displeased at his majesty's conduct, apprehending it calculated to prolong the war, and occasion a difference between the two nations; which was certainly intended, as appears by the king's letter to the Duke of Ormond, in which he says he had good security that he and his adherents should be safe in their persons, honours, and consciences in the Scots army, and that they would join with him, and employ their forces to obtain a happy and well-grounded peace: whereas the Scots commissioners, in their letter to the House of Peers, aver, "they had given no assurance, nor made any capitulation for joining forces with the king, or combining against the two houses, or any other private or public agreement whatsoever, between the king on one part, and the kingdom of Scotland, their army, or any in their names, and having power from them, on the other part;" and they called the contrary assertion a damnable untruth; and add, "that they never expect a blessing from God any longer than they continue faithful to their Covenant."‡ So that this must be the ar-

---

me," says Mr. Granger, "that she should have gone distracted for the loss of her husband, if she had been without Mr. Dod's Sayings in the house."—*History of England*, vol. i., p. 370, 8vo.—ED.

* Fuller's Ch. Hist., p. 220.   † Rapin, p. 320.
‡ Rushworth, vol. vi., p. 215, 216.

* Vol. iv., p. 626.
† Rapin, vol. ii., p. 523. Rushworth, vol. vi., p. 268, 273, 274, 303, 304.
‡ Dr. Grey, to confute these declarations, which

tifice of Montreville, the French ambassador, who undertook to negotiate between the two parties, and drew the credulous and distressed king into that snare, out of which he could never escape.

His majesty surrendered his person to the Scots, and sending orders to the governors of Newark, Oxford, and all his other garrisons and forces, to surrender and disband, concluded the first civil war; upon which most of the officers, with Prince Rupert and Maurice, retired beyond sea; so that by the middle of August all the king's forces and castles were in the Parliament's hands, Ragland Castle being the last; which was four years, wanting three days, from the setting up the royal standard at Nottingham.

Some time before the king left Oxford,* he had commissioned the Marquis of Ormond to conclude a peace with the Irish papists, in hopes of receiving succours from thence, which gave great offence to the Parliament; but though his majesty, upon surrendering himself to the Scots, wrote to the marquis, June 11,† not to proceed, he ventured to put the finishing hand to the treaty, July 28, 1646, upon the following scandalous articles,‡ among others, which surely the marquis durst not have consented to, without some private instructions from the king and queen.

1. "That the Roman Catholics of that kingdom shall be discharged from taking the oath of supremacy.

2. "That all acts of Parliament made against them shall be repealed; that they be allowed the freedom of their religion, and not be debarred from any of his majesty's graces or favours.

3. "That all acts reflecting on the honour of the Roman Catholic religion, since August 7, 1641, be repealed.

4. "That all indictments, attainders, outlawries, &c., against them, or any of them, be vacated and made void.

5. "That all impediments that may hinder their sitting in Parliament, or, being chosen burgesses, or knights of the shire, be removed.

6. "That all incapacities imposed upon the nation be taken away, and that they have power to erect one or more inns of court in or near the city of Dublin; and that all Catholics educated there be capable of taking their degrees without the oath of supremacy.

7. "That the Roman Catholics shall be empowered to erect one or more universities, and keep free-schools for the education of their youth, any law or statute to the contrary notwithstanding.

8. "That places of command, honour, profit, and trust, shall be conferred on the Roman Catholics, without making any difference between them and Protestants, both in the army and in the civil government.*

9. "That an act of oblivion shall be passed in the next Parliament, to extend to all the Roman Catholics, and their heirs, absolving them of all treasons and offences whatsoever, and particularly of the massacre of 1641,† so that no person shall be impeached, troubled, or molested, for anything done on one side or the other.

10. "That the Roman Catholics shall continue in possession of all those cities, forts, garrisons, and towns that they are possessed of, till things are come to a full settlement."‡

Was this the way to establish a good understanding between the king and his two houses? or could they believe that his majesty meant the security of the Protestant religion, and the extirpation of popery in England, when his general consented to such a peace in Ireland, without any marks of his sovereign's displeasure? nay, when, after a long treaty with the Parliament commissioners, he refused to deliver up the forts and garrisons into their hands, insomuch that, after six weeks' attendance, they were obliged to return to their ships, and carry back the supplies they had brought for the garrisons,§ having only published a declaration that

---

Mr. Neal has brought forward, quotes several affidavits and assertions of Dr. Hudson: the substance of which is, that the Scots agreed to secure the person and honour of the king; to press him to nothing contrary to his conscience; to protect Mr. Ashburnham and himself; and if the Parliament refused to restore the king, upon a message from him, to his rights and prerogatives, to declare for him, and take all his friends into their protection. But the doctor omits to observe, that Hudson spoke on the authority of the French agent, one Montreville, who negotiated the business between the king and the Scots; and who, it appears, promised to the king more than he was empowered, and was recalled and disgraced.—*Rapin*, vol. ii., p. 523, 524. It is more easy to conceive that Montreville exceeded his commission, as, according to Hudson's confession, quoted by Dr. Grey, the Scots would not give anything under their hands.—ED.

* It was before leaving Oxford that Charles wrote to Lord Digby, in which he says, "*I desire you to assure my friends that if I cannot live as a king, I shall die like a gentleman*, without doing that which may make honest men blush for me." His course with the commissioners hardly accorded with this profession.—C.

† Lord Digby wished to have it understood that this letter was surreptitious, or a forged one from his majesty, and most contrary to what he knew to be his free resolution and unconstrained will and pleasure.—*Dr. Grey.*—ED.

‡ Mr. Neal, as Dr. Grey observes, gives only a very concise abridgment of these articles, which were thirty in number, and, as they stand in Rushworth, take up almost twelve pages in folio. But Mr. Neal's view of some of them, though the doctor calls it curtailing them, is sufficient to show the tenour and spirit of the whole.—ED.

* Rushworth, part iv., vol. i., p. 402.

† But it was provided that such barbarities as should be agreed on by the lord-lieutenant and the Lord-viscount Mountgarret, or any five or more of them, should be tried by such indifferent commissioners as they should appoint.—*Dr. Grey.*—ED.

‡ Our author having called the preceding propositions "scandalous articles," Dr. Grey appeals from his sentence to the remonstrance of the Protestant archbishops, bishops, and inferior clergy of the kingdom of Ireland to the lord-lieutenant, on the 11th and 13th of August, 1646, in which they express a strong and grateful sense of obligation for the peace established among them. But it will still remain a question, whether the sentiment of these prelates and clergy were disinterested and judicious.—ED.

§ Our author incurs here the censure of Dr. Grey for not "affording us any authority in proof of this assertion." The editor confesses that he cannot supply the omission. Dr. Grey confronts Mr. Neal with large quotations from Lord Clarendon's History of the Rebellion in Ireland, p. 53, 54, 65, 66, 73–75. But they appear not to the point for which they are produced. The purport of them is, "That the Mar-the Parliament of England would take all the Protestants of Ireland into their protection, and send over an army to carry on the war against the papists with vigour.

The king being now in the hands of the Scots, the English Presbyterians at London resumed their courage, concluding they could not fail of a full establishment of their discipline, and of bringing the Parliament at Westminster to their terms of uniformity; for this purpose, they framed a bold remonstrance in the name of the lord-mayor, aldermen, and common council, and presented it to the House, May 26, complaining,* "that the reins of discipline were let loose; that particular congregations were allowed to take up what form of Divine service they pleased, and that sectaries began to swarm by virtue of a toleration granted to tender consciences. They put the Parliament in mind of their Covenant, which obliged them to endeavour the extirpation of popery, prelacy, superstition, heresy, schism, profaneness, and whatsoever else was found contrary to sound doctrine; and, at the same time, to preserve and defend the person and authority of the king; they therefore desired, since the whole kingdom was now in a manner reduced to the obedience of the Parliament, that all separate congregations may be suppressed; that all such separatists who conform not to the public discipline may be declared against; that no person disaffected to the Presbyterial government sent forth by Parliament may be employed in any place of public trust;† that the House will endeavour to remove all jealousies between them and the Scots, and hasten their propositions to the king for a safe and well-grounded peace."‡

This remonstrance was supported by the whole Scots nation, who acted in concert with their English brethren, as appears by a letter of thanks to the lord-mayor, aldermen, and common council, from the General Assembly, dated June 10, 1646, within a month after the delivery of the remonstrance:§ the letter commends their courageous appearance against

quis of Ormond resolved not to proceed to any conjunction with the commissioners without his majesty's express directions, for which he privately despatched several expresses; that, in consequence of this, the commissioners, not obtaining possession of the garrisons, returned with all their supplies to their ships; that the marquis received his majesty's order not to deliver up the garrisons, if it were possible to keep them under the same entire obedience to his majesty; but should there be a necessity, to put them into the hands of the English, rather than of the Irish." The rest of the quotation describes the difficulties and distresses under which the marquis laboured, which drove him at last to make a disadvantageous agreement with the commissioners. The reader will judge whether, by these references, Mr. Neal's assertions are not, instead of being confuted, established.—See, also, Mrs. Macaulay, vol. iv., p. 250, note (†).—ED. * Vol. Pamp., No. 34.

† Presbyterianism thus displayed the same intolerance as Episcopacy had done. "Religious tyranny," observes Mr. Robinson, "subsists in various degrees, as all civil tyrannies do. Popery is the consummation of it, and Presbyterianism a weak degree of it. But the latter has in it the essence of the former, and differs from it only as a kept-mistress differs from a street-walker, or as a musket differs from a cannon."—Plan of Lectures, 5th edition, p. 38.—ED. (TOULMIN). ‡ Whitelocke's Memorials, p. 212. § Rushworth, p. 306.

sects and sectaries; their firm adherence to the Covenant, and their maintaining the Presbyterial government to be the government of Jesus Christ. It beseeches them to go on boldly in the work they had begun, till the three kingdoms were united in one faith and worship. At the same time, they directed letters to the Parliament, beseeching them, also, in the bowels of Jesus Christ, to give to him the glory that is due to his name, by an immediate establishing of all his ordinances in their full integrity and power, according to the Covenant. Nor did they forget to encourage the Assembly at Westminster to proceed in their zeal against sectaries, and to stand boldly for the sceptre of Jesus Christ against the encroachments of earthly powers. These letters were printed, and dispersed over the whole kingdom.

The wise Parliament received the lord-mayor and his brethren with marks of great respect and civility; for neither the Scots nor English Presbyterians were to be disgusted while the prize was in their hands for which both had been contending; but the majority of the Commons were displeased with the remonstrance, and the high manner of enforcing it, as aiming, by a united force, to establish a sovereign despotic power in the Church, with a uniformity to which themselves, and many of their friends, were unwilling to submit; however, they dismissed the petitioners, with a promise to take the particulars into consideration.

But the Independents and sectarians in the army, being alarmed at the impending storm, procured a counter petition from the city with great numbers of hands, "applauding the labours and successes of the Parliament in the cause of liberty, and praying them to go on with managing the affairs of the kingdom according to their wisdoms, and not suffer the freeborn people of England to be enslaved upon any pretence whatsoever; nor to suffer any set of people to prescribe to them in matters of government or conscience, and the petitioners will stand by them with their lives and fortunes." Mr. Whitelocke says the hands of the Royalists were in this affair, who, being beaten out of the field, resolved now to attempt the ruin of the Parliament, by sowing discord among their friends.*

The houses were embarrassed between the contenders for liberty and uniformity, and endeavoured to avoid a decision till they saw the effect of their treaty with the king. They kept the Presbyterians in suspense, by pressing the Assembly for their answer to the questions relating to the jus divinum of Presbytery already mentioned, insinuating that they themselves were the obstacles to a full settlement, and assuring them, when this point was agreed, they would concur in such an ordinance as they desired. Upon this the Assembly appointed three committees to take the questions into consideration; but the Independents took this opportunity to withdraw, refusing absolutely to be concerned in the affair.

The first committee was appointed to determine whether any particular church government was jure divino, and to bring their proofs from Scripture. But here they stumbled at the

* Oldmixon's History of the Stuarts, p. 308. Memorials, p. 213.

very threshold, for the Erastians divided them, and entered their dissent, so that when the answer was laid before the Assembly, it was not called the answer of the committee, but of some brethren of the committee; and when the question was put, they withdrew from the Assembly, and left the high Presbyterians to themselves, who agreed, with only one dissenting voice, that Jesus Christ, as king of the Church, hath himself appointed a church government distinct from the civil magistrate. The names of those who subscribed this proposition were,

Rev. Mr. White.	Rev. Dr. Staunton.
Mr. Palmer.	Dr. Hoyle.
Dr. Wincop.	Mr. Bayly.
Mr. Ley.	Mr. Taylor.
Dr. Gouge.	Mr. Young.
Mr. Walker.	Mr. Cawdrey.
Mr. Sedgwick.	Mr. Ash.
Mr. Marshal.	Mr. Gibson.
Mr. Whitaker.	Mr. Good.
Mr. Newcomen.	Mr. Vines.
Mr. Spurstow.	Mr. Seaman.
Mr. Delmy.	Mr. Chambers.
Mr. Calamy.	Mr. Corbet.
Mr. Proffet.	Mr. Dury.
Mr. Perne.	Mr. Salway.
Mr. Scuddir.	Mr. Hardwicke.
Mr. Carter, Sen.	Mr. Langley.
Mr. Caryl.	Mr. Simpson.
Mr. Woodcocke.	Mr. Conant.
Mr. Carter, Jun.	Mr. De la March.
Mr. Goodwin.	Mr. Byfield.
Mr. Nye.	Mr. Herle.
Mr. Greenhill.	Mr. De la Place.
Mr. Valentine.	Mr. Wilison.
Mr. Price.	Mr. Reyner.
Dr. Smith.	Mr. Gower.

The divine who entered his dissent was Mr. Lightfoot, with whom Mr. Colman would have joined, if he had not fallen sick at this juncture, and died.

The discussing the remaining questions engaged the Assembly from May till the latter end of July, and even then they thought it not safe to present their determinations to Parliament, for fear of a premunire; upon which the city divines at Sion College took up the controversy in a treatise entitled " The Divine Right of Church Government," by the London ministers. Wherein they give a distinct answer to the several queries of the House of Commons, and undertake to prove every branch of the Presbyterial discipline to be *jure divino*, and that the civil magistrate had no right to intermeddle with the censures of the Church.

And to show the Parliament they were in earnest, they resolved to stand by each other, and not comply with the present establishment, till it was delivered from the yoke of the civil magistrate; for which purpose they drew up a paper of reasons, and presented it to the lord-mayor, who, having advised with the common council, sent a deputation to Sion College, offering to concur in a petition for redress, which they did accordingly, though without effect; for the Parliament, taking notice of the combination of the city ministers, published an order June 9, requiring those of the province of London to observe the ordinance relating to church government, enjoining the members for the city to send copies thereof to their several parishes, and to take effectual care that they were immediately put in execution. Upon this the ministers of London and Westminster met again at Sion College June 19, and being a little more submissive, published certain considerations and cautions, according to which they agree to put the Presbyterial government in practice according to the present establishment. Here they declare, "that the power of church censures ought to be in church officers, by the will and appointment of Jesus Christ, but then they are pleased to admit that the magistracy ought to be satisfied in the truth of the government they authorize; and though it be not right in every particular, yet church officers may act under that rule, provided they do not acknowledge the rule to be right in all points; therefore, though they conceive the ordinances of Parliament already published are not a complete rule, nor in all points satisfactory to their consciences, yet because in many things they are so, and provision being made to enable the elderships, by their authority, to keep away from the Lord's Supper all ignorant and scandalous persons; and a farther declaration being made, that there shall be an addition to the scandalous offences formerly enumerated, therefore they conceive it their duty to put in practice the present settlement, as far as they conceive it correspondent with the Word of God; hoping that the Parliament will in due time supply what is lacking to make the government entire, and rectify what shall appear to be amiss." Thus reluctantly did these gentlemen bend to the authority of the Parliament!*

The kingdom of England, instead of so many dioceses, was now divided into a certain number of provinces, made up of representatives from the several classes within their respective boundaries; every parish had a congregational or parochial presbytery for the affairs of the parish; the parochial presbyteries were combined into classes; these returned representatives to the Provincial Assembly, as the Provincial did to the National; for example, the province of London being composed of twelve classes, according to the following division, each classis chose two ministers and four lay-elders, to represent them in a Provincial Assembly, which received general appeals from the parochial and classical presbyteries, as the National Assembly did from the Provincial.

THE DIVISION OF THE PROVINCE OF LONDON.

The first classis to contain the following parishes:

1. Allhallows, Bread-street.	6. St. John Evangelist.	11. St. Mary Aldermary.
2. Andrew's Wardrobe.	7. Margaret Moses.	12. St. Mary le Bow.
3. Bennet, Paul's Wharf.	8. St. Martin, Ludgate.	13. St. Matthew, Friday-street.
4. Faith's.	9. St. Anne, Blackfriars.	14. Mildred, Bread-st., St. Paul's.
5. St. Gregory.	10. St. Austin's.	15. St. Peter's, Paul's Wharf.

---

* It would be difficult for Mr. Hetherington to justify the presumptuous slur with which he alludes to Neal at this passage. The history of the Assembly seems to be faithfully reported by the historian of the Puritans.—C.

The second classis.

1. St. Antholine.	6. St. Mary Magdal., Old Fish-st.	11. St. Nicholas, Old Abby.
2. Bennet Sheerhog.	7. St. Mary, Somerset.	12. St. Nicholas Olives.
3. St. James, Garlickhithe.	8. St. Mary Mounthaw.	13. Pancras, Soper's Lane.
4. St. John Baptist.	9. St. Micnael, Queenhithe.	14. St. Thomas Apostle.
5. Martin the Vintry.	10. St. Michael Royal.	15. Trinity.

The third classis.

1. Allhallows the Greater.	5. Lawrence Pountney.	9. St. Mary Woolnoth.
2. Allhallows the Less.	6. St. Mary Abchurch.	10. St. Nicholas Aaron.
3. Allhallows, Lombard-street.	7. St. Mary Bothaw.	11. St. Stephen's, Walbrook.
4. St. Edmund, Lombard-street.	8. St. Mary Woolchurch.	12. St. Swithin's.

The fourth classis.

1. St. Andrews Hubbert.	6. St. George, Botolph Lane.	11. St. Mary Hill.
2. St. Bennet, Grace Church.	7. St. Leonard, Eastcheap.	12. St. Michael, Crooked Lane.
3. St. Botolph, Billingsgate.	8. St. Magnus.	13. St. Michael, Cornhill.
4. St. Clement, Eastcheap.	9. St. Margaret, New Fish-street.	14. St. Peter, Cornhill.
5. Dionis Back-church.	10. St. Martin Orgars.	

The fifth classis.

1. St. Anne, Aldersgate.	5. Christ Church.	9. St. Michael in the Corn, vulgo
2. St. Botolph, Aldersgate.	6. St. John Zachary.	in the Querne.
3. St. Bride's.	7. St. Leonard, Foster Lane.	10. St. Olave, Silver-street.
4. Bridewell.	8. St. Mary Staynings.	11. St. Peter, Cheap.
		12. St. Foster, alias Vedast.

The sixth classis.

1. St. Alban, Wood-street.	6. St. Lawrence, Jewry.	10. St. Mary Colechurch.
2. Allhallows, Honey Lane.	7. St. Martin, Ironmonger Lane.	11. St. Michael, Wood-street.
3. St. Alphage.	8. St. Mary, Aldermanbury.	12. St. Mildred, Poultry.
4. St. Giles, Cripplegate.	9. St. Mary Magdalen, Milk-street.	13. St. Olave, Jewry.
5. St. James's Chapel.		

The seventh classis.

1. Allhallows in the Wall.	4. St. Botolph, Bishopsgate.	7. St. Michael, Bassishaw.
2. St. Bartholomew, Exchange.	5. St. Christopher's.	8. St. Peter Poor.
3. St. Bennet Finck.	6. St. Margaret, Lothbury.	9. St. Stephen, Coleman-street.

The eighth classis.

1. St. Andrew Undershaft.	5. St. Helen's.	8. St. Leonard, Shoreditch.
2. St. Botolph, Aldgate.	6. St. James, Duke Place.	9. St. Martin, Outwich.
3. St. Ethelburga.	7. St. Katherine, Creechurch.	10. St. Mary, Stoke-Newington.
4. St. John, Hackney.		

The ninth classis.

1. Allhallows Barking.	6. St. Katherine, Tower.	10. Stepney.
2. Allhallows Steyning.	7. St. Margaret Pattoons.	11. Trinity, Minories.
3. St. Dunstan in the East.	8. St. Olive, Hart-street.	12. Wapping.
4. St. Gabriel, Fenchurch.	9. St. Peter in the Tower.	13. Whitechapel.
5. St. Katherine, Coleman.		

The tenth classis.

1. St. George, Southwark.	4. St. Mary Overies.	7. Rotherhithe.
2. Lambeth.	5. Newington Butts.	8. St. Thomas's Hospital.
3. St. Mary Magdalen, Bermond-sey.	6. St. Olave, Southwark.	9. St. Thomas's, Southwark.

The eleventh classis.

1. St. Clement Danes.	4. St. Margaret, Westminster.	7. St. Peter, Westminster.
2. St. Giles in the Fields.	5. St. Martin in the Fields.	8. St. Paul, Covent Garden.
3. Knightsbridge.	6. New Church.	

The twelfth classis.

1. St. Andrew, Holborn.	4. Charter House.	7. St. Mary, Islington.
2. St. Bartholomew the Greater.	5. St. Dunstan in the West.	8. St. Sepulchre's.
3. St. Bartholomew the Less.	6. St. James's, Clerkenwell.	

Thus the Presbyterian ecclesiastical government began to appear in its proper form; but new obstructions being raised by the ministers to the choice of representatives, the Provincial Assembly did not meet till next year, nor did it ever obtain except in London and Lancashire. The Parliament never heartily approved it, and the interest that supported it being quickly disabled, Mr. Echard says, the Presbyterians never saw their dear presbytery settled in any one part of England.* But Mr. Baxter, who is a much better authority, says the ordinance was executed in London and Lancashire, though it

remained unexecuted in almost all other parts. However, the Presbyterian ministers had their voluntary associations for church affairs in most counties, though without any authoritative jurisdiction.

To return to the king, who marched with the Scots army from Newark to Newcastle, where he continued about eight months, being treated with some respect, but not with all the duty of subjects to a sovereign. The first sermon that was preached before him gave hopes* that they

* Echard, p. 634.

* Mr. Whitelocke informs us (Memorials, p. 234), " that a Scotch minister preached boldly before the king, December 16, 1646, at Newcastle, and after his

would be mediators between him and the Parliament ; it was from 2 Sam., xix., 41–43, " And behold, all the men of Israel came to the king, and said to the king,- Why have the men of Judah stolen thee away ? And all the men of Judah answered the men of Israel, Because the king is near of kin to us ; wherefore then be ye angry for this matter ? have we eaten at all of the king's cost ? or hath he given us any gift ? And the men of Israel answered the men of Judah, and said, We have ten parts in the king ; and we have also more right in David than ye ; why then did ye despise us, that our advice should not be first had, in bringing back our king ? And the words of the men of Judah were fiercer than the words of the men of Israel." But it quickly appeared that nothing would be done except upon condition of the king's taking the Covenant, and establishing the Presbyterial government in both kingdoms. When the king was pressed upon these heads, he pleaded his conscience, and declared that, though he was content the Scots should enjoy their own discipline, he apprehended his honour and conscience were concerned to support Episcopacy in England, because it had been established from the Reformation, and that he was bound to uphold it by his coronation oath ; however, he was willing to enter into a conference with any person whom they should appoint, protesting he was not ashamed to change his judgment or alter his resolution, provided they could satisfy him in two points :

1st. That the Episcopacy he contended for was not of Divine institution. 2dly. That his coronation oath did not bind him to support and defend the Church of England as it was then established.

To satisfy the king in these points, the Scots sent for Mr. Alexander Henderson from Edinburgh, pastor of a church in that city, rector of the university, and one of the king's chaplains, a divine of great learning and abilities, as well as discretion and prudence. Mr. Rushworth says that he had more moderation than most of his way ; and Collyer adds, that he was a person of learning, elocution, and judgment, and seems to have been the top of his party.* The debate was managed in writing : the king drew up his own papers, and gave them Sir Robert Murray to transcribe, and deliver to Mr. Henderson ;† and Mr. Henderson's hand not being so legible as his, Sir Robert, by the king's appointment, transcribed Mr. Henderson's papers for his majesty's use.‡

sermon called for the fifty second Psalm, which be-

 ' Why dost thou, tyrant, boast thyself,
  Thy wicked works to praise ?'
His majesty thereupon stood up and called for the fifty-sixth Psalm, which begins,
 ' Have mercy, Lord, on me I pray,
  For men would me devour.'
The people waived the minister's psalm, and sung that which the king called for."—ED.
 * Collyer, p. 848.
 † Duke of Hamilton's Memoirs, 277.
 ‡ Dr. Grey blames Mr. Neal here for omitting Bishop Burnet's account of the king's superiority in this controversy. " Had his majesty's arms," says the bishop, " been as strong as his reason was, he had been every way unconquerable, since none have the disingenuity to deny the great advantage his maj-

The king, in his first paper of May 29, declares his esteem for the English Reformation, because it was effected without tumult, and was directed by those who ought to have had the conduct of such an affair.* He apprehends they kept close to apostolical appointment, and the universal custom of the primitive Church ; that therefore the adhering to Episcopacy must be of the last importance, as without it the priesthood must sink, and the sacraments be administered without effect ; for these reasons he conceives Episcopacy necessary to the being of a church, and also, that he is bound to support it by his coronation oath. Lastly, his majesty desires to know of Mr. Henderson what warrant there is in the Word of God for subjects to endeavour to force their king's conscience, or to make him alter laws against his will.

Mr. Henderson, in his first paper of June 3, after an introduction of modesty and respect, wishes, when occasion requires, that religion might always be reformed by the civil magistrate, and not left either to the prelates or the people ; but when princes or magistrates are negligent of their duty, God may stir up the subject to perform this work.† He observes, that the Reformation of King Henry VIII. was very defective in the essentials of doctrine, worship, and government ; that it proceeded with a Laodicean lukewarmness ; that the supremacy was transferred from one wrong head to another, and the limbs of the anti-Christian hierarchy were visible in the body. He adds, that the imperfection of the English Reformation had been the complaint of many religious and godly persons ; that it had occasioned more schism and separation than had been heard of elsewhere, and had been matter of unspeakable grief to other churches. As to the king's argument, that the validity of the priesthood, and the efficacy of the sacraments, depended upon Episcopacy, he replies, that Episcopacy cannot make out its claim to apostolical appointment ; that, when the apostles were living, there was no difference between a bishop and a presbyter ; no inequality in power or degree, but an exact parity in every branch of their character ; that there is no mention in Scripture of a pastor or bishop superior to other pastors. There is a beautiful subordination in the ministry of the New Testament ; one kind of ministers being placed in degree and dignity above another, as first apostles, then evangelists, then pastors and teachers, but in offices of the same rank and kind we do not find any preference ; no apostle is constituted superior to other apostles ; no evangelist is raised above other evangelists ; nor has any pastor or deacon a superiority above others of their order.

Farther, Mr. Henderson humbly desires his majesty to take notice, that arguing from the

esty had in all these writings ; and this was when the help of his chaplains could not be suspected, they being so far from him ; and that the king drew with his own hand all his papers without the help of any, is averred by the person who alone was privy to the interchanging of them, that worthy and accomplished gentleman, Robert Murray." The bishop's opinion may be justly admitted as a testimony to the ability with which the king handled the question ; and yet some allowance should be made for the bias with which this prelate would naturally review arguments in favour of *his own sentiments and rank*.—ED.
 * Bibl. Reg., p. 296. † Ibid., p. 312, &c.

practice of the primitive Church, and the con-sent of the Fathers, is fallacious and uncertain, and that the law and testimony of the Word of God are the only rule. The practice of the primitive Church, in many things, cannot certainly be known, as Eusebius confesses that even in the apostles' time Diotrephes moved for the pre-eminence, and the mystery of iniquity began to work; and that, afterward, ambition and weakness quickly made way for a change in church government.

Mr. Henderson hopes his majesty will not deny the lawfulness of the ministry, and due administration of the sacraments, in those Reformed churches where there are no diocesan bishops; *that it is evident from Scripture, and confessed by many champions for Episcopacy, that presbyters may ordain presbyters*; and to disengage his majesty from his coronation oath, as far as relates to the Church, he conceives, when the formal reason of an oath ceases, the obligation is discharged; when an oath has a special regard to the benefit of those to whom the engagement is made, if the parties interested relax upon the point, dispense with the promise, and give up their advantage, the obligation is at an end. Thus, when the Parliaments of both kingdoms have agreed to the repealing of a law, the king's conscience is not tied against signing the bill, for then the altering any law would be impracticable. He concludes with observing, that King James never admitted Episcopacy upon Divine right; and that, could his ghost now speak, he would not advise your majesty to 'run such hazards, for men [prelates] who would pull down your throne with their own, rather than that they perish alone.'

The king, in his second paper* of June 6, avers no reformation is lawful, unless under the conduct of the royal authority; that King Henry VIII.'s reformation being imperfect, is no proof of defects in that of King Edward VI. and Queen Elizabeth; that Mr. Henderson can never prove God has given the multitude leave to reform the negligence of princes; that his comparing our Reformation to the Laodicean lukewarmness, was an unhandsome way of begging the question, for he should have first made out that those men [the Puritans] had reason to complain, and that the schism was chargeable upon the conformists. His majesty is so far from allowing the Presbyterian government to be practised in the primitive times, that he affirms that it was never set up before Calvin; and admits that it was his province to show the lawfulness, and uninterrupted succession, and, by consequence, the necessity of Episcopacy; but that he had not then the convenience of books, nor the assistance of such learned men as he could trust, and therefore proposes a conference with his divines. And whereas Mr. Henderson excepts to his reasoning from the primitive Church and consent of the fathers, his majesty conceives his exception indefensible; for if the sense of a doubtful place of Scripture is not to be governed by such an authority, the interpretation of the inspired writings must be left to the direction of every private spirit, which is contrary to St. Peter's doctrine, 2 Pet., i., 20, "No prophecy of Scripture is of private interpretation;" it is likewise the source of all

sects, and, without prevention, will bring these kingdoms into confusion. His majesty adds, that it is Mr. Henderson's part to prove that presbyters without a bishop may ordain other presbyters. As to the administration of the sacraments, Mr. Henderson himself will not deny a lawfully-ordained presbyter's being necessary to that office; so that the determination of this latter question will depend in some measure on the former. With regard to oaths, his majesty allows Mr. Henderson's general rule, but thinks he is mistaken in the application; for the clause touching religion in the coronation oath was made only for the benefit of the Church of England; that, therefore, it is in the power of the two houses of Parliament to discharge the obligation of this oath, without their consent. That this Church never made any submission to the two houses, nor owned herself subordinate to them; that the Reformation was managed by the king and clergy, and the Parliament assisted only in giving a civil sanction to the ecclesiastical establishment. These points being clear to his majesty, it follows, by necessary consequence, that it is only the Church of England, in whose favour he took this oath, that can release him from it, and that, therefore, when the Church of England, lawfully assembled, shall declare his majesty discharged, he shall then, and not till then, reckon himself at liberty.*

Mr. Henderson, in his reply to this second paper of June 17, agrees with the king, that the prime reforming power is in kings and princes, but adds, that in case they fail of their duty, this authority devolves upon the inferior magistrate, and upon their failure, to the body of the people, upon supposition that a reformation is necessary, and that people's superiors will by no means give way to it; he allows that such a reformation is more imperfect with respect to the manner, but commonly more perfect and refined in the product and issue. He adds, that the government of the Church of England is not supposed to be built on the foundation of Christ and his apostles, by those who confess that church government is mutable and ambulatory, as was formerly the opinion of most of the English bishops; that the Divine right was not pleaded till of late by some few; that the English Reformation has not perfectly purged out the Roman leven, but rather depraved the discipline of the Church by conforming to the civil polity, and adding many supplemental officers to those instituted by the Son of God. To his majesty's objections, that the Presbyterian government was never practised before Calvin's time, he answers, that it is to be found in Scripture; and the Assembly of Divines at Westminster had made it evident that the primitive Church at Jerusalem was governed by a presbytery; that the church at Jerusalem consisted of more congregations than one; that all these congregations were combined under one Presbyterial government, and made but one church; that this church was governed by elders of the same body, and met together for functions of authority, and that the apostles acted not in quality of apostles, but only as elders, Acts, xv.; that the same government was settled in the churches of Ephesus, Corinth, Thessalonica, and continued

* Bib. Reg., p. 320, 322, &c.

* Bib. Reg., p. 325.

many years after; and at last, when one of the presbytery presided over the rest with the style of bishop, even then, as St. Jerome says, churches were governed with the joint consent of the presbytery, and it was custom, rather than Divine appointment, which raised a bishop above a presbyter. To his majesty's argument, that where the meaning of Scripture is doubtful, we must have recourse to the fathers, Mr. Henderson replies, that notwithstanding the decrees of councils, and the resolutions of the fathers, a liberty must be left for a judgment of discretion, as had been sufficiently shown by Bishop Davenant and others. To prove presbyters may ordain other presbyters without a bishop, he cites St. Paul's advice to Timothy, 1 Tim., iv., 14, not to neglect the gift that was given him by the laying on of the hands of the presbytery; but granting bishops and presbyters to be distinct functions, it will not follow that the authority and force of the presbyter's character were derived from the bishop; for though the evangelists and seventy disciples were inferior to the apostles, they received not their commission from the apostles, but from Christ himself.

Concerning the king's coronation oath, Mr. Henderson apprehends nothing need be added. As to the supremacy, he thinks such a headship as the kings of England claim, or such a one as the two houses of Parliament now insist on, that is, an authority to receive appeals from the supreme ecclesiastical judicatures, in things purely spiritual, is not to be justified; nor does he apprehend the consent of the clergy to be absolutely necessary to church reformation, for if so, what reformation can be expected in France, in Spain, or in Rome itself? It is not to be imagined that the pope or prelates will consent to their own ruin. His majesty had said, that if his father, King James, had been consulted upon the question of resistance, he would have answered, that prayers and tears are the Church's weapons. To which Mr. Henderson replies, that he could never hear a good reason to prove a necessary defensive war, a war against unjust violence, unlawful; and that Bishop Jewel and Bilson were of this mind. To the question, What warrant there was in Scripture for subjects to endeavour to force their king's conscience? he replies, that when a man's conscience is mistaken, it lies under a necessity of doing amiss; the way, therefore, to disentangle himself is to get his conscience better informed, and not to move till he has struck a light and made farther discoveries.* ∴

The king, in his answer of June 22, to Mr. Henderson's second paper, still insists that inferior magistrates and people have no authority to reform religion. If this point can be proved by Scripture, his majesty is ready to submit; but the sacred history in the Book of Numbers, chap. xvi., is an evidence of God's disapproving such methods. Private men's opinions disjoined from the general consent of the Church signify little, for rebels, says his majesty, never want writers to maintain their revolt. Though his majesty has a regard for Bishop Jewel and Bilson's memories, he never thought them infallible; as for Episcopal government, he is ready to prove it an apostolical institution, and that it

has been handed down through all ages and countries till Calvin's time, as soon as he is furnished with books, or such divines, as he shall make choice of; he does not think that Mr. Henderson's arguments to prove the Church of England not built on the foundation of Christ and his apostles are valid, nor will he admit that most of the prelates, about the time of the Reformation, did not insist upon the Divine right. The king adds, Mr. Henderson would do well to show where our Saviour has prohibited the addition of more church officers than those named by him; and yet the Church of England has not so much as offered at this, for an archbishop is not a new officer, but only a distinction in the order of government, like the moderator of assemblies in Scotland. His majesty denies that bishops and presbyters always import the same thing in Scripture, and when they do, it only respects the apostles' times, for it may be proved that the order of bishops succeeded that of the apostles, and that the title was altered in regard to those who were immediately chosen by our Saviour. As for the several congregations in Jerusalem, united in one church, his majesty replies, Are there not many parishes in one diocess? And do not the deans and chapters, and sometimes the inferior clergy, assist the bishop? So that, unless some positive and direct proof can be brought of an equality between the apostles and other presbyters, all arguments are with him inconclusive. The king confesses, that in case he cannot prove from antiquity that ordination and jurisdiction are peculiar branches of authority belonging to bishops, he shall begin to suspect the truth of his principles. As for Bishop Davenant's testimony, he refuses to be governed by that; nor will he admit of Mr. Henderson's exception against the fathers, till he can find out a better rule of interpreting Scripture. And whereas Mr. Henderson urged the precedent of foreign Reformed churches in favour of presbytery, his majesty does not undertake to censure them, but supposes necessity may excuse many things which would otherwise be unlawful; the Church of England, in his majesty's judgment, has this advantage, that it comes nearest the primitive doctrine and discipline; and that Mr. Henderson has failed in proving presbyters may ordain without a bishop, for it is evident St. Paul had a share in Timothy's ordination, 2 Tim., i., 6. As to the obligation of the coronation oath, the king is still of opinion none but the representative body of the clergy can absolve him; and as for the impracticableness of reformation upon the king's principles, he cannot answer for that, but thinks it sufficient to let him know, that incommodum non solvit argumentum. His majesty then declares, that as it is a great sin for a prince to oppress the Church, so, on the other hand, he holds it absolutely unlawful for subjects to make war (though defensively) against their lawful sovereign, upon any pretence whatsoever.

Mr. Henderson, in his third paper of July 2, considers chiefly the rules his majesty had laid down for determining the controversy of church government, which are the practice of the primitive Church, and the universal consent of the fathers; and affirms, there is no such primitive testimony, no such universal consent in favour of modern Episcopacy; the fathers very often

---

* Bib. Reg., p. 337, &c.

contradicting one another, or at least not concurring in their testimony. But to show the uncertainty of his majesty's rule for determining controversies of faith, Mr. Henderson observes,

1. That some critics joined the Word of God and antiquity together; others make Scripture the only rule, and antiquity the authentic interpreter. Now he thinks the latter a greater mistake than the former, for the papists bring tradition no farther than to an equality of regard with the inspired writings, but the others made antiquity the very ground of their belief of the sense of Scripture, and by that means exalt it above the Scripture; for the interpretation of the fathers is made the very formal reason why I believe the Scripture interpretable in such a sense; and thus, contrary to the apostle's doctrine, our faith must stand in the wisdom of man, and not in the power of God.

2. He observes, that Scripture can only be authentically interpreted by Scripture itself. Thus the Levites had recourse only to one part of Scripture for the interpreting another, Neh., viii., 8. So, likewise, our Saviour interprets the Old Testament, by comparing Scripture with Scripture, and not having recourse to the rabbies. This was likewise the apostles' method. Besides, when persons insist so much upon the necessity of the fathers, they are in danger of charging the Scriptures with obscurity or imperfection.

3. The fathers themselves say, that Scripture is not to be interpreted but by Scripture.

4. Many errors have passed under the shelter of antiquity and tradition; Mr. Henderson cites a great many examples under this head.

And, lastly, He insists that the universal consent and practice of the primitive Church are impossible to be known; that many of the fathers were no authors; that many of their tracts are lost; that many performances which go under their names are spurious, especially upon the subject of Episcopacy, and that therefore they are an uncertain rule.

The king, in his papers* of July 3 and 16, says, no man can reverence Scripture more than himself; but when Mr. Henderson and he differ about the interpretation of a text, there must be some judge or umpire, otherwise the disputes can never be ended; and when there are no parallel texts, the surest guide must be the fathers. In answer to Mr. Henderson's particulars, his majesty answers, that if some people overrate tradition, that can be no argument against the serviceableness of it; but to charge the primitive Church with error, and to call the customs and practices of it unlawful, unless the charge can be supported from Scripture, is an unpardonable presumption. Those who object to the ancient rites and usages of the Church must prove them unlawful, otherwise the practice of the Church is sufficient to warrant them. His majesty denies it is impossible to discover the universal consent, and understand the practice, of the primitive Church; and concludes with this maxim, that though he never esteemed any authority equal to the Scriptures, yet he believes the unanimous consent of the fathers, and the universal practice of the primitive Church, the best and most authentic interpreters, and by consequence the best-qualified judges between himself and Mr. Henderson.

One may learn, from this controversy, some of the principles in which King Charles I. was instructed; as,

(1.) The Divine right of Diocesan Episcopacy.

(2.) The uninterrupted succession of bishops, rightly ordained, from the time of the apostles; upon which the whole validity of the administration of the Christian sacraments depends.

(3.) The necessity of a judge of controversies, which his majesty lodges with the fathers of the Christian Church, and by that means leaves little or no room for private judgment.*

(4.) The independency of the Church upon the State.

(5.) That no reformation of religion is lawful but what arises from the prince or Legislature; and this only in cases of necessity, when a general council cannot be obtained.

(6.) That the multitude or common people may not in any case take upon them to reform the negligence of princes. Neither,

(7.) May they take up arms against their prince, even for self-defence, in cases of extreme necessity.

How far these principles are defensible in themselves, or consistent with the English Constitution, I leave with the reader; but it is very surprising that his majesty should be so much entangled with that part of his coronation oath which relates to the Church, when for fifteen years together he broke through all the bounds of it with relation to the civil liberties of his subjects, without the least remorse.

Upon the close of this debate, and the death of Mr. Henderson, which followed within six weeks, the king's friends gave out that his majesty had broke his adversary's heart.† Bishop Kennet and Mr. Echard have published the following recantation, which they would have the world believe this divine dictated or signed, upon his deathbed:

"I do declare before God and the world, that, since I had the honour and happiness to converse and confer with his majesty with all sorts

---

* Bib. Reg., p. 351–353.

In addition to the encomium bestowed by Bishop Burnet on the king's papers, which we have already quoted, it may be subjoined, that Sir Philip Warwick also extolled them, as his majesty's "great ability and knowledge, when he was destitute of all aids." Yet it is remarkable, as observes Dr. Harris, who had turned over Stillingfleet's Irenicum, and Unreasonableness of Separation, Hoadly's Defence of Episcopal Ordination, and many other volumes, these royal "papers have been little read, and are seldom or never quoted on the subject of Episcopacy." So that it is "possible these learned churchmen had not so great an opinion of the arguments made use of by Charles in these papers as the historians (viz., Burnet and Sir P. Warwick) I have quoted."—Life of Charles I., p. 101.—ED.

* The monarch would have seen little to object against in the Oxford Tracts, had they appeared in his day.—C.

† This effect was ascribed to his majesty's arguments by Bishop Kennet and Lord Clarendon, who certainly were a little too hasty in this judgment; for, as it is well observed by Dr. Harris, "disputants, veteran ones, as Henderson was, have generally too good a conceit of their own abilities to think themselves overcome; and though the awe of majesty may silence, it seldom persuades them."—The Life of Charles I., p. 99, 100. Some said Mr. Henderson died of grief, because he could not persuade the king to sign the propositions.—Whitelocke's Memorials, p. 225.—ED.

of freedom, especially in matters of religion, whether in relation to the Kirk or State, that I found him the most intelligent man that I ever spoke with, as far beyond my expression as expectation. I profess that I was oftentimes astonished with the solidity and quickness of his reasons and replies; and wondered how be, spending his time so much in sports and recreations, could have attained to so great knowledge; and must confess ingenuously, that I was convinced in conscience, and knew not how to give him any reasonable satisfaction; yet the sweetness of his disposition is such, that whatsoever I said was well taken. I must say, I never met with any disputant of that mild and calm temper, which convinced me the more, and made me think that such wisdom and moderation could not be without an extraordinary measure of Divine grace. I had heard much of his carriage towards the priests in Spain, and that King James told the Duke of Buckingham, upon his going thither, that he durst venture his son Charles with all the Jesuits in the world, he knew him to be so well grounded in the Protestant religion, but could never believe it before. I observed all his actions, more particularly those of devotion, which I must truly say are more than ordinary: if I should speak of his justice, magnanimity, charity, sobriety, chastity, patience, humility, and of all his other Christian and moral virtues, I should run myself into a panegyric; no man can say there is conspicuously any predominant vice in him; never man saw him passionately angry; never man heard him curse, or given to swearing; or heard him complain in the greatest durance of war or confinement. But I should seem to flatter him, to such as do not know him, if the present condition that I lie in did not exempt me from any suspicion of worldly ends, when I expect every hour to be called from all transitory vanities to eternal felicity, and the discharging of my conscience before God and man did not oblige me to declare the truth simply and nakedly, in satisfaction of that which I have done ignorantly, though not altogether innocently."* The declaration adds, that he was heartily sorry for the share he had had in the war; that the Parliament and Synod of England had been abused with false aspersions of his majesty; and that they ought to restore him to his just rights, and his crown and dignity, lest an indelible character of ingratitude lie upon him.

Mr. Echard confesses† he had been informed that this declaration was spurious,‡ but could

find no authority sufficient to support such an assertion. It will be proper, therefore, to trace the history of this imposture, and set it in a clear and convincing light, from a memorial sent me from one of the principal Scots divines, Professor Hamilton, of Edinburgh. The story was invented by one of the Scots Episcopal writers, who had fled to London, and was first published in the beginning of the year 1648, in a small pamphlet in quarto, about two years after Mr. Henderson's death. From this pamphlet Dr. Heylin published it as a credible report. Between thirty and forty years after Heylin had published it, viz., 1693, Dr. Hollingsworth, in his character of King Charles I., republished the paper above mentioned, entitled "The Declaration of Mr. Alexander Henderson, principal Minister of the Word of God at Edinburgh, and chief Commissioner of the Kirk of Scotland to the Parliament and Synod of England;" which paper the doctor says he had from Mr. Lamplugh, son to the late Archbishop of York of that name, from whom the historians above mentioned, and some others, have copied it; but, says the memorial, upon publishing the aforesaid story to the world, the assembly of the Kirk of Scotland appointed a committee to examine into the affair, who, after a full inquiry, by their act of August 7, 1648, declared the whole to be a forgery, as may be seen in the printed acts of the General Assembly for that year, quarto, page 420, &c., in which they signify their satisfaction and assurance that Mr. Henderson persisted in his former sentiments to his death;* that when he left the king at Newcastle, he was greatly decayed in his natural strength; that he came from thence by sea in a languishing condition, and died within eight days after his arrival at Edinburgh;† that he was not able to frame such a declaration as is palmed upon him, and that all he spoke upon his deathbed showed his judgment was the same as it ever had been about church reformation. This was attested before the Assembly by several ministers who visited him upon his deathbed, and particularly by two who constantly attended him from the time he came home till the time he expired. After this, and a great deal more to the same purpose, "they declare the above-mentioned paper, entitled 'A Declaration of Mr. Alexander Henderson's,' &c., to be forged, scandalous, and false,‡ and the author and contriver of the same to be void of charity and a good conscience; a gross liar and

great advocate for the king, had it not been a forgery, would not have failed to publish it; that it is not found in King Charles's works, though all that passed between the king and Mr. Henderson is there recited; that Mr. Henderson was a Scotchman, whereas the words, style, and matter are plainly and elegantly English, and not Scottish; but the great stress is laid on the inscription on his monument, and on the Assembly's declaration, to which Mr. Neal refers, and which Dr. Grey treats as spurious. These papers, as Ludlow's tract is scarce, shall be given in the Appendix, No. 10.—ED.
* Appendix, No. 10.
† History of the Stuarts, p. 310.
‡ If this character of Charles, ascribed to Mr. Henderson, were genuine, "it would (as Ludlow observes) avail very little; being the single sentiment of a stranger, that could not have had much experience of him."—*Truth brought to Light*, p. 6.—ED.

* Compl. Hist., p. 190. Bennet's Def. of his Mem., p. 130. † Echard, p. 526, ed. 3d.
‡ Dr. Grey sneers here at Mr. Neal for not referring to the place where Mr. Echard makes this confession, and for keeping out of view the name of the memorialist on whose authority he speaks. He then spends nearly five pages in cavilling at this authority, and in strictures on that of Mr. Burnet; through these I am not properly qualified to follow the doctor, as I have not Mr. Bennet's Defence of his Memorial; and it is unnecessary, for the question concerning the spuriousness of this piece had been discussed in 1693, ere Neal or Burnet had written, by Lieutenant-general Ludlow, in a tract against Dr. Hollingworth, entitled "Truth brought to Light." Ludlow argues against its authenticity on these grounds: that Archbishop Lamplugh, the

a calumniator, and led by the spirit of the accuser of the brethren."*

While the king was debating the cause of Episcopacy, the Parliament were preparing their propositions for a peace, which were ready for the royal assent by the 11th of July. The Scots commissioners demurred to them for some time, for not coming up fully to their standard, but at length acquiescing, they were engrossed, and carried to the king by the Earl of Pembroke, and Montgomery and the Earl of Suffolk, of the House of Peers; and by Sir Walter Erle, Sir John Hippisly, Robert Goodwin, and Luke Robertson, Esq., of the House of Commons; the Earls of Argyle and Loudon were commissioners for Scotland, and the Rev. Mr. Marshal was ordered to attend as their chaplain.† The commissioners arrived at Newcastle, July 23; next day they waited upon his majesty, and having kissed his hand, Mr. Goodwin delivered the following propositions:

Those relating to the civil government were,

(1.) That the king should call in all his declarations against the Parliament.

(2.) That he should put the militia into their hands, for twenty years, with a power to raise money for their maintenance.

(3.) That all peerages since May 21, 1642, should be made void.

(4.) That the delinquents therein mentioned should undergo the penalties assigned in the bill. And,

(5.) That the cessation with the Irish be disannulled, and the management of the war left to the Parliament.

The propositions relating to religion were,

1. "That his majesty, according to the laudable example of his father, would be pleased to swear and sign the late solemn League and Covenant, and give his consent to an act of Parliament enjoining the taking it throughout the three kingdoms, under certain penalties, to be agreed upon in Parliament.

2. "That a bill be passed for the utter abolishing and taking away all archbishops, bishops, their chancellors, commissaries, deans, sub-deans, deans and chapters, archdeacons, canons, and prebendaries, and all chanters, chancellors, treasurers, sub-treasurers, succentors, sacrists, and all vicars and choristers, old vicars, and new vicars of any cathedral or collegiate church, and all other under-officers, out of the Church of England, and out of the Church of Ireland, with such alterations as shall agree with the articles of the late treaty of Edinburgh, November 29, 1643, and the joint declaration of both kingdoms.

3. "That the ordinance for the calling and sitting of the Assembly of Divines be confirmed.

4. "That reformation of religion, according to the Covenant, be settled by act of Parliament in such manner as both houses have agreed, or shall agree, after consultation with the Assembly of Divines.

5. "Forasmuch as both kingdoms are obliged, by covenant, to endeavour such a uniformity of religion as shall be agreed upon by both houses of Parliament in England, and by

the Church and kingdom of Scotland, after consultation had with the divines of both kingdoms assembled, that this be confirmed by acts of Parliament of both kingdoms respectively.

6. "That for the more effectual disabling Jesuits, priests, papists, and popish recusants from disturbing the state and eluding the laws, an oath be established by act of Parliament, wherein they shall abjure and renounce the pope's supremacy, the doctrine of transubstantiation, purgatory, worshipping of the consecrated host, crucifixes, and images, and all other popish superstitions and errors; and the refusal of the said oath, legally tendered, shall be a sufficient conviction of recusancy.

7. "That an act of Parliament be passed for educating of the children of papists by Protestants, in the Protestant religion.

8. "That an act be passed for the better levying the penalties against papists; and another for the better preventing their plotting against the state; and that a stricter course may be taken to prevent saying or hearing of mass in the court, or any other part of the kingdom; the like for Scotland, if the Parliament of that kingdom shall think fit.

9. "That his majesty give his royal assent to an act for the due observation of the Lord's Day; to the bill for the suppression of innovations in churches and chapels in and about the worship of God; to an act for the better advancement of the preaching of God's holy Word in all parts of the kingdom; to the bill against pluralities of benefices and non-residency; and, to an act to be framed for the reforming and regulating both universities, and the colleges of Westminster, Winchester, and Eton:"

About sixty persons were by name excepted out of the general pardon;* besides,

(1.) All papists that had been in the army.

(2.) All persons that had been concerned in the Irish rebellion.

(3.) Such as had deserted the two houses at Westminster and went to Oxford.

(4.) Such members of Parliament as had deserted their places, and borne arms against the two houses. And,

(5.) Such bishops or clergymen, masters or fellows of colleges, or masters of schools or hospitals, or any ecclesiastical living, who had deserted the Parliament, and adhered to the enemies thereof, were declared incapable of any preferment or employment in Church or Commonwealth; all their places, preferments, and promotions were to be utterly void, as if they were naturally dead; nor might they be permitted to use their function of the ministry, without advice and consent of both houses of Parliament; provided that no lapse shall incur by this vacancy till six months after notice thereof.

When Mr. Goodwin had done, the king asked the commissioners if they had power to treat, to which they replied, that they were only to receive his majesty's answer; then said the king, "Saving the honour of the business, a trumpeter might have done as well;"† the very same language as at the treaty of Oxford; but the Earl of Pembroke told his majesty they must receive his peremptory answer in ten days, or return without it.

* Vide Bennet's Def. of his Mem., p. 134.
† Rushworth, vol. vi., p. 309, 311. Rapin, vol. ii., p. 524, fol. edit.

* Remonstrance, vol. vi., p. 315.
† Whitelocke's Memorials, p. 223.

Great intercessions were made with the king to comply with these proposals,* particularly in the point of religion, for without full satisfaction in that nothing would please the Scots nation, nor the city of London, by whom alone his majesty could hope to be preserved; but if this was yielded, they would interpose for the moderating other demands; the Scots general, at the head of one hundred officers, presented a petition upon their knees, beseeching his majesty to give them satisfaction in the point of religion, and to take the Covenant. Duke Hamilton, and the rest of the Scots commissioners, pressed his majesty, in the most earnest manner, to make use of the present opportunity for peace.† The lord-chancellor for that kingdom spoke to this effect: " The differences between your majesty and your Parliament are grown to such a height, that after many bloody battles, they have your majesty, with all your garrisons and strongholds, in their hands, and the whole kingdom at their disposal; they are now in a capacity to do what they will in Church and State; and some are so afraid, and others so unwilling, to submit to your majesty's government, that they desire not you, nor any of your race, longer to reign over them; but they are unwilling to proceed to extremities, till they know your majesty's last resolutions. Now, sir, if your majesty shall refuse to assent to the propositions, you will lose all your friends in the houses and in the city, and all England will join against you as one man; they will depose you, and set up another government; they will charge us to deliver your majesty to them, and remove our armies out of England; and, upon your refusal, we shall be constrained to settle religion and peace without you, which will ruin your majesty and your posterity. We own the propositions are higher in some things than we approve of, but the only way to establish your majesty's throne is to consent to them at present, and your majesty may recover, in a time of peace, all that you have lost in this time of tempest and trouble."‡

This was plain dealing: the king's best friends prayed his majesty to consider his present circumstances, and not hazard his crown for a form of church government; or, if he had no regard to himself, to consider his royal posterity; but the king replied, his conscience was dearer to him than his crown; that till he had received better satisfaction about the Divine right of Episcopacy, and the obligation of his coronation oath, no considerations should prevail with him; § he told the officers of the army he neither could nor would take the Covenant, till he had heard from the queen.‖ Which was only an excuse to gain time to divide his enemies, for the king had then actually heard from his queen by Monsieur Bellievre, the French ambassador, who pressed his majesty, pursuant to positive instructions given him for that pur-

pose, as the advice of the King of France, of the queen, and of his own party, to give the Presbyterians satisfaction about the Church.* Bellievre, not being able to prevail, despatched an express to France, with a desire that some person of more weight with the king might be sent. Upon which Sir William Davenant came over, with a letter of credit from the queen, beseeching him to part with the Church for his peace and security. When Sir William had delivered the letter, he ventured to support it with some arguments of his own, and told his majesty, in a most humble manner, that it was the advice of Lord Culpeper, Jermyn, and of all his friends; upon which the king was so transported with indignation, that he forbid him his presence. When, therefore, the ten days for considering the propositions were expired, instead of consenting, his majesty gave the commissioners his answer in a paper, directed to the speaker of the House of Peers, to this effect: " That the propositions contained so great alterations both in Church and State, that his majesty could not give a particular and positive answer to them;" but, after some few concessions, hereafter to be mentioned, " he proposes to come to London, or any of his houses thereabout, and enter upon a personal treaty with both houses; and he conjures them, as Christians and subjects, and as men that desire to leave a good name behind them, to accept of this proposal, that the unhappy distractions of the nation may be peaceably settled."†

When this answer was reported to the House, August 12, it was resolved to settle accounts with the Scots, and to receive the king into their own custody; but in the mean time his majesty attempted to bring that nation over to his interest by playing the Independents against them, and telling them the only way to destroy the sectarians was to join with the Episcopalians, and admit of the establishment of both religions.‡ " I do by no means persuade you," says the king, " to do anything contrary to your Covenant, but I desire you to consider whether it be not a great step towards your reformation (which I take to be the chief end of your Covenant), that the Presbyterial government be legally settled. It is true, I desire that the liberty of my own conscience, and those who are of the same opinion with myself, may be preserved, which I confess does not as yet totally take away Episcopal government. But then consider, withal, that this will take away all the superstitious sects and heresies of the papists and Independents, to which you are no less obliged by your Covenant than to the taking away of Episcopacy. And this that I demand is likely to be but temporary, for if it be so clear, as you believe, that Episcopacy is unlawful, I doubt not but God will so enlighten my eyes that I shall soon perceive it, and then I promise to concur with you fully in matters of religion; but I am sure you cannot imagine that there are any hopes of converting or silencing the Independent party, which undoubtedly will get a toleration in religion from the Parliament of England, unless

---

* The commissioners of both kingdoms, on their knees, begged of him to do it.— *Whitelocke's Memoirs.* p. 223.—ED.

† Hamilton's Memoirs, p. 281, 285.

‡ Rapin, vol. ii., p. 524; and Rushworth, vol. vi., p. 319.   § Duke of Hamilton's Memoirs, p. 281.

‖ This clause is not in the Memoirs of the duke; and, as Mr. Neal has not particularly referred to his authority for it, Dr. Grey expressed his fears that it is an interpolation.—ED.

Vol. II.—E

* Clarendon, vol. iii., p. 29, 31, 32.

† Dr. Grey gives the king's answer at length from MS. collections of Dr. Philip Williams, president of St. John's College, Cambridge.—ED.

‡ Duke of Hamilton's Memoirs, p. 286, 287.

you·join with me in that way that I have propo-sed for·the ·establishing of my crown ; or, at least, that you do. not press me to do this (which is·yet against my conscience) till I·may do it without sinning,·which, as I am confident none of you will persuade me· to. do, so I hope you have.so much ·charity as' not to put things to such·a desperate issue as to hazard the loss of all, because· for the present you cannot have full satisfaction from.me in point of religion, not considering that, besides the other mischiefs that may happen, it will infallibly set up the. innu-merable sects of the Independents, nothing be-ing more against your Covenant than the suffer-ing those schisms to increase."*· His majesty then added, "that he should be content· to re-strain Episcopal goverñment to the diocesses of Oxford, Winchester, Bath and Wells; and Ex-eter, leaving all the rest of England fully to the Presbyterial discipline, with the strictest ´claus-es that could be thought of in an act of Parlia-ment against the papists and Independents." But the Scots would abate· nothing in the arti-cles of religion, even for the overthrow of the sectaries. Duke Hamilton left no methods un-attempted· to· persuade his majesty to comply, but without effect.†·

When·the king could not gain the· commis-sioners, he applied by his friends to the Kirk, who laid his proposals before the Geríeral·As-sembly; with his offer to make any declaration they should· desire against the· Independents, and that;really, without. any reserve or equivo-cation·; but the Kirk were as peremptory as the commissioners; they said the king's heart was not with·them, nor could they depend upon his promises any longer than·it was not in his pow-er to set them·aside.‡ ·

In the mean time,·the· English ·Parliament were debating·with the Scots commissioners at London, the right of disposing of the king's per-son, the latter claiming ´an equal right to him with the former ; and the Parliament voted that the kingdom·of Scotland had no joint right to dispose of the person of the king in the kingdom of England. 'To which the. Scots would hardly have submitted had it·not been for. fear of ·en-gaging in a new war, and losing all their arrears. His majesty would willingly have retired into Scotland, but the clergy of that nation. would not·receive him, as appears ·by their solemn warning to all estates ·and degrees of persons throughout the land, dated December 17, 1646, in which; they say, " So· long as his ·majesty does not approve in his heart, and seal with his hand, the League and Covenant,·we cannot but apprehend that; according to his former princi-ples, he· will walk contrary to it,·and study to draw us into the violation of it.· Besides, our receiving his·majesty into Scotland at this time will confirm the suspicion of the English nation of our underhand dealing with·him· before he came·into our army. · Nor do we see how it is consistent with our Covenant and treaties ; but, on the contrary, it would involve us in the guilt of perjury, and expose us to the hazard of a bloody war. We are bound by our Covenant to defend, the king's person and authority, in the defence and preservation öf the;true religion,

and the liberties of the kingdom, and so far·as· his majesty is for these we will be for him ; but if his majesty will not satisfy the·just desires. of his people, both nations are engaged to pur-sue the ends thereof, against all lets and imped-iments ; we therefore desire that those who are· intrusted with the public affairs of this kingdom would still insist upon·his majesty's settling re-ligion according to· the Covenant, as the only means of preserving himself, his crown, and posterity." Upon ·reading this. admonition of the Kirk, the Scots Parliament resolved that his. majesty be desired to grant the whole proposi-tions; that in case of refusal, the kingdom should: be secured without·him. They declared, far-ther, ·that·the kingdom of Scotland could not· lawfully engage for the king as long as he refü-sed to take the Covenant, and give them satis-faction in point of religion.* Nor would they admit him to· come into Scotland unless he· gave a satisfactory answer to the proposition· lately presented· to him in the name of both. kingdoms. ·

The resolutions above· mentioned were not· communicated in·form to the king till the begin-ning of January, when the Scots commissioners, pressing him again in the most humble and im-· portunate·manner to give them satisfaction, at least·in the point of religion, his majesty re-mained.immovable; which being reported back to Edinburgh, the question was put in that Par-·liament, whether they should leave the king in· England to his two houses of Parliament 1 and· it was carried in the affirmative. January 16 a declaration .was published in the name of the whole kingdom of Scotland, wherein they say,. ." that when his majesty came to their army be-· fore Newark, he professed that·he absolutely resolved to comply with his Parliaments in ev-erything for· settling· of truth· and peace ; in· confidence. whereof the committees of the king-· dom of Scotland declared to himself, and to the· kingdom of England, that they ·received him· into their· protection· only upon these terms;. since which time propositions of peace have· been presented. to his ·majesty for the royal as-sent, with earnest supplications to the same· purpose, but without· effect. The Parliament of Scotland therefore being now to recall their· army out of England, considering that his maj-esty in several messages has desired to be near· his two houses of Parliament; and that the Par-· liament has appointed his majesty to reside at Holmby House with safety to his royal person ; and in regard of his majesty's not giving a sat-isfactory· answer to the propositions for peace ; and from a desire to preserve a right under-standing between the two kingdoms, and for. preventing new troubles, the States of Párlia-ment of the kingdom of Scotland do declare· their concurrence for the king's majesty's going· to Holmby House, to remain there till he give· satisfaction about the propositions for peace ;. and that, in the mean time, there be no harm, prejudice, injury, or violence done to his royal· person; that there be no change of government ;· and that his posterity be no way prejudiced in their lawful succession to the crown and gov-ernment of these kingdoms."† ·

While the Parliament and Kirk of Scotland were debating the king's·proposals, his majesty

* Rushworth, p. 328.
† Duke of Hamilton's Memoirs, p. 288.
‡ Hamilton's Memoirs, p. 298. Rushworth, p. 380.

* Rushworth, p. 392,   † Ibid., p. 396.

wrote to the Parliament of England, in the most pressing terms, for a personal treaty at London: "It is your king," says he in his letter of December 10, " that desires to be heard, the which, if refused to a subject by a king, he would be thought a tyrant; wherefore I conjure you, as you would show yourselves really what you profess, good Christians and good subjects, that you accept this offer." But the houses were afraid to trust his majesty in London, and therefore appointed commissioners to receive him from the Scots,* and convoy him to Holmby House in Northamptonshire, where he arrived February 6, 1646-7.† The sum of £200,000, being half the arrears due to the Scots army, having been paid them by agreement before they marched out of Newcastle, it has been commonly said, They sold their king. An unjust and malicious aspersion! It ought to be considered, that the money was their due before the king delivered himself into their hands; for that, in settling the accounts between the two nations, his majesty's name was not mentioned ;‡ that it was impossible to detain him without a war with England; and that the officers of the army durst not carry the king to Edinburgh, because both Parliament and Kirk had declared against receiving him.§

* The king happened to be playing at chess when he was informed of the resolution of the Scots nation to deliver him up ; but, such command of temper did he enjoy, he continued his game without interruption, and none of the by-standers could perceive that the letter which he perused had brought him news of any consequence. He admitted the English commissioners who, some days after, came to take him into custody, to kiss his hands, and received them with the same grace and cheerfulness as if they had travelled on no other errand but to pay court to him.—*Hume's History of England*, vol. vii., 8vo, 1763, p. 81, 82.—Ed.

† Holmby House was one of his nineteen palaces. When Duke of York, it had been purchased for him by his mother, Anne of Denmark, who little anticipated that it would ever become the prison of her favourite child. It was soon after pulled down by a decree of the Parliament.—C.

‡ *Vide* Rapin, vol. ii., p. 325, folio edition.

§ Mr. Neal is supported in his account of this transaction by General Ludlow, who farther says, that the condition on which the money was paid was, to deliver up (not the king, but) Berwick, Newcastle, and Carlisle to the Parliament ; that it was far from truth that this was the price of the king, for the Parliament freely granted to the Scots that they might carry him, if they pleased, to Edinburgh, but they refused it ; and that it was the king's desire to be removed into the southern parts of England. The Scots nation, however, underwent, and still undergo, the reproach of selling their king, and bargaining their prince for money. It has been argued that the Parliament would never have parted with so considerable a sum had they not been previously assured of receiving the king. It is a very evident fact, that while the Scots were demanding the arrears due to them, another point of treaty between them and the Parliament, if it were not the explicit and avowed condition of complying with that requisition, was the delivering up the king. The unhappy monarch was considered and treated as the prisoner of those to whom he fled for protection. Instead of declining to receive him, or afterward permitting him to take his own steps, they retained him, and disposed of him as a captive, as their interest or policy dictated. Was honour or justice in this case consulted? Alas ! they are seldom consulted by political parties.—*A Letter from General Ludlow to Dr. Hollingworth*, 4to, 1662, p.

But how amazing was his majesty's conduct ! What cross and inconsistent proposals did he make at this time ! While he was treating with the Scots, and offering to concur in the severest measures against the Independents, he was listening to the offers of those very Independents to set him upon the throne, without taking the Covenant, or renouncing the liturgy of the Church, provided they might procure a toleration for themselves. This agreeing with the king's inclinations, had too great a hearing from him, says Bishop Burnet, till Lauderdale wrote from London; "that he was infallibly sure they designed the destruction of monarchy, and the ruin of the king and his posterity ; but that if he would consent to the propositions, all would be well, in spite of the devil and the Independents too."* If his majesty had in good earnest fallen in with the overtures of the army at this time, I am of opinion they would have set him upon the throne, without the shackles of the Scots Covenant.

While the king was at Holmby House, he was attended with great respect,† and suffered to divert himself at bowls with gentlemen in the neighbouring villages, under a proper guard. The Parliament appointed two of their clergy, viz., Mr. Caryl and Mr. Marshal, to preach in the chapel, morning and afternoon, on the Lord's Day, and perform the devotions of the chapel on week-days, but his majesty never gave his attendance.‡ He spent his Sundays in private ; and though they waited at table, he would not so much as admit them to ask a blessing.

Before the king removed from Newcastle, the Parliament put the finishing hand to the destruction of the hierarchy, by abolishing the very names and titles of archbishops, bishops, &c., and alienating their revenues for payment of the public debts. This was done by two ordinances, bearing date October 9, and November 16, 1646, entitled " Ordinances for abolishing archbishops and bishops, and providing for the payment of the just and necessary debts of the kingdom, into which the same has been drawn by a war, mainly promoted by and in favour of the said archbishops, bishops, and other their adherents and dependants." The ordinance appoints, " that the name, title, style, and dignity of Arch-

67. *Mrs. Macaulay's History*, vol. iv., p. 271, 8vo. *Hume's History of England*, vol. vii., 8vo, 1763, p. 79-81 ; and *Whitelocke's Memorials*, p. 240. Dr. Grey has bestowed thirteen pages on this point, chiefly to show that £400,000 could not be due as arrears to the Scots, and to advance against them the charge of selling the king. He informs us, that the £200,000 immediately paid to them was borrowed of the Goldsmiths' Company. To Mr. Neal's reflection on the imputation cast on the Scots of selling their king, that it is an unjust and malicious aspersion, Bishop Warburton retorts, " The historian, before he said this, should have seen whether he could answer these two questions in the affirmative, Would the English have paid the arrears without the person of the king ? Would the Scots have given up the king if they could have had the arrears without ?"—Ed.

* Hamilton's Memoirs, p. 288.

† But his situation here, independently of confinement, was made unpleasant to him, as his old servants were dismissed, and he was not allowed the attendance of his own chaplains. His majesty remonstrated on this last circumstance in a letter to the House of Peers, but without effect.—*Clarendon*, vol. iii., p. 39.—Ed.   ‡ Clarendon, vol. iii., p. 38.

bishop of Canterbury, Archbishop of York, Bishop of Winchester, Bishop of Durham, and all other bishops of any bishoprics within the kingdom of England and dominion of Wales, be, from and after September 5, 1646, wholly abolished and taken away ; and all and every person and persons are to be thenceforth disabled to hold the place, function, or style of archbishop or bishop of any church, see, or diocess, now established or erected within the kingdom of England, dominion of Wales, or town of Berwick-on-Tweed ; or to use, or put in use, any archiepiscopal or episcopal jurisdiction or authority whatsoever, any law, statute, usage, or custom to the contrary notwithstanding."*

By the ordinance of November 16, it is farther ordained, " that all counties palatine, honours, manors, lordships, styles, circuits, precincts, castles, granges, messuages, mills, lands, tenements, meadows, pastures, parsonages, appropriate tithes, oblations, obventions, pensions, portions of tithes, vicarages, churches, chapels, advowsons, donations, nominations, rights of patronage and presentations, parks, woods, rents, reversions, services, annuities, franchises, liberties, privileges, immunities, rights of action and of entry, interests, titles of entry, conditions, commons, court-leets and court-barons, and all other possessions and hereditaments whatsoever; which now are, or within ten years before the beginning of the present Parliament were, belonging to the said archbishops and bishops, archbishoprics or bishoprics, or any of them, together with all chattels, deeds, books, accompts, rolls, and other writings and evidences whatsoever, concerning the premises, which did belong to any of the said archbishops, bishops, &c.,† are vested and settled, adjudged and deemed to be, in the real and actual possession and seizin of the twenty-four trustees mentioned in the ordinance, their heirs and assigns, upon trust that they shall dispose of the same, and the rents and profits thereof, as both houses of Parliament shall order and appoint, i. e., for payment of the public debts, and other necessary charges occasioned by the war, promoted chiefly by and in favour of the said hierarchy, saving and excepting all tithes appropriate, oblations, obventions, and portions of tithes, &c., belonging to the said archbishops, bishops, and others of the said hierarchy; all which, together with £30,000 yearly rent belonging to the crown, they reserve for the maintenance of preaching ministers. The trustees are not to avoid any lease made for three lives, or twenty-one years, provided the said lease or leases were not obtained since the month of December, 1641. They are empowered to appoint proper officers to survey, and take a particular estimate of all the bishops' lands, to receive the rents and profits of them, and to make a sufficient title to such as shall purchase them, by order of Parliament."‡ By virtue of this ordinance, the trustees were empowered to pay, or cause to be paid, to the Assembly of Divines, their constant salary allowed them by a former order of Parliament, with all their arrears, out of the rents, revenues, and profits belonging to the late Archbishop of Canterbury, till such time as the said lands and revenues shall happen to be sold. These church-

lands were at first mortgaged as a security for several large sums of money, which the Parliament borrowed at eight per cent. interest. Several members of Parliament, and officers of the army, afterward purchased them at low rates, but the bargain proved dear enough in the end. And surely it was wrong to set them to sale ; the lands having been originally given for the service of religion, ought to have been continued for such uses, and the substance of the donors' intentions pursued, unless it appeared that too great a proportion of the national property had been settled in mortmain. But herein they followed the ill examples of the kings and queens of England at the Reformation.

The Presbyterians were now in the height of their power, the hierarchy being destroyed, the king their prisoner, and the best, if not all, the livings in the kingdom distributed among them ; yet still they were dissatisfied for want of the top-stone to their new building, which was church power; the pulpits and conversation of the city were filled with invectives against the men in power, because they would not leave the Church independent on the State ; the Presbyterian ministers were very troublesome, the Parliament being teased every week with church grievances of one kind or another ; December 19, the lord-mayor and his brethren went up to Westminster with a representation of some of them, and a petition for redress. The grievances were,

1. " The contempt that began to be put upon the Covenant, some refusing to take it, and others declaiming loudly against it ; they therefore pray that it may be imposed upon the whole nation, under such penalties as the houses shall think fit ; and that such as refuse it be disqualified from all places of profit and trust.

2. " The growth of heresy and schism ; the pulpits having been often usurped by preaching soldiers, who infected all places where they came with dangerous errors ; they therefore pray that all such persons may be forbid to preach as have not taken the Covenant, and been regularly ordained, and that all separate congregations, the very nurseries of damnable heretics, may be suppressed ; that an ordinance be made for the exemplary punishment of heretics and schismatics, and that all godly and orthodox ministers may have a competent maintenance, many pulpits being vacant of a settled minister for want of it ; and here," say they " we would lay the stress of our desires, and the urgency of our affections." They complain, farther, of the " undue practices of country committees, of the threatening power of the army, and of some breaches in the Constitution ; all which they desire may be redressed, and that his majesty's royal person and authority may be preserved and defended, together with the liberties of the kingdom, according to the Covenant."

To satisfy the petitioners, the House of Commons published a declaration, December 31, " wherein they express their dislike of lay-preachers, and their resolution to proceed against all such as shall take upon them to preach or expound the Scriptures in any church or chapel, or any other public place, except they be ordained either here or in some other Reformed Churches ; likewise against all such ministers

---

* Husband's Collection, p. 922.
† Rushworth, p. 377.   ‡ Scobel, p. 100, 102, 103.

and others as shall publish, or maintain by preaching, writing, printing, or any other way, anything against or in derogation of the church government which is now established by authority of Parliament ; and also against all and every person or persons who shall willingly or purposely interrupt or disturb a preacher in the public exercise of his functions ; and they command all officers of the peace, and officers of the army, to take notice of this declaration, and by all lawful means to prevent offences of this kind, to apprehend offenders, that a course may be speedily taken for a due punishment to be inflicted upon them." The House of Lords published an order, bearing date December 22, requiring the headboroughs and constables, in the several parishes of England and Wales, to arrest the bodies of such persons as shall disturb any minister in holy orders, in the exercise of his public calling, by speech or action, and carry them before some justice of peace, who is required to put the laws in execution against them. February 4, they published an ordinance to prevent the growth and spreading of errors, heresies, and blasphemies ; but these orders not coming up to their Covenant uniformity, the lord-mayor and common council presented another petition to the two houses March 17, and appointed a committee to attend the Parliament from day to day, till their grievances were redressed, of which we shall hear more under the next year.

We have already accounted for the unhappy rise of the sectarians in the army when it was new-modelled, that were now grown so extravagant as to call for some proper restraint, the mischief being spread not only over the whole country, but into the city of London itself: it was first pleaded in excuse for this practice, that a gifted brother had better preach and pray to the people than nobody ; but now learning, good sense, and the rational interpretation of Scripture, began to be cried down, and every bold pretender to inspiration was preferred to the most grave and sober divines of the age ; some advanced themselves into the rank of prophets, and others uttered all such crude, undigested absurdities as came first into their minds, calling them the dictates of the Spirit within them ; by which the public peace was frequently disturbed, and great numbers of ignorant people led into the belief of the most dangerous errors. The Assembly of Divines did what they could to stand in the gap, by writing against them, and publishing a Detestation of the Errors of the Times. The Parliament also appointed a fast on that account February 4, 1645-6, and many books were published against the Antinomians, Anabaptists, Seekers, &c., not forgetting the Independents, whose insisting upon a toleration was reckoned the inlet to all the rest.

The most furious writer against the sectaries was Mr. Thomas Edwards,[*] minister of Christ-

---

* He was originally of the University of Cambridge, but in 1623 was incorporated at Oxford. At the beginning of the civil wars he joined the Parliament, embarked all that was dear to him in the cause of the people, whom he excited to prosecute the war by the strain of his prayers and sermons, and advanced money to carry it on.—*Wood's Athenæ Oxonienses*, vol. i., p. 846.—ED.

Church, London, a zealous Presbyterian, who became remarkable by a book entitled Gangræna, or a catalogue of many of the errors, heresies, blasphemies, and pernicious practices of this time ; in the epistle dedicatory he calls upon the higher powers to rain down all their vengeance upon these deluded people, in the following language : " You have done worthily against papists, prelates, and scandalous ministers, in casting down images, altars, crucifixes, throwing out ceremonies, &c., but what have you done," says he, " against heresy, schism, disorder, against Seekers, Anabaptists, Antinomians, Brownists, Libertines, and other sects? You have made a reformation, but with the reformation have we not worse things come upon us than we had before, as denying the Scriptures, pleading for toleration of all religions and worships ; yea, for blasphemy, and denying there is a God ? You have put down the Common Prayer, and there are many among us that are for putting down the Scriptures. You have broken down the images of the Trinity, and we have those who oppose the Trinity. You have cast out bishops and their officers, and we have many that cast down to the ground all ministers. You have cast out ceremonies in the sacraments, as the cross, kneeling at the Lord's-Supper, and many cast out the sacraments themselves. You have put down saints' days, and many make nothing of the Lord's Day. You have taken away the superfluous maintenance of bishops and deans, and we have many that cry down the necessary maintenance of ministers. In the bishops' days we had singing of psalms taken away in some places, conceived prayer, preaching, and in their room anthems, stinted forms, and reading brought in ; and now singing of psalms is spoken against, public prayer questioned, and all ministerial preaching denied. In the bishops' time popish innovations were introduced, as bowing at altars, &c., and now we have anointing the sick with oil ; then we had bishoping of children, now we have bishoping of men and women, by laying on of hands. In the bishops' days we had the fourth commandment taken away, and now all ten are taken away by the Antinomians. The worst of the prelates held many sound doctrines and had many commendable practices, but many of our sectaries deny all principles of religion, are enemies to all holy duties, order, learning, overthrowing all, being whirligig spirits, and the great opinion of a universal toleration tends to the laying all waste, and dissolution of all religion and good manners. Now," says our author, " a connivance at, and suffering without punishment, such false doctrines and disorders, provokes God to send judgments. A toleration doth eclipse the glory of the most excellent Reformation, and makes these sins to be the sins of the Legislature that countenances them. A magistrate should use coercive power to punish and suppress evils, as appears from the example of Eli. Now, right honourable, though you do not own these heresies, but have put out several orders against them, yet there is a strange, unheard-of suffering of them, such a one as there hardly ever was the like under any orthodox Christian magistrate and state. Many sectaries are countenanced and employed in places of trust : there has not been any exemplary restraint of the sectaries, by virtue of any of your ordinances, but they are slighted and scorned ; preaching of laymen was never more in request than since your ordinance against it ; Presbyterial government never more preached and printed against than since it was established. Our dear brethren of Scotland stand amazed, and are astonished at these things ; the orthodox ministers and people both in city and country are grieved and discouraged, and the common enemy scorns and blasphemes ; it is high time, therefore, for your honours to suffer no longer these sects and schisms, but to do something worthy of a Parliament against them, and God will be with you.".

After this dedication there are one hundred and seventy-six erroneous passages collected from sundry pamphlets printed about this time, and from the reports of friends in all parts of the kingdom, to whom he sent for materials to fill up his book ; however, the heretics are at length reduced under sixteen general heads. . ¨

1. Independents. 6. Arminians. 11. Perfectists.
2. Brownists. 7. Libertines. 12. Socinians.
3. Millenaries. 8. Familists. 13. Arians.
4. Antinomians. 9. Enthusiasts. 14. Antitrinitarians.
5. Anabaptists. 10. Seekers. 15. Antiscripturists.
  16. Skeptics.

The industrious writer might have enlarged his catalogue with papists and prelates, Deists, Ranters, Behemenists, &c., &c., or, if he had pleased, a less number might have served his turn, for very few of these sectaries were collected into societies ; but his business was to blacken the adversaries of Presbyterian uniformity, that the Parliament might crush them by sanguinary methods. Among his heresies there are some which do not deserve that name ; and among his errors, some that never grew into a sect, but fell occasionally from the pen or lips of some wild enthusiast, and died with the author. The Independents are put at the head of the sectaries, because they were for toleration of all Christians who agreed in the fundamentals of religion ; to prove this, which they never denied, he has collected several passages out of their public prayers ; one Independent minister (says he) prayed that Presbytery might be removed and the kingdom of Christ set up ; another prayed two or three times that the Parliament might give liberty to tender consciences ; another thanked God for the liberty of conscience granted in America ; and said, Why, Lord, not in England ? Another prayed, Since God had delivered both Presbyterians and Independents from prelatical bondage, that the former might not be guilty of bringing their brethren into bondage. The reader will judge of the spirit of this writer by the foregoing specimen of his performance, which I should not have thought worth remembering, if our church writers had not reported the state of religion from his writings. " I knew Mr. Edwards very well," says Fuller,* " my contemporary in Queen's College, who often was transported beyond due bounds with the keenness and eagerness of his spirit, and therefore I have just cause in some things to suspect him." He adds, farther, " I am most credibly informed, by such who I am confident will not abuse me and posterity therein, that

* Appeal, p. 58.

Mr. Herbert Palmer (an anti-Independent to the height), being convinced that Mr. Edwards had printed some falsehoods in one sheet of his Gangræna, proffered to have the sheet reprinted at his own charge, but some accident obstructed it." However, our author went on publishing a second and third Gangræna, full of most bitter invectives and reproaches, till his own friends were nauseated with his performances.

The Reverend Mr. Baxter, who attended the victorious army, mentions the Independents, Anabaptists, and Antinomians, as the chief separatists, to whom he adds some other names, as Seekers, Ranters, Behemenists, Vanists, all which died in their infancy, or united in the people afterward known by the name of Quakers ; but when he went into the army he found " almost one half of the religious party among them orthodox, or but very lightly touched with the above-mentioned mistakes, and almost another half honest men, that had stepped farther into the contending way than they ought, but with a little help might be recovered ; a few were fiery, self-conceited men among them, kindled the rest, and made all the noise and bustle ; for the greatest part of the common soldiers were ignorant men, and of little religion ; these would do anything to please their officers, and were instruments for the seducers in their great work, which was to cry down the Covenant, to vilify parish ministers, and especially the Scots and the Presbyterians." Mr. Baxter observes,* that " these fiery, hot men were hatched among the old Separatists ; that they were fierce with pride, and conceit, and uncharitableness, but many of the honest soldiers, who were only tainted with some doubts about liberty of conscience and independency, would discourse of the points of sanctification and Christian experience very savourily ; the seducers above mentioned were great preachers and fierce disputants, but of no settled principles of religion ; some were of levelling principles as to the state, but all were agreed that the civil magistrate had nothing to do in matters of religion, any farther than to keep the peace, and protect the Church liberties." The same writer adds, " To speak impartially, some of the Presbyterian ministers frightened the sectaries into this fury, by the unpeaceableness and impatience of their minds ; they ran from libertinism into the other extreme, and were so little sensible of their own infirmity, that they would not have them tolerated who were not only tolerable, but worthy instruments and members in the churches." Lord Clarendon says, that Cromwell and his officers preached and prayed publicly with their troops, and admitted few or no chaplains in the army, except such as bitterly inveighed against the Presbyterian government, as more tyrannical than Episcopacy ; and that the common soldiers, as well as the officers, did not only pray and preach themselves, but went up into the pulpits in all churches, and preached to the people, who quickly became inspired with the same spirit ; women as well as men taking upon them to pray and preach ; which made as great a noise and confusion in all opinions concerning religion as there was in the civil government of the state.

Bishop Bramhall, in one of his letters to Archbishop Usher, writes, that " the papists took

* Baxter's Life, p. 53.

advantage of these confusions, and sent over above one hundred of their clergy, that had been educated in France, Italy, and Spain, by order from Rome. In these nurseries the scholars were taught several handicraft trades and callings, according to their ingenuities, besides their functions in the Church ; they have many yet at Paris," says the bishop, "fitting up to be sent over, who twice in the week oppose one the other; one pretending Presbytery, the other Independency ; some Anabaptism, and others contrary tenets. The hundred that went over this year," according to the bishop, " were most of them soldiers in the Parliament army."* But Mr. Baxter,† after a most diligent inquiry, declares " that he could not find them out ;" which renders the bishop's account suspected. " The most that I could suspect for papists among Cromwell's soldiers," says he, " were but a few that began as strangers among the common soldiers, and by degrees rose up to some inferior officers, but none of the superior officers seemed such." The body of the army had a vast aversion to the papists; and the Parliament took all occasions of treating them with rigour ; for, June 30, Morgan, a priest, was drawn, hanged, and quartered, for going out of the kingdom to receive orders from Rome, and then returning again. However, without all question, both Church and State were in the utmost disorder and confusion at the close of this year [1646].

Among the illustrious men of the Parliament's side who died about this time, was Robert D'Evereux, earl of Essex, son of the famous favourite of Queen Elizabeth ; he was educated to arms in the Netherlands, and afterward served the King and Queen of Bohemia for the recovery of the Palatinate. King Charles I. made him lieutenant of his army in his expedition against the Scots, and lord-chamberlain of the household ; but the earl, being unwilling to go into the arbitrary measures of the court in favour of popery and slavery, engaged on the side of the Parliament, and accepted of the commission of captain-general of their forces, for which the king proclaimed him a traitor. He was a person of great honour, and served the Parliament with fidelity ; but being of opinion that the war should be ended rather by treaty than by conquest, did not always push his successes as far as he might. Upon the new modelling of the army, the cautious general was dismissed with an honourable pension for his past services; after which he retired to his house at Eltham, in Kent, where he died of a lethargy, occasioned by overheating himself in the chase of a stag in Windsor Forest, September 14, 1646, in the fifty-fifth year of his age.‡ He was buried with great funeral solemnity in Westminster Abbey, October 22, at the public expense, both houses of Parliament attending the procession. His effigy was afterward erected in Westminster Hall, but some of the king's party found means in the night to cut off the head, and break the sword, arms, and escutcheons. Mr. Vines preached his funeral sermon, and gave him a very high encomium, though Lord Clarendon has stained his charac-

ter for taking part with the Parliament, which he says was owing to his pride and vanity. The earl's countenance appeared stern and solemn, but to his familiar acquaintance his behaviour was mild and affable. Upon the whole, he was a truly great and excellent person ; his death was an unspeakable loss to the king, for he was the only nobleman, perhaps, in the kingdom who had interest enough with both parties to have put an end to the civil war, at the very time when Providence called him out of the world.

Among the remarkable divines may be reckoned the reverend and learned Mr. Thomas Colman, rector of St. Peter's Church in Cornhill : he was born at Oxford, and entered in Magdalen College in the seventeenth year of his age ; he afterward became so perfect a master of the Hebrew language, that he was commonly called Rabbi Colman. In the beginning of the civil war he left his rectory of Blyton in Lincolnshire, being persecuted from thence by the cavaliers. Upon his coming to London, he was preferred to the rectory of St. Peter's, Cornhill, and made one of the Assembly of Divines. Mr. Wood says he behaved modestly and learnedly in the Assembly; and Mr. Fuller gives him the character of a modest and learned divine ;* he was equally an enemy to Presbytery and prelacy, being of Erastian principles ; he fell sick while the Assembly was debating the *jus divinum* of Presbytery ; and when they sent some of their members to visit him, he desired they would not come to an absolute determination till they heard what he had to offer upon the question ; but his distemper increased, he died in a few days, and

---

* Parr's Life of Usher, p. 611.
† Baxter's Life, p. 78.
‡ Ludlow, p. 186, or 4to edition, 1771, p. 79.

---

* Colman preached a sermon before the House of Commons, 30th July, 1645, on the Unity of the Church and how to promote it. For this he gives several directions, of which the following are the chief : "1. Establish as few things *jure divino* as can well be. Hold out the practice, but not the ground. 2. Let all precepts held out as Divine institutions have clear Scriptures; an occasional practice, a phrase upon the by, a thing named, are too weak grounds to uphold such a building. I could never yet see how two co-ordinate governments, exempt from superiority and inferiority, can be in one state ; and in Scripture no such thing is found that I know of. 3. Lay no more burden of government upon the shoulders of ministers than Christ hath plainly laid upon them ; let them have no more hand therein than the Holy Ghost clearly gives them. The ministers will have other work to do, and such as will take up the whole man. I ingenuously profess I have a heart that knows not how to be governed than to govern; I fear an ambitious ensnarement, and I have cause. I see what raised prelacy and papacy to such height, and what their practices were, being so raised. Give us doctrine; take you the government. Give me leave to make this request, in the name of the ministry ; give us two things, and we shall do well : give us learning, and give us a competency. 4. A Christian magistrate, as a Christian magistrate, is a governor in the Church. All magistrates, it is true, are not Christians ; but that is their fault: all should be ; and when they are, they are to manage their office under and for Christ. Christ hath placed governments in his Church. Of other governments besides magistracy I find no institution ; of them I do. I find all government given to Christ, and to Christ as mediator; and Christ, as head of these, given to the Church. To rob the kingdom of Christ of the magistrate and his governing power, I cannot excuse, no, not from a kind of sacrilege, if the magistrate be His."—C.

the whole Assembly did him the honour to attend his funeral in a body, March 30, 1646.*

About the middle of July. died the learned Doctor William Twisse, vicar of Newbury, and prolocutor of the Assembly of Divines; he was born at Speenham-Land, near Newbury, in Berkshire; his father was a substantial clothier in that town, and educated his son at Winchester School, from whence be was translated to New College, in Oxford, of which he was fellow; here he employed himself in the study of divinity, with the closest application, for sixteen years together. In the year 1604 he proceeded master of arts; about the same time he entered into holy orders, and became a diligent and frequent preacher; he was admired by the universities for his subtle wit, exact judgment, exemplary life and conversation, and many other valuable qualities which became a man of his function. In the year 1604 he proceeded doctor of divinity, after which he travelled into Germany, and became chaplain to the princess palatine, daughter of King James I. After his return to England, he was made vicar of Newbury, where he gained a vast reputation by his useful preaching and exemplary living. His most able adversaries have confessed that there was nothing then extant more accurate and full, touching the Arminian controversy, than what he published; and hardly any who have written upon this argument since the publishing of Dr. Twisse's works but have made an honourable mention of him.† The doctor was offered the prebend of Winchester, and several preferments in the Church of England; the States of Friesland invited him to the professorship of divinity in their University of Franeker, but he refused all. In the beginning of the civil war he was forced from his living at Newbury by the cavaliers, and upon convening the Assembly of Divines, was appointed by Parliament their prolocutor, in which station he continued to his death, which happened, after a lingering indisposition, about the 20th of July, 1646, in the seventy-first year of his age. He died in very necessitous circumstances, having lost all his substance by the king's soldiers, insomuch that, when some of the Assembly were deputed to visit him in his sickness, they reported that he was very sick and in great straits. He was allowed to be a person of extensive knowledge in school divinity, a subtle disputant,‡ and, withal, a modest, humble, and religious person. He was buried, at the request of the Assembly, in the collegiate church of St. Peter's, Westminster, near the upper end of the poor folks' table, next the vestry, July 24, and was attended by the whole Assembly of Divines: there his body rested till the restoration of King Charles II., when his bones were dug up by order of council, September 14, 1661, and

thrown, with several others, into a hole in the churchyard, of St. Margaret's, before the back door of the lodgings of one of the prebendaries.

Towards the end of the year died the reverend and pious Mr. Jeremiah Burroughs; he was educated in Cambridge, but obliged to quit the university and kingdom for nonconformity in the late times.* Upon his leaving England he was chosen minister of an English congregation at Rotterdam, with which he continued till the year 1642, when he returned to England, and became preacher to two of the largest and most numerous congregations about London, viz., Stepney and Cripplegate. He was one of the dissenting brethren in the Assembly, but was a divine of great candour, modesty, and charity. He never gathered a separate congregation, nor accepted of a parochial living, exhausting his strength in continual preaching, and other services of the Church. He was an excellent scholar, a good expositor, a popular preacher; he published several treatises while he lived, and his friends have published many others since his death, which have met with a general acceptance. It was said the divisions of the times broke his heart, because one of the last subjects he preached upon, and printed, was his Irenicum, or an attempt to heal divisions among Christians: Mr. Baxter used to say, if all the Presbyterians had been like Mr. Marshal, and the Independents like Mr. Burroughs, their differences might easily have been compromised. He died of a consumptive illness, November 14, 1646, about the forty-seventh year of his age.

CHAPTER VIII.

PROCEEDINGS OF THE ASSEMBLY UPON THEIR CONFESSION OF FAITH AND CATECHISMS.—PROVINCIAL ASSEMBLIES OF LONDON.—THE KING TAKEN OUT OF THE PARLIAMENT'S CUSTODY, AND CONVEYED TO THE ARMY.—CONTROVERSY BETWEEN THE PARLIAMENT AND ARMY.—HIS MAJESTY'S CONDUCT.—HE ESCAPES FROM HAMPTON COURT, AND IS CONFINED IN THE ISLE OF WIGHT.

THE Rev. Mr. Charles Herle succeeded to the prolocutor's chair by order of Parliament, July 22, 1646, in the room of the late Dr. Twisse, when the discipline of the Church being pretty well settled, it was moved to finish their confession of faith. The English divines would have been content with revising and explaining the Thirty-nine Articles of the Church of England, but the Scots insisting on a system of their own, a committee was appointed to prepare materials for this purpose May 9, 1645; their names were, Dr. Gouge, Dr. Hoyle, Mr. Herle, Gataker, Tuckney, Reynolds, and Vines, with the Scots divines, who, having first settled the titles of the several chapters, as they now stand in their confession of faith, in number thirty-two, distributed them, for greater expedition, among several sub-committees, which sat two

* Church History, b. ix., p. 213. Wood's Athen. Oxon., vol. ii., p. 62.

† Anthenæ Oxon., vol. ii., p. 40, 41.

‡ He distinguished himself by his writings against Arminianism. The most learned of that party confessed that there was nothing more accurate, exact, and full, on that controversy, than his works. His plain preaching was esteemed good; his solid disputations were accounted, by some, better; and his pious way of living was reckoned by others, especially the Puritans, best of all.—Wood's Athenæ Oxon., vol. ii., p. 40.—ED.

* He for some time sheltered himself under the hospitable roof of the Earl of Warwick.—Granger's History of England, vol. ii., p. 193, 8vo. This nobleman was a great patron of the Puritan divines; and not contented with hearing long sermons in their congregations only, would have them repeated at his own house.—Ibid., 116.—ED.

days every week, and then reported what they had finished to the committee, and so to the Assembly, where it was debated paragraph by paragraph. The disputes about discipline had occasioned so many interruptions, that it was a year and a half before this work was finished; but on November 26, 1646, the prolocutor returned thanks to the several committees, in the name of the Assembly, for their great pains in perfecting the work committed to them. At the same time, Dr. Burges was appointed to get it transcribed, in order to its being presented to Parliament, which was done December 11, by the whole Assembly in a body, under the title of "The Humble Advice of the Assembly of Divines and others, now, by the authority of Parliament, sitting at Westminster, concerning a Confession of Faith." The House of Commons having voted the Assembly thanks, desired them to insert the proofs of the several articles in their proper places, and then to print six hundred copies,* and no more, for the perusal of the houses. The Rev. Mr. Wilson, Mr. Byfield, and Mr. Gower, were appointed, January 6, to be a committee to collect the Scriptures for confirmation of the several articles; all which, after examination by the Assembly, were inserted in the margin. And then the whole confession was committed once more to a review of the three committees, who made report to the Assembly of such farther amendments as they thought necessary; which being agreed to by the House, it was sent to the press, May 11, 1647. Mr. Byfield, by order of the House of Commons, delivered to the members the printed copies of their confession of faith, with Scripture notes, signed,

Charles Herle, prolocutor;

Corn. Burges, Herbert Palmer, assessors;

Henry Roborough, Adoniram Byfield, scribes. And because no more were to be given out at present, every member subscribed his name to the receipt thereof.

The House of Commons began their examination of this confession May 19, when they considered the whole first chapter article by article; but the disturbances which arose between the Parliament and army interrupted their proceeding the whole summer; but when these were quieted they resumed their work, and October 2, ordered a chapter of the confession of faith at least to be debated every Wednesday, by which means they got through the whole before the end of March following; for at a conference with the House of Lords March 22, 1647-8, the Commons presented them with the confession of faith as passed by their house, with some alterations: they agreed with the Assembly in the doctrinal part of the confession; and ordered it to be published, June 20, 1648, for the satisfaction of the foreign churches, under the title of "Articles of Religion approved and passed by both Houses of Parliament, after Advice had with an Assembly of Divines called to-

gether by them for that Purpose."* The Parliament not thinking it proper to call it a confession of faith, because the sections did not begin with the words I confess; nor to annex matters of church government, about which they were not agreed, to doctrinal articles; those chapters, therefore, which relate to discipline, as they now stand in the Assembly's confession, were not printed by order of the House, but recommitted, and at last laid aside; as the whole thirtieth chapter, of church censures, and of the power of the keys; the thirty-first chapter, of synods and councils, by whom to be called, and of what force in their decrees and determinations; a great part of the twenty-fourth chapter, of marriage and divorce, which they referred to the laws of the land; and the fourth paragraph of the twentieth chapter, which determines what opinions and parties disturb the peace of the Church, and how such disturbers ought to be proceeded against by the censures of the Church, and punished by the civil magistrate. These propositions, in which the very life and soul of Presbytery consists, never were approved by the English Parliament, nor had the force of a law in this country; but the whole confession, as it came from the Assembly, being sent into Scotland, was immediately approved by the General Assembly and Parliament of that kingdom, as the established doctrine and discipline of their kirk; and thus it has been published to the world ever since, though the chapter above mentioned, relating to discipline, received no parliamentary sanction in England; nevertheless, as the entire confession was agreed to by an assembly of English divines, I have given it a place in the Appendix.§

Nor is it to be supposed that the confession of faith itself, which determines so many abstruse points of divinity, should have the unanimous and hearty assent of the whole Assembly or Parliament: for though all the divines were in the anti-Arminian scheme, yet some had a greater latitude than others. I find in my MS. the dissent of several members against some expressions relating to reprobation, to the imputation of the active as well as passive obedience of Christ, and to several passages in the chapters of liberty of conscience and church discipline; but the confession, as far as related to articles of faith, passed the Assembly and Parliament by a very great majority.∥

Various censures have been passed by learned men upon this laboured performance; some have loaded it with undeserved reproaches; and others, perhaps, have advanced its reputation too high. Mr. Collyer condemns it for determining in favour of the morality of the Sabbath; for pronouncing the pope to be antichrist; and for maintaining the Calvinian rigours of absolute predestination, irresistible grace, and the impotency of man's will; doctrines, in his opinion, inconsistent with Christianity.¶ But then, he observes very justly, that it falls very short of the Scots claim in points of discipline; it

---

* The MSS. to which Mr. Neal refers, though supported by the authority of Rushworth, made a mistake here; for by a copy of the original order, given by Dr. Grey in his Appendix, No. 71, it appears that the order of the House was for printing five hundred copies, and no more, of "The Humble Advice," &c.—See, also, *Whitelocke's Memorials*, p. 233. —ED. † Rushworth, part iv., vol. i., p. 482.

* Rushworth, part iv., vol. i., p. 1035.
† Savoy Conf., Pref., p. 18, 19.
‡ Savoy Conf., Pref., p. 20. § Appendix, No. 8.
∥ Hetherington's history of the Assembly may be consulted advantageously upon the events connected with the preparation and adoption of the confession of faith.—C. ¶ Eccl. Hist., vol. ii., p. 842.

yields the magistrate a power of convening church assemblies, and of superintending their proceedings; it is silent as to the independency of the Church, and the Divine right of presbytery, &c. Upon the whole, the Assembly's confession, with all its faults, has been ranked by very good judges among the most perfect systems of divinity* that have been published upon the Calvinistic or anti-Arminian principles in the last age.

While the confession was carrying through the Assembly, committees were appointed to reduce it into the form of catechisms; one larger, for the service of a public exposition in the pulpit, according to the custom of foreign churches; the other smaller, for the instruction of children; in both which the articles relating to church discipline are entirely omitted.† The larger catechism is a comprehensive system of divinity, and the smaller, a very accurate summary, though it has by some been thought a little too long, and in some particulars too abstruse for the capacities of children. The shorter catechism was presented to the House of Commons, November 5, but the larger, by reason of the marginal references to Scripture, which the houses desired might be inserted, was not ready till the 14th of April, 1648, when the House ordered six hundred copies to be printed for the service of the members; and having examined and approved it, they allowed it to be printed by authority, for public use, September 15, 1648. The king, after many solicitations, at the treaty of the Isle of Wight, offered to license a shorter catechism with a suitable preface; but that treaty proving unsuccessful, it was not accomplished.‡

The chief affairs committed to the Assembly being thus finished, Mr. Rutherford, one of the Scots divines, moved, October 24, 1647, that it might be recorded in the scribes' books, that the Assembly had enjoyed the assistance of the honourable, reverend, and learned commissioners of the Church of Scotland, during all the time they had been debating and perfecting these four things mentioned in the Covenant, viz., their composing a directory for public worship; a uniform confession of faith; a form of church government and discipline; and a public catechism, some of their number having been present during the whole of these transactions; which being done, about a week after, he and the rest of the commissioners took their leave and returned home; upon which occasion, Mr. Herle, the prolocutor, rose up, and, in the name of the Assembly, "thanked the honourable and reverend commissioners for their assistance; he excused, in the best manner he could, the Directory's not being so well observed as it ought, and lamented that the Assembly had not power to call offenders to an account: he confesses that their affairs were very much embarrassed, and that they were still in

a chaos of confusion [the king being now taken out of the hands of the Parliament, and in custody of the army]; he takes notice of what distresses the Parliament were in, while the common enemy was high and strong; and adds, that their extraordinary successes hitherto were owing to the prayers of their brethren in Scotland, and other Protestants abroad, as well as to their own. He then mentions with concern some other restraints the Assembly lay under, but that this was not a proper season for redress."

The commissioners went home under a very heavy concern for the storm that was gathering over England, and for the hardships the Presbyterians lay under with respect to their discipline; and having obtained the establishment of the Directory, the Confession of Faith and Catechisms, the Presbyterian Discipline, and Rouse's Psalms in Metre, for the service of their Kirk, they appointed a general fast, to lament their own defection from the solemn League and Covenant, and the distressed condition of their brethren in England, who were zealous for carrying on the work of God, but were now oppressed, under pretence of liberty, when no less was aimed at than tyranny and arbitrary power.

If the Parliament had dissolved the Assembly at this time, as they ought to have done, they had broke up with honour and reputation, for after this they did little more than examine candidates for the ministry, and squabble about the *jus divinum* of Presbytery; the grand consultations concerning public affairs, and practising upon the new establishment, being translated to the provincial assemblies and weekly meetings of the London clergy at Sion College.*

* Rapin, vol. ii., p. 297, note. That the reader may form a judgment of what was intended to be established in England, it may not be improper to set before him, in one view, the discipline that was then settled in the Kirk of Scotland, and subsists at this time. "In Scotland there are eight hundred and ninety parishes, each of which is divided, in proportion to its extent, into particular districts, and every district has its own ruling elders and deacons; the ruling elders are men of the principal quality and interest in the parish, and the deacons are persons of a good character for manners and understanding. A consistory of ministers, elders, and deacons is called a kirk session, the lowest ecclesiastical judicatory, which meets once a week, to consider the affairs of the parish. The minister is always moderator, but without a negative; appeals lie from hence to their own presbyteries, which are the next higher judicatories. Scotland is divided into sixty-nine presbyteries, each consisting of from twelve to twenty-four contiguous parishes. They meet in the head town and choose their moderator, who must be a minister, half-yearly; from hence appeals lie to provincial synods, which are composed of several adjacent presbyteries; two, three, four, to eight—there are fifteen in all. The members are a minister and a ruling elder out of every parish. These synods meet twice a year at the principal town of their bounds. They choose a moderator, who is their prolocutor. The acts of the synods are subject to the review of the General Assembly, the dernier resort of the Kirk of Scotland. It consists of commissioners from presbyteries, royal burghs, and universities. A presbytery of twelve ministers sends two ministers and one ruling elder; a presbytery of between twelve and eighteen sends three, and one ruling elder; of between eighteen and twenty-four, sends four, and two ruling elders; of twenty-four,

* Here may be introduced, as it escaped our recollection in the more proper place, the remark made by Mr. Robinson on the Directory. "The best state instructions to preachers were given in the Directory by the Assembly of Divines; but even these," he properly adds, "include the great, the fatal error, the subjection of God's Word to human laws."—*Translation of Claude on the Composition of a Sermon*, vol. ii., Prefatory Dissertation, p. 63.—ED.

† Rushworth, p. 888, 1060.   ‡ Ibid., p. 1326.

Though the city and suburbs of London had been formed into a province, and divided into twelve classical Presbyteries (as has been remembered under the last year), new complaints were still made to the Parliament of certain obstructions to their proceedings.; upon which the houses published their resolutions of April 22d, 1647, entitled "Remedies for removing some Obstructions in Church Government;"* in which they ordered letters to be sent from the speakers of both houses to the several counties of England, immediately to divide themselves into distinct presbyteries and classes; "they then appoint the elders and ministers of the several classes of the province of London, to hold their provincial assembly in the Convocation House of St. Paul's in London, upon the first Monday in May next ensuing, and to adjourn their meetings de die in diem, and conclude them with adjournment to the next opportunity, according to the ordinance of Parliament; but that no act shall pass or be valid in the said province of London, except it be done by the number of thirty-six present, or the major part of them, whereof twelve to be ministers, and twenty-four ruling elders. That in the classical meetings, that which shall be done by the major part present shall be esteemed the act of the whole; but no act done by any classes shall be valid, unless it be done by the number of fifteen present, or the major part of them, whereof five be ministers and ten ruling elders." So that the number of lay-elders in these assemblies was double to the number of ministers.

According to this appointment, the first Provincial Assembly met at the Convocation House of St. Paul's, May 3, consisting of three ministers and six ruling elders from the several classes, in all about one hundred and eight persons; at their first session they chose the Rev. Dr. Gouge prolocutor, who opened the Assembly with a sermon at his own church in Blackfriars ; the Rev. Mr. Thomas Manton, Mr. Ralph Robinson, and Mr. Cardel, being appointed scribes. After their return to the Convocation House, a committee of seven ministers and fourteen ruling elders were chosen to consider of the business of the province.

The ministers were,

Rev. Mr. Whitaker,	Rev. Mr. Spurstow,
Dr. Seaman,	Mr. Tuckney,
Mr. Ed. Calamy,	Mr. Proffet,
Rev. Mr. Jackson.	

The ruling elders were,

Sir Edward Popham,	Mr. Houghton,
Dr. Clarke,	Mr. Eyres,
Dr. Bastwicke,	Mr. Vaughan,
Dr. Brinley,	Mr. Webbe,
Mr. Bence,	Mr. English,
Mr. Russel,	Col. Sowtonstall,
Mr. Bains,	Mr. ——.

Any six to be a quorum, provided there be two ministers and four ruling elders. Their

___

sends five, and two elders; every royal burgh sends one elder, and Edinburgh two; every university sends one commissioner, usually a minister. The General Assembly meets once a year, in the month of May, and is opened and adjourned by the king's royal commissioner appointed for that purpose."
* Vol. Pamp., No. 4.

next meeting to be at Sion College, May 6, at two in the afternoon.

At the second sessions, it was moved that application be made to Parliament for liberty to remove the Assembly from the Convocation House to some other place ; and, accordingly, they were allowed to adjourn to any place within the city or liberties of London, upon which they agreed upon Sion College, where they continued to meet twice a week to the end of the year 1659, as appears by a manuscript of the late Mr. Grange, now in Sion College library. Before the adjournment from the Convocation House at St. Paul's, they came to the following resolutions : Resolved,

1. That the Provincial Assembly shall meet twice every week, Mondays and Thursdays.

2. That the moderator for the time being shall begin and end every session with prayer.

3. When a new moderator is to be chosen, the senior minister shall preside.

4. The moderator shall be subject to the censure of the majority of the Assembly, in case of complaint, and shall leave the chair while the complaint is debating, and the senior minister shall preside.

5. Every one that speaks shall direct his speech to the moderator, and be uncovered.

6. No man shall speak above three times to the same question at one sessions.

7. When any business is before the Assembly relating to any particular member, he shall withdraw, if desired by the majority.

8. After the Assembly is set, no member shall withdraw without leave.

9. The names of the members present shall be recorded by the scribes.

Every Provincial Assembly was dissolved in course at the end of six months, when notice was given to the several classes to return new representatives; but it was an ill omen upon them, that their meetings were interrupted almost the whole summer, by reason of the distraction of the times.

The second Provincial Assembly met November 8, Dr. Seaman moderator, and presented a petition to the Parliament in a body, January 11, in which they humbly pray,

1. "That the number of delegates to the Provincial Assembly may be enlarged, because they found it difficult sometimes to make up the number of thirty-six.

2. "That the houses would quicken the settlement of those classes [in London] that were not yet formed, which they say were four.

3. "That some more effectual encouragement may be provided for a learned ministry.

4. "That effectual provision may be made against clandestine marriages, for the punishment of fornication, adultery, and such uncleanness as is not fit to be named.

5. "That church censures may be so established that scandalous persons may be effectually excluded from church communion."

The Parliament received them with respect, and promised to take the matter of the petition into consideration, which was all that was done in the affair.

But, besides the Provincial Assembly, it has been remembered that the London clergy had their weekly meetings at Sion College, to consult about church affairs, in one of which they

10. "That the children of believers ought not to be baptized, nor baptism continued among Christians; that the meaning of the Third Commandment is, Thou shalt not forswear thyself.*

11. "That persons of the next kindred may marry; and that indisposition, unfitness, or contrariety of mind, arising from natural causes, are a just reason of divorce.†

12. "That the soul of man is mortal; that it sleeps with the body; and that there is neither heaven nor hell till the day of judgment."‡

The last error they witness against, and in which all agree, is called the "error of toleration,§ patronising and promoting all other errors, heresies, and blasphemies whatsoever, under the grossly abused notion of liberty of conscience;" and here they complain, as a very great grievance, "that men should have liberty to worship God in that way and manner as shall appear to them most agreeable to the Word of God; and no man be punished or discountenanced by authority for the same; and that an enforced uniformity of religion throughout a nation or state confounds the civil and religious, and denies the very principles of Christianity and civility."||

They then bear their testimony to the Covenant, and to the Divine right of Presbytery. They lament the imperfect settlement of their discipline by the Parliament, and lay the foundation of all their calamities in the countenancing of a public and general toleration, and conclude thus : "Upon all these considerations, we, the ministers of Jesus Christ, do hereby testify to our flocks, to all the kingdom, and to the Reformed world, our great dislike of prelacy, Erastianism, Brownism, and Independency; and our utter abhorrence of anti-Scripturism, popery, Arianism, Socinianism, Arminianism, Antinomianism, Anabaptism, Libertinism, and Familism ; and that we detest the forementioned toleration, so much pursued and endeavoured in this kingdom, accounting it unlawful and pernicious." What sad work would these divines have made, had the sword of the magistrate been at their disposal !¶

The principal authors from whom these errors

* Tombes. † Saltmarsh, Ham. Milton, p. 19.
‡ P. 20, Man's Mortality, by R. O.
§ Mr. Emlyn justly observes, "That the principle of the admired Assembly's larger catechism, under the second commandment, is, that it forbids toleration of all false religion."—*Emlyn's Works*, vol. i., p. 60, of the narrative edition of 1746.—ED.
|| Bloody Tenet. Five Holland Ministers, p. 22.
¶ It deserves to be mentioned here, as a fact remarkable in itself, and honourable to the Assembly at Westminster, that, notwithstanding the zeal expressed against toleration, the confession of faith it drew up was not made the legal standard of orthodoxy. It was not subscribed by any member of that Assembly, except by the prolocutor, assessors, and clerks. Nor till forty years after was a subscription or assent to it required of any layman or minister as a term of Christian communion. And Mr. Nye, a member of the Assembly, informs us, when the Scots commissioners proposed that the answers in the shorter catechism should be subscribed by all the members, the motion was rejected, after a considerable number in the Assembly had shown it was an unwarrantable imposition. — *Conscientious Nonconformity*, printed for *Noon*, 1737, p. 77. *The Religious Establishment in Scotland Examined*, 1771, p. 104.—ED

were collected are mentioned in the margin; two of whom determined to vindicate the citations out of their books : Dr. Hammond published a vindication of three passages in his Practical Catechism, from the censures of the London ministers ; in which he very justly complains of the hard names with which the ministers load the opinions they reject, as "abominable errors, damnable heresies, horrid blasphemies, many of which are destructive of the fundamentals of Christianity, and all of them repugnant to the Holy Scriptures, the scandal and offence of the Reformed churches abroad, and the unparalleled reproach of this Church and nation ; and, in a word, the dregs and spawn of those old cursed heresies which have been already condemned." The doctor then recites his three passages : the first, concerning universal redemption ; the second, concerning faith's being the condition of our justification ; and the third, concerning the interpretation of the third commandment ; and avers them all to be true, and agreeable to the doctrine of the Church of England. In conclusion, the doctor desires this favour, that either the first subscriber, Mr. J. Downham, who licensed his catechism for the press, or else Dr. Gouge or Mr. Gataker, who are foremost in the second rank, or some other persons of learning, Christianity, and candour, would afford him their patience, personally and by fair discourse, or any other Christian way, to debate the truth of these assertions, for which he will wait their leisure. Dated from Oxford, January 24, 1647–8, but nobody thought fit to accept the challenge.

Mr. John Goodwin was a learned divine, and a smart disputant; but of a peculiar mould, being a republican, and a thorough Arminian ; he had been Vicar of Coleman-street, whence he was ejected, in the year 1645, by the committee for plundered ministers, because he refused to baptize the children of his parishioners promiscuously, and to administer the sacrament to his whole parish. He had published several large and learned books ; as, the Divine Authority of the Scriptures ; Redemption Redeemed ; A Treatise of Justification ; and An Exposition of the Ninth Chapter to the Romans, out of which the above-mentioned exceptions were taken. This divine, taking it amiss to be marked for a heretic, challenged any of the London clergy to a disputation, as thinking it a very unrighteous method to condemn opinions before they had been confuted. Mr. William Jenkins, at that time a warm and zealous Presbyterian, though afterward softened into more catholic principles, entered the lists with our author, in a pamphlet entitled "The Busy Bishop." To which the other replied, in a book entitled "The Novice Presbyter Instructed." By some passages in which, one may discover the angry spirit of the times.

Mr. Jenkins had complained that the orthodox clergy had short commons, and were under the cross, whereas the sectaries met with the greatest encouragement. To which Mr. Goodwin replies, "If by orthodox ministers he means those of the adored order of Presbytery, with what face can he say that they are under the cross ? Is not the whole English element of church-livings offered up by the state to their service ? Are not all the benefices of the king-

dom appropriated to their order ? And all others thrust out of doors to make room for them ? Must they feed with hecatombs every day, or else complain of short commons ? Or is Mr. Jenkins of Mar. Crassus's mind, who would have no one accounted rich unless he could maintain an army with his revenue ? In what sense can he affirm the Presbyterian clergy to be under the cross ? Are they under the cross who are scarce under the crown ? who are carried by authority upon eagles' wings : over whom the Parliament itself rejoices to do good ; heaping ordinance upon ordinance to advance both them and their livings together. But certainly there is something that Mr. Jenkins calls a cross which few men know by that name, but those who are baptized into the spirit of high Presbytery ; for the cross he speaks of is no other than this, that his orthodox brethren have not the power to do all the evil that is in their hearts against a quiet, peaceable, harmless generation of men, of whom they are jealous, lest they should take their kingdom from them. How can this writer say that the Independent preachers meet with encouragement, and are under worldly glory ? Does he account it matter of worldly glory to be discountenanced by the State, to be declared incapable of those favours and privileges which other ministers in the land enjoy ; to be sequestered from their livings, and to be thrust into holes and corners ; to be represented, both to the magistrate and people, as sectaries, schismatics, erroneous, heretical, factions, troublesome, dangerous to the State, and what not ! If this be worldly glory, then may the preachers against whom Mr. Jenkins writes be truly said to be under worldly glory." Old Mr. Vicars and some others carried on the controversy, but their writings are not worth remembering ; especially since the English Presbyterians of the present age have openly renounced and disavowed their principles.

To return to more public affairs. Hitherto the army had acted in perfect subordination to the Parliament ; but the war being over, and the king a prisoner, the great difficulty was to settle the nation upon such a foot as might content the several parties, or bring them at least to acquiesce ; this was the rock upon which they split, and which in the end proved the ruin of their cause. To give light to this affair, it will be proper to consider the separate views of the king, the Parliament, and the army.

The royal party being broken, and the king a prisoner, his majesty had no prospect of recovering his throne but by dividing his enemies, in order to the making the best terms with them he could ; the Presbyterians being in league with the Scots nation, were most numerous and powerful ; but that which rendered their agreement with the king impracticable, was his majesty's zealous attachment to this point, that Episcopal government was essential to Christianity, and that he was bound by his coronation oath to maintain it ; whereas the others held themselves equally bound by their solemn League and Covenant to abolish Episcopacy, and establish Presbytery in its room. Both parties were immovable, and therefore irreconcilable. His majesty's agreement with the army was more open and practicable, because they would have set aside the Covenant, and obliged the Parliament to tolerate Episcopal government as well as the sectaries ; but the king could never forgive those officers who had destroyed his armies, and driven him out of the field : though he dreaded their military·valour, he had a very mean opinion of their politics, and therefore affected to play them against the Parliament, hoping to take advantage of their divisions and establish himself upon the ruins of both ; for it was his majesty's maxim, which he did not scruple to avow, that neither party could·subsist without him, and that those must be ruined whom he abandoned.   By which unhappy principle he lost his interest both in the Parliament and army, and (as Bishop Kennet observes) laid the foundation of his ruin:

The Presbyterians were no less·unhappy in an imagination, that as the majority of the House of Commons, with the city of London, and the whole Scots nation, were firmly attached to their interest, no opposition could stand before them, and therefore would abate nothing of their demands, nor hearken to any other terms of accommodation with the king than those of the Covenant, which were the entire abolishing of prelacy, and the establishing Presbyterian uniformity throughout both kingdoms, with an absolute extirpation of all sectaries whatsoever. This was not only an effectual bar to their union with the king (as has been observed), but awakened the jealousy of the army, who were thoroughly·convinced that, when the Presbyterians were in the legal possession of their demands, they would exercise equal tyranny over the consciences of men with the bishops ; and, indeed, nothing less was to be expected, considering their steady adherence to the Covenant in all their treaties, their efforts in Parliament·to get the power of the keys into their own hands, their frequent addresses for the suppressing all sectaries by the civil authority, and their declarations, both from the pulpit and the press, against toleration and liberty of conscience.· In all their treaties with the king, even to that in the Isle of Wight (except when the army was in possession of the cities of London and Westminster), this was one article of peace, " That an effectual course be taken by act of Parliament, and all other ways needful or expedient, for suppressing the opinions of the Independents; and all other sectaries." To which his majesty had agreed in his· private treaty with the Scots in the Isle of Wight, signed December 27, so that the army was left unsatisfied.

For although there were some few Presbyterians in the army, the greatest part consisted of Independents, Anabaptists, and men of unsettled principles in religion, who, for want of regular chaplains to their regiments, had used their own talents among themselves in religious exercises. The Scots treaty of the Isle of Wight says the army was made up of Anti-Trinitarians, Arians, Socinians, Anti-Scripturists, Anabaptists, Antinomians, Arminians; Familists, Brownists, Separatists, Independents, · Libertines, Seekers, &c.·

Mr. Rapin, contrary to the testimony of all other writers, calls them all Independents, and represents the controversy between the Parliament and them as a dispute, Whether Presbytery or Independency· should be uppermost ; whereas the grand controversy was, Presbytery

with a toleration, or without one.· The army· consented that Presbytery should be the national religion, but insisted upon a toleration of all· Christians in the enjoyment of all their civil and religious rights.   This, says Lord Clarendon, was their great charter, and till they had obtained it by·a legal settlement, they agreed not to lay down their arms : they had fought the Parliament's battles, and therefore thought it unreasonable to be told openly, if they could not comply with the Presbyterian settlement, they must expect to be punished as sectaries, and driven out of the land. To avoid this, they treated separately with the king, both before and after they had· him in their hands ;·and, when they apprehended he did not deal sincerely with them, they made proposals·to the Parliament to establish the Presbyterian discipline, with a toleration to all Protestants, without him ; but when they found the Presbyterians, even in their last treaty with the king, in the year 1648, insisted upon the Presbyterian uniformity, without making the least provision for that liberty of conscience they had been contending for, they were exasperated, and grew outrageous ; they seized his majesty's person a second time, and having purged the House of Commons, in a most arbitrary manner, of all who were not disposed to their desperate measures, they blew up the whole Constitution, and buried king, Parliament, and Presbytery in its ruins.   This was not in their original intention, nor the result of any set of religious principles they embraced, as Rapin insinuates, but, was a violence resulting from despair, to which they had been driven by a series of disappointments, and a train of mistaken conduct in the Royalists and Presbyterians.

We left the king, the beginning of the spring, at his house at Holmby, where he continued under an easy restraint from the 16th of February to the 4th of June following. The war being ended, the houses attempted to get rid of the army, by offering six months' pay, and six weeks' advance to as many as would go over to Ireland ; and by voting that the remainder should be disbanded, with an act of indemnity for all hostilities committed by them, in pursuance of the powers vested in them by Parliament ; but the army, being apprehensive that the Presbyterians would make peace with the king, upon the foot of Covenant uniformity, and without a toleration, resolved to secure this as a kind of preliminary point ; for which purpose they chose a council of officers, and a committee of agitators, consisting of two inferior officers out of each regiment, to manage their affairs ; these met in distinct bodies, like the two houses of Parliament, and came to the following resolutions, which they sent to Westminster by three of their number, who delivered them in at the bar of the House : " That they would not disband without their arrears, nor without full provision for liberty of conscience ; that they did not look upon themselves as a band of janizaries, but as volunteers that had been fighting for the liberties of the nation, of which they were a part, and that they were resolved to see those ends secured."*   It was moved in the House that the messengers might

* Rushworth, vol. vi., p 485, 498. Rapin, vol. ii., p. 529, folio ed.

be committed to the Tower ; but, after a long debate, they were dismissed only with a reprimand for meddling in affairs of state, and for presuming to offer a petition to Parliament without their general. Upon this, the officers sent their petition by the general himself, but the Parliament, instead of taking it into consideration, ordered, May 21, that all who would not list for the Irish service should be immediately paid off and disbanded ; upon which, the officers, seeing the snare that was laid for them, bound themselves and the army by an engagement, May 29, not to disband till the grievances above mentioned were redressed. Whereupon the two houses ordered Lieutenant-general Cromwell, who was then in town, and suspected to be at the head of these counsels, to be seized ; but being advertised of the design, he made his escape to the army. They then voted the petition seditious, and all those traitors who had promoted it ; and having sent a message to the general to remove the army farther from London, they raised the city train-bands, and determined to put an end to the power of the army by a speedy conclusion of peace with the king.

His majesty's answer to the propositions at Newcastle were read in the House, May 18, in which " he agrees to settle the Presbyterian government for three years—to ratify the Assembly of Divines at Westminster, proposing a few of his own clergy to consider what government to settle afterward—he yields the militia for ten years—desires ministers of his own to satisfy him about the Covenant—consents to the act against papists, and to an act of oblivion—and desired to come to London, in order to give the Parliament satisfaction upon the other articles." Two days after, the Lords voted that the king be removed to his house at Oatlands, and that it be immediately fitted for his reception.

Things being come to this crisis, the agitators considered that, the king being the prize contended for, whoever had him in their power must be masters of the peace, and make their own terms ; they therefore resolved, by the advice and direction of Lieutenant-general Cromwell, to get possession of his majesty's person, which they accomplished by a bold stratagem, in the night of June 4, with very little opposition from his attendants or guards ; Cornet Joyce, at the head of fifty resolute horse, having secured the avenues to Holmby House, entered with two or three of his company, and going to the king's chamber, acquainted him with his design of carrying him to the army at Newmarket ; his majesty, being surprised at so unexpected a visit, and so late at night, asked for his commission, who pointed to his troops drawn up before the gates ; his majesty answered, it was very legible ; and finding it in vain to resist, consented to go with the cornet next morning,* on promise of safety to his person, and that he should not be forced to anything against his conscience ; the chief officers of the army met his majesty at Childerley, four miles from Cambridge, and were admitted to

kiss his hand ; from thence he was removed to Newmarket, where he took the diversion of the heath, had the liberty of four of his own chaplains to wait upon him, and was attended with all due ceremony and respect ; Cromwell being heard to say among his friends, that " now he had got the king into his hands, he had the Parliament in his pocket."*

The two houses received the news of the king's being carried off to the army with the utmost surprise and astonishment ; the whole city was in confusion, and all persons within the lines of communication ordered to arms ; the lobby at Westminster was thronged with the disbanded officers of the Earl of Essex's army offering their service to the Parliament, for every one imagined the army would be at the gates of the city in a few hours ; when their panic was a little abated, commissioners were sent to the general, not to advance within forty miles of London ; but being already at St. Alban's, the general promised not to march his army nearer without due notice,† and assured the two houses that they would not oppose the Presbyterial government, nor set up the Independent ; but only insisted that some effectual course might be taken that such who, upon conscientious grounds, differed from the establishment, might not be debarred from the common rights, liberties, or benefits belonging equally to all, while they lived soberly and inoffensively towards others, and peaceably and faithfully towards the state.‡ June 10, another letter was sent to the lord-mayor, aldermen, and common council of London, signed by Fairfax,§ Cromwell, and twelve other officers, assuring them " they intended no alteration of the civil government ; nor to interrupt the settlement of presbytery ; nor to introduce a licentious liberty, under colour of obtaining ease for tender consciences, but that, when the state had made a settlement, they would submit or suffer. They wished that every peaceable subject might have liberty and encouragement, for the obtaining which," say they, "we are drawing near the city. We seek the good of all, and shall wait for a time to see if these things may be settled without us, and then we will embark for Ireland."‖

The Commons took no notice of these remonstrances, but declared, in print, that his majesty was a prisoner, and barbarously used, because their commissioners could have no access to him but in the presence of some officers ; the army replied, " that all suggestions of that na-

---

* He was attended in the same coach by three of the commissioners, the Earls of Pembroke and Denbigh and Lord Montague, the rest on horseback, and, according to Herbert, who was present, the king was the *merriest* person of the party.—*Herbert*, p. 26.—C.

* Rushworth, p. 545, 549. Rapin, vol. ii., p. 530, folio ed. Echard, vol. ii., p. 575.—C.
† Rushworth, p. 546, 561, 589, &c.
‡ Rapin, vol. ii., p. 379, 531.
§ Fairfax was ignorant of the design to seize the king. On being informed of it, he sent Col. Whalley, with two regiments of horse, to recover him from the custody of Joyce, and to bring him back to Holmby, but the king positively refused to return. He was glad to escape from the strict vigilance of the parliamentary commissioners, and hoped to profit by the distractions of his enemies. The general summoned a council of war, " to proceed against Joyce for this high offence and breach of the articles of war ; but the officers," he tells us, " whether for fear of the distempered soldiers, or, rather (as I suspected), a secret allowance of what was done, made all my efforts ineffectual."—*Fairfax's Memoirs, Masere's Tracts*, vol. ii., 447, 488.—C.
‖ Rushworth, p. 554.

ture were absolutely false, and contrary to their principles, which are most clearly for a general right and just freedom to all men, and therefore upon this occasion they declare to the world, that they desire the same for the king, and others of his party, so far as can consist with common right and freedom, and with the security of the same for the future. And we do clearly profess," say they, "that we do not see how there can be any peace to this kindom firm or lasting, without a due provision for the rights, quiet, and immunity of his majesty, his royal family, and his late partakers; and herein we think, that tender and equitable dealings (as supposing their cases had been ours), and a spirit of common love and justice diffusing itself to the good and preservation of all, will make the most glorious conquest over their hearts, to make them, and the whole people of the land, lasting friends."*

The leading members of the Presbyterian party in the House of Commons could not contain themselves within any reasonable bounds at these proceedings; they said it was insufferable that the Parliament, instead of treating with the king, should be obliged to treat with their own servants, and therefore advised raising a new army, and opposing force with force, till those who had the king in their custody should submit to their superiors, and deliver him back. On the other hand, the officers and agitators resolved to get rid of these resolute gentlemen, and therefore impeached eleven of the members of high treason, June 16, for obstructing the business of Ireland; for acting against the army and against the laws and liberties of the subject, &c.; and desired they might be suspended from the House till they were legally acquitted;† their names were Denzil Hollis, Esq., Sir Phil. Stapleton, Sir William Lewis, Sir John Clotworthy, Sir William Waller, Sir John Maynard, Major-general Massey, Mr. Glyn, recorder, Colonel Walter Long, Colonel Edward Hartley, Anthony Nichols, Esq. The Commons not only rejected their impeachment, but ordered the king to be brought to Richmond, and that four full companies of the militia should guard the two houses. This quickened the resentments of the army, who sent the following proposals, among others, June 23: "That the king's coming to Richmond be suspended; that no place be appointed for his residence nearer London than the Parliament will allow the quarters of the army; that the impeached members be sequestered the House; that the multitude of soldiers that flock together about the city be dispersed; and that no new forces be raised, nor any preparations made for a new army."‡ If these particulars are not complied with in a week's time, they declare they will march to London, and do themselves justice. The houses, being terrified with the approach of the army, agreed to content them for the present, in order to gain time; and the impeached members having desired leave to withdraw, retired first into the city, and after some time left the kingdom. The other requests of the army were also complied with; whereupon, after returning thanks to the houses, they retreated to Wickham, and ap-

pointed commissioners to settle all remaining differences with the Parliament.*

But the city of London, by the influence of the impeached members, kindled into a flame; for the Parliament, by an ordinance of May 4, having put the nomination of the officers of the militia into the hands of the common council, these had discharged the old ones, and put in such as they could confide in for opposing the army, and establishing uniformity according to the Covenant; the officers, in order to defeat their design, insisted that the ordinance of May 4 be repealed, and the militia put into the hands of those who had conducted it during the course of the late war.† The houses, with much reluctance, consented to the repeal July 23, which alarmed the citizens, and occasioned those tumults which brought upon them the very mischiefs they were afraid of. Denzil Hollis, with the other impeached members who were retired into the city, prevailed with the common council to oppose the repeal, and petition the House that the ordinance of May 4 might remain in full force. At the same time some citizens met at Skinner's Hall, and subscribed a solemn engagement to endeavour, with the hazard of their lives, to procure a "personal treaty" with the king; that he might return to his two houses with honour and safety; that his majesty's concessions of May 11 might be confirmed, and the militia continue in the hands of the present committee."‡ How vain was all this bustle, when they knew the king was in the custody of those who would pay no regard to their demands! The houses, indeed, forbade the signing of the engagement by sound of trumpet; but such was the misguided zeal of the citizens, that they held assemblies, enlisted soldiers, and gave them orders to be ready on the first notice.

The Parliament was now in great perplexity, considering the impossibility of contenting the Presbyterians and the army at the same time; while the citizens, resolved to carry their point by one method or another, went up to Westminster July 26, with such a number of apprentices and young men, as terrified the houses by their tumultuous and insolent behaviour; for they would scarce suffer the door to be shut; some thrust themselves into the House with their hats on, crying out, Vote, vote; and when the speaker would have left the chair to put an end to the confusion, they obliged him to return, till the militia was settled to their mind, and the king voted to come to London.§ This, says Mr. Baxter, looked like a riot upon the Parliament; and, indeed, both houses were so terrified and pressed between the city Presbyterians on one side, and the army on the other, that they adjourned immediately from Monday to Friday, in which interval the Earl of Manchester, speaker of the House of Lords, with eight peers and the speaker of the House of Commons, with about a hundred members,‖ withdrew privately from the city, and joined the army; a surprising event in their favour! The officers received them with the utmost satisfac-

---

* Rushworth, p. 589, 590.
† Ibid., p. 570, 572. Rapin, vol. ii., p. 531.
‡ Rushworth, p. 585.

* Whitelocke, p. 264. Rapin, vol. ii., p. 532.
† Rapin, vol. ii., p. 533.
‡ Rushworth, p. 637. Rapin, vol. ii., p. 533, 534.
§ Rushworth, p. 642. Rapin, vol. ii., p. 534.
‖ Dr. Zach. Grey says there were but fifty-nine, but I do not know his authority.—ED.

tion and transport, paying them all imaginable honours, and assuring them that they would re-establish them in their full power; or die in the attempt. There must surely have been some very pressing reasons for this conduct,* other-wise so many zealous Presbyterians, as were most of the members who quitted the Parliament House, would not have had recourse to the protection of the army. Lord Clarendon believes that they apprehended the army design-ed to restore the king to all his rights at this time, and that they were willing to avoid his majesty's vengeance, by concurring with them in his restoration, which is not unlikely, if they could have brought him to their terms.

However, the Presbyterian members that re-mained in London assembled on Friday accord-ing to adjournment, and having chosen a new speaker, voted that the king should come to London; that the eleven impeached members should be restored; that a committee of safety should join the city militia; and that forces should be immediately raised under the com-mand of Waller, Massey, and Poyntz; in all which they appeared so resolute, that no man could imagine but either that they had the king at their disposal, or intended a brave and val-iant defence of the city.† The common coun-cil gave orders for the trained-bands to repair to the works; and for all capable of bearing arms to appear at the places of rendezvous. Massey, Waller, and Poyntz were also busy in forming regiments and companies; and the committee of the militia were empowered to punish such as did not repair to their colours. At the same time, they wrote to their brethren in Scotland to return with their army immedi-ately to their assistance; but, alas! they were at too great a distance; however, they pub-lished a declaration in the name of the Kirk and whole kingdom, August 13, wherein they engage, by a solemn oath, to establish the Presbyterian government in England; to re-deem his majesty out of the hands of schismat-ics, and place him at the head of his Parlia-ment with honour; to vindicate the honour of the eleven impeached members, and to settle the privileges of Parliament against the over-

* Rapin, as well as Mr. Neal, expresses his sur-prise at this secession of these members of Parlia-ment: he supposes that it proceeded from a disap-probation of the measures pursued by their brethren and the Common Council of London, and from an apprehension that they would be infallibly oppressed by the army. By joining the army, they sought their security from the ruin which threatened their own party; and, says Mr. Hume, "paid their court in time to that authority which began to predominate in the nation." What Whitelocke reports concerning the reason which the Earls of Warwick, Manchester, &c., assigned for their conduct, appears to have esca-ped the attention of these writers. He says that they sent to the general to acquaint him "that they had quitted the Parliament, for that there was no free-sitting for them, and they cast themselves into his protection."—*Memorials*, p. 265. Dr. Grey, in his Appendix, No. 72, has confirmed this account of the matter, by giving at length their letter to Sir Thom-as Fairfax, signed by the Speaker of the House of Lords and eight peers, and by the speaker and fifty-eight of the Commons. Mr. Neal, and since him Mrs. Macaulay, says a hundred Commoners seceded. All, probably, did not sign the letter. Dr. Grey is rather severe here upon our author.—ED.

† Rapin, vol. ii., p. 399, 534. Rushworth, p. 737.
VOL. II.—G

awing power of the army. A little after they declared against toleration and liberty of con-science, resolving to the last man to stand by the Covenant, whatever the English Parliament might submit to.

Pursuant to the order of the two houses, the general had removed his headquarters above forty miles from the city, till, upon the repre-sentation of the members who fled to them for protection from the outrageous violence of the mob, they resolved to push their advantage, and bring the mutineers to justice; according-ly, they resolved to march to London; and ren-dezvous the whole army on Hounslow Heath, August 3, to the number of twenty thousand men, with a suitable train of artillery, accompa-nied with fourteen peers, and about one hun-dred members of the House of Commons.* The citizens were no sooner informed of this, than their courage sunk at once, and, instead of defending the city, they ordered the militia to retire from the lines, and sent their submis-sion to the general, promising to open their passes, and give all assistance to the replacing of those members who had withdrawn to the army. August 6, being appointed for this ser-vice, the mayor and aldermen met the general at Hyde Park with a present of a gold cup, be-seeching him to excuse what had been amiss; but his excellency refused the present, and hav-ing dismissed them with very little ceremony, conducted the members to their seats in Parlia-ment, who immediately voted all proceedings in their absence void, and gave thanks to the army for their safe-conduct.† Next day the army marched through the city without any disorder, and constituted Colonel Titchburn lieu-tenant of the Tower, contrary to the request of the lord-mayor and citizens; the militia was changed, and put into the hands of the old offi-cers who had conducted it before; the fortifi-cations and lines of circumvallation about the city were levelled, and sundry peers, who had been at the head of the late tumults, were im-peached of high treason, as the Earl of Suffolk, Middlesex, Lincoln, Lord Willoughby of Par-ham, Hudson, &c.; the lord-mayor and some of the principal citizens were sent to the Tow-er; and it was resolved to purge the House of all who had been active in the late unhappy riot; which put a full period to the Presbyteri-an power for the present; and the army being quartered near the city all the next winter, there was a council of officers at their headquarters at Putney, whose debates and resolutions had, no doubt, a very powerful influence upon the resolutions of the two houses.

The odium of this grand revolution, by which the army became masters of the city of London, and of the Parliament itself, fell chiefly on the Presbyterians themselves, whose intemperate zeal for Covenant uniformity carried them to very impolitic excesses. The sermons of their ministers were filled with invective against the army while at a distance; in their public prayers they entreated the Almighty to incline the hearts of the Scots to return to their relief; and the conversation of their people was riotous and dis-orderly; however, lest the weight of this rev-olution should fall too heavily on the London

* Rushworth, p. 745, 750. † Ibid., p. 751, 756.

ministers,* as the chief incendiaries of the people, they wisely prepared a vindication of themselves, and published it four days before the army entered the city; it was dated from Sion College, August 2, 1647, and is to this purpose: "We, the ministers of London, whose names are subscribed, do profess, in the presence of the Searcher of all hearts,

1. "That we have never done anything purposely and wittingly to engage the city against the army, or the army against the city, but have sincerely and faithfully endeavoured to prevent it.

2. "That seeing both the Parliament and city have declared the necessity of putting the city into a present posture of defence, yet protesting against any desires of a new war, and thereupon have called upon us to stir up the people to prepare for their defence; we accordingly have done and shall do our duty therein, that the people may be encouraged to their own just and necessary preservation.

3. "But withal, we profess our abhorrence of the shedding any blood on either side; and we humbly pray all whom it may concern, that they will be very careful in preventing it by a seasonable treaty."

Signed by about twenty of the London ministers, and presented to a committee of both houses, sitting at Guildhall.

Let the reader now pause a little, and judge of the authors of this grand revolution, which brought the Parliament under the power of the army, and how far the Presbyterian ministers were concerned in it. Mr. Baxter, in a very angry style, lays all the blame at the door of the Independents. "A few dissenting members of the Westminster Synod," says he, "began all this, and carried it far on. Afterward they increased, and others joined them, who, partly by stiffness, and partly by policy, increased our flames, and kept open our wounds, as if there had been none but they considerable in the world; and having an army, and city agents fit to second them, effectually hindered all remedy, till they had dashed all into pieces as a broken glass. One would have thought that, if all their opinions had been certainly true, and their church order good, yet the interests of Christ and the souls of men, and of greater truths, should have been so regarded by the dividers in England, as that the safety of all these should have been preferred, and not all ruined, rather than their way should want its carnal arm and liberty; and that they should not tear the government of Christ all to pieces rather than it should want their lace."† I am far from clearing the Independents from all manner of blame in their conduct; their principles might be too narrow and mistaken in some points, and their zeal for Christian liberty betray them into some imprudences. But on which side was the stiffness? on theirs who only desired a peaceable toleration; or on theirs who were determined to make the whole nation stoop to Presbyterian uniformity? Were not these the men who kept open the Church's wounds? Had their discipline been ever so good, yet certainly they might

have had some regard to men of piety and virtue, who had not equal discernment with themselves; could they not be content with being the established religion, and having most of the livings of the kingdom divided among them, without trampling on the religious rights of mankind, by enforcing an absolute uniformity, which can never be maintained but on the ruins of a good conscience, and, therefore, is no means of promoting the true interest of Christ and salvation of souls? Mr. Baxter had milder sentiments, in his latter days; and it is for the honour of the present generation of those commonly called Presbyterians, that they have not only abandoned and renounced these servile doctrines,* but have appeared in defence of the civil and religious liberties of mankind, upon the most solid and generous principles.

His majesty was obliged, all this time, to attend the removes of the army: from Newmarket he came to Royston, June 24; from thence to Hatfield; from thence to Windsor, and two days after to Caversham, where he had the pleasure of conversing with his children. But when the city of London threatened a new war, his majesty was removed to a greater distance; about the middle of July he was at Maidenhead; and towards the end of the month at Latimer's, in Buckinghamshire; when the army had got possession of the city they brought his majesty back to Oatlands, August 14, and two days after to Hampton Court, where he appeared in state and splendour about three months, being attended by the proper officers of the court, and a vast resort of people, both from city and country.

While the king was with the army, Lieuten-

---

* The Assembly of Divines also, Dr. Grey informs us, presented a petition for peace, which he has preserved, from the MSS. of Dr. Williams, No. 74 of his Appendix.—ED.   † Abridg., p. 97.

* "To know whether the Presbyterians have indeed abandoned their persecuting principles," says Bishop Warburton, "we should see them under an establishment. It is no wonder that a tolerated sect should espouse those principles of Christian liberty which support their toleration. Now the Scottish Presbyterians are established, and we find they still adhere to the old principle of intolerance." His lordship's reflections are too well founded in fact and experience. The recent persecution of Dr. M'Gill for his valuable and guarded Essay on the Death of Christ, may be adduced as a new proof of the intolerance of Scotch Presbyterianism. But, strictly speaking, Presbyterianism hath no existence among the English Dissenters, who form so many independent societies. The name is, indeed, applied to one part of them; but they are invested with no power but what arises from the management of a fund for the assistance of small congregations. This they are known to direct on a truly liberal plan, without demanding subscription to any articles, or making any inquisition into the sentiments, on doctrine or discipline, of the ministers or churches to whom they grant exhibitions. And the writings of those who have been called Presbyterians, the bishop could not but know, were most able vindications of the principles of liberty. In this cause did a Browne, an Evans, a Grosvenor, a Chandler, and many others, argue and plead. His lordship's argument, I would add, applies to an extent to which it is conceived he did not wish to have it carried; it more than implies, that toleration and an establishment are incompatible; that when once the tolerated are possessed of power, they of course become intolerant. If so, an establishment cannot exist without being inimical to the interests of truth and the rights of conscience. Could a severer reflection be passed on establishments than is here conveyed by an Episcopal pen?—ED.

ant-general Cromwell and Ireton took sundry opportunities to confer with his majesty privately about his restoration. They offered to set him upon the throne with the freedom of his conscience upon the point of Episcopacy, or lose their lives in the attempt; if he would consent to their proposals to the Parliament, and bestow some particular preferments on themselves and a few of their friends, wishing that God would deal with them and their families according to their sincerity.* Nay, they engaged to indemnify his whole party if they would be quiet.† Sir J. Berkley, the king's agent, entreated his majesty in the most importunate and submissive manner, considering the state of his affairs, to accept of the said proposals; but the king treated them with a haughty reserve, and said, if they intended an accommodation, they would not impose such conditions upon him. Sir J. Berkley said, he should suspect they designed to abuse him if they had demanded less; and that a crown so near lost was never recovered on easier terms. But Mr. Ashburnham, who came with instructions from France, fell in with the king's humour, and encouraged him to stand his ground, relying upon an ill-judged maxim which his majesty had imbibed, and which his best friends could not make him depart from, viz., that it was in his power to turn the scale, and that the party must sink which he abandoned.‡ This sealed his ruin, and made him play between both, till neither would trust him. When the Parliament brought their propositions, he put them in mind of the offers of the army; and when the proposals of the latter were tendered in the most respectful manner, he put on a frown, and said, "I shall see you glad, ere long, to accept more equal terms; you cannot be without me; you will fall to ruin if I do not sustain you; no man shall suffer for my sake; the Church must be established according to law." The officers were confounded at this language. "Sir," says Sir J. Berkley, "you speak as if you had some secret strength, which, since you have concealed from me, I wish you had concealed from these men."§ After divers conferences of this kind to no purpose, Cromwell told him plainly, "Sir, we perceive you have a design to be arbitrator between the Parliament and us; but we now design to be the same between your majesty and the Parliament." This fluctuating temper (says Bishop Kennet) was the king's ruin, which he repented of when it was too late. Mr. Whitelocke says, the king's bishops persuaded him against what he was inclined to in his own judgment, and thereby ruined him and themselves.||

When the officers found they could make no impression on the king, and had discovered his secret correspondence with the queen, they withdrew from court, which raised suspicions in his majesty's mind of a secret design against his life, and put him on attempting to escape

out of their hands. It is very certain that Cromwell withdrew his parole of honour for the king's safety, and sent him word, a few days before he left Hampton Court, that he would not be answerable any longer for what might befall him, which was owing to a discovery he had made of the king's insincerity in treating with him. Mr. Coke says, there was a report at that time, and he is confident that in time it will appear, that in the army's treaty with the king, Cromwell had made a private article of advantage for himself,* but his majesty not allowing himself to conclude anything without the queen, wrote her word, "that if he consented to those proposals, it would be easier to take off Cromwell afterward, than now he was at the head of the army."† Which letter Cromwell intercepted.‡ Bishop Kennet says, "that

* Detect., p. 323. † Complete History, p. 270.

‡ This very important point in vindication of Cromwell's conduct towards the false-hearted Charles has been too much overlooked, and yet it is a circumstance thoroughly substantiated. Mr. Baron Maseres, in a note to his publication of tracts relative to these times, referring to Cromwell's abandonment of the treaty with the king, which, he observes, he had been carrying on for more than five months (from the beginning of June to the end of November, 1647), for restoring him to the exercise of his royal authority, observes, that Sir John Berkley's account is so clear and circumstantial, and supported by the testimony of so many respectable persons who were concerned in the management of it, that it seems highly deserving of credit without seeking any other motive for this change of his (Cromwell's) conduct towards the king, besides the fear of losing his influence over the army if he should persist in his endeavour to restore him to his authority, after a great part of the army had resolved to act against him. The baron then gives the copy of the supposed letter (said to have been the cause of the death of the king), of which the writer he mentions gives the following account: That Lord Bolingbroke told them (Mr. Pope and Lord Marchmont), June 12, 1742, that Lord Oxford (the second Earl of Oxford) had often told him that he had seen, and had in his hands an original letter that the king wrote to the queen, in answer to one of hers that had been intercepted, and then forwarded to him; wherein she had reproached him for having made those villains too great concessions, viz., that Cromwell should be lord-lieutenant for life without account; that that kingdom (Ireland) should be in the hands of the party, with an army there kept which should have no head but the lieutenant; and that Cromwell should have a garter, &c.; that in this letter of the king's it was said, that she should leave him to manage, who was better informed of all circumstances than she could be; but that she might be entirely easy as to whatever concessions he should make them; for that he should know in due time how to deal with the rogues, who, instead of a silken garter, should be fitted with a hempen cord; that she the letter ended; which answer, as they waited for, so they intercepted accordingly; and that it determined his fate; and for which letter Lord Oxford said he had offered five hundred pounds. This letter seems to be the same as is referred to in the following passage from the Memoirs of Lord Broghell, afterward Earl of Orrery, written by his chaplain: it is related to be the subject of a conversation between his lordship, and Cromwell, and Ireton, respecting and after the king's death; in which Cromwell is stated to have said, that if the king had followed his own mind, and had had trusty servants about him, he had fooled them all; and added, that once they had a mind to have closed with him; but upon something that happened, they fell off from that design; that, in answer to a question of his lordship, why they once would have closed with the king, and

<hr>

* Dr. Grey fills, here, four pages with authorities to prove the insincerity and hypocrisy of Cromwell and Ireton; by which nothing that Mr. Neal had advanced above is invalidated.—ED.

† Dugdale's Troubles of England, p. 264.

‡ Rushworth, p. 807, 810.

§ History of the Stuarts, p. 570.

|| Memorials, p. 271.

it was reported that Cromwell was to have £10,000 and a garter; and that the bargain had certainly taken effect, if the king had not made an apology to the queen, and sufficiently implied that he did it by constraint, and that when he was at liberty, and in power, he should think himself discharged from the obligation. This letter was sewed up in the skirt of a saddle to be sent to France; but Cromwell and Ireton, having information of it, went to an inn in Holborn, and seized the letter." Dr. Lane, of the Commons, frequently declared, "that he had seen this original letter, that he knew it to be the king's own hand, and that the contents were as above." Another writer says, that the letter mentioned his majesty's being courted by the Scots Presbyterians as well as the army, and that they that bid fairest for him should have him.* Upon the discovery of this letter, Cromwell went to Mr. Ashburnham, who attended the king's person, and told him that he was now satisfied the king could not be trusted; that he had no confidence in the army, but was jealous of them and their officers; that he had treaties with the city Presbyterians, and with the Scots commissioners, to engage the nation again in blood, and that, therefore, he could not be answerable if anything fell out contrary to expectation. Sir Richard Baker, Mr. Coke, and others, are of opinion that, till this time, Cromwell and Ireton were hearty and zealous for restoring the king, and opposing the Levellers who began to arise in the army, but that after this discovery they forsook him, as did the rest of the chief officers, who seldom came to court: the guards also changed their language, and said that God had hardened the king's heart and blinded his eyes.

Under these circumstances the infatuated king left Hampton Court, November 11, at night, and having crossed the Thames, took horse in company with Sir J. Berkley, Mr. Leg, and Mr. Ashburnham; and next morning arrived at Titchfield House, where he stayed while Leg went over to the Isle of Wight, to treat with

why they did not, Cromwell is stated to have said, that they would have closed with the king, because they found that the Scots and the Presbyterians began to be more powerful than themselves, and that, if they made up matters with the king, they (Cromwell and his party) would have been left in the lurch; that, therefore, they thought it best to prevent them, by offering, first, to come into any reasonable condition; but that, while they were busied in these thoughts, there came a letter from one of their spies, acquainting them that on that day their final doom was decreed, referring to a letter sent from the king to the queen; which the spy described as sewed up in the skirt of a saddle, to be taken that night to the Blue Boar Inn, in Holborn, to be taken from thence to Dover. Then follows the particulars of finding the letter in the saddle by Cromwell and Ireton, who attended there for that purpose in the habits of troopers: that by this letter they found that the king had acquainted the queen that he was then courted by both the factions; but that he thought he should close with the Scotch sooner than the other; that upon this, added Cromwell, we took horse and went to Windsor, and finding we were not likely to have any tolerable terms from the king, we immediately, from that time forward, resolved his ruin.—See *Memoirs of Oliver Cromwell and of his Sons Richard and Henry, by Oliver Cromwell, Esq., a descendant of the family,* 2 vols. 8vo, London, 1822, vol. ii., p. 82.—C.

* History of the Stuarts, p. 390.

Colonel Hammond, the governor, about the safety of his person, who, without any treaty, brought the governor to the house where his majesty was, upon which the king said he was betrayed; as, indeed, he was in all his affairs.* Hammond carried him over to the Isle November 13, and after some time shut him up in Carisbrook Castle, where his majesty remained almost a year with one or two servants only, having little conversation with the world, and time sufficient to contemplate on the uncertainty of all human affairs, and on the miserable circumstances to which Divine Providence had suffered his own imprudent conduct to reduce him.†

Let us now attend to the projects of the several parties for restoring the public tranquillity. As soon as the army had got possession of the city of London, they made the following proposals to the two houses. With regard to religion, " That an act be passed to take away all coercive power and jurisdiction of bishops extending to any civil penalties upon any. That there be a repeal of all acts, or clauses of acts, enjoining the use of the Common Prayer, and imposing any penalty for neglect thereof, and for not coming to church, or for meeting elsewhere. That the taking of the Covenant be not enforced upon any; but that all orders and ordinances tending to that purpose be repealed." With regard to the state, " That the militia and great officers be disposed of by Parliament for ten years, and after that the houses to nominate three, out of which the king to choose one. That there be acts of indemnity and revocation

* Rushworth, p. 920, 960.
† A "pretty summer house" was erected for Charles on the ramparts, whither he often retired to commune with his own thoughts. The bowling green on the barbican at Carisbrook, with its turf steps, is as perfect at the present time as if it had been laid down but yesterday. When at Carisbrook, Charles clothed his melancholy feelings in poetry. The verses in question, which extend to a considerable length, were omitted in the collection of the king's works, but were printed shortly afterward by his biographer, Perinchief. Burnet says, " The mighty sense and great piety of them will be found to be beyond all the sublimities of poetry, which are not yet wanting here." Even Walpole condescends to speak well of them: he says, " The poetry is uncouth and inharmonious; but there are strong thoughts in them, some good sense, and a strain of majestic piety.". It may be doubted if too high praise has not been passed upon this production: the following verses are certainly far from happy:

Tyranny bears the title of taxation,
Revenge and robbery are reformation;
Oppression gains the name of sequestration.

My loyal subjects, who in this bad season
Attend (by the law of God and reason),
They dare impeach and punish for high treason.

Next at the clergy do their furies frown;
Pious Episcopacy must go down;
They will destroy the crosier and the crown.

Churchmen are chained and schismatics are freed,
Mechanics preach, and holy fathers bleed;
The crown is crucified with the Creed.

The Church of England doth all faction foster,
The pulpit is usurped by each impostor;
Extempore excludes the *Pater Noster*.

Jesse's Court of the Stuarts, vol. ii., p. 146.—C.

of all declarations against the proceedings of Parliament. That the present unequal, and troublesome, and contentious way of ministers' maintenance by tithes be considered of, and some remedy applied. That none may be obliged to accuse themselves or relations in criminal causes; and no man's life taken away under two witnesses. That consideration be had of all statutes, laws, or customs of corporations, imposing any oaths tending to molest or ensnare religious and peaceable people merely for nonconformity in religion. That the arbitrary power given to committees and deputy-lieutenants be recalled."*

After several debates upon these proposals with regard to religion, the Lords agreed, October 13, "that the king be desired to give his consent to the settling the Presbyterial government for three years, with a provision, that no person shall be liable to any penalty for nonconformity to the said government, or form of Divine service; but such persons shall have liberty to meet for the service and worship of God, and for exercise of religious duties and ordinances in any fit and convenient places, so as nothing be done by them to the disturbance of the peace of the kingdom. Provided this shall not be construed to extend to a toleration of the popish religion, nor to exempt popish recusants from any penalties imposed upon them for the exercise of the same. Nor shall it extend to the toleration of anything contrary to the principles of the Christian religion contained in the Apostles' Creed, as it is expounded in the first fifteen articles of the Church of England, as they had been cleared and vindicated by the Assembly of Divines now sitting at Westminster; nor of anything contrary to such points of faith; for the ignorance whereof men are to be kept from the sacrament, according to the ordinance of October 20, 1645. Nor shall it extend to excuse any persons from the penalties of 1 Elizabeth, cap. ii., for not coming to hear the Word of God on the Lord's Day in any parish church or chapel, unless he can show a reasonable cause for his absence, or that he was present to hear the Word of God preached or expounded elsewhere."†

The Commons likewise agreed, "that Presbytery be established till the end of the next sessions of Parliament, or till the second sessions; that the tenths, and all other maintenance belonging to any church or chapel, shall be only for the use of them who can submit to the Presbyterial government, and none other. The liberty of conscience shall extend to none who shall print, preach, or publish, contrary to the first fifteen articles of the thirty-nine, except the eighth, relating to the three creeds. That nothing contained in this ordinance shall extend to popish recusants."‡ October 14, they agreed farther, "that such tender consciences should be freed, by way of indulgence; from the penalty of the statute for the Presbyterian government, for their nonconformity, who do meet in some other congregation for the worship of God on the Lord's Day, and do nothing against the laws and peace of the kingdom, and that none others shall be freed from the penalty of the statute of Eliz., cap. ii.". October 16, the

Commons voted, "that the indulgence granted to tender consciences should not extend to tolerate the use of common prayer in any part of the kingdom."* Which was against the sense of the army, who were for a general indulgence, as appears from the declaration of the agitators, dated November 1, in which they say that "matters of religion and the ways of God's worship are not at all intrusted by us to any human power, because therein we cannot omit or exceed a tittle of what our consciences dictate to be the mind of God, without wilful sin; nevertheless, the public way of instructing the nation, so it be not compulsive, is left to their discretion."† Here was a fair plan of accommodation, but no ordinance was brought into the House to confirm these resolutions. November 8, both houses agreed to the addition of some new propositions. As,

1. "For the due observation of the Lord's Day.

2. "Against innovations in religion.

3. "A new oath for the conviction of papists.

4. "For the education of the children of papists in the Protestant religion.

5. "Against pluralities."

The proposals of the Presbyterians were the same with those of Newcastle already mentioned; but whereas the king declined to accept them without a personal treaty, they determined in the House of Commons to reduce them into four bills, which, if his majesty refused to sign as preliminaries, they resolved to settle the nation without him; but before they were perfected, the king withdrew from Hampton Court, and was secured in the Isle of Wight, where the commissioners from the two houses waited on him, and tendered him the following bills, December 24: the first, was settling the militia, as has been related; the second, for calling in all his majesty's declarations and proclamations against the two houses, and those that adhered to them; the third, to disqualify those peers from sitting in the House that had been created after the great seal had been conveyed to Oxford; the fourth, to empower the two houses to adjourn, as they should think fit. In matters of religion, they insisted peremptorily on the establishment of the Presbyterian Church government upon the ruins of the prelatical; upon the extirpation of all sectaries; and upon Covenant uniformity in both nations, as will appear more fully hereafter. But the king, instead of signing the preliminaries, insisted strenuously on a personal treaty, which it was hardly reasonable for him to expect, when he had so lately attempted to escape out of their hands, and now refused to yield anything in a way of condescension.

It had not been possible to unriddle the mystery of this escape, if it had not appeared, soon after, that the king was at that very time throwing himself into the hands of the Scots, who, being offended with the Parliament (now under the influence of the army) for not acting in concert with them in the present treaty, according to their Covenant, determined on a separate negotiation for themselves; and accordingly, by the mediation of some of their own nation, they concluded a secret treaty with the king, which was begun before his majesty left Hampton

* Rushworth, p. 736. Rapin, vol. ii., p. 538, 539.
† Rushworth, p. 840.   ‡ Ibid., p. 841.

* Rushworth, p. 842.   † Ibid., p. 160.

Court, but not signed till the 27th of December following, three days after his majesty's refusal of the Parliament's four bills. ".This alliance," says Lord Clarendon,[*] "was most scandalous, and derogatory to the honour and interest of the English nation, and would have been abominated if known and understood by all men." But Rapin thinks it not so criminal on the part of the Scots as his lordship represents, since they yielded to the establishment of their beloved Presbytery in England only for three years; however, it laid the foundation of the king's ruin with the army.

In the preamble his majesty gives "a favourable testimony to the solemn League and Covenant, and to the good intentions of those that entered into it." In the treaty "he obliges himself to confirm the Covenant by act of Parliament as soon as he can do it with honour and freedom in both kingdoms; with a proviso, that none that were unwilling should be obliged to take it for the future. He engages, farther, to confirm by act of Parliament the Presbyterial government in England, the Directory for public worship, and the Assembly of Divines, for three years only, with liberty for himself and his household to use that form of Divine service they had formerly practised; and that during the three years there should be a consultation with the Assembly of Divines, to whom twenty of the king's nomination should be added, and some from the Church of Scotland, to determine what form of church government should be established afterward."[†] Then follows a scourge for the army: "That an effectual course should be taken to suppress the opinions of the Anti-Trinitarians, Arians, Socinians, Arminians, Independents, Brownists, Antinomians, Anabaptists, Separatists, Seekers; and, in general, all blasphemy, heresy, schism, and other doctrines contrary to the known principles of Christianity, whether concerning faith, worship, conversation, or the power of godliness, or which may be destructive to order and government, or to the peace of the Church and kingdom."

In return for these concessions, "the Scots engaged to raise an army to deliver his majesty out of captivity, to assert his right to the militia, the great seal, the negative voice in Parliament; and, in a word, to restore him to his throne with honour and freedom;" which occasioned a second civil war the next year.

As soon as his majesty arrived in the Isle of Wight from Hampton Court, he sent a letter to the Speaker of the House of Lords, to be communicated to the Commons, with the following concessions on his part, very inconsistent with the treaty last mentioned: "For the abolishing archbishops, bishops, &c., his majesty clearly professeth, that he cannot consent to it either as a Christian or a king; for the first he avows, that he is satisfied in his judgment that this order was placed in the Church by the apostles themselves, and ever since their time has continued in all Christian churches throughout the world till this last century; and in this church, in all times of change and reformation, it has been upheld, by the wisdom of his ancestors, as the great preserver of doctrine, discipline, and order, in the service of God. As a king, at his coronation he not only swore to maintain this

order; but his majesty and his predecessors, in their confirmations of the great charter, have inseparably woven the rights of the Church into the liberty of the subject; and yet he is willing that it be provided, that particular bishops perform the several duties of their callings, both by their personal residence and frequent preaching; that in their personal exercise no act of jurisdiction or ordination be without consent of their presbyters; and will consent, that in all things their powers be so limited that they may not be grievous to the tender consciences of others; his majesty sees no reason why he alone, and those of his judgment, should be pressed to a violation of theirs.

"Nor can his majesty consent to the alienation of church lands, because it cannot be denied to be the sin of sacrilege; as, also, that it subverts the intentions of so many pious donors, who have laid a heavy curse upon all such profane violations. And, besides, his majesty believes it to be a prejudice to the public good, many of his subjects having the benefit of renewing leases at much easier rates than if those possessions were in the hands of private men; not omitting the discouragement it will be to learning and industry, when such eminent rewards shall be taken away; yet, considering the present distempers concerning church discipline, and that the Presbyterian government is now in practice, his majesty, to avoid confusion as much as may be, and for the satisfaction of his two houses, is content that the same government be legally permitted to stand in the same condition it now is for three years, provided that his majesty, and those of his judgment, or any others who cannot in conscience submit thereunto, be not obliged to comply with the Presbyterial government, but have free practice of our own profession, without any prejudice thereby; and that free consultation be had with the divines at Westminster, twenty of his majesty's nomination being added to them, to consider how to settle the Church afterward, with full liberty to all those who shall differ upon conscientious grounds from that settlement; always provided, that nothing aforesaid be understood to tolerate those of the popish profession, or exempt them from penal laws; or to tolerate the public profession of atheism or blasphemy, contrary to the doctrine of the apostles, the Nicene and Athanasian Creeds; they having been received by, and had in reverence of, all Christian churches; and more especially the Church of England since the Reformation."[*] This was inserted to cajole the army, and was entirely reversed by the Scots treaty five weeks after.

From these inconsistent views of the contending parties, we may easily discern the precarious situation of the public tranquillity, especially as there was a general distrust on all sides, and each party resolved to carry their point without any abatements: the king was held by ties of conscience and honour (as he said) to preserve Episcopacy; the Scots and English Presbyterians, though divided at present, thought themselves equally bound to stand by their solemn League and Covenant; and the army was under a solemn engagement to agree with neither without a toleration. If the king could have submitted to Covenant uniformity, he might have been restored by the Presbyterians, or, if either king or Parliament would have declared heartily for a toleration, they might have established themselves by the assistance of the military power; but his majesty seems to have been playing an unsteady, if not a double game. The reader will judge of the equity of the several proposals, and of the prudential conduct of each party, from the respective circumstances in which they stood: the king was a prisoner; the Parliament in possession of the whole legislative authority; but the sword was in the hands of the army, who were determined not to sheath it till they had secured to themselves that liberty for which they had been fighting; this they had in vain solicited from the king, and were next determined to try their interest with the Parliament.

The houses being informed of the king's design to make his escape out of the Isle of Wight, ordered the governor to put away his servants, and confine him a close prisoner in the castle, so that no person might be admitted to speak to him without leave. His majesty having also declared, when he rejected the Parliament's four bills, that nothing which could befall him could ever prevail with him to consent to any one act till the conditions of the whole peace were concluded, they began to despair of an accommodation. In this juncture, the officers of the army sent a message to the houses, assuring them that they would live and die with them in settling the nation, either with or without the king, and leave all transactions of state for the future to them alone.*

However, after the seclusion of the eleven impeached members, and the quartering the army in the neighbourhood of the city, the Parliament, either from interest or fear, had a great regard to the opinion of those officers who were members of the House. Upon a motion that no more addresses be made to the king from the Parliament, nor any messages received from him, Ireton and Cromwell opened themselves very freely: Ireton said, "Subjection to the king was but in lieu of protection from him, which being denied, we may settle the kingdom without him. Let us, then, show our resolution," says he, "and not desert those valiant men who have engaged for us beyond all possibility of retreat." Cromwell said, "That the Parliament should govern by their own power, and not teach the people any longer to expect safety from an obstinate man, whose heart God had hardened. The army will defend you against all opposition. Teach them not, by neglecting yours and the kingdom's safety, in which their own is involved, to think themselves betrayed, and left hereafter to the rage and malice of an irreconcilable enemy, whom they have subdued for your sake, lest despair teach them to seek their safety by some other means than adhering to you [there he put his hand to his sword]; and how destructive such a resolution will be," says he, "I tremble to think, and leave you to judge!" The question being then put, it was carried by a majority of fifty voices; yeas one hundred and forty-one, noes ninety-one. January 17, the Lords concurred with the Commons in their votes of

non-addresses. Till this very time, says Lord Clarendon, no man mentioned the king's person without duty and respect. But now a new scene was opened, and some of their officers, at their meetings at Windsor, began to talk of deposing the king, or prosecuting him as a criminal, of which his majesty was advertised by Watson the quartermaster, but it made no impression upon him.

The two houses having concurred in their votes for non-addresses, the army agreed to stand by the Parliament in settling the nation without the king; and that the people might be satisfied with the reasons of their proceedings, a remonstrance was published by order of Parliament, February 15, in which they recapitulate all the errors of his majesty's government; his insincerity in the several treaties of peace he had entered into with them; and that though they had applied to him seven times with propositions, in all which the Scots had concurred except the last, yet he had never complied with any; from whence they conclude, either that the nation must continue under the present distractions, or they must settle it without him. In the posthumous works of Lord Clarendon,* there is a large reply to this remonstrance, in which his lordship endeavours to vindicate the king and throw all the blame upon the Parliament; but though there were ill instruments on both sides, and there might be no real occasion to rip up the misdemeanors of the king's government from the beginning, yet it is hardly possible for the art of man to justify his majesty's conduct before the war, or to vindicate his prudence and sincerity in his treaties afterward; the design of commencing a new war being evidently at this time concerted and agreed upon, with his majesty's allowance, in pursuance of the Scots treaty, while he was amusing both the Parliament and army with overtures of peace.

Among the ordinances that passed this year for reformation of the Church, none occasioned so much noise and disturbance as that of June 8, for abolishing the observation of saints' days, and the three grand festivals of Christmas, Easter, and Whitsuntide; the ordinance says, "Forasmuch as the feast of the nativity of Christ, Easter, Whitsuntide, and other festivals, commonly called holydays, have been heretofore superstitiously used and observed; be it ordained, that the said feasts, and all other festivals, commonly called holydays, be no longer observed as festivals; any law, statute, custom, constitution, or canon, to the contrary in anywise notwithstanding.†

"And that there may be a convenient time allotted for scholars, apprentices, and other servants, for their recreation, be it ordained, that all scholars, apprentices, and other servants, shall, with the leave of their masters, have such convenient, reasonable recreation, and relaxation from labour, every second Tuesday in the month throughout the year, as formerly they used to have upon the festivals; and masters of scholars, apprentices, and servants, shall grant to them respectively such time for their recreation, on the aforesaid second Tuesday in the month, as they may conveniently spare from their extraordinary necessary service and occasions; and if any difference arise between mas-

---

* Rushworth, p. 951, 953, 962. Rapin, vol. ii., p. 545.

* Vol. iii., p. 92, 93.   † Scobel, p. 128.

ters and servants concerning the liberty hereby granted, the next justice of peace shall reconcile it."

The king was highly displeased with this ordinance; and therefore, while the affair was under debate, he put this query to the Parliament commissioners at Holmby House, April, 23, 1647.

I desire to be out-resolved of this question, Why the new reformers discharge the keeping of Easter? My reason for this query is, "I conceive the celebration of this feast was instituted by the same authority which changed the Jewish Sabbath into the Lord's Day or Sunday, for it will not be found in Scripture where Saturday is discharged to be kept, or turned into the Sunday; wherefore it must be the Church's authority that changed the one and instituted the other; therefore my opinion is, that those who will not keep this feast may as well return to the observation of Saturday, and refuse the weekly Sunday. When anybody can show me that herein I am in an error, I shall not be ashamed to confess and amend it; till when you know my mind.* C. R."

Sir James Harrington presented his majesty with an answer to this query, in which he denies that the change of the Sabbath was from the authority of the Chnrch, but derives it from the authority and example of our Saviour and his apostles in the New Testament; he admits that, if there was the like mention of the observation of Easter, it would be of Divine or apostolical authority; but as the case stands, he apprehends, with great reason, that the observation of the Christian Sabbath, and of Easter, stands upon a very different footing.

The changing the festival of Christmas into a fast last winter was not so much taken notice of, because all parties were employed in acts of devotion; but when it returned this year, there appeared a strong propensity in the people to observe it; the shops were generally shut, many Presbyterian ministers preached; in some places the common prayer was read, and one or two of the sequestered clergy getting into pulpits, prayed publicly for the bishops; several of the citizens of London, who opened their shops, were abused; in some places there were riots and insurrections, especially in Canterbury, where the mayor, endeavouring to keep the peace, had his head broke by the populace, and was dragged about the streets; the mob broke into divers houses of the most religious in the town, broke their windows, abused their persons, and threw their goods into the streets, because they exposed them to sale on Christmas Day.† At length, their numbers being increased to above two thousand, they put themselves into a posture of defence against the magistrates, kept guard, stopped passes, examined passengers, and seized the magazine and arms in the town-hall, and were not dispersed without difficulty. The like disorders were at Ealing, in Middlesex, and in several other counties. The Parliament was alarmed at these disorders, and therefore commanded all papists and delinquent clergymen to retire without the lines of communication, and punished some of the principal rioters as a terror to the rest, it being apparent that the king's party took ad-

vantage of the holydays to try the temper of the people in favour of his release, for during the space of the following twelve years, wherein the festivals were laid aside, there was not the least tumult on account of the holydays, the observation of Christmas being left as a matter of indifference.

The war being thought to be at an end, many of the clergy who had followed the camp returned home, and endeavoured to repossess themselves of their sequestered livings, to the prejudice of those whom the Parliament had put into their places; they petitioned the king while he was with the army, and in a state of honour and dignity, to take their poor distressed condition into his gracious consideration. His majesty recommended them to the general, at the very time when the difference between the Parliament and army was subsisting, upon which they represented their grievances to him in a petition, showing, that "whereas for divers years they had been outed of their livings, contrary to the fundamental laws of the land, by the arbitrary power of committees, whose proceedings have usually been by no rule of law, but by their own wills; most of them having been turned out for refusing the Covenant, or adhering to the king, and the religion established, and of those, divers never called to answer, and scarce one had articles proved by oath; or other legal process; by which means your petitioners are reduced to extreme want and misery; and whereas, those who are put into our places labour to stir up the people to involve the kingdom in a new war, and are generally men ignorant and unable to instruct the people; and many of them scandalous in their practices, if impartially examined, and divers of them hold three or four of the best benefices, while divers other churches are void, and without any constant preacher. And forasmuch as the main profit of our benefices consists in the harvest which is now at hand, which many of the present possessors, if they could receive, would presently be gone, whereby the burden of the cure will lie upon your petitioners, having nothing to live upon the next year. Your petitioners therefore pray that your excellency would make stay of the profits of the harvest, that those of us that are charged with any legal scandal may come to a just trial, and if we are found innocent, may enjoy our rights, according to the known laws of the land."*

By this bold petition, it is evident these gentlemen were encouraged to hope that the army would carry their resentments so far as to unravel all they had been doing for five years; that they would not only renounce the Covenant, but disclaim the proceedings of their committees, and even countenance the clergy's adhering to the king; and no doubt, if his majesty had complied with the proposals of the army, he might have made good terms for them; for the general received them with respect, and, having debated their address in council, proposed it to the Parliament that the estates of all sequestered persons, including the clergy, should remain in the hands of the tenants till a general peace. Upon which the old incumbents grew very troublesome, forbidding the parishioners to pay their tithes, and threatening the present pos-

---

* Relig. Car., p. 370.   † Rushworth, p. 948.   * Sufferings of the Clergy, p. 140.

sessors of their livings with legal prosecutions.

On the other hand, the Presbyterian clergy addressed the general, August 12, a few days after the Parliament and army were united, with a complaint that "divers delinquent ministers, who had been put out of their livings, did now trouble and seek to turn out those ministers whom the Parliament had put in; and particularly, that Dr. Layfield, by a counterfeit warrant from the general, had endeavoured to remove a minister from his benefice in Surrey." The general and his council declared their dislike of these proceedings, and promised to write to the Parliament that such offenders may be brought to punishment, which he did accordingly. The difference between the Parliament and army being now in a manner compromised, which cut off the expectations of the clergy, August 19, the Lords and Commons acquainted the general that they would take care for the punishment of those delinquent ministers and others, by whose practices ministers put into livings by the Parliament had been disquieted and turned out; and on the 23d of the same month they passed an ordinance, setting forth " that whereas divers ministers in the several counties had been displaced by authority of Parliament, for notorious scandals and delinquency, and godly, learned, and orthodox ministers had been placed in their room; and whereas the said scandalous and delinquent ministers, by force or otherwise, had entered upon the churches, and gained possession of the tithes, &c., the Lords and Commons did therefore ordain, that all sheriffs, mayors, committees, &c., do forthwith apprehend such ministers, and all such persons as have been aiding and abetting to them, and commit them to prison, there to remain till those they have thus dispossessed and molested should receive satisfaction for their damages ; and that the said sheriffs, &c., do restore those molested ministers to the quiet possession of their respective places, and do, in case of need, raise the trained-bands to put this ordinance in execution ; and do also take effectual course that the tithes, profits, &c., be for the future duly paid to those ministers put in by Parliament, &c. And if any such disturbance should hereafter be given, the offender was to suffer for every such disturbance one month's imprisonment."

However, some small favour was shown, about this time, to those bishops and others who had lived peaceably, and been little more than spectators of the distracting miseries of their country ; the committee was ordered to make payment of the £800 per year granted to the Bishop of Durham ; the real estate of the pious Bishop Hall, who had lately published his Hard Measure, was discharged ; Archbishop Usher had an allowance of £400 per annum, till he could be otherwise provided for, and was soon after allowed to be preacher at Lincoln's Inn, only upon taking the negative oath. But the bishops were not much considered in these donations. The commissioners of the great seal were ordered to fill up the vacant livings in the gift of the crown, without obliging the incumbents to take the Covenant ; but the new disturbances which arose in favour of the captive king brought down new severities upon

Vol. II.—H

the Episcopal clergy before the end of the following year.*

CHAPTER IX.

THE VISITATION OF THE UNIVERSITY OF OXFORD.
—STATE OF RELIGION AT THE END OF THE YEAR
1647.

SAD and deplorable was the condition of the University of Oxford when it fell into the hands of the Parliament ; the colleges and halls were gone to ruin, five of them perfectly deserted, and the rest in a very shattered condition. The public acts had been discontinued for some years, the schools were turned into magazines for the king's army, and the chambers filled with officers and soldiers, or let out to townsmen : there was little or no instruction for youth, nor hardly the face of a university ; poverty, desolation, and plunder, the sad effects of war, were to be seen in every corner ; the bursaries were emptied of the public money, the plate melted down for the king's service, and the colleges involved in debts which they were not able to satisfy ; there were few heads of colleges or scholars remaining, except such as were strongly prejudiced against the Parliament, having employed their wits, during the course of the war, in writing weekly mercuries and satirical pamphlets, in which they aspersed the proceedings of the two houses, and treated their divines as the most infamous, ignorant, and hypocritical traitors ; nor were their tempers in the least softened, though their lives and fortunes were in the hands of their adversaries. It was therefore thought necessary to put the education of youth into such hands as the Parliament could confide in, a power being reserved for that purpose in the articles of surrender.

But before they proceeded to extremes, the two houses, about the beginning of September, 1646, appointed seven of their most popular divines to repair to Oxford, with authority to preach in any pulpits of the university for six months, in order to soften the spirits of the people,† and give them a better opinion of their cause, viz., the Reverend Mr. Robert Harris, or Hanwell, Oxfordshire ; Mr. Edward Reynolds, afterward Bishop of Norwich ; Mr. Henry Wilkinson, of Magdalen College ; Mr. Francis Cheynel, Mr. Edward Corbet, of Merton College ; Mr. Henry Cornish, of New Inn, and Mr. Henry Langley, of Pembroke College ; men of reputation and character,‡ sober divines and popular preachers, though A. Wood, the Oxford historian, is pleased to say, "Their sermons were the contempt and scorn of the university, because they were too long and had too little learning ; because they prayed very coldly for

* Rushworth, p. 831, 937, 948, 958.
† Suff. Cler., p. 125.
‡ Dr. Grey would impeach the truth of this eulogium, and refers to Anthony Wood to support his invidious reflections on these men. The names and characters of Mr. Robert Harris, Dr. Reynolds, Mr. F. Cheynel, and Mr. Corbet, will again come before the reader in Mr. Neal's next volume ; and we would refer him to Dr. Calamy, or Mr. Palmer's Nonconformist's Memorial, for biography.—ED.

the king, but were very earnest for a blessing upon the councils and arms of the Parliament, and did not always conclude with the Lord's Prayer; because they reflected on some of the heads of the university, calling them dumb dogs, having a form of religion without the power; and because their manner of delivery was rather theatrical than serious: nevertheless, their auditories were crowded, though none of the heads of colleges or senior scholars attended."

The ministers were very diligent in the discharge of their trust, preaching twice every Lord's Day; and that they might gain the affections of the people, set up a weekly conference every Thursday, in which they proposed to solve such objections as should be raised against their new confession of faith and discipline, and to answer any other important cases in divinity: the question or case was to be propounded the week before, that it might be well considered; a moderator also was appointed to keep order, who began and concluded with a short prayer, and the whole was conducted with decency and gravity.* But several of the scholars ridiculed their proceedings, and, by way of contempt, called their place of meeting the scruple shop; however, it was frequented by great numbers of people, some of whom were prevailed with to renounce the Oxford oath, and others to take the solemn League and Covenant. They met with some little disturbance from one Erbury, a turbulent Antinomian, and chaplain in the garrison; but upon the whole, when the ministers returned to London, they declared the citizens showed them a great deal of respect, although the university poured all the contempt upon them imaginable, so that they apprehended themselves to have the same lot as Saint Paul had at Athens, Acts, xvii., 32, 34: "Some mocked them, others slighted them, but certain clave to them, and believed."†

There being no prospect of reforming the university by these methods, the two houses resolved to proceed upon a visitation, which they apprehended they might undertake without the king, by virtue of the fourteenth article of their recapitulation, which says "that the chancellor, masters, and scholars of the university, and all heads, governors, masters, fellows, and scholars of the colleges, halls, bodies corporate, and societies of the said university, and the public professors, readers, and orators thereof, and all other persons belonging to the said university, shall and may, according to their statutes, charters, and customs, enjoy their ancient form of government, subordinate to the immediate authority and power of Parliament, and that all the rights, privileges, franchises, lands, tenements, houses, rents, revenues, libraries, debts, goods, and chattels, &c., belonging to the said university, shall be enjoyed by them respectively as aforesaid, free from sequestrations, fines, taxes, and all other molestations whatsoever under colour of anything relating to the present war. And if any removal shall be made by the Parliament of any head or other members of the university, that they shall enjoy their profits for six months after the surrendering of Oxon, and shall have convenient time allowed them for the removal of themselves and their

goods; provided that this shall not extend to retard any reformation there intended by the Parliament, or give them any liberty to intermeddle with the government."* But the heads of colleges did not think themselves obliged by this capitulation, nor anything contained in it, because they were not made parties, nor called upon to give their separate consent to the articles, though they took advantage of everything that was stipulated in their favour.†

May 1, 1647, an ordinance passed both houses for visiting the university, and nominating the following gentlemen, lawyers, and divines, for that service, viz. :‡

Sir Nath. Brent.	Mr. George Greenwood.
Sir William Cobb.	Mr. John Packer.
William Prynne, of Lincoln's Inn, Esq.	Mr. William Cope.
	Mr. John Heling, of Gray's Inn.
John Pulliston, of Lincoln's Inn, Esq.	Rev. Dr. John Wilkinson.
Barth. Hall, of the Middle Temple, Esq.	" Mr. Henry Wilkinson.
Tho. Knight, of Lincoln's Inn, Esq.	" Mr. Edw. Reynolds.
Samuel Dunch, Esq.	" Mr. Rob. Harris.
William Draper, of Lincoln's Inn, Esq.	" Mr. Edw. Corbet.
	" Mr. Fran. Cheynel.
Gabriel Beck, of Lincoln's Inn, Esq.	" Mr. John Wilkinson.
	" Mr. John Mills.
John Cartwright, Esq.	" Mr. Christopher Rogers.
Mr. William Tripping.	

The ordinance empowers the visiters, or any five of them, "to hear and determine all crimes, offences, abuses, and disorders which, by the laws and statutes of this realm, or by the customs and statutes, rightly established, of that university, or by the several statutes of the respective colleges or halls, may lawfully be inquired of, heard, or determined, in the course and way of visitation of the university, or of the colleges, halls, masters, scholars, fellows, members, and officers, or any of them, respectively. They are more particularly to inquire by oath concerning those that neglect to take the solemn League and Covenant, and the negative oath, being tendered to them by such as are authorized by Parliament; and concerning those who oppose the execution of the ordinance of Parliament, concerning the discipline and Directory; and those who shall teach or write against any point of doctrine, the ignorance whereof doth exclude from the Lord's Supper. They are likewise to inquire, upon oath, concerning all such who have taken up arms against the Parliament. And they are to certify to a committee of the House of Lords and Commons, mentioned in the ordinance, what masters, scholars, fellows, members, or officers have committed any of the offences above mentioned, and the quality and condition of the offenders, that such farther proceedings may be had thereupon as the committee of Lords and Commons shall think fit. The visiters are farther empowered to examine and consider, all such oaths as are enjoined by the statutes of the university, or any of the halls and colleges, as are not fit to be taken, and present their opinion to the committee above mentioned; provided, always, that if any of the masters, scholars, fellows, &c., shall find themselves aggrieved by any sentence given by the visiters, it shall be lawful for them to ap-

---

* Suff. Cler:, p. 125. Minist. Account, p. 5. Vol. Pamph., No. 282.   † Minist. Account, p. 52.

* Rushworth, p. 283.   † Fuller's Appeal, p. 70   ‡ Scobel's Collect., part i., p. 116.   Suff. Cler., p. 126.

peal to the committee of Lords and Commons, who are authorized finally to hear and determine every such case brought before them."

Before the visitation could take place, the vice-chancellor, Dr. Fell, summoned a convocation [June 1], wherein it was agreed not to submit to the Parliament visiters. A paper of reasons against the Covenant,[*] the negative oath, and the Directory, drawn up chiefly by Dr. Sanderson, was also consented to, and ordered to be published to the world both in Latin and English, against the time the visiters were to come down, under the title of "Reasons of the present Judgment of the University of Oxford, concerning the solemn League and Covenant, the Negative Oath, and the Ordinances concerning Discipline and Worship, approved by general consent in a full Convocation, June 1, 1647," an abstract of which I shall now set before the reader.[†]

To the Preface of the Covenant [transcribed under the year 1643].[‡]

They declare, "We cannot say the rage, power, and presumption of the enemies of God (in the sense there intended) are increased. Nor that we have consented to any supplica-

*. Dr. Sanderson methodized and put into form this paper, or manifesto, and added what referred to reason and conscience. The law part was drawn up by Dr. Zouch, a civilian. But, on the whole, twenty delegates, by the appointment of the university, were concerned in this composition; among whom were Dr. Sheldon, afterward Archbishop of Canterbury, Dr. Hammond, Dr. Sanderson, and Dr. Morley, afterward Bishop of Winchester.—*Walton's Life of Sanderson*, 1678, p. 78, 79.—Ed.

† Bp. Sanderson's Life, Appendix, p. 169.

‡ Clarendon exults in the intrepidity of the Oxford men on this occasion. "To their eternal renown," he says, "being at the same time under a strict and strong garrison, put over them by the Parliament—the king in prison, and all their hopes desperate—they passed a public act and declaration against the Covenant, with such invincible arguments of the illegality, wickedness, and perjury entertained in it, that no man of the contrary opinion, nor the Assembly of Divines, ever ventured to make any answer to it; nor is it, indeed, to be answered, but must remain, to the world's end, as a monument of the learning, courage, and loyalty of that excellent place, against the highest malice and tyranny that was ever exercised in or over any nation."—*History of the Revolution*, vol. v., p. 481. This language was not unnatural from the eulogist of Charles and his party, but it is due to historical fidelity to state, that there was no such heroism in the conduct of the Oxford divines as Clarendon alleges.

The influence of the Parliament was rapidly declining before that of the army, and its commissioners might therefore be resisted without the alternative of martyrdom being chosen. The soldiers within sight of the university openly resisted the visiters, and the king's person was seized by a detachment from the army within two days of the Oxford "Reasons" being drawn up. It is only to suppose that the heads of colleges participated in the hopes of the monarch, and their conduct will appear much less marvellous than Clarendon represents.

When the enthusiasm of loyalty was at its height, subsequent to the restoration of the Stuarts, the Commons ordered a vote of thanks to be given to the vice-chancellor, and other members of the university, for their "remarkable loyalty," and "for the illustrious performance they printed" on this occasion. —*Price's History of Nonconformity*, vol. ii., p. 390. —C.

tion or remonstrance to the purposes therein expressed. We do not think the taking the Covenant to be a lawful and probable means to preserve ourselves and our religion from ruin; nor do we believe it to be according to the commendable practice of these kingdoms, or the example of God's people in other nations."

To the Covenant in general.

"We are of opinion that a covenant ought to be a voluntary contract, and not imposed. Now we cannot voluntarily consent to this Covenant without betraying our liberties, one of which is, not to be obliged to take any oath but what is established by act of Parliament; and without acknowledging in the imposers a greater power than has been challenged in former time, or can subsist with our former protestation. But if the Covenant were not imposed, but only recommended, we apprehend the taking it to be inconsistent with our loyalty to the king, especially since he has, by proclamation, forbid it."

Objections to the several Articles of the Covenant.

To the first Article.

"We cannot swear to preserve the religion of another kingdom (Scotland), whereof we have very little understanding, which, as far as we are acquainted with it, is much worse than our own in worship, discipline, and government, and in doctrine not at all better; wherein there are some things so far tending to superstition and schism, that it seems reasonable to us that we should call upon them to reform, rather than we should be bound to preserve it entire.

"Neither are we satisfied in the present reformation of religion in our own kingdom, in doctrine, worship, and discipline, because, (1.) It gives a manifest scandal to the papist and separatist, by giving up the cause for which the martyrs and bishops have contended since the Reformation; by justifying the papists in their recusancy, who reproach us by saying, we know not what religion we are of; nor where to stop, since we have left them; and that ours is a Parliamentary religion. Besides, this would be a tacit acknowledgment that there has been something in the Church of England not agreeable to the Word of God, and so justify the separation, and condemn all the penal laws that have been made to oblige people to conform.[*] (2.) By the intended reformation we should wrong ourselves, by swearing to reform that which we have formerly by our subscriptions approved, and which we do still believe to be more agreeable to the Word of God than that which by this Covenant we must swear to preserve; and to which, by the laws still in being, every clerk, at his admission to a benefice, is bound to give his consent. (3.) Besides, we would be in danger of perjury; because it is contrary to our former protestation, which obliges us to maintain the doctrine of the Church of England, which may take in the whole establishment; and it is contrary to the oath of supremacy, which gives the sole power to the king in matters ecclesiastical."

* Bishop Sanderson's Life, Appendix, p. 179.

Objections to the second Article.

"We are very much grieved to see the prelacy of the Church of England ranked with popery, superstition, heresy, schism, and profaneness, with an intimation that it is contrary to sound doctrine or the power of godliness.* Nor can we swear to the extirpation of it, because, (1.) We believe it to be of apostolical institution. Or, (2.) At least, that Episcopal aristocracy hath a fairer claim to a Divine institution than any other form of church government. (3.) That Episcopal government has continued in the Church, without interruption, for fifteen hundred years; therefore, to extirpate it, would give advantage to the papists, who are wont to charge us with a contempt of antiquity, and love of novelty, and it would diminish the just authority due to the consent and practice of the Catholic Church. (4.) Besides, we cannot swear to the extirpating this government, because we have subscribed the Thirty-nine Articles, one of which says, the book containing the form of consecration has nothing in it contrary to the Word of God. We have been ordained by bishops; we have petitioned the Parliament for the continuance of them; and some of us hold our livelihoods by the titles of deans, deans and chapters, &c. (5.) We are not satisfied that the inconveniences of the new government will be less than the old, the House of Commons having remonstrated [December 15, 1641], that it was far from their purpose to abolish this government, but only to regulate it, and that it was a sign of malignancy to infuse into the people that they had any other meaning. Lastly, in respect of our obligation to his majesty, having acknowledged him to be supreme governor in all causes ecclesiastical, we cannot endeavour to extirpate this government without the royal assent, which we are so far from desiring, that we are continually praying that the king may not be prevailed with to do an act so prejudicial to his conscience and honour, and which, by his coronation oath, he is bound to preserve.† By the laws of the land, there are sundry privileges and emoluments arising to the crown from the ecclesiastical estate, which are a considerable part of the revenue, which, by the extirpation of prelacy, will be cut off; whereas we are bound by the oath of allegiance to maintain the king's honour and estate. And, after all, the prelatical government is best suited to monarchy, insomuch that King James used to say, No bishop, no king."

Objections to the third Article.

"We are dissatisfied with the limitation of our loyalty in these words, ' in the preservation and defence of the true religion and liberties of the kingdom;' because no such limitation is to be found in the oath of allegiance, nor in the Word of God; because it leaves the duty of the subject loose, and the safety of the king uncertain. The conscience of a papist or sectary may swallow an oath with such a limitation, but the conscience of a good Protestant cannot but strain at it."‡

Objections to the fourth Article.

They reply, "That the imposing the Covenant in this article may lay a necessity upon the son to accuse the father, in case he be a malignant, which is contrary to religion, nature, and humanity; or it may open a way for children that are sick of their fathers, to effect their unlawful intentions, by accusing them of malignancy; besides, the subjecting ourselves to an arbitrary punishment, at the sole pleasure of such uncertain judges as may be deputed for that effect, is betraying the liberty of the subject."*

Objections to the fifth Article.

"We cannot acknowledge the happiness of such a peace as in the article is mentioned, for no peace can be firm and well grounded, unless the respective authority, power, and liberty of king, Parliament, and subject, be preserved full and entire, according to the known laws and respective customs of the kingdom before the beginning of these distractions."†

Objections to the sixth Article.

They say, "We are not satisfied that the cause of our joining in covenant for the prosecution of the late war was the cause of religion, liberty, and peace of the kingdom, or that the glory of God and the honour of the king were concerned in it. And if it was, we are not satisfied that it ought to be supported and carried on by such means as are destitute of all warrant from the Word of God, or the laws of the realm."‡

In conclusion, say they, " Our hearts tremble to think that we should be required to pray that other Christian churches may be encouraged by our example to join in the like covenant to free themselves from the antichristian yoke, for we do not know any antichristian yoke we were under; nor do we yet see such good fruits of this Covenant among ourselves as to invite us to pray that other churches should follow our example; it is as if we should pray that the God of love and peace would take away all love and peace, and set the Christian world in a combustion; that he would render the Reformed religion odious to the world; that Christian princes might be provoked to use more severity towards those of the Reformed religion, if not to root it out of their dominions; for the yoke of antichrist, if laid upon subjects by their lawful sovereigns, is to be thrown off by Christian boldness in confessing the truth, and suffering for it, not by taking up arms, or violent resisting of the higher powers."

After these remarks upon the several articles, they take notice,

(1.) Of the following seeming contradictions in that Covenant; as, "The preserving and yet reforming one and the same reformed religion. The reforming church government according to the Word of God, and yet extirpating that government which we apprehend agreeable to it. The extirpating heresy and schism, and yet dissolving that government in the Church, the want of the due exercise of which has been the occasion of the growth of these evils. The preserving the liberties of the kingdom, and yet submitting to a covenant and oath not established by law."§

---

* Bishop Sanderson's Life, Appendix, p. 184.
† Ibid., p. 197.   ‡ Ibid., p. 201.

* Bishop Sanderson's Life, Appendix, p. 203.
† Ibid., p. 206.   ‡ Ibid., p. 207.   § Ibid., p. 243.

(2.) They observe some dark and doubtful expressions which they do not well understand; as, "Who are the common enemies? Which are the best Reformed churches? Who are malignants? How far the hindering reformation may be extended, &c."*

(3.) By the use that has been made of the Covenant, they apprehend "the conduct of the Parliament to be contrary to the meaning of it, for instead of reforming the worship and service of the Church, they have quite abolished it; instead of reforming the discipline of the Church, it is quite destroyed, or put upon such a foot as is not agreeable to the Word of God, or the example of any church since the creation. Instead of extirpating heresy and profaneness, little or nothing has been done towards it, but only the extirpation of prelacy, and something else that looks so like sacrilege (say they) that we do not venture upon it. And as for the preservation of the king's honour and estate in defence of the true religion and liberties of the kingdom, though we apprehend all other things should be subordinate to it, yet by some bold speeches that have been made we are afraid nothing less is intended."

Of the Salvoes for taking the Covenant.

(1.) "It has been said that we may take it in our own sense. But this we apprehend contrary to the nature and end of an oath; contrary to the end of speech; contrary to the design of the Covenant, and contrary to the solemn profession at the conclusion of it, viz., That we shall take it with a true intention to perform the same, as we shall answer it to the Searcher of all hearts at the great day. Besides, this would be Jesuitical; it would be taking the name of God in vain; and it would strengthen the objection of those who say, There is no faith to be given to Protestants.†

(2.) "It has been said, we may take the Covenant with these salvoes expressed, So far as lawfully I may, so far as it is agreeable to the Word of God, and the laws of the land, saving all oaths by me formerly taken, &c., which is no better than vile hypocrisy; for by the same rule one might subscribe to the Council of Trent, or the Turkish Alcoran.

(3.) "It is said that we may take the Covenant in our present circumstances, notwithstanding our allegiance to the king, because protection and subjection are relatives, and the king, being unable to protect us any longer, we are free from subjection to him. But we answer, that the king's inability to perform his duty does not discharge the subject from his, as long as he is able; much less when the non-protection on the king's part is not from want of will, but of power.

(4.) "It is said that the Parliament being the supreme judicatory of the kingdom, wheresoever the king is in person he is always present with his Parliament in power; as what is done in courts of justice is not done without the king, but by him, though not personally present. But we deny the king to be always present with his Parliament in power, for then his actual royal assent would not be necessary to the making of laws, but only a virtual assent included in

* Sanderson's Life, Appendix, p. 213.
† Ibid., p. 221, &c.

the votes of both houses: the houses need not, then, desire the royal assent, nor can the king be supposed to have a negative voice. Besides, the statute which provides that the king's assent to any bill signified under his great seal shall be as valid as if he were personally present, imports that the king's power is not present with his two houses, otherwise than it appears in his person, or under his great seal. As to the analogy of other courts, we conceive it of no consequence; in other courts the judges are the king's servants, and do all in his name, and by his authority; they sit there not by any proper interest of their own, but in right of the king, whose judges they are; but the Parliament is the king's council, and have their several proper rights and interests distinct from the king's, by virtue of which they are distinct orders and conservators of their several interests. Besides, the judges of other courts are bounded by the laws in being, and therefore the king's personal presence is not necessary; but the case is quite different in making new laws, for the making new laws is the exercise of a legislative rather than a judicial power; now no act of legislative power can be valid, unless it be confirmed by such person or persons as the sovereignty of that community resideth in. Upon the whole, since all judicial power is radically in the king, who is therefore called the fountain of justice, it seems to us, that neither the judges in inferior courts, nor the Lords and Commons assembled in Parliament, may exercise any other power over the subjects of this realm than such as by their respective patents and writs issued from the king, or by the established laws of the land, formerly assented to by the kings of this realm, does appear to be derived from them; by which writs, patents, and laws, it does not appear that the two houses of Parliament have any power without the king to order, command, or transact; but only with him to treat, consult, and advise concerning the great affairs of the kingdom."

Concerning the Negative Oath.

They say, "We cannot take it without giving up our liberties, without abusing our natural allegiance, and without diminution of his majesty's just power and greatness."*

Concerning the Discipline and Directory.

"We are not satisfied to submit to the ordinance for establishing the Directory, because it has not the royal assent, and yet abrogates acts of Parliament made by the joint consent of king, Lords, and Commons, especially one which annexes the whole power of ordering all ecclesiastical matters forever to the imperial crown of this realm; now we are not satisfied that a less power can have a just right to abrogate a greater.

"If under the title of discipline be comprehended the government of the Church also, we declare we cannot consent to the eradication of a government of such reverend antiquity, which has from time to time been confirmed by the laws of the kingdom, and which the kings, at their successive coronations, have sworn to preserve. If the word discipline be distinguished from government, as in the first article of

* Sanderson's Life, Appendix, p. 243.

the Covenant, yet are we not satisfied to place so much power in the hands of persons (many of whom may be of mean quality) for the keeping back thousands of well-meaning Christians from the blessed Sacrament, when St. Paul, in a church abounding with sundry errors and corruptions in faith and manners, satisfies himself with a general declaration of the danger of unworthy communicating, and enjoins every particular person a self-examination; without empowering either ministers or lay-elders to exclude any from the communion upon their examination.

"As to the Directory itself, we cannot, without regret of conscience, and during the continuance of the present laws, consent to the taking away the Book of Common Prayer, which we have subscribed, and solemnly promised to use no other ; which we believe contains in it nothing but what is justly defensible; and which we think ourselves able to justify against all papists and sectaries. Besides, we look upon the statute enjoining the use of the Common Prayer to be still in force, and will always remain so, till it shall be repealed by the same good and full authority by which it was made ; that is, by the free consent of king, Lords, and Commons."[*]

By comparing these reasons with those of the Parliament divines for taking the Covenant, the reader will be capable of judging how far they are conclusive. Many of them are unquestionably good, and had the Constitution remained entire, and the laws had their free and ordinary course, as in times of peace, most of them would have been conclusive ; but how far the necessity of the war, and the right of self-defence, will vindicate the extraordinary proceedings of Parliament, I shall not take upon me to determine for others. *I am no advocate for the particulars of the Covenant, any more than for the high and arbitrary principles of government contained in the university's reasons.* The consciences of men are not under the direction of their wills, but of their judgments, and therefore ought not to be constrained by oaths, protestations, or covenants, to attempt those things in matters of religion for which their own hearts must condemn them. Religion and civil government stand upon a distinct foundation, and are designed for very different ends ; the magistrate may demand security for men's peaceable submission to the civil government, but ought not to force them to be active against the light of their consciences in matters of religion. The university's reasons are not built upon these principles ; for those gentlemen were as much for the coercive power of the magistrate in cases of conscience as the Puritans ; and whereas they say, the allegiance of the subject, and the protection of the king, are not relatives ; and that the king's inability to discharge his duty does not absolve the subject from his, I shall only observe, that upon these principles the crown can never be forfeited ; a coronation oath is of very little significance ; nor may a nation submit to a conqueror even when they can resist no longer. Inability alone in the prince, I grant, may not in all cases absolve us from our allegiance ; but tyranny, oppression,

and open attempts to subvert the whole Constitution and laws of the country, certainly may ; upon what other ground can we justify the late revolution, and the present happy establishment of the Protestant succession ? When the Oxford divines, at the period of the revolution, had taken the oath of allegiance to King James III., and the corporation oath, which says, " It is not lawful to resist or take up arms against the king upon any pretence whatsoever ;" what could absolve them from these engagements, or justify their joining the Prince of Orange with a foreign force against a king upon the throne ? However, the stand now made by the university was a bold and adventurous attempt, for which they received the applause of the Oxford Parliament in the year 1665, when it was resolved, " that the thanks of the House of Commons be returned to the chancellor, masters, and scholars of the University of Oxford, for their bold opposition to the rebellious visiters ; for refusing to submit to their League and Covenant ; and, lastly, for the illustrious performance they printed, entitled 'The Judgment of the University,' &c., in which they have learnedly maintained the king's cause." This was the fashionable doctrine of King Charles II.'s reign, when the laws were suspended and infringed, and arbitrary power in the prince rose to such a height as in the next reign issued in a revolution of government. The University of Oxford did all they could to countenance the triumphs of the prerogative ; for in the year 1663 they passed a decree in full convocation, affirming the necessity of passive obedience and non-resistance in the strongest terms ; but how soon were the tables turned ! when within five years these very gentlemen thought fit to enter into an association to adhere to the Prince of Orange against the king upon the throne, and have since had the mortification to see that same decree burned by the hands of the common hangman.

To return to the visitation. May 15, a citation was issued in the names of ten of the visiters then in London, to the proctors and heads of houses, or their vice-principals, requiring them and all the officers, scholars, &c., to appear in the Convocation House, on Friday, June 4, between the hours of nine and eleven in the morning, and to bring with them a list of the several names of those who were absent, and of the colleges to which they belonged. At the time appointed the Reverend Mr. Harris, Mr. Reynolds, Mr. Rogers, Mr. Henry Wilkinson, Mr. Cheynel, Mr. John Wilkinson, Mr. Dunce, and Mr. Draper, &c., opened the visitation with prayers and a sermon at St. Mary's Church, from whence they proceeded to the Convocation House, where the vice-chancellor [Dr. Fell] and a few of the scholars had been waiting a considerable time ; but perceiving the visiters were like to outstay the precise hour of summons, he ordered the sexton to set the clock exactly with the sun, and as soon as it struck eleven he dismissed the scholars, marching away with the beadles before him ; the visiters met them in their return at the *proscholium*, where the passage being narrow, the beadle cried out, " Make way for Mr. Vice-chancellor," which the visiters did. And the vice-chancellor having moved his hat as he passed by, said,

---

* Bishop Sanderson's Life; Appendix, p. 244.

"How do ye, gentlemen? it is past eleven o'clock." But the visiters went forward, and having consulted about an hour upon the vice-chancellor's behaviour, resolved to adjourn till Michaelmas, and return to London, in order to obtain farther powers from the Parliament. In the mean time, Dr. Fell summoned a committee of the heads of the several colleges, who came to the following resolutions :

1. That no man should appear before the visiters unless the summons had five names.

2. That no one should appear upon a holy-day.

3. That he should demand by what authority he was summoned ; and, if denied an answer, should presently depart.

4. That if they declared their authority, he should answer with a *salvis juribus regni, academiæ et collegii,* &c.

5. That he should demand his accusation in writing, as also time to put in his answer, and should return it in writing, and no otherwise. Lastly, That he should utterly refuse to answer on oath, because that would be to accuse himself, and would plainly revive the oath *ex officio.*

Such was the stout behaviour of these few academics, "who (according to Dr. Walker) poured upon the visiters all manner of contempt and scorn, though they knew their very lives and fortunes were at their disposal. The university," says he, "held out a siege of more than a year and a half; the Convocation House proved a citadel, and each single college a fort not easy to be reduced ;"* a clear evidence of the humanity of the visiters, and an unanswerable demonstration of the necessity of the Parliament's acting with greater vigour.

The two houses having resolved to support their visiters, and enable them to go through their work, passed an ordinance, August 26, empowering them "to administer the Covenant and the negative oath ; to demand the perusal of the statutes, registers, accompts, &c., and of all other papers of the university, and of the respective colleges and halls ; and to seize and detain in custody any person who, after a personal citation, refused to appear and produce their books and papers after a second citation :" a jury was also to be empannelled, of members of the university, above the age of twenty-one, to inquire by oath on the articles contained in the ordinance of visitation ;"† and a new commission was drawn up by Mr. Attorney-general St. John, with the great seal affixed to it, September 27, authorizing the persons above named to visit the university without any farther warrant ; the commission began in the usual form, "Charles, by the grace of God, &c., to our trusty and well-beloved Sir Nath. Brent, &c. Know ye that we, intending the regulation and reformation of our University of Oxford, &c.," which was a very strange style considering the king was never consulted about the visitation, much less gave any consent ; but the houses affected this form, from a mistaken supposition that the king was always present with his Parliament, in his legislative capacity ; though it served no other purpose than giving the adversary an opportunity to expose their

proceedings, and charge them with assuming and acting under a forged authority.

Furnished with these new powers, the visiters returned to Oxford the latter end of September; the mayor, sheriffs, and other magistrates being commanded to aid and assist them as there should be occasion. On Michaelmas Day a paper was fixed to the door of University Church, giving notice that the visitation would now proceed *de die in diem.** Next day a citation was issued to all the heads of houses, requiring them to bring in their statutes, registers, accompts, and all their public writings, to the warden's lodgings at Merton College. The vice-chancellor was ordered to appear at the same time, to answer to such questions as should be demanded of him, and to send by the hands of the persons who served those orders all the books and acts belonging to the university. The proctors were likewise enjoined to bring in their books, keys, and other public things in their custody. But it is not enough to say, says the Oxford antiquary, that every one of these orders was disobeyed ; they were also despised and contemned. However, the vice-chancellor and heads of colleges condescended to appear at the second summons, October 6, when, instead of bringing their books and papers, they demanded to know by what authority they were summoned ; upon which the visiters produced their commission under the broad seal, at the same time serving them with a third citation to appear four days after with their books and papers, or with their reasons in writing why they refused so to do. Next day they sent for the keys of the Convocation House and school, and for the beadles' staves, but they were denied. The day following the proctors appeared, and delivered a protestation, attested by a public notary, in the name of the vice-chancellor, delegates, and all the scholars, to this purpose, that "they could not own any visiter but the king, and that, having sworn to maintain his right, they could not, without perjury, submit themselves to acquaint the Parliament."† Hereupon Dr. Fell, the vice-chancellor, the very same day, was deprived of his vice-chancellorship, and public notice was given to the proctors and other officers of the university, not to obey him any longer under that character ; but the doctor, without regard to his deprivation, or to the prorogation of the term, which the visiters had adjourned from the 10th to the 15th instant, proceeding on the 11th to hold a congregation, and open the term as usual, was taken into custody, and some time after, by order of Parliament, brought to London ; immediately under which, Dr. Potter, president of Trinity College, ordered the beadles with their staves to attend him as pro-vice-chancellor. November 2 and 4, the several heads of colleges then present appeared before the visiters, but without their statute-books and papers, and being called in severally, were asked in their turns, Whether they approved of the *judicium universitatis,* or the reasons of the university above mentioned ? Whether they owned the power of the visiters ? Or whether they approved of the answer of the proctors in the name of the whole university ?‡ And refusing to give a direct answer, were

---

* Sufferings of the Clergy, p. 122, 123, 128, &c.
† Ibid., p. 128.

* Wood's Antiq. Oxon., p. 388. † Ibid., p. 389, 390.
‡ Suff. Cler., p. 130.

served with a citation to appear before the Committee for the Reformation of the University at Westminster the 11th instant, which they did accordingly; and having owned their approbation of the answer of the proctors in the name of the university, they tendered a paper to the committee in the name of all who had been cited, setting forth, "that what they had done was not out of obstinacy, but from conscience; and praying that in an affair of so much consequence they might be allowed time to advise with counsel." Their request being readily granted, two gentlemen of the long robe of their own nomination, viz., Mr. Hale and Mr. Chute, were appointed their counsel. The day of hearing was December 9; the position they offered to maintain was, that it was one of the privileges of the university to be subject only to a royal visitation: the counsel for the university made a learned argument upon this head; but, as Mr. Collyer observes, this question had been debated before the king in council in the year 1637, when Archbishop Laud claimed a right of visiting the two universities *jure metripolitico.*[*] It was then admitted that the king might visit when he pleased; yet, after a full hearing, his majesty, with the advice of his council, declared and adjudged the right of visiting both universities, as universities, to belong to the archbishop and metropolitan church of Canterbury, by themselves or commissaries, and that the universities should from time to time be obedient thereunto. Which determination of his majesty the archbishop moved might be drawn up by counsel learned in the law, and put under the broad seal, to prevent disputes for the future. And the same was accordingly done; the university, therefore, lost their question in this committee. The counsel for the visiters were farther of opinion, that the kingly power was always virtually present with his great council of Parliament, and that therefore they might visit; but supposing this to be a mistake, they affirmed that the Parliament had an undoubted right to reform the university by the articles of capitulation, in which they had expressly reserved this power to themselves. After a full hearing on both sides, the committee voted that the answer of the several heads of houses, and of others of the university, was derogatory to the authority of Parliament.

The Oxford divines, not satisfied with this determination, appealed soon after to the public in a letter to the learned Mr. Selden, representative for the university, entitled "The Case of the University of Oxford; or, the Sad Dilemma that all the Members thereof are put to, to be perjured or destroyed."[†] The letter says, "that the only question proposed by the visiters to every single person in the university is, Whether he will submit to the power of the Parliament in this visitation? To which they reply, that unless they have the personal consent of the king, they cannot submit to any visitation without danger or perjury; as appears by the words of the oath, which are, 'You shall swear to observe all the statutes, liberties, privileges, and customs of the university;' to which the scholar answers, 'I swear.' Now it being one of our

privileges to be visited by none but the king, or by the Archbishop of Canterbury, the archbishop, op being dead, it follows we can be visited by none but the king; to submit, therefore, to another visitation, must be a breach of our liberties, and, consequently, downright perjury. They urged, farther, that the statutes of their several colleges, which bind them to certain rules in their electing of proctors, in the calling and meeting of convocations, in the choice of several officers in case of a vacancy, all which, instead of being referred to the members of the university, is now done by the arbitrary power of the visiters. Nothing," say they, "can be alleged in answer to this, but the pretended sovereign power of the two houses to make and abolish laws, which we absolutely disbelieve. Upon the whole, they appeal to any divine whether they ought to submit to the visitation as long as they believe their oaths to be in full force, and are confident that the two houses cannot dispense with them? And, consequently, whether they ought to be turned out of their freeholds on this account?"

The committee at London, having waited till the end of the month of December to see if any of the heads of colleges would submit, voted Dr. Fell out of his deanery of Christ Church for contumacy;[*] and passed the same sentence upon

Dr. Oliver, President of Magdalen College.
Dr. Potter, " Trinity.
Dr. Bayly, " St. John's.
Dr. Radcliffe, Principal of Brazen Nose.
Dr. Gardner, }
Dr. Iles, } Canons of Christ Church.
Dr. Morley, }

When these resolutions were sent to Oxford, the proper officers refused to publish them, and when they were pasted upon the walls of colleges, they were torn down, and trampled under foot; upon which the pro-vice-chancellor and the two proctors were ordered into custody; but they absconded, and Dr. Oliver assumed the office of pro-vice-chancellor. The Parliament, provoked at this usage, passed an ordinance, January 22, 1647-8, constituting the Earl of Pembroke chancellor of Oxford, and March 8, they ordered him to repair thither in person, to support the visiters, and place the several persons whom the committee had chosen in the respective chairs of those they had ejected.[†]

April 11, the chancellor made his public entrance into the city, attended with a great number of clergy and gentlemen of the country, and about one hundred horse out of Oxford itself; the mayor welcomed him at his entrance into the city with a congratulatory speech; and when he came to his lodgings, Mr. Button, one of the new proctors, made a speech to him in Latin, but not one of the heads of colleges came near him; the insignia of the university were not to be found, and the scholars treated the chancellor and his retinue with all that rudeness they had been taught to express towards all who adhered to the Parliament.

Next morning, the earl, attended with a guard of soldiers, went to Christ Church, and having in vain desired Mrs. Fell, the dean's

---

* Ecclesiastical History, p. 766.
† Sufferings of the Clergy, p. 133. Vol. Pamp., No. 34.

* Sufferings of the Clergy, p. 131.
† Whitelocke, p. 290.

wife, to quit the lodgings peaceably, he commanded the soldiers to break open the doors, and carry her out into a chair in the middle of the quadrangle ;* he then put the new-elected dean, Mr. Reynolds, afterward Bishop of Norwich, into possession ; from thence his lordship, with the visiters, went to the hall, and having got the Buttery Book, struck out Dr. Fell's name, and inserted that of Mr. Reynolds ; the like they did by Dr. Hammond, sub-dean and public orator ; by Dr. Gardner, Dr. Rayne, Dr. Iles, and Dr. Morley,† placing in their stead Mr. Corbet, who was made public orator ; Mr. Rogers, Mr. Mills, Mr. Cornish, Mr. Henry Wilkinson, Sen., and Mr. Langley ; Dr. Sanderson being spared, because he was out of town when the last summons was issued.

In the afternoon they held a convocation, which was opened with an elegant Latin oration, pronounced by Mr. Corbet, their new orator.‡ When the chancellor had taken the chair in the Convocation House, he declared Mr. Reynolds vice-chancellor, to whom an oath was administered that he would observe the statutes and privileges of the university, subject to the authority of Parliament. Mr. Button and Mr. Cross were declared proctors, and all three returned their thanks to the chancellor in Latin speeches. On this occasion, degrees were conferred upon divers learned men. Mr. Chambers, Mr. Gallicott, and Mr. Harris, were made doctors of divinity ; Mr. Palmer, doctor of physic ; Mr. J. Wilkins [afterward bishop], Mr. Langley, Mr. Cornish, and Mr. Cheynel, bachelors of divinity ; the young Earl of Carnarvon, the chancellor's two youngest sons, and several other gentlemen, masters of arts.§

Next morning, April 13, the chancellor and visiters, with a guard of musketeers, went to Magdalen College, and having broke open the doors of the president's lodgings [Dr. Oliver], who was out of the way, they gave Dr. Wilkinson possession. In the afternoon they went to All-Souls, where Dr. Sheldon, the warden, appearing, and refusing to submit, returned to his lodgings, and locked the doors ; which being broke open, the doctor was taken into custody for contempt, and Dr. Palmer put in his place ; from thence they went to Trinity College, and having broke open the lodgings, Dr. Harris was put into possession in the room of Dr. Potter. In like manner, Dr. Cheynel had possession given him of St. John's, in the room of Dr. Bayly ; Mr. Wilkins was appointed President of Wadham College, in the room

* Sufferings of the Clergy, p. 133.
† Dr. Grey, on the authority of Bishop Sanderson's biographer and Mr. Wood, says that Dr. Morley was not turned out. Dr. Richardson says that, being deprived of all his ecclesiastical benefices in 1648, he withdrew into the kingdom, first to the Hague, and then to Antwerp.—*De Præsulibus Angliæ Commentarius*, p. 244. Dr. Grey appears to have mistaken the passage in Sanderson's Life, which relates only the steps that a friend would have taken to secure Dr. Morley's continuance in the university, and concludes with his memorable and generous reply, which shows that he declined availing himself of his friend's kindness, saying, "that when all the rest of the college were turned out except Dr. Wall, he should take it to be, if not a sin, yet a shame, to be left alive with him only."—ED.
‡ Rushworth, p. 1364.
§ Sufferings of the Clergy, p. 133, 134.

of Dr. Pit ; and Mr. Greenwood was put into possession of Brazen Nose College, in the room of Dr. Radcliffe, allowing those they displaced a month's time to remove their effects. But some of the students of Christ Church having got the Buttery Book, impudently cut out the names of those whom the visiters had inserted ; so that they were forced to return the next day, and write over again the names of their new deans and canons.* The heads of colleges being thus fixed in their several stations, the chancellor took leave of the university and departed for London ; and having reported his conduct, April 21, received the thanks of the two houses.

But Dr. Wilkinson, Sen., and Mr. Cheynel, who returned with the chancellor, having represented to the Parliament that the fellows, scholars, and under officers still refused to submit to their orders, it was resolved "that the visiters should cite all the officers, fellows, and scholars before them, and that such as refused to appear, or upon appearance did not submit, should be suspended from their places, and their names returned to the committee, who were authorized to expel them from the university ; and the new heads (on signification of such sentence from the committee), in conjunction with the visiters, were empowered to put others in their places. They resolved, farther, that the bursars should make no dividend of money till they had orders from the committee ; and that the tenants should pay their rents to none but the heads appointed by the authority of Parliament."†• But the bursars absconded, and were not to be found.

By virtue of these orders, the visiters cited the fellows, scholars of houses, gentlemen-commoners, and servitors to appear before them at several times ; the only question demanded of them was, Will you submit to the power of the Parliament in this visitation ? To which they were to give their answer in writing, and according to it were confirmed or, displaced. Great numbers were absent from the university, and did not appear ; others, who disowned the power of the Parliament at first, afterward submitted, but the main body stood it out to the last : Dr. Walker says that one hundred and eighty withdrew ;‡ that of about six hundred and seventy-six who appeared, five hundred and forty-eight refused at first to own the authority of the visitation, but that afterward many submitted and made their peace.§ In another place he supposes one fourth submitted, and makes the whole number of fellows and scholars deprived three hundred and seventy-five ; and then, by a list of new elections in some following years, reduces them to three hundred and fifty-six ; but considering that some may have been omitted, he guesses the whole to be about four hundred. The Oxford historian, Mr. Wood, says the number of those that refused to submit was about three hundred and thirty-four, but that they were not presently expelled ; for though the visiters were obliged to return their names to the committee, and were empowered to expel them, yet they deferred the execution

* Sufferings of the Clergy, p. 134.
† Ibid., p. 134.   ‡ Life of Mr. Phil. Henry, p. 12.
§ Sufferings of the Clergy, part i., p. 135 ; and part ii., p. 138, 139.

of their power, in hopes that time might bring them to a compliance; which it is very likely it did, because it appears by the register, that in the eight succeeding years, i. e., between the years 1648 and 1656, there were no more than three hundred and ninety-six new elections, which, allowing for deaths and removals, must infer the deprivations at this time could not be very considerable; however, had their numbers been much greater than they really were, the Parliament were obliged, in their own defence, to dispossess them.* · ·

The few scholars that remained in the university treated the visiters with insufferable rudeness; scurrilous and invective satires, equal if not superior in raillery and ill language to Martin Mar-Prelate, and the rest of the Brownistical pamphlets in the reign of Queen Elizabeth, were dispersed in the most public places of the city every week; as Mercurius Academicus; Pegasus, or the Flying Horse from Oxon; Pegasus taught to dance to the Tune of Lachrymæ; News-from Pembroke and Montgomery, or Oxford Manchestered; the Owl at Athens, or the Entrance of the Earl of Pembroke into Oxford, April 11; the Oxford Tragicomedy, in heroic Latin verse; Lord have mercy upon us!—which is the inscription put upon houses that have the plague; and many others, which the visiters took no farther notice of than to forbid the booksellers to print or sell the like for the future.† If the Puritans had published such pamphlets against the exorbitances of the High Commission Court in the late times, the authors or publishers must have lost their ears, as the Brownists did their lives towards the latter end of Queen Elizabeth; and surely the university might have evinced their loyalty without offering such unmannerly provocations to gentlemen, who were disposed to behave towards them with all gentleness and moderation. The visiters being informed that an insurrection was designed among the scholars in favour of the king, and in concert with the loyalists in other parts of the kingdom, acquainted the commanding officers of the garrison, who gave im-

* Some of the Episcopal clergy were men of learning, and of estimable character, and the sufferings consequent upon their expulsion were deeply to be deplored. But the majority of those whom the commissioners drove from the university were distinguished only by their reckless loyalty, and a contumelious resistance to the will of Parliament. To have permitted such to retain stations of authority and influence, would have been to arm their enemies against themselves, and to have perpetuated in the rising generation the same spirit and principles as actuated the men of their day. The Parliament was perfectly right in demanding from the university submission to its authority; but was wrong in making a *religious creed* the test of obedience, and the badge of patriotism. Having established its own supremacy, it was entitled to require submission from all corporate bodies, and to eject from places of honour and emolument those who refused it. So far its proceedings coincided with the obvious necessities of the case, and required no apology; but when the Covenant was enforced as the pledge of civil obedience, a course was ad pted which, however analogous to that of the bishops, admits of no extenuation or defence. The rights of conscience were invaded by the exercise of an authority unsanctioned by the Christian system.—*Price's History of Nonconformity*, vol. ii., p. 30.

† Sufferings of the Clergy, p. 135.

mediate orders to search the colleges for arms;: and on the 26th of May, 1648, the visiters ordered all the members of the university to deliver a peremptory answer in writing within seven days, whether they would submit to the authority of the Parliament in this visitation or not; and that none should depart the university without leave from the pro-vice-chancellor. The day following both houses of Parliament passed an order, " that forasmuch as many doctors, and other members of the university, notwithstanding the example that had been made of some of them, did still persist in their contempt of the authority of Parliament, which might be of dangerous consequence; therefore the committee for reforming the university should have power to send for them under the custody of a guard, and commit them to prison." When this order came to Oxford, the visiters declared that whosoever should not plainly, and without reserve, declare his submission to the visitation, should be deemed as flatly denying its authority, and be taken into custody; and that whosoever laid claim to any place in the university, should within fifteen days declare his submission, or be deprived; accordingly, at the expiration of the time, such as did not appear were deprived of their fellowships, and expelled the university: but still the scholars would not remove, being too stubborn to be evicted by votes at London, or papers and programmes at Oxford. The visiters, therefore, after having waited above six months, were obliged to proceed to the last extremity; and July 5, 1649, ordered a sergeant, attended with some files of musketeers, to publish by beat of drum before the gates of the several colleges, that "if any of those who had been expelled by the visiters should presume to continue any longer in the university, they should be taken into custody, and be made prisoners by the governor." This not answering the proposed end, the Oxford historian adds, that four days after they published a farther order by beat of drum before the gate of every college, "that if any one who had been expelled did presume to tarry in the town, or was taken within five miles of it, he should be deemed as a spy, and punished with death." And to enforce this order, General Fairfax, who was then in the field, gave public notice that he would proceed accordingly with such as did not depart in four days, unless they obtained leave from the vice-chancellor and visiters to continue longer. At length their courage cooled, and the young gentlemen were prevailed on to retire. Thus the University of Oxford was cleared of the Royalists, and the visiters at liberty to fill up their vacancies in the best manner they could; in all which one cannot tell which most to admire, the unparalleled patience and forbearance of a victorious Parliament for almost two years, or the stubborn perverseness and provoking behaviour of a few academics, against a power that could have battered their colleges about their ears, and buried them in their ruins in a few days. About ten of the old heads of colleges and professors of sciences submitted to the visiters, and kept their places, and about nineteen or twenty were expelled. Those who submitted were,

Dr. Langbain, provost of Queen's ⎫
Dr. Hood, rector of Lincoln ⎪
Dr. Saunders, provost of Oriel ⎪
Dr. Hakewell, rector of Exeter ⎬ College.
Sir Nath. Brent, warden of Merton ⎪
Dr. Zouch, principal of Alban Hall ⎪
Dr. Lawrence, master of Baliol ⎭
Dr. Pocock, Arabic professor:
Dr. Clayton, anatomy professor..
Mr. Philips, music professor.

The following characters of these gentlemen, with those of their predecessors and successors, I have taken, for the most part, from writers not to be suspected of partiality in favour of the Puritans.

Dr. Gerard Langbain, provost of Queen's College, was a great ornament to his college; he was elected keeper of the archives or records of the university, being in general esteem for his great learning and honesty. He was an excellent linguist, an able philosopher and divine, a good common lawyer, a public-spirited man, a lover of learning and learned men, beloved of Archbishop Usher, Selden, and the great Goliaths of literature. He was also an excellent antiquary, indefatigable in his studies, and of immense undertakings. He died February 10, 1657-8, and was buried in the inner chapel of Queen's College.*

Dr. Paul Hood, rector of Lincoln College, had been many years governor of this house, and continued in it through all changes till his death; he was vice-chancellor of the university in the year 1660, when he conformed to the Established Church, and died in the year 1668.†

Dr. John Saunders, provost of Oriel College, disowned the authority of the visiters at first, but afterward complied; for, as Dr. Walker observes, there was no other provost till after his death, which was in the year 1652.‡

Dr. George Hakewell, rector of Exeter College, had been chaplain to Prince Charles and Archdeacon of Surrey; upon the promotion of Dr. Prideaux to the See of Worcester, he was chosen rector of this college, but resided little there, retiring during the war to his Rectory of Heanton, in Devon, where he led a recluse life, and died in April, 1649. He was, according to Dr. Walker, a great divine, a very good philosopher, and a noted preacher.§

Sir Nathaniel Brent, warden of Merton College, was probationer fellow in the year 1594, and proctor of the university in 1607; he afterward travelled into several parts of the learned world, and underwent dangerous adventures in Italy to procure the history of the Council of Trent, which he translated into English, and therefore, says Mr. Wood,‖ deserves an honourable mention. By the favour of Archbishop Abbot he was made commissary of the Diocess of Canterbury, and vicar-general to the archbishop, being doctor of laws, and at length judge of the prerogative. In 1629 he was knighted at Woodstock, and at the commencement of the civil war took part with the Parliament, for which reason he was ejected his wardenship of this college, but restored again when it came into the Parliament's hands in 1646. He was one of the

visiters of the university, and esteemed a very learned and judicious civilian. He resigned his wardenship in the year 1650, and died in London in 1652, after he had lived seventy-nine years.

Richard Zouch, LL.D., principal of Alban Hall, was of noble birth, and served in Parliament, for the borough of Hythe, in Kent. He was chancellor of the Diocess of Oxon, principal of St. Alban Hall in 1625, and at length judge of the High Court of Admiralty; he was very able and eminent in his own profession, a subtle logician, an expert historian, and for the knowledge and practice of the civil law the chief person of his time. As his birth was noble, says Mr. Wood,* so was his behaviour and discourse; and as he was personable and handsome, so naturally sweet, pleasing, and affable, he kept his principalship and professorship till his death, which happened March 1, 1660-1.

Dr. Thomas Lawrence, master of Baliol College, and Margaret professor of divinity, had been chaplain to King Charles I. and prebendary of Litchfield, and by the interest of Archbishop Laud, preferred to the mastership of this college in 1637. He submitted to the authority of the visiters, and had a certificate under their hands, dated August 3, 1648, wherein they attest, that he had engaged to observe the Directory in all ecclesiastical administrations, to preach practical divinity to the people, and to forbear preaching any of those opinions that the Reformed church had condemned.† Dr. Walker says he resigned all his preferments in the university in the year 1650, but does not say upon what occasion; only that he grew careless, and did much degenerate in his life and manners; that he died in the year 1657, but that if he had lived three years longer, he would, notwithstanding, have been consecrated an Irish bishop.‡

The professors of sciences who submitted to the visiters, and were continued, were,

Dr. Edward Pocock, professor of the Hebrew and Arabic languages; one of the most learned men of his age, and justly celebrated at home and abroad for his great skill in the Oriental languages, and for many works that he published. He was afterward ejected from his canonry of Christ Church for refusing the engagement, 1651,§ but was suffered to enjoy his professorship of Arabic and Hebrew; he conformed in the year 1660, and lived in great reputation till the year 1691.‖

Thomas Clayton, M.D., king's professor of anatomy, which professorship he resigned to Dr.

<hr/>

* Wood's Athen., vol. ii., p. 140.
† Wood's Fasti, p. 127. ‡ Walker, p. 131.
§ Ibid., p. 114. ‖ Athen. Oxon., vol. ii., p. 92.

* Athen. Oxon., vol. ii., p. 166. † Ibid., p. 135.
‡ Sufferings of the Clergy, p. 100.
§ He was very near being ejected from his living of Childrey "for ignorance and insufficiency;" but Dr. Owen, the learned Independent, interested himself in his behalf, and prevented his ejectment. When he was in the East, into which he made two voyages, the Mufti of Aleppo laid his hand upon his head, and said, "This young man speaks and understands Arabic as well as the Mufti of Aleppo." He was the first Laudean professor of Arabic.—*Granger's History of England*, vol. iii., p. 270, 8vo.—Ed. This "ignorance and insufficiency" sounds strangely, after reading that he was "one of the most learned men of his age;" if his ignorance had been that of theology, that good man, Dr. Owen, would hardly have been his advocate.—C. ‖ Athen. Oxon., p. 868.

William Petty in January, 1650. He was made warden of Merton College upon the resignation of Dr. Reynolds, March 26, 1661, and the next day was knighted by the interest of his brother-in-law, Sir Charles Cotterel.

Mr. Arthur Philips, professor of music, of whom I have met with no account.

The heads of colleges ejected by the visiters, with their successors, may be seen in the following table:

Heads of Colleges turned out.	Colleges.	Succeeded by.
Dr. Fell, vice-chancellor, from	Deanery of Christ Church,	Dr. Reynolds, afterward Bishop of Norwich.
Dr. Pit, warden of	Wadham College,	Dr. J. Wilkins, afterward Bishop of Cnester.
Dr. Walker,	University College,	Dr. Joshua Hoyle.
Dr. Radcliffe,	Brazen Nose College,	Dr. D. Greenwood.
Dr. Sheldon,	All-Souls College,	Dr. Palmer; M.D.
Dr. Newlin,	Corpus Christi College,	Dr. Ed. Staunton.
Dr. Bayly,	St. John's College,	Dr. Cheynel.
Dr. Oliver,	Magdalen College,	Dr. John Wilkinson.
Dr. Han. Potter,	Trinity College,	Dr. Robert Harris.
Dr. Mansell,	Jesus College,	Dr. Mic. Roberts.
Mr. Wightwick, B.D.,	Pembroke College,	Dr. H. Langley.
Dr. Stringer, Prof. Gr. Lang.	New College,	{ Mr. Geo. Marshall. { Mr. Harmar; Prof. Gr. Lang.

Professors of Sciences turned out.	Professorships.	Succeeded by:—
Dr. Robt. Sanderson,	Reg. Pr. of Div.,	Dr. Crosse.
Mr. Birkenhead, A.M.,	M. Philos. Prof.,	Dr. Hen. Wilkinson, Jun.
Mr. Rob. Warin,	Camd. Hist. Prof.,	Dr. L. du Moulin.
Dr. Jn. Edwards,	Nat. Phil. Prof.,	Dr. Joshua Crosse.
Dr. Turner, M.D.,	Savil. Prof. Geo.,	Dr. John Wallis.
Mr. J. Greaves, A.M.,	Profess. Astron.,	{ Dr. Ward, afterward Bishop of Salisbury.
Dr. Henry Hammond,	University Orator,	{ Mr. Burton, A.M. { Mr. Corbet, who quitted.

Dr. Gilbert Sheldon, warden of All-Souls College, was ejected April 3, 1648, and lived retired with his friends in Staffordshire till 1659, when he was restored to his wardenship upon the death of Dr. Palmer. After the Restoration he was successively Bishop of London, Chancellor of Oxford, and Archbishop of Canterbury; he built the noble theatre at Oxford, and did a great many other works of charity,* but never gave any great specimens of his piety or learning to the world.†

Dr. Samuel Fell, vice-chancellor of the university, and dean of Christ Church, dispossessed of his deanery April 12, 1648.‡ He gave the visiters all the disturbance he could, and was therefore taken into custody for a time, but being quickly released, he retired to his rectory at Sunningwell, in Berkshire, where he died February 1, 1648-9. He had been a Calvinist, but changed his sentiments, and after great creepings and cringings to Archbishop Laud, says Mr. Wood,§ he became his creature, and if the rebellion had not broke out, would no doubt have been made a bishop. He left no remarkable traces of his learning behind him.

Dr. Samuel Radcliffe, principal of Brazen Nose College, was elected to his headship 1614, and was in an infirm condition when he was ejected for disowning the authority of the visiters, April 13, 1648; and died the June following.‖ Neither Mr. Wood nor Walker says anything of his learning, nor are his works extant.

Dr. Robert Newlin, president of Corpus

Christi College, and pro-vice-chancellor in the year 1648. He was restored to his president-ship again in the year 1660, and died in it 1687. But neither Wood nor Walker has given him any character.*

Dr. Richard Bayly, president of St. John's College, a kinsman of Archbishop Laud, and one of his executors; he had been president of this college twenty years when he was ejected; but was restored in 1660, and died at Salisbury 1667.† He was hospitable and charitable, but very faulty, says Mr. Wood; in using some kind of oaths in common conversation.‡ I do not know that he published anything.

Dr. John Oliver, president of Magdalen College, had been domestic chaplain to Archbishop Laud, and was a man, says Dr. Walker,§ of great learning and sound principles in religion (that is, of the principles of the archbishop); he was restored to his preferments 1660, but died soon after, October 27, 1661.

Dr. Hannibal Potter, president of Trinity College, elected 1643, and turned out with the rest who disowned the authority of the visiters, April 13, 1648. He afterward accepted of a curacy in Somersetshire, and was ejected for insufficiency; but Dr. Walker says‖ it was because he used part of the church service. He was restored in 1660, and died in 1664.

Dr. John Pit, warden of Wadham College, elected April 16, 1644, after that city was garrisoned for the king; he behaved very refractorily towards the visiters, and died soon after his ejectment.¶

Dr. Francis Mansell, principal of Jesus College, elected to this principalship in the year 1630, and ejected May 22, 1648. He was re-

---

* His benefactions, public and private, amounted to £66,000. Much of this money was appropriated to the relief of the necessitous in the time of the plague, and to the redemption of Christian slaves. The building only of the theatre in Oxford cost him £16,000.—*Granger's History of England*, vol. iii., p. 231, 8vo.—Ed.

† Walker's Sufferings of the Clergy, p. 98.
‡ Walker, p. 102. § Athen. Oxon., vol. ii., p. 94.
‖ Walker, p. 101.

* Walker, p. 111. † Ibid., p. 116.
‡ Dr. Grey asks, "Where does Wood say this? Nowhere that I can meet with." Nor can I find the passage.—Ed. § Walker, p. 122.
‖ Ibid., p. 133. ¶ Ibid., p. 136.

stored again in 1660, and died 1665, having been an eminent benefactor,to his college.

Dr. Thomas Walker, master of University College, elected 1632, and dispossessed by the visiters July 10, 1648. He was restored in the year 1660, and died in 1665. He was related to Archbishop Laud, and was one of his executors, and, according to Lloyd, a deserving, modest man, and a great sufferer.*

Mr. Henry Wightwick, B.D., elected to the mastership of Pembroke College in direct opposition to the order of Parliament, July 13, 1647, for which reason he was soon after removed. In the year 1660 he was restored, but turned out again in 1664, for what reasons Dr. Walker says he does not know. He died in Lincolnshire 1671.†

Dr. Henry Stringer, elected to the wardenship of New College, after the same manner, in direct opposition to the visiters, November 18, 1647, for which reason he was deprived August 1, 1648. He was professor of the Greek language, but resigned, and died at London 1657.‡

The professors ejected by the visiters were,

Dr. Robert Sanderson, regius professor of divinity ; a very learned man, and an excellent casuist ;§ he was nominated one of the Assembly of Divines, but did not sit among them. He had a very considerable hand in drawing up the reasons of the university against the Covenant and the negative oath. After his ejectment he retired to his living at Boothby, where he continued preaching, though not without some difficulties, till the Restoration, when he was preferred to the Bishopric of Lincoln, and died 1662-3.||

Mr. John Birkenhead, A.M., moral philosophy reader ; he was employed by the court to write the Mercurius Aulicus, a paper filled with most bitter invectives against the Parliament, for which he was rewarded with this lectureship. After his ejectment he lived privately till the Restoration, when he was knighted, and chosen burgess in Parliament for the borough of Wilton. He was also created LL.D. and master of the faculties, and died in 1679, leaving behind him, according to Wood, a very sorry character.¶

Mr. Robert Waring, Camden history professor ; he bore arms for the king in the garrison at Oxford, and was not elected to this professorship till after the visitation began. He was reckoned, says Wood, among the wits of the university, and was a good poet and orator. He died 1658.**

John Edwards, M.D., natural philosophy lec-

turer, who behaved rudely towards the visiters, and was therefore not only dispossessed of his preferment, but expelled the university ;* but neither Wood nor Walker gives any character of him.

Peter Turner, M.D., Savilian professor of geometry ; he served his majesty as a volunteer under the command of Sir J. Byron, and being a zealous Loyalist, was expelled the university by the visiters, after which he retired to London, and died 1650. He was a good mathematician, well read in the fathers, an excellent linguist, and highly esteemed by Archbishop Laud.†

John Greaves, A.M., professor of astronomy, was sent by Archbishop Laud to travel into the eastern parts of the world to make a collection of books in those languages.‡ After his return he was preferred to this professorship, but was ejected by the visiters, and November 9, 1648, expelled the university, for sending the college treasure to the king, and other offences of the like nature. He died at London 1652, with the reputation of a good scholar, having been well respected by Mr. Selden and others.§

Dr. Henry Hammond, university orator, was a very learned man and a great divine, highly esteemed by King Charles I. He assisted at the Treaty of Uxbridge, and attended the king as his chaplain when he was permitted. After his ejectment he retired to the house of Sir John Packington, of Worcestershire, where he employed his time in writing several valuable and learned treatises in defence of the hierarchy of the Church of England, and in the study of the New Testament. He died April 25, 1660.||

The heads of colleges who succeeded those that were ejected by authority of Parliament were,

Dr. Edward Reynolds, vice-chancellor of the university, and dean of Christ Church in the place of Dr. Fell ; he was probationer-fellow of Merton College in the year 1620, which he obtained by his uncommon skill in the Greek tongue ; he was a good disputant and orator, a popular divine, and in great esteem in the city of London, being preacher to the honourable society of Lincoln's Inn. Mr. Wood confesses¶ he was a person of excellent parts and endowments, of a very good wit, fancy, and judgment, and much esteemed by all parties for his florid style. Sir Thomas Brown adds, that he was a divine of singular affability, meekness, and humility ; of great learning, a frequent preacher, and a constant resident. He conformed at the Restoration, and was made Bishop of Norwich, and died 1676.

Dr. John Wilkins, promoted to the warden-

* Walker, p. 114. † Ibid., p. 132. ‡ Ibid., p. 127.
§ "He was, especially in the former part of his life, remarkable for his excessive modesty ; an infirmity," observes my author, " oftener seen in men of the quickest sensibility, and of the best understanding, than in the half-witted, the stupid, and the ignorant."—*Granger's History of England,* vol. iii., p. 238, 239, 8vo. He disapproved of and wrote against the usual mode of lending money on interest. But he adopted another way of advancing it more advantageous to the lender, and sometimes to the borrower. He would give £100 for £20, for seven years.—*Calamy's Church and Dissenters compared as to Persecution,* p. 30.—ED. Bishop Sanderson's most celebrated work is entitled " A Preservative against Schism and Rebellion," &c., 3 vols. 8vo, 1722.—C.
|| Athen. Oxon., vol. ii., p. 376. ¶ Ibid.
** Walker, p. 106. Athen. Oxon., vol. ii., p. 143.

* Walker, p. 118. † Wood, vol. ii., p. 84.
‡ This he did with indefatigable industry, and at the peril of his life. He also collected for Archbishop Laud many Oriental gems and coins. He took a more accurate survey of the pyramids than any traveller who went before him. During his stay at Rome, on his return from the East, he made a particular inquiry into the true state of the ancient weights and measures. He was a great man.—*Granger's History of England,* vol. iii., p. 119, 120, 8vo.—ED. § Walker, p. 125.
|| This is the divine whose discourses were so highly admired by Dr. Johnson that he often gave them to young clergymen.—C.
¶ Athen. Oxon., vol. ii., p. 421.

ship of Wadham College in the place of Dr. Pit. He was educated in Magdalen Hall, and was chaplain to Charles. count-palatine of the Rhine. A little before the Restoration he came to Lon- don, and was minister of St, Lawrence Jewry, and preacher to the society at Lincoln's Inn. Mr. Wood admits* that he was a person of rare gifts, a noted theologian and preacher, a curious critic, an excellent mathematician, and as well seen in mechanism and the new philosophy as any in his time. In the year 1656 he married the sister of O. Cromwell, then lord-protector of England, and had the headship of Trinity College in Cambridge conferred upon him, which is the best preferment in that university. He was afterward a member of the Royal Soci- ety, to which he was a considerable benefactor. Dr. Burnet says that Bishop Wilkins was a man of as great a mind, as true a judgment, of as eminent virtue, and as good a soul, as any he ever knew. Archbishop Tillotson gives him an equal character ; and several members of the Royal Society acknowledge him to have been an ornament to the university and the English nation. He was created Bishop of Chester in the year 1668, and died of the stone, in the house of Dr. Tillotson, 1672.†

Dr. Joshua Hoyle, preferred to the headship of University College in the room of Dr. Walk- er ; he was educated at Magdalen Hall, Oxford, but being invited into Ireland, became fellow of Trinity College, and professor of divinity in the University of Dublin. In the beginning of the Irish rebellion he came over to England, and was made vicar of Stepney, a member of the Assembly of Divines, and at length master of this college, and king's professor of divinity in the room of Dr. Sanderson. Mr. Wood says‡ he was a person of great reading and memory, but of less judgment. He was exactly acquaint- ed with the schoolmen, and so much devoted to his book that he was in a manner a stranger to the world ; he was indefatigably industrious,

* Athen. Oxon., vol. ii., p. 371.

† To Mr. Neal's character of Bishop Wilkins it may be added, that he was a man of an enlarged and liberal mind, which showed itself in his great moder- ation on the points agitated beween the Conformists and Nonconformists, and in his free, generous way of philosophizing. He disdained to tread in the beat- en track, but struck out into the new road pointed out by the great Lord Bacon, He formed institu- tions for the encouragement of experimental philos- ophy, and the application of it to affairs of human life, at each university; and was the chief means of establishing the Royal Society. His chimeras were those of a man of genius. Such was his attempt to show the possibility of a voyage to the moon ; to which the Duchess of Newcastle made this objec- tion : " Doctor, where am I to find a place for baiting at in the way up to that planet ?" " Madam," said he, " of all the people in the world I never expected that question from you, who have built so many cas- tles in the air, you that may lie every night at one of your own."—Granger, ut supra, the note. His char- acter was truly exemplary as well as extraordinary. His great prudence never failed in any undertaking. Sincerity was natural to him. With a greatness of mind, he looked down upon wealth as much as others admire it. What he really received from the Church he bestowed in its services; and made no savings from his temporal estate, acting up to his frequent declaration, " I will be no richer."—Birch's Life of Tillotson, p. 405, 406. Granger's History of England, vol. iii., p. 247, 248, 8vo; and Lloyd's Funeral Sermon, p. 41-43.—ED. ‡ Athen. Oxon., vol. ii., p. 113.

and as well qualified for an academic as any person of his time. He died 1654.

Dr. Daniel Greenwood, principal of Brazen Nose College, in the room of Dr. Radcliffe ; he had been fellow of the college for a considerable time, and had the reputation of a profound scholar and divine. Mr. Wood says* he was a severe and good governor, as well in his vice- chancellorship as in his principalship ; he con- tinued in his college with an unspotted charac- ter till the Restoration, when he was ejected by the king's commissioners, after which he lived privately till 1673, when he died.

Dr. John Wilkinson had been principal of Magdalen Hall before the civil wars, but when that university was garrisoned by the king he fled into the Parliament's quarters, and was succeeded by Dr. Thomas Read, who was ad- mitted by the king's mandate, October 16, 1643, but in 1646 Dr. Wilkinson was restored. The year following (1647) he was made president of Magdalen College in the room of Dr. Oliver ; he was a learned and pious man, died January 2, 1649, and was buried in the church of Great Milton, Oxfordshire.

Dr. Henry Wilkinson, Junior, commonly called Dean Harry, principal of Magdalen Hall ; he was a noted tutor and moderator in his college before the commencement of the civil wars, upon the breaking out of which he left Oxford and came to London, but when that city was surrendered to the Parliament he returned to the university, and was created D.D., made principal of his hall, and moral philosophy pro- fessor in the room of Mr. Birkenhead. Mr. Wood says† that he took all ways imaginable to make his house flourish with young students ; that he was a frequent and active preacher, and a good disciplinarian; for which reason the heads of the university persuaded him earnestly to conform at the Restoration, that they might keep him among them, but he refused. After his ejectment, he suffered for his nonconformi- ty, by imprisonments, mulcts, and the loss of his goods and books ; though, according to the same author, he was very courteous in speech and carriage, communicative of his knowledge, generous, charitable to the poor, and so public- spirited that he always regarded the common good more than his own private concerns. He published several learned works, and died 1690, aged 74.

Dr. Robert Harris, president of Trinity Col- lege in the room of Dr. Potter, was educated in Magdalen Hall, and had been a famous preacher in Oxfordshire for about forty years ; upon the breaking out of the war he came to London, where he continued till appointed one of the visiters of the university, and head of this col- lege, over which he presided ten years, though he was now seventy. He was a person of great piety and gravity, an exact master of the He- brew language, and well versed in chronology, church history, the councils, and fathers. He governed his college with great prudence, and gained the affections of all the students, who reverenced him as a father, though he had been stigmatized by the Royalists as a notorious plu- ralist. To which the writer of his life replies, that whatever benefices he might have been

* Wood's Fasti, vol. iii., p. 770.

† Athen. Oxon., vol. ii., p. 646.

nominated to, he declared he did not receive the profits of them. The inscription upon his tombstone says that he was "præses æternum celebrandus; perspicacissimus indolum scrutator, potestatis arbiter mitissimus, merentium fautor integerrimus," &c. He died 1658.*

Dr. Henry Langley, master of Pembroke College in the room of Mr. Wightwick, was originally fellow of his college, and made master of it in 1647. He kept his place till the Restoration, after which he set up a private academy among the Dissenters; having the character of a solid and judicious divine, and being a frequent preacher. He died 1679.†

Dr. Francis Cheynel, president of St. John's College in the room of Dr. Bayly, was probationer-fellow of Merton College in the year 1629, and afterward rector of Petworth, a member of the Assembly of Divines, and this year made president of that college, and Margaret professor in the room of Dr. Lawrence, both which he quitted after some time for refusing the engagement, and retired to his living at Petworth, from whence he was ejected at the Restoration. He was a person of a great deal of indiscreet zeal, as appears by his behaviour at the funeral of the great Mr. Chillingworth, already mentioned. Bishop Hoadly says he was exactly orthodox, and as pious, honest, and charitable as his bigotry would permit; and Mr. Echard adds, that he was of considerable learning and great abilities.‡

Dr. Michael Roberts, principal of Jesus College in the room of Dr. Mansell, was a good scholar, and would, no doubt, have conformed at the Restoration, had he been inclined to have accepted any preferment; but he had resigned his principalship into the hands of the protector, 1657, and, being rich, chose a private life.§ He published a Latin elegy upon General Monk, duke of Albemarle, and died in Oxford, 1679.

Dr. Edmund Staunton, president of Corpus-Christi College in the room of Dr. Newlin, was admitted fellow of this college 1616, and afterward minister of Kingston-upon-Thames. He took the degrees in divinity 1634, and was afterward one of the Assembly of Divines. He kept his principalship till he was ejected by the king's commissioners at the Restoration; he was a diligent, popular preacher, a good scholar, and continued his labours among the Nonconformists till his death, which happened 1671.‖

John Palmer, M.D., warden of All-Souls in the room of Dr. Sheldon, had been bachelor of physic of Queen's College, and was now created M.D. in presence of the chancellor; he was a learned man, and held his preferment till his death, which happened March 4, 1659; at which time, there being a near prospect of the Restoration, Dr. Sheldon was restored to his wardenship.¶

Upon the death of Dr. Pink, the visiters nominated old Mr. White, of Dorchester, to succeed

him, but I think he refused it, being very much advanced in years.*

The professors of sciences who succeeded the ejected ones were,

Dr. Seth Ward, professor of astronomy in the place of Dr. Greaves, and, according to Mr. Wood, the most noted mathematician and astronomer of his time; he was educated in Sidney College, Cambridge, and in the year 1643 ejected for adhering to the king, but having afterward changed his mind, he made friends to the committee for reforming the University of Oxford, and was nominated to this preferment; he was afterward master of Trinity College, and upon his majesty's restoration preferred, first to the bishopric of Exeter, and then to that of Salisbury, where he died 1668.‡

Dr. John Wallis, Savilian professor of geometry in the room of Dr. Turner: the fame of this gentleman's learning is well known to the world; he was of Emanuel College, Cambridge, and afterward fellow of Queen's College, in the same university, then minister of St. Martin's, Ironmonger Lane, London, one of the scribes in the Assembly of Divines, and now, by the appointment of the committee, geometry professor;§ he conformed at the Restoration, and maintained his post, and was an ornament to the university to a very advanced age.‖

Lewis du Moulin, M.D., of the University of Leyden, Camden professor of history in the place of Mr. Robert Waring, was incorporated in the same degree at Cambridge, 1634; he was son of the famous Peter du Moulin, the French Protestant, and kept his preferment till the Restoration, when he was turned out by his majesty's commissioners, and persisted in his nonconformity till his death. He was a valuable and learned man, as appears by his writings; but Mr. Wood observes¶ he was a violent Independent, and ill-natured; he died in London 1680.

Joshua Crosse, LL.D., natural philosophy reader in the room of Dr. Edwards; and one of the proctors of the university; he was fellow of

---

* Wood's Fasti, p. 68.

† He was the first who brought mathematical learning into vogue in the University of Cambridge. He was a close reasoner and an admirable speaker, having in the House of Lords been esteemed equal, at least, to the Earl of Shaftesbury. He was a great benefactor to both his bishoprics; as by his interest the deanery of Berïen, in Cornwall, was annexed to the former, though it has been since separated from it, and the chancellorship of the garter to the latter. He was polite, hospitable, and generous. He founded in his lifetime the College of Salisbury, for the reception and support of ministers' widows; and the sumptuous hospital at Buntingford, in Hertfordshire, the place of his nativity.—*Granger's History of England*, vol. iii., p. 244, 245, 8vo.—ED.

‡ Athen. Oxon., vol. ii., p. 627, 628.

§ Wood's Fasti, p. 72, 106.

‖ Mathematical science is greatly indebted to Dr. Wallis for several important improvements and inventions. The modern art of deciphering was his discovery; and he was the author of the method of teaching deaf and dumb persons to speak, and to understand a language. His English grammar, in which many things were entirely his own, showed at once the grammarian and the philosopher.—*Granger's History of England*, vol. iii., p. 286, 8vo. He is said to have applied his art of deciphering to the king's letters taken at Naseby.—ED.

¶ Wood's Fasti, vol. ii., p. 753, 754.

---

* Clarke's Lives, p. 314. His works are very valuable: they are chiefly sermons in one volume folio. He must have been one of the best preachers of the age.—C.

† Wood's Fasti, vol. ii., p. 747, 771.

‡ Athen. Oxon., vol. ii., p. 245.

§ Fasti, vol. ii., p. 752.

‖ Athen. Oxon., vol. ii., p. 352, 353.

¶ Fasti, vol. ii., p. 747.

HISTORY OF THE PURITANS.

Magdalen College, and kept his reader's place till the Restoration, after which he lived privately in Oxford till his death, which happened in 1676. He was a gentleman much honoured for his becoming conversation.*

Ralph Button, A.M., university orator in the room of Dr. Hammond, and one of the proctors of the university; he was originally of Exeter College, where he made so great a progress in philosophy, and other literature, that when he was only bachelor of arts he was recommended by Dr. Prideaux to stand for a fellowship in Merton College, and was accordingly chosen 1633. He was afterward a celebrated tutor in his house, but was obliged to quit Oxford in the beginning of the civil wars, because he would not bear arms for the king. When the war was over he resumed his employment as tutor, and upon the refusal of Edward Corbet was made canon of Christ Church, and university orator; he was ejected at the Restoration, and afterward taught academical learning at Islington, near London, till 1680, when he died. He was an excellent scholar, a most humble, upright man, and a great sufferer for nonconformity.†

Mr. John Harmon, A.M., professor of the Greek language in the room of Dr. Stringer, was educated in Magdalen College, and took his degrees 1617; he was afterward master of the free school at St. Alban's, and one of the masters of Westminster school; from thence he was removed to the Greek professorship in this university. He was, says Mr. Wood,‡ a great philologist, a tolerable Latin poet, and one of the most excellent Grecians of his time, but otherwise an honest, weak man. He was turned out at the Restoration, and afterward lived privately at Steventon, in Hampshire, till the year 1670, when he died.

These were all the changes that were made among the heads of colleges and professors at this time; and, upon the whole, though it must be allowed that many of the ejected Loyalists were men of learning and great merit, it is certain those that kept their places, and the successors of such as were ejected, were men of equal probity and virtue, and no less eminent in their several professions, as appears by the monuments of their learning, some of which are remaining to this day.

The very enemies of the new heads of colleges have confessed that they were strict in the government of their several houses, that they kept a more than common watch over the morals of the students, and obliged them to an exact compliance with their statutes. The professors were indefatigable in instructing their pupils both in public and private; drunkenness, oaths, and profanation of the Lord's Day were banished; strict piety, and a profession of religion, were in fashion; the scholars often met together for prayer and religious conference; so that, as Mr. Philip Henry, who lived then in the university, observes, "If those of the old spirit and way were at first the better scholars, these were the better men."

Let the reader now judge of the *spirit and candour* of those writers who insinuate "that the new professors could neither pronounce Latin nor write English; that in the room of the

* Calamy's Abridg., p. 58.   † Ibid., p. 60.
‡ Athen. Oxon., vol. ii., p. 347, 348.

ejected Loyalists there succeeded an illiterate rabble, swept up from the plough-tail, from shops, and grammar-schools, and the dregs of the neighbouring university; that the muses were driven from their ancient seats; that all loyalty, learning, and good sense were banished; and that there succeeded in their room nothing but barbarism, enthusiasm, and ignorance, till the dawn of the Restoration."* Lord Clarendon was a declared enemy to these changes, and has painted them in the most odious colours, yet the force of truth has obliged him to confess that, "though it might have been reasonably expected that this wild and barbarous depopulation," as he calls it, "would have extirpated all the learning, religion, and loyalty which had flourished there, and that the succeeding ill husbandry and unskilful cultivation would have made it fruitful only in ignorance, profaneness, atheism, and rebellion; yet, by God's wonderful providence, that fruitful soil could not be made barren by all that stupidity and negligence; it choked the weeds, and would not suffer the poisonous seeds, that were sown with industry enough, to spring up, but after several tyrannical governors mutually succeeding each other, and with the same malice and perverseness endeavouring to extinguish all good literature and allegiance, it yielded a harvest of extraordinary good knowledge in all parts of learning; and many who were wickedly introduced applied themselves to the study of good learning, and the practice of virtue, and had inclinations to that duty and obedience they had never been taught, that when it pleased God to bring King Charles II. back to his throne he found the university abounding in excellent learning, and devoted to duty and obedience little inferior to what it was before its desolation." Considering the ill-nature that runs through this paragraph, it must be acknowledged to be an *unanswerable testimony* to the learning and application of the new professors, and with equal justice it may be added, that the university was in a much better state for learning, religion, and good sense at the Restoration than before the civil wars, as all the eminent philosophers and divines of the establishment, who did so much honour to their country in the three succeeding reigns, owed their education to these professors, viz., the Tillotsons, Stillingfleets, Patricks, Souths, Caves, Sprats, Kidders, Whitbys, Bulls, Boyles, Newtons, Lockes, and others. The university was in high reputation in foreign parts, and produced as many learned performances as in any former period. So that, admitting the new professors were not introduced into their places in a legal way, according to the statutes, because of the necessity of the times, yet it is certain they proved wise and watchful governors, strict observers of their statutes, and industrious promoters of piety and the liberal arts; and were far from deserving the brand of "ignorant, illiterate, hypocritical blockheads, enemies to the legal Constitution of their country," or of being pronounced unworthy the high preferments they enjoyed.

There were, no doubt, at first, very considerable vacancies in the several colleges; many of the fellows and scholars being dead, or killed in the king's service, and others having resigned

* Walker's Suff. Cler., p. 140.

their places in the university for benefices in the Church, besides those who were expelled by the visiters as already mentioned; but to supply the deficiency of fellows and tutors, the committee encouraged several learned graduates in the University of Cambridge to translate themselves to Oxford, and accept of preferments according to their merits. Many who had deserted the university when it became a garrison for the king returned to their colleges, and were promoted according to their seniority. Great numbers of youths, who had been kept at home because of the public commotions, were now sent to Oxford by their parents to perfect their education; and if it be considered, farther, that there had been no admissions from Westminster, Eton, St. Paul's, Merchant Tailors', and other public schools, for five or six years past, it is not to be wondered that there was an unusual flow of youth to the university at this time, so that the damage occasioned by this revolution of affairs was quickly repaired, and the muses returned to their ancient seats.

The long interruption of education in the university produced a very great scarcity of orthodox and learned ministers in the counties, some being silenced for refusing the Covenant, and others dispersed or killed in the wars. Many pulpits, also, w$_{ere}$ vacant by reason of the scandal or insufficiency of the incumbents, which was one occasion of the increase of lay-preachers, for the country people would go to hear anybody rather than have no sermons; besides, the Presbyterian clergy would authorize none to preach except such as would take the Covenant, and consent to their discipline. To remedy these evils, the northern counties petitioned the houses to erect a new university in the city of York, but the confusion of the times prevented their prosecuting the design. The Independents, who were less zealous about clerical orders, encouraged, or, at least, connived at the lay-preachers, apprehending that, in cases of necessity, pious men of good natural parts might exercise their gifts publicly to the edification of the Church; till, under this cover, they saw every bold enthusiast almost begin to usurp the office of a teacher. To bring things, therefore, into a little better order, the following petition was presented to both houses of Parliament, October 6, under the title of "The humble Petition of many Citizens of London, and others."

"Your petitioners are deeply sensible of the extreme want of preaching the Gospel throughout this kingdom, there being many hundreds of towns and villages altogether destitute of any preaching ministers, and many others are not well supplied; by reason whereof ignorance, drunkenness, profaneness, disaffection to the Parliament, and to others in authority, everywhere abound, there being scarce so much as the face of religion in many places. There is a great cry of people, from several counties of the kingdom, for men to preach to them the word of eternal life; and there are many men of competent gifts and abilities, of good life and honest conversation, who, being willing to employ their talents in the Lord's work, and to submit themselves for approbation to moderate and judicious men, are yet, by occasion of some scruples about ordination, discouraged from en-

gaging in this work of publishing the Gospel, wherein they might be helpful to many. And seeing that in the days of Queen Elizabeth, upon occasion of people's necessities, many such men were sent forth to publish the Gospel who had no formal act of ministerial ordination passed upon them, whose endeavours the Lord blessed to the good of many souls, and the furthering of the kingdom's peace; and since also we nothing doubt but the propagation of the Gospel throughout this kingdom, and the information of men in the things of their peace, and the peace and safety of the kingdom, are worthy of your greatest zeal, and are not the least of your care.:

"Therefore your petitioners humbly pray, that those who shall be approved of as men meet to dispense the mysteries of the Gospel, by such judicious, moderate, and able men, whom you in wisdom shall appoint thereunto, may receive from this honourable House encouragement and protection in preaching the Gospel in any place in this kingdom, or dominion of Wales, where need requires, that so the Word of the Lord may have free course and be glorified; ignorant men may be instructed; drunkenness, profaneness, and disaffection to the Parliament, and to others in authority, may be abandoned; and both the temporal and spiritual peace and prosperity of all sorts of men be the more advanced."[*]

The houses thanked the petitioners for their good affection, but did nothing upon it.

By an ordinance of February 11, this year, "all stage-players were declared to be rogues, punishable by the acts of the 39th of Queen Elizabeth and 7th of King James, notwithstanding any license they might have from the king or any other person. All stage galleries, seats, and boxes, are ordered to be pulled down by warrant of two justices of peace; all actors in plays for time to come being convicted shall be publicly whipped, and find sureties for their not offending in like manner for the future; and all spectators of plays for every offence are to pay five shillings."[†]

The controversies about church government, and liberty of conscience, ran still as high as ever; the Presbyterians, who had the government of the city of London in their hands, were for pressing Covenant uniformity in their sermons, which the Independents, and others of more catholic principles, endeavoured to oppose with all their might. Lord Clarendon is pleased to represent this in a ludicrous manner: "The pulpit skirmishes," says his lordship, "were now higher than ever, the Presbyterians in those fields losing nothing of their courage; having a notorious power in the city, notwithstanding the emulation of the Independents, who were more learned and rational, who, though they had not so great congregations of the common people, yet infected and were followed by the most substantial citizens, and by others of better condition. To these men Cromwell and most of the officers of the army adhered; but the divinity of the times was not to be judged by the preaching and congregations in churches, which were now thought not to be the fit and proper places of devotion and religious exercises, where the bishops had exer-

VOL. II.—K

* Rushworth, p. 834.   † Scobel, p. 143.

cised such unlimited tyranny, and which had been polluted by their consecrations. Liberty of conscience was now become the great charter, and men who were inspired preached and prayed when and where they would. Anabaptists grew very numerous, with whom the Independents concurred, so far as to join with them for the abolishing of tithes, as of Judaical institution. If any honest man could have been at so much ease as to have beheld the prospect with delight, never was such a scene of confusion as had spread itself at this time over the whole kingdom."* And yet it is certain that the laws against vice and immorality were strictly executed, the Lord's Day was duly observed, the churches were crowded with attentive hearers, family devotion was in repute, neither servants nor children being allowed to walk in the fields or frequent the public-houses. In a word, notwithstanding the difference of men's opinions and political views, there was a zeal for God, and a much greater appearance of sobriety, virtue, and true religion, than before the civil war, or after the blessed Restoration.

Among the Puritan divines who died this year, was the Reverend Mr. Herbert Palmer, B.D., of whom mention has been made among the Cambridge professors; his father was Sir Thomas Palmer, of Wingham, in Kent; his mother, the eldest daughter of Herbert Pelham, of Sussex, Esq.† Our divine was born at Wingham, and baptized there March 29, 1601; he had a polite education in his father's house, and learned the French language almost as soon as he could speak. In the year 1615 he was admitted fellow-commoner in St. John's College, Cambridge. In 1622 he took the degree of M.A. In 1623 he was chosen fellow of Queen's College in that university; the year following he was ordained to the ministry, to which he had devoted himself from his infancy: his first exercise was at a lecture in the city of Canterbury, where he preached once a week, till it was put down with the rest of the afternoon sermons. In the year 1632 he was presented by Archbishop Laud to the vicarage of Ashwell, in Hertfordshire, where he preached twice every Lord's Day, and catechized the children of his parishioners. The same year he was chosen one of the university preachers of Cambridge, by which he had authority to preach, as he should have occasion, in any part of England. In the year 1640, he and Dr. Tuckney were chosen clerks of the convocation for the diocess of Lincoln. In the year 1643 he was called to be a member of the Assembly of Divines at Westminster, and after some time chosen one of their assessors, in which place he behaved with great wisdom and integrity. April 11, 1644, he was constituted master of Queen's College, Cambridge, by the Earl of Manchester; here he set himself industriously to the promoting of religion and learning, being very solicitous that none should be admitted to a scholarship or fellowship in his college but such as were qualified in both these respects, the good effects of which appeared in the reputation and credit of that society, beyond most others of the university in his time. Mr. Palmer was a gentleman of a low stature, and a weakly constitution, but indefatigable in busi-

ness; his leisure was employed in works of devotion and charity, and as he had a competent estate, and chose a single life, he had an opportunity of doing a great deal of good; he maintained several poor scholars at his own expense in the college, and when he died left a considerable benefaction to the same purpose. His last sickness was not long, his constitution being spent, but his behaviour was uncommon; he looked the king of terrors in the face with an unshaken resolution, and resigned his life this summer with a firm expectation of the mercy of God to eternal life, in the forty-sixth year of his age, and was buried at the new church at Westminster.   -

Mr. Henry Wilkinson, B.D., was born in Yorkshire, and educated at Merton College, Oxford. In the year 1586 he was chosen probationer-fellow, and proceeded in arts; after some time he was made B.D., and in the year 1601 became pastor of Waddesdon, in Bucks. He was a person of considerable learning and piety, and being an old Puritan, says Mr. Wood,* was elected one of the Assembly of Divines in 1643, but he spent the chief of his time and labours among his parishioners at Waddesdon, where he died in a very advanced age, March 19, 1647-8, and lies buried in his own church.

Mr. John Saltmarsh, descendant of an ancient family in Yorkshire, was educated in Magdalen College, Cambridge, and graduated there; he was esteemed a person of a fine, active fancy, no contemptible poet, and a good preacher; he was first minister at Northampton, afterward at Braisted, in Kent, and at length chaplain in Sir Thomas Fairfax's army, where he always preached up love and unity; he meddled not with Presbytery or Independency, but laboured to draw souls from sin to Christ. He published some treatises, by which it appears he was of Antinomian principles. The manner of his death was extraordinary: December 4th, 1647, being at his house at Ilford, in Essex, he told his wife he had been in a trance, and received a message from God which he must immediately deliver to the army. He went that night to London, and next day to Windsor: being come to the council of officers, he told them that the Lord had left them; that he would not prosper their consultations, but destroy them by divisions among themselves, because they had sought to destroy the people of God, those who had stood by them in their greatest difficulties. He then went to the general, and without moving his hat, told him that God was highly displeased with him for committing of saints to prison. The like message he delivered to Cromwell, requiring him to take effectual means for the enlargement of the members of the army, who were committed for not complying with the general council. He then took his leave of the officers, telling them he had now done his errand, and must never see them any more. After which he went to London, and took leave of his friends there, telling them his work was done, and desiring some of them to be careful of his wife. Thursday, December 9, he returned to Ilford in perfect health; next day he told his wife that he had now finished his work, and must go to his Father. Saturday morning, De-

---

* Clarendon, vol. v., p. 115, 116.
† Clarke's Lives in his Martyrology, p. 183.

* Athen. Oxon., vol. ii., p. 59.

cember 11, he was taken speechless, and about four in the afternoon he died.*

◆

CHAPTER X.

THE SECOND CIVIL WAR. — THE CONCLUSION OF THE ASSEMBLY OF DIVINES. — THE PROGRESS OF PRESBYTERY. — THE TREATY OF THE ISLE OF WIGHT.—DEATH AND CHARACTER OF KING CHARLES I.—HIS WORKS, AND THE AUTHORS OF HIS UNHAPPY SUFFERINGS.—ANNO 1648.

THE king was all last winter in a close prisoner in Carisbrook Castle, attended only by two servants of his own, and debarred of all other conversation, without the knowledge of the governor ; nevertheless, by the assistance of some particular friends, he sent and received several letters from the queen, though his correspondence was discovered oftener than he was aware. His majesty made several attempts to escape, but was always prevented ; Captain Burley attempted to raise the island for him, but was apprehended and executed. However, in pursuance of the secret treaty with the Scots, already mentioned, an army was raising in that kingdom, to be commanded by Duke Hamilton ; but the English cavaliers, impatient of delay, without concerting proper measures among themselves, or with the Presbyterians, took up arms in several counties, to deliver the king from his confinement, and to restore him without any treaty with his Parliament. The Welsh appeared first, under Major-general Langhorn, Colonel Poyer, and Powel, three officers in the Parliament army, who had privately accepted commissions from the Prince of Wales.† These were followed by others in Dorsetshire, Devonshire, Sussex, Surrey, Lincolnshire, Norfolk, Kent, Northamptonshire, Essex, and in the city of London itself. The insurrection in the city began on Sunday, April 9, in Moorfields, by a company of young fellows with clubs and staves crying out for God and King Charles. But after they had done some mischief in the night, and frighted the mayor into the Tower, they were dispersed next morning by the general at the head of two regiments. The Kentish men, under the Earl of Norwich, having plundered some houses, were defeated near Maidstone, and having a promise of pardon, the main body laid down their arms ; notwithstanding which, the earl, with five hundred resolute men, crossed the Thames at the Isle of Dogs, and came as far as Mile End Green, expecting assistance from the city ; but being disappointed, he joined the Essex cavaliers under Sir Charles Lucas and Lord Capel, who surprised the Parliament's committee at Chelmsford, and then shut themselves up in Colchester, where they maintained themselves against General Fairfax for ten weeks, till, being reduced to the last extremity, they were forced to surrender at discretion, August 28 ;‡ after which the general marched

round about the country, and having quieted all insurrections in those parts, returned to his headquarters at St. Alban's about Michaelmas. While Fairfax was in Kent and Essex, Lieutenant-general Cromwell reduced the Welsh about the end of June. At the same time, the Earl of Holland and Duke of Buckingham appeared at the head of five hundred horse and some foot near Kingston-upon-Thames, but they were soon dispersed ; the earl was taken prisoner at St. Neot's, in Huntingdonshire, by Colonel Scroop, and the Duke of Buckingham, with great difficulty, escaped into the Low Countries. About the same time, several of the Parliament's ships revolted to the Prince of Wales, then in Holland, who went on board, and with Prince Rupert, Lord Hopton, and others, sailed to the coast of England, with a design to relieve Colchester; but, although disappointed, he landed five hundred men about Deal and Sandwich, and blocked up the Thames' mouth ; but when the Earl of Warwick came up with the Parliament's fleet, he sailed back to Holland, and most of the ships returned to the obedience of Parliament.

It was not without great difficulty that the king's friends in Scotland prevailed with the Parliament of that kingdom to consent to the raising an army against England, the commissioners of the Kirk and the whole body of their ministers being vehemently against it ; and when it was put to the vote, eighteen lords and forty commoners entered their protests, from a strong suspicion that, by the vast resort of Loyalists to Edinburgh, there was a private agreement between Hamilton and that party to lay aside the Covenant, and restore the king without any conditions; to prevent which, the Scots Parliament gave express orders that none should be received into their army, or join with them at their entrance into England, except such as should take the Covenant; but Hamilton, who betrayed their cause, found means to evade the order, by which means he ruined himself, and the party he intended to serve.*

claimed against this as an unusual piece of severity; and some historians have censured it as a bloody step. Mrs. Macaulay represents it as an instance of the humanity of the general, that, though he had been provoked by many irritating circumstances in the conduct of the besieged, he selected the two chief commanders only, to avenge the innocent blood they had caused to be spilt. The fact was, that these two gentlemen had shown themselves most implacable ; had prevented the soldiers from accepting terms of indemnity offered by the Parliament in the beginning ; that the besieged had been exposed to the utmost extremities of famine; and that the Independents regarded the engaging the kingdom in a second war as an unpardonable crime. When Sir Charles Lucas urged that the sentence of the general was unprecedented, a Parliament soldier standing by told him, "that he had put to death with his own hand some of the Parliament's soldiers in cold blood." At which he was dismayed. A few days after, a gentleman in mourning for Sir Charles Lucas appearing in his presence, the king wept.—*Mrs. Macaulay's History*, vol. iv., p. 362, 363.— *Whitlocke's Memorials*, p. 328–330.—ED. * Rapin, vol. ii., p. 550, 553, folio. Hamilton's Memoirs, p. 339. Bishop Burnet endeavours to exculpate the duke from such a charge, and imputes the miscarriage of the expedition, in which he was leader, to his yielding to the counsels of others. The bishop sets against the report of his betraying the army several instances of his generous and disinter-

---

* Rushworth, p. 944.   † Ibid., p. 1007.
‡ Dr. Grey is displeased with Mr. Neal that he does not inform his readers what use General Fairfax made of the power with which this unconditional surrender invested him. He seized Sir Charles Lucas and Sir George Lisle, and made them instant sacrifices to military justice. All the prisoners ex-

The Scots army entered England, July 11th, to the number of twenty thousand foot* and six thousand horse, under the command of Duke Hamilton, and were afterward joined by Sir Marmaduke Langdale at the head of four thousand foot and seven or eight hundred horse; but these being Englishmen and cavaliers who had not taken the Covenant, were not incorporated with the Scots forces, but were obliged to march a day before them, which was Hamilton's contrivance to evade his orders; nevertheless, they composed one army, Langdale being to receive all his orders from Hamilton, and to act only by his directions. But though there was a private understanding between the generals, the subalterns and soldiers of both parties were not acquainted with it, and had the same incurable jealousy of each other as formerly; from the same motive the Presbyterians in the Parliament at Westminster commissioned their army to oppose the Scots, though they came into England with an avowed intention of restoring the king upon the terms of the Covenant, which was the supreme object of their wishes.

It may seem surprising, however, that there was no good understanding between the two Parliaments, when those of England sent commissioners to Edinburgh to accomplish it; but the Scots, being strongly persuaded that the Parliament at Westminster was still governed by an army of Independents, all that Mr. Marshall and the rest could say was not sufficient to divert them from their enterprise, which is the easier accounted for, when the strength of the Hamiltonian faction, and their obligations to the king by their secret treaty, are considered. This engagement appears from the duke's letter to Lambert, in which he acquaints him, that he was commanded to enter England with an army, for maintaining the solemn League and Covenant; for settling religion; for delivering the king from his base imprisonment; and freeing the Parliament from the constraint put upon them.† The state of affairs had undergone a considerable change by the rising of the English cavaliers; the army was in the field, and divided into several distant parts of the kingdom, and the Presbyterians in as full possession of the government as ever; they were renewing the treaty with the king, and sending propositions to the Scots to join with them; but the good understanding between the two nations having been interrupted last winter, by the growing influence of the army, who were no friends to Covenant uniformity, the Scots would not be satisfied with the present diminution of their power, unless they were entirely disbanded, and

therefore had not changed the instructions to their general. On the other hand, the Parliament could not with safety disband their army while the cavaliers were in the field; nor could they forbid their opposing the Scots, who had joined the common enemy, and were marching into England with an armed force, to deliver the king from his imprisonment, although they had concerted no measures with the two houses, or communicated their secret treaty with his majesty in the Isle of Wight. Thus the two Parliaments of England and Scotland opposed each other, when both had the same views, and were actuated by the same principles. If the Scots army had been commanded by a general the Presbyterians could have confided in, and had marched directly for London without joining the cavaliers, the Parliament of England would have gladly received them, and the citizens of London have opened their gates; for the English Presbyterians wished them well; but by joining the common enemy, who were in arms all over the kingdom, they were staggered; and Duke Hamilton, who betrayed their cause by trifling away a whole month in the north, gave the English army, which was distributed into various parts, time to reunite and defeat all their enterprises.*

The Scots, invading England in this hostile manner, and in the midst of so many insurrections, awakened men's fears, and made them apprehend the cause was to be fought over again. And while the Parliament was alarmed on every side, the English army gave them strong assurances they would stand by them, and march wheresoever the committee of the two houses (appointed to manage their motions) should direct. However, General Fairfax, who engaged heartily against the cavaliers, refusing to march against the Scots, because they had openly declared for the Covenant, Colonel Lambert was ordered into the north, with a flying squadron, to harass them, till Lieutenant-general Cromwell could come out of Wales to his assistance. The Scots having been joined by Sir Marmaduke Langdale, who had seized the important town of Berwick, marched through Cumberland and Westmoreland into Lancashire, without opposition; but upon the 17th of August, Cromwell, having joined Lambert, and refreshed his troops, faced them near Preston with eight or ten thousand men, and after a sharp engagement with the cavaliers under Sir Marmaduke Langdale, who were almost a day's march before the duke, routed the whole Scots army, and took eight or nine thousand prisoners, with all their artillery and baggage; Hamilton fled with three thousand horse, but was so closely pursued by Lambert, that he surrendered without striking another stroke, and all his men were dispersed or made prisoners. Cromwell after this action pursued his victory, marching directly for Edinburgh, which opened its gates; and having entered the city and changed the magistracy to his mind, he left three regiments of horse to keep the country quiet, and returned into England October 11, laden with martial glory and renown.†

ested conduct, in his care to preserve the army and to act for the king's advantage, at the risk of his own liberty and safety.—*Memoirs of the Duke of Hamilton,* p. 365.—Ed.

* Dr. Grey here censures Mr. Neal for often speaking at random: because Bishop Burnet, on the authority of Turner, the adjutant-general, says that "the forces of the Scots amounted only to ten thousand foot and four thousand horse."—*Memoirs of Hamilton,* p. 356. But it may afford a sanction to Mr. Neal's representation, that since he wrote, Mrs. Macaulay and Mr. Hume have given the same estimate of the army led by Duke Hamilton into England. With these agrees Whitelocke, *Memoirs,* p. 327.—Ed.

† Rushworth, p. 1194.

* Hamilton's Memoirs, p. 337, 345, 353, &c.

† "So he did," says Dr. Grey, "but it was in the same sense that a company of highwaymen or banditti would return laden with martial glory and hon-

Before the army left London, and while their influence over the Parliament continued, the Commons, having taken into consideration the affair of settling the government, voted unanimously, that the government of the kingdom should be still by king, Lords, and Commons, and that the propositions at Hampton Court should be the ground-work for a settlement, which shows that there was no design, as yet formed, of changing the government into a commonwealth; at least nothing appeared, though the agitators, who were the chief managers of the army, began to mutter, that if the king could not be brought to reason he must be set aside, and the Duke of Gloucester, or one of his younger children, placed on the throne.[*]

The army had no sooner left the neighbourhood of the city but the Presbyterians resumed the management of public affairs. May 5, the Parliament resolved to maintain the solemn League and Covenant, and to unite with the kingdom of Scotland upon the propositions of Hampton Court.[†] The militia of the city of London was restored to the lord-mayor and common council; the eleven impeached members, and the seven peers, were discharged; and, in short, all that had been done against the Presbyterian greatness by the influence of the army last winter was reversed; so that, as from August 6, 1647, to the beginning of May, 1648, the Parliament may be supposed to have lain under some restraint from the army; from that time to the end of the treaty of the Isle of Wight, it was at full liberty, and entirely under Presbyterian direction.[‡] Petitions came now from divers counties, and from the city of London itself, for a personal treaty with the king; upon which the Commons set aside their votes of non-addresses, and, at the request of the Lords, consented to treat with the king, without his signing any preliminary propositions; hoping, as matters then stood, his majesty would not delay a moment to grant their demands, that he might be released from his confinement, and placed upon his throne, before the army should be at leisure to throw farther obstacles in the way; but here was the fatal oversight: the king and his friends would not condescend, nor the Presbyterians relax, till both were driven out of the field, and the army became irresistible.

Let the reader pause a little, and reflect with grief upon the miserable distractions of this unhappy kingdom; in this crisis were three or four powerful parties with separate views striving for mastery. The king, a close prisoner in the Isle of Wight, was the prize contended for; he had little or no weight to throw into either scale, though, by signing the Scots treaty, he was reputed the author of that invasion, and of the second civil war; the cavaliers were in arms to preserve the Episcopal Church of England; but having concerted no measures among themselves, were easily dispersed. The Scots came into England in pursuance of the Cove-

nant, and the secret treaty in the Isle of Wight, but two mistakes ruined their enterprise; one was, their not communicating the contents of that treaty to the English Presbyterians, which they might have done by their commissioners without the knowledge of the English army, before they had marched into England; the other was, Duke Hamilton's acting in concert with the English cavaliers, allowing them, to march in the van, who gave their enemies in the Parliament at Westminster a fair opportunity of engaging the whole military power of England against them; for, without all doubt, if the duke had prevailed, not only the Independent, but the Presbyterian cause had been betrayed into the hands of the cavaliers, which must, in the end, have been equally fatal to both parties, and lost them all the advantages of the war. This fatal conjunction broke the strength of the English Presbyterians, and played the game into the hands of a third party, who destroyed the other two. The army, with whom were the Independents, Anabaptists, and other sectaries, was governed by the agitators, who had given up the king, and had an incurable aversion to the cavaliers, and all who adhered to them, as their most determined enemies; nor could they confide in the Presbyterians, because in all their past treaties they had seen themselves made a sacrifice to Covenant uniformity. Upon the whole, all parties were stiff in their demands, disunited in their councils, and infinitely jealous of each other. Among the Presbyterians, some were for fighting only with the cavaliers, and others for opposing the Scots as invaders. Some of the cavaliers were for restoring the king by their own valour, and others for availing themselves of the assistance of the Scots. The army was no less distracted; those who served under General Fairfax were unwilling to march against the Scots Presbyterians; those under Cromwell were for encountering every power that would not secure them: that liberty of conscience for which they had been contending; and despairing of this, not only from the king, but from the Scots and English Presbyterians, they unhappily ran upon those extravagant measures which ended in the destruction of the king and overthrow of the whole Constitution.

Tantum religio potuit suadere malorum!

But to return: the Assembly of Divines having finished their main business, was reduced to a small number, most of the country ministers having returned home, and those who remained about London were employed chiefly in the examination of such ministers as presented themselves for ordination, or induction into livings; thus they subsisted till February 22, 1648-9, about three weeks after the king's death, having sat five years, six months, and twenty-two days, in which time they had one thousand one hundred and sixty-three sessions. They were afterward changed into a committee for the purposes last mentioned, and met every Thursday morning till March 25, 1652, when the Long Parliament being turned out of the House by Oliver Cromwell, they broke up without any formal dissolution.[*]

The works of the Assembly, besides some

---

our, after obtaining a good booty from the lawful owners of it." This remark shows the strain and spirit of Dr. Grey's Examination of Mr. Neal. Lord Clarendon, speaking of this transaction, with more truth and candour calls it " this great victory."—ED.

[*] Rushworth, p. 1074
[†] Rapin, p. 504, 508, 511, 518.
[‡] Rushworth, p. 1127.

[*] MS., *penes me.*

letters to foreign churches, and occasional admonitions, were,

1. Their humble Advice to the Parliament for Ordination of Ministers and Settling the Presbyterian Government.

2. A Directory for Public Worship.

3. A Confession of Faith.

4. A Larger and Shorter Catechism.

5. A Review of some of the Thirty-nine Articles.

The annotations on the Bible, which go under their name, were neither undertaken nor revised by them, but by a committee of Parliament, who named the commentators, and furnished them with books; nor were they all members of the Assembly, as appears by the following list.

Those with asterisks were not of the Assembly.

	WAS WRITTEN BY
The Commentary on the five Books of Moses,	Rev. Mr. Ley, subdean of Chester.
The two Books of Kings, The two Books of Chronicles. Ezra, Nehemiah, Esther,	Dr. Gouge.
The Psalms,	*Mr. Meric Casaubon.
Proverbs,	Mr. Francis Taylor.
Ecclesiastes,	Dr. Reynolds.
Solomon's Song,	*Mr. Sinalwood, recommended by Archbishop Usher.
Isaiah, Jeremiah, Lamentations,	Mr. Gataker.
Ezekiel, Daniel, and the smaller Prophets,	*Mr. Pemberton in the first edition. *Bishop Richardson in the second.
Matthew, Mark, Luke, John,	Mr. Ley.
St. Paul's Epistles,	Dr. D. Featly; but his notes are broken and imperfect, the author dying before he had revised them.

There were two other persons concerned in this work, who might probably have the other parts of Scripture allotted them, not here mentioned, viz., Mr. Downham and Mr. Reading.

When posterity shall impartially review the labours of this Assembly of Divines, and consider the times in which they sat, they will have a just veneration for their memory; for though their sentiments in divinity were in many instances too narrow and contracted, yet with all their faults, among which their persecuting zeal for religion was not the least, they were certainly men of real piety and virtue, who meant well, and had the interest of religion at heart; and most of them possessed as much learning as any of their contemporaries; the names of Lightfoot, Selden,* Gataker, Greenhill, Arrowsmith, Twisse, Bishop Reynolds, Wallis, &c., will always meet with esteem from the learned world; and had they not grasped at coercive power, or jurisdiction over the consciences of men, their characters would have been unblemished. Mr. Baxter, who knew most of them, says, "They were men of eminent learning, godliness, ministerial abilities, and fidelity; and being not worthy to be one of them myself,"

says he, "I may more fully speak the truth which I know, even in the face of malice and envy, that, as far as I am able to judge by the information of history, and by any other evidences, *the Christian world, since the days of the apostles, had never a synod of more excellent divines than this synod, and the Synod of Dort.*"* The Divine right of the Presbyterian government first threw them into heats, and then divided them, engaging them first with the Parliament, and then with the Independents and Erastians; their opposing a toleration raised them a great many enemies, and caused a secession in their own body: for after they had carried the question of Divine right, the Independents and Erastians deserted them, after which they found it very difficult to muster as many as would make a house. Had the Parliament dissolved them at that juncture, they had separated with honour, but they dwindled by degrees, as has been related, the business of the Church being now translated to the Provincial Assemblies.

We have already remembered the two former of these assemblies; the third met May 3, this year, and chose the Rev. Mr. Whitaker moderator. In the fourth session they agreed to present a second petition to the Parliament in the name of the province, humbly to desire, "1. That they would renew the consideration of their former petition. 2. That they would establish the two catechisms of the Assembly of Divines, and appoint them to be publicly taught throughout the kingdom. 3. That they would add their civil sanction to the new confession of faith. 4. That the Directory for public worship may be better observed; and that better care may be taken for the observation of the Lord's Day." In their twelfth session, October 6, they agreed to the report of their committee concerning the cause of the decay of religion, which they say was chiefly owing to the want of able and settled ministers, there being above forty parish churches and congregations within the province which had no ministers settled among them by allowance of authority, a catalogue of which churches were subjoined. The reason of this defect being chiefly want of maintenance, they pray the houses "to agree upon some method that the dean and chapter lands, and the impropriations belonging to bishops, lying within this province, may be applied for the augmentation of the clergy's maintenance; and that there may be a fixed maintenance in every parish recoverable by the incumbent."

The fourth Provincial Assembly met November 3, the Rev. Mr. Edmund Calamy moderator. In their third session, November 23, they ordered that the several ministers of the province of London do begin the work of catechising; that they use the Assembly's catechism, and no other; that the persons to be catechised be children and servants not admitted to the Lord's Table; that the time be in the afternoon before sermon; and that they exhort their parishioners to encourage it. In their fourth session, November 30, they resolved that the twelve classes of the province of London observe their course for ordination of ministers; and that at the close of every public ordination notice be given which classis is to ordain next. But the nation being in confusion, and the clouds gathering thick over their heads, they did little more this winter than keep a weekly fast* among themselves, to avert the judgment of God, which threatened the life of the king, and the dissolution of the whole government.

The county of Lancaster being formed into another Presbyterian province this year, assembled at Preston, February 7, 1648, and published a kind of pastoral letter, or solemn exhortation to the several churches within their province, to the practice of those duties that were requisite to the supporting and carrying on the Presbyterian discipline, subscribed by the reverend

Mr. James Hyatt, *Moderator.*
Mr. Thomas Johnson, *Assessor.*
Mr. Edward Gee, *Scribe.*†

They likewise appointed a committee to examine the paper called The Agreement of the People [hereafter to be mentioned], and tendered to the consideration of the nation by the officers of the army, with a desire that they would by subscription declare their concurrence to it; but it was carried in the negative.‡ The design of this paper was, to change the form of government into a kind of commonwealth, without a king or House of Lords. It was published by way of probation, that they might learn the sense of the nation; but the article relating to religion being peculiar, and giving great offence to the Presbyterian clergy, shall be transcribed entire : "We do not empower our representatives," say they, "to continue in force, or make any laws, oaths, or covenants, whereby to compel by penalties, or otherwise, any person to anything, in or about matters of faith, religion, or God's worship; or restrain any person from professing his faith, or exercise of his religion according to his conscience, in any house or place, except such as are or shall be set apart for the public worship. Nevertheless, the instruction or direction of the nation in a public way, for matters of faith, worship, or discipline, so it be not compulsive, or express popery, is referred to their discretion." The Agreement adds, "It is intended that the Christian religion be held forth and recommended as the public profession in this nation, which we desire may, by the grace of God, be reformed to the greatest purity in doctrine, worship, and discipline, according to the Word of God. The instructing the people thereunto in a public way, provided it be not compulsive ; as, also, the maintaining of able teachers for that end, and for the confutation and discovery of heresy, error, and whatsoever is contrary to sound doctrine, is allowed to be provided by our representatives ; the maintenance of teachers may be out of a treasury, and we desire not by tithes." But, besides these, "all who profess

faith in God by Jesus Christ, however differing in judgment from the doctrine, discipline, and worship, publicly held forth, shall be protected in the profession of their faith, and exercise of their religion according to their consciences, so as they abuse not this liberty to the civil injury of others, or the disturbance of the public peace." These were just and generous sentiments ; however, the synod forbade their people to subscribe them, not only because the Agreement imported a change in the civil government, but because of the mischiefs that would attend a toleration ; their reasons for which they published to the world March 6, 1648, subscribed by fifty-nine ministers.

The Provincial Assemblies of London met regularly every half year, to the year 1655, when, finding themselves without power, and not being willing to apply* to the protector and his Parliament for support, they desisted ; but there were none legally formed in any other counties of England. However, the country ministers entered into voluntary associations, and erected a sort of classes for ordination of ministers, and promoting friendship and peace among themselves; many of the Independent ministers joining with them ; the associations met once a month; at one or other church in the county, and after prayers and a sermon, conferred upon the state of religion, and gave their advice upon such cases as were brought before them in a neighbourly and friendly manner.

To return to the Parliament, which was now recruited with such Presbyterian members as had absconded, or deserted their stations, while the army was quartered in the neighbourhood of the city ; these gentlemen, finding they had the superiority in the House, resumed their courage, and took the opportunity of discovering their principles and spirit, in passing such a law against heretics as is hardly to be paralleled among Protestants.† It had been laid aside by the influence of the army for above nine months, till May 1, when it was voted that all ordinances concerning church government referred to committees be brought in and debated ; and that the ordinance concerning blasphemy and heresy be now determined, which was done accordingly. This was one of the most shocking laws I have met with in restraint of religious liberty, and shows that the governing Presbyterians would have made a terrible use of their power, had they been supported by the sword of the civil magistrate.‡ The ordinance is dated May

---

* Bishop Warburton's remark on this is: "These were glorious saints, that fought and preached for the king's destruction ; and then fasted and prayed for his preservation, when they had brought him to the foot of the scaffold !" This remark goes on the supposition that, to oppose the king's arbitrary views and measures, was to fight and preach for his destruction. If it eventually proved so, from whence could it arise but from his adherence to his designs, till concessions came too late ?—ED.   † Vol. Pamph., No. 73.
‡ Rushworth, p. 1259.

* Bishop Warburton says that they did apply to the protector, "and received such an answer as they deserved." A deputation of the London ministers went to him to complain that the cavalier Episcopal clergy got their congregations from them, and debauched the faithful from their ministers. "Have they so ?" said the protector: "I will take an order with them ;" and made a motion, as if he was going to say something to the captain of the guards ; when turning short, "But, hold !" said he, "after what manner do the cavaliers debauch your people ?" "By preaching," replied the ministers. "Then preach back again," said this able statesman ; and left them to their own reflections.—ED.
† Scobel's Collect., cap. 114, p. 149.
‡ Mr. Neal has done himself honour by the strong terms of reprobation in which he speaks of this intolerant, iniquitous, and cruel ordinance. It cannot be condemned in too severe terms : though Dr. Grey insinuates that there was occasion for it in the

2, 1648, and ordains, "that all persons who shall willingly maintain, publish, or defend, by preaching or writing, the following heresies with obstinacy, shall, upon complaint, and proof, by the oaths of two witnesses, before two justices of the peace, or confession of the party, be committed to prison, without bail or mainprize, till the next jail delivery; and in case the indictment shall then be found, and the party upon his trial shall not abjure his said error, and his defence and maintenance of the same, he shall suffer the pains of death,* as in case of felony, without benefit of clergy; and if he recant or abjure, he shall remain in prison till he find sureties that he will not maintain the same heresies or errors any more; but if he relapse, and is convicted a second time, he shall suffer death as before. The heresies, or errors, are these following:

1. "That there is no God.
2. "That God is not omnipresent, omniscient, almighty, eternal, and perfectly holy.
3. "That the Father is not God, that the Son is not God, that the Holy Ghost is not God, or that these three are not one eternal God; or, that Christ is not God equal with the Father.
4. "The denial of the manhood of Christ, or that the Godhead and manhood are distinct natures; or that the humanity of Christ is pure and unspotted of all sin.
5. "The maintaining that Christ did not die, nor rise again, nor ascend into heaven bodily.
6. "The denying that the death of Christ is meritorious on the behalf of believers, or that Jesus Christ is the Son of God.
7. "The denying that the Holy Scriptures of the Old and New Testament are the Word of God.
8. "The denying of the resurrection of the dead, and a future judgment."

The ordinance proceeds to specify some other errors of less demerit, and says, "that whosoever shall maintain or defend them, shall, upon conviction by the oaths of two witnesses, or by his own confession before two justices of peace, be ordered to renounce the said error or errors in the public congregation of the parish from whence the complaint comes, or where the offence was committed; and in case of refusal, he shall be committed to prison till he find sureties that he shall not publish or maintain the

said error or errors any more. The errors are these following:

1. "That all men shall be saved.
2. "That man by nature hath free will to turn to God.
3. "That God may be worshipped in or by pictures or images.
4. "That the soul dies with the body, or after death goes neither to heaven nor hell, but to purgatory.
5. "That the soul of man sleeps when the body is dead.
6. "That the revelations or workings of the Spirit are a rule of faith, or Christian life, though diverse from or contrary to the written Word of God.
7. "That man is bound to believe no more than by his reason he can comprehend.
8. "That the moral law contained in the Ten Commandments is no rule of the Christian life.
9. "That a believer need not repent or pray for pardon of sin.
10. "That the two sacraments, of baptism and the Lord's Supper, are not ordinances commanded by the Word of God.
11. "That the baptism of infants is unlawful and void; and that such persons ought to be baptized again.
12. "That the observation of the Lord's Day, as enjoined by the ordinances and laws of this realm, is not according, or is contrary to the Word of God.
13. "That it is not lawful to join in public or family prayer, or to teach children to pray.
14. "That the churches of England are no true churches, nor their ministers and ordinances true ministers and true ordinances; or, that the church government by presbyters is antichristian or unlawful.
15. "That magistracy, or the power of the civil magistrate, by law established in England, is unlawful.
16. "That all use of arms, though for the public defence (and be the cause never so just), is unlawful."

This black list of heresies was taken from the speeches or writings of the papists, Arminians, Antinomians, Arians, Baptists, and Quakers, &c., of these times. The ordinance was a comprehensive engine of cruelty,* and would have tortured great numbers of good Christians and good subjects. The Presbyterians of the present age are not only thankful that the confusion of the times did not permit their predecessors to put this law into execution, but wish also that it could be blotted out of the records of time, as it is impossible to brand it with the censure equal to its demerits.

June 21, the army being still in the field, and the Parliament at liberty, the ordinance for the more effectual settling the Presbyterian government, without limitation of time, was read the second time and committed, and on the 29th of August it was perfected, and received the sanction of both houses, under the title of "A Form of Church Government to be used in the Church-

---

"monstrous opinions," as he calls them, which prevailed in those times; and for which he refers to Edwards's Gangræna. "Besides the severity of the penalties which this ordinance denounced, the mode of process which it appointed," as I have observed in another place, "was arbitrary and repugnant to the Constitution of this country in particular, as well as opposite to the general principles of equity and justice; for it allowed neither the privilege of a jury, nor the liberty of an appeal. Such is the operation of religious bigotry."—See a *Review of the Life, Character, and Writings of the Rev. John Biddle*, p. 52. The nature of this ordinance is fully considered from p. 48 to 56.—ED.

* Death, under Constantius, the son of Constantine, was made the punishment of idolatry: the like sentence is here inflicted upon the worshippers of the only living and true God, the creator and governor of the world. "How fluctuating and convertible," observes an excellent writer, "are all penal laws in religion!"—*Dr. Disney's Life of Dr. Jortin*, p. 136, 137. —ED.

* The indignation which the liberal mind feels at the principles and spirit of those who, themselves recently suffering under the hard hand of intolerance, could frame and pass such a law, is somewhat relieved by finding that it did not pass without much opposition.—*Whitelocke's Memoirs*, p. 302.—ED.

es England and Ireland."* It is a collection of the several ordinances, for establishing the branches of Presbyterial government already mentioned, and ordains that " all parishes and places whatsoever within England and Wales shall be under the government of congregational, classical, provincial, and national assemblies, except the houses or chapels of the king and his children, and of the peers of the realm, which are to continue free for the exercise of divine duties, according to the Directory, and not otherwise; it gives directions for the choice of ruling elders in every parish, and for proper persons to be judges of the qualifications of the persons chosen; it appoints commissioners to divide the whole kingdom into distinct classical presbyteries; it gives direction about the con stituting of provincial and national synods, with the extent of their several powers; it determines the method of ordination of ministers, of dispensing church censures, and suspension from the sacrament; and, last of all, it gives direction for excommunication and absolution," but lays no penalty upon recusants or such as do not come to the sacrament, or submit to their discipline; which was the utmost length that Presbytery obtained in this kingdom.

The Parliament having agreed to treat with the king without any preliminary conditions, sent the Earl of Middlesex, Sir John Hippisly, and Mr. Bulkely, to acquaint his majesty with their resolutions, and to desire him to appoint what place he pleased in the Isle of Wight for the congress; his majesty seemed pleased with the message, and sent a letter to the two houses August 10, desiring them to recall their votes, which forbade the access of his friends, and to direct that men of necessary use in this affair may be permitted to assist him, and that the Scots be parties in the treaty.† His majesty then appointed Newport, in the Isle of Wight, for the place of conference. To all which the Lords agreed without any restriction; but the Commons insisted that no person lately in arms against the Parliament be of the number; that the Scots be not included; and that if his majesty be at liberty as at Hampton Court, he pass his royal word not to go out of the island during the treaty, nor twenty-eight days after, without consent of Parliament.

Upon these conditions his majesty was conducted to Newport, and left at liberty upon his parole of honour. Several noblemen, gentlemen, divines, and lawyers were appointed to assist him in the treaty, who were to stand behind his majesty's chair and hear the debates, but not to speak, except when the king withdrew into another room for their advice; the names of his divines were,‡ Dr. Juxon, bishop

of London, Dr. Duppa, bishop of Salisbury, Dr. Sheldon, Dr. Hammond, Dr. Oldisworth, Dr. Sanderson, Dr. Turner, Dr. Haywood; and towards the end of the treaty, Dr. Usher, archbishop of Armagh, Dr. Bramhall, Dr. Prideaux, Dr. Warner, Dr. Ferne, and Dr. Morely; Dr. Brownrigge, bishop of Exter, was also sent for, but he was under restraint; and Dr. Sheldon, Dr. Hammond, and Dr. Oldisworth, being also under restraint, were not permitted to stand.

The Parliament appointed five noblemen and ten commoners, with four divines, to assist them in their debates touching religion, viz., Mr. Vines, Mr. Caryl, Dr. Seaman, and Mr. Marshall. The treaty was to continue forty days, and to proceed upon the propositions of Hampton Court.* September 12, the Parliament observed a day of public fasting and prayer, for a blessing; and some days after the king and his household did the like, when, after the public service, the following prayer was read, drawn up by his majesty's direction:

" O most merciful Father, Lord God of peace and truth, we, a people sorely afflicted by the scourge of an unnatural war, do earnestly beseech thee to command a blessing from heaven upon this present treaty, begging for the establishment of a happy peace. Soften the most obdurate hearts with a true Christian desire of saving those men's blood for whom Christ himself hath shed his; or if the guilt of our great sins cause this treaty to break off in vain, Lord, let the truth clearly appear who those men are who, under pretence of the public good, do pursue their own private ends; that this people may be no longer so blindly miserable as not to see, at least in this their day, the things that belong to their peace. Grant this, gracious God, for his sake, who is our peace itself, even Jesus Christ our Lord. Amen."

The conferences opened on Monday, September 18, about nine in the morning, at the house of Sir William Hodges. The first day the commissioners presented the king with a draught of three bills: the first to establish the Presbyterian government† forever in the Church of England; the second to relinquish the militia to the two houses for thirty years; and the third to recall all his majesty's declarations against the Parliament. To the last of these the king readily consented, but excepted to the preamble, in which were these words: " that the two houses of Parliament had been necessitated to enter into a war in their just and lawful defence."‡ Instead of which, the king proposed an act of indemnity; but the commissioners insisting peremptorily upon the words as those without

* Scobel, cap. 117, p. 175.
† Rushworth, vol. ii., p. 1236.
‡ According to Dr. P. Williams's MS. collections, to which Dr. Grey pays great deference, the order was limited to Dr. Juxon and Dr. Duppa; and Dr. Sheldon, Dr. Hammond, and Dr. Oldsworth were not permitted to go to the king, being under restraint. But Mr. Neal's list, except as to these three, is confirmed by Whitelocke, with this difference, that Dr. Usher, Bambridge, Prideaux, Warner, Ferne, and Morely were not included in the first appointment, but were allowed to attend the king in consequence of a message from him on the 3d of November.—Memor., p. 341.—ED.

* Rapin, vol. ii., p. 559.
† " The utter extinction of Episcopacy, and their setting up their own idol in its stead, was the superior consideration for which, it is plain, the Presbyterians had entered into the hazard of war : this was the chief cause of their quarrel with their old associates, the Independents; and the not being fully gratified on this article by the king was, in their eyes, losing the best fruits of their success. The Parliament's commissioners with earnestness, and even tears, assured the king that all his concessions would be useless, unless he gave up the point of Episcopacy : he absolutely refused farther yielding on this article, and the Parliament voted his concessions unsatisfactory."—Macaulay's History of England, 8vo, vol. iv., p. 365, 366.—ED.
‡ Rushworth, p. 1263.

which they could not be safe, his majesty with great reluctance consented, having first protested in writing, that no concession of his should be binding if the treaty broke off without effect. His majesty yielded the militia to the Parliament for twenty years, and the management of the Irish war.* He conceded to vacate those titles of honour that had been conferred since the carrying away the great seal, and to confirm the Parliament's great seal. He agreed to the payment of the public debts, provided they were stated within two years ; to confirm the charter of the city of London ; to empower the Parliament to confer offices, and constitute magistrates for twenty years; and to take away the Court of Wards, provided he might have £50,000 a year in lieu of it.† His majesty consented, farther, that those of his party whom they call delinquents‡ should submit to a fine or be proscribed the court, if the Parliament saw fit ; but he abhorred the thought of charging them with treason who had acted by his commission, and therefore absolutely refused to consent to it.

With regard to religion, his majesty agreed, October 2d, that " the Assembly of Divines at Westminster be confirmed for three years ; that the Directory and Presbyterian government be confirmed for the same time, provided that neither himself nor those of his judgment be obliged to comply with it; that a consultation, in the mean time, be had with the Assembly, and twenty divines of his majesty's nomination, as to what form of church government shall be established afterward, with a clause for the

* The utter faithlessness of Charles destroyed all confidence in his promises. It was the one quality which was perpetually evinced in all seasons, and under all circumstances. *The day* on which he assented to the Parliament's proposition respecting the military power, he wrote thus to Sir W. Hopkins : " To deal freely with you, the great concession I made *this day* was merely in order to my escape, of which if I had not hope, I would not have done it. For then I could have returned to my state prison without reluctance ; but now I confess it would break my heart, having done that which only an escape can justify." Next day he wrote to Ormond, then in Ireland, " Wherefore I must command you two things : first, to obey all my wife's commands; then, not to obey any public commands of mine, until I send you word I am free from restraint. Lastly, be not alarmed at my great concessions concerning Ireland, for they will come to nothing." Towards the end of the month he again wrote to Ormond, " Though you will hear that this treaty is near, or at least most likely to be concluded, yet believe it not, but pursue the way you are in with all possible vigour. Deliver also that my command to all your friends, but not in a public way."—*Godwin's Hist. of the Commonwealth,* vol. ii., p. 615, 616.—C.

† It appears, by Dr. Grey's authority, Williams's MS. collection, whose account is confirmed by the representations which Mr. Hume and Mrs. Macaulay give of this matter, that Mr. Neal is mistaken about the sum granted in lieu of the Wards; which was not £50,000, but £100,000. Since this was written, I find the matter put out of all doubt by Whitelocke, p. 341, who says that £100,000 was the sum.—ED.

‡ Dr. Grey has given at length the act proposed by the Parliament's commissioners relative to delinquents, whom the king absolutely refused to give up. " The severe repentance which he had undergone for abandoning Strafford, " remarks Mr. Hume, " confirmed him in the resolution never again to be guilty of the like error."—ED.

ease of tender consciences. His majesty consented, farther, that legal estates for lives, or for a term of years not exceeding ninety-nine, should be made out of the bishop's lands and revenues, for the satisfaction of them that have purchased them, provided that the inheritance may still remain to the Church, and the rest be preserved for their maintenance. His majesty will consent, farther, to an act for the better observation of the Lord's Day ; for suppressing innovations in churches and chapels ; for the better advancing of preaching God's Holy Word ; and against pluralities and nonresidence. To an act for regulating and reforming the universities and the colleges of Westminster, Winchester, and Eton ; for the better discovery of papists, and for the educating their children in the Protestant religion. To an act for better putting the laws in execution against papists, and to prevent the hearing and saying mass ; but as to the Covenant, his majesty is not as yet satisfied to sign or swear to it, or consent to impose it on the consciences of others."*

These concessions about church government being declared not satisfactory, as amounting only to a sort of interim, his majesty desired to confer with the Parliament divines for the satisfaction of his conscience, having been bred and instructed (as he said) in the way he stands for, by his father, the wisest king and best man in the world, and therefore could not easily yield. There is hardly anything to be met with in this conference but what has been already taken notice of in his majesty's debate with Mr. Henderson, and in the answer of the Smectymnuan divines to Bishop Hall, in the first volume of this history ; and therefore it will be the less necessary to enter into the particulars of the debate. His majesty proposed some scruples in law about the obligation of his coronation oath, which the commissioners undertook to answer themselves ; but the papers relating to the unalterable institution of Episcopacy were referred to the divines on both sides, and were as follow :

The King's first Paper.

" Newport, October 2, 1648.

" CHARLES REX :

" I conceive that Episcopal government is most consonant to the Word of God, and of an apostolical institution, as it appears by the Scripture to have been practised by the apostles themselves, and by them committed and derived to particular persons as their substitutes or successors therein (as for ordaining presbyters and deacons, giving rules concerning Christian discipline, and exercising censures over presbyters and others),† and has ever since, till these last times, been exercised by bishops in all the churches of Christ ; and, therefore, I cannot in conscience consent to abolish the said government.

" Notwithstanding this my persuasion, I will be glad to be informed if our Saviour and his apostles did so leave the Church at liberty, as they might totally alter or change the church government at their pleasure, which if you can make appear to me, then I will confess that one

* Rushworth, p. 1281.
† Acts, vi., 6 ; xiv., 23. 1 Cor., v., 3 ; xiv. and xvi., 1. 3 John, ix., 10. 1 Tim., v., 19, 22. Titus, i., 5 ; iii., 10. Rev., ii., 3.

of my great·scruples is clean ·taken away,· and then there only remains, ·

"·That being by my coronation oath obliged to ·maintain Episcopal· government, as I ·found it settled· to my ·hands, whether I ·may consent to the abolishing thereof until the same shall be evidenced·to me to be contrary to the Word of God."* .

The Parliament divines, in answer to the first part of his majesty's paper, admit that the apostles did exercise the extraordinary powers his majesty mentions; but deny that they conferred them upon any particular persons as their substitutes or successors, and insist that in Scripture there are only two orders of officers, viz., bishops and deacons : Phil., i., 1, "To the saints at Philippi that are in Christ Jesus, with the bishops and deacons;" and that the name, office, and work of a bishop and presbyter are the same, as in Titus, i., 5 and 7: " For this cause I left thee in Crete—that thou shouldst ordain presbyters in every city; for a bishop must be blameless." Acts, xx., 27, 28' Paul called the presbyters together, and charged them to "take heed to the flock over which the Holy Ghost had made them bishops."† 1 Pet., v., 1, 2 : " The presbyters among you, I exhort, who also am a presbyter, feed the flock of God among you, performing the office of bishops."‡ As the apostles were extraordinary officers, so were Timothy and Titus, viz., evangelists, but neither of them are called bishops in Scripture, much less were they fixed to Ephesus or Crete, but travelled up and down to settle churches in several countries. They observe, farther, that in the same order of officers there was not any one superior to another; no apostle above an apostle, no presbyter above a presbyter, nor one deacon above another: They add, that the angels of the churches in the Revelation are never called bishops, nor is the word used in any of St. John's writings, who calls himself a presbyter ; from whence they argue the identity of these offices in Scripture, and the equality of the officers. They admit that, not long after the apostles' times, bishops are reported to have some superiority above presbyters; but this was not a Divine, but an ecclesiastical institution, as is evident from the testimony of the most ancient fathers, and the most considerable writers in the Romish Church ; to which they add the suffrage of the first Reformers in King Henry VIII.'s reign. The Erudition of a Christian Man, printed 1643, says expressly, that the Scripture mentions but two orders, i. e., bishops or priests, and deacons. They conclude with observing that the modern Episcopacy is very different from that which began to obtain in the second and third ages of the Church, insomuch that the present hierarchy, being a human institution, might be abolished, and the other remain.

After three days, his majesty, with the assist-. ance of his learned divines, replied to the foregoing paper, and acknowledges, "that the words bishop and presbyter are sometimes confounded in Scripture ; he admits that presbyters are episcopi gregis, bishops of the flock ; but that bishops are episcopi gregis et pastorum within their several precincts, i. e., bishops of the

flock and of the pastors too ; and that; soon after, common usage appropriated bishop to the ecclesiastical governor, leaving presbyter to signify the ordinary minister or priest, as appears from the ancient fathers and councils. He admits the calling of the apostles and their gifts to be extraordinary; but adds, that their mission to govern and teach was ordinary and perpetual; that the bishop succeeded them in the former, and presbyters in the latter function.*

His majesty still insists " that Timothy and Titus were bishops, as appears from antiquity, and by a catalogue of twenty-seven bishops of Ephesus lineally descending from Timothy, as is avouched by Dr. Reynolds against Hart ; and therefore the distinction between an evangelist and a bishop is without foundation, the work of an evangelist being no more than diligence in preaching the Word, notwithstanding all impediments, according to the apostle, 2 Tim., ii.,. 4, 5. : His majesty observes,· that the Parliament divines had said nothing to prove that the ' angels of the churches' were not persona singulares, and such as had a prelacy over pastors,. i. e., bishops, but that they dealt only in generals, and seemed unwilling to speak their opinions about them."

His majesty affirms "that bishops are the successors of the apostles in all things not extraordinary, such as teaching and governing ; and the reasons why they are not mentioned as a distinct order in the New Testament, are, 1. Because the apostles reserved to themselves the government of those churches where they appointed presbyters, and so it is probable the Philippians had no bishop when Paul wrote to them. 2. Because, in the Epistles to Timothy and Titus, the persons to whom he wrote, being themselves bishops, there was no need to write about the qualifications of any other officers than those they wanted, which were presbyters and deacons only."

His majesty admits, concerning the ages after the apostles, " that they are but a human testimony, and yet may be infallible in matter of fact, as we infallibly know that Aristotle was a Greek philosopher, &c. ; he avers the genuineness of those epistles of Ignatius, which gave testimony to the superiority of a bishop above a presbyter ; and though his majesty's royal progenitors had enlarged the power and privileges of bishops, he conceives the government to be substantially the same."

Eleven days after the Parliament divines replied to the king's second paper, in which they say that they can find no such partition of the apostolical office in Scripture as his majesty mentions, viz., that the governing part should be committed to bishops, the teaching and administering the sacraments to presbyters ; but that the whole work, per omnia, belongs to presbyters, as appears from the two words used in the Acts of the Apostles and St. Peter's Epistle, ποιμαίνειν, and ἐπισκοπεῖν, under the force of which words the bishops claim their whole right of government and jurisdiction ; and when the Apostle Paul was taking leave of the Ephesian presbyters and bishops, he commits the government of the church not to Timothy; who. was then at his elbow, but to the presbyters,. under the name of bishops made by the Holy

---

* Rel. Carol., vol. ii., p. 245.   † Ἐπισκοπούς.
‡ Ἐπισκοποῦντες.

* Rel. Carol., p. 260.

Ghost : from whence they conclude that bishops and presbyters must be only two names of the same order.* They observe, that the obscurity of church history in the times succeeding the apostles made the catalogue-makers take up their succession upon report ; and it is a blemish to their evidence, that the nearer they come to the days of the apostles, they are the more doubtful and contradictory. These divines are therefore of opinion that human testimony on both sides ought to be discharged, and the point in debate be determined only by Scripture. And here they take hold of his majesty's concession, that in Scripture the names of bishops and presbyters are not distinguished ; and that there is no mention but of two orders, bishops and deacons. They desire his majesty to show them where the Scripture has assigned any particular work or duty to a bishop that is not common to a presbyter, for they apprehend his majesty's asserting that a bishop is an ecclesiastical governor, and a presbyter an ordinary minister, is without any demonstration or evidence ; a few clear passages of Scripture for the proof of this (they say) would bring the point to an issue. They deny his majesty's distinction of *episcopi gregis et pastorum*, bishops of sheep and shepherds, as being the point in question, and affirmed without any evidence. That the office of teaching and governing was ordinary in the apostles, because continued in the Church, we crave leave to say, is that great mistake which runs through the whole file of your majesty's discourse ; for though there be a succession in the work of teaching and governing, there is no succession in the commission or office, by which the apostles performed them ; a succession may be to the same work, but not to the same commission ; and since your majesty cannot produce any record from Scripture warranting the division of the office of teaching and governing into two hands, we must look upon it as an invention of men to get the power into their own hands.

These divines go on with a long proof that Timothy and Titus were evangelists ; that is, not fixed to one place, but travelling with the apostles from one country to another to plant churches, and accordingly have drawn out an account of their travels from the Acts of the Apostles and St. Paul's Epistles. They observe the weakness of his majesty's reasons, why bishops are not mentioned as a distinct order in Scripture, and add a third of their own, viz., because really they were not. As for the apostles reserving to their own hands the power of governing, they admit that they could no more part with it than with their apostleship. Had they set up bishops in all churches, they had no more parted with their power of governing than in setting up presbyters ; presbyters being called rulers, governors, and bishops ; nor could the apostles reasonably be supposed to commit the government of the Church of Ephesus to the presbyters, when he was taking his last farewell of them, and yet reserve the power of governing, in ordinary, to himself. His majesty's other reason, they say, is inconclusive, and, in short, begging the question. They add, that it is very unaccountable, that if there had been two sorts of bishops, one over presbyters and the other

over the flock, that there should be no mention, no mark of difference, no distinct method of ordination, by which they might be distinguished, throughout the whole New Testament.

As to the ages after the apostles, they admit there were presbyter-bishops, but not of Divine institution ; that the catalogues of succession are undoubtedly defective, but if they were not, it remains still to be proved that the bishops in the catalogue were vested with the jurisdiction which the modern bishops claim.

These divines profess to honour the pious intentions of his majesty's ancestors, and admit that ornamental accessions to the person make no substantial change in the office, but that the primitive episcopacy, and the present hierarchy, are essentially different. They acknowledge a subordination of the exercise of jurisdiction to the civil power and the laws of the land ; and conclude with thanks to his majesty's condescension, in allowing them to examine his learned reply, clothed in such excellence of style, and pray that a pen in the hand of such abilities may ever be employed on a subject worthy of it.

Some days after his majesty offered his last paper, wherein "he acknowledges the great pains of these divines to inform his judgment, and takes particular notice of the decency of their manner, and of their respectful address to him upon this occasion, but says they mistook him when they spoke of a writ of partition of the episcopal office ; whereas his meaning was, that the office of teaching was common both to the bishop and presbyter, but that government was peculiar to the bishop."* His majesty declines answering to all the particulars, because he would not draw out the dispute into a greater length, but seems unconvinced by anything that had been offered ; he affirms that Timothy and Titus were *episcopi pastorum*, bishops over presbyters ; and that Timothy had a distinct work from presbyters, that is, that he might know how to behave himself in the exercise of his episcopal office. His majesty relies on the numerous testimonies of ancient and modern writers for the Scripture original of bishops, and adds, that the testimonies of an equal number of equal credit to the contrary will signify nothing, because one witness for the affirmative ought to be of more value than ten for the negative. In conclusion, his majesty put them upon evidencing one of these three things : (1.) Either that there is no form of church government prescribed in Scripture. Or, (2.) If there be, that the civil power may change it as they see cause. Or, (3.) If it be unchangeable, that it was not episcopal, but some other that they will name, for till this is done he shall think himself excusable for not consenting to the abolishing that government which he found settled at his coronation ; which is so ancient, has been so universally received in the Christian world, has been confirmed by so many acts of Parliament, and subscribed by all the clergy of the Church of England. But the ministers declined entering into so large a field, which must have brought on a debate concerning the whole ecclesiastical polity of the Church.

These were all the papers which passed on both sides, and deserve the notice of those who would enter into this controversy. His majesty saying that one witness for the affirmative that Episcopacy is of Divine institution ought to be of more value than ten for the negative, is, I apprehend, one of the weakest and most frivolous arguments of his letter; for it is only changing the form of the question, and making the Presbyterians say that Presbytery is of Divine institution, and then asking his majesty, or any Episcopal divine, whether one affirmative testimony ought not to be of more value than ten negative ones of equal merit. His majesty's style is strong and masculine, and that of the Parliament divines decent and respectful. Sir Philip Warwick read the king's papers before the commissioners, and Mr. Vines those of the ministers; all was managed with the greatest propriety, which makes it hard to excuse Lord Clarendon's account of the behaviour of these divines, who says,* "They all behaved with that rudeness, as if they meant to be no longer subject to a king any more than to a bishop; that they inveighed bitterly against the pride and lustre of lord-bishops; that two of them very plainly and fiercely told the king, that if he did not consent to the utter abolishing of bishops, he would be damned; these men were Spurstow and Jenkins, who, after the return of King Charles II., according to the modesty of that race of people, came to kiss his majesty's hand." And yet neither of the divines above mentioned was nominated to assist at the treaty, nor had any share in the debates. Mr. Baxter says, all the Parliament divines came off with great honour. But such is his lordship's, or his editor's, candour towards anything that looks like a Presbyterian!

The king's second difficulty, relating to his coronation oath, by which he apprehended himself bound to maintain Episcopal government as he found it settled when he received the crown, the commissioners did not think so proper for the discussion of divines, because it depended upon the law of the land, and therefore took this part of the debate upon themselves. The king conceived that the consent of the clergy themselves, in convocation assembled, was necessary, before they could be deprived of those possessions and privileges of which they were legally possessed. But the commissioners maintained that the Legislature alone was to determine in this case, as it had done at the Reformation; that it was not to be supposed that any body of men would consent to part with their possessions if they could keep them; but if the Legislature judged any part of the king's coronation oath hurtful to the public, it was certainly in their power, with the consent of the king, to alter or annul it. One may justly ask how this branch of the coronation oath should stick so much with the king, when it was notorious that his government, for almost fifteen years, had been one continued breach of Magna Charta, and an encroachment upon the civil liberties of his subjects.

But neither party would accede to the other, though the article of religion was almost the only point that hindered the conclusion of the treaty: his majesty wondered at the shyness and reluctance of the Parliament divines to debate his three questions, and told them plainly, that their endeavours to give him satisfaction in them would have added to the reputation of their ingenuity in the whole undertaking, it not being probable that they should work much upon his judgment, while they were fearful to declare their own; or possible to relieve his conscience but by a free declaring of theirs.* But what was all this to the point? the only question before them was, whether diocesan Episcopacy was of Divine institution? if they had satisfied his majesty in that, they had discharged their duty; to launch out farther was to lose time, and protract the treaty beyond its limits. If diocesan Episcopacy was not scriptural, it might be abolished, as whether Parliament contended for at present.† But the king's divines encouraged him to dispute every inch of ground, and instead of yielding any one point to the ministers, to start new difficulties, till his ruin was inevitable. However, towards the close of the treaty, when the victorious army was returning towards London, and things almost come to an extremity, his majesty told the commissioners, "that though he could not with a good conscience consent to the abolishing of Episcopacy, because he believed the substance of it to be of apostolical institution, he was willing to reduce it to the primitive usage; and if his two houses should so advise, he would be content to lessen the extent and multiply the number of dioceses. He still apprehended the entire alienation of the bishop's lands by sale to be sacrilege. He was willing to assent to the calling and sitting of the Assembly of Divines, as desired. He would also confirm the public use of the Directory in all churches and chapels, and would repeal so much of all statutes as concerned the Book of Common Prayer only; provided the use thereof might be continued in his majesty's chapel for himself and his household; and that the same [i. e., the Directory] should be confirmed by act of Parliament for three years, provided a consultation be had in the mean time with the Assembly of Divines as before mentioned. Touching the articles of religion [the Assembly's confession], his majesty desired farther time to examine them before he bound up himself and his subjects in matters of faith and doctrine. His majesty will consent to an act for better observation of the Lord's Day, and to prevent saying of mass. But as to the Covenant, his majesty was not satisfied to take it, nor to impose it on others."

These concessions being voted unsatisfactory by the two houses at Westminster, his majesty consented farther, October 21, "1. That archbishops, chancellors, deans, and the whole hierarchy, be abolished except bishops. 2. That none but the Presbyterian government be exercised for three years. 3. That in case no settlement should be agreed upon within that time, that then for the future the power of ordination should not be exercised by bishops without the counsel and assistance of presbyters; that no other Episcopal jurisdiction should be exercised but such as should be agreed upon in Parliament; and if within that time his majesty should be convinced that Episcopacy is not agreeable to the Word of God, or that Christ commanded any other government, he will embrace it, and take Episcopacy quite away." The houses being still dissatisfied with these con-

---

* Vol. iii., p. 216.

* Rushworth, p. 1291. † Ibid., p. 1301, 1302.

cessions, his majesty added, November 4, "that he would make no new b'shops for three years; and for the farther satisfaction of the Parliament, he would not insist upon the use of the Common Prayer in his own chapel for that time, but would make use of some other form of Divine service for himself, and forbid mass to be said in the queen's chapel." This was his majesty's final answer, which the Commons voted unsatisfactory, and ordered the commissioners to acquaint him with their votes.

The treaty was prolonged three weeks after this, in which time the commissioners did all that was in their power to obtain his majesty's consent, beseeching him with tears upon their bended knees, since matters were brought to so narrow a compass, to yield up the point of religion. In their last paper of November 20, they beseech him to consider, "that it is not the apostolical bishops which the Parliament desire him to abolish, but that Episcopacy which was formerly established by law in this kingdom, and has been found by experience to be a hinderance to piety, a grievance to the subject, an encroachment upon the power of the civil magistrate, and so a burden to the persons, purses, and consciences of men. They do not meddle with the apostolical bishop, nor determine what that bishop was whom the apostles mention in the Scripture; but they are for putting him down by a law who was set up by a law; and certainly nothing can be more proper for parliaments than to alter, repeal, or make laws, which appear to them for the good of the commonwealth.

"But admitting apostolical bishops were within the purport of this bill, we humbly conceive it does not follow that therefore in conscience it must not be passed, for we may not grant that no occasion can make that alterable which has foundation only in the practice of the apostles, and not in a precept.* Some things have certainly been altered which the apostles practised; circumstances many times change the nature of moral actions; for the attaining a great good, or the avoiding a great evil, that which singly considered is not fit to be done, and perhaps would be a fault if it were, may become a duty, and a man may be bound in conscience to do it. And if ever circumstances could have a more powerful and considerable influence than in this juncture, we leave to your majesty's consideration. But this is said only for argument's sake, admitting, but not granting the grounds on which your majesty is pleased to go, in refusing to pass this bill."† The strength of the commissioners' reasoning upon this head may be seen at once in this short syllogism: Whatsoever is not of Divine institution may be very lawfully altered, changed, or reversed. But the Episcopacy which is established in the Church of England is not that Episcopacy mentioned in Scripture; therefore the laws which established it may take it away.

The commissioners go on, "As for the sale of bishops' lands, which your majesty conceives to be sacrilege, we humbly offer that, bishoprics being dissolved, their lands revert to the crown, which is their foundation and patron, and heretofore held it no sacrilege to dispose of bishops'

lands to its own or other uses by act of Parliament, which was an ordinary parctice in your majesty's predecessors, kings and queens of this nation. Besides, in all ages, even under the ceremonial law, imminent and urgent necessity has dispensed with the alienation of consecrated things.*

"Your majesty is pleased to say, 'You cannot communicate in a public form of Divine service, where it is uncertain what the minister will offer to God.' But we beseech your majesty to be informed that the Directory sets down the matter of the prayer which the minister is to use, words and expressions for enlargement being left to his discretion. But give us leave to add, that this ought to be no objection with your majesty, for then one must not hear any prayer before sermon, for every minister has a several form, which he varies according to occasion.

"Upon the whole, therefore, we humbly hope that your majesty, after a most serious consideration, will discern the just cause which the two houses have for remaining unsatisfied with your majesty's concessions with relation to the Church, for they are apprehensive that, after the expiration of the three years in which Episcopal government is to be suspended, a bishop so qualified as your majesty expresses will rise again; for if you should not, in the mean time, agree with your Parliament upon any other form of government, which depends wholly upon your majesty's pleasure, no other government can be set up; and then this Episcopacy will return with so great power, that the bishop may choose whether any minister at all shall be made in the Church of England, and those that shall must be at his devotion, he having the negative voice in ordination, which we humbly conceive is no where declared in Scripture to be the prerogative of an apostolical bishop.

"We humbly say, farther, that the charging bishops' lands with leases for ninety-nine years is not sufficient, because there is a rent reserved to the bishop, and the property will continue as before; so that it cannot be expected that the Presbyterian government should be complied with, and exercised with profit or comfort to the Church, as long as a door is left open for the return of a superior power upon the first opportunity.

"We hope your majesty will pardon our pressing in this manner; our intention is not to offer violence to your majesty's conscience, but to endeavour to inform it in a matter that appears to the two houses of so great consequence. We again humbly beseech your majesty to review our former papers; call to mind those reasons and arguments which in debate have been used upon this subject, with such others as your own wisdom shall suggest, and then be pleased to give your royal consent to the particulars above specified, that both yourself and your people may have cause to rejoice."

The committee of states in Scotland joined with the Parliament commissioners in beseeching his majesty to accede to the proposition about religion, which they understood to be the point his majesty most stuck at, and which

* For the king's answer, see Dr. Grey's Examination, p. 342, &c.—ED.

† Rushworth, p. 1335. Whitelocke, p. 351.

* Dr. Grey, p. 345, has given his majesty's reply.—ED.

they in honour and interest were obliged most to insist upon, and without which, they add, his throne cannot be established in righteousness.* They also wrote to the Prince of Wales to mediate with his father. The General Assembly, and the commissioners of the Kirk of Scotland, sent at the same time two angry letters, for it was said they would speak more plainly in the name of their master than the commissioners of estates would venture to do in their own. But his majesty was deaf to all remonstrances and persuasions, being determined, if his two houses did not think fit to recede from the rigour of their demands in these particulars, to cast himself, as he said, on his Saviour's goodness to support and defend him from all afflictions, how great soever, which might befall him, rather than, upon politic considerations, deprive himself of the tranquillity of his mind; and therefore, excepting his majesty's consent to license the Assembly's lesser catechism with a proper preface, in all other matters in difference he resolved to abide by his former answers.†

At the close of the treaty the king made a short speech to the commissioners, in which he reminds them how far he had condescended for the sake of peace. He desired them to put a good interpretation on his vehement expressions in some part of the debates, there being nothing in his intentions but kindness; and that, as they had used a great deal of freedom, and showed great abilities in their debates, which had taken him off from some of his opinions, that they would use the same freedom with his two houses, to press them to an abatement of those things in which his conscience was not yet satisfied, which more time might do, his opinions not being, like the laws of the Medes and Persians, unalterable or infallible; adding his very hearty thanks for the pains they had taken to satisfy him, professing that he wanted eloquence to commend their abilities.‡ He desired them candidly to represent all the transactions of the treaty to his two houses, that they might see nothing of his own interest, how near or dear soever (but that wherein his conscience is not satisfied), can hinder, on his part, a happy conclusion of the treaty.

The king's concessions were certainly a sufficient foundation for peace with the Presbyterians, if they could have been relied upon, and were so voted by the Parliament when it was too late. His majesty had given up the main pillars of the hierarchy, by consenting to abolish archbishops, deans, and chapters, and that a bishop should not act without his presbyters; which was Archbishop Usher's scheme, and all that the Puritans at first contended for; but the Scots and the English Presbyterians, grown lofty in power, and being less apprehensive of danger from the army than they ought, concluded they could not fail of their whole establishment in a few weeks, though there was not the least provision for liberty of conscience for dissenters, which they might have been sensible would occasion high discontents in the army. The commissioners were disposed to an accommodation, and took all opportunities to assure his majesty that, if he would but yield for a

* Rushworth, p. 1301.
† Clarendon, p. 224. Rushworth, p. 1326, 1334.
‡ Vol. Pam., No. 83.

time, things should be made easy to him afterward. But the truth is, as the king would not trust the Parliament, so neither would they the king, because they observed, (1.) His dilatoriness in the treaty, as if he waited for some advantageous turn of affairs to revoke his concessions. (2.) His resolute disputing every inch of ground without yielding a single proposition, or none of any considerable moment. (3.) His majesty's maxim, that what was yielded out of necessity was not binding when the restraint was taken off. (4.) They suspected his sincerity, because the Duke of Ormond was at this very time treating with the Irish rebels by his majesty's commission, which he would not recall.* (5.) They remembered his majesty's

* The preceding assertions of Mr. Neal much displease Dr. Grey; he contradicts them, and endeavours to confront them with facts. He challenges Mr. Neal to produce one single well-attested fact to support his reflection on the king's sincerity. The appeal for the truth of the charge may be made to the reader, who has accompanied Charles through his reign, and observed his conduct on various occasions. The appeal may be made to the facts that have been collected in Dr. Harris's Historical and Critical Account of Charles I., p. 72–83, and in An Essay towards a True Idea of the Character of King Charles I., p. 93–102. We may also refer to what has before been advanced on this point. It suffices to add here the authority of Ludlow only, who says "that the duplicity of the king's dealings with the Parliament manifestly appeared in his own papers, taken at the battle of Naseby and elsewhere."—Ludlow's Memoirs, 4to, 1771, p. 114. Dr. Grey asserts against Mr. Neal, that "from the MS. treaty it is manifest that there was not the least delay on the king's part." But he forgets the duration of the treaty, which was to continue forty days only; and, commencing on the 18th of September, did not close till towards the end of November; and would not have ended then, if the army had not seized his majesty; for the answers of the king were voted "to be a ground only for the House to proceed on to settle the peace of the kingdom."—Whitelocke's Memoirs, p. 353. But the length of the treaty could arise only from the king's not at first yielding to the propositions made by the commissioners. Mr. Neal's next assertion, that the king "disputed every inch of ground" is implied in the duration of the treaty, and it is proved by the quotation which Mr. Neal, a little farther on, makes from Whitelocke. But Dr. Grey attempts to disprove it, by bringing forward three concessions made in one day, the 21st of October, by the king. The reader will determine whether an exception drawn from the transactions of one day can disprove an assertion which applies to a treaty depending more than seventy days; and those concessions, he will consider, were not yielded till the forty days originally appointed for the continuance of the treaty were drawing to an end. In opposition to our author's fourth reason, Dr. Grey produces from Williams's MS. collections a letter of the king, 25th of November, to the commissioners, in which he informs them (sending, at the same time, the letter itself for their perusal) that he had written to the Marquis of Ormond, "acquainting him with such informations as he had received from the two houses concerning his proceedings in that kingdom, and requiring him to desist from any farther prosecution of the same. And in case he shall refuse, his majesty will then make such public declaration against his powers and proceedings as is desired." Notwithstanding this, Mr. Neal spoke on authority; for on the 21st of November, the House received letters from the Isle of Wight, "that the king refused to pass anything against the Marquis of Ormond, until the treaty be wholly ended."—Whitelocke's Mem., p. 350. See also Lord Clarendon, vol. iii., p. 222.—ED.

artful manner of interpreting away his concessions. (6.) They gave out that he was not his
own master, but that his conscience was under
the direction of his divines, who would put him
upon all extremes for their support. (7.) They
were incensed at the murders and depredations
of the cavalier soldiers, even after they were
beaten out of the field, and were afraid of their
recovering the management of public affairs.
And, lastly, They were as firmly persuaded of
the Divine institution of Presbytery, and the obligation of the Covenant, as the king and his
divines were of the *jus divinum* of Episcopacy.

Yet, under all these propossessions, Lord Clarendon* observes, some of the commissioners
found means to advertise the king, in private,
"that they were of his majesty's judgment
about church government, which they hoped
might be preserved, but not by the method his
majesty pursued; that all the reasonable hope
of preserving the crown was in dividing the
Parliament and the army, which could be done
no other way than by giving satisfaction with
reference to the Church. This might probably
unite the Parliament and the city of London,
and enable them to bring his majesty to London with honour, where he might have an opportunity of gaining more abatements than he
could ever expect by refusing to sign the preliminaries. Many advertisements came from
his majesty's friends in London, and other places, that it was high time the treaty was at an
end, before the army drew nearer London,
which it would shortly do, as soon as those in
the north had finished their works." Sir J.
Browning entreated his majesty, in his closet,
to make all his concessions in one declaration,
at one instant, and in one day. The Parliament commissioners were no less importunate
with the king, but he was inflexible, and usually out of humour. Remarkable are the words
of Mr. Whitelocke, speaking of the above-mentioned concessions: "More than this could not
be obtained, though most earnestly begged of
his majesty by some of the commissioners
(great persons) with tears, and upon their
knees, particularly as to the proposition concerning religion, wherein church government,
public worship, and chiefly the revenues of the
Church, swayed more with the king's chaplains
then about him; and they more with his majesty (continually whispering matters of conscience to him) than the Parliament, and all
their commissioners, could prevail with him for
an agreement, though possibly his own judgment (which was above all theirs) might not
be so fully convinced by his eager divines about
him."† But these had possession of his majesty's conscience, and directed his answers;‡
and though they abhorred the thoughts of deposing the king, or putting him to death, it

ought to be considered whether their stiff and
imprudent behaviour did not manifestly contribute to that catastrophe.

His majesty being thus entangled, was pleased, before the breaking up of the treaty, to send
for Archbishop Usher, and asked him this question, "Whether he found, in all antiquity, that
presbyters alone ordained any?" To which
the archbishop replied frankly, that "*he could
show his majesty more than that, even that presbyters alone had successively ordained bishops,*" and
instanced in St. Jerome's words, in his Epist.
ad Evagrium, where he says the presbyters of
Alexandria chose and made their own bishops
from the days of Mark the apostle till Héraclus
and Dionysius.* At the same time the archbishop offered his own scheme for the reduction
of Episcopacy to the form of Presbytery, which
his majesty had formerly rejected, but was now
at length willing to accept, as the archbishop
himself told Mr. Baxter; but the Scots and
English Presbyterians were grown so stubborn
that they would not acquiesce.

Though the commissioners had no power to
recede from their instructions, the treaty was
prolonged from time to time, in hopes that
something or other might gain upon the king;
but his majesty was frequently out of temper,
and treated the commissioners with no degree
of confidence. The forty days to which the
treaty was limited being ended October 28, it
was enlarged for fourteen days, and then for
seven, and so on to the 28th of November, for
which, says Lord Clarendon,† his majesty was
nothing glad; nor did his friends in the House
desire the prolongation, it being moved by those
that wished the treaty might have no good effect, to give the army time to finish their summer's work, and return to London. On the last
day of the treaty, when the commissioners
pressed his majesty to consider that there was
not one whole day to determine the fate of the
kingdom, and that nothing could save his majesty from the growing power of the army but
giving his two houses satisfaction in the particular of the Church, "then," says Lord Clarendon,‡ "his majesty's own council, and the divines, besought him to consider the safety of
his person, even for the Church's sake, which
had no prospect of being preserved but by his
life, that the unavoidable necessity that lay upon
him obliged him to do anything that was not
sin." And why did they not do this sooner?
However, it seems they could only prevail for a
suspension of the Episcopal power in point of
ordination and jurisdiction, till he and the two
houses should agree what government should be
established for the future. Which was the substance of all his majesty intended by his concessions. After supper the commissioners took
their leave, and having kissed his majesty's
hand, began their journey next morning towards
London. It is intrepid language that Mr. Warwick puts into the king's mouth on this occasion: his majesty said to him one night, "I am
like a captain that has defended a place well,
and his superiors not being able to relieve him,
he had leave to surrender it; but though they
cannot relieve me in the time, let them relieve
me when they can, else," says he, "I will hold

---

* Book xi., p. 217.   † Whitelocke's Memoirs, p. 325.
‡ Dr. Grey is displeased with this representation,
and impeaches the truth of it. He says, that when
Mr. Vines took the freedom to observe "that possibly his majesty's scruples were not so much his own
as other men's," the king a little warmly replied,
"that it was a mistake; for his scruples were really
his own, and contained in his first paper." The
doctor did not reflect that few men are willing to
have it supposed, and more unwilling to own, that
they are led. But however this was, Mr. Neal is
supported by the authority of Whitelocke.—ED.

---

* Baxter's Life, p. 206.   † Vol. iii., p. 322.
‡ Book xi., or vol. iii., p. 227.

it out till I make some stone in this building my tombstone; and so I will do by the Church of England."

Lord Clarendon is of opinion "that the major part of both houses, as well as the commissioners, were at this time so far from desiring the execution of all their concessions, that if they had been able to have resisted the wild fury of the army, they would themselves have been suiters to have declined the greatest part of them." And were not the king's counsellors and divines sensible of this? Why, then, did they trifle away a month in fruitless debates, when it was evident to all men that the king's condition became more desperate every day?

Thus ended the famous treaty at Newport; which, like all the former, proved unsuccessful, chiefly from an incurable jealousy between the contending parties, which, how reasonable it was on either side, must be left with the reader.

The noble historian observes,* that the king sent the Prince of Wales a journal of the proceedings of the treaty, and an exact copy of all the papers that had passed to the 29th of November, together with a letter of six sheets of paper written with his majesty's own hand, containing the reasons and motives of all his concessions. The conclusion of the letter, his lordship says, deserves to be preserved in letters of gold, as it gives the best character of that excellent prince; but the copy does not, in my opinion, resemble the original. Some passages of it are these: "We have laboured long in search of peace, do not you be disheartened to tread in the same steps. Prefer the way of peace—conquer your enemies by pardoning rather than by punishing—never affect more greatness, or prerogative, than that which is really and intrinsically for the good of your subjects, not the satisfaction of favourites. You may perceive that all men intrust their treasure where it returns them interest. If princes, like the sea, receive, and repay all the fresh streams the rivers intrust with, they will not grudge, but pride themselves to make them up an ocean: if God restore you to your right, whatever you promise keep: don't think anything in this world worth obtaining by false and unjust means." These are excellent maxims of government; and if his majesty had conducted himself by them, he could not have been reduced to such a low and destitute condition, as to have hardly a place in the world to hide himself in; "for," says Lord Clarendon,† "there was at that time no court in Christendom so honourably or generously constituted, that it would have been glad to have seen him, and they who wished him well did not wish his escape, because they imagined imprisonment was the worst that could befall him."

I am unwilling to suspect the genuineness of this letter, though there were so many forgeries obtruded upon the world about this time to advance his majesty's piety and virtue, that one can hardly feel the ground he treads on. If such a letter was sent to the prince, it is very strange he should never see it; or that his lordship, who lived in the prince's family, and extracted his account of the treaty of Newport from these papers, as he declares, should never show it his master; and yet these are the

words of Bishop Burnet, in the History of his Life and Times: "The Duke of York suffered me to talk very freely to him about religion, and he told me, among other things, that the letter to the Prince of Wales was never brought to him."

The army had been six months in the field this summer, engaged against the cavaliers and Scots, who, being now reduced and subdued, they began to express a high dissatisfaction with the present treaty, because no provision had been made for their darling point, liberty of conscience. Here they had just reason of complaint, but ought not to have relieved themselves by the methods and at the expense they did. They were thoroughly incensed against the king and his cavaliers on one hand, and the high Presbyterians on the other. It appeared to them that the king's sentiments in religion and politics were not changed; that he would always be raising new commotions till things returned to their former channel; and in the present treaty, he had yielded nothing but through constraint; and that when he was restored to his throne, after all the blood that had been shed, they should be safe neither in their lives nor fortunes. On the other hand, if Presbyterian uniformity should take place by virtue of the present treaty, their condition would be little mended; for, said they, if the king himself cannot obtain liberty to have the Common Prayer read privately in his own family, what must the Independents and sectaries expect? What have we been contending for, if, after all the hazards we have run, Presbytery is to be exalted, and we are to be banished our country or driven into corners?

While the resentments of the army were thus inflamed, their officers, who were high enthusiasts, though men of unblemished morals,* observed several days of fasting and prayer at their headquarters at St. Alban's, till at length, in a kind of despair, and under the influence of a religious phrensy, they entered upon the most desperate measures, resolving to assume the sovereign power into their own hands, to bring the king to justice, to set aside the Covenant, and change the government into a commonwealth. To accomplish these monstrous resolutions, which were founded, as they alleged, upon self-preservation, though prosecuted by measures subversive not only of the rights of Parliament, but of the fundamental laws of society, the officers agreed upon a remonstrance, which was presented to the Parliament by six of their council, November 20, eight days before the expiration of the treaty with the king, together with a letter from General Fairfax to the House, desiring it might have a present reading.

The remonstrance sets forth the miscarriages of the king's government,† and his double and

---

* The character of virtuous morals, Bishop Warburton considers as inconsistent with their being, as Mr. Neal says, "high enthusiasts; when," his lordship adds, "they all acted, as almost all enthusiasts do, on this maxim, that the end sanctifies the means, and that the elect, of which number they reckoned themselves chief, are above ordinances." Mr. Neal, I presume, is to be understood as speaking of their personal virtue, with regard to sensual indulgences, in opposition to drunkenness and debauchery.—ED.

† Lieutenant-general Ludlow apprehended that the dispute between the king's party and the Parlia-

dilatory proceedings in treaties, particularly in that now on foot, and then desires the House to return to their votes of non-addresses; to lay aside that bargaining proposition, of compounding with delinquents, and bring them to punishment; and among these offenders, they propose, "(1.) That the king he brought to justice, as the capital cause of all. (2.) That a day be set for the Prince of Wales and the Duke of York to surrender themselves, or be declared incapable of the government; and that, for the future, no king be admitted but by the free election of the people."*

The Commons, upon reading this remonstrance, were struck with surprise, and, being in the utmost consternation, deferred the debate for ten days, i. e., to the end of the treaty. But the officers, being apprehensive of what might happen in that time, sent Colonel Ewer to the Isle of Wight with a party of horse to secure the person of the king, and ordered Colonel Hammond to leave the island, and attend the council of officers at their headquarters at Windsor; the king was secured the very day after the expiration of the treaty, and next morning [November 30] conveyed by a party of horse to Hurst Castle, where he continued till he was conducted by Colonel Harrison to Windsor, in order to his trial. The same day the officers sent a declaration to the House to enforce their late remonstrance, complaining that they were wholly neglected, and desiring the majority of the House to exclude from their councils such as would obstruct justice, or else withdraw from them.† This occasioned warm debates among the members, and a motion that the principal officers who had a share in the remonstrance might be impeached of high treason.‡ Upon which the army marched directly to London, with General Fairfax at their head, who wrote to the lord-mayor and common council that he was marching to Westminster in pursuance of the late remonstrance, and desired £40,000 of the city, in part of their arrears. December 2, he quartered his troops about Whitehall, the Mews, Covent Garden, and St. James's, assuring the citizens that they should disturb no man in his property.

Though the houses were now environed with an armed force, they had the courage to vote that the seizing of the person of the king, and carrying him prisoner to Hurst Castle, was without their advice and consent; and next day, after having sat all night [December 5], it was carried, without a division, that the king's concessions to the Parliament's propositions were a sufficient ground for the houses to proceed upon for settling the peace of the kingdom, two hundred and forty-four members be-

ing present. But the officers being determined to carry their point, discharged the city trainedbands, and placed a regiment of horse and another of foot, the very next day, at the door of the Parliament House, and Colonel Pride, having a list of the disaffected members in his hand, took about forty of them into custody, and denied entrance to about a hundred more, which determined several others to withdraw, insomuch that the House of Commons was left in the possession of about one hundred and fifty or two hundred persons, most of them officers of the army, who conducted everything according to the plan concerted in their council at St. Alban's. Oliver Cromwell was not yet come to London from his northern expedition, but wrote from Knottingsley, November 20, that the officers of his regiments were deeply sensible of the miseries of the kingdom, and had a great zeal for impartial justice to be done on offenders, with whom he concurred. December 6, he came to London, and next day had the thanks of the House thus garbled for his faithful services to the public.* December 11, a paper called the Agreement of the People was presented to the general and council of officers, as a rule for future government. It was supposed to be drawn up by Ireton, and proposed a dissolution of the present Parliament, and a new one to be chosen, consisting of three hundred members,† who were to elect a council of state from among themselves, for the management of all public affairs, under certain restrictions; one of which is, that they do not lay any restraints on the consciences of men for religious differences (as has been mentioned), but no proceedings were had upon it, nor did it ever take place.

In the mean time, the House of Commons (if they now deserved that name) voted his majesty's concessions at the Isle of Wight not satisfactory,‡ and "that no member who had been absent when that vote was passed should sit again in the House till he had subscribed it;§ that no more addresses be made to the king for the future;‖ that no malignant, who had assisted against the Parliament in the first or second civil war, or that had abetted the late tumults, should be capable of being chosen lord-mayor or alderman of the city of London, or be capable of any place of profit or trust, or so much as of giving his vote for choosing persons into such offices, for the space of one year."¶ The secluded members published a protestation**

* Dugdale, p. 363.
† According to the authority, Williams's MS. Collections, on which Dr. Grey relies, it was proposed that the representatives should be four hundred; and the ground of the motion was, that the people of England being very unequally distributed by boroughs for election of their representatives) were indifferently proportioned.—ED.
‡ They also reversed the vote of the 5th of December, viz., "that the king's answer was a ground on which to proceed upon for the settlement of peace of the kingdom," as dishonourable to Parliament, destructive to the peace of the kingdon, and tending to the breach of the public faith of the kingdom.—Dr. Grey, p. 357.—ED.
§ Rushworth, p. 1300.   ‖ Ibid., 1365.
¶ Clarendon, p. 240.
** Bishop Warburton observes, "that these very secluded members had voted the bishops guilty, of high treason, for protesting in the same manner, when under the like force." The reader will turn back to

ment turned upon this simple question, "Whether the king should govern as a god by his will, and the nation be governed by force like beasts; or whether the people should be governed by laws made by themselves, and live under a government derived from their own consent?"—Ludlow's Memoirs, 4to, 1771, p. 114. On this point rests the difference between free and despotic governments, and in the degree in which a government deviates from the former, it approximates to the latter state.—ED.
* Clarendon, vol. iii., p. 236. Rapin, vol. ii., p. 564, folio.
† Rushworth, p. 1341. Rapin, vol. ii., p. 565, folio.
‡ Clarendon, vol. iii., p. 237.

against all these proceedings as null and void till they were restored to their places; but the lords and commons who remained in the houses voted their protestation false, scandalous, and seditious.

The army, having vanquished all opposition, went on with irresistible violence to change the whole frame of government;* and, to make way for it, determined to impeach the king of high treason, as having been the cause of all the blood that had been spilt in the late war.† This unheard-of motion met with some opposition even in that packed assembly;‡ Oliver Cromwell was in doubt, and said, "If any man moved this of choice or design, he should think him the greatest traitor in the world; but since Providence or necessity had cast them upon it; he should pray God to bless their councils, though he was not provided on the sudden to give them advice." Some said there was no need to bring the king to a trial; others, that there was no law to try him, nor any judicatory to call him to account; but all this was overruled; and because the Lords rejected the ordinance for the king's trial, Lord Clarendon tells us, they shut up their doors; but Mr. Whitelocke says, they entered their house, and although several ordinances passed, the Commons would not own them any longer. Thus the Constitution was dissolved, and all that ensued must be considered as effected by the military power.§

Though some few petitions had been procured from divers counties, and even from the common council of London, that justice might be done upon the authors of our troubles and bloodshed, in an exemplary way, and without respect to persons, yet the general voice of the nation was against such violence, as appears by the petitions and protestations of all orders of people.

The prelatical clergy lay still, either because they could not assemble in a body, or because they apprehended they could do no service by appearing; but Dr. Gauden, afterward Bishop of Exter, published "A Protestation against the declared Purposes and Proceedings of the Army, and others, about trying and destroying our Sovereign Lord the King," dated January 5, and sent it to a colonel to be presented to Lord Fairfax at the council of war. Dr. Hammond sent an humble address to the general and council of war, to prevent the horrid design of putting the king to death, dated January 16. Both these papers insisted on the Divine right of kingly government, and that to call the king before the tribunal of the people was contrary to the laws of the land. The famous Mr. Prynne, one of the secluded members, published "A brief Memento to the pretent unparliamentary Junto, touching their present Intentions and Proceedings to depose and execute Charles Stuart, their lawful King of England," dated from the King's Head in the Strand, January 1, 1648.

The officers of the army attempted by their creatures to gain over the London ministers to their measures, or at least to persuade them to a neutrality. Hugh Peters, one of their chaplains, was sent to the remains of the Assembly of Divines at Westminster for this purpose, but they declared unanimously for the release of the king. He then invited several of the London ministers, as Mr. Marshal, Calamy, Whitaker, Sedgwick, Ash, &c., to a conference with some officers of the army, upon the subject of the coercive power of the magistrate in matters of religion, which was foreign to the present purpose; but instead of meeting them, these divines assembled with their brethren at Sion College, and published a paper entitled "A serious and faithful Representation of the Judgment of the Ministers of the Gospel within the Province of London, whose Names are subscribed, contained in a Letter to the General, and his Council of War, delivered to his Excellency by some of the Subscribers," January 18, 1648.

In this address, after assigning reasons why they would not consult with the officers upon matters of religion, they complain of their imprisoning the members of Parliament: "We remember," say they,* "that when the king with a multitude of armed men demanded but a small number of the members of Parliament, it was deemed an unparalleled breach of the privilege of Parliament, and was one reason that an army was raised by their authority, and for their preservation; but that this very army should so far exceed that act, which was then esteemed without parallel, is what we could not believe, had not our eyes been witnesses of it!

"And though both houses of Parliament saw reason to take up arms in their own defence, and in defence of the Protestant religion, and the fundamental laws of their country, yet this cannot be pleaded in justification of your usurping an authority over king and Parliament, who are but so many private persons, and no part of the Legislature.

"Moreover, though the Parliament took up arms in defence of the laws, it was never their intention to do violence to the person of the king, or divest him of his royal authority, much less to overthrow the whole Constitution.

"We therefore think ourselves bound by our protestation, and by our solemn League and Covenant, to appear for our excellent Constitution against arbitrary and tyrannical power in the king, on the one hand, and against the illegal proceedings of private persons, tending to subvert the Constitution and introduce anarchy and confusion, on the other.

"Instead, therefore, of consulting with you, we earnestly entreat you, as the ambassadors of Christ, that you would consider of the evil of your present ways, and turn from them. You cannot but know that the Word of God commands obedience to magistrates, and consonant to this Scripture has been the judgment of Protestant divines at home and abroad, with whom we concur; disclaiming, detesting, and abhorring the practices of Jesuits, concerning the opposing of lawful magistrates by any private persons, and the murdering of kings by any, though under the most specious and colourable pretences. Examine your consciences,

---

Vol. ii., p. 404–407, compare the two cases, and decide whether they were entirely similar. Not but it is too common for men not to discern the nature of oppression till they come to feel it; and to condemn in others what they allow in themselves.—ED.

* Rushworth, p. 1363. † Rapin, vol. ii., p. 567.
‡ Dugdale, p. 366. § Memor., p. 361.

* Vol. Pamph., No. 52.

if any number of persons of different principles from yourselves had invaded the rights of Parliament, imprisoned the king, and carried him about from place to place, and attempted the dissolution of the whole government, whether you would not have charged them with the highest crimes.

"We desire you not to infer the justice of your proceedings from the success, but to distinguish between God's permission and approbation, and that God's suffering men to prosper in their evil courses is one of the severest judgments; the providence of God, therefore, which is so often pleaded in justification of your actions, is no safe rule to walk by, in such actions which the Word of God condemns.

"Nor is it safe to be guided by the impulses of the spirit, when they are contrary to the written Word of God; we are to try the spirits, and to have recourse to the law and the testimony; if they speak not according to them, there is no light in them.

"If you plead necessity for doing that which yourselves confess to be irregular, we answer, no necessity can oblige men to sin; besides, it is apparent you were under no necessity, the Parliament (till forced by you) being full and free; besides, you have engaged by oath to preserve his majesty's person, and the privileges of Parliament, and no necessity can justify perjury, or dispense with lawful oaths.

"We therefore beseech you to recede from this your evil way, and learn John Baptist's lesson to soldiers, Do violence to no man, neither accuse any man falsely, and be content with your wages. But if you persist in this way, be sure your sin will find you out. If our exhortation prevail not, we have discharged our duty, and we hope delivered our own souls. If it be our portion to suffer, as we are told, we trust we shall suffer as Christians; but. we hope better things of you, and subscribe ourselves your servants in the Lord,

James Nalton, pastor, Foster Lane.
Thomas Cawton, St. Bartholomew Exchange.
John Fuller, Bishopsgate.
Francis Roberts, St. Austin.
William Jenkins, Christ Church.
Elidad Blackwell, Alhallows Undershaft.
William Harrison, Grace Church.
John Sheffield, St. Swithin's.
Matthew Haviland, Trinity.
George Smalwood, Poultry.
William Taylor, Coleman-street.
Christopher Love, Aldersgate.
Robert Mercer, St. Bride's.
Thomas Gataker, Rotherhithe.
George Walker, St. John Evangelist.
Arthur Jackson, M. Wood-street.
Charles Offspring, St. Antholin's.
Henry Rodborough, Eastcheap.
Nicholas Profet, Foster Lane.
Thomas Case, Milk-street.
Stanly Gower, Ludgate.
Andrew Janeway, Alhallows-on-the-Wall.
Samuel Clark, St. Bene't Fink.
Thomas Clenden, Alhallows Barking.
John Wale, St. M. Cornhill.
James Crawford, St. Christopher.
Ralph Robinson, pastor, St. Mary Woolnoth.
William Blackmore, St. Peter, Cornhill.
Francis Peck, St. Nicholas Acorns.
Stephen Watkins, St. Saviour, Southwark.
William Wickers, St. Andrew Hubbard.
John Wallis, Ironmonger Lane.

Thomas Manton, Stoke Newington.
Thomas Gouge, St. Sepulchre's.
Thomas Watson, Walbrook.
Nathaniel Staniforth, St. Mary Bothaw
John Halk, Alhallows-on-the-Wall.
John Glascock, St. Andrew Undershaft.
Thomas Whately, St. Mary Woolchurch.
Jacob Tice, Billingsgate.
Jonathan Lloyd, Garlickhithe.
John Morton, Newington Butts.
Joshua Kirby.
Arther Barham, St. Helen's.
Benjamin Needler, St. Margaret Moses.
John Wells, St. Olave Jury.
Robert Matthew, St. Andrew Wardrobe."

Notwithstanding their seasonable and explicit remonstrance, the Episcopal divines, *in order to throw off the guilt of the king's misfortunes from themselves, who, by their obstinate behaviour, had in reality reduced him to the last extremity,* resolved to fix it upon the Presbyterians; *as their successors have done even till this day.* It was therefore given out among the people, that the Presbyterians had brought the king to the block, and that the Independents would cut off his head.* To wipe away this calumny, the Pres-

* The execution of Charles has generally been attributed by Royalist writers to the malecontent religionists of the day. Court divines and mercenary scribblers sought, after the Restoration, to inflame the worst passions of a licentious court by loading the Nonconformists with the guilt of the king's death; and their representations have been handed down to the present day. The persecutions of the son were stimulated and justified by the alleged murder of the father. In that age of reckless profligacy and fierce intolerance, the most virtuous class of English subjects were exposed to cruel exactions and protracted imprisonments as the representatives of a set of tyrannicides. Their personal virtues, their ministerial diligence, their services at the Restoration, and their peaceful submission to the new order of things, pleaded ineffectually on their behalf. They were condemned without a hearing, and pined in solitude and penury, the victims of a revengeful and selfish faction. The calmer judgment of posterity is now doing them justice, and their faults are, in consequence, partially forgotten in the recollection of their many virtues.

The death of Charles was not the work of any religious party. It was brought about by a rare concurrence of circumstances, and was effected by a combination of men of every variety and shade of religious faith. It is a palpable violation of the rules of historic evidence, to attribute it either to the Presbyterians or to the Independents. Rapin affirms that the Rump Parliament, which passed the ordinance for the king's trial, was composed exclusively of Independents; but no evidence of the fact is adduced. No one sect possessed the power, or were animated with the resolution of perpetrating the deed. Individuals belonging to each afforded their sanction, but the several parties, so far as their sentiments could be ascertained, were thoroughly hostile to it. This was emphatically the case with the Presbyterians, whose infatuated loyalty towards the House of Stuart was subsequently evinced at the sacrifice of themselves, and of the kingdom's liberty. So soon as the purpose of the army to bring the king to trial was ascertained, the London ministers, to the number of forty-seven, drew up and published an address, entitled "A serious and faithful Representation of the Judgment of the Ministers of the Gospel within the Province of London," in which they strongly condemned the proceedings of the officers, and plead the cause of the king, contending that they were bound by their solemn League and Covenant to appear "against arbitrary and tyrannical power in the king, on the one hand, and against the illegal pro-

byterian clergy published another paper, entitled "A Vindication of the London Ministers from the unjust Aspersions cast upon their former Actings for the Parliament, as if they had promoted the bringing of the King to Capital Punishment." It was addressed to the people, and after they had repeatedly declared their dislike of the proceedings at Westminster against the king, they conclude in words to this purpose: " Therefore, according to our Covenant, we do, in the name of the great God, warn and exhort all that belong to our respective charges, or to whom we have administered the said Covenant, to abide by their vow, and not suffer themselves to be persuaded to subscribe the Agreement of the People, which is subversive of the present Constitution, and makes way for the toleration of all heresies and blasphemies, and will effectually divide the two kingdoms of England and Scotland. We earnestly beseech them to mourn for the sins of the Parliament and city, and for the miscarriages of the king himself in his government, which have cast him down from his excellency into a horrid pit of misery, almost beyond example ; and to pray that God would give him effectual repentance, and sanctify the bitter cup of Divine displeasure which Divine Providence has put into his hands; and that God would restrain the violence of men, that they may not dare to draw upon themselves and the kingdom the blood of their sovereign."

This was signed by fifty-seven ministers, among whom were the following nineteen, whose names were not to the above-mentioned representation : .

Cornelius Burges, D.D., at St. Paul's.
William Gouge, D.D., Blackfriars.
Edmund Stanton, D.D., Kingston.
Thomas Temple, D.D., Battersea.
Edmund Calamy, B.D., Aldermanbury.

ceedings of private individuals, tending to subvert the Constitution and introduce anarchy and confusion, on the other." The document thus published breathes the free spirit which had formerly struggled against the usurpations of Charles, and should have served to screen its authors from the charge which has been preferred against them. "Examine your consciences," say the ministers, addressing the men before whom Parliament had quailed, "if any number of persons, of different principles from yourselves, had invaded the rights of Parliament, imprisoned the king, and carried him about from place to place, and attempted the dissolution of the whole government, whether you would not have charged them with the highest crimes."

Another paper was subsequently drawn up by the Presbyterian ministers, and signed by fifty seven, including nineteen who had not subscribed the former, in which the members of their respective congregations were entreated, among other things, to pray " that God would restrain the violence of men, that they may not dare to draw upon themselves and the kingdom the blood of their king." Burnet expressly excepts the Presbyterians from any share in the king's death, declaring " *that they and the body of the city were much against it, and were everywhere fasting and praying for the king's preservation.*"—*History of his own Times,* i., p. 85. Baxter bears a similar testimony. He says, " They preached and prayed against disloyalty ; they drew up a writing to the lord-general, declaring their abhorrence of all violence against the person of the king, and urging him and his army to take heed of such an unlawful act ; they presented it to the general when they saw the king in danger, but pride prevailed against their counsels."—*Sylvester's Baxter,* pt. i., p. 64.—C.

Jeremiah Whitaker, St. Mary Magdalen, Bermondsey.
Daniel Cawdrey, St. Martin in the Fields.
William Spurstow, D.D., Hackney.
Lazarus Seaman, Bread-street.
Simeon Ash, Bassishaw.
Thomas Thoroughgood, of Crayford.
Edward Corbet, Croydon.
John Viner, Aldgate.
John Crosse, Friday-street.
Peter Witham, St. Alban, Wood-street.
John Stileman, Rotherhithe.
Josias Ball, North Grey.
Jonathan Devereux, late of St. Andrew, Holborn.
Paul Russel, Hackney.

It was not possible for the few Independent ministers in London to join the Presbyterians in these addresses, (1.) Because they were not possessed of parochial livings, nor members of the Provincial Assembly of London, nor admitted to their weekly consultations at Sion College, but were a sort of dissenters from the public establishment: (2.) Because they did not believe themselves so far bound by the Covenant as to oppose a toleration, nor to support any constitution that was not consistent with Christian liberty, which the Presbyterians would not admit. None of their ministers that I know of declared their approbation of the proceedings of the council of officers in the trial of the king, except Mr. Hugh Peters and Mr. John Goodwin: Some of the Independent ministers in the country joined the Presbyterians in protesting against it; those of Oxford and Northampton of both denominations published their humble advice and earnest desire, presented to General Fairfax and the council of war, January 25, subscribed by nineteen or twenty names, in which they declare their utter disapprobation of all proceedings against his majesty's crown and life, as contrary to Scripture, to the laws of the land, the solemn League and Covenant, and tending to destroy the Constitution, and involve the nation in a war with their neighbours. They declare their dissent from the late violence upon the Parliament ; but with reference to religion they say, " Though our souls abhor that grand design of the devil and his agents to decry all religious and zealous professors under the names of sectaries and Independents, we willingly grant, and heartily desire, that the interest of all godly and honest men may be carefully provided for, as far as is consistent with the Word of God, our Covenant, and the public peace ; and that men of different apprehensions in matters of religion may not be utterly incapable of all offices of power and trust, though we cannot agree to a universal toleration." They conclude with beseeching the general to suspend all farther prosecutions against the king, and to endeavour a right understanding between the king, Parliament, and army ; but if they cannot prevail, they desire to wash their hands of the blood of their dread sovereign, and to approve themselves innocent of all that confusion and misery in which the deposing and taking away his majesty's life will involve them, their posterity, and all men professing godliness in the three kingdoms.[*]

It must be confessed the Independents were a sort of malecontents, and had reason to be dissatisfied with the treaty of Newport, because

[*] Vol. Pamph., 108.

they were not only excluded the new establishment, but debarred of a toleration; and yet, as Mr. Echard and Dr. Bates the physician observe, several of them joined with their brethren in declaring against the design of putting the king to death, in their sermons from the pulpit, in conferences, monitory letters, petitions, protestations, and public remonstrances.* The Scots Kirk, by their commissioners, declared and protested against the putting the king to death, as absolutely inconsistent with their solemn League and Covenant. They published a protestation, directed to the ministers of the province of London meeting at Sion College, January 25, 1648-9, with a letter, exhorting them to courage and constancy in their opposition to the proceedings of the House of Commons, and to a universal toleration.

Sundry foreign princes and states, by their ambassadors, interceded for the king; some from their respect to his person, and others from a regard to the honour that was due to crowned heads. But it was impossible to stop the impetuous wildfire of the army, who, having brought the king from Hurst Castle to Windsor, obtained a vote in the Parliament (if we may so call it) that all ceremonies due to a crowned head be laid aside; and then came to the following resolutions, January 4: "First, that the people, under God, are the original of all just power. Secondly, that the House of Commons are the supreme power of the nation. Thirdly, that whatever is declared for law by the Commons in Parliament is valid, though the consent of the king and the House of Peers be not had thereto."† The House of Lords, which was reduced to sixteen peers, having unanimously rejected the ordinance of the Commons for the king's trial, and adjourned for a fortnight, the Commons resolved to act without them, and, having named a committee of thirty-eight persons to receive informations, and draw up a charge against the king, they constituted a high court of justice for his trial,‡ consisting of one hundred and forty-five persons, of whom twenty or more might proceed to business; but

* Ech., Hist., p. 654, Elench. Cot. Nar., 1ma., p. 118.   † Rapin, vol. ii., p. 568, folio.

‡ The reader may be amused by the relation of an accident which befell the king at Oxford, which appeared to affect his spirits, and may be deemed, by superstition, a prognostic of the calamities that befell him, and were now thickening on him. On visiting the public library, he was showed, among other books, a Virgil, nobly printed and exquisitely bound. Lord Falkland, to divert him, would have his majesty make trial of his fortune by the Sortes Virgilianæ; a kind of augury in use for some ages. On the king's opening the book, the period which presented itself was Dido's imprecation on Æneas, thus translated by Mr. Dryden:

" Yet let a race untamed and haughty foes
His peaceful entrance with dire arms oppose;
Oppress'd with numbers in th' unequal field,
His men discouraged, and himself expell'd,
Let him for succour sue from place to place,
Torn from his subjects, and his son's embrace.
First let him see his friends in battle slain,
And their untimely fate lament in vain;
And when at length the cruel war shall cease,
On hard conditions may he buy his peace.
Nor let him then enjoy supreme command,
But fall untimely by some hostile hand,
And lie unburied on the barren land."
Welwood's Memoirs, p. 90, 91.—ED.

not above one half would act under this authority: Mr. Sergeant Bradshaw was president; Mr. Cook, solicitor-general; and Mr. Steel, Mr. Dorislaus, and Mr. Aske were to support the charge. The form of process being settled by the commissioners, the king, who had been conducted to St. James's, January 15, appeared before his judges in Westminster Hall the first time on Saturday, January 20, 1648, when, being seated at the bar in a chair of crimson velvet, and covered, as were all his judges, Mr. Cook, the solicitor, exhibited a charge of high treason against him; which being read, the king, instead of pleading to the charge, excepted to the jurisdiction of the court, which was overruled, the president replying that they would not suffer their authority to be disputed, and therefore required the king to think better of it against Monday; but his majesty persisting in his refusal to plead both on Monday and Tuesday, the clerk was ordered to record the default; Wednesday the court sat in the Painted Chamber, and examined witnesses against the king;* Thursday and Friday they consulted how to proceed; and on Saturday his majesty was brought the last time to the bar, when, persisting to disown the jurisdiction of the court, he desired to be heard in the Painted Chamber by the Lords and Commons, but his request was denied, and the president pronounced sentence of death against him as a traitor, fifty-nine being present, and signifying their concurrence by standing up, as had been agreed. Sundry indignities and insults were offered to the king by the soldiers as he passed along Westminster Hall, but the far greater number of people deplored his unhappy condition. Tuesday, January 30, being appointed for his execution, his majesty was offered the assistance of Mr. Calamy, Vines, Caryl, Dell, and Goodwin, but he refused them, and chose Dr. Juxon, bishop of London, who, according to Bishop Burnet, performed his office with such a dry coldness as could not raise the king's devotion.† On the fatal day he was conducted on foot by a strong guard through St. James's Park, to a scaffold erected in the open street before the banqueting house at Whitehall, where he made

* The evidence of Henry Goode, on the examination, proved the king's insincerity in the treaty of Newport; for he deposed that, on observing to his majesty, to whom he had access, that he had justified the Parliament's taking up arms, the king replied, that though he was contented to give the Parliament leave to call their own war what they pleased, yet he neither did then, nor should, decline the justice of his own cause.—Rushworth in Macaulay's History, vol. iv., p. 388, note.—ED.

† It ought to be mentioned that Hugh Peters' obtained for the king the attendance of Bishop Juxon. "What a contrast to the treatment of his grandmother, the unfortunate Queen of Scots, by Burleigh and Walsingham, whose cruel bigotry, or policy, if possible, more inhuman, deprived her of an auxiliary so consoling to human infirmity in the agony of the last moments, religious communion; by Fletcher, dean of Peterborough, who outraged her feelings, and assailed her fortitude with all the terrors which the imagination of a bigot could supply to the hatred of a theologian. But Burleigh and Walsingham are canonized politicians; Fletcher was an orthodox divine — censure must not approach them; while Cromwell, Ireton, Harrison, and Peters are to be named only with reprobation and reviling."—Contin. of Mackintosh's History, vol. vi., p. 122.—C.

a short speech to the people, in which he made no acknowledgment of the mistakes of his government, but declared himself a martyr for the laws and liberties of the people; after which he laid down his head on the block, which was severed from his body at one blow* by some bold executioner in a mask, in the forty-ninth year of his age, and twenty-fourth of his reign. His body was interred privately at Windsor, February 28 following, without ceremony, and with no other inscription on the coffin than "King Charles, 1648."†

* Mr. Philip Henry was a spectator of this event, and noticed two remarkable circumstances which attended it. One was, that at the instant when the blow was given, there was such a dismal, universal groan among the thousands of people that were within sight of it (as it were with one consent) as he never heard before, and desired he might never hear the like again. The other was, that immediately after the stroke was struck, there was, according to order, one troop marching from Charing Cross towards King-street, and another from King-street towards Charing Cross, purposely to disperse and scatter the people, and to divert the dismal thoughts which they could not but be filled with, by driving them to shift every one for his own safety.—P. Henry's Life, p. 16.—ED.

† Had he died a martyr, he could not have maintained a more composed or befitting aspect; so anomalous are the exhibitions of human character, so complex and ill-assorted the attributes which may pertain to the same man. It is not the province of the historian to pronounce on the future, or to limit the range of Divine mercy. Charity will hope that the closing hours of a life distinguished by falsehood, tyranny, and other crimes, was visited by that benign and purifying power which alone can renovate the heart, and prepare for everlasting peace. It would be beside the province of this work to enter on the several questions to which the execution of Charles has given rise. It was, undoubtedly, an unconstitutional and disastrous event, in which the genius of the commonwealth's men was signally at fault. No provision has been made by English law for the punishment of a king convicted of an attempt to subvert the Constitution and annihilate the liberties of the people. Of this crime, however, Charles was guilty; and the men whom he had sought to crush appealed, in justification of his death, to the first principles of justice, and the acknowledged purposes of human society.

"Whatever the matter was," says Milton, "whether we consider the magistrates or the body of the people, no men ever undertook with more courage, and, which our adversaries themselves confess, in a more sedate temper of mind, so brave an action— an action which might have become those famous heroes of whom we read in former ages; an action by which they ennobled not only laws and their execution, which seems for the future equally restored to high and low against one another, but even justice, and to have rendered it, after so signal a judgment, more illustrious and greater than in its own self." That the transaction was illegal, is universally admitted; but it was *an act of substantial justice due*—if death can ever be so—*to the crimes which had been perpetrated*, and demanded, apparently, by the necessities of the state. "It is much to be doubted," says Mr. Fox, "whether this singular proceeding has not, as much as any other circumstance, served to raise the character of the English nation in the opinion of Europe in general. He who has read, and, still more, he who has heard in conversation discussions upon this subject by foreigners, must have perceived that, even in the minds of those who condemn the act, the impression made by it has been far more that of respect and admiration than that of disgust and horror. The truth is, that the guilt of the action, that is to say, the taking away the life of the

The reader will collect the character of this unfortunate prince rather from the preceding facts, than from the keen reflections of his determined enemies, or the flattering encomiums of his friends and admirers, which latter, in their anniversary sermons,* have almost equalled his sufferings with those of our blessed Saviour. It must be admitted that King Charles I. was sober, temperate, chaste, an enemy to debauchery and lewdness, and very regular in his devotions. But these excellent qualities were balanced with some of a very different nature; his temper was distant and reserved to a fault; he was far from being generous, and when he bestowed any favour, did it in a very disagreeable and uncourtly manner; his judgment in affairs of government was weak and unsteady, and generally under the direction of a favourite. In his treaties with the Parliament, he was chargeable with great insincerity, making use of evasive and ambiguous terms, the explication of which he reserved for a proper place and season. He had lofty notions of the absolute power of princes, and the unlimited obedience of subjects; and though he was very scrupulous about his coronation oath in regard to the Church, yet he seems to have paid little attention to it as it respected the laws and liberties of his subjects, which he lived in the constant violation of for fifteen years.† He was a perfect dupe to his queen, who had too much the direction of public affairs both in Church and State; no wonder, therefore, that he had a determined aversion to the Puritans, and leaned so much to the pomp and ceremony of the Church of Rome, that though a Protestant in judgment, he was for meeting the papists half way, and for establishing one motley religion throughout Great Britain, in which both parties might unite. He told Dr. Sanderson, that if God ever restored him to his crown, he would go barefoot from the Tower of London, or Whitehall, to St. Paul's, by way of penance for consenting to the Earl of Strafford's death, and to the abolishing of Episcopacy in Scotland, and desire the people to intercede with God for his pardon.‡ Such was his majesty's superstition! Upon the whole, though King Charles I. had virtues that might have rendered him amiable as a private gentleman, his foibles were so many as en-

king, is what most men in the place of Cromwell and his associates would have incurred; what there is of splendour and of magnanimity in it, I mean the publicity and solemnity of the act, is what few would be capable of displaying. It is a degrading fact to human nature, that the sending away of the Duke of Gloucester was an instance of generosity almost unexampled in the history of transactions of this nature."—*Fox's Hist. of James II.*, p. 16. *Price's Hist. of Nonconformity*, vol. ii., p. 429–30. *Milton's Defence of the People of England.*—C.

*. It is the remark of Bishop Warburton, that "blackened characters on the one hand, and impious comparisons on the other, equally offensive to charity and religion, in the early days of this returning solemnity, turned an act of worship into a day of contention. But these," he adds, "were the unruly workings of a storm just then subsided. Time, which so common, ly corrupts other religious institutions, hath given a sobriety and a purity to the returning celebrations of this."—*Sermon on the 30th of January, 1760, to the House of Lords*, p. 7, 8.—ED.

† Clarendon's Hist., p. 430.

‡ Life of Sanderson, p. 79.

title him to the character of a very weak and impolitic prince ; far from appearing truly great in any one scene of his whole life except the last. Mr. Coke says,* he was wilful and impatient of contradiction ;. his actions sudden and inconsiderate, and his councils without secrecy. He would never confess any of his irregularities in government, but justified them all to his death. If any gave him advice contrary to his inclination, he would never be friends with him again. He was unaffable and difficult of address, requiring such strained submissions as were not usual to his predecessors. The sincerity of his promises and declarations was suspected by his friends as well as enemies,† so that he fell a sacrifice to his arbitrary principles, the best friends of the Constitution being afraid to trust him. Bishop Burnett adds, "that he affected, in his behaviour, the solemn gravity of the court of Spain, which was sullen even to moroseness ; this led him to a grave, reserved deportment, in which he forgot the civilities and affabilities which the nation naturally loved ; nor did he, in his outward deportment, take any pains to oblige any persons whatsoever. He had such an ungracious way of showing a favour, that the manner of bestowing it wa salmost as mortifying as the favour was obliging., He loved high and rough measures, but had neither skill to conduct them, nor height of genius to manage them. He hated all that offered prudent and moderate counsels, and even when it was necessary to follow such advices, he hated those that gave them. His whole reign, both in peace and war, was a continued series of errors, so that it does not appear that he had a true judgment of things. He was out of measure set upon following his humour, but unreasonably feeble to those whom he trusted, chiefly to the queen, and (it may be added also) to the clergy. He had a high notion of the regal power, and thought that every opposition to it was rebellion. He minded little things too much, and was more concerned in drawing up a paper than in fighting a battle. He had a firm aversion to popery, but was much inclined to a middle way between Protestants and papists, by which he lost one without gaining the other. At his death he showed a calm and composed firmness which amazed all people, and so much the more, because it was not natural to him, and was, therefore, by his friends, imputed to an extraordinary measure of supernatural assistance."

After his majesty's death, the Episcopal clergy did all they could to canonize him for a martyr ; they printed his sayings, his prayers, his meditations, and forms of devotion under his sufferings, and drew his portrait in the most devout and heavenly attitude. His works, consisting of sundry declarations, remonstrances, and other papers, have been published in a most pompous and elegant form ; among which one is of very suspected authority, if not absolutely spurious, I mean his 'Εικων Βασιλικη, i. e., " Ei-

* Detect., p. 336.
† Bishop Warburton grants that "the king made his concessions with so ill a grace, that they only served to remind the public of his former breaches of faith, and to revive their diffidence in the royal word."—*Sermon before the House of Lords*, 30th of January, 1760, p. 16.—Ed.
‡ His Life, vol. i., p. 23, 64, Edin. ed.—Ed.

koon Basilikè, or the Portraiture of his sacred Majesty in his Solitude and Sufferings," said to be written with the king's own hand ; it was first printed in the year 1649, and passed through fifty editions in divers languages within twelve months.* No book ever raised the king's reputation so high as this, which obliged the new council of state to employ the celebrated Milton to destroy its credit, which he attempted in a treatise under the title of 'Εικων Κλαστης [Eikono Clastese], or an answer to a book entitled Eikoon Basilikè, printed by Du Garde, 1652 ; but the fraud was not fully detected till some years after.

The grounds and evidences of the spuriousness of this book are these : 1. That Lord Clarendon, in his history of the grand rebellion, makes no mention of it.† 2. Bishop Burnet says,‡ the Duke of York, afterward King James II., told him in the year 1673, that the book called Eikoon Basilikè was not of his father's writing, but that Dr. Gauden wrote it ; that after the Restoration, the doctor brought the Duke of Somerset to the king and to the Duke of York, who both affirmed they knew it to be his [the doctor's] writing, and that it was carried down by the Earl of Southampton, and showed the king during the treaty of Newport, who read and approved it. 3. The Earl of Anglesey gave it under his hand, that King Charles II. and the Duke of York declared to him, in the year 1675, that 'they were very sure the said book was not written by the king their father, but by Dr. Gauden, bishop of Exeter. 4. Dr. Gauden himself, after the Restoration, pleaded the merit of this performance in a letter to Lord-chancellor Hyde, who returned for answer that the particular he mentioned [i. e., of his being the author of that book] was communicated to him as a secret ; I am sorry, says his lordship, that it was told me, for when it ceases to be a secret, it will please nobody but Mr. Milton.§ 5. Dr. Walker, a clergyman of the Church of England, after invoking the great God, the searcher of hearts, to witness to the truth of what he declares, says, in his treatise entitled "A True Account of the Author of Eikoon Basilikè," "I know and believe the book was written by Dr. Gauden, except chap. xvi. and xxiv., by Dr. Duppa. Dr. Gauden," says he, "acquainted me with this design, and showed me the heads of several chapters,

* It has gone through forty-seven impressions in England. The number of copies are said to have been forty-eight thousand five hundred. It produced, at home and abroad, the most favourable impressions for the king's piety and memory. Lord Shaftesbury supposed that it contributed, in a great measure, to his glorious and never-fading titles of saint and martyr. Dr. Grey is displeased with Mr. Neal for suspecting the authenticity of the book, and has bestowed ten pages to establish the king's right to be considered as its author. Since Dr. Grey and Mr. Neal wrote, the evidence for and against its spuriousness has been fully stated by Dr. Harris, in his Critical History, p. 106, 116. Mr. Hume's remark with regard to the genuineness of that production is, that " it is not easy for an historian to fix any opinion which will be entirely to his own satisfaction." He afterward adds, " Many have not scrupled to ascribe to that book the subsequent restoration of the royal family."—*History of Great Britain*, vol. vii., 8vo, 1763, p. 159, 160.—Ed.
† Vide Bayle's Dict., title Milton.
‡ His Life, p. 51.   § Crit. Hist., p. 191.

and some of the discourses. Some time after the king's death, I asked him whether his majesty had ever seen the book? He replied, I know it certainly no more than you; but I used my best endeavours that he might, for I delivered a copy of it to the Marquis of Hertford when he went to the treaty of the Isle of Wight."* Dr. Gauden delivered the MS. to this Walker, and Walker carried it to the press; it was copied by Mr. Gifford, and both the doctor's son and his wife affirm that they believe it was written in the house where they lived.

Notwithstanding all this evidence, Mr. Archdeacon Echard says, the book is incontestably the king's; and Bishop Kennet adds, that those who pretend Eikoon Basilikè was a sham put upon the world, are a set of men that delight to judge and execute the royal martyr over again by murdering his name. Dr. Hollingworth, Dugdale, Wagstaff, and others, have endeavoured to invalidate the above-mentioned authorities, by showing that Dr. Gauden was not capable of writing such a book; but surely the evidence already procured is as strong and convincing as anything of this nature can possibly be.†

The king's trial and execution, in such an illegal and unheard-of manner, struck the whole Christian world with astonishment. The Prince of Wales, then in Holland, encouraged the learned Salmasius to write a Latin treatise, entitled Defensio Regis, or a Defence of King Charles I., dedicated to his son, Charles II., which was answered by Milton, in a book entitled Defensio pro Populo Anglicano; or, A Defence of the People of England, written in an elegant, but severe style. This book, says Mr. Bayle, made the author's name famous over all the learned world. Another performance appeared about the same time, entitled, Clamor Regii Sanguinis ad Cœlum; or, The Cry of the King's Blood to Heaven. It was written in Latin by Peter du Moulin, Junior, and answered by Milton in the same language. But to satisfy the English reader, Mr. John Goodwin published a small treatise, which he called "A Defence of the Sentence passed upon the late King by the High Court of Justice; wherein the Justice and Equity of the said Sentence are demonstratively asserted, as well from clear Texts of Scripture as Principles of Reason, Grounds of Law, Authorities and Precedents, as well Foreign as Domestic;" a very weak and inconclusive performance! for, admitting our author's principles, that the original of government is from the people, and that magistrates are accountable to them for administration, they are not applicable to the present case, because the officers of the army had nei-

ther the voice of the people, nor of their representatives in a free Parliament; the House of Commons was purged, and the House of Peers dispersed, in order to make way for this outrage upon the Constitution. Our author was so sensible of this objection, that, in order to evade it, he advances this ridiculous conclusion, that "though the erecting a high court of justice by the House of Commons alone be contrary to the letter, yet, it being for the people's good, it is sufficient that it is agreeable to the spirit of the law."* But who gave a few officers of the army authority to judge what was for the people's good, or to act according to the spirit of a law in contradiction to the letter? This would expose every man's life and estate to the will, and pleasure of an arbitrary tyrant, and introduce a rule of government, so justly complained of in the former part of this reign, in opposition to a rule of law. The President Bradshaw, in his speech at pronouncing sentence, goes upon the same general topics, that the people are the origin of civil power, which they transfer to their magistrates under what limitations they think fit, and that the king himself is accountable to them for the abuse of it; but if this were true, it is not to the present purpose, because, as has been observed, the king's judges had not the consent of the people of England in their diffusive or collective capacity. His majesty's own reasons against this high court of justice, which he would have given in court if he might have been heard, are, in my opinion, a sufficient answer to all that can be said on the other side. "Admitting, but not granting," says his majesty, "that the people of England's commission could grant your pretended power, I see nothing you can show for that, for certainly you never asked me the question of the tenth man of the kingdom; and in this way you manifestly wrong even the poorest ploughman, if you demand not his free consent; nor can you pretend any colour for this, your pretended commission, without consent, at least, of the major part of the people of England, of whatsoever quality, or condition, which I am sure you never went about to seek, so far are you from having it. Nor must I forget the privileges of both houses of Parliament, which this day's proceedings do not only violate, but likewise occasion the greatest breach of the public faith that I believe ever was heard of, with which I am far from charging the two houses. Then, for anything I can see, the higher house is totally excluded; and for the House of Commons, it is too well known that the major part of them are detained, or deterred from sitting. And, after all, how the House of Commons can erect a court of judicature, which was never one itself, as is well known to all lawyers, I leave to God and the world to judge."§ King Charles, therefore, died by the hands of violence, or by the military sword, assumed and managed in an arbitrary manner by a few desperate officers of the army and their dependants,† and of sundry denominations as to religion,

---

* Crit. Hist., p. 189. Hist. Stuarts, p. 283.

† "There is full as strong evidence on the other side," says Bishop Warburton, "all of which this honest historian conceals; evidence of the king's bedchamber, who swear they saw the progress of it; saw the king write it; heard him speak of it as his; and transcribed parts of it for him." It seems that Mr. Neal considered the evidences of its spuriousness to be so strong, as to supersede entering into a detail of the evidences for its authenticity. The bishop, it is to be remarked, though he judges the strongest and most unexceptionable evidence is on that side which gives it to the king, yet owns that the question "is the most uncertain matter he ever took the pains to examine." No such great blame, then, can lie on Mr. Neal for taking the other side of the question.—Ed.

VOL. II.—N

* P. 20.

† They have been described as "a third party rising out of the ferment of the self-denying ordinance; a swarm of armed enthusiasts, who outwitted the patriots, outprayed the Puritans, and outfought the cavaliers." — Bishop Warburton's Sermon before the House of Lords, 30th of January, 1760, p. 22.—Ed.

without any regard to the ancient Constitution of their country, or the fundamental laws of society ; for, by the former, the king cannot be tried for his life before any inferior court of justice ; nor could they feign any pretence for the latter, without the express consent of the majority of the nation, in their personal or representative capacities, which these gentlemen never pretended. But since all, parties have endeavoured to throw off the odium of this fatal event from themselves, it may not be improper to set before the reader the sentiments of our best historians upon this head, leaving every one to draw what conclusion from them he pleases.

Not to insist upon the king's servile fondness for his queen and her friends ; his resolute stiffness for his old principles of government in Church and State ; his untimely and ungracious manner of yielding to what he could not avoid ; his distant and reserved behaviour towards those who only were capable of serving him ; and his manifest doubling between the Parliament and army, which some very reasonably apprehend were the principal causes of all his misfortunes, Mr. Whitelocke and Mr. Coke lay a good deal of blame upon his majesty's chaplains : the latter reproaches them with insisting peremptorily to the last upon the Divine right of Episcopacy ; and the former for continual whispering in the king's ears the importance of preserving the revenues of the Church, to the hazard of his person and kingdom ; and, surely, if these warm and eager divines could have disentangled his majesty's conscience (which Mr. Whitelocke apprehends was not fully satisfied), as soon as the cavaliers had been dispersed, and the Scots beaten out of the field, the mischief that followed might have been prevented. I will not take upon me to say how far their influence might reach, though his majesty's profound deference to their judgment was notorious ; but the conviction does not seem impracticable, when it is remembered the king was of opinion that what he yielded through the necessity of his affairs was not binding when he should be at liberty ; but neither his majesty nor his clergy foresaw the issue.*

Most of the writers on the king's side, as well as the preachers since the Restoration, in their anniversary sermons, have with great injustice charged the Presbyterians with bringing the king to the block, contrary to the strongest and most convincing evidence ; for though their stiffness for the Divine right of Presbytery, and their antipathy to liberty of conscience, are not to be vindicated, yet I apprehend enough has been said in the foregoing pages to clear them from this unrighteous charge ;† if the zeal of the

Presbyterians for their discipline and Covenant were culpable, the behaviour of the king and his divines in the opposition was no less so, considering he was a prisoner, and in the hands of a victorious Parliament ; neither side were sensible of the danger till it was too late, but when the storm was ready to burst on their heads, I do not see what men could do more in their circumstances to divert it than the Presbyterians did ; they preached and prayed, and protested against it in the most public manner ; many of them resigned their preferments because they would not take the engagement to the new commonwealth ; they groaned under all the preceding changes of government, and had a principal share in the restoration of the royal family in the year 1660, without which these anniversary declaimers would never have had an opportunity of pelting them with their ecclesiastical artillery, in the unwarrantable manner they have done.

The forementioned writers, together with Mr. Rapin, in his late History of England, load the Independents, as a religious sect, with all the guilt of cutting off the king's head ; and with being in a plot, from the commencement of the civil war, to destroy equally king, monarchy, Episcopacy, and Presbyterianism ; but this last-named writer, not being acquainted with their religious principles, constantly confounds the Independents with the army, which was compounded of a number of sectaries, the majority of whom were not of that denomination. There were no doubt among the Independents, as well as among other parties, men of republican principles, who had a large share in the reproach of this day ; but besides what has been observed, of some of their number joining with the Presbyterians in protesting against the king's execution, the divines of this persuasion had no difference with the Presbyterians or moderate Episcopalians about forms of civil government ; the leading officers would have contributed their part towards restoring his majesty to his throne, when he was with the army, upon more equal terms than some other of his adversaries, had they not discovered his designs to sacrifice them when it should be in his power. In their last propositions they consented to the restoring the king, upon the foot of a toleration for themselves and the Episcopal party, leaving the Presbyterians in possession of the establishment. Both Whitelocke* and Welwood† observe, that at the very time of the king's trial, the prevailing party were not determined what form of government to set up, "many having thoughts of making the Duke of Gloucester king ;" which his majesty being informed of, forbade the duke, in his last interview, to accept the crown while his elder brothers were living. And though Mr. Rapin says, that after the force put upon the members of Parliament on the 6th and 7th of December, the House consisted of none but Independent members, it is certain to a demonstration, that there were then remaining in the House men of all parties, Episcopalians, Presbyterians, Independents, Anabaptists, and

---

* Whitelocke's Mem., p. 335. Coke's Detect., p. 331, 332.

† Bishop Warburton, with Mr. Neal, acquits the Presbyterians from being parties in the execution of the king ; but then he will not allow them merit or virtue in this instance, but would ascribe it to their not uniting with the Independents in other matters, and the opposition which that party made to their two darling points, the Divine right of Presbytery, and the use of force in religious matters. The reader will judge how far this is a candid construction of the conduct and motives of the Presbyterians ; and, at the same time, he will lament that there should have been any ground for the severe reflection which the

bishop subjoins : "Those who were capable of punishing Arians with death, were capable of doing any wickedness for the cause of God."—ED.

* Memor., p. 358.

† Ibid., p. 90 ; vol. ii., p. 367, folio.

others : so little foundation is there for this writer's conclusion, that the Independents, and these only, put the king to death.

Dr. Lewis du Moulin, history professor in Oxford, who lived through these times, says that "*no party of men, as a religious body*, were the actors of this tragedy, but that it was the contrivance of an army, which, like that of King David's in the wilderness, was a medley or collection of all parties that were discontented ; some courtiers, some Presbyterians, some Episcopalians ; few of any sect, but most of none, or else of the religion of Thomas Hobbes and Dr. Scarborough ; not to mention the papists, who had the greatest hand in it of all."[*] The same learned professor, in his book entitled "The Conformity of the Independent Discipline with that of the Primitive Christians," published in 1680, had a chapter entitled "An Answer to those who accuse the Independents for having an immediate hand in the Death of King Charles I."[†] But the times were such that the author was advised not to publish it.[†]

Mr. Baxter says, " Many that minded no side in religion thought it was no policy to trust a conquered king, and therefore were wholly for a parliamentary government without a king ; of these," says he, " some were for an aristocracy, and others for a Democracy, and some thought they ought to judge the king for all the blood that had been shed ; the Vanists, the Independents, and other sects, with the Democratical party, being left by Cromwell to do the business under the name of the Parliament of England."[‡]

Bishop Burnet says, that " Ireton was the person that drove it on, for Cromwell was all the while in suspense about it ; Ireton had the principles and temper of a Cassius ; he stuck at nothing that might turn England into a commonwealth ; Fairfax was much distracted in his mind, and changed purposes every day ; the Presbyterians and the body of the city were much against it, and were every day fasting and praying for the king's preservation. There were not above eight thousand of the army about the town, but those were the most engaged in enthusiasm, and were kept at prayer in their way almost day and night, except when they were upon duty, so that they were wrought up to a pi c of fury which struck terror into all people.[§]

Mr. Echard and some others are of opinion that great numbers of papists, under hopes of liberty of conscience, or of destroying Episcopacy, joined with foreign priests and Jesuits against the king. The celebrated author of Foxes and Firebrands has this remarkable passage :[‖] " Let all true Protestants, who desire sincerely to have a happy union, recollect what a blemish the emissaries of Rome have cast upon those Protestants named Presbyterian and

Independent, Rome saying the Presbyterians brought Charles the First's head to the block, and the Independents cut it off ; whereas it is certain that the members and clergy of Rome, under dissenting shapes, contrived this murder. Nay, the good king himself was informed that the Jesuits in France, at a general meeting, resolved to bring him to justice, and to take off his head by the power of their friends in the army."[*] Bishop Bramhall, in a letter to Archbishop Usher, dated July 20, 1654, adds, " Thus much to my knowledge have I seen and heard since my leaving your lordship, which I myself could hardly have credited, had not mine eyes seen sure evidence of the same, viz., that when the Romish orders, which were in disguise in the Parliament army, wrote to their several convents, and especially to the Sorbonists, about the lawfulness of taking away the king's life, it was returned by the Sorbonists, that it was lawful for any Roman Catholic to work a change in governments for the mother-church's advancement, and chiefly in an heretical kingdom, and, so lawful to make way with the king."[†] Mr. Prynne adds, " that Mr. Henry Spotswood saw the queen's confessor on horseback among the crowd in the habit of a trooper, with his drawn sword, flourishing it over his head in triumph, as others did, when the king's head was just cut off ; and being asked how he could be present at so sad a spectacle, answered, there were above forty more priests and Jesuits there besides himself, and when the fatal blow was given, he flourished his sword and said, Now the greatest enemy we have in the world is dead." But this story does not seem to me very probable, nor is it easy to believe that the papists should triumph in the death of a king who was their friend and protector in prosperity, and whose sufferings are, in a great measure, chargeable upon his too great attachment to their interests.[‡]

But the strongest and most unexceptionable testimony is the act of attainder of the king's judges passed upon the restoration of King Charles II., the preamble to which sets forth, that the " execrable murder of his royal father was committed by a party of wretched men, desperately wicked, and hardened in their impiety, who, having first plotted and contrived the ruin of this excellent monarchy, and with it of the true Protestant religion, which had long flourished under it, found it necessary, in order to carry on their pernicious and traitorous designs, to throw down all the bulwarks and fences of law, and to subvert the very being and constitution of Parliament. And for the more easy effecting their attempts on the person of the king himself, they first seduced some part of the then army into a compliance, and then kept the rest in subjection, partly for hopes of preferment, and chiefly for fear of losing their employments and arrears, till by these, and other more odious arts and devices, they had fully strengthened themselves in power and faction ; which being done, they declared against all manner of treaties with the person of the king, while a treaty with him was subsisting ; they remonstrated against the Parliament for their proceedings ; they seized upon his royal person

---

[*] " There is doubtless," says Bishop Warburton, " a great deal of truth in all this. *No party of men, as a religious body,* farther than as they were united by one common enthusiasm, were the actors in this tragedy." See what Burnet says : " But who prepared the entertainment, and was at the expense of the exhibition, is another question."—ED.

[†] Vind. Prot. Relig., p. 53, 59.
[†] Baxter's Life, p. 63.
[§] Hist. Life and Times, vol. i., p. 63, Edin. edition.
[‖] Part iii., p. 188.

[*] Part iii., p. 168, 160. [†] Necess. Vind., p. 45.
[‡] Foxes and Firebrands, part ii., p. 86.

while the commissioners were returned to London with his answers, which were voted a sufficient foundation for peace; they then secluded and imprisoned several members of the House of Commons, and then, there being left but a small number of their own creatures (not a tenth part of the whole), they sheltered themselves under the name and authority of a Parliament, and in that name prepared an ordinance for the trial of his majesty; which, being rejected by the Lords, they passed alone in the name of the Commons of England, and pursued it with all possible force and cruelty till they murdered the king before the gates of his own palace. Thus," say they, "the fanatic rage of a few miscreants, who were neither true Protestants nor good subjects, stands imputed by our adversaries to the whole nation; we therefore renounce, abominate, and protest against it."*

If this be a true state of the case, it is evident, from the highest authority in this kingdom, that the king's death was not chargeable upon any

* 12 Cor. II., cap. xxx.

religious party or sect of Christians; nor upon the people of England assembled in a free Parliament, but upon the council of officers and agitators, who, having become desperate by the restless behaviour of the cavaliers, and ill conduct of the several parties concerned in the treaty of Newport, plotted the overthrow of the king and Constitution, and accomplished it by an act of lawless violence; that it was only a small part of the army who were seduced into a compliance, and these kept the rest in subjection till the others had executed their desperate purposes; so that, though the wisdom of the nation has thought fit to perpetuate the memory of this fatal day by an anniversary fast, as that which may be instructive both to principes and subjects, yet, if we may believe the declaration of his majesty at his trial, or of the act of Parliament which restored his family, the king's murder was not the act of the people of England, nor of their legal representatives, and therefore ought not to be lamented as a national sin.

PREFACE

TO VOL. IV. OF THE ORIGINAL EDITION.

THIS volume brings the History of the Sufferings of the Puritans down to its period ;* for though the Protestant Dissenters have since complained of several difficulties and discouragements, yet most of the penal laws have been suspended ; the prosecutions of the spiritual courts have been considerably restrained by the kind interposition of the civil powers, and liberty of conscience enjoyed without the hazard of fines, imprisonments, and other terrors of this world.

The times now in review were stormy and boisterous : upon the death of King Charles I., the Constitution was dissolved : the men at the helm had no legal authority to change the government into a commonwealth, the protectorship of Cromwell was a usurpation, because grafted only on the military power, and so were all the misshapen forms into which the administration was cast till the restoration of the king. In order to pass a right judgment upon these extraordinary revolutions, the temper and circumstances of the nation are to be duly considered ; for those actions which in some circumstances are highly criminal, may, in a different situation of affairs, become necessary. The parties engaged in the civil wars were yet living, and their resentments against each other so much inflamed as to cut off all hopes of a reconciliation ; each dreaded the other's success, well knowing they must fall a sacrifice to those who should prevail. All present views of the king's recovering his father's throne were defeated at the battle of Worcester, the Loyalists being then entirely broken and dispersed ; so that if some such extraordinary genius as Cromwell's had not undertaken to steer the nation through the storm, it had not been possible to hold the government together till Providence should open a way for restoring the Constitution, and settling it on its legal basis.

The various forms of government (if they deserve that name) which the officers of the army introduced after the death of Cromwell, made the nation sick of their phrensies; and turned their eyes towards their banished sovereign, whose restoration, after all, could not be accomplished without great imprudence on one part, and the most artful dissimulation on the other. The Presbyterians, like weak politicians, surrendered at discretion, and parted with their power on no other security than the royal word, for which they have been sufficiently reproached ; though I am of opinion, that if the king had been brought in by a treaty, the succeeding Parliament would have set it aside. On the other hand, nothing can be more notorious than the deep hypocrisy of General Monk, and the solemn assurances given by the bishops and other Loyalists, and even by the king himself, of burying all past offences under the foundation of the Restoration ; but when they were lifted into the saddle, the haste they made to show how little they meant by their promises exceeded the rules of decency as well as honour. Nothing would satisfy till their adversaries were disarmed, and in a manner deprived of the protection of the government : the terms of conformity were made narrower and more exceptionable than before the civil wars, the penal laws were rigorously executed, and new ones framed almost every sessions of Parliament for several successive years, the Nonconformist ministers were banished five miles from all the corporations in England, and their people sold for sums of money to carry on the king's unlawful pleasures, and to bribe the nation into popery and slavery, till the House of Commons, awakened at last with a sense of the

* The reader will observe that the period here referred to is the passing the Act of Toleration, with which Mr. Neal's fourth volume concludes. But the additions to the original work, by notes and supplements in this edition, have necessarily extended it to a fifth volume, which comprehends the author's last two chapters, the papers that form the Appendix to each of his volumes, and other papers.—ED.

threatening danger, grew intractable, and was therefore dissolved. His majesty, having in vain, attempted several other representatives of the people, determined, some time before his death, to change the Constitution, and govern by his sovereign will and pleasure, that the mischiefs which could not be brought upon the nation by consent of Parliament, might be introduced under the wing of the prerogative; but the Roman Catholics, not satisfied with the slow proceedings of a disguised Protestant, or apprehending that the discontents of the people and his own love of ease might induce him some time or other to change measures, resolved to have a prince of their own religion and more sanguine principles on the throne, which hastened the crisis of the nation, and brought forward that glorious revolution of King William and Queen Mary, which put a final period to all their projects.

The nature of my design does not admit of a large and particular relation of all the civil transactions of these times, but only of such a summary as may give light to the affairs of religion; and I could have wished that the memory of both had been entirely blotted out of the records of time, if the animosities of the several parties and their unchristian principles had been buried with them; but as the remembering them may be a warning to posterity, it ought to give no offence to any denomination of Christians in the present age, who are noways answerable for the conduct of their ancestors, nor can otherwise share in a censure of it, than as they maintain the same principles, and imitate the same unchristian behaviour. At the end of each year I have added the characters of the principal Nonconformist ministers as they died, partly from the historians of those times, but chiefly from the writings of the late Reverend Dr. Calamy, whose integrity, moderation, and industry deserve a peculiar commendation. My design was to preserve the memory of the reverend assembly of divines at Westminster, as well as the little army of confessors, who afterward suffered so deeply in the cause of nonconformity.

In passing a judgment on the several parties in Church and State, I have carefully distinguished between those who went into all the arbitrary measures of the court, and such as stood firm by the Protestant religion and the liberties of their country; for it must be allowed, that in the reign of King Charles II. there were even among the clergy some of the worst as well as best of men, as will appear to a demonstration in the course of this history; but I desire no greater stress may be laid upon facts or characters than the quality of the vouchers in the margin will support. Where these have been differently related, I have relied on the best authorities, and sometimes reported from both sides, leaving the reader to choose for himself; for if facts are fairly represented, the historian is discharged. I am not so vain as to imagine this history free from errors; but if any mistakes of consequence are made to appear, they shall be acknowledged with thankfulness to those who shall point them out in a civil and friendly manner; and as I aim at nothing but truth, I see no reason to engage in a warm defence of any parties of Christians who pass before us in review, but leave their conduct to the censure of the world. Some few remarks of my own are here and there interspersed, which the reader will receive according as he apprehends them to follow from the premises; but I flatter myself, that when he has carefully perused the several volumes of this history, he will agree with me in the following conclusions:

1st. That uniformity of sentiments in religion is not to be attained among Christians; nor will a comprehension within an establishment be of service to the cause of truth and liberty, without a toleration of all other dutiful subjects. Wise and good men, after their most diligent searches after truth, have seen things in a different light, which is not to be avoided as long as they have liberty to judge for themselves. If Christ had appointed an infallible judge upon earth, or men were to be determined by an implicit faith in their superiors, there would be an end of such differences; but all the engines of human policy that have been set at work to obtain it have hitherto failed of success. Subscriptions, and a variety of oaths and other tests, have occasioned great mischiefs to the Church: by these means men of weak morals and ambitious views have been raised to the highest preferments, while others of stricter virtue and superior talents have been neglected and laid aside; and power has been lodged in the hands of those who have used it in an unchristian manner, to force men to an agreement in sounds and outward appearances, contrary to the true conviction and sense of their minds, and thus a lasting reproach has been brought on the Christian name, and on the genuine principles of a Protestant Church.

2dly. All parties of Christians, when in power, have been guilty of persecution for conscience' sake. The annals of the Church are a most melancholy demonstration of this truth. Let the reader call to mind the bloody proceedings of the popish bishops in Queen Mary's reign, and the account that has been given of the Star Chamber and High Commission Court in later times ; what numbers of useful ministers have been sequestered, imprisoned, and their families reduced to poverty and disgrace, for refusing to wear a white surplice, or to comply with a few indifferent ceremonies ! What havoc did the Presbyterians make with their covenant uniformity, their *jure divino* discipline, and their rigid prohibition of reading the old service-book ! And though the Independents had a better notion of the rights of conscience, how defective was their instrument of government under Cromwell ! how arbitrary the proceedings of their triers ! how narrow their list of fundamentals ! and how severe their restraints of the press ! And though the rigorous proceedings of the Puritans of this age did by no means rival those of the prelates before and after the civil wars, yet they are so many species of persecution, and not to be justified even by the confusion of the times in which they were acted.

3dly. It is unsafe and dangerous to intrust any sort of clergy with the power of the sword : for our Saviour's kingdom is not of this world ; " if it were," says he, " then would my servants fight, but now is my kingdom not from hence." The Church and State should stand on a distinct basis, and their jurisdiction be agreeable to the nature of their crimes ; those of the Church purely spiritual, and those of the State purely civil ; as the king is supreme in the State, he is also head, or guardian, of the Church in those spiritual rights that Christ has intrusted it with. When the Church in former ages first assumed the secular power, it not only rivalled the State, but in a little time lifted up its head above emperors and kings, and all the potentates of the earth : the thunder of its anathemas was heard in all nations, and in her skirts was found the blood of the prophets and saints, and of all that were slain upon the earth. And whenever it recovers the wound that was given it at the Reformation, it will undoubtedly resume the same absolute coercive dominion. It is therefore the interest of all sovereign princes to keep their clergy within the limits that Christ has prescribed for them in the New Testament, and not to trust them with the power of inflicting corporeal pains or penalties on their subjects, which have no relation to the Christian methods of conversion.

4thly. Reformation of religion, or a redress of grievances in the Church, has not, in fact, arisen from the clergy. I would not be thought to reflect upon that venerable order, which is of great usefulness and deserved honour, when the ends of its institution are pursued ; but so strange has been the infatuation, so enchanting the lust of dominion and the charms of riches and honour, that the propagation of piety and virtue has been very much neglected, and little else thought of but how they might rise higher in the authority and grandeur of this world, and fortify their strongholds against all that should attack them. In the dawn of the Reformation the clergy maintained the pope's supremacy against the king, till they were cast in a præmunire. In the reign of Queen Elizabeth there was but one of the whole bench who would join in the consecration of a Protestant bishop ; and when the Reformation was established, how cruelly did those Protestant bishops, who themselves had suffered for religion, vex the Puritans, because they could not come up to their standard ! How unfriendly did they behave at the Hampton Court Conference ! At the restoration of King Charles II., and at the late revolution of King William and Queen Mary ! when the most solemn promises were broken, and the most hopeful opportunity of accommodating differences among Protestants lost, by the perverseness of the clergy towards those very men who had saved them from ruin. So little ground is there to hope for a union among Christians, or the propagation of truth, peace, and charity, from councils, synods, general assemblies, or convocations of the clergy of any sort whatsoever.

5thly. Upon these principles, it is evident that freedom of religion, in subordination to the civil power, is for the benefit of society, and noways inconsistent with a public establishment. The king may create dignitaries, and give sufficient encour-

agement to those of the public religion, without invading the liberties of his dissenting subjects. If religious establishments were stripped of their judicial processes
and civil jurisdiction, no harm could be feared from them. And as his majesty is
defender of the faith in Scotland as well as England, and equally the guardian of both
churches, he will no doubt hold the balance, and prevent either from rising to such
a pitch of greatness as to act independently on the State, or become formidable and
oppressive to their neighbours: the former would create *imperium in imperio ;* and
there is but one step between the Church's being independent on the State, and the
State becoming dependant on the Church. Besides, as freedom of religion is for the
true honour and dignity of the crown, it is no less for the service of the community ;
for the example of the neighbouring nations may convince us, that uniformity in the
Church will always be attended with absolute and despotic power in the State. The
meetings of dissenting Protestants were formerly called seditious, because the peace
of the public was falsely supposed to consist in uniformity of worship ; but long experience has taught us the contrary ; for though the Nonconformists, in those times,
gave no disturbance to the administration, the nation was far from being at peace ;
but when things came to a crisis, their joining with the Church, against a corrupt
court and ministry, saved the religion and liberties of the nation. It must therefore
be the interest of a free people to support and encourage liberty of conscience, and
not to suffer any one great and powerful religious body to oppress, devour, and swallow up the rest.

Finally. When Protestant Dissenters recollect the sufferings of their fathers in the
last age for the freedom of their consciences, let them be thankful that their lot is
cast in more settled times. The liberties of England are the price of a great deal of
blood and treasure ; wide breaches were made in the Constitution in the four reigns
of the male line of the Stuarts ; persecution and arbitrary power went hand in hand ;
the Constitution was often in convulsive agonies, when the patrons of liberty appeared boldly in the noble cause, and sacrificed their estates and lives in its defence.
The Puritans stood firm by the Protestant religion, and by the liberties of their country, in the reigns of King Charles II. and King James II., and received the fire of
the enemy from all their batteries, without moving sedition, or taking advantage of
their persecutors, when it was afterward in their power. Some amendments, in my
humble opinion, are still wanting to settle the cause of liberty on a more equal basis,
and to deliver wise and good men from the fetters of oaths, subscriptions, and religious tests of all sorts. But whether such desirable blessings are in reserve for this
nation, must be left to the determination of an all-wise Providence. In the mean
time, may Protestant Dissenters express their gratitude for the protection and ease
they enjoy at present, by an undissembled piety towards God ! by a firm and unshaken loyalty to his majesty's person and wise administration ! by avoiding everything that tends to persecution or censoriousness for mere differences in religion !
and by the integrity of their own lives and manners ! And while they think it their
duty to separate from the national establishment, may they distinguish themselves by
the exercise of all social virtues, and stand fast in the liberty wherewith the providence of God has made them free ! By such a conduct they will preserve their
characters with all sober persons, and will transmit the blessings of the present
age to their latest posterity.

                                                           DANIEL NEAL.

London, March 1, 1737-8.

ADVERTISEMENT

TO VOL. IV. OF DR. TOULMIN'S EDITION.

THE volume of Mr. Neal's History of the Puritans now presented to the public, besides the additions made to it in the form of notes, is considerably enlarged by supplemental chapters. These comprise the continued history of the English Baptists and Quakers, and furnish the reader with the substance of Mr. Crosby's history of the former, and a full abstract of Mr. Gough's work concerning the latter sect. The editor hopes that in this part of his undertaking he has not only done justice and showed respect to two denominations who, in the last century, were treated neither with humanity nor equity, but afforded the reader information and entertainment.

Where he has seen reason to animadvert on and correct Mr. Neal, it were sufficient to rest his justification on the plea of impartiality and the love of truth. But to the honour of his author he can add, he has only done what was wished by him, who, in his preface to the first volume, has said,* " I shall be always thankful to any that will convince me of my mistakes in a friendly manner;" and in that to the third volume he has more fully expressed himself in this manner : " In historical debates nothing is to be received upon trust; but facts are to be examined, and a judgment formed upon the authority by which those facts are supported ; by this method we shall arrive at truth ; and if it shall appear that, in the course of this long history, there are any considerable mistakes, the world may be assured I will take the first opportunity to retract or amend them."†

The editor can declare, that it has been his own aim to do full justice to the sects and characters of those who have, in this work, come before him in review, and he can boldly appeal to his pen itself to prove the sincerity of his declaration. He scarcely would have thought of making this appeal, if, in an early stage of his undertaking, it had not been insinuated that it was his design to make this work a vehicle for conveying particular opinions in theology, and that his own sentiments made him an unfit person for the task. He has, indeed, sentiments of his own, but he can estimate goodness and worth wherever they are found. He has sentiments of his own, but he rejoices in the consciousness of a disposition to grant to others a full liberty to avow, defend, and disseminate their sentiments, though opposite to his own, and can give them the praise due to their abilities and characters.

It is a pleasure to him, that the examination of the writers who have censured Mr. Neal with severity has eventually established the authenticity of the history, and the candour and impartiality of the author in all the main parts of his work. It reflects high and lasting honour on this ecclesiastical history, that if the author were convicted by a Warburton, a Maddox, and a Grey, of partiality, it could be only such a partiality as might arise from a zeal against tyrants and oppressors. The work has, on the whole, a liberal cast ; it is on the side of civil and religious liberty ; it is in favour of the rights of Englishmen, against unconstitutional prerogative ; it is in favour of the rights of conscience, against an imperious and persecuting hierarchy, whether Episcopal or Presbyterian ; it is in favour of the great interests of mankind, and, to adopt the words of a most able and liberal writer,‡ " A history that is written without any regard to the chief privileges of human nature, and without feelings, especially of the moral kind, must lose a considerable part of its instruction and energy."

* P. x.   † P. xxiv.
‡ Dr. Kippis: Preface to the first volume of the second edition of the Biographia Britannica, p. 21.

PART IV.

CHAPTER I.

FROM THE DEATH OF KING CHARLES I. TO THE
CORONATION OF KING CHARLES II. IN SCOT-
LAND—1648.

UPON the death of the late king, the legal
constitution was dissolved, and all that followed till the restoration of King Charles II. was
no better than a usurpation, under different
shapes; the House of Commons, if it may deserve that name, after it had been purged of a
third part of its members,* relying on the Act
of Continuation, called themselves the supreme
authority of the nation, and began with an act
to disinherit the Prince of Wales, forbidding all
persons to proclaim him King of England, on
pain of high treason. The House of Lords was
voted useless; and the office of a king unnecessary, burdensome, and dangerous. The form
of government for the future was declared to be
a free commonwealth; the executive power
lodged in the hands of a council of state of forty
persons,† with full powers to take care of the
whole administration for one year; new keepers of the great seal were appointed, from whom
the judges received their commissions, with the
name, style, and title of *custodes libertatis Angliæ authoritate Parliamenti*, i. e., keepers of the
liberties of England by authority of Parliament.
The coin was stamped on one side with the
arms of England between a laurel and a palm,
with this inscription, "The Commonwealth of
England;" and on the other, a cross and harp,
with this motto, "God with us."‡ The oaths
of allegiance and supremacy were abolished,
and a new one appointed, called the Engagement, which was, to be true and faithful to the
government established, without king or House
of Peers. Such as refused the oath were declared incapable of holding any place or office of
trust in the commonwealth; but as many of the
excluded members of the House of Commons
as would take it resumed their places.§

* According to Echard, not above a fifth part of
the Commons were left. On account of the reduced
and mutilated state of the House, they were called
the Rump Parliament. This name was first given to
them by Walker, the author of the History of Independency, by way of derision, in allusion to a fowl,
all devoured but the rump; and they were compared
to a man "who would never cease to whet and whet
his knife, till there was no steel left to make it useful."—*Dr. Grey*, and *Rapin*.—ED.
† According to Whitelocke, who gives their names,
the council consisted of thirty-eight persons only.
—ED.
‡ On which a man of wit observed, "That God
and the commonwealth were not both on a side."—
Dr. Grey.—ED.
§ In one respect the superiority of the new rulers
over those whom they displaced was very apparent.
A new oath of fidelity to the commonwealth was devised, and ordered to be taken by the public func-
tionaries of government, and subsequently by all

Such was the foundation of this new Constitution, which had neither the consent of the people of England, nor of their representatives in a
free Parliament. "And if ever there was an
usurped government mutilated, and founded
only in violence," says Rapin,* "it was that of
this Parliament." But though it was unsupport-
ed by any other power than that of the army, it
was carried on with the most consummate wisdom, resolution, and success, till the same military power that set it up was permitted, by
Divine Providence, with equal violence to pull
it down.

The new commonwealth in its infant state
met with opposition from divers quarters : the
Levellers in the army gave out that the people
had only changed their yoke, not shaken it off;
and that the Rump's little finger (for so the
House of Commons was now called) would be
heavier than the king's loins. The agitators
therefore petitioned the House to dissolve themselves, that new representatives might be chosen. The Commons, alarmed at these proceedings, ordered their general officers to cashier
the petitioners, and break their swords over
their heads, which was done accordingly. But
when the forces passed under a general review
at Ware, their friends in the army agreed to
distinguish themselves by wearing something
white in their hats;† which Cromwell having
some intelligence of beforehand, commanded
two regiments of horse, who were not in the
secret, to surround one of the regiments of
foot; and having condemned four of the ringleaders in a council of war, he commanded two
of them to be shot to death by their other two
associates, in sight of the whole army; and to
break the combination, eleven regiments were
ordered for Ireland; upon which great numbers
deserted, and marched into Oxfordshire; but
Generals Fairfax and Cromwell, having overtaken them at Abingdon, held them in treaty
till Colonel Reynolds came up, and after some
few skirmishes dispersed them.

The Scots threatened the commonwealth
with a formidable invasion, for upon the death

members of Parliament, magistrates, military officers,
and clergymen. It was framed in a spirit of liberality hitherto unknown to English statesmen, and *presented no bar to the occupation of office by religionists of
all complexions and parties*. It provided simply for the
civil obedience of the subject—offering no violence to
conscience, and presenting no temptation to hypocrisy. It imposed no religious test as a qualification
for civil office, but left unimpaired the natural right
of every human being to adopt whatever form of religious faith he pleased. Dr. Walker calls this oath
the "Independent Covenant," but fails to establish
the analogy which his language suggests.—*Clarendon*, vol. vi., p. 21. *Parliamentary Hist.*, vol. iii., p.
1334. *Price's Hist. Nonconformity*, vol. ii., p. 440.—C.
* Vol. ii., p. 573, folio.
† Whitelocke, p. 387, 389.

of King Charles I. they proclaimed the Prince of Wales king of Scotland, and sent commissioners to the Hague to invite him into that kingdom, provided he would renounce popery and prelacy, and take the solemn League and Covenant. To prevent the effects of this treaty, and cultivate a good understanding with the Dutch, the Parliament sent Dr. Dorislaus,* an eminent civilian, concerned in the late king's trial, agent to the States-General ; but the very first night after his arrival, May 3, 1649, he was murdered in his own chamber by twelve desperate cavaliers in disguise, who rushed in upon him while he was at supper, and with their drawn swords killed him on the spot.† Both the Parliament and States of Holland resented this base action‡ so highly, that the young king thought proper to remove into France, from whence he went to the Isle of Jersey, and towards the latter end of the year fixed at Breda, where the Scots commissioners concluded a treaty with him, upon the foot of which he ventured his royal person into that kingdom the ensuing year.

But, to strike terror into the cavaliers, the Parliament erected another high court of justice, and sentenced to death three illustrious noblemen, for the part they had acted in the last civil war : Duke Hamilton, the Earl of Holland, and Lord Capel, who were all executed March 9, in the Palace-yard at Westminster : Duke Hamilton declared himself a Presbyterian, and the Earl of Holland was attended by two ministers of the same persuasion ; but Lord Capel was a thorough Loyalist, and went off the stage with the courage and bravery of a Roman.

But the chief scene of great exploits this year was in Ireland, which Cromwell, a bold and enterprising commander, had been appointed to reduce ; for this purpose he was made lord-lieutenant for three years, and having taken

leave of the Parliament, sailed from Milford-Haven* about the middle of August, with an army of fourteen thousand men of resolute principles, who before the embarcation observed a day of fasting and prayer ; in which, Mr. Whitelocke remarks, after three ministers had prayed, Lieutenant-general Cromwell himself, and the Colonels Gough and Harrison, expounded some parts of Scripture excellently well, and pertinently to the occasion. The army was under a severe discipline ; not an oath was to be heard throughout the whole camp, the soldiers spending their leisure hours in reading their Bibles, in singing psalms, and religious conferences.

Almost all Ireland was in the hands of the Royalists and Roman Catholics, except Dublin and Londonderry ; the former of these places had been lately besieged by the Duke of Ormond with twenty thousand men,† but the garrison being recruited with three regiments from England, the governor, Colonel-Jones, surprised the besiegers, and after a vigorous sally stormed their camp, and routed the whole army, which dispersed itself into Drogheda, and other fortified places. Cromwell, upon his arrival, was

* Neal is at fault, I imagine, both *in fact and date,* in stating that Cromwell sailed from Milford-Haven. Jesse says " his departure, and the stateliness of his cavalcade," are announced in the Moderate Intelligencer, July 10, 1649 : " This evening, about five of the clock, the Lord-lieutenant of Ireland began his journey the way of Windsor, and so to Bristol. He went forth in that state and equipage as the like hath hardly been seen ; himself in a coach with six gallant Flanders mares, whitish gray, divers coaches accompanying him, and very many officers of the army : his life-guard consisting of eighty gallant men, the meanest whereof a commander or esquire, in stately habit, with trumpets sounding almost to the shaking of Charing Cross, had it been now standing ; of his life-guard many are colonels, and I believe it is such a guard as is hardly to be paralleled in the world." And I find in the city records of Bristol the following entry : " July, 1649, Lieut.-gen. Oliver Cromwel lcame to Bristol, and thence passed to Ireland." Cromwell entered Dublin the 15th of August.—*Seyer's Memoirs of Bristol,* quarto, vol. ii., p. 469.—C.

† Dr. Grey controverts Mr. Neal's account of the number of the Duke of Ormond's army, on the authority of Lord Clarendon and Mr. Carte ; the former says that Jones sallied out with a body of six thousand foot and one thousand nine hundred horse, and that the army encamped at Rathmines was not so strong in horse and foot : the latter, that Jones's forces amounted to only four thousand foot and one thousand two hundred horse, which was a body nearly equal to the whole Irish army, if it had been all engaged. These authorities are set against Mr. Neal. On the other hand, Whitelocke informs us that, previously to this defeat, letters from Ireland represented the Duke of Ormond as approaching Dublin with twelve thousand foot and two thousand four hundred horse ; and letters from Chester reported him forty thousand strong before Dublin. Ludlow says that his forces were double in number to those of Jones. Borlase says that Jones, with very few forces, comparatively, fell on the besiegers, killed four thousand, and took two thousand five hundred and seventeen prisoners. The plunder of the field, we are told, was so rich, that the camp was like a fair, presenting for sale cloth, silk, and all manner of clothes. The Parliament settled £1000 per annum in land on Jones for his services.—*Whitelocke's Memorials,* p. 393, 401, 404. *Ludlow's Memoirs,* p. 101, 4to ed. ; and *Harris's Life of Cromwell,* p. 228.—ED.

* This person was a native of Holland, and doctor of the civil law at Leyden. On his coming to England he was patronised by Fulk, Lord Brook, who appointed him to read lectures on history in Cambridge. But as, in the opening of his course, he decried monarchy, he was silenced ; he then resided some time near to Maldon, in Essex, where he had married an English woman. He was afterward a judge-advocate, first in the king's army, and then in the army of the Parliament, and, at length, one of the Judge's of the Court of Admiralty. The Parliament ordered £250 for his funeral ; settled on his son £200 per annum for his life, and gave £500 apiece to his daughters.—*Wood's Athenæ Oxon.,* vol. ii., p. 228 ; and *Whitelocke's Memorials,* p. 390.—ED.

† Whitelocke, p. 386.

‡ Dr. Grey cannot easily believe that the murder of Dr. Dorislaus was resented by the States of Holland, because they had bravely remonstrated, by their two ambassadors, against the king's death ; he cannot, therefore, be easily induced to think that, after this, they could resent the death of one of his execrable murderers. But Dr. Grey does not consider what was due in this case to the honour of their own police, and to the reputation and weight of their own laws. Mr. Neal is justified in his representations by Whitelocke, who says, " that letters from the Hague reported that the States caused earnest inquisition to be made after the murderers of Dr. Dorislaus ; promised one thousand guilders to him who should bring any of them ; and published it death to any who should harbour any one of them."—*Memorials,* p. 390.—ED.

received with the acclamations of a vast concourse of people, to whom he addressed himself from a rising ground, with hat in hand, in a soldierlike manner, telling them "he was come to cut down and destroy the barbarous and bloodthirsty Irish, with all their adherents;* but that all who were for the Protestant religion, and the liberties of their country, should find suitable encouragement from the Parliament of England and himself, in proportion to their merits." Having refreshed his forces, he marched directly to Drogheda, which was garrisoned with two thousand five hundred foot and three hundred horse, and was therefore thought capable of holding out a month; but the general, neglecting the common forms of approach, battered the walls with his cannon, and having made two accessible breaches, like an impetuous conqueror entered the town in person, at the head of Colonel Ewer's regiment of foot, and put all the garrison to the sword. From thence he marched to Wexford, which he took likewise by storm, and, after the example of Drogheda, put the garrison to the sword; the general declaring that he would sacrifice all the Irish papists to the ghosts of the English Protestants whom they had massacred in cold blood.† The conquest of these places

* Dr. Grey spends here more than ten pages in detailing, from Lord Clarendon, various acts of oppression, cruelty, and murder perpetrated by individuals of Cromwell's army, to show that they were not less barbarous and bloodthirsty than the inhuman wretches concerned in the Irish massacre. Such deeds, undoubtedly, shock humanity, and ought to shock every party. But the guilt lieth originally at the door of those who were the first aggressors, whose conduct furnished the precedent, and provoked retaliation.—ED.

† Great reproach, on this account, has fallen on the name of Cromwell. He reconciled himself to the execution of such severe orders, for putting to the sword and giving no quarter, by considering them as necessary to prevent the effusion of blood for the future, and as the instrument of the righteous judgment of God upon those barbarous wretches who had imbrued their hands in so much innocent blood. If ever such measures are justifiable, "it is in such a case as this," observes Dr. Harris, "where the known disposition and behaviour of the sufferers are remarkably barbarous, inhuman, and cruel." Such horror, we are told, had the barbarities committed by the Irish, in the beginning of the rebellion and during the course of the war, impressed on every English breast, that even the humane and gentle Fairfax expressed in warm and severe terms his disapprobation of granting them quarter.—*Harris's Life of Cromwell,* p. 229; and *Macaulay's History of England,* vol. v., p. 15, note, 8vo ed.—ED.

"It is worthy of remark, that not a voice was heard against this tremendous act of oppression, such horror had the Irish massacre excited, and so irreclaimable, in the judgment of all men, was the nature of the inhabitants; even when new settlers established themselves there, 'through what virtues of the soil,' says Harrington, ' or vice of the air soever it be, they came still to degenerate;' and of the descendants of English colonists there it was said, in Elizabeth's time, they were *Hibernis ipsis Hiberniores.* So little were their rights, or even their existence, taken into the account, that Harrington thought the best thing the commonwealth could do with Ireland was to farm it to the Jews forever, for the pay of an army to protect them during the first seven years, and two millions a year from that time forward! What was to be done with the Irish, whether they were to be made hewers of wood and drawers of

struck such a terror into the rest, that they surrendered upon the first summons; the name of Cromwell carrying victory on its wings before himself appeared, the whole country was reduced by the middle of May, except Limerick, Galway, and one or two other places, which Ireton took the following summer. Lord Inchequin deserted the remains of the royal army, and Ormond fled into France. Lieutenant-general Cromwell being called home to march against the Scots, arrived at London about the middle of May, and was received by the Parliament and city with distinguished respect and honour, as a soldier who had gained more laurels, and done more wonders, in nine months, than any age or history could parallel.

It is a remarkable account the lieutenant-general gives in one of his letters, of the behaviour of the army after their arrival in Ireland : "Their diligence, courage, and behaviour are such," says he, "through the providence of God, and strict care of the chief officers, that never men did obey orders more cheerfully, nor go upon duty more courageously. Never did greater harmony and resolution appear to prosecute this cause of God, than in this army. Such a consent of hearts and hands ; such a sympathy of affections, not only in carnal, but in spiritual bonds, which tie faster than chains of adamant ! I have often observed a wonderful consent of the officers and soldiers upon grounds of doing service to God, and how miraculously they have succeeded. The mind of man being satisfied, and fixed on God, and that his undertaking is for God's glory, it gives the greatest courage to those men, and prosperity to their actions."*

To put the affairs of Ireland together : The Roman Catholics charged the ill success of their affairs upon the Duke of Ormond, and sent him word " that they were determined not to submit any longer to his commands, it not being fit that a Catholic army should be under the direction of a Protestant general ; but that if he would depart the kingdom, they would undertake of themselves to drive Ireton out of Dublin." After this they offered the kingdom to the Duke of Lorrain, a bigoted papist, who was wise enough to decline the offer,† and then quarrelling among themselves, they were soon driven out of all the strongholds of the kingdom, and forced to submit to the mercy of the conqueror. All who had borne arms in the late insurrection were shipped away into France, Spain, or Flanders, never to return on pain of death. Those who had a hand in murdering the Protestants at the time of the massacre

water, or to become Jews by compulsion, he has not explained. *For the sufferings of the Irish, however, Cromwell is not responsible, and under the order which he established, if it had continued for another generation, the island would have been in a better state than any which its authentic history has yet recorded ; for there, as in Scotland, a more equitable administration was introduced than that which had been destroyed."—London Quarterly,* vol. xxv., p. 341.—C.

* Whitelocke, p. 434.
† Dr. Grey insinuates here a reflection on Mr. Neal's veracity, by remarking that he produces no authority for the assertion. But that Ireland was offered to the guardianship of the Duke of Lorrain has been since mentioned, as an incontrovertible fact, by Dr. Harris and Mrs. Macaulay.—ED.

were brought from several parts of the country, and after conviction upon a fair trial were executed. The rest of the natives, who were called Tories, were shut up in the most inland counties, and their lands given partly in payment to the soldiers who settled there, and the rest to the first adventurers.* Lord Clarendon relates it thus : " Near one hundred thousand of them were transported into foreign parts, for the service of the Kings of France and Spain ; double that number were consumed by the plague, famine, and other severities exercised upon them in their own country ; the remainder were by Cromwell transplanted into the most inland, barren, desolate, and mountainous part of the province of Connaught, and it was lawful for any man to kill any of the Irish that were found out of the bounds appointed them within that circuit. Such a proportion of land was allotted to every man as the Protector thought competent for them ; upon which they were to give formal releases of all their titles to their lands in any other provinces ; if they refused to give such releases, they were still deprived, and left to starve within the limits prescribed them, out of which they durst not withdraw ; so that very few refused to sign those releases, or other acts, which were demanded. It was a considerable time before these Irish could raise anything out of their lands to support their lives ; but necessity was the spring of industry." Thus they lived under all the infamy of a conquered nation till the restoration of King Charles II., a just judgment of God for their barbarous and unheard-of cruelties to the Irish Protestants !

To return to England :— The body of the Presbyterians acted in concert with the Scots, for restoring the king's family upon the foot of the Covenant ; several of their ministers carried on a private correspondence with the chiefs of that nation, and instead of taking the engagement to the present powers, called them usurpers, and declined praying for them in their churches ; they also declared against a general toleration, for which the army and Parliament contended.

When Lieutenant-general Cromwell was embarking for Ireland, he sent letters to the Parliament, recommending the removal of all the penal laws relating to religion ; upon which the House ordered a committee to make report concerning a method for the ease of tender consciences, and an act to be brought in to appoint commissioners in every county, for the approbation of able and well-qualified persons to be made ministers, who cannot comply with the present ordinance for ordination of ministers.†

August 16, General Fairfax and his council of officers presented a petition to the same purpose, praying " that all penal statutes formerly made, and ordinances lately made, whereby many conscientious people were molested, and the propagation of the Gospel hindered, might be removed. Not that they desired this liberty should extend to the setting up popery, or the late hierarchy ; or to the countenancing any sort of immorality or profaneness ; for they earnestly desired that drunkenness, swearing, uncleanness, and all acts of profaneness, might be vig-

orously prosecuted in all persons whatsoever."* The House promised to take the petition into speedy consideration, and after some time passed it into a law.

But to bring the Presbyterian clergy to the test, the Engagement, which had been appointed to be taken by all civil and military officers within a limited time, on pain of forfeiting their places, was now required to be sworn and subscribed by all ministers, heads of colleges and halls, fellows of houses, graduates, and all officers in the universities ; and by the masters, fellows, schoolmasters, and scholars of Eton College, Westminster, and Winchester schools ; no minister was to be admitted to any ecclesiastical living, no clergyman to sit as member of the Assembly of Divines, nor be capable of enjoying any preferment in the Church, unless he qualified himself by taking the Engagement within six months, publicly in the face of the congregation.†

November 9, it was referred to a committee, to consider how the Engagement might be subscribed by all the people of the nation, of eighteen years of age and upward. Pursuant to which a bill was brought in, and passed, January 2, to debar all who should refuse to take and subscribe it from the benefit of the law ; and to disable them from suing in any court of law or equity.

This was a severe test on the Presbyterians, occasioned by the apprehended rupture with the Scots ; but their clergy inveighed bitterly against it in their sermons, and refused to observe the days of humiliation appointed by authority for a blessing upon their arms. Mr. Baxter says‡ that he wrote several letters to the soldiers, to convince them of the unlawfulness of the present expedition ; and in his sermons declared it a sin to force them to pray for the success of those who had violated the Covenant, and were going to destroy their brethren. That he both spoke and preached against the Engagement, and dissuaded men from taking it. At Exeter, says Mr. Whitelocke, the ministers went out of town on the fast-day, and shut up the church doors ; and all the magistrates refused the Engagement. At Taunton, the fast was not kept by the Presbyterian ministers ; and at Chester they condemned the Engagement to the pit of hell ; as did many of the London ministers, who kept days of private fasting and prayer, against the present government. Some of them (says Whitelocke) joined the Royalists, and refused to read the ordinances of Parliament in their pulpits, as was usual in those times ; nay, when the Scots were beaten, they refused to observe the day of thanksgiving,§ but shut up their churches and went out of town ; for which they were summoned before the committee and reprimanded ; but the times being unsettled, no farther notice was taken of them at present.

---

* Carrington's Life of Cromwell, p. 155. Clarendon, p. 153.   † Whitelocke, p. 405.

* Whitelocke. p. 404.   † Walker, p. 146.
‡ Life, p. 64, 66.
§ Lord Grey, at the desire of some who were zealously attached to the Parliament, complained, in a letter to the Lord-president of the Council of State, of the neglect of the ministers, in Leicestershire and another county, in this instance; and urged the importance of noticing their contempt of the thanksgiving-day, expressed by their non-observance of it.— *Dr. Grey's Appendix, No. 8.*—ED.

Most of the sectarian party, says Mr. Baxter,[*] swallowed the Engagement; and so did the king's old cavaliers, very few of them being sick of the disease of a scrupulous conscience: some wrote for it, but the moderate Episcopal men and Presbyterians generally refused it. Those of Lancashire and Cheshire published the following reasons against it:

(1.) " Because they apprehended the Oath of Allegiance, and the solemn League and Covenant, were still binding.

(2.) " Because the present powers were no better than usurpers.

(3.) " Because the taking of it was a prejudice to the right heir of the crown, and of the ancient legal Constitution."

To which it was answered, " that it was absurd to suppose the Oath of Allegiance, or the solemn League and Covenant, to be in force after the king's death; for how could they be obliged to preserve the king's person, when the king's person was destroyed, and the kingly office abolished? and as to his successor, his right had been forfeited and taken away by Parliament." With regard to the present powers, it was said, " that it was not for private persons to dispute the rights and titles of their supreme governors. Here was a government de facto, under which they lived; as long, therefore, as they enjoyed the protection of the government, it was their duty to give all reasonable security that they would not disturb it, or else to remove." The body of the common people, being weary of war, and willing to live quiet, under any administration, submitted to the Engagement, as being little more than a promise not to attempt the subversion of the present government, but many of the Presbyterian clergy chose rather to quit their preferments in the Church and university than comply; which made way for the promotion of several Independent divines, and among others, of Dr. Thomas Goodwin, one of the dissenting brethren in the Assembly, who, by order of Parliament, January 8, 1649-50, was appointed president of Magdalen College, Oxford, with the privilege of nominating fellows and demies in such places as should become vacant by death, or by the possessors refusing to take the Engagement.[†]

The Parliament tried several methods to reconcile the Presbyterians to the present administration; persons were appointed to treat with them, and assure them of the protection of the government, and of the full enjoyment of their ecclesiastical preferments according to law; when this could not prevail, an order was published, that ministers in their pulpits should not meddle with state affairs. After this the celebrated Milton was appointed to write for the government, who rallied the seditious preachers with his satirical pen in a severe manner; at length, when all other methods failed, a committee was chosen to receive informations against such ministers as in their pulpits vilified and aspersed the authority of Parliament, and an act was passed that all such should be sequestered from their ecclesiastical preferments.[‡]

The Presbyterians supported themselves under these hardships by their alliance with the Scots, and their hope of a speedy alteration of affairs by their assistance; for, in the remonstrance of the General Assembly of that Kirk, dated July 27, they declare that " the spirit which has acted in the councils of those who have obstructed the work of God, despised the Covenant, corrupted the truth, forced the Parliament, murdered the king, changed the government, and established such an unlimited toleration in religion, cannot be the spirit of righteousness and holiness. They therefore warn the subjects of Scotland against joining with them, and in case of an invasion, to stand up in their own defence. The English have no controversy with us," say they, " but because the Kirk and State have declared against their unlawful Engagement; because we still adhere to our Covenant, and have borne our testimony against their toleration, and taking away the king's life."[*] But they then warn their people also against malignants, "who value themselves upon their attachment to the young king; and if any from that quarter should invade the kingdom before his majesty has given satisfaction to the Parliament and Kirk, they exhort their people to resist them, as abetters of an absolute and arbitrary government."

About two months after this the Parliament of England published a declaration on their part, wherein they complain of the revolt of the English and Scots Presbyterians, and of their taking part with the enemy, because their discipline was not the exact standard of reformation. " But we are still determined," say they,[†] " not to be discouraged in our endeavours to promote the purity of religion, and the liberty of the commonwealth; and for the satisfaction of our Presbyterian brethren, we declare that we will continue all those ordinances which have been made for the promoting a reformation of religion, in doctrine, worship, and discipline, in their full force; and will uphold the same in order to suppress popery, superstition, blasphemy, and all kinds of profaneness. Only we conceive ourselves obliged to take away all such acts and ordinances as are penal, and coercive in matters of conscience. And because this has given so great offence, we declare, as in the presence of God, that by whomsoever this liberty shall be abused, we will be ready to testify our displeasure against them by an effectual prosecution of such offenders."

The Scots commissioners were all this while treating with the king in Holland, and insisting on his subscribing the solemn League and Covenant; his establishing the Westminster Confession, the Directory, and the Presbyterian government in both kingdoms. The king, being under discouraging circumstances, consented to all their demands with regard to Scotland, and as to England, referred himself to a free Parliament; but the Scots, not satisfied with his majesty's exceptions as to England, replied, that " such an answer as this would grieve the whole Kirk of Scotland, and all their covenanting brethren in England and Ireland who, under pain of the most solemn perjury, stand bound to God and one another, to live and die by their Covenant, as the chief security of their religion and liberties against popish and prelatical malignants. Your majesty's father," say they, " in his last message to our Kirk, offered to rat-

---

* Life, p. 64, 65. † Whitelocke, p. 453.
‡ Whitelocke, p. 387.

* Vol. Pamph., No. 34, p. 6. † Ibid., No. 34.

.ify the solemn League and Covenant. · He offered, likewise, at the Isle of Wight, to confirm
the Directory, and the Presbyterial government
in England and Ireland till he and his. Parliament should agree upon a settled order of the
Church. · Besides, your majesty having offered
to confirm the abolishing of Episcopacy, and the
service-book in Scotland, it cannot certainly be
against your conscience to do it in England."
But the king would advance no farther till he
had heard from the queen-mother, who sent him
word that it was the opinion of the council of
France that he should agree with the Scots
upon the best terms he was able, which he did
accordingly, as will be related the next year.· ·
· The fifth Provincial Assembly of London met
the beginning of May [1649] at Sion College,
the Rev. Mr. Jackson, of St. Michael Wood-
street, moderator. A committee was appointed
to prepare materials for proof of the Divine
right of Presbyterial church government. The
proofs were examined and approved by this, and
the Assembly that met in November following, of
which Mr. Walker was moderator, Mr. Calamy
and Mr. Jackson assessors, and Mr. Blackwell
scribe. The treatise was printed, and asserts,
  (1.) That there is a church government of
Divine institution. · ·
  (2.) That the civil magistrate is not the origin or head of church government. And,
  (3.) That the government of the Church by
synods and classes is the government that
Christ appointed. It maintains separation from
their churches to be schism ; that ministers
formerly ordained by bishops need not be reordained ; and for private Christians in particular churches to assume a right of sending persons forth to preach, and to administer the sac-
, raments, is, in their opinion, insufferable.
  The Parliament did all they could to satisfy.
the malecontent Presbyterians, by securing them
in their livings, and by ordering the dean and
chapter lands to be sold,* and their names to be
extinct, except the deanery of Christ Church,
and the foundations of Westminster, Winchester, and Eton schools. The bishops' lands,
which had been sequestered since the year 1646,
were now, by an ordinance of June 8, 1649,
vested in the hands of new trustees, and appropriated to the augmentation of poor livings
in the Church.† The first-fruits and tenths of
all ecclesiastical livings, formerly payable to the
crown, were vested in the same hands, free
from all encumbrances, on trust, that they
should pay yearly all such salaries, stipends, allowances, and provisions, as have been settled
and confirmed by Parliament, for preaching
ministers, schoolmasters, or professors in the
universities; provided the assignment to any one
do not exceed £100. It is farther provided that
the maintenance of all incumbents shall not be
less than £100 a year, and the commissioners
of the great seal are empowered to inquire into
the yearly value of all ecclesiastical livings to

which any cure of souls is annexed ; and to certify into the Court of Chancery the names of
the present incumbents who supply the cure,
with their respective salaries ; how many chapels belong to parish churches, and how the several churches and chapels are supplied with
preaching ministers ; that so some course may
be taken for providing for a better maintenance
where it is wanting. Dr. Walker says,* the
value of bishops' lands forfeited and sold amounted to a million of money ; but though they sold
very cheap, they that bought them had a very
dear bargain in the end.
  Upon debate of an ordinance concerning public worship and church government, the House
declared that the Presbyterial government
should be the established government, but
upon the question whether tithes should be continued, it was resolved that they should not be
taken away till another maintenance equally
large and honourable should be substituted in
its room.
  The inhabitants of the principality of Wales
were destitute of the means of Christian knowledge, the language was little understood, their
clergy were ignorant and idle ; so that they had
hardly a sermon from one quarter of a year
to another. The people had neither Bibles nor
catechisms ; nor was there a sufficient maintenance for such as were capable of instructing
them. The Parliament taking the case of these
people into consideration, passed an act, February 22, 1649, for the better propagation and
preaching of the Gospel in Wales, for the ejecting scandalous ministers and schoolmasters, and
redress of some grievances ; to continue in force
for three years. What was done in pursuance
of this ordinance will be related hereafter ; but
the Parliament were so intent upon the affair of
religion at this time, that, Mr. Whitelocke says,
they devoted Friday in every week to consult
ways and means for promoting it.
  Nor did they confine themselves to England,
but as soon as Lieutenant-general Cromwell had
reduced Ireland, the Parliament passed an ordinance, March 8, 1649, for the encouragement of
religion and learning in that country ; " they
invested all the manors and lands late of the.
Archbishop of Dublin, and of the dean and
chapter of St. Patrick, together with the parsonage of Trym, belonging to the bishopric of
Meath, in the hands of trustees, for the maintenance and support of Trinity College, in Dublin ; and for the creating, settling, and maintaining another college in the said city, and for
a master, fellows, scholars, and public professors ; and also for erecting a free-school, with
a master, usher, scholars, and officers, in such
manner as any five of the trustees, with the
consent of the lord-lieutenant, shall direct and
appoint. The lord-lieutenant to nominate the
governor, masters, &c., and to appoint them
their salaries ; and the trustees, with the consent of the lord-lieutenant, shall draw up statutes
and ordinances, to be confirmed by the Parliament of England." ·
  The University of Dublin being thus revived,
and put upon a new foot, the Parliament sent
over six of their most acceptable preachers to
give it reputation, appointed them £200 a year
out of the bishops' lands ; and till that could be

* The money raised by the sale of those lands
amounted to a very considerable sum. The return
of the value of the lands, contracted for the 29th of
August, 1650, made to the committee for the sale of
them, fixed it at the sum of £948,409 18s. 2¼d., of
which, on the 31st of August, the total of the purchasers' acquittances amounted to £658,501 2s. 9d.
—Dr. Grey, vol. iii., Appendix, p. 18.—ED. · ,
† Scobel, p. 41, 113.

* P. 14.

duly raised, to be paid out of the public revenues; and for their farther encouragement, if they died in that service, their families were to be provided for. By these methods learning began to revive, and in a few years religion appeared with a better face than it had ever done before in that kingdom.

A prospect being opened for spreading the Christian religion among the Indians, upon the borders of New-England, the Parliament allowed a general collection throughout England, and erected a corporation for this service, who purchased an estate in land of between 5 and £600 a year; but on the restoration of King Charles II. the charter became void, and Colonel Bedingfield, a Roman Catholic officer in the king's army, of whom a considerable part of the land was purchased, seized it for his own use, pretending he had sold it under the real value, in hopes of recovering it upon the king's return. In order to defeat the colonel's design, the society solicited the king for a new charter, which they obtained by the interest of the lord-chancellor. It bears date February 7, in the fourteenth year of his majesty's reign, and differs but little from the old one. The honourable Robert Boyle, Esq., was the first governor. They afterward recovered Colonel Bedingfield's estate, and are at this time in possession of about £500 a year, which they employ for the conversion of the Indians in America.

But all that Parliament could do was not sufficient to stop the mouths of the Loyalists and discontented Presbyterians; the pulpit and press sounded to sedition; the latter brought forth invectives every week against the government; it was therefore resolved to lay a severe fine upon offenders of this kind, by an ordinance bearing date September 20, 1649, the preamble to which sets forth, that "Whereas divers scandalous and seditious pamphlets are daily printed, and dispersed with officious industry, by the malignant party both at home and abroad, with a design to subvert the present government, and to take off the affections of the people from it, it is therefore ordained,

"That the author of every seditious libel or pamphlet shall be fined ten pounds, or suffer forty days' imprisonment. The printer five pounds, and his printing-press to be broken. The bookseller forty shillings; the buyer twenty shillings, if he conceals it, and does not deliver it up to a justice of peace. It is farther ordained, that no newspaper shall be printed or sold without license, under the hand of the clerk of the Parliament, or the secretary of the army, or such other person as the Council of State shall appoint. No printing-presses are to be allowed but in London and in the two universities. All printers are to enter into bonds of three hundred pounds, not to print any pamphlet against the state without license, as aforesaid, unless the author's or licenser's name, with the place of his abode, be prefixed. All importers of seditious pamphlets are to forfeit five pounds for every such book or pamphlet. No books are to be landed in any other port but that of London, and to be viewed by the master and wardens of the Company of Stationers. This act to continue in force for two years."*

But the pulpit was no less dangerous than the

* Scobel, p. 88, cap. 60.

Vol. II.—P

press; the Presbyterian ministers, in their public prayers and sermons, especially on fast-days, keeping alive the discontents of the people. The government, therefore, by an ordinance, abolished the monthly fast, which had subsisted for about seven years, and had been in a great measure a fast for strife and debate; but declared, at the same time, that they should appoint occasional fasts, from time to time, for the future, as the providences of God should require.*

In the midst of all these disorders, there was a very great appearance of sobriety both in city and country; the indefatigable pains of the Presbyterian ministers in catechising, instructing, and visiting their parishioners, can never be sufficiently commended. The whole nation was civilized, and considerably improved in sound knowledge, though Bishop Kennet and Mr. Echard are pleased to say that heresies and blasphemies against Heaven were swelled up to a most prodigious height. "I know," says Mr. Baxter,[†] "you may meet with men who will confidently affirm, that in these times all religion was trodden under foot, and that heresy and schism were the only piety; but I give warning to all ages, that they take heed how they believe any, while they are speaking for the interest of their factions and opinions against their real or supposed adversaries." However, the Parliament did what they could to suppress and discountenance all such extravagances; and even the officers of the army, having convicted one of their quartermasters of blasphemy in a council of war, sentenced him to have his tongue bored through with a hot iron, his sword broken over his head, and to be cashiered the army.

But Bishop Kennet says, even the Turkish Alcoran was coming in; that it was translated into English, and said to be licensed by one of the ministers of London! Sad times! Was his lordship, then, afraid that the Alcoran should prevail against the Bible? or that the doctrines of Christ could not support themselves against the extravagant follies of an impostor? But the book did no harm, though the Commons immediately published an order for suppressing it; and since the restitution of monarchy and Episcopacy, we have lived to see the life of Mohammed and his Koran published without mischief or offence.

His lordship adds, that the papists took advantage of the liberty of the times, who were never more numerous and busy; which is not very probable, because the Parliament had banished all papists twenty miles from the city of London, and excepted them out of their acts of indulgence and toleration; the spirit of the people against popery was kept up to the height; the mob carried the pope's effigy in triumph, and burned it publicly on Queen Elizabeth's birthday; and the ministers in their pulpits pronounced him antichrist; but such is the zeal of this right reverend historian![‡]

* Whitelocke, p. 383.   † Life, p. 86.
‡ In this place we may notice that Colonel Lilburne, who in the reign of Charles I. felt the severe effects of regal and episcopal anger, now incurred the displeasure of a republican government. On October 26, 1646, he was tried for transgressing the new statute of treasons enacted by the commonwealth. He was acquitted by the jury, and Westminster Hall, on the verdict being given, resounded with the accla-

The beginning of this year, the Marquis of Montrose was taken in the north of Scotland by Colonel Straughan* with a small body of troops, and hanged at Edinburgh on a gallows thirty feet high ; his body was buried under the gallows, and his quarters set upon the gates of the principal towns in Scotland ; but his behaviour was great and firm to the last. The marquis appeared openly for the king in the year 1643, and having routed a small party of Covenanters in Perthshire, acquired considerable renown ; but his little successes were very mischievous to the king's affairs, being always magnified beyond what they really were ; if his vanity was the occasion of breaking off the treaty of Uxbridge, and his fears lest King Charles II. should agree with the Scots, and revoke his commission before he had executed it, now hurried him to his own ruin.

The young king being in treaty with the Scots Covenanters at Breda, was forced to stifle his

mations of the people. A print was struck on the occasion representing him standing at the bar on his trial ; at the top of it was a medal of his head, with this inscription, "John Lilburne, saved by the power of the Lord, and the integrity of his jury, who are judges of law as well as fact, October 6, 1646." On the reverse were the names of the jury. He was a very popular character, as appears from the many petitions presented to the House in his favour during his imprisonment, one of which came from a number of women. When some were sent to seize his books, he persuaded them " to look to their own liberties, and let his books alone ;" and on his trial he behaved with singular intrepidity. After he was discharged by the jury, he was, by the order of Parliament, committed to the Tower. He seems to have been a bold and consistent oppugner of tyranny, under whatever form of government it was practised. He died a Quaker, at Eltham, August 28, 1658. The following character was given of him by Sir Thomas Wortley, in a song, at a feast kept by the prisoners in the Tower, in August, 1647 :

John Lilburne is a stirring blade,
  And understands the matter ;
He neither will king, bishops, lords,
  Nor th' House of Commons flatter.

John loves no power prerogative,
  But that derived from Sion ;
As for the mitre and the crown,
  Those two he looks awry on.

—Granger's History of England, vol. iii., p. 78, 8vo. Whitelocke's Mem., p. 383, 384, and 405. Dr. Grey, vol. i. p. 167, and vol. iii., p. 17.—ED.

* This is not accurate. Colonel Straughan's forces, in conjunction with others, fell on Lord Montrose's party, routed them, and took six hundred prisoners ; but the marquis himself escaped, though with difficulty, for his horse, pistols, belt, and scabbard were seized ; and two or three days after the fight he was taken, sixteen miles from the place of engagement, in a disguise, and sorely wounded, having been betrayed, some say, by Lord Aston, but, according to Bishop Burnet, by Mackland, of Assin.
—Dr. Grey, and Whitelocke's Memorials, p. 438, 439.—ED.

† If his successes were magnified beyond the truth, his character has also been handed down with the highest eulogiums. The Marquis of Montrose (says Mr. Granger) was comparable to the greatest heroes of antiquity. We meet with many instances of valour in this active reign, but Montrose is the only instance of heroism. Among other circumstances of indignity which accompanied his execution, the book of his exploits, a small octavo written in elegant Latin, which is now very scarce, was tied appendant to his neck.—Dr. Grey, and Granger's History of England, vol. ii., p. 245, 246, 8vo.—ED.

resentments for the death of the marquis, and submit to the following hard conditions : -
(1.) " That all persons excommunicated by the Kirk should be forbid the court.
(2.) " That the king by his solemn oath, and under his hand and seal, declare his allowance of the Covenant.
(3.) " That he confirm those acts of Parliament which enjoin the Covenant. That he establish the Presbyterian worship and discipline, and swear never to oppose or endeavour to alter them.
(4.) " That all civil matters be determined by Parliament ; and all ecclesiastical affairs by the Kirk.
(5.) " That his majesty ratify all that has been done in the Parliament of Scotland, in some late sessions, and sign the Covenant upon his arrival in that kingdom, if the Kirk desired it."*

The king arrived in Scotland June 23 ; but before his landing, the commissioners insisted on his signing the Covenant, and upon parting with all his old councillors, which he did, and was then conducted by the way of Aberdeen and St. Andrew's to his house at Faulkland. July 11, his majesty was proclaimed at the Cross at Edinburgh, but the ceremony of his coronation was deferred to the beginning of the next year. In the mean time, the English commonwealth was providing for a war which they saw was unavoidable ; and General Fairfax refusing to act against the Scots, his commission was immediately given to Cromwell, with the title of captain-general in chief of all the forces raised, and to be raised by authority of Parliament, within the commonwealth of England. Three days after, viz., June 29, he marched with eleven thousand foot and five thousand horse towards the borders of Scotland, being resolved not to wait for the Scots invading England; but to carry the war into their country. The Scots complained to the English Parliament of this conduct, as a breach of the Act of Pacification, and of the Covenant ; but were answered that they had already broken the peace by their treaty with Charles Stuart, whom they had not only received as their king, but promised to assist in recovering the crown of England. Their receiving the king was certainly their right as an independent nation ; but whether their engaging to assist him in recovering the crown of England was not declaring war, must be left to the reader.

July 22, the general crossed the Tweed, and marched his army almost as far as Edinburgh without much opposition, the country being deserted by reason of the terror of the name of Cromwell, and the reports that were spread of

*. Besides taking the Covenant, it was exacted of the king also to acknowledge twelve articles of repentance, in which were enumerated the sins of his father and grandfather, and idolatry of his mother ; and in which were declarations, that he sought the restitution of his rights for the sole advantage of religion, and in subordination to the kingdom of Christ.
—Mrs. Macaulay's History of England, vol. v., p. 62, 8vo.—ED. It is asserted by Jesse, in his " Court of England under the Stuarts," that the Scotch had the brutality to affix to the house in which Charles was lodged in Edinburgh one of the quarters of his adherent, the gallant Montrose. — Vol iii., p. 227. —C.

his cruelty in Ireland. Not a Scotsman appeared under sixty, nor a youth above six years old, to interrupt his march. All provisions were destroyed or removed to prevent the subsistence of the army, which was supplied from time to time by sea; but the general having made proclamation that no man should be injured in his person or goods who was not found in arms, the people took heart, and returned to their dwellings.

The Scots army, under the command of General Lesley, stood on the defensive, and watched the motions of the English all the month of August; the main body being intrenched within six miles of Edinburgh, to the number of thirty thousand of the best men that ever Scotland saw; General Cromwell did everything he could to draw them to a battle, till, by the fall of rain and bad weather, he was obliged to retreat to Musselborough, and from thence to Dunbar, where he was reduced to the utmost straits, having no way left but to conquer or die.* In this extremity he summoned the officers to prayer; after which he bid all about him take heart, for God had heard them; then walking in the Earl of Roxborough's gardens, that lay under the hill upon which the Scots army was encamped, and discovering by perspective glasses that they were coming down to attack him, he said God was delivering them into his hands. That night proving very rainy, the general refreshed his men in the town, and ordered them to take particular care of their firelocks, which the Scots neglected, who were all the night coming down the hill. Early next morning, September 3, the general, with a strong party of horse, beat their guards, and then advancing with his whole army, after about an hour's dispute, entered their camp and carried all before him: about four thousand Scots fell in battle, ten thousand were made prisoners, with fifteen hundred arms, and all their artillery and ammunition; the loss of the English amounting to no more than about three hundred men.

It is an odd reflection Lord Clarendon† makes upon this victory: "Never was victory obtained," says his lordship, "with less lamentation; for as Cromwell had great argument of triumph, so the king was glad of it, as the greatest happiness that could befall him, in the loss of so strong a body of his enemies."‡ Such was the encouragement the Scots had to fight for their king!

Immediately after this action, the general took possession of Edinburgh, which was, in a manner, deserted by the clergy; some having shut themselves up in the castle, and others fled with their effects to Stirling; the general, to deliver them from their fright, sent a trumpet to the castle, to assure the governor that the ministers might return to their churches,

and preach without any disturbance from him, for he had no quarrel with the Scots nation on the score of religion.* But the ministers replied that, having no security for their persons, they thought it their duty to reserve themselves for better times. Upon which the general wrote to the governor,

"That his kindness offered to the ministers in the castle was without any fraudulent reserve; that if their Master's service was their principal concern, they would not be so excessively afraid of suffering for it. That those divines had misreported the conduct of his party, when they charged them with persecuting the ministers of Christ in England; for the ministers in England (says he) are supported, and have liberty to preach the Gospel, though not to rail at their superiors at discretion; nor, under a pretended privilege of character, to overtop the civil powers, or debase them as they please. No man has been disturbed in England or Ireland for preaching the Gospel; nor has any minister been molested in Scotland since the coming of the army hither; speaking truth becomes the ministers of Christ; but when ministers pretend to a glorious reformation, and lay the foundation thereof in getting to themselves power, and can make worldly mixtures to accomplish the same, such as the late agreement with their king, they may know that the Sion promised is not to be built with such untempered mortar. And for the unjust invasion they [the ministers] mention, time was when an army out of Scotland came into England, not called by the supreme authority: we have said in our papers with what hearts and upon what account we came, and the Lord has heard us, though you would not, upon as solemn an appeal as any experience can parallel. I have nothing to say to you but that I am,

"Sir, your humble servant,
"O. Cromwell."†

The Scots ministers, in their reply to this letter, objected to the general his opening the pulpit-doors to all intruders, by which means a flood of errors was broke in upon the nation.‡ To which the general replied, "We look on ministers as helpers of, not lords over, the faith of God's people: I appeal to their consciences, whether any denying of their doctrines, or dissenting from them, will not incur the censure of

---

* Life of Cromwell, p. 178. Burnet's Hist., vol. i., p. 74, Edinb. edit. † Vol. iii., p. 377. ‡ Dr. Grey adds the reason which Lord Clarendon assigns for the king's rejoicing in this victory; which was, his apprehension that if the Scots had prevailed, they would have shut him up in prison the next day; whereas, after this defeat, they looked upon the king as one they might stand in need of, gave him more liberty than they had before allowed, permitted his servants to wait on him, and began to talk of a Parliament and of a time for his coronation. —ED.

* It is a proof of this, that while Oliver Cromwell was at Edinburgh, he attended Divine worship in the great church there, when Mr. William Derham preached, and called Oliver a usurper to his face. He was so far from resenting this, that he invited Mr. Derham to visit him in the evening, when they supped together in great harmony. Oliver observed, however, "that it was well known to him how much he and his brethren disliked him; but they might assure themselves that, if any of the Stuart line came to the throne, they would find their little fingers greater than his loins."—Dr. Gibbon's Account of the Cromwell Family, annexed to his Funeral Sermon for William Cromwell, Esq., p. 47.—ED.

† Life of Cromwell, p. 182.

‡ The Scotch clergy protested against the preaching of laymen, which was allowed by the English general; and claimed for their own order the exclusive right of ordaining to the ministry. This was assailing the stronghold of Cromwell's tolerant policy, and he met it with an indignant refutation.—Price's Hist. of Nonconformity, vol. ii., p. 454.—C.

a sectary; and what is this but to deny Christians their liberty, and assume the infallible chair? Where do you find in Scripture that preaching is included within your function? Though an approbation from men has order in it, and may be well, yet he that hath not a better than that, hath none at all.

"I hope He that ascended up on high may give his gifts to whom he pleases; and if those gifts be the seal of mission, are not you envious, though Eldad and Medad prophesy? You know who has bid us covet earnestly the best gifts, but chiefly, that we may prophesy; which the apostle explains to be a speaking to instruction, edification, and comfort, which the instructed, edified, and comforted can best tell the energy and effect of.

"Now, if this be evidence, take heed you envy not for your own sakes, lest you be guilty of a greater fault than Moses reproved in Joshua, when he envied for his sake. Indeed, you err through mistake of the Scriptures. Approbation is an act of convenience in respect of order, not of necessity, to give faculty to preach the Gospel.

"Your pretended fear lest error should step in, is like the man that would keep all the wine out of the country, lest men should be drunk. It will be found an unjust and unwise jealousy to deny a man the liberty he hath by nature, upon a supposition he may abuse it. When he doth abuse it, then judge."*

The governor complained to the general that the Parliament at Westminster had fallen from their principles, not being true to the ends of the Covenant. And then adds, with the ministers, that men of secular employments had usurped the office of the ministry, to the scandal of the Reformed churches.

In answer to the first part of this expostulation, General Cromwell desired to know whether their bearing witness to themselves was a good evidence of their having prosecuted the ends of the Covenant? "To infer this," says he, "is to have too favourable an opinion of your own judgment and impartiality. Your doctrines and practice ought to be tried by the Word of God, and other people must have a liberty of examining them upon these heads, and of giving sentence."†

As to the charge of indulging the use of the pulpit to the laity, the general admits it, and adds, "Are ye troubled that Christ is preached? does it scandalize the Reformed churches, and Scotland in particular? is it against the Covenant? away with the Covenant, if it be so. I thought the Covenant and these men would have been willing that any should speak good of the name of Christ; if not, it is no Covenant of God's approving; nor the kirk you mention so much the spouse of Christ."

The general, in one of his letters, lays considerable stress upon the success of their arms, after a most solemn appeal to God on both sides. To which the Scots governor replied, "We have not so learned Christ, as to hang the equity of a cause upon events." To which Cromwell answers, "We could wish that blindness had not been upon your eyes to those marvellous dispensations which God has lately

wrought in England. But did you not solemnly appeal and pray? Did not we do so too? And ought not we and you to think with fear and trembling on the hand of the great God in this mighty and strange appearance of his, and not slightly call it an event? Were not your expectations and ours renewed from time to time, while we waited on God to see how he would manifest himself upon our appeals? And shall we, after all these our prayers, fastings, tears, expectations, and solemn appeals, call these bare events? The Lord pity you."

From this correspondence the reader may form a judgment of the governing principles of the Scots and English at this time; the former were so inviolably attached to their Covenant, that they would depart from nothing that was inconsistent with it. The English, after seeking God in prayer, judged of the goodness of their cause by the appearance of Providence in its favour; most of the officers and soldiers were men of strict devotion, but went upon this mistaken principle, that God would never appear for a bad cause after a solemn appeal to him for decision. However, the Scots lost their courage, and surrendered the impregnable Castle of Edinburgh into the hands of the conqueror, December 24, the garrison having liberty to march out with their baggage to Burnt Island in Fife; and soon after the whole kingdom was subdued.

The Provincial Assembly of London met this year, as usual, in the months of May and November, but did nothing remarkable; the Parliament waited to reconcile them to the Engagement, and prolonged the time limited for taking it; but when they continued inflexible, and instead of submitting to the present powers, were plotting with the Scots, it was resolved to clip their wings, and make some examples, as a terror to the rest. June 21, the committee for regulating the universities was ordered to tender the Engagement to all such officers, masters, and fellows as had neglected to take it, and upon their refusal, to displace them. Accordingly, in the University of Cambridge, Mr. Vines, Dr. Rainbow, and some others, were displaced, and succeeded by Mr. Sydrach Sympson, Mr. Jo. Sadler, and Mr. Dell. In the University of Oxford, Dr. Reynolds, the vice-chancellor, refused the Engagement, but after some time offered to take it, in hopes of saving his deanery of Christ Church; but the Parliament resenting the example, took advantage of his forfeiture, and gave the deanery to Dr. John Owen, an Independent divine, who took possession of it March 18, 1650–1.*

Upon the resignation of the vice-chancellor, Dr. Daniel Greenwood, principal of Brazen Nose College, and a Presbyterian divine, was appointed his successor, October 12, and on the 15th of January following, Oliver Cromwell, now in Scotland, was chosen unanimously, in full convocation, chancellor of the university, in the room of the Earl of Pembroke, lately deceased.‡ When the doctor and masters who were sent to Edinburgh acquainted him with the choice, he wrote a letter to the university, in which, after a modest refusal of their favour, he adds, "If

---

* Whitelocke, p. 458. Collyer's Ecclesiastical History, p. 863.   † Ibid., p. 864.

* Baxter's Life, p. 64.

† Wood's Fasti, p. 92; or Athen. Oxon., vol. ii., p. 772.

these arguments prevail not; and that I must continue this honour till I can personally serve you, you shall not want my prayers that piety and learning may flourish among you, and be rendered useful and subservient to that great and glorious kingdom of our Lord Jesus Christ; of the approach of which so plentiful an effusion of the Holy Spirit upon those hopeful plants among you is one of the best presages." When the general's letter was read in convocation, the House resounded with cheerful acclamations. Dr. Greenwood continued vice-chancellor two years, but was then displaced for his *disaffection to the government*, and the honour was conferred on Dr. Owen. Thus by degrees the Presbyterians lost their influence in the universities, and delivered them up into the hands of the Independents.

To strengthen the hands of the government yet farther, the Parliament, by an ordinance bearing date September 20, took away all the penal statutes for religion.* The preamble sets forth, "that divers religious and peaceable people, well-affected to the commonwealth, having not only been molested and imprisoned, but brought into danger of abjuring their country, or, in case of return, to suffer death, as felons, by sundry acts made in the times of former kings and queens of this nation, against recusants not coming to church, &c., they therefore enact and ordain,

"That all the clauses, articles, and provisoes in the ensuing acts of Parliament, viz., 1 Eliz., 23 Eliz., 35 Eliz., and all and every branch, clause, article, or proviso, in any other act or ordinance of Parliament, whereby any penalty or punishment is imposed, or meant to be imposed on any person whatsoever, for not repairing to their respective parish churches, or for not keeping of holydays, or for not hearing Common Prayer, &c., shall be, and are hereby wholly repealed and made void.

"And to the end that no profane or licentious persons may take occasion, by the repeal of the said laws, to neglect the performance of religious duties, it is farther ordained that all persons not having a reasonable excuse, shall, on every Lord's Day, and day of public thanksgiving or humiliation, resort to some place of public worship; or be present at some other place, in the practice of some religious duty, either of prayer or preaching, reading or expounding the Scriptures."

By this law the doors were set open, and the state was at liberty to employ all such in their service as would take the oaths to the civil government, without any regard to their religious principles.

Sundry severe ordinances were made for suppressing of vice, error, and all sorts of profaneness and impiety.† May 10, it was ordained

"that incest and adultery should be made felony; and that fornication should be punished with three months' imprisonment for the first offence; and the second offence should be felony without benefit of clergy. Common bawds, or persons who keep lewd houses, are to be set in the pillory; to be whipped, and marked in the forehead with the letter B, and then committed to the House of Correction for three years for the first offence; and, for the second, to suffer death, provided the prosecution be within twelve months."*

June 28, it was ordained "that every nobleman who shall be convicted of profane cursing and swearing, by the oath of one or more witnesses, or by his own confession, shall pay for the first offence thirty shillings to the poor of the parish; a baronet or knight, twenty shillings; an esquire, ten shillings; a gentleman, six shillings and eightpence; and all inferior persons, three shillings and fourpence. For the second offence they are to pay double, according to their qualities above mentioned. And for the tenth offence they are to be judged common swearers and cursers, and to be bound over to their good behaviour for three years. The like punishment for women, whose fines are to be determined according to their own or their husbands' quality."†

August 9, an ordinance was passed for punishing blasphemous and execrable opinions. The preamble takes notice that, "though several laws had been made for promoting reformation in doctrines and manners, yet there were divers men and women who had lately discovered monstrous opinions, even such as tended to the dissolution of human society; the Parliament, therefore, according to their declaration of September 27, 1649, in which they said they should be ready to testify their displeasure against such offenders, by strict and effectual proceedings against them who should abuse and turn into licentiousness the liberty given in matters of religion, do therefore ordain and enact,

"That any persons not distempered in their

they were not sufficiently mindful of the delicate nature of their task. Their vocation was high and holy, but the mode in which they sought to accomplish their object frequently tended to its defeat, rather than its furtherance. Men are not to be drilled into morality—they cannot be made virtuous by laws. Vice may be driven from the walks of public life, but unless the sentiments of a community be improved—unless its moral judgments be rectified, the same propensities will be indulged under other forms—forms less obtrusive, but not less fatal. The unnatural restraint under which the people were held during the ascendency of the Parliament, formed an artificial character, and reacted with fearful energy at the Restoration. At the same time, it should in fairness be remembered, that the men who now ruled the nation combined, with laws against specific vices, a vigorous and effective course of religious training. The result of the two processes was a mixed state of things. There was much of good, and much of evil in the existing condition of society. The elements of light and darkness were strangely blended; religious principles were gathering strength for the conflict they subsequently sustained; while hypocrisy was preparing a large portion of the people for the infidelity and licentiousness which flourished under the patronage of the Second Charles. — *Dr. Price's Hist. Nonconformity*, vol. ii., p. 459.—C.

* Scobel, p. 121.　　　　　† Ibid., p. 123.

---

* Scobel, p. 131.

† The present rulers of the nation were engaged in an enterprise of unparalleled difficulty, and could only hope to succeed as they invigorated and raised the tone of public feeling. Having demolished the ancient landmarks of English sympathy and action, they were concerned to generate a new order of sentiments, nobler in its character, and more ample in its range. For this purpose, they sought to banish vice from the walks of public life—to brand it with infamy—to coerce it from society, as its weakness, no less than its disgrace. In pursuing this object,

brains, who shall maintain any mere creature to be God, or to be infinite, almighty, &c., or that shall deny the holiness of God; or shall maintain that all acts of wickedness and unrighteousness are not forbidden in Holy Scripture; or that God approves them : any one who shall maintain that acts of drunkenness, adultery, swearing, &c., are not in themselves shameful, wicked, sinful, and impious; or that there is not any real difference between moral good and evil, &c., all such persons shall suffer six months' imprisonment for the first offence; and for the second 'shall be banished; and if they return without license, shall be treated as felons."*

Though several ordinances had been made heretofore for the strict observation of the Lord's Day, the present House of Commons thought fit to enforce them by another, dated April 19, 1650, in which they ordain "that all goods cried or put to sale on the Lord's Day, or other days of humiliation and thanksgiving appointed by authority, shall be seized. No wagoner or drover shall travel on the Lord's Day, on penalty of 10s. for every offence. No persons shall travel in boats, coaches, or on horses, except to church, on penalty of 10s. The like penalty for being in a tavern. And where distress is not to be made, the offender is to be put into the stocks six hours. All peace-officers are required to make diligent search for discovering offenders; and in case of neglect, the justice of peace is fined £5, and every constable 20s." Such was the severity of these times.†

The Parliament having ordered the sale of bishops' lands, and the lands of deans and chapters, and vested the money in the hands of trustees, as has been related, appointed this year, April 5, part of the money to be appropriated for the support and maintenance of such late bishops, deans, prebendaries, singing-men, choristers, and other members, officers, and persons destitute of maintenance, whose respective offices, places, and livelihoods were taken away and abolished, distributing and proportioning the same according to their necessities. How well this was executed I cannot determine; but it was a generous act of compassion, and more than the Church of England would do for the Nonconformists at the Restoration.‡

A motion being made in the House about translating all law-books into the English language, Mr. Whitelocke made a learned speech on the argument, wherein he observes, that "Moses read the law to the Jews in the Hebrew language; that the laws of all the Eastern nations were in their mother tongue; the laws of Constantinople were in Greek; at Rome they were in Latin; in France, Spain, Germany, Sweden, Denmark, and other places, their laws are published in their native language. As for our own country," says he, "those who can read the Saxon character may find the laws of our ancestors in that language. Pursuant to this regulation, William, duke of Normandy, commonly called the Conqueror, commanded the laws to be published in English, that none might pretend ignorance. He observes farther, that by 36 Eliz., cap. iii., it was ordered that all

pleadings should be in English; and even in the reigns of those princes, wherein our statutes were enrolled in French, the sheriffs were obliged to proclaim them in English, because the people were deeply concerned to know the laws of their country, and not to be kept in ignorance of the rule by which their interests and duty were directed."*

The arguments in this speech were so forcible that the House agreed unanimously to a bill, wherein they ordain, "that all books of law be translated into English; and all proceedings in any court of justice, except the Court of Admiralty, after Easter term, 1651, shall be in English only; and all writs, &c., shall be in a legible hand, and not in court-hand, on forfeiture of £20 for the first offence, half to the commonwealth, and the other half to them that will sue for the same."† And though this regulation ceased at the Restoration, as all other ordinances did that were made in these times, the late Parliament has thought fit to revive it.

From this time we may date the rise of the people called Quakers, in whom most of the enthusiasts of these times centred; their first leader was George Fox, born at Drayton in Lancashire, 1624; his father, being a poor weaver,‡ put him apprentice to a country shoemaker, but having a peculiar turn of mind for religion, he went away from his master, and wandered up and down the country like a hermit, in a leathern doublet; at length his friends, hearing he was at London, persuaded him to return home, and settle in some regular course of employment; but after he had been some months in the country, he went from his friends a second time, in the year 1646, and threw off all farther attendance on the public service in the churches: the reasons he gave for his conduct were, because it was revealed to him that a

* Whitelocke, p. 460.   † Scobel, p. 155.

‡ It is to be wished that Mr. Neal had not used this epithet, poor. It is not in the author whom he quotes, was needless, and has the appearance of contempt. The parents of Fox were truly respectable; his father, Christopher Fox, of such a virtuous life, that his neighbours called him righteous Christer; his mother, of the stock of martyrs, and a woman of qualifications superior to the generality of her circumstances in life; they were both members of the National Church, distinguished by piety, and cherished the religious turn of mind which their son discovered in his earliest years. Virtuous and sober manners, a peculiar staidness of mind, and gravity of demeanour, marked his youth. His chief employment under his master, who also dealt in wool and cattle, was to keep sheep, which was well suited to his disposition both for innocence and solitude. He acquitted himself with a fidelity and diligence that conduced much to the success of his master's affairs. It was a custom with him to ratify his dealing with the word *verily*, to which he so firmly and conscientiously adhered, that those who knew him would remark, "If George says *verily*, there is no altering." Mr. Neal's expression, " he went away from his master," may be understood as intimating a clandestine and dishonourable leaving his master's service, which was not the case. He did not begin his solitary travels till after his apprenticeship was finished, and he had returned home to his parents. The leathern dress was adopted by him on account of its simplicity and its durableness, as it required little repairing, which was convenient to him in his wandering and unsettled course of life.—*Sewel's Hist.*, p. 6–12 Eand *Gough's History of the Quakers*, vol. i., p. 60.— D.

* Scobel, p. 124.   † Ibid., p. 119.   ‡ Ibid., p. 111.

learned education at the university was no qualification for a minister, but that all depended on the anointing of the Spirit, and that God, who made the world, did not dwell in temples made with hands. In the year 1647 he travelled into Derbyshire and Nottinghamshire, walking through divers towns and villages, which way soever his mind turned, in a solitary manner. He fasted much (says my author), and walked often abroad in retired places, with no other companion but his Bible. He would sometimes sit in a hollow tree all day, and frequently walked about the fields in the night, like a man possessed with deep melancholy : which the writer of his life calls the " time of the first working of the Lord upon him."* Towards the latter end of this year he began first to set up for a teacher of others, about Duckinfield and Manchester; the principal argument of his discourse being, that people should receive the inward Divine teachings of the Lord, and take that for their rule.

In the year 1648, there being a dissolution of all government, both civil and ecclesiastical, George Fox waxed bold,† and travelled through the counties of Leicester, Northampton, and Derby, speaking to the people in market-places, &c., about the inward light of Christ within them.‡ At this time, says my author,§ he apprehended the Lord had forbid him to put off his hat to any one, high or low ; he was required also to speak to the people, without distinction, in the language of thou and thee. He was not to bid people good-morrow or goodnight ; neither might he bend his knee to the chief magistrate in the nation ; the women‖ that followed him would not make a courtesy to their superiors, nor comply with the common forms of speech. Both men and women affected a plain and simple dress, distinct from the fashion of the times. They neither gave nor accepted any titles of respect or honour, nor would they call any man master on earth. They refused to take an oath on the most solemn occasion. These, and the like peculiarities, he

* Sewel's History of the Quakers, . 6–12.
† The circumstances of this period, as stated by Gough, will show the propriety of our author's language here, and preclude the suspicion that has fallen on him, of intending to insinuate that the boldness of George Fox was criminal, and that the dissolution of government had rendered him licentious. At this time the Independents and Republicans had accomplished their purpose; regal dominion, the peculiar privileges of the nobilty, and the office of bishops were abolished. Their professed principles were in favour of civil and religious liberty. The places of public worship seem, for a season, to have been open to teachers of different denominations, and not uncommonly appropriated to theological discussion and disputation between the teachers or members of various sects. These propitious circumstances furnished Fox and others with opportunities of disseminating their opinions, and a fair opportunity naturally inspirits and imboldens to any undertaking.— Gough's History, vol. i, p. 72.—ED.
‡ The words of Sewel are, " that every man was enlightened by the divine light of Christ." The term used by this historian for the followers of Fox is fellow-believers, without any reference to their sex ; nor does his narrative show that they consisted more of women than men, which Mr. Neal's expression seems to intimate.—ED.
§ History of the Quakers, p. 18.
‖ See note ‡ of this page.

supported by such passages of Scripture as these : " Swear not all ;" " How can ye believe who receive honour one of another, and seek not the honour which comes from God only ?" But these marks of distinction which George Fox and his followers were so tenacious of, unhappily brought them into a great deal of trouble when they were called to appear before the civil magistrate.

In the year 1649 he grew more troublesome, and began to interrupt the public ministers in time of Divine service : his first essay of this kind was at Nottingham, where the minister, preaching from these words of St. Peter, " We have a more sure word of prophecy," &c., told the people that they were to try all doctrines, opinions, and religions by the Holy Scriptures. Upon which, George Fox stood up in the middle of the congregation and said, " Oh no ! it is not the Scripture, but it is the Holy Spirit by which opinions and religions are to be tried ; for it was the Spirit that led people into all truth, and gave them the knowledge of it." And continuing his speech to the disturbance of the congregation, the officers were obliged to turn him out of the church, and carry him to the sheriff's house ; next day he was committed to the castle, but was quickly released without any other punishment.* After this he disturbed the minister of Mansfield in time of Divine service, for which he was set in the stocks, and turned out of the town.† The like treatment he met with

* Mr. Neal's account of this imprisonment of George Fox is censured by a late historian as not strictly true, nor supported by his authority, Sewel and, through a partial bias, a very palliative narration. The fact, more exactly and fully stated, is this : That Fox was not taken immediately from the church to the sheriff's house, but to prison, and put into a place so filthy and intolerably noisome, that the smell thereof was very grievous to be endured. At night he was carried before the mayor, aldermen, and sheriffs of the town, and after examination was recommitted. But one of the sheriffs, whose name was Reckless, being much affected with the sentiments he had advanced, removed him to his own house. During his residence there Mr. Fox was visited by persons of considerable condition ; the sheriff, as well as his wife and family, were greatly affected with his doctrine, insomuch that he and several others exhorted the people and the magistrates to repentance. This provoked the latter to remove Fox back to the common prison, where he lay till the assizes. When he was to have been brought before the judge, the officer was so dilatory in the execution of his business that the court was broken up before he was conducted to it. He was, on this, again ordered into the common jail, and detained there some time longer. As far as appears, he was imprisoned, detained in prison, and released, at the mere will and pleasure of the magistrates of Nottingham, without any legal cause assigned. " Such arbitrary exertion of power," well observes my author, " ill agrees with a regard for cherished privileges and equal liberty."—Gough's Hist. of the Quakers, vol. i., p. 83, 84. Sewel's Hist., p. 21, 22.—ED.
‡ Mr. Neal is considered as passing over this treatment of Fox in too " cursory a manner ;" and is blamed for placing his conduct in the most invidious light it would bear, disturbing the minister. But, surely, if Mr. Fox spoke while the minister was preaching, without waiting till he had finished his discourse, it was disturbing him by an unseasonable interruption. But this circumstance is not to be clearly ascertained by Sewel. The treatment which Fox met with was iniquitous and violent to an ex-

at Market Bosworth, and several other towns.* At length the magistrates of Derby confined him six months in prison, for uttering divers blasphemous opinions,† pursuant to a late act of treme degree. The hearers of the minister " converted the place of Divine worship into a scene of lawless riot, and the time set apart for the service of God into an enormous abuse of a fellow-creature ; manifesting their religion to be such," observes Mr. Gough, with great propriety, " at the time when it should most affect their minds, as admitted of injury, revenge, and violating the peace and order of society. For they assaulted Mr. Fox in a furious manner, struck him down, and beat him cruelly with their hands, Bibles, and sticks, whereby he was grievously bruised. After they had thus vented their rage, they haled him out, and put him into the stocks, where he sat some hours ; and then they took him before a magistrate, who, seeing how grossly he had been abused, after much threatening, set him at liberty. But still the rude multitude, insatiate in abuse, stoned him out of the town, though hardly able to go, or well to stand, by reason of their violent usage." It should be remarked here, that the magistrate's conduct was extremely culpable in not inflicting a punishment on these disturbers of the peace, for this unjust and violent attack on a man who had done them no harm, but meant to do them good, and in not affording to him his protection.—*Gough's History,* vol. i., p. 84–86.—ED.   * Sewel, p. 22.

† This was the language of the mittimus by which Fox and another were committed to the House of Correction ; we regret that Mr. Neal should have adopted it without giving his reader the grounds on which the severe epithet was applied to their opinions. After the service of a lecture, at which Mr. Fox had attended, was finished, he spoke what was on his mind, and was heard without molestation ; when he had done, an officer took him by the hand and carried him before the magistrates. Being asked, " Why he came thither ?" he answered, that " God had moved him to it ;" and added, " that God did not dwell in temples made with hands ; and that all their preaching, baptism, and sacrifices, would never sanctify them ; but that they ought to look unto Christ in them, and not unto him, for it is Christ that sanctifies." As they were very full of words, sometimes disputing and sometimes deriding, he told them " they were not to dispute of God and Christ, but to obey him."- At last they asked him " if he was sanctified ?"-he replied, " Yes :" " if he had no sin ?" his answer was, " Christ, my Saviour, hath taken away my sin, and in him there is no sin." To the next question, " How he and his friends knew Christ was in them ?" he replied, " By his Spirit.' which he had given us." Then they were asked " if any of them were Christ ?" to which insidious query he answered, " Nay, we are nothing ; Christ is all.", He was next interrogated, " If a man steal, is it no sin ?" to which his reply was, " All unrighteousness is sin." With what candour, with what propriety, with what truth, could the charge of blasphemy be grounded on these declarations, especially by the magistrates who examined and committed him ? The names to the mittimus were Ger. Bennet and Nath. Barton ; both of them were Independents, the latter an officer and preacher ; men whose tenets implied a supernatural influence, and admitted no interference of the civil magistrate in spiritual concerns, but were pointed in favour of universal toleration ; one of whom could himself have no commission to preach but on the ground of God's moving him to it. These were the men who accused Fox of blasphemy, and imprisoned him ; " a remarkable instance," observes Mr. Gough, " of the inconsistency of men with themselves in different stations of life ;" a remarkable instance, it may be added, how the law may be wrested, and justice perverted by passion and prejudice. Mr. Neal's manner of relating this transaction unhappily conceals the criminal conduct of these magistrates, and is too much calcu-

Parliament for that purpose. By this time there began to appear some other visionaries, of the same make and complexion with George Fox, who spoke in places of public resort, being moved, as they said, by the Holy Ghost ; and even some women, contrary to the modesty of their sex, went about streets, and entered into churches, crying down the teaching of men, and exhorting people to attend to the light within themselves.

It was in the year 1650 that these wandering lights first received the denomination of. Quakers, upon this ground, that their speaking to the people was usually attended with convulsive agitations and shakings of the body. All their speakers had these tremblings, which they gloried in, asserting it to be the character of a good man to tremble before God. When George Fox appeared before Gervas Bennet, Esq., one of the justices of Derby, October 30, 1650, he had one of his agitations, or fits of trembling, upon him, and with a loud voice and vehement emotion of body, bid the justice and those about him tremble at the Word of the Lord ; whereupon the justice gave him and his friends the name of Quakers, which being agreeable to their common behaviour, quickly became the distinguishing denomination of this people.*

At length they disturbed the public worship by appearing in ridiculous habits, with emblematical or typical representations of some impending calamity ;· they also took the liberty of giving ministers the reproachful names of hire-

lated to perpetuate the prejudice which misled and governed them.—*Sewel's History,* p. 24, and *Gough's History,* vol. i., p. 90–94.—ED.

* The above paragraph has given great offence, and is severely censured by Mr. Gough, as " an opprobrious description, approaching to scurrility." The plain fact, as it stands in Sewel, has none of those circumstances of agitations, a loud voice, and vehement emotions, with which Mr. Neal has described it, and for which he has quoted no authority. Fox, according to Sewel, having bid the justice and those about him to " tremble at the Word of the Lord," Mr. Bennet took hold of this weighty saying with such an airy mind, that from thence he took occasion to call him and his friends, scornfully, Quakers. This name was eagerly taken up and spread among the people. As to the convulsive emotions with which it is said the preaching of these Christians was accompanied, it is but fair to hear their advocate. " We readily admit," says Mr. Gough, " these promulgators of primitive Christianity had no university education, were not trained in schools of oratory. It was plain truth and righteousness they sought to follow and recommend in a plain, simple way, without the studied decorations of fine language, or the engaging attractions of a graceful motion ; they spoke not to the head or to the eye, but to the hearts of their auditors. Being themselves animated, and deeply affected in spirit with the inward feeling of the power of that truth, to the knowledge of which they aimed to bring others, that thereby they might be saved ; an unaffected warmth of zeal in recommending righteousness, and testifying against vice and wickedness, might produce a warmth of expression, and action also, which to an invidious eye might appear convulsive ; but their convulsions did not bereave them of understanding ; they spake with the spirit and with the understanding also, of things which they knew, and testified of things which they had seen. And their doctrine was often effectual to open the understanding of their hearers, to see clearly the state of their minds, both what they were and what they ought to be."— *Gough's History,* vol. i., p. 96, note.—ED.

lings, deceivers of the people, false prophets, &c. Some of them went through divers towns and villages naked, denouncing judgments and calamities upon the nation. Some have famished and destroyed themselves by deep melancholy; and others have undertaken to raise their friends from the dead. Mr. Baxter says* many Franciscan friars and other papists have been disguised speakers in their assemblies; but little credit is to be given to such reports.†

It cannot be expected that such an unsettled people should have a uniform system of rational principles. Their first and chief design, if they had any, was to reduce all revealed religion to allegory; and because some had laid too great stress upon rites and ceremonies, these would have neither order nor regularity, nor stated seasons of worship, but all must arise from the inward impulse of their spirits. Agreeably to this rule, they declared against all sorts of clergy or settled ministers; against people's assembling in steeple-houses; against fixed times‡ of public devotion, and, consequently, against the observation of the Sabbath. Their own meetings were occasional, and when they met, one or another spake as they were moved from within, and sometimes they departed without any one's being moved to speak at all.

The doctrines they delivered were as vague and uncertain§ as the principles from which

---

* Baxter's Life, p. 77.

† If but little credit is to be given to such reports, it may be asked, Why are they introduced, when, if not refuted, they tend to mislead the reader, and to fix a reproach on an innocent people? Is it becoming the candour and dignity of an historian, by recording, to appear to give them a sanction? As to the case in hand, Mr. Baxter, on whose authority Mr. Neal speaks, though he was a great and excellent man, was not entirely exempt from the influence of prejudice and credulity. In general, stories to the discredit of a new, despised, and hated sect, are often eagerly adopted and spread with circumstances of aggravation. So it happened to the first Christians. This has befallen the Methodists in our times. And the Quakers, being particular objects of priestly indignation, had reason to complain of this. They were often confounded with an ephemeron sect, whose principles were totally incompatible with theirs, called Ranters, and whose practices outraged all decency and order. An active preacher among the Quakers, Mr. Edward Burroughs, and the celebrated Barclay, wrote against the practices of these people.—*Gough's History*, vol. i., p. 128, 129, note; and vol. iii., p. 15.—Ed.

‡ This is not accurate, or is applicable only to the infancy of the sect. For, though they did not esteem one house more holy than another, and believed all times equally the Lord's, and that all days should be Sabbaths, or times of continual rest and abstinence from evil, yet, as soon as their numbers were sufficient for the purpose, they held fixed and regular meetings for worship, particularly on the first day of the week, which they chose as more convenient, because more generally accepted than any other. In 1654, meetings were settled in many places in the north, and also in the city of London, which were held in private houses, till the body growing too large to be accommodated in them, a house known by the name of Bull-and-Mouth, in Martin's-le-Grand, near Aldersgate-street, was hired for a meeting-house. And no body of Christians were more open, steady, and regular, than they have been in their public associations for worship or discipline. —*Sewel's History*, p. 80, 84. *Gough's History*, vol. i., p. 144 and 509.—Ed.

§ The account which Mr. Neal gives of the senti-

---

they acted. They denied the Holy Scriptures to be the only rule of their faith, calling it a dead letter, and maintaining that every man had a light within himself, which was a sufficient rule. They denied the received doctrine of the Trinity and incarnation. They disowned the sacraments of baptism and the Lord's Supper; nay, some of them proceeded so far as to deny a Christ without them; or, at least, to place more of their dependance upon a Christ within. They spake little or nothing, says Mr. Baxter,* about the depravity of nature; about the covenant of grace; about pardon of sin, and reconciliation with God; or about moral duties.† But the disturbance they gave to the public religion for a course of years was so insufferable, that the magistrates could not avoid punishing them as disturbers of the peace; though of late they are become a more sober and inoffensive people; and by the wisdom of their managers, have formed themselves into a

ments and practices of the Quakers, in this and the preceding paragraph, being delivered as the assertions of individuals only, and deriving their complexion from their different tastes, capacities, and views, would, to the public eye, wear the aspect of variety and uncertainty. But long before Mr. Neal wrote, their principles had assumed a systematic form. Penn had published his Key, and Robert Barclay his Catechism and Confession of Faith, and that elaborate work, his Apology. The propositions illustrated and defended in this treatise exhibit a concise view of the chief principles of the Quakers, and, that they may speak for themselves, we will give them in the Appendix, No. 12.—Ed.   * Baxter, p. 77.

† This quotation is not correct. Mr. Baxter's words, concerning the strain of their preaching, are these: "They speak much for the dwelling and working of the Spirit in us, but little of justification and the pardon of sin, and our reconciliation with God through Jesus Christ." Here is nothing said about their neglecting to insist on "moral duties." The great object of Fox's zeal, we are told, was a heavenly temper and a life of righteousness, and his endeavours to propagate true religion and righteousness were not confined to public or private meetings, but exerted in other places, as occasion offered; particularly in courts of judicature, to admonish to justice, and caution against oppression; in markets, to recommend truth, candour, and fair dealings, and to bear his testimony against fraud and deceitful merchandise: at public-houses of entertainment, to warn against indulging intemperance, by supplying their guests with more liquor than would do them good; at schools and in private families, to exhort to the training up of children and servants to sobriety, in the fear of their Maker; to testify against vain sports, plays, and shows, as tending to draw people into vanity and libertinism, and from that state of circumspection and attentive consideration wherein our salvation is to be wrought out, forewarning all of the great day of account for all the deeds done in the body. This was certainly insisting on moral duties, and bringing home the principles of righteousness to the various circumstances of human life with much propriety and energy.—*Gough's History*, vol. i., p. 67, 75.—Ed.

,sort of body politic, and are in general very worthy members of society.

CHAPTER II.

FROM THE CORONATION OF KING CHARLES II. IN
SCOTLAND, TO THE PROTECTORSHIP OF OLIVER
CROMWELL.—1651.

THE coronation of King Charles by the Scots,
which had been deferred hitherto, being now
thought necessary to give life to their cause,
was solemnized at Scone on New-Year's day,
1651, with as much magnificence as their circumstances would. admit,* when his majesty
took the following oath: "I, Charles, king of
Great Britain, France, and Ireland, do assure
and declare, by my solemn oath, in the presence
of Almighty God, the searcher of all hearts, my
allowance and approbation of the national Covenant, and of the solemn League and Covenant ;
and faithfully oblige myself to prosecute the
ends thereof in my station and calling ;. and
that I myself and successors shall consent and
agree to all the acts of Parliament enjoining the
national Covenant, and the solemn League and
Covenant, and fully establish Presbyterian government, the Directory of Worship, Confession of
Faith, and Catechisms, in the kingdom of Scotland, as they are approved by the General Assembly of this Kirk, and Parliament of this kingdom; and that I will give my royal word and
assent to all acts of Parliament passed, or to be
passed, enjoining the same in my other dominions ; and that I shall observe these in my own
practice and family, and shall never make opposition to any of these, or endeavour any change
thereof."† . This oath was annexed to the Covenant itself, drawn up on a fair roll of parchment, and subscribed by him in the presence of
the nobility and gentry.‡

His majesty also signed a declaration, in
which he acknowledged the sin of his father in
marrying into an idolatrous family ; and that the
blood shed in the late wars lay at his father's
door.§ He expressed a deep sense of his own
ill education, and of the prejudices he had drunk
in against the cause of God, of which he was
now very sensible. He confessed all the former
parts of his life to have been a course of enmity
to the Word of God. He repented of his commission to Montrose. He acknowledged his
own sins, and the sins of his father's house,
and says he will account them his enemies
who oppose the covenants, both which he had

* The ceremonial of this coronation is given at
length by Dr. Grey, vol. iii., p. 121-124.—ED.
† Jesse says his "coronation at Scone, though
conducted with some magnificence, was, after all,
little better than an insult." Dr. Price, with his usual discrimination, observes, " The scene enacted on
this occasion in perfect keeping with the whole
course of the young prince in Scotland; and was the
most disgracefully hypocritical ever exhibited on the
theatre of human action. * † * * It is needless to
comment on such a farce. It was a worthy commencement of one of the most inglorious careers ever
run by human prince. Had Cromwell been the actor
on this occasion, volumes would have been written
on the depth of his dissimulation and treachery."—C.
‡ Oldmixon's History of the Stuarts, p. 391.
§ History of the Stuarts, p. 387. Burnet, vol. i., p.
78, Edinb. edit.

faken without any sinister intention of attaining his own ends. He declares his detestation and abhorrence of all popery, superstition,
idolatry, and prelacy, and resolves not to tolerate them in any part of his dominions. He acknowledges his great sin in making peace with
the Irish rebels, and allowing them the liberty
of their religion, which he makes void, resolving
for the future rather to choose affliction than
sin ; and though he judges charitably of those
who have acted against the Covenant, yet he
promises not to employ them for the future till
they have taken it. In the conclusion, his majesty confesses over again his own guilt ; and
tells the world the state of the question was not
altered, inasmuch as he had obtained mercy to be
on God's side, and therefore hopes the Lord will
be gracious, and countenance his own cause,
since he is determined to do nothing but with
advice of the Kirk.

Our historians, who complain of the prevari
cation of Cromwell, would do well to find a parallel to this in all history ; the king took the
Covenant three times with this tremendous
oath, ".By the Eternal and Almighty God, who
liveth and reigneth forever, I will observe and
keep all that is contained herein." Mr. Baxter
admits* that the Scots were in the wrong in
tempting the young king to speak and publish
that which they might easily know was contrary
to the thoughts of his heart ; but surely his majesty was no less to blame, to trample upon the
most sacred bonds of religion and society. He
complied with the rigours of the Scots discipline
and worship : he heard many prayers and sermons of great length. "I remember," says
Bishop Burnet,† "in one fast-day, there were six
sermons preached without intermission. He
was not allowed to walk abroad on Sundays ;
and if at any time there had been any gayety at
court, as dancing or playing at cards, he was
severely reproved for it, which contributed not
a little to beget in him an aversion to all strictness in religion." And the Scots were so jealous that all this was from necessity, that they
would suffer none of his old friends to come
into his presence and councils, nor so much as
to serve in the army.

While the Scots were raising forces for the
king's service, a private correspondence was
carried on with the English Presbyterians ; letters were also written, and messengers sent,
from London to the king and queen-mother in
France, to hasten an accommodation with the
Scots, assuring them that the English Presbyterians would then declare for him the first opportunity. Considerable sums of money were
collected privately to forward an expedition into
England ; but the vigilance of the commonwealth discovered and defeated their designs.
The principal gentlemen and ministers concerned in the correspondence were some disbanded
officers who had served the Parliament in the

* "It seemed to me and many others," says Mr.
Baxter, "that the Scots miscarried divers ways: 1.
In imposing laws upon their king, for which they had
no authority : 2. In forcing him to dishonour the memory of his father by such confessions : 3. In tempting
him to speak and publish that which they might easily know was contrary to his heart, and so to take
God's name in vain : 4. And in giving Cromwell occasion to charge them all with dissimulation."—
Baxter's Life, p. 66.—ED.　　　　　　　† P. 73.

late wars, as Major Adams, Alford, and Huntington; Colonel Vaughan, Sowton, Titus, Jackson, Bains, Barton; Captain Adams, Potter, Far, Massey, Starks; and Mr. Gibbons. The ministers were, Dr. Drake, Mr. Case, Watson, Heyrick, Jenkins, Jackson, Jacquel, Robinson, Cawton, Nalson, Haviland, Blackmore, and Mr. Love. These had their private assemblies at Major Adams's, Colonel Barton's, and at Mr. Love's house, and held a correspondence, with the king, who desired them to send commissioners to Breda to moderate the Scots demands, which service he would reward when God should restore him to his kingdoms.

But so numerous a confederacy was hardly to be concealed from the watchful eyes of the new government, who had their spies in all places. Major Adams, being apprehended on suspicion, was the first who discovered the conspiracy to the Council of State. On his information, warrants were issued out for apprehending most of the gentlemen and ministers above mentioned; but several absconded, and withdrew from the storm. The ministers who were apprehended were Dr. Drake, Mr. Jenkins, Jackson, Robinson, Watson, Blackmore, and Haviland, who after some time were released on their petition for mercy, and promising submission to the government for the future; but Mr. Love and Gibbons were made examples, as a terror to others. Mr. Jenkins's petition being expressed in very strong terms,* was ordered to be printed; it was entitled, "The humble Petition of William Jenkins, Prisoner, declaring his unfeigned Sorrow for all his late Miscarriages, and promising to be true and faithful to the present Government; with three Queries, being the Ground of his late Petition, and Submission to the present Powers."

The Reverend Mr. Love was brought before a new high court of justice erected for this purpose, as was the custom of these times for state criminals, when Mr. Attorney-general Prideaux, June 20, exhibited against him the following charge of high treason: "That at several times in the years 1649, 1650, and 1651, and in several places, he, with the persons above mentioned, had maliciously combined and contrived to raise forces against the present government; that they had declared and published Charles Stuart, eldest son of the late king, to be King of England, without consent of Parliament; that they had aided the Scots to invade this commonwealth; that the said Christopher Love, at divers times between the 29th of March, 1650, and the first of June, 1651, at London and other places, had traitorously and maliciously maintained correspondence and intelligence by let-

ters and messages with Charles Stuart, son of the late king, and with the queen his mother, and with sundry of his council; that he did likewise hold correspondence with divers of the Scots nation, and had assisted them with money, arms, and other supplies, in the present war, as well as Colonel Titus and others of the English nation, in confederacy with them, to the hazard of the public peace, and in breach of the laws of the land." To this charge Mr. Love, after having demurred to the jurisdiction of the court, pleaded not guilty. The witnesses against him were eight of the above-mentioned gentlemen. Reverend Mr. Jackson was summoned, but refused to be sworn or give evidence, because he looked on Mr. Love to be a good man; saying, he should have a hell in his conscience to his dying day if he should speak anything that should be circumstantially prejudicial to Mr. Love's life. The court put him in mind of his obligation to the public, and that the very safety of all government depended upon it. But he refused to be sworn, for which the court sent him to the Fleet, and fined him £500.

But it appeared by the other witnesses that Mr. Love had carried on a criminal correspondence both with the king and the Scots. With regard to the king, it was sworn, that about a month after his late majesty's death, several of them met at a tavern at Dowgate, and other places, to concert measures to forward the king's agreement with the Scots, for which purpose they applied by letters to the queen, and sent over Colonel Titus with £100 to defray his expenses. The colonel, having delivered his message, sent back letters by Colonel Alsford, which were read in Mr. Love's house; with the copy of a letter from the king himself, Mr. Love being present. Upon these and such like facts, the council for the commonwealth insisted, that here was a criminal correspondence to restore the king, contrary to the ordinance of January 30, 1648, which says, "that whosoever shall proclaim, declare, publish, or any ways promote Charles Stuart, or any other person, to be King of England, without consent of Parliament, shall be adjudged a traitor, and suffer the pains of death as a traitor."

The other branch of the charge against Mr. Love was his correspondence with the Scots, and assisting them in the war against the Parliament. To support this article, Captain Potter, Adams, and Mr. Jacquel swore, that letters came from Scotland to Colonel Bamfield with the letter L upon them, giving a large narrative of the fight at Dunbar, and of the Scots affairs for three months after till Christmas. There came also letters from the Earl of Argyle, Lothian, and Loudon, who proposed the raising £10,000 to buy arms and to hire shipping, in order to land five thousand men in England. The letters were read at Mr. Love's house; but the proposal being disliked, only £40 was raised for the expenses of the messenger. At another time a letter was read from General Massey, in which he desires them to provide arms, and mentions his own and Colonel Titus's necessities; upon which it was agreed to raise 2 or £300 by way of contribution, and every one present wrote down what he would lend, among whom was Mr. Love, who not only contributed

---

* The most remarkable positions in this petition were: That the Parliament, without the king, were the supreme authority of the nation; that God's providences are antecedent declarations of his will and approbation, and appeared as evidently in removing the king and investing their honours with the government, as in taking away and bestowing any government in any history of any age of the world; that the refusal of subjection to their authority was such an opposing the government set up by the sovereign Lord of heaven and earth, as none can have peace either in acting or suffering for; and that it was a duty to yield to this authority all active and cheerful obedience, in the Lord, for conscience' sake.—*Dr. Grey's Remarks*, vol. iii., p. 127.—ED.

himself, but carried about the paper to encourage others. This was construed, by the council for the commonwealth, sufficient to bring Mr. Love within the ordinance of July 1, 1649, which says, "that if any shall procure, invite, aid, or assist any foreigners or strangers to invade England or Ireland, or shall adhere to any forces raised by the enemies of the Parliament, or commonwealth, or keepers of the liberties of England, all such persons shall be deemed and adjudged guilty of high treason."

Mr. Love, in his defence, behaved with a little too much freedom and boldness; he set too high a value, upon his sacred character, which the court was inclined to treat with neglect. He objected to the witnesses, as being forced into the service to save their lives. He observed, that to several of the facts there was only one witness; and that some of them had sworn falsely, or, at least, their memories had failed them in some things; which might easily happen at so great a distance of time. He called no witnesses to confront the evidence, but at the close of his defence confessed ingenuously that there had been several meetings of the above-named persons at his house, that a commission was read, but that he had dissented from it. He acknowledged, farther, that he was present at the reading of the letters, or of some part of them, "but I was ignorant," says he, "of the danger that I now see I am in. The act of August 2, 1650, makes it treason to hold any correspondence with Scotland, or to send letters thither, though but in a way of commerce, the two nations being at war; now here my council acquaints me with my danger, that I, being present when letters were read in my house, am guilty of a concealment, and therefore as to that, I humbly lay myself at your feet and mercy."

And to move the court to show mercy to him, he endeavoured to set out his own character in the most favourable light: "I have been called a malignant and apostate," says he, "but, God is my witness, I never carried on a malignant interest; I shall retain my covenanting principles, from which, by the grace of God, I will never depart; neither am I an incendiary between the two nations of England and Scotland, but I am grieved for their divisions; and if I had as much blood in my veins as there is water in the sea, I could account it well spent to quench the fire that our sins have kindled between them. I have all along engaged my life and estate in the Parliament's quarrel, against the forces raised by the late king, not from a prospect of advantage, but from conscience and duty; and I am so far from repenting, that were it to do again, upon the same unquestionable authority, and for the same declared ends, I should as readily engage in it as ever; though I wish from my soul that the ends of that just war had been better accomplished.

"Nor have my sufferings in this cause been inconsiderable; when I was a scholar in Oxford and M.A., I was the first who publicly refused to subscribe the canons imposed by the late archbishop, for which I was expelled the Convocation House. When I first came to London, which was about twelve years ago, I was opposed by the Bishop of London, and it was about three years before I could obtain so much as a lecture. In the year 1640, or 1641, I was imprisoned in Newcastle, for preaching against the Service Book, from whence I was removed hither by habeas corpus, and acquitted. In the beginning of the war between the late king and Parliament, I was accused for preaching treason and rebellion, merely because I maintained, in a sermon at Tenderton, in Kent, the lawfulness of a defensive war. I was again complained of by the commissioners at Uxbridge for preaching a sermon, which I hear is lately reprinted; and if it be printed according to the first copy, I will own every line of it. After all this, I have been three times in trouble since the late change of government. Once I was committed to custody, and twice cited before the Committee for plundered ministers, but for want of proof was discharged. And now, last of all, I am arraigned for my life, and like to suffer from the hands of those for whom I have done and suffered so much, and who have lift up their hands with me in the same covenant; and yet I am not conscious of any personal act proved against me, that brings me within any of your laws as to treason.

"Upon the whole, though I never wrote nor sent letters into Scotland, yet I confess their proceedings with the king are agreeable to my judgment, and for the good of the nation; and though I disown the commission and instructions mentioned in the indictment, yet I have desired an agreement between the king and the Scots, agreeably to the Covenant; for they having declared him to be their king, I have desired and prayed, as a private man, that they might accomplish their ends upon such terms as were consistent with the safety of religion and the Covenant."

He concludes with beseeching the court that he may not be put to death for state reasons. He owns he had been guilty of a concealment, and begs the mercy of the court for it, promising for the future to lead a quiet and peaceable life. He puts them in mind, that when Abiathar the priest had done an unjustifiable action, King Solomon said he would not put him to death at that time, because he bore the ark of the Lord God before David his father; and because he had been afflicted in all wherein his father had been afflicted. "Thus," says he, "I commit myself and my all to God, and to your judgments and consciences, with the words of Jeremiah to the rulers of Israel, 'As for me, behold I am in your hands, do with me as seemeth good and meet to you; but know ye for certain, that if ye put me to death, ye shall surely bring innocent blood upon yourselves.' But I hope better things of you, though I thus speak."

The court allowed Mr. Love the benefit of counsel learned in the law, to argue some exceptions against the indictment; but after all that Mr. Hales could say for the prisoner, the court, after six days' hearing, on the 5th of July pronounced sentence of death against him as a traitor.

Great intercessions* were made for the life

* Not only by his wife and friends, says Mr. Granger, but by several parishes in London, and by fifty-

of this reverend person by the chief of the Presbyterian party in London; his wife presented several moving petitions; and two were presented from himself, in one of which he acknowledges the justice of his sentence according to the laws of the commonwealth; in the other, he petitions that, if he may not be pardoned, his sentence may be changed into banishment; and that he might do something to deserve his life, he presented with his last petition a narration of all that he knew relating to the plot, which admits almost all that had been objected to him at his trial.

But the affairs of the commonwealth were now at a crisis, and King Charles II. having entered England at the head of sixteen thousand Scots, it was thought necessary to strike some terror into the Presbyterian party, by making an example of one of their favourite clergymen. Mr. Whitelocke says* that Colonel Fortescue was sent to General Cromwell with a petition on behalf of Mr. Love, but that both the general and the rest of the officers declined meddling in the affair; Bishop Kennet and Mr. Echard say the general sent word in a private letter to one of his confidants, that he was content that Mr. Love should be reprieved, and upon giving security for his future good behaviour, pardoned; but that the post-boy being stopped upon the road by some cavaliers belonging to the late king's army, they searched his packet, and finding this letter of reprieve for Mr. Love, they tore it with indignation, as thinking him not worthy to live, who had been such a firebrand at the treaty of Uxbridge.† If this story be true, Mr. Love fell a sacrifice to the ungovernable rage of the cavaliers, as Dr. Dorislaus and Mr. Ascham had done before.

The mail arriving from Scotland, and no letter from Cromwell in behalf of Mr. Love, he was ordered to be executed upon Tower Hill, August 22, the very day the king entered Worcester at the head of his Scots army. Mr. Love mounted the scaffold with great intrepidity and resolution, and taking off his hat two several times to the people, made a long speech, wherein he declares the satisfaction of his mind in the cause for which he suffered; and then adds, "I am for a regulated, mixed monarchy, which I judge to be one of the best governments in the world. I opposed in my place the forces of the late king, because I am against screwing up monarchy into tyranny as much as against those who would pull it down into anarchy. I was never for putting the king to death, whose person I did promise in my covenant to preserve; and I judge it an ill way of curing the body politic by cutting off the political head. I die with my judgment against the Engagement; I pray God forgive them that impose it, and them that take it, and preserve them that refuse it. Neither would I be looked upon as owning this present government; I die with my judgment against it. And lastly, I die cleaving to all those oaths, vows, covenants, and protestations that were imposed by the two houses of Parliament. I bless God I have not the least trouble on my spirit, but I die with as much

quietness of mind as if I was going to lie down upon my bed to rest. I see men thirst after my blood, which will but hasten my happiness and their ruin; for though I am but of mean parentage, yet my blood is the blood of a Christian, of a minister, of an innocent man, and (I speak it without vanity) of a martyr. I conclude with the speech of the apostle: 'I am now ready to be offered up, and the time of my departure is at hand, but I have finished my course, I have kept the faith: henceforth there is laid up for me a crown of righteousness; and not for me only, but for all them that love the appearance of our Lord Jesus Christ,' through whose blood I expect salvation and remission of sins. And so the Lord bless you all."

After this he prayed with an audible voice for himself and his fellow-sufferer Mr. Gibbon, for the prosperity of England, for his covenanting brethren in Scotland, and for a happy union between the two nations, making no mention of the king. He then rose from his knees, and having taken leave of the ministers, and others who attended him, he laid his head upon the block, which the executioner took off at one blow, before he had attained the age of forty years.* Mr. Love was a zealous Presbyterian, a popular preacher, and highly esteemed by his brethren. His funeral sermon was preached by Dr. Manton, and published under the title of "The Saint's Triumph over Death;" but his memory has suffered very much by Lord Clarendon's character,† who represents him as guilty of as much "treason against the late king as the pulpit could contain; and delighting himself with the recital of it to the last, as dying with false courage, or (as he calls it) in a raving fit of satisfaction, for having pursued the ends of the sanctified obligation, the Covenant, without praying for the king, any farther than he propagated the Covenant."‡

* Mr. Love was born at Cardiff, in Glamorganshire; became a servitor of New Inn, Oxford, 1635, aged seventeen. In 1642 he proceeded master of arts. He was, at the beginning of his ministry, preacher to the garrison of Windsor, then under the command of Colonel John Venn, and was called by the Royalists Venn's principal fireman at Windsor. He was afterward successively minister of St. Ann's, near Aldersgate, and St. Lawrence Jewry, in London. He was the author of sermons and some pieces of practical divinity, which gained him a considerable reputation. He was buried with great lamentation on the north side of the chancel of St. Lawrence Jewry.—*Wood's Athen. Oxon.*, vol. ii., p. 74; and *Granger's History*, vol. iii., p. 48, 8vo.—ED. Mr. Love was an accomplished divine; his most valuable productions are, "The Combat between the Flesh and Spirit," "The Christian's Directory;" "A Treatise on Effectual Calling;" "Heaven's Glory;" "Hell's Terror." These are well worthy of careful study.—C. † Vol. iii., p. 434.

‡ These are heavy charges. But if Mr. Love was guilty of so "much treason," it was in *behalf of the king*, and with a view to promote the royal cause. If Clarendon refers to his preaching at Uxbridge, the charge is asserted without an atom of evidence. With respect to Mr. Love's "speaking with bitterness and animosity against both the king and the bishops" when he was on the scaffold, this charge is entirely without foundation, and stands diametrically opposed to matter of fact, as appears from Love's speech at length. And as to his laying his head on the block "in a raving fit," we are at a loss to understand his lordship's meaning, unless he undesignedly insinuates that Mr. Love died in the enjoyment of

four ministers.—*History of England*, vol. iii., p. 43, 8vo.—ED. * Memorials, p. 474.
† Compl. Hist., P. 202. Echard, vol. ii., p. 706. Kennet's Hist. of Eng., vol. iii., p. 185.—C.

To return to more public affairs. "After the battle of Dunbar, General Cromwell, through the inclemency of the weather, and his great fatigues, was seized with an ague which hung upon him all the spring, but as the summer advanced he recovered, and in the month of July marched his army towards the king's at Stirling; but not thinking it advisable to attempt his camp, he transported part of his forces over the frith into Fife, who, upon their landing, defeated the Scots, killing two thousand, and taking twelve hundred prisoners. After that, without waiting any longer on the king, he reduced Johnstown, and almost all the garrisons in the north."

While the general was employed in these parts, the Scots committee, that directed the marches of their army, fearing the storm would quickly fall upon themselves, resolved to march their army into England, and try the loyalty of the English Presbyterians; for this purpose Colonel Massey was sent before into Lancashire, to prepare them for a revolt; and the king himself entered England by the way of Carlisle, August 6, at the head of sixteen thousand men; but when the committee of ministers that attended the army observed that the king and his friends, upon their entering England, were for dropping the Covenant, they sent an express to Massey without the king's knowledge (says Lord Clarendon*), requiring him to publish a declaration, to assure the people of their resolution to prosecute the ends of the Covenant. The king had no sooner notice of this, but he sent to Massey, forbidding him to publish the declaration, and to behave with equal civility towards all men who were forward to serve him; "but before this inhibition," says his lordship, "the matter had taken air in all places, and was spread over the whole kingdom, which made all men fly from the houses, or conceal themselves, who wished the king well." But his lordship is surely mistaken, for the king's chief hopes under Massey were from the Presbyterians, who were so far from being displeased with his majesty's declaring for the Covenant, that it gave them all the spirit he could wish for; but when it was known that the Covenant was to be laid aside, Massey's measures were broken, many of the Scots deserted and returned home; and not one in ten of the English would hazard his life in the quarrel.† Mr. Baxter,‡ who was a much better judge of the temper of the people than his lordship, says, "the English knew that the Scots coming into England was rather a flight than a march. They considered, likewise, that the implacable cavaliers had made no preparation of the people's minds, by proposing any terms of a future reconciliation; that the prelatical divines were gone farther from the Presbyterians by Dr. Hammond's new way than their prede-

cessors; and that the cause they contended for being not concord, but government, they had given the Presbyterian clergy and people no hopes of finding any abatement of their former burdens; and it is hard to persuade men to venture their lives in order to bring themselves into a prison or banishment." However, these were the true reasons, says Mr. Baxter, that no more came in to bring at present; and had the Presbyterians observed them at the Restoration, they had made better terms for themselves than they did.

The Parliament at Westminster were quickly advised of the march, and by way of precaution, expelled all delinquents out of the city; they raised the militia; they mustered the trained-bands, to the number of fourteen thousand; and in a few weeks had got together an army of near sixty thousand brave soldiers. Mr. Echard* represents the Parliament as in a terrible panic, and projecting means to escape out of the land; whereas, in reality, the unhappy king was the pity of his friends, and the contempt of his enemies. General Cromwell sent an express to the Parliament to have a watchful eye over the Presbyterians, who were in confederacy with the Scots, and told them that the reason of his not interposing between the enemy and England was, because he was resolved to reduce Scotland effectually before winter. He desired the House to collect their forces together, and make the best stand they could till he could come up with the enemy, when he doubted not but to give a good account of them. At the same time he sent Major-general Lambert with a strong body of horse to harass the king's forces, while himself with the body of the army hastened after, leaving Lieutenant-general Monk with a sufficient force to secure his conquests, and reduce the rest of the country, which he quickly accomplished. Bishop Burnet says† there was an order and discipline among the English, and a face of gravity and piety, that amazed all people; most of them were Independents and Baptists, but all gifted men, and preached as they were moved, but never above once disturbed the public worship.

The Earl of Derby was the only nobleman in England who raised fifteen hundred men for the young king, who, before he could join the royal army, was defeated by Colonel Lilburn, near Wigan, in Lancashire, and his forces entirely dispersed. The earl, being wounded, retired into Cheshire, and from thence got to the king, who had marched his army as far as Worcester, which opened its gates, and gave him an honourable reception; from thence his majesty sent letters to London, commanding all his subjects between the age of sixteen and sixty to repair to his royal standard; but few had the courage to appear, the Parliament having declared all such rebels, and burned the king's summons by the hands of the common hangman. His majesty's affairs were now at a crisis. Lambert was in his rear with a great body of horse, and Cromwell followed with ten thousand foot, which, together with the forces that joined him by order of Parliament, made an army of thirty thousand men. The king, being unable to keep the field, fortified the city of Worcester, and encamped almost under the

---

the most happy and exquisite religious feelings. Dr. Calamy assures us "that he died neither timorously nor proudly, but with great alacrity and cheerfulness, as if he had been going to bed." Dr. Manton, who attended Mr. Love upon the scaffold, and who knew him better than the historians who have traduced his character, says "he was a man eminent in grace, of a singular life and conversation, and a pattern of piety most worthy of imitation."—*Clarendon and Whitelocke compared*, p. 303. *Dr. Manton's Funeral Sermon for Mr. Love. Brooks's Lives of the Puritans*, p. 137.—C.

† Rapin, vol. ii., p. 585, folio.   ‡ Life, p. 68.

* Vol. iii., p. 400, 406.

* P. 689.   † P. 80.

walls. September 3, Cromwell attacked Powick Bridge, within two miles of the city, which drew out the king's forces and occasioned a general battle, in which his majesty's army was entirely destroyed; four thousand being slain, seven thousand taken prisoners, with the king's standard, and one hundred and fifty-eight colours. Never was a greater route and dispersion, nor a more fatal blow to the royal cause. The account which the general gave to the Parliament was, "that the battle was fought with various success for some hours, but still hopeful on our part, and in the end became an absolute victory, the enemy's army being totally defeated, and the town in cur possession, our men entering at the enemy's heels, and fighting with them in the streets, took all their baggage and artillery. The dispute was long, and very often at push of pike from one defence to another. There are about six or seven thousand prisoners, among whom are many officers and persons of quality. This, for aught I know, may be a crowning mercy." All possible diligence was used to seize the person of the king; it was declared high treason to conceal him, and a reward of £1000 was set upon his head; but Providence ordained his escape,* for after he had travelled up and down the country six or seven weeks, under various disguises, in company with one or two confidants, and escaped a thousand dangers, he got a passage across the Channel at Brighthelmstone, in Sussex, and landed at Dieppe, in Normandy, October 21, the morning after he embarked; from whence he travelled by land to Paris, where his mother maintained him out of her small pension† from the court of France.‡

* Hobbes, of Malmesbury, in his " Behemoth," attributes Charles's escape to there being none of the enemy's horse in Worcester to follow him : " The plundering foot," he says, " kept the gates shut, lest the horse should enter and have a share of the booty."
—Masere's Tracts, part ii., p. 620.—C.

† This must be understood only of the king's first arrival : for her pension was so small and so ill paid, that when Cardinal de Retz visited her on a time in the month of January, the Princess Henrietta could not rise for want of fire. When her son arrived, she had not money enough to buy him a change of linen for the next day. The French court was obliged to provide for his necessities, and settled on him a pension of six thousand livres per month. — Dr. Grey, vol. iii., p. 134, 135. Clarendon's History, vol. iii., p. 441.—Ed.

‡ The story of the wanderings of the young king, after the fatal battle of Worcester, his hairbreadth escapes, and, eventually, his almost miraculous deliverance, are perhaps unexampled for their stirring interest in the annals of real romance. Attributing to Charles the credit of some slight sympathy with the sufferings of others; admitting that he could not have reflected without some feelings of pity on the scene of slaughter and devastation which he had just quitted, or have heard without a sigh of the death and captivity of his most faithful adherents; allowing, even, that he was alive to the common impressions of fear, suspense, and hunger, and we can imagine nothing more distressing than the condition of the hunted and houseless Charles. Miracles have not been wrought openly in our time, nor in that of our immediate forefathers; besides, we are unwilling to reconcile with the fortunes of a profligate an especial departure of Providence from its settled rules; nevertheless, in reviewing the circumstances of the king's wonderful deliverance, we can scarcely doubt that Providence was about his path

The hopes of the Royalists were now expiring, for the islands of Guernsey and Jersey, with all the British plantations in America, were reduced this summer to the obedience of the Parliament, insomuch that his majesty had neither fort nor castle, nor a foot of land in all his dominions. The liturgy of the Church of England was also under a total eclipse, the use of it being forbid, not only in England, but even to the royal family in France, which had hitherto an apartment in the Louvre separated to that purpose; but after the battle of Worcester, an order was sent from the queen-regent to shut up the chapel; it being the king's pleasure not to permit the exercise of any religion but the Roman Catholic in any of his houses; nor could Chancellor Hyde obtain more than a bare promise that the Queen of England would use her endeavours that the Protestants of the family should have liberty to exercise their devotions in some private room belonging to the lodgings.

Upon the king's arrival in France, he immediately threw off the mask of a Presbyterian, and never went once to the Protestant church at Charenton, though they invited him in the most respectful manner; but Lord Clarendon dissuaded him, because the Huguenots had not been bearty in his interest, and because it might look disrespectful to the old Church of England. In truth, there being no farther prospect of the king's restoration by the Presbyterians, the eyes of the court were turned to the Roman Catholics, and many of his majesty's retinue changed their religion, as appears by the Legenda Lignea, published about this time, with a list of fifty-three new converts, among whom were the following names in red capitals : the Countess of Derby, Lady Kilmichin, Lord Cottington, Sir Marm. Langdale, Sir Fr. Doddington, Sir Theoph. Gilby, Captain Tho. Cook, Tho. Vane, D.D., De Cressy, prebendary of Windsor, Dr. Bayley, Dr. Cosins, Junior, D. Goffe, and many others, not to mention the king himself, of whom Father Huddleston, his confessor, writes, in his treatise entitled "A short and plain Way to the Faith of the Church," published 1685, that he put it into the king's hands in his retirement, and that when his majesty had read it, he declared he could not see how it could be answered.* Thus early, says a learned prelate of the Church of England, was the king's advance towards popery, of which we shall meet with a fuller demonstration hereafter.†

General-Monk, whom Cromwell left in Scotland with six thousand men, quickly reduced that kingdom, which was soon after united to the commonwealth of England, the deputies of the several counties consenting to be governed by authority of Parliament, without a king or House of Lords.‡ The power of the Kirk was likewise restrained within a narrow compass; for though they had liberty to excommunicate offenders, or debar them the communion, they

and around his bed; that it led him forth from the land of captivity, and sheltered and preserved him for the furtherance of its ends.—See Jesse's Court of England, &c., vol. iii., p. 235.—C,

* Clarendon, vol. iii., p. 444.
† Kennet, p. 200, 210. Rapin, vol. ii., p. 586, folio.
‡ Whitelocke, p. 498, 503, 504.

might not seize their estates, or deprive them of their civil rights and privileges. No oaths or covenants were to be imposed but by direction from Westminster; and as all fitting encouragement was to be given to the ministers of the established Kirk, so others, not satisfied with their form of church government, had liberty to serve God after their own manner; and all who would live peaceably, and yield obedience to the commonwealth, were protected in their several persuasions. This occasioned a great commotion among the clergy, who complained of the loss of their Covenant and church discipline; and exclaimed against the toleration, as opening a door to all kinds of error and heresy; but the English supported their friends against all opposition.

The Laird of Drum, being threatened with excommunication for speaking against the Kirk, and for refusing to swear that its discipline was of Divine authority, fled to the English for protection, and then wrote the Assembly word that their oppression was equal to that of the late bishops, but that the commonwealth of England would not permit them to enslave the consciences of men any longer. The Presbytery would have proceeded to extremities with him, but Monk brandished his sword over their heads, and threatened to treat them as enemies to the state, upon which they desisted for the present.*

Soon after this, commissioners, chiefly of the Independent persuasion, were sent into Scotland, to visit the universities, and to settle liberty of conscience in that kingdom, against the coercive claim of the Kirk, by whose influence a declaration was presented to the Assembly at Edinburgh, July 26, in favour of the Congregational discipline, and for liberty of conscience; but the stubborn assemblymen, instead of yielding to the declaration, published a paper called a "Testimony against the present Encroachments of the Civil Power upon the Ecclesiastical Jurisdiction," occasioned by a proclamation of the English commissioners appointing a committee for visiting their universities, which they take to be a special flower of the Kirk prerogative. The Synod of Fife also protested against the public resolutions of the civil power; but the sword of the English kept them in awe; for when the Synod of Perth cited before them several persons for slighting the admonitions of the Kirk, Mr. Whitelocke says† that, upon the day of appearance, their wives, to the number of about one hundred and twenty, with clubs in their hands, came and besieged the church where the synod sat; that they abused one of the ministers who was sent out to treat with them, and threatened to excommunicate them; and that they beat the clerk and dispersed the assembly; upon which thirteen of the ministers met at a village about four miles distant, and having agreed that no more synods should be held in that place, they pronounced the village accursed. When the General Assembly met again at Edinburgh next summer, and were just entering upon business, Lieutenant-colonel Cotterel went into the church, and standing up upon one of the benches, told them that no ecclesiastical judicatories were to sit there but by authority of the Parliament of England; and

without giving them leave to reply, he commanded them to retire, and conducted them out of the west gate of the city with a troop of horse and a company of foot; and having taken away the commissioners from their several classes, enjoined them not to assemble any more above three in a company.

But with all these commotions, Bishop Burnet observes,* that the country was kept in great order; the garrisons in the Highlands observed an exact discipline, and were well paid, which brought so much money into the kingdom, that it continued all the time of the usurpation in a flourishing condition; justice was carefully administered, and vice was suppressed and punished; there was a great appearance of devotion; the Sabbath was observed with uncommon strictness; none might walk the streets in time of Divine service, nor frequent public-houses; the evenings of the Lord's Days were spent in catechising their children, singing psalms, and other acts of family devotion, insomuch that an acquaintance with the principles of religion; and the gift of prayer, increased prodigiously among the common people.†

The war being now ended, the Parliament published an act of indemnity for all crimes committed before June 30, 1648, except pirates, Irish rebels, the murderers of Dr. Dorislaus and Mr. Ascham, and some others, provided they laid hold of it and took the Engagement before February 1, 1652. In the course of the year they chose a new council of state out of their own body for the next year, and continued themselves, instead of dissolving and giving way to a new Parliament; the neglect of which was their ruin.

On the 26th of September, Lieutenant-general Ireton died at Limerick in Ireland, after he had reduced that city to the obedience of the commonwealth. He was bred to the law, and was a person of great integrity, bold and intrepid in all his enterprises, and never to be diverted from what he thought just and right by any arguments or persuasions. He was a thorough commonwealth's man. Bishop Burnet says he had the principles and temper of a Cassius,‡ and was most liberal in employing his purse and hazarding his person in the service of the public. He died in the midst of life, of a burning fever,§ after ten days' sickness. His body be-

---

* History, vol. i., p. 84, Edin. edition. † Speaking of Scotland at this time, an historian writes, " *I verily believe that there were more souls converted to Christ in that short period of time than in any season since the Reformation, though of triple its duration.* Nor was there ever greater purity and plenty of the means of grace than was in their time. Ministers were powerful, people were diligent; and if a man had seen one of their solemn communions, where many congregations met in great multitudes—some dozens of ministers used to preach, and the people continued, as it were, in a kind of trance (so serious were they in spiritual exercises) for three days at least—he would have thought it a solemnity unknown to the rest of the world. At the king's return every parish had a minister, every village a school, every family almost a Bible, for in most of the country all the children could read the Scriptures."—*Kirkton's History of the Church of Scotland,* p. 54.—C.   ‡ History, vol. i., p. 63, Edin. ed. § Lord Clarendon ascribes the death of Ireton to the infection of the plague, which was gotten into his army. He was of Trinity College in Oxford, and

iag brought over into England, was laid in state at Somerset House, and buried in Westminster Abbey with a pomp and magnificence suited to the dignity of his station ; but after the Restoration of the royal family, his body was taken out of the grave with Cromwell's, and buried under the gallows.

About the same time died Mr. Francis Woodcock, born in Chester, 1613, and educated in Brazen Nose College, Oxford, where he took a degree in arts, entered into orders, and had a cure of souls bestowed upon him.* In the beginning of the civil wars he sided with the Parliament, and was one of the Assembly of Divines, being then lecturer of St. Lawrence Jewry. He was afterward, by ordinance of Parliament dated July 10, 1646, made parson of St. Olave's, Southwark, having the esteem of being a good scholar, and an excellent preacher. He died in the midst of his days and usefulness, ætatis thirty-eight.

Mr. George Walker proceeded B.D. in St. John's College, Cambridge. He was famous for his skill in the Oriental languages, and was an excellent logician and theologist; being very much noted for his disputations with the Jesuit Fisher, and others of the Romish Church, and afterward for his strict Sabbatarian principles. He was a member of the Assembly of Divines, where he gained great reputation by his munificent and generous behaviour.†

on leaving the university he studied at the Middle Temple. He and Lambert distinguished themselves at the battle of Naseby, and were both concerned in drawing up the remonstrance of the army to the Parliament. Ireton had the greatest hand in preparing the ordinance for the king's trial, and the precept for proclaiming the High Court of Justice, in which he sat as a judge. His authority was so great, that he was entirely submitted to in all the civil as well as martial affairs ; though his parts were considered by some as more fitted for modelling a government than for the conduct of an army. The Oxford historian describes him as of a turbulent and saucy disposition, nurtured to mischief, and a profound, thorough-paced dissembler under the mask of religion. His corpse was carried from the ship in which it was brought to Bristol in a hearse of velvet, attended by the mayor, aldermen, and council, in their formalities, and the governor and officers, to the castle, from whence it was removed to London with great pomp. The Parliament settled on his widow and children £2000 per annum, out of the lands belonging to George, duke of Bucks. His daughter, who married Thomas Bendish, Esq., of Gray's Inn, was a most singular character, and bore a greater resemblance, in countenance and dispositions, to her grandfather, Oliver Cromwell, than did any of his descendants. A curious sketch of her character, drawn by the Rev. Samuel Say, is preserved in the second volume of " Letters", published by Mr. Duncombe.—*Dr. Grey*, vol. iii., p. 141, &c. *Lord Clarendon's History*, vol. iii., p. 467. *Wood's Athen. Oxon.*, p. 81, 82. *Whitelocke's Mem.*, p. 491, 494 ; and *Granger's History*, vol. ii., p. 259, and vol. iii., p. 16, 17.—ED.

* *Athen. Oxon.*, vol. ii., p. 81, 82. Mr. Woodcock was proctor to the University of Cambridge. His principal works were upon " The Two Witnesses," Rev., ii., and " Lex talionis," or " God paying every Man in his own Coin :" this last was a fast sermon before the House of Commons.—C.

† Mr. Walker was born in Lancashire, 1581. In 1614 he became Rector of St. John the Evangelist in Watling St., London, where he continued 40 years, refusing all preferments offered him. At this time he was chaplain to Dr. Felton, bishop of Ely. He was often engaged in controversy with the Romish

VOL. II.—R

Mr. Thomas Wilson was born in Cumberland, 1601, and educated in Christ's College, Cambridge, where he proceeded in arts. He was first minister of Capel in Surrey, and after several other removes, fixed at Maidstone in Kent, where he was suspended for refusing to read the Book of Sports, and not absolved till the Scots troubles in 1639. In 1643 he was appointed one of the Assembly of Divines, at Westminster, being reputed a good linguist, and well read in ancient and modern authors. He was of a robust constitution, and took vast pains in preaching and catechising ; he had a great deal of natural courage, and was in every respect a cheerful and active Christian, but he trespassed too much upon his constitution, which wore him out when he was little more than fifty years old. He died comfortably and cheerfully, towards the end of the year 1651. Sir Edward Deering gave him this character in the House of Commons : " Mr. Wilson is as orthodox in doctrine, and laborious in preaching ; as any we have, and of an unblemished life."*

The terms of conformity in England were now lower than they had been since the beginning of the civil wars ; the Covenant was laid aside, and no other civil qualification for a living required but the Engagement, so that many Episcopal divines complied with the government ; for though they might not read the liturgy in form, they might frame their prayers as near it as they pleased. Many Episcopal assemblies were connived at, where the liturgy was read, till they were found plotting against the government ; nor would they have been denied an open toleration, if they would have given security for their peaceable behaviour, and not meddling with politics.

The Parliament having voted, in the year 1649, that tithes should be taken away as soon as another maintenance for the clergy could be agreed upon, several petitions came out of the country, praying the House to bring this affair to an issue : one advised that all the tithes over the whole kingdom might be collected into a treasury, and that the ministers might be paid their salaries out of it. Others, looking upon tithes as unlawful, would have the livings valued, and the parish engaged to pay the minister. This was suspected to come from the sectaries, and awakened the fears of the established clergy. Mr. Baxter printed the Worcester petition on the behalf of the ministers,† which was presented to the House by Colonel Bridges and Mr. Foley ; and Mr. Boreman, B.D., and fellow of Trinity College, Cambridge, published " The

clergy ; his dispute with Smith was published. In 1638 he was prosecuted in the infamous Star Chamber, before which he was cited by Laud for the strictness of his opinions in favour of the Sabbath, and his declaring Christ's authority to be above that of the temporal monarch. His punishment was fine and imprisonment ; after two years, he was liberated by an order of Parliament. Mr. Walker was a witness in the trial of Laud. All his writings are valuable, especially his controversial works, and his treatise upon " The Holy Weekly Sabbath," 1641.—*Brooks's Lives*, &c., vol. iii., p. 140.—C.

* Mr. Wilson was a Baptist, and in 1638 joined Mr. Spilsbury's church. He was author of a sermon entitled " Jerichoe's Downfall," 1643.—C.

† Baxter's Life, p. 115.

Countryman's Catechism, or the Church's Plea for Tithes," dedicated to the nobility, gentry, and commons of the realm, in which he insists upon their Divine right. But the clergy were more afraid than hurt; for though the Commons were of opinion, with Mr. Selden, that tithes were abolished with the old law, yet the committee not agreeing upon an expedient to satisfy the lay-impropriators, the affair was dropped for the present.

Upon complaint of the expense and tediousness of lawsuits, it was moved in the House that courts of justice might be settled in every county, and maintained at the public charge; and that all controversies between man and man might be heard and determined free, according to the laws of the land; and that clerks of all courts and committees might do their duty without delay, or taking anything more than their settled fees. Accordingly, a committee was appointed to consider of the inconveniences and delays of lawsuits, and how they might be remedied. The committee came to several resolutions upon this head; but the dissolution of the Parliament, which happened the next year, prevented their bringing it to perfection.

An act had passed, in the year 1649, for propagating the Gospel in Wales; and commissioners were appointed for ejecting ignorant and scandalous ministers, and placing others in their room; pursuant to which, Mr. Whitelocke writes,* " that by this time there were one hundred and fifty good preachers in the thirteen Welsh counties, most of whom preached three or four times a week; that in every market town there was placed one, and in most towns two schoolmasters, able, learned, and university men; that the tithes were all employed to the uses directed by act of Parliament; that is, to the maintenance of godly ministers; to the payment of taxes and officers; to schoolmasters; and the fifths to the wives and children of the ejected clergy:" of which we shall meet with a more particular relation in its proper place.

The commonwealth was now very powerful, and the nation in as flourishing a condition, says Mr. Rapin,† as under Queen Elizabeth. The form of government, indeed, was altered contrary to law, and without consent of the people, the majority of whom were disaffected, preferring a mixed monarchy to an absolute commonwealth; but the administration was in the hands of the ablest men England had beheld for many years; all their enemies were in a manner subdued, and the two kingdoms incorporated into one commonwealth; but still there were two things that gave them uneasiness: one was the growing power of the army, who were now at leisure, and expected rewards suitable to their successes; the other, the necessity they were under to dissolve themselves in a little time, and put the power into other hands.

With regard to the army, it was resolved to reduce the land-forces, and augment the fleet with them, in order to secure the nation against the Dutch; for the Parliament having a desire to strengthen their hands, by uniting with the commonwealth of Holland, sent over Oliver St. John and Sir Walter Strickland with proposals for this purpose; but the Dutch treated them

---

with neglect,* as their younger sister, which the Parliament resenting, demanded satisfaction for the damages the English had sustained at Amboyna, and other parts of the East Indies; and to cramp them in their trade, passed the famous Act of Navigation, prohibiting the importing goods of foreign growth in any but English bottoms, or such as were of the country from whence they came. Upon this the Dutch sent over ambassadors, desiring a clause of exception for themselves, who were the carriers of Europe; but the Parliament, in their turn, treated them coldly, and put them in mind of the murder of their envoy, Dr. Dorislaus. Both commonwealths being dissatisfied with each other, prepared for war; and Van Trump, the Dutch admiral, with a convoy of merchantmen, meeting Admiral Blake in the Channel, and refusing him the flag, an engagement ensued May 17, which continued four hours, till the night parted them. The Dutch excused the accident, as done without their knowledge; but the Parliament was so enraged, that they resolved to humble them. In these circumstances, it was thought reasonable to augment the fleet out of the land-forces, who had nothing to do, and would in a little time be a burden to the nation.

Cromwell, who was at the head of the army, quickly discovered that the continuance of the war must be his ruin, by disarming him of his power, and reducing him from a great general to the condition of a private gentleman. Besides, Mr. Rapin observes, that he had secret information of a conspiracy against his life; and without all question, if the army had not agreed to stand by their general, his ruin would have been unavoidable; the officers, therefore, determined to combine together, and not suffer their men to be disbanded or sent to sea till the arrears of the whole army were paid; for this purpose, they presented a petition to the House, which they resented, and instead of giving them soft language, and encouragement to hope for some suitable rewards for their past services, ordered them to be reprimanded, for presuming to meddle in affairs of state that did not belong to them. But the officers proving as resolute as their masters, instead of submitting, presented another petition, in which, having justified their behaviour, they boldly strike at the Parliament's continuance, and put them in mind how many years they had sat; that they had engrossed all preferments and places of profit to

* Dr. Grey, evidently with a view to controvert Mr. Neal's representation, as well as from prejudice against these ambassadors and the power from whom they received their commission, says, " the States of Holland treated them with much more regard and civility than was due to them;" and gives, as proofs of this, two of their own letters, in his Appendix, No. 50 and 51. But all which these letters prove is, that the first reception given to these gentlemen was both respectful and pompous. Mr. Neal is to be understood of the attention paid to their proposals, with respect to their conduct of the Dutch was cold and evasive. And even the persons of the ambassadors did not escape insults, which the States did not properly resent. Mr. Strickland's life was threatened. A plot was formed to assassinate Mr. St. John; and an affront was offered to him by Prince Edward, one of the Palatinate, as he was passing the streets.—*Mrs. Macaulay's History*, vol. v., p. 83, 84, note; and *Ludlow's Memoirs*, 4to, 1771, p. 148.—ED.

---

* Memoirs, p. 518.

† Vol. ii., p. 586, folio edition.

themselves and their friends; that it was a manifest injury to the gentlemen of the nation to be excluded the service of their country, and an invasion of the rights of the people to deprive them of the right of frequent choosing new representatives; they therefore insist upon their settling a new council of state for the administration of public affairs; and upon their fixing a peremptory day for the choice of a new Parliament.

This was a new and delicate crisis; the civil and military powers being engaged against each other, and resolved to maintain their respective pretensions: if Cromwell, with the sword in his hand, had secured the election of a free representative of the people, and left the settlement of the nation to them, all men would have honoured and blessed him, for the people were certainly weary of the Parliament. But when the officers had destroyed this form of government, they were not agreed what to establish, whether a monarchy or a new republic; the general, being for a mixed monarchy, had, no doubt, some ambitious views to himself, and therefore called together some select friends of several professions to advise on the affair, when Sir Thomas Widdrington, Lord-chief-justice St. John, and the rest of the lawyers, declared for monarchy, as most agreeable to the old Constitution, and proposed the Duke of Gloucester for king; but the officers of the army then present declared for a republic. Cromwell himself, after much hesitation, gave his opinion for something of a monarchical power, as most agreeable to the genius of the English, if it might be accomplished with safety to their rights and privileges as Englishmen and Christians.

Some time after, Cromwell desired Mr. Whitelocke's opinion upon the present situation of affairs : "My lord," says he, "it is time to consider of our present danger, that we may not be broken in pieces by our particular quarrels after we have gained an entire conquest over the enemy." Whitelocke replied, "that all their danger was from the army, who were men of emulation, and had now nothing to do." Cromwell answered, "that the officers thought themselves not rewarded according to their deserts; that the Parliament had engrossed all places of honour and trust among themselves; that they delayed the public business, and designed to perpetuate themselves; that the officers thought it impossible to keep them within the bounds of justice, law, or reason, unless there was some authority or power to which they might be accountable." Whitelocke said, "he believed the Parliament were honest men, and designed the public good, though some particular persons might be to blame, but that it was absurd for the officers, who were private men, and had received their commissions from the Parliament, to pretend to control them." "But," says Cromwell, "what if a man should take upon him to be king?" Whitelocke answered, "that the remedy was worse than the disease; and that the general had already all the power of a king, without the envy, danger, and pomp of the title." "But," says he, "the title of king would make all acts done by him legal; it would indemnify those that should act under him, at all events, and be of advantage to curb the insolence of those whom the present powers could

not control." Whitelocke agreed to the general's reasons, but desired him to consider "whether the title of king would not lose him his best friends in the army, as well as those gentlemen who were for settling a free commonwealth; but if we must have a king," says he, "the question will be, whether it shall be Cromwell or Stuart?"[*] The general asking his opinion upon this, Whitelocke proposed a private treaty with the king of the Scots, with whom he might make his own terms, and raise his family to what pitch of greatness he pleased; but Cromwell was so apprehensive of the danger of this proposal, that he broke off the conversation with some marks of dissatisfaction, and never made use of Whitelocke with confidence afterward.

Thus things remained[†] throughout the whole winter; the army, having little to do after the battle of Worcester, drew near to London, but there was no treaty of accommodation between them and the Parliament; one would not disband without their full pay; nor the other dissolve by the direction of their own servants, but voted the expediency of filling up their numbers, and that it should be high treason to petition for their dissolution. When the general heard this, he called a councill of officers to Whitehall, who all agreed that it was not fit the Parliament should continue any longer. This was published in hopes of frightening the House to make some advances towards a dissolution; but when Colonel Ingoldsby informed the general, next morning, that they were concluding upon an act to prolong the session for another year, he rose up in a heat, and with a small retinue of officers and soldiers marched to the Parliament House, April 20, and having placed his men without doors, went into the House, and heard the debates. After some time he beckoned to Colonel Harrison, on the other side of the House, and told him in his ear, that he thought the Parliament was ripe for dissolution, and that this was the time for doing it. Harrison replied that the work was dangerous, and desired him to think better of it. Upon this he sat down about a quarter of an hour, and then said, This is the time, I must do it; and, rising up in his place, he told the House that he was come to put an end to their power, of which they had made so ill a use; that some of them were whoremasters, looking towards Harry Martin and Sir Peter Wentworth; others were drunkards, and some corrupt and unjust men, who had not at heart the public good, but were only

---

[*] Whitelocke, p. 523, &c.

[†] Here may be inserted, from Whitelocke, two anecdotes, which afford a pleasing specimen of the temper of the Quakers under ill treatment. February 3, 1653, they were assaulted and beaten by some people in the north. February 13, 1654, a similar outrage was offered to others of them, at Hasington in Northumberland, for speaking to the ministers on the Sabbath Day, so that one or two of them were almost killed. The Quakers fell on their knees and prayed God to forgive the people, as those who knew not what they did; and remonstrated with them so as to convince them of the evil of their conduct, on which they ceased from their violence, and began to reproach each other with being the occasion of it; and, in the last instance, beat one another more than they had before the Quakers.—*Memorials*, p. 564, 599.—ED.

for perpetuating their own power. Upon the whole, he thought they had sat long enough, and therefore desired them to retire and go away. When some of the members began to reply, he stepped into the middle of the House, and said, " Come, come, I will put an end to your prating ; you are no Parliament ; I say you are no Parliament ;" and, stamping with his foot, a file of musketeers entered the House, one of whom he commanded to take away that fool's bawble, the mace ; and Major Harrison taking the speaker by the arm, conducted him out of the chair. Cromwell, then seizing upon their papers, obliged them to walk out of the House ; and having caused the doors to be locked upon them, returned to Whitehall.*

In the afternoon the general went to the Council of State, attended by Major-general Lambert and Harrison, and as he entered the room, said, "Gentlemen, if you are met here as private persons you shall not be disturbed, but if as a Council of State, this is no place for you ; and since you cannot but know what was done in the morning, so take notice the Parliament is dissolved." Sergeant Bradshaw replied, " Sir, we have heard what you did in the morning, but you are mistaken to think the Parliament is dissolved, for no power can dissolve them but themselves ; therefore, take you notice of that." But the general not being terrified with big words, the Council thought it their wisest way to rise up and go home.

Thus ended the commonwealth of England, after it had continued four years, two months, and twenty days, which, though no better than a usurpation, had raised the credit of the nation to a very high pitch of glory and renown ; and with the commonwealth ended the remains of the Long Parliament for the present ; an assembly famous throughout all the world for its undertakings, actions, and successes :† " the acts of this Parliament," says Mr. Coke,‡ " will hard-

* The character of the Long Parliament has been very differently sketched, just as the passions of men have prompted their pens. Nor is it easy to do justice to the theme. The assembly possessed no uniform character, but changed its complexion with the progress of events, and the introduction of new members. In the earlier periods of its existence, it was calm and dignified ; an honourable emblem of the national intellect and heart. Subsequently it was torn by factions, and, mangled by military violence. Its deliberations were characterized by passion, and its votes, became indicative of the departure of its master spirits. It lost the amplitude, and range, and generosity of its designs, and looked to the triumph of a party rather than to the interest of the commonwealth.—C.

† Mrs. Macaulay, after quoting the high eulogiums made on the government of this Parliament, adds, " It is to be remembered, that to them is due the singular praise of having pursued the true interest of their country in attending particularly to its maritime strength, and carrying on its foreign wars by its naval power. This example, which raised England to so great a height of glory and prosperity, has never yet been followed, and in all probability never will, by the succeeding monarchs. The aim of princes is to make conquests on their subjects, not to enlarge the empire of a free people. A standing army is a never-failing instrument of domestic triumph ; and it is very doubtful whether a naval force could be rendered useful in any capacity but that of extending the power and prosperity of the country."—Hist. of England, vol. v., p. 106, note, 8vo.—ED.

‡ Detect., p. 363.

ly find belief in future ages ; and to say the truth, they were a race of men most indefatigable and industrious in business, always seeking men fit for it, and never preferring any for favour or importunity : you hardly ever heard of any revolt from them, no soldiers or seamen being ever pressed. And as they excelled in civil affairs, so, it must be confessed, they exercised in matters ecclesiastical no such severities as others before them did upon such as dissented from them."

But their foundation was bad, and many of their actions highly criminal ; they were a packed assembly, many of their members being excluded by force, before they could be secure of a vote to put the late king to death ; they subverted the Constitution, by setting up themselves, and continuing their sessions after his majesty's demise ; by erecting high courts of justice of their own nomination for capital offences ; by raising taxes, and doing all other acts of sovereignty without consent of the people ; all which they designed to perpetuate among themselves, without being accountable to any superior, or giving place to a new body of representatives. If, then, it be inquired, What right or authority General Cromwell and his officers had to offer violence to this Parliament ? it may be replied, 1. The right of self-preservation, the ruin of one or the other being unavoidable. 2. The right that every Englishman has to put an end to a usurpation when it is in his power, provided he can substitute something better in its room ; and if Cromwell could by this method have restored the Constitution, and referred the settlement of the government to a free and full representative of the people, no wise man would have blamed him. It was not, therefore, his turning out the old Parliament that was criminal, but his not summoning a new one, by a fair and free election of the people ; and yet Mr. Rapin* is of opinion that even this was impracticable, there being three opposite interests in the nation : the Republicans, who were for an absolute commonwealth ; the Presbyterians, who were for restoring things to the condition they were in 1648 ; and the Cavaliers, who were for setting the king upon the throne ; as before the civil wars ; it was by no means possible (says he†) to reconcile the three parties, and if they had been let loose, they would have destroyed each other, and thrown the whole nation into blood and confusion ; nothing, therefore, but giving a forcible superiority to on was capable to hold the other two in subjection. The king was now no way interested in the change, for it was not Charles Stuart, but a republican usurpation, that was dispossessed of the supreme power. If the general had failed in his design, and lost his life in the attempt, the king would have received no manner of advantage, for the nation was by no means disposed to restore him at this time. Supposing, then, it was not practicable to choose a free Parliament, nor fit to let the old one perpetuate themselves, Oliver Cromwell had no other choice but to abandon the state, or to take the administration upon himself ; or put it into the hands of some other person who had no better title. How far private ambition took place of the public good in the choice, must be left to the judgment of

* Vol. ii., p. 289, folio edition.　　† Rapin, p. 140

every reader; but if it was necessary that there should be a supreme authority, capable of enforcing obedience, it cannot be denied but that General Cromwell was more capable of governing the state in such a storm than any man then living. No objection can be raised against him, which might not with more justice have been urged against any other single person, or body of men in the nation, except the right heir. However, all the three parties, of Cavaliers, Presbyterians, and Republicans, were displeased with his conduct, loaded him with invectives, and formed conspiracies against his person, though they could never agree in any other scheme which, in the present crisis, was more practicable.

The Parliament being thus violently dispersed, the sovereign power devolved on the council of officers, of which Cromwell was head, who published a declaration, justifying his dissolution of the late Parliament, and promising to put the administration into the hands of persons of approved fidelity and honesty, and leave them to form it into what shape they pleased. Accordingly, April 30, another declaration was published, signed by Oliver Cromwell and thirty of his officers, nominating a new council of state to take care of the government, till a new representative body of men could be called together; and June 8, the general, by the advice of his council, sent the following summons out of the one hundred and forty select persons, out of the several counties of England, to meet at Westminster, in order to settle the nation: "I, Oliver Cromwell, captain-general, &c., do hereby summons and require you, ——, being one of the persons nominated by myself, with the advice of my council, personally to appear at the Council Chamber at Whitehall, upon the fourth of July next ensuing the date hereof, to take upon you the trust of the affairs of the commonwealth; to which you are hereby called and appointed to serve as a member for the county of —— ; and hereof you are not to fail. Given under my hand this eighth of June, 1653.
"O. CROMWELL."

These were high acts of sovereignty, and not to be justified but upon the supposition of extreme necessity. The dissolution of the Long Parliament was an act of violence, but not unacceptable to the people, as appeared by the numerous addresses from the army, the fleet, and other places, approving the general's conduct, and promising to stand by him and his council in their proceedings; but then for the general himself, and thirty officers, to choose representatives for the whole nation, without interesting any of the counties or corporations of England in the choice, would have deserved the highest censure under any other circumstances.

About one hundred and twenty of the new representatives appeared at the time and place appointed, when the general, after a short speech, delivered them an instrument in parchment under his hand and seal, resigning into their hands, or the hands of any forty of them, the supreme authority and government of the commonwealth, limiting the time of their continuance to November 3, 1654, and empowering them, three months before their dissolution, to make choice of others to succeed them for a

year, and they to provide for a future succession. It was much wondered, says Whitelocke,[*] that these gentlemen, many of whom were persons of fortune and estate,[†] should accept of the supreme authority of the nation upon such a summons, and from such hands. Most of them were men of piety, but no great politicians, and were therefore in contempt called sometimes the Little Parliament; and by others, Barebones' Parliament, from a leather-seller of that name,[‡] who was one of the most active members. When the general was withdrawn,

* Memoirs, p. 534.

† Dr. Grey, after Lord Clarendon and others, and Mr. Hume since them, have spoken in severe and contemptuous terms of this assembly and their proceedings. "The major part of them," says his lordship, "consisted of inferior persons, of no quality or name, artificers of the meanest name, known only by their gifts in praying and preaching." But many of Cromwell's after-councillors, many of the chief officers of the army, were in this assembly. They were treated as the supreme authority of the nation by sovereign princes, and had the most humble applications made to them by the chief cavaliers, as by the Earls of Worcester, Derby; and Shrewsbury, Lord Mansfield; and the Countess of Derby; and they were, during their short session, employed about points of the highest national concernment; such as abolishing the Court of Chancery on account of its expensiveness and delays, the forming a new body of the law, the union of Scotland with England, the regulation of marriages, and the investing the solemnization and cognizance of them in the civil magistrate, with other matters of moment.—Harris's Life of Oliver Cromwell, p. 335–337.—ED.

‡ There were three brothers of this family, each of whom had a sentence for his name, viz. "Praise God, Barebone; Christ came into the world to save Barebone; and, if Christ had not died, thou hadst been damned, Barebone." In this style were the Christian names of very many persons formed in the times of the civil wars: It was said that the genealogy of our Saviour might be learned from the names in Cromwell's regiments; and that the muster-master used no other list than the first chapter of Matthew. A jury was returned in the county of Sussex of the following names:

Accepted, Trevor, of Norsham.
Redeemed, Compton, of Battle.
Faint not, Hewet, of Heathfield.
Make-peace, Heaton, of Hare.
God-reward, Smart, of Fivehurst.
Stand fast on high, Stringer, of Crowhurst.
Earth, Adams, of Warbleton.
Called, Lower, of ditto.
Kill Sin, Pimple, of Witham.
Return, Spelman, of Watling.
Be faithful, Joyner, of Britling.
Fly Debate, Robert, of ditto.
Fight the good Fight of Faith, White, of Emer.
More Fruit, Fowler, of East-Hadley.
Hope for, Bending, of ditto.
Graceful, Harding, of Lewes.
Weep not, Billings, ditto.
Meek, Brewer, of Okeham.
—Granger's History of England, vol. iii., p. 68, 8vo, note; and Dr. Grey, p. 286, 287, note. Mr. Hume has also given this list of the Sussex jury. But the ridicule which falls on this mode of naming children belongs not to these times only, for the practice was in use long before.—Harris's Life of Oliver Cromwell, p. 342, the note.—ED. "Praise God" is scarcely more fanatical than that of Deodatus, which is to be found in the records of most of the countries of Europe." I quote the language of Godwin, and this admirable historian rejects the account of this same Sussex jury, as totally undeserving of credit.—Hist. of the Commonwealth, vol. iii., p. 524.—C.

they chose Mr. Rouse, an aged and venerable man, member in the late Parliament for Truro in Cornwall, their speaker, and then voted themselves the Parliament of the commonwealth of England. Mr. Baxter* places them in a contemptible light, and says, "They intended to eject all the parish ministers, and to encourage the gathering Independent churches; that they cast out all the ministers in Wales, which, though bad enough for the most part, were yet better than none, or the few itinerants they set up in their room; and that they attempted, and had almost accomplished, the same in England." But nothing of this appears among their acts. When the city of London petitioned that more learned and approved ministers might be sent into the country to preach the Gospel; that their settled maintenance by law might be confirmed, and their just properties preserved; and that the universities might be zealously countenanced and encouraged, the petitioners had the thanks of that House; and the committee gave it as their opinion, that commissioners should be sent into the several counties, who should have power to eject scandalous ministers, and to settle others in their room. They were to appoint preaching in all vacant places, that none might live above three miles from a place of worship. That such as were approved for public ministers should enjoy the maintenance provided by the laws; and that if any scrupled the payment of tithes, the neighbouring justices of peace should settle the value, which the owner of the land should be obliged to pay; but as for the tithes themselves, they were of opinion that the incumbents and impropriators had a right in them, and therefore they could not be taken away till they were satisfied.

July 23, it was referred to a committee, to consider of a repeal of such laws as hindered the progress of the Gospel; that is (says Bishop Kennet), to take away the few remaining rules of decency and order; or, in other language, the penal laws. This was done at the instance of the Independents, who petitioned for protection against the presbyteries; upon which, it was voted that a declaration should be published for giving proper liberty to all that feared God, and for preventing their imposing hardships on one another.

Mr. Echard, and others of his principles, write, that this Parliament had under deliberation the taking away the old English laws, as badges of the Norman conquest, and substituting the Mosaic laws of government in their place; and that all schools of learning and titles of honour should be extinguished, as not agreeing with the Christian simplicity. But no such proposals were made to the House, and therefore it is unjust to lay them to their charge.

The solemnizing of matrimony had hitherto been engrossed by the clergy; but this convention considered it a civil contract, and put it into the hands of justices of peace, by an ordinance, which enacts "that after the 29th of September, 1653, all persons who shall agree to be married within the commonwealth of England, shall deliver in their names and places of abode, with the names of their parents, guardians, and overseers, to the registrar of the parish where each party lives, who shall publish the

* P. 70, 180.

bans in the church or chapel three several Lord's Days, after the morning service; or else in the market-place three several weeks successively, between the hours of eleven and two, on a market day, if the party desire it. The registrar shall make out a certificate of the due performance of one or the other, at the request of the parties concerned, without which they shall not proceed to marriage.

"It is farther enacted, that all persons intending to marry shall come before some justice of peace within the county, city, or town corporate where publication has been made as aforesaid, with their certificate, and with sufficient proof of the consent of the parents, if either party be under age, and then the marriage shall proceed in this manner:

"The man to be married shall take the woman by the hand, and distinctly pronounce these words: I, A. B., do here, in the presence of God, the Searcher of all hearts, take thee, C. D., for my wedded wife; and do also, in the presence of God, and before these witnesses, promise to be to thee a loving and faithful husband.

"Then the woman, taking the man by the hand, shall plainly and distinctly pronounce these words: I, C. D., do here, in the presence of God, the Searcher of all hearts, take thee, A. B., for my wedded husband; and do also, in the presence of God, and before these witnesses, promise to be to thee a loving, faithful, and obedient wife.

"After this, the justice may and shall declare the said man and woman to be from henceforth husband and wife; and from and after such consent, so expressed, and such declaration made of the same (as to the form of marriage), it shall be good and effectual in law; and no other marriage whatsoever, within the commonwealth of England, after the 29th of September, 1653, shall be held or accounted a marriage according to the law of England."

This ordinance was confirmed by the protector's Parliament in the year 1656, except the clause, "that no other marriage whatsoever within the commonwealth of England shall be held or accounted a legal marriage;" and it was wisely done of the Parliament, at the Restoration, to confirm these marriages, in order to prevent illegitimacy, and vexatious lawsuits in future times. But the acts of this convention were of little significance, for when they found the affairs of the nation too intricate, and the several parties too stubborn to yield to their ordinances, they wisely resigned, and surrendered back their sovereignty into the same hands that gave it them, after they had sat five months and twelve days.

The general and his officers finding themselves reinvested with the supreme authority, by what they fancied a more parliamentary delegation, took upon them to strike out a new form of government, a little tending towards monarchy, contained in a large instrument of forty-two articles, entitled "The Government of the Commonwealth of England, Scotland, and Ireland." It appoints the government to be in a single person; that the single person be the General Oliver Cromwell, whose style and title should be his highness, lord-protector of the commonwealth of England, Scotland, and Ireland, and of the dominions thereunto belonging;

that the lord-protector should have a council, consisting of no more than twenty-one persons, nor less than thirteen, to assist him in the administration. A Parliament was to be chosen out of the three kingdoms every three years at longest, and not to be dissolved, without their consent, in less than five months. It was to consist of four hundred members for England and Wales; thirty for Scotland, and thirty for Ireland; whereof sixty were to make a house. The counties of England and Wales were to choose two hundred and thirty-nine; the other elections to be distributed among the chief cities and market-towns, without regard to ancient custom. The county of Dorset was to choose eleven members; Cornwall eight; Bedfordshire five; the several ridings of Yorkshire fourteen; Middlesex four; the city of London six; Westminster two; the whole number of cities and boroughs which had the privilege of election were one hundred and ten, and the number of representatives to be chosen by them one hundred and sixty. If the protector refused to issue out writs, the commissioners of the great seal, or the high-sheriff of the county, was to do it, under pain of treason; none to have votes but such as were worth £200. This regulation, being wisely proportioned, met with universal approbation. Lord Clarendon says it was fit to be more warrantably made, and in a better time; all the great offices of state, as chancellor, treasurer, &c., if they became vacant in time of Parliament, to be supplied with their approbation; and in the intervals, with the approbation of the council; such bills as were offered to the protector by the Parliament, if not signed in twenty days, were to be laws without him, if not contrary to this instrument. In the present crisis, the protector and his council might publish ordinances, which should have force till the first sessions of Parliament; the protector was to have power to make war and peace, to confer titles of honour, to pardon all crimes except treason and murder; the militia was intrusted with him and his council, except during the sessions of Parliament, when it was to be jointly in both. In short, the protector had almost all the royalties of a king; but, then, the protectorship was to be elective, and no protector after the present to be general of the army. The articles relating to religion were these:

Art. 35. "That the Christian religion contained in the Scriptures be held forth and recommended as the public profession of these nations, and that, as soon as may be, a provision less subject to contention, and more certain than the present, be made for the maintenance of ministers; and that, till such provision be made, the present maintenance continue.

Art. 36. "That none be compelled to conform to the public religion by penalties or otherwise; but that endeavours be used to win them by sound doctrine, and the example of a good conversation.

Art. 37. "That such as profess faith in God by Jesus Christ, though differing in judgment from the doctrine, worship, or discipline publicly held forth, shall not be restrained from, but shall be protected in the profession of their faith and exercise of their religion, so as they abuse not this liberty to the civil injury of others, and to the actual disturbance of the public peace on their parts: provided this liberty be not extended to popery or prelacy, or to such as, under a profession of Christ, hold forth and practise licentiousness.

Art. 38. "That all laws, statutes, ordinances, and clauses, in any law, statute, or ordinance, to the contrary of the aforesaid liberty, shall be esteemed null and void."

The protector was installed with great magnificence, December 16, 1653, in the Court of Chancery, by order of the council of officers, in presence of the lord-mayor and aldermen of London, the judges, the commissioners of the great seal, and other great officers, who were summoned to attend on this occasion. Oliver Cromwell, standing uncovered on the left hand of a chair of state set for him, first subscribed the instrument of government in the face of the court, and then took the following oath:

"Whereas the major part of the last Parliament (judging that their sitting any longer as then constituted would not be for the good of the commonwealth) did dissolve the same; and by a writing under their hands, dated the 12th of this instant December, resigned to me their powers and authorities. And whereas it was necessary, thereupon, that some speedy course should be taken for the settlement of these nations upon such a basis and foundation as, by the blessing of God, might be lasting, secure property, and answer those great ends of religion and liberty so long contended for; and upon full and mature consideration had of the form of government hereunto annexed, being satisfied that the same, through Divine assistance, may answer the ends afore-mentioned; and having also been desired and advised, as well by several persons of interest and fidelity in the commonwealth as the officers of the army, to take upon me the protection and government of these nations in the manner expressed in the said form of government, I have accepted thereof, and do hereby declare my acceptance accordingly; and do promise, in the presence of God, that I will not violate or infringe the matters and things contained therein, but to my power observe the same, and cause them to be observed; and shall in all other things, to the best of my understanding, govern these nations according to the laws, statutes, and customs, seeking their peace, and causing justice and law to be equally administered."

After this he sat down in the chair of state covered, and the commissioners delivered him the great seal, and the lord-mayor his sword and cap of maintenance; which he returned in a very obliging manner. The ceremony being over, the soldiers, with a shout, cried out, "God bless the lord-protector of the commonwealth of England, Scotland, and Ireland!" In their return to Whitehall, the lord-mayor carried the sword before his highness uncovered, and presently after he was proclaimed in the city of London, and throughout all the British dominions.[*]

---

[*] Cromwell understood well the intrinsic value of outward state; he was aware that, taken abstractedly, a monarch is but a ceremony, and so we find him affecting greater magnificence as he increased in years. A full narration of the ceremonial connected with his inauguration may be seen in Jesse's Court of the Stuarts.—C.

Thus did this wonderful man, by surprising management, supported only by the sword, advance himself to the supreme government of three kingdoms without consent of Parliament or people. His birth seemed to promise nothing of this kind; nor does it appear that he had formed the project till after the battle of Worcester, when he apprehended the Parliament had projected his ruin by disbanding the army, and perpetuating their authority among themselves : which of the two usurpations was most eligible must be left with the reader; but how he brought the officers into his measures, and supported his sovereignty by an army of enthusiasts, Anabaptists, fifth monarchy men, and Republicans, will be the admiration of all posterity; and though by this adventurous act he drew upon himself the plots and conspiracies of the several factions in the nation, yet his genius and resolution surmounted all difficulties, his short empire being one continued blaze of glory and renown to the British isles, and of terror to the rest of Europe.

The reader will make his own remarks upon the new instrument of government, and will necessarily observe that it was a creature of Cromwell's and his council of officers, and not drawn up by a proper representative of the people. How far the present circumstances of the nation made this necessary, must be concluded from the remarks we have made upon the change of government; but the articles relating to religion can hardly be complained of, though they disgusted all that part of the clergy who were for church power; the Presbyterians preached and wrote against the 36th and 37th articles, as inconsistent with their establishment, and sinking it almost to a level with their sectaries. The Republicans were dissatisfied because the Engagement, by which they had sworn fidelity to a commonwealth, without a single person, or House of Lords, was set aside. Bishop Kennet is angry with the protector's latitude, because there was no test or barrier to the establishment. "How little religion was the concern, or so much as any longer the pretence of Cromwell and his officers," says his lordship, "appears from hence, that in the large instrument of the government of the commonwealth, which was the Magna Charta of the new Constitution, there is not a word of churches or ministers, nor anything but the Christian religion in general, with liberty to all differing in judgment from the doctrine, worship, or discipline publicly held forth." Strange, that this should displease a Christian bishop! But his lordship should have remembered, that this liberty was not to extend to any kinds of immoralities, nor to such as injured the civil rights of others, nor to such as disturbed the public peace. And do the Scriptures authorize us to go farther? The sixth article provides, "that the laws in being relating to the Presbyterian religion were not to be suspended, altered, abrogated, or repealed; nor any new law made, but by consent of Parliament." The 36th adds, "that until a better provision can be made for the encouragement and maintenance of able and painful teachers, the present maintenance shall not be taken away nor impeached." And triers were appointed soon after for preventing scandalous and unlearned persons invading the

pulpit. This part of the instrument is, in my opinion, so far from being criminal, that it breathes a noble spirit of Christian liberty, though it was undoubtedly faulty, in putting popery, prelacy, and licentiousness of manners upon a level. The open toleration of popery is hardly consistent with the safety of a Protestant government; otherwise, considered merely as a religious institution, I see not why it should be crushed by the civil power; and licentiousness of manners is not to be indulged in any civilized nation; but if the Episcopalians would have given security for their living peaceably under their new masters, they ought undoubtedly to have been protected; however, the protector did not in every instance adhere strictly to the instrument.

But though, in point of policy, the Episcopalians were at this time excepted from a legal toleration, their assemblies were connived at; and several of their clergy indulged the public exercise of their ministry without the fetters of oaths, subscriptions, or engagements; as Dr. Hall, afterward Bishop of Chester, Dr. Wild, Pearson, Ball, Hardy, Griffith, Farringdon, and others. Several of the bishops, who had been kept from public service by the Covenant and Engagement, preached again publicly in the city, as Archbishop Usher, Bishop Brownrigge, and others. Mr. Baxter, who was very far from being a friend of the protector's, says " that all men were suffered to live quietly, and enjoy their properties under his government; that he removed the terrors and prejudices which hindered the success of the Gospel, especially considering that godliness had countenance and reputation as well as liberty, whereas before, if it did not appear in all the fetters and formalities of the times, it was the way to common shame and ruin. It is well known that the Presbyterians did not approve of the usurpation, but when they saw that Cromwell's design was to do good in the main, and encourage religion as far as his cause would admit, they acquiesced." And then, comparing these times with those after the Restoration, he adds, " I shall for the future think that land happy where the people have but bare liberty to be as good as they are willing; and if countenance and maintenance be but added to liberty, and tolerated errors and sects be but forced to keep the peace, I shall not hereafter much fear such a toleration, nor despair that truth will bear down its adversaries."* This was a considerable testimony to the protector's administration from the pen of an adversary.

The protector's first council were, Major-general Lambert, Lieutenant-general Fleetwood, Colonel Montague, afterward Earl of Sandwich; Philip Lord-viscount Lisle, since Earl of Leicester; Colonel Desborough, Sir Gilbert Pickering, Sir Anthony Ashley Cooper, afterward Earl of Shaftesbury; Sir Charles Woolsley, Major-general Skippon, Mr. Strictland, Colonel Sydenham, Colonel Jones, Mr. Rouse, Mr. Lawrence, and Mr. Major : men of great name in those times, some of whom made a considerable figure after the Restoration. The protector's wise conduct appeared in nothing more than his unwearied endeavours to make all religious parties easy. He indulged the army in

* Life, p. 86, 87.

their enthusiastic raptures, and sometimes joined in their prayers and, sermons. He countenanced the Presbyterians, by assuring them he would maintain the public ministry, and give them all due encouragement. He supported the Independents, by making them his chaplains; by preferring them to considerable livings in the Church and universities; and by joining them in one commission with the Presbyterians as triers of all such as desired to be admitted to benefices. But he absolutely forbade the clergy of every denomination dealing in politics, as not belonging to their profession; and when he perceived the managing Presbyterians took too much upon them, he always found means to mortify them; and would sometimes glory that he had curbed that insolent sect, that would suffer none but itself.

It was happy for the wise and moderate Presbyterians that the protector disarmed their discipline of its coercive power; for he still left them all that was sufficient for the purposes of religion; they had their monthly or quarterly classical Presbyteries in every county, for the ordination of ministers, by imposition of hands, according to the Directory, to whom they gave certificates, or testimonials, in the following words: " We, the ministers of the Presbytery of ——, having examined Mr. —— according to the tenour of the ordinance for that purpose, and finding him duly qualified and gifted for that holy office and employment (no just exception having been made to his ordination); having approved him, and accordingly, on the day and year hereafter expressed, have proceeded solemnly to set him apart to the office of a preaching presbyter, and work of the ministry, with fasting and prayer, and imposition of hands; and do hereby actually admit him (as far as concerns us) to perform all the offices and duties of a faithful minister of Jesus Christ. In witness whereof, we have hereunto subscribed our names, this —— day of September, 1653."

Other testimonials were in this form:
" We, the ministers of Christ, who are called to watch over this part of his flock in the city of ——, with the assistance of some others, that we might not be wanting to the service of the Church in its necessity, having received credible testimonials, under the hands of divers ministers of the Gospel, and others, of the sober, righteous, and godly conversation of ——, as also concerning his gifts for the ministry, have proceeded to make farther trial of his fitness for so great a work; and being in some good measure satisfied concerning his piety and ability, have, upon the —— day of ——, 1653, proceeded solemnly to set him apart to the office of a presbyter, and work of the ministry, by laying on our hands with fasting and prayer; by virtue whereof we do esteem and declare him a lawful minister of Christ, and hereby recommend him to the Church of ——. In witness whereof, we have set our hands," &c.

When the Presbyterians found that their classes could obtain no power to inflict pains and penalties on those who refused to submit to their discipline, the ministers of the several denominations in the country began to enter into friendly associations for brotherly counsel and advice. Mr. Baxter, and his brethren of Worcestershire, formed a scheme upon such general principles as all good men were agreed in, which he communicated to the Reverend Mr. Vines and Gataker; and when he had drawn up articles of concord, he submitted them to the correction of Archbishop Usher, and other Episcopal divines, who agreed with him, that no more discipline should be practised than the Episcopalian, Presbyterian, and Independent divines agreed in; that they should not meddle with politics or affairs of civil government, in their assemblies, nor pretend to exercise the power of the keys, or any church censures; but only to assist, advise, and encourage each other in propagating truth and holiness, and in keeping their churches from profane and scandalous communicants.* Their meetings were appointed to be once a month in some market-town, where there was a sermon in the morning; and after dinner the conversation was upon such points of doctrine or discipline as required advice; or else an hour was spent in disputing upon some theological question which had been appointed the preceding month. Doctor Warmestry, afterward Dean of Worcester, and Dr. Good, one of the prebendaries of Hereford, sent Mr. Baxter a letter dated September 20, 1653, wherein they testify their approbation of the association above mentioned, and of the articles of concord.†

In the west of England, Mr. Hughes, of Plymouth, and Mr. Good, of Exeter, prevailed with the ministers of the several persuasions in those parts to follow the example of Worcestershire; accordingly, they parcelled themselves into four divisions, which met once a quarter; and all four had a general meeting for concord once a year: the Reverend Mr. Hughes presided in those of 1655 and 1656. The moderator began and ended with prayer, and several of the Episcopal divines of the best character, as well as Independents, joined with them; "the chief of the Presbyterian and Independent divines, who were weary of divisions, and willing to strengthen each other's hands, united in these assemblies, though the exasperated prelatists, the more rigid Presbyterians, and severer sort of Independents, kept at a distance: but many remarkable advantages," says Mr. Baxter, "attended these associations;" they opened and preserved a friendly correspondence among the ministers; they removed a great many prejudices and misunderstandings, insomuch that the controversies and heats of angry men began to be allayed, their spirit bettered, and the ends of religion more generally promoted.

But these country associations were not countenanced by the more zealous Presbyterians of London, who met weekly at Sion College; they could hardly digest a toleration of the sectaries, much less submit to a coalition, but resolved to keep close to the ordinances of Parliament, and to the acts of their provincial assembly: they wanted the sword of discipline, and were impatient under the present restraint; and nothing but the piercing eye of the protector, whose spies were in every corner, kept them from preaching, praying, and plotting against the government. However, the country ministers being easy in their possessions, cultivated good neigh-

* Baxter's Life, part ii., p. 147, &c., p. 167., &c.
† Ibid., p. 149.

bourhood, and spread the associations through Wiltshire, Essex, Hampshire, Dorsetshire, Cumberland, Westmoreland, and other parts ; that if I am not misinformed, there are the like brotherly associations among the Dissenters in several counties to this day.

This year died old Dr. William Gouge, born at Stratford-le-Bow in the year 1575, and educated at King's College, Cambridge, of which he was fellow. He entered into orders 1607, and the very next year was settled at Blackfriars, London, where he continued to his death. He commenced doctor of divinity in the year 1628, about which time he became one of the feoffees for buying up impropriations, for which he was ordered to be prosecuted in the Star Chamber. In the year 1643 he was nominated one of the Assembly of Divines, and was in such reputation, that he often filled the moderator's chair in his absence. He was a modest, humble, and affable person, of strict and exemplary piety, a universal scholar, and a most constant preacher, as long as he was able to get up into the pulpit. For many years he was esteemed the father of the London ministers, and died comfortably and piously December 12, 1653, in the seventy-ninth year of his age, having been minister of Blackfriars almost forty-six years.*

Doctor Thomas Hill, of whom mention has been made before, was born in Worcestershire, and educated in Emanuel College, Cambridge, of which he was a fellow, and tutor to young scholars for many years. He was afterward preferred to the living of Tichmarsh in Northamptonshire, and was chosen into the Assembly of Divines for that county. While he was at London he preached every day at St. Martin's-in-the-Fields, and was one of the morning lecturers at Westminster Abbey. He was afterward chosen to be master of Emanuel College, Cambridge, and from thence removed to Trinity College ; in which stations he behaved with great prudence and circumspection. He was a good scholar, and very careful of the antiquities and privileges of the university ; a strict Calvinist, a plain, powerful, and practical preacher, and of a holy and unblamable conversation. He died of a quartan ague December 18, 1653, at an advanced age, very much lamented by his acquaintance and brethren.†

* He spent nine years at King's College, and was never absent from public prayers at the chapel, and constantly read fifteen chapters in the Bible every day. He was the laborious, exemplary, and much-loved minister, of whom none thought or spoke ill, says Mr. Granger, "but such as were inclined to think or speak ill of religion itself." He refused the provostship of King's College in Cambridge ; and had eight children, who lived to man's and woman's estate.—*Clarke's Lives in his General Martyrology*, p. 234; and *Granger's History of England*, vol. ii., p. 179, 8vo.—Ed. Dr. Gouge's great effort seems to have been *usefulness ;* he used to say, "It is my highest ambition to go from Blackfriars to heaven." He regularly read fifteen chapters of the Bible a day. Laud and Neile both persecuted him for his opposition to Arminianism and ceremonies; Dr. Gouge was regarded as the oracle of his time. Wood and Granger both testify to his worth and learning. Bishop Wilkins classes Dr. Gouge's sermons as among the best of his time, and Wood styles his Commentary on Hebrews a learned and useful work.—C.

† Dr. Hill used to lay his hand upon his breast, and say, "Every true Christian hath something here

CHAPTER III.

If the reader, will carefully review the divided state of the nation at this time, the strength of the several parties in opposite interests, and almost equal in power, each sanguine for his own scheme of settlement, and all conspiring against the present, he will be surprised that any wise man should be prevailed with to put himself at the head of such a distracted body ; and yet more, that such a genius should arise, who, without any foreign alliances, should be capable of guarding against so many foreign and domestic enemies, and of steering the commonwealth through such a hurricane, clear of the rocks and quicksands which threatened its ruin.

This was the province that the enterprising Oliver undertook, with the style and title of lord-protector of the commonwealth of England, Scotland, and Ireland. He assumed all the state and ceremony of a crowned head ; his household officers and guards attended in their places, and his court appeared in as great splendour, and more order, than had been seen at Whitehall since Queen Elizabeth's reign. His first concern was to fill the courts of justice with the ablest lawyers ; Sir Matthew Hale was made Lord-chief-justice of the Common Pleas ; Mr. Maynard, Twisden, Newdigate, and Windham, sergeants at law ; Mr. Thurloe, secretary of state; and Monk, governor of Scotland. His next care was to deliver himself from his foreign enemies ; for this purpose he gave peace to the Dutch, which the fame of his power enabled him to accomplish without the ceremony of a formal treaty ; he therefore sent his Secretary Thurloe, with the conditions to which they were to submit ; the Dutch pleaded for abatements, but his highness was at a point, and obliged them to deliver up the island of Polerone in the East Indies ; to pay £300,000 for the affair of Amboyna; to abandon the interests of King Charles II.; to exclude the Prince of Orange from being stadtholder, and to yield up the sovereignty of the seas.

When this was accomplished, most of the sovereign princes in Europe sent to compliment his highness upon his advancement, and to cultivate his friendship: the King of Portugal asked pardon for receiving Prince Rupert into his ports ; the Danes got themselves included in the Dutch treaty, and became security for £140,000 damages done to the English shipping ; the Swedes sued for an alliance, which was concluded with their ambassador ; the crown of Spain made offers which the protector rejected ; but the address of the French ambassador was most extraordinary ; the protector received him in the Banqueting House at Whitehall, with all the state and magnificence of a crowned head ; and the ambassador, having made his obeisance, acquainted his highness with the king his master's desire to establish a correspondence between his dominions and England. He mentioned the value of the friendship of France, and how much it was courted by the greatest potentates of the earth ; "but," says the am-

that will frame an argument against Arminianism." Dr. Grey railed against this good man, yet I can see nothing but his piety to which he could object.—C.

bassador, "the king my master communicates his resolutions to none with so much joy and cheerfulness, as to those whose virtuous actions and extraordinary merits render them more conspicuously famous than the largeness of their dominions. His majesty is sensible that all these advantages do wholly reside in your highness, and that the Divine Providence, after so many calamities, could not deal more favourably with these three nations, nor cause them to forget their past miseries with greater satisfaction, than by subjecting them to so just a government."

The protector's most dangerous enemies were the Royalists, Presbyterians, and Republicans, at home; the former menaced him with an assassination, upon which he declared openly, that though he would never begin so detestable a practice, yet, if any of the king's party should attempt it and fail, he would make an assassinating war of it, and exterminate the whole family, which his servants were ready to execute; the terror of this threatening was a greater security to him than his coat of mail or guards. The protector had the skill always to discover the most secret designs of the Royalists by some of their own number, whom he spared no cost to gain over to his interests. Sir Richard Willis was Chancellor Hyde's chief confidant, to whom he wrote often, and in whom all the party confided, as in an able and wise statesman; but the protector gained him with £200 a year, by which means he had all the king's party in a net, and let them dance in it at pleasure.* He had another correspondent in the king's little family, one Manning, a Roman Catholic, who gave Secretary Thurloe intelligence of all his majesty's councils and proceedings. But though the king's friends were always in one plot or other against the protector's person and government, he always behaved with decency towards them, as long as they kept within tolerable bounds; and without all question, the severe laws that were made against the Episcopal party were not on the account of religion, but of their irreconcilable aversion to the government.

The whole body of the Presbyterians were in principle for the king and the Covenant, but after the battle of Worcester, and the execution of Mr. Love, they were terrified into a compliance with the commonwealth, though they disallowed their proceedings, and were pleased to see them broken in pieces; but the surprising advancement of Cromwell to the protectorship filled them with new terrors, and threatened the overthrow of their church power, for they considered him not only as a usurper, but a sectarian, who would countenance the free exercise of religion to all that would live peaceably under his government; and though he assured them he would continue religion upon the footing of the present establishment, yet nothing would satisfy them as long as their discipline was disarmed of its coercive power.

But the protector's most determined adversaries were the commonwealth party; these were divided into two branches; one had little or no religion, but were for a democracy in the state, and universal liberty of conscience in religion; the heads of them were Deists, or, in the language of the protector, Heathens, as Algernon Sidney, Henry Neville, Martin, Wildman, and Harrington. It was impossible to work upon these men, or reconcile them to the government of a single person, and therefore he disarmed them of their power. The others were high enthusiasts, and fifth monarchy men, who were in expectation of King Jesus, and of a glorious thousand years' reign of Christ upon earth. They were for pulling down churches, says Bishop Burnet,* for discharging tithes, and leaving religion free (as they called it), without either encouragement or restraint. Most of them were for destroying the clergy, and for breaking everything that looked like a national establishment. These the protector endeavoured to gain, by assuring them, in private conversation, "that he had no manner of inclination to assume the government, but had rather have been content with a shepherd's staff, were it not absolutely necessary to keep the nation from falling to pieces, and becoming a prey to the common enemy; that he only stepped in between the living and the dead, as he expressed it, and this only till God should direct them on what bottom to settle, when he would surrender his dignity with a joy equal to the sorrow with which he had taken it up." With the chiefs of this party he affected to converse upon terms of great familiarity, shutting the door, and making them sit down covered in his presence, to let them see how little he valued those distances he was bound to observe for form's sake with others; he talked with them in their own language, and the conversation commonly ended with a long prayer.

The protector's chief support against these powerful adversaries were the Independents, the city of London, and the army; the former looked upon him as the head of their party, though he was no more theirs than as he was averse to church power, and for a universal toleration. He courted the city of London with a decent respect, declaring, upon all occasions, his resolution to confirm their privileges, and consult measures for promoting trade and commerce. These, in return, after his instalment, entertained him at dinner in a most magnificent and princelike manner, and by degrees modelled their magistrates to his mind. But his chief dependance was upon the army, which, being made up of different parties, be took care to reform by degrees, till they were in a manner entirely at his devotion. He paid the soldiers well, and advanced them according to their merits and zeal for his government, without regard to their birth or seniority.

It was the protector's felicity that the parties above mentioned had as great an enmity to each other as to him; the Cavaliers hated the Presbyterians and Republicans, as these did the Cavaliers; the Royalists fancied that all who were against the protector must join with them in restoring the king; while the Presbyterians were pushing for their Covenant uniformity, and the Republicans for a commonwealth. Cromwell had the skill not only to keep them divided, but to increase their jealousies of each other, and by that means to disconcert all their measures against himself. Let the reader recollect what a difficult situation this was; and

* Burnet, p. 91, vol. i., Edin. edit.

* Vol. i., p. 93.

what a genius it must require to maintain so high a reputation abroad, in the midst of so many domestic enemies, who were continually plotting his destruction.

In pursuance of the instrument of government, the protector published an ordinance, April 12, to incorporate the two kingdoms of Scotland and England. The ordinance sets forth, " that whereas the Parliament in 1651 had sent commissioners into Scotland to invite that nation to a union with England under one government ; and whereas the consent of the shires and boroughs was then obtained, therefore, for completing that work, he ordains that the people of Scotland, and all the territories thereunto belonging, shall be incorporated into one commonwealth with England, and that in every Parliament to be held successively for the said commonwealth, thirty members shall be called from thence to serve for Scotland." Shortly after, Ireland was incorporated after the same manner ; and from this time the arms of Scotland and Ireland were quartered with those of England.

But the protector was hardly fixed in his chair before an assassination-plot of the Royalists was discovered, and three of the conspirators, viz., Mr. Fox, Mr. Gerhard, and Mr. Vowel, were apprehended, and tried before a high court of justice, for conspiring to murder the lord-protector as he was going to Hampton Court, to seize the guards, and the Tower of London, and to proclaim the king. Mr. Fox, who confessed most of what was alleged against him, pleaded guilty, and was reprieved ; but the other two, putting themselves on their trial, though they denied the jurisdiction of the court, were convicted, and executed July 10. Gerhard, a young, hot-headed ensign in the late king's army, was beheaded ; and Vowel, a schoolmaster at Islington, hanged at Charing Cross : Gerhard confessed he knew of the plot, but Vowel was silent.* These commotions were the occasion of the hardships the Royalists underwent some time after.

Don Pantaleon Sa, brother of the Portuguese ambassador, was beheaded the same day, upon account of a riot and murder in the New Exchange. Pantaleon had quarrelled with the above-mentioned Gerhard, and to revenge himself, brought his servants next day, armed with swords and pistols, to kill him ; but instead of Gerhard, they killed another man, and wounded several others. The Portuguese knight and his associates fled to his brother the ambassador's house for sanctuary, but the mob followed them, and threatened to pull down the house, unless they were delivered up to justice. The protector, being informed of the tumult, sent an officer with a party of soldiers to demand the murderers. The ambassador pleaded his public character, but the protector would admit of no

* Mr. Neal's account, as Dr. Grey remarks, does not agree with Lord Clarendon, who represents Vowel as earnestly and pathetically addressing the people and the soldiers, exhorting them to loyalty ; and Gerhard as declaring " that he was innocent, and had not entered into or consented to any plot, nor given any countenance to any discourse to that purpose." Whitelocke says, that when they were brought before the high court, they both denied all the charges alleged against them.—*Clarendon's History*, vol. iii., p. 492. *Whitelocke's Memoirs*, p. 575.—ED.

excuse ; and therefore, being forced to deliver them up, they were all tried and convicted, by a jury. half English and half foreigners ; the servants (says Whitelocke*) were reprieved and pardoned ; but the ambassador's brother, who was the principal, notwithstanding all the intercession that could be made for his life, was carried in a mourning coach to Tower Hill, and beheaded. This remarkable act of justice raised the people's esteem of the protector's resolution, and of the justice of his government.

In order to a farther settlement of the nation, the protector summoned a Parliament to meet at Westminster, September 3 ; which being reckoned one of his auspicious days, he would not alter, though it fell on a Sunday ; the House met accordingly, and having waited upon the protector in the Painted Chamber, adjourned to the next day, September 4, when his highness rode from Whitehall to Westminster with all the pomp and state of the greatest monarch : some hundreds of gentlemen went before him uncovered ; his pages and lackeys in the richest liveries ; the captains of his guards on each side of his coach, with their attendants, all uncovered ; then followed the commissioners of the treasury, master of ceremonies, and other officers. The sword, the great seal, the purse, and four maces, were carried before him by their proper officers.

After a sermon preached by Dr. Thomas Goodwin, his highness† repaired to the Painted Chamber,‡ and being seated in a chair of state, raised by sundry steps, he made a speech to the members, in which he complained of the levellers and fifth monarchy men, who were for subverting the established laws, and for throwing all things back into confusion. He put them in mind of the difficulties in which the nation was involved at the time he assumed the government. " That it was at war with Portugal, Holland, and France ; which, together with the divisions among ourselves," says he, " begat a confidence in the enemy that we could not hold out long. In this heap of confusion, it was necessary to apply some remedy, that the nation might not sink ; and the remedy," says he, "is this government, which is calculated for the interest of the people alone, without regard to any other, let men say what they will ; I can speak with comfort before a greater than you all as to my own intention. Since this government has been erected, men of the most known integrity and ability have been put into seats of justice. The Chancery has been reformed. It has put a stop to that heady way for every man that will to make himself a preacher, by settling a way for approbation of men of piety and fitness for the work. It hath taken care to expunge men unfit for that work ; and now, at length, it has been instrumental of calling a free Parliament.

" A peace is now made with Sweden and with the Danes ; a peace honourable to the nation and satisfactory to the merchants. A peace is made with the Dutch and with Portugal ; and

* Mem., p. 577.   † Whitelocke, p. 582.
‡ This is, I think, Cromwell's best speech, and has strong marks of the ability which he possessed as a statesman. No royal address ever delivered to Parliament has the force and power of this production. Whitelocke calls it "a large and subtle speech."—C.

such a one that the people that trade thither have liberty of conscience, without being subject to the bloody Inquisition." He then advises them to concert measures for the support of the present government, and desires them to believe that he spoke to them not as one that intended to be a lord over them, but as one that was resolved to be a fellow-servant with them for the interest of their country; and then, having exhorted them to unanimity, he dismissed them to their house to choose a speaker.

William Lenthal, Esq., master of the rolls, and speaker of the Long Parliament, was chosen without opposition. The first point the House entered on was the instrument of government, which occasioned many warm debates, and was like to have occasioned a fatal breach among them. To prevent this, the protector gave orders, September 12, that as the members came to the House, they should be directed to attend his highness in the Painted Chamber, where he made the following remarkable speech, which is deserving the reader's careful attention: "Gentlemen, I am surprised at your conduct, in debating so freely the instrument of government; for the same power that has made you a Parliament has appointed me protector, so that if you dispute the one, you must disown the other."* He added, "that he was a gentleman by birth, and had been called to several employments 'in Parliament, and in the wars, which being at an end, he was willing to retire to private life, and prayed to be dismissed, but could not obtain it. That he had pressed the Long Parliament, as a member, to dissolve themselves; but finding they intended to continue their sessions, he thought himself obliged to dismiss them, and to call some persons together from the several parts of the nation, to see if they could fall upon a better settlement. Accordingly, he resigned up all his power into their hands, but they, after some time, returned it back to him. After this," says he, "divers gentlemen having consulted together, framed the present model without my privity, and told me that, unless I would undertake the same, blood and confusion would break in upon them; but I refused again and again, till, considering that it did not put me into a higher capacity than I was in before, I consented; since which time I have had the thanks of the army, the fleet, the city of London, and of great numbers of gentry in the three nations. Now the government being thus settled, I apprehend there are four fundamentals which may not be examined into or altered. (1.) That the government be in a single person and a Parliament. (2.) That Parliaments be not perpetual. (3.) The article relating to the militia. And, (4.) A due liberty of conscience in matters of religion. Other things in the government may be changed as occasion requires. Forasmuch, therefore, as you have gone about to subvert the fundamentals of this government, and throw all things back into confusion, to prevent the like for the future, I am necessitated to appoint you a test or recognition of the government, by which you are made a Parliament, before you go any more into the House."† Accordingly, at their return, they found a guard at the door.denying entrance to any who would

not first sign the following engagement: "I, A. B., do hereby freely promise and engage to be true and faithful to the lord-protector of the commonwealth of England, Scotland, and Ireland, and will not propose or give my consent to alter the government, as it is settled in one single person and a Parliament." About three hundred of the members signed the recognition, and having taken their places in the House, with some difficulty confirmed the instrument of government almost in everything but the right of nominating a successor to the present protector, which they reserved to the Parliament. They voted the present lord-protector to continue for life. They continued the standing army of ten thousand horse and twenty thousand foot, and £60,000 a month for their maintenance. They gave the protector £200,000 a year for his civil list, and assigned Whitehall, St. James's, and the rest of the late king's houses for his use; but they were out of humour, and were so far from showing respect to the court, that they held no manner of correspondence with it; which, together with their voting that no one clause of what they had agreed upon should be binding unless the whole were consented to, provoked the protector,* as derogating from his power of consenting to or refusing particular bills; and therefore, having discovered several plots against his government ready to break out, in which some of the members were concerned, he sent for them into the Painted Chamber, January 22 ‡, and after a long and intricate speech, in which, after some strong expressions in favour of liberty to men of the same faith, though of different judgments in lesser matters, he complained that they had taken no more notice of him, either by message or address, than if there had been no such person in being; that they had done nothing for the honour and support of the government, but spent their time in fruitless debates of little consequence, while the nation was bleeding to death; and instead of making things easy, that they had laid a foundation for future dissatisfactions; he therefore dissolved them, without confirming any of their acts, after they had sat five months, according to the instrument of government, reckoning twenty-eight days to a month. This was deemed an unpopular action, and a renouncing the additional title the Parliament would have given him; but this great man, with the sword in his hand, was not to be jostled out of the saddle with votes and resolutions; and if one may credit his speech, his assuming the government was not so much the effect of his own ambition, as of a bold resolution to prevent the nation's falling back into anarchy and blood.

Upon the rising of the Parliament, Major-general Harrison, one of the chiefs of the Republicans, was taken into custody;† and Mr.

---

* Dugdale's Late Troubles, p. 426, &c.
† Whitelocke, p. 587.

* Life of Cromwell, p. 291.
† The Republicans were divided into two branches, the political and the religious, the former headed by Vane, Bradshaw, and Scott; the latter, by Harrison and others. Some of these leaders partook of the qualities which distinguished both parties. Vane was at once a statesman and mystic; while Harrison combined military qualities of a high order, with an enthusiasm as ardent and visionary as any of his soldiers. Few men have had more reason to complain of the judgment of posterity than Harrison.

John Wildman, who had been expelled the House, was apprehended as he was drawing up a paper, entitled "A Declaration of the free and well-affected People of England now in Arms against the Tyrant Oliver Cromwell;" which prevented the rising of that party.*

The Royalists were buying up arms at the same time, and preparing to rise in several parts of the kingdom.† They had procured commissions from the young king at Cologne, and desired his majesty to be ready on the seacoast by the 11th of March, when there would be a revolt in the army, and when Dover Castle would be delivered into their hands. The king, accordingly, removed to Middleburgh in Zealand; but the protector had intelligence of it from his spies, and declared it openly as soon as he was arrived, which intimidated the conspirators, and made them fear they were discovered: however, about the time appointed, some small parties of Royalists got together in Shropshire with an intent to surprise

He committed some errors, and who that has acted a prominent part in times of revolution has done otherwise? But take him as a whole, he was a man of whom England may well be proud. Honest, undaunted, and of acknowledged military genius, he was inferior only to Cromwell in the army. His character is ably vindicated by Mr. Godwin, in his History of the Commonwealth, vol. iv., p. 379–387. The policy of Vane and his associates was decided, yet cautious. They bore a public testimony against the usurper by retiring from his councils, &c., while they prudently refused to mix themselves up with the conspiracies that were afloat. But the party which Harrison represented was not to be thus restrained. His own conduct was unexceptionable—frank, but prudent; true to his avowed principles, yet tempered by a just sense of the evil which another revolution would bring on the country. But the fifth monarchy men were in the calm spirit, and on the prudential considerations of Vane and Bradshaw. They saw in the protector a second Antichrist; a power opposed to the setting up of that kingdom in the triumphs of which they were to share. With them it was a question of conscience, and admitted of no delay. They were the chosen heralds of Messiah, the liege subjects of the Prince of Heaven. The voice of the eternal God summoned them to bear witness on his behalf before an apostate generation. Faithful among the faithless, they stood alone to achieve the mighty enterprise of stemming the torrent of a nation's corruption—of throwing back the polluted waters which threatened to deluge their Zion; and on the fair face of a renovated creation, to stamp the characters of paradise. Such was their faith: ethereal, yet earthly; high-minded, but visionary; having its origin in some of the noblest aspirations of the human mind, yet incrusted with the prejudices and passions of the channel through which it passed. Their proceedings were, consequently, a strange mixture of wisdom and folly, of power and weakness. Some of the fifth monarchy men were distinguished by an exalted and blameless piety. Their visionary scheme arose out of the *stimulating events of the day*. Applying the splendid visions of prophecy to the passing circumstances of their times, they looked for the speedy annihilation of all anti-Christian powers, and the establishment of a universal monarchy, under the immediate auspices and personal superintendence of the Messiah. The extravagances of the more violent members of the sect have, with glaring injustice, been attributed by our historians to the whole, and infidelity and a cold-hearted formalism have thus sought to throw discredit upon religion.—*Dr. Price's History of Nonconformity*, vol. ii., p. 556–7.—C. * Whitelocke, p. 600.

† Clarendon, vol. iii., p. 551.

Shrewsbury and Chirk Castle. A cart-load of arms was brought to a place of rendezvous for the northern parts, where they were to be headed by Wilmot, earl of Rochester; but they no sooner met but they dispersed, for fear of being fallen upon by the regular troops. In the west, Sir Joseph Wagstaffe, Colonel Penruddock, Captain Hugh Grove, Mr. Jones, and others, entered the city of Salisbury, with two hundred horse well armed, in the time of the assizes, and seized the Judges Rolls and Nichols, with the sheriff of the county, whom they resolved to hang. They proclaimed the king, and threatened violence to such as would not join them; but the country not coming in according to their expectations, they were intimidated, and after five or six hours marched away into Dorsetshire, and from thence to Devonshire, where Captain Crook overtook them, and with one single troop of horse defeated and took most of them prisoners; penruddock and Grove were beheaded at Exeter; and some few others were executed at Salisbury, the place where they had so lately triumphed.

The vigilance of the protector on this occasion is almost incredible; he caused a great many suspected lords and gentlemen to be secured; he sent letters to the justices of peace in every county, whom he had already changed to his mind, commanding them to look out, and secure all persons who should make the least disturbance. And his private intelligence of people's discourse and behaviour, in every corner of the land, never failed.*

If the reader will duly consider the danger arising from these commotions, and the necessity of striking some terror into the authors of them, he will easily account for the protector's severity against the Royalists; when, therefore, the insurrection was quashed, he resolved to make the whole party pay the expense; and accordingly, with the consent of his council, published an order, "that all who had been in arms for the king, or had declared themselves of the Royal party, should be decimated; that is, pay a tenth part of their estates to support the charge of such extraordinary forces as their turbulent and seditious practices obliged him to keep up; for which purpose commissioners were appointed in every county, and considerable sums were brought into the treasury." To justify this extraordinary procedure, the protector published another declaration; in which he complains of the irreconcilableness of those who had adhered to the king, towards all those who had served their country on the side of the Parliament; that they were now to be looked upon as public enemies, and to be kept from being able to do mischief, since it sufficiently appeared that they were always disposed to do all they could. Upon these accounts, he thought it highly reasonable, and declares it to be his resolution, that if any desperate attempts were undertaken by them for the future, the whole party should suffer for it.

To return to the affairs of religion: though the Presbyterian discipline was at a low ebb, it was still the established religion of the nation. The Provincial Assembly of London continued their sessions at Sion College every half year, and endeavoured to support the dignity of the

* Whitelocke, p. 602.

ministerial office. Complaint having been made that the pulpit doors were set open to laymen and gifted brethren, they appointed a committee to collect materials for the vindication of the ministerial character, which, being revised by the synod, was published this summer, under the title of "Jus Divinum Ministerii Evangelici; or, the Divine Right of an Evangelical Ministry, in two Parts. By the Provincial Assembly of London. With an Appendix, of the Judgment and Practice of Antiquity."

In the debates of Parliament upon the instrument of government, it was observed that, by the thirty-seventh article, all who professed faith in God by Jesus Christ should be protected in their religion.*/ This was interpreted to imply an agreement in fundamentals. Upon which it was voted, that all should be tolerated or indulged who professed the fundamentals of Christianity; and a committee was appointed to nominate certain divines to draw up a catalogue of fundamentals to be presented to the House: the committee being above fourteen, named each of them a divine; among others, Archbishop Usher was nominated, but he declining the affair, Mr. Baxter was appointed in his room; the rest who acted were,

Dr. Owen.	Mr. Nye.
Dr. Goodwin.	Mr. Sydrach Simpson.
Dr. Cheynel.	Mr. Vines.
Mr. Marshal.	Mr. Manton.
Mr. Reyner.	Mr. Jacomb.

Mr. Baxter† would have persuaded his brethren to offer the committee the Apostles' Creed, the Lord's Prayer, and the Ten Commandments alone, as containing the fundamentals of religion; but it was objected, that this would include Socinians and papists. Mr. Baxter replied that it was so much fitter for a centre of unity or concord, because it was impossible, in his opinion, to devise a form of words which heretics would not subscribe, when they had perverted them to their own sense. These arguments not prevailing, the following articles were presented to the committee, but not brought into the House,‡ under the title of "The Principles of Faith, presented by Mr. Thomas Goodwin, Mr. Nye, Mr. Sydrach Simpson, and other Ministers, to the Committee of Parliament for Religion, by way of Explanation to the Proposals for propagating the Gospel."

1st. That the Holy Scripture is that rule of knowing God and living unto him, which whoso does not believe, cannot be saved.—2 Thes., ii., 10–12, 15. 1 Cor., xv., 1–3. 2 Cor., i., 13. John, v., 39. 2 Peter, ii., 1.

2dly. That there is a God, who is the creator, governor, and judge of the world, which is to be received by faith, and every other way of the knowledge of him is insufficient.—Heb., xi.,

3, 6. Rom., i., 19–22. 1 Cor., i., 21. 2 Thess., i., 8.

3dly. That this God, who is the creator, is, eternally distinct from all creatures in his being and blessedness.—Rom., i., 18, 25. 1 Cor., viii., 5, 6.

4thly. That this God is one in three persons or subsistences.—1 John, v., 5–9, compared with John, viii., 17–19, 21. Matt., xxviii., 19, compared with Ephesians, iv., 4–6. 1 John, ii., 22, 23. 2 John, 9, 10.

5thly. That Jesus Christ is the only mediator between God and man, without the knowledge of whom there is no salvation.—1 Tim., ii., 4–6. 2 Tim., iii., 15. 1 John, ii., 22. Acts, iv., 10, 12. 1 Cor., iii., 10, 11.

6thly. That this Jesus Christ is the true God.—1 John, v., 29. Isaiah, xlv., 21–25.

7thly. That this Jesus Christ is also true man.—1 John, iv., 2, 3. 2 John, 7.

8thly. That this Jesus Christ is God and man in one person.—1 Tim., iii., 16. Matt., xvi., 13–18.

9thly. That this Jesus Christ is our Redeemer, who, by paying a ransom and bearing our sins, has made satisfaction for them.—Isaiah, liii., 11. 1 Pet., ii., 24, 25. 1 Cor., xv., 2, 3. 1 Tim., ii., 4–6.

10thly. That this same Lord Jesus Christ is he that was crucified at Jerusalem, and rose again, and ascended into heaven.—John, viii., 24. Acts, iv., 10–12. Acts, x., 38–43. 1 Cor., xv., 2–8. Acts, xxii., 2. Acts, ii., 36.

11thly. That this same Jesus Christ, being the only God and man in one person, remains forever a distinct person from all saints and angels, notwithstanding their union and communion with him.—Col., ii., 8–10, 19. 1 Tim., iii., 16.

12thly. That all men by nature are dead in sins and trespasses; and no man can be saved unless he be born again, repent and believe.—John, iii., 3, 5–7, 10. Acts, xvii., 30, 31. Acts, xxvi., 17–20. Luke, xxiv., 47. Acts, xx., 20, 21. John, xxiv., 25.

13thly. That we are justified and saved by grace and faith in Jesus Christ, and not by works.—Acts, xv., 24, compared with Gal., i., 6–9. Gal., v., 2, 4, 5. Rom., ix., 31–33. Rom., x., 3, 4. Rom., i., 16, 17. Gal., iii., 11. Ephes., ii., 8–10.

14thly. That to continue in any known sin, upon what pretence or principle soever, is damnable.—Rom., i., 32. Rom., vi., 1, 2, 15, 16. 1 John, i., 6, 8, and iii., 3–8. 2 Pet., ii., 19, 20. Rom., viii., 13.

15thly. That God is to be worshipped according to his own will; and whosoever shall forsake and despise all the duties of his worship, cannot be saved.—Jer., x., 15. Psalm xiv., 4. Jude, 18–21. Rom., x., 13.

16thly. That the dead shall rise; and that there is a day of judgment, wherein all shall appear, some to go into everlasting life, and some into everlasting condemnation.—1 Tim., i., 19, 20, compared with 2 Tim., ii., 17, 18. Acts, xvii., 30, 31. John, v., 28, 29. 1 Cor., xv., 19.

Mr. Baxter* says Dr. Owen worded these articles; that Dr. Goodwin, Mr. Nye, and Mr. Simpson, were his assistants; that Dr. Cheynel was scribe; and that Mr. Marshal, a sober, worthy man, did something; but that the rest

---

* Baxter's Life, part ii., p. 197.
† Life, part ii., p. 198.
‡ Neal represents these articles as consisting of only sixteen, and says they were not brought into the House; but the testimony of Baxter, and the following entry on the journals, proves him to be inaccurate on both these points: "Sir William Marsham reports from the committee empowered to confer with divines touching articles of faith, twenty articles, with the proofs thereof from Scripture. Resolved, that three hundred copies of these articles be printed, only for the service of the House," &c.— *Burton's Diary, Introduction,* p. 119.—C

* Life, p. 205.

were little better than passive. He adds, that twenty of their propositions we,e printed, though in my copy, licensed by Scobel, there are only sixteen : however, the Parliament being abruptly dissolved, they were all buried in oblivion.

It appears by these articles, that these divines intended to exclude, not only Deists, Socinians, and papists, but Arians, Antinomians, Quakers, and others. Into such difficulties do wise and good men fall when they usurp the kingly office of Christ, and pretend to restrain that liberty which is the birthright of every reasonable creature! *It is an unwarrantable presumption for any number of men to declare what is fundamental in the Christian religion, any farther than the Scriptures have expressly declared it.** It is one thing to maintain a doctrine to be true, and another to declare that without the belief of it no man can be saved : *none may say this but God himself.* Besides, why should the civil magistrate protect none but those who profess faith in God by Jesus Christ? If a colony of English merchants should settle among the Mohammedans or Chinese, should we not think that the government of those countries ought to protect them in their religion as long as they invaded no man's property, and paid obedience and submission to the government under which they lived? Why, then, should Christians deny others the same liberty?

The protector and his council were in more generous sentiments of liberty, as will appear hereafter.† Mr. Baxter says the protector and his friends gave out that they could not understand what the magistrates had to do in matters of religion ; they thought that all men should be left to the liberty of their own consciences, and that the magistrate could not interpose without ensnaring himself in the guilt of persecution. And were not these just and noble sentiments, though the Parliament would not accept them? His highness, therefore, in his speech at their dissolution, reproaches them in these words :§ " How proper is it to labour for liberty, that men should not be trampled upon for their consciences! Have we not lately laboured under the weight of persecution ; and is it fit, then, to sit heavy upon others? Is it ingenuous to ask liberty, and not to give it? What

greater hypocrisy, than for those who were oppressed by the bishops to become the greatest oppressors themselves, so soon as their yoke is removed? I could wish that they who call for liberty now also, had not too much of that spirit, if the power were in their hands. As for profane persons, blasphemers, such as preach sedition, contentious railers, evil-speakers, who seek by evil words to corrupt good manners, and persons of loose conversation, punishment from the civil magistrate ought to meet with them ; because, if these pretend conscience, yet walking disorderly, and not according, but contrary, to the Gospel and natural light, they are judged of all, and their sins being open, make them the subject of the magistrates' sword, who ought not to bear it in vain."

Agreeably to these principles, Dr. George Bates, an eminent Royalist, and a great enemy of Cromwell's, writes, " that the protector indulged the use of the Common Prayer in families, and in private conventicles ; and though the condition of the Church of England was but melancholy, yet," says the doctor, " it cannot be denied but they had a great deal more favour and indulgence than under the Parliament; which would never have been interrupted had they not insulted the protector, and forfeited their liberty by their seditious practices and plottings against his person and government."

The approbation of public ministers had been hitherto reserved to the several presbyteries in city and country ; but the protector observing some inconvenience in this method, and not being willing to intrust the qualification of candidates all over England to a number of Presbyterians only, who might admit none but those of their own persuasion, contrived a middle way of joining the several parties together, and intrusting the affair with certain commissioners of each denomination, men of as known abilities and integrity as any the nation had.* This was done by an ordinance of council, bearing date March 20, 1653-4 ; the preamble to which sets forth, " that whereas for some time past there had not been any certain course established for supplying vacant places with able and fit persons to preach the Gospel, by reason whereof the rights and titles of patrons were prejudiced, and many weak, scandalous, popish, and ill-affected hands had intruded themselves, or been brought in ; for remedy of which it is ordained by his highness the lord-protector, by and with the consent of his council, that every person who shall, after the 25th of March, 1654, be presented, nominated, chosen, or appointed to any benefice with care of souls, or to any public settled lecture in England or Wales, shall, before he be admitted, be examined and approved by the persons hereafter named, to be a person, for the grace of God in him, his holy and unblamable conversation, as also for his knowledge and utterance, able and fit to preach the Gospel."† Among the commissioners were eight or nine laymen, the rest ministers ; their names were, -

Francis Rouse, Esq.	John Sadler, Esq.
Alderman Tichbourne.	William Goffe, Esq.
Mark Hildesly, Esq.	Thomas St. Nicholas, Esq.
Thomas Wood, Esq.	William Packer, Esq.

---

* Mr. Orme urges in vindication of the divines, that " they were called together to state what in their opinion was fundamental in Christianity. With the propriety," he adds, " of tolerating those who differed from them on the points of their declaration, they had nothing to do. The use to be made of these papers was no concern of theirs, and to the question proposed to them they religiously adhered, as they gave no opinion of any kind on the subject of religious liberty." " This defence," says Dr. Price, " is more specious than just. The divines were well informed of the temper which originated their appointment, and of the use which would be made of their labours. They ought to have declined the invidious task, and to have enforced a more enlarged and tolerant policy ; advocates of toleration themselves, they were placed in the disreputable position of aiding the intolerance of others."—*Orme's Life of Owen,* p. 115. C.

† " Bigotry," says Dr. Harris, " made no part of Cromwell's character ;" and he proves the truth of his assertion by a full elucidation and a minute detail. —*Life of Cromwell,* p. 37–45.—Ed.

‡ Life, p. 193.   § Life of Cromwell, p. 307.

* Baxter's Life, p. 72.   † Scobel, p. 279.

Edward Cresset, Esq.	Rev. Mr. Stephen Marshall.
Rev. Dr. John Owen.	" John Tombes, B.D.'
" Dr. Thomas Goodwin.	" Mr. Walter Craddock.
" Dr. Arrowsmith.	" Mr. Samuel Fairclough.
" Dr. Tuckney.	" Mr. Hugh Peters. '
" Dr. Horton.	" Mr. Peter Sterry.
" Thankful Owen, M.A.	" Mr. Samuel Bamford.
" Mr. Joseph Caryl.	" Thomas Valentine, of
" Mr. Philip Nye.	Chaford, B.D.
" Mr. William Carter.	" Mr. Henry Jesse.
" Mr. Sydrach Simpson.	" Mr. Obadiah Sedgwick.
" Mr. William Greenhill.	" Mr. Nicholas Lockyer.'
" Mr. William Strong.	" Mr. Dan. Dike.
" Mr. Thomas Manton.	" Mr. James Russel.
" Mr. Samuel Slater.	" Mr. Nath. Campfield.
" Mr. William Cooper.	

These were commonly called triers; in all, thirty-eight; of whom some were Presbyterians, others Independents, and two or three were Baptists. Any five were sufficient to approve; but no number under nine had power to reject a person as unqualified. In case of death, or removal of any of the commissioners, their numbers were to be filled up by the protector and his council; or by the Parliament, if sitting. But some of the Presbyterian divines declined acting, for want of a better authority; or because they did not like the company; though the authority was as good as any these times could produce till the next sessions of Parliament.* By an ordinance of September 2, 1654, I find the Rev. Mr. John Rowe, Mr. John Bond, Mr. George Griffith of the Charter House, Mr. John Turner, and Godfrey Bosville, Esq., added to the commissioners above mentioned.

To such as were approved, the commissioners gave an instrument in writing under a common seal for that purpose, by virtue of which they were put into as full possession of the living to which they were nominated or chosen as if they had been admitted by institution and induction.

It was farther provided, that all who presented themselves for approbation should produce a certificate signed by three persons at least, of known integrity, one of whom to be a preacher of the Gospel in some settled place, testifying on their personal knowledge the holy and good conversation of the person to be admitted; which certificate was to be registered and filed. And all penalties for not subscribing or reading the articles of religion, according to the act of 13 Eliz., were to cease and be void.

And forasmuch as some persons might have been preferred to livings within the last twelvemonth, when there was no settled method of approbation, the ordinance looks back, and ordains " that no person who had been placed in any benefice or lecture since April 1, 1653, should be allowed to continue in it, unless he got himself approved by the 24th of June, or at farthest the 23d of July, 1654."

It is observable that this ordinance provides no security for the civil government, the commissioners not being empowered to administer an oath of allegiance or fidelity to the protector. By this means, some of the sequestered clergy, taking advantage of the Act of Oblivion in 1651, passed their trials before the commissioners, and returned to their livings. The protector being advised of this defect, by advice of his council, published an additional ordinance, September 2, 1654, requiring the commissioners not to give admission to any who had been sequestered

from their ecclesiastical benences for delinquency, till, by experience of their conformity, and submission to the present government, his highness and his council should be satisfied of their fitness to be admitted into ecclesiastical promotions; and the same to be signified to the said commissioners.* Both these ordinances were confirmed by Parliament in the year 1656, with this proviso, " that the commissioners appointed by his highness in the intervals of Parliament should afterward be confirmed by the succeeding Parliament." Another defect in the ordinance was, that it did not appoint some standard or rule for the triers to go by; this would have taken off all odium from themselves, and prevented a great many needless disputes; but, as matters now stood, men's qualifications were perhaps left too much to the arbitrary opinions and votes of the commissioners. After examination, they gave the candidate a copy of the presentation in these words:† " Know all men by these presents, that the —— day of ——, in the year ——, there was exhibited to the commissioners for examination of public ministers a presentation of Mr. —— to the rectory of ——, in the county of ——, made to him by Mr. ——, the patron thereof, under his hand and seal, together with a testimony of his holy and godly conversation. Upon perusal, and due consideration of the premises, and finding him to be a person qualified, as in and by the ordinance for such qualifications is required, the commissioners above mentioned have adjudged and approved the said Mr. —— to be a fit person to preach the Gospel, and have granted him admission, and do admit the said Mr. —— to the rectory of —— aforesaid, to be full and perfect possessor and incumbent thereof; and do hereby signify to all persons concerned therein, that he is hereby entitled to all the profits and perquisites, and to all rights and dues incident and belonging to the said rectory, as fully and effectually as if he had been instituted and inducted according to any such laws and customs as have in this case formerly been made or used in this realm. In witness whereof, they have caused the common seal to be hereunto affixed, and the same to be attested by the hand of the registrar, by his highness in that behalf appointed. Dated at ——, the —— day of ——, in the year ——.

" (L.S.) John Nye, Reg."

Loud complaints have been made against these triers; Mr. Collyer objects to there being eight laymen among the commissioners, and that any five having power to act, it might sometimes happen that none but secular men might determine the qualifications of such who were to preach and administer the sacraments.

Mr. John Goodwin, an Independent divine of Arminian principles, observes, the triers made their own narrow Calvinian sentiments in divinity the door of admission to all church preferments; and that their power was greater than the bishops', because the laws had provided a remedy against their arbitrary proceedings, by a quare impedit; or if the bishop might determine absolutely of the qualifications of the candidate or clerk to be admitted into a living, yet these qualifications were sufficiently specified,

---

Vol. II.—T   * Scobel, p. 366.

* Scobel, p. 366.   † Calamy, vol. ii., p. 247.

and particularized in the ecclesiastical laws or canons, and the bishop might be obliged, by due course of law, to assign the reasons of his refusal; whereas the determinations of these commissioners for approbation were final; nor were they obliged so much as to specify any reason for their rejecting any person, but only their vote, *not approved*.

It was farther complained of as a very great hardship, that " there was but one set of triers for the whole nation, who resided always at London, which must occasion great expense and long journeys to such as lived in the remoter counties.' But to remedy this inconvenience, Dr. Walker says* they appointed sub-commissioners in the remoter counties. And, according to Mr. Baxter, if any were unable to come to London, or were of doubtful qualifications, the commissioners of London used to refer them to some ministers in the county where they lived; and under their testimonial they approved or rejected them. Amid such variety of sentiments, it was next to impossible to please all parties; when there were no triers, the complaint was, that the pulpit doors were left open to all intruders, and " now they cannot agree upon any one method of examination." And it must be left to every one's judgment, whether a bishop and his chaplain, or a classis of presbyters, or the present mixture of laity and clergy, be most eligible.

The chief objections against these triers has been to the manner of executing their powers. Bishop Kennet says† "that this holy inquisition was turned into a snare to catch men of probity, and sense, and sound divinity, and to let none escape but ignorant, bold, canting fellows; for these triers," says the bishop, "asked few or no questions in knowledge or learning, but only about conversation, and the grace of God in the heart, to which the readiest answers would arise from infatuation in some, and the trade of hypocrisy in others. By this means the rights of patronage were at their pleasure, and the character and abilities of divines whatever they pleased to make them, and churches were filled with little creatures of the state."‡ But the bishop has produced no examples of this; nor were any of these canting little creatures turned out for insufficiency at the Restoration. Dr. George Bates, an eminent Royalist, with a little more temper and truth, says, " that they inquired more narrowly into their affection to the present government, and into the eternal marks and character of the grace of God in their heart, than into their learning; by which means many ignorant laics, mechanics, and pedlers were admitted to livings, when persons of greater merit were rejected." But it may be observed again, that, ignorant as they were, not one of the mechanics or pedlers who conformed at the Restoration *was ejected for insufficiency*. When the commissioners had to do with per-

sons of known learning, sobriety, reputed or thodoxy, and a peaceable behaviour, they made but little inquiry into the marks of their conversation; as appears from the example of Mr. Fuller the historian, who, being presented to a living, was approved by the triers, without giving any other evidence of the grace of God in him than this, that he made conscience of his thoughts.

Dr. Walker has published the examinations of two or three clergymen, who were notorious for their malignity and disaffection to the government, whom the commissioners puzzled with dark and abstruse questions in divinity, that they might set them aside, without encountering their political principles; for when they had private intimations of notorious malignants to come before them, they frequently had recourse to this method; though it is not unlikely that, upon some other occasions, they might lay too great stress upon the internal characters of regeneration, the truth of which depends entirely upon the integrity of the respondent. But I believe not a single instance can be produced of any who were rejected for insufficiency without being first convicted either of immorality, of obnoxious sentiments in the Socinian or Pelagian controversy, or of disaffection to the present government. Mr. Sadler, who was presented to a living in Dorsetshire, but rejected by the triers, published his examination in a pamphlet, which he calls Inquisitio Anglicana; wherein he endeavours to expose the commissioners in a very contemptuous manner; but Mr. John Nye, clerk to the commissioners, followed him with an answer, entitled " Sadler examined; or, his Disguise discovered;" showing the gross mistakes and most notorious falsehoods in his dealings with the commissioners for approbation of public preachers,* in his Inquisitio Anglicana. To which Mr. Sadler never replied.

Dr. George Bates and Dr. Walker have charged the triers with simony, upon no other proof, but that Hugh Peters said once to Mr. Camplin, a clergyman of Somersetshire, upon his applying to him, by a friend, for despatch, " Has thy friend any money?" a slender proof of so heavy a charge. They who are acquainted with the jocose conversation of Hugh Peters, will not wonder at such an expression. But I refer the reader back to the names and characters of the commissioners, most of whom were men of unquestionable probity, for a sufficient answer to this calumny.

No doubt the triers did commit sundry mistakes, which it was hardly possible to avoid in their station. I am far from vindicating all their proceedings; they had a difficult work on their hands, lived in times when the extent of Christian liberty was not well understood, had to deal with men of different principles in religion and politics; and those who were not approved would, of course, complain. Had this power been lodged with the bishops of these times or their chaplains, or with the high Presbyterians, would they not have had their shibboleth, for which ill-natured men might have called them a holy inquisition? But Mr. Baxter has given a very fair and candid account of

* Walker, p. 172.   † Complete History, p. 209.
‡ After reading the catalogue of worthies who

Bishop Kennet? No doubt they made *mistakes*, but the *general tendency* of their labours was most salutary. Owen, Goodwin, Caryl, Simpson, Manton, and Strong, had no greater affinity for vice and ignorance than their right reverend slanderer.—C

* Athen. Oxon., vol. ii., p. 370.

them; his words are these: "Because this assembly of triers is most heavily accused and reproached by some men, I shall speak the truth of them, and suppose my word will be taken, because most of them took me for one of their boldest adversaries : the truth is, though their authority was null, and though some few over-rigid and over-busy Independents among them were too severe against all that were Arminians, and too particular in inquiring after evidences of sanctification in those whom they examined, and somewhat too lax in admitting of unlearned and erroneous men, that favoured Antinomianism and Anabaptism, yet, to give them their due, they did abundance of good to the Church. They saved many a congregation from ignorant, ungodly, drunken teachers, that sort of men who intend no more in the ministry than to say a sermon, as readers say their common prayers on a Sunday, and all the rest of the week go with the people to the ale-house, and harden them in sin ; and that sort of ministers who either preached against a holy life, or preached as men that were never acquainted with it; these they usually rejected, and in their stead admitted of any that were able, serious preachers, and lived a godly life, of what tolerable opinion soever they were; so that though many of them were a little partial for the Independents, separatists, fifth-monarchy men, and Anabaptists, and against the prelatists and Arminians, yet so great was the benefit above the hurt which they brought to the Church, that many thousands of souls blessed God for the faithful ministers whom they let in, and grieved when the prelatists afterward cast them out again."*

The commissioners were not empowered to look farther back than one year before the date of the ordinance which constituted them.† All who were in possession of their livings before that time were out of their reach ; nor would the protector have given these any disturbance, had he not received certain information of their stirring up the people to join the insurrection that was now on foot for the restoration of the king. They continued sitting at Whitehall till the protector's death, or the year 1659, and were then discontinued.

But to humble the clergy yet farther, and keep them within the bounds of their spiritual function, his highness, by the advice of his council, published an ordinance, bearing date August 28, 1654, entitled "An Ordinance for ejecting scandalous, ignorant, and insufficient Ministers and Schoolmasters." The ordinance appoints and nominates certain lay-commissioners for every county, and joins with them ten or more of the gravest and most noted ministers, their assistants, and empowers any five or more of them to call before them any public preacher, lecturer, parson, vicar, curate, or schoolmaster, who is or shall be reputed ignorant, scandalous, insufficient, or negligent ; and to receive all articles or charges that shall be exhibited against them on this account ; and to proceed to the examination and determination

of such offences, according to the following rules :*

"Such ministers and schoolmasters shall be accounted scandalous in their lives and conversations, as shall hold or maintain such blasphemous or atheistical opinions as are punishable by the act entitled ' An Act against several Blasphemous and Atheistical Opinions,' &c., or that shall be guilty of profane swearing and cursing, perjury, and subornation of perjury ; such as maintain any popish opinions required to be abjured by the oath of abjuration ; or are guilty of adultery, fornication, drunkenness, common haunting of taverns or ale-houses; frequent quarrellings or fightings ; frequent playing at cards or dice ; profaning the Sabbath ; or that do allow and countenance the same in their families, or in their parishes. Such as have frequently read or used the Common Prayer Book in public since the first of January last, or shall at any time hereafter do the same. Such as publicly and profanely scoff at the strict profession or professors of godliness. Such as encourage or countenance Whitsun-ales, wakes, morrice-dancing, May-poles, stage plays, or such like licentious practices. Such as have declared, or shall declare, by writing, preaching, or otherwise publishing, their disaffection to the present government.

"Such ministers shall be accounted negligent as omit the public exercise of preaching and praying on the Lord's Day (not being hindered by necessary absence or infirmity of body), or that are or shall be nonresidents. Such schoolmasters shall be accounted negligent as absent themselves from their schools, and wilfully neglect to teach their scholars.

"Such ministers or schoolmasters shall be accounted ignorant and insufficient as shall be so declared and adjudged by the commissioners in every county, or any five of them, together with five of the ministers mentioned in the ordinance."

The lay-commissioners were to proceed upon oath, both for and against the person accused ; but in cases of ignorance or insufficiency, they were to be joined by five of the assistant clergy at least ; and if ten of the commissioners, whereof five to be ministers, gave it under their hands that the party was ignorant or insufficient, then the said minister or schoolmaster was to be ejected, and the said judgment entered in a register book, with the reason thereof. After ejectment, the party might not preach or teach school in the parish from whence he was ejected ; but convenient time was to be allowed for his removal, and the fifths reserved for the support of his family. The rightful patron was to present to the vacant living an approved preacher ; and in case of lapse, it fell to the protector and his council.

This ordinance being confirmed by the Parliament of 1656, gave great offence to the old clergy ; Mr. Gatford, the sequestered rector of Denington, published a pamphlet, entitled "A Petition for the Vindication of the Use of Common Prayer," &c., occasioned by the late ordinance for ejecting scandalous ministers ; as also thirty-seven queries concerning the said ordinance, which he presented to the Parlia-

---

* Baxter's Life, part i., p. 72.
† Their duty was *prospective*. It respected the future rather than the past, and was designed for the prevention, and not for the cure of evils.—*Price*, vol. ii., p. 535.—C.

* Scobel, p. 335, 340.

ment, which met September 3, 1654; but they took no notice of it.

Mr. Gatford observes, that the protector and his council had no legal authority to make this or any other ordinance without consent of a Parliament; whereas the instrument of government empowered them to provide for the safety of the state, by making laws till the Parliament should meet. He observes farther, that such a proceeding must justify his late majesty and council in all their illegal proceedings before the civil wars; that it would justify the High Commission Court; and that, by the same authority, an ordinance might be published to eject freeholders out of their estates.

He complains that the power of the commissioners is final, and admits of no appeal; that it looks back to crimes antecedent to the law for a twelvemonth; whereas it ought only to declare that for the future such offences shall be punished with deprivation.

That the commissioners who were to sit in judgment upon the clergy were all laymen, the ministers being called in only in cases of ignorance and insufficiency; that the ordinance admits of the oath of one witness, provided it be supported with other concurrent evidence, which is contrary to the laws of God and man.

That some crimes in the ordinance were none at all, and others of a very doubtful nature; as how often a minister omitting to pray and preach in his pulpit should render him negligent, and what should be deemed nonresidence. Above all, he complains that the public reading of the Common Prayer should be ranked with the sins of swearing and drunkenness, and be an evidence of a scandalous life and conversation; which observation was unquestionably just.

To give the reader an example or two of the proceedings of the commissioners: those for Berkshire summoned Dr. Pordage, rector of Bradfield, to appear before them at Speenhamland, near Newbury, to answer to divers articles of blasphemy and heresy. After several days' hearing, and witnesses produced on both sides, the commissioners determined, December 8, 1654, that the said doctor was guilty of denying the Deity of Christ; the merits of his precious blood and passion; and several other such like opinions. It is farther declared, under the hands of six of the commissioners, and a sufficient number of ministers, their assistants, that the said doctor was ignorant, and insufficient for the work of the ministry; it is therefore ordered, that the said doctor be and he is hereby ejected out of the rectory of Bradfield, and the profits thereof; but the said commissioners do grant him time, till the 2d of February, to remove himself, his family, his goods and chattels, out of the said parsonage-house; and farther time to remove his corn out of the barns, till the 23d of March.

The Oxford historian says this Pordage was a doctor by Charientismus, and had been preacher of St. Lawrence Church in Reading before he came to Bradfield.* That he was a mystic enthusiast, and used to talk of the fiery Deity of Christ dwelling in the soul and mixing itself with our flesh.† He dealt much in astrology,

* Athen. Oxon., vol. ii., p. 450.
† Mr. Neal is not correct here; for, as Dr. Grey

and pretended to converse with the world of spirits. After his ejectment he wrote against the commissioners a pamphlet, entitled "Innocency Appearing," which was answered by Mr. Christopher Fowler, vicar of St. Mary, Reading, in his Dominium Meridianum. However, the doctor was restored to his living at Bradfield, at the Restoration.

The Wiltshire commissioners summoned Mr. Walter Bushnel, vicar of Box, near Malmesbury, before them, to answer to a charge of drunkenness, profanation of the Sabbath, gaming, and disaffection to the government;* and, after a full hearing, and proof upon oath, they ejected him. The vicar prepared for the press "A Narrative of the Proceedings of the Commissioners appointed by O. Cromwell for ejecting scandalous and ignorant Ministers, in the case of Walter Bushnel," &c.; but it was not printed till the king's restoration; and even then the commissioners did themselves justice in a reply, which they entitled "A Vindication of the Marlborough Commissioners, by the Commissioners themselves." And Dr. Chambers, who was reproached by the said Bushnel, did himself justice in a distinct vindication. However, the vicar was restored to his vicarage in a lump with the rest at the Restoration.

Upon the whole, the industrious Dr. Walker says he can find no footsteps of the numbers of the clergy that were ejected by the commissioners, though he imagines they might be considerable.† But I am well satisfied there were

observes, this passage is not in the Oxford historian. It is probable that Mr. Neal took this charge against Dr. Pordage, either from his narrative of the proceedings of the commissioners, or from Mr. Fowler's animadversions; but though, by not specifying his name, the reader is led to suppose that the whole paragraph is grounded on the representation of the Oxford historian. He, it should be also noticed, does not ascribe a skill in astrology to Dr. Pordage, but says that "Mr. Ashmole commended him for his knowledge in, and so great affection to, astronomy."—ED.

* This last, Dr. Grey supposes, was the main reason; for Wood says, "he continued at Box in good esteem the greatest part of the interrupted times; but was at length ejected from his living in the reign of Oliver."—Athen. Oxon., vol. ii., p. 2.—ED.

† "At the commencement of the civil war, the mass of the clergy were thoroughly secular, and a large number of them immoral. They had been thinned by successive ejectments, but ignorance and consequent inefficiency, accompanied, in some cases, by open vice, were still the characteristics of many. It is easier, therefore, to impugn the judgments of the commissioners in particular cases, than to disprove the necessity for some such tribunal as they constituted. * * * The influence of the least qualified among them was tempered by the better spirit and more enlightened views of their associates. The case of Dr. Pococke, the professor of Arabic at Oxford, may serve as a specimen. He held the living of Childrey, in Berkshire, and being summoned before the commissioners for that county, was in danger of being ejected. Dr. Owen was, at the time, the vice-chancellor of the university, and though his political views differed greatly from Pococke's, he keenly felt the injustice which was threatened to his associate, and the dishonour which must accrue from its being perpetrated. He accordingly wrote to Thurloe, and his letter is, happily, preserved. 'There are in Berkshire,' says the Independent divine, 'some few men of mean quality and condition, rash, heady, enemies of tithes, who are the commissioners for the ejecting of ministers; * * * they intend next week to eject Pococke, a man of as unblamable

none of any considerable character ; for there were not a great many zealous Loyalists in livings at this time ; and those that were had the wisdom to be silent about public affairs, while they saw the eyes of the government were upon them in every corner of the land. The commissioners continued to act till some time after the protector's death, and were a greater terror to the *fanatics* and *visionaries of those times, than to the regular clery of any denomination.**

conversation as any I know living, of repute for learning throughout the world, being the professor of Hebrew and Arabic in our university. If anything could be done to cause them to suspend acting until this storm be over, I cannot but think it would be good service to his highness and the commonwealth to do it.' Not content with this appeal, Owen repaired, in company with Drs. Ward, Wilkins, and Wallace, to the meeting of the commissioners, and warmly expostulated with them on the injustice and absurdity of their proceedings, &c. ; his appeal was irresistible.

"There are many instances, however, which show that their scrutiny was often less severe, and their decision more charitable than their enemies allow. An instance of this is furnished in the case of Fuller, the Church historian, whose quaint humour and ever-flowing wit were happily chastened by the mild and catholic spirit of Christianity. Having been cited before the commissioners, Fuller was alarmed for the result, and applied to his friend John Howe for advice. 'You may observe, sir,' was his characteristic remark to Howe, 'that I am a pretty corpulent man, and I am to go through a passage that is very strait: I beg you will be so kind as to give me a shove, and help me through.' Howe's advice is not recorded, but its soundness is evidenced in the simple reply which his alarmed friend made to the inquiry of the commissioners, 'Whether he had ever had any experience of a work of grace on his heart?' Fuller, instead of perplexing himself by a minute detail of the history and marks of his conversion, gravely replied, that he made conscience of his very thoughts ; and this reply, though vague, was received as satisfactory by the examiners."—*Price's Hist. Noncon.*, vol. ii., p. 537. *Orme's Owen*, p. 118. *Calamy's Life of Howe*, p. 20.—C.

* Baxter bears full testimony to the labours of the commissioners, and was too honest to resist the evidence of facts. "For all the faults that are now among us, I do not believe that ever England had so able and faithful a ministry since it was a nation as it hath at this day ; and I fear that few nations on earth, if any, have the like. Sure I am the change is so great within these twelve years, that it is one of the greatest joys that ever I had in the world to behold it. Oh, how many congregations are now plainly and frequently taught, that lived then in great obscurity! How many able, faithful men are there now in a county, in comparison of what were then! How graciously hath God prospered the studies of many young men that were little children in the beginning of the late troubles, so that now they cloud the most of their seniors! How many miles would I have gone twenty years ago, and less, to have heard one of those ancient, reverend divines, whose congregations are now grown thin, and their parts esteemed mean by reason of the notable improvement of their juniors! And, in particular, how mercifully hath the Lord dealt with this poor county (Worcestershire), in raising up so many of these that do credit to their sacred office, and self-denying, and freely, zealously, and unweariedly lay out themselves for the good of souls! I bless the Lord that hath placed me in such a neighbourhood, where I may have the brotherly fellowship of so many able, humble, unanimous, peaceable, and faithful men. Oh, that the Lord would long continue this admirable mercy to this unworthy country! I hope I shall rejoice in God while I have a being for

The protector and his council passed another ordinance, August 30, for the service of Wales, appointing Sir Hugh Owen, and about eighteen other commissioners, for the six counties of South Wales, with the county of Monmouth ; and Matthew Morgan, with about twelve other commissioners, for the six counties of North Wales ; any three of which were empowered to call before them all such who, by authority of the act for propagating the Gospel in Wales, had received or disposed of any of the profits of the rectories, vicarages, &c., in that principality ; and to give an account, upon oath, of all such rents and profits ; and the surplus money, in the hands of the commissioners, to be paid into the exchequer.*

To set this affair before the reader in one view : the principality of Wales, by reason of the poverty of the people, and the small endowments of church livings, was never well supplied with a learned or pious clergy ; the people were generally very ignorant, and only one remove from heathens. In 1641, a petition was presented to the king and Parliament, which declares that there were not so many conscientious and constant preachers in Wales as there were counties ; and that these were either silenced or much persecuted.† The civil wars had made their condition worse ; for as they generally adhered to the king, received great numbers of Irish papists into their country, their preachers went into his majesty's service, or fled from their cures, when the Parliament forces took possession of it. After the king's death, the Parliament passed the ordinance already mentioned, for the better propagating of the preaching of the Gospel in Wales, and for ejecting scandalous ministers and schoolmasters, and for redress of some grievances ; it bears date February 22, 1649, and empowers the commissioners therein mentioned, or any twelve of them, to receive and

the common change in other parts that I have lived to see ; that so many hundred faithful men are so hard at work for the saving of souls, '*frementibus licet et frendentibus inimicis ;*' and that more are springing up apace. I know there are some men whose parts I reverence, who being, in point of government, of another mind from them, will be offended at my very mention of this happy alteration ; but I must profess, if I were absolutely prelatical, if I knew my heart, I could not choose, for all that, but rejoice. What! not rejoice at the prosperity of the Church, because men differ in opinion about its order! Should I shut my eyes against the mercies of the Lord? The souls of men are not so contemptible to me that I should envy them the Bread of Life because it is broken to them by a hand that had not the prelatical approbation. Oh, that every congregation were thus supplied! But all cannot be done at once. They had a long time to settle a corrupted ministry ; and when the ignorant and scandalous are cast out, we cannot create abilities in others for the supply ; we must stay the time of their preparation and growth ; and then, if England drive not away the Gospel by their abuse, even by their wilful unreformedness and hatred of the light, they are likely to be the happiest nation under heaven. For, as for all the sects and heresies that are creeping in daily and troubling us, I doubt but the free Gospel, managed by an able, self-denying ministry, will effectually disperse and shame them all."—*Baxter's Reformed Pastor, Works,* vol. xiv., p. 152.—C.   * Scobel, p. 347.
† Calamy's Com. of Church and Dissenters, p. 47, *note.*

dispose of all and singular rents, issues, and profits, of all ecclesiastical livings, impropriations, and glebe lands, within the said counties, which then were or afterward should be under sequestration, or in the disposal of the Parliament, and out of them to order and appoint a constant yearly maintenance for such persons as should be recommended, and approved for the work of the ministry, or education of children ; and for such other ministers as were then residing in the said counties. The ordinance to continue in force for three years, from March 25, 1650.

By virtue of this ordinance, many clergymen were ejected, but not all, for in Montgomeryshire eleven or twelve remained, as did several in other counties ; but all who were ejected were so for manifest scandal.* Afterward, complaints being made that the people were turning papists or heathens for want of the Word of God, several were sent into Montgomeryshire, where there were at least sixteen preachers, of which ten were university men, the meanest of whom were approved and settled in parishes at the Restoration. The commissioners were empowered to examine into the behaviour of such as were reputed ignorant, insufficient, nonresident, scandalous, or enemies to the present government. And it being impossible to fill up the vacant livings with such as could preach in the Welsh language, the revenues were to be collected and brought into a common treasury, out of which £100 per annum was to be given to sundry itinerant preachers in each county.

Dr. Walker says that, from the account drawn up by the commissioners themselves in April, 1652, it appears that there had been ejected in South Wales and Monmouthshire one hundred and seventy-five ministers ; that is, fifty-six from the year 1645 to the time when this act took place, and one hundred and nineteen by the present commissioners. Mr. Vavasor Powel, who had a chief hand in the sequestrations, says that, by virtue of this act, between fifty and sixty of the old clergy were dispossessed of their livings when he wrote. Upon the whole, the commissioners, who continued to act as long as the protector lived, charged themselves with between three hundred and twenty and three hundred and thirty several and distinct livings ; but there could not be an equal number of sequestered clergymen, because in the compass of seven years a great many must die ; some fled or were killed in the wars ; in many parishes the tithes were not duly paid by reason of the confusion of the times, and the livings being but from 5 to 10 or £20 a year, most of the incumbents were pluralists. It is computed that about one half of the Church lands and revenues in the principality of Wales, by the several accidents of death, desertion, sequestration, &c., fell into the hands of the government before the expiration of this ordinance in 1653, the profits of which, if duly collected and paid, must amount to a very considerable sum. There were thirteen counties in North and South Wales within the limits of the commission ; but the largest sum that the sequestrators and agents charge themselves with for the county of Brecknock, in any one year, till

* Calamy's Com. of Church and Dissenters, p. 47.

the year 1653, when the propagation had suosisted eight years, is £1543, by which the reader may make a tolerable computation of the whole ; and if we may believe Mr. Whitelocke,* who lived through these times, in the year 1653 there were one hundred and fifty good preachers in the thirteen Welsh counties, most of whom preached three or four times a week ; that in every market town there was a schoolmaster, and in most great towns two able, learned, and university men ; and that the tithes were all employed to the uses directed by act of Parliament,† there can be no great reason to complain of the negligence of the commissioners.

The crimes for which the old clergy were ejected were malignancy, insufficiency, drunkenness, and negligence of their cures. Mr. Vavasor Powel says, that of all the men they had put out in North Wales, he knew not any that had the power of godliness, and very few the form ; but that most of them were unpreaching curates, or scandalous in their morals. The commissioners affirm, that of the sixteen they had dispossessed in Cardiganshire, there were but three that were preachers, and those most scandalous livers. And Mr. Baxter admits that they were all weak, and bad enough for the most part. But the writers on the other side say that the commissioners had no regard to ability in preaching or sobriety in conversation. And Dr. Walker thinks the sequestered Welsh clergy need no other vindication than to let the world know that many of them were graduates in the university ; as if every graduate must of course be possessed of all ministerial qualifications. There might possibly be some few pious and industrious preachers among the ejected Welsh clergy ; but they who will argue very strenuously in favour of the body of them, must know very little of the country, or their manner of life.

It was not in the power of the commissioners to find a succession of pious and learned preachers in the Welsh language ; but, to remedy this in the best manner they could, they appointed six university preachers of university education for each county, to whom they allowed £100 a year ; besides which, they sent out thirty-two ministers, of whom twenty-four were university men, and some of the rest good scholars; but these were too few for the work, though they were indefatigable in their labours. To supply what was farther wanting, they approved of several gifted laymen, members of churches, to travel into the neighbourhood, and assist the people's devotions, and to these they allowed from 17 to £20 per annum. In an article of the sequestrators' accounts, there appears £340 per annum distributed among godly members

* Memor., p. 518.

† These uses and the proportions of the appropriation were as follows, viz. : The tithes were divided into six parts; one of which went to the ejected ministers ; a second to other settled and itinerant ministers ; a third to maintain schools, of which the ejected ministers and their sons were masters ; a fourth to the widows and children of the ejected ministers ; a fifth to under-officers, as treasurers, solicitors, sequestrators, &c. ; and a sixth to the widows of deceased ministers. — *Whitelocke's Mem.*, p. 518. *Calamy's Church and Dissenters Compared*, p. 47, note.—ED.

of the Church of Lanvacles, and Mynthists Loyn, who had been sent out to exercise their gifts among the Welsh mountaineers, and to help forward the work of the Lord. Many others of the same quality were approved by the commissioners, who went through great difficulties and hardships in their work. Mr. Powel says that some hundreds, if not thousands, had been converted and reformed by the propagators.* But, after all, it must be confessed that at first the number of itinerants, both scholars and others, was by no means equal to their work; the parishes in that mountainous country are large and wide, and there being but one itinerant to several of those parishes, the people must have been neglected, and their children too much without instruction; but this was owing to the necessity of the times.

When the commissioners had acted about two years, a petition was presented to the Parliament by the inhabitants of South Wales, signed by above a thousand hands, in favour of the old ejected clergy, setting forth the numbers that had been dispossessed, and the want of a competent number of preachers in their places, upon which account the country was reduced to a very miserable condition. They therefore pray the House to take some course for a future supply of godly and able preachers, and to call those persons to account who had received all the profits of church livings into their hands.† The House received the petition, and referred it to the committee for plundered ministers, who were empowered to examine witnesses, and to authorize other commissioners in the country to examine witnesses upon oath touching the matters contained in the petition. The committee ordered the commissioners to bring in their accounts in a month's time, which they did accordingly. And the petitioners were ordered to deliver in the particulars on which the desired witnesses might be examined within two days; but not being provided, they desired liberty to make their allegations in the country, to which the commissioners willingly agreed. But this taking up some time, the Long Parliament was dissolved, and the prosecution of this inquiry suspended for the present; but as soon as the protector was fixed in his government, he published an ordinance, August 20, 1654, to bring the propagators to an account; pursuant to which, the sequestrators and treasurer for South Wales delivered in their accounts for the years 1650, 1651, 1652, which was all the time the ordinance continued in force; and the commissioners appointed by the protector having received and examined them, after a full inquiry, allowed and passed them, August 10, 1655.

It is hard to read with temper the reproaches cast upon these commissioners by our angry historians, who have charged them with all manner of corruption, as if they had got great estates out of the revenues of the Church, though without producing a single example. Mr. Powel, who took more pains among them than any man of his time, declares that he never received for all his preaching in Wales, by salary, above 6 or £700; that he never had anything from the tithes. And whereas it was said that he had enriched himself by purchasing some thousands a year of crown-lands, he protests that he

never purchased above £70 a year, which he lost at the Restoration.* And if Mr. Powel did not enrich himself, I apprehend none of his brethren could. Besides, if this had been true, the protector's commissioners would have discovered them; or, if they had escaped the protector's inquiry, their enemies would have exposed them at the Restoration, when King Charles appointed a commission to make the strictest inquiry into their management. "All persons who had acted as commissioners for propagating the Gospel were, by his majesty's instructions, to be summoned before his commissioners; and all that had acted under them as farmers, tenants, &c; all that had succeeded in the sequestered livings, or received any of the profits; all parishioners who had kept any of the tithes in their hands; the heirs, executors, or administrators of any of the aforesaid persons; and all credible persons, who could give evidence of any of these matters. They were likewise to inquire after books and writings; and to signify to all persons concerned, that if they would forthwith apply to his majesty's commissioners, they might compound for what they stood charged with, and so avoid the expense of a lawsuit." But after all this mighty outcry and scrutiny, nothing of any consequence appeared, and therefore it was thought proper to drop the commission, and bury the whole affair in silence. Mr. Vavasor Powel, above mentioned, was cruelly handled by the Welsh clergy, but he did himself justice in a pamphlet, entitled Examen et Purgamen Vavasoris, published 1653, wherein he vindicates his proceedings in the propagation.† And when he was in the Fleet after the Restoration, he published a brief narrative concerning the proceedings of the commissioners in Wales against the ejected clergy, occasioned by a report that he had been thrown into that prison for some of the revenue, which was never answered.

By an ordinance of September 2, commissioners were appointed to inquire into the yearly value of all ecclesiastical livings and benefices without cure of souls; what person or persons received the profits, and who was the patron; and to certify the same into Chancery; and if, upon a careful consideration of things, it shall be found convenient and advantageous to unite two parishes or more into one, and that the whole ecclesiastical revenues, tithes, and profits belonging to the said parishes so united should be applied for a provision for one godly and painful minister to preach in the said united parishes, that the trustees or commissioners appoint-

---

* Mr. Powel vindicated his character in two publications: one entitled Examen et Purgamen Vavasoris, 1653, wherein he was cleared by the authentic certificates of persons of great credit, and many of them gentlemen of good landed property; the other called "The Bird in the Cage chirping; or, a Brief Narrative of the former Propagation and late Restriction of the Gospel in Wales," 12mo, 1661. The author of his life, in 1671, says "that he received nothing from the churches in Wales but neighbourly and brotherly kindness. The Parliament ordered him £100 per annum out of a sinecure, whereof he received about £60 for seven or eight years: many considerable gifts he refused; and never did he get anything by the act for the propagation of the Gospel in Wales."—Life, p. 112. Calamy's Church and Dissenters compared, p. 47, 48, note.—ED.

* Calamy's Comp., p. 48.   † Walker, p. 169.   † Walker, p. 149.

ed by this act shall represent the same to his highness and council, upon whose approbation they shall, by an instrument under the hands and seals of any five or more of them, declare that they do thereby unite such parishes into one; which instrument being enrolled in Chancery, the said parishes from thenceforth shall be adjudged and taken to be consolidated into one. If there happen to be more patrons than one in the parishes thus united, the patrons shall present by turns; but the union shall not take place till the avoidance of one of the livings by the death of the incumbent.*

On the other hand, where parishes were too large, the trustees for the augmentation of poor livings were empowered to divide them into two or more, upon their avoidance by death.

Farther, if, when two or more parishes were united into one, the income or salary did not amount to £100 per annum, the trustees for receiving impropriations, tithes, first-fruits, and tenths, &c., were directed to make up the deficiency; and where there was a considerable surplus, they might take off the augmentations formerly granted: provided this ordinance be not construed to restrain the said trustees from granting augmentations to preachers in cities and market-towns, where there shall be cause, to a greater proportion, with the consent of the protector and his council. This was a noble and generous design; and if the protector had lived to have seen it executed, must have been of general service to the body of the clergy.

Though his highness himself was no great scholar, he was a patron of learning and learned men.† He settled £100 a year on a divinity professor in Oxford; and gave twenty-four rare manuscripts to the Bodleian Library. He erected and endowed a college in Durham for the benefit of the northern counties, Mr. Falkland, M.A., being one of the first fellows. But these, and some other designs that he had formed for the advancement of learning, died with him.‡

In order to secure the education of youth, he took care to regulate both universities, by appointing new visiters, the former ceasing with the dissolution of the Long Parliament, viz.:

For the University of Oxford.§

The vice-chancellor for the time being.
Dr. Harris, president of Trinity College.
Dr. Rogers, principal of New Inn Hall.
Dr. T. Goodwin, president of Magdalen College.
Dr. John Owen, dean of Christ Church.
Dr. Henry Wilkinson, Margaret-professor of divinity.
Dr. Peter French, prebend of Christ Church.
Dr. John Conant, rector of Exeter College.
Dr. John Goddard, warden of Merton College.

Mr. Thankful Owen, president of St. John's.
Mr. Stephens, principal of Hart Hall.
Mr. James Baron, of Magdalen College.
Mr. Francis Howel, fellow of Exeter College.
William, viscount Say and Seal.
Nathaniel Fiennes, Esq.
Bulstrode Whitelocke, comm. of the great seal.
Samuel Dunch, Esq.
Sir John Dryden.
Richard Ingoldsly, ⎫
John Crew, ⎪
George Fleetwood, ⎬ Esqrs.
John Bright, ⎪
—— Jenkinson, ⎪
—— Greenfield,* ⎭

For the University of Cambridge.

The vice-chancellor for the time being.
Dr. Tuckney, master of St. John's College.
Dr. Arrowsmith, master of Trinity College.
Dr. Horton, president of Queen's College.
Dr. Samuel Bolton, master of Christ's College.
Dr. Law. Seaman, master of Peter House.
Dr. Lightfoot, master of Katherine Hall.
Mr. John Sadler, master of Magdalen College.
Dr. Whichcote.
Dr. Cudworth.
Mr. Worthington, master of Jesus College.
Mr. Dillingham, master of Emm. College.
Mr. Simpson, master of Pembroke Hall.
Mr. Templer, fellow of Trinity College.
Mr. Mowbrey, fellow of St. John's College.
Mr. William Moses, fellow of Pembroke Hall.
Mr. Wood, fellow of Magdalen College.
Henry Cromwell.
Henry Lawrence, lord-president of his highness's council.
J. Lambert, ⎫
J. Desborough, ⎬ Esqrs
Sir Gilbert Pickering.
Col. Ed. Montague.
Francis Rouse, Esq.
Oliver St. John, lord-chief-justice of the Common Pleas.
J. Thurloe, ⎫
Robert Castle, ⎪
Tho. Bendish, ⎬ Esqrs.
Rob. Viner, ⎪
Griffith Lloyd, ⎭
Sir William Strickland.

Any seven or more of the commissioners above named were authorized to visit all colleges and halls within their respective universities; to examine what statutes were fit to be abrogated, altered, or added, and to exhibit the same to his highness and the Parliament. They are farther authorized to explain such statutes as are ambiguous and obscure; to determine appeals; and are to be assisted upon all occasions by the mayor, sheriffs, and justices of peace. The said visiters, or any four of them, are authorized to visit Westminster School, Winchester School, Merchant Tailors' School, and Eton College; and to consider of such statutes of the said schools as are fit to be abrogated, and of others that may be proper to be added, for the well-government of the said schools and colleges.

The visiters discharged their duty with great fidelity, and the heads of colleges had a watchful eye over their several houses; drunkenness, swearing, gaming, and all kinds of immorality, were severely punished; all students, graduates, and others, were obliged to be at home in proper hours; the public-houses were searched, and the practice of religion in the several col-

---

* Scobel, p. 353.

† To the proofs which Mr. Neal produces of the patronage Cromwell afforded to learning, may be added, that he permitted the paper of Dr. Walton's Polyglot to be imported free of duty; and that when, through his pre-engagement to another, Dr. Seth Ward, afterward Bishop of Exeter, lost the principalship of Jesus College in Oxford, 1657, on being informed of his merit and learning, he promised him an annuity equal to the value of the principalship.—*Dr. Harris's Life of Oliver Cromwell,* p. 429–431 ; and *Calamy's Life of Mr. Howe,* p. 19.—Ed. Manton tells us that his library was well selected, and it is enough to say that Thurloe and Milton were his secretaries, and Hugh Peters his favourite preacher.—C.

‡ Whitelocke, p. 588.   § Scobel, p. 366.

* Add, from Dr. Grey, Sir Charles Wolseley, Bart., and Humphrey Mackworth, Esq.

... ere fit to be
... and to exhibit the
... and the Parliament. They
... to explain such statutes
... ous and obscure; to determine
... mayor sheriff
... The said visitor
... authorize...

pe...
ed
yglo.
throug.
Ward, an..
ship of Jes...
formed of his ,
annuity equal to
Harris's Life of Ol... ...
amy's Life of Mr. H..., ...—Ed. Manton tells
us that his library was well selected, and it is enough
to say that Thurloe and Milton were his secretaries,
and Hugh Peters his favourite preacher.—C.

‡ Whitelocke, p. 588.   § Scobel, p. 366.

... y with at at
... had a watch-
; drunkenness
... of immorality.
... dents, gradu-
... ...e be at home in
proper hours; the public-houses were searched,
and the practice of religion in the several col-

* Add, from Dr. Grey, Sir Charles Wolseley, Bart.,
and Humphrey Mackworth, Esq.

Engraved by Rasher, from an Original

STEPHEN CHARNOCK, B.D.

leges enforced with rigour. One of the professors writes, that there was more frequent practical preaching in the colleges than ever had been known. On the Lord's Day, at different hours, there were three or four sermons in several churches ; and on the week days, lectures on Tuesdays, Thursdays, Fridays, and Saturdays. The tutors were very diligent in discharge of their duty ; the public lectures were well attended, and the students under strict discipline ; learning revived, and the Muses returned to their seats, as appears by the number of learned men that flourished in the reign of King Charles II., who owed their education to these times.*

The protector's zeal for the welfare of the Protestant churches abroad deserves a particular notice, and was highly valued by all the reformed in foreign countries.† He took all imaginable care to appear at the head of that interest on all occasions, and to show his power in protecting them. The Prince of Tarente having written a respectful letter to the protector, his highness returned him the following answer : " That it was with extreme pleasure he had learned by letters his inviolable zeal and attachment to the Reformed churches, for which his praise was the greater, inasmuch as he showed that zeal at a time and in a place where such flattering hopes were given to persons of his rank if they would forsake the orthodox faith, and where those who continued steadfast are threatened with so many troubles. He rejoices that his own conduct in religion was so pleasing to him ; he calls God to witness, that he desired nothing so much as an opportunity to answer the favourable opinion the churches have of his zeal and piety, by endeavouring to propagate the true faith, and procure rest and peace for the Church. He exhorts the prince to hold out firm to the end in the orthodox religion which he received from his fathers ; and adds, that nothing would bring him greater glory than to protect it as much as lay in his power." What projects the protector formed for this purpose will be seen hereafter.

But the royal interest abroad was inclining towards popery ; the Duke of York was already perverted to the Romish faith :‡ no attempts were unessayed by the queen-mother, the Queen of France, and others, to gain the young Duke of Gloucester, who had been under the instruction of parliamentary tutors till the last year ;§ but this young prince was too well established in his religion to be perverted at present,|| upon

which the queen forbade him her presence ; and the Marquis of Ormond conducted him to his brother at Cologne. The king was a man of no religion, and having little to do, devoted his leisure hours to the ladies, and other private pleasures. His majesty had some trial (says Bishop Kennet*) of his conscience and courage in resisting the little arguments, or, rather, importunities, of popery. The papists put him in mind that all his hopes from the Protestant party were at an end ; that the bishops were dead, except a very few ; and the church-lands sold ; and that, since the late defeat at Worcester, the Presbyterian power was destroyed ; all his hopes, therefore, must be from the Roman Catholics, from whose assistance only he could now hope for his restoration. But the prospect was so distant, that the king, by advice of Lord Clarendon, was prevailed with not to declare himself openly at present.

On the last of November died the learned Mr. John Selden, the glory of the English nation :† he was born in Sussex, December 6, 1584, and educated in Hart Hall, Oxford ; after which he was transplanted to the Inner Temple, where he became a prodigy in the most uncommon parts of science. He was a great philologist, antiquary, herald, linguist, statesman, and lawyer, but seldom appeared at the bar. He was chosen burgess for several parliaments, where he displayed his profound erudition in speeches and debates in favour of the liberties of his country ; for which he was imprisoned, and severely fined with Mr. Pym in the Parliament of 1618 and 1628. He was chosen again in the Long Parliament, and appeared against the prerogative, as he had formerly done. He was one of the lay-members of the Assembly of Divines, and by his vast skill in the Oriental learning and Jewish antiquities, frequently silenced the most able divines. He wrote on various subjects, which gained him the title among foreigners of the dictator of learning in the English nation.‡ Among other remarkable pieces, we may reckon his History of Tithes, published 1618, in which he proves them not to be due to the Christian clergy by Divine institution : for this he was summoned before the High Commission Court, and obliged to make a public recantation.§ But after some time his reputation

---

* If the High Church accounts of the ignorance and fanaticism of the Puritan party be true, how can it be accounted for that such an *unequalled* amount of talent issued from the universities in this period ? For a list of the eminent men who filled the chairs of Oxford, or were trained in its schools, see Orme's Life of Owen, p. 133-142 ; also Dr. Owen's Testimony in Favour of the State of Learning and Piety, p. 137.—C.   † History of the Stuarts, p. 423.
‡ Compl. Hist., p. 203. § Kennet's Chron., p. 599.
|| The manner of expression used by Mr. Neal may lead the reader, Dr. Grey observes, to think that the Duke of Gloucester was at last perverted, which he apprehends was not the case. For Echard affirms that the duke was an invincible assertor of his father's faith ; and Carte represents him as withstanding the arguments of the Abbot of Pontoise, and rejecting the offers of a cardinal's hat, and even the promise of placing him on the throne. But, on the

other hand, Oldmixon assures his reader, on the authority of a minister of state, a man of known wisdom and probity, who was a particular favourite with the Prince of Orange, at the Hague, from whose mouth he had the information, that the duke *was* afterward reconciled to the Church of Rome.—*Grey,* vol. iii., p. 175. *History of the Stuarts,* p. 489.—ED.
* Compl. Hist., p. 213.
† Athenæ Oxon., vol. ii., p. 107, 108.
‡ It does honour to Grotius, his antagonist, that he pronounced Mr. Selden to be " the glory of the English nation." Like a man of genius, he was for striking out new paths of learning, and enlarging the territories of science. The greater part of his works are on uncommon subjects. But towards the close of his life he saw the emptiness of all human learning ; and owned that, out of the numberless volumes he had read and digested, nothing stuck so close to his heart, or gave him such solid satisfaction, as a single passage of Paul's Epistles : Tit., ii., 11-14.—*Granger's History of England,* vol. ii., p. 228, 229, 8vo.—ED.
§ It is judiciously remarked by Le Clerc, that it was great impolicy in the Church and court party to

VOL. II.—U

was so great, that it was thought worth while to gain him over to the court ; and upon the new civilities he received at Lambeth, he was prevailed with to publish his Mare Clausum against Hugo Grotius, which was esteemed such an invaluable treasure, that it was ordered to be laid up in the Court of Records. The archbishop offered him preferments, but he would accept of nothing. Upon the first pressures against the bishops, he published his Eutychius in Greek and Latin, with notes, in which he proves that bishops and presbyters differ only in degree. He afterward answered his majesty's declaration about the commission of array, and was made master of the rolls by the Long Parliament. He had a large and curious library of books ; in the frontispiece of each he used to write this motto, Περὶ παντὸς ἐλευθερίαν : Above all, liberty. At length, being worn out with age and hard study, he died at his house in the Whitefriars, aged seventy years, and was magnificently interred in the Temple Church on the south side of the round walk, according to the Directory, in the presence of all the judges, some Parliament-men, benchers, and great officers. His funeral sermon was preached by Archbishop Usher, who acknowledged he was not worthy to carry his books after him. His works are lately collected, and printed together in six volumes folio.

Mr. Thomas Gataker was born in London 1574, and was educated in St. John's College, Cambridge, where he proceeded M.A., and was afterward removed to Sidney College, where he became remarkable for his skill in the Hebrew and Greek languages.* After his ordination he was chosen minister of Lincoln's Inn, and occupied that station ten years ; but in the year 1611 he was presented to the rectory of Rotherhithe, where he continued till his death. In the year 1643 he was chosen a member of the Assembly of Divines, and was an ornament and reputation to it. When the Earl of Manchester visited and reformed the University of Cambridge, he offered Mr. Gataker the mastership of Trinity College, but he refused it on account of his health. Mr. Gataker was a very learned man, and a considerable critic and linguist, as appears by his writings, which were very numerous, considering his infirm state of health. He was a constant preacher, of a most holy and exemplary deportment, but withal of great modesty. It is hard, says Mr. Echard, to say which

offend and irritate such a man as Selden : a man of deep learning, not in Jewish antiquities only, but in those of his own country, the laws of which he understood to their first grounds. Such persons ought at all times to be courted and favoured, on account of the great use which may be made of them on all occasions ; but especially in seasons of public discontents, when they can turn the balance on the side which they join. Whereas it generally happens that they are ill treated, and the court favours are bestowed on those only who are fit for nothing but to feed on a great benefice or a good pension. It would have been more wise to have secured Selden, since he was by no means a fanatic, as many places in his Table-Talk show ; and even was partial to the old ecclesiastical government, in opposition to those who often set it at naught.—*Bibliothèque Ancienne et Moderne*, tom. vi., p. 253.—ED.

* Clarke's General Martyrology, p. 248, &c., of the Lives.

was most remarkable, his exemplary piety and charity, his polite literature, or his humility and modesty in refusing preferments. He maintained a correspondence with Salmasius, Hornbeck, and other learned foreigners, and was in high esteem both at home and in the Low Countries, where he had travelled. He died of age, and a complication of infirmities, July 27, 1654, in the eightieth year of his age.*

Mr. William Strong was educated in Katherine Hall, Cambridge, of which he was a fellow. He was afterward rector of More Crichel in Dorsetshire, where he continued till he was forced to fly from the Cavaliers ; † he then came to London, and was chosen one of the Assembly of Divines, and minister of St. Dunstan's in the West. After some time he became preacher at Westminster Abbey, where he died suddenly in the vigour of life, and was buried in the Abbey Church, July 4, 1654. His funeral sermon was preached by Mr. Ob. Sedgwick, who says that he was so plain in heart, so deep in judgment, so painful in study, so exact in preaching, and, in a word, so fit for all the parts of the ministerial service, that he did not know his equal. But after the Restoration his bones were dug up, and removed to St. Margaret's churchyard, with those of other eminent Presbyterian divines. He published several sermons and theological treatises in his lifetime ; and after his death there was a posthumous one upon the Covenants, in the preface to which Mr. Theophilus Gale observes, that the author was a wonder of nature for natural parts, and a miracle of grace for his deep insight into the more profound mysteries of the Gospel. His thoughts were sublime, but clear and penetrating, especially in interpreting difficult texts.‡

Mr. Andrew Pern was educated in Cambridge, and from thence removed to Welby in Northamptonshire, where he maintained the character of a zealous, laborious, and successful preacher for twenty-seven years. In the year 1643 he was chosen a member of the Assembly of Divines at Westminster. When he was at London he was offered several considerable preferments, but refused them, resolving to return to his people at Welby, who honoured him as a father ; for by his awakening sermons, and exemplary life and conversation, he accomplished

* The most celebrated of his works is a valuable edition of Marcus Antoninus, with a Latin translation and commentary, and a preliminary discourse on the philosophy of the Stoics, which is much esteemed. His house was a private seminary for divers young gentlemen of this nation, and many foreigners resorted to him, and lodged at his house in order to receive from him advice in their studies.—*British Biography*, vol. iv., p. 354, note.—ED. In obedience to his appointment by the General Assembly, he wrote the annotations upon Isaiah, Jeremiah, and Lamentations, published in the "*Assembly's Annotations on the Bible.*"—C.   † Athenæ Oxon., p. 218.

‡ Among Mr. Strong's other publications was a volume of thirty-one sermons published in 1656, with a preface by Dr. Manton, and one by Dr. Wilkinson, dean of Christ Church. Dr. Wilkinson says "there is an excellent vein in his sermons ; the farther you search, the richer treasure you are like to find. *** He was well studied in the soul's anatomy, and could dexterously dissect the old man." The careful perusal of Strong's discourses on the two Covenants will satisfy the judicious reader that the author was one of the greatest divines of his age.—C.

a 'great reformation of manners in that town. He was full of spiritual warmth, says the preacher of his funeral sermon, filled with a holy indignation against sin, active in his work, and never more in his element than in the pulpit. As his life was holy, so his death was comfortable. He blessed God that he was not afraid to die; nay, he earnestly desired to be gone, often crying out, in his last sickness, "When will that hour come? One assault more, and this earthen vessel will be broken, and I shall be with God." He died the beginning of December, 1654, before he was arrived to the age of sixty.

Dr. Samuel Bolton was educated in Cambridge, and from thence removed to the living of St. Martin's, Ludgate. Upon his coming to the city he was chosen one of the additional members of the Assembly of Divines, being a person of great name and character for learning and practical preaching. He was a burning and shining light, says Mr. Clarke,* an interpreter one of a thousand, an amiable preacher, and his life was an excellent commentary upon his sermons. Upon the death of Dr. Bainbrigge he was chosen master of Christ's College, Cambridge, which he governed with great wisdom and prudence till his death, which happened about the 10th of October, 1654. He was buried with great solemnity in his parish church of Ludgate on the 16th of the same month, very much lamented by the London clergy of those times.†

Mr. Jer. Whitaker was born at Wakefield in Yorkshire, 1599, and educated in Sidney College, Cambridge, where he proceeded in arts. He taught the free-school at Okeham in Rutlandshire seven years, and then became minister of Stretton, in the same county, where he continued thirteen years. In 1643 he was nominated one of the Assembly of Divines at Westminster, which brought him to London, where he was chosen to the rectory of St. Mary Magdalen, Bermondsey, in Southwark. He preached three or four sermons every week; two in Southwark, one at Westminster, and one at Christ Church, London. He never withdrew from any opportunity of preaching if he was in health; and though he preached often, his sermons were solid and judicious. He was a universal scholar, both in arts and languages; well acquainted with the fathers and schoolmen, an acute disputant, and inferior to none in his acquaintance with the Holy Scriptures.‡ He was of the Presbyterian persuasion, and had a chief hand in composing the Defence of the Gospel Ministry, published this year by the Provincial Synod of London. He refused the Engagement, and lamented the wars between England, Scotland, and Holland. No man was more beloved by the Presbyterian ministers of London than Mr. Whitaker. When he was seized with the

violent and acute pain of the stone, about the beginning of November, many days of prayer and fasting were observed for his recovery, but the distemper was incurable. He bore his pains with uncommon patience, fearing nothing more than to dishonour God by unreasonable complaints. When his distemper was most violent he would desire his friends to withdraw, that they might not be affected with his roarings. At length, nature being quite spent, he cheerfully resigned his soul into the hands of his Redeemer, about the fifty-fifth year of his age. His funeral sermon was preached by Mr. Calamy, who gave him a large and deserved encomium.

Mr. Richard Vines, of whom mention has been made already, was born at Blazon in Leicestershire, and educated in Magdalen College, Cambridge, where he commenced M.A. He was first schoolmaster at Hinckley, then minister of Weddington in Warwickshire. At the beginning of the civil war he was driven from his parish, and forced to take shelter in Coventry. When the Assembly of Divines was convened, he was chosen one of their number; and, as Fuller says,* was the champion of their party. While he was at London he became minister of St. Clement's Danes; afterward he removed to Watton in Hertfordshire, and was chosen master of Pembroke Hall in Cambridge, but resigned that, and his living of St. Lawrence Jewry, on account of the Engagement. He was a son of thunder, and therefore compared to Luther; but moderate and charitable to those who differed from him in judgment. The Parliament employed him in all their treaties with the king; and his majesty, though of a different judgment, valued him for his ingenuity, seldom speaking to him without touching his hat, which Mr. Vines returned with most respectful language and gestures. He was an admirable scholar; holy and pious in his conversation, and indefatigable in his labours, which wasted his strength, and brought him into a consumption, when he had lived but about fifty-six years. He was buried in his own parish church, February 7, 1655, his funeral sermon being preached by Dr. Jacomb, who gave him his just commendation. He was a perfect master of the Greek tongue, a good philologist, and an admirable disputant. He was a thorough Calvinist, and a bold, honest man, without pride or flattery.† Mr. Newcomen

---

* Lives of Eminent Persons, p. 43.

† He gave orders in his last will and testament, to be interred as a private Christian, and not with the outward pomp of a doctor; "because," as he observed, "he hoped to rise in the day of judgment, and appear before God, not as a *doctor*, but as an *humble Christian*." When he perceived any symptoms of his approaching dissolution, he rejoiced exceedingly, calling them the little crevices through which his soul peeped.—C.

‡ Clarke's General Martyrol. in the Lives, p. 264.

* Fuller's Worthies, p. 134.

† Dr. Grey insinuates a reflection on Mr. Vines's simplicity and integrity, by a story of his praying in the morning of an Easter Sunday, before the Marquis of Hertford, for the king's restoration to his throne and legal rights; but in the afternoon, when the marquis was absent, and Lord Fairfax came to church, praying, in *stylo parliamentario*, that God would turn the heart of the king, and give him grace to repent of his grievous sins, especially all the blood shed in those civil, uncivil wars. On which it was observed, that Mr. Vines was much more altered between the forenoon and afternoon than the difference between an English marquis and an Irish baron. The reader, perhaps, will think that each prayer might very consistently be formed by the same person. Not a week before Mr. Vines's death, as he was preaching at St. Gregory's, a rude fellow cried out to him, "Lift up your voice, for I cannot hear you;" to whom Mr. Vines returned, "Lift up your ears, for I can speak no louder."—*Fuller's Worthies,* p. 446, 8vo edition, 1684.—ED.

calls him " disputator acutissimus, concionator felicissimus, theologus eximius." Many funeral poems and elegies were published on his death.*

.The protector having dissolved his second Parliament without confirming their acts, was obliged still to rely on the military arm ; this, together with the insurrections in several parts of the country, induced him, for his greater se curity, to canton the nation into eleven districts, and place over them major-generals, whose commission it was to inspect the behaviour of the inferior commissioners within their districts ; to commit to prison all suspected persons ; to take care of collecting the public taxes ; and to sequester such as did not pay their decimation. They were to inquire after all private assemblies of suspected persons, and after such as bought up arms ; after vagabonds and idle persons ; after such as lived at a higher rate than they could afford ; after such as frequented taverns and gaming-houses, and after scandalous and unlearned ministers and schoolmasters ; and there was no appeal from them but to the protector and his council. They were ordered to list a body of reserves, both horse and foot, at half pay, who were to be called together upon any sudden emergency, and to attend so many days at their own expense, but if they were detained longer, to have full pay ; by which means the protector had a second army in view, if any disaster should befall the first ; but these officers became so severe and arbitrary, that his highness found it necessary, after some time, to reduce their power, and when affairs were a little more settled, to dissolve them.

Having provided for the security of his government at home, the protector concluded an alliance with France, October 23, in which it is remarkable that Louis XIV. is not allowed to style himself King of France, but King of the French, his highness claiming the protectorship of that kingdom among his other titles ; and, which is more surprising, the name of Oliver stands in the treaty before that of the French king. At the same time, he sent Admiral Blake with a fleet into the Mediterranean, who spread the terror of the English name all over Italy, even to Rome itself ; processions being made, and the Host exposed for forty hours, to avert the judgments of Heaven, and preserve the patrimony of the Church. But Blake's commission was only to demand £60,000 of the Duke of Tuscany, for damages sustained by the English merchants while he harboured Prince Rupert, which he paid immediately. The admiral released all the English slaves on the coast of Barbary, to the number of four hundred, and obtained satisfaction for the ships taken by the pirates of Algiers, Tunis, &c. Upon the whole, he brought home sixteen ships laden with booty, which sailed up the River Thames to the port of London, as a grateful spectacle of triumph to the people.

While Blake was in the Mediterranean, Admiral Penn and Venables, with thirty men-of-war and some land-forces, sailed to the West Indies,

with a design to surprise the town of Hispaniola ; but, miscarrying in the attempt, they re-embarked and took possession of the island of Jamaica, which is in possession of the crown of Great Britain to this day.

The protector did not commission Blake to assault the Spanish coasts in the Mediterranean, because there was no open rupture between the two nations in Europe ; but the West Indies not being included in the treaty, he thought himself at liberty in those parts : which occasioned a declaration of war, on the part of Spain, with all the English dominions ; upon which, Blake was ordered to cruise upon the Spanish coasts, and to wait for the return of the Plate fleet, of which he gave a very good account the next summer.

To support these additional expenses, the protector, by advice of his council, raised some extraordinary taxes before the Parliament met, which he knew to be illegal, and did not pretend to justify upon any other foot than "the absolute necessity of the public safety ; the distracted condition of the nation ; that it was impracticable, in the present juncture, to call a Parliament, or to proceed in the ordinary course of law ; and that in extraordinary cases, where-in all was at stake, some extraordinary methods were allowable." How far this reasoning will excuse the protector, or vindicate his conduct, must be left with the reader. But it is agreed on all hands, that in things that did not affect the very being of his government, he never interposed, but let the laws have their free course. He had a zeal for trade and commerce beyond all his predecessors, and appointed a standing committee of merchants for advancing it, which met for the first time in the Painted Chamber, November 27, 1655, and continued to his death.

The Provincial Assembly of London, finding their attempts to establish their discipline ineffectual, employed themselves this year in promoting the religious education of youth ; for which purpose they published an exhortation to catechising, with the following directions for the more orderly carrying it on :

1. "That the ministers, on some Lord's Day, prove in their sermons the necessity and usefulness of such a work, and exhort all parents and masters of families to prepare their children and servants for it, by catechising them at home, that they may more readily make their answers in public.

2. "That the catechism to be used be the lesser catechism of the Assembly of Divines. This catechism excelling all others in this respect, that every answer is a perfect proposition without the question.

3. "That the persons to be catechised be children and servants that have not been admitted to the Lord's Supper by the eldership.

4. "That the time of catechising be on the Lord's Day in the afternoon, before the sermon, to the end that the whole congregation may receive benefit thereby.

5. "That the catechism may be explained briefly at the first going over, that the people may in a short time have a notion of the whole body of divinity.

6. "That the parish be desired, at the common charge, to provide catechisms for the poor

* Clarke's Lives of Eminent Persons, p. 48.—There are few things more to be desired than a judicious biography of these glorious pulpit giants : how few of the present generation know their worth, and appreciate their claims !—C.

er sort, who cannot well provide for themselves, and that the distribution of them be referred to the respective ministers.

7. "It is desired that an account in writing, what progress is made in the premises, may be returned from the classes to the Provincial Assembly within forty days after the receipt hereof.

"Signed in the name and by the appointment of the assembly,

"Edmund Calamy, *Moderator.*

"William Harrison, } *Scribes.*"
"William Blackmore, }

These instructions were sent to the several classes of London; and after their example, the associated ministers in the several counties of England published the like exhortations to their brethren.

The occasion of this proceeding was the publishing two catechisms of Mr. John Biddle, a Socinian, one called a Scripture Catechism, and the other a Brief Scripture Catechism, for the Use of Children. Complaints of which being made to the last Parliament, they were ordered to be burned by the hands of the common hangman, and the author to be imprisoned in the Gate-house. Mr. Biddle had been in custody for his opinions before the late king's death. While he was there, he had published twelve questions or arguments against the Deity of the Holy Spirit, in quarto, 1647, which were answered by Mr. Pool, and the book ordered to be burned. Next year, being still in prison, he published seven articles against the Deity of Christ, with the testimonies of several of the fathers on this head; upon which, some zealous in the assembly moved that he might be put to death as a heretic; but he went on, and being set at liberty, in the year 1651 he composed and published the catechisms above mentioned, in which he maintains, "(1.) That God is confined to a certain place. (2.) That he has a bodily shape. (3.) That he has passions. (4.) That he is neither omnipotent nor unchangeable. (5.) That we are not to believe three persons in the Godhead. (6.) That Jesus Christ has not the nature of God, but only a Divine lordship. (7.) That he was not a priest while upon earth, nor did reconcile men to God. And, (8.) That there is no Deity in the Holy Ghost." These propositions* were condemned by the Parliament, and the author committed to the Gate-house. But as soon as the protector had dissolved his Parliament, he gave him his liberty.

After this, being of a restless spirit,† he challenged Mr. Griffin, a Baptist preacher, to dispute with him in St. Paul's Cathedral on this question: "Whether Jesus Christ be the Most High, or Almighty God?" This occasioning new disturbances, the council committed him to Newgate; but the protector thought it best to send him out of the way, and accordingly transported him to Scilly, and allowed him one hundred crowns à year for his maintenance. Here he remained till the year 1658, when, the noise being over, he was set at liberty; his catechisms having been answered by Dr. Owen, in a learned and elaborate treatise, entitled "Vindiciæ Evangelicæ," &c.

After the protector's death, Biddle set up a private conventicle in London, which continued till the Restoration, when the Church being restored to its coercive power, he was apprehended while preaching, and committed to prison, where he died in September, 1662, and was buried in the burying-ground in Old Bedlam. He had such a prodigious memory (says Wood), that he could repeat all St. Paul's Epistles in Greek, and was reckoned by those of his persuasion a sober man, and so devout, that he seldom prayed without lying prostrate on the ground.

Though it was well known by this, as well as other examples, that the protector was averse to all acts of severity on the account of religion, yet such was the turbulent behaviour of the Royalists, who threatened an assassination,* published the most daring libels against the government, and were actually in arms, that he thought it necessary to crush them, and therefore an order was published November 24,† "That no persons after January 1, 1655–6, shall keep in their houses or families, as chaplains or schoolmasters for the education of their children, any sequestered or ejected minister, fellow of a college, or schoolmaster, to have their children to be taught by such. That no such persons shall keep school either publicly or privately, nor preach in any public place, or private meeting, of any others than those of his

in this manner of one who thought it his duty, by the fair and peaceable means of preaching and writing, to advance and disseminate sentiments which he judged to be the truths of Scripture, and only called men to inquire and examine. Such language fixes a stigma upon the honest advocate for truth, and is the illiberal cry of those who cannot bear to have established opinions attacked. The first teachers of Christianity were reproached as men of restless spirits; as men who "would turn the world upside down."—Acts, xvii., 6. In the present case, the term was not deserved; Mr. Neal has misstated the transaction. Mr. Biddle was not the first in the business. The challenge came from Mr. Griffin, and Mr. Biddle waived accepting it, and declined the disputation for some time; and when he entered the lists, there were in the auditory many of his bitter and fiery adversaries.—See *Review of his Life*, p. 117, 118; or a modern *Collection of Unitarian Tracts*, in 12mo, vol. iv., p. 91.—ED. (TOULMIN).

* It is not generally known that a proclamation, dated Paris, 3d May, 1654, was issued by the exile king, in which he promised an annuity of £500 to any person, and his heirs forever, who would take away the life of the protector. In this proclamation Charles talks of "a certain mechanic fellow, by name Oliver Cromwell," &c.—*Jesse's Court*, &c., vol. iii., p. 114.—C.

† The date, as given by Evelyn, is 27th November.—*Harleian Miscellany*, vol. vi., p. 420.—C.

---

* Mr. Biddle was a pious, holy, and humble man; a conscientious sufferer for what appeared to him Divine and important truth. The propositions objected to him above do not appear in his catechisms under the form of principles which he asserts, but of questions which he proposes, and the answers to which are numerous texts of Scripture, that appear to speak to the point. E. g., The first proposition is this question: "Is not God, according to the current of the Scripture, in a certain place, namely, in beaven?" The answer consists of twenty-nine passages of Scripture, which represent God as "looking from heaven, as our Father who art in heaven," and the like. For a full account of these catechisms, I would refer the reader to my Review of the Life, Character, and Writings of Mr. John Biddle, section 8.—ED. (TOULMIN).

† It is to be regretted that Mr. Neal should speak

own family; nor shall administer baptism, or the Lord's Supper, or marry any persons, òr use the Book of Common Prayer, or the forms of prayer therein contained, on pain of being prosecuted, according to the orders lately published by his highness and council, for securing the peace of the commonwealth. Nevertheless, his highness declares that towards such of the said persons as have, since their ejectment or sequestration, given, or hereafter shall give, a real testimony of their godliness, and good affection to the present government, so much tenderness shall be used as may consist with the safety and good of the nation."*

This was a severe and terrible order† upon the Episcopalians, and absolutely unjustifiable in itself; but the title of the act, which is "An Ordinance for securing the Peace of the Commonwealth," as well as the last clause, shows it was made for the safety of the government, against a number of men who were undermining it, and was published chiefly *in terrorem, for no person was prosecuted upon it*; and the Parliament which met next year not confirming it, it became absolutely void.‡

Dr. Gauden presented a petitionary remonstrance to the protector against this order; and Archbishop Usher was desired to use his interest with his highness in behalf of the Episcopal clergy; upon which, says the writer of the archbishop's life,§ the protector promised either to recall his declaration, or prevent its being put in execution, provided the clergy were inoffensive in their language and sermons, and stood clear in meddling with matters of state. His highness, accordingly, laid the matter before his

council, who were of opinion* that it was not safe for him to recall his declaration, and give open liberty to men who were declared enemies to his government, but that he should suspend the execution of it as far as their behaviour should deserve; so that in the event there was no great cause of complaint; for notwithstanding this ordinance, the sober Episcopal clergy preached publicly in the churches, at London and in the country, as Dr. Hall, afterward Bishop of Chester, Dr. Ball, Dr. Wild, Dr. Hardy, Dr. Griffith, Dr. Pearson, bishop of Chester, and others. Remarkable are the words of Bishop Kennet to this purpose: "It is certain," says his lordship, "that the protector was for liberty, and the utmost latitude to all parties, so far as consisted with the peace and safety of his person and government, and therefore he was never jealous of any cause or sect on the account of heresy and falsehood, but on his wiser accounts of political peace and quiet; and even the prejudice he had against the Episcopal party *was more for their being Royalists, than for being of the good old Church.* Dr. Gunning, afterward Bishop of Ely, kept a conventicle in London, in as open a manner as Dissenters did after the toleration; and so did several other Episcopal Divines."†

For the same reasons, his highness girt the laws close upon the papists, not on account of their religion, but because they were enemies to his government; for, in the month of May, a proclamation was published for the better executing the laws against Jesuits and priests, and for the conviction of popish recusants; the reasons of which the protector gives in his declaration of October 31, published with the advice of his council, in these words: "Be-

---

* Hughes's Exact Abridgment of Public Acts and Ordinances, 4to, p. 597.

† "It would be useless," says Dr. Harris, "to spend words in exposing the cruelty of this declaration. Persecution is written on the face of it, nor is it capable of a vindication."—*Life of Oliver Cromwell,* p. 438.—ED.

‡ This ordinance was designed to terrify rather than injure, and was, in point of fact, as Mr. Hallam remarks, "so far from being rigorously observed, that Episcopalian conventicles were openly kept in London." "It was one of the unhappy features of these times, that religion and politics were so intimately blended as to admit of no practical disjunction. Cromwell was desirous of extending toleration to all; to the Catholic as well as to the Protestant; to the Episcopalian equally with the Presbyterian and Independent. From this generous policy he was compelled partially to swerve, in the case of the Episcopalians and Catholics. These parties had sunk into two sections of one political faction, whose imbittered hostility to his government was the prominent and most practical article of their creed. Their religion was the rallying-point of disaffection; the perpetual incentive to revolt; he must have been more of a philosopher than is usual with statesmen, if he had not sought to discourage their religious faith. * * It *was not* against Episcopacy that Cromwell warred, but against the politics—ever restless and plotting—with which its profession was associated." Hallam says, "It is somewhat bold in Anglican writers to complain, as they do, of the persecution they suffered at this period, when we consider *what had been the conduct of the bishops before, and what it was afterward.* I do not know that any member of the Church of England was imprisoned under the commonwealth, except for *some political reason*; certain it is, *the jails were not filled with them,*" as in prelatical persecutions.—*Const. Hist.,* vol. ii., p. 428, note.—C.

§ Parr's Life of Usher, p. 75.

* On this ground, when the lord-primate went to him a second time to get the promise which the protector on the first application had made of taking off these restraints ratified and put into writing, he retracted his engagement, which both grieved and irritated the archbishop. He had, indeed, good reason to be displeased. By this it appears that Mr. Neal's statement above is not accurate. The ordinance was executed; and though some worthy Episcopalians were permitted to officiate, it cannot be doubted but many innocent and worthy men must have received very hard measure. The ordinance was marked with horrid severity; and it is "a barbarous thing to prohibit men the use of those forms of address to the Deity which they imagine are most honourable and acceptable to him." Besides, men ought not to suffer in their most valuable and inalienable rights on suspicion; and instead of being amenable for overt acts, be punished, as it were, for crimes they have never committed. This is injustice and cruelty; has its origin in fear and the consciousness of oppressive government; and tends to make the government, which it would protect from danger, odious and hateful.—*Grey's Remarks,* vol. iii., p. 177, 178. *Harris's Life of O. Cromwell,* p. 438, 439.—ED.

† Conf. Plea, part iv., p. 510. Compl. Hist., p. 223. Baxter, in his True History of Councils, makes a statement greatly adapted to diminish sympathy with the Episcopalians of that period. "In the days of the usurper," he says, "I moved for a petition that when they granted liberty of conscience for so many others, they would grant liberty for the full exercise of the Episcopal government to all that desired it. But the Episcopal party that I spake to would not endure it, as knowing what bare liberty would be to their cause, unless they could have the sword to suppress   se that yielded not to their reason."—P. 131.—Cho.

cause it was not only commonly observed, but there remains with us somewhat of proof, that Jesuits have been found. among discontented parties of this nation, who are observed to quarrel and fall out with every form of administration in Church and State."* The protector gave notice of the like kind to the Republicans, fifth monarchy men, Levellers, and to the Presbyterians, that they should stand upon the same foot with Royalists, in case of any future deliuquencies.

Such was the protector's latitude, that he was for indulging the Jews, who petitioned for liberty of their religion, and for carrying on a trade in London. Manasseh Ben Israel, one of their chief rabbies, with some others, came from Amsterdam to Whitehall for this purpose, whom the protector treated with respect, and summoned an assembly of divines, lawyers, and merchants to consult upon the affair.† The divines were to consider it as a case of conscience; the lawyers to report how far it was consistent with the laws of England; and the merchants, whether it was for the advantage of trade and commerce. Bishop Burnet apprehends that the protector designed the Jews for spies in the several nations of Europe; however, he was of opinion that their admission, under certain limitation, might be for the advantage of commerce; and told the divines that, since there was a promise in Holy Scripture of the conversion of the Jews, he did not know but the preaching of the Christian religion, as it was then in England, without idolatry or superstition, might conduce to it. But the assembly not agreeing in their opinions, the affair was dropped, and the petitioners returned to Holland, where Manasseh Ben Israel wrote a handsome letter, now before me, which he calls "An Answer to certain Questions propounded by a noble and learned Gentleman, touching the Reproaches cast upon the Nation of the Jews, wherein all Objections are candidly and fully stated." The famous Mr. Prynne, and Mr. Dury, a Presbyterian minister, wrote fiercely against the admission of the Jews; but other divines, whom the protector consulted, were for admitting them with some limitations. I shall report their resolution on this point in their own language.

Question, Whether the Jews, at their desire, may be admitted into this nation to traffic and dwell among us, as Providence shall give occasion?

The answer of those who were against it was, that they could not think it lawful for the following reasons.

1. "Because the motives on which Manasseh Ben Israel, in his book lately printed, desires their admission into this commonwealth, are such as we conceive to be very sinful.

2. "The danger of seducing the people of this nation, by their admission, is very great.

3. "Their having synagogues, or any public meetings for the exercise of their religion, is not only evil in itself, but likewise very scandalous to other Christian churches.

4. "Their customs and practices concerning marriage and divorce are unlawful, and will be of very evil example among us.

5. "The principles of not making conscience of oaths made, and injuries done to Christians in life, chastity, goods, or good name, have been very notoriously charged upon them by valuable testimony.

6. "Great prejudice is like to arise to the natives of this commonwealth in matters of trade, which, besides other dangers here mentioned, we find very commonly suggested by the inhabitants of the city of London."

Other divines were of opinion that the civil magistrate might tolerate them under the following limitations:

1. "That they be not admitted to have any public judicatories, civil or ecclesiastical.

2. "That they be not permitted to speak or do anything to the defamation or dishonour of the names of our Lord Jesus Christ, or of the Christian religion.

3. "That they be not permitted to do any work, or anything, to the open profanation of the Lord's Day, or Christian Sabbath.

4. "That they be not permitted to have any Christians dwell with them as their servants.

5. "That they have no public office or trust in this commonwealth.

6. "That they be not allowed to print anything in our language against the Christain religion.

7. "That so far as may be, they be not suffered to discourage any of their own from using any proper means, or applying themselves to any who may convince them of their error; and turn them to Christianity. And that some severe penalty be imposed upon them who shall apostatize from Christianity to Judaism."

Mr. Archdeacon Echard says,* "The Jews offered the protector £200,000 provided they might have St. Paul's Cathedral for a settlement." And he adds the following malicious reflection, that "the money made his highness look upon it as the cause of God, but that both the clergy and laity so declaimed against them, that the religious juggle would not take place." This the archdeacon himself could not believe, as being quite out of character, for he knew that the protector did not enrich his family, nor value money, but for the public service. He concludes that "the Jews could never be permitted to live long in a well-settled monarchy." What, then, does he call the monarchy of England, where the Jews have been indulged in the free exercise of their religion, without doing any damage to the religion or commerce of the nation, for above sixty years?

The protector's zeal for the Reformed religion made him the refuge of persecuted Protestants in all parts of the world. The Duke of Savoy, at the instance of his duchess, sister to the Queen of England, determined to oblige his reformed subjects in the valleys of Piedmont to embrace the Roman Catholic religion or depart the country. For this purpose, he quartered an army upon them, which ate up their substance. The Protestants making some little resistance to the rudeness of the soldiers, the duke gave

---

* Compl. Hist., p. 225, in marg.

† It is a proof of the protector's good dispositions towards this business. and of his respect for the rabbi who came to negotiate it, that, by an order of the 24th of March, 1655, he directed £200 to be paid to him out of the treasury.— *Whitelocke's Memorials,* p. 673.—Ed.

* P. 716.

orders that all the Protestant families in the valley of Lucerne should go into banishment, which some obeyed, while the rest sent deputies to the court of Turin to implore mercy; but the pope and the princes of Italy advised the duke to improve the present opportunity for extirpating the Reformed, and making all his subjects of one religion. The duke accordingly sent express orders to his general to drive them all out of the country, with their wives and children, and to put to death such as should remain. This was executed with great severity, April 20, 1655. Those who escaped the sword fled into the mountains, from whence, being ready to perish with hunger and cold, they sent their agents to the Lord-protector of England, and other Protestant powers, for relief. It was the beginning of May when his highness was first made acquainted with their distress, whereupon he appointed a general fast, and charitable contributions throughout all England for their present assistance; and such was the compassion of the people, that the collection amounted to £37,097 7s. 3d. About £30,000 was remitted to their deputies at several payments, in this and the next year; but the confusions which followed upon the protector's death prevented the clearing the whole account till the Convention Parliament at the Restoration, who ordered the remaining £7000 to be paid. The protector applied to the Protestant kings of Sweden and Denmark; to the States of Holland, the cantons of Switzerland, and the Reformed churches of Germany and France; and by his powerful instances procured large contributions from those parts. He wrote to the King of France, and to Cardinal Mazarine; and being glad of an opportunity to strike terror into the Roman Catholic powers, he sent Samuel Moreland, Esq., with a letter to the Duke of Savoy, in which, having represented the cruelty and injustice of his behaviour towards the Protestants in the valleys, he tells him, "that he was pierced with grief at the news of the sufferings of the Vaudois, being united to them not only by the common ties of humanity, but by the profession of the same faith, which obliged him to regard them as his brethren; and he should think himself wanting in his duty to God, to charity, and to his religion, if he should be satisfied with pitying them only (whose miserable condition was enough to raise compassion in the most barbarous minds), unless he also exerted himself to the utmost of his ability to deliver them out of it." This awakened the popish powers, insomuch that Mazarine wrote in the most pressing language to the court of Turin to give the protector immediate satisfaction; with which the duchess reproached him, because he had made no terms for the English papists;* but his eminence replied, "We must leave to God the care of defending the Catholics, whose cause is most just; but that of the heretics needs for its support the clemency of princes." Upon this the persecution immediately ceased: the duke recalled his army out of the valleys, and restored their goods; the poor people returned to their houses, and recovered all their ancient rights and privileges. But to strike some farther terror into

the pope and the little princes of Italy, the protector gave out that, forasmuch as he was satisfied they had been the promoters of this persecution, he would keep it in mind, and lay hold of the first opportunity to send his fleet into the Mediterranean to visit Civita Vecchia, and other parts of the ecclesiastical territories; and that the sound of his cannon should be heard in Rome itself. He declared publicly that he would not suffer the Protestant faith to be insulted in any part of the world; and therefore procured liberty to the Reformed in Bohemia and France; nor was there any potentate in Europe so hardy as to risk his displeasure by denying his requests.*

The charitable society for the relief of the widows and children of clergymen, since known by the name of the Corporation for the Sons of the Clergy, had its beginning this year; the first sermon being preached by the Reverend Mr. George Hall, son of the famous Joseph Hall, bishop of Exeter, then minister of Aldersgate, afterward Archdeacon of Canterbury, and Bishop of Chester. The sermon was entitled "God's appearing for the Tribe of Levi, improved in a Sermon preached at St. Paul's, November 8, 1655, to the Sons of Ministers then solemnly assembled," from Numb., xvii., 8, "The rod of Aaron budded, and bloomed blossoms, and yielded almonds." The preacher's design was to enforce the necessity and usefulness of a settled ministry; and though there were some passages that discovered him to be a prelatist, the main part of the sermon breathes moderation. "Let those ill-invented terms," says he, "whereby we have been distinguished from each other, be swallowed up in that name which will lead us hand in hand to heaven, the name of Christians. If my stomach, or any of yours, rise against the name of brotherly communion, which may consist with our several principles retained, not differing in substantials, God take down that stomach, and make us see how much we are concerned to keep the unity of the Spirit in the bond of peace. Why should some, in the height of their zeal for a liturgy, suppose there can be no service of God but where that is used? Why should others, again, think their piety concerned and trespassed upon, if I prefer and think fit to use a set form? There must be abatements and allowances of each other; a coming down from our punctilios, or we shall never give up a good account to God."† From this time sermons have been preached annually, and large contributions made for the service of this charity. In the reign of King Charles II. they became a body corporate; and their present grandeur is sufficiently known to the whole nation.

On the 21st of March, this year, died the most reverend and learned Archbishop Usher, born in Dublin, 1580, and educated in Trinity Col-

---

* Burnet, vol. i., p. 108, Edin. edit.

* Mr. Neal's statement of Cromwell's interference in behalf of the Waldenses is, in general, correct; but when he says "the poor people returned to their houses *and recovered all their ancient rights and privileges*," his representation is not borne out by facts. If the reader wishes a more detailed and correct account of this tragical affair, he should consult *Jones's History of the Christian Church*, vol. ii., c. vi., sect. vi., p. 358–398.—C.

† How rarely are these admirable sentiments to be heard from the advocates of prelacy!—C.

lege.* 'He proceeded M.A. in the year 1600, and next year was ordained deacon and priest by his uncle, Henry Usher, then Archbishop of Armagh. In the year 1620 he was made Bishop of Meath, and, four years after, Archbishop of Armagh; in which station he remained till the dissolution of the hierarchy during the civil wars. In his younger years he was a Calvinist, but in his advanced age he embraced the middle way between Calvin and Arminius. He was one of the most moderate prelates of his time, and allowed of the ordinations of foreign Protestants, which none but he and Bishop Davenant, and one or two more among the bishops of those times, would admit.† The archbishop having lost all his revenues by the Irish rebellion, the king conferred upon him the bishopric of Carlisle, in commendam. In 1643 he was nominated one of the Assembly of Divines at Westminster, but did not appear among them. As long as the king was at Oxford he continued with him, but, when the war was ended, he returned to London and lived privately, without any molestation. He assisted at the treaty of the Isle of Wight, but could do no service, the contending parties being then at too great a distance to be reconciled. A little before the king's death, the archbishop was chosen preacher to the honourable society of Lincoln's Inn, preaching constantly all term-time, till his eyes failing, he quitted that post, about a year and a half before his death, and retired with the Countess of Peterborough to her house at Ryegate. The protector had a high esteem for this excellent prelate, and consulted him about proper measures for advancing the Protestant interest at home and abroad : he allowed him a pension, and promised him a lease of part of the lands of his archbishopric in Ireland for twenty-one years; but his death prevented the accomplishment of his design. About the middle of February the archbishop went down to Ryegate, and on the 20th of March was seized with a pleurisy, of which he died the next day, in the seventy-sixth year of his age, having been fifty-five years a preacher, four years Bishop of Meath, and thirty-one years Archbishop of Armagh. The archbishop was one of the most learned men of his age; he had a penetrating judgment, a tenacious memory; above all, he was a most pious, humble, exemplary Christian.‡ His body was of the smaller size, his

complexion sanguine, but his presence always commanded reverence. The protector did him the honour of a public funeral, and buried him at his own expense,* in King Henry VII.'s chapel.†

Stephen Marshall, B.D., was born at Godmanchester in Huntingdonshire, and was educated in Cambridge, and afterward beneficed at Finchingfield in Essex, where he acquired such reputation by his preaching, that he was often called to preach before the Long Parliament, who consulted him in all affairs relating to religion. He was one of the Assembly of Divines, and employed in most, if not all, the treaties between the king and Parliament : Mr. Echard, according to his usual candour, calls him "a famous incendiary, and assistant to the Parliamentarians, their trumpet in their fasts, their confessor in their sickness, their counsellor in their assemblies, their chaplain in their treaties, and their champion in their disputations;"‡ and

---

Passion, pride, self-will, or the love of the world, seemed not to be so much as in his nature. He had all the innocence of the dove in him. But no man is entirely perfect. He was not made for the governing part of his function. His soul was too gentle to manage the rough work of reforming abuses ; therefore, he left things as he found them. He saw the necessity of cutting off many abuses, and hoped for a time of reformation, yet he did not exert himself to correct or remove those corruptions which he apprehended would bring a curse and ruin upon the Church. It seems that this sat heavy upon his mind in his last illness ; for he prayed often, and with great humility, that God would forgive his sins of omission, and his failings in his duty."—*Life of Bishop Bedel*, p. 86, 87.—ED.

* Here Mr. Neal was, it seems, in a mistake. The protector, though he directed that this prelate should be buried with great pomp at Westminster Abbey, bore but half the expense of the funeral ; the other half fell very heavily upon his relations. His Annals of the Old and New Testament is esteemed the most valuable of his numerous works ; and the first draught of this work was drawn up by him when he was only fifteen years of age. The Western world owes its first acquaintance with the Samaritan Bible to this prelate. Four copies were procured for him by a factor, and sent to him from Syria, in 1625. He gave one copy to the library at Oxford ; a second he lodged in Sir Robert Cotton's library ; he sent a third to Leyden, and reserved the fourth to himself. The Old Testament in Syriac was obtained for him not long after.—*Clarke's Martyrology*, in the *Lives*, p. 280 and 292. *Granger's Hist. of Eng.*, vol. iii., p. 27, 8vo.

Cromwell prevented the sale of Archbishop Usher's valuable library of prints and manuscripts to foreigners ; and caused it to be purchased and sent over to Dublin, with an intention to bestow it on a new college, or hall, which he proposed to build and endow there. The lease, which, as Mr. Neal says, Cromwell promised to the archbishop, was never executed ; and it admits a doubt whether the pension was ever enjoyed.—*Dr. Grey*, on the authority of *Dr. Parr*, the primate's biographer.—ED.

† Clarke's General Martyrology, p. 277, &c., of the Lives.

‡ The words of Mr. Echard are almost verbatim borrowed from Fuller. Dr. Grey, to confute the character given of Mr. Marshall as an admired preacher, quotes some passages from his sermons, which certainly are not in the taste of modern eloquence ; but they had a point in them, and abounded in antitheses and comparisons, which, it is easy to conceive, might gain admiration. Besides, compositions should be, in part at least, judged of by the spirit and taste of the age to which they were adapted.—ED.

---

* It is a curious and singular circumstance, that Archbishop Usher received his first elements of learning from two aunts, who were both born blind, yet found out a method of teaching him to read English. These ladies had vast memories, and could repeat most part of the Scriptures by heart distinctly and without mistake. When it was debated whether Dr. Usher should be nominated one of the assembly at Westminster, Mr. Selden is reported to have said, "that they had as good inquire whether they had best admit Inigo Jones, the king's architect, to the company of mousetrap-makers."—*British Biography*, vol. iv., p. 336, 350.—ED.

† He was not so severe in his judgment about Episcopacy as to disown other Reformed churches, but declared that he loved and honoured them as true members of the Church universal, and was ready for the ministers of Holland, France, &c., to testify his communion with them.—*Clarke's Life of Usher*, edition 1662, p. 239.—C.

‡ "With his great and vast learning (it is said), no man had a better soul, and a more apostolical mind.

then adds, "This great Shimei, being taken with a desperate sickness, departed the world.mad and raving." An unjust aspersion !· for he was a person of sober and moderate principles, inasmuch that Mr. Baxter used to say, that if all the bishops had been of the spirit and temper of Archbishop Usher, the Presbyterians of the temper of Mr. Marshall, and the Independents like Mr. Jer. Burroughs, the divisions of the Church would have been easily compromised. When he was taken ill, and obliged to retire into the country for the air, and spent the last said he was distracted, and in his rage constantly cried out, that he was damned for adhering to the Parliament in their war against their king. But he lived to confute the calumny, and published a treatise to prove the lawfulness of defensive arms in cases of necessity. He was an admired preacher, and far from running into the extremes of the times. In the decline of his life he retired from the city, and spent the last two years of his life in Ipswich. The Reverend Mr. G. Firmin, in a preface to one of Mr. Marshall's posthumous sermons, writes, that he had left few labourers like himself behind him ; that he was a Christian by practice as well as profession ; that he lived by faith, and died by faith, and was an example to the believers in word, in conversation, in charity, in faith, and purity. That when he and others were talking with Mr. Marshall about his death, he replied, "I cannot say, as he, I have not so lived that I should now be afraid to die ; but this I can say, I have so learned Christ, that I am not afraid to die." He enjoyed the full use of his understanding to the last ; but lost the use of his hands and appetite, insomuch that he could eat nothing for some months before he died. Mr. Fuller says that he performed his exercise for bachelor of divinity with general applause ; that he was a good preacher, but so supple, that he brake not a joint in all the alteration of the times ; and although some suspected him of deserting his Presbyterian principles, yet upon his deathbed he gave them full satisfaction that he had not.* His remains were solemnly interred in Westminster Abbey, but were dug up again at the Restoration.†

The protector having as yet no better than a military title to his high dignity, resolved to obtain a more legal one as soon as the times would admit. He had now cut his way through a great many difficulties, and the success of his arms this summer having raised his reputation to an uncommon pitch of greatness, he resolved to summon a new Parliament, to meet at Westminster, September 17, 1656, to confirm his title to the protectorship ;· and the Republicans being his most dangerous enemies, the protector sent for Sir H. Vane and Major-general Ludlow, to give security not to act against the present government.‡ He asked Ludlow what made him uneasy, or what he would have ? Ludlow answered, He would have the nation governed by its own consent. I am, said the protector, as much for a government by consent as any man ; but where shall we find that consent :

among the Prelatical, Presbyterian, Independent, Anabaptist, or Levelling parties ? The other replied, Among those of all sorts who have acted with fidelity and affection to the public. The protector, apprehending that he was for throwing all things back into confusion, told him that all men now enjoyed as much liberty and protection as they could desire, and that he was resolved to keep the nation from being imbrued again in blood. "I desire not," says he, "to put any more hardships upon you than upon myself ; nor do I aim at anything by this proceeding but the public quiet and security. As to my own circumstances in the world, I have not much improved them, as these gentlemen (pointing to his council) well know." But Ludlow, Sir Henry Vane, and Colonel Rich persisting in their refusal to give security, were taken into custody. Bishop Burnet says that others solicited him to restore the young king, and that the Earl of Orrery told him he might make his own terms ; but that Cromwell replied, "that the son could never forgive his father's blood ; and that he was so debauched he would undo everything." It was therefore resolved to set him aside, and proceed upon the present plan.

When the Parliament met according to appointment, the Reverend Dr. Owen preached before them ; his text was Isa., xiv., 32 : "What shall one then answer the messengers of the nation ? That the Lord hath founded Zion, and the poor of his people shall trust in it." From the Abbey, the protector went with the members to the Painted Chamber, where he made a speech, and then dismissed them to their house ;· but to prevent their entering into debates about his title, a guard was placed at the door, with a paper of recognition for each member to subscribe, wherein they promised not to act anything prejudicial to the government as it was established under a protector. Upon their subscribing this, if they were under no disqualification, they had a certificate of their return, and of their being approved by his highness and council.* This measure was certainly inconsistent with the freedom of Parliaments : for if the crown has a negative upon the return of the members, they are tools of the crown, and not representatives of the people ; because, though they are legally chosen and returned by the proper officer, a superior tribunal may set them aside. Besides, if the Parliament was to give a sanction to the new government, the recognition was absurd, because it obliged them to consent to that which they had no liberty to debate. It must therefore be allowed, that Cromwell's protectorship was built solely upon the authority of the council of officers, this being one of those fundamentals which his highness would not suffer any of his Parliaments to debate. But it is highly probable that these stretches of power might be absolutely unavoidable, at this time, to maintain government under any form ; and that without them the several parties would have fallen to pieces, and involved the nation in confusion and a new war. The Parliament, in their humble petition and advice, guarded against the exclusion of their members for the future, except by a vote of the House, which the protector freely consented to ; so that this was

---

* Fuller's Worthies, book ii., p. 53.
† Mr. Marshall was one of the authors of the work written by Smectymnuus, 1641, in reply to Bishop Hall's "Humble Remonstrance to Parliament."—C.
‡ Life of Cromwell, p. 340.

* Whitelocke, p. 639.

only a temporary expedient, and not to be made a precedent of: but at present almost one hundred members refused to subscribe, and were therefore excluded. These presented a petition to the sitting members for redress; and were answered, that the protector had promised to relieve them if they could show cause of complaint. But instead of this, they appealed to the people in a severe remonstrance, charging his highness with invading their fundamental rights and liberties, and preventing the free meeting of the representatives of the people in Parliament. To which it was replied, that if they would not so much as own the protector, they had no colour or pretence to call themselves members of Parliament.

The sitting members having chosen Sir Thoman Widdrington their speaker, approved of the war with Spain, and voted supplies to support his highness in the prosecution of it. They renounced and disannulled the title of Charles Stuart; and passed an act, making it high treason to compass or imagine the death of the lord-protector. They reviewed the orders and ordinances of the protector and his council in the intervals of Parliament, and confirmed most of them. They abrogated the authority and power of the major-generals, conceiving it inconsistent with the laws of England and liberties of the people. These, and some other acts hereafter mentioned, were presented to his highness, November 27, for confirmation; and as he was pleased to confirm them all, he told them, that as it had been the custom of the chief governors to acknowledge the care and kindness of the Commons upon such occasions, so he did very heartily and thankfully acknowledge their kindness therein. But the Parliament continued sitting till next year, when we shall meet with more important transactions.

The act for security of the protector's person was no sooner passed than a plot was discovered against his life. Miles Syndercomb, a Leveller, a bold, resolute man, having been disbanded in Scotland, combined with one Cecil, and another of the protector's lifeguards, to assassinate him as he was going to Hampton Court; but being disappointed once and again by some unexpected accidents, the other conspirators betrayed the design. Syndercomb put himself on his trial, and was condemned on the statute 25th of Edward III., the Chief-justice Glynne declaring that, by the word king in the statute, any chief magistrate was understood. But Syndercomb prevented the execution; for the very morning he was to suffer, he was found dead in his bed; whereupon his body was tied to a horse's tail, and dragged naked to the scaffold on Tower Hill, and then buried with a stake driven through it. However, a day of public thanksgiving was appointed for the protector's deliverance, February 20, when his highness gave the speaker and members of Parliament a splendid entertainment at the Banqueting House.

The war with Spain this summer was attended with vast success, for no sooner had the King of Spain seized the effects of the English merchants in his country, than the protector ordered his admirals, Blake and Montague, to block up the harbour of Cadiz, and look out for the Plate fleet, which Captain Stayner, who was left with seven men-of-war upon the coast, while

the admirals were gone to Portugal for fresh water, discovered, consisting of eight men-of-war, making directly for Cadiz; Stayner bore up to them with all the sail he could make, and engaged them within four leagues of their port; the Spanish admiral ran his ship ashore with six hundred thousand pieces of eight; but the vice-admiral, with twelve hundred thousand pieces of eight, and another galleon, were fired and sunk; the rear-admiral, with two millions of plate in her, was taken; and, upon the whole, six of the eight ships were destroyed; the plate, to the value of two millions, was brought to Portsmouth, and conveyed in carts to London, and carried through the city to the Tower to be coined. Admiral Blake, with the rest of the fleet, wintered upon the coast of Spain, and destroyed another fleet of much greater value the next summer.

After the discovery of Syndercomb's plot, the Prelatists, Presbyterians, and Levellers, were pretty quiet, but the Quakers began to be very troublesome. The reader has been informed, under the year 1650, that George Fox travelled the countries, declaiming in the market-places, and in churches, against all ordained ministers; and placing the whole of religion in an inward light, and an extraordinary impulse of the Holy Spirit. In the year 1652, the Quakers set up separate assemblies in Lancashire and the adjacent parts. In 1654, they opened the first separate meeting of the people called Quakers in the house of Robert Dring, in Watling-street, London. These unwary people, by interrupting public worship, and refusing to pay any respect to the magistrate, frequently exposed themselves to sufferings.* One of them, in a letter to the protector, says, "that though there are no penal laws in force obliging men to comply with the established religion, yet the Quakers are exposed upon other accounts; they are fined and imprisoned for refusing to take an oath; for not paying their tithes; for disturbing the public assemblies, and meeting in the streets, and places of public resort; some of them have been whipped for vagabonds, and for their plain speeches to the magistrates." But the Quakers were so far from being discouraged, that they

* Gough says, " that mostly (though not always) they waited till the worship was ended." The Quakers, he observes, were not singular concerning Gospel-liberty of prophesying. The Baptists and Independents adopted the opinion that ordained ministers had not; either from the appointment of Christ, or the practice of the primitive Christians, an exclusive right of speaking in the Church; but that all properly gifted might speak one by one. During the civil wars it had been usual for laymen, soldiers, and others, with the connivance, if not with the approbation of the ruling powers, to speak or preach in the public places of worship, or elsewhere. Oliver Cromwell, in his correspondence with the ministers of Scotland, in 1650, had vindicated the practice. The members of this infant society, who thought it their duty to declare the burden of the Word on their minds, were sanctioned by the opinions and manners of the age. They were reprehensible only when the impetuosity of their zeal interrupted the service as it was proceeding. And then the irregularity and rudeness of this conduct did not justify the violence and outrage with which they were often treated, as contrary to humanity and civilization as to the professed principles of religious liberty.—*Gough's History of the Quakers*, vol. i., p. 87.—ED.

opened a public meeting under favour of the toleration, at the Bull-and-Mouth Inn, in Aldersgate-street, where women as well as men spake as they were moved ; and when none were moved, there was no speaking at all.* The novelty of this assembly drew great numbers of people thither out of curiosity ; nor did any give them disturbance, as long as they continued quiet within themselves ; but in several places where they had no business, the extravagance of their speakers was insufferable ; one of them interrupted the minister in Whitechapel Church, and disturbed the whole assembly. A female came into Whitehall Chapel stark naked, in the midst of public worship,† the lord-protector himself being present. Another came into the Parliament House with a trenchard in her hand, which she broke in pieces, saying, " Thus shall ye be broke in pieces." Thomas Aldam, having complained to the protector of the imprisonment of some friends in the country, and not finding redress, took off his cap and tore it in pieces, saying, " So shall thy government be torn from thee and thy house." Several pretending an extraordinary message from Heaven, went about the streets of London denouncing the judgments of God against the protector and his council. One came to the door of the Parliament House with a drawn sword, and wounded several who were present, saying " he was inspired by the Holy Spirit to kill every man that sat in the House."‡ Others, in their prophetic raptures, denounced judgments on the whole nation, and frequently disturbed the public assemblies where the chief magistrate himself was present. Many opened their shops on the Lord's Day, in defiance of the laws, and were so very obstinate and intractable, that it was impossible to keep the peace without some marks of severity.

But the most extravagant Quaker that appeared at this time was James Naylor,◊ formerly an officer in Major-general Lambert's troops in

* Sewel's History, p. 84.
† It does not appear on what authority Mr. Neal brings forward this story. It is not to be met with in Sewel, who does relate the two following facts, p. 144. If it were a well-authenticated fact, and if this female were a Quaker, the impropriety and indecency of her conduct ought not to be imputed to the society, unless it directly arose from their avowed principles, and had been sanctioned by their approbation. Mr. Neal, farther on, speaks of " other extravagances of this people, recorded by our historians about that time." The matter of inquiry will be whether these historians wrote on good evidence, and were candid and fair in their representations. He says that " the protector was continually teased with their importunities :" others may applaud the firmness and perseverence with which their remonstrances, on the persecutions they suffered, here called teasing importunities, were renewed. " Fox and others," he adds, " wrote letters to him, filled with denunciations of the Divine judgments." If we may judge by the specimens of these letters which Sewel and Gough have given us, the candid reader will find reason rather to applaud the honest simplicity and undisguised plaindealing in them, than contempt of authority, or bitter invectives.—ED.
‡ Whitelocke, p. 502.
◊ There is so much of painful interest connected with the delusion and sufferings of this man, and nearly all his history being unknown to the largest part of this community, that I shall give his history and tortures at length in the Appendix, copied from a rare work.—C.

Scotland, a man of good natural parts, and an admired speaker among these people ; some of whom had such a veneration for him, that they styled him, in blasphemous language, the " everlasting Son of righteousness ; the Prince of peace ; the only-begotten Son of God ; the fairest among ten thousand." Some of the friends kissed his feet in the prison at Exeter, and after his release went before him into the city of Bristol, after the manner of our Saviour's entrance into Jerusalem ; one walked bareheaded ; another of the women led his horse ; others spread their scarfs and handkerchiefs before him in the way, crying continually as they went on, "Holy, holy, holy is the L$_{\text{ord}}$ God of hosts : Hosanna in the highest ; holy, holy is the Lord God of Israel."* Upon this the magistrates of Bristol caused him to be apprehended, and sent up to the Parliament, who appointed a committee to examine the witnesses against him, upon a charge of blasphemy : (1.) For admitting religious worship to be paid to him ; and, (2.) For assuming the names and incommunicable titles and attributes of our blessed Saviour, as the name Jesus, the fairest among ten thousand, the only-begotten Son of God, the Prophet of the Most High, the King of Israel, the everlasting Sun of righteousness, the Prince of peace." All which he confessed,† but alleged in his own defence that these honours were not paid to him, but to Christ who dwelt in him.

* The story of James Naylor was too remarkable, both on account of the extravagant delusions which misled him and his admirers, and the severe and illegal sentence under which he suffered, not to be recorded. But to give it as a picture of Quakerism is not fair or candid ; for not only Sewel himself condemns the behaviour of Naylor and his followers, and resolves it into his being stupified in his understanding, and beguiled by the wiles of Satan, but informs us that the Quakers in general spoke against him and his doings. They disowned him and his adherents. Gough, therefore, not without reason, complains that this has been passed over unnoticed, while the enormities of this man, instead of being overlooked, have been rather exaggerated. The reflection he makes on this is just, and deserves serious attention. " There seems to be a pride and malignity in human nature, while unreformed by religion, diametrically opposite to Christian charity, which, unconscious of sublime virtue in itself, and aiming to depress the rest of mankind below its own level, delights to dwell on the dark side of characters, to magnify the failings of men, and draw a suspicious shade over their virtues, or the mitigating circumstances of their defects ; and this malevolent disposition receives new force from the spirit of party, which peculiarly characterized this age, and raged with unabated violence against the Quakers." It may be added, though it should be with deep concern, that even good and liberal minds do not always rise wholly superior to the influence of these dispositions.—Gough's History, vol. i., p. 247, 248, 251. Sewel's History, p. 143, 150.—ED. A reference to the Appendix will show that this is disputed ; and though it is no disgrace to Quakerism now, that Naylor was one, I am well satisfied that Neal did him nor the body any injustice in calling him one. He was hardly inferior in celebrity to Fox himself, and both before and after his mania he was identified with them.—C.
† This is not accurate. When the speaker, Widdrington, was going to pronounce the sentence, J. Naylor said " he did not know his offence." To which the speaker replied, " he should know his offence by his punishment." The trial was published, but the extravagance of the sentence countenances the suspicion that the account was partially taken

The committee asked him why he came in so extraordinary a manner into Bristol. To which he replied, that he might not refuse any honours which others who were moved by the Lord gave him. Being farther asked whether he had reproved the persons who gave him those titles and attributes, he answered, "If they had it from the Lord, what had I to do to reprove them? If the Father has moved them to give these honours to Christ, I may not deny them; if they have given them to any other but to Christ, I disown them." He concluded his defence thus : " I do abhor that any honours due to God should be given to me, as I am a creature; but it pleased the Lord to set me up as a sign of the coming of the righteous one, and what has been done to me passing through the town, I was commanded by the power of the Lord to suffer to be done to the outward man, as a sign; but I abhor any honour as a creature."

From the committee, he was brought to the bar of the House, where the report being read, he confessed it; upon which the House voted him guilty of blasphemy, and ordered him to be set in the pillory two hours at Westminster, and two hours at the Old Exchange; that he should be whipped through the streets from Westminster to the Old Exchange ; that his tongue should be bored through with a hot iron, and his forehead stigmatized with the letter B; he was afterward to be sent to Bristol, and to ride through the city with his face to the horse's tail, and to be whipped the next market day after he came thither. Last of all, he was to be committed to Bridewell, in London, to be restrained from company, and to be put to hard labour till he should be released by Parliament; during which time he was to be debarred from pen, ink, and paper, and to have no sustenance* but what he got by his hard labour. A sentence much too severe for such a wrong-headed, obstinate creature.†

and published to justify the cruelty of it. Some of his answers were innocent enough; some not clear, and some wrested and aggravated by his adversaries: they reported the worst, and more than was true; adding and diminishing, it is said, as they were minded, and leaving out much of what was spoken to the committee. His words were perverted, and ensnaring questions proposed to him.—*Sewel's History*, p. 139, note, and p. 140 ; or *Gough*, vol. i., p. 237, 238, note.—ED.

* It ought to be mentioned, to the honour of humanity, and as a proof that some persons of equity and moderation existed in those times, that several persons of different persuasions had offered petitions to Parliament on his behalf, but it was resolved not to read them till sentence had been passed : when, by the execution of the first part of it, he was reduced to a state of extreme weakness, many again interposed in his behalf by a petition, which was presented to the House by more than a hundred on behalf of the subscribers, while the execution of the remaining part was respited for a week, pleading that this respite had refreshed the hearts of many thousands altogether unconcerned in his practice, and praying that it might be wholly remitted. But intolerance and vindictiveness resisted these solicitations. The protector was then addressed, on which he wrote a letter to the House ; but this, though it occasioned some debate, obtained no resolution in favour of the prisoner. On this the petitioners presented a second address to the protector; but it is said the public preachers, by their influence, prevented its effect.— *Sewel*, p. 141 ; and *Gough*, vol. i., p. 240, 241.—ED.

† Mr. Neal's censure of this sentence is too gentle.

December 18, James Naylor stood in the pillory in the Palace-yard, Westminster, and was whipped to the Old Exchange ; the remainder of the sentence being respited for a week, in which time the Reverend Mr. Caryl, Manton, Nye, Griffith, and Reynolds went to him, in order to bring him to some acknowledgment of his crime ;* but not being able to reclaim him, the remainder of his sentence was executed December 27, when some of his followers licked his wounds, and paid him other honours, both ridiculous and superstitious. He was afterward sent to Bristol, and whipped from the middle of Thomas-street, over the bridge, to the middle of Broad-street. From Bristol he was brought back to Bridewell, London, where he remained sullen for three days, and would not work, but then begged for victuals, and was content to labour.

At length, after two years' imprisonment, he recanted his errors so far as to acknowledge that the honours he received at his entrance into Bristol were wrong ; " and all those ranting, wild spirits which gathered about me," says he, " at that time of darkness, with all their wild acts and wicked works, against the honour of God and his pure Spirit and people; I renounce. And whereas I gave advantage, through want of judgment, to that evil spirit, I take shame to myself." After the protector's death, James Naylor was released out of prison, and wrote several things in defence of the Quakers, who owned him as a friend, notwithstanding his extravagant behaviour ;† but he did not long survive.

It was repugnant to humanity, equity, and wisdom ; for though the religious extravagances of Naylor might reasonably shock pious and sober minds, his criminality ought to have been estimated, not by the sound of the titles and claims he assumed or which were given to him, but by the delusion and phrensy which had seized his brain; and on this ground he was an object of pity, not of indignation ; and he should have been assigned over to a physician for a cure of his madness, and not to the executioner of public justice to be punished. His features, we are told, bore a near resemblance to the common pictures of Christ ; which is candidly mentioned by Mr. Granger to account for his imagining that he was transformed into Christ; and which circumstance ought to have had its influence with his judges.—*History of England*, vol. iii., p. 149, 8vo.—ED.

* These gentlemen, in many respects excellent characters, did not manage this interview in a manner worthy of themselves, or honourable to their memory; for they would admit no friend of his, nor any other person, into the room, although requested. When Naylor insisted that what had passed should be put in writing, and a copy left with him or the jailer, they consented ; but on his remarking afterward, in the course of the conversation, on perceiving they meant to wrest his words, "how soon they forgot the work of the bishops who were now treading the same steps, seeking to ensnare the innocent," they rose up in a rage, and burned what they had written.—*Sewel*, p. 142. *Gough*, vol. i., p. 242.—ED.

† The reflections insinuated here against the Quakers might have been well spared ; and it would have been more handsome in our author to have stated the matter as Sewel has : " James Naylor," says he, " came to very great sorrow and deep humiliation of mind ; and therefore, because God forgives the transgressions of the penitent, and blotteth them out, and remembereth them no more, so could James Naylor's friends do no other than forgive his crime, and thus take back the lost sheep into their society."— *Sewel's History*, p. 153.—ED.

vive his enlargement, for, retiring into Hunting-donshire; he died there towards the latter. end of the year 1660, about the forty-fourth year of his age.* Mr. Whitelocke observes, very justly, that many thought he was too furiously prosecuted by some rigid men.†

Other extravagances of this people about this time are recorded by our historians. The protector was continually teased with their importunities ; they waited for him on the road, and watched about his palace, till they got an opportunity to speak to him. George Fox and others wrote letters filled with denunciations of Divine judgments, unless he would pull down the remains of antichrist, by which they understood church ministers and church maintenance : to which the protector paid no regard.

As new inroads were made upon the ordinances for observation of the Sabbath, the Parliament took care to amend them. This year they ordained, that "the Sabbath should be deemed to extend from twelve of the clock on Saturday night, to twelve of the clock on the Lord's Day night ; and within that compass of time they prohibited all kinds of business and diversions, except works of necessity and mercy. No election of magistrates is to be on the Lord's Day ; no holding of courts or return of writs, but if, according to their charters, they fall upon the Lord's Day, they are to be deferred to Monday.

* The expressions uttered by James Naylor, about two hours before his death, both in justice to his name, and on account of their own excellence, deserve to be preserved here. "There is a spirit which I feel," he said, "that delights to do no evil, nor to revenge any wrong, but delights to endure all things, in hopes to enjoy its own to the end : its hope is to outlive all wrath and contention, and to weary out all exaltation and cruelty, or whatever is of a nature contrary to itself. It sees to the end of all temptation : as it bears no evil in itself, so it conceives none in thought to any other ; if it be betrayed, it bears it ; for its ground and spring are the mercies and forgiveness of God ; its crown is meekness, its life is everlasting love unfeigned, and takes its kingdom with entreaty, and not with contention, and keeps it by lowliness of mind. In God alone it can rejoice, though none else can regard it, or can own its life : it is conceived in sorrow, and brought forth without any pity to it ; nor doth it murmur at grief and oppression. It never rejoiceth but through sufferings, for with the world's joy it is murdered : I found it alone, being forsaken ; I have fellowship therein with them who lived in dens and desolate places in the earth, who through death obtained this resurrection and eternal life." After his fall James Naylor was a man of great self-denial, and very diffident and jealous of himself.—Sewel, p. 159. Gough's History, vol. i., p. 246.—Ed.

† Whitelocke's observation on Naylor's sentence, just as it is, is not sufficiently strong and poignant. In its cruelty, this sentence bore a great resemblance to that passed on Dr. Leighton by the infamous court of Star Chamber ; and it vied with it in illegality, for the House of Commons, as Gough remarks, is no court of judicature, nor hath any power to inflict a punishment beyond imprisonment during its session. —Hist. of the Quakers, vol. i., p. 239. It ought not to be omitted, that many of the members were very averse to the severity of the measures taken against this persecuted man, whom a temporary phrensy misled. Though it may be added here, the recantation of this bewildered victim was not published till after his release, yet, that and other pieces were written by him while he was in prison ; during which period he recovered a sound state of mind, and repented of his errors.—Sewel, p. 144.—Ed.

It is farther enacted, That all persons not having a reasonable excuse, to be allowed by a justice of peace, shall resort to some church or chapel, where the true worship of God is performed, or to some meeting-place of Christians not differing in matters of faith from the public profession of the nation, on a penalty of two shillings and sixpence for every offence. It is farther ordered, that no minister shall be molested or disturbed in the discharge of his office on the Lord's Day, or any other day when he is performing his duty, or in going and coming from the place of public worship. Nor shall any wilful disturbance be given to the congregation, on penalty of five pounds, or being sent to the workhouse for six months, provided the information be within one month after the offence is committed."* This ordinance to be read in every church or chapel of this nation annually, the first Lord's Day in every March.

The oath of abjuration, for discovering popish recusants, not being effectual, it was now farther ordained, "that all justices of peace, at the quarter-sessions, should charge the grand juries to present all persons whom they suspected to be popishly affected ; and that every such person should appear at the next quarter-sessions, and take and subscribe the following oath of abjuration, on penalty of being adjudged popish recusants convict, to all intents and purposes whatsoever :

"I, A. B., do abjure and renounce the pope's supremacy and authority over the Catholic Church in general, and over myself in particular. And I do believe the Church of Rome is not the true Church ; and that there is not any transubstantiation in the sacrament of the Lord's Supper, or in the elements of bread and wine after consecration thereof, by any person whatsoever. And I do also believe that there is not any purgatory ; and that consecrated hosts, crucifixes, or images, ought not to be worshipped ; neither that any worship is due unto them. And I also believe that salvation cannot be merited by works. And I do sincerely testify and declare, that the pope, neither of himself, nor by any authority of the Church or See of Rome, or by any other means, with any other, hath any power or authority to depose the chief magistrate of these nations, or to dispose of any of the countries or territories thereunto belonging ; or to authorize any foreign prince or state to invade or annoy him or them ; or to discharge any of the people of these nations from their obedience to the chief magistrate ; or to give license or leave to any of the said people to bear arms, raise tumults, or to offer any violence or hurt to the person of the said chief magistrate, or to the state or government of these nations, or to any of the people thereof. And I do farther swear, that I do from my heart abhor, detest, and abjure this damnable doctrine and position, that princes, rulers, or governors, which be excommunicated or deprived by the pope, may, by virtue of such excommunication or deprivation, be killed, murdered, or deposed from their rule or government ; or any outrage or violence done to them by the people that are under them ; or by any other whatsoever upon such pretence. And I do farther swear, that I do believe that the pope, or Bishop of Rome, hath no authority, power,

* Scobel, p. 438.

or jurisdiction whatsoever within England, Scotland, and Ireland, or any or either of them, or the dominions or territories thereunto belonging, or any or either of them. And all doctrines in affirmation of the same points I do abjure and renounce, without any equivocation, mental reservation, or secret evasion whatsoever, taking the words by me spoken according to the common and usual meaning of them. And I do believe no power derived from the pope or Church of Rome, or any other person, can absolve me from this mine oath. And I do renounce all pardons and dispensations to the contrary. So help me God."*

Upon refusal of this oath, the protector and his successors might, by process in the exchequer, seize upon two thirds of their estates, both real and personal, for the use of the public, during the time of their recusancy ; but after their decease, the same were to return to the right heir, provided they took the above-mentioned oath. It was farther ordained, " that no subject of this commonwealth shall at any time be present at mass, in the house of any foreign ambassador or agent, or at any other place, on penalty of £100 and imprisonment for six months, half to the protector, and half to the informer."

How far these severities were needful.or justifiable I leave with the judgment of the reader.

The protector had an opportunity this year of appearing for the Protestants of France,† as he had done last year for those of the Valleys ; there happened a quarrel between the burghers of Nismes, who were mostly Huguenots, and the magistrates and bishop of the city ; the intendant of the province being informed of it, repaired thither to prevent an insurrection ; but the burghers, standing in their own defence, raised a tumult, of which the intendant sent an account to court. The burghers, being soon sensible of their folly, submitted, and begged pardon ; but the court, laying hold of the opportunity, resolved to ruin them. Upon which, they despatched a messenger privately to Cromwell, and begged his interposition. The protector, having heard the whole account, bid the messenger stay and refresh himself, and before he could return to Paris, his business should be done. Accordingly, an express was immediately despatched with a letter to the King of France; under cover of the following to Cardinal Mazarine :

" To his Eminence the Lord Cardinal Mazarine.

"Having thought necessary to despatch this gentleman to the king with the enclosed letter, I commanded him to salute your eminence on my part ; and having charged him to communicate to you certain affairs which I have intrusted him with, I therefore pray your highness to

give credit to what he shall say, having an entire confidence in him.

" Your eminence's most affectionate,

" O. CROMWELL, protector of the

" Commonwealth of England, &c.

" Whitehall, December 28th, 1656."

The protector added the following postscript with his own hand : " I have been informed of the tumult at Nismes : I recommend to your highness the interest of the reformed." And in his instructions to his ambassador Lockhart, he commanded him to insist peremptorily that the tumult of Nismes be forgiven, or else to leave the court immediately. Mazarine complained of this usage as too high and imperious ; but his eminence stood in too much awe of the protector to quarrel with him, and therefore sent orders to the intendant to make up the matter as well as he could. Mr. Welwood says, the cardinal would change countenance whenever he heard the name of the protector, insomuch that it became a proverb in France, that 'Mazarine was not so much afraid of the devil as of Oliver Cromwell. Such was the terror of this great man's name in the principal courts of Europe !

This year* died the right reverend and pious Dr. Joseph Hall, bishop of Norwich, whose practical works have been in great esteem among the Dissenters. He was born at Ashby-de-la-Zouch in Leicestershire, and educated in

* In September, this year [1656], there happened at Abingdon, in Berkshire, a tumult, which was attended with singular circumstances, expressive of the political as well as religious phrensy of the times. It was occasioned by the burial of Mr. Pendarvis, the pastor of the Baptist church in that town, who died in London, and was brought down to Abingdon by water, in a sugar-cask filled up with sand, to be interred. As he was one of the fifth-monarchy men, and the people to whom he ministered were of that stamp, and famous among the party in general, his interment drew together so vast a concourse of people, even from the remotest parts of the kingdom, that the governing powers took notice of it, and sent Major-general Bridges with a party of soldiers to attend on the occasion. Several days were spent by the people in religious exercises, in which were thrown out many railing accusations against the existing government, and exhortations to "arise and fight the Lord's battles," &c. At last the major-general sent an order to dissolve the meeting in these words : " It is the order of the state that you depart to your habitations." They refused to obey this order, and persisted in their exercises. A guard was then set upon the house where they were assembled. On this, they repaired to the market-place, and continued in the most insolent manner to rail at the protector and abuse the soldiers, crying out, "Now, Lord, appear ; down with the priests," &c., the very women exciting the men to violence. The soldiers at last pulled down the men from their stools. A fray ensued, and swords and canes were brandished together in the greatest confusion, and some few slightly hurt. The major-general then entered the town with his whole brigade of horse. The ringleaders were apprehended and brought before him, with whom he reasoned and expostulated in the most friendly manner, but without success, for none of them would own their fault, or acknowledge the existing government, nor even promise to behave peaceably, saying, "they knew not how soon they might be called forth to do the Lord's work." However, five only were committed to prison, and they were soon afterward released.—*Thompson's Collections, under word Abingdon MSS.*—ED.

* Scobel, p. 444.

† The conduct of Cromwell in this instance does him the more honour, as, unhappily for the suffering Protestants of France, it is unparalleled. It was not formed on any precedent ; nor has his generous example been followed. "When an opportunity," observes an ingenious writer, "offered for doing something for them at the peace of Ryswick, in 1697 ; and again at Utrecht, 1713, at which time four hundred were still groaning on board the galleys, or perishing in dungeons, there was not one stipulation in their favour."—*Bicheno's Signs of the Times,* part i., p. 46, note.—ED.

Emanuel College, Cambridge. When he left the university, he travelled with Sir Edmund Bacon to the Spa in Germany. Upon his return, he was taken into the service of Prince Henry, and preferred to the rectory of Waltham in Essex, which he held twenty-two years. King James sent him to the Synod of Dort with other English divines, where he preached a Latin sermon, but was forced to retire to England before the synod broke up, on the account of his health. Some time after his return, he was preferred to the bishopric of Exeter, and from thence translated to Norwich. At the beginning of the troubles between the king and Parliament, the bishop published several treatises in favour of diocesan Episcopacy, which was answered by Smectymnuus, as has been already related. He was afterward imprisoned in the Tower with the rest of the protesting bishops; upon his release he retired to Norwich, the revenues of which bishopric being soon sequestered, together with his own real and personal estate, he was forced to be content with the fifths. The soldiers used him severely, turning him out of his palace, and threatening to sell his books, if a friend had not given bond for the money at which they were appraised. The bishop complained very justly of this usage in a pamphlet entitled Hard Measure. At length the Parliament, to make him some amends, voted him £40 per annum; and when the war was ended, in the year 1647, they took off the sequestration from his estate, and the bishop lived peaceably upon it afterward, spending his solitude in acts of charity and divine meditation. He was a learned and pious man, and of great humility and goodness in conversation; but being the tool of Archbishop Laud in supporting the Divine right of diocesan Episcopacy, lessened him in the esteem of the Parliament. Mr. Fuller says* he was frequently called our English Seneca, for the pureness, plainness, and fulness of his style.† He was more happy in his practical than polemical writings. There is one remarkable passage in his will, which is this:- after having desired a private funeral, he adds, " I do not hold God's house a meet repository for the dead bodies of the greatest saints." In his last sickness he was afflicted with violent pains of the stone and strangury, which he bore with wonderful patience, till death put an end to all his troubles, September 8, 1656, in the eighty-second year of his age.

Towards the latter end of this year died the Reverend Mr. Richard Capel, born at Gloucester, 1586, and educated in Magdalen College, Oxon, where he proceeded M.A.‡ His eminence in the university, says the Oxford historian, was great; he had divers learned men for his pupils, who were afterward famous in the Church, as Accepted Frewen, archbishop of York, William Pemble, and others. He left the university for the rectory of Eastington in his

own county, where he became celebrated for his painful and practical preaching, as well as for his exemplary life. When the Book of Sports came out, 1633, he refused to read it, but resigned his rectory and commenced physician. In 1641 he closed with the Parliament, and was chosen one of the Assembly of Divines, but declined sitting among them, choosing to reside at his living at Pitchcomb, near Stroud, where he was in great reputation as a physician and divine, preaching gratis to his congregation. He published several valuable treatises, and, among others, a celebrated one, Of Temptations, their Nature, Danger, and Cure. He was a good old Puritan, of the stamp of Mr. Dod, Cleaver, and Hildersham; and died at Pitchcomb, in Gloucestershire, September 21, 1656, aged seventy-two years.*

* Mr. Neal has passed over here a name of great worth and eminence, which ought not to be forgotten in a history of the progress of religious liberty—that of the "ever-memorable" John Hales, of Eaton, as he has been usually called, who died on the 19th of May, 1656, aged seventy-two years: whose writings, though not numerous, especially his Discourse on Schism, have much contributed to promote just sentiments and a liberality of spirit. He was born at Bath in 1584, and made so early a proficiency in grammar-learning, that at thirteen years of age he was sent to Corpus-Christi College in Oxford, and studied under George Abbot, afterward Archbishop of Canterbury, under whom he imbibed an attachment to the doctrines of Calvinism. In 1605, by the interest of Sir Henry Saville, warden of Merton College, whose notice and patronage his merit and learning had attracted, he was chosen fellow of the same; and his assistance was engaged in the excellent edition of Chrysostom's work by Sir Henry, which is the best printed Greek book England can boast, and cost the learned editor several thousand pounds.— *Harwood's View of the Editions of the Classics, second edition,* p. 143. Mr. Hales was also appointed to read the Greek lecture in his college, and in 1612 he was elected Greek professor to the university. In 1612–13 he was called upon to compose and speak the funeral oration for Sir Thomas Bodley, founder of the Bodleian library, whose corpse the university determined to inter in the most solemn manner. On the 24th of May in that year, he was admitted fellow of Eton College, being then in holy orders. In 1618 he accompanied Sir Dudley Carleton, King James's ambassador to the States of Holland, as his chaplain; and was present at many of the sessions of the Synod of Dort, from whence he returned an Arminian: " There," he said, " I bid John Calvin good-night." On the 27th of June, 1639, by the interest of Archbishop Laud, he was installed a canon of Windsor; but he enjoyed this preferment, which he reluctantly accepted, little more than two years, till the beginning of the civil wars in 1642. About the beginning of 1645 he retired into a private chamber at Eton, where he remained a quarter of a year in a very obscure manner, and he is said, during that time, to have lived only upon bread and beer. His fellowship was continued, though he refused to sign the Covenant; but he was rejected from it on refusing to take the oath of fidelity to the commonwealth. His necessities at length obliged him to sell his admirable library for £700, which had cost him £2500. His love of retirement and study induced him to decline a generous offer of one of the Seldian family. When he held the fellowship and bursar's place of his college, he was wont to say, they were worth to him £50 a year more than he could spend. His body, it is reported, was well proportioned, and his motion brisk and lively; his countenance was sanguine, cheerful, and full of air. His parts were great; his genius acute and piercing, his judgment profound; his learning various, polite, and universal; so that he

---

* Fuller's Worthies, book ii., p. 130.

† In his younger years he composed a book of satires, and was the first writer in that kind of our English poets. Mr. Pope said high things of this performance.—*Granger's History of England,* vol. ii., p. 157, 8vo.—Ed. Hall's Contemplations are among the best practical works of theology afforded by the English Church. All his works (reprinted) are well worthy of a place in the library of every Christian minister.—C.

‡ Fuller's Worthies, p. 260.

The Parliament which met September 17 continued sitting till the next year, having before them an affair of the greatest consequence, which was confirming the government under Cromwell as lord-protector, or changing it for the title of king. Colonel Jephson, one of the members from Ireland, moved that the protector might have the title of king, and was seconded by Alderman Pack, one of the representatives for the city of London; but the Republicans in the House opposed it with great vehemence; however, upon putting the question, it was carried for a king, most of the lawyers, as Sergeant Glyn, Maynard, Fountain, St. John, and others, being on that side.* April 4, a petition was presented to the protector, recommending the title and office of a king as best fitted to the laws and temper of the people of England; and upon his desiring time to consider of it, a committee was appointed to give him satisfaction in any difficulties that might arise, who urged, that "the name of protector was unknown to our English Constitution; that his highness had already the office and power of a king, and therefore the dispute was only about a name. That his person would never be secure till he assumed it, because the laws did not take notice of him as chief magistrate, and juries were backward to find persons guilty of treason where there was no king. They urged the advantages of a mixed monarchy, and insisted on the safety and security of himself and his friends. That, by the laws of Edward IV.

was called "a walking library." His manners were most amiable and engaging. He was most exemplarily meek and humble, and beyond all example charitable; of great candour and moderation; judging for himself, but not others; none more studious of the knowledge of the Gospel, or more curious in the search; of the strictest integrity, and sincerely pious. He had a great detestation of an imposing, censorious, and intolerant spirit; and would often say, that "*he would renounce the religion of the Church of England to-morrow, if it obliged him to believe that any other Christians would be damned; and that nobody would conclude another man to be damned who did not wish him so.*" The force, eloquence, and simplicity with which he wrote to Archbishop Laud, give a picture of his mind, as well as convey excellent instruction. "The pursuit of truth," says he, "has been my only care ever since I understood the meaning of the word. For this I have forsaken all hopes, all friends, all desires which might bias me, and hinder me from driving right at what I aimed. For this I have spent my money, my means, my youth, my age, and all that I have. If, with all this cost and pains, my purchase is but error, I may safely say, to err has cost me more than it has many to find the truth; and truth shall give me this testimony at last, that if I have missed of her, it is not my fault, but my misfortune." He was buried, according to his desire, in Eton College churchyard, on the day after his death; and a monument was erected over his grave by Mr. Peter Curwen. A complete edition of his work was, for the first time, offered to the public, from the press of the Foulis at Glasgow, 1765, in three volumes 12mo, undertaken with the approbation of Dr. Warburton, the bishop of Gloucester. "The greatness of his character," observes Mr. Granger, "has stamped a value upon some of his compositions, which are thought to have but little merit in themselves."—*History of England,* vol. ii.. 8vo, p. 172. *British Biography,* vol. iv., p. 368–375; and *Works,* vol. i. *Testimonies prefixed,* and p. 137, 138. —Ed.

* Clarke's General Martyrology, p. 303, of the annexed Lives.—Ed.

Vol. II.—Y

and Henry VII., whatever was done by a king in possession, with the consent of a House of Lords and Commons, was valid, and all that served under him were exempt from punishment. That without this title all the grants and sales that had been made were null and void; and all who had collected the public moneys were accountable. In short, that the inclinations of the nation were for a king. That his not accepting the office would occasion the changing many ancient laws, customs, and formalities. That there would be no lasting settlement till things reverted to this channel. To all which they added, that it was the advice and opinion of the representatives of the three nations; and since the Parliament of England, Scotland, and Ireland advised and desired him to accept the title, he ought not, in reason or equity, to decline it."*

The protector attended to these arguments, and would no doubt have complied if he could have relied upon the army; but the chief officers remonstrated strongly against it, and many of his old friends, among whom was his own son-in-law Fleetwood, threatened to lay down their commissions. All the Republicans declaimed loudly against his accepting the crown, and presented a petition to the House against it, drawn up by Dr. Owen, and presented by Lieutenant-general Mason: they said, "they had pulled down monarchy with the monarch, and should they now build it up? They had appealed to God in the late war, who had answered in their favour, and should they now distrust him? They had voted to be true to the commonwealth, without king or kingship, and should they break their vows, and go back to Egypt for security? They thought it rather their happiness to be under a legal danger, which might make them more cautious and diligent. Some said, if they must have a king, why not the legal one?"† Upon these grounds they stood out, and rejected with scorn all limitations of the prerogative under monarchy. So that, whatever might be the protector's inclination,‡ he judged it most prudent to decline the crown at present: and accordingly, May 8, he sent for the House, and acquainted them that, as the circumstances of affairs then stood, he could not undertake the government with the title of king.§

Some have been of opinion that the protector's great genius forsook him in this affair; but it is impossible, at this distance of time, to judge of the strength of the reasons that determined him the other way. Had he assumed the title of king, the army would have revolted; the Cavaliers would have joined the Republicans to have pulled him down from the throne, the

---

* Whitelocke, p. 646.
† Burnet, vol. i., p. 98, 12mo, Edinb. edition.
‡ The inclinations of Cromwell were strongly in favour of kingship: for he used all possible means to prevail with the officers of the army to concur with his scheme of royalty. With this view he invited himself to dine with Colonel Desborough, and carried Lieutenant-general Fleetwood with him, as he knew the influence of those officers, and their aversion to his wearing the crown. He then even stooped to solicit their indulgence: "It is but a feather in a man's cap," said he, "and therefore he wondered that men would not please children, and permit them to enjoy their rattle."—*Ludlow's Memoirs;* 4to, p. 248.—Ed.
§ Whitelocke, p. 646.

whole nation would in all probability have been thrown into confusion, and himself have been the sacrifice. The protector had made large advances in power already, and he might apprehend it not worth while at present to risk the whole for the sake of a name; though I make no question, but if he had lived to see his government established, and the spirits of the people calmed, he would in a proper time have accepted of the style and title, as he had already done the office, of king. Nay, Mr. Welwood* says that a crown was actually made, and brought to Whitehall for that purpose.

Upon Cromwell's declining the title of king, the Parliament concluded upon an humble petition and advice, which was presented to the protector May 25, containing, among others, the following articles: "That his highness would exercise the office of chief magistrate of this nation under the title of lord-protector; and that during life he would declare his successor. That for the future he would be pleased to call Parliaments, consisting of two houses, to meet once in three years, and oftener, if there be occasion. That the ancient liberties of Parliament may be preserved; and that none who are chosen may be excluded but by the judgment and consent of the house of which they are members. That no papist, no person that has borne arms against the Parliament, unless he has since given proof of his good affection to the commonwealth; no clergyman, no atheist, or openly profane person, be qualified to be chosen member of Parliament. That the other House of Parliament be not more than seventy, nor less than forty, of which twenty-one to make a house. That they may not vote by proxy. That as any of them die, no new ones be admitted but by consent of the House itself, but the nomination to be in the protector; and that they may not proceed in any criminal causes but by impeachment of the Commons. That no laws be abrogated, suspended, or repealed but by act of Parliament; and that no person be compelled to contribute to any gift, loans, benevolences, or taxes, without consent of Parliament. That the number of his highness's council be not more than twenty-one, of which seven to be a quorum; and that no privy councillor be removed but by consent of Parliament; though, in the intervals of Parliament, they may be suspended. That the chancellor, or keeper of the great seal, the commissioners of the treasury, and other chief officers of state, may be approved by both houses of Parliament."

The article relating to religion was in these words: "That the Protestant Christian religion contained in the Holy Scriptures of the Old and New Testament, and no other, be asserted and held forth, as the public profession of this nation; and that a confession of faith, to be agreed upon by your highness and this present Parliament, be asserted, and recommended to the people of the nation; and that none shall be permitted by opprobrious words or writings to revile or reproach the said confession. That such who profess faith in God the Father, and in Jesus Christ his eternal Son, the true God, and in the Holy Ghost, God coequal and coeternal with the Father and the Son, one God blessed forever, and do acknowledge the Holy Scriptures of the

Old and New Testament to be the revealed will and Word of God, though in other things they may differ in word and doctrine, or discipline, from the public profession held forth, shall not be compelled by penalties or restraints from their profession, but shall be protected from all injuries and molestations in the profession of their faith, and exercise of their religion, while they abuse not this liberty to the civil injury of others, or the disturbance of the public peace; provided this liberty do not extend to popery or prelacy, or to the countenance of such who publish horrid blasphemies; or who practise or hold forth licentiousness or profaneness, under the profession of Christ; and those ministers, or public preachers, who agree with the public profession aforesaid in matters of faith, though they differ in matters of worship or discipline, shall not only have protection in the way of their churches or worship, but shall be deemed equally fit and capable (being otherwise qualified) of any trust, promotion, or employment in this nation, with those who agree with the public profession of faith, only they shall not be capable of receiving the public maintenance appointed for the ministry. And all ministers shall remain disqualified from holding any civil employment according to the act for disabling all persons in holy orders to exercise any temporal jurisdiction and authority; which is hereby confirmed."*

The protector having consented to these, and some other articles, to the number of eighteen, an oath was appointed to be taken by all privy councillors and members of Parliament for the future, "to maintain the Protestant religion; to be faithful to the lord-protector; and to preserve the rights and liberties of the people;" and a few days after Oliver Cromwell was proclaimed a second time lord-protector in the cities of London and Westminster, this being esteemed a new and more parliamentary title; and if the House had been full and free it might have been so, but the council's assuming a power to approve or disapprove of the members after they were returned—their forbidding them to debate the fundamentals of the new government, and obliging them to sign a recognition of it before they entered the House, looks like a force, or taking the election out of their hands. But, lame and imperfect as the protector's title may seem, it was as good as that of the Roman emperors, or the original claims of many of the royal houses of Europe; and, in the present disjointed state of the English nation, not only necessary, but it may be the best thing that could be done; for if the protectorship had been set aside, there was hardly a man in the House who would have ventured to vote for the king; an absolute commonwealth could not have been supported, and therefore anarchy would inevitably have ensued.

This being the last settlement of government in the protector's time, the reader will observe that the four fundamental articles already mentioned, viz., (1.) That the government be in a single person and a Parliament; (2.) that Parliaments be not perpetual; (3.) the militia; and (4.) liberty of conscience in matters of religion, were not suffered to be examined or altered, but were supposed as the basis upon which the

* Memoirs, p. 111.

* Whitelocke's Memoirs, p. 678.

new government was founded. That, though Oliver's title to the government had the sanction and confirmation of the present Parliament, it was derived originally from the choice of the council of officers, and was never suffered to be debated in the House afterward. That the humble petition and advice approaches nearer the old legal Constitution, by appointing two houses of Parliament, and would most likely, in time, have been converted into it. That the regulations it makes in the Constitution are for the most part reasonable. That the Presbyterians were still left in possession of all the ecclesiastical revenues of the kingdom, though an open and free liberty was granted to all Christians, except papists and Prelatists, who were excluded for reasons of state; and the penal laws made against the latter were dropped by the Parliament's not confirming them. Remarkable are the words of the Lord-commissioner Fiennes, at the opening of the second session of this Parliament, in which he "warns the houses of the rock on which many had split, which was a spirit of imposing upon men's consciences in things wherein God leaves them a latitude, and would have them free. The prelates and their adherents, nay, and their master and supporter, with all his posterity, have split upon it. The bloody rebels in Ireland, who would endure no religion but their own, have split upon it; and we doubt not but the prince of those satanical spirits will in due time split upon it, and be brought to the ground with his bloody inquisition. But as God is no respecter of persons, so he is no respecter of forms; but, in what form soever the spirit of imposition appears, he would testify against it. If men, though otherwise good, will turn ceremony into substance, and make the kingdom of Christ consist in circumstances, in discipline, and in forms; and if they carry their animosities to such a height, that if one says Sibboleth instead of Shibboleth, it shall be accounted ground enough to cut his throat; if they shall account such devils, or the seed of the serpent, that are not within such a circle or of such an opinion, in vain do they protest against the persecution of God's people, when they make the definition of God's people so narrow, that their persecution is as broad as any other, and usually more fierce, because edged with a sharp temper of spirit. Blessed, therefore, be God, who, in mercy to us and them, has placed the power in such hands as make it their business to preserve peace, and hinder men from biting and devouring one another. It is good to hold forth a public profession of the truth, but not so as to exclude those that cannot come up to it in all points from the privilege that belongs to them as Christians, much less from the privilege that belongs to them as men."[*]

His highness having now a more parliamentary title, it was thought proper that he should have a more solemn inauguration, which was accordingly appointed to be celebrated on June 26, in Westminster Hall, which was adorned and beautified for this purpose as for a coronation. At the upper end there was an ascent of two degrees covered with carpets, in the midst of which there was a rich canopy, and under it a chair of state. Before the canopy there was

a table and chair for the speaker,[*] and on each side seats for the members of Parliament, for the judges, for the lord-mayor and aldermen of London. The protector was conducted from the House of Lords with all the state and grandeur of a king, and being seated under the canopy of state, the speaker of the Parliament, the Earl of Warwick, and Commissioner Whitelocke, vested him with a purple velvet robe lined with ermine; they delivered into one of his hands a Bible richly gilt, and embossed with gold, and into the other a sceptre of massy gold; and, lastly, they girt him with a rich sword; after this they administered an oath to the protector, to govern according to law. The solemnity concluded with a short prayer, pronounced by Dr. Manton; and then the herald having proclaimed his highness's titles, the people shouted, with loud acclamations, "Long live the lord-protector !" &c., and the day concluded with feastings, and all other kinds of public rejoicing.

The protector having waded through all these difficulties to the supreme government of these nations, appeared on a sudden like a comet or blazing star,[†] raised up by Providence to exalt this nation to a distinguished pitch of glory, and to strike terror into the rest of Europe.[‡] His management for the little time he survived was the admiration of all mankind; for though he would never suffer his title to the supreme government to be disputed, yet his greatest enemies have confessed that, in all other cases, distributive justice was restored to its ancient splendour. The judges executed their duty according to equity, without partiality or bribery; the laws had their full and free course without impediment or delay; men's manners were wonderfully reformed, and the protector's court kept under an exact discipline. Trade flourished, and the arts of peace were cultivated throughout the whole nation; the public money was managed with frugality, and to the best advantage; the army and navy were well paid, and served accordingly.§ As the protector proceeded with great steadiness and resolution against the enemies of his government, he was no less generous and bountiful to those of all parties who submitted to it; for as he would not declare himself of any particular sect, he gave out that "it was his only wish that all would gather into one sheepfold, under one shepherd, Jesus Christ, and love one another." He respected the clergy in their places, but confined them to their spiritual function. Nor was he jealous of any who did not meddle in politics, and endeavour to raise disturbances in the state;

<hr/>

[*] Whitelocke's Memoirs, p. 93.

[*] Dr. Grey gives at length the speech with which the speaker, Lord Widdrington, addressed the protector.—ED.

[†] Echard, p. 719. [‡] Complete Hist., p. 223.

§ Dr. Grey controverts the truth of this representation of the happy state of things under Cromwell's government : though Mr. Neal quotes Echard and Kennet, whose authority Dr. Grey does not attempt to invalidate. He refers principally to a speech of Cromwell, 25th January, 1657, complaining that the army was unpaid, and that Ireland and Scotland were suffering by poverty. For a review of the administration of Cromwell, the reader is referred to *Dr. Harris's Life of Cromwell*, p. 412–475, and *Mrs. Macaulay's History of England*, vol. v., 8vo, p. 194–203, who is by no means partial to the protector.—ED.

even the prejudice he had against the Episcopal party, says Bishop Kennet, was more for their being Royalists than being of the Church of England. But when one party of the clergy began to lift up their heads above their brethren, or to act out of their sphere, he always found means to take them down. He had a watchful eye over the Royalists and Republicans, who were always plotting against his person and government; but his erecting a House of Lords, or upper house, so quickly after his instalment, roused the malecontents, and had like to have subverted his government in its infancy.

The protector was in high reputation abroad, and carried victory with his armies and navies wherever they appeared. There had been a negotiation with France concerning an alliance against Spain, begun at London, 1655, but not concluded till March 13, 1657, by which the protector obliged himself to join six thousand men with the French army, and to furnish fifty men-of-war to conquer the maritime towns belonging to Spain in the Low Countries, on this condition, that Dunkirk and Mardyke should be put into his hands, and the family of the Stuarts depart the territories of France. That which determined him to join with France rather than Spain, was the numerous parties that were against him at home; for if the young king, assisted by France, should have made a descent upon England with an army of French Protestants, it might have been of fatal consequence to his infant government; whereas the Spaniards were at a distance, and having no Protestant subjects, were less to be feared. Upon the conclusion of this treaty, King Charles entered into an alliance with the Spaniards, who allowed him a small pension, and promised him the command of six thousand men as soon as he was possessed of any seaport in England. In consequence of this treaty, most of the Royalists enlisted in the Spanish service. But the protector's six thousand men in Flanders behaved with undaunted bravery, and took St. Venant, Mardyke, and some other places from the Spaniards this summer.*

Admiral Blake was no less successful at sea; for, having received advice of the return of the Spanish West India fleet, he sailed to the Canaries with twenty-five men-of-war, and on the 20th of April arrived at the Bay of Santa Cruz, in the island of Teneriffe, where the galleons, to the number of sixteen, richly laden, lay close under a strong castle, defended by seven forts mounted with cannon; the admiral, finding it impossible to make them prize, had the good fortune to burn and destroy them all, only with the loss of one ship, and one hundred and sixty men. When the news of this success arrived in England, a day of thanksgiving was appointed, and a rich present ordered the admiral upon his return; but this great sea-officer, having been three years at sea, died as he was entering Plymouth Sound, August 17, in the sixty-seventh year of his age.† He was of the ancient family of the Blakes, of Planchfield, Somersetshire, and was educated in Wadham College, Oxford.‡ He was small of stature, but

the bravest and boldest sailor that England ever bred, and consulted the honour of his country beyond all his predecessors. When some of his men, being ashore at Malaga, refused to do honour to the host as it passed by, one of the priests raised the mob upon them. Upon which Blake sent a trumpet to the viceroy to demand the priest, who, saying he had no authority to deliver him up, the admiral answered, that if he did not send him aboard in three hours, he would burn the town about their ears: upon which he came, and begged pardon; the admiral, after a severe reprimand, told him that, if he had complained to him of his sailors, he would have punished them, but he would have all the world know that an Englishman was only to be punished by an Englishman, and so dismissed him, being satisfied with having struck terror into the priest, and had him at his mercy. When Oliver read this passage of Blake's letter in council, he said, "he hoped to make the name of an Englishman as great as ever that of a Roman had been."* The admiral preserved an exact discipline in the fleet, and taught his men to despise castles on shore as well as ships at sea.† Valour seldom missed its reward with him, nor cowardice its punishment. He had a noble public spirit; for, after all his services for his country, and opportunities of acquiring immense riches from the Spaniards, he died not £500 richer than his father left him. His body was brought by water to Greenwich, and deposited, in a most magnificent manner, in a vault made on purpose, in King Henry VII.'s chapel, at the public expense; but at the Restoration his body was taken out of the grave, and flung, with others, into a common pit;‡ and his brother, being a Dissenter, suffered so many hardships for religion in King Charles II.'s reign, that he was obliged to sell the little estate the admiral left him, and transport himself and children to Carolina.

By the second article of the humble advice, which appoints all future Parliaments to consist of two houses, the form of the present government began to change in favour of the ancient Constitution. The protector, pursuant to the powers given him, made several promotions

* Burnet, vol. i., p. 113, 114.
† It is remarkable that Blake did not take the command of the fleet till he was above fifty years of age. "His want of experience," says Mr. Granger, "seems to have been of great advantage to him; he followed the light of his own genius only, and was presently seen to have all the courage, the conduct, and precipitancy of a good sea-officer."—Ed.
‡ Bishop Kennet, whom Dr. Grey quotes here, being ashamed, it is probable, of the base contempt with which the body of Blake was treated, says, "It was taken up and buried in the churchyard." But Wood plainly says that his body, with others, by his majesty's express command sent to the Dean of Westminster, was taken up and buried in a pit in St. Margaret's churchyard. The other bodies treated thus ignominiously were Admiral Dean's, a brave man, who lost his life in the service of his country; Colonel Humphrey Mackworth's; Sir W. Constable's; Colonel Boscawen's, a Cornish gentleman of a family distinguished by its constant attachment to liberty; and many others, too long to be here mentioned. "Such," observes Dr. Harris, "was the politeness and humanity introduced by the Restoration!"—Life of Cromwell, p. 400. Wood's Athen. Oxon., vol. i., p. 285, 286.

* Burnet, p. 73.
† Other accounts say in the fifty-ninth year of his age.—Ed.   ‡ Echard, p. 725.

of knights and lords, and in the month of December issued out writs, by advice of his council, to divers lords and gentlemen to sit as members of the other House,* at the next session of Parliament, January 20. His intention was to have this house considered as a House of Peers, though he declined giving it that name till a more favourable conjuncture. Some declined the honour, and chose to sit in the Lower House, but between fifty and sixty appeared, among whom were seven or eight of the ancient peers, divers knights and gentlemen of good families, and some few chief officers of the army. They met in the House of Lords, whither his highness came at the time of their meeting, and, according to ancient custom, sent the usher of the black rod to bring up the Commons, to whom he made a short speech from the throne, beginning with the usual form, "My lords, and you the knights, citizens, and burgesses," &c., and then, as our kings used to do, he referred them to the Lord-commissioner Fiennes, who tired them with a long and perplexed harangue before they entered upon business.

This hasty resolution of the protector and his council had like to have subverted the infant government, for many of the protector's best friends being called out of the Lower House to the Upper, the balance of power among the Commons was changed; whereas, if he had deferred the settling of the Upper House till the present Parliament had been dissolved, they would have gone through their business without interruption; but the Lower House was now in a flame, some being disappointed of their expectations, and others envied for their advancement, insomuch that, as soon as they returned to their house, they called for the third article of the humble advice, which says, that no "members legally chosen shall be excluded from performing their duty but by consent of the house of which they are members;" and then, to strengthen their party, they ordered all those who had been excluded last sessions, because they would not recognise the new government, to return to their places; which was no sooner done, than they began to call in question the authority and jurisdiction of the other house, though themselves had advised it, and though there was almost as good reason for their being an upper, as for the other being a lower house; but these gentlemen were determined to erect an absolute commonwealth on the ruins of the present family. Many degrading speeches were made in the Lower House against the persons who had been thus promoted, who were no less resolute in defending their honours and characters; so that there was no prospect of an agreement till the protector himself appeared, and having sent for them to Whitehall, spoke with such an accent in favour of the other house, that they returned and acknowledged it; but then they went on to re-examine the validity of the whole instrument of government, as being made when many members were excluded. Upon which, the protector, being out of all patience, went to the

House and dissolved them, after they had sat about fifteen days.

The protector's speech upon this occasion will give the reader the best idea of the state of the nation: "I had comfortable expectations that God would make the meeting of this Parliament a blessing for the improvement of mercy, truth, righteousness, and peace. I was drawn into this office of protector by your petition and advice: there is not a man living that can say I sought it; but after I was petitioned and advised to take the government upon me, I expected that the same men that made the frame should make it good to me. I told you at a conference that I would not accept the government unless there might be some persons to interpose between me and the House of Commons, and it was granted I should name another house, which I did, of men of your own rank and quality, who will shake hands with you while you love the interest of England and religion. Again, I would not have accepted the government unless mutual oaths were taken to make good what was agreed upon in the petition and advice; and God knows, I took the oath upon the condition expressed, and thought we had now been upon a foundation and bottom, otherwise we must necessarily have been in confusion. I do not say what the meaning of the oath was to you—that were to go against my own principles; but God will judge between us; but if there had been any intention in you of a settlement, you would have settled on this basis.

"But there have been contrivances in the army against this settlement by your consent. I speak not this to the gentlemen or lords (pointing to his right hand), whatsoever you will call them, of the other house, but to you; you advised me to accept of this office, and now you dispute the thing that was taken for granted, and are in danger of running the nation back into more confusion within these fifteen days you have sat, than it has been in since the rising of the last session, from an immoderate design of restoring a commonwealth, that some people might be the men that might rule all, and they are endeavouring to engage the army in the design, which is hardly consistent with the oath you have taken to the present government. Has that man been true to the nation, whosoever he is, that has taken an oath thus to prevaricate! These things are not according to truth, pretend what you will, but tend to play the King of Scots' game, which I think myself bound before God to do what I can to prevent. There are preparations of force to invade us; the King of Scots has an army at the water-side, ready to be shipped for England. I have it from those who have been eyewitnesses of it; and while this is doing, there are endeavours of some, not far from this place, to stir up the people of this town into tumulting—what if I had said rebellion? and I hope to make it appear no better, if God assist me. You have not only endeavoured to pervert the army while you have been sitting, but some of you have been listing persons by commission from Charles Stuart to join with any insurrection that may be made; and what is like to be the end of this but blood and confusion! Now, if this be the case, I think it high time to put an end to your sitting, and I do

---

* Dr. Grey gives a catalogue of the names of the persons whom the writ summoned, with degrading anecdotes of some of them.—ED.

accordingly dissolve this Parliament; and let God judge between me and you."*.

The protector, being now convinced that the disturbances in Parliament arose from the chief officers of the army, who clogged his affairs in order to introduce a commonwealth government, resolved to clear his hands of them at once; Harrison and Ludlow were laid aside; Fleetwood was recalled from his government in Ireland; Major-general Lambert was ordered to surrender his commission; and the rest were obliged to take an oath not to oppose the present government. By such methods he went on purging the army and navy; and if he had lived a little longer, would have had none in power but such as were thoroughly attached to his person and government. It was observed, after this, that all things succeeded at home and abroad according to his wish; and that his power and greatness were better established than ever, though there were a few malecontents who were hardy enough to attempt some little disturbances; but the disasters that befell the protector's family soon after broke the firmness of his constitution, and hastened his end.

It was his highness's ambition not only to set himself at the head, but to strengthen the whole body of the Protestant interest, and unite its several members, so that it might maintain its ground against the Church of Rome. Bishop Burnet† informs us, that he had projected a sort of general council, to be set up in opposition to the congregation de Propaganda Fide at Rome: it was to consist of seven councillors, and four secretaries for different provinces; the first was for France, Switzerland, and the Valleys; the second for the Palatinate, and other Calvinists; the third for Germany, for the North, and for Turkey; the fourth for the East and West Indies. The secretaries were to have £500 a year each, and to hold a correspondence everywhere, to acquaint themselves with the state of religion all over the world, that so all good designs for the welfare of the whole, and of the several parts, might by their means be protected and encouraged. They were to have a fund of £10,000 a year, and to be farther supplied as occasion should require. Chelsea College was to be fitted up for them. This was a noble project, says the bishop, and must have been attended with extraordinary effects under the protection of a power which was formidable and terrible to all nations to whom it was known.

About the beginning of this year, Dr. Bryan Walton, afterward Bishop of Chester, published the Biblia Polyglotta, in six volumes in folio, wherein the sacred text is printed in the Vulgar Latin, Hebrew, Greek, Syriac, Chaldee, Samaritan, Arabic, Ethiopic, and Persic languages, each having its peculiar Latin translation, with an apparatus for the better understanding those tongues. This laborious performance, by the assistance of several who engaged in it, was completed in about four years, and was reckoned the most absolute edition of the Bible that the world had ever seen. Several learned persons, both Puritans and others, assisted in correcting the press and in collating the copies. Many noblemen and gentlemen of quality con-

tributed to the expense of printing this work, without which it could not have seen the light.* After the Restoration, the doctor presented King Charles II. with the six volumes, which his majesty received very graciously, and rewarded the author with the bishopric of Chester.†

The learned Dr. Owen made some remarks on the prolegomena of this work; but, after a high commendation of the performance in general, complains that he had weakened the certainty of the sacred text, (1.) By maintaining that the points or vowels of the Hebrew language were of novel invention. (2.) By producing a great number of various readings from the ancient copies of little moment. (3.) By his own critical remarks and amendments, not supported by ancient authorities. The doctor maintains, on the other hand, the antiquity of the Hebrew points, and their absolute necessity to fix the determinate sense of Scripture; that the various readings are of little consequence, and that conjectural amendments ought not to be admitted without the authority of ancient copies. The doctor writes with great modesty, but the validity of his arguments must be submitted to the learned reader.

On the 3d of July the protector resigned his chancellorship of Oxford, and upon the 18th day of the same month his eldest son Richard was chosen his successor, and installed‡ at Whitehall on the 29th. About six weeks after, the new chancellor dismissed Dr. Owen, who had been vice-chancellor of the university about five years, and appointed Dr. John Conant, rector of Exeter College, to succeed him. This gentleman, says the Oxford historian,§ was a good Latinist and Grecian, a profound theologian, a learned, pious, and meek divine, and an excellent preacher. He had been one of the Assembly of Divines, and was elected rector of this college upon the death of Dr. Hakewell, in June, 1649. In the latter end of the year 1654 he became king's professor of divinity in the room of Dr. Hoyle. He continued the vice-chancellorship two years with due commendation, keeping a severe discipline in his college, as did all the heads of colleges in these times. He was ejected out of everything in 1662 for nonconformity; but some time after, being persuaded to comply with the establishment, he became vicar of All Saints in Northampton, archdeacon of Norwich, and prebendary of Worcester, which places he held till his death, which did not happen till 1693.

* "This," Mr. Granger says, "was the first book published in England by subscription. The design of this great work was formed in 1645. Dr. Walton died 1661."—*Hist. of Eng.*, vol. iii., p. 29, 8vo.—ED.

† A seventh volume of the Polyglott was prepared for the press by Dr. Samuel Clarke, including the Targum of Rabbi Joseph on the Chronicles, and several Arabic and other versions of other parts of the Sacred Scriptures, but it was never printed, owing to the death of Bishop Walton. It is deposited in the Bodleian Library. Cromwell not only suffered the paper for this great work to be imported duty free, but contributed £1000 to commence the undertaking. For a full account of Bishop Walton, and interesting details respecting the individuals who aided him in his learned labours, see *Lloyd's Memoirs of the Worthies of Charles I.*, folio 1668.—C.

‡ The ceremonial of the instalment may be seen in Dr. Grey, vol. iii., p. 200, note.—ED.

§ Athen. Oxon., vol. ii., p. 785.

* Rapin, vol. ii., p. 598, folio.
† Burnet, vol. i., p. 109, 12mo.

.. November 24, his highness signed a commission, appointing his younger son Henry to be Lord-lieutenant of Ireland, with a power of conferring the honour of knighthood. Henry was a wise and discreet governor, and by his prudent behaviour kept the Irish in awe, and brought the nation into a flourishing condition. Upon the accession of Richard to the protectorship, he advised him to abide by the Parliament, and have a watchful eye over the army, whom he suspected to be designing mischief (as appears by his letters now before me). Nay, he offered to come over to his assistance, but was forbid till it was too late. When Richard was deposed, his brother Henry laid down his charge, and came over to England, and lived privately upon an estate of his own of about £600 a year, at Spinny Abbey in Cambridgeshire, not far from Newmarket, till his death. While he was in Ireland he behaved with such a generous impartiality as gained him the esteem even of the Royalists themselves, and after his retirement King Charles II. did him once the honour of a visit; he had a son, Henry, who was bred to arms, and had a major's commission, and died in the service of the crown about the year 1711, and left behind him several children; some of the sons are yet living in good reputation in the city of London, and are the only male descendants of the Protector Cromwell, the posterity of Richard being extinct.

The Royal Society, which has been the ornament of the English nation, by the vast improvement it has made in natural and experimental philosophy, was formed at Oxford in these times, which some have represented as covered with ignorance, barbarism, and pedantry ; the words of Bishop Sprat,* their historian, are these : " It was some space after the end of the civil wars at Oxford, in Dr. Wilkins's lodgings, in Wadham College, which was then the place of resort for virtuous and learned men, that the first meetings were made which laid the foundation of all that followed. The university had, at that time, many members of its own who had begun a free way of reasoning, and was also frequented by some gentlemen of philosophical minds, whom the misfortune of the kingdom, and the security and ease of a retirement among gownsmen, had drawn thither. The principal and most constant of them were, Dr. Seth Ward, Mr. Boyle, Dr. Wilkins, Sir William Petty, Dr. Matthew Wren, Dr. Wallis, Dr. Goddard, Dr. Willis, Dr. Bathurst, Dr. Christopher Wren, and Mr. Rook, besides several others who joined them on occasions. Their meetings were as frequent as their occasions would permit ; their proceedings were upon some particular trials in chemistry or mechanics, which they communicated to each other. They continued without any great interruption till the death of the protector, when their meetings were transferred to London." Here they began to enlarge their designs, and formed the platform of a philosophical college, to inquire into the works of nature ; they set up a correspondence with learned foreigners, and admitted such into their numbers without distinction of names or parties in religion, and were at length incorporated by the royal patent or charter in the year 1663.

This year [1657] died Mr. John Langley, the

noted master of St. Paul's School, London ; he was born near Banbury in Oxfordshire, and became a commoner or brother of Magdalen Hall about 1612 ; was also prebendary of Gloucester, where he kept the college-school for twenty years. In the year 1640 he succeeded Dr. Gill, chief master of St. Paul's School, where he educated many who were afterward eminent in Church and State. He was a universal scholar, an excellent linguist, grammarian, historian, cosmographer, a most judicious divine, and so great an antiquarian, says the Oxford historian, that his delight and acquaintance in antiquity deserve greater commendation than can be given in a few lines.* He was esteemed by learned men, and particularly by Mr. Selden ; but was not regarded by the clergy, because he was a Puritan, and a witness against Archbishop Laud at his trial. He was a member of the Assembly of Divines,† and died at his house next adjoining to St. Paul's School, September 13, 1657. Dr. Reynolds preached his funeral sermon, and gave him a very high encomium.‡

Mr. Obadiah Sedgwick was born at Marlborough in the year 1600, and educated in Magdalen College, Oxford, where he took the degrees in arts, and was afterward chaplain to Sir Horatio Vere, with whom he travelled into the Low Countries. After his return he became reader of the sentences, 1629, and was afterward chosen preacher to the inhabitants of St. Mildred, Bread-street, London; but being driven from thence by the severity of the governors of the Church, he retired to Coggeshall in Essex, where he continued till the breaking out of the civil wars. In 1643 he was chosen a member of the Assembly of Divines. In 1646 he became a preacher at St. Paul's, Covent Garden : he often preached before the Parliament, and was esteemed an orthodox, as well as an admired preacher.§ In the year 1653 he was appointed one of the triers, and the year after, one of the commissioners, for ejecting scandalous ministers ; but, finding his health declining, he resigned his preferments, and retired to his native town of Marlborough, where he died the beginning of January, 1657.‖

Mr. Edward Corbet was born in Shropshire, and educated in Merton College, Oxford, where he took the degrees in arts, and was made probationer fellow of his college.¶ In 1638 he was

---

* Wood's Athen. Oxon., vol. ii., p. 135.

† Wood says it was a man of another name who sat in the Assembly.—*Athenæ*, vol. ii., p. 135.—C.

‡ Dr. Fuller calls him "The able and religious schoolmaster." He had a very awful presence and speech, that struck a mighty respect and fear in his scholars ; yet his behaviour towards them was such, that they both loved and feared him. When he was buried, all the scholars attended his funeral, walking before the corpse, hung with verses instead of escutcheons, with white gloves, as he died a single man, from the school through Cheapside to Mercer's Chapel, where he was buried. He was so much in favour with the worshipful Company of Mercers, that they accepted his recommendation of his successor. —*Knight's Life of Dr. John Colet*, p. 379, &c.—ED.

§ All the writings of Mr. Sedgwick are valuable, and deserving of reprint. His " Shepherd of Israel" and " The Humble Sinner Resolved" are admirable performances. He was succeeded at St. Paul's by the celebrated Dr. Thomas Manton.—C.

‖ Wood's Athen. Oxon., vol. ii., p. 138.

¶ Ibid., p. 749.

* P. 53, 57. ..

one of the proctors of the university; but, being a Puritan divine, was denied the rectory of Chatham by Archbishop Laud, then in the Tower; upon which an ordinance of Parliament came out, May. 17, 1643, appointing him rector of Chatham. He was a member of the Assembly of Divines, a witness against the archbishop at his trial, one of the preachers appointed to reconcile the Oxford scholars to the Parliament, and afterward one of the visiters, orator, and canon of Christ Church, in the room of Dr. Hammond, which he soon after quitted, and became rector of Great Hasely, in Oxfordshire, where he continued to his death. He was a very considerable divine, a valuable preacher, and a person of remarkable integrity and steadiness of conscience.

Mr. James Cranford was born in Coventry, and some time master of the free-school there: he was educated in Baliol College, Oxford, where he took the degrees in arts, and was at length rector of St. Christopher's-le-Stocks, near the Old Exchange, London.* He was an exact linguist, well acquainted with the fathers and schoolmen, as well as with the modern divines; a zealous Presbyterian, and a laborious preacher. Mr. Fuller adds,† that he was a subtle disputant, orthodox in judgment, and a person of great humility, charity, and moderation towards all men. In the beginning of the civil wars he was appointed licenser of the press in London, which gave him an occasion to write several epistles before books, besides some treatises that he published of his own. He died April 27, 1657, aged about fifty-five years.‡

The protector's arms were no less successful this summer than they had been the last, for in the month of June, Marshal Turenne, in conjunction with the English forces, laid siege to Dunkirk, then in possession of the Spaniards, which brought on an engagement between the two armies: the Spanish forces consisted of thirty thousand men, but Major-general Morgan, who covered the siege, attacked the right wing of the Spanish army which came to relieve it with six thousand English, who routed the whole army, which was followed with the surrender of the town, June 25. The French looked on, and said they never saw a more glorious action in their lives.§ Cardinal Mazarine intended to keep this important place in French hands, contrary to the late treaty; of which his highness being informed, acquainted the ambassador; but his excellency denying any such intended breach of contract, the protector pulled out of his pocket a copy of the cardinal's private order, and desired him to let his eminence know, that if the keys of Dunkirk were not de-

livered to Lockhart within an hour after it was taken, he would come in person, and demand them at the gates of Paris;* and the cardinal had too great a dread of the name of Cromwell to deny anything he required. By this conquest the protector gained immortal glory, because it gave the English a settlement on the Continent, and made them masters of both sides of the Channel.† How basely it was sold by Lord Clarendon to the French, will be seen hereafter.

The enthusiastic Republicans, or fifth-monarchy men, having failed in their design in Parliament, agreed, to the number of three hundred, to attempt a revolution of government by force, and having killed the protector, to proclaim King Jesus; but Secretary Thurloe, who never spared expense to gain intelligence, had a spy among them, who discovered their intrigues, and seized their arms and ammunition in Shoreditch, with their standard, containing a lion couchant, alluding to the lion of the tribe of Judah, with this motto, Who will rouse him up? The chief of the conspirators, as Venner, Grey, Hopkins, &c., were imprisoned in the Gate-house till the protector's death, with their accomplices, Major-general Harrison, Colonel Rich, Colonel Danvers, and others, after which they created new disturbances, which hastened their own destruction soon after the king's restoration.

But the most formidable conspiracy against the government was a new one of the Cavaliers, with which the protector acquainted the lord-mayor and common council of the city in a speech, wherein he takes notice, that the Marquis of Ormond had been privately in London three weeks,‡ to promote the king's affairs,

---

* Dr. Grey, while he grants that Cromwell was a vain man, very much questions the truth of what is said above, as it does not agree with what Whitelocke says concerning the surrender of Dunkirk. The story Mr. Neal relates is the same we find in Welwood's Memoirs, p. 97, 6th edition. Dr. Harris treats it as all falsehood and invention, and as authoritatively confuted by Thurloe's State Papers, vol. vii., p. 173, where Lockhart, in his letter to Thurloe written the day before the surrender of Dunkirk, has these expressions: "To-morrow, before five of the clock at night, his highness's forces under my command will be possessed of Dunkirk. I have a great many disputes with the cardinal about several things; nevertheless, I must say, I find him willing to hear reason; and though the generality of court and arms are even mad to see themselves part with what they call un si bon morceau, or so delicate a bit, yet he is still constant to his promises. and seems to be as glad, in the general (notwithstanding our differences in little particulars), to give this place to his highness, as I can be to receive it. The king is also exceedingly obliging and civil, and hath more true worth in him than I could have imagined."—Life of Cromwell, p. 402, 403.—ED.

† Compl. Hist., p. 223. Echard, p. 730.

‡ A remarkable instance of the accuracy of Cromwell's information is related, which shows how almost impossible it was to escape his vigilance. Ormond had visited London. Cromwell was aware of his presence, and traced him from place to place. Having learned his business, and who were his accomplices, he took this magnanimous mode to induce him to depart. "An old friend of yours is come to town;" said Cromwell, in a jocular strain, to Lord Broghill. The latter asked, "Who?" Cromwell replied, "The Marquis of Ormond." Broghill protested his ignorance of the fact, which Cromwell admitted, adding, " He lodges at —— ; and if you have

---

* Wood's Athen. Oxon., vol. ii., p. 133.

† Fuller's Worthies, book iii., p. 128.

‡ Mr. Cranford was the author of a very interesting volume, entitled "the Tears of Ireland, wherein is represented the unheard-of Cruelties of the Blood-thirsty Jesuits, and the Popish Faction," 1642.—C.

§ Dr. Grey, though he allows that Mr. Neal had the authority of Echard for the merit which he imputes to the English forces in the siege of Dunkirk, yet contends that the French had their share in the glories of the day; and, to prove this, he gives a full detail of the action from the History of Visc. Turenne.—Impartial Examination, vol. iii., p. 207, 213.—ED

who lay ready on the coast with an army of eight thousand men and twenty-two ships; that there was a design to seize the Tower; and that several ill-affected persons were endeavouring to put themselves in arms for that purpose; he therefore desired them to put the city into a posture of defence, professing a more passionate regard for their safety than his own. The citizens returned his highness thanks, and in an address, promised to defend his person and government with their lives and fortunes. The like addresses came from several of the regiments at home, and from the English army in Flanders. This was the plot the protector mentioned in his speech to the Parliament, and was discovered by one Stapley, whose father had been one of the king's judges. Immediately after the dissolution of the Parliament, three of the conspirators were apprehended, and tried before a high court of justice, according to the late act for the security of his highness's person. Mr. Mordaunt, youngest son and brother of the Earl of Peterborough, was acquitted by one vote; but the other two, Sir Henry Slingsby and Dr. Hewet, were condemned. The doctor was indicted for holding correspondence with Charles Stuart, for publishing him to be King of England, Scotland, and Ireland, and for sending him money. He behaved with great boldness towards his judges, keeping his hat upon his head while the indictment was reading; but an officer being sent to take it off, he saved him the trouble. The doctor then refused to plead three times, disowning the jurisdiction of the court; but, though they read the clause in the late act by which they were empowered to be his judges, he continued mute; upon which one of the judges summed up the charge, and was going to pronounce sentence, when he offered to put himself upon his trial, but was told it was then too late, so judgment was given against him as a mute. The doctor had prepared a plea and demurrer to the jurisdiction and proceedings of the court, and exceptions to their judgment, drawn up in form by counsel, and ready to be engrossed, but was not suffered to have them argued. However, he had the favour of being beheaded on Tower Hill, June 8, 1658, being attended by Dr. Wild, Dr. Warmestry, and Dr. Barwick.* His funeral sermon was preached the Sunday following, by Mr. Nath. Hardy, at St. Dionis Backchurch, in Lime-street; and soon after, both the sermon and the doctor's intended defence were published, entitled "Beheaded Dr. John Hewet's Ghost crying for Justice," containing his legal plea, demurrer, and exceptions to the jurisdiction of the court, &c., drawn up by his counsel, Mr. William Prynne. The doctor was a Cambridge divine, but lived at Oxford and in the army till the end of the war, when he came to London, and was permitted to preach in the Church of St. Gregory's, London, though he was known to be a malignant. After his conviction, the Lady Claypole and Lady Falconbridge, the protector's daughters, interceded

a mind to save an old friend, let him know that I am aware where he is and what he is doing."
There was no thirsting for blood in the heart of Cromwell; he never took the life of an enemy but from a conviction of *absolute necessity.*—See *Godwin,* vol. iv., p. 507.—C.   * Life of Barwick, p. 175.
Vol. II.—Z

with their father for his life; but because he disputed the authority of the court, which struck at the very life of his government, the protector would not pardon him. He told Dr. Manton, one of his chaplains, that if Dr. Hewet had shown himself an ingenuous person, and would have owned what he knew was his share in the design against him, he would have spared his life; but he said he would not be trifled with, and the doctor was of so obstinate a temper that he was resolved he should die; and the protector *convinced* Dr. Manton, before they parted, that he knew, without his confession, how far he was engaged in the plot. Three more of the conspirators were executed in other parts of the city, but the rest were pardoned.

A little before the protector's death, the Independents petitioned his highness for liberty to hold a synod, in order to publish to the world a uniform confession of their faith. They were now become a considerable body, their churches being increased both in city and country,* by the addition of great numbers of rich and substantial persons; but they were not agreed upon any standard of faith or discipline. The Presbyterians in the Assembly of Divines had urged them to this, and their brethren in New-England had done it ten years ago; nor were the

* The number of these churches was, proportionally, much greater in the two counties of Norfolk and Suffolk than in most other parts of the kingdom. This was owing to the particular intercourse which those counties have with the city of Rotterdam and Holland, where the more rigid Puritans, who were driven out of England by the severities of the times, before the civil wars began, had taken refuge, and formed several Congregational churches. On the return of the English exiles to England, at the commencement of those dissensions, they brought with them their sentiments on church government, and formed churches on the Independent plan. Of these the most ancient was the church of Yarmouth, consisting of members resident in that town and at Norwich; and the Lord's Supper was administered alternately at the two places. This, after a time, was found very troublesome, and by a majority of votes the seat of the church was fixed at Yarmouth. This new arrangement was attended with great inconvenience to those who lived at Norwich. They therefore, with the consent of the other part who resided at Yarmouth, formed a separate church, June 10, 1644. This consent was given with expressions of the most tender and endeared affection, as having been, many of them, "companions together in the patience of our Lord Jesus in their own and in a strange land, and having long enjoyed sweet communion together in Divine ordinances." On these models other churches were settled through these counties. As at Denton, in May or June of the year 1655. At Tunstead, North Walsham, Wymondham, and Guestwick, in 1652. In the same year was laid the foundation of the Congregational Church of Beccles, in Suffolk, by nine persons joining together in church-fellowship, and by July 29, 1653, their number was increased to forty. The church at Walpole was settled into fellowship in the year 1647. That of St. Edmund's Bury, in 1648. That of Woodbridge, in 1651. That at Wattesfield, May 2, 1678. That of Wrentham was first gathered February 1, 1649, under Mr. John Philip, and one of its first members was Francis Brewster, Esq., lord of the manor of Wrentham, who gave the church-plate, which bears his arms; and some considerable legacies were left by him and different branches of his family. The hall was a place of refuge and concealment for the ministers or any of the people in time of persecution.—*Mr. Thompson's MS. Collections, under the words Norfolk and Suffolk.*—Ed.

English Independents insensible of the defect; for hitherto, say they, there have "been no association of our churches, no meetings of our ministers to promote the common interest; our churches are like so many ships launched singly, and sailing apart and alone in the vast ocean of these tumultuous times, exposed to every wind of doctrine; under no other conduct than the Word and Spirit, and their particular elders and principal brethren, without associations among themselves, or so much as holding out a common light to others, whereby to know where they were."* To remedy this, some of their divines and principal brethren in London met together, and proposed that there might be a correspondence among their churches in city and country for counsel and mutual edification; and forasmuch as all sects and parties of Christians had published a confession of their faith, they apprehended the world might reasonably expect it from them; for these reasons, they petitioned the protector for liberty to assemble for this purpose. This was opposed by some of the court, as tending to establish a separation between them and the Presbyterians; nor was the protector himself fond of it; however, he gave way to their importunity; and, as Mr. Echard represents that matter, when he was moved upon his deathbed to discountenance their petition, he replied, "They must be satisfied, they must be satisfied, or we shall all run back into blood again."

However, the protector did not live to see the fruits of this assembly, which was appointed to be held at the Savoy, October 12, 1658, where ministers and messengers from above one hundred Congregational churches met together, of which the majority were laymen, the rest pastors in churches, and some younger divines about the court, as the reverend and learned Mr. John Howe, at that time chaplain to the young protector, and others.† They opened their synod with a day of fasting and prayer, and after some debate whether they should adopt the doctrinal articles of the Westminster Assembly for their own, with some amendments and additions, it was thought more advisable to draw up a new confession, but to keep as near as possible to the method and order of the other. A committee of the most eminent divines was chosen for this work, viz., Dr. Thomas Goodwin, Dr. Owen, Mr. Phil. Nye, Mr. William Bridge, of Yarmouth, Mr. Jos. Caryl, and Mr. William Greenhill. While these were employed in preparing and putting together the articles of their confession, the synod heard complaints and gave advice in several cases which were brought before them, relating to disputes or differences in their churches. The particular heads of doctrine agreed to by the committee were presented to the synod every morning, and read by the Reverend Mr. George Griffith, their scribe. There were some speeches and debates upon words and phrases, but at length all acquiesced, and the whole was soon after published in quarto, under the title of "A Declaration of the Faith and Order owned and practised in the Congregational Churches in England, agreed upon and consented unto by their Elders and Messengers, in their Meeting at the Savoy, Oc-

tober 12, 1658." Next year it was translated into Latin by Professor Hornbeck, and published at the end of his Epistola ad Duræum de Independentissimo. Some imputed their unanimity to the authority and influence of Dr. Owen, Mr. Nye, and the rest of the elder divines over the younger; but they themselves, in their preface, "look upon it as a great and special work of the Holy Ghost, that so numerous a company of ministers and other principal brethren should so readily, speedily, and jointly give up themselves to such a whole body of truths as is there collected." They add, farther, "that this agreement of theirs fell out without their having held any correspondence together or prepared consultation, by which they might be advised of one another's minds," which I confess is very extraordinary, considering the confession consists of thirty-three chapters, in which are almost two hundred distinct articles of faith and discipline, and that the whole time of the synod's sessions or continuance was not above eleven or twelve days.

The Savoy confession proceeds upon the plan of the Westminster Assembly, which made the work very easy, and in most places retains their very words. They tell the world, in their preface, that they fully consent to the Westminster confession for the substance of it, but have taken liberty to add a few things, in order to obviate some erroneous opinions that have been more boldly maintained of late than in former times. They have likewise varied the method in some places, and have here and there expressed themselves more clearly, as they found occasion. They have omitted all those chapters in the Assembly's confession which relate to discipline, as the thirtieth and thirty-first,. with part of the twentieth and twenty-fourth, relating to the power of synods, councils, church censures, marriage and divorce, and the power of the civil magistrate in matters of religion. These (say they) were such doubtful assertions, and so unsuited to a confession of faith,. that the English Parliament would never ratify them, there being nothing that tends more to heighten dissensions among brethren than to place these doubtful speculations under so high a title as a confession of faith. After the nineteenth chapter of the Assembly's confession, of the law, the Savoy divines have added an entire chapter, of the Gospel, in which what is dispersed up and down the Assembly's confession is collected and put together. Upon the whole, the difference between these two confessions, in points of doctrine, is so very small, that the modern Independents have in a manner laid aside the use of it in their families, and agreed with the Presbyterians in the use of the Assembly's catechism.

At the end of the Savoy confession there is a chapter of discipline, entitled "Of the Institution of Churches, and the Order appointed in them by Jesus Christ," in which they assert, ·

"That every particular society of visible professors agreeing to walk together in the faith and order of the Gospel is a complete church, and has full power within itself to elect and ordain all church-officers, to exclude all offenders, and to do all other acts relating to the edification and well-being of the church. · ·

"That the way of ordaining officers, that is,

* Confess., Pref., p. 6.
† Calamy's Abridg., vol. ii., p. 444.

pastors, teachers, or elders, is, after their election, by the suffrage of the church, to set them apart with fasting and prayer, and imposition of the hands of the eldership of the church, though, if there be no imposition of hands, they are nevertheless rightly constituted ministers of Christ; but they do not allow that ordination to the work of the ministry, though it be by persons rightly ordained, does convey any office power, without a previous election of the church.

"That no persons may administer the sacrament but such as are ordained and appointed thereunto. Nor are the pastors of one church obliged to administer the sacraments to any other than to the members of that church to whom they stand related in that capacity. Nor may any person be added to the church as a private member, but* by the consent of the church, after a confession of his faith, declared by himself, or otherwise manifested.

"They disallow the power of all stated synods, presbyteries, convocations, and assemblies of divines, over particular churches; but admit that, in cases of difficulty, or difference relating to doctrine or order, churches may meet together by their messengers in synods or councils, to consider and give advice, but without exercising any jurisdiction.

"And, lastly, they agree that churches, consisting of persons sound in the faith and of good conversation, ought not to refuse communion with each other, though they walk not in all things according to the same rule of church order; and if they judge other churches to be true churches, though less pure, they may receive to occasional communion such members of those churches as are credibly testified to be godly, and to live without offence.

"These opinions," say they, "may appear new to a great many people, because they have not been openly and publicly professed in the English nation; but we are able to trace the footsteps of an Independent congregational way in the ancientest practice of the Church, and in the writings of the soundest Protestant divines." They add, "that their principles do not in the least interfere with the authority of the civil magistrate, nor do they concern themselves upon any occasion with him, any farther than to

* It was also a practice of the Independents, at the first formation of their churches, to sign an agreement, or covenant, which they entered on their church books. This sometimes ran out into various articles, expressive of their devotedness to the service of God, their trust in Christ, their determination to study the Scriptures, and to form their faith and worship by them, of their mutual engagement to keep the Christian ordinances, to watch over one another in the Lord, to bear one another's burdens, and to preserve union and love, and of their resolutions to persevere in a course of faith and holiness. Of these forms of agreement, one of the most simple is that which was adopted by the church at Wattesfield, in Suffolk. It was in these words: "We do covenant or agree, in the presence of God, through the assistance of his Holy Spirit, to walk together in all the ordinances of the Lord Jesus, as far as the same are made clear unto us, endeavouring the advancement of the glory of our Father, the subjection of our will to the will of our Redeemer, and the mutual edification of each other in his most holy faith and fear."—*Mr. Thompson's MS. Collections, under the name Wattesfield.*—ED.

implore his protection for the preservation of the peace and liberty of their churches." They glory in this, that ever since they appeared in the world, they have distinguished themselves in the cause of Christian liberty. "We have always," say they, "maintained this principle, that among all Christian states and churches, there ought to be a forbearance and mutual indulgence to Christians of all persuasions, that keep to and hold fast the necessary foundations of faith and holiness. This principle we have maintained for the sake of others, when we ourselves had no need of it." They conclude with thankfulness to their present governors for permitting those who could not comply with the Presbyterian establishment to enjoy the liberty of their consciences, and equal encouragement and protection with others; and that this liberty is established by law, as long as they disturb not the public peace. This should engage us (say they) to promote the honour and prosperity of such a government, to be peaceably disposed one towards another, and to love as brethren; forasmuch as the differences between Presbyterians and Independents are differences between fellow-servants, neither of them having authority, from God or man, to impose their opinions upon one another.*

Mr. Baxter, in the main a very peaceable and candid divine, loses all temper when he speaks of this assembly; he finds fault with their definition of justification, and makes these remarks: "They thought it not enough expressly to contradict St. James, and to say unlimitedly that we are justified by the righteousness of Christ only, and not by any works, but they contradicted St. Paul also, who says, that 'faith is imputed for righteousness;' and not only so, but they asserted that we have no other righteousness but that of Christ. A doctrine abhorred by all the Reformed and Christian churches, and which," says he, "would be an utter shame of the Protestant name, if what such men held and did were imputable to sober Protestants." But is it possible that Mr. Baxter could believe that the Savoy divines denied the necessity of sanctification, or personal holiness? when they have a whole chapter in their Confession upon sanctification, another upon repentance and good works, and a third upon the moral law, which they declare does forever bind all men to obedience, both justified and unjustified. When Mr. Baxter asked some honest men who joined them whether they subscribed the Confession, they said no; he then inquired why they did not contradict this? To which they answered, because the meaning was, that they had no other righteousness but that of Christ to be justified by, which is certainly the doctrine of the Westminster Assembly. What does Mr. Baxter reply to this? Why nothing, but adds, very uncharitably, "that the Independent confessions are like such oaths as speak one thing and mean another; so much could two men [Dr. Owen and Goodwin] do with many honest, tractable young men, who had more zeal for separating strictness than judgment to understand the Word

* Dr. Price observes, "The views maintained on the constitution of the Christian Church are precisely those still held by the whole body of Congregationalists" (in England).—*Hist. Nonconformity, vol. ii., p. 621.*—C.

of God, the interest of the churches and of themselves."* And yet there were in that assembly many divines of as great age and learning as himself; their design was not to *undervalue* the Westminster Confession, but rather to *answer the desires of that assembly, by publishing to the world such a declaration of their faith and discipline as they had demanded.* And the Confession was so far from raising any new divisions, that Mr. Philip Henry observes, upon the death of Cromwell, that there was a great change in the tempers of good people throughout the nation, and a mighty tendency to peace and unity, as if they were by consent weary of their long clashings. However, the Independents lost their best friend in the protector, who was not only their patron upon the principle of liberty, but a balance to the Presbyterian pretences to ecclesiastical power.

The hierarchy of the Church of England was now at a very low ebb, and, in danger of being lost beyond recovery ; for if the bishops, who were now very ancient, had all died off before others had been consecrated, '*the line of succession* must have failed ; for the Church of Rome was so far from supporting it, that they published a treatise this year, Of the Nature of the Catholic Faith, and of Heresy ; in which they endeavour to invalidate the English ordinations, and revived the story of the Nag's-head Club, for the truth of which they appealed to Dr. Moreton, the ancient Bishop of Durham, who, in a solemn speech made in full Parliament (say they), declared in express words, that our first bishops after the Reformation had been consecrated in a tavern ; and that this was so far from being doubted, that it was a fact most notorious to all the world ; adding, that the rest of the bishops present rather approved than in the least opposed what he had said. The bishop, then in the ninety-fourth year of his age, being advised of this calumny, sent for a public notary from London, and in the presence of proper witnesses, made a solemn protestation of the falsehood of this   , and signed it in due form, July 17, 1658 stoke then sent his chaplain, Dr. Barwick,† to all the lords spiritual and temporal then alive, who had sat in that Parliament, desiring that if they believed him undeservedly aspersed, they would attest it by subscribing their names ; which was done by six bishops and fourteen temporal lords, and by the several clerks and registrars of the House. The bishop died soon after, but his protestation, with the proofs, was afterward published by Dr. Bramhal, bishop of Derry, in a treatise entitled "The Consecration and Succession of Protestant Bishops Justified ; the Bishop of Duresme Vindicated ; and the Fable of the Ordination of the Nag's-head Club clearly Confuted." This awakened the clergy to enter upon measures for the continuance of a succession of bishops, though they could not be regularly chosen, lest the validity of the Episcopal ministry should cease ; which will come under consideration in the transactions of the next year.

Lord Clarendon mentions an address of the Anabaptists to the king, who, being disappointed in their expectations of a commonwealth, threw themselves at his majesty's feet, offering their assistance to pull down the present government.

In their address they say, "they took up arms in the late war for liberty and reformation, but assure his majesty that they were so far from entertaining any thoughts of casting off their allegiance, or extirpating the royal family, that they had not the least intent to abridge him of his just prerogatives, but only the restraining those excesses of government, which were nothing but the excrescences of a wanton power, and were rather a burden than an ornament to the royal diadem." They then go on to declaim against the protector, calling him that grand impostor, that loathsome hypocrite, that detestable traitor, the prodigy of nature, the opprobrium of mankind, a landskip of iniquity, a sink of sin, a compendium of baseness. And then, begging pardon for their former offences, they promise to sacrifice their lives and fortunes for his majesty's restoration, provided his majesty would be so gracious as to restore the remains of the Long Parliament ; to ratify the treaty of the Isle of Wight ; to establish liberty of conscience ; to take away tithes, and provide some other maintenance for the national clergy ; and to pass an act of oblivion for all who had been in arms against his father and himself, except those who should adhere to that ungodly tyrant who calls himself protector. His lordship adds, that the messenger that brought these propositions, asking the sum of £2000 to carry on the project, his majesty dismissed him with civil expressions, telling him he had no design to trouble any man for his opinion. However, if there had been such an address from the body of the Anabaptists, it is a little strange that after the Restoration it was not remembered to their advantage. But his lordship seems to have had no great acquaintance with these men, when he says they always pretended a just esteem and value for all men who faithfully adhered to the king ; whereas they were of all sects the most zealous for a commonwealth, and were enemies to the protector for no other reason but because he was for government by a single person. In truth, this whole affair seems no more than an artifice to get a little money out of the poor king's purse.*

The protector's health was now declining, through his advanced age and excessive toils and fatigues. The restless spirits of the Royalists and Republicans put him upon his guard, insomuch that he usually wore under his clothes a piece of armour, or a coat of mail. The loss of his beloved daughter Claypole, who died this summer, had also a very sensible influence on his health. About the middle of August he was seized with a slow fever, which turned to a tertian ague ; but the distemper appeared so favourable for a while, that he walked abroad in the gardens at Hampton Court. Ludlow says, the protector had a humour in his leg, which he desired the physicians to disperse, by which means it was thrown into his blood ; at length his pulse began to intermit, and he was advised to keep his bed ; and his ague fits growing stronger, it was thought proper to remove him to Whitehall, where he began to be light-headed ; upon which his physicians declared his life

---

* Life, p. 104   † Ibid., p. 40.

* Notwithstanding the suspicions which rest upon this affair, Crosby has seen fit to preserve the address, propositions, and letter, in the Appendix to his first volume, No. 5.—ED.

in danger, and the council being summoned to desire him to nominate his successor, be appointed his eldest son Richard. In the intervals of his fits he behaved with great devotion and piety, but manifested no remorse for his public actions ; he declared, in general, that he designed the good of the nation, and to preserve it from anarchy and a new war. He once asked Dr. Goodwin, who attended at his bedside, and is said to have expressed an unbecoming assurance* to Almighty God in prayer of his recovery, whether a man could fall from grace? which the doctor answering in the negative, the protector replied, " Then I am safe, for I am sure I was once in a state of grace."† About twelve hours before he died be lay very quiet, when Major Butler, being in his chamber, says he heard him make his last prayer to this purpose : " Lord, I am a poor foolish creature ; this people would fain have me live ; they think it best for them, and that it will redound much to thy glory, and all the stir is about this. Others would fain have me die ; Lord, pardon them, and pardon thy foolish people ; forgive their sins, and do not forsake them, but love and bless, and

* The language of Dr. Goodwin was thus extravagant : " Lord, we beg not for his recovery, for that thou hast already granted and assured us of ; but for his speedy recovery." And when news was brought of his death, Mr. Peter Sterry stood up, and desired them not to be troubled. " For," said he, " this is good news : because, if he was of great use to the people of God when he was among us, now he will be much more so, being ascended to heaven to sit at the right hand of Jesus Christ, there to intercede for us, and to be mindful of us on all occasions."—Ludlow's Memoirs, 4to, p. 258, 259. Dr. Grey does not fail to notice these strange flights. And Sewel the historian's reflection on this last instance of the flattery, or phrensy, of these courtiers, was just. " Oh, horrid flattery ! Thus I call it, though he had been the greatest saint on earth ; which he came much short of, though he was once endued with some eminent virtues."—History of the Quakers, p. 189.—ED. The abundant knowledge that we possess of Dr. Goodwin from his works, and the character ascribed to him by his cotemporaries, furnish conclusive evidence of the falsity of this version of his prayer for Cromwell. Sir Phillip Warwick's account of Cromwell's last sickness is manifestly unworthy of credit. The phrensied speeches and prayers attributed to his chaplains by Echard, and such writers, are gross caricatures, unworthy of a place in any work pretending to historical fidelity. The language of Dr. Goodwin reported by Ludlow, and improved on by subsequent writers, is fairly susceptible of an interpretation against which no valid objection can be urged. Thurloe's letter to Henry Cromwell proves that there was a period of the protector's illness when his disorder was thought to have yielded to the remedies which had been employed. Only let it be supposed that it was at this period—and there is nothing against the supposition—that the prayer referred to was uttered, and what is there in the following sentence to call for the pious horror which has been expressed ? " Lord, we beg not for his recovery, for that thou hast already granted and assured us of ; but for his speedy recovery." It requires little but candour and fair dealing to interpret Goodwin's language by the light which is thus incidentally obtained. The danger was believed to be past, and speedy restoration to health was therefore implored. Dr. Owen was charged with similar language, but his brief and conclusive reply was, " Mentitur impudentissime, for I saw him not in his sickness, nor in some long time before."—Owen's Works, vol. xxi., p. 566. South's sermons abound in slanders of this kind: see volume i., p. 65.—C. † Baxter's Life, p. 98.

give them rest, and bring them to a consistency, and give me rest, for Jesus Christ's sake, to whom, with thee and thy Holy Spirit, be all honour and glory, now and forever, Amen."* The protector died September 3, 1658, about three in the afternoon, the day on which he had triumphed in the battles of Marston Moor,† Dunbar, and Worcester, when he had lived fifty-nine years, four months, and eight days : four years and eight months after he had been declared protector by the instrument of government, and one year and three months after his confirmation by the humble petition and advice. As he had lived most part of his life in a storm, his death was attended with one of the greatest hurricanes that had been known for many years.‡ Some have said, that next night after his death his body was wrapped up in lead, and buried in Naseby field, according to his desire. Others, more probably, that it was deposited privately in a vault in King Henry VII.'s chapel, some time before the public funeral, which was performed November 23, with all imaginable grandeur and military pomp,§ from Somerset House, where he had lain in state, to the Abbey Church

* Thurloe, his secretary, would be more likely to furnish an accurate form of Cromwell's prayer than the major, and he sent it to Henry in Ireland, inscribed, " His Highnesse's Prayer, Sept. 2, being the night before he departed." " Lord, although I am a wretched and miserable creature, I am in covenant with thee through grace ; and I may, I will come to thee for my people : thou hast made me a mean instrument to doe them some good, and thee sarves, and many of them have sett too high a value upon me, though others wishe, and would be glad of my death ; but, Lord, however thou shall dispose of me, continue and goe on to doe good for them ; give them consistency of judgment, mutual love, and one harte ; goe on to deliver them, and with the work of reformation, and make the name of Christ great and glorious in the world ; teach those who looke too much upon thy instruments to depend more upon thyselfe. Pardon such as desire to trample upon the dust of a poore worme, for they are thy people too ; and pardon the folly of this short prayer, for Jesus Christ his sake, and give us a good night if it be thy pleasure."—Cromwell's Memoirs of Oliver Cromwell, vol. ii., p. 366.—C.

† This, as Dr. Grey notices, is an error ; the battle of Marston Moor was fought on the 2d of July, 1644.—ED.

‡ Dr. Grey tells us, also, that on the day his coffin was taken up and hung at Tyburn, almost as remarkable a storm rose in the northern parts of the kingdom: Superstition and a hatred of Cromwell construed these circumstances as appearances of nature or the God of nature, by physical phenomena, expressing an abhorrence of his character. But sound philosophy sees nothing but a singular coincidence of events, happening together, but without any correspondence in their causes ; and will reflect how many storms disturb the elements, when no wicked tyrant dies in the political world !—ED.

§ The expenses of Cromwell's funeral amounted to £60,000. The body was laid in a more private apartment till the 1st of November ; in imitation of the solemnities used upon the like occasion for Philip II., king of Spain, who was then represented to be in purgatory for two months. It was then removed into the great hall of Somerset House ; the part where the bed stood was railed in, and the rails and ground within covered with crimson velvet. Four or five hundred candles, set in flat shining candlesticks, were so placed round near the roof of the hall, that the light they gave seemed like the rays of the sun ; by all which he was represented to be in a state of glory.—Ludlow's Memoirs, 4to, p. 260.—ED.

in Westminster, where a fine 'mausoleum was erected for him, on which his effigy was placed, and exhibited to the view of all spectators for a time ; but after the king's restoration, his coffin was taken out of the vault, and drawn upon a sledge to Tyburn, where he was hanged up till sunset, and then buried under the gallows.*

Thus died the mighty Oliver Cromwell, the greatest soldier and statesman of his age, after he had undergone excessive fatigues and labours in a long course of warlike actions, and escaped innumerable dangers from the plots and conspiracies of domestic enemies. Few historians have spoken of him with temper, though no other genius, it may be, could have held the reins, or steered the commonwealth through so many storms and hurricanes, as the factions of these times had raised in the nation. He was born at Huntingdon, April 25, 1599, and descended of the family of Williams, of Glamorgan in Wales, which assumed the name of Cromwell by marrying with a daughter of Cromwell, earl of Essex, in the reign of King Henry VIII. The seat of the eldest branch of the family was called Hinchinbrook, now belonging to the Earl of Sandwich, who were reputed to possess an estate of £30,000 a year. Oliver, who was descended of a younger branch, was educated in Cambridge, and from thence became a student in Lincoln's Inn, being a wild and extravagant youth till about the thirty-fifth year of his age, when he quitted his irregular life, and became remarkably sober. In the year 1640 he was chosen representative in Parliament for the town of Cambridge, and sat two years undistinguished in the House, as a mere country gentleman, appearing, says Sir Philip Warwick, in a plain cloth suit of clothes made by a country tailor, his linen not very clean, his band un-fashionable, his hat without a hat-band, and his sword close by his side ; his countenance was swollen and reddish, his voice hoarse and untunable ; but his elocution was full of fervour and warmth, and he was well heard in the House. His person somewhat exceeded the middle stature,† but was well proportioned,

compact, and strong. He had a masculine countenance, a sparkling eye, a manly, stern look, a vigorous constitution, and was an enemy to ease and excess ; the motto upon his coat of arms was, *Pax quæritur bello.*

Upon the breaking out of the civil war he took arms for the Parliament, and though he was forty-three years of age before he drew a sword, he soon became colonel of a regiment of chosen men, who declared they fought not for gain, but for the cause of religion and liberty. He always went to prayer before battle, and returned solemn thanks for his success afterward. He was careful to promote an exact discipline in the army, and would not have pardoned his own brother, says my author,* if he had found him plundering the country people. The army had not an officer who faced danger with greater intrepidity, or more eagerly sought occasions to distinguish his personal valour. He had a great presence of mind in the heat of action, and taught his soldiers to fight in a more desperate manner than usual, not allowing them to discharge their muskets till they were so near the enemy as to be sure of doing execution. His reputation rose so fast, that he quickly became a major-general, then lieutenant-general, under Fairfax, and at last supplanted him. His troops believed themselves invincible under his conduct ; he never lost a battle where he had the chief command. The victory of Marston Moor was chiefly ascribed to his valour. The reduction of Ireland in less than a year made him the terror of his enemies ; and the battles of Dunbar and Worcester completed his martial glory.

How far his usurping the protectorship of the three nations, without the previous consent of a free Parliament, was the result of, ambition or necessity, has been considered already ; but if we view him as a statesman, he was an able politician, a steady, resolute governor ; and though he had more numerous and powerful enemies than any man of the age, he was never intimidated, having a peculiar art of keeping men quiet, and giving them, by turns, hopes of his favour. He had a wonderful knowledge of mankind, and an inimitable sagacity and penetration. If there was a man in England who excelled in any faculty or science, he would find him out, and reward him according to his merit. In nothing was his good understanding better discovered, says Bishop Burnet, than in seeking out able and worthy men for all employments, which gave a general satisfaction. By these methods, in the space of four or five years he carried the reputation and glory of the English nation as high as it was capable of being raised. He was equally dreaded by France, Spain, and the United Provinces, who condescended to servile compliances to obtain his friendship ; Charles Gustavus, king of Sweden, thought himself honoured by his alliance ; and Cardinal Mazarine said that nothing but the

* The reader is referred, for very curious and minute information upon this much-disputed subject, the disposal of the protector's body, to *Noble's House of Cromwell*, vol. ii., p. 288-291.—C.

† Sir John Reresby calls Cromwell "one of the greatest and bravest men, had his cause been good, the world ever saw. His figure did not come up to his character ; he was, indeed, a likely person, but not handsome, nor had he a very bold look with him. He was plain in his apparel, and rather negligent than not. Tears he had at will, and was, doubtless, the greatest dissembler on earth."—*Memoirs,* p. 2. Since Mr. Neal wrote, various historians have reviewed the actions and character of Cromwell, among whom the faithful and judicious Dr. Harris deserves particular mention. The candid and copious account of this extraordinary man in the first edition of the Biographia Britannica has been enriched with new and curious matter by the learned and accurate pen which has conducted the second edition. The history of the Cromwell family has been accurately investigated by Mr. Noble, in his Memoirs of the Protectoral House of Cromwell ; not to mention other writers who have elucidated this subject. To other particulars with which Dr. Kippis has improved the article Cromwell in the Biogr. Britan., is added an ample exhibition of the characters of him drawn by foreigners and natives.—Ed. Since Dr. Toul-

min wrote this note, other lives of Cromwell have appeared. The best, undoubtedly, that has appeared, is entitled "Memoirs of Oliver Cromwell and his Sons, by Oliver Cromwell, Esq.," 3d edition, London, 1822. Russell's Life in the Family Library is a high church libel upon that great man.—C.

* Carrington's Life of Cromwell, p. 243. Welwood's Mem., p. 104.

King of France's having the smallpox could have hindered him from coming over to England, that he might have the honour of waiting on one of the greatest men.

The protector had an uncommon command of his passions, and knew how to behave in character upon all occasions, though in private life he would be jocose and merry with his inferiors; yet no prince was more jealous of his dignity on public occasions. His ambassadors in foreign courts had all the respects paid them that our kings ever had. All Europe trembled at his name! And though he could converse with no foreigners but in broken Latin, yet no man ever had better intelligence, nor understood the views and interest of the several courts of Europe better than himself. He had spies at Madrid and Paris, and was so happy as to fix upon persons who never failed him. Mr. Algernon Sydney, who was not inclined to think or speak well of kings, commended him to Bishop Burnet, as one who had just notions of public liberty; and though he made some severe and cruel laws against the Episcopal clergy, it was not for their religion, but because they were open and declared enemies to his person and government.

The protector was a Protestant, but affected to go under no denomination or party; he had chaplains of all persuasions; and though he was by principle an Independent, he esteemed all Reformed churches as part of the Catholic Church; and without aiming to establish any tenets by force or violence, he witnessed, on all occasions, an extreme zeal for the Protestant religion, and a just regard for liberty of conscience.

As to his moral character, his greatest enemies have not charged him with any public vices. Dr. Welwood admits that he was not addicted to swearing, gluttony, drunkenness, gaming, avarice, or the love of women, but kept close to his marriage-bed. Nor is he chargeable with covetousness, for it has been computed, says the writer of his life,* that he distributed £40,000 a year out of his privy purse to charitable uses.† He promoted virtuous men, and was inflexible in his punishment of ill actions. His court was regulated according to a most strict discipline, says Mr. Echard, where every vice was banished or severely punished. He maintained a constant appearance of piety, and was regular in his private and public devotions: he retired constantly every day to read the Scriptures and prayer; and some who watched him narrowly have reported, that after he had read and expounded a chapter, he prostrated himself with his face on the ground, and, with tears, poured out his soul to God for a quarter of an hour. He was a strict observer of the Sabbath, and an encourager of goodness and austerity of life.‡ Mr. Baxter admits that "he kept as

much honesty and godliness as his cause and interest would allow; that he had a zeal for religion, meant honestly in the main, and was pious in the main course of his life,* till prosperity corrupted him."

But, with all these good qualities, it is certain the protector was a strong enthusiast, and did not take up his religion upon rational or solid principles, which led him into sundry mistakes, not supported by reason or Scripture. One of his favourite principles was, a particular faith; that is, if anything was strongly impressed upon his mind in prayer, he apprehended it came immediately from God, and was a rule of action; but if there were no impressions, but a flatness in his devotions, it was a denial. Upon this maxim he is said to have suffered the late king to be put to death in an arbitrary and illegal manner. Another maxim was, that "in extraordinary cases, something extraordinary, or beyond the common rules of justice, may be done; that the moral laws, which are binding in ordinary cases, may then be dispensed with; and that private justice must give way to public necessity." Which was the protector's governing principle in all his unwarrantable stretches of power. A third principle by which the protector was misled was, his determining the goodness of a cause by its success. An appeal to the sword was with him an appeal to God; and as victory inclined, God owned or discountenanced the cause. It is impossible that a man's conduct could be just or consistent while it was directed by such mistaken principles.

It has been farther objected to the protector's character, that he was notoriously guilty of hypocrisy and dissimulation both to God and man! that he mocked God by the pretence of piety and devotion, and by long prayers full of hypocritical zeal. But who can penetrate the heart, to see whether the outward actions flow from an inward principle? With regard to men, it is certain the protector knew how to address their passions, and talk to them in their own way; and if in his devotions he uttered with his mouth what his heart never meant, no one can vindicate him: but men are not slightly to be arraigned, says Rapin, for the inward motions of their heart, which pass all human knowledge. Besides, it is not easy to conceive the watchful eyes that were upon him, and the vast difficulties he had to contend with. Queen Elizabeth's dissimulation has been extolled for the very same reason that the protector's is condemned; if, therefore, such a conduct was necessary to govern the several parties, there is nothing

theatrical exhibitions. There was, indeed, a remarkable exception, in his permitting, from hatred to the Spaniards, the representation of a performance entitled "The Cruelty of the Spaniards in Peru."—*Roscius Anglicanus*, p. 29, in the *Literary Museum*, 8vo, printed in 1792.—ED.

* That his religious character was not originally assumed, however it might afterward be abused, to carry political views, and was prior to his dignity and power, it has been observed, is evinced from his letters written long before that period, and from what Milton says of him: "that, being arrived to manly and mature age, which he spent as a private person, and noted for nothing more than the cultivation of pure religion and integrity of life, he was grown wealthy in retirement at home."—*Gibbon's Funeral Sermon for William Cromwell*, p. 47, 48.—ED.

---

* Carrington, p. 248.

† An observation of Dr. Gibbons, as just in itself and doing honour to Cromwell, deserves to be mentioned here. It is this: "that it does not appear that, in the height of his power, he ever diverted any part of the national property to the private emolument of himself or family, as he left them possessed of the small estates only which he enjoyed before he arrived to the protectorate."—*Funeral Sermon for William Cromwell*, p. 48.—ED.

‡ To this must be ascribed his prohibition of all

greatly blameworthy in it, says the same author, unless it was a crime in him not to put it into the power of his enemies to destroy him with the greater ease.

Ambition and thirst of glory might sometimes lead the protector aside, for he imagined himself to be a second Phineas, raised up by Providence to be the scourge of idolatry and superstition; and in climbing up to the pinnacle of supreme power, he did not always keep within the bounds of law and equity: to this passion some have ascribed his assuming the protectorship, and putting himself at the head of three kingdoms; though others are of opinion it was owing to hard necessity and self-preservation. I will not venture to decide in this case; possibly there might be a mixture of both. When he was in possession of the sovereign power, no man ever used it to greater public advantage, for he had a due veneration for the laws of his country in all things wherein the life of his jurisdiction was not concerned; and though he kept a standing army, they were under an exact discipline, and very little burden to the people.

The charge of cruelty, which is brought against him for having put some men to death for conspiring against his person and government, deserves no confutation, unless they would have had him sit still till some conspiracy or other had succeeded. Cruelty was not in his nature;[*] he was not for unnecessary effusion of blood. Lord Clarendon assures us that, when a general massacre of the Royalists was proposed by the officers in council, he warmly opposed and prevented it.

Dr. Welwood[†] compares the protector to an unusual meteor, which with its surprising influence overawed not only three kingdoms, but the most powerful princes and states about us. A great man he was, says he, and posterity might have paid a just homage to his memory, if he had not imbrued his hands in the blood of his prince, and trampled upon the liberties of his country.

Upon the whole, it is not to be wondered that the character of this great man has been transmitted down to posterity with some disadvantage; by the several factions of Royalists, Presbyterians, and Republicans, because each were disappointed, and enraged to see the supreme power wrested from them: but his management is a convincing proof of his great abilities: he was at the helm in the most stormy and tempestuous season that England ever saw; but, by his consummate wisdom and valour, he disconcerted the measures and designs of his enemies, and preserved both himself and the commonwealth from shipwreck. I shall only observe farther, with Rapin, that the confusions which prevailed in England after the death of Cromwell clearly evidence the necessity of this

* Such was the sensibility of his spirit, that if an account were given him of a distressed case, the narration would draw tears from his eyes. It speaks strongly in favour of his temper and his domestic deportment, that the daughter of Sir Francis Russel, married to his second son Henry, who, before her marriage, had entertained an ill opinion of her father Oliver, upon her coming into the family felt all her prejudice removed, and changed into a most affectionate esteem for her father-in-law, as the most amiable of parents.—*Gibbon's Funeral Sermon for William Cromwell, Esq.*, p. 46.—ED.   † P. 102.

usurpation, at least till the Constitution could be restored. After his death his great achievements were celebrated in verse by the greatest wits of the age, as Dr. Sprat, afterward Bishop of Rochester, Waller, Dryden, and others, who in their panegyrics outdid everything which till that time had been written in the English language.*

Four divines of the assembly died this year; Dr. John Harris, son of Richard Harris, of Buckinghamshire, born in the parsonage house of Hardwick in the same county, educated in Wickham school near Winchester, and in the year 1606 admitted perpetual fellow of New College. He was so admirable a Grecian and eloquent a preacher, that Sir Henry Saville called him a second St. Chrysostom. In 1619 he was chosen Greek professor of the university. He was afterward prebendary of Winchester, rector of Meonstoke in Hampshire, and in the year 1630, warden of Wickham College, near Winchester; in all which places he behaved with great reputation. In the beginning of the civil wars he took part with the Parliament, was chosen one of the Assembly of Divines, took the Covenant, and other oaths, and kept his wardenship till his death; he published several learned works,[†] and then died at Winchester, August 11, 1658, aged seventy years.

Mr. Sydrach Sympson, a meek and quiet divine of the Independent persuasion, was educated in Cambridge, but forced to fly his country for nonconformity in the times of Archbishop Laud. He was one of the dissenting brethren in the Assembly, and behaved with great temper and moderation.[‡] Bishop Kennet says he was silenced for some time from preaching, because he differed in judgment from the Assembly in points of church discipline, but was restored to his liberty October 28, 1646. He afterward gathered a congregation in London, after the manner of the Independents, which met in Ab Church, near Cannon-street. Upon the resignation of Mr. Vines in the year 1650, for refusing the Engagement, he was by the visiters made master of Pembroke Hall, Cambridge. He was a divine of considerable learning, and of great piety and devotion. In his last sickness he was under some darkness and melancholy apprehensions: upon which account some of his friends and brethren assembled in his own house, to assist him with their prayers; and in the evening, when they took their leave, he thanked them, and said he was now satisfied

* The reader is referred to the Appendix for a view of the character of Oliver Cromwell, drawn from various works.—C.

† His principal work was "A View of the Life of Dr. Arthur Lake, Bishop of Bath and Wells, 1629."—C.

‡ Dr. Grey calls Mr. Sympson a celebrated preacher of *rebellious principles*; which is plain, he says, from the following extract from one of his discourses: "Reformation is liable to inhuman treacheries. Pharaoh's dealing was very treacherous. He bade the people go; gave them liberty by proclamation; and when he had got them at an advantage, he brought up an army to cut them off. The reforming of the Church will meet with such kind of enemies." If Dr. Grey had not been *accustomed* to ascribe rebellion to *all the Puritan divines*, he would have been unable to find rebellious doctrine in this passage. Brooks says it would puzzle both the universities to detect the treason.—C.

in his soul; and lifting up his hands towards heaven, said, "He is come, he is come;" and that night died.

Dr. Robert Harris was born at Broad Camden in Gloucestershire, 1578, and educated in Magdalen College, Oxon. He preached for some time about Oxford, and settled afterward at Hanwell, in the place of famous Mr. Dodd, then suspended for nonconformity;* here he continued till the breaking out of the civil wars, when by the king's soldiers he was driven to London. He was appointed one of the Assembly of Divines, and minister of St. Botolph, Bishopsgate. In the year 1646 he was one of the six preachers to the University of Oxford, and next year one of their visiters, when he was created D.D. and made president of Trinity College, and rector of Garlington, near Oxford, which is always annexed to it. Here he continued till his death, governing his college with a paternal affection, being reverenced by the students as a father. The inscription over his grave gives him a great character; but the Royalists charge him, and I believe justly, with being a notorious pluralist.‡ He died December 11, 1658, in the eightieth year of his age.†

Mr. William Carter was educated in Cambridge, and afterward a very popular preacher in London. He was a good scholar, of great seriousness, and though a young man, appointed one of the Assembly of Divines. After some time he joined the Independents, and became one of the dissenting brethren in the Assembly. He had offers of many livings, but refused them, being dissatisfied with the parochial discipline of those times; nevertheless, he was indefatigable in his ministry, preaching twice every Lord's Day to two large congregations in the city, besides lectures on the week days; this wasted his strength, and put an end to his life about midsummer, 1658, in the fifty-third year of his age. His family were afterward great sufferers by the purchase of bishops' lands.

CHAPTER IV.

THE INTERREGNUM FROM THE DEATH OF OLIVER CROMWELL TO THE RESTORATION OF KING CHARLES II. AND THE RE-ESTABLISHMENT OF THE CHURCH OF ENGLAND. 1659.

Upon the death of the protector, all the discontented spirits who had been subdued by his administration resumed their courage, and within the compass of one year revived the confu-

---

sions of the preceding ten. Richard Cromwell being proclaimed protector upon his father's decease, received numberless addresses from all parts,* congratulating his accession to the dignity of protector, with assurances of lives and fortunes cheerfully devoted to support his title. He was a young gentleman of a calm and peaceable temper, but had by no means the capacity or resolution of his father, and was therefore unfit to be at the helm in such boisterous times. He was highly caressed by the Presbyterians, though be set out upon the principles of general toleration, as appears by his declaration of November 25, entitled "A Proclamation for the better encouraging godly Ministers and others;" and for their enjoying their dues and liberties, according to law, without being molested with indictments for not using the Common Prayer Book.†

* Of these addresses Dr. Grey says, "Nothing ever exceeded them in point of flattery, except those canting addresses of the Dissenters to King James, upon his indulgence;" and he gives several at length, as specimens of the strain of adulation in which they were drawn up, from different corporations; from which the reader will see that mayors, recorders, and aldermen of that day could rival the Independent ministers, whom the doctor reproaches as "most foully guilty," in their effusions of flattery. In truth, all were paying their devoirs to the rising sun.—ED.

† "The Presbyterian discipline and synodical government," says Mr. Hallam, "were very partially introduced; and, upon the whole, the church, during the suspension of the ancient laws, was rather an assemblage of congregations than a compact body, proving little more unity than resulted from their common dependancy on the temporal magistrate. In the time of Cromwell, who favoured the Independent sectaries, some of that denomination obtained livings; but very few, I believe, comparatively, which had not received either Episcopal or Presbyterian ordination. The right of private patronage to benefices, and that of tithes, though continually menaced by the more violent party, subsisted without alteration."—Const. History, vol. ii., p. 427. The anomalous condition of the ecclesiastical affairs led to the possession of church livings by a few Independent and Baptist ministers. The fact is notorious, and cannot be reconciled with the principles of the parties in question. Independency is founded on the voluntary character of religion. This is the element in which it lives, and moves, and has its being. It is its universal and all-pervading attribute; the simple but majestic doctrine which it lisped in its infancy, and the distinct enunciation of which constitutes the glory of its manhood. It is, therefore, matter of surprise that any Congregationalist should so far have forgotten what was due to their own consistency as to have received the constrained report of their people. The violation of their principles in this case was as real as in the more palpable forms sometimes assumed by the coercive principle when it had dictated the modes of religious worship, and furnished the slightest departure from an established creed and ritual. To compel others to support religion is to admit the seminal principle of persecution; while it subjects the recipients of such tribute to a host of noxious influences, from which no personal excellences can wholly protect them. Nor can the consistency of the parties in question be defended on the ground that, though they occupied the edifices, and received the stipend allotted by the state, they did not regard themselves as parochial ministers. The churches which they formed approximated, it is true, more nearly to the Congregational than to any other model; but there were incongruous elements in their constitution, which, had time permitted, could not fail to have produced the most lamentable results: Like the image of Nebuchadnezzar, the system was

---

* Dr. Harris did not conceive any one external form to be so essential to a church, but that it might still deserve that name, though under a Presbyterian, or Independent, or Episcopal form, so long as it was kept within the bounds of those general rules laid down in the Scriptures.—Life of Dr. Harris, p. 318.—C.

† Against this charge, if the truth of it should be admitted, ought to be set his charity, which, we are told, exceeded the ordinary proportion of his revenues. —ED. Dr. Walker, that most mendacious of all historians, rests the evidence of this accusation on the authority of a scurrilous letter, published to pour contempt upon the Puritans.—See Brooks's Lives of the Puritans, vol. iii., p. 307.—C.

‡ Clarke's Lives, in his Martyrology, p. 314-339.

VOL. II —A A

The young protector summoned a Parliament to meet on the 27th of January, 1658-9. The elections were not according to the method practised by his father, but according to the old Constitution, because it was apprehended that the smaller boroughs might be more easily influenced than cities and counties ; but it was ill judged to break in upon the instrument of government, by which he held his protectorship. The Parliament met according to appointment, but did little business, the Lower House not being willing to own the Upper. The army was divided into two grand factions : the Wallingford House party, which was for a commonwealth ; and the Presbyterian, which, with the majority of the Parliament, was for the protector. The Wallingford House party, of which Fleetwood and Desborough were the head, invited Dr. Owen and Dr. Manton to their consultations. Dr. Owen went to prayer before they entered on business, but Dr. Manton, being late before he came, heard a loud voice from within saying, He must down, and he shall down. Manton knew the voice to be Dr. Owen's, and understood him to mean the deposing of Richard, and therefore would not go in. But the writer of Dr. Owen's life discredits this story ; though, in my opinion, it is very probable, for the doctor inclined to a Republican government ; he sided with the army, and drew up their address against Oliver's being king ; upon which, he declined in the protector's favour, and as soon as Richard became chancellor of Oxford, he turned him out of the vice-chancellorship. The cabinet-council at Wallingford House having gained over several to their party, prevailed with Richard to consent to their erecting a general council of officers, though he could not but know they designed his ruin, being all Republicans ; and therefore, instead of supporting the protector, they presented a remonstrance, complaining of the advancement of disaffected persons, and that the good old cause was ridiculed. Richard, sensible of his fatal mistake, by the advice of Lord Broghill dissolved the council, and then the Parliament voted they should meet no more ; but the officers bid him defiance, and like a company of sovereign dictators armed with power, sent the protector a peremptory message to dissolve the Parliament, telling him that it was impossible for him to keep both the army and Parliament at his devotion, but that he might choose which he would prefer ; if he dissolved the Parliament, he might depend upon the army ; but if he refused, they would quickly pull him out of Whitehall. Upon this, the timorous gentleman being at a plunge, and destitute of his father's courage, submitted to part with the only men who could support him.

After the dissolution of the Parliament, Richard became a cipher in the government ; Lord Broghill, afterward Earl of Orrery, advised him to the last to support the Parliament and declare against the council of officers ; and if he had allowed the captain of his guard at the same time to have secured Fleetwood and Desborough, as he undertook to do with the hazard of his life, he might have been established ; but the poor-spirited protector told him that he was afraid of blood ; upon which the captain, Lord Howard, made his peace with the king.* The officers at Wallingford House, having carried their point, published a declaration about twelve days after, without so much as asking the protector's leave, inviting the remains of the Long Parliament to resume the government, who immediately declared their resolutions for a commonwealth without a single person, or House of Peers. Thus was the grandeur of Cromwell's family destroyed by the pride and resentment of some of its own branches ; Fleetwood had married the widow of Ireton, one of Oliver's daughters, and being disappointed of the protectorship by his last will, was determined that no single person should be his superior. Desborough, who had married Oliver's sister, joined in the fatal conspiracy. Lambert, whom Oliver had dismissed the army, was called from his retirement to take his place among the council of officers. These, with Sir H. Vane, and one or two more behind the curtain, subverted the government, and were the springs of all the confusions of this year, as is evident by the letters of Mr. Henry Cromwell, lord-lieutenant of Ireland, now before me, who saw farther into their intrigues at that distance, than the protector, who was upon the spot. I shall take the liberty to transcribe some passages out of them to my present purpose.

Upon the surprising news of Oliver's death, he writes to his brother, September, 18, 1658,

---

partly gold and partly clay, imposing and beautiful it may be to the eye, but destined speedily to become "like the chaff of the summer threshing-floor." Milton's keen vision detected and exposed the inconsistency. "Independency and state hire in religion," he remarks, "can never consist long or certainly together ; for magistrates, at some time or other, will pay none, but such whom, by their committees of examination, they find conformable to their interests and opinions. And hirelings will soon frame themselves to that interest, and those opinions which they see best pleasing to their paymasters ; and, to seem right themselves, will force others as to the truth." Such is the testimony of Dr. Price upon the state of the Church at this period. Yet the inconsistency was more apparent than real, in some cases at least. The Independent or Baptist minister consented to occupy the vacant pulpit of a parish, but threw himself entirely on the voluntary support of the people. This appears to have been the case with John Goodwin, who replied in the following language to a violent attack upon his character by the celebrated Prynne : "I am charged with receiving their tithes. My answer is, that I demand no tithes of any of them, nor ever had any right to do it. Nor have I ever received any tithes from them in the nature of tithes, but as their voluntary contribution. The parsonage is impropriate in the parishioners' hands ; the vicarage is only endowed with eleven pounds per annum. For the last half year I have received little above twenty pounds, excepting only one half of the yearly rent of a small house, let sometimes but for twelve pounds, and never for above fourteen pounds a year. Out of which sum, twelve pounds ten shillings being deducted for the rent of my house, the remainder is of as low a proportion as envy herself can desire for the maintenance of a minister, his wife, and seven children, in such an expensive place as this city. If Mr. Prynne knew how small a portion of subsistence I receive, and what my labour and pains are, I verily believe that, instead of upbraiding me with 'receiving tithes,' he would pity me that I received no more."—Jackson's Life of Goodwin, p. 68.—C.

* See the dialogue between Richard and Howard, marked SS., in Noble's House of Cromwell, vol. i., p. 330.—C.

"I am so astonished at the news of my dear father's sickness and death, that I know not what to say or write on so grievous an occasion ; but the happy news of leaving your highness his successor gives some relief, not only on account of the public, but of our poor family, which the goodness of God has preserved from the contempt of our enemies. I may say, without vanity, that your highness has been proclaimed here with as great joy and general satisfaction (I believe) as in the best-affected places of England ; and I make no doubt of the dutiful compliance of the army. Now, that the God of your late father and mine, and your highness's predecessor, would support you, and pour down a double portion of the same spirit that was so eminently in him, and would enable you to walk in his steps, and do worthily for his name, namesake, and people, and continually preserve you in so doing, is the prayer of

"Yours, &c., H. C.".

In another letter of the same date, sent by an express messenger, he writes, that "he had caused a very dutiful address to be sent to the army, which had been already signed by several of the field officers, and when perfected, should be sent to him as a witness against any single officer that should hereafter warp from his obedience ; so that I may and do assure your highness of the active subjection of this army to your government, and will answer for it with my life."

In his letter of October 20, 1658, he says, "If the account be true which I have received of the state of affairs in England, I confess it is no more than I looked for, only I had some hopes it might have been prevented by keeping all officers at their respective charges ; but, as things now stand, I doubt the flood is so strong you can neither stem it nor come to an anchor, but must be content to go adrift and expect the ebb. I thought those whom my father had raised from nothing would not so soon have forgot him, and endeavour to destroy his family before he is in his grave. Why do I say I thought, when I know ambition and affection of empire never had any bounds? I cannot think these men will ever rest till they are in the saddle ; and we have of late years been so used to changes, that it will be but a nine days' wonder ; and yet I fear there is no remedy, but what must be used gradually and pedetentim. Sometimes I think of a Parliament, but am doubtful whether sober men will venture to embark themselves when things are in so high a distraction ; or if they would, whether the army can be restrained from forcing elections. I am almost afraid to come over to your highness, lest I should be kept there, and so your highness lose this army, which, for aught I know, is the only stay you have, though I cannot but earnestly desire it. I also think it dangerous to write freely to you, for I make no question but all the letters will be opened that pass between us, unless they come by a trusty messenger. I pray God help you, and bless your councils.

"I remain yours, &c. H. C."

In a letter of the same date to his brother-in-law Fleetwood, he writes : —

"Dear Brother,

"I received your account of the petition of the officers ; but pray give me leave to expostulate with you : How came these two or three hundred officers together ? If they came of their own heads, their being absent from their charge without license would have flown in their face when they petitioned for a due observance of martial discipline. If they were called together, were they not also taught what to say and do ? If they were called, was it with his highness's privity ? If they met without leave in so great a number, were they told of their error ? I shall not meddle with the matter of their petition ; but, dear brother, I must tell you, I hear that dirt was thrown upon his late highness at that great meeting ; that they were exhorted to stand up for that good old cause which had long lain asleep. I thought my father had pursued it to the last. He died praying for those that desired to trample on his dust. Let us, then, not render evil for good, and make his memory stink before he is under ground. Let us remember his last legacy, and for his sake render his successor considerable, and not make him vile, a thing of naught, and a by-word. Whither do these things tend ! What a hurly-burly is there ! One hundred Independent ministers called together ; a council, as you call it, of two or three hundred officers of a judgment. Remember what has always befallen imposing spirits. Will not the loins of an imposing Independent or Anabaptist be as heavy as the loins of an imposing prelate or presbytery ? And is it a dangerous opinion, that dominion is founded in grace, when it is held by the Church of Rome, and a sound principle when it is held by the fifth-monarchy men ? Dear brother, let us not fall into the sins of other men, lest we partake of their plagues. Let it be so carried, that all the people of God, though under different forms ; yea, even those whom you count without, may enjoy their birthright and civil liberty ; and that no one party may tread upon the neck of another. It does not become the magistrate to descend into parties ; but can the things you do tend to this end ! Can these things be done, and the world not think his highness a knave or a fool, or oppressed with mutinous spirits ? Dear brother, my spirit is sorely oppressed with the consideration of the miserable state of the innocent people of these nations : what have these sheep done that their blood should be the price of our lust and ambition ! Let me beg you to remember how his late highness loved you ; how he honoured you with the highest trust, by leaving the sword in your hand, which must defend or destroy us. And his declaring his highness his successor shows that be left it there to preserve him and his reputation. O brother! use it to curb extravagant spirits and busy-bodies, but let not the nations be governed by it. Let us take heed of arbitrary power ; let us be governed by the known laws of the land ; and let all things be kept in their proper channels ; and let the army be so gorverned, that the world may never hear of them unless there be occasion to fight. And truly, brother, you must pardon me if I say God and man may require this duty at your hand, and lay all miscarriages of the army, in point of discipline, at your door. You see I deal freely and plainly with you, as becomes your friend and a good subject ; and the great God, in whose presence I speak, knows that I do it not to reproach you, but out of my tender affection and faithfulness to you. And you may rest assured that you shall always find me your true friend and loving brother.

"H. C."

In other letters to Lord Broghill, afterward Earl of Orrery, with whom he maintained an intimate correspondence, "he complains of his being forbid to come over into England; and that the clause in his new commission was left out; namely, the power of appointing a deputy, or juries, in order to prevent his coming over to England, which he hopes his highness will permit, there being much more cause to press it now than ever." "I find," says he, in a letter to the protector, "that my enemies have sentenced me to an honourable banishment; I am not conscious of any crime which might deserve it; but if they can denounce judgment upon my innocence, they will easily be able to make me criminal. They have already begot a doubt among my friends whether all be right; but I will rather submit to any sufferings with a good name, than be the greatest man upon earth without it." In a letter to Secretary Thurloe, he writes, "that since he was not allowed to leave Ireland, he could do no more than sit still and look on. The elections for Parliament are like to be good here," says he, "though I could wish the writs had come timely, that the members might have been there before they had been excluded by a vote, which, it is said, will be the first thing brought upon the stage." From these, and some other of his letters, it is natural to conclude that Lieutenant-general Fleetwood was at the head of the councils which deposed Richard, which might be owing either to his Republican principles, or to his disappointment of the protectorship. However, when he found he could not keep the army within bounds, who were for new changes, he retired from public business, and spent the remainder of his life privately among his friends at Stoke Newington, where he died soon after the Revolution, being more remarkable for piety and devotion than for courage and deep penetration in politics.*

To return: After the Rump Parliament had sat about a week, the officers petitioned, "1. That the laws might have their free course. 2. That all public debts unsatisfied might be paid. 3. That all who profess faith in the holy Trinity, and acknowledge the Holy Scriptures to be the revealed will of God, may have protection and encouragement in the profession of their religion, while they give no disturbance to the state, except papists, Prelatists, and persons who teach licentious doctrines. 4. That the two universities, and all schools of learning, may be countenanced. 5. That those who took part with the king in the late wars, or are notoriously disaffected to the Parliament's cause, may be removed from all places of trust. 6. That

the protector's debts be paid, and an allowance of £10,000 per annum be allowed to Richard and his heirs forever. 7. That there may be a representative of the people, consisting of one house, successively chosen by the people; and that the government of the nation may be placed in such a representative body, with a select senate co-ordinate in power; and that the administration of all executive lower of government may be in a council of state, consisting of a convenient number of persons eminent for godliness, and who are in principle for the present cause."

The Parliament thanked the officers for their petition, but postponed the affair relating to Richard till he should acquiesce in the change of government. The protector, having parted with the Parliament, who were his chief support, had not the resolution to strike a bold stroke for three kingdoms, but tamely submitted to resign his high dignity,* by a writing under his hand, after he had enjoyed it eight months. How little the soul of Oliver survived in his son Richard may be seen by this conduct! His brother Henry,† who was at the head of an army in Ireland, offered to come immediately to his assistance, but was forbid, and the timorous young gentleman returned to a private life with more seeming satisfaction than he had accepted the sovereignty.‡ Upon his quitting White-,

---

* Richard Cromwell has been reproached as "extremely pusillanimous," as "a fool and a sot," and "a titmouse prince," because he yielded to the times, and relinquished power and royalty. "But, in the name of common sense," says Dr. Harris, with virtuous animation, "what was there weak and foolish in laying down a burden too heavy for the shoulders? What in preferring the peace and welfare of men to blood and confusion, the necessary consequences of retaining the government? Or what, in a word, in resigning the power to such as, by experience, had been found fully equal to it, and intent on promoting the common welfare? Ambition, glory, fame, sound well in the ears of the vulgar; and men, excited by them, have seldom failed to figure in the eyes of the world: but the man who can divest himself of empire for the sake of his fellow-men, must, in the eye of reason, be entitled to a much higher renown than the purpled hero who leads them on to slaughter, though provinces or kingdoms are gained to him thereby."

Ambition, cease : the idle contest end ;
'Tis but a kingdom thou canst win or lose.
And why must murder'd myriads lose their all
(If life be all) ; why desolation lour
With famish'd frown on this affrighted ball,
That thou mayst flame the meteor of an hour !—MASON.

—*Harris's Life of Charles II.*, vol. i.; p. 214.—ED.

† Had Henry been the first-born of his father, probably Charles II. would never have succeeded to the throne of his ancestors. Henry is said to have resembled his father not only in person, but in mind. —C.

‡ For his conduct at this period, Richard has been accused of feebleness and pusillanimity. Mrs. Hutchinson says in her Memoirs, "He was a meek, temperate, and quiet man, but had not a spirit fit to succeed his father or to manage such a perplexed government." Certainly, had he plunged the nation into a war, and had he put to death two or three of his most factious opponents, he might possibly have remained in power for a longer season. He entertained, however, a strong disinclination to shed blood ; and rather than owe his aggrandizement to crime, returned peaceably to the private station from which he had sprung, and for the enjoyment of which his nature was peculiarly adapted. By the Cavaliers

---

* "He thought that prayers superseded the use of carnal weapons, and that 'it was sufficient to trust in the hand of Providence, without exerting the arm of flesh.' He would fall on his knees and pray when he heard of a mutiny among the soldiers; and was with the utmost difficulty roused to action on several emergencies."—*Granger's History of England*, vol. iii., 8vo, p. 17.—ED

hall, and the other royal palaces, the Parliament voted him a maintenance, but refused to concern themselves with his father's debts,* the payment whereof swept away the greatest part of his estate, which was far from being large, considering the high preferments his father had enjoyed for several years. This was a farther contempt thrown upon the protector's memory; former obligations were forgotten, and a new council of state being chosen, the nation seemed to slide peaceably into a commonwealth government...

The Presbyterians would have been content with Richard's government; but seeing no likelihood of restoring the Covenant, or coming into power, by the Rump Parliament, which was chiefly made up of enthusiasts and declared enemies to monarchy, they entered into a kind of confederacy with the Royalists to re-

and Republicans, the course adopted by Richard was of course ridiculed, and affected to be despised. Such terms as "Queen Dick," "Tumble-down Dick," and "the meek knight," were plenteously bestowed upon him. Heath styles him a "milksop;" Lord Clarendon, a "poor creature;" and Bishop Warburton, a "poltroon." Of his true character and of the real motives of his conduct, historians probably will ever remain divided in opinion. Richard resided on the Continent till 1680, principally in Paris. On his return, he settled, under the name of Richard Clarke, at Cheshunt. Here, with the exception of exchanging occasional visits with a few friends, he passed the remainder of his long life in peace and seclusion. Dr. Watts, who was one of his most favoured intimates, used to mention that only on one occasion had he heard any allusion from the recluse as to his former greatness, and then but in an indirect manner.

Allusion has been made to the many fulsome addresses which were poured upon the new protector on his first accession to power. They flew to him, says Anthony Wood, "from all parts of the three nations to salute and magnify his assumption to the sovereignty, wherein he was celebrated for the excellence of his wisdom and nobleness of his mind," &c. On his expulsion from Whitehall, Richard, showing particular anxiety about the safety of two old trunks, a friend, somewhat surprised, inquired the reason of this extraordinary interest. ' "They contain," said the ex-protector, "no less than the lives and fortunes of the people." The fact is, they were the addresses which he had received in the zenith of his glory, in which he was spoken of as the saviour of his country, and as the person on whom alone depended the lives and liberties of the three kingdoms.

Richard died at Cheshunt, 1712, in his 86th year; he seems to have been a religious character, and attended service alternately at the Established Church and at the Baptist meeting in Romsey.—*Jeses's Court of the Stuarts*, vol. iii., p. 170-2. *Noble*, vol. i., p. 183. —C.

* The Parliament instituted, however, an inquiry into the debts of Richard Cromwell, and a schedule of them was given in; by which it appeared that Richard, even after having reduced his father's debts from £28,000 to £23,550, owed £29,640. It was resolved to acquit Richard Cromwell from this debt, and to provide for the payment of it by the sale of the plate, hangings, goods, and furniture in Whitehall and Hampton Court, belonging to the state, which could be conveniently spared. It was also resolved to settle on him an annuity of £8700, so as to make to him with his own fortune a yearly income of £10,000. But, through the changes that followed, Richard Cromwell derived no benefit from these resolutions.—*Grey's Examination*, vol. iii., p. 241. *Dr. Harris's Life of Charles II.*, vol. i., p. 108, &c.—ED.

store the king and the old Constitution. The particulars of this union (says Rapin) are not known, because the historians who write of it, being Royalists, have not thought fit to do so much honour to the Presbyterians. But it is generally agreed that from this time the Presbyterians appeared no longer among the king's enemies, but very much promoted his restoration. Upon the foundation of this union an insurrection was formed in several parts of the country, which was discovered by Sir Richard Willis, a correspondent of Secretary Thurloe's, so that Sir George Booth, a Presbyterian, had an opportunity of appearing about Chester, at the head of five or six hundred men, declaring for a free Parliament, without mentioning the king; but he and Sir Thomas Middleton, who joined him, were defeated by Lambert, and made prisoners.* The king and Duke of York came to Calais, to be in readiness to embark in case it succeeded, but upon the news of its miscarriage they retired, and his majesty, in despair, determined to rely upon the Roman Catholic powers for the future. Several of the Presbyterian ministers appeared in this insurrection, as the Reverend Mr. Newcombe, of Manchester, Mr. Eaton, of Walton, and Mr. Finch, chaplain to Sir George Booth, all afterward ejected by the Act of Uniformity.

The Parliament, to secure the Republican government, first appointed an oath of abjuration, whereby they renounced allegiance to Charles Stuart, and the whole race of King James, and promised fidelity to the commonwealth, without a single person or the House of Peers. They then attempted the reduction of the army, which had set them up, depending upon the assurances General Monk had given them from Scotland, of his army's entire submission to their orders; but the English officers, instead of submitting, stood in their own defence, and presented another petition to the House, desiring their former address from Wallingford House might not lie asleep, but that Fleetwood, whom they had chosen for their general, might be confirmed in his high station. The House demurred upon the petition, and seeing there was like to be a new contest for dominion, endeavoured to divide the officers, by cashiering some, and paying others their arrears. Upon this, the officers presented a third petition to the same purpose; but the Parliament, being out of all patience, told them their complaints were without just grounds, and cashiered nine of their chiefs, among whom were Lieutenant-general Fleetwood, Lambert, Desborough, Berry, Kelsey, Cobbet, and others of the first rank: by means whereof things were brought to this crisis, that the army must submit to the Parliament, or instantly dissolve them. The discarded officers resolved on the latter, for which purpose, October 13, Lambert with his forces secured all the avenues to the Parliament House, and as the speaker passed by Whitehall, he rode up to his coach, and having told him there was nothing to be done at Westminster, commanded Major Creed to conduct him back to his house. At the same time all the members were stopped in their passage, and prevented from ta-

* The Parliament so much resented this insurrection, that they disfranchised the city of Chester.— *Dr. Grey's Examination*, vol. iii., p. 242.—ED.

king their seats in Parliament, Fleetwood having placed a strong guard at the door of the Parliament House for that purpose. Thus, the remains of the Long Parliament, after they had sat five months and six days, having no army to support them, were turned out of their house a second time by a company of headstrong officers, who knew how to pull down, but could not agree upon any form of government to set up in its place.

There being now a perfect anarchy, the officers, who were masters of the nation, first appointed a council of ten of their own body to take care of the public, and having restored their general officers, they concluded upon a select number of men to assume the administration, under the title of a Committee of Safety, which consisted of twenty-three persons, who had the same authority and power that the late council of state had, to manage all public affairs, till they could agree upon a new settlement. The people of England were highly disgusted with these changes, but there was no Parliament or king to fly to; many of the gentry, therefore, from several parts, sent letters to General Monk in Scotland, inviting him to march his army into England to obtain a free Parliament, and promising him all necessary assistance.

The Committee of Safety, being aware of this, attempted an accommodation with Monk by Clarges his brother-in-law, but without success; for they had not sat above a fortnight before they received letters from Scotland full of reproaches for their late violation of faith to the Parliament, and of the general's resolution to march his army into England to restore them. Upon this Lambert was sent immediately to the frontiers, who, quartering his soldiers about Newcastle, put a stop to Monk's march for about a month. In the mean time, the general, in order to gain time, sent commissioners to London, to come to terms with the Committee of Safety, who were so supple, that a treaty was concluded November 15, but when it was brought to Monk he pretended his commissioners had exceeded their instructions, and refused to ratify it. The Council of State, therefore, which sat before the Rump Parliament was interrupted, taking advantage of this, resolved to gain over Monk to their party, and, being assembled privately, sent him a commission, constituting him general of the armies of England, Scotland, and Ireland, which was the very thing he desired.

At this juncture died Sergeant Bradshaw, who sat as-judge and pronounced sentence of death on King Charles at his trial: he died with a firm belief of the justice of putting his majesty to death in the manner it was done, and said that if it were to do again, he would be the first man that should do it: he was buried in a very pompous manner in Westminster Abbey, being attended by most of the members of the Long Parliament, and other gentlemen of quality, November 22, 1659, but his body was not suffered to rest long in its grave.*

* At the Restoration Bradshaw was exhumed, and, with Cromwell, hanged on a gallows; and on the 30th of January, 1660, the anniversary of Charles I.'s death, their heads were set upon poles on the top of Westminster Hall, where they remained twenty years.— Noble's House of Cromwell, vol. i., p. 290.—C.

The general having secured Scotland, and put garrisons into the fortified places, marched to the borders with no more than five thousand men; but while Lambert was encamped about Newcastle to oppose his progress, it appeared that the nation was sick of the phrensies of the officers, and willing to prefer any government to the present anarchy; Portsmouth and part of the fleet revolted, and declared for a free Parliament, as did several of the detachments of the army; upon which Lambert retired towards London, and made way for Monk's entering England. The Committee of Safety, seeing all things in confusion, and not knowing whom to trust, resigned their authority, and restored the Parliament, which met again December 26, and would now have been glad to have had Monk back again in Scotland: for this purpose, they sent letters to acquaint him with their restoration, and that now he might return to his government in Scotland; but the general, having entered England January 2, continued his march towards London, designing a new as well as a free Parliament. When he came to York, Lord Fairfax received him into that city, and declared for a new and free Parliament; as did the London apprentices, and great numbers of all ranks and orders of men, both in city and country. The Rump being suspicious that Monk had some farther design, either of establishing himself after the example of Cromwell, or of restoring the king, obliged him to take the oath of abjuration of Charles Stuart, already mentioned, and to swear that, by the grace and assistance of Almighty God, he would be true, faithful, and constant to the Parliament and commonwealth; and that he would oppose the bringing in or setting up any single person or House of Lords in this commonwealth. They also sent Mr. Scot and Robinson to be spies upon his conduct, who came to him at Leicester, where he received addresses from divers parts, to restore the secluded Presbyterian members of 1648, which was the first step towards the king's restoration. Thus a few giddy politicians at the head of an army, through ambition, envy, lust of power, or because they knew not what to carve out for themselves, threw the whole kingdom back into confusion, and made way for that restoration they were most afraid of, and which, without their own quarrels, and insulting every form of government that had been set up, could not have been accomplished.

When the general came to St. Alban's, he sent a message to desire the Parliament to remove the regiments quartered in the city to some distance, which they weakly complied with, and made way for Monk's entrance with his forces in a sort of triumph, February 3, 1659–60. Being conducted to the Parliament House, the speaker gave him thanks for his great and many services; and the general having returned the compliment, acquainted the House that several applications had been made to him, in his march from Scotland, for a full and free Parliament; for the admission of the secluded members in 1648, without any previous oath or engagement, and that the present Parliament would determine their sitting. To all which he had replied, that they were now a free Parliament, and had voted to fill up their house in order to their being a full Parliament; but to restore the secluded members without a previous oath to the present government, is what had never been done in England ; but he took the liberty to add, that he was of opinion that the fewer oaths the better, provided they took care that neither the Cavaliers nor fanatics should have any share in the administration."

The citizens of London being Presbyterians, fell in with Monk, in hopes of a better establishment, and came to a bold resolution in common council, February 17, to pay no more taxes till the Parliament was filled up. Upon this, the House, to show their resentment, ordered the general to march into the city; to seize eleven of the most active common councilmen, and to pull down their gates, chains, and portcullisses. This was bidding them defiance at a time when they ought to have courted their friendship. Monk, having arrested the common councilmen, prayed the Parliament to suspend the execution of the remaining part, but they insisting upon his compliance, he obeyed. The citizens were enraged at this act of violence; and Monk's friends told him that his embroiling himself with the city in this manner would inevitably be his ruin, for without their assistance he could neither support himself nor obtain another Parliament; people being now generally of opinion with Oliver Cromwell, that the Rump Parliament was designed to be perpetual, and their government as arbitrary as the most despotic king. Monk, therefore, convinced of his mistake, resolved to reconcile himself to the magistracy of the city, in order to which, he sent his brother Clarges to assure them of his concern for what he had done; and having summoned a council of officers in the night, he sent a letter to the Parliament, insisting upon their issuing out writs to fill up their house, and, when filled, to rise at an appointed time, and give way to a full and free Parliament. Upon reading this letter, the House voted him thanks, and sent to acquaint him that they were taking measures to satisfy his request; but the general, not willing to trust himself in their hands, broke up from Whitehall, and having been invited by the Lord-mayor of London, and the chief Presbyterian ministers, marched his whole army into the city; and a common council being called, he excused his late conduct, and acquainted them with the letter he had sent to the House, assuring them that he would now stand by them to the utmost of his power. This appeased the angry citizens, and caused them to treat him as their friend, notwithstanding what had happened the day before. When the news of this reconciliation was spread through the town, the Parliament were struck with surprise; but there was a perfect triumph among the people; the bells rung, bonfires were made, and numbers of rumps thrown into them; in contempt of the Parliament.

The general, being now supported by the citizens, proceeded to restore the secluded members of 1648 who were of the Presbyterian party :* for this purpose, he appointed a conference between them and some of the sitting members, which miscarried, because the sitting members could not undertake that the Parliament would stand to their agreement. Upon

which, Monk resolved to restore them immediately by force, lest the Parliament and their army should come to an accommodation, and dislodge him from the city. Accordingly, he summoned the secluded members to Whitehall, February 24, and having acquainted them with his design, exhorted them to take care of the true interest of the nation, and told them "that the citizens of London were for a commonwealth, the old foundations of monarchy being so broken that it could not be restored but upon the ruins of the people, who had engaged for the Parliament; for if the king should return," says he, "he will govern by arbitrary will and power. Besides, if the government of the State be monarchical, the Church must follow, and prelacy be brought in, which I know the nation cannot bear, and have sworn against it; and therefore a moderate, not a rigid Presbyterian government, with liberty of conscience, will be the most acceptable way to the Church's settlement."* He then obliged them to subscribe the following articles : " 1. To settle the armies so as to preserve the peace. 2. To provide for their support; and pay their arrears. 3. To constitute a council of state for Scotland and Ireland. And, 4. To call a new Parliament and dissolve the present." And so dismissed them with a strong party of guards to see them take their places in the House. This speech was very different from what is pretended the general had in view, and seems to have been drawn up by some of the more moderate Presbyterians, with whom he kept a close correspodence. And though he did not turn the members out of the House as Cromwell did, yet his discharging the Parliament-guards, and placing a strong body of his own horse at the House, without leave of the Parliament, gave them sufficiently to understand what would be the consequence of their making opposition.

The House, thus enlarged, became entirely Presbyterian. They ratified the vote of December, 1648, viz., that the king's concessions at the Isle of Wight were a sufficient ground for peace. They annulled the Engagement of 1649. They put the militia into new hands, with this limitation, that none should be employed in that trust but who would first declare, under their hands, that they believed the war raised by both houses of Parliament against the king was just and lawful, till such time as force and violence were used upon the Parliament, in 1648. They repealed the oath of abjuration of Charles Stuart. They appointed a new council of state, and declared for a free commonwealth; for a learned and pious ministry; for the continuance of tithes, and for the augmentation of smaller livings by the tenths and first-fruits. They resolved to encourage the two universities, and all other schools of learning. And, to content the Independents, they voted that provision should be made for a due liberty of conscience in matters of religion, according to the Word of God.

Thus all things seemed to return to the condition they were in at the treaty of the Isle of Wight. The Presbyterians being now again in the saddle, a day of thanksgiving was kept; after which, the city ministers petitioned for the redress of sundry grievances ; as, 1. "That a

---

* Dr. Grey has given a list of those secluded members.—*Examination*, vol. iii., p. 250.—ED.

* Kennet's Chron., p. 63, 64.

more effectual course be taken against the papists. 2. That the Quakers be prohibited opening their shops on the Sabbath-day. 3. That the public ministers may not be disturbed in their public services." They requested the House to establish the Assembly's Confession of Faith, Directory, and Catechisms ; to appoint persons for approbation of ministers, till the next Parliament should take farther order ; and to call another Assembly, of Divines, to be chosen by the ministers of the several counties, to heal the divisions of the nation.*

In answer to these requests, the House agreed to a bill, March 2, for approbation of public ministers, according to the Directory, and named Dr. Manton, and several others of the Presbyterian persuasion, for that service ; which passed into an act March 14. They declared for the Assembly's Confession of Faith, except the thirtieth and thirty-first chapters of the discipline, and appointed a committee to prepare an act, declaring it to be the public confession of faith of the Church of England. The act passed the House March 5, and was ordered to be printed ; Dr. Reynolds, Dr. Manton, and Mr. Calamy, to have the care of the press. On the same day they ordered the solemn League and Covenant to be reprinted, and set up in every church in England, and read publicly by the minister once every year.

Thus Presbytery was restored to all the power it had ever enjoyed ; and the ministers of that persuasion were in full possession of all the livings in England. A reform was made in the militia ; and the chief places of profit, trust, and honour were put into their hands. The army was in disgrace, the Independents deprived of all their influence, and all things managed by the Presbyterians, supported by Monk's forces. After this the Long Parliament passed an act for their own dissolution, and for calling a new Parliament to meet April 25, 1660, the candidates for which were to declare, under their hands, that the war against the late king was just and lawful ;† and all who had assisted in any war against the Parliament since January 1, 1641, they and their sons were made incapable of being elected, unless they had since manifested their good affection to the Parliament.‡ They then appointed a new council of state, consisting of thirty-one persons, to take care of the government ; and dissolved themselves March 16, after they had sat, with sundry intermissions, nineteen years, four months, and thirteen days.

We are now come to the dawn of the Restoration, of which General Monk has had the reputation of being the chief instrument. This gentleman was the son of Sir Thomas Monk, of Potheridge in Devonshire, and served the king in the wars for some years; but, being taken prisoner, he changed sides, and acted for the Parliament. He afterward served Oliver Cromwell, and was by him left commander-in-chief

of the forces in Scotland, from whence he now marched into England to restore the Parliament. Lord Clarendon and Echard say " he was of a reserved nature, of deep thoughts, and of few words ; and what he wanted in fine elocution, he had in sound judgment. That he had a natural secrecy in him, prevalent upon all his qualifications of a soldier ; a strong body, a mind not easily disordered, an invincible courage, and a sedate and uniform contempt of death, without any phrensy of fanaticism or superstition to turn his head." This is the language of flattery. Others have set him forth in a very different light ; they admit that he was bold and enterprising, but had nothing of the gentleman, nor had any depth of contrivance ; that he was perpetually wavering, and betrayed all whom he served but Cromwell. Ludlow says he was a man of covetous temper, and of no principles ; of a vicious life and scandalous conversation. Father Orleans says that he was a man of slow understanding. And Whitelocke reports that the French ambassador said he had neither sense nor breeding. The truth is, he had a cloudy head, and in no action of his life discovered a quick or fine genius. In the latter part of his life he was sordidly covetous, and sunk into most of the vices of the times. No man ever went beyond him in dissimulation and falsehood, as appears in this very affair of the king's restoration. He took the abjuration oath once under Oliver, and again this very year, whereby he renounced the title of Charles Stuart, and swore to be true to the commonwealth, without a single person or House of Lords.* And yet, in his first message to the king by Sir John Grenville, he assures his majesty that his heart had been ever faithful to him, though he had not been in a condition to serve him till now.† When he came with his army to London, he assured the Rump Parliament of his cheerful obedience to all their commands, and desired them to be very careful that the Cavalier party might have no share in the civil or military power. When he restored the secluded members, he promised the Parliament to take effectual care that they should do no hurt. When the commonwealth's men expressed their fears, and asked the general whether he would join with them against the king, he replied, " I have often declared my resolution so to do ;" and taking Sir Arthur Haslerigge by the hand, he said, " I do here protest to you, in the presence of all these gentlemen, that I will oppose to the utmost the setting up of Charles Stuart, a single person, or a House of Peers." He then expostulated with them about their suspicions : " What is it I have done in bringing these members into the House ?" says he. " Are they not the same that brought the king to the block, though others cut off his head, and that justly ?" And yet this very man, within six months, condemned these persons to the gallows. Nay, farther, the general sent letters to all the regiments, assuring them that the government should continue a commonwealth, that they had no purpose to return to their old bondage, that is, monarchy ; and if any made disturbances in favour of Charles Stuart, he desired they might be secured. So that, if this gentleman was in

---

* Kennet's Chron., p. 52, 75.

† This was the requisition put to such as sought a commission in the army, rather than to candidates for a seat in Parliament; though Kennet, in his margin, applies it to the eligibility of members. He says nothing of the candidates being obliged to sign the declaration. So that Mr. Neal is not quite accurate in his statement of this matter.—ED.

‡ Kennet's Chron., p. 85

---

* Welwood's Mem., p. 117, &c.

† History of the Stuarts, p. 459.

the secret of restoring the king from his entrance into England, or his first coming to London, I may challenge all history to produce a scene of hypocrisy and dissimulation equal to his conduct. Dr. Welwood adds,* that he acted the part of a politician much better than that of a Christian, and carried on the thread of dissimulation with 'wonderful dexterity.' Bishop Burnet differs from the doctor, and says, that "though he had both the praise and the reward, yet a very small share of the restoration belonged to him. The tide ran so strong that the general only went into it dexterously enough to get much fame and great rewards. If he had died soon after, he might have been more justly admired; but he lived long enough to make it known how false a judgment men are apt to make upon outward appearance."†

But before we relate the particulars of the Restoration, it will be proper to consider the abject state of the Church of England, and the religion of the young king. If Cromwell had lived ten or twelve years longer, Episcopacy might have been lost beyond recovery, for by that time the whole bench of bishops would have been dead, and there would have been none to consecrate or ordain for the future, unless they could have obtained a new conveyance from the Church of Rome, or admitted the validity of Presbyterian ordination. This was the case in view, which induced some of the ancient bishops to petition the king to fill up the vacant sees with all expedition, in which they were supported by Sir Edward Hyde, chancellor of the exchequer, who prevailed with his majesty to nominate certain clergymen for those

high preferments, and sent over a list of the names to Dr. Barwick, to be communicated by him to the Bishops of London, Ely, Sarum, and others who were to be concerned in the consecration. It was necessary to carry on this design with a great deal of secrecy, lest the governing powers should secure the bishops, and by that means put a stop to the work. It was no less difficult to provide persons of learning and character who would accept the charge, when it would expose them to sufferings, as being contrary to the laws in being, and when there was no prospect of restoring the Church. But the greatest difficulty of all was, how to do it in a canonical manner, when there were no deans and chapters to elect, and, consequently, no persons to receive a congé d'elire, according to ancient custom.

Several expedients were proposed for removing this difficulty. Sir Edward Hyde was of opinion that the proceeding should be by a mandate from the king to any three or four bishops, by way of collation, upon the lapse, for the dean and chapters' non-election. But it was objected, that the supposal of a lapse would impair the king's prerogative more than the collation would advance it, because it would presuppose a power of election pleno-jure in the deans and chapters; which they have only de facultate regia; nor could they petition for such a license, because most of the deans were dead, some chapters extinguished, and all of them so disturbed that they could not meet in the Chapter House, where such acts regularly are to be performed.

Dr. Barwick,* who was in England, and cor-

---

* Memoirs, p. 117, 120,
† Burnet's History, vol. i., p. 126, 12mo. I subjoin the following from another source : "George Monk was a gentleman by birth, being descended of a very ancient and respectable family in Devonshire: he was related to the blood royal by his great-grandmother, daughter of Arthur Plantagenet, Viscount Lisle. He was at first a Royalist, but happening to become a prisoner to the Parliamentarians, they converted him to their sentiments; he was an able officer, and as such, rose in their army. The elder protector trusted him much, though he suspected him of being inclined to the interests of Charles Stuart, but he was a good subject to both Oliver and Richard : after the ruin of the latter, he was at a loss which side to declare for, and had thoughts of seating himself in the protectorship, as France offered to support him; but he was ordered to espouse the royal interest by his wife, who had been his mistress, and is said to have been the daughter of a blacksmith, to whom he bore an implicit obedience ; therefore, at the expense of a thousand perjuries, he was the main instrument in seating Charles upon the throne of his ancestors; at least, in causing his return without any conditions; a great misfortune to the royal family, as well as these kingdoms. He was rewarded with the title of Duke of Albemarle, honoured with the garter, and as many other titles and places as he would accept. The dukedom became extinct in his son. He himself died January 4, 1670, and was buried in Westminster Abbey at the public expense, and almost in regal style. His duchess died January 23, a few days after him. She retained that vulgarity when duchess which she had early imbibed; she was a most turbulent woman, and Monk was more fearful of her than an army. It is said she would even give him manual correction. The duke was awkward and stupid in a drawing-room, and respectable only in the camp."—Noble's Memoirs of House of Cromwell, vol, i., p. 389.—C.

VOL. II.—B B

* The Dr. Barwick to whom Mr. Neal refers was a singular and eminent character at this period : an active and zealous adherent to the Kings Charles I. and II. He managed with great address and dexterity the correspondence of the first with the city of London, when he was at Oxford. He corresponded with the second while he was abroad; and was sent by the bishops, as will afterward appear, with their instructions to him at Breda, where he preached before him, and was made one of his chaplains. He had the chief hand in the Querela Cantabrigiensis, and wrote against the Covenant. It was much owing to his influence that the Cambridge plate was presented to the king; and he is said to have furnished Lord Clarendon with a great part of the materials for his history. He was so dexterous in all his communications as to elude the vigilance of Thurloe. He was born April 20, 1612, at Wetherslack in Westmoreland, and received his classical learning at Sedberg School in Yorkshire, where he distinguished himself by acting the part of Hercules in one of Seneca's tragedies. In the eighteenth year of his age he was sent to St. John's College, Cambridge; where, so eminent were his abilities and attainments, that he was chosen, when he was little more than twenty, by the members of his college, to be their advocate in a controverted election of a master, which was heard before the privy council. He resided some time in Durham House in London, as chaplain to the bishop, Dr. Morton, who bestowed on him a prebend in his cathedral, and the rich rectories of Wolsingham and of Houghton-in-le-Spring. In 1660, Charles II. promoted him to the deanery of Durham ; and before the end of the year he was removed from that dignity to the deanery of St. Paul's. On the 18th of February, 1661, he was chosen prolocutor of the Convocation. He died in the year 1664, aged fifty-two. He united in his character, with his loyalty, sincere devotion with sanctity of manners, and an undaunted spirit under his sufferings in the royal

responded with the chancellor, proposed that his majesty should grant his commissions to the bishops of each province, respectively assembled in provincial council, or otherwise, as should be most convenient, to elect and consecrate fit persons for the vacant sees, with such dispensative clauses as should be found necessary upon the emergency of the case, his majesty signifying his pleasure concerning the persons and the sees, which commission may bear date before the action, and then afterward upon certificate, and petition to have his majesty's ratification—and confirmation of the whole process, and the register to be drawn up accordingly by the chief actuary, who may take his memorials ,hence, and make up the record there.*

Dr. Bramhall, bishop of Derry, was for the Irish way, where the king has an absolute power of nomination ; and, therefore, no way seemed to him so safe as consecrating the persons nominated to void sees in Ireland, and then removing them to others in England, which he apprehended would clearly elude all these formalities, which seemed to perplex the affair ; but this was thought an ill precedent, as it opened a door for destroying the privileges of the Church of England in their capitular elections. The old Bishop of Ely was so far from wishing, with Dr. Bramhall, that the Irish method might be introduced into England, that he said, if he should live to see the Church restored, he would be an humble suiter to his majesty, that the privileges of the English Church, in their elections of bishops, might be introduced into Ireland.

Dr. Wren, bishop of Ely, and Dr. Cosins, of Peterborough, were for an expedient something like the second, to which the court agreed, and Mr. Chancellor Hyde wrote to Dr. Barwick for the form of such a commission—as they judged proper, and urged that it might be despatched with all possible, expedition. The chancellor had this affair very much at heart, but the old bishops were fearful lest it should be discovered, in which case they were sure to be the sufferers. Dr. Brownrigge, of Exeter, and Dr. Skinner, of Oxford, declined meddling in the affair; the rest declared their willingness to advance the work, but lived in hopes there might be no occasion for the hazard. The chancellor, in one of his letters, says the king was much troubled that no more care was taken of the Church by those who should be the guardians of it. He censures the slowness of the clergy, and says it was very indecent, when their afflicted mother was in extremity, any of her sons should be timorous and fearful. Such were the chancellor's narrow principles, who seemed to lay the essence of Christianity, and the virtue of all Divine ordinances, upon the conveyance of ecclesiastical power by an uninterrupted succession from the apostles.

The nonjurors had the like case in view after

cause, for which he was imprisoned in a dungeon in the Tower. He was then far gone in a consumption ; but living upon gruel and vegetables, he, after some time, recovered to a miracle.—*See his Life*; and *Granger's History of England*, vol. iii., p. 257, 8vo.—ED.

* Life of Barwick, p. 204. Kennet's Chron., p. 14, 15.

the Revolution, and provided for it in the best manner they could. But is not the Christian world in a sad condition, if the Christian bishop cannot be chosen or consecrated without a royal mandate, and the suffrage of *a dean and chapter,. when there were no such officers in the Church for three hundred years after the apostles ?* and if the validity of all sacerdotal ministrations must depend on a regular uninterrupted succession from St. Peter ! especially as Baronius, a popish historian, confesses that, in a succession of fifty popes, not one pious or virtuous man sat in the chair ; that there had been no popes for some years together ; and at other times two or three at once ; and when the same writer admits between twenty and thirty schisms, one of which continued fifty years, the Popes of Avignon and Rome excommunicating each other, and yet conferring orders upon their several clergy. How impossible is it to trace the right line through so much confusion !*

But with regard to the king, his concern for the regular consecration of Protestant bishops was a mere farce ; for if he was not a papist before this time, it is certain he was reconciled to the Church of Rome this year, at the Pyrenean treaty concluded between France and Spain at Fontarabia, whither he had repaired *incognito* to engage them in his interest. Here the king stayed twenty days, in which time his majesty, with the Earl of Bristol, and Sir H. Bennet, embraced the Roman Catholic religion. The secret of this affair was well known to Lord Clarendon, though he is pleased to mention it with great tenderness. "It is believed," says his lordship, "by wise men, that in that treaty somewhat was agreed to the prejudice of the Protestant interest ; and that in a short time there would have been much done against it, both in France and Germany, if the measures they had then taken had not been shortly broken, chiefly by the surprising revolution in England, which happened the next year, and also by the death of the two great favourites of the two crowns,. Don Lewis de Haro, and Cardinal Mazarine, who both died not long after it."† But the secret of the king's reconciliation to the Church of Rome has been more fully acknowledged, of late years, by the eldest son of Lord Clarendon, and by the Duke of Ormond, who declared to several persons of honour, that " he himself, to his great surprise and concern, accidentally, in a morning early, saw the king in the great church on his knees before the high altar, with several priests and ecclesiastics about him. That he was soon after confirmed in his sentiments by Sir Henry Bennet and the Earl of Bristol, who both owned the king to be a Catholic as well as themselves ; but it was agreed that this change should be kept as the greatest secret imaginable." There is another story, says Bishop Kennet, which I have reason

* It seems almost impossible that American ministers can be so infatuated as to swallow the absurdities of this same Divine apostolical succession! But Prelacy is one and the same thing in all ages, and the world over. The claims of the Bishop of London are not a jot more revolting than those of our Right Reverend Fathers in God, who forbid laymen to speak in conventions, or dare to question their apostolic movements.—C.

† Echard, p. 751.

to think true : "Sir H. Bennet was soon after seen to wait on the king from mass, at which sight the Lord Culpeper had so much indignation, that he went up to Bennet and spoke to this effect : 'I see what you are at'; is this the way to bring our master home to his three kingdoms? Well, sir, if ever you and I live to see England together, I will have your head, or you shall have mine;' which words struck such terror upon Sir Harry Bennet, that he never durst set his foot in England till after the death of Lord Culpeper, who met with a very surprising end soon after the king's return."*

But, though the prime ministers of France and Spain were now first witnesses of his majesty's abjuring the Protestant religion, there are strong presumptions that he was a papist long before, even before his brother James, if we may credit the testimony of his confessor, Father Huddleston.† To the proofs of this fact, already mentioned under the year 1652, I would add the testimony of the author of the Mystery of Iniquity, printed 1689, who writes thus: "The king's [Charles II.'s] apostacy is not of so late a date as the world is made commonly to believe, for though it was many years concealed, and the contrary pretended and dissembled, yet it is certain he abjured the Protestant religion soon after the exilement of the royal family, and was reconciled to the Church of Rome at St. Germains in France. Nor were several of the then suffering bishops and clergy ignorant of this, though they had neither integrity nor courage to give the nation warning of it."‡ Bishop Burnet, in the History of his Life and Times, confirms this testimony from the cardinal minister, who sent an advertisement of it to the bishop himself; for he says, "that before the king left Paris (which was in June, 1654) he changed his religion, but by whose persuasion is not yet known; only Cardinal de Retz was in the secret, and Lord Aubigny had a great hand in it. Chancellor Hyde had some suspicion of it, but would not suffer himself to believe it quite."§ And Sir Allen Broderick declared upon his deathbed that King Charles II. made profession of the popish religion at Fontainebleau before he was sent out of France to Cologne.

The Dutch Protestants suspected the change, but the king denied it in the most public manner; for when he was at Brussels in the year 1658, he wrote the following letter to the Reverend Mr. Cawton, the Presbyterian minister of the English congregation at Rotterdam :

"CHARLES REX.

"Trusty and well beloved, we greet you well. We have received so full testimony of your affection to our person, and zeal for our service, that we are willing to recommend an affair to you in which we are much concerned. We do not wonder that the malice of our enemies should continue to lay all manner of scandals upon us, but are concerned that they should find credit with any to make our affection to the Protestant religion suspected, since the world cannot but take notice of our constant and uninterrupted profession of it in all places. No

man has or can more manifest his affection to, and zeal for the Protestant religion, than we have done. Now, as you cannot but have much conversation with the ministers of the Dutch Church, we presume and expect that you will use your utmost diligence and dexterity to root out those unworthy aspersions so maliciously and groundlessly laid upon us by wicked men; and that you assure all that will give credit to you, that we value ourselves so much upon that part of our title, of being defender of the faith, that no worldly consideration can ever prevail with us to swerve from it, and the Protestant religion in which we have been bred, the propagation whereof we shall endeavour with our utmost power. Given at Bruxels, November 7, in the tenth year of our reign."

To carry on the disguise, Dr. Morley, afterward Bishop of Winchester, was employed to write an apologetical letter to Dr. Trigland, the Dutch minister at the Hague, to assert and prove the king's steadfastness to the Reformed faith and communion. The letter was dated June 7, 1659, a little before the king's going to the Pyrenean treaty, to engage the Roman Catholic powers for his restoration:*

But to confirm the Presbyterians farther, and to put an end to all suspicions of his majesty's being turned papist, Sir Robert Murray and the Countess of Balcarras were employed to engage the most eminent Reformed ministers in France to write to their Presbyterian brethren in England, and assure them of the king's steadfastness in the Protestant faith, and to excuse his not joining with the church at Charenton. Accordingly, these credulous ministers, not being acquainted with the secret, wrote to their brethren at London to the following purpose:

Monsieur Raymond Gaches, pastor of the Reformed Church at Paris, to the Rev. Mr. Baxter, March 23, 1659–60: "I know what odium has been cast upon the king; some are dissatisfied in his constancy to the true religion. I will not answer what truly may be said, that it belongs not to subjects to inquire into the prince's religion; be he what he will, if the right of reigning belongs to him, obedience in civil matters is his due. But this prince never departed from the public profession of the true religion; nor did he disdain to be present at our religious assemblies at Roan and Rochelle, though he never graced our church at Paris with his presence, which truly grieved us."†

Monsieur Drelincourt, another of the French pastors at Paris, writes, March 24, "A report is here, that the thing which will hinder the king's restoration is the opinion conceived by some of his being turned Roman Catholic, and the fear that in time he will ruin the Protestant religion. But I see no ground for the report, his majesty making no profession of it, but, on the contrary has rejected all the aids and advantages offered him upon that condition. Charity is not jealous, and if it forbids us to suspect on slight grounds private persons, how can it approve jealousies upon persons so sacred! Besides, there are in the king's family, and among his domestics, some gentlemen of our religion, and my old friends, who at several times have given me assurances of the piety of this prince, and his stability in the profession he makes.

---

* Kennet, p. 238. † Welwood's Memoirs, p. 126.
‡ Kennet's Chron., p. 598.
§ Burnet, vol. i., p. 103, 104, 12mo.

* Kennet's Chron., p. 95. † Ibid., p. 91, 92.

Your Presbyterians are now intrusted with the honour of our churches; if they recall this prince without the intervening of any foreign power, they will acquire to themselves immortal 'glory, and stop their mouths forever, who charge us falsely as enemies to royalty, and make appear that the maxim, No bishop, no king, is falsely imputed to us."

The famous Monsieur Daillé, of Paris, in his letter of April 7, 1660, writes to the same purpose : "I know it is reported that the king has changed his religion ; but who can believe a thing so contrary to all probability? Nothing of this appears to us ; on the contrary, we well know that, when he has resided in places where the exercise of his religion is not permitted, he has always had his chaplains with him, who have regularly performed Divine service. Moreover, all Paris knows the anger the king expressed at the endeavours that were used to pervert the Duke of Gloucester. And though it is objected that he never came to our church at Charenton, yet, as we are better informed of this than any one, we can testify that religion was not the cause of it, but that it was upon political and prudential considerations, which may be peculiar to our church, for he has gone to sermon in Caen and some other towns ; and in Holland he heard some sermons from the famous Monsieur More, our present colleague. Thus, sir, it is more clear than the day, that whatsoever has been reported till this time of the change of this prince's religion, is a mere calumny."*

Monsieur de l'Angle, minister of the Protestant Church at Rouen, wrote upon the same subject to his friend in London, more fully to evidence the king's steadfastness in the Protestant religion. These letters were printed and industriously spread over the whole kingdom.

The king himself, in his letter to the House of Commons, says, "Do you desire the advancement of the Protestant religion? We have, by our constant profession and practice, given sufficient testimony to the world that neither unkindness of those of the same faith towards us, nor the civilities and protestations of those of a contrary profession, could in the least degree startle us, or make us swerve from it."†

* Kennet's Chron., p. 94, 95.

† The reader will find very curious information respecting Charles's religious opinions in Jesse's Court of the Stuarts. He will probably gather, from those passages, that Charles, from his earliest exile, held himself ready to confess himself a convert to that faith which was the most likely to assist his restoration. The earliest intimation of Charles's conversion to popery is on the authority of the Duke of Ormond. At Fontarabia, in 1659, the duke, we are told, to his great surprise and concern, accidentally, one morning early, saw the king in the great church on his knees before the high altar, with several priests and ecclesiastics about him ; that he was soon after confirmed in his sentiments by Sir Henry Bennet and the Earl of Bristol, who both owned the king to be a Catholic as well as themselves ; the former was of opinion that the king ought, in policy, to declare his religion as the most hopeful method to recover his dominions. But the latter looked upon it as the most dangerous advice that could be given, such as would be the ruin of the king's cause ; and it was finally agreed by the majority of the little court there, that this change should be kept as the greatest secret imaginable. After perusing this pas-

It is a surprising reflection of Mr. Baxter,* upon occasion of these letters : " These divines," says he, " knew nothing of the state of affairs in England. They knew not those men who were to be restored with the king. They pray," says he, " for the success of my labours, when they are persuading me to put an end to my labours by setting up those prelates, who will silence me and many hundreds more. They persuade me to that which will separate me from my flock, and then pray that I may be a blessing to them ; and yet," says he, " I am for restoring the king, that when we are silenced, and our ministry at an end, and some of us lie in prisons, we may there, and in that condition, have peace of conscience in the discharge of our duty, and the exercise of faith, patience, and charity in our sufferings." Was there ever such reasoning as this? But the reader will make his own remarks upon these extraordinary paragraphs.

To return back to General Monk in Scotland. As long as the army governed affairs at Westminster, the general was on their side, and entertained Mr. John Collins, an Independent minister, for his chaplain ; but upon the quarrel between the army and Parliament, and Monk's declaring for the latter, it was apprehended he had changed sides, and would fall in with the Presbyterians ; upon which, Mr. Caryl and Barker were sent to Scotland with a letter from Dr. Owen, expressing their fears of the danger of their religious liberties upon a revolution of government. The general received them with all the marks of esteem ; and after a few days returned the following answer, in a letter directed to Dr. Owen, Mr. Greenhill, and Mr. Hook, to be communicated to the churches in and about London :

" Honourable and dear Friends,

" I received yours, and am very sensible of your kindness expressed to the army in Scotland, in sending such honourable and reverend persons, whom we received with thankfulness and great joy as the messengers of the churches, and the ministers of Christ in these three nations. I do promise you for myself, and the rest of the officers here, that your interest, liberty, and encouragement shall be very dear to us. And we shall take this as a renewed obligation to assert to the utmost what we have already declared to the churches of Jesus Christ. I doubt not but you have received satisfaction of our inclinations to a peaceable accommodation. I do hope that, some differences being obviated, we shall obtain a fair composure. I do assure you that the great things that have been upon my heart to secure and provide for, are our liberties and freedom, as the subjects and servants of Jesus Christ, which we have conveyed to us in the covenant of grace, as-

sage, it is amusing to turn to the pages of the obsequious Fuller. "During the king's continuance beyond the seas," says that writer, "great were the proffers tended to him of forsaking the Protestant religion. But, alas! as soon might the impotent waves remove the most sturdy rocks, as they once unfix him : such his constancy, whom neither the frowns of his affliction, nor smiles of secular advantage, could make to warp from his first principles." "This," says Jesse, "is nonsense, and Dr. Fuller probably knew as much; at all events, he could not have been in ignorance of Charles's character."—C.

* Life, part ii., p. 210.

sured in the promises purchased by the blood of our Saviour for us, and given as his great legacy to his Church and people ; in comparison of which, we esteem all other things as dung and dross, but as they have a relation to, and dependance upon this noble end. The others are our laws and rights as men, which must have their esteem in the second place ; for which many members of churches have been eminent instruments to labour in sweat and blood for these eighteen years last past, and our ancestors for many hundred years before ; the substance of which may be reduced to a parliamentary government, and the people's consenting to the laws by which they are governed. That these privileges of the nation may be so bounded that the churches may have both security and settlement, is my great desire, and of those with me ; so that I hope you will own these just things, and give us that assistance that becomes the churches of Christ, in pursuance of this work. And we do assure you we shall comply as far as possible, with respect had to the security and safety of the nation, and the preservation of our ancient birthright and liberties. And we shall pray that we may be kept from going out of God's way in doing God's work.

"I do, in the name of the whole army and myself, give all our affectionate thanks for this your work of love ; and though we are not able to make such returns as are in our hearts and desires to do, yet we shall endeavour, by all ways and means, to express our care and love to the churches, and shall leave the reward to him who is the God of peace, and has in special assured all blessings to the peacemakers. I conclude with the words of David, 1 Sam,. xxv., 32, 'Blessed be the Lord God of Israel, and blessed be your advice,' and blessed be you all. Now the Lord God be a wall of fire round about you, and let his presence be in his churches, and they filled with his glory. I have no more, but to entreat your prayers for a happy issue of this unhappy difference ; which is the prayer of him who is, reverend sirs and dear friends, your very affectionate brother and servant,

" G. MONK.

"Edinburgh, Nov. 23, 1659."

In one of the general's letters to the Parliament, written about June, 1659, he declares strongly for liberty of conscience, and an absolute commonwealth, in language which in another would be called the fumes of fanaticism. "You are the people," says he, "who have filled the world with wonder, but nothing is difficult to faith ; and the promises of God are sure and certain. We acknowledge that we ourselves have very much contributed to the Lord's departing from our Israel, but we see God's hour is come, and the time of the people's deliverance, even the set time, is at hand. He cometh skipping over all the mountains of sin and unworthiness, &c. We humbly beseech you not to heal the wounds of the daughter of God's people slightly, but to make so sure and lasting provision for both Christian and civil rights, as both this and future generations may have cause to rise up and call you blessed, and the blackest of designs may never be able to cast dirt in your faces any more."* He then desires them

to encourage none but godly ministers and magistrates, that no yoke may be imposed upon conscience but what is agreeable to the Word of God, and that they would establish the government in a free state or commonwealth. Signed by General Monk and twenty-five of his chief officers.

Upon the general's coming to London, he was transformed at once into a zealous Presbyterian, and thought no more of the Independent churches ; he received the sacrament at Mr. Calamy's church, and would suffer none to preach before him but whom he approved. He consulted the Presbyterian ministers, and asked their advice in all important affairs. It seems these were the gentlemen that beat him out of his commonwealth principles, if we may believe the Reverend Mr. Sharp, afterward Archbishop of St. Andrew's, whose words are these, in one of his letters to the Reverend Mr. Douglas in Scotland : " Sunday last, March 11, the general sent his coach for Mr. Calamy, Mr. Ash, and me ; we had a long conversation with him in private, and convinced him that a commonwealth was impracticable ; and, to our sense, beat him off that sconce he has hitherto maintained. We urged upon him that the Presbyterian interest, which he had espoused, was much concerned in keeping up this house, and settling the government upon terms. But the subtle general replied, that in regard he had declared so lately against a House of Lords, and the continuing this House of Commons, he could not so reputably do it."* Afterward, when some gentlemen of quality, suspecting the king to be at the bottom, were earnest with the general, that if the king must be brought in by the next Parliament, it might be upon the terms of his late majesty's concessions at the Isle of Wight, the general at first recoiled, and declared he would adhere to a commonwealth ; but at last, seeming to be conquered into a compliance, he intimated to them that this was the utmost line he could or would advance in favour of the king ; and yet, when this was moved in the Convention Parliament by Sir Matthew Hale, the general stood up, and declared against all conditions, and threatened them that should encourage such a motion with all the mischiefs that might follow. Thus the credulous Presbyterians were gradually drawn into a snare, and made to believe that Presbytery was to be the established government of the Church of England under King Charles II.

The Scots were equally concerned in this affair, and much more zealous for their discipline. The general, therefore, sent letters to the Kirk, with the strongest assurances that he would take care of their discipline.† But the Scots, not willing to trust him, commissioned Mr. Sharp to be their agent, and gave him instructions to use his best endeavours that the Kirk of Scotland might, without interruption or encroachment, enjoy the freedom and liberty of her established judicatories, and to represent the sinfulness and offensiveness of a toleration in that kingdom. Sharp was to concert measures with Mr. Calamy, Ash, Manton, and Cowper ; but these gentlemen being not very zealous for the discipline, Sharp informed his principals that it was feared the king would come

* Welwood's Memoirs Appendix No. ii.

* Kennet's Chron., p. 81. † Ibid p. 50.

in, and with him moderate Episcopacy, at least in England, but that the more zealous party were doing what they could to keep on foot the Covenant. To which Douglas replied, "It is best that the Presbyterian government be settled simply, for you know that the judgment of honest men here is for admitting the king on no other but covenant terms."

The Independents and Baptists were in such disgrace, that their leaders had not the honour of being consulted in this weighty affair. General Monk and the Presbyterians were united, and had force sufficient to support their claims; the tide was with them, and the Parliament at their mercy. The Independents offered to stand by their friends in Parliament, and to raise four new regiments from among themselves, to force the general back into Scotland. Dr. Owen and Mr. Nye had frequent consultations with Mr. Whitelocke and St. John; and at a private treaty with the officers at Wallingford House, offered to raise £100,000 for the use of the army, provided they would protect them in their religious liberties, which they were apprehensive Monk and the Presbyterians designed to subvert; but those officers had lost their credit; their measures were disconcerted and broken; one party was for a treaty; and another for the sword, but it was too late; their old veteran regiments were dislodged from the city, and Monk in possession. In this confusion, their general, Fleetwood, who had brought them into this distress, retired, and left them a body without a head, after which they became insignificant,' and in a few months quite contemptible. Here ended the power of the army and of the Independents.

Being now to take leave of this people, it may be proper to observe, that the Independents sprang up and mightily increased in the time of the civil wars, and had the reputation of a wise and politic people : they divided from the Presbyterians upon the foot of discipline, and fought in the Parliament's quarrel, not so much for hire and reward, as from a real belief that it was the cause of God ; this inspired their soldiers with courage, and made them face death with undaunted bravery, insomuch that, when the army was new modelled, and filled up with men of this principle, they carried all before them. When the war was ended, they boldly seized the person of the king, and treated him with honour till they found him unsteady to his promises of a toleration of their principles, and then they became his most determined enemies; when they were assured afterward, by the treaty of the Isle of Wight, that they were to be crushed between both parties, and to lose their religious liberty, for which they had been fighting, they tore up the government by the roots, and subverted the whole Constitution. This they did, not in consequence of their religious principles, but to secure their own safety and liberty. After the king's death they assumed the chief management of public affairs, and would not part with it on any terms, lest they should be disbanded and called to account by a parliamentary power, and therefore they could never come to a settlement, though they attempted it under several forms : the first was an absolute commonwealth, as most agreeable to their principles ; but when the commonwealth began to

clip their military wings, they dispossessed them, and set up their own general, with the title of protector, who had skill enough to keep them in awe, though they were continually plotting against his government. After his death they dispossessed his son, and restored the commonwealth. When these again attempted to disband them, they turned them out a second time, and set up themselves under the title of a Committee of Safety ; but they wanted Oliver's head, their new general, Fleetwood, having neither courage nor conduct enough to keep them united. Thus they crumbled into factions, while their wanton sporting with the supreme power made the nation sick of such distractions, and yield to the return of the old Constitution.

The officers were made up chiefly of Independents and Anabaptists, most of them of mean extraction, and far from being as able statesmen as they had been fortunate soldiers ; they were brave and resolute men, who had the cause of religion and liberty at heart ; but they neglected the old nobility and gentry so much, that when they fell to pieces, there was hardly a gentleman of estate or interest in his county that would stand by them. As to their moral character, they seem to have been men of piety and prayer ; they called God into all their councils, but were too much governed by the false notions they had imbibed, and the enthusiastic impulses of their own minds. I do not find that they consulted any number of their clergy, though many of the Independent ministers were among the most learned and eminent preachers of the times, as, Dr. Goodwin, Owen, Nye, and Greenhill, &c., some of whom had no small reputation for politics ; but their pulling down so many forms of government, without adhering steadily to any, issued in their ruin. Thus, as the army and Independents outwitted the Presbyterians in 1648, the Presbyterians, in conjunction with the Scots, blew up the Independents at this time ; and the next year the Episcopal party, by dexterous management of the credulous Presbyterians, undermined and deceived them both.[*]

This year died Dr. Ralph Brownrigge, bishop of Exeter, born at Ipswich in the year 1592, educated at Pembroke Hall, Cambridge, and at length chosen master of Katherine Hall in that university.[†] He was also prebendary of Dur-

*An admirable testimony has been borne by an Episcopalian historian to the liberal policy of the Independents ; and I cite the testimony with pleasure, because it is in strong contrast to the bigotry and ignorance so frequently evinced on the subject. " At the Restoration fell, ultimately, the power of the Independents. With their management of civil matters I shall not now concern myself ; *but all the world will allow that, in point of religious liberty, their conduct when in power (and would that the same could be averred of all other religious bodies !) fulfilled the promises made when they were in obscurity.* They exhibited a noble and memorable example of a sect who, in possessing the citadel of establishment, forgot and forgave the injuries they had sustained, abused not their authority by the oppression of their brethren, and were content to hold the second place, preferring others before themselves in honour and emoluments."—*History of the English Church and Sects, by the Rev. Johnson Grant,* vol. ii., p. 435.—C.

† He was esteemed one of the greatest ornaments of his time to this seminary. He was one of those excellent men with whom Archbishop Tillotson cul-

ham, and rector of Barly in Hertfordshire. In the year 1641 he was nominated to the see of Exeter, and installed June 1, 1642, but the wars between the king and Parliament did not allow him the enjoyment of his dignity. He was nominated one of the Assembly of Divines, and was vice-chancellor of the University of Cambridge in the year 1644, when the Earl of Manchester visited it ; and complied so far as to keep his mastership till the next year, when he was deprived for a sermon he preached upon the anniversary of his majesty's inauguration. He was no favourer of Archbishop Laud's innovations ;* for while he was vice-chancellor he sent for one of Mr. Barwick's pupils, and said to him, " I wonder your tutor, no ill man in other respects, does not yet abstain from that form of worship [bowing down towards the east] which he knows is disagreeable to our excellent Parliament, and not very acceptable to God himself ;† but be you careful to steer your course clear of the dangerous rock of every error, whether it savour of the impiety of Arminianism, or of the superstition of popery."‡

He was succeeded by Dr. Spurstow, and suffered in common with the rest of the bishops ; but being a Calvinist, and a person of great temper and moderation, he was allowed by the Protector Cromwell to be a preacher at the Temple, in which employment he died, December 7, 1659, about the sixty-seventh year of his age. Dr. Gauden says he was a person of great candour, sweetness, gravity, and solidity of judgment. He was consulted by Mr. Baxter and others in several points of controversy, and was indeed a most humble Christian, and very patient under most severe fits of the stone, which were very acute and tedious for some time before his death.

The Reverend Mr. Charles Herle, some time prolocutor of the Assembly of Divines at Westminster, was born of honourable parents at Prideaux Herle, near Lostwithyel in Cornwall, in the year 1598.§ He was educated in Exeter College, Oxon. In the year 1618 he took

tivated an acquaintance at his first coming to London, and by whose preaching and example he formed himself. · His sermons were not exceeded by any published in that period ; and they derived great advantage, in the delivery, from the dignity of his person and the justness of his elocution.—*Granger's History of England*, vol. ii., p. 161, 8vo.—ED.

* Dr. Grey neglects not to inform the reader, on the authority of Dr. Gauden, that Bishop Brownrigge was tenacious of the doctrine, worship, devotion, and government of the Church of England, " which," he said, " he liked better and better as he grew older." He seems to have been very free in his advice to Cromwell ; for when the protector, with some show of respect to him, demanded his judgment in some public affairs, then at a nonplus, Bishop Brownrigge, with his wonted gravity and freedom, replied, " My lord, the best counsel I can give you is that of our Saviour, Render unto Cæsar the things that are Cæsar's, and unto God the things that are God's :" with which free answer the protector rested rather silenced than satisfied.—*Dr. Grey's Examination*, vol. iii., p. 258.—ED.

† This form still exists in the Episcopal Church, and bowing and courtesying to the east may be seen at the present day. So far from the Church having thrown off her points of semblance to popery, she seems at the present day to be studiously keeping them in repair.—C.

‡ Life of Barwick, p. 17.
§ Wood's Athenæ Oxon. vol. ii., p. 151 152.

the degrees in arts, and was afterward rector of Winwick in Lancashire, one of the richest livings in England, and was always esteemed a Puritan. When the wars broke out, he took part with the Parliament, was elected one of the members of the Assembly of Divines, and upon the death of Dr. Twisse in 1646, was appointed prolocutor. After the king's death he retired to his living at Winwick, and was in very high esteem with all the clergy in that country.· In the year 1654 he was appointed one of the assistant commissioners for ejecting scandalous ministers, together with Mr. Isaac Ambrose and Mr. Gee. He was a moderate Presbyterian, and left behind him some practical and controversial writings. Mr. Fuller says* he was so much of a Christian, scholar, and gentleman, that he could agree in affection with those who differed from him in judgment. He died at his parsonage at Winwick, in the sixty-first year of his age, and was buried in his own church. September 29, 1659.

The Reverend Mr. Thomas Cawton, born at Raynham in Norfolk, and educated in Queen's College, Cambridge ; he was afterward minister of Wivenhoe in Essex, 1637, and at last of St. Bartholomew behind the Exchange. He was, says the Oxford historian,† a learned and religious Puritan, driven into exile for preaching against the murder of King Charles I., and for being in the same plot with Mr. Love, for raising money to supply the army of King Charles II., when he was coming into England to recover his right. He fled to Rotterdam, and became preacher to the English church there, where he died August 7, 1659, in the fifty-fourth year of his age.‡

The new year [1660] began with the Restoration of King Charles II. to the throne of his ancestors. The Long Parliament dissolved themselves March 16, and while the people were busy in choosing a new one, General Monk was courted by all parties. The Republicans endeavoured to fix him for a commonwealth ; the French ambassador offered him the assistance of France if he would assume the government either as king or protector, which, it is said, he would have accepted, if Sir Anthony Ashley Cooper had not prevented it, by summoning him before the council, and keeping the doors locked till he had taken away the commissions from some of his most trusty officers, and given them to others of the council's nomination. But·be this as it will, it is certain Monk had not yet given the king any encouragement to rely upon him ; though his majesty had sent him a letter as long ago as July 21, 1659, by an express messenger, with the largest offers of reward.

* Fuller's Worthies, p. 305.
† Wood's Athenæ Oxon., vol. ii.; p. 432.
‡ Mr. Cawton had few equals in learning, and scarcely a superior in piety. Those great works, the Polyglot Bible, and Dr. Castle's Polyglot Lexicon, owed much to his encouragement and exertions. It showed a most deep seriousness of spirit, though probably mingled with superstitious notions of the Lord's Supper, that he fainted when he first received it ; and he ever afterward expressed at that solemnity the profoundest reverence and most elevated devotion.—*Granger's History of England*, vol. iii., 8vo, p. 47.—ED. The Reverend Mr. Thomas Cawton ejected in 1662 was his son. In that year he published the life of his father, with his sermon, entitled "Good Rule for a Godly Life," from Phil., i., 27.—C.

The Presbyterians were now in possession of the whole power of England; the Council of State, the chief officers of the army and navy, and the governors of the chief forts, and garrisons were theirs; the clergy were in possession of both universities, and of the best livings in the kingdom. There was hardly a Loyalist or professed Episcopalian in any post of honour or trust; nor had the king any number of friends capable of promoting his restoration, for there was a disabling clause in the Qualification Act, that all who had been in arms against the Long Parliament should be disqualified from serving in the next. The whole government, therefore, was with the Presbyterians, who were shy of the Independents, as a body of men more distant from the Church, and more inclined to the commonwealth. They were no less vigilant to keep out of Parliament the Republicans of all sorts, some of whom, says Burnet,[*] ran about everywhere like men that were giddy or amazed, but their time was past. On the other hand, they secretly courted the Episcopalians, who dispersed papers among the people, protesting their resolutions to forget all passed injuries, and to bury all rancour, malice, and animosities, under the foundation of his majesty's restoration. "We reflect," say they; "upon our sufferings as from the hand of God, and therefore do not cherish any violent thoughts or inclinations against any persons whatsoever who have been instrumental in them; and if the indiscretion of any particular persons shall transport them to expressions contrary to this general sense, we shall disclaim them."[†] This was signed by eighteen noblemen, and about fifty knights and gentlemen.[‡] Dr. Morley and some of his brethren met privately with the Presbyterian ministers, and made large professions of lenity and moderation, but without descending to particulars. The king and Chancellor Hyde carried on the intrigue. The chancellor, in one of his letters from Breda, dated April 20, 1660, says that "the king very well approved that Dr. Morley and some of his brethren should enter into conferences, and have frequent conversation with the Presbyterian party, in order to reduce them to such a temper as is consistent with the good of the Church; and it may be no-ill expedient," says he, " to assure them of present good preferments; but, in my opinion, you should rather endeavour to win over those who, being recovered, will both have reputation, and desire to merit from the Church, than be over-solicitous to comply with the pride and passion of those who propose extravagant things."[§] Such was the spirit or professions of the Church party, while they were decoying the others into the snare! The Presbyterian ministers did not want for cautions from the Independents and others not to be too forward in trusting their new allies, but they would neither hear, see, nor believe, till it was too late. They valued themselves upon their superior influence; and from an ambitious desire of grasping all the merit and glory of the Restoration to themselves, they would suffer none to act

openly with them, but desired the Episcopal clergy to lie still for fear of the people, and leave the conducting this great affair to the hands it was in.

Accordingly, the Presbyterian ministers wrote to their friends in their several counties to be careful that men of republican principles might not be returned to serve in the next Parliament, so that in some counties the elections fell upon men void of all religion; and in other places the people broke through the disabling cause. Dr. Barwick says they paid no regard to it, and Monk declared, that if the people made use of their natural rights in choosing whom they thought fit, without reserve, no injury should be done them. So that when the houses met, it was evident to all wise men it would be a court Parliament.

. But the Scots were more steady to the Covenant, and sent over the Reverend Mr. James Sharp, with the Earls of Crawford and Lauderdale, to Holland, humbly to put his majesty in mind that the Kirk of Scotland expected protection upon the footing of the Presbyterian establishment, without indulgence to sectaries. Their brethren in the north of Ireland joined in the address to the same purpose: and some of the English Presbyterians were of the same mind; ten of whom met the Scots commissioners at London, and made earnest applications to the general not to restore the king but upon the concessions made by his father in the Isle of Wight.[*] But this was only the resolution of a few; the majority, says Mr. Sharp, were for moderate Episcopacy, upon the scheme of Archbishop Usher, and therefore willing to hearken to an accommodation with the Church. Dr. Barwick adds,[†] "What the Presbyterians aimed at, who were now superior to the Independents, was, that all matters should be settled according to the treaty of the Isle of Wight," which gave the court a fair opportunity of referring all church matters to a conciliatory synod, the divines of each party to be summoned when the king should be settled on his throne. This was the bait that was laid for the Presbyterians, and was the ruin of their cause. The Scots Kirk stood to their principles, and would have bid defiance to the old clergy, but Mr. Calamy, Manton, and Ash informed them, in the name of the London ministers, that the general stream and current being for the old prelacy in its pomp and height, it was in vain to hope for establishing Presbytery, which made them lay aside the thoughts of it, and fly to Archbishop Usher's moderate Episcopacy.[‡] Thus they were beaten from their first works.

But if the tide was so strong against them, should they have opened their sluices, and let in the enemy at once, without a single article of capitulation? It is hard to account for this conduct of the Presbyterians, without impeaching their understandings. Indeed, the Episcopal clergy gave them good words, assuring them that all things should be to their minds when the king was restored; and that their relying upon the royal word would be a mark of confidence which his majesty would always remember, and would do honour to the king, who had

* History, vol. i., p. 123, 12mo.
† Baxter, p. 216, 218. History of the Stuarts, p. 458.
‡ Kennet's Chronicle, p. 121, 144. Baxter's Life, part ii., p. 217.   § Life of Barwick, p. 525.

* Kennet's Chron., p. 101, 104, 110.
† Life, p. 256.   ‡ Kennet's Chron., p. 228.

been so long neglected. But should this have induced the ministers to give up a cause that had cost so much treasure, and blood, and become humble petitioners to those who were now almost at their mercy? For they could not but be sensible that the old Constitution must return with the king, that diocesan episcopacy was the only legal establishment, that all which had been done in favour of presbytery not having had the royal assent, was void in law, therefore they and their friends who had not Episcopal ordination and induction into their livings, must be looked upon as intruders, and not legal ministers of the Church of England. But, notwithstanding this infatuation and vain confidence in the court and the clergy, Mr. Echard would set aside all their merit by saying, "Whatever the Presbyterians did in this affair, was principally to relieve themselves from the oppression of the Independents, who had wrested the power out of their hands, and not out of any affection to the king and Church." Directly contrary to his majesty's declaration concerning ecclesiastical affairs, which says, " When we were in Holland we were attended with many grave and learned ministers of the Presbyterian persuasion, whom, to our great satisfaction and comfort, we found to be full of affection to us, of zeal for the peace of the Church and State, and neither enemies (as they have been given out to be) to episcopacy nor liturgy." Bishop Burnet acknowledges* that many of the Presbyterian ministers, chiefly in the city of London, had gone into the design of the Restoration in so signal a manner, and with such success, that they had great merit, and a just title to very high preferments. Mr. Baxter† gives the following reasons of their conduct : " The Presbyterians," says he, " were influenced by the Covenant, by which, and by the oaths of allegiance to the king and his heirs, they apprehended themselves bound to do their utmost to restore the king, let the event be what it will." But then he adds, " Most of them had great expectations of favour and respect ; and because the king had taken the Covenant, they hoped he would remove subscriptions, and leave the Common Prayer and ceremonies indifferent, that they might not be cast out of the churches. Some, who were less sanguine, depended on such a liberty as the Protestants had in France ; but others, who were better acquainted with the principles and tempers of the prelates, declared that they expected to be silenced, imprisoned, and banished, but yet they would do their parts to restore the king, because no foreseen ill consequence ought to hinder them from doing their duty." Surely, these were better Christians than casuists ! When the ministers waited on his majesty in Holland, he gave them such encouraging promises, says Mr. Baxter, as raised in some of them high expectations. When he came to Whitehall he made ten of them his chaplains ; and when he went to the House to quicken the passing the Act of Indemnity, he said, " My lords, if you do not join with me in extinguishing this fear, which keeps the hearts of men awake, you keep me from performing my promise, which if I had not made, neither I nor you had been now here. I pray let us not deceive those who brought or permit-

ted us to come hither." Here is a royal declaration, and yet all came to nothing. The reader will judge hereafter who were most to blame, the Episcopal party, for breaking through so many solemn vows and protestations ; or the Presbyterians, for bringing in the king without a previous treaty, and trusting a set of men whom they knew to be their implacable enemies. I can think of no decent excuse to the former ; and the best apology that can be made for the latter is, that most of them lived long enough to see their error and heartily repent it.

In the interval between the dissolution of the Long Parliament and the meeting of the convention which brought in the king, General Monk, seeing which way the tide ran, fell in with the stream, and ventured to correspond more freely with the king by Sir J. Grenville, who brought the general a letter, and was sent back with an assurance that he would serve his majesty in the best manner he could. He desired the king to remove out of the Spanish dominions, and promised that, if his majesty wrote letters to the Parliament, he would deliver them at the opening of the sessions. Bishop Burnet says that he had like to have let the honour slip through his fingers, and that a very small share of it really belonged to him.*

The convention met. April 25, the Earl of Manchester being chosen speaker of the House of Peers, and Sir Harbottle Grimstone of the Commons. At the opening the sessions, Dr. Reynolds preached before the houses. April 30 was appointed for a fast, when Dr. Reynolds and Mr. Hardy preached before the Lords, and Dr. Gauden, Mr. Calamy, and Baxter, before the Commons ; all except Gauden of the Presbyterian party. Lord Clarendon says the Presbyterian party in the House were rather troublesome than powerful ; but others, with great probability, affirm that the body of the Commons were at first of that party. Next day after the fast, the king, by the advice of the general, having removed privately to Breda, and addressed letters to both houses, the general stood up and acquainted the speaker that one Sir J. Grenville had brought him a letter from the king, but that he had not presumed to open it ; and that the same gentleman attended at the door with another to the House. Sir John was immediately called in, and having delivered his letter at the bar, withdrew, and carried another to the Lords.† The letter contained an earnest invitation to the Commons to return to their duty, as the only way to a settled peace ; his majesty promising an act of oblivion for what was past, and all the security they could desire for their liberties and properties, and the rights of Parliament, for the future.

Under the same cover was enclosed his majesty's declaration from Breda, granting " a general pardon to all his loving subjects who should

* Burnet, vol. i., p. 123.

† Two days after Sir John Grenville received the thanks of the House for delivering the king's letter, in a high strain of joy and adulation ; and the House voted him £500 to buy a jewel, as a badge of the honour due to the person whom " the king had honoured to be the messenger of his gracious message." The city of London also presented to him and Lord Mordaunt, who brought them his majesty's letter, £300 to buy them rings.—Dr. Grey's Examination, vol. iii., p. 260, 261, and note (o).—ED.

lay hold of it within forty days, except such who should be excepted by Parliament. Those only excepted," says he, "let all our subjects, how faulty soever, rely upon the word of a king solemnly given, that no crime committed against us or our royal father shall ever be brought into question to the prejudice of their lives, estates, or reputation. We do also declare a liberty to tender consciences; and that no man shall be disquieted or called in question for differences of opinion in matters of religion, which do not disturb the peace of the kingdom. And we shall be ready to consent to such an act of Parliament as, upon mature deliberation, shall be offered to us for the full granting that indulgence." Upon reading these letters, the Commons voted that, according to the ancient Constitution, the government of this kingdom is, and ought to be, by kings, lords, and commons; and a committee was appointed to draw up a dutiful letter, inviting his majesty to return to his dominions: money was voted to defray his expenses; a deputation of lords and commons was sent to attend his majesty; and the fleet was ordered to convey him home. Sir Matthew Hale moved that a committee might be appointed to review the propositions of the Isle of Wight, and was seconded in the motion; but Monk, who was prepared for such a motion, stood up and said, "The nation was now quiet, but there were many incendiaries upon the watch, trying where they could first raise a flame; that he could not answer for the peace of the kingdom or army, if any delays were put to the sending for the king. What need is there of it," says he, "when he is to bring neither arms nor treasure along with him?" He then added, "That he should lay the blame of all the blood and mischief that might follow on the heads of those who should insist upon any motion that might retard the present settlement of the nation,"* which frightened the House into a compliance. And this was all the service General Monk did towards the king's restoration, for which he was rewarded with a garter, a dukedom, a great estate in land, and with one of the highest posts of honour and profit in the kingdom.

Thus was the king voted home in a hurry, which was owing to the flattering representations made by Lord Clarendon in his letters of the king's good nature, virtue, probity, and application to business;† so that when the Earl of Southampton saw afterward what the king was like to prove, he said once, in great wrath, to the chancellor, "that it was to him they owed all they either felt or feared; for if he had not possessed them in all his letters with such an opinion of the king, they would have taken care to have put it out of his power either to do himself or them any mischief, which was like to be the effect of their trusting him so entirely." To which Hyde answered, that "he thought the king had so true a judgment, and so much good nature, that when the age of pleasure should be over, and the idleness of his exile, which made him seek new diversions for want of other employment, was turned to an obligation to mind affairs, then he would have

* Burnet, vol. i., p. 123, 124, 12mo.
† Clarendon, p. 88, 89.

shaken off these entanglements." But here t e chancellor was mistaken.

When the Lords and Commons sent over a deputation to the king at Breda, the London ministers moved that a pass might be granted to some of their number, to wait upon his majesty with an address from their brethren; accordingly, Dr. Reynolds, Dr. Spurstow, Mr. Calamy, Mr. Hall, Mr. Manton, and Mr. Case were delegated, who went over with three or four attendants, and had an audience May 17, wherein, according to Lord Clarendon, "they magnified their own, and the affection of their friends, who had always wished his majesty's restoration, according to the Covenant, and had lately informed the people of their duty to invite him home. They thanked God for his majesty's constancy to the Protestant religion, and declared themselves no enemies to moderate episcopacy, only they desired that such things might *not be pressed upon them in God's worship, which in their judgments that used them were indifferent, but by others were held to be unlawful.*"* But the tables were now turned: the king spoke kindly to them, and acknowledged their services, but told them he would refer all to the wisdom of the Parliament. At another audience (if we may believe the noble historian) they met with very different usage; for when they entreated his majesty at his first landing not to use the Book of Common Prayer entire and formally in his chapel, it having been long laid aside, the king replied with some warmth, "that while he gave them liberty, he would not have his own taken away. That he had always used that form of service, which he thought the best in the world, and had never discontinued it in places where it was more disliked than he hoped it was by them. That when he came into England, he should not severely inquire how it was used in other churches, but he would have no other used in his own chapel."† They then besought him, with more impunity, that the use of the surplice might be discontinued by his chaplains, because it would give offence; but the king was as inexorable in that point as the other, and told them that it was a decent habit, and had been long used in the Church; that it had been still retained by him, and that he would never discountenance that good old practice of the church in which he had been bred. Mr. Baxter says, the king gave them such encouraging promises of peace, as raised some of them to high expectations. He never refused them a private audience when they desired it; and to amuse them farther, while they were once waiting in an antechamber, his majesty said his prayers with such an audible voice in the room adjoining, that the ministers might hear him; "he thanked God that he was a covenanted king; that he hoped the Lord would give him an humble, meek, forgiving spirit; that he might have forbearance towards his offending subjects, as he expected forbearance from offended Heaven." Upon hearing which old Mr. Case lifted up his hands to heaven,‡

* Kennet's Chron., p. 139.   Compl. Hist., p. 247.
† Kennet's Chron., p. 152.
‡ Mr. Daniel Dyke, who, soon after the Restoration, voluntarily resigned the living of Hadham-Magna in Hertfordshire, showed more discernment and judgment. For when Mr. Case, to induce him to

and blessed God, who had given them a praying king.

Though the bishops held a private correspondence with Chancellor Hyde, and by him were assured of the king's favour, they were not less forward than the Presbyterians in their application to his majesty himself; for while he remained at Breda, Mr. Barwick was sent over with the following instructions:

1. He was to wait upon the right honourable the Lord-chancellor of England, and beg his lordship's assistance to present a most humble petition to his majesty in the name of the bishops, and then to deliver their lordships' letters to the chancellor, to the Lord-lieutenant of Ireland, and to the secretary of state, wherein they returned those great men their most thankful acknowledgments for their piety and affection to the Church in the late most afflicted state.

2. He was then to give his majesty a distinct account of the present state of the Church in all the particulars wherein his majesty desired to be informed; and to bring the bishops back his majesty's commands, with regard to all that should be thought proper for them, or any of them, to do.

3. He was humbly to ask his majesty's pleasure with regard to some of the bishops waiting on the seacoast to pay their duty to his majesty, when, by God's blessing, he should soon land in England; and whether it was his royal pleasure that they should attend him there in their Episcopal habits; and at what time, and place, and how many, and which of them his majesty pleased should wait his arrival.

4. He was also to inquire concerning the number of his majesty's chaplains; whether any of them, besides those in waiting, should attend his arrival upon the coast; and to beg that his majesty would vouchsafe to appoint how many, and who.

5. He was most humbly to beseech his majesty, that if Dr. Lushington, formerly the king's chaplain, should offer to officiate in that capacity, his majesty would be pleased not to indulge him in that favour till inquiry should be made concerning his suspected faith and principles. [He was a Socinian.]

6. Since it has been customary for our kings to celebrate public thanksgivings in St. Paul's Cathedral, he was humbly to beseech his majesty to signify what was his royal pleasure in this behalf, considering the ruinous estate of that church.

7. His last instruction was to give a just and due account to his majesty why the affair of filling up the vacant sees had met with no better success.

continue in it, related the king's behaviour, and argued what a hopeful prospect it gave them, Mr. Dyke wisely answered, "that they did but deceive and flatter themselves; that if the king was sincere in his show of piety and great respect for them and their religion, yet, when he came to be settled, the party that had formerly adhered to him, and the creatures that would come over with him, would have the management of public affairs, and would circumvent all their designs, and in all probability not only turn them out, but take away their liberty too."—*Crosby's History of the Baptists*, vol. i., p. 357; and *Palmer's Nonconformists' Memorial* vol. ii., p. 43. —ED

Mr. Barwick was most graciously received by the king and his ministers, and the Sunday after his arrival at Breda was appointed to preach before his majesty.* The court was as yet very much upon their guard with respect to the Presbyterians; but the flames began to kindle at home, the Episcopal clergy not observing any measures of prudence in their sermons; Dr. Griffith, having preached an angry sermon before the general at Mercers' Hall, March 25, on Prov., xxiv., 21, "My son, fear thou the Lord and the king, and meddle not with them that are given to change," was for a pretence confined to Newgate, but in a few days was released, and published his sermon, with a dedication to the general. Others, in their sermons, began to threaten those who had hitherto had the power in their hands; of which the king being advised, commanded Chancellor Hyde to acquaint his correspondents that he was extremely apprehensive of inconvenience and mischief to the Church and himself from offences of that kind, and ordered him to desire Mr. Barwick and Dr. Morley to use their credit and authority with such men, and to let them know from his majesty the tenderness of the conjuncture. The chancellor accordingly, in his letter from Breda, April 16, 1660, wrote the king's sense, and added, that if occasion required, they were to speak to the Bishops of Ely and Salisbury to interpose their authority to conjure these men to make a better judgment of the season, and not to awaken those jealousies and apprehensions which all men should endeavour to extinguish. "And truly I hope," says the chancellor, "if faults of this kind are not committed, that both the Church and the kingdom will be better dealt with than is imagined; and I am confident these good men will be more troubled that the Church should undergo a new suffering by their indiscretion, than for all that they have suffered hitherto themselves."

The clouds gathering thus thick over the late managers, every one began to shift for himself. Richard Cromwell resigned his chancellorship of the University of Oxford the very day the king was invited home, and retired beyond sea: he had offered to relinquish it when he was divested of the protectorship, as appears by his letter on that occasion, which says, "You should have had fuller experience of my high esteem for learning and learned men, if Providence had continued me in my high station; but as I accepted of the honour of being your chancellor in order to promote your prosperity, I assure you I will divest myself of the honour when it will contribute to your advantage."†

Accordingly, as soon as the king's return was voted, he sent them the following resignation:

"Gentlemen,

"I shall always retain a hearty sense of my former obligations to you, in your free election of me to the office of your chancellor; and it is no small trouble to my thoughts, when I consider how little serviceable I have been to you in that relation. But since the all-wise providence of God, which I desire always to adore and bow down unto, has been pleased to change my condition, that I am not in a capacity to an-

---

* Life of Barwick, p. 519, note.
† Kennet's Chron., o. 141.

swer the ends of the office, I do therefore most freely resign and give up all my right and interest therein, but shall always retain my affection and esteem for you, with my prayers for your continual prosperity, that, amid the many examples of the instability and revolutions of human affairs, you may still abide flourishing and fruitful.

"Gentlemen,
"Your affectionate friend and servant,
"RICH. CROMWELL.
"Hursley, May 8, 1660."

Thus Richard went off the stage of public action. "As he was innocent of all the evil his father had done," says Burnet,* "so there was no prejudice laid against him. Upon his advancement to the protectorship, the city of London, and almost all the counties of England, sent him addresses of congratulation; but when he found the times too boisterous, he readily withdrew, and became a private man; and as he had done no hurt to anybody, so nobody ever studied to hurt him." A rare instance of the instability of human greatness, and of the security of innocence! In his younger years he had not all that zeal for religion as was the fashion of the times; but those who knew him well in the latter part of life have assured me that he was a perfect gentleman in his behaviour, well acquainted with public affairs, of great gravity, and real piety; but so very modest, that he would not be distinguished or known by any name but the feigned one of Mr. Clarke.† He died at Theobalds about the year 1712.

The king landed at Dover‡ May 26, and came the same night to Canterbury, where he rested the next day, and on Tuesday, May 29, rode in triumph, with his two brothers, through the city of London to Whitehall, amid the acclamations of an innumerable crowd of spectators.§ As he passed along, old Mr. Arthur Jackson, an eminent Presbyterian minister, presented his majesty with a book embossed Bible, which he was pleased to receive, and to declare it his resolution to make that book the rule of his conduct.‖

Two days after the king's arrival at Whitehall, his majesty went to the House of Peers, and after a short congratulatory speech, passed

---

* Vol. i, p. 116, 117.

† Under this name he lived, for some years, privately at Hursley, about seven miles from Romsey, now the seat of Sir Thomas Heathcote, Bart., and attended the meeting-house in Romsey. The pew in which he used to sit is still in being, and preserved entire at the church's removal to their new house, as a relic worthy of notice.—*Mr. Thomson's MS. Collections*, under the word *Romsey*.—ED.

‡ "I conversed," says an anonymous writer, "with some of our seamen who brought over King Charles in the Naseby, and they told me that the first time they had ever heard the Common Prayer and God damn ye, was on board that ship as she came home with his majesty."—*Inquiry into the Causes of our Naval Miscarriages, London*, 1707.—C.

§ Dr. Grey gives, from Echard and Heath, a description of the procession.—ED.

‖ Baxter's Life, p. 218. Jesse, in his Court of the Stuarts, says, "Charles displayed his gratitude to Heaven for his wonderful restoration, by passing the night of his return with Mrs. Palmer (afterward the celebrated Duchess of Cleveland), at the house of Sir Samuel Morland."—Vol. iii., p. 308.—C.

---

an act turning the present convention into a Parliament. After which the houses, for themselves and all the commons of England, laid hold of his majesty's most gracious pardon, and appointed a committee to prepare an act of indemnity for all who had been concerned in the preceding commotions, except the late king's judges, and two or three others.

Had the directions given for the choice of this Parliament been observed, no Royalist could have sat in the House; however, their numbers were inconsiderable; the convention was a Presbyterian Parliament, and had the courage to avow the justice and lawfulness of taking arms against the late king till the year 1648;* for when Mr. Lenthall, speaker of the Long Parliament, in order to show the sincerity of his repentance, had said, that he that first drew his sword against the late king, committed as great an offence as he that cut off his head, he was brought to the bar, and received the following reprimand from the present speaker, by order of the House:

"Sir,
"The House has taken great offence at what you have said, which, in the judgment of the House, contains as high a reflection upon the justice of the proceedings of the lords and commons of the last Parliament, in their actings before 1648, as could be expressed. They apprehend there is much poison in the said words, and that they were spoken out of design to inflame, and to render them who drew the sword to bring delinquents to punishment, and to vindicate their just liberties, into balance with them who cut off the king's head; of which they express their abhorrence and detestation. Therefore I am commanded to let you know, that had these words fallen out at any other time in this Parliament but when they had considerations of mercy and indemnity, you might have expected a sharper and severer sentence. Nevertheless, I am, according to command, to give you a sharp reprehension, and I do as sharply and severely as I can reprehend you for it."

But it was too little purpose to justify the civil war, when they were yielding up all they had been contending for to the court;† for though they stopped short of the lengths of the next Parliament, they increased his majesty's revenues so much, that if he had been a frugal prince, he might have lived without Parliaments for the future. The restoring the king after this manner without any treaty, or one single article for the securing men in the enjoyment of their *religious and civil liberties*, was, as Bishop Burnet observes,‡ the foundation of all the misfortunes of the nation under this reign. And as another right reverend prelate observes, the restoration of the king in this high and absolute manner laid the foundation of all the king's future miscarriages; so that if the revolution by King William and Queen Mary had not taken place, the Restoration had been no blessing to the nation.§

---

* Echard, p. 765. † Rapin, p. 258. ‡ Page 126.

§ Let those who take so much pleasure in casting blame upon Cromwell and the judges of Charles I., remember that all their work had to be done over again in 1688! How can men who glory in the revolution of 1688, or in that of 1776, find fault with the

But it ought to be remembered, that this was not a legal Parliament, for the Rump had no power to appoint keepers of the liberties of England ; nor had the keepers a right to issue out writs for election of a new Parliament ; nor could the king's writ, without the subsequent choice of the people, make them so. All the laws, therefore, made by this convention, and all the punishments inflicted upon offenders in pursuance of them, were not strictly legal ; which the court were so apprehensive of, that they prevailed with the next Parliament to confirm them. When this convention-Parliament had set about eight months, it was dissolved, December 29, partly because it was, not legally chosen, and because it was too much Presbyterian ; the prime minister [Hyde] having now formed a design, in concert with the bishops, of evacuating the Church of all the Presbyterians.

The managing Presbyterians still buoyed themselves up with hopes of a comprehension within the Church, though they had parted with all their weight and influence ; and from directors, were become humble supplicants to those very men who, a few months before, lay at their feet. They had now no other refuge than the king's clemency, which was directed by Chancellor Hyde and the bishops ; but to keep them quiet, his majesty condescended, at the instance of the Earl of Manchester, to admit ten of their number into the list of his chaplains in ordinary, viz., Dr. Reynolds, Spurstow, Wallis, Manton, Bates ; Mr. Calamy, Ashe, Case, Baxter, and Woodbridge.*

But none of these divines were called to preach at court, except Dr. Reynolds, Dr. Spurstow, Mr. Calamy, and Mr. Baxter, each of them once. Here, again, the Presbyterians were divided in their politics, some being for going as far as they could with the court, and others for drawing back. Of the former sort were, Mr. Calamy, Dr. Reynolds, and Mr. Ashe, who were entirely directed by the Earl of Manchester, and had frequent assemblies at his house ; to them were joined Dr. Bates, Dr. Manton, and most of the city ministers ; but Dr. Seaman, Mr. Jenkins, and others, were of another party : these were a little estranged from the rest of their brethren, and meddled not with politics, says Mr. Baxter,† because the court gave them no encouragement, their design being only to divide them ; but the former had more confidence in their superiors, and carried on a treaty, till, by force and violence, they were beaten out of the field.

Upon the king's arrival at Whitehall, the liturgy of the Church of England was restored to his majesty's chapel, and in several churches both in city and country ; for it was justly observed, that all acts and ordinances of the Long Parliament which had not the royal assent were in themselves null, and, therefore, prelacy was still the legal establishment, and the Common Prayer the only legal form of worship, and that they were punishable by the laws of the land who officiated by any other. The king, in his declaration, had desired that the Presbyterians

would read so much of the liturgy as they themselves had no exception against, but most of them declined the proposal.* But, to set an example to the rest of the nation, the House of Peers, two days after the king was proclaimed, appointed Mr. Marston to read Divine service before them, in his formalities, according to the Common Prayer Book ; and the Sunday following Dr. Gauden preached and administered the sacrament to several of the peers, who received it kneeling. On the 31st of May they ordered that the form of prayers formerly used should be constantly read in their House, provided that no prejudice, penalty, or reflection shall be on any who are not present. The House of Commons followed the example of the Lords ; and before the end of the year many of the parochial clergy, who scrupled the use of the Service Book, were prosecuted for offending against the statutes made in that behalf ; the justices of the peace and others insisting that the laws returned with the king, and that they ought not to be dispensed with in the neglect of them.

The old sequestered clergy flocked in great numbers about the court, magnifying their sufferings, and making interest for preferment ; every one took possession of the living from which he had been ejected ; by which means some hundreds of the Presbyterian clergy were dispossessed at once. Upon this, the heads of that party waited upon the king, and prayed that, though all who had lost their livings for malignancy, or disaffection to the late powers, were restored, yet that those ministers who succeeded such as had been ejected for scandal, might keep their places ; but the court paid no regard to their petitions. However, where the incumbent was dead, his majesty yielded that the living should be confirmed to the present possessor.

The heads of colleges and fellows who had been ejected in the late times were no less forward in their applications to be restored ; upon which the Parliament appointed a committee to receive their petitions. Dr. Goodwin having resigned his presidentship of Magdalen College, the Lords ordered " that Dr. Oliver be restored in as full and ample manner as formerly he enjoyed it, till the pleasure of his majesty be farther known. And the three senior fellows were appointed to put this order in execution."† The ejected fellows of New College, Oxon, petitioned, at the same time, to be restored ; upon which the Lords ordered, May 19, that " Robert Grove, John Lampshire, &c., late fellows of New College, Oxon, and all others who were unjustly ejected out of their fellowships, be forthwith restored ; and that all such fellows as have been admitted contrary to the statute be forthwith ejected ; and that no new fellows be admitted contrary to the statutes."‡ And to prevent farther applications of this kind, the Lords passed this general order, June 4 : " that the chancellors of both universities shall take care that the several colleges in the said universities shall be governed according to their respective statutes ; and that such persons who have been unjustly put out of their headships, fellowships, or other offices relating to the several colleges or universities, may be restored

opposition of their forefathers to the pranks of royalty and prelacy in the civil war ?—C.

* Kennet's Chron., p. 162.
† Baxter's Life, p. 229.

* Kennet's Chron., p. 432.   † Ibid., p. 152.
‡ Ibid., p. 153.

according to the said statutes of the university, and founders of colleges therein."*.

Pursuant to this order, there followed a very considerable change in both universities, commissioners being appointed by the king to hear and determine all causes relating to this affair,

who, in the months of August and September, restored all such as were unmarried to their respective places. In the University of Oxford, besides Dr. Oliver, already mentioned, the following heads of colleges were restored, and the present possessors ejected :

Heads of Colleges restored, August 3.   *President of.*   *In the place of heads ejected.*

Dr. Hannibal Potter,	Trinity College,	Dr. Seth Ward.
Dr. Richard Bayly,	St. John's College,	Mr. Thank Owen.
Dr. Francis Mansel,	Jesus College,	Mr. Francis Howel.
Dr. Robert Newlin,	Corpus Christi College,	Dr. Edward Staunton.
Dr. Gilbert Sheldon,	All Souls College,	Dr. Meredith, dec.
Dr. Thomas Yate,	Brazen Nose College,	Dr. D. Greenwood.
Mr. Henry Wightwick,	Pembroke College,	Dr. Henry Langley.

N. B. This Mr. Wightwick was ejected a second time, 1664.

Mr. Henry Wightwick,	St. Mary's Hall,	Mr. Thomas Cole.
Dr. Robert Saunderson,	Regius Professor in Divinity,	Dr. John Conant.
Dr. Thomas Willis,	Natural Philosophy reader,	Dr. Josh. Crosse.
Dr. John Fell,		
Dr. Robert South,	Canon of Christ Church and University orator,	Mr. Ralph Button.
Dr. Thomas Barlow,	Canon of Christ Church and Margaret Prof.,	Dr. H. Wilkinson, Sen.

Besides these, all surviving ejected fellows of colleges were restored without exceptions, and such as had been nominated by the commissioners in 1648, or elected in any other manner than according to the statutes, were ejected, and their places declared vacant.

The like alterations were made in the University of Cambridge. The Earl of Manchester, chancellor, was obliged to send the following letter to the university, dated August 3, for restoring Dr. Martin to the mastership of Queen's College, whom he had ejected for scandal, by letters under his hand, dated March 13, 1643 :

"Whereas I am informed that Dr. Ed. Martin has been wrongfully put out of his mastership : these are to signify to all whom it may concern, that I do, by virtue of an authority given to me, by the Lords assembled in Parliament, restore him to his said mastership, together with all lodgings, &c., appertaining to his place, from henceforth to have and enjoy all profits, rights, privileges, and advantages belonging thereunto, unless cause be shown to the contrary within ten days after the date hereof."* This gentleman was accordingly restored, and with him several others; as,

Heads of Colleges restored.   *Master of.*   *In place of heads ejected.*

Dr. J. Cosins,	Peter House,	Dr. Lazarus Seaman.
Dr. Thomas Paske,	Clare Hall,	Resigned to Dr. The. Dillingham.
Dr. Benjamin Laney,	Pembroke Hall,	Mr. William Moses.
Dr. Robert King,	Trinity Hall,	Mr. Bond.
Dr. Richard Sterne,	Jesus College,	Mr. J. Worthington.
Dr. Edw. Rainbowe,	Magdalen College, ejected for refusing Eng.,	Mr. John Sadleir.

All the surviving fellows unmarried were restored, as in the other university, by which means most of the Presbyterians were dispossessed, and the education of youth taken out of their hands.† To make way for the filling up these and other vacancies in the Church, the honours of the universities were offered to almost any, who would declare their aversion to Presbytery, and hearty affection for Episcopal government.‡ It was his majesty's pleasure, and the chancellor's, that there should be a creation in all faculties of such as had suffered for the royal cause, and had been ejected from the university by the visiters in 1648. Accordingly, between seventy and eighty masters of arts were created this year ; among whom, says the Oxford historian, some that had not been sufferers thrust themselves into the crowd for their money ; others, yet few, were gentlemen, and created by the favour of the chancellor's letters only ; eighteen were created bachelors of divinity, seventy doctors of divinity, twenty-two doctors of physic, besides doctors of laws. The creations in the University of Cambridge were yet more numerous. On Midsummer-day, a grace passed in the university in favour of some

candidates for degrees.† August 2, the king sent letters to Cambridge for creating nine or ten persons doctors of divinity ;‡ and on the 5th of September there were created, by virtue of his majesty's mandamus, no less than seventy-one doctors of divinity, nine doctors of civil law, five doctors of physic, and five bachelors of divinity. So that, within the compass of little more than six months, the universities conferred one hundred and fifty doctors of divinity degrees, and as many more in the other faculties. Some of these were deserving persons, but the names of most of them are nowhere to be found but in the university-registers. Had the Parliament visiters in 1648, or Oliver Cromwell in his protectorship, made so free with the honours of the universities, they might justly have been supposed to countenance the illiterate, and prostitute the honour of the two great luminaries of this kingdom ; but his majesty's promoting such numbers in so short a time by a royal mandamus, without inquiring into their qualifications, or insisting upon their performing any academical exercise, must be covered with a veil, because it was for the service of the church. In the midst of these promotions, the Marquis of Hertford, chancellor of

---

* Kennet's Chron., p. 173.   † Fasti, p. 120.
‡ Kennet's Chron., p. 220, 221, &c.

* Kennet's Chron., p. 221, 222.
† Ibid., p. 189.   ‡ Ibid., p. 220, 251.

the University of Oxford, died, and was succeeded by Sir Edward Hyde, now Lord-chancellor of England, and created about this time Earl of Clarendon. He was installed November 15, and continued in this office till he retired into France in the year 1667;

These promotions made way for filling up the vacancies in cathedrals ; July 5, Drs. Killigrew, Jones, Doughty, and Busby, were installed prebendaries of Westminster ; and within a month or six weeks four more were added.* In the months of July and August, all the dignities in the Cathedral of St. Paul's were filled up, being upward of twenty. July 13, twelve divines were installed prebendaries in the Cathedral of Canterbury ; and before the end of the year, all the dignities in the Cathedrals of Durham, Chester, Litchfield, Bristol, Hereford, Worcester, Gloucester, &c., were supplied with younger divines, who ran violently in the current of the times.† There were only nine bishops alive at the king's restoration, viz. :

Dr. William Juxon,   Bishop of London.
Dr. William Pierse,   "   Bath and Wells.
Dr. Matthew Wren,   "   Ely.
Dr. Robert Skinner,   "   Oxford.
Dr. William Roberts ,   "   Bangor.
Dr. John Warner,   "   Rochester.
Dr. Bryan Duppa,   "   Sarum.
Dr, Henry King,   "   Chichester.
Dr. Accepted Frewen,   "   Litchfield and Coventry.‡

In order to make way for a new creation, some of the bishops above mentioned were translated to better sees ; as,

Dr. Juxon, bishop of London, to Canterbury, who was promoted more out of decency, says Bishop Burnet,§ as being the eldest and most eminent of the surviving bishops ; he never was a great divine, but was now superannuated.

Dr. Accepted Frewen was translated to York, September 22, and confirmed October 4. He was the son of a Puritanical minister, and himself inclined that way, till some time after the beginning of the civil wars, when he became a great Loyalist, and was promoted in the year 1644 to the see of Litchfield and Coventry : he made no figure in the learned world,‖ and died in the year 1664.

Dr. Bryan Duppa was translated to Winchester, and confirmed October 4. He had been the king's tutor, though no way equal to the service. He was a meek, humble man, and much beloved for his good temper, says Bishop Burnet,¶ and would have been more esteemed if he had died before the Restoration, for he made not that use of the great wealth that flowed in upon him as was expected.**

* Kennet's Chron., p. 199.   † Ibid., p. 204.
‡ Ibid., p. 252.   § Vol. i., p. 257.
‖ Dr. Grey observes, however, on the authority of Wood, that Dr. Frewen, though he published only a Latin oration, with some verses on the death of Prince Henry, was esteemed a general scholar and a good orator. He was buried in his cathedral church, and a splendid monument was erected over his grave. He bequeathed £1000 to Magdalen College, Oxon, of which he had been president.—*Wood's Athenæ Oxon.*, vol. ii., p. 663, 664. *Godwinus de Præsulibus, curâ Richardson*, p. 714.—Ed.   ¶ Page 258.
** Dr. Grey censures Mr. Neal for adopting this mistake of Bishop Burnet, and says that Dr. Duppa's charities were extraordinary. He gave for redeem-

To make way for the election of new bishops in a *regular* and *canonical manner, it was first necessary to restore to every cathedral a dean and chapter ;* which being done,

Dr. Gilbert Sheldon was advanced to the see of London ; he was esteemed a learned man before the civil wars, but had since engaged so deep in politics, says Bishop Burnet,† that scarce any prints of what he had been remained ; he was a dexterous man in business, and treated all men in an obliging manner, but few depended much on his professions of friendship. He seemed not to have a deep sense of religion, if any at all ; and spoke of it most commonly as an engine of government, and a matter of policy, for which reason the king looked upon him as a wise and honest clergyman. He was one of the most powerful and implacable adversaries of the Nonconformists.

Dr. Henchman was consecrated Bishop of Sarum, and Dr. George Morley Bishop of Worcester, October 28; December 2, seven bishops were consecrated together in St. Peter's, Westminster, viz. :

Dr. John Cosins,   Bishop of Durham.
Dr. William Lawes,   "   St. David's.
Dr. Benjamin Laney,   "   Peterborough.
Dr. Hugh Lloyd,   "   Landaff.
Dr. Richard Sterne,   "   Carlisle.
Dr. Bryan Walton,   "   Chester.
Dr. John Gauden,   "   Exeter.

On the 6th of January following four other bishops were consecrated, viz :

Dr. Gilbert Ironside,   Bishop of Bristol.
Dr. Edward Reynolds,   "   Norwich.
Dr. Nicholas Monk,   "   Hereford.
Dr. William Nicholson,   "   Gloucester.

Four or five sees were kept vacant for the leading divines among the Presbyterians, if they would conform ; but they declined, as will be seen hereafter. In Scotland and Ireland things were not quite so ripe for execution ; the Scots Parliament disannulled the Covenant, but Episcopacy was not established in either of the kingdoms till next year.

ing of captives, building and endowing almshouses, with other charitable deeds, in benevolences, repairs, &c., £16,000, and was so good to his tenants as to abate £30,000 in fines. Richardson says that during the two years he lived after his translation to the see of Winchester, he expended great sums in public services, and was meditating more undertakings. He built an almshouse at Richmond, and endowed it by his will with £1500. He bequeathed £200 to the almshouse at Pembridge in Herts ; and, to omit private donations, he left to the Church of Salisbury £500, of Winchester £200, of St. Paul's, London, £300, and of Cirencester 200.—*Grey's Examination*, vol. iii., p. 276 ; and *Godwin, de Præsulibus*, p. 243.—Ed.

.* *All these are not to be found in the New Testament.* No bishop of the English Church can be made without them. That Church declares no minister can be scripturally ordained but by these bishops so *un-scripturally* made. How long will it be before we have deans and chapters in this country ? Certain bishops among us have already taken their titles as Bishop of States, and applications have been made to legislatures to incorporate "the Church," this, and the other matter. Perhaps Episcopacy at first will be content to be acknowledged as *the court* religion. The chaplains of the army and navy are nearly all appointed from this division of the Christian Church. —C.   † Page 257.

The English hierarchy being restored to its former pre-eminence, except the peerage of the bishops, it remained only to consider what was to be done with the malecontents; the Independents and Anabaptists petitioned the king only for a toleration;* and the English papists, depending upon their interest at court, offered his majesty £100,000, before he left Breda, to take off the penal laws, upon which his majesty ordered the chancellor to insert the following clause in his declaration concerning ecclesiastical affairs: That others also be permitted to meet for religious worship, so be it they do it not to the disturbance of the peace; and that no justice of peace offer to disturb them.† When this was debated in the king's presence after the Restoration, the bishops wisely held their peace; but Mr. Baxter, who was more zealous than prudent, declared plainly his dislike of a toleration of papists and Socinians; which his majesty took so very ill, that he said the Presbyterians were a set of men who were only for setting up themselves. These still flattered themselves with hopes of a comprehension, but the Independents and Baptists were in despair.

And here was an end of those distracted times, which our historians have loaded with all the infamy and reproach that the wit of man could invent. The Puritan ministers have been decried as ignorant mechanics, canting preachers, enemies to learning, and no better than public robbers. The universities were said to be reduced to a mere Munster; and that if the Goths and Vandals, and even the Turks, had overrun the nation, they could not have done more to introduce barbarism, disloyalty, and ignorance; and *yet in these times, and by the men who then filled the university chairs, were educated the most learned divines and eloquent preachers of the last age, as the Stillingfleets, Tillotsons, Bulls, Burrows, Whitbys, and others, who retained a high veneration for their learned tutors after they were rejected and displaced.* The religious part of the common people have been stigmatized with the character of hypocrites; their looks, their dress, and behaviour have been represented in the most odious colours; and yet one may venture to challenge these declaimers to produce any period of time since the Reformation wherein there was less open profaneness and impiety, and more of the spirit as well as appearance of religion. Perhaps there was too much rigour and preciseness in indifferent matters; but the lusts of men were laid under a visible restraint; and though the legal constitution was unhappily broken, and men were governed by false politics, yet better laws were never made against vice, or more vigorously executed. The dress and conversation of people were sober and virtuous, and their manner of living remarkably frugal; there was hardly a single bankruptcy to be heard of in a year; and in such a case the bankrupt had a mark of infamy set upon him that he could never wipe off. Drunkenness, fornication, profane swearing, and every kind of debauchery, were justly deemed infamous, and unfavourably discountenanced. The clergy were laborious to excess in preaching and praying, and catechising youth, and visiting their parishes. The

magistrates did their duty in suppressing all kind of games, stage-plays, and abuses in public houses. There was not a play acted on any theatre in England for almost twenty years. The Lord's Day was observed with unusual reverence; and there were a set of as learned and pious youths training up in the university as had ever been known. So that if such a reformation of manners had obtained under a legal administration, they would have deserved the character of the best of times.

But when the legal constitution was restored, there returned with it a torrent of debauchery and wickedness. The times which followed the Restoration were the reverse of those that preceded it; for the laws which had been enacted against vice for the last twenty years being declared null, and the magistrates changed, men set no bounds to their licentiousness. A proclamation, indeed, was published against those loose and riotous Cavaliers whose loyalty consisted in drinking healths and railing at those who would not revel with them; but in reality the king was at the head of these disorders, being devoted to his pleasures, and having given himself up to an avowed course of lewdness; his bishops and chaplains said that he usually came from his mistresses' apartments to church, even on sacrament days.* There were two play-houses erected in the neighbourhood of the court. Women-actresses were introduced into the theatres, which had not been known till that time; the most lewd and obscene plays were brought on the stage; and the more obscene, the king was the better pleased, who graced every new play with his royal presence. Nothing was to be seen at court but feasting, hard drinking, revelling, and amorous intrigues, which engendered the most enormous vices. From court the contagion spread like wildfire among the people, insomuch that men threw off the very profession of virtue and piety, under colour of drinking the king's health; all kinds of old cavalier rioting and debauchery revived; the appearances of religion which remained with some, furnished matters of ridicule to libertines and scoffers;† some, who had been concerned in the former changes, thought they could not redeem their credit better than by deriding all religion, and telling or making stories to render their former party ridiculous. To appear serious, or make conscience either of words or actions, was the way to be accounted a schismatic, a fanatic, or a sectarian; though, if there was any real religion during the course of this reign, it was chiefly among those people. They who did not applaud the new ceremonies were marked out for Presbyterians, and every Presbyterian was a rebel. The old clergy who had been sequestered for scandal, having taken possession of their livings, were intoxicated with their new felicity, and threw off all the restraints of their order. Every week, says Mr. Baxter,‡ produced reports of one or other clergyman who was taken up with the watch drunk at night, and mobbed in the streets. Some were taken with lewd women; and one was reported to be drunk in the pulpit.§ Such was the general

<hr>

* Kennet's Chron., p. 142. † Compl. Hist., p. 258.

* Kennet's Chron., p. 167.   † Ibid., p. 493.
‡ Life, part ii. p. 288.
§ Dr. Grey questions the truth of the above charge

dissoluteness of manners which attended the deluge of joy which overflowed the nation upon his majesty's restoration !

About this time died the Reverend Mr. Francis Taylor, some time rector of Clapham in Surry, and afterward of Yalden, from whence he was called to sit in the Assembly of Divines at Westminster, and had a considerable share in the annotations which go under their name. From Yalden Mr. Taylor removed to Canterbury, and became preacher of Christ Church in that city, where I presume he died, leaving behind him the character of an able critic in the Oriental languages, and one of the most considerable divines of the Assembly. He published several valuable works, and among others, a translation of the Jerusalem Targum on the Pentateuch out of the Chaldee into Latin, dedicated to the learned Mr. Gataker, of Rotherhithe, with a prefatory epistle of Selden's and several others, relating to Jewish antiquities. Among the letters to Archbishop Usher there is one from Mr. Taylor, dated from Clapham, 1635. He corresponded also with Boetius, and most of the learned men of his time. He left behind him a son who was blind,* but ejected for nonconformity in the year 1662, from St. Alphage Church in Canterbury, where he lies buried.

CHAPTER V.

FROM THE RESTORATION OF KING CHARLES II. TO THE CONFERENCE AT THE SAVOY. 1660.

BEFORE we relate the conference between the Episcopal and Presbyterian divines in order to a comprehension, it will be proper to represent the views of the court, and of the bishops, who had promised to act with temper, and to bury all past offences under the foundation of the Restoration. The point in debate was, "Whether concessions should be made, and pains taken, to gain the Presbyterians ?" The king seemed

But whoever reads Mr. Baxter's account of the matter, and of the conduct of himself and some of his brethren on the report of it, which rang through the city, will scarcely doubt the fact. But there is force and candour in what Dr. Grey adds concerning the reply of Mr. Selden to an alderman of the Long Parliament on the subject of episcopacy. The alderman said, "that there were so many clamours against such and such prelates, that they would never be quiet till they had no more bishops." On this Mr. Selden informed the House what grievous complaints there were against such and such aldermen; and therefore, by parity of reasoning, it was his opinion, he said, that they should have no more aldermen. Here was the fault transferred to the office, which is a dangerous error; for not only government, but human society itself, may be dissolved by the same argument, if the frailties or corruptions of particular men shall be revenged upon the whole body.—*Grey's Examination*, vol. iii., p. 267.—ED.

* He lost his sight by the smallpox, but pursued his studies by the aid of others who read to him. His brother, who was also blind, he supported, and took great pains to instruct and win over to sober religion, but not with all the success he desired; he was a man of good abilities, and noted for an eloquent preacher; and his ministry was much valued and respected. He did not long survive the treatment he met with in being seized and carried to prison; but was cheerful in all his afflictions.—*Palmer's Nonconformists' Memorial*, vol. ii., p. 57, 58.—ED.

VOL. II.—D d

to be for it; but the court-bishops, with Lord Clarendon at their head, were absolutely against it ; Clarendon was a man of high and arbitrary principles, and gave himself up to the bishops, for the service they had done him in reconciling the king to his daughter's clandestine marriage with the Duke of York. If his lordship had been a friend to moderate measures, the greatest part of the Presbyterians might have been gained; but he would not disoblige the bishops; the reasons of whose angry behaviour were, "1. Their high notions of the Episcopal form of government, as necessary to the very essence of a Christian church. 2. The resentments that remained in their breasts against all who had engaged with the Long Parliament, and had been the cause of their sufferings. 3. The Presbyterians being legally possessed of most of the benefices in Church and State, it was thought necessary to dispossess them; and if there must be a schism, rather to have it out of the Church than within it;" for it had been observed that the half conformity of the Puritans before the war had, in most cities and corporations, occasioned a faction between the incumbents and lecturers, which latter had endeavoured to render themselves popular at the expense of the hierarchy. 4. Besides, they had too much influence in the election of representatives to serve in Parliament; therefore, instead of using methods to bring them into the Church, says Bishop Burnet,* they resolved to seek the most effectual ones for casting them out. Here was no generosity or spirit of catholicism, no remembrance of past services, no compassion for weak or prejudiced minds, but a fixed resolution to disarm their opponents at all events; so that the ensuing conferences with the Presbyterians were no other than an amusement to keep them quiet till they could obtain a law for their utter expulsion.

The king was devoted to his pleasures, and had no principles of real religion ; his grand design was to lay asleep the former controversies, and to unite both Protestant and papist under his government; with this view he submitted to the scheme of the bishops, in hopes of making it subservient to a general toleration ; which nothing could render more necessary than having great bodies of men shut out of the Church, and put under severe penal laws, who must then be petitioners for a toleration, which the Legislature would probably grant ; but it was his majesty's resolution that, whatsoever should be granted of that sort, should pass in so limited a manner, that papists as well as other sectaries should be comprehended within it. The Duke of York and all the Roman Catholics were in this scheme; they declared absolutely against a comprehension, but were very much for a general toleration, as what was necessary for the peace of the nation, and promoting the Catholic cause.

The well-meaning Presbyterians were all this while striving against the stream, and making interest with a set of men who were now laughing in their sleeves at the abject condition to which their egregious credulity had reduced them. They offered Archbishop Usher's model of primitive Episcopacy as a plan of accommodation; that the surplice, the cross in baptism,

* Vol. i., p. 259, 260, 12mo.

and kneeling at the communion, should be left indifferent.* They were content to set aside the Assembly's confession, and let the articles of the Church of England take place with some few amendments. . About the middle of June, Mr. Calamy, Dr. Reynolds, Mr. Ashe, Mr. Baxter, Dr. Wallis, Dr. Manton, and Dr. Spurstow waited upon the king, being introduced by the Earl of Manchester, to crave his majesty's interposition for reconciling the differences in the Church, that the people might not be deprived of their faithful pastors. Honest Mr. Baxter told his majesty that the interest of the late usurpers with the people arose from the encouragement they had given religion ; and he hoped the king would not undo, but rather go beyond, the good which Cromwell or any other had done.† They laid a good deal of stress on their own loyalty, and carefully distinguished between their own behaviour and that of other sectaries, who had been disloyal and factious. The king replied that " he was glad to hear of their inclinations to an 'agreement ; that he would do his part to bring them together, but this must not be by bringing one party over to another, but by abating somewhat on both sides, and meeting in the midway ; and that if it were not accomplished, it should not be his fault; nay, he said, he was resolved to see it brought to pass."‡ Accordingly, his majesty required them to draw up such proposals as they thought meet for an agreement about church government, and to set down the most they could yield ; promising them a meeting with some Episcopal divines in his majesty's presence, when the proposals were ready. Upon this they summoned the city ministers to meet and consult at Sion College, not excluding such of their country brethren as would attend, that it might not be, said afterward they took upon themselves the concluding so weighty an affair.§ After two or three weeks' consultation, they agreed upon a paper to the following purpose, drawn up chiefly by Dr. Reynolds, Dr. Worth, and Mr. Calamy, which, together with Archbishop Usher's reduction of Episcopacy, they offered to the king, with the following address :

"May it please your most excellent majesty, "We, your majesty's most loyal subjects, cannot but acknowledge it is a very great mercy of God, that immediately after so wonderful and peaceable restoration to your throne and government (for which we bless his name), he has stirred up your royal heart, as to a zealous testimony against profaneness, so to endeavour a happy composing of the differences, and healing the sad breaches which are in the Church. And we shall, according to our bounden duty, become humble suiters to the throne of grace, that the God of peace, who has put such a thing as this into your majesty's heart, will, by his heavenly wisdom and Holy Spirit, assist you herein, that you may bring your resolutions to a perfect effect and issue.

"In humble conformity to your majesty's Christian designs, we, taking it for granted that there is a firm agreement between our brethren and us in the doctrinal truths of the Reformed religion, and in the substantial parts of Divine worship, humbly desire,

First, "That we may be secured of those things in practice of which we seem to be agreed in principle ; as,

1. "That those of our flocks that are serious in matters of their salvation may not be reproachfully handled by words of scorn, or any abusive language, but may be encouraged in their duties of exhorting and provoking one another in their most holy faith, and of furthering one another in the ways of eternal life.

2. "That each congregation may have a learned, orthodox, and godly pastor, that the people may be publicly instructed by preaching every Lord's Day, by catechising, by frequent administering the Lord's Supper and baptism ; and that effectual provision by law may be made that such as are insufficient, negligent, or scandalous, may not officiate.

3. "That none may be admitted to the Lord's Supper till they personally own their baptismal covenant by a credible profession of faith and holiness, not contradicted by a scandalous life. That to such only confirmation may be administered ; and that the approbation of the pastor to whom the instructing those under his charge doth appertain, may be produced before any person receives confirmation.

4 "That an effectual course be taken for the sanctification of the Lord's Day, appropriating the same to holy exercises both in public and private, without any unnecessary divertisements."

"Then for matters in difference, viz., church government, liturgy, and ceremonies, we humbly represent,

"That we do not renounce the true ancient primitive episcopacy or presidency, as it was balanced with a due commixtion of presbyters. If, therefore, your majesty, in your grave wisdom and moderation, shall constitute such an episcopacy, we shall humbly submit thereunto. And in order to an accommodation in this weighty affair, we desire humbly to offer some particulars which we conceive were amiss in the Episcopal government as it was practised before the year 1640.

1. "The great extent of the bishop's diocess, which we apprehend too large for his personal inspection.

2. "That, by reason of this disability, the bishops did depute the administration, in matters of spiritual cognizance, to commissaries, chancellors, officials, whereof some are secular persons, and could not administer that power that originally belongs to the officers of the Church.

3. "That the bishops did assume the sole power of ordination and jurisdiction to themselves.

4 "That some of the bishops exercised an arbitrary power, by sending forth articles of visitation, inquiring unwarrantably into several things, and swearing church-wardens to present accordingly. Also, many innovations and ceremonies were imposed upon ministers and people not required by law.

"For remedy of these evils we crave leave to offer,

1. "The late most reverend primate of Ireland, his reduction of episcopacy into the form of synodical government.

2. "We humbly desire that the suffragans,

or chorepiscopi, may be chosen by the respect-ive synods.

3. " That no oaths, or promises of obedience to the bishops, nor any unnecessary subscrip-tions or engagements, be made necessary to or-dination, institution, or induction, ministration, communion, or immunities of ministers; they being responsible for any transgression of the law. And that no bishops or ecclesiastical gov-ernors may exercise their government by their private will or pleasure, but only by such rules, canons, and constitutions as shall be establish-ed by Parliament.

Secondly, " Concerning liturgy.

1. " We are satisfied in our judgments con-cerning the lawfulness of a liturgy, or form of worship, provided it be for matter agreeable to the Word of God, and suited to the nature of the several ordinances and necessities of the Church, neither too tedious, nor composed of too short prayers or responsals, not dissonant from the liturgies of other Reformed churches, nor too rigorously imposed, nor the minister confined thereunto, but that he may also make use of his gifts for prayer and exhortation.

2. " Forasmuch as the ·Book' of Common Prayer is in some things justly offensive, and needs amendment, we most humbly pray that some learned, godly, and moderate divines of both persuasions, may be employed to compile such a form as is before described, as much as may be in Scripture words ; or at least to revise and reform the old : together with an addition of other various forms in Scripture phrase, to be used at the minister's choice.

Thirdly, " Concerning ceremonies.

" We hold ourselves obliged, in every part of Divine worship, to do all things decently and in order, and to edification ; and are willing to be determined by authority in such things as, being merely circumstantial, or common to human actions and societies, are to be ordered by the light of nature and human prudence.

" As to divers ceremonies formerly retain-ed in the Church of England, we do, in all hu-mility, offer to your majesty the following con-siderations :

" That the worship of God is in itself pure and perfect, and decent, without any such cer-emonies. That it is, then, most pure and ac-ceptable when it has least of human mixtures. That these ceremonies have been imposed and advanced by some, so as to draw near to the significancy and moral efficacy of sacraments. That they have been rejected by many of the Reformed churches abroad, and have been ever the subject of contention and endless disputes in this church ; and therefore, being in their own nature indifferent and mutable, they ought to be changed, lest in time they should be ap-prehended as necessary, as the substantials of worship themselves.

" May it therefore please your majesty gra-ciously to grant that kneeling at the Lord's Supper, and such holydays as are but of human institution, may not be imposed on such as scruple them. That the use of the surplice and cross in baptism, and bowing at the name of Jesus, may be abolished. And forasmuch as erecting altars and bowing towards them, and such like (having no foundation in the law of the land), have been introduced and imposed,

we humbly beseech your majesty that such in-novations may not be used or imposed for the future.".

When the Presbyterian divines came to court with these proposals, the king received them favourably, and promised to bring both parties together. His majesty expressed a satisfaction in hearing they were disposed to a liturgy and forms of prayer, and that they were willing to yield to the essence of episcopacy, and there-fore doubted not of procuring an accommoda-tion. The ministers expected to have met the bishops with their papers of proposals, but none of them appeared, having been better instructed in a private conference with Lord-chancellor Hyde, who told them it was not their business to offer proposals, because they were in posses-sion of the laws of the land ; that the hierarchy and Service Book, being the only legal estab-lishment, ought to be the standard of agree-ment ; and therefore their only concern was to answer the exceptions of the ministers against it. Accordingly, instead of a conference, or paper of proposals, which the ministers expect-ed, the bishops, having obtained a copy of the paper of the Presbyterians, drew up an answer in writing, which was communicated to their ministers, July 8.

In this answer, the bishops take notice of the ministers' concessions in their preamble, as that they agree with them in the substantials of doctrine and worship ; and infer from thence, that their particular exceptions are of less im-portance, and ought not to be stiffly insisted on to the disturbance of the peace of the Church.*

To the particulars they answer,

1. Concerning church government, "That they never heard any just reasons for a dissent from the ecclesiastical hierarchy of this king-dom, which they believe in the main to be the true primitive episcopacy, which was more than a mere presidency of order. Nor do they find that it was balanced by an authoritative commixtion of presbyters, though it has been in all times exercised with the assistance and counsel of presbyters in subordination to bish-ops. They wonder that they should, except against the government by one single person, which, if applied to the civil magistrate, is a most dangerous insinuation."†

As to the four particular instances of things amiss.

1. " We cannot grant the extent of any dio-cess is so great but that a bishop may well per-form his duty, which is not a personal inspec-tion of every man's soul, but the pastoral charge, or taking care that the ministers, and other ecclesiastical officers within their diocess, do their duties ; and if some diocesses should be too large, the law allows suffragans.

2. " Concerning lay-chancellors, &c., we con-fess the bishops did depute part of their eccle-siastical jurisdiction to chancellors, commissa-ries, officials, &c., as men better skilled in the civil and canon laws ; but as for matters of mere spiritual concernment, as excommunica-tion, absolution, and other censures of the Church, we conceive they belong properly to the bishop himself, or his surrogate, wherein, if

---

* Kennet's Chron., p. 200.   Baxter's Life, part ii., p. 242.   † Baxter, p. 243.

anything has been done amiss, we are willing it should be reformed.

3. "Whether bishops are a distinct order from presbyters or not, or whether they have the sole power of ordination, is not now the question; but we affirm that the bishops of this realm have constantly ordained with the assistance of presbyters, and the imposition of their hands together with the bishops, and for this purpose the colleges of deans and chapters are instituted.

4. "As to Archbishop Usher's model of church government, we decline it, as not consistent with his other learned discourses on the original of episcopacy, and of metropolitans; nor with the king's supremacy in causes ecclesiastical."

II. Concerning Liturgy.

"We esteem the liturgy of the Church of England, contained in the Book of Common Prayer, and by law established, to be such a one as is by them desired, according to the qualifications which they mention; the disuse of which has been the cause of the sad divisions of the Church, and the restoring it may be, by God's blessing, a special means of making up the breach. Nor can the imposition of it be called rigorous, as long as clergymen have the liberty of using their gifts before and after sermon. Nevertheless, we are not against revising the liturgy by such discreet persons as his majesty shall think fit to employ therein.

III. Of Ceremonies.

"Lawful authority has already determined the ceremonies in question to be decent and orderly, and for edification, and, consequently, to be agreeable to the general rules of the Word. We allow the worship of God is in itself perfect in essentials, but still the Church is at liberty to improve it with circumstantials for decency and order. Ceremonies were never esteemed to be sacraments, nor imposed as such; they are retained by most Protestant churches; and that they have been the subject of contention is owing to men's weakness, and their unwillingness to submit their private opinions to the public judgment of the Church. We acknowledge that these things are in their nature mutable, but we can by no means think it expedient to remove them. However, as we are no way against such a tender and religious compassion in things of this nature, as his majesty's piety and wisdom shall think fit to extend, so we cannot think that the satisfaction of some private persons is to be laid in the balance against the public peace and uniformity of the Church.

"As for kneeling at the Lord's Supper, it is a gesture of the greatest reverence and devotion, and so most agreeable to that holy service.

"Holydays of human institution having been observed by the people of God in the Old Testament, and by our blessed Saviour himself in the Gospel, and by all the churches of Christ in the primitive and following times, as apt means to preserve the memorials of the chief mysteries of the Christian religion; and such holydays also being fit times for the honest recreation of the meaner sort of people, for these reasons we humbly desire they may be continued in the Church.

"As for the three other ceremonies, the surplice, the cross after baptism, and bowing at the name of Jesus, though we see not any sufficient reason why they should be utterly abolished, nevertheless, how far forth, in regard of tender consciences, a liberty may be thought fit to be indulged to any, his majesty is best able to judge."

They conclude thus : "We are so far from believing that his majesty's condescending to the ministers' demands will take away not only our differences, but the roots and causes of them, that we are confident it will prove the seminary of new differences, both by giving dissatisfaction to those that are well pleased with what is already established, who are much the greatest part of his majesty's subjects; and by encouraging unquiet spirits, when these things shall be granted, to make farther demands; there being no assurance by them given what will content all dissenters, than which nothing is more necessary for settling a firm peace in the Church."

About a week after, the Presbyterian divines sent the bishops a warm remonstrance and defence of their proposals, drawn up chiefly by Mr. Baxter, to the following purpose:

Concerning the Preamble.

"We are not insensible of the danger of the Church, through the doctrinal errors of those with whom we differ about points of government and worship; but we choose to say nothing of the party that we are agreed with in doctrinals, because we both subscribe the same Holy Scriptures, articles of religion, and books of homilies; and the contradictions to their own confessions, which too many are guilty of, we did not think just to charge upon the whole."[*]

Concerning Church Government.

"Had you read Gerson, Bucer, Parker, Baynes, Salmasius, Blondel, &c., you would have seen just reason given for our dissent from the ecclesiastical hierarchy, as stated in England."

Instances of Things amiss.

"You would easily grant that dioceses are too great, if you had ever conscionably tried the task which Dr. Hammond describeth as the bishop's work; or had ever believed Ignatius, and other ancient descriptions of a bishop's church. You cannot be ignorant that our bishops have the sole government of pastors and people; that the whole power of the keys is in their hands, and that their presbyters are but ciphers."

Concerning Ceremonies.

"These divines argue for leaving them indifferent for the peace of the Church, as being not essential to the perfection of Christian worship, especially when so many looked upon them as sinful."

They conclude thus : "We perceive your counsels against peace are not likely to be frustrated. Your desires concerning us are likely to be accomplished. You are like to be gratified with our silence and ejection; and yet we will believe that 'Blessed are the peace-makers;' and though we are prevented by you in our pursuits of peace, and are never like thus publicly to seek it more, yet are we resolved, as much as possible, to live peaceably with all men."

---

* Kennet's Chron., p. 205. Baxter, part ii., p. 248.

The eyes of the Presbyterians were now opened, and they began to discern their weakness in expecting an agreement with the bishops, who appeared to be exasperated, and determined to tie them down to the old establishment. The former severities began already to be revived, and the laws were put in execution against some who did not make use of the old liturgy. Many were suspended and turned out of their livings on this account; upon which the leading Presbyterians applied to the king, and humbly requested,

1. "That they might with all convenient speed see his majesty's conclusions upon the proposals of mutual condescensions, before they pass into resolves.

2. "That his majesty would publicly declare his pleasure for the suspension of all proceedings upon the Act of Uniformity, against nonconformists to the liturgy and ceremonies, till they saw the issue of their hoped-for agreement.

3. "That, until the said settlement, there may be no oath of canonical obedience, nor subscription to the liturgy and ceremonies required, nor renunciation of their ordination by mere presbyters, imposed as necessary to institution, induction, or confirmation.

4. "That his majesty would cause the broad seal to be revoked, where persons had been put into the possession of the livings of others not void by sequestration, but by the death of the former incumbents.

5. "That a remedy may be provided against the return of scandalous ministers into the places from whence they had been ejected."*

His majesty gave them a civil audience, and told them he would put what he thought fit to grant them into the form of a declaration, which they should have the liberty of perusing before it was made public. A copy of this was accordingly delivered by the chancellor to Mr. Baxter, and other Presbyterian divines, September 4, with liberty to make exceptions, and give notice of what they disliked.† These divines petitioned for some farther amendments and alterations; upon which the king appointed a day to hear what could be said on both sides, and came to the chancellor's house, October 22, attended by the Dukes of Albemarle and Ormond, the Earls of Manchester, Anglesea, and Lord Hollis. On the part of the bishops were,

Dr. Sheldon, Bishop of London.
Dr. Morley, " Worcester
Dr. Henchman, " Salisbury.
Dr. Cosins, " Durham.
Dr. Gauden, " Exeter.
Dr. Hacket, } " Litchfield and Coventry.
Dr. Barwick, } Dean of St. Paul's; Dr. Gunning, &c.

On the side of the Presbyterians were,

Dr. Reynolds, Dr. Manton,
Mr. Calamy, Mr. Baxter,
Dr. Spurstow, Dr. Wallis.
Mr. Ashe,

As the chancellor read over the declaration, each party were to allege their exceptions, and the king to determine. The chief debates were on the high power of the bishops, and the necessity of reordination. Bishop Morley and Dr.

Gunning spoke most on one side; and Mr. Calamy and Baxter on the other.* Upon hearing the whole, his majesty delivered his judgment as to what be thought proper should stand in the declaration; and appointed Bishop Morley and Henchman, Dr. Reynolds and Mr. Calamy, to express it in proper words; and if they disagreed, the Earl of Anglesea and Lord Hollis to decide.

At length the declaration, with such amendments as the king would admit, was published under the following title:

"His Majesty's Declaration to all his loving Subjects of his Kingdom of England and Dominion of Wales, concerning Ecclesiastical Affairs. Given at our Court at Whitehall, October 25, 1660, in the twelfth Year of our Reign."

The declaration being long,† and to be met with in most of our historians, I shall give the reader only an abstract of it.

"CHARLES REX.

"In our letter from Breda, we promised in due time to propose something to the world for the propagation of the Protestant religion; and we think ourself more competent to propose, and, with God's assistance, determine many things now in difference, from the experience we have had in most of the Reformed churches abroad, where we have had frequent conferences with the most learned men, who have unanimously lamented the distempers and too notorious schisms in matters of religion in England.

"When we were in Holland, we were attended by many grave and learned ministers from hence of the Presbyterian opinion, and, to our great satisfaction, we found them full of affection to us, no enemies to Episcopacy or liturgy (as they have been reported to be); but modestly desiring such alterations as, without shattering foundations, might give ease to the tenderness of some men's consciences. For the doing of this we intended to have called a synod of divines, but observing the over-passionate and turbulent way of proceeding of some persons, and the impatience of others for a speedy determination of these matters, we have been prevailed with to invert the method we proposed, and to give some determination ourself to the matters in difference, till such a synod may be called as may, without passion or prejudice, give us such farther assistance towards a perfect union of affections, as well as submission to authority, as is necessary.

"We must, for the honour of all with whom we have conferred, declare, that the professions and desires of all for the advancement of piety and true godliness are the same; their professions of zeal for the peace of the Church, and of affection and duty to us, the same; they all approve Episcopacy and a liturgy, and disapprove of sacrilege, and the alienation of the revenues of the Church."‡

His majesty then declares his high esteem and affection for the Church of England, and

---

* Baxter's Life, part ii., p. 241.
† Kennet's Chron., p. 246. Baxter's Life part ii., p. 275, 276.

* Baxter's Life, part ii., p. 278.
† This declaration was drawn up by Lord-chancellor Hyde, but many of the evasive clauses were suggested by some of the king's more secret advisers. —*Secret History of the Court and Reign of Charles II.*, vol. i., p. 93.—ED.
‡ Comp. Hist., vol. iii., p. 246. Baxter's Life, part ii., p. 259. Kennet's Chron., p. 289.

that his esteem of it is not lessened by his condescending to dispense with some particular ceremonies, and then proceeds to his concessions.

1. " We declare our purpose and resolution is, and shall be, to promote the power of godliness, to encourage the public and private exercises of religion, to take care of the due observation of the Lord's Day, and that insufficient, negligent, and scandalous ministers be not permitted in the Church. We shall take care to prefer none to the Episcopal office and charge but men of learning, virtue, and piety; and we shall provide the best we can, that the bishops be frequent preachers, and that they do often preach in some church or other of their diocess.

2. " Because some diocesses may be of too large extent, we will appoint such a number of suffragans as shall be sufficient for the due performance of their work.

3. " No bishop shall ordain or exercise any part of jurisdiction which appertains to the censures of the Church, without advice and assistance of the presbyters. No chancellors, commissaries, or officials shall excommunicate, absolve, or exercise any act of spiritual jurisdiction, wherein any of the ministry are concerned with reference to their pastoral charge. Nor shall the archdeacon exercise any jurisdiction without the advice and assistance of six ministers of his archdeaconry; three to be nominated by the bishop, and three by the suffrage of the presbyters within the archdeaconry.

4. " We will take care that the preferment of deans and chapters shall be given to the most learned and pious presbyters of the diocess, and that an equal number (to those of the chapter) of the most learned and pious presbyters of the same diocess, annually chosen by the major vote of all the presbyters of that diocess present at such elections, shall be always advising and assisting, together with those of the chapter, in all ordinations, at all church censures, and other important acts of ecclesiastical jurisdiction wherein any of the ministry are concerned. Provided, that at all such meetings, the number of ministers so elected, and those of the chapter present, be equal; and to make the numbers equal, the juniors of the exceeding number shall withdraw to make way for the more ancient. Nor shall any suffragan bishop ordain or exercise any jurisdiction without the advice and assistance of a sufficient number of presbyters annually chosen as before. And our will is, that ordination be constantly and solemnly performed by the bishop and his aforesaid presbyters at the four set times appointed by the Church for that purpose.

5. " Confirmation shall be rightly and solemnly performed, by the information and with the consent of the minister of the place, who shall admit none to the Lord's Supper till they have made a credible profession of their faith, and promised obedience to the will of God, according to the rubric before the catechism; and all diligence shall be used for the instruction and reformation of scandalous offenders, whom the minister shall not suffer to partake of the Lord's Supper till they have openly declared their repentance, and resolutions of amendment; provided there be place for appeals to superior powers. Every rural dean to be nominated by

the bishop as heretofore), with three or four ministers of that deanery chosen by the major part of all the ministers within the same, shall meet once a month to receive complaints from the ministers or church-wardens of parishes, and to compose such differences as shall be referred to them for arbitration, and to reform such things as are amiss, by their pastoral reproofs and admonitions, and what they cannot reform are to be presented to the bishop. Moreover, the rural dean and his assistants are to take care of the catechising children and youth, and that they can give a good account of their faith before they are brought to the bishop to be confirmed.

6. " No bishop shall exercise any arbitrary power, or impose anything upon his clergy or people, but according to the law of the land.

7. " We will appoint an equal number of divines of both persuasions to review the liturgy of the Church of England, and to make such alterations as shall be thought necessary ; and some additional forms in the Scripture phrase, as near as may be, suited to the nature of the several parts of worship, and that it be left to the minister's choice to use one or the other at his discretion. In the mean time, we desire that the ministers in their several churches will not wholly lay aside the use of the Common Prayer, but will read those parts of it against which they have no exception ; yet our will and pleasure is, that none be punished or troubled for not using it till it be reviewed and effectually reformed.

8. Lastly, " Concerning ceremonies, if any are practised contrary to law, the same shall cease. Every national church has a power to appoint ceremonies for its members, which though before they were indifferent, yet cease to be so when established by law. We are therefore content to indulge tender consciences, so far as to dispense with their using such ceremonies as are an offence to them, but not to abolish them: We declare, therefore, that none shall be compelled to receive the sacrament kneeling, nor to use the cross in baptism, nor to bow at the name of Jesus, nor to use the surplice, except in the royal chapel, and in cathedral and collegiate churches. Nor shall subscription, nor the oath of canonical obedience, be required at present, in order to ordination, institution, or induction, but only the taking the oaths of allegiance and supremacy ; nor shall any lose their academical degrees, or forfeit a presentation, or be deprived of a benefice, for not declaring his assent to all the Thirty-nine Articles, provided he read and declare his assent to all the doctrinal articles, and to the sacraments. And we do again renew our declaration from Breda, that no man shall be disquieted or called in question for differences of opinion in matters of religion which do not disturb the peace of the kingdom."

His majesty concludes " with conjuring all his loving subjects to acquiesce and submit to this declaration, concerning the differences that have so much disquieted the nation at home, and given offence to the Protestant churches abroad."

Though this declaration did not satisfy all the ministers, yet the greatest numbers were content ; but because it proceeded upon the plan of diocesan Episcopacy which they had covenanted against, others were extremely uneasy; some ventured upon a second address to the king, in which they renew their requests for Archbishop Usher's scheme of primitive Episcopacy, as most agreeable to Scripture, most conducive to good discipline, and as that which would save the nation from the violation of a solemn League and Covenant, which, whether it were lawfully imposed or no, they conceive now to be binding.

Concerning the preamble of his majesty's declaration they tender these requests: .

1. "That as they are persuaded it is not in his majesty's thoughts to intimate that they are guilty of the offences therein mentioned; they hope it will be a motive to hasten the union.

2. "Though they detest sacrilege, yet they will not determine whether, in some cases of superfluities of revenues, and the necessity of the Church, there may not be an alienation, which is no sacrilege.

3. "His majesty having acknowledged their moderation, they still hope they may be received into the settlement, and continue their stations in the Church.

4. "Since his majesty has declared that the essence of Episcopacy may be preserved, though the extent of the jurisdiction be altered, they hope his majesty will consent to such an alteration as may satisfy their consciences."

They then renew their requests for promoting of piety; of a religious and diligent ministry; of the requisites of church communion; and for the observation of the Sabbath. They complain that parish discipline is not sufficiently granted in his majesty's declaration, that inferior synods are passed by, and that the bishop is not *episcopus præses,* but *episcopus princeps,* endued with sole power of ordination and jurisdiction. They therefore pray again that Archbishop Usher's form of church government may be established, at least in these three points :[*]

1. "That the pastors of parishes may be allowed to preach, catechise, and deny the communion of the Church to the impenitent, scandalous, or such as do not make a credible profession of faith and obedience to the commands of Christ.

2. "That the pastors of each rural deanery may meet once a month, to receive presentments and appeals, to admonish offenders, and, after due patience, to proceed to excommunication.

3. "That a diocesan synod of the delegates of rural synods may be called as often as need requires; that the bishop may not ordain or exercise spiritual censures without the consent of the majority; and that neither chancellors, archdeacons, commissaries, nor officials may pass censures purely spiritual; but for the exercise of civil government coercively by mulcts, or corporeal penalties, by power derived from your majesty, as supreme over all persons and things ecclesiastical, we presume not at all to interpose."

" *As to the Liturgy.*

" They rejoice that his majesty has declared that none should suffer for not using the Com-

mon Prayer and ceremonies; but then it grieves us," say they, " to hear that it is given in charge to the judges at the assizes to indict men upon the Act of Uniformity for not using the Common Prayer. That it is not only some obsolete words and phrases that are offensive, but that other things need amendment; therefore, we pray that none may be punished for not using the book, till it be reformed by the consent of the divines of both parties."

" *Concerning Ceremonies.* .

" They thank his majesty for his gracious concessions, but pray him to leave out of his declaration these words, ' that we do not believe the practice of the particular ceremonies excepted against unlawful,' because we are not all of that opinion; but we desire that there may be no law nor canon for or against them (being allowed by our opponents as indifferent), as there is no canon against any particular gesture in singing psalms, and yet there is an uninterrupted unity."

" *For particular Ceremonies.*

1. " We humbly crave that there may be liberty to receive the Lord's Supper either kneeling, standing, or sitting. 2. That the observation of holydays of human institution may be left indifferent. 3. We thank your majesty for liberty as to the cross in baptism, the surplice, and bowing at the name of Jesus; but we pray that this liberty may extend to colleges and cathedrals, for the benefit of youth as well as elder persons, and that the canons which impose these ceremonies may be repealed.

" We thank your majesty for your gracious concession of the forbearance of subscription; though we do not dissent from the doctrinal articles of the Church of England; nor do we scruple the oaths of allegiance and supremacy, nor would we have the door left open for papists and heretics to come in. .

" But we take the liberty to represent to your majesty, that, notwithstanding your gracious concessions, our ministers cannot procure institution without renouncing their ordination by presbyters, or being reordained, nor without subscription and the oaths of canonical obedience. And we are apprehensive that your majesty's indulgence does not extend to the abatement of reordination, or subscription, or the oath of canonical obedience. We therefore earnestly crave that your majesty will declare your pleasure, 1. That ordination, and institution, and induction, may be confirmed without the said subscription and oath. 2. That none may be urged to be reordained, or denied institution for want of ordination by prelates that have been ordained by presbyters. 3. That none may forfeit their presentation or benefice for not reading those articles of the thirty-nine that relate to government and ceremonies."

However, if the king's declaration, without any amendments, had passed into a law, it would have prevented in a great measure the separation that followed; but neither the court nor ministry intended it, if they could stand their ground upon the foot of the old establishment. A reverend prelate of the Church of England confesses, " that this declaration has in it a spirit of true wisdom and charity above any one public confession that was ever made in matters

---

[*] Hist. of the Noncon., p. 14. Baxter, part ii., p. 268.

of religion. It shows the admirable temper and prudence of the king and his council in that tender juncture of affairs; it proves the.charity and moderation of the suffering bishops, in thinking such concessions just and reasonable for peace and unity ; and it shows a disposition in the other party to have accepted the terms of union consistent with our Episcopacy and liturgy. It condemns the unhappy ferment that soon after followed for want of this temper ; and it may stand for a pattern to posterity, whenever they are disposed to restore the discipline. and heal the breaches of the Church." Another conformist writer adds, "If ever a divine sentence was in the mouth of any king, and his mouth erred not in judgment, I verily believe it was thus with our present majesty when he composed that admirable declaration, which, next to the Holy Scriptures, I adore, and think that the united judgment of the whole nation cannot frame a better or a more unexceptionable expedient, for a firm and lasting concord of these distracted churches."

The Presbyterians about London were so far pleased, that they drew up the following address of thanks, in the name of the city ministers, and presented it to the king. November 16, by the hands of the Reverend Mr. Samuel Clarke :

"Most dread Sovereign !

"We, your majesty's most dutiful and loyal subjects, ministers of the Gospel in your city of London, having perused your majesty's late declaration, and finding it so full of indulgence and gracious condescension; we cannot but judge ourselves highly obliged, first, to render our unfeigned thanks to God, and, next, our most hearty and humble acknowledgments to your majesty, that we may testify to your royal self, and all the world, our just sentiments of your majesty's great goodness and clemency therein expressed."*

The address then recites the several condescensions of his majesty in the declaration, and concludes thus : " We crave leave to profess, that though all things in this frame of government be not exactly suited to our judgments, yet your majesty's moderation has so great an influence on us, that we shall to the utmost endeavour the healing of the breaches, and promoting the peace and union of the Church. We would beg of your majesty, with all humility, upon our knees, that reordination, and the surplice in colleges, might not be imposed ; and we hope God will incline your majesty's heart to gratify us in these our desires also."

Signed by

Samuel Clarke,	Jo. Rawlinson,	Thomas Lye,
William Cooper,	Jo. Sheffield;	John Jackson,
Thomas Case,	Thomas Gouge,	John Meriton,
Jo. Gibbon,	Gab. Sanger,	William Bates,
William Whitaker,	El. Pledger.	With many others.
Thomas Jacomb,	Matth. Pool,	

The king having received the address, returned this answer :† "Gentlemen, I will endeavour to give you all satisfaction, and to make you as happy as myself."‡

* Baxter's Life, part ii., p. 279, 284. Kennet's Chron., p. 311.　　† Kennet's Chron., p. 315.
‡ December 11, 1729.—Waiting on Arthur Onslow, Esq., speaker of the honourable House of Commons, he was pleased to suffer me to peruse, and afterward to transcribe, a marginal note, which he had

Upon the terms of this declaration Dr. Reynolds accepted of the bishopric of Norwich ; Mr. Baxter was offered the bishopric of Hereford, but refused upon other reasons ; and Mr. Calamy declined the bishopric of Litchfield and Coventry, till the king's declaration should be passed into a law. Dr. Manton, having been presented to the living of Covent Garden by the Earl of Bedford, accepted it upon the terms of the declaration, and received Episcopal institution from Dr. Sheldon, bishop of London, January 10, 1660-61. Having first subscribed the doctrinal articles of the Church of England only, and taken the oaths of allegiance and supremacy, and of canonical obedience in all things lawful and honest, the doctor was also content, that the Common Prayer should be read in his church. Dr. Bates was offered the deanery of Litchfield ; Dr. Manton the deanery of Rochester ; and Mr. Bowles that of York ; but finding how things were going at court, after some time, refused.

The Lords and Commons, upon reading the king's declaration, agreed to wait upon his majesty in a body, and return him thanks ; and the Commons ordered a bill into their house to pass it into a law ; but when the bill had been read the first time, the question being put for a second reading, it passed in the negative ; one of the secretaries of state opposing it, which was a sufficient indication, says Dr. Bates, of the king and court's aversion to it.* Sir Matthew Hale, who was zealous for the declaration, at that very juncture was taken out of the House of Commons, and made lord-chief-baron of the exchequer, that he might not oppose the resolutions of the ministry. Strange! that a House

written with his own hand to pages 152, 153, and 154, of the first volume of my Abridgment of Mr. Baxter's Life, where the subject of which I was treating was King Charles's celebrated declaration for ecclesiastical affairs, which bore date October 25, 1660.

I had said, that the concessions there made were so highly pleasing, that an address of thanks was drawn up and signed by many of the dissenting members in and about London, &c.

The marginal note before mentioned was in the words following :

"Both houses of Parliament did also severally present to the king an address of thanks for this declaration ; and in the House of Commons, November 6, 1660, a committee was appointed to bring in a bill to make the declaration effectual, and the person first named of the committee was Sergeant Hale, who was therefore very probably the first mover of this bill. And as he was the next day (I think it was so soon) made chief-lord-baron, it is not unlikely that he was desirous to leave the House of Commons with this mark of his moderation as to the religious differences of that time, and what he thought would be the proper means to heal them. But his endeavours did not succeed ; for on the 28th of November following, the bill being read the first time, and a question put that the bill be read a second time, it passed in the negative : the yeas one hundred and dred and fifty-seven, the noes one hundred and eighty-three. The tellers for the yeas were Sir Anthony Joby and Sir George Booth ; for the noes, Sir Solomon Swale and Mr. Palmer."

Note. "Sir. Solomon Swale was afterward discharged being a member of the House of Commons, for being a popish recusant convict."—Dr. Calamy's History of his own Life.

I here insert this for the use of posterity.

* Kennet's Chron., p. 358.

of Commons, which on the 9th of November, had given the king thanks for his declaration by their speaker *nem contradicente*, should on the 28th of the same month reject it before a second reading. This blasted all the expectations of the Presbyterian clergy at once. It was now apparent that the court did not design the declaration should be carried into execution, but only serve as a temporary expedient to keep them quiet till the Church should be in circumstances to bid them defiance. While the diocesan doctors, were at Breda (says Mr. Baxter), they did not dream that their way to the highest grandeur was so fair; then they would have been glad of the terms of the declaration of Breda ; when they came in they proceeded by slow degrees, that they might feel the ground under them ; for this purpose they proposed the declaration, which, being but a temporary provision, must give place to laws ; but when they found the *Parliament and populace ripe for anything they should propose,* they dropped the declaration, and all farther thoughts of accommodation.†

The court and bishops were now at ease, and went on briskly with restoring all things to the old standard ; the doctrines of passive obedience and non-resistance were revived ; men of the highest principles, and most inveterate resentments, were preferred to bishoprics, by which they were more than compensated for their sufferings by the large sums of money they raised on the renewal of leases,‡ which, after so long an interval, were almost expired ; but what a sad use they made of their riches, I choose rather to relate in the words of Bishop Burnet than my own. "What the bishops did with their great fines was a pattern to all their lower dignitaries, who generally took more care of themselves than of the Church ; the men of service were loaded with many livings and many dignities. With this accession of wealth, there broke in upon the Church a great deal of luxury and high living, on pretence of hospitality ; and with this overset of wealth and pomp that came upon men in the decline of their age, they who were now growing into old age became lazy and negligent in all the true concerns of the Church."§

From this time, says Bishop Kennet, Presbyterians began to prepare for the cry of persecution, and not without reason, for March 23, Mr. Zach. Crofton, minister of Aldgate, was sent to the Tower for writing in favour of the Covenant ; where he lay a considerable time at great expense, and was at last turned out of his parish without any consideration, though he had a wife and seven children, and had been very zealous for the king's restoration.* Mr. Andrew Parsons, rector of Wem in Shropshire, a noted Loyalist, was fetched from his house in the month of December by six soldiers, for seditious preaching and nonconformity to the ceremonies ; for which he was fined £200, and to continue in prison till it was paid.

Spies were sent into all the congregations of Presbyterians throughout England, to observe and report their behaviour to the bishops ; and if a minister lamented the degeneracy of the times, or expressed his concern for the ark of God, if he preached against perfidiousness, or glanced at the vices of the court, he was marked for an enemy to the king and government. Many eminent and loyal Presbyterians were sent to prison upon such informations; among whom was the learned and prudent Mr. John Howe ; and when they came to their trials, the court was guarded with soldiers, and their friends not suffered to attend them. Many were sequestered from their livings, and cited into the ecclesiastical courts, for not using the surplice and other ceremonies, while the discipline of the Church was under a kind of suspension. So eager were the spiritual courts to renew the exercise of the sword ; and so fiercely was it brandished against the falling Presbyterians !

The convention Parliament passed sundry acts with relation to the late times, of which these following deserve to be remembered : An act for the confirming and restoring of ministers, which enacts, among other things, "that every sequestered minister, who has not justified the late king's murder, or declared against infant baptism, shall be restored to his living before the 25th of December next ensuing, and the present incumbent shall peaceably quit it,

---

* Life, p. 287.

† How very apostolical and peaceable were these successors of the apostles who were on the bench at this period !—C.

‡ The terms on which these leases were renewed were high and oppressive, and the bishops incurred the severe censure of the Presbyterian ministers, and raised against themselves the clamour of the subordinate and dependant clergy. The fines raised by renewing the leases amounted to a million and a half. In some sees they produced 40. or £50,000, which were applied to the enriching the bishops, families.—*Secret History of the Court and Reign of King Charles II.*, vol. i., p. 350–354 ; and *Burnet's History of his Own Times*, vol. i., p. 271, 12mo.—Ed.

§ Dr. Grey endeavours to show that Bishop Burnet's representation, quoted above, was founded in a mistake ; and with this view he states the benefactions and charities of some of the bishops, deans, and chapters. According to his authorities, besides the expenditures of Bishop Duppa, which we have mentioned before, Dr. Juxon, archbishop of Canterbury, gave to various purposes and public works £48,000, and abated in fines £16,000. Dr. Sheldon, while Bishop of London, expended £40,000, and abated to his tenants £17,000. Dr. Frewen, archbishop

VOL. II.—E E

of York, disbursed in public payments, besides abatements to tenants, £15,000. Dr. Cosins's (bishop of Durham) expenditures in building and repairing public edifices and in charities amounted to £44,000. Dr. Warner, bishop of Rochester, though his fines were small, gave in royal presents, benevolences, and subsidies, and redeeming captives, £25,000. The liberalities of various deans and chapters made the sum of £191,300. These expenditures bespeak munificence and generosity ; and they appear to take off much of the edge of Bishop Burnet's censure. He allows that "some few exceptions are to be made ; but, so few (he adds), that if a new set of men had not appeared of another stamp, the Church had quite lost her esteem over the nation." The reader will also reflect, that the proportion not of the number of dignitaries only, who made a display of charity or liberality, but of the sums they expended to the accession of wealth, is to be taken into the account. The above sums fall more than a million short of the amount of the fines that were raised : to these must be added the annual incomes of the ecclesiastical estates to which they were preferred.—*Grey's Examination*, vol. iii., p. 269–274. *Burnet's History*, vol. i., p. 271.—Ed.

* Kennet's Chron., p. 397. Conf. Plea, p. 34.

and be accountable for dilapidations, and all arrears of fifths not paid." By this act some hundreds of Nonconformist ministers were dispossessed of their livings, before the Act of Uniformity was penned. Here was no distinction between good or bad ; but if the parson had been Episcopally ordained, and in possession, he must he restored, though he had beed ejected upon the strongest evidence of immorality or scandal.

The act for confirmation of marriages was very expedient for the peace of the kingdom, and the order and harmony of families. It enacts, "that all marriages since May 1, 1642, solemnized before a justice of peace, or reputed justice ; and all marriages since the said time, had or solemnized according to the direction of any ordinance, or reputed act or ordinance of one or both houses of Parliament, shall be adjudged and esteemed to be of the same force and effect as if they had been solemnized according to the rites and ceremonies of the Church of England."

An act for the attainder of several persons guilty of the horrid murder of his late sacred majesty King Charles I., and for the perpetual observation of the 30th of January.* This was the subject of many conferences between the two houses, in one of which Chancellor Hyde declared that the king having sent him in embassy to the King of Spain, charged him to tell that monarch expressly, "that the horrible murder of his father ought not to be deemed as the act of the Parliament or people of England, but of a small crew of wretches and miscreants who had usurped the sovereign power, and rendered themselves masters of the kingdom ;"† for which the Commons sent a deputation with thanks to the king. After the preamble, the act goes on to attaint the king's judges, dead or alive, except Colonel Ingoldsby‡ and Thompson, who, for their late good services, were pardoned, but in their room were included Colonel Lambert, Sir Harry Vane, and Hugh Peters,

* The service for this day, it has been remarked, was framed on the *jure divino* plan, consequently on principles inconsistent with those of the Revolution. It was drawn up by Archbishop Sancroft, whose influence procured it to be adopted and published by the king's authority, though another of a more moderate strain was at first preferred to it. When Sancroft himself was laid aside for adopting or adhering to principles suitable to his style, what had we to do any longer with Sancroft's office?—*Letters and Essays in favour of Public Liberty*, vol. i., p. 32.—ED.

† This plea, it has been observed by a late writer, would have been precluded, had the Parliament of 1641 proceeded against the king by way of attainder, about the time that Strafford and Laud were impeached. For then they were constitutionally invested with the legislative and judicial powers of a national representative ; and they had sufficient overt acts before them to convict him of the blackest treason against the majesty of the people of England.— *Memoirs of Hollis*, vol. ii., p. 591.—ED.

‡ Dr. Grey observes, on the authority of Lord Clarendon, that the case of Colonel Ingoldsby was singular. He was drawn into the army about the time when he came first of age by Cromwell, to whom he was nearly allied. Though appointed to it, he never sat with the judges of the king ; and his signature to the warrant for the king's death was obtained by violence ; Cromwell seized his hand, put the pen between his fingers, and with his own hand wrote Richard Ingoldsby, he making all the resistance he could.—*Clarendon's History*, vol. iii., p. 763.

who were not of the judges. On the 30th of January this year, the bodies of O. Cromwell, Bradshaw, and Ireton were taken out of their graves, and drawn upon hurdles to Tyburn, where they were hung up from ten in the morning till sunset of the next day, after which their heads were cut off, and their trunks buried all together in one hole under the gallows.* Colonel Lambert was sent to the Isle of Jersey, where he continued shut up as a patient prisoner almost thirty years ; nineteen made their escape beyond sea ; seven were made objects of the king's clemency ; nineteen others, who surrendered on the king's proclamation of June 6, had their lives saved after trial, but underwent other penalties, as imprisonment, banishment, and forfeiture of estates ; so that ten only were executed in the month of October, after the new sheriffs were entered upon their office, viz., Colonel Harrison, Mr. Carew, Cook, Hugh Peters, Mr. Scot, Clement, Scroop, Jones, Hacker, and Axtel.†

Bishop Burnet says,‡ "The trials and executions of the first that suffered were attended by vast crowds of people. All men seemed pleased with the sight ; but the firmness and show of piety of the sufferers, who went out of the world with a sort of triumph in the cause for which they suffered, turned the minds of the populace, insomuch that the king was advised to proceed no farther." The prisoners were rudely treated in court, the spectators, with their noise and clamour, endeavouring to put them out of countenance. None of them denied the fact, but all pleaded "Not guilty to the treason," because, as they said, they acted by authority of Parliament ; not considering that the House of Commons is no court of judicature ; or if it was, that it was packed and purged before the king was brought to his trial. Those who guarded the scaffold, pleaded that they acted by command of their superior officers, who would have cashiered or put them to death if they had not obeyed. They were not permitted to enter into the merits of the cause between the king and Parliament, but were condemned upon the statute of the 25th Edward III., for compassing and imagining the king's death.

The behaviour of the regicides at their execution was bold and resolute ; Colonel Harrison declared at the gibbet that he was fully persuaded that what he had done was the cause and work of God, which he was confident God would own and raise up again, how much soever it suffered at that time. He went through all the indignities and severities of his suffering with a calmness, or rather cheerfulness, that astonished the spectators ; he was turned off, and cut down alive ; for, after his body was opened, he raised himself up, and gave the executioner a box on the ear.§ When Mr. Solicitor Cook and Hugh Peters went into the sledge, the head of Major-general Harrison was put upon it, with the face bare towards them ; but, notwithstanding this, Mr. Cook went out of the world with surprising resolution, blessing

* This was done, says Dr. Grey, upon a 30th of January ; a circumstance which Mr. Neal might probably think below his notice.—ED.
† Kennet's Chron., p. 367.   ‡ Vol. i., p. 234.
§ State Trials, p. 404.

God that he had a clear conscience. Hugh Peters was more timid; but after he had seen the execution and quartering of Mr. Cook, he resumed his courage at length (which some said was artificial), and said to the sheriff, " Sir, you have here slain one of the servants of the Lord; and made me behold it, on purpose to terrify and discourage me ; but God has made it an ordinance for my strengthening and encouragement."* Mr. Scot was not allowed to speak to the people, but said in his prayer, " that he had been engaged in a cause not to be repented of ; I say in a cause not to be repented of." Carew appeared very cheerful as he went to the gibbet, but said little of the cause for which he suffered. Clements also said nothing. Colonel Jones justified the king and court in their proceedings ; but added, that they did not satisfy him in so great and deep a point. Colonel Scroop was drawn in the same sledge, whose grave and venerable countenance, accompanied with courage and cheerfulness, raised great compassion in some of the spectators, though the insults and rudeness of others were cruel and barbarous : he said he was born and bred a gentleman, and appealed to those who had known him for his behaviour ; he forgave the instruments of his sufferings, and died for that which he judged to be the cause of Christ. Colonel Axtel and Hacker suffered last ; the former behaved with great resolution, and, holding the Bible in his hand, said, " The very cause in which I was engaged is contained in this Book of God ; and having been fully convinced in my conscience of the justness of the war, I freely engaged in the Parliament's service, which, as I do believe, was the cause of the Lord, I ventured my life freely for it, and now die for it." Hacker read a paper to the same purpose ; and after having expressed his charity towards his judges, jury, and witnesses, he said, " I have nothing lies upon my conscience as guilt whereof I am now condemned, and do not doubt but to have the sentence reversed."

Few, if any, of these criminals were friends of the Protector Cromwell, but gave him all possible disturbance in favour of a commonwealth. Mr. H. Cromwell, in one of his letters from Ireland, 1657–8, says, " It is a sad case, when men, knowing the difficulties we labour under, seek occasions to quarrel and unsettle everything again ; I hear Harrison, Carew, and Okey, have done new feats. I hope God will infatuate them in their endeavours to disturb the peace of the nation ; their folly shows them to be no better than abusers of religion, and such whose hypocrisy the Lord will avenge in due time."

The regicides certainly confounded the cause of the Parliament, or the necessity of entering into a war to bring delinquents to justice, with the king's execution ; whereas they fall under a very distinct consideration ; the former might be necessary, when the latter had neither law nor equity to support it :† for admitting, with

them, that the king is accountable to his Parliament, the House of Commons alone is not the Parliament ; and if it was, it could not be so after it was under restraint, and one half of the members forcibly kept from their places by the military power. They had no precedent for their conduct, nor any measure of law to try and condemn their sovereign ; though the Scripture says, " He that sheds man's blood, by man shall his blood be shed," yet this is not a rule of duty for private persons, when there is a government subsisting. If the king had fallen in battle, it had been a different case ; but how criminal soever his majesty might be in their apprehensions, they had no warrant to sit as his judges ; and, therefore, could have no right by their verdict or sentence to put him to death.

There was another act passed this session for a perpetual anniversary thanksgiving on the 29th of May, for his majesty's happy restoration ; upon which occasion the bishops were commanded to draw up a suitable form of prayer ; and Mr. Robinson, in the preface to his Review of the Case of Liturgies, says that in their first form, which is since altered, there are these unwarrantable expressions, which I mention only to show the spirit of the times : " We beseech thee to give us grace to remember and provide for our latter end, by a careful and studious imitation of this thy blessed saint and martyr, and all other thy saints and martyrs that have gone before us, that we may be made worthy to receive the benefit by their prayers, which they, in communion with thy Church catholic, offer up unto thee for that part of it here militant, and yet in sight with and danger from the flesh."*

The books of the great Milton, and Mr. John Goodwin, published in defence of the sentence of death passed upon his late majesty, were called in by proclamation. And upon the 27th of August, Milton's Defensio pro Populo Anglicano contra Salmasium, and his answer to a book entitled The Portraiture of his sacred Majesty in his Solitude and Sufferings, were burned by the hands of the common hangman ; together with Mr. John Goodwin's book, entitled The Obstructers of Justice ; but the authors absconded till the storm was over. It was a surprise to all that they had escaped

---

* I propose to afford the reader an opportunity of understanding Hugh Peters's character, by annexing an historical and critical account of this much-slandered man in the Appendix.—C.

† A distinguished writer, who now ranks a peer, delivers a different opinion from our author. " If a

king deserves," says he, " to be opposed by force of arms, he deserves death ; if he reduces his subjects to that extremity, the blood spilled in the quarrel lies on him ; the executing him afterward is a mere formality."—Walpole's Royal and Noble Authors, vol. ii., p. 69, as quoted by Dr. Harris, Life of Charles II., vol. i., p. 262. A sentiment of this last writer, which carries truth and force in it, may be properly brought forward in this connexion. " The depriving of the people of their rights and liberties, or the arguing for the expediency and justice of so doing, is a crime of a higher nature than the murdering, or magnifying the murder, of the wisest and best prince under heaven. The loss of a good prince is greatly to be lamented ; but it is a loss which may be repaired : whereas the loss of a people's liberties is seldom or ever to be recovered ; consequently, the foe to the latter is much more detestable than the foe to the former."— Historical and Critical Account of Hugh Peters, p. 49, 50.— Ed.

* Dr. Grey asks, " What is there blameable in all this ? Here is no praying to saints ; and nothing but what was thought warrantable by the fathers, long before popery had a being."—Ed.

prosecution. None but Goodwin and Peters had magnified the king's execution in their sermons; but Goodwin's being a strenuous Arminian procured him friends.† Milton had appeared so boldly, though with much wit, and so great purity and elegance of style, upon the argument of the king's death, that it was thought a strange omission not to except him out of the Act of Indemnity;† but he lived many years after, though blind, to acquire immortal renown by his celebrated poem of Paradise Lost.‡

The tide of joy which overflowed the nation at the king's restoration brought with it the return of popery, which had been at a very low ebb during the late commotions: great numbers of that religion came over with his majesty, and crowded about the court, magnifying their sufferings for the late king. A list of the lords, gentlemen, and other officers, who were killed in his service, was printed in red letters, by which it appeared that several noblemen, ten knights and baronets, fourteen colonels, seven lieutenant-colonels, fourteen majors, sixty-six captains, eighteen lieutenants and cornets, and thirty-eight gentlemen, lost their lives in the civil war, besides great numbers who were wounded, and whose estates were sequestered. The queen-mother came from France, and resided at Somerset House with her Catholic attendants, both religious and secular. Several Romish priests who had been confined in Newgate, Lancaster, and other jails, were by order of council set at liberty. Many popish priests were sent over from Douay into England, as missionaries for propagating that religion; and their clergy appeared openly in defiance of the laws; they were busy about the court and city in dispersing popish books of devotion; and the king gave open countenance and protection to such as had been serviceable to him abroad, and came over with him, or soon followed him,

which, Bishop Kennet says, his majesty could not avoid. Upon the whole, more Roman Catholics appeared openly this year than in all the twelve years of the interregnum.

In Ireland the papists took possession of their estates, which had been forfeited by the rebellion and massacre, and turned out the purchasers; which occasioned such commotions in that kingdom, that the king was obliged to issue out a proclamation, commanding them to wait the determination of the ensuing Parliament. The body of their clergy, by an instrument bearing date January 1, 1660, O. S., signed and sealed by the chief prelates and officials of their religion, ventured to depute a person of their own communion to congratulate his majesty's restoration, and to present their humble supplications for the free exercise of their religion, pursuant to the articles of 1648, whom the king received very favourably, and encouraged to hope for an accomplishment of their requests in due time. Such amazing changes happened within nine months after the king's arrival at Whitehall.

The only persons who, under pretence of religion, attempted anything against the government, were a small number of enthusiasts, who said they were for King Jesus; their leader was Thomas Venner, a wine cooper, who, in his little conventicle in Coleman-street, warmed his admirers with passionate expectations of a fifth universal monarchy, under the personal reign of King Jesus upon earth, and that the saints were to take the kingdom to themselves. To introduce this imaginary kingdom, they marched out of their meeting-house towards St. Paul's churchyard, on Sunday, January 6, to the number of about fifty men well armed, and with a resolution to subvert the present government or die in the attempt. They published a declaration of the design of their rising, and placed sentinels at proper places: The lord-mayor sent the trained-bands to disperse them, whom they quickly routed, but in the evening retired to Cane Wood, between Highgate and Hampstead. On Wednesday morning they returned, and dispersed a party of the king's soldiers in Threadneedle-street. In Wood-street they repelled the trained-bands, and some of the horse-guards; but Venner himself was knocked down, and some of his company slain; from hence the remainder retreated to Cripplegate, and took possession of a house, which they threatened to defend with a desperate resolution, but nobody appearing to countenance their phrensy, they surrendered after they had lost about half their number; Venner and one of his officers were hanged before their meeting-house door in Coleman-street, January 19, and a few days after nine more were executed in divers parts of the city.*

* Burnet, vol. i., p. 236, 237, 12mo edit.

† "And so, indeed, it was," says Dr. Grey, "he being the most pestilent writer that appeared at that time in defence of the regicides, Peyton and John Goodwin excepted." Milton's safety, it is said, was owing to the powerful intercession and interest of Secretary Morrice, Sir Thomas Clarges, and Andrew Marvel; but principally to the influence and gratitude of Sir William Davenant, whose release Milton had procured when he was taken prisoner in 1650. Nor was Charles II., says Toland, such an enemy to the muses as to require his destruction.—*British Biography*, vol. v., p. 313, 314; and *Dr. Grey's Examination*, vol. iii., p. 298.—ED.

‡ The only avenue to royal favour at the Restoration was to defame the character of all who had been active in behalf of the rights of the people. We ought to receive the *biography of that period* with many grains of allowance. Take, for an example, the following life of John Milton, taken literally and without abridgment from William Winstanley's Lives of the most famous English Poets, licensed for printing June 16, 1686.

"John Milton was one whose natural parts might deservedly give him a place among the principal of our English poets, having written two heroic poems and a tragedy; viz., Paradise Lost, Paradise Regained, and Samson Agonistes; but his fame is gone out like a candle in a snuff, and his memory will always stink, which might have ever lived in honourable repute, had he not been a notorious traitor, and most impiously and villanously belied that blessed martyr, King Charles I."—P. 195.—C.

* It plainly appeared, on the examination of these insurgents, that they had entered into no plot with any other conspirators. The whole transaction was the unquestionable effect of the religious phrensy of a few individuals. Yet it was the origin of a national burden and evil felt to this day. At the council, on the morning after the insurrection was quelled, the Duke of York availed himself of the opportunity to push his arbitrary measures. On the pretext that so extravagant an attempt could not have arisen from the rashness of one man, but was the result of a plot formed by all the sectaries and fanatics to overthrow the present government, he moved "to suspend, at

This mad insurrection gave the court a handle for breaking through the late declaration of indulgence within three months after it was published ; for January 2 there was an order of council against the meetings of sectaries in great numbers, and at unusual times ; and on the 10th of January a proclamation was published, whereby his majesty forbids the Anabaptists, Quakers, and fifth-monarchy men to assemble or meet together under pretence of worshipping God, except it be in some parochial church or chapel, or in private houses by the persons there inhabiting.* All meetings in other places are declared to be unlawful and riotous. And his majesty commands all mayors, and other peace-officers, to search for such conventicles, and cause the persons therein to be bound over to the next sessions. Upon this, the Independents, Baptists, and Quakers, who dissented from the establishment, thought fit publicly to disown and renounce the late insurrection.

The Independents, though not named in the proclamation, were obnoxious to the government, and suspected to concur in all designs that might change the constitution into a commonwealth : to wipe off this odium, there was published "A Renunciation and Declaration of the Congregational Churches and public Preachers of the said Judgment, living in and about the City of London, against the late horrid Insurrection and Rebellion acted in the said City."† Dated January, 1660. In this declar-

such an alarming crisis, the disbanding of General Monk's regiment of foot ;" which had the guard of Whitehall, and was, by order of Parliament, to have been disbanded the next day. Through different causes the motion was adopted, and a letter was sent to the king to request him to approve and confirm the resolution of the council, and to appoint the continuance of the regiment till farther order. To this the king consented ; and, as the rumours of fresh conspiracies were industriously kept up, those troops were continued and augmented, and a way was prepared for the gradual establishment of a standing army under the name of guards. This should be a memento to future ages how they credit reports of plots and conspiracies thrown out by a minister, unless the evidence of their existence be brought forward. The cry of conspiracies has been frequently nothing more than the chimera of fear, or the invention of a wicked policy to carry the schemes of ambition and despotism.—*Secret History of the Court and Reign of Charles II.*, vol. i., p. 346, 347.—ED.

* Kennet's Chron., p. 357.

† " This proclamation," Mr. Gough well observes, "appears to be drawn up with more art and fallacy than sound judgment and equity ; while it reaches all the different sects of Dissenters, all who do not assemble for worship in some parochial church or chapel, as rioters, it distinguishes only those looked upon as the most insignificant, and least formidable for their numbers or abilities. The Presbyterians are passed over in silence, for they could not, with any colour of decency, be pointed at as foes to the government they had just before been conducive to establishing. The Independents are also unnoticed, probably for fear of awakening the exertion of that vigour and of those abilities, the effects whereof were yet recent in the memory of the present administration. The Anabaptists and Quakers, as new or weaker sects, are treated with less ceremony, and are ranked with the wild disturbers of the public peace : wherein justice, the characteristic virtue of good government, was designedly violated by involving the innocent with the guilty in one confused mass."—*Hist. of the Quakers*, vol. I., p. 443, 444.—ED.

ation they disown the principles of a fifth monarchy, or the personal reign of King Jesus on earth, as dishonourable to Him, and prejudicial to His Church ; and abhor the propagating this or any other opinion by force or blood. They refer to their late meeting of messengers from one hundred and twenty churches of their way, at the Savoy, in which they declare (chap. xxiv. of their Confession) that civil magistrates are of Divine appointment, and that it is the duty of all subjects to pray for them, to honour their persons, to pay them tribute, to obey their lawful commands, and to be subject to their authority ; and that infidelity, or indifference in religion, does not make void the magistrates' just and legal authority, nor free the people from their obedience. Accordingly, they cease not to pray for all sorts of blessings, spiritual and temporal, upon the person and government of his majesty, and by the grace of God will continue to do so themselves; and persuade others thereunto. And with regard to the late impious and prodigiously-daring rebellion, they add, " Cursed be their anger, for it was fierce ; and their wrath, for it was cruel : O my soul ! come, not thou into their secret, but let God divide them in Jacob, and scatter them in Israel." Signed by

Jos. Caryl,	Samuel Slater,	William Greenhil,
George Griffiths,	George Cockyan,	Matth. Barker,
Richard Kenrick,	Thomas Goodwin,	Tho. Malory,
Robert Bragge,	Thomas Brooks,	John Loder,
Ralph Venning,	Corn. Helme,	John Yates,
John Oxenbridge,	John Hodges,	Thomas Owen,
Philip Nye,	John Rachiler,	Nath. Mather,
John Rowe,	Seth Wood,	Will. Stoughton.
Thomas Weld,		

The Baptists published an apology* in behalf of themselves and their brethren of the same judgment, with a protestation against the late wicked and most horrid treason and rebellion in this city of London ; in which they avow their loyalty to the king, and promise that their practice shall be conformable ; subscribed by William Kiffen, Henry Den, John Batty, Thomas Lamb, Thomas Cowper, and about twenty-nine or thirty other names. They also addressed the king, that the innocent might not suffer with the guilty ; protesting in the most solemn manner, that they had not the least knowledge of the late insurrection, nor did, directly or indirectly, contrive, promote, assist, or approve of it. They offered to give security for their peacea-

* This was subscribed by thirty ministers and principal members of the Baptist congregations. It was accompanied by another paper, called also an " Apology," which had been presented to the king some months before Venner's insurrection, declaratory of their sentiments concerning magistracy, and of their readiness to obey the king and all in authority in all things lawful. Mr. Jessey, preaching soon after, declared to his congregation, that Venner should say, " that he believed there was not one Baptist among his adherents ; and that if they succeeded, the Baptists should know that infant baptism was an ordinance of Jesus Christ." In farther vindication of this people, and to show that they were unjustly charged with opposing magistracy and government, there was published about this time a small treatise entitled " Moderation ; or, Arguments and Motives tending thereto ; humbly tendered to the honourable Members of Parliament." Copious extracts from this piece may be seen in *Crosby's History of the English Baptists*, vol. ii., p. 42, 83.—ED. (TOULMIN).

ble behaviour, and for their supporting his majesty's person and government. But notwithstanding this, their religious assemblies were disturbed in all places, and their ministers imprisoned ;* great numbers were crowded into Newgate and other prisons, where they remained under close confinement till the king's coronation, when the, general pardon published on that occasion set them at liberty.

---

*. Divers pious persons were haled out of their houses ; four hundred were committed to Newgate ; others to Wood-street Compter ; and many to other prisons. The first and most violent persecution was chiefly levelled against them. Among others who suffered on this occasion was Mr. Hanserd Knollys. Mr. Vavasor Powel was, early in the morning, taken from his house by a company of soldiers, and carried to prison; from whence he was conducted to Salop, and committed with several others to the custody of a marshal; where they were detained nine weeks, till they were released by an order of the king and council. Mr. John Bunyan was apprehended at a meeting and committed to prison, though he offered bail, till the next sessions. He was then indicted for "devilishly and perniciously abstaining from coming to church to hear Divine service ; and as a common upholder of several unlawful meetings and conventicles, to the distraction of the good subjects of this kingdom, contrary to the laws of our sovereign lord the king." He frankly owned being at the meeting. The justices took this for a confession of the indictment ; and; because he refused to conform, sentenced him to perpetual banishment, on an act made by the then Parliament. Though the sentence of banishment was never executed upon him, he was kept in prison twelve years and a half, and suffered much under cruel and oppressive jailers. Above sixty Dissenters were imprisoned with him, among whom were Mr. Wheeler and Mr. Dun, two eminent ministers well known in Bedfordshire. Mr. Bunyan was at last liberated, on the importunity of Dr. Barlow, bishop of Lincoln.—*Crosby's History of the Baptists,* vol. ii., p. 91–93 ; *Vavasor Powel's Life,* p. 129 ; and *Robinson's Translation of Claude,* vol. ii., p. 228. —Ed.

I cannot resist the desire I have to gratify the reader with Mr. Robinson's remarks on *the bill of indictment* against John Bunyan. "The two facts are these : Bunyan *did not* worship Almighty God in the parish meeting-house. Bunyan *did* worship God in a farmhouse. Now these two facts are innocent in themselves, inoffensive to society, and altogether unconnected with plots of subverting civil government ; consequently, the citizen who did them ought not to have been criminated for these actions. But see what rhetoric can do ! Call the parish meeting house *the church ;* name the ceremonies performed there *service ;* assert the book that contains them to be *Divine ;* make the whole of religion to consist in *hearing* a priest *read* it ; affirm that a *devil* or a *devilkin* comes from hell to persuade Bunyan not to hear it ; say that Bunyan's absence is of so much consequence as to be *pernicious* or destructive to the Divine Book ; call the farmer's parlour, held in fee simple, a *conventicle* or meeting-place ; say if sixteen harvestmen and their wives meet there on the 20th of August and get drunk at harvest home, the parlour is a *lawful* conventicle ; and that if they meet there on the 21st of August to repent of drunkenness, and get Bunyan to pray to God there to accept their repentance, and to tell them out of the book whether God will accept it, that then it is an unlawful conventicle ; say that the prayers and tears of these poor wretches *disturb* and *distract* all the good subjects of the kingdom, who may happen to be at the very time extremely merry at operas; play-houses, taverns, ale-houses, and other places, and know nothing about it ; bedizen all this with the name of *our sovereign lord the king ;* and lo ! this rhetorical objection shall send Bunyan to jail for 12 years and 6 months."—C.

The Quakers also addressed the king upon this occasion in the following words :*
"Oh King Charles !
"Our desire is, that thou mayest live forever in the fear of God and thy council. We beseech thee and thy council to read these following lines, in tender bowels, and compassion for our souls, and for our good.
"And this consider : we are about four hundred imprisoned in and about this city, of men and women from their families ; besides, in the country jails above ten hundred. We desire that our meetings may not be broken up, but that all may come to a fair trial, that our innocency may be cleared up.
"London, 16th day eleventh month, 1660."†

On the 28th of the same month, they published the declaration referred to in their address, entitled " A Declaration from the harmless and innocent People of God called Quakers, against all Sedition, Plotters and Fighters in the World, for removing the Ground of Jealousy and Suspicion from both Magistrates and People in the Kingdom, concerning Wars and Fightings." Presented to the king the 21st day of the eleventh month, 1660.‡ Upon which, his majesty promised them, on the word of a king, that they should not suffer for their opinions as long as they lived peaceably ; but his promises were little regarded.§

The Presbyterian clergy were in some degree affected with these commotions, though envy itself could not charge them with guilt ; but it was the wish and desire of the prelatical party that they might discover their uneasiness in such a manner as might expose them to trouble; for their ruin was already determined, only some pretexts were wanting to cover the design, particularly such as affected the peace of the kingdom, and might not reflect on his majesty's declaration from Breda, which promised that no

---

* Mr. Neal, a respectable person of the society informs me, has given two short paragraphs only of an address containing seven quarto pages of close letter-press. It underwent, it seems, several editions, not fewer than eight or ten ; for, being fraught with much pertinent, solid matter, as persecution continued, it was made very public. Mr. Neal, or his author Kennet, is charged with having mutilated the paragraphs which he quotes. For the second sentence stands in the original thus : " We beseech thee and thy council to read these following lines ; and in tender bowels and compassion to read them over, for we write in love and compassion to your souls, and for your good." And after families should be added, "in close holes and prisons."—Ed.
† Kennet's Chron., p. 361.   ‡ Ibid., p. 366.
§ Dr. Grey impeaches here the candour and fidelity of Mr. Neal as an historian ; and adds, " Sewel, a Quaker, speaks more favourably." This writer, as Dr. Grey quotes him, does say, that at this time the king showed himself moderate. for, at the solicitation of some, he set at liberty about seven hundred of the people called Quakers ; and that they were acquitted from any hand in Venner's plot, and that, being continually importuned, the king issued forth a declaration that the Quakers should be set at liberty without paying fees. But though Sewel states these facts, Dr. Grey either overlooked, or forgot to inform his reader, that Mr. Neal, in charging the king with the breach of his promise, speaks on the authority of Sewel, who says "the king seemed a good-natured prince, yet he was so misled, that in process of time he seemed to have forgot what he so solemnly promised on the word of a king."—*History of the Quakers,* p. 257.—Ed.

person should be molested purely for religion.* But they were insulted by the mob in the streets; when their families were singing psalms in their houses, they were frequently interrupted by blowing of horns or throwing stones at the windows. The Presbyterian ministers made the best retreat they could, after they had unadvisedly delivered themselves up into the hands of their enemies; for while they were careful to maintain an inviolable loyalty to his majesty's person and government, they contended for their religious principles in the press; several new pamphlets were published, and a great many old ones reprinted, about the magistrates' right of imposing things indifferent in the worship of God; against bowing at the name of Jesus; the unlawfulness of the ceremonies of the Church of England; the Common Prayer Book unmasked; grievances and corruptions in church government, &c., most of which were answered by divines of the Episcopal party.

But the most remarkable treatise that appeared about this time, and which, if it had taken place, must have prevented the mischiefs that followed,† was that of the Reverend Dr. Edward Stillingfleet, rector of Sutton in Bedfordshire, and afterward the learned and worthy Bishop of Worcester, who first made himself known to the world at this time by his "Irenicum; or, A Weapon Salve for the Church's Wounds," printed 1661, in which he attempts to prove that no form of church government is of Divine right, and that the Church had no power to impose things indifferent. I shall beg the reader's attention to a few passages out of his preface. "The design of our Saviour," says he, "was to ease men of their former burdens, and not to lay on more; the duties he required were no other but such as were necessary, and, withal,

* Rapin, vol. ii., p. 624, folio.

† A conciliating and liberal design formed by two respectable men deserves to be mentioned here. "Soon after the Restoration, the honourable Mr. Boyle and Sir Peter Pett were discoursing of the severities practised by the bishops towards the Puritans in the reign of Charles I., and of those which were returned on the Episcopal divines during the following usurpations; and being apprehensive that the restored clergy might be tempted by their late sufferings to such a vindictive retaliation as would be contrary to the true measures of Christianity and politics, they came, at last, to an agreement that it would tend to the public good to have something written and published in defence of liberty of conscience. Sir Peter Pett engaged to write on the political part of the question. Mr. Boyle undertook to engage Dr. Thomas Barlow to treat of the theological part; and he also prevailed on Mr. John Drury, who had spent many years in his travels, and had taken an active part in a scheme for reconciling the Lutherans and Calvinists, to state the fact of the allowance of liberty of conscience in foreign parts. Sir Peter Pett's and Mr. Drury's tracts were printed in 1660. But, for particular reasons, the publication of Dr. Barlow's piece did not take place; but it was published after his death.

"Dr. Barlow had given offence by writing, just before the Restoration, a letter to Mr. Tombs, and expressing in it some prejudice against the practice of infant baptism, and by refusing, even after the Restoration, to retract that letter. This refusal was a noble conduct, for the doctor was in danger by it of losing his station in the University of Oxford, and all his hopes of future preferment." This shows how obnoxious was the sect of the Baptists.—*Birch's Life of Boyle*, p. 299, 300.—ED.

very just and reasonable; he that came to take away the insupportable yoke of Jewish ceremonies, certainly did never intend to gall the necks of his disciples with another instead of it; and it would be strange the Church should require more than Christ himself did, and make other conditions of her communion than our Saviour did of discipleship. What possible reason can be assigned or given why such things should not be sufficient for communion with the Church which are sufficient for eternal salvation? And certainly those things are sufficient for that which are laid down as the necessary duties of Christianity by our Lord and Saviour in his Word. What ground can there be why Christians should not stand upon the same terms now which they did in the time of Christ and his apostles? Was not religion sufficiently guarded and fenced in then? Was there ever more true and cordial reverence in the worship of God? What charter hath Christ given the Church to bind men up to more than himself hath done? Or to exclude those from her society who may be admitted into heaven? Will Christ ever thank men at the great day for keeping such out from communion with his Church who he will vouchsafe, not only crowns of glory too, but it may be aureolæ too, if there be any such things there? The grand commission the apostles were sent out with was only to teach what Christ had commanded them; not the least intimation of any power given them to impose or require anything beyond what himself had spoken to them, or they were directed to by the immediate guidance of the Spirit of God. It is not, whether the things commanded and required be lawful or not? It is not, whether indifferences may be determined or no? It is not how far Christians are bound to submit to a restraint of their Christian liberty, which I now inquire after, but whether they consult the Church's peace and unity who suspend it upon such things. We never read of the apostles making laws but of things necessary, as Acts, xv., 19. It was not enough with them that the things would be necessary when they had required them; but they looked upon an antecedent necessity either absolute or for the present state, which was the only ground of their imposing these commands upon the Gentile Christians. But the Holy Ghost never thought those things fit to be made matters of law to which all parties should conform. All that the apostles required as to this was mutual forbearance and condescension towards each other in them. The apostles valued not indifferences at all; and those things they accounted as such which were of no concernment to their salvation. And what reason is there why men should be tied up so strictly to such things which they may do or let alone, and yet be very good Christians? Without all controversy, the main inlet of all the distractions, confusions, and divisions of the Christian world, has been by adding other conditions of church communion than Christ has done. Would there ever be the less peace and unity in a church, if a diversity were allowed as to practices supposed indifferent? Yea, there would be so much more, as there was a mutual forbearance and condescension as to such things. The unity of the Church is a unity of love and affection, and not a bare uniformity of practice and opinion. There is nothing in the primitive Church more deserving our imitation than that admirable, temper, moderation, and condescension, which was used in it towards its members. It was never thought worth the while to make any standing laws for rites and customs that had no other original but tradition, much less to suspend men from her communion for not observing them."*

The doctor's proposals for an accommodation were, "1. That nothing be imposed as necessary but what is clearly revealed in the Word of God. 2. That n_{othing} be required or determined but what is sufficiently known to be indifferent in its own nature. 3. That whatever is thus determined be in order only to a due performance of what is in general required in the Word of God, and not to be looked upon as any part of Divine worship or service. 4. That no sanctions be made, nor mulcts or penalties be inflicted; on such who only dissent from the use of some things whose lawfulness they at present scruple, till sufficient time and means be used for their information of the mature and indifferency of these things. I am sure," says the doctor, "it is contrary to the primitive practice, and the moderation then used, to suspend or deprive men of their ministerial function for not conforming in habits and gestures, or the like. Lastly, that religion be not clogged with ceremonies; for when they are multiplied too much, though they eat out the heart, heat, life, and vigour of Christianity."† If the doctor had steadily adhered to those principles, he could hardly have subscribed the Act of Uniformity next year, much less have written so warmly against the Dissenters, as he did twenty years afterward.‡ But all he could say or do at present availed nothing; the Presbyterians were in disgrace, and nothing could stem the torrent of popular fury that was now coming upon them.

[In the year 1660, April 25, died, when the king designed to advance him to the see of Worcester, the learned Dr. Henry Hammond. In addition to the short account given of him by Mr. Neal, in a former volume, some other particulars may be subjoined here. He was born 18th August, 1605, at Chertsey in Surrey; and was the youngest son of Dr. John Hammond, a physician. He received his grammar learning at Eton School, and in 1618 was sent to Magdalen College in Oxford, of which he was elected fellow in July, 1625, and entered into

holy orders in 1629. The rectory of Penshurst was bestowed upon him by the Earl of Leicester in 1633. In 1640 he was chosen one of the members of the Convocation; in 1643 made Archdeacon of Chichester, and the same year was named one of the Assembly of Divines, but never sat among them. He was distinguished in his youth for the sweetness of his carriage, and, at the times allowed for play, would steal from his fellows into places of privacy to pray; omens of his future pacific temper and eminent devotion. When he was at the university he generally spent thirteen hours of the day in study. Charles I. said "he was the most natural orator he had ever heard." He was extremely liberal to the poor; and was used to say, that "it was a most unreasonable and unchristian thing to despise any one for his poverty, and it was one of the greatest sensualities in the world to give." He gave it as a rule to his friends of estate and quality, "to treat their poor neighbours with such a cheerfulness, that they might be glad to have met with them." The alms of lending had an eminent place in his practice. He was accustomed strongly to recommend to others "to be always furnished with something to do," as the best expedient both for innocence and pleasure. Devoted as he was to his studies, he would never suffer anybody to wait that came to speak to him; and to the poor he came with peculiar alacrity.—British Biography, vol. v., p. 219, 225.—Ed.]

The Earl of Clarendon, lord-chancellor, was prime minister, and at the head of the king's councils. The year [1661] began with new scenes of pleasure and diversion, occasioned by the king's marriage with the infanta of Portugal, which was consummated April 30. The match was promoted by General Monk and Lord Clarendon, if, according to the Oxford historian, the latter was not the first mover of it.* And it was reckoned very strange that a Protestant chancellor should advise the king to a popish princess, when a Catholic king proposed at the same time a Protestant consort. But his lordship had farther views; for it was generally talked among the merchants that the infanta could have no children, in which case the chancellor's daughter, who had been privately married to the king's brother, must succeed, and her issue by the Duke of York become heirs to

---

* Irenicum, p. 8–10.   † Ibid., p. 66, 67.
‡ "If Mr. Neal," says Dr. Grey, "would allow a man to retract his mistakes upon discovering them, he would not find fault with Bishop Stillingfleet." He then quotes the bishop's apology for his conduct, from the preface to the Unreasonableness of Separation. "If anything in the following treatise be found different from the sense of that book, I entreat them to allow me that which I heartily wish to them, that in twenty years' time we may arrive to such a maturity of thoughts as to see reason to change our opinion of some things, and I wish I had not cause to add, of some persons." But notwithstanding the force of the bishop's plea, it will not, I conceive, be deemed a fortunate or honourable change, if a man's views and spirit, instead of enlarging and becoming more liberal, are contracted, and grow narrow and partial: if, instead of being the advocate for generous and conciliating measures, he should argue for oppression and intolerance.—Ed.

* Dr. Grey observes that Mr. Neal antedates this marriage somewhat above a year; the king met the infanta at Portsmouth the 21st of May, 1662, and was then privately married to her by Dr. Sheldon, bishop of London. The doctor, on the authority of Echard, endeavours to invalidate the imputation which lies on Lord Clarendon of being the promoter, if not the first mover, of this marriage. Mr. Neal is supported in his representation of the affair by the testimony of Sir John Reresby, who says, "It is well known that the lord-chancellor had the blame of this unfruitful match." He adds, that the queen was said to have had a constant fluor upon her, which rendered her incapable of conception. Though, on this occasion (says Sir John), everything was gay, and splendid, and profusely joyful, it was easy to discern that the king was not excessively charmed with his new bride, who was a very little woman, with a pretty tolerable face. She neither in person nor manners had any one article to stand in competition with the charms of the Countess of Castlemain, afterward Duchess of Cleveland, the finest woman of her age.—Memoirs, p. 9, 10.—Ed.

the throne ; which happened accordingly, in the persons of Queen Mary II. and Queen Anne. Such were the aspiring views of this great man, which, together with his haughty behaviour, in the end proved his ruin.

The convention Parliament being dissolved, a new one was elected, and summoned to meet May 8. The House of Commons, by the interest of the court party,* had a considerable majority of such as were zealous enemies of the Presbyterians, and abetters of the principles of Archbishop Laud ; many of whom, having impaired their fortunes in the late wars, became tools of the ministry in all their arbitrary and violent measures. The court kept above one hundred of them in constant pay, who went by the name of the club of voters, and received large sums of money out of the exchequer, till they had almost subverted the Constitution ; and then, because they would not put the finishing hand to what they had unadvisedly begun, they were disbanded.

The king acquainted the houses, at the opening of the session,† that " he valued himself much upon keeping 'his word, and upon making good whatsoever he had promised to his subjects."‡ But the chancellor, who commented upon the king's speech, spoke a different language, and told the House, " that there were a sort of patients in the kingdom that deserved their utmost severity, and none of their lenity ; these 'were the seditious preachers, who could not be contented to be dispensed with for their full obedience to some laws established, without reproaching and inveighing against those laws, how established soever, who tell their auditories, that when the apostle bid them stand to their liberties, he bid them stand to their arms, and who, by repeating the very expressions and teaching the very doctrines they set on foot in the year 1640, sufficiently declare that they have no mind that twenty years should put an end to the miseries we have undergone. What good Christians can think, without horror, of these ministers of the Gospel, who by their function should be messengers of peace, but are in their practice only the trumpets of war, and incendiaries towards rebellion ? And if the persons and place can aggravate their offence, so

no doubt it does before God and man. Methinks the preaching rebellion and treason out of the pulpit should be as much worse than advancing it in the market, as poisoning a man at a communion would be worse than killing him at a tavern." His lordship concludes thus : " If you do not provide for the thorough quenching these firebrands, king, lords, and commons shall be the meaner subjects, and the whole kingdom will be kindled in a general flame."* This was a home-thrust at the Presbyterians ; the chancellor did not explain himself upon the authors of these seditious sermons, his design being not to accuse particular persons, but to obtain a general order which might suppress all teachers who were not of the Church of England ; and the Parliament was prepared to run blindfold into all the court measures ; for in this session the militia was given absolutely to the king ; the solemn League and Covenant was declared void and illegal ; the act for disabling persons in holy orders to exercise temporal jurisdiction was repealed ; the bishops were restored to their seats in Parliament ; the old ecclesiastical jurisdiction was revived by the repeal of the 17th of Charles I., except the oath ex officio ; and it was made a premunire to call the king a papist.†

The storm was all this while gathering very black over the Presbyterians ; for when the Parliament met a second time, November 20, the king complimented the bishops, who appeared now again in their places among the peers, and observed in his speech, that it was a felicity he had much desired to see, as the only thing wanting to restore the old Constitution. He then spoke the language of the chancellor, and told the Commons " that there were many wicked instruments who laboured night and day to disturb the public peace. That it was worthy of their care to provide proper remedies for the diseases of that kind ; that if they found new diseases, they must find new remedies. That the difficulties which concerned religion were too hard for him, and therefore he recommended them to their care and deliberation who could best provide for them." The tendency of this speech was to make way for breaking through the Breda declaration, and to furnish the Parliament with a pretence for treating the Nonconformists with rigour, to which they were themselves too well inclined.

---

* There were only fifty-six members of the Presbyterian party returned, notwithstanding their great interest in almost all the corporations. But in the interval between the two Parliaments the court party had been active, and the hints given at the dissolution of the late Parliament by the chancellor had great weight. He recommended that " such persons should be returned as were not likely to oppose the king, but had already served him, and were likely to serve him with their whole heart, and to gratify him in all his desires."—*Secret History of the Court and Reign of Charles II.*, vol. i., p. 171 and 406. Had the people been alive to a just sense of the design of representation and the nature of the Constitution, they would have received these hints with indignant contempt.—ED.

† The king went to the House of Lords, to open the session, with almost as much pomp and splendour as had been displayed on the coronation day ; and, says my author, for the same reasons, to dazzle the mob, and to impress on the minds of the people very exalted notions of the dignity of regal government.—*Secret History of the Court and Reign of Charles II.*, vol. i., p. 407, note.—ED.

‡ Kennet's Chron., p. 434.
Vol. II.—F F

* Kennet's Chron., p. 510, 511.

† To Mr. Neal's detail of the acts of this session, it should be added, that the Commons voted that all their members should receive the sacrament according to the prescribed liturgy, before a certain day, under penalty of expulsion. This was intended as a test of their religious sincerity. Besides repealing the solemn League and Covenant, they ordered it to be taken out of all the courts and places where it was recorded, and to be burned by the common hangman. To the same sentence were doomed all acts, ordinances, or engagements which had been dictated by a republican spirit during the late times. And they enervated the right of petitioning by various restrictions ; limiting the number of signatures to twenty; unless with the sanction of three justices, or the major part of the grand Jury; and of those who should present a petition to the king or either House of Parliament to ten persons, under the penalty of a fine of £100 and three months' inprisonment. —*Secret History of the Court and Reign of Charles II.*, vol. i., p. 412–414.—ED.

Lord Clarendon, in a conference between the two houses, affirmed positively that there was a real conspiracy against the peace of the kingdom ; and though it was disconcerted in the city, it was carried on in divers counties ; a committee was therefore appointed to inquire into the truth of the report ; but, after all their examinations, not one single person was convicted, or so much as prosecuted for it.* Great pains were taken to fasten some treasonable designs on the Presbyterians ; letters were sent from unknown hands to the chiefs of the party in several parts of the kingdom, intimating the project of a general insurrection, in which their friends were concerned, and desiring them to communicate it to certain persons in their neighbourhood, whom they name in their letters, that they may be ready at time and place. A letter of this kind was directed to the Reverend Mr. Sparry, in Worcestershire, desiring him and Captain Yarrington to be ready with money, and to acquaint Mr. Oatland and Mr. Baxter with the design. This, with a packet of the same kind, was said to be left under a hedge by a Scots pedler ; and as soon as they were found, they were carried to Sir J. Packington, who immediately committed Sparry, Oatland, and Yarrington to prison. The militia of the county was raised, and the city of Worcester put into a posture of defence ; but the sham was so notorious, that the Earl of Bristol, though a papist, was ashamed of it ; and after some time the prisoners, for want of evidence, were released. The members for Oxfordshire, Herefordshire, and Staffordshire informed the Commons that they had rumours of the like conspiracies in their counties. Bishop Burnet says "that many were taken up, but none tried ; that this was done to fasten an odium on the Presbyterians, and to help to carry the penal laws through the House ; and there were appearances of foul dealing," says he, "among the fiercer sort." Mr. Locke adds, that the reports of a general insurrection were spread over the whole nation, by the very persons who invented them ; and though Lord Clarendon could not but be acquainted with the farce, he kept it on foot to facilitate passing the severe laws that were now coming upon the carpet.† The government could not with decency attack the Nonconformists purely on account of their religion ; the declaration from Breda was too express on that article ; they were therefore to be charged with raising disturbances in the state. But supposing the fact to be true, that some few malecontents had been seditiously disposed, which yet was never made out, what reason can be assigned why it should be charged upon the principles of a whole body of men, who were unquestionably willing to be quiet ?

It was nevertheless on this base and dishonourable suggestion that the first penal law which passed against the Nonconformists this session was founded,‡ entitled,

"An Act for the well-governing and regulating Corporations ;" which enacts, "that within the several cities, corporations, boroughs, cinque-ports, and other port-towns within the kingdom of England, dominion of Wales, and

town of Berwick-upon-Tweed, all mayors, aldermen, recorders, bailiffs, town-clerks, common councilmen, and other persons bearing any office or offices of magistracy, or places, or trusts, or other employment, relating to or concerning the government of the said respective cities, corporations, and boroughs, and cinque-ports, and their members, and other port-towns, shall take the oaths of allegiance and supremacy, and this oath following :

"'I, A. B., do declare and believe that it is not lawful, upon any pretence whatsoever, to take arms against the king ; and that I do abhor that traitorous position of taking arms by his authority against his person, or against those that are commissioned by him.'*

"They shall also subscribe the following declaration :

"'I, A. B., do declare that there lies no obligation upon me from the solemn League and Covenant, and that the same was an unlawful oath imposed on the subject against the laws and liberties of the kingdom.'

"Provided, also, and be it enacted by the authority aforesaid, that no person shall hereafter be elected or chosen into any of the offices or places aforesaid, that shall not have, within one year next before such election or choice, taken the sacrament of the Lord's Supper according to the rites of the Church of England ; and that every person so elected shall take the aforesaid oaths, and subscribe the said declaration at the same time when the oath for the due execution of the said places and offices shall be respectively administered."

Thus all Nonconformists were turned out of all the branches of magistracy at once, and rendered incapable of serving their country in the offices of a common councilman, or a burgess or bailiff of the smallest corporation. The oath imposed in this act robbed them of their right as subjects. Mr. Echard confesses that it seems at once to give up the whole Constitution ; and no wonder, says he, if many of the clergy as well as laity, on the account of this act, espoused a doctrine which, if rigidly taken, was hard to be reconciled to the great deliverance afterward. Mr. Rapin adds,† that to say that it is not lawful on any pretence whatever to resist the king, is, properly speaking, to deliver up the liberties of the nation into his hands. The High-churchmen had then elevated ideas of the royal authority. But even this Parliament did not think fit afterward to admit the dangerous consequences of their own maxims.

Commissioners were appointed and employed during this and the following year to visit the several corporations in England, and to turn out of office such as were in the least suspect-

---

* Kennet's Chron., p. 602.
† Rapin, vol. ii., p. 627.
‡ Kennet's Chron., p. 602.

* "One would suppose (it has been well remarked) that the Parliament who prescribed such an oath must have been as near-sighted and as stupid as they were servile and corrupt. Such a maxim of nonresistance to the king, on any pretence, was directly subversive of their own consequence, as well as of civil and religious liberty. The extent to which this principle might be carried was put to the proof by James II., but the people of England rent asunder the chains which had been forged for them by their perfidious representatives."—*Secret History of the Court and Reign of Charles II.*, vol i., p. 428, note.—ED.   † Vol. ii., p. 628.

ed ; who executed their commissions with so much rigour, that the corporations had not one member left who was not entirely devoted to the king and the Church.

CHAPTER VI.

FROM THE CONFERENCE AT THE SAVOY TO THE ACT OF UNIFORMITY. 1661.

ACCORDING to his majesty's declaration of October 25, 1660, concerning ecclesiastical affairs, twelve bishops* and nine assistants were appointed on the part of the Episcopal Church of England, and as many ministers on the side of the Presbyterians, to assemble at the Bishop of London's lodgings at the Savoy, " to review the Book of Common Prayer, comparing it with the most ancient and purest liturgies ; and to take into their serious and grave consideration the several directions and rules, forms of prayer, and things in the said Book of Common Prayer contained, and to advise and consult upon the same, and the several objections and exceptions which shall now be raised against the same ; and if occasion be, to make such reasonable and necessary alterations, corrections, and amendments, as shall be agreed upon to be needful and expedient for giving satisfaction to tender consciences, and the restoring and continuance of peace and unity in the churches under his majesty's government and direction." They were to continue four months from the 25th of March, 1661, and then present the result of their conferences to his majesty under their several hands.

The names of the Episcopal divines on the side of the Establishment at the Savoy Conference were,

The Most Rev. Dr. Accepted Frewen, Archbishop of York.
The Right Rev. Dr. Gilbert Sheldon, Bishop of London.
 "   "   Dr. John Cosins, Bishop of Durham.
 "   "   Dr. John Warner, Bishop of Rochester.
 "   "   Dr. Henry King, Bishop of Chichester.
 "   "   Dr. Humph. Henchman, Bishop of Sarum.
 "   "   Dr. George Morley, Bishop of Worcester.
 "   "   Dr. Robert Saunderson, Bishop of Lincoln.
 "   "   Dr. Benj. Laney, Bishop of Peterborough.
 "   "   Dr. Bryan Walton, Bishop of Chester.
 "   "   Dr. Richard Sterne, Bishop of Carlisle.
 "   "   Dr. John Gauden, Bishop of Exeter.

Their Assistants.

John Earle, D.D., Dean of Westminster.
Peter Heylin, D.D.   John Pearson, D.D.
John Hacket, D.D.   Thomas Pierce, D.D.
John Barwick, D.D.   Anthony Sparrow, D.D
Peter Gunning, D.D.   Herbert Thorndike, B.D.

The names of the Presbyterian divines, or those who were for alterations in the hierarchy of the Church at the Savoy Conference, were,

The Right Rev. Edward Reynolds, Bishop of Norwich.
The Rev. Anthony Tuckney, D.D.M., St. John's College, Cambridge.
 "   John Conant, D.D., Regius Professor, Oxon.
 "   William Spurstow, D.D., Vicar, Hackney.
 "   John Wallis, D.D., Sav. Professor Geometry.
 "   Thomas Manton, D.D., Master of Covent Garden.
 "   Edmund Calamy, B.D., of Aldermanbury.
 "   Mr. Richard Baxter, Clerk; late of Kidderminster.
 "   Mr. Arthur Jackson, Clerk, of St. Faith's.

* Dr. Nichols reckons twelve bishops, but has left out the Bishop of Chichester, and named Edward, Bishop of Norwich. Dr. Kennet names thirteen bishops, among whom are the Bishops of Chichester and Norwich.—*Dr. Grey's Examination,* vol. iii., p. 308.—ED.

The Rev. Mr. Thomas Case, Clerk, Rector of St. Giles.
 "   Mr. Samuel Clarke, Clerk, of St. Bene't Fink.
 "   Mr. Matthew Newcomen, Clerk, of Dedham.

Their Assistants.

Rev. Thomas Horton, D.D.   Rev. John Collins, D.D.
 "   Thomas Jacomb, D.D.   "   Benj. Woodbridge, B.D
 "   William Bates, D.D.   "   Mr. John Rawlinson,
 "   William Cooper, D.D.   Clerk.
 "   John Lightfoot, D.D.   "   Mr. Wm. Drake, Clerk.

When the commissioners* were assembled the first time, April 15, the Archbishop of York stood up and said he knew little of the business they were met about, and therefore referred it to Dr. Sheldon, bishop of London, who gave it as his opinion, that the Presbyterians having desired this conference, they [the bishops] should neither say nor do anything till the others had brought in all their exceptions and complaints against the liturgy, in writing, with their additional forms and amendments.† The Presbyterians humbly moved for a conference according to the words of the commission, but the Bishop of London insisting peremptorily upon his own method, the others consented to bring in their exceptions at one time, and their additions at another. For this purpose, Bishop Reynolds, Dr. Wallis, and the rest of the Presbyterian party, met from day to day to collect their exceptions ;‡ but the additions, or drawing up a new form, was intrusted with Mr. Baxter alone. " Bishop Sheldon saw well enough," says Burnet,§ " what the effect would be of obliging them to make all their demands at once; that the number would raise a mighty outcry against them, as a people that could never be satisfied." On the other hand, the Presbyterians were divided in their sentiments ; some were for insisting only on a few important things, reckoning that if they were gained, and a union followed, it might be easier to obtain others afterward. But the majority, by the influence of Mr. Baxter, were for extending their desires to the utmost, and thought themselves bound by the words of the commission to offer everything they thought might conduce to the peace of the Church, without considering what an aspect this would have with the world, or what influence their numerous demands might have upon the minds of those who were now their superiors in numbers and strength ;|| but

* " Though the Baptists in England were at this time very numerous, and as famous men among them for learning and piety as most in the commission, yet to regard was had to their case, nor any one of that persuasion appointed to have any share in it. They did not design to reform so far; for if they could but bring the Presbyterian party in, which was the most numerous of the Dissenters, that might be sufficient to secure their power ; though, by the consequence of this proceeding, it seems probable there was no design of reformation, but only to quiet the minds of the people till they could gain time."— *Crosby,* vol. ii., p. 84, 85.—ED.

† Baxter's Life, part ii., p. 305.
‡ Ibid., p. 306.   § P. 262.
|| " This," observes a late writer, " was precisely what the advocates for persecution desired : they could say that the king had taken every step which the best policy and the tenderest concern for the happiness of all his subjects could suggest to gain over and compose the jarring sects into a system of perfect harmony, but that all his wise and benevolent endeavours were defeated by the wilful obstinacy and perverseness of the Nonconformists ; and that he must therefore now pursue such measures as the safety both of the Church and State required."--St.

when they were put in mind that the king's commission gave them no power to alter the government of the Church, nor to insist upon Archbishop Usher's model, nor so much as to claim the concessions of his majesty's late declaration, they were quite heartless; for they were now convinced that all they were to expect was a few amendments in the liturgy and Common Prayer Book. This was concluded beforehand at court, and nothing more intended than to drop the Presbyterians with a show of decency.

The ministers were under this farther hardship, that they were, to transact for a body of men from whom they had no power, and therefore could not be obliged to abide by their decisions; they told the king and the prime minister that they should be glad to consult their absent brethren, and receive from them a commission in form, but this was denied, and they were required to give in their own sense of things, to which they consented, provided the bishops, at the same time, would bring in their concessions; but these being content to abide by the liturgy as it then stood, had nothing to offer, nor would they admit of any alterations but what the Presbyterians should make appear to be necessary. With this dark and melancholy prospect the conference was opened.* It would interrupt the course of this history too much to insert all the exceptions of the Presbyterians to the present liturgy; and the papers which passed between the commissioners, with the letter of the Presbyterian ministers to the archbishop and bishops, and the report they made of the whole to the king. I shall only take notice in this place, that, instead of drawing up a few supplemental forms, and making some amendments to the old liturgy, Mr. Baxter composed an entire new one in the language of Scripture, which he called the Reformed Liturgy; not with a design entirely to set aside them old one, but to give men liberty to use either as they approved. It was drawn up in a short compass of time, and after it had been examined, and approved by his brethren, was presented to the bishops in the conference, together with their exceptions to the old liturgy. This gave great offence, as presuming that a liturgy drawn up by a single hand in fourteen days was to be preferred, or stand in competition with one which had been received in the Church for a whole century. Besides, it was inconsistent with the commission and the bishops' declaration of varying no farther from the old standard than should appear to be necessary; and therefore the Reformed Liturgy, as it was called, was rejected at once, without being examined.

When the Presbyterians brought in their exceptions to the liturgy, they presented at the same time a petition for peace, beseeching the bishops to yield to their amendments; to free them from the subscriptions and oaths in his majesty's late declaration; and not to insist upon the reordination of those who had been ordain-

cret *History of the Court and Reign of Charles II.*, vol. i., p. 349, 350.—Ed.

* N.B. All the papers relating to the conference at the Savoy are collected in a book, entitled "The History of the Nonconformity," as it was argued and stated by commissioners on both sides appointed by his majesty King Charles II. in the year 1661. Octavo, second edit., 1708.—See, also, *Sylvester's Life of Baxter, folio.*—C.

ed without a diocesan bishop, nor upon the surplice, the cross in baptism, and other indifferent ceremonies; for this purpose they make use of various motives and arguments, sufficient, in my judgment, to influence all who had any concern for the honour of God and the salvation of souls. The bishops gave a particular answer to these exceptions; to which the Presbyterians made such a reply as, in the opinion of their adversaries, showed them to be men of learning, and well versed in the practice of the ancient Church; however, the bishops would indulge nothing to their prejudices; upon which they sent them a large expostulatory letter, wherein, after having repeated their objections, they lay the wounds of the Church at their door. The term for the treaty being almost spun out in a paper controversy,* about ten days before the commission expired, a disputation was agreed on to argue the necessity of alterations in the present liturgy.† Three of each party were chosen to manage the argument: Dr. Pearson, Gunning, and Sparrow, on one side; and Dr. Bates, Jacomb, and Mr. Baxter, on the other. The rest were at liberty to withdraw if they pleased. Mr. Baxter was opponent, and began to prove the sinfulness of impositions; but, through want of order, frequent interruptions, and personal reflections, the dispute issued in nothing; a number of young divines interrupting the Presbyterian ministers, and laughing them to scorn. At length Bishop Cosins produced a paper‡ containing an expedient to shorten the debate, which was, to put the ministers on distinguishing between those things which they charged as sinful, and those which were only inexpedient. The three disputants on the ministers' side were desired to draw up an answer to this paper, which they did, and charged the rubric and injunctions of the Church with eight things flatly sinful, and contrary to the Word of God.§

1. That no minister be admitted to baptize without using the sign of the cross

2. That no minister be admitted to officiate without wearing a surplice.

3. That none be admitted to the Lord's Supper without he receive it kneeling.

4. That ministers be obliged to pronounce all baptized persons regenerated by the Holy Ghost, whether they be the children of Christians or not.

5. That ministers be obliged to deliver the sacrament of the body and blood of Christ to the unfit both in health and sickness, and that, by personal application, putting it into their hands, even those who are forced to receive it against their wills, through consciousness of their impenitency.

* In the course of this controversy, many points connected with the doctrine and manner of baptism came into discussion: such as, the right of the children of heathens, or of the excommunicated, to baptism; the efficacy of children's baptism; the qualifications of this ordinance; the use of godfathers and godmothers, and of the sign of the cross, and other questions; on which, it is said, contributed much to encourage and promote what was called Anabaptism.—*Crosby's History of the Baptists,* vol. ii., p. 85, 86.—Ed.

† Baxter's Life, part ii., p. 337.

‡ Kennet's Chronicle, p. 504.

§ Baxter's Life, part ii., p. 341.

6. That ministers are obliged to absolve the unfit, and that in absolute expressions.

7. That ministers are forced to give thanks for all whom they bury, as brethren whom God has taken to himself.

8. That none may be preachers who do not subscribe that there is nothing in the Common Prayer Book, Book of Ordination, and the Thirty-nine Articles, contrary to the Word of God.

After a great deal of loose discourse, it was agreed to debate the third article, of denying the communion to such as could not kneel. The ministers proved their assertion thus, that it was denying the sacrament to such whom the Holy Ghost commanded us to receive, Rom., xiv., 1–3 : " Him that is weak in the faith receive ye, but not to doubtful disputations : one believes he may eat all things ; another, that is weak, eateth herbs : let not him that eateth, despise him that eateth not ; and let not him that eateth not, judge him that eateth, for God has received him." The Episcopal divines would not understand this of the communion: They also distinguished between things lawful in themselves, and things both lawful in themselves and required by lawful authority. In the former case they admit a liberty, but the latter being enjoined by authority, become necessary. The ministers replied, that things about which there is to be a forbearance ought not to be enjoined by authority, and made necessary ; and for governors to reject men by this rule is to defeat the apostle's reasoning, and so contradict the law of God. But when Dr. Gunning had read certain citations* and authorities for the other side of the question, Bishop Cosins, the moderator, called out to the rest of the bishops and doctors, and put the question, " All you that think Dr. Gunning has proved that Romans xiv. speaketh not of receiving the sacrament, say Ay." Upon which there was a general cry among the hearers, Ay, ay, the Episcopal divines having great numbers of their party in the hall ; whereas the ministers had not above two or three gentlemen and scholars who had the courage to appear with them. Nevertheless, they maintained their point, and, as Bishop Burnet observes, insisted upon it, that a " law which excludes all from the sacrament who dare not kneel, was unlawful, as it was a limitation in point of communion put upon the laws of Christ, which ought to be the only condition of those that have a right to it."

At length, the Episcopal divines became opponents upon the same question, and argued thus : " That command which enjoins only an act in itself lawful is not sinful." Which Mr. Baxter denied. They then added, " That command which enjoins only an act in itself lawful, and no other act or circumstance unlawful, is not sinful." This, also, Mr. Baxter denied. They then advanced farther. " That command which enjoins only an act in itself lawful, and no other act whereby an unjust penalty is enjoined, or any circumstance whence directly or per accidens any sin is consequent which the commander ought to provide against, hath in it all things requisite to the lawfulness of a command, and particularly cannot be charged with

enjoining an act per accidens unlawful, nor of commanding an act under an unjust penalty." This also was denied, because, though it does not command that which is sinful, it may restrain from that which is lawful, and it may be applied to undue subjects. Other reasons were assigned ;* but the dispute broke off with noise and confusion, and high reflections upon Mr. Baxter's dark and cloudy imagination, and his perplexed, scholastic, metaphysical manner of distinguishing, which tended rather to confound than to clear up that which was doubtful ; and Bishop Saunderson being then in the chair, pronounced that Dr. Gunning had the better of the argument.

Bishop Morley said that Mr. Baxter's denying that plain proposition was destructive of all authority human and Divine ; that it struck the Church out of all its claims for making canons, and for settling order and discipline ; nay, that it took away all legislative power from the king and Parliament, and even from God himself ; for no act can be so good in itself, but may lead to a sin by accident ; and if to command such an act be a sin, then every command must be a sin.

Bishop Burnet adds,† " that Baxter and Gunning spent several days in logical arguing, to the diversion of the town, who looked upon them as a couple of fencers engaged in a dispute that could not be brought to any end. The bishops insisted upon the laws being still in force ; to which they would admit of no exception, unless it was proved that the matter of them was sinful. They charged the Presbyterians with making a schism for that which they could not prove to be sinful. They said there was no reason to gratify such men ; that one demand granted would draw on many more ; that all authority in Church and State was struck at by the position they had insisted on, namely, that it was not lawful to impose things indifferent, since these seemed to be the only matters in which authority could interfere." Thus ended the disputation.

From arguments the ministers descended to entreaties, and prayed the bishops to have compassion on scrupulous minds, and not despise their weaker brethren. If the Nonconformists should be ejected, they urged that there would not be clergymen enough to fill the vacant pulpits ; they put them in mind of their peaceable behaviour in the late times ; what they had suffered for the royal cause, and the great share they had in restoring the king ; they pleaded his majesty's late declaration, and the design of the present conference. To all which the bishops replied, that they were only commissioned to make such alterations in the liturgy as should be necessary, and such as should be agreed upon. The ministers replied, that the word necessary must refer to the satisfying tender consciences ; but the bishops insisted that they saw no alterations necessary, and, therefore, were not obliged to make any till they could prove them so. The ministers prayed them to consider the ill consequence that might follow upon a separation. But all was to no purpose ; their lordships were in the saddle, and, if we may believe Mr. Baxter, would not abate the smallest ceremony, nor correct the grossest

---

* Kennet's Chron., p. 506.

* Kennet's Chron., p. 505.   † Vol. i., p. 264.

error, for the peace of the Church.' Thus the king's commission expired July 25, and the conferences ended without any prospect of accommodation.

It was agreed, at the conclusion, that each party might represent to his majesty that they were all agreed upon the ends of the conference, which were the Church's welfare, unity, and peace; but still disagreed as to the means of procuring them. The bishops thought they had no occasion to represent their case in writing; but the Presbyterian commissioners met by themselves, and drew up an account of their proceedings, with a petition for that relief which they could not obtain from the bishops.* They presented it to the king by Bishop Reynolds, Dr. Bates, Dr. Manton, and Mr. Baxter;† but received no answer.

Before we leave this famous conference at the Savoy, it will not be amiss to remark the behaviour of the commissioners on both sides, some of whom seldom or never appeared, as, Dr. King, bishop of Chichester, Dr. Heylin, Barwick, and Earle ;‡ Sheldon, bishop of London, came but seldom, though he, with Henchman and Morley, had the chief management of affairs ;§ others who were present, but did not much concern themselves in the debate, as, Dr. Frewen, archbishop of York ; Lucy, of St. David's ; Warner, of Rochester ; Saunderson, of Lincoln ; Laney, of Peterborough ; Walton, of Chester ; Sterne, of Carlisle ; Dr. Hacket and Dr. Sparrow. On the side of the Presbyterians, Dr. Horton never appeared, nor Dr. Drake, because of a misnomer in the commission ; Dr. Lightfoot, Tuckney, and Mr. Woodbridge were present only once or twice.

Among the bishops, Dr. Morely was the chief

speaker ; his manner was vehement, and he was against all abatements. He frequently interrupted Mr. Baxter ;* and when Dr. Bates said, " Pray, my lord, give him leave to speak," he could not obtain it.

Bishop Cosins was there constantly, and though he was inclined to moderate measures, said some very severe things. When the ministers prayed the bishops to have some compassion on their brethren, and not cast such great numbers unnecessarily out of the ministry, he replied, " What, do you threaten us with numbers ? For my part, I think the king would do well to make you name them all." Again, when the members complained that, after so many years' calamity, the bishops would not yield to that which their predecessors offered them before the war, Bishop Cosins replied, " Do you threaten us, then, with a new war ? It is time for the king to look to you."

Bishop Gauden often took part with the Presbyterian divines, and was the only moderator among the bishops, except Bishop Reynolds, who spoke much the first day for abatements and moderation ; but afterward, sitting among the bishops, he only spoke now and then a qualifying word, though he was heartily grieved for the fruitless issue of the conference.

Of the disputants, it is said Dr. Pearson, afterward Bishop of Chester, disputed accurately, soberly, and calmly. The Presbyterian ministers had a great regard for him, and believed, that if he had been an umpire in the controversy, his concessions would have greatly relieved them.

Dr. Gunning was the most forward speaker, and stuck at nothing. Bishop Burnet says† that all the arts of sophistry were used by him in as confident a manner as if they had been sound reasoning ; that he was unweariedly active to very little purpose, and being very fond of the popish rituals and ceremonies, he was very much set upon reconciling the Church of England to Rome.

On the side of the Presbyterians, Dr. Bates and Manton behaved with great modesty : the most active disputant was Mr. Baxter, who had a very metaphysical head and fertile invention, and was one of the most ready men of his time for an argument, but too eager and tenacious of his own opinions. Next to him was Mr. Calamy, who had a great interest among the Presbyterian ministers in city and country, and for his age and gravity was respected as their father.

Among the auditors, Mr. Baxter observes,‡ there was with the bishops a crowd of young divines, who behaved indecently ; but mentions only two or three scholars and laymen who, as auditors, came in with the Presbyterians, as Mr. Miles, Mr. Tillotson, &c.

This Mr. Tillotson was afterward the most reverend and learned Archbishop of Canterbury, one of the most celebrated divines and preachers of the age. We shall have frequent occasion to mention him hereafter, and, therefore, I shall give a short account of him in this place. He was born in Yorkshire, 1630, and received his first education among the Puritans ; and, though he had freer notions, he still stuck to

* Mr. Crosby says, "he had been informed, that when the Presbyterians were pleading hard for such concessions from his majesty as they thought would bring about a union, the lord-chancellor told them his majesty had received petitions from the Anabaptists, who desired nothing more than to have liberty to worship God according to their consciences. At which they were all struck dumb, and remained in a long silence." Mr. Baxter places this matter in another light : that petitions having been received from the Independents and Anabaptists, the chancellor proposed to add a clause to the king's declaration, permitting others besides the Presbyterians to meet, if they did it peaceably, for religious worship, secure from molestation by any civil officer. On this the bishops and the Presbyterians, seeing it would operate in favour of the papists, were silent : till Mr. Baxter, judging that consenting to it would bring on them the charge of speaking for the toleration of papists and sectaries, and that opposing it would draw on them the resentment of all sects and parties as the causes of their sufferings, said, " that as they humbly thanked his majesty for his indulgence to themselves, so they must distinguish the tolerable parties from the intolerable : that for the former that they craved favour and lenity ; but that they could not request the toleration of the latter, such as the papists and Socinians, whom Dr. Gunning, speaking against the sects, had then 'named." To this his majesty said, " that there were laws enough against the papists." Mr. Baxter replied, " They understood the question to be, whether those laws should be executed on them or not." And so his majesty broke up the meeting of that day.—*Crosby's History of the Baptists*, vol. ii., p. 87–89. *Baxter's Life*, part ii., p. 277.—ED.

† Baxter's Life, part ii., p. 366.   ‡ Ibid., p. 307.
§ Kennet's Chronicle, p. 507.

* Baxter's Life, part ii., p 363.   † Page 263, 264.
‡ Baxter's Life, p. 337.

the strictness of life to which he was bred, and retained. a just value and a due tenderness for men of that persuasion. He was admitted student of Clare Hall, in Cambridge, under the tuitiou of Mr. David Clarkson, in the year 1647. He was bachelor of arts 1650, and within the compass of a year was elected fellow. ,He had then a sweetness of temper which. he retained as long as he lived ; and in those early years was respected as a person of very great parts and prudence.* In the year 1661 he continued a Nonconformist, and has a sermon in the morning exercises on Matt., vii., 12. He appeared with the Presbyterians at the Savoy disputation ; and though he conformed upon the Act of Uniformity in 1662, he was always inclined to the Puritans, never fond of the ceremonies of the Church, but would dispense sometimes with those who could not conscientiously submit to them. He owned the Dissenters had some plausible objections against the Common Prayer ; and, in the opinion of some, persuaded men rather to bear with the Church, than he zealous for it. In the year 1663 he was preferred to the Rectory of Keddington, in Suffolk, vacant by the. nonsubscription of Mr. Samuel Fairclough. Next year he was chosen preacher to Lincoln's Inn, and lecturer of St. Lawrence's Church, in London, where his excellent sermons, delivered in a most graceful manner, drew the attention of great numbers of the quality, and most of the divines and gentlemen in the city. In 1669 he was made canon of Christ Church, in Canterbury ; and, in 1672, dean of that church, and residentiary ; but rose no higher till the revolution of King William and Queen Mary, when he was first made clerk of the closet, and then advanced at once to the Archbishopric of Canterbury, in the room of Dr. Sancroft, a nonjuror. He was a divine of moderate principles to the last, and always disposed to promote a toleration, and, if possible, a comprehension of the Dissenters within the Church. Upon the whole, he was a second Cranmer, and one of the most valuable prelates that this, or it may be any other, church ever produced.

 Various censures were passed within doors upon the Savoy Conference ; the Independents were disgusted, because none of them were consulted, though it does not appear to me what concern they could have in it, their views being only to a toleration, not a comprehension. Some blamed their brethren for yielding too much, and others thought they might have yielded more ; but when they saw the fruitless end of the treaty, and the papers that were published, most of them were satisfied. Bishop Burnet says† the conference did rather hurt than good ; it heightened the sharpness which was already on people's minds to such a degree, that it needed no addition to raise it higher. Mr. Robinson says,‡ " It was notorious that the business of the Episcopal party was not to consult the interest of religion, but to cover a political design, which was too bad to appear at first ; nor did they mean to heal the Church's wounds, so much as to revenge their own. When they knew what the Presbyterians scrupled, they said, now they knew their minds they would have matters so fixed that not one of that sort

should be able to keep his living. They did not desire, but rather fear, their compliance."* Nay, so unacceptable was the publishing the papers relating to the conference, that Bishop Saunderson and some of his brethren cautioned their clergy against reading them. From this time the Presbyterians were out of the question, and the settlement of the Church referred entirely to the Convocation and Parliament. It had been debated in council whether there should be, a convocation while the conference at the Savoy was depending ; but, at the intercession of Dr. Heylin and others, the court was prevailed with to consent that there should ; and such care was taken in the choice of members, as Bishop. Burnet observes, that everything went among them as was directed by Bishop Sheldon and Morley. If a convocation had been holden with the convention Parliament, the majority would have been against the hierarchy ; but it is not to be wondered they were otherwise now, when some hundreds of the Presbyterian clergy, who were in possession of sequestered livings, had been dispossessed ; and the necessity of ordination by a bishop being urged upon those who had been ordained by presbyters only, great numbers were denied their votes in elections. Nevertheless, the Presbyterian interest carried it in London for Mr. Baxter and Calamy, by three voices ; but the Bishop of London, having a power of choosing two out of four, or four out of six, within a certain circuit, left them both out ; by which means the city of London had no clerks in the Convocation. The author of the Conformists' Pleat says, " That to frame a convocation to their mind, great care and pains were used to keep out, and to get men in, by very undue proceedings ; and that protestations were made against all incumbents not ordained by bishops." The Savoy Conference having ended without success, the king sent a letter to the Convocation, November 20, commanding them to review the Book of Common Prayer, and make such additions and amendments‡ as they thought neces-

* When the lord-chamberlain, Manchester, told the king (while the Act of Uniformity was under debate) that he was afraid the terms were so hard that many of the late ministers could not comply with them, Bishop Sheldon, being present, replied, 'I am afraid they will.' —Dr. Bates's Funeral Sermon for Mr. Baxter. " Hence it is plain the design of the bishops was to shut them out of the Church, and then to reproach and punish them for not coming in. It is evident, also, that the ministers were honester men than the bishops feared they were."—Prot. Dissenters' Catechism, p. 15.—C.   † Page 35.
 ‡ It was required "that all proposed alterations should be exhibited and presented for his majesty's farther allowance and confirmation : this was accordingly done. He was finally to pronounce on the propriety and truth of the proposed alterations. All the debates, investigations, and decisions of the clergy and bishops, had no efficacy without the sanction of the king. They might be mistaken, but he could not. There is an absurdity in ascribing infallibility to any human being, necessarily liable to imperfect views, to prejudices, and to error. ' But, if possible, the absurdity is greater in attributing it to the sceptred, rather than to the mitred sovereign. The former is not educated to a religious profession ; and his time, from the moment he fills the throne, that is, from the moment he becomes infallible, must be constantly employed in civil concerns : but yet, as the head of the Church, to him all truth is known ; to

* Athen. Oxon., p. 968.   † Page 265.
‡ Answer to Bennet, of Liturgies, p. 382.

sary. Letters to the same purpose were sent to the Archbishop of York, to be communicated to the clergy of his province, who, for the greater expedition, sent proxies with procuratorial letters to those of Canterbury, and obliged themselves to abide by their votes under forfeiture of their goods and chattels.

"It is inconceivable," says Dr. Nichols, "what difficulties the bishops had to contend with about making these alterations; they were not only to conquer their own former resentments, and the unreasonable demands of Presbyterians, but they had the court to deal with, who pushed them on to all acts of severity."* Whereas, on the contrary, the tide was strong on their side; the bishops pushed on the court, who were willing to give them the reins, that when the breach was made as wide as possible, a door might be opened for the toleration of papists. The review of the Common Prayer Book engaged the Convocation a whole month; and on the 20th of December it was signed, and approved by all the members of both houses.

The alterations were these :†

1. The rubric for singing of lessons,‡ &c., was omitted, the distinct reading of them being thought more proper.

2. Several collects for Sundays and holydays complained of, were omitted; and others substituted in their room.

3. Communicants at the Lord's Supper were enjoined to signify their names to the curate some time the day before.

4. The preface to the Ten Commandments was restored.§

5. The exhortations to the holy communion were amended.

6. The general confession in the communion office was appointed to be read by one of the ministers.

7. In the office for Christmas Day the words "this day" were changed for "as at this time."

8. In the prayer of consecration the priest is directed to break the bread.

9. The rubric for explaining the reason of kneeling at the sacrament was restored.

10. Private baptism is not to be administered but by a lawful minister.

11. The answer to the question in the catechism, "Why, then, are children baptized?" is thus amended : "Because they promise them both by their sureties; which promise, when they come to age, themselves are bound to perform."

12. In the last rubric before the catechism these words are expunged, "And that no man shall think that any detriment shall come to children by deferring of their confirmation," &c.

him all appeals from the ecclesiastical courts must be made.'"—*A Treatise on Heresy*, p. 73, 74.—ED.

* Kennet's Chron., p. 574. † Ibid., p. 585.

‡ The rubric in King James's Review directed, also, the two lessons to be distictly read, but added, "To the end the people may better hear, in such places where they do sing, there shall the lessons be sung in a plain tune, after the manner of distinct reading, and likewise the Epistle and Gospel."—*Grey's Examination*, p. 308.—ED.

§ "So, indeed, says Bishop Kennet," remarks Dr. Grey; "but they are both mistaken. The commandments were not in King Edward's first liturgy, but in King Edward's, 1552, and in the Reviews of Queen Elizabeth and King James."—*Grey's Examination*, p. 309.—ED

13. It is appointed that the curate of every parish shall either bring or send in writing, with his hand subscribed thereunto, the names of all such persons within his parish as he shall think fit to be presented to the bishop to be confirmed.

14. The rubric after confirmation was thus softened : "None shall be admitted to the communion till such time as he be confirmed, or be ready and desirous to be confirmed."

15. In the form of matrimony, instead of, "till death us depart," it is, "till death us do part."

16. In the rubrics after the form of matrimony, it is thus altered : "After which, if there be no sermon declaring the duties of man and wife, the minister shall read as followeth :" and instead of the second rubric, it is advised to be convenient, that the new-married persons should receive the communion at the time of marriage, or at the first opportunity afterward.

17. In the order for visitation of the sick it is thus amended : " Here the sick person shall be moved to make special confession of his sins, if he feel his conscience troubled with any weighty matter; after which the priest shall absolve him, if he humbly and heartily desire it, after this sort."

18. In the communion for the sick the minister is not enjoined to administer the sacrament to every sick person that shall desire it, but only as he shall judge expedient.

19. In the order for the burial of the dead it is thus altered : The priests and clerks meeting, the corpse at the entrance of the churchyard, and going before it either into the church, or towards the grave, shall say or sing, In the office itself, these words, "In sure and certain hope of resurrection to eternal life," are thus altered : "in sure and certain hope of *the* resurrection to eternal life;" and to lessen the objection of "God's taking to himself the soul of this our dear brother departed," &c., the following rubric is added : "Here is to be noted, that the office ensuing is not to be used for any that die unbaptized or excommunicate, or who have laid violent hands upon themselves."

20. In the churching of women, the new rubric directs that the woman, at the usual time after her delivery, shall come into the church decently apparelled, and there shall kneel down in some convenient place, as has been accustomed, or as the ordinary shall direct, and the hundred and sixteenth or hundred and seventeenth Psalm shall be read.

Dr. Tenison, afterward Archbishop of Canterbury, says, "They made about six hundred small alterations or additions ;" but then adds, "If there was reason for these changes, there was equal, if not greater reason for some farther improvements. If they had foreseen what is since come to pass, I charitably believe they would not have done all they did, and just so much and no more ; and yet I also believe, if they had offered to move much farther, 'a stone would have been laid under their wheel, by a secret but powerful hand ;' for the mystery of popery did even then work."* Bishop Burnet confesses that no alterations were made in favour of the Presbyterians, for it was resolved to gratify them in nothing.

But besides the alterations and amendments already mentioned, there were several additi-

* Compl. Hist., p. 252, in marg.

tional forms of prayer,* as for the 30th of January and the 29th of May ; forms of prayer to be used at sea; and a new office for the administration of baptism, to grown persons.† Some corrections were made in the calendar. Some new holydays were added, as the conversion of St. Paul and St. Barnabas.‡ More new lessons were taken out of the Apocrypha, as, the story of Bel and the Dragon, &c. But it was agreed that no Apocryphal lessons should be read on Sundays. These were all the concessions the Convocation would admit ;§ and this was all the fruit of the conference at the Savoy, by which, according to Mr. Baxter and Bishop Burnet, the Common Prayer Book was rendered more exceptionable, and the terms of conformity much harder than before the civil war.

The Common Prayer Book thus altered and amended was sent up to the king and council, and from thence transmitted to the House of Peers, February 24, with this message : That his majesty had duly considered of the alterations, and does, with the advice of his council, fully approve and allow the same ; and doth recommend it to the House of Peers, that "the said books of Common Prayer, and of the forms of ordination, and consecration of bishops, priests, and deacons, with those additions and alterations that have been made, and presented to his majesty by the Convocation, be the book which in and by the intended Act of Uniformity shall be appointed to be used by all that officiate in all cathedral and collegiate churches, and chapels, &c., and in all parish churches of England and Wales, under such sanctions or penalties as the Parliament shall think fit."‖ When the Lords had gone through the book, the Lord-chancellor Hyde, by order of the House, gave the bishops thanks, March 15, for their care in this business,¶ and desired their lordships to give the like thanks to the lower house of convocation, and acquaint them that their amendments were well received and approved, though some of them met with a considerable opposition. From the Lords they were sent down to

* Besides the new forms specified by Mr. Neal, there were also added, Dr. Grey says, the prayer for the High Court of Parliament, the prayer for all conditions of men, and the general thanksgiving.—*Examination*, p. 310.—ED.

† This service was added because, on account of the spread of Baptistical sentiments, there were now many grown up too old to be baptized as infants, whose duty it was to make a profession of their own faith.—*Wall's Hist. of Infant Baptism*, vol. ii., p. 215.—ED.

‡ These two holydays, though then first appointed by act of Parliament, were not now added to the calendar ; for they stand in the liturgy of Edward VI. by Whitchurch, 1549 ; in his Review, 1552; in Queen Elizabeth's Review, 4to, 1601 ; in King James's Review, 1609; and in the Scotch liturgy at Edinburgh, folio, 1637.—*Grey's Examination*, p. 311. It may be added, they are, with suitable collects, in the liturgy printed by Bonham Norton and John Bill, 1629, *penes me.*—ED.

§ There is one alteration not mentioned by Mr. Neal. In the second collect, in the visitation of the sick, these words are omitted : "Visite him. O Lord, as thou didst Peter's wive's mother, and the captain's servant :" which were in King Edward's, Queen Elizabeth's, and King James's Review.—*Id.*, p. 311. —ED. ‖ Kennet's Chronicle, p. 633.

¶ Id., p. 642, 643.
VOL. II.—G G

the Commons, and inserted in the Act of Uniformity, as will be seen under the next year.

But before this famous act had passed either house, the Presbyterians were reduced to the utmost distress. In the month of March, 1661-2,* the grand jury at Exeter found above forty bills of indictment against some eminent Nonconformist ministers for not reading the Common Prayer according to law. They likewise presented the travelling about of divers itinerant preachers, ejected out of sequestered livings, as dangerous to the peace of the nation. They complained of their teaching sedition and rebellion in private houses, and other congregations, tending to foment a new war. They also presented such as neglected their own parish churches, and ran abroad to hear factious ministers ; and such as walked in the church-yards, or other places, while Divine service was reading ; all which were the certain forerunners of a general persecution.

In Scotland the court carried their measures with a high hand ; for, having got a Parliament to their mind,† the Earl of Middleton, a most notorious debauchee, opened it, with presenting a letter of his majesty's to the House ; after which they passed an act, declaring all leagues not made with the king's authority illegal. This struck at the root of the covenant made with England in 1643.‡ They passed another act rescinding all acts made since the late troubles, and another empowering the king to settle the government of the Church as he should please. It was a mad, roaring time, says the bishop, and no wonder it was so, when the men of affairs were almost perpetually drunk. The king hereupon directed that the Church should be governed by synods, presbyters, and kirk-sessions, till he should appoint another government, which he did by a letter to his council of Scotland, bearing date August 14, 1661, in which he recites the inconveniences which had attended the Presbyterian government for the last twenty-three years, and its inconsistency with monarchy. "Therefore," says he, "from our respect to the glory of God, the good and interest of the Protestant religion, and the better harmony with the government of the Church of England, we declare our firm resolution to interpose our royal authority for restoring the Church of Scotland to its right government by bishops, as it was before the late troubles. And our will and pleasure is, that you take effectual care to restore the rents belonging to the several bishoprics ; that you prohibit the assembling of ministers in their synodical meetings till our farther pleasure ; and that you keep a watchful eye over those who, by discourse or preaching, endeavour to alienate the affections of our people from us or our government." Pursuant to these directions, the lords of the council ordered the heralds to make public proclamation at the market-cross in Edinburgh, September 6, of this his majesty's royal will and pleasure. In the month of December a commission was issued out to the Bishops of London and Worcester§ to ordain and consecrate, according to the rites and ceremonies of the Church of England, Mr. James Sharp, arch-

* Kennet's Chronicle, p. 647.
† Burnet, vol. i., p. 161. ‡ Ibid., p. 166.
§ Ibid., p. 133, 134.

bishop of St. Andrew's, Mr. Andrew Fairfoul, archbishop of Glasgow, Mr. Robert Leighton, bishop' of Dunblain, and Mr. James Hamilton, bishop of Galloway. A very bad choice, says Bishop Burnet. Sharp was one of the falsest and vilest dissemblers in the world. Fairfoul was next akin to a natural. Leighton was an excellent prelate; but Hamilton's life was scarce free from scandal.* He had sworn to the Covenant, and when one objected to him, that it went against his conscience, he said,' " Such medicines as could not be chewed must be swallowed whole."† The English bishops insisted upon their renouncing their Presbyterian orders, which they consented to, and were, in one and the same day, ordained first deacons, then priests, and last of all bishops, according to the rites of the Church of England.

Bishop Burnet says, that though the king had a natural hatred to Presbytery, he went very coldly into this design; nay, that he had a visible reluctancy against it, because of the temper of the Scots nation, and his unwillingness to involve his government in new troubles; but the Earl of Clarendon‡ pushed it forward with great zeal; and the Duke of Ormond said that Episcopacy could not be established in Ireland, if Presbytery continued in Scotland. The Earls of Lauderdale and Crawford, indeed, opposed it, but the councils of Scotland not protesting, it was determined; but it was a large strain of the prerogative for a king by a royal proclamation to alter the government of a church established by law, without consent of Parliament, convocation, or synod, of any kind whatsoever; for it was not until May the next year that this affair was decided in Parliament.

Some of the Scots ministers preached boldly against this change of government; and, among others, Mr. James Guthrie, minister of Stirling, for which, and some other things, he was convicted of sedition and treason. Bishop Burnet,§ who saw him suffer, says that he expressed a contempt of death; that he spoke an hour upon the ladder with the composure of a man that was delivering a sermon rather than his last words; that he justified all he had done, exhorting all people to adhere to the Covenant, which he magnified highly. He was executed June 14, 1661, and concluded his dying speech with these words :‖ " I take God to record upon my soul, that I would not exchange this scaffold with the palace or mitre of the greatest prelate

---

* Burnet., p. 191; 192.

† It is here, as Dr. Grey remarks, that Mr. Neal has strangely confounded two characters: ascribing to Bishop Hamilton what Bishop Burnet has applied to Bishop Fairfoul. It is singular that Dr. Grey has, in the next paragraph, committed a similar mistake; for, quoting Mr. Neal's account of the death of Mr. James Guthrie, who, on the authority of Burnet, he says, "spoke an hour before his execution with great composedness," he admits the correctness of this passage: but adds, that Burnet, but two pages before, said that Mr. Guthrie spoke for half an hour with great appearance of serenity; and observes, "so consistent was this great man with himself in the compass of two pages." Now the inconsistency is in Dr. Grey, and not Bishop Burnet, who speaks, in the first place, not of Mr. Guthrie, but of the Marquis of Argyle, vol. i., p. 179.—ED.

† Hist., p. 130, 131. Kennet's Chron., p. 577.

§ Hist. of the Stuarts, p. 144.

‖ Kennet's Chron., p. 459. Burnet, p. 181.

in Britain. Blessed be God, who hath showed mercy to such a wretch, and hath revealed his Son in me, and made me a minister of the everlasting Gospel; and that he has designed, in the midst of such contradiction from Satan and the world, to seal my ministry upon the hearts of not a few of this people, and especially in the congregation and presbytery of Stirling." There was with him on the same scaffold young Captain Govan, whose last words were these : " I bear witness with my blood to the persecuted government of this Church, by synods and presbyteries. I bear witness to the solemn League and Covenant, and seal it with my blood. I likewise testify against all popery, prelacy, idolatry, superstition, and the Service Book, which is no better than a relic of the Romish idolatry."* Soon after this the rights of patronages were restored, and all the Presbyterian ministers silenced, though the court had not a supply of men of any sort to fill up their vacancies.

The account that Bishop Burnet gives of the old Scots Presbyterian ministers, who were possessed of the church livings before the Restoration, is very remarkable, and deserves a place in this history. " They were,'' says he, "a brave and solemn people ; their spirits were eager, and their tempers sour, but they had an appearance that created respect ; they visited their parishes much, and were so full of Scripture, and so ready at extempore prayer, that from that they grew to practise sermons ; for the custom in Scotland was, after dinner or supper, to read a chapter in the Bible, and when they happened to come in, if it was acceptable, they would on a sudden expound the chapter ; by this means the people had such a vast degree of knowledge, that the poor cottagers could pray extempore. Their preachers went all in one track in their sermons, of doctrine, reason, and use ; and this was so methodical, that the people could follow a sermon quite through every branch of it. It can hardly be imagined to what a degree these ministers were loved and reverenced by their people. They kept scandalous persons under severe discipline ; for breach of the Sabbath, for an oath, or drunkenness, they were cited before the kirk-sessions, and solemnly rebuked for it; for fornication they stood on the stool of repentance in the Church, at the time of worship, for three days, receiving admonition, and making profession of repentance, which some did with many tears, and exhortations to others to take warning by them ; for adultery they sat in the same place six months covered with sackcloth. But with all this," says the bishop, "they had but a narrow compass of learning, were very affected in their deportment, and were apt in their sermons to make themselves popular by preaching against the sins of princes and courts, which the people delighted to hear, because they had no share in them."†

The bishops and clergy who succeeded the Presbyterians were of a quite different stamp ; most of them were very mean divines, vicious in their morals, idle and negligent of their cures; by which means they became obnoxious to the whole nation, and were hardly capable of supporting their authority through the reign of King Charles II., even with the assistance of the

---

* Burnet, p. 152, 153.   † Ibid., p. 226, 227.

civil power. Bishop Burnet adds,* that they were mean and despicable in all respects; the worst preachers he ever heard; ignorant to a reproach, and many of them openly vicious; that they were a disgrace to their order, and to the sacred functions, and were, indeed, the dregs and refuse of the northern parts. The few who were above contempt or scandal were men of such violent tempers, that they were as much hated as the others were despised. ' '

In Ireland the hierarchy was restored after the same manner as in Scotland; the king, by his letters patent, in right of his power to appoint bishops to the vacant sees, issued his royal mandate to Dr. Bramhall, archbishop of Armagh, and Dr. Taylor, bishop of Down and Connor, by virtue of which they consecrated two archbishops and ten bishops in one day.† His grace insisted on the reordination of those who had been ordained in the late times without the hands of a bishop, but with this softening clause in their orders: "Non annihilantes priores ordines (si quos habuit) nec validitatem aut invaliditatem eorundem determinantes, multo minus omnes ordines sacros ecclesiarûm forinsecarum condemnantes, quos propriô judicio relinquimus: sed solummodo supplentes quicquid prius defuit per canones ecclesia Anglicanæ requisitum:" i. e., "Not annihilating his former orders (if he had any), nor determining concerning their validity or invalidity, much less condemning all the sacred ordinations of foreign churches, whom we leave to their own judge, but only supplying what was wanting according to the canons of the Church of England." Without such an explication as this, few of the clergy of Ireland would have kept their stations in the Church.‡ On the 17th of May, the lords spiritual and temporal, and the commons in Parliament assembled in Ireland, declared their opinion and high esteem of Episcopal government, and of the Book of Common Prayer, according to the use of the Church of England; and thus the old constitution in Church as well as State was restored in the three kingdoms.

The French ministers, who had been tools to persuade the English Presbyterians to restore the king without a treaty, went along with the torrent, and complimented the Church of England upon her re-establishment; they commended the liturgy, which they formerly treated with contemptuous language. Some few of them pretended to bemoan the want of Episcopacy among themselves, and to wonder that any of the English Presbyterians should scruple conformity.§ The French Church at the Savoy submitted to the rites and ceremonies of the English hierarchy; and M. du Bosc, minister of Caen, writes to the minister of the Savoy, that he was as dear to him under the surplice of England as under the robe of France.‖ So complaisant were these mercenary divines towards those who disallowed their orders, disowned their churches, and the validity of all their administrations.

Lord Clarendon and the bishops having got over the Savoy Conference, and carried the Service Book with the amendments through the Convocation, were now improving the present temper of the Parliament to procure it the sanc-

tion of the Legislature; for this purpose the king, though a papist, is made to speak the language of a zealous churchman. In his speech to the Parliament, March 1st, he has these words: "Gentlemen, I hear you are zealous for the Church, and very solicitous, and even jealous, that there is not expedition enough used in that affair. I thank you for it, since I presume it proceeds from a good root of piety and devotion; but I must tell you, that I have the worst luck in the world, if, after all the reproaches of being a papist, while I was abroad, I am suspected of being a Presbyterian now I am come home. I know you will not take it unkindly if I tell you I am as zealous for the Church of England as any of you can be, and am enough acquainted with the enemies of it on all sides. I am as much in love with the Book of Common Prayer as you can wish, and have prejudices enough against those who do not love it; who I hope, in time, will be better informed, and change their minds. And you may be confident I do as much desire to see a uniformity settled as any among you; and pray trust me in that affair, I promise you to hasten the despatch of it with all convenient speed; you may rely upon me in it. I have transmitted the Book of Common Prayer, with the amendments, to the House of Lords; but when we have done all we can, in time, will be settling that affair will require great prudence and discretion, and the absence of all passion and precipitation."*

The reason of the king's requiring discretion in the Parliament, and the absence of passion, was not in favour of the Presbyterians, but the papists, who went all the lengths of the prerogative, and published a remonstrance about this time, "wherein they acknowledge his majesty to be God's vicegerent upon earth in all temporal affairs; that they are bound to obey him under pain of sin, and that they renounce all foreign power and authority, as incapable of absolving them from this obligation." It was given out that they were to have forty chapels in and about the city of London, and much more was understood by them, says Archbishop Tenison, who have penetrated into the designs of a certain paper, commonly called the Declaration of Somerset House; but the design miscarried, partly by their divisions among themselves, and partly by the resoluteness of the prime minister, who charged them with principles inconsistent with the peace of the kingdom.† Father Orleans says, " There were great debates in this Parliament about liberty of conscience. The Catholic party was supported by the Earl of Bristol, a man in great repute; the Protestant party by Chancellor Hyde, chief of an opposite faction, and a person of no less consideration, who, putting himself at the head of the prevailing Church of England party in that Parliament, declared not only against the Roman Catholics, but against the Presbyterians, and all those the Church of England call Nonconformists.' The king, who was no good Christian in his actions, but a Catholic in his heart, did all that could be expected from his easy temper to maintain the common liberty, that so the Catholics might

---

* Page 229.   † Kennet's Chron., p. 440, 441.
‡ Ibid., p. 449.   § Ibid., p. 462.   ‖ Ibid., p. 475.

* Rapin, vol. ii., p. 628, folio.
† Compl. Hist., p. 252. Kennet's Chron., p. 482, 498.

have a share in it ; but the Church of England and Chancellor Hyde were so hot upon that point, that his majesty was obliged to yield rather to the chancellor's importunity than to his reason."* However, by the favour of the queen-mother, swarms of papists came over into England, and settled about the court ; they set 'up private seminaries for the education of youth ; and though they could not obtain an open toleration, they multiplied exceedingly, and laid the foundation of all the dangers which threatened the Constitution and Protestant religion in the latter part of this and in the next reign.

Towards the latter end of this year, the court and bishops, not content with their triumphs over the living Presbyterians, descended into the grave, and dug up the bodies of those who had been deposited in Westminster Abbey in the late times, lest their dust should one time or other mix with the Loyalists ; for besides the bodies of Cromwell, and others already mentioned, his majesty's warrant to the dean and chapter of Westminster was now obtained to take up the bodies of such persons who had been unwarrantably buried in the chapel of King Henry VII. and in other chapels and places within the collegiate church of Westminster since the year 1641, and to inter them in the churchyard adjacent ; by which warrant they might have taken up all the bodies that had been buried there for twenty years past. Pursuant to these orders, on the 12th and 14th of September they went to work, and took up about twenty,† among whom were,

* Kennet's Chron., p. 498.
† Among the following names, the reader will find some who have not been noticed in the preceding history, or in the notes. The mother of Oliver Cromwell was by no means deserving of the malevolence and indignity with which her memory was treated. For, though she lavished the greatest fondness on her only son, she was averse to his protectorate, seldom troubled him with her advice, and with reluctance partook of the pageantry of sovereignty. She was an amiable and prudent woman, who, to make up the deficiency of a narrow income, undertook and managed the brewing trade on her own account, and from the profits of it provided fortunes for her daughters sufficient to marry them into good families. Her anxiety for her son's safety kept her in such constant alarm, that she was discontented if she did not see him twice a day. The report of a gun was never heard by her without her crying out, " My son is shot." It ought to have softened the resentment of the Royalists against Mrs. Claypole, though the daughter of Cromwell, that she had importunately interceded for the life of Dr. Hewett ; and the denial of her suit had so afflicted her, that it was reported to have been one cause of her death, and was the subject of her exclamations to her father on her dying bed. Thomas May, Esq., whose name appears in the following list, was a polite and classical scholar, the intimate friend of the greatest wits of his time, and ranked in the first class of them. He was the author of several dramatic pieces, and of two historical poems of the reigns of Henry II. and Edward III. But his principal work was a "Translation of Lucan's Pharsalia," and a continuation of it. Colonel, or Sir John Meldrum, a Scotsman, displayed his military prowess in the west, defeated the Earl of Newcastle before Hull, with the assistance of Sir Thomas Fairfax took the strong town of Gainsborough and the isle of Axholm, conquered the forces of the Lords Byron and Molyneux, near Ormskirk, and took the

The body of Eliz. Cromwell, mother of Oliver, daughter of Sir Richard Stewart, who died November 18, 1654, and was buried in Henry VII.'s chapel.

The body of Eliz. Claypole, daughter of Oliver, who died August 7, 1658, and was buried in a vault made for her in Henry VII.'s chapel.

The body of Robert Blake, the famous English admiral, who, after his victorious fight at Santa Cruz, died in Plymouth Sound, August 7, 1657, and was buried in Henry VII.'s chapel : a man whose great services to the English nation will be an everlasting monument of his renown.

The body of the famous Mr. John Pym, a Cornish gentleman, and member of the Long Parliament, who was buried in the year 1643, and attended to his grave by most of the Lords and Commons in Parliament.

The body of Dr. Dorislaus, employed as an assistant in drawing up the charge against the king, for which he was murdered by the Royalists, when he was ambassador to the States of Holland in 1649.

The body of Sir William Constable, one of the king's judges, governor of Gloucester, and colonel of a regiment of foot, who died 1655.

The body of Colonel Edward Popham, one of the admirals of the fleet, who died 1651·

The body of William Stroud, Esq., one of the five members of Parliament demanded by King Charles I.

The body of Colonel Humphrey Mackworth, one of Oliver Cromwell's colonels, buried in Henry VII.'s chapel, 1654.

The body of Dennis Bond, Esq., one of the Council of State, who died August 8, 1658.

The body of Thomas May, Esq., who compiled the history of the Long Parliament with great integrity, and in a beautiful style. He died in the year 1650.

The body of Colonel John Meldrum, a Scotsman, who died in the wars.

The body of Colonel Boscawen, a Cornish man.

To these may be added several eminent Presbyterian divines ; as,

The body of Dr. William Twisse, prolocutor of the Assembly of Divines, buried in the south cross of the Abbey Church, July 24, 1645.

The body of Mr. Stephen Marshall, buried in the south aisle, November 23, 1655.

The body of Mr. William Strong, preacher in the Abbey Church, and buried there July 4, 1654. These, with some others of lesser note, both men and women, were thrown together into one pit in St. Margaret's churchyard, near the back door of one of the prebendaries ; but the work was so indecent, and drew such a general odium on the government, that a stop was put to any farther proceedings.

Among others who were obnoxious to the ministry, were the people called Quakers, who, having declared openly against the lawfulness of making use of carnal weapons, even in self-defence, had the courage to petition the House of Lords for a toleration of their religion, and for a dispensation from taking the oaths, which

town and castle of Scarborough.—*Biogr. Britan.*, vol. iv., p. 517. *Ludlow's Memoirs*, 4to, p. 257. *Granger's History of England*, vol. iii., p. 94, and vol. ii., p. 265.—ED.	* Kennet's Chron., p. 536.

they held unlawful, not from any disaffection to the government, or a belief that they were less obliged by an affirmation, but from a persuasion that all oaths were unlawful ; and that swearing, upon the most solemn occasions, was forbidden in the New Testament. The Lords, in a committee, rejected their petition, and, instead of granting them relief, passed the following act* May 2, the preamble to which sets forth, "That whereas sundry persons have taken up an opinion that an oath, even before a magistrate, is unlawful, and contrary to the Word of God. And whereas, under pretence of religious worship, the said persons do assemble in great numbers in several parts of the kingdom, separating themselves from the rest of his majesty's subjects, and from the public congregations, and usual places of Divine worship ; be it therefore enacted, that if any such persons after the 24th of March, 1661-2, shall refuse to take an oath when lawfully tendered, or persuade others to do it, or maintain, in writing or otherwise, the unlawfulness of taking an oath ; or if they shall assemble for religious worship to the number of five or more, of the age of fifteen, they shall for the first offence forfeit £5 ; for the second, £10 ; and for the third shall abjure the realm, or be transported to the plantations ; and the justices of peace, at their open sessions, may hear and finally determine in the affair." The act was passed by commission, and had a dreadful influence upon that people, though it was notorious they were far from sedition or disaffection to the government. G. Fox, in his address to the king, acquaints his majesty, that three thousand and sixty-eight of their friends had been imprisoned since his majesty's restoration ; that their meetings were daily broken up by men with clubs and arms, and their friends thrown into the water, and trampled under foot, till the blood gushed out, which gave rise to their meeting in the open streets. Another narrative was printed, signed by twelve witnesses, which says that more than four thousand two hundred Quakers were imprisoned ; and of them five hundred were in and about London and the suburbs, several of whom were dead in the jails.† But these were only the beginning of sorrows.

* Some of the society, getting early intelligence of this bill, interfered to stop its progress. Edward Burrough, Richard Hubberthorn, and George Whitehead, attended the Parliament to solicit against passing it into an act ; and were admitted, but without success, to offer their reasons against it, at the bar of the House. "But political considerations, party animosity, and bigoted, exasperated zeal for the church (so called), were the moving causes of action with the majority. Appeals to their reason and humanity were vain." It aggravated the injustice and severity of this act, that it was framed, notwithstanding a paper, containing the sentiments of the Quakers respecting oaths, had been lately presented to the king and council by Edward Burrough, entitled "A Just and Righteous Plea :" which stated their conscientious scruples, expressed in strong terms their loyalty, and declared, "that it had ever been with them an established principle, confirmed by a consonant practice, to enter into no plots, combinations, or rebellions against government, nor to seek deliverance from injustice or oppression by any such means."—Gough's History of the Quakers, vol. i., p. 499, &c.—ED.

† Sewel, p. 346. Kennet's Chron., p. 651. "Some were put into such noisome prisons, as

Religion, which had been in vogue in the late times, was now universally discountenanced ; the name of it was hardly mentioned but with contempt, in a health or a play. Those who observed the Sabbath, and scrupled profane swearing and drinking healths, were exposed under the opprobrious names of Puritans, Fanatics, Presbyterians, Republicans, seditious persons, &c. The Presbyterian ministers were everywhere suspended or deprived, for some unguarded expressions in their sermons or prayers. Lord Clarendon was at the head of all this madness, and declared in Parliament "that the king could distinguish between tenderness of conscience and pride of conscience ; that he was a prince of so excellent a nature, and of so tender a conscience himself, that he had the highest compassion for all errors of that kind, and would never suffer the weak to undergo its punishment ordained for the wicked." Such was the deep penetration of the chancellor ; and such the reward the Presbyterians received for their past services !

The profligate manners of the court, at the same time, spread over the whole land, and occasioned such a general licentiousness, that the king took notice of it in his speech at the end of this session of Parliament. "I cannot but observe," says his majesty, "that the whole nation seems to be a little corrupted in their excess of living ; sure all men spend much more in their clothes, in their diet, and all other expenses, than they have been used to do ; I hope it has been only the excess of joy after so long suffering, that has transported us to these other excesses, but let us take heed that the continuance of them does not indeed corrupt our natures. I do believe I have been faulty myself ; I promise you I will reform, and if you will join with me in your several capacities, we shall, by our examples, do more good both in city and country than any new laws would do." This was a frank acknowledgment and a good resolution, but it was not in the king's nature to retrench his expenses, or control his vices, for the public good.*

were owned not fit for dogs. Some prisons so crowded that the prisoners had not room to sit down altogether. In Cheshire, sixty-eight persons were thus locked up in a small room. No age or sex found any commiseration. Men of sixty, seventy, or more years of age, were, without pity or remorse, subjected to all the rigours of such imprisonments under the infirmities of a natural decline ; many times they were forced to lie on the cold ground, without being permitted the use of straw, and kept many days without victuals. No wonder that many grew sick and died by such barbarous imprisonments as these." —Gough, vol. i., p. 538.—ED.

* In the preceding year died, on the 22d of December, aged seventy-two years, Mr. Thomas Lushington, a scholar of eminence, and a favourer of the sentiments of Socinus ; who translated into English and published, Crellius's Commentary on the Epistle to the Galatians, and a commentary on that to the Hebrews from the Latin of the same author, or some other Unitarian writer. He published, among other works, two sermons on Matt., xxviii., 13, and Acts, ii., 1, entitled "The Resurrection rescued from the Soldier's Calumnies." He was reckoned more ingenious than prudent, and was more apt to display his fancy than to proceed upon solid reason. At one time he personated in his sermon a Jewish Pharisee and persecutor of Christ, descanting on the whole life of our Saviour in a way suited to draw scorn and

Though the revenues of the crown were augmented above double what they had been at any time since the Reformation; and though the king had a vast dowry with his queen, whom he married this spring, yet all was not sufficient to defray the extravagance of the court; for besides the king's own expenses, the queen-mother maintained a splendid court of Roman Catholics at Somerset House, and might have done so as long as she had lived, if she could have kept within moderate bounds; but her conduct was so imprudent and profuse, that she was obliged to return to France after three or four years, where she died in the year 1669. A lady of such bigotry in religion,* and intrigue in

aversion on him and his attendants: he then changed his character, and speaking as a disciple of Christ, he answered the cavils and invectives before thrown out with such dexterity, that his hearers broke into such loud and repeated applauses, as hindered him for a good space from proceeding in his sermon. He was a native of Sandwich, and matriculated at Broadgate's Hall, in Oxford, when he was seventeen, in 1606-7. He graduated, as master of arts, in Lincoln College, in 1618. In 1631, Bishop Corbet gave him the prebendal stall of Bemister Secunda in the church of Salisbury; and afterward bestowed on him the rectory of Burnham Westgate, in Norfolk. In the rebellion he lost his spiritualities, but on the return of Charles II. was restored to them. He died and was buried at Sittingbourne, near Milton, in Kent.—*Wood's Athen. Oxon.*, vol. ii., p. 71, 72.—Ed.

In the year 1661, or soon after the Restoration, died also Mr. Henry Denne, whom we have mentioned before. He began his ministry in the Church of England, and in 1641 drew great attention by a sermon which he preached at Baldock, in Hertfordshire; in this discourse he freely exposed the sin of persecution, and inveighed against the pride and covetousness of the clergy, their pluralities and nonresidences, and the corrupt practices of the spiritual courts. He was reckoned by one, who had a great hand in the public affairs of the age, "to be the ablest man in the kingdom for prayer, expounding, and preaching." When the government declared their design to reform religion, Mr. Denne and many others were led to extend their inquiries after religious truth to points which before they had only taken for granted; and it appearing to him, in his researches, that the practice of baptizing children was without any foundation in Scripture, or the writings of three Christians for the first two ages, he publicly professed himself a Baptist, and was baptized by immersion at London in 1643. This exposed him to the resentment of those who sat at the helm of ecclesiastical affairs; but notwithstanding this, he obtained the parish of Elsly in Cambridgeshire. Meeting with opposition and persecution, he quitted his living and went into the army, and gained reputation in the military line. In 1658 he held a public disputation concerning infant baptism with Dr. Gunning, in St. Clement's Church, Temple Bar, in which he is said to have afforded strong proofs of his abilities and learning as a good scholar and complete disputant. Mr. Edwards gives him the character of "a very affecting preacher." A clergyman put on his grave this epitaph:

" To tell his wisdom, learning, goodness, unto men,
　I need say no more, but here lies Henry Denne."

—*Crosby's History of the English Baptists*, vol. i., p. 297, &c.—Ed. For a much more full and satisfactory account of this able divine, consult "Brook's Lives of the Puritans," vol. iii., p. 376, 380.—C.

* It was the grand argument with the Duke of York, for his adherence to the tenets of popery, that his mother had, upon her last blessing, commanded him to be firm and steadfast thereto.—*Reresby's Memoirs*, p. 16.

politics, that her alliance to this nation was little less than a judgment from Heaven.

To procure more ready money for these extravagances, it was resolved to sell the town of Dunkirk to the French, for £500,000. The Lord-chancellor Clarendon was the projector of this vile bargain,* as appears by the letters of Count d'Estrades, published since his death, in one of which his lordship acknowledges that the thought came from himself.† Several mercenary pamphlets were dispersed to justify this sale; but the wars with France, in the reigns of King William and Queen Anne, have sufficiently convinced us that it was a fatal stab to our trade and commerce: insomuch, that even the queen's last ministry durst not venture to make a peace with France, till the fortifications of it were demolished.

But to divert the people's eyes to other objects, it was resolved to go on with the prosecution of state criminals, and with humbling and crushing the Nonconformists: three of the late king's judges being apprehended in Holland, by the forward zeal of Sir G. Downing, viz., Colonel Okey, Corbet, and Berkstead, were brought over to England by permission of the States, and executed on the Act of Attainder, April 19. They died with the same resolution and courage as the former had done, declaring they had no malice against the late king, but apprehended the authority of Parliament sufficient to justify their conduct.

Before the Parliament rose, the House addressed the king to bring Colonel Lambert and Sir Henry Vane, prisoners in the Tower, to their trial; and accordingly, June 4, they were arraigned at the King's Bench bar; the former for levying war against the king, and the latter for compassing his death. Lambert was convicted, but for his submissive behaviour was pardoned as to life, but confined in the Isle of Guernsey, where he remained a patient prisoner till his death, which happened about thirty years after. Sir Henry Vane had such an interest in the Convention Parliament, that both Lords and Commons petitioned for his life, which his majesty promised; and yet, afterward, at the instigation of the present House of Commons, he

* Dr. Grey is much displeased with Mr. Neal for imputing the sale of Dunkirk to Lord Clarendon; and remarks on it, that "had the Count d'Estrades declared positively that the Lord Clarendon had no concern therein, it is probable that his authority would have been rejected or passed over in silence. But Lord Clarendon was a great friend to monarchy and Episcopacy, and therefore Lord Clarendon's character must at all adventures he run down." The reader will determine concerning the candour and fairness of this censure. The passages in which D'Estrades ascribes this transaction to Lord Clarendon *are to be seen in Rapin, and in Dr. Harris's Life of Charles II.*, vol. ii., p. 192-198. Dr. Grey, on the other hand, refers to Kennet and Roger Coke, Esq., as acquitting his lordship from advising the sale of Dunkirk. Bishop Burnet, it may be added, says, on the information of his lordship's son, "that he kept himself out of that affair entirely." To reconcile the nation to the sale of Dunkirk, the king promised to lay up all the money in the Tower, and that it should not be touched but upon extraordinary occasions. But in violation of his word and of decency, it was immediately squandered away among the creatures of his mistress, Barbara Villiers.—*Burnet's History of his Own Times*, vol. i., p. 251.—Ed.

† Rapin, p. 630, 631.

was tried and executed. Sir Harry made a brave defence, but it was determined to sacrifice him to the ghost of the Earl of Strafford; and when his friends would have had him petition for his life, he refused, saying, if the king had not a greater regard for his word and honour than he had for his life, he might take it. Nevertheless, Bishop Burnet says,[*] " He was naturally a fearful man, and had a head as dark in the notions of religion; but when he saw his death was determined; he composed himself to it with a resolution that surprised all who knew how little of that was natural to him. He was beheaded on Tower Hill, June 14, where a new and very indecent practice was begun; it was observed that the dying speeches of the regicides had left impressions on the hearers that were not at all to the advantage of the government; and strains of a peculiar nature being expected from him, drummers were placed under the scaffold, who, as soon as he began to speak to the public, upon a sign given, struck up with their drums. But this put him into no disorder; he desired they might be stopped, for he knew what was meant by it. Then he went to his devotion; and as he was taking leave of those about him, he happened to say something again with relation to the times, when the drums struck up a second time; so he gave over, saying, it was a sorry cause that would not bear the words of a dying man; and died with so much composedness, that it was generally thought the government lost more than it gained by his death." The Oxford historian says he appeared on the scaffold like an old Roman, and died without the least symptoms of concern or trouble.[†]

But the grand affair that employed the Parliament this spring was the famous Act of Uniformity of Public Prayers, &c., designed for the enclosure of the Church, and the only door of admission to all ecclesiastical preferments. The review of the Common Prayer had been in convocation three or four months,[‡] and was brought into Parliament, with their alterations and amendments, before Christmas;[§] the bill was read the first time in the House of Commons January 14, and passed, after sundry debates; but by six voices, yeas 186, noes 180; but met with greater obstacles among the Lords, who offered several amendments, which occasioned conferences between the two houses. The Lords would have exempted schoolmasters, tutors, and those who had the education of youth; and in the disabling clause, would have included only livings with cure.[‖] But the Commons being supported by the court, would abate nothing,[¶] nor consent to any provision for such

as should be ejected. They would indulge no latitude in the surplice or cross in baptism, for fear of establishing a schism, and weakening the authority of the Church as to her right of imposing indifferent rites and ceremonies.[*] And the court were willing to shut out as many as they could from the Establishment, to make a general toleration more necessary. When the Lords urged the king's declaration from Breda, the Commons replied, that it would be strange to call a schismatical conscience a tender one; but suppose this had been meant (say they), his majesty can be guilty of no breach of promise, because the declaration had these two limitations, a reference to Parliament, and so far as was consistent with the peace of the kingdom. May 8, the result of the conference with the House of Commons being reported to the Lords, the House laid aside their objections and concurred with the Commons, and the bill passed; but, as Bishop Burnet observes, with no great majority. May 19 it received the royal assent, and was to take place from the 24th of August following. This act being prefixed to the Book of Common Prayer, and lying open to public view, I shall only give the reader an abstract of it. It is entitled,

"An Act for the Uniformity of Public Prayers, and Administration of Sacraments, and other Rites and Ceremonies; and for establishing the Forms of making, ordaining, and consecrating Bishops, Priests, and Deacons in the Church of England."

The preamble sets forth, " That from the first of Queen Elizabeth, there had been one uniform order of common service and prayer enjoined to be used by act of Parliament, which had been very comfortable to all good people, until a great number of the people in divers parts of the realm, living without knowledge and the due fear of God, did wilfully and schismatically refuse to come to their parish churches upon Sundays, and other days appointed to be kept as holydays. And whereas, by the scandalous neglect of ministers in using the liturgy during the late unhappy troubles, many people have been led into factions and schisms, to the decay of religion and the hazard of many souls; therefore, for preventing the like for time to come, the king had granted a commission to review the Book of Common Prayer to those bishops and divines who met at the Savoy; and afterward his majesty required the clergy in convocation to revise it again; which alterations and amendments having been approved by his majesty and both houses of Parliament, therefore, for setting the peace of the nation, for the honour of religion, and to the intent that every person may know the rule to which he is to conform in public worship, it is enacted by the king's most excellent majesty, &c.,

" That all and singular ministers shall be bound to say and use the morning prayer, evening prayer, and all other common prayers, in such order and form as is mentioned in the book; and that every parson, vicar, or other minister whatsoever, shall before the feast of St. Bartholomew, which shall be in the year of our Lord 1662, openly and publicly, before the congregation assembled for religious worship, declare his unfeigned assent and consent to the

---

*. Burnet, p. 237, 238.

† See Upham's admirable Life of Sir Henry Vane. Sylvester's Life of Baxter, part i., p. 75. Granger's Biog. Dict., vol. ii., p. 213; vol. iii., p. 109.—C.

‡ Dr. Grey is at a loss to understand how the Act of Uniformity could come into the Convocation, and continue there for three or four months: for the two houses never send their bills thither for their perusal and approbation. He thinks, therefore, that Mr. Neal's mistake must be owing to their review of the Common Prayer.—Examination, vol. iii. p. 320.—ED.

§ Kennet's Chron., p. 604.   ‖ Ibid., p. 677.

¶ The reason for extending it to schoolmasters was, we are told, to guard against the influence and force of education.—Examination, p. 321.—ED.

+ Kennet's Chron., p. 679.

use of all things contained and prescribed in the said book, in these words, and no other :

. " I, A. B., do declare my unfeigned assent and consent to all and everything contained and prescribed in and by the book entitled 'The Book of Common Prayer, and Administration of Sacraments, and other Rites and Ceremonies of the Church, according to the Use of the Church of England, together with the Psalter or Psalms of David, pointed as they are to be sung or said in Churches ;' and the form and manner of making, ordaining, and consecrating of bishops, priests, and deacons."*

The penalty for neglecting or refusing to make this declaration is deprivation, *ipso facto*, of all his spiritual promotions.

" And it is farther enacted, that every dean, canon, and prebendary ; all masters, heads, fellows, chaplains, and tutors, in any college, hall, house of learning, or hospital ; all public professors, readers in either university, and in every college and elsewhere ; and all parsons, vicars, curates, lecturers ; and every schoolmaster keeping any public or private school ; and every person instructing youth in any private family, shall, before the feast of St. Bartholomew, 1662, subscribe the following declaration, viz. :

" I, A. B., do declare that it is not lawful, upon any pretence whatsoever, to take arms against the king ; and that I do abhor that traitorous position of taking arms by his authority, against his person, or against those that are commissioned by him ; and that I will conform to the liturgy of the Church of England, as it is now by law established. And I do hold that there lies no obligation upon me, or on any other person, from the oath commonly called the solemn League and Covenant, to endeavour any change or alteration of government, either in Church or State, and that the same was in itself an unlawful oath, and imposed upon the subjects of this realm against the known laws and liberties of this kingdom."

This declaration is to be subscribed by the persons above mentioned, before the archbishop, bishop, or ordinary of the diocess, on pain of deprivation, for those who were possessed of livings ; and for schoolmasters or tutors, three months' imprisonment for the first offence ; and for every other offence, three months' imprisonment, and the forfeiture of five pounds to his majesty. Provided, that after the 25th of March, 1682, the renouncing of the solemn League and Covenant shall be omitted.

" It is farther enacted, that no person shall be capable of any benefice, or presume to consecrate and administer the holy sacrament of the Lord's Supper, before he be ordained a priest by Episcopal ordination, on pain of forfeiting for every offence one hundred pounds.†

" No form or order of common prayer shall be used in any church, chapel, or other place of public worship, or in either of the universities, than is here prescribed and appointed.

" None shall be received as lecturers, or be permitted to preach, or read any sermon or lecture in any church or chapel, unless he be approved and licensed by the archbishop or

bishop, and shall read the Thirty-nine Articles of Religion, with a declaration of his unfeigned assent and consent to the same : and unless, the first time he preaches any lecture or sermon, he shall openly read the Common Prayer, and declare his assent to it ; and shall, on the first lecture day of every month afterward, before lecture or sermon, read the Common Prayer and service, under pain of being disabled to preach ; and if he preach while so disabled, to suffer three months' imprisonment for every offence.

" The several laws and statutes formerly made for uniformity of prayer, &c., shall be in force for confirming the present Book of Common Prayer, and shall be applied for punishing all offences contrary to the said laws, with relation to the said book, and no other.

" A true printed copy of the said book is to be provided in every parish church, chapel, college, and hall, at the cost and charge of the parishioners or society, before the feast of St. Bartholomew, on pain of forfeiting three pounds a month for so long as they shall be unprovided of it."*

It was certainly unreasonable in the Legislature to limit the time of subscription to so short a period,† it being next to impossible that the clergy in all parts of the kingdom should read and examine the alterations within that time. The dean and prebendaries of Peterborough declared that they could not obtain copies before August 17, the Sunday immediately preceding the feast of St. Bartholomew ; so that all the members of that cathedral did not and could not read the service in manner and form as the act directs, and therefore they were obliged to have recourse to the favour of their ordinary to

---

* This form of subscription and solemn declaration was inserted by the Lords, with whom this Act of Uniformity began.—ED.

† This clause was also inserted by the Lords.—ED.

* "The Act of Uniformity and the Corporation Act," Mr. Gough observes, "did not in themselves materially affect the Quakers, who aspired to no places of honour or profit, and who testified against preaching for hire, and sought for no more than a toleration and protection in their religious and civil rights, to lead a quiet and peaceable life in all godliness and honesty ; yet the Corporation Act in its consequences did affect them, by filling the city and country with persecuting magistrates."—*History of the Quakers*, vol. i., p. 469.—ED.

† Dr. Grey argues that this objection is taken off by a clause exempting from the penalties of the act those who were prevented subscribing within the limited time by some lawful impediment allowed and approved by the ordinary of the place, and complying with its requisition within a month after such impediment was removed ; and the doctor adds, that, in pursuance of this clause, Dr. Laney, the Bishop of Peterborough, dispensed with the dean and chapter of that church. He farther alleges a public advertisement given in London, 6th of August, 1662, declaring that the Book of Common Prayer was then perfectly and exactly printed, and books in folio were provided for all churches and chapels in the kingdom ; which left a space of eighteen days for conveying them through the country. But the doctor did not calculate how many of these days would be run out before this notice had circulated through the nation, and had reached the remoter parts and country parishes lying at a distance from the great post-roads. Bishop Burnet says, " The vast number of copies, being many thousands, that were to be wrought off for all the parish churches of England, made the impression go on so slowly that there were few books set out to sale when the day came."—*Burnet*, vol. i., p. 269. *Examination*, vol. i., p. 420-423 ; and vol. iii., p. 322, 323.—ED.

dispense with their default; however, their prefermènts were then legally forfeited, as appears by the act of the 15th of Charles II., cap. vi., entitled " An Act for the Relief of such as, by Sickness or other Impediments, were disabled from subscribing the Declaration of the Act of Uniformity ;" which says, that those who did not subscribe within the time limited were utterly disabled, and *ipso facto* deprived, and their benefices void, as if they were naturally dead. And if this was the case at Peterborough, what must be the condition of the clergy in the more northern counties? In fact, there was not one divine in ten, that lived at any considerable distance from London, who did peruse it within that time; but the matter was driven on with so much precipitancy, says Bishop Burnet,* that it seems implied, that the clergy should subscribe implicitly to a book they had never seen; and this was done by too many, as by the bishops themselves, confessed.

The terms of conformity now were,
(1.) Reordination, if they had not been Episcopally ordained before.†
(2.) A declaration of their unfeigned assent and consent to all and everything prescribed and contained in " The Book of Common Prayer, and Administration of Sacraments, and other Rites and Ceremonies of the Church of England, together with the Psalter," and the form and manner of making, ordaining, and consecrating of bishops, priests, and deacons:
(3.) To take the oath of canonical obedience.
(4.) To abjure the solemn League and Covenant, which many conscientious ministers could not disentangle themselves from.
(5.) To abjure the lawfulness of taking arms against the king, or any commissioned by him, on any pretence whatsoever.

It appears from hence, that the terms of conformity were higher than before the civil wars, and the Common Prayer Book more exceptionable; for, instead of striking out the Apocryphal lessons, more were inserted, as the story of Bel and the Dragon; and some new holydays were added, as St. Barnabas; and the conversion of St. Paul; a few alterations and new collects were made by the bishops themselves, but care was taken, says Burnet,‡ that nothing should be altered as was moved by the Presbyterians. The validity of Presbyterian ordination was renounced, by which the ministrations of the foreign churches were disowned. Lecturers and schoolmasters were put upon the same foot with incumbents as to oaths and subscriptions. A new declaration was invented, which none who understood the Constitution of England could safely subscribe; and to terrify the clergy into a compliance, no settled provision was made for those who should be deprived of their livings, but all were referred to the royal clemency.§ A severity, says Bish-

op Burnet, neither practised by Queen Elizabeth in enacting the liturgy, nor by Cromwell in ejecting the Royalists; in both which a fifth of the benefice was reserved for their subsistence.

Mr. Rapin has several remarks on this act: if we compare it with the king's declaration from Breda, says he,* it will easily be seen what care the ministers about the king, who were the real authors or promoters of this act, had for his honour and promise; though some, therefore, may look upon this act as the great support and bulwark of the Church, others, no less attached to its interests, will perhaps look upon it as her disgrace and scandal. His second remark is, for the reader to take notice of the amount of the promises made to the Presbyterians by the king's party, upon the assurance of which they had so cheerfully laboured for his restoration, and followed the directions transmitted by his friends. His third remark is, that by an artifice, the most gross conspiracies were invented, which had no manner of reality; or supposing they had, could no ways be charged on the Presbyterians, who were not to answer for the crimes of other sects.

On the other band, Bishop Kennet says,† " The world has reason to admire, not only the wisdom of this act, but even the moderation of it, as being effectually made for ministerial conformity alone, and leaving the people unable to complain of any imposition. And it would certainly have had the desired and most happy effect, of unity and peace," says his lordship, " if the government had been in earnest in the execution of it." Must the blessings of unity and peace, then, be built on the foundation of persecution, plunder, perfidy, and the wastes of conscience? If his majesty's declaration concerning ecclesiastical affairs breathed the spirit of true wisdom and charity, and ought to stand for a pattern to posterity, whenever they are disposed to heal the breaches of the Church, as the bishop has elsewhere declared,‡ where could be the wisdom and moderation of this act, which turned out two thousand ministers into the world to beg their bread upon such severe terms? And whereas the bishop says the people had no reason to complain of imposition, was it no hardship to be obliged to go to church, and join in a form of worship that went against their consciences? Does not the act revive and confirm all the penal laws of Queen Elizabeth and King James, in these words : " Be it farther enacted, that the several good laws and statutes of this realm, which have been formerly made, and are now in force for the uniformity of prayers and administration of the sacraments within this realm of England and places aforesaid, shall stand in full force and strength to all

Lords, " that such persons as have been put out of their livings by virtue of the Act of Uniformity, may have such allowances out of their livings for their subsistence as his majesty shall think fit."—*Grey's Examination*, vol. i., p. 423. A feeble, inefficient proviso, permitting the king to be kind, but leaving it to his option to be unjust and cruel; tantalizing distress, rather than relieving it.—ED.
* Vol. ii., p. 629, folio.
† The references are, I apprehend, to the bishop's Complete History. There is a passage correspondent to the first in the Chronicle, p. 712.—ED.
‡ Kennet's Chron., p. 246.

---

* Page 269.
† It is not only an absurdity, but a profane playing with holy things, for a man to profess to be moved by the Holy Ghost to take upon him the office of deacon, who is conscious that he is already in a higher and nobler office. And it is another absurdity to ordain a man to the office of a deacon, who is never intended to do the work of a deacon, *serving tables*, but the work of a bishop, to teach and watch over souls.—C.   ‡ Page 267.
§ This was done by a proviso, drawn up by the

intents and purposes whatsoever, and shall be applied, practised, and be put in use, for the punishing all offences contrary to the said law." Surely this must affect the laity! it is more to be admired, in my opinion, that the clergy of England, and all officers, both civil and military, could subscribe a declaration which gave up the whole Constitution into the bands of an arbitrary prince ; for, if the king had abolished the use of Parliaments, and commanded his subjects to embrace the popish religion, which way could they have relieved themselves, when they had sworn that it was not lawful to take up arms against the king, or any commissioned by him, on any pretence whatsoever, on pain of high treason ? It is hard to reconcile this doctrine with the revolution of King William and Queen Mary. I shall only add, that many of the, most learned and judicious divines of the Church have wished, for their own sakes, that the act might be amended and altered.

Mr. Collyer, a nonjuring clergyman, who suffered for his principles, speaks more like a gentleman and a Christian than the bishop : " The misfortune of the Presbyterians," says he, "cannot be remembered without regret ; those who quit their interest are certainly in earnest, and deserve a charitable construction. Mistakes in religion are to be tenderly used, and conscience ought to be pitied when it cannot be relieved."

It is fit the authors and promoters of this memorable act, which broke the peace of the Church and established à separation, should stand upon record. Among these the Earl of Clarendon deserves the first place, who was once for moderate measures, but afterward altered his conduct, says Bishop Burnet,* out of respect to bishops. " The rhetoric and interest of this great minister," says Collyer,† " might possibly make an impression upon both houses, and occasion the passing the Act of Uniformity in the condition it now stands." He entertained the Presbyterians with hopes, while he was cutting away the ground from under their feet. Strange! that one and the same band could, consistently with conscience and honour, draw up the king's declaration from Breda, and his late declaration concerning ecclesiastical affairs, and this severe Act of Uniformity.

Next to Chancellor Hyde was Dr. Sheldon, bishop of London, and afterward Archbishop of Canterbury, of whom notice has been already taken; he was a facetious man, says Burnet,‡ but of no great religion. When the Earl of Manchester told the king he was afraid the terms of conformity were so hard that many ministers would not comply, the bishop replied he was afraid they would, but now we know their minds, says he, we will make them all knaves if they conform. And when Dr. Allen said, " It is pity the door is so strait," he answered, " It is no pity at all ; if we had thought so many of them would have conformed, we would have made it straiter."§ And Mr. Bax-

ter adds, that as far as he could perceive, it was by some designed it should be so.

Next to Bishop Sheldon was Bishop Morley, a pious man, says Burnet, but extremely passionate, and very obstinate. Morley was thought the honester man, but Sheldon the abler states-man. To these may be added, Dr. Gunning, bishop of Ely ; Henchman, of London ; Dolbert, of Rochester ; Stern, of York ; Dr. Pierce, Sparrow, and Barwick, all creatures of the court, and tools of the prerogative.

But neither the courtiers nor bishops could have accomplished their designs without tampering with the Parliament. Care was therefore taken of the best speakers, and men of influence among the Commons. The Parliament was undoubtedly actuated by a spirit of revenge, says Rapin,* and being of principles directly opposite to the Presbyterians, who were for reducing the royal power within certain limits, they resolved to put it out of their power forever to restrain the prerogative, or altar the government of the Church ; and the king, being in continual want of money, was content to sacrifice the Presbyterians for a large supply of the nation's money, especially when he knew he was serving the cause of popery at the same time, by making way for a general toleration.

The Presbyterian ministers had only three months to consider what to do with themselves and their families. There were several consultations both in city and country to know each other's sentiments ; and it happened here, as it did afterward about taking the oaths to King William and Queen Mary ; some, who persuaded their brethren to dissent, complied themselves, and got the others' livings. It is not to be supposed they had all the same scruples. Bishop Kennet says,† that renouncing the Covenant was the greatest obstacle of conformity to the Presbyterians. But his lordship is mistaken ; for if abjuring the Covenant had been omitted, they could not have taken the corporation oath. Some could not in conscience comply with the very form of the hierarchy. Great numbers scrupled the business of reordination, which implied a renouncing the validity of their former ministrations. But that which the dissenters of all denominations refused, was giving their assent and consent to all and everything contained in the Book of Common Prayer. This they apprehended to be more than was due to any human composure.

Mr. Echard represents them as under great difficulties : " Some," says he, " were positive against any compliance, but great numbers were doubtful and uncertain, and had great struggles between the attractions of conscience and honour, interest and humour. The act was strictly penned, and pressed hard upon late principles and practices. A continual inter-course of letters passed between those in the city and the rest in the countries, how to pro-

_____

* Page 270. , † Page 88. ‡ Page 257.
§ It reflects some honour on the name of Bishop Saunderson, that he spoke of this act in a milder strain. To a worthy clergyman who was with him the evening after the king passed it, he said "that more was imposed on ministers than he wished had been." On passing the act, he sent to Mr. Matthew Sylvester, whose living was in his diocess, and treating him

with great civility, earnestly pressed him not to quit his living, and patiently heard him state his difficulties; and when he found that he could not obviate them to his satisfaction, he lamented it, and at last signified a concern that some things were carried so high in the ecclesiastical settlement ; which, he said, should not have been if he could have prevented it.—*Calamy's History of His Own Life*, vol. ii., p. 111, MS. ; and *Church and Dissenters Compared*, p. 81.
—ED.   * Page 632, &c.   † Page 471

ceed in this nice affair. Sometimes the chief of them were for compliance, as I have been assured," says he, " by the best hands, and then, upon farther consideration, they changed their minds. They were under considerable temptations on both sides : on one side their livings and preferments were no small inducement towards their compliance ; on the other side, besides their consciences, they were much encouraged by the greatness of their numbers, and were made to believe, that if they unanimously stood out, the Church must come to them, since the people would never bear so shocking a change. Besides, they had great expectations from several friends at court, and particularly the popish party, who gave them great encouragement, not only by a promise of pensions to some, but also by a toleration, and a suspension of the act itself, which not long after was partly made good. No doubt but the noncompliance of several proceeded purely from a tender conscience, and in that case ought not only to be pitied, but rather applauded than condemned." Bishop Burnet adds, that the leaders of the Presbyterian party took great pains to have them all stick together : they said that if great numbers stood out, it was more likely to produce new laws in their favour ; so it was thought, says his lordship, that many went out in the crowd to keep their friends company.

It is possible some noblemen, and others who were in the interest of the Presbyterians, might advise them to adhere to each other ; but it is hardly credible that men of abilities and good sense should throw up their livings, sacrifice their usefulness, and beggar their families, for the sake of good company.

Some of the Nonconformists quitted their stations in the Church before the 24th of August, as Mr. Baxter and others, with an intent to let all the ministers in England know their resolution beforehand.* Others about London preached their farewell sermons the Sunday before Bartholomew Day ; several of which were afterward collected into a volume, and printed with their effigies in the title-page ; as the Reverend Dr. Manton, Bates, Jacomb, Calamy, Matth. Mead, and others. The like was done in several counties of England ; and such a passionate zeal for the welfare of their people ran through their sermons as dissolved their audiences into tears.

At length the fatal St. Bartholomew came, when about two thousand relinquished their preferments in the Church, or refused to accept of any upon the terms of the Act of Uniformity ; an example hardly to be paralleled in the Christian world ! It raised a grievous cry over the nation, for here were many men much valued, says Bishop Burnet,† and distinguished by their abilities and zeal, now cast out ignominiously; reduced to great poverty, provoked by such spiteful usage, and cast upon those popular practices, which both their principles and their circumstances seemed to justify, of forming separate congregations, and of diverting men from the public worship. This begot esteem, and raised compassion, as having a fair appearance of suffering persecution for conscience. Mr.

* Baxter's Life, part ii., p. 384.
† Page 270, 280.

Locke calls them *worthy, learned, pious, orthodox divines*, who did not throw themselves out of service, but were forcibly ejected. Nor were they cast out because there was a supply of ministers to carry on the work of religion, for there was room for the employment of more hands, if they were to be found.

At the reformation from popery by Queen Elizabeth, there were not above two hundred deprived of their livings ; besides, they were treated with great mildness, and had some allowances out of their livings ; whereas these were teated with the utmost severity, and cast entirely upon Providence for a supply. They were driven from their houses, from the society of their friends, and, what was yet more affecting, from all their usefulness, though they had merited much from the king, and laboured indefatigably for his restoration. The former were men of another faith, and owned a foreign head of the Church ; whereas these were of the same faith with the Established Church, and differed only about rites and ceremonies. It had been said that greater numbers were ejected in the late times upon the foot of the Covenant ;* but if this were true, it was in a time of war, when the civil and religious differences between the king and Parliament were so intermixed that it was impossible to separate one from the other ; the whole nation was in confusion, and those who suffered by the Covenant, suffered more for their loyalty than their religion ; for when the war was ended, the Covenant was relaxed, and such as would live peaceably returned to their vacant cures, or were admitted to others.

Besides, the ingratitude of the High-churchmen upon this occasion ought to be taken notice of. " Who can answer for the violence and injustice of actions in a civil war ?" says a divine of the Church of England. " Those sufferings were in a time of general calamity, but these were ejected not only in a time of peace, but a time of joy to all the land, and after an act of oblivion, when all pretended to be reconciled and made friends, and to whose common rejoicings these suffering ministers had contributed their earnest prayers and great endeavours."† Another divine of the same church

* Dr. Grey asserts this ; and there was a laboured attempt by Dr. Walker to prove that the clergy ejected or suffering in the civil wars exceeded in numbers those whom the Act of Uniformity ejected or silenced ; and that the sufferings of the former surpassed in nature and severity those of the latter. The publication, which endeavoured to establish these points, was a folio, in small print, entitled " An Attempt towards recovering an Account of the Numbers and Sufferings of the Clergy of the Church of England, Heads of Colleges, Fellows, Scholars, &c., who were sequestered, harassed, &c., in the late Times of the Grand Rebellion : occasioned by the ninth Chapter (now the second volume) of Dr. Calamy's Abridgment of the Life of Mr. Baxter; together with an Examination of that Chapter." The public was at first amused with so large a work, but by degrees began to speak freely of it in conversation, where it had the fate of other performances. It received from the press two able replies : one by Mr. John Withers, a judicious and worthy dissenting minister in Exeter ; the other by Dr. Calamy, in a tract entitled " The Church and Dissenters Compared as to Persecution." On this subject we would refer the reader back to Mr. Neal, vol. i., p. 497.—ED.   † Conf. Plea for Nonconformity, p. 12, 13.

writes, "I must own, that in my judgment, however, both sides have been excessively to blame; yet, that the severities used by the Church to the Dissenters are less excusable than those used by the Dissenters to the Church. My reason is, that the former were used in times of peace and a settled government, whereas the latter were afflicted in a time of tumult and confusion.; so that the plunderings and ravagings endured by the church ministers were owing (many, of them, at least) to the rudeness of the soldiers and the chances of war; they were plundered, not because they were conformists, but Cavaliers, and of the king's party. The allowing of the sequestered ministers a fifth part of their livings was a Christian act,* and what, I confess, I should have been glad to have seen imitated at the Restoration. But no mercy was to be shown to these unhappy sufferers, though it was impossible on a sudden to fill up the gap that was made by their removal."

Bishop Burnet says the old clergy, now much enriched, were despised, but the young clergy who came from the university did good service. But, though all the striplings in both universities were employed, a great many poor livings in the country had no incumbents for a considerable time. The author of The Five Groans of the Church, a very strict conformist, complains, with great warmth, of above three thousand ministers admitted into the Church, who were unfit to teach because of their youth; of fifteen hundred debauched men ordained; of one thousand three hundred forty-two factious ministers, a little before ordained; and that, of twelve thousand church livings, or thereabout, three thousand or more being impropriate; and four thousand one hundred sixty-five sinecures, there was but a poor remainder left for a painful and honest ministry.

Such were the spoils of uniformity! and, though Mr. Echard says there was more sense and sound doctrine preached in one twelvemonth after the Presbyterian ministers were turned out than in nigh twenty years before; yet another church writer, who knew them better, calls the young clergy "florid and genteel preachers, of a more romantic than true majestic and divine style; who tickled and captivated people at first, but did little service to the souls of men, and in process of time had fewer admirers and friends than at first." He adds, that "in the late times they all spake the same

things, and carried on the same work, which was the instruction, conversion, consolation, and edification of souls; not biting one another, nor grudging at one another. I never heard," says he, "in many hundreds of sermons, diversities of opinions either set up by some or pulled down by others; we heard, indeed, that some were Independents, others Presbyterians, and others Episcopal, but we heard no such things from the pulpits. Some men think that the preaching of those days was mere fanaticism, blessing the usurpation, railing against bishops, or deifying Calvin with an infallibility; but Calvin was preached no farther than Christ spake in him: 'Non Calvinum sed Christum prædicabant.' "*

The truth of this observation will appear farther, by mentioning the names of some of those ministers, whose learning and piety were universally acknowledged, and who were capable of preaching and writing as good sense, and to as good purpose, as most of their successors; as Dr. Gilpin, Bates, Manton, Jacomb, Owen, Goodwin, Collins, Conant, Grew, Burgess, and Annesly; Mr. Bowles, Baxter, Clarkson, Woodbridge, Newcomen, Calamy, Jackson, Pool, Caryl, Charnock, Gouge, Jenkins, Gale, Corbet, Cradock, Matth. Mead, Howe, Kentish, Alsop, Vincent, Greenhill, S. Clark, Flavel, Phil. Henry, and others of like character, "whom I have heard vilified, and represented according to the fancies, passions, or interests of men," says a learned Conformist; "but I dare not but be just to them, as to eminent professors of the Christian faith, and think that common Christianity has suffered much by their silencing and disparagement. A great part of the world is made to believe that the Nonconformists are not fit to be employed in the Church, nor trusted by the State; but what they are God knows, and the world may know, if they please to consult their writings. They are not, to them that know them, what they are reported by them that know them not. I know them sufficiently to make me bewail their condition, and the vast damage to thousands of souls by their exclusion, not only in the outskirts, but in the very heart of England, who are committed in many parts to them that neither can nor will promote their everlasting interests."† Upon the whole, though I do not pretend that all the ejected ministers were equally learned, pious,‡ and deserving, yet, upon a calm and sedate view of things, I cannot help concluding that, in the main, they were a body of as eminent confessors for truth and liberty as this or any other nation has produced.

Many complied with the terms of conformity, not because they approved them, but for the sake of their families, or because they were unwilling to be buried in silence, as Bishop Reynolds, Wilkins, Hopkins, Fowler, &c. Several young students, who were designed for the pul-

---

* Dr. Grey quotes here, from Dr. Fuller (Church Hist., book xi., p. 230), a long detail of the evasions on which many of the sequestered clergy were refused their fifths. Dr. Walker has also complained, that scarcely one in ten ever had them without trouble, and to the full value. "This is a case in which," as Dr. Calamy observes, "it is no easy thing to make calculation." Supposing it to have been paid ever so indifferently, it was certainly a better provision than was made by the Act of Uniformity for those who were ejected and silenced. It afforded the sufferers, to a degree, a legal remedy for their calamities; and would doubtless, in many instances, be efficient. Dr. Fuller speaks of it as an instance of "the pitiful and pious intentions of Parliament; which, no doubt, desired to be like the best of beings, who as closely applieth his lenitive as corrosive plasters, and that his mercy may take as true effect as his justice." But this matter has been before stated by Mr. Neal, vol. i., p. 489.—ED.

* Conformist Plea, part i., in pref., and p. 53.
† Conform. Plea, in pref., part i.
‡ To suppose that more than two thousand men could be equal in worth and piety, would be to admit an impossibility; but it deserves notice, that Bishop Kennet is so candid as to limit the charge of scandalous lives and characters, or of a conduct which was, at least, no credit to the cause for which they suffered, to some few only.—Grey's Examination, p. 332.—Ed.

pit, applied themselves to law or physic, or diverted to some secular employment. Bishop Kennet, in order to extenuate their calamities,* has taken pains to point out the favours the ejected ministers received from private persons.† "Some," says he, "found friends among the nobility and gentry, who relieved their necessities; some were taken as chaplains into good families, or officiated in hospitals, prisons, or chapels of ease; some became tutors or schoolmasters; some who went beyond sea were well received in foreign parts; some became eminent physicians and lawyers; some had good estates of their own, and others married great fortunes;" but how does this extenuate the guilt of the Church or Legislature, who would have deprived them of these retreats if it had been in their power? The bishop adds, "Therefore we do ill to charge the Church with persecution, when the laws were made by the civil government with a view to the peace and safety of the State, rather than to any honour or interest of the Church." It seems, therefore, the load of persecution must lie wholly upon the Legislature; but had the bishops and clergy no hand in this affair? did they not push the civil government upon these extremities, and not only concur, but prosecute, the penal laws with unrelenting rigour throughout the greatest part of this reign? The Church and State are said to be so incorporated as to make but one constitution, and the penal laws are shifted from one to the other till they are quite lost; the Church cannot be charged with persecution, because it makes no laws; nor can the civil government be charged with it, because it makes them not against conscience, but with a view to the safety of the State. With such idle sophisms are men to be amused, when it is to cover a reproach!

Dr. Bates says, "They (the ministers) fell a sacrifice to the wrath and revenge of the old clergy, and to the servile compliance of the young gentry with the court, and their distaste of serious religion.‡ That this is no rash imputation upon the ruling clergy is evident," says the doctor, "not only from their concurrence in passing these laws (for actions have a language as convincing as those of words), but from Dr. Sheldon, their great leader, who expressed his fears to the Earl of Manchester, lest the Presbyterians should comply. The act was passed after the king had engaged his faith and honour, in his declaration from Breda, to preserve liberty of conscience inviolable, which promise opened the way for his restoration, and after the Royalists had given public assurance that all former animosities should be laid aside as rubbish, under the foundation of universal concord."

Sad were the calamities of far the greater part of these unhappy sufferers, who, with their

families, must have perished, if private collections in London, and divers places in the country, had not been made for their subsistence.* Bishop Burnet says, they cast themselves on the providence of God and the charity of friends. The reverend and pious Mr. Thomas Gouge, late of St. Sepulchre's, was their advocate, who, with two or three of his brethren, made frequent application to several worthy citizens, of whom they received considerable sums of money for some years, till that charity was diverted into another channel; but, nevertheless, "many hundreds of them," according to Mr. Baxter,† "with their wives and children, had neither house nor bread;‡ the people they left were not able to relieve them, nor durst they if they had been able, because it would have been called a maintenance of schism or faction. Many of the ministers, being afraid to lay down their ministry after they had been ordained to it, preached to such as would hear them, in fields and private houses, till they were apprehended and cast into jails, where many of them perished. The people were no less divided: some conformed, and others were driven to a greater distance from the Church, and resolved to abide by their faithful pastors at all events: they murmured at the government, and called the bishops and conforming clergy cruel persecutors; for which, and for their frequenting the private assemblies of their ministers, they were fined and imprisoned, till many families left their native country and settled in the plantations."

The Presbyterian ministers, though men of gravity and far advanced in years, were rallied in the pulpits under the opprobrious names of Schismatics and Fanatics; they were exposed in the playhouse and insulted by the mob, insomuch that they were obliged to lay aside their habits and walk in disguise. "Such magistrates were put into commission as executed the penal laws with severity. Informers were encouraged and rewarded. It is impossible," says the Conformist Plea for the Nonconformist,§ "to relate the number of the sufferings both of ministers and people; the great trials, with hardships upon their persons, estates, and families, by uncomfortable separations, dispersions, unsettlements, and removes; disgraces, reproaches, imprisonments, chargeable journeys, expenses in law, tedious sicknesses, and incurable diseases ending in death; great disquietments and frights to the wives and families, and their doleful effects upon them. Their congregations had enough to do, besides a small maintenance, to help them out of prisons, or maintain them there. Though they were as frugal as possible, they could hardly live: some lived on little more than brown bread and wa-

---

* Kennet's Chron., p. 888, &c.
† Dr. Grey has given this passage of Bishop Kennet at length, which Mr. Neal has here noticed. But the amount of the bishop's statement, which runs out into thirty-one particulars, only shows that some men were more equitable and kind than was the Legislature; and that they who suffered under the operation of an iniquitous law, met with relief from the kind disposals of Divine Providence.—ED.
‡ Baxter, p. 101.

* Kennet's Chron., p. 838, 192.
† Life, part ii., p. 385.
‡ The observation made, not long before he died, by the excellent Mr. Philip Henry, who survived these times, deserves to be mentioned here. It was, that "though many of the ejected ministers were brought very low, had many children, were greatly harassed by persecution, and their friends generally poor and unable to support them, yet, in all his acquaintance, he never knew, nor could remember to have heard of, any Nonconformist minister in prison for debt."—P. Henry's Life, p. 74, second edition.—ED.
§ Part iv., p. 40.

ter; many had but £8 or £10 a year to maintain a family, so that a piece of flesh has not
come to one of their tables in six weeks' time.;
their allowance could scarcely afford them bread
and cheese.   One went to plough six days and
preached on the Lord's Day.   Another was
forced to cut tobacco for a livelihood., The
zealous justices of peace knew the calamities
of the ministers, when they issued out warrants
upon some of the hearers, because of the poverty of the preachers. Out-of respect to the worth
and modesty of some of them," says my author,* "I forbear their names." Upon these
foundations, and with these, triumphs, was the
present constitution of the Church of England
restored. I shall make no farther remarks upon
it, but leave it to the censure of the reader.'

Among the Presbyterian divines who died
this year was Mr. John Ley, M.A., born at
Warwick, February 4, 1583, and educated in
Christ Church, Oxford, where he took the degrees in arts, and was presented to the living
of Great Budworth in Cheshire. He was afterward prebendary of Chester, and sub-dean and
clerk of the Convocation once or twice. In the
year 1641 he took part with the Parliament,
was one of the Assembly of Divines, chairman
of the committee for examination of ministers,
and president of Sion College. In the year
1645 he succeeded Dr. Hyde in the rich parsonage of Brightwell, Berks., In 1653 he was
one of the triers, and at length obtained the
rectory of Solyhull, in Warwickshire, but having broken a vein by overstraining himself in
speaking, he resigned his living, and retired to
Sutton Colfield, where he died, May 16, 1662,
in the seventy-ninth year of his age. He was
a very learned person, well read in the fathers
and councils, a popular preacher, a pious and
devout Christian, and one of the main pillars
(says Mr. Wood†) of the Presbyterian cause.‡

Mr. Henry Jeanes, M.A., was born in Somersetshire about the year 1611, and educated in
New Inn, and afterward in Hart Hall, Oxon,
where he took the degrees in arts, and entered
into holy orders. ' He was an admired preacher
in the university, and was quickly preferred to
the rectory of Beercrocomb, and the vicarage
of Kingston in Somersetshire. In the year
1641 he closed with the Parliament, and became
rector of Chedsoy, near Bridgewater. Here he
took into his family several young persons, and
instructed them in the liberal arts and sciences ;
he was a most excellent philosopher, a noted
metaphysician, and well versed in polemical divinity. With all these qualifications (says Mr.
Wood§), he was a contemner of the world, generous, free-hearted, jolly, witty, and facetious.
He wrote many books,‖ and died in the city of
Wells a little before the fatal day of St. Bartholomew, and was buried in the cathedral
church there, ætatis fifty-two.

Dr. Humphrey Chambers was born in Somer-

setshire, and educated in University College,
Oxon. In the year 1623 he was made rector
of Claverton in Somersetshire, but was afterward silenced by his diocesan, Bishop Piers,
for preaching up the morality of the Sabbath,
and imprisoned for two years. He was created
one of the Assembly of Divines. In the year
1648 he was created D.D., and had the rich rectory of Pewsey given him by the Earl of Pembroke. After the king's restoration he kept his
living till the very day the Act of Uniformity
took place, when, having preached his farewell
sermon on Psal. cxxvi., 6, he went home, fell
sick and died, and was buried in his church at
Pewsey, September 8, without the service of
the church, which had just then taken place.*

Mr. Simeon Ash was educated in 'Emanuel
College, Cambridge. His first station in the
Church was in Staffordshire, where he contracted an acquaintance with the most eminent Puritans. He was displaced from his living for refusing to read the Book of Sports, and not conforming to the ceremonies. After some time
he got liberty to preach in an exempt church at
Wroxhall, under the protection of Sir John Bur-
goign ; and elsewhere, under the Lord Brook,
in Warwickshire. Upon the breaking out of
the civil war he became chaplain to the Earl of
Manchester, and had a considerable part in the
Cambridge visitation. After the king's death
he vigorously opposed the new commonwealth,
and declaimed publicly against the Engagement.
He was concerned in all the designs for bringing in the king, and went with other London
divines to congratulate his majesty at Breda.
He was a Christian of primitive simplicity, and
a Nonconformist of the old stamp, being eminently sincere, charitable, holy, and of a cheerful spirit. He had a good paternal estate, and
was very hospitable, his house being much frequented by his brethren, by whom he was highly esteemed.† He died in an advanced age on
the very evening before Bartholomew Day, in a
cheerful and firm expectation of a future happiness.‡

Mr. Edward Bowles, M.A., born 1613, and
educated in Katherine Hall, Cambridge, under
Dr. Sibbes and Dr. Brownrigge. He was first
chaplain to the Earl of Manchester, and upon
the reduction of York to the Parliament, settled
in that city. He was a wise and prudent man,
having a clear head and a warm heart; an excellent scholar, and a useful preacher. He attended Lord Fairfax when General Monk passed
through Yorkshire, and presented an address to
the general for a free Parliament. He was very
zealous and active in promoting the king's restoration, and waited on his majesty with Lord
Fairfax at Breda. It is credibly reported that
the deanery of York was offered to him, but
not being satisfied with conformity, he was excluded the minister, though he continued preaching at Allhallows, and afterward at St. Martin's,

---

*. Conformist Plea, part iv., p. 43.
† Athen. Oxon., vol. ii., p. 190–4.
‡ Mr. Ley was a voluminous writer. There are
twenty-nine pieces of his extant. His best works
are on the Sabbath, and annotations upon the Pentateuch and four evangelists, in the Assembly's annotations.—C.   § Athen. Oxon., vol. ii., p. 195.
‖ One of his most famous pieces is entitled
"Want of Church Government no Warrant for a
total Omission of the Lord's Supper."—C.

* Calamy, vol. ii., p. 754; or Palmer's Nonconf.
Memorial, vol. ii., p. 509.
† Mr. Ash was a member of the Westminster Assembly, and one of the Corn Hill lecturers. His funeral sermons for Whitaker, Ralph Robinson, Gataker, Vines, and the Countess of Manchester are admirable, and his prefaces have been greatly praised,
especially that to Ball's Covenant of Grace.—C.
‡ Calamy, vol. ii., p. 1; or Palmer's Nonncoform.
ists' Memorial, vol. i., p. 85.

as he had opportunity.* When the fatal Bartholomew Day approached he grew sick of the times, and died in the flower of his life, aged forty-nine, and was buried on the eve of St. Bartholomew, 1662.†

[In the preceding year there passed an act for regulating the press, enacting "that no private person or persons should print, or cause to be printed, any book or pamphlet whatsoever, unless the same was first lawfully licensed and authorized to be printed by certain persons appointed by the act to license the same; viz., law-books by the lord-chancellor, or one of the chief-justices, or by the chief baron ; books of history, or concerning state affairs, by one of the principal secretaries of state ; on heraldry, by the earl-marshal ; and all other books, i. e., to say all novels, romances, and fairy tales, and all books about philosophy, mathematics, physic, divinity, or love, by the Lord-archbishop of Canterbury, or the Bishop of London for the time being." . "The framers of this curious act," observes Lord Stanhope, "no doubt, supposing that these right reverend prelates were, of all men in the kingdom, most conversant with all these subjects." This act commenced in June, 1662, and passed only for two years. It was continued by an act of the 16th of Charles II., and by another act of the 17th of the same reign ; and in a few months afterward it expired. We may form some idea of the private instructions given to the licenser, as well as of his excessive caution and ignorant zeal, when we are assured, that on his taking exception to the following lines in Milton's Paradise Lost, that admirable poem had like to have been suppressed.

"As when the sun, new risen,
Looks through the horizontal misty air
Shorn of his beams ; or from behind the moon
In dim eclipse, disastrous twilight sheds
On half the nations, and with fear of change
Perplexes monarchs."

—*Stanhope on the Rights of Juries*, p. 64, &c. *Secret History of the Court and Reign of Charles II.*, vol. i., p. 441, note ; and '*Dr. Harris's Life of Charles II.*, vol. ii., p. 263–274.—ED.]

CHAPTER VII.

FROM THE ACT OF UNIFORMITY TO THE BANISHMENT OF THE EARL OF CLARENDON, IN THE YEAR 1667.

1662.

AT this time, says Bishop Burnet, the name of Puritans was changed into that of Protestant Nonconformists, who were subdivided into Presbyterians, Independents, Anabaptists, and Quakers ; these being shut out of the Establish-

* Calamy, vol. ii., p. 779–782 ; or Palmer's Nonconformists' Memorial, vol. ii., p. 580.
† A MS. of that day has this anecdote. "One evening Mr. Bowles visiting Sir Henry Vane, at his taking leave, Sir Henry followed with a candle in his hand to the head of the stairs. Mr. Bowles desired him not to give himself that trouble. 'Nay, sir,' says Sir Henry, 'I will see you down.' 'Indeed, Sir Henry,' says Mr. Bowles, 'I believe you will *see us down*.' Merrily intending, that if Sir Henry Vane might hold the candle, all ordinances, orders, and forms of worship should go down."—C.

ment, had nothing now in view but a toleration, which the credulous Presbyterians said they had strong assurances of before the Act of Uniformity passed into a law ; but in this they were disappointed, as well as in everything else ; for which the Independents told them they might thank themselves, because their managers had protested against including the papists ; whereas, the Legislature and the bishops were concerned to prevent any mischief from that quarter, and to their care the Presbyterians should have left it.* Some observing how much the court and Parliament were set against them, were for removing, with their ministers, to Holland ; and others proposed New-England ; but the papists, at a meeting at the Earl of Bristol's house, agreed to do whatever they could to keep the Nonconformists in England, and buoy them up with hopes of a toleration.

The king was a concealed Roman Catholic, and had swarms of that persuasion about his person and court, who had fought for his father in the wars, or been civil to him in his exile ; their design was to introduce a toleration of their religion, by the royal indulgence, in common with other Dissenters from the Establishment ; and the king was so far in their measures, that he declared openly he would give liberty to all or none. The court was therefore content that the Act of Uniformity should pass in the severest terms, on purpose to make the number of Dissenters more considerable ; and when this was objected, it was replied, the more Dissenters the better, because it will make a toleration more needful, in which the papists will be included.† The papists had two maxims from which they never departed : one was, to keep themselves united, and promote a general toleration, or a general prosecution. The other, to divide the Protestants as much as possible among themselves. For this reason, the sword was put into the hands of such magistrates as would inflame the differences, and exasperate their spirits one against the other. Nor were there wanting some hot-headed young clergymen, who ran greedily into the snare, and became the tools of popery and arbitrary power, till the Protestant religion was expiring, and must inevitably have been lost, had it not been revived almost by miracle. With a like view, the laws against profaneness and immorality were relaxed, men's morals were neglected, interludes, masquerades, promiscuous dancing, profane swearing, drunkenness, and a universal dissolution of manners, were connived at, and the very name of godliness became a reproach.

The Parliament, being made up of a set of pensioners and mercenaries, went into all the court measures, and enacted more penal laws for religion than, it may be, all the Parliaments put together since the Reformation. They pressed the Act of Uniformity with inflexible rigour, and enforced it with so many other penal laws, that under their wing popery grew to such a height as to threaten the extirpation of the northern heresy. At length, many of the members being dead, and others grown fat with the spoils of the public, they would have retrieved their errors, and distinguished between Protestant Nonconformists and popish recusants,

* Burnet, vol. i., p. 282.   † Ibid., p. 285.

but it was too late ; and the king having found ways and means to subsist without Parliaments, resolved to adhere by his standing maxim, to give ease to all Dissenters or to none. ,

It is impossible to excuse the clergy from their share in the troubles of this reign. If the Convocation of 1662, in their review of the liturgy, had made any amendments for the satisfaction of the Presbyterians, they would undoubtedly have passed both houses of Parliament, and healed, in some measure, the divisions of the Church ; but they were actuated by a spirit of revenge, and not only promoted such laws as might deprive the Presbyterians of the power of hurting them for the future, but assisted in putting them in execution. None had a greater share in inflaming the minds of the people, and in sounding the trumpet to persecution. But here the reader must distinguish between those zealots who, from resentment, bigotry, or sinister views set themselves to encourage and promote all the methods of oppression and tyranny, and those who, though they complied with the terms of conformity themselves, were disposed to an accommodation with the Protestant Nonconformists upon moderate terms.

The bishops were generally of the former sort ; they were old and exasperated, fond of their persecuting principles, and fearful of everything that tended to relieve the Presbyterians. They went with zeal into all the slavish doctrines of the prerogative, and voted with the court in everything they required. But even some of these bishops, who at first were very zealous to throw the Presbyterians out of the Church, afterward grew more temperate. Dr. Laney, bishop of Peterborough, who made a great bustle in the Savoy Conference, was willing at length to wipe his hands of the dirty work, and, to use his own expression, could look through his fingers and suffer a worthy Nonconformist to preach publicly near him for years together. Bishop Saunderson had a roll of Nonconformist ministers under his angry eye, designed for discipline, but when he was near his end, he ordered the roll to be burned, and said he would die in peace. And most remarkable is the passage in the last will and testament of Dr. Cosins, bishop of Durham, a zealous enemy of the Presbyterians, and who had met with ill usage in the late times : " I take it to be my duty," says he, " and that of all the bishops and ministers of the Church, to do our utmost endeavour, that at last an end may be put to the differences of religion, or, at least, that they may be lessened." Such was the different temper of this learned prelate in the vigour of life, and when he came to review things calmly on his dying bed. To these may be added Bishop Gauden, Wilkins, Reynolds, and a few others, who were always moderate, and are said to carry the wounds of the Church in their hearts to the grave ; but the far greater majority of the bench, especially those who frequented the court, were of different principles.

The like may be observed of the inferior clergy, who were divided, a few years after, into those of the court and the country ; the former were of an angry, superstitious spirit, and far more strenuous for a few indifferent ceremonies than for the peace of the Church, or its more important articles ; their sermons were

filled with reverence due to their holy mother, with the sacred dignity of their own indelible characters, with the slavish doctrines of passive obedience and nonresistance, and with the most bitter raillery and invectives against the routed Presbyterians ; they encouraged the enacting severe laws, and carried them into execution as long as their superiors would permit, without any regard to mercy or merit ; but took comparatively little or no care, by their doctrine or example, of the morals of the people, which were shamefully neglected throughout the nation. The clergy of this character were by far the more numerous for twenty years after the Restoration ; the tide of church preferments running in this channel, and their doctrines being the most fashionable.

The country clergy were of a quite different spirit ; they were determined Protestants and true churchmen, but more disposed to a coalition with Protestant Dissenters than with papists : among these were the *Tillotsons*, *Stillingfleets*, *Whichcotes*, *Wilkins*, *Cudworths*, &c., men of the first rank for learning, sobriety, and virtue ; they were the most eminent preachers of the age, whose sermons and writings did honour to the Church of England, and supported its character in the worst of times. They lamented the corruptions and vices of the people, and stood in the gap against an inundation of popery and tyranny ; but their numbers were small, because the road to preferment lay another way ; and when the High-church clergy had betrayed the liberties of their country, and the cause of the Protestant religion into the hands of the papists, these appeared boldly in their defence, disarmed their adversaries, and saved the nation.

When, therefore, we speak of the furious proceedings of the bishops and clergy, it must not be understood of the whole body, but only of those who were tools of a corrupt court and ministry, and who, out of ignorance or other private and personal motives, went blindfold into all their destructive measures.

Bishop Burnet, in his book against the author of Parliamentum Pacificum, has the following remarkable passage : " It is well known that those who were secretly papists, and disguised their religion, as the king himself did, animated the chief men of the Church to carry the points of uniformity as high as possible, that there might be many Nonconformists, and great occasion for a toleration, under which popery might creep in ; for if the king's declaration from Breda had taken place, of two thousand ministers that were turned out, about seventeen hundred had stayed in ; but the practice of the papists had too great an influence on the churchmen, whose spirits were too much soured by their ill usage during the war ; nor were they without success on the Dissenters, who were secretly encouraged to stand out, and were told that the king's temper and principles, and the consideration of trade, would certainly procure them a toleration. Thus they tampered with both parties ; liberty of conscience was their profession ; but when a session of Parliament came, and the king wanted money, then a new severe law against the Dissenters was offered to the angry men of the Church party as the price of it ; and this seldom failed to have its effect : so that they were like the jewels of the crown, pawned when the king needed money, but redeemed at the next prorogation." . The same prelate observes in another performance, "that the first spirit of severity was heightened by the practices of the papists. That many churchmen, who understood not the principles of human society, and the rules of the English government, wrote several extravagant treatises about the measures of submission; that the Dissenters were put to great hardships in many parts of England." But concludes that "he must have the brow of a Jesuit that can cast this wholly upon the Church of England, and free the court of it. Upon the whole matter," says his lordship, "it is evident that the passions and infirmities of some of the Church of England being unhappily stirred up by the Dissenters, they were fatally conducted by the popish party to be the instruments of doing a great deal of mischief."

But to go on with the history: three days after the Act of Uniformity took place, the silenced ministers presented a petition to his majesty for a toleration, by the hands of Dr. Manton, Dr. Bates, and Mr. Calamy, to this effect: "That having had former experience of his majesty's clemency and indulgence, some of the London ministers, who are like to be deprived of all future usefulness by the late Act of Uniformity, humbly cast themselves at his majesty's feet, desiring him of his princely wisdom to take some effectual course that they may be continued in their ministry, to teach his people obedience to God and his majesty; and they doubt not but, by their dutiful and peaceable behaviour, they shall render themselves not altogether unworthy of so great a favour."*
The matter being debated next day in council, his majesty gave his opinion for an indulgence if it was feasible. Others were for conniving at the more eminent divines, and putting curates into their churches to read the service till they should die. off:† this was the opinion of the Earl of Manchester, who urged it with a great deal of earnestness; but Lord Clarendon was for the strict execution of the law: "Surely," says he, "there cannot be too intent a care in kings and princes to preserve and maintain all decent forms and ceremonies both in Church and State, which keeps up the reverence due to religion, as well as the duty and dignity due to the government and the majesty of kings."‡ Bishop Sheldon was of the same side, and declared that if the act was suspended, he could not maintain his Episcopal authority; that this would render the Legislature ridiculous, and be the occasion of endless distractions.§ England is accustomed to obey laws, says he, so that while we stand on that ground we are safe; and, to answer all objections, he undertook to fill the vacant pulpits more to the people's satisfaction. By such arguments, delivered with great earnestness and zeal, they prevailed with the council to let the law take place for the present.

Nevertheless, about four months after, his majesty published a declaration to all his loving subjects, by advice of his privy council, dated

December 26, 1662, in which, after reciting those words of his declaration from Breda relating to his giving liberty to tender consciences, and his readiness to consent to an act of Parliament for that purpose, his majesty adds, "As all these things are fresh in our memory, so are we still firm in the resolution of performing them to the full. But it must not be wondered at, since that Parliament to which those promises were made never thought fit to offer us an act for that purpose, that we, being so zealous as we are (and by the grace of God shall ever be) for the maintenance of the true Protestant religion, should give its establishment the precedency before matters of indulgence to dissenters from it; but that being done, we are glad to renew to all our subjects concerned in those promises of indulgence this assurance, That, as for what concerns the penalties upon those who, living peaceably, do not conform to the Church of England through scruple or tenderness of misguided conscience, but modestly, and without scandal, perform their devotions in their own way, we shall make it our special care, as far as in us lies, without invading the freedom of Parliament, to incline their wisdom at the next approaching sessions, to concur with us in making some act for that purpose, as may enable us to exercise with a more universal satisfaction that power of dispensing which we conceive to be inherent in us; nor can we doubt of their cheerful co-operating with us in a thing wherein we conceive ourselves so far engaged; both in honour, and in what we owe to the peace of our dominions, which we profess we can never think secure while there shall be a colour left to disaffected persons to inflame the minds of so many multitudes upon the score of conscience, with despair of ever obtaining any effect of our promises for their ease."

His majesty then proceeds to obviate the objection of his favouring papists; and, after having avowed to the world the due sense he had of their having deserved well from his royal father, and from himself, and even from the Protestant religion, in adhering to them with their lives and fortunes, for the maintenance of their crown in the religion established, he declares, that "it is not in his intention to exclude them from all benefit from such an act of indulgence, but that they are not to expect an open toleration; but refers the manner to the approaching sessions of Parliament, which he doubts not will concur with him in the performance of his promises." He concludes "with hoping that all his subjects, with minds happily composed by his clemency and indulgence (instead of taking up thoughts of deserting their professions, or transplanting), will apply themselves comfortably, and with redoubled industry, to their several vocations, in such manner as the private interest of every one in particular may encourage him to contribute cheerfully to the general prosperity.

"Given at our court at Whitehall, this 26th of December, in the fourteenth year of our reign."

This declaration was thought to be framed at Somerset House, where the queen-mother kept her court, without the knowledge of Lord Clarendon or Bishop Sheldon; and, according to

---

* Kennet's Chron., p. 753.   † Ibid., p. 730, 742.
‡ Parker's History, p. 29.
§ Burnet, vol. i., p. 279.

Burnet, was the result of a council of papists at the Earl of Bristol's (who were under an oath of secrecy), and of the king himself.* It is modestly expressed ; and, though it carries in it a claim of the dispensing power, and of good-will to popery, yet it refers all to the Parliament. Accordingly, his majesty, in his speech at the opening the next sessions, February 28, 1663, supported his declaration in the following words: "That though he was, in his nature, an enemy to all severity in religion, he would not have them infer from thence that he meant to favour popery, though several of that profession, who had served him and his father well, might justly claim a share in that indulgence he would willingly afford to other Dissenters ; not that I intend them to bold any place in the government," says his majesty, "for I will not yield to any, no, not to the bishops themselves, in my zeal for the Protestant religion, and my liking the Act of Uniformity ; and yet, if the Dissenters will behave themselves peaceably and modestly under the government, I could heartily wish I had such a power of indulgence to use upon all occasions, as might not needlessly force them out of the kingdom, or, staying here, give them cause to conspire against the peace of it." This was the first open claim of a dispensing power, which, the reader will observe, did not propose a law for liberty of conscience, but that his majesty might have a legal power of indulgence vested in himself, which he might use or recall as he thought fit. This alarmed the House of Commons, who voted the thanks of the House for his majesty's resolution to maintain the Act of Uniformity ; but that it was the opinion of the House that no indulgence be granted to dissenters from it ; and an address was appointed to be drawn up, and presented to his majesty, with the following reasons :

"We have considered," say they, "your majesty's declaration from Breda, and are of opinion that it was not a promise, but a gracious declaration to comply with the advice of your Parliament; whereas no such advice has been given.† They who pretend a right to the supposed promise, put the right into the hands of their representatives, who have passed the Act of Uniformity.‡ If any shall say a right to the benefit of the declaration still remains, it tends to dissolve the very bond of government, and to suppose a disability in the whole Legislature to make a law contrary to your majesty's declaration. We have also considered the nature of the indulgence proposed, and are of opinion, 1. That it will establish schism by a law, and make the censures of the Church of no consideration. 2. That it is unbecoming the wisdom of Parliament to pass a law in one session for uniformity, and in another session to pass a

law to frustrate or weaken it, the reasons continuing the same. 3. That it will expose your majesty to the restless importunities of every sect who shall dissent from the Established Church. 4. That it will increase sectaries, which will weaken the Protestant profession, and be troublesome to the government ; and, in time, some prevalent sect may contend for an establishment, which may end in popery. 5. That it is unprecedented, and may take away the means of convicting recusants. 6. That the indulgence proposed will not tend to the peace, but to the disturbance of the kingdom ; the best way, therefore, to produce a settled peace, is to press vigorously the Act of Uniformity."

The reader will judge of the force of these reasons, which, in my opinion, would justify the severest persecution in the world ; however, the king was convinced with a sum of money, and therefore made no other reply, but that he had been ill understood. The House then addressed him to put the laws in execution against papists ; and a proclamation was issued out for that purpose, but little regarded. However, this opposition to the king and the Roman Catholics by Lord Clarendon, and his friends in the House of Commons, laid the foundation of his impeachment the next year, and of his ruin some time after. Bishop Kennet admits that the king was inclined to a general indulgence,* "though, whether it was from his good-nature, or a secret inclination to introduce popery, is not very decent to determine ;" but both he and Echard are of opinion† "that the king's clemency hardened the Dissenters against the Church ; whereas, if they had lost all dependance on a court interest, and had found the king and his ministry intent upon the strict execution of the Act of Uniformity, most of them," say they, "would, at this juncture, have conformed." A notorious mistake ! the contrary to this being evident to a demonstration throughout the course of this reign. The conformity of honest men does not depend up the will, but the understanding, and it is very ungenerous at this distance to impeach men's integrity, who underwent a long course of the severest trials to retain it.

Some of the ejected Presbyterians, who were men of piety and learning, complied as far as they could, and made a distinction between lay conformity and ministerial : they practised the former, and went sometimes to their parish churches before or after the exercise of their ministry in some private houses ; and this they did, not for interest or advantage, but, to all appearance, to express their catholicism and brotherly love.‡ Here was the rise of occasional conformity, practised by Dr. Bates, Mr. Baxter, and others, to their death ; but this, instead of being well taken, was the occasion of bringing some of them into trouble ; for Mr. Calamy, late minister of Aldermanbury, being at his parish church, December 28, the preacher happened to disappoint them ; upon which, by the importunity of the parishioners, Mr. Calamy went up into the pulpit, and preached a sermon upon "Eli's concern for the ark of

---

* Burnet, vol. i., p. 282, 283.
† Rapin, vol. ii., p. 634.
‡ According to this curious mode of reasoning, the authority of a trust justifies the abuse of it, and persons elected for the general welfare are not accountable for acting contrary to the interests of their constituents. Such a position is just as absurd, to use the simile of a late writer, as to imagine "that physicians, chosen to superintend and cure the sick in hospitals, have a right to kill their patients if they please."—*Secret History of the Reign of Charles II.*, vol. ii., p. 7, note.—ED.

* Page 258.
‡ Baxter's Life, part ii., p. 436.
† Echard, p. 806.
Compl. Hist., p. 267.

God;" a subject much upon their thoughts at that time: but this was so highly resented at court, that he was sent to Newgate next week for sedition in breaking the king's laws.* It was done in terrorem, says my author, but there was such a clamour among the people, and such a resort of persons of distinction to visit the prisoner, that his majesty thought fit to release him in a few days; which not being done by due course of law, the Commons resented it, and presented an address that the laws for the future might have their free course. This disgusted the king, who was willing to assert his prerogative, and show some favour to the Presbyterians, that he might cover the papists; but Lord Clarendon, who was their implacable enemy, and at the head of that party which meditated their ruin, opposed the court measures, and encouraged his friends in both houses to abide by the laws.†

The following summer [1663] there was a fresh discourse of liberty for the silenced ministers; and the court was so far in the design as to encourage them to petition for a general toleration, insinuating this to be the only way of relief, and that the Legislature would go on to increase their burdens, and lay them in jails till they complied. The Independents went up to court to speak for themselves, but the Presbyterians refused; upon which Mr. Baxter says, the Independent brethren thought it owing to them that they missed of their intended liberty.‡ The court being displeased, Lord Clarendon and his friends took the opportunity to awaken their resentments, by fathering upon the Nonconformists some new plots against the government. There was said to be a conspiracy in the north among the Republicans and Separatists, to restore the Long Parliament, and put Lambert and Ludlow at their head, though the former was shut up in prison in a remote island, and the other gone into banishment. There had been some unadvised and angry conversation among the meaner sort of people of republican principles, but it was not pretended that any gentleman of character, much less that the body of the English Nonconformists, were acquainted with it; however, about twenty were tried and condemned at York and Leeds, and several executed. Some very mean persons were indicted at the Old Bailey for a branch of the same design, as, Tongue, Phillips, Stubbes, Hind, Sellars, and Gibbes: they were not tried separately, but set at the bar together, and condemned in the lump. It was pretended that the fifth-monarchy men, Anabaptists, Independents, and some Quakers, were consenting to some desperate designs, but the authors were never discovered; however, four of these pretended conspirators were executed, who confessed, at the place of execution, that they had heard some treasonable expressions in company, but denied to the last that they were acquainted with any conspiracy against the king; and whoever reads their trials will be inclined to think that it was a design of those who were at the head of affairs to inflame the populace,

against the Nonconformists, in order to bring on them greater severities.

An act was passed this summer "for the relief of such persons as by sickness, or other impediments, were disabled from subscribing the declaration in the Act of Uniformity, and explanation of the said act." The preamble sets forth, "that divers persons of eminent loyalty, and known affection to the liturgy of the Church of England, were out of the kingdom; and others, by reason of sickness, disability of body, or otherwise, could not subscribe within the time limited, and were therefore disabled, and ipso facto deprived of their prebendaries, or other livings, therefore farther time is given them to the feast of the Nativity of our Lord next ensuing; or if out of England, forty days after their return:"* which shows that the time limited by the Act of Uniformity was not sufficient. The journal of the House of Lords mentions a clause inserted by their lordships, explaining the subscription and declaration to relate only to practice and obedience to the law, which passed the Upper House, though several temporal lords protested against it, as destructive to the Church of England; however, when it came down to the Commons, the clause was rejected, and the Lords did not think fit to insist upon its being restored.†

While the Parliament were relieving the Loyalists, they increased the burdens of the Nonconformists; for under colour of the late pretended plots, they passed an act for suppressing seditious conventicles; the preamble to which having set forth, that the sectaries, under pretence of tender consciences, at their meetings had contrived insurrections, the act declares the 35th of Queen Elizabeth to be in full force, which condemns all persons refusing peremptorily to come to church, after conviction, to banishment, and in case of return, to death without benefit of clergy. It enacts farther,‡ "that if any person above the age of sixteen, after the first of July, 1664, shall be present at any meeting, under colour or pretence of any exercise of religion, in other manner than is allowed by the liturgy or practice of the Church of England, where shall be five or more persons than the household, shall for the first offence suffer three months' imprisonment, upon record made upon oath under the hand and seal of a justice of peace, or pay a sum not exceeding five pounds; for the second offence six months' imprisonment, or ten pounds; and for the third offence the offender to be banished to some of the American plantations for seven years, excepting New-England and Virginia, or pay one hundred pounds; and in case they return, or make their escape, such persons are to be adjudged felons, and suffer death without benefit of clergy. Sheriffs, or justices of peace, or others commissioned by them, are empowered to dissolve, dissipate, and break up, all unlawful conventicles, and to take into custody such of their number as they think fit. They

* Calamy, vol. ii., p. 6.　　† Rapin, p. 312, 313.
‡ Baxter's Life, part ii., p. 430, 433.
§ Kennet's Chron , p. 840, 841. Calamy, vol. i., p. 305. Rapin, p. 635.

* 15 Car. II., cap. vi.
† " Thus it is the declared sense of the Legislature, that the unfeigned assent and consent relates not only to the use, but to the inward and entire approbation of all and everything as expressed in the subscription."—Fowler's French Constitution, p. 352, note.　　‡ 16 Car. II., cap. iv.

who suffer such conventicles in their houses or barns are liable to the same forfeitures as other offenders. The prosecution is to be within three months. Married women taken at conventicles are to be imprisoned for twelve months, unless their husbands pay forty shillings for their redemption. This act to continue in force for three years after the next session of Parliament."

This was a terrible scourge over the laity, put into the hands of a single justice of the peace, without the verdict of a jury, the oath of the informer being sufficient. The design of the Parliament (says Rapin) was to drive them to despair, and to force them into real crimes against the government. By virtue of this act, the jails in the several counties were quickly filled with dissenting Protestants, while the papists had the good fortune to be covered under the wing of the prerogative. Some of the ministers who went to church in sermon time were disturbed for preaching to a few of their parishioners after the public service was over; their houses were broke open, and their hearers taken into custody; warrants were issued out for levying £20 on the minister, £20 upon the house, and 5s. upon each hearer. If the money was not immediately paid, there was a seizure of their effects, the goods and wares were taken out of the shops; and in the country, cattle were driven away and sold for half their value. If the seizure did not answer the fine, the minister and people were hurried to prison, and held under close confinement for three or six months. The trade of an informer began to be very gainful, by the encouragement of the spiritual courts. At every quarter sessions several were fined for not coming to church, and others excommunicated: nay, some have been sentenced to abjure the realm, and fined in a sum much larger than all they were worth in the world.

Before the Conventicle Act took place, the laity were courageous,* and exhorted their ministers to preach till they went to prison; but when, it came home to themselves, and they had been once in jail, they began to be more cautious, and consulted among themselves how to avoid the edge of the law in the best manner they could; for this purpose their assemblies were frequently held at midnight, and in the most private places; and yet, notwithstanding all their caution, they were frequently disturbed; but it is remarkable that, under all their hardships, they never made the least resistance, but went quietly along with the soldiers or officers when they could not fly from them. The distress of so many families made some confine themselves within their own houses, some remove to the plantations, and others have recourse to occasional conformity, to avoid the penalty for not coming to church; but the Independents, Anabaptists, and Quakers declined the practice; for they said, If persecution was the mark of a false church, it must be absolutely unlawful to join with one that was so notoriously guilty.

Indeed, the Quakers gloried in their sufferings, and were so resolute as to assemble openly at the Bull-and-Mouth, near Aldersgate,† from whence the soldiers and other officers drag-

ged them to prison, till Newgate was filled, and multitudes died by close confinement in the several jails. The account published about this time says, there were six hundred of them in prison, merely for religion's sake, of whom several were banished to the plantations. Sometimes the Quakers met and continued silent, upon which it was questioned whether such an assembly was a conventicle for religious exercise; and when some were tried for it in order to banishment, they were acquitted of the banishment, and came off with a fine, which they seldom paid, and were, therefore, continued in prison.* In short, the Quakers about London gave such full employment to the informers, that they had less leisure to attend the meetings of other Dissenters.

So great was the severity of these times, and the arbitrary proceedings of the justices, that many were afraid to pray in their families, if above four of their acquaintance who came only to visit them were present. Some families scrupled asking a blessing on their meat, if five strangers were at table. In London, where the houses join, it was thought the law might be evaded if the people met in several houses, and heard the minister through a window or hole in the wall; but it seems this was overruled, the determination being (as has been observed) in the breast of a single mercenary justice of the peace. And while conscientious people were thus oppressed, the common people gave themselves up to drunkenness, profane swearing, gaming, lewdness, and all kinds of debauchery, which brought down the judgments of Heaven upon the nation.

The first general calamity that befell the kingdom, was a war with the Dutch, which the king entered into this winter by the instigation of the young French monarch, Louis XIV., who, being grown rich by a long peace, sought for an opportunity to make new conquests in the Spanish Flanders; for this purpose, he engaged the maritime powers in a war, that, by weakening each other's hands, they might not be at leisure to assist the Spaniards, whom he intended to attack. The English made complaints of the encroachments of the Dutch upon their trade, and indignities offered to his majesty's subjects in India, Africa, and elsewhere; the French promoted these misunderstandings, and promised to supply the king with what sums of money he wanted; till at length war was proclaimed, February 22, 1664–5, in the course of which sundry bloody engagements happened at sea; the two nations were drained of their blood and their treasure, and the Protestant interest almost ruined, while the French were little more than spectators. The war continued about two years and a half, and then ended with no manner of advantage to either nation.

[In the year 1663 there was obtained, by the interest of Mr. Baxter and Mr. Ashurst with the Lord-chancellor Hyde, a charter for the incorporating "A Society or Company for Propagation of the Gospel in New-England, and the Parts adjacent in America." Such a society had been formed under the sanction of an act of Parliament in 1646; and by a collection made in all the parishes in England, there had been

---

* Baxter's Life, part ii., p. 436.   † Sewel, p. 445.

* Baxter's Life, part ii., p. 436.

raised a sum sufficient to purchase an estate in land of between £500 and £600 a year. Upon the restoration of King Charles II. the charter became void, and Colonel Beddingfield, a Roman Catholic officer in the army, of whom a considerable part of the land was bought, seized it for his own use ; pretending he had sold it under the value, in hopes of recovering it upon the king's return. The society being re-established at great trouble and expense, were again put in possession of the estate by a decree of Chancery, which the Honourable Mr. Boyle was very instrumental in obtaining.* He was appointed the first governor of the company.†

On the 4th of June this year died, aged eighty-one, Dr. William Juxon, archbishop of Canterbury, whose elevation to the post of Lord-high-treasurer of England, and other early preferments, have been mentioned before, vol. i., p. 326. He was born in Chichester, received his grammar learning at Merchant Tailors' School, became fellow of St. John's College, Oxford, in 1598, and bachelor of the civil law in 1603; being about that time a student in Grey's Inn. Soon after he entered into holy orders, and in 1609 was made vicar of St. Giles, Oxford. In 1626 he executed the office of vice-chancellor. After the death of Charles I. he retired to his paternal manor of Little Compton, in Gloucestershire, and devoted himself to liberal studies. On the Restoration he was advanced, September 4, 1660, to the see of Canterbury. He was buried with great funeral pomp in St. John's College, Oxon. He is said to have acted, at a very critical time, with a prudence, moderation, and integrity which enmity could not impeach in his arduous office as high-treasurer. He left many monuments of his munificence and liberality. " The mildness of his temper, the gentleness of his manners, and the integrity of his life," says Mr. Granger,

---

* The Honourable Robert Boyle was a man distinguished alike by birth, genius, and learning, and that which infinitely surpassed them all, by unfeigned and fervent piety. He could not, therefore, be content to live to himself. He was a son of the Earl of Cork, and educated at the University of Oxford, where, after his travels, he fixed his residence, on account of the disorders of the times. Here he collected around him a select circle of men devoted, like himself, to science and philosophy. This society at first styled themselves " the Philosophical College," and from which arose, after the Restoration, " the Royal Society of London." Mr. Boyle wrote numerous valuable treatises on philosophical, critical, moral, and religious subjects. His spirit was truly catholic and Christian ; leading him to esteem as brethren the excellent Nonconformists of his day and the pious Conformists. He was largely imbued with the missionary spirit. To the labours of John Eliot and his colleagues among the Indians at Roxbury, Massachusetts, he contributed between £300 and £400 sterling per annum. At his expense a translation was made of the New Testament into the Malayan tongue. He procured a translation of the New Testament also into the Turkish language, contributed largely to an edition of the Welsh Bible, and gave £700 towards an edition of the Irish Bible. He founded a Lecture in England in defence of the Gospel, against the daring infidels of the reign of Charles II., and, according to Bishop Burnet, who preached his funeral sermon, he devoted more than £1000 a year to advance the interests of pure religion. He died 1691.—C.

† Neal's History of New-England, vol. i., p. 262.

" gained him universal esteem ; and even the haters of prelacy could never hate Juxon."*

Mr. Henry Jessey, an eminent divine among the Puritans, died also on the 4th of September, this year. He was born on the 3d of September, 1601, at West Rowton, near Cleveland in Yorkshire, where his father was minister. At seventeen years of age he was sent to St. John's College in Cambridge ; he continued six years at the university, where he commenced first bachelor, then master of arts. In 1623 died his father, who had hitherto supplied him according to his ability ; which event left him in such strait circumstances that he had not above threepence a day for his maintenance, yet he so economically managed this small pittance as to spare some of it for hiring books. He pursued his studies with diligence, and not contenting himself with the *ipse dixit* of authority, he investigated science freely. He left the university well versed in the Hebrew and the writings of the rabbies, with a knowledge of Syriac and Chaldee. During this period his mind imbibed a strong sense of religion, and he determined to devote himself to the ministry. He spent nine years after leaving the university as chaplain in the family of Mr. Brampton Gurdon, at Assington in Suffolk, improving his time, and, among other studies, giving his attention to physic. In 1627 he received Episcopal ordination, but could not be prevailed upon to accept any promotion until 1633' when the living of Aughton, in Yorkshire, was given to him. But he was removed the very next year for not using the ceremonies, and for taking down a crucifix. On this he was received into the family of Sir Matthew Bointon, in the same county, and preached frequently at two parishes in the neighbourhood. In 1635, accompanying his patron to London, he was invited to be pastor of the congregation formed in 1616 by Mr. Henry Jacob ; this his modesty led him to decline for some time, but, after many prayers and much consideration, he accepted the invitation, and continued in this post until his death. Soon after, the sentiments of the Baptists were embraced by many of this society. This put him upon studying the controversy ; and the result was, that after great deliberation, many prayers, and frequent conferences with pious and learned friends, he altered his sentiments, first concerning the mode, and then the subjects of baptism. But he maintained the same temper of friendship and charity towards other Christians, not only as to conversation, but church communion. When he visited the churches in the north and west of England, he laboured to promote the spirit of love and union among them, and was a principal person in setting up and maintaining for some time a meeting of some eminent men of each denomination in London. He divided his labours according to the liberality of his temper. In the afternoon of every Lord's Day he was among his own people. In the morning he usually preached at St. George's Church, Southwark, and once in the week at Ely House, and at the Savoy to the maimed soldiers. The master study of his life was a new translation of the Bible ; in this de-

* Granger's History of England, vol. ii., p. 109, 154. Wood's Athen. Oxon., vol. ii., p. 662, 663 ; and Richardson, de Præsulibus, p. 162.

sign he engaged the assistance of many persons of note. It was almost completed, when the great turn given to public affairs at the Restoration rendered it abortive.* The benevolence of his exertions formed a most distinguishing trait in his character. He chose a single life, that he might be more at liberty for such labours. Besides his own alms, he was a constant solicitor and agent for the poor, and carried about with him a list and description of the most peculiar objects of charity which he knew. Thirty families had all their subsistence from him. But his charity was not limited to his own congregation; and where he thought it no charity to give, he would often lend without interest or security. One of the most remarkable instances of his charity, which had scarcely a precedent, was what he showed to the Jews at Jerusalem, who, by a war between the Swedes and Poles, which cut off their subsistence from their rich brethren in other countries, were reduced to great extremities. Mr. Jessey collected for them £300, and sent with it letters, with a view to their conversion to Christianity. In the year 1650 he had written a treatise to remove their prejudices, and convince them of the Messiahship of Jesus, recommended by several of the Assembly of Divines, and afterward translated into Hebrew, in order to be dispersed among the Jews of all nations. He was exposed to a great number of visiters, which occasioned him to have it written over his study door,

AMICE, QUISQUIS HUC ADES;
AUT AGITO PAUCIS, AUT ABI,
AUT ME LABORANTEM ADJUVA.

WHATEVER FRIEND COMES HITHER,
DESPATCH IN BRIEF, OR GO,
OR HELP ME BUSIED TOO.   H. J.

When he went long journeys, he laid down rules to regulate the conversation for his fellow-travellers, which were enforced by small pecuniary mulcts on the violation of them. He was meek and humble, and very plain in speech, dress, and demeanour. He was so great a scripturist, that if one began to rehearse any passage, he could go on with it, and name the book, chapter, and verse, where it might be found. The original languages of the Old and New Testament were as familiar to him as his mother tongue. He was several times apprehended at meetings for religious worship. Upon the Restoration he was ejected from his living at St. George's, silenced from his ministry, and committed to prison. About five or six months after his last release, he died full of peace and joy; lamented by persons of different persuasions, several thousands of whom attended his funeral.—*Crosby's History of the Baptists*, vol. i., p. 307-321. *Palmer's Noncon-*

* In reference to his translation he would often exclaim, "Oh that I may see this done before I die!" To show the necessity of amending the common translation, he observed that (as Dr. Hill declared in a great assembly) Archbishop Bancroft, who was a supervisor of this work, *altered it in fourteen places* to make it *speak the prelatical language*. Dr. Smith, also, who was one of the translators of the Bible, and *wrote the preface*, who was afterward made Bishop of Gloucester, complained to a minister of that county of the archbishop's unwarrantable alterations. "But," says he, "he is so potent, there is no contradicting him."—C.

formists' Memorial, vol. i., p. 108-113. The *Life and Death of Mr. Jessey*, 1671; where are the letters written to the Jews, remarks on our translation of the Bible, and rules for a new version.—ED.] (TOULMIN).

The next judgment which befell the nation was the most dreadful plague that had been known within the memory of man. This was preceded by an unusual drought; the meadows were parched and burned up like the highways, insomuch that there was no food for the cattle, which occasioned first a murrain among them, and then a general contagion among the human species, which increased in the city and suburbs of London until eight or ten thousand died in a week.* The richer inhabitants fled into the remoter counties; but the calamities of those who stayed behind, and of the poorer sort, are not to be expressed. Trade was at a full stand; all commerce between London and the country was entirely cut off, lest the infection should be propagated thereby. Nay, the country housekeepers and farmers durst not entertain their city friends or relations till they had performed quarantine in the fields or outhouses. If a stranger passed through the neighbourhood, they fled from him as an enemy. In London the shops and houses were quite shut up, and many of them marked with a red cross, and an inscription over the door, Lord, have mercy upon us! Grass grew in the streets; and every night the bellman went his rounds with a cart, crying, Bring out your dead. From London the plague spread into the neighbouring towns and villages, and continued near three quarters of a year, till it had swept away almost one hundred thousand of the inhabitants.†

Some of the established clergy, with a commendable zeal, ventured to continue in their stations; and preach to their parishioners throughout the course of the plague, as Dr. Walker, Dr. Horton, Dr. Meriton, and a few others;‡ but most of them fled, and deserted

* Dr. Grey has introduced here a full and affecting narrative of the progress of this calamity, and of the mortality it produced; drawn up by the pen of Mr. Vincent, one who charitably gave his assistance at that time, as copied by Dr. Calamy, in his Continuation, p. 33. It was usual for people, as they went about their business, to drop down in the street. A bagpiper, who, excessively overcome with liquor, had fallen down and lay asleep in the street, was taken up and thrown into a cart, and betimes the next morning carried away with some dead bodies. At daybreak he awoke, and, rising, began to play a tune: which so surprised those who drove the cart, and could see nothing distinctly, that in a fright they betook them to their heels, and would have it they had taken up the devil in the disguise of a dead man.—*Sir John Reresby's Memoirs*, p. 10, 11.—ED.

† De Foe has recorded this awful visitation in a most graphic volume.—C.

‡ Baxter's Life, part iii., p. 2. Baxter, in another place, says, "It is scarcely possible for people that live in times of health and security to apprehend the dreadfulness of the pestilence. How fearful were people, even a hundred miles from London, of any thing bought in a draper's shop there, or of any person that came to their houses! How they would shut their doors against their friends, and if men met, one another in the fields, how they would avoid each other." Baxter says that only three Nonconformist ministers died of the plague.—*Baxter's Life*, part ii., p. 448.—C.

their parishes at a time when their assistance was most wanted; upon this some of the ejected ministers ventured to preach in the vacant pulpits, imagining that so extraordinary a case would justify their disregard to the laws. The ministers who embarked in this service were, the Reverend Mr. Thomas Vincent, Mr. Chester, Mr. Janeway, Mr. Turner, Grimes, Franklin, and others. The face of death, and the arrows that fled among the people in darkness at noonday, awakened both preachers and hearers: many who were at church one day were thrown into their graves the next; the cry of great numbers was, "What shall we do to be saved!" A more awful time England had never seen.

But it will amaze all posterity, that in a time both of war and pestilence, and when the Nonconformist ministers were hazarding their lives in the service of the souls of the distressed and dying citizens of London, that the prime minister and his creatures,* instead of mourning for the nation's sins, and meditating a reformation of manners, should pour out all their vengeance upon the Nonconformists, in order to make their condition more insupportable. One would have thought such a judgment from Heaven, and such a generous compassion in the ejected ministers, should have softened the hearts of their most cruel enemies; but the Presbyterians must be crushed, in defiance of the rebukes of Providence. Bishop Kennet and Mr. Echard would excuse the ministry, by alleging that some of the old Oliverian officers were enlisted in the Dutch service,† which, if true, was nothing to the body of the Presbyterians, though Lord Clarendon did what he could to incense the Parliament, and make them believe they were in confederacy with the enemies of the government. In his harangue to the House, he says, "Their countenances were more erect, and more insolent, since the beginning of the war, than before; that they were ready, if any misfortune had befallen the king's fleet, to have brought the war into our fields and houses. The horrid murderers of our late royal master have been received into the most sacred councils in Holland; and other infamous persons of our nation are admitted to a share in the conduct of their affairs, with liberal pensions. Too many of his majesty's subjects have been enlisted in their service for a maintenance. Their friends at home made no doubt of doing the business themselves, if they could pitch upon a lucky day to begin the work. If you carefully provide for suppressing your enemies at home, you will find your enemies abroad more inclined to peace." Is it possible that such a speech could proceed from the lips of a wise and faithful counsellor, who was to ask for money to carry on the war? Could the chancellor think that the way to conquer abroad was to divide and harass the king's subjects at home, in the midst of the distress of a terrible plague? He confessed, afterward, that he was most averse to this war, and abhorred it from his very soul; and yet he makes a handle of it to rain down vengeance on the Presbyterians, who had no concern in it. But it happened to them as in popish countries: when any general calamity befalls the people, it is imputed to too great an

* Baxter's Life, part iii., p. 3.   † Echard, p. 824.

indulgence to heretics, and the vengeance is returned upon their heads.* Bishop Burnet is of opinion that the Oxford act was rather owing to the liberty the Nonconformists took in their sermons to complain of their own hardships, and to lament the vices of the court, as the causes of the present calamities. And supposing this to be true, their complaints were not without reason,

However, the load was to lie on the dissenting ministers, and therefore an act was brought into the House to banish them from their friends, which had the royal assent, October 31, 1665. It was entitled, "An Act to restrain Nonconformists from inhabiting Corporations;" the preamble to which sets forth, "that divers parsons, and others in holy orders, not having subscribed the Act of Uniformity, have taken upon them to preach in unlawful assemblies, and to instil the poisonous principles of schism and rebellion into the hearts of his majesty's subjects, to the great danger of the Church and kingdom. Be it therefore enacted, that all such Nonconformist ministers shall take the following oath: I, A. B., do swear that it is not lawful, upon any pretence whatsoever, to take arms against the king;† and that I do abhor that traitorous position of taking arms by his authority against his person, or against those that are commissioned by him, in pursuance of such commissions; and that I will not at any time endeavour any alteration of government either in Church or State. And all such Nonconformist ministers shall not, after the 24th of March, 1665, unless in passing the road, come, or be within five miles of any city, town corporate, or borough, that sends burgesses to Parliament; or within five miles of any parish, town, or place, wherein they have since the Act of Oblivion been parson, vicar, or lecturer, &c., or where they have preached in any conventicle, on any pretence whatsoever, before they have taken and subscribed the aforesaid oath before the justices of peace at their quarter sessions, for the county, in open court; upon forfeiture for every such offence of the sum of forty pounds, one third to the king, another third to the poor, and a third to him that shall sue for it. And it is farther enacted, that such as shall refuse the oath aforesaid shall be incapable of teaching any public or private schools, or of taking any boarders‡ or tablers to be taught or instructed, under pain of forty pounds, to be distributed as above. Any two justices of peace, upon oath made before them of any offence committed against this act, are empowered to commit the offender to prison for six months, without bail or mainprize."

The Earl of Southampton, Lord Wharton, Ashley, Dr. Earl, bishop of Salisbury, and oth-

* Echard, p. 846.
† A project was formed of imposing this clause on the whole nation, by requiring this oath of every subject. The point was so near carried, that the bill brought in for the purpose was rejected by three voices only.—*Secret History of the Reign of Charles II.*, vol. ii., p. 172, *note.*—Ed.
‡ "This act seemed (it is justly observed) to be the last step in the climax of intolerance; for to deprive men of the means of subsistence implies more deliberate cruelty, though it does not excite so much horror as fire and fagots."—*Secret History of the Reign of Charles II.*, vol. ii., p. 171, *note.*—Ed.

ers, vehemently opposed this bill, out of compassion to the Nonconformists, and as it enforced an unlawful and unjustifiable oath, which (as the Earl of Southampton observed) *no honest man could take*; but the madness of the times prevailed against all reason and humanity.* The promoters of the act were, Lordchancellor Clarendon, Archbishop Sheldon, Ward, the new Bishop of Salisbury, and their creatures, with all that were secret favourites of popery, says Bishop Burnet. It was moved that the word *legally* might be inserted in the oath, before the word "commissioned;" and that before the words "endeavoured to change the government," might be inserted the word *unlawfully*; but all amendments were rejected; † however, Bridgeman, chief justice of the Common Pleas, declaring that the oath must be so understood, Dr. Bates and about twenty others took it, to avoid the imputation of sedition; but they had such a lecture afterward from the bench for their scruples, that they repented of what they had done before they went out of court. Mr. Howe, and about twelve in Devonshire, and a few in Dorsetshire, took the oath, with a declaration in what sense and with what limitations they understood it.‡

But the body of the Nonconformist ministers refused the oath, choosing rather to forsake their habitations, their relations, and friends, and all visible support, than destroy the peace of their consciences. Those ministers who had some little estate or substance of their own, retired to some remote and obscure villages, or such little market-towns as were not corporations, and more than five miles from the places where they had preached; but in many counties it was difficult to find such places of retirement; for either there were no houses untenanted, or they were annexed to farms which the ministers were not capable of using; or the people were afraid to admit the ministers into their houses, lest they should be suspected as favourers of nonconformity.§ Some took advantage of the ministers' necessities, and raised their rents beyond what they could afford to give. Great numbers were thus buried in obscurity, while others, who had neither money nor friends, went on preaching as they could, till they were sent to prison, thinking it more eligible to perish in a jail than to starve out of one; especially when by this means they had some occasional relief from their hearers, and hopes that their wives and children might be supported after their death.‖ Many who lay concealed in distant places from their flocks, in the daytime, rode thirty or forty miles to preach to them in the night, and retired again before daylight. These hardships tempted some few to conform, says Mr. Baxter, contrary to their former judgments; but the body of Dissenters remained steadfast to their principles, and the Church gained neither reputation nor numbers. The informers were very diligent in hunting after their game, and the soldiers and officers behaved with great rudeness and violence. When they missed of the ministers, they went into

the barns and out-houses, and sometimes thrust their swords up to the hilts in the hay and straw, where they supposed they might lie concealed; they made havoc of their goods, and terrified the women and children almost out of their lives. These methods of cruelty reduced many ministers, with their families, to the necessity of living upon brown rye bread and water; but few were reduced to public beggary, says Mr. Baxter,* the providence of God appearing wonderfully for their relief in their greatest extremities.

And as if the judgments of Heaven upon this nation were not heavy enough, nor the Legislature sufficiently severe, the bishops must throw their weight into the scale; for in the very midst of the plague, July 7, 1665, Archbishop Sheldon sent orders to the several bishops of his province to return the names of all ejected Nonconformist ministers, with their places of abode and manner of life; and the returns of the several bishops are still preserved in the Lambeth library.† The design of this inquiry was to gird the laws closer upon the Dissenters, and to know by what means they earned their bread; and if this tender-hearted archbishop could have had his will, they must have starved, or sought a livelihood in foreign countries.

This year put an end to the life of Dr. Cornelius Burgess, a divine of the Puritan stamp,‡

*. Page 4.   † Compl. Hist., vol. iii., p. 279.

‡ "If all the Puritans," says Dr. Grey, "had been of his rebellious stamp, they had certainly been a wicked crew; but there was a great difference in Puritans, some very good, and some very bad, as is justly observed by Mr. Fuller." In his first volume, also, p. 268, the doctor impeaches the character of this divine, in the words of Echard, who calls him "the seditious Dr. Burgess; and one of the greatest boutefeus of the whole party, being the perpetual trumpeter to the most violent proceedings, a great instrument in bringing on the miseries of the nation; who died in great want and poverty, tormented and eaten up by a cancer in his neck and cheek—a fearful instance of rebellion and sacrilege." To these and other invectives of the Archdeacon Echard against Dr. Burgess, Dr. Calamy replied; but the reply goes chiefly to show the archdeacon's partiality, by inveighing in this manner against Burgess, when the characters of some on the other side were open to similar charges. The fact, which seems to bear hard on the name of this divine, is, that though he declared it "by no means lawful to alienate the bishops' lands from public and pious uses, or to convert them to any private person's property," yet he gained so much as to grow rich by the purchase of them. After the Restoration he lost all. This, Dr. Calamy thinks, might be allowed a sufficient punishment without branding his memory. What inconsistency or faults soever might be chargeable on Dr. Burgess, the interpretation which the archdeacon puts on his death deserves severe censure, as "rash and presuming." This method gives a particular and invidious construction to events that arise from general laws, and equally befall the righteous and the wicked; and it shows how they who use it would direct, if it were in their power, the evils and calamities of life. It indicates as much a want of candour and generosity as of sound judgment. It appears from a MS. history drawn up by Dr. Henry Sampson, a noted physician, that Dr. Burgess was deemed a man of solid parts and great learning; that no temptations could induce him to return to the Episcopal side; that in the year 1648 he preached a sermon fuller of loyalty than the boldest at that time would dare to express; that he was against imposing the Covenant, and refused to take it till he was sus-

* Baxter, part iii., p. 3.   Burnet, vol. i., p. 329.
† Baxter's Life, part iii., p. 15.
‡ Howe's Life, p. 41.
§ Baxter, part iii., p. 4.   Burnet, p. 331.
‖ Baxter's Life, part iii., p. 15.

educated at Oxford, and chaplain to King Charles I. He suffered much by the High Commission Court; but, taking part with the Parliament, was chosen one of the pacific divines, who met in the Jerusalem Chamber, to accommodate differences in the Church : he often preached before the House of Commons, and was one of the Assembly of Divines, but refused to take the Covenant till he was suspended. He was ejected at the Restoration from St. Andrew's, in the city of Wells, in Somersetshire, and having laid out all his money in the purchase of bishops' lands, he was reduced to absolute poverty.[*] He appeared at the head of the London divines, against bringing the king to his trial, and was esteemed a very learned and able divine.[†] He died at his house at Watford, June, 1665.

We have already remembered Dr. Cheynel among the Oxford professors, a man of great abilities, and a member of the Assembly of Divines. He quitted his preferments in the University for refusing to take the Engagement, and was ejected from the living of Petworth at the Restoration, without having enriched himself by any of his preferments.[‡] It is reported that he was sometimes disordered in his head, but he was perfectly recovered some years before his death, which happened at his house near Brighthelmstone, in Sussex, September, 1665.[§]

[There died in prison this year, Mr. Samuel Fisher, a man of great parts and literature, eminent piety and virtue, who reflected honour on each denomination of Christians, with which, through the change of his sentiments, he became successively connected. His father was a haberdasher of hats, and Mayor of Northampton. In 1623, at the age of eighteen, he became a student in Trinity College, Oxford, where he took the degree of master of arts, and then removed to New Inn. At the University he distinguished himself, by his application and

pended. He was excellently skilled in the liturgical controversies, and those of church government, and was possessed of all the books of Common Prayer that were ever printed in England, and bestowed them upon Oxford library.—*Dr. Calamy's Letter to Mr. Archdeacon Echard*, p. 107–111.—Ed.

[*] Wood's Athen. Oxon., vol. ii., p. 235. Calamy, vol. ii., p. 586; or Palmer's Nonconformists' Memorial, vol. ii., p. 384.

[†] He was author of many small tracts; one of his works is entitled "*The Baptismal Regeneration of Elect Infants.*" 1629. His sermons were numerous before the House of Commons. He was also the author of a treatise "On the Necessity of Reformation, in Doctrine, Discipline, and Worship:" this was published anonymously, but Baxter says it was his.—*Baxter's Life*, part ii., p. 265.—C.

[‡] For he was remarkable throughout his life for hospitality and contempt of money. Dr. Johnson published an account of this extraordinary man, that appeared first in the Gentleman's Magazine for March and April, 1775; which, Mr. Palmer remarks, is a satire both upon Dr. Cheynel and the times. Dr. Cheynel, this narrative says, "had an intrepidity which was never to be shaken by any danger, and a spirit of enterprise not to be discouraged by difficulty; which were supported by an unusual degree of bodily strength. Whatever he believed he thought himself obliged to profess, and what he professed he was ready to defend."—Ed.

[§] Wood's Athen. Oxon., vol. ii., p. 245. Calamy, vol. ii., p. 675; and Palmer's Nonconformists' Memorial, vol. ii., p. 467.

Vol. II.—K k

proficiency gained an accurate knowledge of Greek and Roman antiquities, and was particularly given to the study of rhetoric and poetry. When he had finished his academic course, he became chaplain to Sir Arthur Haslerigge. In 1632 he was presented to the vicarage of Lidd, in Kent, a living of £500 a year. Here he had the character of a very powerful preacher, united with humility and affability of carriage. While in this situation, in consequence of frequent conversation with a Baptist minister, he was led into an examination of the questions concerning baptism, which ended in his embracing the opinions of the Baptists, being baptized by immersion, and taking the pastoral care of a congregation of that people, having freely resigned his living and returned his diploma to the bishop; which those who differ from him must applaud as a singular instance of sincerity and self-denial. On this he rented a farm and commenced grazier; " by which he procured a decent competency, enhanced," says Mr. Gough, " by the consolation of solid content, and the internal testimony of an approving heart." During his connexion with the Baptists, he baptized some hundreds, and was frequently engaged in public disputes in vindication of their sentiments, to the number of nine, in the course of three years, with several noted ministers, sometimes in the presence of two thousand auditors, and once with Dr. Cheynel. He published also a treatise, entitled "Baby-baptism mere Babism," which is represented as containing the whole state of the controversy as it was then managed. He was deemed an ornament to the sect, and was one of the chief defenders of their doctrine. In 1665 he embraced the principles of the Quakers, and became an active and laborious minister among them. He preached at Dunkirk against the idolatry of the priests and friars; and, in company with another friend, travelled on foot over the Alps to Rome; where they testified against the superstitions of the place, and distributed some books among the ecclesiastics, and left it without molestation. After his return, he suffered among Protestants the persecution he escaped among the Romanists. The great part of the last four years of his life was spent in prison; and, after two years' confinement in the White Lion prison in Southwark, he died "in perfect peace with God; in good esteem both with his friends and many others, on account of the eminence of his natural parts and acquired abilities as a scholar, and of his exemplary humility, social virtues, and circumspect conversation as a Christian; in meekness instructing those who opposed him, and labouring incessantly, by his discourses and by his writings, to propagate and promote true Christian practice and piety."—*Wood's Athen. Oxon.*, vol. ii., p. 243. *Crosby's History of the Baptists*, vol. i., p. 361, &c.; and *Gough's History of the Quakers*, vol. i., p. 163; and vol. ii., p. 141.—Ed.] (Toulmin).

The vices of the nation not being sufficiently punished by pestilence and war, it pleased Almighty God this year to suffer the city of London to be laid in ashes by a dreadful conflagration, which broke out in Pudding Lane behind the Monument, September 2, 1666, and within three or four days consumed thirteen thousand two hundred dwelling-houses, eighty-nine churches, among which was the Cathedral of St. Paul's; many public structures, schools, libraries, and stately edifices. Multitudes lost their goods and merchandise, and the greatest part of their substance, and some few their lives;* the king, the Duke of York, and many of the nobility, were spectators of the desolation, but had not the power to stop its progress, till at length it ceased almost as wonderfully as it began. Moorfields was filled with household goods, and the people were forced to lodge in huts and tents: many families who were last week in prosperity, were now reduced to beggary, and obliged to begin the world again. The authors of this fire were said to be the papists, as appears by the inscription upon the Monument. The Parliament being of this opinion, petitioned the king to issue out a proclamation, requiring all popish priests and Jesuits to depart the kingdom within a month, and appointed a committee who received evidence of some papists who were seen to throw fire-balls into houses, and of others who had materials for it in their pockets; but the men were fled, and none suffered but one Hubert, a French-man, by his own confession.†

In this general confusion, the churches being burned, and many of the parish ministers withdrawn, for want of habitations or places of worship, the Nonconformists resolved again to supply the necessities of the people, depending upon it, that in such an extremity they should escape persecution... Some churches were erected of boards, which they called tabernacles, and the Dissenters fitted up large rooms with pulpits, seats, and galleries, for the reception of all who would come. Dr. Manton had his rooms full in Covent Garden; Mr. Thomas Vincent, Mr. Doolittle, Dr. Turner, Mr. Grimes, Mr. Jenkyns, Mr. Nathaniel Vincent, Dr. Jacomb, Mr. Watson, had their separate meetings in other places. The Independents, also, as Dr. Owen, Dr. Goodwin, Mr. Griffiths, Brooks, Caryl, Baker, Nye, and others, began the same practice; many citizens frequented the meetings, where the liturgy was not read; though the few parish pulpits that remained were filled with very able preachers, as Dr. Tillotson, Stillingfleet, Patrick, White, Gifford, Whichcote, Horton, Meriton, &c. But none of these calamities had any farther influence upon the court prelates, than that they durst not prosecute the preachers so severely for the present.‡

Among the Nonconformist ministers who died this year were the Rev. Mr. Edward Calamy, B.D.,§ the ejected minister of Aldermanbury, born in London, 1600, and bred in Pembroke Hall, Cambridge; he was first chaplain to Dr. Felton, bishop of Ely, and afterward settled at St. Edmundsbury, from whence, after ten years,

he, with thirty other ministers, was driven out of the diocess of Bishop Wren's Visitation Article and the Book of Sports. Upon the death of Dr. Stoughton, 1639, he was chosen to Aldermanbury, where he soon gained a vast reputation. He was one of the divines who met in the Jerusalem Chamber for accommodating ecclesiastical matters in the year 1641. He was afterward a member of the Assembly at Westminster, and an active man in all their proceedings. He was one of the most popular preachers in the city,* and had a great hand in the king's restoration, but soon repented having done it without a previous treaty. He refused a bishopric, because he could not have it upon the terms of the king's declaration; and soon after the Bartholomew Act, was imprisoned in Newgate for preaching an occasional sermon to his parishioners.† He afterward lived pretty much retired till this year, when, being driven in a coach through the ruins of the city of London, it so affected him that he went home and never came out of his chamber more, dying within a month, in the sixty-seventh year of his age.‡

Mr. Arthur Jackson, M.A., the ejected minister of St. Faith's, was born about the year 1593, and educated in Cambridge. He became minister of St. Michael's, Wood-street, in the year 1625, when the pestilence raged in the city, and continued with his parish throughout the whole course of the distemper.§ He was fined

His week-day lecture was constantly attended, for twenty years together, by persons of the greatest quality, there being seldom so few as twenty coaches. He was president in meetings of the city ministers, and qualified, by natural and acquired abilities, to be the leader of the Presbyterians. He never known to be intimidated, where he thought his duty was concerned; of which his grandson gives a remarkable proof. He was one of the writers against the liturgy. The title of one of the answers to him and his brethren is a curious specimen of the taste and spirit of the times. It was called "A Throat Hapse for the Frogs and Toads that crept abroad croaking against the Common Prayer Book."—Granger's History of England, vol. ii., p. 184, octavo, and note.—ED.

† This case has already been alluded to. This confinement made no small noise, Mr. Calamy was a man so generally beloved and respected. Dr. Wilde published a copy of verses on the occasion, which was spread through all parts of the kingdom. And the passage through Newgate-street was obstructed by the coaches of those who visited him in his imprisonment. A popish lady, who had been stopped by them, finding what alarm and disturbance this proceeding against Mr. Calamy had produced, took the first opportunity to wait upon the king at Whitehall, and communicate the whole matter to him, expressing her fear that if such steps as these were taken, he would lose the affections of the city, which might be of very ill consequence. On this remonstrance, and for some other reasons, Mr. Calamy was in a little time discharged by the express order of his majesty.—Memoirs of Dr. Edmund Calamy, MS.
—C.   ‡ Nonconformists' Memorial, vol. i., p. 73.
§ Calamy's Abridgment, vol. ii., p. 3; or Palmer's Nonconformists' Memorial, vol. i., p. 104.

* Preaching before General Monk, soon after the Restoration, having occasion to speak of filthy lucre, he said, "Some men will betray three kingdoms for filthy lucre's sake;" and immediately threw his handkerchief, which he usually waved up and down while he was preaching, towards the general's pew.—Palmer and Granger, ut supra.
—ED.

* It is worthy of notice that only six lives were lost.—See Burnet's Own Times, vol. i., p. 321-326. Hume, vol. vii., p. 415.—C.
† Hubert was a French Huguenot, of Rouen in Normandy. Though he confessed the fact, yet, according to Echard, he suffered unjustly; for he was a sort of lunatic, and had not landed in England till two days after the fire, as appeared by the evidence of the master of the ship who had him on board. —Grey's Examination, vol. iii., p. 439.—ED.
‡ Baxter's Life, part iii., p. 19.
§ Calamy's Abridgment. vol. ii., p. 4.

£500 for refusing to give evidence against Mr. Love, and committed prisoner to the Fleet, where he remained seventeen weeks. At the Restoration he was chosen, by the Provincial Assembly of London, to present a Bible to the king at his public entrance.* He was afterward one of the commissioners of the Savoy; and when the Uniformity Act took place, being old, he retired to a private life, and died with great satisfaction in his nonconformity, August 5, 1665, in the seventy-fourth year of his age.†

' Dr. William Spurstow, the ejected minister of Hackney, was some time master of Katherine Hall, Cambridge, but ejected for refusing the Engagement. He was one of the authors of Smectymnuus, a member of the Assembly of Divines, and afterward one of the commissioners of the Savoy; a man of great learning, humility, and charity, and of a cheerful conversation : he lived through the sickness-year, but died the following, in an advanced age.‡

This year was memorable for the fall of the great Earl of Clarendon, lord-high-chancellor of England, who attended the king in his exile, and upon his majesty's restoration was created a peer, and advanced to the high dignity of Chancellor of England. He governed with a sovereign and absolute sway as prime minister for about two years; but, in the year 1663, he was impeached of high treason by the Earl of Bristol, and, though the impeachment was dropped for want of form, his interest at court declined from that time, and, after the Oxford Parliament of 1665, his lordship was out of all credit. This summer the king took the seals from him, and, on the 12th of November, Sir Edward Seymour impeached him of high treason at the bar of the House of Peers, in the name of all the commons of England, for sundry arbitrary and tyrannical proceedings contrary to law, by which he had acquired a greater estate than could be honestly gotten in that time; for procuring grants of the king's lands

to his relations, contrary to law; for corresponding with Cromwell in his exile;* for advising and effecting the sale of Dunkirk; for issuing out quo warrantos to obtain great sums of money from the corporations; for determining people's title to their lands at the council-table, and stopping proceedings at law, &c. The earl had made himself obnoxious at court by his magisterial carriage to the king,† and was grown very unpopular by his superb and magnificent palace at St. James's, erected in the time of war and pestilence, which cost him £50,000.‡ Some called it Dunkirk House, as being built with his share of the price of that fortress; and others Holland House, as if he had received money from the king's enemies in time of war. The king's second marriage, which proved barren, was laid to his charge, and said to be contrived for the advancement of his grandchildren by the Duchess of York, who was the earl's daughter. When his majesty inclined to part with his queen, and, if possible, to legitimate his addresses to Miss Steward, the chancellor got her married privately to the Duke of Richmond, without the king's knowledge, which his majesty was told was to secure the succession of the crown to his own family. This intriguing, together with his high opposition to the Roman Catholics, and to all who were not of his principles, procured him many enemies, and struck him quite out of the king's favour. The earl did not think fit to abide the storm, but withdrew to France, leaving a paper behind him, in which he denies almost every article of his charge;§ but the Par-

* Dr. Grey supposes that Mr. Neal could not but know that Lord Clarendon had cleared himself from this charge to the king's satisfaction during his exile, who declared "that he was sorry that he was not in a condition to do him more justice than to declare him innocent, which he did, and commanded the clerk of the council to draw up a full order for his justification, which his majesty himself would sign."—ED. † Burnet, p. 365, 369, 370.

‡ Mr. Echard says that this palace was built in the absence of the chancellor, principally at the expense of the Vintners' Company; and that, when he came to see the case of it, he rather submitted than consented, and with a sigh said, "This house will one day be my ruin."—Grey's Examination, vol. iii., p. 352, note. The doctor fills two pages here with quoting Lord Clarendon's vindication of himself.—ED.

§ The articles of the charge stated by Mr. Neal were, if you credit Dr. Welwood; the ostensible causes only of the chancellor's fall. The true reason why he was abandoned to his enemies was, that he secretly opposed the design of the Parliament to settle such a revenue upon the king during life as would place him beyond the necessity of asking more, except on some extraordinary occasion; and he drew the Earl of Southampton into his views, urging that he knew the king so well, that if such a revenue were once settled upon him for life, neither of them two would be of any farther use; and there would be no probability of seeing many more sessions of Parliament during that reign. This came to the king's ears.—Memoirs, p. 109, 110, sixth edition. Lord Cornbury, in a letter to the Duke of Ormond, preserved by Carte, said that his father never stirred as long as he saw any probability of being brought to his trial in Parliament, though all his friends persuaded him to leave the kingdom, fearing that his innocence would not protect him against the malice of his enemies. When he found that there was a design to prorogue the Parliament on purpose to try

* "There was," Mr. Granger observes, "a particular propriety in assigning this office to him; as he had written a commentary on several parts of the Bible." He was a man of prodigious application; at the university he studied fourteen or sixteen hours a day, and to the day of his death constantly rose, summer and winter, at three or four o'clock in the morning.—Granger's History of England, vol. iii., p. 43, octavo.—ED.

† Not long after his coming to London the Clothworker's Company, of which his father and uncle were members and governors, chose him to be their chaplain, to whom he preached once every quarter, where, also, he sometimes dispensed the communion on a turn-up table, which was used at other times for different purposes. Laud, then Bishop of London, hearing of this, sent for Mr. Jackson, and expressed his dislike of it, saying, "I know not what you young divines think, but, for my own part, I know no other place of residence that God hath on earth but the high altar;" forgetting the doctrines of Scripture, and of the homily concerning the bodies and souls of true Christians as the special temples of God.—Palmer's Nonconformists' Memorial, vol. i., p. 121. His works are Annotations on parts of the Bible, in four volumes, quarto.—C.

‡ Calamy, vol. ii., p. 471; or Palmer's Nonconformists' Memorial, vol. ii., p. 173. Dr. Spurstow was chaplain to the regiment commanded by John Hampden, and attended that pious patriot on his deathbed.—Forster's Statesmen of the Commonwealth, vol. ii., p. 373.—C.

liament voted his defence scandalous, and ordered it to be burned by the hands of the common hangman. December 18, his lordship was banished the king's dominions for life by act of Parliament. He spent the remaining seven years of his life at Rouen in Normandy, among papists and Presbyterians, whom he would hardly suffer to live in his own country, and employed the chief of his time in writing the History of the Grand Rebellion,* which is in every one's hands.

The Earl of Clarendon was a Protestant of Laudean principles in Church and State; and at the head of all the penal laws against the Nonconformists to this time. Bishop Burnet says,† "He was a good chancellor,‡ but a little too rough; that he meddled too much in foreign affairs, which he never understood well; that he had too much levity in his wit, and did not observe the decorum of his post." Mr. Rapin adds,§ " that from him came all the blows aimed at the Nonconformists since the beginning of this reign. His immoderate passion against Presbyterianism was this great man's foible.‖ He gloried in his hatred of that people; and, perhaps, contributed more than any other person to that excess of animosity which subsists against them at this day among the followers of his maxims and principles." Mr. Echard says, " His removal was a great satisfaction to the Dissenters (directly contrary to Mr. Baxter); who observes a remarkable providence of God, that he who had dealt so cruelly by the Nonconformists should be banished by his own friends,

him by a jury of peers, by which means he might fall into the hands of the protesting lords, he resolved to avail himself of an opportunity of going over to Calais.—*Grey's Examination*, vol. iii., p. 355, 356.—ED.
* He also read over Livy and Tacitus, and almost all Tully's works; and " was a much greater, perhaps a happier man, alone and in exile," says Mr. Granger, " than Charles II. upon his throne."—*History of England*, vol. iii., p. 360, and vol. iv., p. 64, note.—ED.
† Page 33.
Dr. Grey gives Bishop Burnet's character of the lord-chancellor more at length, and perfixes another character of his lordship drawn by the pen of Mr. Carte, to " obviate (as he expresses himself) the ill-natured reflection cast upon him by Mr. Neal, because he adhered to the interest of his king and country, and would not give up the Church established into the hands of unreasonable fanatics."—ED.
‡ A domestic incident, related by Bishop Burnet, is supposed to have fixed and heightened the chancellor's zeal for the constitutional liberties of his country, in civil matters. On a visit which he paid to his father, a gentleman of Wiltshire, when he began to grow eminent in his profession, as they were walking one day in a field, his father observed to him, " that men of his profession did often stretch law and prerogative to the prejudice of the liberty of the subject, to recommend and advance themselves;" and charged him, that he should " never sacrifice the laws and liberties of his country to his own interest, or to the will of a prince." He repeated this twice, and immediately fell into a fit of apoplexy, of which he died in a few hours.—*Burnet's History of his Own Times*, vol. i., p. 231.
§ Vol. ii., p. 650, folio edition.
‖ Clarendon was banished in 1667, and observes himself, that his " affairs never prospered after the Oxford Act." No one should read his history without remembering that he was the arch-enemy of the Nonconformists, and that his works afford about as faithful a picture of those good men, as Bonner would have drawn of the Reformers.—C.

while the others, whom he had persecuted, were most moderate in his case, and many of them for him. It was a great ease that befell good men by his fall," says he, " for his way was to decoy men into conspiracies, or pretended plots, and upon those rumours innocent people were laid in prison, so that no man knew when he was safe; whereas, since his time, though the laws have been made more severe, yet men are more safe."* His lordship was undoubtedly a person of very considerable abilities, which have been sufficiently celebrated by his admirers, but I have not been able to discover any great or generous exploits for the service of the public; and how far his conduct with regard to the Nonconformists was consistent with humanity, religion, or honour, must be left with the reader.

CHAPTER VIII.

FROM THE BANISHMENT OF THE EARL OF CLARENDON TO THE KING'S DECLARATION OF INDULGENCE IN THE YEAR 1672.

1667.

UPON the fall of the Earl of Clarendon, the discourse of a toleration began to revive ; the king, in his speech to his Parliament, February 10, has this passage : " One thing more I hold myself obliged to recommend to you at this present, that is, that you would seriously think of some course to beget a better union and composure in the minds of my Protestant subjects' in matters of religion, whereby they may be induced not only to submit quietly to the government, but also cheerfully give their assistance to the support of it."† Sundry pamphlets were published upon this head ; and the Duke of Buckingham being now prime minister, the Nonconformists about London were connived at, and people went openly and boldly to their meetings.

But the House of Commons, who were yet influenced by the pernicious maxims of the late chancellor, petitioned the king to issue out his proclamation for enforcing the laws against conventicles, and for preserving the peace of the kingdom against unlawful assemblies of papists and Nonconformists. Accordingly, his majesty issued out his proclamation, that " upon consideration of the late petition, and upon information that divers persons in several parts of the realm (abusing his clemency, even while it was under consideration to find out a way for the better union of his Protestant subjects) have, of late, frequently and openly, in great numbers, and to the great disturbance of the peace, held unlawful assemblies and conventicles, his majesty declares that he will not suffer such notorious contempt of the laws to go unpunished, but requires, charges, and commands all officers to be circumspect and vigilant in their several jurisdictions, to enforce and put the laws in execution against unlawful conventicles, commanding them to take particular care to preserve the peace."

The sufferings of the Dissenters began to excite compassion in the minds of the people, insomuch that their numbers visibly increased,

* Baxter, part iii., p. 20, 21.
† Calamy's Abridgment, vol. i., p. 316.

partly through the indulgence of the court, and the want of churches since the fire in London, and partly through the poverty of the common people, who, having little to lose, ventured to go publicly to meetings in defiance of the laws. The indolence of the established clergy, and the diligence of the Nonconformist ministers, contributed very much to the increase of Nonconformists: Bishop Burnet says,[*] "The king was highly offended at the behaviour of most of the bishops; Archbishop Sheldon and Morley, who kept close by Lord Clarendon, the great patron of persecuting power, lost the king's favour; the former never recovered it, and the latter was sent from court into his diocess. When complaint was made of some disorders and conventicles, the king said *the clergy* were chiefly to blame; for if they had lived well,[†] and gone about their parishes, and taken pains to convince the Nonconformists, the nation might have been well settled; but they thought of nothing but to get good benefices, and keep a good table." In another conversation with the bishop, about the ill state of the Church,[‡] his majesty said, " If the clergy had done their parts, it had been easy to run down the Nonconformists, but they will do nothing," says the king, " and will have me do everything; and *most of them do worse than if they did nothing.* I have a very honest chaplain," says he, "to whom I have given a living in Suffolk, but he is a very great blockhead, and yet has brought all his parish to church; I cannot imagine what he could say to them, for he is a very silly fellow; but he has been about from house to house, and I suppose his nonsense has suited their nonsense; and in reward of his diligence I have given him a bishopric in Ireland." About this time Ralph Wallis, a cobbler of Gloucester, published an account of a great number of scandalous Conformist ministers, and enumerated their scandals, to the great displeasure of the clergy; and I fear, says Mr. Baxter,[§] to the temptation of many Nonconformists, who might be glad of anything to humble the Prelatists.

The learned Dr. Lazarus Seaman, the ejected minister of Allhallows, Bread-street, died this year, of whom we have given some account among the Cambridge professors; he was educated in Emanuel College, and by his indefatigable industry rose to high reputation in the learned world for his exact acquaintance with the Oriental languages; he was an able divine, an active member of the Assembly at Westminster, and was taken notice of by King Charles I. at the treaty of the Isle of Wight, for his singular abilities in the debates about church government.[‖] He was also master of Peter House, Cambridge, but lost all at the Restoration; he underwent strong pains with admirable patience, and at length died in peace in the month of September, 1667.[¶]

Mr. George Hughes, B.D., the ejected minister of Plymouth, born in Southwark,[*] and educated in Corpus Christi College, in Cambridge. He was called to a lecture in London; but was silenced for nonconformity by Archbishop Laud. After some time he went to Tavistock, and, last of all, settled at Plymouth, having institution and induction from Dr. Brownrigge, bishop of Exeter, in the year 1644. Here he continued till the year 1662, whence he was ejected a week before the Act of Uniformity took place. He was afterward imprisoned in St. Nicholas Island, where he contracted an incurable scurvy and dropsy, which at length put an end to his life. He was well read in the fathers, an acute disputant, a most faithful pastor to a large flock under his care, and a most holy, pious, and exemplary Christian. He had the greatest interest and influence of any minister in the west country, and refused a rich bishopric at the Restoration. He was both charitable and hospitable when it was in his power, and died at length in most heavenly manner, in the month of July, 1667, and in the sixty-fourth year of his age.[†] The Reverend Mr. John Howe, his son-in-law, composed a Latin epitaph for him, which is inscribed on his tomb.[‡]

The kingdom was at this time full of factions and discontents, arising from the late calamities of fire and plague, as well as the burden of the Dutch war; trade was, at a stand, and great numbers of his majesty's subjects were both dispirited and impoverished by the penal laws; but that which struck all considerate men with a panic, was the danger of the Protestant interest, and the liberties of Europe, from the formidable progress of the French armies, which this very summer overrun the Spanish Flanders, and took the strong towns of Charleroy, Bergues, Ath, Douay, Tournay, Audenard, Lisle, Courtray, Furnes, &c., which, with their dependances, were yielded in full sovereignty to France by the treaty of Aix-la-Chapelle. The English court seemed unconcerned at the French conquests, till they were awakened by the clamours of the whole nation; upon this, Sir William Temple was sent into Holland, who in a few weeks concluded a triple alliance between England, Holland, and Sweden, which strengthened the Protestant interest while it subsisted; but the French mistresses and money could dissolve the strongest bonds.

In this critical situation of affairs abroad, some attempts were made to quiet the minds of his majesty's Protestant subjects at home, for men began to think it high time for Protestants to put a stop to the pulling down their neighbours' houses, when the common enemy was threatening the destruction of them all; therefore, Lord-keeper Bridgman, Lord-chief-justice Hales, Bishop Wilkins, Reynolds, Dr. Burton, Tillotson, Stillingfleet, and others, set on foot a comprehension of such as could be brought into the Church by some abatements,

---

* Vol. i., p. 371, 379.

† The very charge of the Nonconformists is here granted and confessed!—C.

‡ Page 380.　　§ Life, part iii., p. 23.

‖ Calamy, vol. ii., p. 17; and Palmer's Nonconformists' Memorial, vol. ii., p. 76.

¶ He left a very valuable library, which yielded £700, and was the first sold by auction in England.—Ed. The catalogue of this library is preserved in the Library and Museum of the Baptist College, Bristol, England.—C.

* In 1603, when his mother, who had never had a child before, though she was now married to her fourth husband, was fifty-two years of age. She lived to her ninety-sixth year.—Ed.

† The slanders of Wood against this excellent minister are amply refuted by Dr. Calamy (*Account*, p. 228-231).—C.

‡ Calamy, vol. ii., p. 222; or Palmer's Nonconformists' Memorial, vol. i., p. 387.

and a toleration for the rest., But the project was blasted by the court bishops, and Lord Clarendon's friends, who took the alarm, and raised a mighty outcry of the danger of the Church.* Nobody (say they) knows where the demands of the Presbyterians will end ; the cause of the hierarchy will be given up, if any of those points are yielded which have been so much contested ; besides, it is unworthy of the Church to court or even treat with her enemies; when there is so little reason to apprehend that we should gain any considerable numbers thereby.. But to this it was replied, that the prodigious increase of popery and infidelity was a loud call of Providence, to attempt everything that could be done without sin for healing our divisions. That though the Nonconformists could not legally meet together to bring in their concessions in the name of the body, it was well enough known what they scrupled, and what would bring most of them into the Church. That a compliance in some lesser matters of indifference would be no reproach, but an honour to the Church, how superior soever she might be in argument or power.†

The proposals were drawn up by Bishop Wilkins and Dr. Burton, and communicated by the lord-keeper to Dr. Bates, Manton, and Baxter, and by them to their brethren, under the following particulars :

1. That such ministers who in the late times had been ordained only by presbyters, should have the imposition of the hands of a bishop, with this form of words : "Take thou authority to preach the Word of God, and administer the sacraments in any congregation of the Church of England, when thou shalt be lawfully appointed thereunto."

2. That instead of all former subscriptions, after the oaths of allegiance and supremacy, they subscribe the following declaration : I, A. B., do hereby profess and declare that I approve the doctrine, worship, and government established in the Church of England, as containing all things necessary to salvation ; and that I will not endeavour, by myself or any other, directly or indirectly, to bring in any doctrine contrary to that which is so established. And I do hereby promise that I will continue in the communion of the Church of England, and will not do anything to disturb the peace thereof.

3. That the gesture of kneeling at the sacrament, the cross in baptism, and bowing at the name of Jesus, be left indifferent, or taken away.

4. That if the liturgy and canons be altered in favour of Dissenters, then every preacher, upon his institution, shall declare his assent to the lawfulness of the use of it, and promise that it shall be constantly used at the time and place accustomed.

The alterations proposed to be made in the liturgy were these :

To read the Psalms in the new translation.

To appoint lessons out of the canonical Scripture instead of the Apocrypha.

Not to enjoin godfathers and godmothers, when either of the parents are present in baptism. To omit that expression in the prayer, " By spiritual regeneration." To change the question, " Wilt thou be baptized?" into, " Wilt thou have this child baptized ?" To omit those words in the thanksgiving, " To regenerate this infant by the Holy Spirit, and to receive him for thy child by adoption." And the first rubric after baptism, " It is certain by God's Word," &c. In the exhortation after baptism, instead of, " Regenerate and grafted into the body," to say, " Received into the Church of Christ." No part of the office of baptism to be repeated in public when the child has been lawfully baptized in private.

To omit this passage in the office of confirmation : " After the example of thy holy apostles, and to certify them by this sign of thy favour and gracious goodness towards them." And instead of, " Vouchsafe to regenerate," read, " Vouchsafe to receive into thy Church by baptism."

To omit the expressions in matrimony, " With my body I thee worship ;" and that in the Collect, " Thou hast consecrated," &c.

In the visitation of the sick, ministers to be allowed to make use of such prayers as they judge expedient.*

In the burial of the dead, instead of, " Forasmuch as it has pleased Almighty God, of his great mercy, to take unto himself," &c., read, " Forasmuch as it hath pleased Almighty God to take out of this world the soul," &c. Instead of, " In sure and certain hope," to read, " In a full assurance of the resurrection by our Lord Jesus Christ." To omit the following words : " We give thee hearty thanks, for that it has pleased thee to deliver this our brother out of the miseries of this sinful world ;" and these other, " As our hope is this our brother doth."

In the communion service, to change, " That our sinful bodies may be made clean by his body," into, " Our sinful souls and bodies may be cleansed by his precious body and blood."

The commination not to be enjoined.

The liturgy to be abbreviated, especially as to the morning service, by omitting all the responsal prayers, from " O Lord, open thou," &c., to the litany ; and the litany, and all the prayers, from, " Son of God, we beseech thee," &c., to, " We humbly beseech thee, O Father."

The Lord's Prayer not to be enjoined more than once, viz., after the absolution, except after the minister's prayer before sermon.

The Gloria Patri to be used but once, after reading the Psalms.

The Venite exultemus to be omitted, unless it be thought fit to put any or all of the first seven among the sentences at the beginning.

The communion service to be omitted when there are no communion days, except the Ten Commandments, which may be read after the Creed ; and enjoining the prayer, " Lord, have mercy upon us, and incline our hearts to keep these laws," only once, at the end.

The Collects, Epistles, and Gospels to be omitted; except on particular holydays.

The prayers for the Parliament to be inserted immediately after the prayer for the royal family, in this or the like form : " That it may please thee to direct and prosper all the consultations of the high court of Parliament, now advantage of thy glory, the good of the Church, the safety, honour, and welfare of our sovereign and his kingdoms."

*. Burnet, vol. i., p. 380, &c.
† Baxter's Life, part iii., p. 25.

* Baxter's Life, p. 34.

To omit the two hymns in the consecration of bishops and ordination of priests. In the catechism, after the first question, "What is thy name?" it may follow, "When was this name given thee?" After that, "What was promised for you in baptism?" Answer, "Three things were promised for me." In the question before the commandments, it may be altered thus: "You said it was promised for you." To the fourteenth question, "How many sacraments hath Christ ordained?" the answer may be, "Two only, baptism and the Lord's Supper."

Mr. Baxter proposed, farther, that the subscription might be only to the doctrinal articles of the Church. That the power of bishops, and their courts, to suspend and silence men, might be limited. That the baptismal covenant might be explicitly owned by all who come to the sacrament. But it was replied, that more than what was above mentioned would not pass with the Parliament.

The proposals for a toleration were communicated by Mr. Baxter to the Presbyterians, to the Independents by Dr. Owen, and were to the following effect :

1. That such Protestants who could not accept of the proposals for a comprehension, might have liberty for the exercise of their religion in public, and to build or to procure places for their public worship at their own charges, either within or near towns, as shall be thought most expedient.

2. That the names of all such persons who are to have this liberty to be registered, together with the congregations to which they belong, and the names of their teachers.

3. That every one admitted to this liberty be disabled from bearing any public office, but shall fine for offices of burden.

4. Upon showing a certificate of being listed among those that are indulged, they shall be freed from such legal penalties as are to be inflicted on those who do not frequent their parish churches.

5. Such persons so indulged shall not, for their meeting in conventicles, be punished by confiscation of estates.

6. Provided they pay all public duties to the parish where they inhabit, under penalty of

7. This indulgence to continue three years.*

According to these heads of agreement, a bill was prepared for the Parliament by Lord-chief-justice Hales ; but Bishop Wilkins, an honest and opened-hearted man, having disclosed the affair to Bishop Ward, in hopes of his assistance, alarmed the bishops, who, instead of promoting the design, concerted measures to defeat it ; for as soon as the Parliament met, notice was taken that there were rumours without doors of an act to be offered for comprehension and indulgence, upon which a vote was passed, that no man should bring such an act into the House. And, to crush the Nonconformists more effectually, Archbishop Sheldon wrote a circular letter to the bishops of his province, dated June 8, to send him a particular account of the conventicles in their several dioceses, and of the numbers that frequented them ; and whether they thought they might

be easily suppressed by the civil magistrate.* When he was provided with this information, he went to the king, and obtained a proclamation to put the laws in execution against the Nonconformists, and particularly against the preachers, according to the statute of 17th King Charles II., which forbids their inhabiting corporations.

Thus the persecution was renewed ; and the Parliament, still bent on severities, appointed a committee to inquire into the behaviour of the Nonconformists, who reported to the House that divers conventicles, and other seditious meetings, were held in their very neighbourhood, in defiance of the laws, and to the danger of the peace of the kingdom.† General Monk, who was near his end, and sunk almost into contempt, was employed to disperse them, and received the thanks of the House for his zeal in that important service, wherein he was sure to meet with no opposition. They also returned his majesty thanks for his proclamation for suppressing conventicles, desiring him to take the same care for the future. By this means the private meetings of the Dissenters, which had been held by connivance, were broken up again. Mr. Baxter was committed to Clerkenwell prison for preaching to his neighbours in his own house at Acton, and for refusing the Oxford oath ; but upon demanding a habeas corpus, his mittimus was declared invalid for want of naming the witnesses.‡ The justices would have mended their mittimus, and sent him to Newgate, but Mr. Baxter, being released, wisely kept out of the way. Mr. Taverner, of Uxbridge, was sentenced to Newgate for teaching a few children at Brentford. Mr. Button, late university orator, was sent to prison for teaching two knights' sons in his own house ; and multitudes in many counties had the like usage, suffering imprisonment for six months.§

But this was contrary to the king's inclinations, who was only for playing the Dissenters against the Parliament for a sum of money ; when the House, therefore, was up, his majesty ordered some of the Nonconformists to be told that he was desirous to make them easy, and that if they would petition for relief, they should be favourably heard.‖ Sir J. Barber, secretary of state, acquainted Dr. Manton with the king's intention, upon which an address was drawn up and presented to his majesty at the Earl of Arlington's lodgings by Dr. Jacomb, Manton, and Bates ; the king received them jealously, and promised to do his utmost to get them comprehended within the Establishment. He wished there had been no bars at all, but that he was forced to comply for peace' sake, and that he would endeavour to remove them, though it was a work of difficulty. He complained of the umbrage that their numerous assemblies gave to clamorous people, and advised them to use their liberty with more discretion hereafter. When the ministers promised obedience, and assured his majesty of their steady loyalty, and constant prayers for the prosperity of his person and government, he dismissed them with a smile, and told them that he was against persecution, and hoped ere long to be

---

* Baxter's Life part iii., p. 25.

* Burnet, vol. i., p. 382.   † Ibid. vol. i., p. 139.
‡ Baxter's Life, part iii., p. 49.   § Ibid., p. 36.
‖ Ibid. part iii., p. 37, 87.

able to stand upon his own legs.' But his majesty's promises were always to be bought off by a sum of money to support his pleasures.

The controversy of the reasonableness of toleration was now warmly debated without doors; many ill-natured books were written to expose the doctrine of the Presbyterians, as leading to Antinomianism and licentiousness of manners.* Others exposed their characters and manner of preaching. Among these must be reckoned the Friendly Debate, which, though written by a good man, says Bishop Burnet,† had an ill effect in sharpening people's spirits too much against the Dissenters: the author was Dr. Simon Patrick, afterward Bishop of Ely, but now in the heat of his youth, who, by aggravating some weak and unguarded expressions, endeavoured to expose the whole body of Nonconformist ministers to contempt. But I must do this prelate so much justice as to inform the reader, that in his advanced age he expressed his dissatisfaction with this part of his conduct; and, in a debate in the House of Lords about the Occasional Bill, declared, "he had been known to write against the Dissenters with some warmth in his younger years, but that he had lived long enough to see reason to alter his opinion of that people, and that way of writing." A rare instance of ingenuity and candour! We shall have occasion to mention Sir Roger l'Estrange hereafter.

But one of the most virulent writers of his time, under the form of a clergyman, was Samuel Parker, afterward Bishop of Oxford, a man of considerable learning and great smartness, but of no judgment, and as little virtue; and as to religion, says Bishop Burnet,‡ rather impious than otherwise.§ At length, Andrew Marvel, the liveliest wit of the age, attacked him in a burlesque strain, and with so peculiar and entertaining an address, that from the king down to the tradesman, his books were read with the highest pleasure. He had all the men of wit on his side, and not only humbled Parker more than the serious and grave writings of Dr. Owen, but silenced the whole party; one of whom concludes his letter to Mr. Marvel with these words: "If thou darest to print or publish any lie or libel against Dr. Parker, by the Eternal God I will cut thy throat." Subscribed J. G.

All sober men were of opinion that it was ungenerous and cruel to treat a number of peaceable men, whom the laws had put almost out of their protection, in so ludicrous a manner.‖ Religion itself suffered by it. I remember, says Lord-chief-justice Hales, that when Ben Jonson, in his play of the Alchymist, introduced Anartus in derision of the Puritans, with many of their phrases taken out of Scripture, in order to render that people ridiculous, the play was detested and abhorred, because it seemed to reproach religion itself; but now, when the Presbyterians were brought upon the stage in their peculiar habits, and with their distinguishing phrases of Scripture, exposed to the laughter of spectators, it met with approbation and applause.

But such was the complexion of the court, that they bid defiance to virtue, and even to decency, giving countenance to all manner of licentiousness. The play-houses were become nests of prostitution, says Burnet,* and the stage was defiled beyond example; the king, queen, and courtiers went about in masks, and came into citizens' houses unknown, where they danced with a great deal of wild frolic, and committed indecencies not to be mentioned. They were carried about in hackney-chairs, and none could distinguish them except those who were in the secret. Once the queen's chairman, not knowing who she was, left her to come home in a hackney-coach, some say in a cart.† Buckingham, who gloried in his debaucheries, and Wilmot, earl of Rochester, the greatest wit and libertine of his age, were the principal favourites. To support these extravagances, the House of Commons supplied the king with what money he wanted, and were themselves so mercenary, that the purchase of every man's vote was known; for as a man rose in credit in the House, he advanced his price, and expected to be treated accordingly.

The university was no less corrupt; there was a general licentiousness of manners among the students: the sermons of the younger divines were filled with encomiums upon the Church, and satires against the Nonconformists; the evangelical doctrines of repentance, faith, charity, and practical religion were unfashionable. The speeches and panegyrics pronounced by the orators and terræ filii, on public occasions, were scurrilous, and little less than blasphemous; as appears by the letter in the margin from Mr. Wallis to the Honourable Robert Boyle, Esq.,‡ of the proceed-

---

* Burnet, p. 267, 386.   Rapin, p. 652.
† A sad picture of Charles's court, and the general morals of the courtiers, is furnished by Jesse, in his Court of the Stuarts. See vol. iii.—C.
‡ A Letter from Mr. John Wallis to the Honourable Robert Boyle, Esq., dated from Oxford, July 17, 1669.

SIR—After my humble thanks for the honour of yours of July 3, I thought it not unfit to give you some account of our late proceedings here. Friday, July 9, was the dedication of our new theatre. In the morning was held a convocation in it, for enter-ing upon the possession of it; wherein was read, first, the archbishop's instrument of donation (sealed with his archiepiscopal seal) of the theatre, with all its furniture, to the end that St. Mary's Church may not be farther profaned by holding the act in it. Next, a letter of his, declaring his intention to lay out £2000 for a purchase to endow it. Then a letter of thanks to be sent from the university to him, where-in he is acknowledged to be both our creator and redeemer, for having not only built a theatre for the act, but, which is more, delivered the Blessed Virgin from being so profaned for the future: he doth, as the words of the letter are, "non tantum condere, hoc est creare, sed etiam redimere." These words, I confess, stopped my mouth from giving a placet to that letter when it was put to the vote. I have since desired Mr. Vice-chancellor to consider whether they were not liable to a just exception. He did at first excuse it; but, upon farther thoughts, I suppose he will think fit to alter them, before the letter be sent and registered. After the voting of this letter, Dr. South, as university orator, made a long oration; the first part of which consisted of satirical invectives against Cromwell, fanatics, the Royal Society, and new philosophy. The next, of encomiastics, in

---

* Baxter's Life, part iii., p. 39.
† Vol. i., p. 382.   ‡ Page 582.
§ This was no hinderance to his imparting a holy apostolical succession!—C.   ‖ Rapin, p. 406.

ings at the opening of Archbishop Sheldon's theatre, which is copied verbatim from the original under his own hand. About this time died the Reverend Mr. Matthew Newcomen, M.A., the ejected minister of Dedham, in Essex; he was educated in St. John's College, Cambridge, and succeeded the famous Mr. John Rogers. He was a most accomplished scholar and Christian, a member of the Assembly of Divines, and, together with Dr. Arrowsmith and Tuckney, drew up their catechism.* He was one of the commissioners of the Savoy, and had many offers of preferment in the late times, but would not desert his church at Dedham, till he was displaced by the Act of Uniformity; after which he retired to Holland, and became pastor of the English

praise of the archbishop, the theatre, the vice-chancellor, the architect, and the painter. The last, of execrations, against fanatics, conventicles, comprehension, and new philosophy; damning them, *ad inferos ad gehennam.* The oration being ended, some honorary degrees were conferred, and the convocation dissolved. The afternoon was spent in panegyric orations, and reciting of poems in several sorts of verse, composed in praise of the archbishop, the theatre, &c., and crying down fanatics. The whole action began and ended with a noise of trumpets; and twice was interposed variety of music, vocal and instrumental, purposely composed for this occasion. On Saturday and Monday, those exercises appertaining to the act and Vespers, which were wont to be performed in St. Mary's Church, were had in the theatre; in which, besides the number of proceeding doctors (nine in divinity, four in law, five in physic, and one in music), there was little extraordinary; but only that the *terræ filii* for both days were abominably scurrilous; and so suffered to proceed without the least check or interruption from vice-chancellor, pro-vice-chancellors, proctors, curators, or any of those who were to govern the exercises; which gave so general offence to all honest spectators, that I believe the university hath thereby lost more reputation than they have gained by all the rest; all or most of the heads of houses, and eminent persons in the university, with their relations, being represented as a company of whoremasters, whores, and dunces. And, among the rest, the excellent lady, which your letter mentions, was, in the broadest language, represented as guilty of those crimes, of which (if there were occasion) you might not stick to be her compurgator; and (if it had been so) she might (yet) have been called whore in much more civil language: During this solemnity (and for some days before and since) have been constantly acted (by the vice-chancellor's allowance) two stage-plays in a day (by those of the Duke of York's house) at a theatre erected for that purpose at the town-hall; which (for aught I hear) was much the more innocent theatre of the two. It hath been here a common fame for divers weeks (before, at, and since the act) that the vice-chancellor had given £300 bond (some say £500 bond) to the *terræ filii,* to save them harmless, whatever they should say, provided it were neither blasphemy nor treason. But this I take to be a slander. A less encouragement would serve the turn with such persons. Since the act (to satisfy the common clamour) the vice-chancellor hath imprisoned both of them; and it is said he means to expel them.

I am, sir, your honour's very humble and affectionate servant, JOHN WALLIS.

* I have by me a copy of Mr. Neal's History, which was formerly the property of the Rev. John Waldron, a dissenting minister in Exeter, who has written in the margin, here, this note: "I have been assured by Mr. Edward Parr, an ejected minister, who lived with Dr. Gouge, that he drew up the catechism. J. W."—ED.

VOL. II.—L L

church at Leyden, where he died about this time, universally lamented by the professors for his humble and pleasant conversation, as well as his universal learning and piety.* Mr. Joseph Allein, the ejected minister† of Taunton, and author of the Call to the Unconverted, was born at Devizes, in Wiltshire, and educated in Lincoln College, Oxon.. He was public preacher in the church of Taunton about seven years, and was universally beloved for his great piety and devotion. After his ejectment, he preached as he had opportunity six or seven times a week. May 26, 1663, he was committed to Ilchester jail for singing psalms in his own house, and preaching to his family, others being present; here he continued a year, but upon his enlargement he returned again to his work, which he followed with unwearied diligence. July 10, 1665, he was committed a second time to jail, with several other ministers, and forty private persons; where he contracted such distempers and weaknesses as brought him to his grave before he was thirty-six years of age.‡ He was an awakening, lively preacher, zealous and successful in his Master's work, and withal of a peaceable and quiet spirit. He died in the year 1668 or 1669.§

The tide in the House of Commons still ran very strong on the side of persecution, as appears by two extraordinary clauses added to the Conventicle Act, which, having expired some time since, was now revived by the Parliament which met October 19. The court went into it with a view of reducing the Presbyterians to the necessity of petitioning for a general toleration. "If we would have opened the door to let in popery," says Mr. Baxter,‖ "that their toleration might have been charged upon us, as done for our sakes, and by our procurement, we might in all likelihood have had our part in

* Calamy, vol. ii., p. 594. Palmer's Nonconformists' Memorial, vol. i., p. 503. Mr. Newcomen was the author of Irenicum, a work which received great commendation. He was eminent for his gift in prayer. Mr. Fairfax preached his funeral sermon, and entitled it "The Dead Saint Speaking."—C.
† To speak with accuracy, Mr. Allein was only assistant to Mr. George Newton, the minister of Taunton.—Dr. Grey.—ED.
‡ Calamy, vol. ii., p. 574. Palmer, vol. ii., p. 377.
§ Mr. Allein was so covetous of time that he could scarcely spare any for sleep, so neither for food. During the time of his health, he rose constantly at about four o'clock. He would be much troubled if he heard any smiths, shoemakers, &c., at work in their trades before he was in his duties with God, saying, "Oh! how the noise shames me. Doth not my Master deserve more than theirs?" He would often say, "Give me that Christian that accounts his time more precious than gold." When he had left the University and was married, an intimate friend of his, who had thoughts of changing his condition, wrote to him for the inconveniences of marriage, to whom he merrily returned this answer: "Thou wouldst know the inconveniences of a wife, and I will tell thee some of them: whereas thou now risest constantly at about four o'clock in the morning, a wife will keep thee till about six; whereas thou usest to study about fourteen hours a day, she will bring thee to eight or nine; and whereas thou art wont to forbear one meal a day at least for thy studies, she will bring thee to thy meat; and if these be not mischiefs enow to affright thee from marriage, I know not what will."—Clark's Lives, folio, 1673, p. 138, 157.—C.
‖ Part iii., p. 36.

HISTORY OF THE PURITANS.

it; but I never shall be one of them who, by any new pressures, shall consent to petition for the papists' liberty; no craft of Jesuits or prelates shall make me believe that it is necessary for the Nonconformists to take this odium upon themselves."* The court bishops were for the bill, but the moderate clergy were against it. Bishop Wilkins spoke against it in the House; and, when the king desired him in private to be quiet, he replied that he thought it an ill thing both in conscience and policy; therefore, as he was an Englishman and a bishop, he was bound to oppose it; and since, by the laws and Constitution of England, and by his majesty's favour, he had a right to debate and vote, he was neither afraid nor ashamed to own his opinion in that matter. However, the bill passed both houses, and received the royal assent April 11, 1670.† It was to the following effect: "That if any persons upward of sixteen years shall be present at any assembly, conventicle, or meeting, under colour or pretence of any exercise of religion, in any other manner than according to the liturgy and practice of the Church of England, where there are five persons or more present, besides those of the said household, in such cases the offender shall pay five shillings for the first offence, and ten shillings for the second. And the preachers or teachers in any such meetings shall forfeit twenty pounds for the first, and forty for the second offence. And lastly, those who knowingly suffer any such conventicles in their houses, barns, yards, &c., shall forfeit twenty pounds. Any justice of peace, on the oath of two witnesses, or any other sufficient proof, may record the offence under his hand and seal, which record shall be taken in law for a full and perfect conviction, and shall be certified at the next quarter sessions. The fines above mentioned may be levied by distress and sale of the offender's goods and chattels; and, in case of the poverty of such offender, upon the goods and chattels of any other person or persons, that shall be convicted of having been present at the said conventicle, at the discretion of the justice of peace, so as the sum to be levied on any one person, in case of the poverty of others, do not amount to above ten pounds for any one meeting: the constables, headboroughs, &c., are to levy the same by warrant from the justice, and to be divided, one third for the use of the king, another third for the poor, and the other third to the informer or his assistants, regard being had to their diligence and industry in discovering, dispersing, and punishing the said conventicles. The fines upon ministers for preaching are to be levied also by distress; and, in case of poverty, upon the goods and chattels of any other present; and the like upon the house where the conventicle is held, and the money to be divided as above.

"And it is farther enacted, that the justice or justices of peace, constables, headboroughs, &c., may, by warrant, with what aid, force, and assistance they shall think necessary, break open and enter into any house or place where they shall be informed of the conventicle, and take the persons into custody. And the lieutenants, or other commissioned officers of the militia, may get together such force and assistance as

they think necessary, to dissolve, dissipate, and disperse such unlawful meetings, and take the persons into custody." Then follow two extraordinary clauses: "That if any justice of peace refuse to do his duty in the execution of this act, he shall forfeit five pounds.

"And be it farther enacted, that all clauses in this act shall be construed most largely and beneficially for the suppressing conventicles, and for the justification and encouragement of all persons to be employed in the execution thereof. No warrant or mittimus shall be made void, or reversed, for any default in the form; and if a person fly from one county or corporation to another, his goods and chattels shall be seizable wherever they are found. If the party offending be a wife cohabiting with her husband, the fine shall be levied on the goods and chattels of the husband, provided the prosecution be within three months."

The wit of man could hardly invent anything, short of capital punishment, more cruel and inhuman.* One would have thought a prince of so much clemency as Charles II., who had often declared against persecution, should not have consented to it, and that no Christian bishop should have concurred in the passing it. Men's houses are to be plundered, their persons imprisoned, their goods and chattels carried away, and sold to those who would bid for them. Encouragement is given to a vile set of informers, and others, to live upon the labour and industry of their conscientious neighbours.† Multitudes of these infamous wretches spent their profits in ill houses, and upon lewd women, and then went about the streets again to hunt for farther prey. The law is to be construed in their favour, and the power to be lodged in the hand of every individual justice of peace, who is to be fined £5 if he refuses his warrant. Upon this, many honest men, who would not be the instruments of such severities, quitted the bench. Mr. Echard, being ashamed to ascribe these cruelties to the influence of the bishop, says, "that this and all the penal laws made against the Dissenters were the acts of Parliament, and not of the Church, and were made more on a civil and political, than upon a moral or religious account; and always upon some fresh provocation in reality or appearance." This is the language by which the patrons of High-church cruelty endeavour to excuse themselves from the guilt of persecution; but it must fall somewhere; and that it may not fall too heavy upon the Church, it is artfully, and with great good manners, cast entirely upon the Legislature, and put upon the score of sedi-

---

* This iniquitous law, by the power with which it invested a single justice, destroyed the bulwark of English liberty, the trial by jury. It punished the innocent for the guilty, by subjecting the husband to a penalty for the conduct of the wife, and the goods of any person present to fines, which other offenders were incompetent to discharge. The mode of conviction was clandestine. Its natural tendency was to influence magistrates to partiality in judgment, and to reverse the scriptural qualification for magistracy to the encouragement of evildoers, and the punishment of those who do well; by the fines it imposed on justices and on officers, and by the sanction it gave to informers.—*Gough's History of the Quakers,* vol. ii., p. 298, 299.—Ed.

---

* Burnet, vol. i., p. 400.   † Rapin, p. 655.   † Burnet, p. 398.

HISTORY OF THE PURITANS. 267

tion, whereas it was well known the Dissenters behaved peaceably, and were very far from disturbing the State. Nor does the preamble to the act charge them with disloyalty, but only says, "That for the providing speedy remedies against the practice of seditious *sectaries*, and others, who, under pretence of tender consciences, have, or may at their.meetings contrive insurrections,* be it enacted," &c. ; as if it was possible to do this in the company of *women* and *servants*, who were always present in their assemblies. It is therefore evident that the act was levelled purely against *liberty of conscience*, and was so severely executed that, as Sir Harry Capel observes, there was hardly a conventicle to be heard of all over England. The two houses, says our Church historian,† were express for the execution of these laws ; the *bishops and clergy* were sincerely zealous in it, and the honest justices and magistrates, as he calls them, bore the more hard upon them, because they saw them so bold in despising and evading the justice of the nation.

Great numbers were prosecuted on this act, and many industrious families reduced to poverty. Many ministers were confined in jails and close prisons ; and warrants were issued out against them and their hearers, whereby great sums of money were levied. In the diocess of Salisbury the persecution was hottest, by the instigation of Bishop Ward ; many hundreds being pursued with great industry, and driven from their families and trades.‡ The act was executed with such severity in Starling's mayoralty, that many of the trading men in the city were removing, with their effects, to Holland, till the king put a stop to it.§ Informers were everywhere at work, and having crept into religious assemblies in disguise, levied great sums of money upon ministers and people. Soldiers broke into the houses of honest farmers, under pretence of searching for conventicles, and where ready money was wanting, they plundered their goods, drove away their cattle, and sold them for half price. Many were plundered of their household furniture ; the sick had their beds taken from under them, and themselves laid on the floor. Should I sum up all the particulars, and the accounts I have received, says Mr. Sewel,‖ it would make a volume of itself. These vile creatures were not only encouraged, but pushed on vehemently by their spiritual guides: for this purpose, Archbishop Sheldon sent another circular letter to all the

* "These words, as late experience has shown, were slyly omitted," says Dr. Grey, who adds, "Here he (Mr. Neal) injuriously lays the blame upon the bishops, as if the king and the two houses were wholly under their direction and influence ; and treats Mr. Archdeacon Echard not over-civilly for being of a contrary opinion." The first censure in this paragraph is not very civil in Dr. Grey ; nor does it appear well grounded, since Mr. Neal has inserted so much of the paragraph as charges the sectaries with having contrived insurrections. Nor does Mr. Neal lay the whole blame upon the bishops, for he says, "the two houses were for the execution of these laws ;" though it is true, indeed, he is not willing that the guilt should be cast entirely upon the Legislature ; for " *the bishops and clergy were sincerely zealous in this business of persecution.*"—ED.
† Page 286.
‡ Calamy's Abridgment, vol. i., p. 332.
§ Burnet, p. 398. ‖ Sewel, p 493.

bishops in his province, dated May 7, 1670, in which he directs all ecclesiastical judges and officers " to take notice of all Nonconformists, holders, frequenters, maintainers, and abettors of conventicles, especially of the preachers or teachers in them, and of the places wherein they are held ; ever keeping a more watchful eye over the cities and greater towns, from whence the mischief is for the most part derived, unto the lesser villages and hamlets. And wheresoever they find such wilful offenders, that then, with a hearty affection to the worship of God, the honour of the king and his laws, and the peace of the king and his laws, and the peace of the Church and kingdom, they do address themselves to the civil magistrate, justices, and others concerned, imploring their help and assistance for preventing and suppressing the same, according to the late act in that behalf made and set forth. And now, my lord, what the success will be we must leave to God Almighty ; yet, my lord, I have this confidence under God, that if we do our parts now at first seriously, by God's help, and the assistance of the civil power, considering the abundant care and provision the act contains for our advantage, we shall in a few months see so great an alteration in the distraction of these times, as that the seduced people, returning from their seditious and self-seeking teachers to the unity of the Church, and uniformity of God's worship, it will be to the glory of God, the welfare of the Church, the praise of his majesty and government, and the happiness of the whole kingdom."‖ Can this be the language of a Christian and Protestant bishop ; or is it not more like a father of the Inquisition, or the dragooning commission of Lewis XIV. when he revoked the Edict of Nantz?*

Copies of this letter were sent by the archdeacons to the officers of the several parishes within their jurisdictions, earnestly exhorting them to take especial care to perform whatsoever is therein required, and to give an account at the next visitation. Many of the bishops chose to lie behind the curtain, and throw off the odium from themselves to the civil magistrate ; but some of the more zealous could not forbear appearing in person, as Bishop Ward, already mentioned, and Bishop Gunning,† who often disturbed the meetings in person ; once finding the doors shut, he ordered the constable to break them open with a sledge ; another time he sat upon the bench at the quarter sessions, upon which the chairman desired his lordship to give the charge, which he refusing, received a very handsome rebuke ; it being hardly consistent with one that is an ambassador of the Prince of Peace to sit in judgment upon the conscien-

* Calamy's Abridg., vol. i., p. 328.
† Henshaw, the bishop of Peterborough, declared publicly in the church at Rowel, after he had commanded the officers to put this act in execution, "Against all fanatics it hath done its business, except the Quakers ; but when the Parliament sits again, a stronger law will be made, not only to take away their lands and goods, but also to sell them for bondslaves." On this, Mr. Gough properly asks, "Who can acquit the Church, so called, of their share in the persecution, when the *rulers* thereof were so intemperately warm and active in it, and still insatiate with all these severities, inhumanly planning more and greater?"—*History*, vol. ii., p. 303.—ED.

ces of his poor countrymen and neighbours, in order to plunder and tear them to pieces.* The bishop was so zealous in the cause, that he sunk his character by giving a public challenge to the Presbyterians, Independents, Anabaptists, and Quakers, and appointed three days for the disputation; on the first of which his lordship went into the pulpit in the church, where was a considerable congregation, and charged the former with sedition and rebellion out of their books, but would hear no reply.† When the day came to dispute with the Quakers, they summoned their friends, and when the bishop railed, they paid him in his own coin; and followed him to his very house; with repeated shouts, "The hireling flieth."

The Nonconformist ministers did what they could to keep themselves within the compass of the law; they preached frequently twice a day in large families, with only four strangers, and as many under the age of sixteen as would come; and at other times, in places where people might hear in several adjoining houses; but, after all, infinite mischiefs ensued, families were impoverished and divided; friendship between neighbours was interrupted; there was a general distrust and jealousy of each other; and sometimes, upon little quarrels, servants would betray their masters, and throw their affairs into distraction. Among others that suffered at this time was Dr. Manton, who was apprehended on a Lord's Day in the afternoon, just as he had done sermon; the door being opened to let a gentleman out, the justice and his attendants rushed in, and went up stairs; they staid till the doctor had ended his prayer, and then wrote down the names of the principal persons present, and took the doctor's promise to come to them at a house in the piazzas of Covent Garden, where they tendered him the Oxford oath, upon his refusal of which, he was committed prisoner to the Gate-house, where he continued till he was released by the indulgence. At another time his meeting-house in White Hart Yard was broken up; the place was fined £40 and the minister £20, which was paid by Lord Wharton, who was then present; they also took down the names of the hearers, for the benefit of the justices of peace and spiritual courts.

The behaviour of the Quakers was very extraordinary, and had something in it that looked like the spirit of martyrdom.‡ They met at the same place and hour as in times of liberty, and when the officers came to seize them, none of them would stir; they went all together to prison; they stayed there till they were dismissed, for they would not petition to be set at liberty, nor pay the fines set upon them, nor so much as the prison fees. When they were discharged, they went to their meeting-house again, as before; and when the doors were shut up by order, they assembled in great numbers in the street before the doors, saying, they would not be ashamed nor afraid to disown their meeting together in a peaceable manner to worship God; but, in imitation of the Prophet Daniel, they would do it more publicly, because they were forbid. Some called this obstinacy, others firmness, but by it they carried their

point, the government being weary of contending against so much perverseness.* On the 1st of September, 1670, two of their principal speakers, Wm. Penn and Wm. Mead, were tried at the Old Bailey for an unlawful and tumultuous assembly in the open street, wherein they spake or preached to the people, who were assembled in Gracechurch-street, to the number of three or four hundred, in contempt of the king's laws, and to the disturbance of the peace. The prisoners pleaded Not Guilty, but met with some of the severest usage that has been known in an English court of justice. They were fined forty marks apiece for coming into court with their hats on, though it was not done out of contempt, but from a principle of their religion. It appeared by the witnesses, that there was an assembly in Gracechurch-street, but there was neither riot, nor tumult, nor force of arms. Mr. Penn confessed they were so far from recanting, or declining to vindicate the assembling themselves to preach, pray, or worship the eternal, holy, just God, that they declared to all the world, they believed it to be their duty, and that all the powers on earth should not be able to divert them from it. When it was said they were not arraigned for worshipping God, but for breaking the law, William Penn affirmed he had broken no law, and challenged the recorder to tell him upon what law he was prosecuted. The recorder answered, upon the common law, but could not tell where that common law was to be found. Penn insisted upon his producing the law, but the court overruled him, and called him a troublesome fellow. Penn replied, "I design no affront to the court, but if you deny to acquaint me with the law you say I have broken, you deny me the right that is due to every Englishman, and evidence to the whole world that your designs are arbitrary." Upon which he was haled from the bar into the bail-dock. As he was going out he said to the jury, "If these fundamental laws which relate to liberty and property must not be indispensable maintained, who can say he has a right to the coat upon his back? Certainly, then, our liberties are openly to be invaded, our wives to be ravished, our children enslaved, and our estates led away in triumph, by every sturdy beggar and malicious informer, as their trophies."

William Mead being left alone at the bar, said, "You men of the jury, I am accused of meeting by force of arms, in a tumultuous manner. Time was when I had freedom to use a carnal weapon, and then I feared no man; but now I

---

* Calamy, vol. ii., p. 692.   † Ibid., vol. ii., p. 334.
‡ Burnet, p. 308.

* A respectable member of the society of Quakers has remarked, with propriety and force, on this language of Bishop Burnet, "that had he concluded with the word perseverance instead of perverseness, his description had been less objectionable, as being nearer the truth. The prejudice discovered by that dignified prelate against this people tarnished his reputation as a faithful historian and as a man; as a true son of the Church, it is not much to be wondered, when it is considered that they, rejecting its honours and its revenues, struck at the root of the hierarchy: while other Dissenters, in general, contending chiefly about rites and ceremonies, manifested little or no objection to that grand support, pecuniary emolument; as their practice in common, particularly during the interregnum, incontestably proved."
—A Letter to the Editor.—Ed.

fear the living God, and dare not make use thereof, nor hurt any man. I am a peaceable man, and therefore demand to know upon what law my indictment is founded; if the recorder will not tell what makes a riot, Coke will tell him that it is when three or more are met together to beat a man, or to enter forcibly into another man's lands to cut his grass or wood, or break down his pales." Upon this the recorder, having lost all patience, pulled off his hat, and said, I thank you, sir, for telling me what the law is. Mead replied, Thou mayest put on thy hat, I have no fee for thee now. The Mayor Starling told him he deserved to have his tongue cut out, and ordered him likewise to be carried to the bail-dock.

When the prisoners were gone, the recorder gave the jury their charge, upon which William Penn stood up, and with a loud voice said, " I appeal to the jury, and this great assembly, whether it be not contrary to the undoubted right of every Englishman to give the jury their charge in the absence of the prisoners?" The recorder answered, with a sneer, Ye are present; ye do hear, do ye not? Penn answered, "No thanks to the court; I have ten or twelve material points to offer in order to invalidate the indictment, but am not heard." The recorder said, " Pull him down ; pull the fellow down." Mead replied, these were barbarous and unjust proceedings; and then they were both thrust into the hole.

After the jury had withdrawn an hour and a half, the prisoners were brought to the bar to hear their verdict ; eight of them came down agreed, but four remained above, to whom they used many unworthy threats, and in particular to Mr. Bushel, whom they charged with being the cause of the disagreement. At length, after withdrawing a second time, they agreed to bring them in guilty of speaking in Gracechurch-street ; which the court would not accept for a verdict, but after many menaces told them they should be locked up without meat, drink, fire, or tobacco ; nay, they should starve, unless they brought in a proper verdict. William Penn being at the bar, said, " My jury ought not to be thus threatened. We were by force of arms kept out of our meeting-house, and met as near it as the soldiers would give us leave. We are a peaceable people, and cannot offer violence to any man." And looking upon the jury, he said, " You are Englishmen, mind your privilege, give not away your right." To which some of them answered, " Nor will we ever do it." Upon this they were shut up all night without victuals or fire, or so much as a chamber-pot, though desired. Next morning they brought in the same verdict ; upon which they were threatened the utmost resentments. The mayor said he would cut Bushel's throat as soon as he could. The recorder said he never knew the benefit of an inquisition till now ; and that the next sessions of Parliament, a law would be made, wherein those that would not conform should not have the benefits of the law * The court

having obliged the jury to withdraw again, they were kept without meat and drink till next morning, when they brought in the prisoners not guilty ; for which they were fined forty marks a man, and to be imprisoned till paid. The prisoners were also remanded to Newgate for their fines in not pulling off their hats.* The jury, after some time, were discharged by habeas corpus returnable in the Common Pleas, where their commitment was judged illegal. This was a noble stand for the liberty of the subject in very dangerous times, when neither law nor equity availed anything. The Conventicle Act was made to encourage prosecutions ; and a narrative was published next year, of the oppressions of many honest people in Devonshire, and other parts, by the informers and justices ; but the courts of justice outran the law itself.

Hitherto the king and Parliament had agreed pretty well by means of the large supplies of money the Parliament had given to support his majesty's pleasures ; but now having assurances of large remittances from France, his majesty resolved to govern by the prerogative, and stand upon his own legs.† His prime counsellors were Lord Clifford, Anthony Ashley Cooper, afterward Lord Shaftesbury, the Duke of Buckingham, Earl of Arlington, and Duke Lauderdale, who, from the initial letters of their names, were called the CABAL. Lord Clifford was an open papist, and the Earl of Arlington a concealed one. Buckingham was a debauchee, and reputed a downright Atheist ; he was a man of great wit and parts, and of sounder principles in the interests of humanity, says Mr. Baxter, than the rest of the court. Shaftesbury had a vast genius; but, according to Burnet, at best was a Deist ; he had great knowledge of men and things, but would often change sides as his interest directed. Lauderdale was a man of learning, and from an almost Republican was become a perfect tool of the prerogative, and would offer at the most desperate councils. He had scarcely any traces of religion remaining, though he called himself a Presbyterian, and had

---

* This speech of the recorder, it appears by a quotation from the "State Trials" in a late publication, was fuller and stronger than Mr. Neal's abridged form represents it. " Till now," said this advocate for arbitrary power, " I never understood the reason of the policy and prudence of the Spaniards in suffer-

ing the Inquisition among them, and certainly it will never be well with us till something like the Spanish Inquisition be in England."—*Stuart's Peace and Reform against War and Corruption*, p. 63, note; and *Gough's History of the Quakers*, vol. ii., p. 336—ED.

* The prisoners excepted to this fine, as being arbitrarily imposed, in violation of the great charter of England, which saith, " No man ought to be amerced but by the oath of good and lawful men of the vicinage." The name of the judge before whom the case of the jury was solemnly argued in the Court of Common Pleas, and by whom it was judged illegal, was Sir John Vaughan, then chief-justice : a name which deserves to be mentioned in this connexion with peculiar respect, and to be perpetuated by Englishmen with gratitude ; for this adjudication confirmed in the strongest manner the rights of juries, and secured them from the attack of arbitrary and unprincipled judges. Sir John Vaughan was a man of excellent parts, and not only versed in all the knowledge requisite to make a figure in his profession, but he was also a very considerable master of the politer kinds of learning. He was the intimate friend of the great Selden, and was buried in the Temple Church, as near as possible to his remains. He died in 1674. His son published his Reports, in which is the above case.—*Gough*, vol. ii., p. 336. *British Biography*, vol. vii., p. 130, 131 ; and *Granger's History*, vol. iii., p. 369.—ED.

† Echard, p. 864. Rapin, p. 655.

an aversion to King Charles I. to the last. By these five ministers of state the king and Duke of York drove on their designs of introducing popery and arbitrary power ; in order to which, a secret treaty was concluded with France ; the triple alliance was broken, and a new war declared with the Dutch to destroy their commonwealth, as will be seen presently. By this means the king had a plausible pretence to keep up a standing army, which might secure him in the exercise of an absolute authority over his subjects, to set aside the use of Parliaments, and settle the Roman Catholic religion in the three kingdoms. These were the maxims the court pursued throughout the remaining part of this reign.

In the beginning of this year died Dr. Anthony Tuckney,* born in September, 1599, and educated in Emanuel College, Cambridge. He was afterward Vicar of Boston in Lincolnshire, where he continued till he was called to sit in the Assembly of Divines at Westminster. In the year 1645 he was made master of his college, and in the year 1648, being chosen vice-chancellor, he removed to-Cambridge with his family. He was afterward master of St. John's and regius professor, which he held to the Restoration, when the king sent him a letter, desiring him to resign his professorship, which if he did, his majesty, in consideration of the great pains and diligence of the said doctor in the discharge of his duty, would oblige his successor to give him sufficient security in law; to pay him £100 a year during his natural life. Upon this notice the doctor immediately resigned, and had his annuity paid him by Dr. Gunning, who succeeded him. After the coming out of the Five-mile Act he shifted about in several counties, and at last died in Spittle-yard, London, February, 1669, in the seventy-first year of his age, leaving behind him the character of an eminently learned and pious man, an indefatigable student, a candid disputant, and an earnest promoter of truth and godliness.†

---

* To what is said concerning Dr. Tuckney by Mr. Neal, and before in the note to p. 255, vol. ii., it is proper to add two facts which are much to his honour. One is, that in his elections at St. John's, when the president, according to the language and spirit of the times, would call upon him to have regard to the godly, his answer was, "No one should have a greater regard to the truly godly than himself; but he was determined to choose none but scholars;" adding very wisely, "They may deceive me in their godliness ;. they cannot in their scholarship." The other fact is, that though he is said to have had a great hand in composing the Confession and Catechisms of the Assembly at Westminster, and in particular drew up the exposition of the commandments in the larger Catechism, yet he voted against subscribing or swearing to the Confession, &c., set out by authority. This conduct the more deserves notice and commendation, because the instances of a consistent adherence to the principles of religious liberty among those who were struggling for liberty were so few and rare in that age. In the year 1753, Dr. Samuel Salter, prebendary of Norwich, published a correspondence between Dr. Tuckney and Dr. Benjamin Whichcote, on several very interesting subjects. — See *Whichcote's Moral and Religious Aphorisms, Preface the second,* p. 15.—ED.

† Calamy, vol. ii., p. 77; or Palmer's. Nonconformists' Memorial, vol. i., p. 205. Many of the an-

About the same time died Mr. William Bridge, M.A., the ejected minister of Yarmouth ; he was student in Cambridge thirteen years, and fellow of Emanuel College. He afterward settled in Norwich, where he was silenced by Bishop Wren for nonconformity, 1637. He was afterward excommunicated ; and when the writ *de excommunicato capiendo* came out against him he withdrew to Holland, and became pastor to the English church at Rotterdam, where Mr. Jer. Burroughs was preacher. In 1642 he returned to England, and was one of the dissenting brethren in the Assembly of Divines. He was chosen after some time minister of Great Yarmouth, where he continued his labours till the Bartholomew Act ejected him with his brethren.* He was a good scholar, and had a well-furnished library,† was a hard student, and rose every morning, winter and summer, at four of the clock. He was also a good preacher, a candid and charitable man, and did much good by his ministry.‡ He died at Yarmouth, March 12, 1670, ætat. seventy.§

While the Protestant Dissenters were harassed in all parts of the kingdom, the Roman Catholics were at ease under the wing of the prerogative ; there were few or no processes against them, for they had the liberty of resorting to mass at the houses of foreign ambassadors, and other chapels, both in town and country : nor did the bishops complain of them in the House of Lords, by which means they began in a few years to rival the Protestants both in strength and numbers. The Commons represented the causes of this misfortune in an address to the king, together with the remedies, which, if the reader will carefully consider, he will easily discover the different usage of Protestant Nonconformists and popish recusants.‖

The causes of the increase of popery were, 1. The great number of Jesuits who were all over the kingdom. 2. The chapels in great towns for saying mass, besides ambassadors' houses, whither great numbers of his majesty's subjects resorted without control. 3. The fraternities or convents of priests and Jesuits at St. James's, and in several parts of the kingdom, besides their schools for the educating youth. 4. The public sale of popish catechisms, &c. 5. The general remissness of magistrates, and

---

swers in the larger Catechism are his, particularly on the commandments.—C.

* Calamy, vol. ii., p. 478. Palmer, vol. ii., p. 208.

† This library is spoken of by his personal friends as rich in the fathers and schoolmen.—C.

‡ In Peck's Desiderata Curiosa is a letter of William Bridge to Henry Scobel, Esq., clerk of the council, about augmenting the income of preachers, with the names of the Independent ministers of prime note in the county of Norfolk. This shows that he was a leading man among the Independents.—*Granger's History of England,* vol. iii., p. 44. Dr. Grey imputes to Mr. Bridge a republican spirit, because, in a sermon before the Commons, he said, "The king must not only command according to God's law, but man's laws ; and if he don't so command, resistance is not resistance of power, but of will. To say that such resistance must only be defensive, is nonsense ; for so a man may be ever resisting, and never resist."—*Grey,* vol. i., p. 187.—ED.

§ Two of his works, two volumes in 4to, were published in 1657, and he was author of more than thirty sermons.—C.   ‖ Rapin, vol. ii., p. 658.

other officers, in not convicting papists according to. law.   6. Suspected recusants enjoying offices by themselves or their deputies. 7. Presentations to livings by popish recusants, or by others as they direct.   8. Sending youth beyond sea under tutors, to be educated in the popish religion. 9. The few. exchequer processes that have been issued forth, though many have been certified thither.   10. The great insolence of papists in Ireland, where archbishops and bishops of the pope's creation appear publicly, mass being said openly in Dublin and other parts of the kingdom.

The remedies which the House proposed against these growing mischiefs were,

1. That a proclamation be issued out to banish all popish priests and Jesuits out of the realm, except such as attend the queen and foreign ambassadors. 2. That the king's subjects he forbid going to hear mass and other exercises of the Romish religion. 3. That no office or employment of public authority be put into the hands of popish recusants. 4. That all fraternities, convents, and popish schools be abolished, and the Jesuits, priests, friars, and schoolmasters, punished. 5. That his majesty require all the officers of the exchequer to issue out processes against popish recusants convict, certified thither. 6. That Plunket, the pretended primate of Ireland, and Talbot, archbishop of Dublin, be sent for into England, to answer such matters as should be objected against them.

The king promised to consider the address, but hoped they would allow him to distinguish between new converts, and those who had been bred up in the popish religion, and served him and his father in the late wars. After some time a proclamation was issued, in which his majesty declares that he had always adhered to the true religion established in this kingdom against all temptations whatsoever; and that he would employ his utmost care and zeal in its defence. But the magistrates, knowing his majesty's inclinations, took no care of the execution of it. Nay, the Duke of York, the king's brother, having lately lost his duchess, Lord Clarendon's daughter, who died a papist;* made a formal abjuration of the Protestant religion at this time before Father Simon, an English Jesuit, publicly declaring himself a Roman Catholic; the reason of which was, that the present queen having no children, the papists gave the duke to understand that they were capable to effect his majesty's divorce, and to set aside his succession, by providing him with

* This Dr. Grey is unwilling to admit, though he owns that Monsieur Mainborough published, in French, her declaration for renouncing the Protestant religion, and he quotes largely from Dr. Richard Watson, a celebrated English divine, who published an answer to it. The amount of his defence of the duchess, as it appears in this quotation, is, that when, on account of her illness, the worship of her oratory had been deserted, it was renewed again by her order, and the doors of her chamber, which were adjoining to it, were opened that she might hear the prayers; and that the Bishop of Oxford was sent for to administer the sacrament to her. In opposition to this, which rises to presumptive evidence only, and in support of Mr. Neal, it may be added, that Sir John Reresby says that she died with her last breath declaring herself a papist."—*Memoirs*, p. 19.—ED.

another queen, which they would certainly attempt unless he would make an open profession of the Roman Catholic religion, which he did accordingly.

The House of Commons was very lavish of the nation's money this session, for though there was no danger of an invasion from abroad, they voted the king £2,500,000, with which his majesty maintained a standing army, and called the Parliament no more together for almost two years. After the houses were up, the Cabal began to prosecute their scheme of making the king absolute; in order to which, besides the £2,500,000 granted by Parliament, they received from France the sum of £700,000 in two years, which not being sufficient to embark in a war with the Dutch, the king declared in council, by the advice of Clifford, that he was resolved to shut up the exchequer, wherein the bankers of London (who had furnished the king with money on all occasions at great interest) had lodged vast sums of other people's cash deposited in their hands. By this means the bankers were obliged to make a stop, which interrupted the course of trade, and raised a great clamour over the whole kingdom. The king endeavoured to soften the bankers, by telling them it should be only for a year, and that he would pay the arrears out of the next subsidies of Parliament; but he was worse than his word; so that great numbers of families and orphans were reduced to beggary, while the king gained about £1,400,000.

A second advance of the Cabal towards arbitrary power was to destroy the Dutch commonwealth; for this purpose the triple alliance was to be broken, and pretences to be found out for quarrelling with that trading people. The Earl of Shaftesbury used this expression in his speech to the Parliament for justifying the war: *Delenda est Carthago;* that is, "The Dutch commonwealth must be destroyed:" but an occasion was wanting to justify it to the world. There had been a few scurrilous prints and medals struck in Holland, reflecting on the king's amours, below the notice of the English court, which the Dutch, however, caused to be destroyed. Complaints were also revived of the insolence of the Dutch in the East Indies, and of the neglect of striking the flag in the narrow seas to the king's yacht, passing by the Dutch fleet. The Cabal managed these complaints like men who were afraid of receiving satisfaction, or of giving the adversary any umbrage to prepare for the storm. The Dutch, therefore, relying on the faith of treaties, pursued their traffic without fear; but when their rich Smyrna fleet of merchantmen, consisting of seventy-two sail under convoy of six men-of-war, passed by the Isle of Wight, the English fleet fell upon them and took several of their ships, without any previous declaration of war; a breach of faith, says Burnet, which Mohammedans and pirates would have been ashamed of.*

Two days after the attempt upon the Smyrna fleet, the Cabal made the third advance towards popery and absolute power, by advising the king to suspend the penal laws against all sorts of Nonconformists. It was now resolved to set

* Vol. ii., p. 16, 12mo.

the Dissenters against the Church, and to offer them the protection of the crown to make way for a general toleration. Lord Shaftesbury first proposed it in council, which the majority readily complied with, provided the Roman Catholics might be included; but when the declaration was prepared, the lord-keeper, Bridgman, refused to put the seal to it, as judging it contrary to law, for which he was dismissed, and the seals given to the Earl of Shaftesbury, who maintained that the indulgence was for the service of the Church of England.* "As for the Church," says his lordship, "I conceive the declaration is extremely for their interest; for the narrow bottom they have placed themselves upon, and the measures they have proceeded by, are contrary to the properties and liberties of the nation, must needs in a short time prove fatal to them;—whereas, this leads them into another way, to live peaceably with the Dissenting and different Protestants, both at home and abroad;" which was true if both had not been undermined by the papists.† Archbishop Sheldon, Morley, and the rest of their party, exclaimed loudly against the indulgence, and alarmed the whole nation, insomuch that many sober and good men, who had long feared the growth of popery, began to think their eyes were open; and that they were in good earnest; but it appeared afterward that their chief concern was for the spiritual power; for, though they murmured against the dispensing power, they fell in with all their other proceedings; which, if Providence had not miraculously interposed, must have been fatal to the Protestant religion and the liberties of Europe.

At length, the declaration having been communicated to the French king, and received his approbation, was published, bearing date March 15, 1671-2, to the following effect:‡

"CHARLES REX.

"Our care and endeavours for the preservation of the rights and interests of the Church have been sufficiently manifested to the world, by the whole course of our government since our happy restoration, and by the many and frequent ways of coercion that we have used for reducing all erring or dissenting persons, and for composing the unhappy differences in matters of religion, which we found among our subjects upon our return : but it being evident, by the sad experience of twelve years, that there is very little fruit of all these forcible courses, we think ourselves obliged to make use of that

*. History of the Stuarts, p. 566.
† Des Maiz. Col., p. 677, &c.
  The bishops took the alarm at this declaration, and charged their clergy to preach against popery. The pulpits were full of a new strain ; it was everywhere preached against, and the authority of the laws was magnified. The king complained to Sheldon that controversy was preached, as if on purpose to inflame the people, and alienate them from him and his government ; and Sheldon, apprehensive that the king might again press him on this subject, convened some of the clergy, to consult with them what answer to make to his majesty. Dr. Tillotson suggested this reply : "That since the king himself professed the Protestant religion, it would be a thing without a precedent that he should forbid his clergy to preach in defence of a religion which they believed, while he himself said he was of it."—*Burnet's History*, vol. ii., p. 17, 12mo ed. ; and *Birch's Life of Tillotson*, p. 41.—ED.

supreme power in ecclesiastical matters, which is not only inherent in us, but hath been declared and recognised to be so by several statutes and acts of Parliament ; and therefore we do now, accordingly issue this our declaration, as well for the quieting of our good subjects in these points, as for inviting strangers in this conjuncture to come and live under us ; and for the better encouragement of all to a cheerful following of their trades and callings, from whence we hope, by the blessing of God, to have many good and happy advantages to our government ; as, also, for preventing for the future the danger that might otherwise arise from private meetings and seditious conventicles.

"And, in the first place, we declare our express resolution, meaning, and intention, to be, that the Church of England be preserved, and remain entire in its doctrine, discipline, and government, as now it stands established by law ; and that this be taken to be, as it is, the basis, rule, and standard of the general and public worship of God, and that the orthodox conformable clergy do receive and enjoy the revenues belonging thereunto, and that no person, though of a different opinion and persuasion, shall be exempt from paying his tithes, or other dues whatsoever. And farther we declare, that no person shall be capable of holding any benefice, living, or ecclesiastical dignity or preferment of any kind, in this our kingdom of England, who is not exactly conformable.

"We do, in the next place, declare our will and pleasure to be, that the execution of all, and all manner of penal laws in matters ecclesiastical, against whatsoever sort of Nonconformists or recusants, be immediately suspended, and they are hereby suspended ; and all judges, judges of assize, and jail delivery, sheriffs, justices of peace, mayors, bailiffs, and other officers whatsoever, whether ecclesiastical or civil, are to take notice of it, and pay due obedience thereto.

"And that there may be no pretence for any of our subjects to continue their illegal meetings and conventicles, we do declare that we shall, from time to time, allow a sufficient number of places, as they shall be desired, in all parts of this our kingdom, for the use of such as do not conform to the Church of England, to meet and assemble in order to their public worship and devotion, which places shall be open and free to all persons.

"But to prevent such disorders and inconveniences as may happen by this our indulgence, if not duly regulated, and that they may be the better protected by the civil magistrate, our express will and pleasure is, that none of our subjects do presume to meet in any place, until such places be allowed, and the teacher of that congregation be approved by us.

"And lest any should apprehend that this restriction should make our said allowance and approbation difficult to be obtained, we do farther declare, that this our indulgence, as to the allowance of the public places of worship, and approbation of the preachers, shall extend to all sorts of Nonconformists and recusants except the recusants of the Roman Catholic religion, to whom we shall in nowise allow public places of worship, but only indulge them their share in the common exemption from the penal laws, and the exercise of their worship in their private houses only.

"And if, after this our clemency and indulgence, any of our subjects shall pretend to abuse this liberty, and shall preach seditiously, or to the derogation of the doctrine, discipline, or government of the Established Church, or shall meet in places not allowed by us, we do hereby give them warning, and declare we will proceed against them with all imaginable severity. And we will let them see we can be as severe to punish such offenders, when so justly provoked, as we are indulgent to truly tender consciences.

"Given at our court at Whitehall, this 15th day of March, in the four-and-twentieth year of our reign."

The Protestant Nonconformists had no opinion of the dispensing power, and were not forward to accept of liberty in this way; they were sensible the indulgence was not granted out of love to them, nor would continue any longer than it would serve the interest of popery. "The beginning of the Dutch war," says one of their writers, "made the court think it necessary to grant them an indulgence, that there might be peace at home while there was war abroad, though much to the dissatisfaction of those who had a hand in framing all the severe laws against them."[*] Many pamphlets were written for and against the Dissenters accepting it, because it was grafted on the dispensing power. Some maintained that it was setting up altar against altar, and that they should accept of nothing but a comprehension. Others endeavoured to prove that it was the duty of the Presbyterians to make use of the liberty granted them by the king, because it was their natural right, which no legislative power upon earth had a right to deprive them of, as long as they remained dutiful subjects; that meeting in separate congregations, distinct from the parochial assemblies, in the present circumstances, was neither schismatical nor sinful.[†] Accordingly, most of the ministers, both in London and in the country, took out licenses, a copy of which I have transcribed from under the king's own hand and seal in the margin.[‡] Great numbers of people attended the meetings, and

* Baxter, part iii., p. 99. Welwood's Mem., p. 190.
† Baxter, part iii., p. 99. Welwood's Mem., p. 102.*
‡ CHARLES REX.
CHARLES, by the grace of God, King of England, Scotland, France, and Ireland, defender of the faith, &c., to all mayors, bailiffs, constables, and others; our officers and ministers, civil and military, whom it may concern, greeting: In pursuance of our declaration of the 15th of March, 1671-2, we do hereby permit and license G. S——, of the Congregational persuasion, to be a teacher of the congregation allowed by us, in a room or rooms of his house in ——, for the use of such as do not conform to the Church of England, who are of that persuasion commonly called Congregational, with farther license and permission to him, the said G. S——, to teach in any place licensed and allowed by us, according to our said declaration.
Given at our court at Whitehall, the second day of May, in the twenty-fourth year of our reign, 1672. By his majesty's command. ARLINGTON.

* The editor cannot meet with these passages in Welwood's Memoirs, 6th edition.
VOL. II.—M M.

a cautious and moderate address of thanks was presented to the king for their liberty, but all were afraid of the consequences.

It was reported, farther, that the court encouraged the Nonconformists, by some small pensions of £50 and £100 to the chief of their party; that Mr. Baxter returned the money, but that Mr. Pool acknowledged he had received £50 for two years, and that the rest accepted it.[*] This was reported to the disadvantage of the Dissenters, by Dr. Stillingfleet and others, with an insinuation that it was to bribe them to be silent, and join interest with the papists; but Dr. Owen, in answer to this part of the charge, in his preface to a book entitled "An Inquiry, &c., against Dr. Stillingfleet," declares, that "it is such a frontless, malicious lie, as impudence itself would blush at; that, however the Dissenters may be traduced, they are ready to give the highest security that can be of their stability in the Protestant cause; and for myself," says he, "never any person in authority, dignity, or power in the nation, nor any from them, papist or Protestant, did ever speak or advise with me about any indulgence or toleration to be granted to papists; and I challenge the whole world to prove the contrary." From this indulgence Dr. Stillingfleet dates the beginning of the Presbyterian separation.

This year died Dr. Edmund Staunton, the ejected minister of Kingston-upon-Thames, one of the Assembly of Divines, and some time president of Corpus Christi College, in Oxford. He was son of Sir Francis Staunton, born at Woburn, in Bedfordshire, 1601, and educated in Wadham College, of which he was a fellow.[†] Upon his taking orders, he became minister of Bushy, in Hertfordshire, but changed it afterward for Kingston-upon-Thames. In 1634 he took the degrees in divinity, and in 1648 was made president of Corpus Christi College, which he kept till he was silenced for nonconformity. He then retired to Rickmansworth, in Hertfordshire, and afterward to a village in that county called Bovingden, where he preached as often as he had opportunity. He was a learned, pious, and peaceable divine. In his last sickness he said he neither feared death nor desired life, but was willing to be at God's disposal. He died July 14, 1671, and was buried in the church belonging to the parish.[‡]

Mr. Vavasor Powell was born in Radnorshire, and educated in Jesus College, Oxon. When he left the university, he preached up and down in Wales, till, being driven from thence for want of Presbyterial ordination, which he scrupled, he came to London, and soon after settled at Dartford, in Kent. In the year 1646 he obtained a testimonial of his religious and blameless conversation, and of his abilities for the work of the ministry, signed by Mr. Herle and seventeen of the Assembly of Divines. Furnished with these testimonials, he returned to Wales,

* Burnet, vol. ii., p. 16, 17.
† Dr. Staunton, in 1615, became a commoner of Wadham College; on the 4th of October, in the same year, was admitted scholar of Corpus Christi College; and afterward fellow, and A.M.— Wood's Athen. Oxon., vol. ii., p. 352; and Dr. Grey.—ED.
‡ Calamy's Abridg., vol. ii., p. 63. Palmer's Nonconformists' Mem., vol. i., p. 173. Clarke's Lives, 1673, folio, p. 160.—C.

and became a most indefatigable and active instrument of propagating the Gospel in those
parts. There were few, if any, of the churches
or chapels in Wales in which he did not preach;
yea, very often he preached to the poor Welsh
in the mountains, at fairs, and in market-places;
for which he had no more than a stipend of
£100 per annum, besides the advantage of some
sequestered livings in North Wales (says my author), which, in those times of confusion, turned
but to a very poor account. Mr. Powell was a
bold man, and of Republican principles, preaching against the protectorship of Cromwell, and
wrote letters to him, for which he was imprisoned, to prevent his spreading disaffection in
the state. At the dawn of the Restoration, being known to be a fifth-monarchy man, he was
secured first at Shrewsbury, afterward in Wales,
and at last in the Fleet. In the year 1662 he
was shut up in South-Sea Castle, near Portsmouth, where he continued five years. In 1667
he was released, but venturing to preach again
in his own country, he was imprisoned at Cardiff, and in the year 1669 sent up to London,
and confined a prisoner in the Fleet, where he
died, and was buried in Bunhill Fields, in the
presence of an innumerable crowd of Dissenters, who attended him to his grave. He was
of an unconquerable resolution, and of a mind
unshaken under all his troubles. The inscription on his tomb calls him "a successful teacher of the past, a sincere witness of the present,
and a useful example to the future age; who,
in the defection of many, found mercy to be
faithful, for which, being called to many prisons,
he was there tried, and would not accept deliverance, expecting a better resurrection." He
died October 27, 1671, in the fifty-third year of
his age, and the eleventh year of his imprisonment.*

* To Mr. Neal's account of Mr. Vavasor Powell
it may be added, that he was born in 1617, and descended from an ancient and honourable stock: on
his father's side, from the Powells of Knocklas in
Radnorshire; and on his mother's, from the Vavasors,
a family of great antiquity, that came out of Yorkshire into Wales, and was related to the principal
gentry in North Wales. So active and laborious
was he in the duties of the ministry, that he frequently preached in two or three places in a day, and,
was seldom two days in the week, throughout the
year, out of the pulpit. He would sometimes ride a
hundred miles in the week, and preach in every
place where he could gain admittance, either by
night or day. He would often alight from his horse,
and set on it any aged person whom he met with on
the road on foot, and walk by the side for miles together. He was exceedingly hospitable and generous, and would not only entertain and lodge, but
clothe the poor and aged. He was a man of great
humility, very conscientious and exemplary in all relative duties, and very punctual to his word. He
was a scholar, and his general deportment was that
of a gentleman. His sentiments were those of a Sabbatarian Baptist. In 1642, when he left Wales, there
was not then above one or two gathered churches;
but before the Restoration, there were above twenty
distinct societies, consisting of from two to five hundred members, chiefly planted and formed by his
care and industry, in the principles of the Baptists.
They were also for the ordination of elders, singing
of psalms and hymns in public worship; laying on of
hands on the newly baptized, and anointing the sick
with oil, and did not limit their communion to an
agreement with them in their sentiments on baptism.
He bore his last illness with great patience, and

CHAPTER IX.

FROM THE KING'S DECLARATION OF INDULGENCE
TO THE POPISH PLOT IN THE YEAR 1678.

1672.

THE French king having prevailed with the
English court to break the triple alliance, and
make war with the Dutch, published a declaration at Paris, signifying that he could not, without diminution of his glory, any longer dissem-
ble the indignation raised in him by the unhandsome carriage of the States-General of the United Provinces, and therefore proclaimed war
against them both by sea and land. In the beginning of May, he drew together an army of one
hundred and twenty thousand men, with which
he took the principal places in Flanders, and
with a rapid fury overran the greatest part of the
Netherlands. In the beginning of July he took
possession of Utrecht, a city in the heart of the
United Provinces, where he held his court, and
threatened to besiege Amsterdam itself. In
this extremity the Dutch opened their sluices,
and laid a great part of their country under water; the populace rose, and having obliged the
states to elect the young Prince of Orange stadtholder, they fell upon the two brothers Cornelius and John de Wit, their late pensionary, and
tore them to pieces in a barbarous manner.
The young prince, who was then but twenty-
two years old, used all imaginable vigilance and
activity to save the remainder of his country;
and like a true patriot, declared he would die in
the last dike rather than become tributary to
any foreign power. At length, their allies came
to their assistance, when the young prince, like
another Scipio, abandoning his own country,
besieged and took the important town of Bonn,
which opened a passage for the Germans into
Flanders, and struck such a surprise into the
French, whose enemies were now behind them,
that they abandoned all their conquests in Holland, except Maestricht and Grave, with as
much precipitance as they had made them.

These rapid conquests of the French opened
people's mouths against the court, and raised
such discontents in England, that his majesty
was obliged to issue out his proclamation to
suppress all unlawful and undutiful conversation, threatening a severe prosecution of such
who should spread false news, or intermeddle
with affairs of state, or promote scandal against
his majesty's counsellors, by their common discourse in coffee-houses or places of public resort. He was obliged, also, to continue the exchequer shut up, contrary to his royal promise,
and to prorogue his Parliament till next year,
which, he foresaw, would be in a flame at their
meeting.

During this interval of Parliament, the declaration of Indulgence continued in force, and the
Dissenters had rest; when the Presbyterians
and Independents, to show their agreement
among themselves, as well as to support the

under the acutest pains would bless God, and say,
"he would not entertain one hard thought of God
for all the world," and could scarcely be restrained
from acts of devotion, and from expressing his sentiments of zeal and piety. Dr. Grey, after Wood, has
vilified Mr. Powell by retailing the falsehoods of a
piece entitled Strena Vavasoriensis.—Crosby's History, vol. i., p. 373, &c. Life and Death of Vavasor
Powell.—ED. (TOULMIN).

doctrines of the Reformation against the prevailing errors of popery, Socinianism, and infidelity, set up a weekly. lecture at Pinners'. Hall, in Broad-street, on Tuesday mornings, under the encouragement of the principal merchants and tradesmen of their persuasion in the city.' Four Presbyterians were joined by two Independents, to preach by turns, and, to give. it the greater reputation, the principal ministers for learning and popularity were chosen as lecturers; as Dr. Bates, Dr. Manton, Dr. Owen, Mr. Baxter, Mr. Collins, Jenkins, Mead, and, afterward, Mr. Alsop, Howe, Cole, and others ; and, though there were some little misunderstandings at their first setting out, about some high points of Calvinism, occasioned by one of Mr. Baxter's first sermons, yet the lecture continued in this form till the year 1695, when it split upon the same rock, occasioned by the reprinting Dr. Crisp's works. The four Presbyterians removed to Salters' Hall, and set up a lecture on the same day and hour. The two Independents remained at Pinners' Hall, and, when there was no prospect of an accommodation, each party filled up their numbers out of their respective denominations, and they are both subsisting to this day.

Among the Puritan divines who died this year, Bishop Wilkins deserves the first place. He was born at Fawsley, in Northamptonshire, in the house of his mother's father, Mr. J. Dod, the decalogist, in the year 1614, and educated in Magdalen Hall under Mr. Tombes.* He was some time warden of Wadham College, Oxford, and afterward master of Trinity College, Cambridge, of which he was deprived at the Restoration, though he conformed. He married a sister of the protector's, Oliver Cromwell, and complied with all the changes of the late times, being, as Wood observes, always Puritanically affected ; but, for his admirable abilities and extraordinary genius, he had scarce his equal. He was made Bishop of Chester 166 ; and surely, says Mr. Echard, the court could not have found out a man of greater ingenuity and capacity, or of more universal knowledge and understanding in all parts of polite learning. Archbishop Tillotson and Bishop Burnet, who were his intimates, give him the highest encomium ; as, that he was a pious Christian, an admirable preacher, a rare mathematician, and mechanical philosopher ; and a man of as great a mind, as true judgment, as eminent virtues, and of as great a soul, as any they ever knew. He was a person of universal charity and moderation of spirit ; and was concerned in all attempts for a comprehension with the Dissenters. He died of the stone, in Dr. Tillotson's house in Chancery Lane, November 19, 1672, in the fifty-ninth year of his age.

Mr. Joseph Caryl, M.A., the ejected minister of St. Magnus, London Bridge, was born of genteel parents in London, 1602, educated in Exeter College, and afterward preacher of Lincoln's Inn ; he was a member of the Assembly of Divines, and afterward one of the triers for approbation of ministers ; in all which stations he appeared a man of great learning, piety, and modesty. He was sent by the Parliament to attend the king at Holmby House, and was one of their commissioners in the treaty of the Isle

* Athen. Oxon., p. 505.

of Wight. After his ejectment in 1662, he lived privately in London, and preached to his congregation as the times would permit ; he was a moderate Independent, and distinguished himself by his learned exposition upon the Book of Job.* He died, universally lamented by all his acquaintance, February 7, 1672-3, and in the seventy-first year of his age.†

Mr. Philip Nye, M.A., was a divine of a warmer spirit. He was born of a genteel family, 1596, and was educated in Magdalen College,‡ Oxford, where he took the degrees. In 1630 he was curate of St. Michael's, Cornhill, and three years after fled from Bishop Laud's persecution into Holland, but returned about the beginning of the Long Parliament, and became minister. of Kimbolton in Huntingdonshire. He was one of the dissenting brethren in the Assembly, one of the triers in the protector's time, and a principal manager of the meeting of the Congregational ministers at the Savoy. He was a great politician, insomuch that it was debated in council, after the Restoration, whether he should not be excepted for life ;§ and it was concluded, that if he should accept or exercise any office, ecclesiastical or civil, he should, to. all intents and purposes in law, stand as if he had been totally excepted. He was ejected from St. Bartholomew behind the Exchange, and preached privately, as opportunity offered, to a congregation of Dissenters till the present year, when he died in the month of September, about seventy-six years old, and lies buried in the church of St. Michael's, Cornhill, leaving behind him the character of a man of uncommon depth, and of one who was seldom if ever outreached.‖

When the king met his Parliament February 4, 1673, after a recess of a year and nine months, he acquainted them with the reasonableness and necessity of the war with the Dutch, and having asked a supply, told them, " he had found the good effect of his indulgence to Dissenters, but that it was a mistake in those who said more liberty was given to

* This work was printed in two volumes folio, consisting of upward of six hundred sheets: and there was also an edition in twelve volumes 4to. " One just remark," says Mr. Granger, " has been made on its utility, that it is a very sufficient exercise for the virtue of patience, which it was chiefly intended to inculcate and improve."—*Granger's History of England*, vol. iii., p. 313, 8vo, note.—ED. It is not amiss to add, that very few works of equal magnitude contain so much piety and good sense. This commentary, for such it may be termed, is highly prized, and a copy is never to be met with in a London catalogue but at a very high price. It is one of the scarcest theological books, and, on account of its size, not likely to meet a reprint.—C.

† Calamy, vol. ii., p. 7. Palmer's Noncon. Mem., vol. i., p. 121.

‡ Mr. Nye was entered a commoner of Brazen Nose July, 1615, aged about nineteen years ; but making no long stay there, he removed to Magdalen Hall, not Magdalen College.—*Dr. Grey ;* and *Wood's Athen. Oxon.*, vol. ii., p. 368.—ED.

§ With John Goodwin and Hugh Peters. Soon after the Restoration, there was an order of Parliament for lodging his papers with the Archbishop of Canterbury at Lambeth, where they yet remain. Mr. Nye had drawn up a complete history of the old Puritan Dissenters, but the MS. was, unfortunately, burned in the fire of London.—C.

‖ Calamy, vol. ii., p. 29. Palmer, vol. i., p. 86.

papists than others, because they had only freedom in their own houses, and no public assemblies ; he should therefore take it ill to receive contradiction in what he had done ; and to deal plainly with you," said his majesty, "I am resolved to stick to my declaration." Lord-chancellor Shaftesbury seconded the king's speech, and having vindicated the indulgence, magnified the king's zeal for the Church of England and the Protestant religion. But the House of Commons declared against the dispensing power, and argued that though the king had a power to pardon offenders, he had not a right to authorize men to break the laws, for this would infer a power to alter the government ; and if the king could secure offenders by indemnifying them beforehand, it was in vain to make any laws at all, because, according to this maxim, they had no force but at the king's discretion. But it was objected, on the other side, that a difference was to be made between penal laws in spiritual matters and others ; that the king's supremacy gave him a peculiar authority over these, as was evident by his tolerating the Jews, and the churches of foreign Protestants. To which it was replied, that the intent of the law in asserting the supremacy was only to exclude all foreign jurisdiction, and to lodge the whole authority with the king ; but that was still bounded and regulated by law ; the Jews were still at mercy, and only connived at, but the foreign churches were excepted by a particular clause in the Act of Uniformity ; and therefore, upon the whole, they came to this resolution February 10, "That penal statutes in matters ecclesiastical cannot be suspended but by act of Parliament ; that no such power had ever been claimed by any of his majesty's predecessors, and therefore his majesty's indulgence was contrary to law, and tended to subvert the legislative power, which had always been acknowledged to reside in the king and his two houses of Parliament." Pursuant to this resolution, they addressed the king February 19, to recall his declaration. The king answered, that he was sorry they should question his power in ecclesiastics, which had not been done in the reigns of his ancestors ; that he did not pretend to suspend laws wherein the properties, rights, or liberties of his subjects were concerned, nor to alter anything in the established religion, but only to take off the penalties inflicted on Dissenters, which he believed they themselves would not wish executed according to the rigour of the law.* The Commons, perceiving his majesty was not inclined to desist from his declaration, stopped the money bill,† and pre-

sented a second address, insisting upon a full and satisfactory assurance that his majesty's conduct in this affair might not be drawn into example for the future, which at length they obtained.

The Parliament was now first disposed to distinguish between Protestant Dissenters and Popish recusants, and to give ease to the former without including the latter, especially when the Dissenters in the House disavowed the dispensing power, though it had been exercised in their favour. Alderman Love, member for the city of London, stood up, and in a handsome speech declared, "that he had rather go without his own desired liberty, than have it in a way so destructive of the liberties of his country and the Protestant interest ; and that this was the sense of the main body of Dissenters :" which surprised the whole House, and gave a turn to those very men who, for ten years together, had been loading the Nonconformists with one penal law after another : but things were now at a crisis ; Popery and slavery were at the door ; the triple alliance broken ; the Protestant powers ravaging one another ; the exchequer shut up ; the heir presumptive of the crown an open papist ; and an army encamped near London under popish officers ready to be transported into Holland to complete their ruin. When the Dissenters, at such a time, laid aside their resentments against their persecutors, and renounced their own liberty, for the safety of the Protestant religion and the liberties of their country, all sober men began to think it was high time to put a mark of distinction between them and the Roman Catholics.

But the king was of another mind ; yet, being in want of money, he was easily persuaded by his mistresses to give up his indulgence ; contrary to the advice of the Cabal, who told him, if he would make a bold stand for his prerogative, all would be well. But he came to the House March 8, and having pressed the Commons to despatch the money bill, he added, "If there be any scruple yet remaining with you touching the suspension of the penal laws, I here faithfully promise you that what has been done in that particular shall not for the future be drawn into example and consequence ; and as I daily expect from you a bill for my supply, so I assure you I shall as willingly receive and pass any other you shall offer me, that may tend to the giving you satisfaction in all your just grievances." Accordingly, he called for the declaration, and broke the seal with his own hands, by which means all the licenses for meeting-houses were called in. Our historians* observe, that this proceeding of the king made a surprising alteration in Lord Shaftesbury, who had been the soul of the Cabal, and the master-builder of the scheme for making the king absolute ;

---

* Echard, p. 889. Burnet, vol. ii., p. 72, 73.
† The remarks of Mr. Gough here are just and weighty : "The conduct of the Commons in this case hath procured the general voice of our historians in their favour ; and it must be acknowledged that they acted consistently with their duty in opposing the infringement of the Constitution. Yet, as the king's apparent inclination to have the Dissenters exempted from penal laws would have merited praise, if it had been sincere, and attempted in a legal way, so the opposition of the Parliament would have been entitled to the claim of greater merit, if it had not originated, with many of them, in an aversion to the principles of the declaration (impunity to the Nonconformists) as much as the grounds upon which it

was published ; and if they had not laid the foundations for this contest in the various penal laws, which, under the influence of party pique, they had universally enacted and received ; and on all occasions manifested a determined enmity to all dissenters from the established religion ; for if they had not an aversion to the principles of the declaration, they had now a fair opportunity of legalizing it, by converting it into an act of Parliament."—*History of the Quakers*, vol. ii., p. 374.—ED.

* Echard, p. 891. Burnet, vol. ii., p. 75.

but that when his majesty was so unsteady as to desert him in the project of an indulgence after he had promised to stand by him, he concluded the king was not to be trusted, and appeared afterward at the head of the country party.

The Nonconformists were now in some hopes of a legal toleration by Parliament, for the Commons resolved, *nemine contradicente,* that a bill be brought in for the ease of his majesty's Protestant subjects, who are dissenters in matters of religion from the Church of England. The substance of the bill was,

" 1. That ease be given to his majesty's Protestant subjects dissenting in matters of religion, who shall subscribe the articles of the doctrine of the Church of England, and shall take the oaths of allegience and supremacy.* 2. That the said Protestant subjects be eased from all pains and penalties for not coming to church. 3. That the clause in the late Act of Uniformity for declaring the assent and consent be taken away by this bill. 4. That the said Protestant subjects be eased from all pains and penalties, for meeting together for performance of any religious exercises. 5. That every teacher shall give notice of the place where he intends to hold such his meetings to the quarter sessions, where in open court he shall first make such subscription, and take such oaths as aforesaid, and receive from thence a certificate thereof, where all such proceedings shall remain upon record. 6. That any such teacher may exercise as aforesaid, until the next respective quarter sessions, and no longer, in case he shall not first take the oaths, and make such subscription before two of the neighbouring justices of the peace, and shall first give them notice of the place of his intended meeting, and take a certificate thereof under the said justices' hands, a duplicate whereof they are to return into the next quarter sessions. 7. The doors and passages of all houses and places where the said Dissenters do meet shall be always open and free during the time of such exercise. 8. If any Dissenter refuses to take the church-wardens' oath, he shall then find another fit person, who is not a Dissenter, to execute that office, and shall pay him for it." But though all agreed in bringing in a bill, there was neither time nor unanimity enough in the House this sessions to agree upon particulars ; for according to Bishop Burnet, it went no farther than a second reading. Mr. Echard says it was dropped in the House of Lords on account of some amendments, till the Parliament was prorogued ; but Mr. Coke says, more truly, that it was because the dead weight of bishops joined with the king and the caballing party against it.†

While this was depending, the Commons addressed the king against papists and Jesuits, expressing their great concern to see such persons admitted into employments and places of great trust and profit, and especially into military commands, and therefore pray that the laws against them may be put in execution. Upon which a proclamation was issued, though to very little purpose, enjoining all popish priests and Jesuits to depart the realm, and the laws to be put in execution against all popish recusants.

But his majesty making no mention of removing them from places of profit and trust, the Commons, knowing where their strength lay, suspended their money bill, and ordered a bill to be brought in to confine all places of profit and trust to those only who are of the communion of the Church of England : this is commonly called the Test Act, and was levelled against the Duke of York and the present ministry, who were chiefly of his persuasion. When it was brought into the House, they opposed it with all their might, and endeavoured to divide the church party, by proposing that some regard might be had to Protestant Dissenters, hoping by this means to clog the bill, and throw it out of the House; upon which Alderman Love, a Dissenter, and representative for the city, stood up again, and said he hoped the clause in favour of Protestant Dissenters would occasion no intemperate heats ; and moved that since it was likely to prove so considerable a barrier against popery, the bill might pass without any alteration, and that nothing might interpose till it was finished ; and then (says the alderman) we [Dissenters] will try, if the Parliament will not distinguish us from popish recusants, by some marks of their favour ; but we are willing to lie under the severity of the laws for a time, rather than clog a more necessary work with our concerns. These being the sentiments of the leading Dissenters both in the House and without doors, the bill passed the Commons with little opposition ; but when it came to be debated in the House of Peers, in the king's presence, March 15, the whole court was against it, except the Earl of Bristol ; and maintained that it was his majesty's prerogative to employ whom he pleased in his service. Some were for having the king stand his ground against the Parliament. The Duke of Buckingham and Lord Berkley* proposed bringing the army to town, and taking out of both houses the members who made opposition. Lauderdale offered to bring an army from Scotland ; and Lord Clifford told the king that the people now saw through his designs, and therefore he must resolve to make himself master at once, or be forever subject to much jealousy and contempt. But the Earl of Shaftesbury, having changed sides, pressed the king to give the Parliament full content, and then they would undertake to procure him the supply he wanted. This suited the king's easy temper, who, not being willing to risk a second civil war, went into these measures, and, out of mere necessity for money, gave up the papists, in hopes that he might afterward recover what in the present extremity he was forced to resign. This effectually broke the Cabal, and put the Roman Catholics upon pursuing other measures to introduce their religion, which was the making way for a popish successor of more resolute principles ; and from hence we may date the beginning of the popish plot, which did not break out till 1678, as appears by Mr. Coleman's letters. The bill received the royal assent March 25, together with the money bill of £1,200,000, and then the Parliament was prorogued to October 20, after a short session of seven weeks.

The Test Act is entitled, " An Act to prevent

---

* Echard, p. 889.   † Detect., p. 490.   * Burnet, vol. ii., p. 75, 76.

Dangers which happen from Popish Recusants." It requires, " that all persons bearing any office of trust or profit shall take the oaths of supremacy and allegiance in public and open court, and shall also receive the sacrament of the Lord's Supper, according to the usage of the Church of England,' in some parish church, on some Lord's Day, immediately after Divine service and sermon, and deliver a certificate of having so received the sacrament, under the hands of the respective ministers and church-wardens, proved by two credible witnesses upon oath, and upon record in court. And that all persons taking the said oaths of supremacy and allegience shall likewise make and subscribe this following declaration : ' I, A.B., do declare that I believe there is no transubstantiation in the sacrament of the Lord's Supper, or in the elements of bread and wine, at or after the consecration thereof by any person whatsoever.' The penalty of breaking through this act is a disability of suing in any court of law or equity, being guardian of any child, executor or administrator to any person, or of taking any legacy, or deed of gift, or of bearing any public office : besides a fine of five hundred pounds."

Mr. Echard observes well, that this act was principally, if not solely, levelled at the Roman Catholics, as appears from the title ; and this is farther evident from the disposition of the House of Commons at this time to ease the Protestant Dissenters of some of their burdens. If the Dissenters had fallen in with the court measures, they might have prevented the bill's passing. But they left their own liberties in a state of uncertainty, to secure those of the nation. However, though the intention was good, the act itself is, in my opinion, very unjustifiable, because it founds dominion in grace. A man cannot be an exciseman, a custom-house officer, a lieutenant in the army or navy, no, not so much as a tide-waiter, without putting on the most distinguishing badge of Christianity, according to the usage of the Church of England. Is not this a strong temptation to profanation and hypocrisy ? Does it not pervert one of the most solemn institutions of religion to purposes for which it was never intended ? And is it not easy to find securities of a civil nature sufficient for the preservation both of Church and State ? When the act took place, the Duke of York, lord-high-admiral of England, lord Clifford, lord-high-treasurer, and a great many other popish officers, resigned their preferments ; but not one Protestant Dissenter, there not being one such in the administration : however, as the Church party showed a noble zeal for their religion, Bishop Burnet observes, that the Dissenters got great reputation by their silent deportment ; though the king and the court bishops resolved to take their skirts.*

This being the last penal law made against the Nonconformists in this reign, it may not be improper to put them all together, that the reader may have a full view of their distressed circumstances : for besides the penal laws of Queen Elizabeth, which were confirmed by this Parliament, one of which was no less than banishment, and another a mulct on every one for not coming to church,

There were in force,

* Vol. ii., p. 80.

1st. An act for well governing and regulating corporations, 13 Car. II., c. i. Whereby all who bear office in any city, corporation, town, or borough, are required to take the oaths and subscribe the declaration therein mentioned, and to receive the sacrament of the Lord's Supper according to the rites of the Church of England. This effectually turned the Dissenters out of the government of all corporations.

2d. The Act of Uniformity, 14 Car. II., c. iv. Whereby all parsons, vicars, and ministers who enjoyed any preferment in the Church, were obliged to declare their unfeigned assent and consent to everything contained in the Book of Common Prayer, &c., or be ipso facto deprived ; and all schoolmasters and tutors are prohibited from teaching youth without license from the archbishop or bishop, under pain of three months' imprisonment.

3d. An act to prevent and suppress seditious conventicles, 16 Car. II., c. iv. Whereby it is declared unlawful to be present at any meeting for religious worship, except according to the usage of the Church of England, where five besides the family should be assembled ; in which case the first and second offences are made subject to a certain fine, or three months' imprisonment, on conviction before a justice of the peace on the oath of a single witness ; and the third offence, on conviction at the sessions, or before the justices of assize, is punishable by transportation for seven years.

4th. An act for restraining Nonconformists from inhabiting in corporations, 17 Car. II., c. ii. Whereby all dissenting ministers, who would not take an oath therein specified against the lawfulness of taking up arms against the king on any pretence whatsoever, and that they would never attempt any alteration of government in Church and State, are banished five miles from all corporation towns, and subject to a fine of £40 in case they should preach in any conventicle.

5th. Another act to prevent and suppress seditious conventicles, 22 Car. II., c. v. Whereby any persons who teach in such conventicles are subject to a penalty of £20 for the first, and £40 for every subsequent offence ; and any person who permits such a conventicle to be held in their house, is liable to a fine of £20 ; and justices of peace are empowered to break open doors where they are informed such conventicles are held, and take the offenders into custody.

6th. An act for preventing dangers which may happen from popish recusants, commonly called the Test Act, whereby (as afore-mentioned) every person is incapacitated from holding a place of trust under the government, without taking the sacrament according to the rites of the Church of England.

By the rigorous execution of these laws, the Nonconformist ministers were separated from their congregations, from their maintenance, from their houses and families, and their people reduced to distress and misery, or obliged to worship God in a manner contrary to the dictates of their consciences, on a penalty of heavy fines, or of being shut up in a prison among thieves and robbers. Great numbers retired to the plantations ; but Dr. Owen, who was shipping off his effects for New-England, was forbid to leave the kingdom by express orders from

King Charles himself. If there had been treason or rebellion in the case, it had been justifiable; but when it was purely for nonconformity to certain rites and ceremonies, and a form of church government, it can deserve no better name than that of persecution.

The House of Commons, from their apprehensions of the growth of popery and of a popish successor to the crown, petitioned the king against the duke's second marriage with the Princess of Modeha, an Italian papist, but his majesty told them they were too late. Upon which the Commons stopped their money bill, voted the standing army a grievance, and were proceeding to other vigorous resolutions, when the king sent for them to the House of Peers, and with a short speech prorogued them to January 7, after they had sat only nine days. In the mean time the duke's marriage was consummated, with the consent of the French king, which raised the expectation of the Roman Catholics higher than ever.

This induced the more zealous Protestants to think of a firmer union with the Dissenters; accordingly, Mr. Baxter, at the request of the Earl of Orrery, drew up some proposals for a comprehension, agreeably to those already mentioned.* "He proposed that the meeting-houses of Dissenters should be allowed as chapels, till there were vacancies for them in the churches; and that those who had no meeting-houses should be schoolmasters or lecturers till such time; that none should be obliged to read the Apocrypha; that parents might have liberty to dedicate their own children in baptism; that ministers might preach where somebody else who had the room might read the Common Prayer; that ministers be not obliged to give the sacrament to such as are guilty of scandalous immoralities, nor to refuse it to those who scruple kneeling; that persons excommunicated may not be imprisoned and ruined; and that toleration be given to all conscientious Dissenters." These proposals being communicated to the Earl of Orrery, were put into the hands of Bishop Morley,† who returned them without yielding to anything of importance. The motion was also revived in the House of Commons, but the shortness of the sessions put a stop to its progress. Besides, the court bishops seemed altogether indisposed to any concessions.‡

This year put an end to the lives of two considerable Nonconformist divines: Mr. William Whitaker, the ejected minister of St. Mary Magdalen, Bermondsey, son of Mr. Jer. Whitaker, a divine of great learning in the Oriental languages. He was an elegant preacher, and a good man from his youth. While he was at Emanuel College, he was universally beloved; and when he came to London, generally esteemed for his sweet disposition. He was first preacher at Hornchurch, and then at the place from whence he was ejected. He afterward preached to a separate congregation, as the times would permit, and died in the year 1673.§

Mr. James Janeway, M.A., was born in Hertfordshire, and a student of Christ Church, Oxford. He was afterward tutor in the house of Mr. Stringer at Windsor; but not being satisfied with conformity, he opened a separate meeting at Rotherhithe, where he preached to a numerous congregation with great success.* He was a zealous preacher, and fervent in prayer; but being weakly, his indefatigable labours broke his constitution, so that he died of a consumption March 16, 1673-4, in the thirty-eighth year of his age.†

The revocation of the indulgence, and the displeasure of the court against the Dissenters for deserting them in their designs to prevent the passing the Test Act, let loose the whole tribe of informers. The papists being excluded from places of trust, the court had no tenderness for Protestant Nonconformists; the judges, therefore, had orders to quicken the execution of the laws against them. The estates of those of the best quality in each county were ordered to be seized. The mouths of the High-church pulpiteers were encouraged to open as loud as possible; one, in his sermon before the House of Commons, told them that the Nonconformists ought not to be tolerated, but to be cured by vengeance. He urged them to set fire to the fagot, and to teach them by scourges or scorpions, and open their eyes with gall. The king himself issued out a proclamation for putting the penal laws in full execution, which had its effect.‡

Mr. Baxter was one of the first upon whom the storm fell, being apprehended as he was preaching his Thursday lecture at Mr. Turner's. He went with a constable and Keting the informer to Sir William Pulteney's, who demanding the warrant, found it signed by Henry Montague, Esq., bailiff of Westminster. Sir William told the constable that none but a city justice could give a warrant to apprehend a man for preaching in the city, whereupon he was dismissed.§ Endeavours were used to surprise Dr. Manton, and send him to prison upon the Oxford or Five-mile Act, but Mr. Bedford preaching for him was accidentally apprehended in his stead; and though he had taken the oath in the Five-mile Act, was fined £20, and the place £40, which was paid by the hearers.||

The like ravages were made in most parts of England; Mr. Joseph Swaffield, of Salisbury, was seized preaching in his own house, and bound over to the assizes, and imprisoned in the county jail almost a year. Twenty-five persons, men and women, were indicted for a riot, that is, for a conventicle, and suffered the penalty of the law.¶ The informers were Roman Catholics, one of whom was executed for treason in the popish plot. At East Salcomb, in Devononshire, lived one Joan Boston, an old blind widow, who, for a supposed conventicle held at her house, was fined £12, and for nonpayment of it threatened with a jail. After some weeks, the officers broke open her doors, and carried away

---

* Baxter, part iii., p. 110.   † Page 100.
‡ Ibid., part iii., p. 140.
§ Calamy, vol. ii., p. 25. Palmer, vol. i., p. 157.
—Dr. Annesley preached his funeral sermon, and Dr. Jacomb wrote an account of his life. He printed two sermons in the morning exercises.—C.

* Calamy, vol. ii., p. 838. Palmer, p. 684.
† Mr. Janeway had four brothers who were ejected in Hertfordshire; they were all consumptive, and died under forty.—C.
‡ State Tracts, vol. iii., p. 42. Baxter, part iii., p. 153.   § State Tracts. part iii., p. 155.
|| Conf. Plea, part iv., p. 75. ¶ Ibid., part iv., p. 75.

her goods to above the value of the fine.' They sold as many goods as were worth £13 for 50s.; six hogsheads valued at 40s. for 9s.; and pewter, feather-beds, &c., for 20s., besides the rent which they demanded of her tenants. Mr. John Thompson, minister in Bristol, was apprehended, and refusing to take the Oxford oath, was committed to prison, where he was seized with a fever through the noisomeness of the place: a physician being sent for, advised his removal; and a bond of £500 was offered the sheriff for his security: application was also made to the bishop without success; so he died in prison, March 4, declaring, that if he had known when he came to prison that he should die there, he would have done no otherwise than he did. Numberless examples of the like kind might be produced during the recess of the Parliament. But the king's want of money, and the discontents of his people, obliged him to put an end to the war with the Dutch, with no other advantage than a sum of 2 or £3000 for his expenses.

His majesty was unwilling to meet his Parliament, who were now full of zeal against popery, and began to consider the Nonconformists as auxiliaries to the Protestant cause; but necessity obliged him to covene them; and as soon as they met, January 7, 1674, they addressed his majesty to banish all papists, who were not housekeepers nor menial servants to peers, ten miles from London; and to appoint a fast for the calamities of the nation. They attacked the remaining members of the Cabal, and voted an address for removing them from his majesty's council; upon which the king prorogued them for above a year, after they had sat six weeks, without giving any money, or passing one single act: which was an indication of ill blood between the king and Parliament, and a certain forerunner of vengeance upon the Dissenters. But, to stifle the clamours of the people, his majesty republished his proclamation,* forbidding their meddling in state affairs, or talking seditiously in coffee-houses; and then commanded an order to be made public, " that effectual care be taken for the suppressing of conventicles: and whereas, divers pretend old licenses from his majesty, and would support themselves by that pretence, his majesty declares that all his licenses were long since recalled, and that no conventicle has any authority, allowance, or encouragement from him."†

This year put an end to the life of that great man, John Milton, born in London, and educated in Christ College, Cambridge, where he discovered an uncommon genius, which was very much improved by his travels. He was Latin secretary to the Long Parliament, and wrote in defence of the murder of King Charles I., against Salmasius and others, with great spirit, and in a pure and elegant Latin style. He was afterward secretary to the Protector Cromwell, and lost the sight of both his eyes by hard study. At the Restoration some of his books were burned, and himself in danger; but he was happily included in the Act of Indemnity, and spent the remainder of his life in retirement. He was a man of an unequalled genius, and acquired immortal fame by his incomparable poem of Paradise Lost; in which he manifested such a sublimity of thought, and such elegance of diction,

as perhaps were never exceeded in any age or nation of the world. His daughters read to him, after he was blind, the Greek poets, though they understood not the language. He died in mean circumstances, at Bunhill Row, London, in the sixty-seventh year of his age.*

Though the Protestant religion stood in need of the united strength of all its professors against the advances of popery, and the Parliament had moved for a toleration of Protestant Dissenters, yet the bishops continued to prosecute them in common with the papists. Archbishop Sheldon directed circular letters to the bishops of his province, enjoining them to give directions to their archdeacons and commissaries to procure particular information from the church-wardens of their several parishes on the following inquiries, and transmit them to him after the next visitation: 1. What number of persons are there, by common estimation, inhabiting with in each parish subject to your jurisdiction? 2. What number of popish recusants, or persons suspected of recusancy, are resident among the inhabitants aforesaid? 3. What number of other Dissenters are there in each parish, of what sect soever, which either obstinately refuse or wholly absent themselves from the communion of the Church of England, at such times as by law they are required? Some of the clergy were grieved at these proceedings, and Dr. Tillotson and Stillingfleet met privately with Dr. Manton, Bates, Pool, and Baxter, to consider of terms of accommodation, which, when they had agreed upon and communicated to the bishops, they were disallowed; so that, when Tillotson saw how things were going, he cautiously withdrew from the odium, and wrote the following letter to Mr. Baxter, April 11, 1675: " That he was unwilling his name should be made public in the affair, since it was come to nothing: not but that I do heartily desire an accommodation," says he, " and shall always endeavour it; but I am sure it will be a prejudice

* It is but a piece of justice to the memory and virtues of some of the most distinguished characters of the Conformists and Nonconformists of this period, to record here their pious exertions for the religious instruction of the Welsh. A subscription was opened, and an association was formed for the distribution of Bibles, Testaments, and practical treatises, and for opening schools in the principality of Wales. At the head of this institution was Dr. Tillotson, then Dean of Canterbury. The gentlemen who were the chief contributors to this design were, Whichcote, Ford, Bates, Outram, Patrick, Durham, Stillingfleet, Meriton, Burton, Baxter, Gouge, Poole, Fowler, Newman, Reading, Griffith, Short, Gape, and the beneficent Firmin. From Midsummer, 1674, to Lady Day, 1675, they had distributed thirty-two Welsh Bibles, which were all that could be procured in Wales or London; two hundred and forty New Testaments, and five hundred Whole Duty of Man, in Welsh. In the preceding year eight hundred and twelve poor children had, by the charity of others, been put to school in fifty-one of the chief towns in Wales. The distribution of these books provoked others to that charitable work, so that the children placed at schools by these gentlemen, and others, from their own purse, amounted to one thousand eight hundred and fifty. It appears as if this undertaking gave birth to an edition of the Bible and liturgy in the Welsh tongue, in which Mr. Gouge had a principal concern, and to which Dr. Tillotson gave £50. The impression extended to eight thousand copies.—*Life of Mr. James Owen*, p. 10–12; and *Life of Mr. Thomas Firmin*, p. 50.—Ed.

* Gazette, No. 883   † Ibid., No. 962, 965.

to me, and signify nothing to the effecting the thing, which, as circumstances are, cannot pass in either House without the concurrence of a considerable part of the bishops, and the countenance of his majesty, which at present I see little reason to expect."*

But the bishops' conduct made them unpopular, and drew on them many mortifications. People's compassion began to move towards their dissenting brethren, whom they frequently saw carried in great numbers to prison, and spoiled of their goods, for no other crime than a tender conscience. The very name of an informer became as odious as their behaviour was infamous. The aldermen of London often went out of their way when they heard of their coming; and some denied them their warrants, though by the act they forfeited £100. Alderman Forth bound over an informer to his good behaviour, for breaking into his chamber without leave.† When twelve or thirteen bishops came into the city to dine with Sir Nathaniel Herne, one of the sheriffs of London, and exhorted him to put the laws in execution against the Nonconformists, he told them plainly, they could not trade with their fellow-citizens one day and put them in prison the next.

The moderate churchmen showing a disposition to unite with the Nonconformists against popery, the court resolved to take in the old ranting Cavaliers, to strengthen the opposition; for this purpose, Morley and some other bishops were sent for to court, and told it was a great misfortune that the Church party and Dissenters were so disposed to unite, and run into one; the court was therefore willing to make the Church easy, and to secure to the king the allegiance of all his subjects at the same time; for this purpose a bill was brought into the House of Lords, entitled, "An Act to prevent the Dangers that may arise from Persons disaffected to the Government;" by which all such as enjoyed any beneficial office or employment, ecclesiastical, civil, or military; all who voted in elections of Parliament men; all privy counsellors, and members of Parliament themselves, were under a penalty to take the following oath, being the same as was required by the Five-mile Act: "I, A. B., do declare that it is not lawful, upon any pretence whatsoever, to take up arms against the king; and that I do abhor that traitorous position of taking arms by his authority against his person, or against those that are commissioned by him in pursuance of such commission. And I do swear that I will not at any time endeavour the alteration of the government either in Church or State. So help me God." The design of the bill was to enable the ministry to prosecute their destructive schemes against the Constitution and the Protestant religion, without fear of opposition even from the Parliament itself.‡ The chief speakers in the bill were, the lord-treasurer and the lord-keeper, Lord Danby and Finch, with Bishop Morley and Ward; but the Earl of Shaftesbury, Duke of Buckingham, Lord Hollis, and Halifax, laid open the mischievous designs and consequences of it; it was considered as disinheriting men of their birthright to shut them out from the right of election by an insnaring oath, as well as destructive of the privilege of Parliament, which was to vote freely in all cases without any previous obligation; that the peace of the nation would be best secured by making good laws; and that oaths and tests without these would be no real security; scrupulous men might be fettered by them, but that the bulk of mankind would boldly take any test, and as easily break through it; as had appeared in the late times. The bill was committed, and debated paragraph by paragraph, but the heats occasioned by it were so violent, that the king came unexpectedly to the House June 9, and prorogued the Parliament;* so the bill was dropped; but the debates of the Lords upon the intended oath being made public, were ordered to be burned. Two proclamations were republished on this occasion; one to prevent seditious discourses in coffee-houses, the other to put a stop to the publishing seditious libels.

The court had reason to desire the passing this bill, because the oath had been already imposed upon the Nonconformists; and the court clergy had been preaching in their churches, for several years, that passive obedience and nonresistance were the received doctrines of the Church of England; the bishops had possessed the king and his brother with the belief of it, and if it had now passed into a law, the whole nation had been bound in chains, and the court might have done as they pleased. But the Parliament saw through the design; and Dr. Burnet says,† he opened the reserve to the Duke of York, by telling him "that there was no trusting to disputable opinions; that there were distinctions and reserves in those who had maintained these points; and that when men saw a visible danger of being first undone, and then burned, they would be inclined to the shortest way of arguing, and save themselves the best way they could; interest and self-preservation being powerful motives." This might be wholesome advice to the duke, but implies such a secret reserve as may cover the most wicked designs, and is not fit for the lips of a Protestant divine, nor even of an honest man.

The daring insolence of the papists, who had their regular clergy in every corner of the town, was so great, that they not only challenged the Protestant divines to disputations, but threatened to assassinate such as preached openly against their tenets; which confirmed the Lords and Commons in their persuasion of

* Baxter, part iii., p. 157, 158.
† Compl. History, p. 338.
‡ Baxter's Life, part iii., p. 167. Burnet, vol. ii., p. 130–134.
Vol. II.—N N

* The immediate occasion of the king's breaking up the sessions was a dispute concerning privilege between the two houses, to which another question gave birth, while the bill for the new test was pending. Of this bill it was justly said, "No conveyancer could have drawn up a dissettlement of the whole birthright of England in more compendious terms." The debate on it lasted five several days, in the House of Lords, before the bill was committed to a committee of the whole House, and eleven or twelve days afterward; and the House sat many days till eight or nine at night; and sometimes till midnight. But, through the interruption given to it by the matter just mentioned, the bill was never reported from the committee to the House; a most happy escape!— Burnet's History, vol. ii., p. 133; and Dr. Calamy's Historical Account of his own Life, MS., p. 63.—ED.
† Page 91.

the absolute necessity of entering into more moderate and healing measures with Protestant Dissenters, notwithstanding the inflexible steadiness of the bishops against it. Upon this occasion, the Duke of Buckingham, lately commenced patriot, made the following speech in the House of Lords, which is inserted in the Commons' journal: "My lords, there is a thing called liberty, which, whatsoever some men may think, is that the people of England are fondest of, it is that they will never part with, and is that his majesty, in his speech, has promised to take particular care of. This, my lords, in my opinion, can never be done without giving an indulgence to all Protestant Dissenters. It is certainly a very uneasy kind of life to any man, that has either Christian charity, humanity, or good-nature, to see his fellow-subjects daily abused, divested of their liberty and birthrights, and miserably thrown out of their possessions and freeholds, only because they cannot agree with others in some opinions and niceties of religion, which their consciences will not give them leave to consent to, and which, even by the confession of those who would impose them, are noways necessary to salvation.

"But, my lords, besides this, and all that may be said upon it, in order to the improvement of our trade and increase of the wealth, strength, and greatness of this nation (which, with your leave, I shall presume to discourse of some other time), there is, methinks, in this notion of persecution, a very gross mistake both as to the point of government and the point of religion: there is so as to the point of government, because it makes every man's safety depend upon the wrong place; not upon the governors, or man's living well towards the civil government established by law, but upon his being transported with zeal for every opinion that is held by those that have power in the Church that is in fashion; and I conceive it is a mistake in religion, because it is positively against the express doctrine and example of Jesus Christ. Nay, my lords, as to our Protestant religion, there is something in it yet worse; for we Protestants maintain that none of those opinions which Christians differ about are infallible, and therefore in us it is somewhat an inexcusable conception, that men ought to be deprived of their inheritance, and all the certain conveniences and advantages of life, because they will not agree with us in our uncertain opinions of religion.

"My humble motion, therefore, to your lordships is, that you will give leave to bring in a bill of indulgence to all Protestant Dissenters. I know very well that every peer in this realm has a right to bring into Parliament any bill he conceives to be useful to his nation; but I thought it more respectful to your lordships to ask your leave before; and I cannot think the doing it will be any prejudice to the bill, because I am confident the reason, the prudence, and the charitableness of it, will be able to justify it to this House, and to the whole world." Accordingly, the House gave his grace leave to bring in a bill to this purpose; but this, and some others were lost by the warm debates which arose in the House upon the impeachment of the Earl of Danby, and which occa-

sioned the sudden prorogation of the Parliament June 9, without having passed one public bill; after which his majesty, upon farther discontent, prorogued them for fifteen months, which gave occasion to a question in the ensuing session, whether they were not legally dissolved.

From this time to the discovery of the Popish Plot, Parliaments were called and adjourned, says Mr. Coke, by order from France to French ministers and pensioners, to carry on the design of promoting the Catholic cause in masquerade.[*] The king himself was a known pensioner of Louis XIV., who had appropriated a fund of twenty millions of livres for the service of these kingdoms, out of which the Duke of York, and the prime ministers and leaders of parties, received the wages of their commission, according as the French ambassador represented their merit. The pensioners made it their business to raise the cry of the Church's danger, and of the return of forty-one. This was spread over the whole nation in a variety of pamphlets and newspapers, &c., written by their own hirelings; and if they met with opposition from the friends of the country, the authors and printers were sure to be fined and imprisoned. A reward of £50 was offered for the printer of a pamphlet supposed to be written by Andrew Marvel, entitled "An Account of the Growth of Power, and a seasonable Argument to all Grand Juries;" and £100 for the persons who conveyed it to the press. No man could publish anything on the side of liberty and the Protestant religion but with the hazard of a prison and a considerable fine; nor is this to be wondered at, considering that Sir Roger l'Estrange was the sole licenser of the press.

This gentleman was a pensioner of the court, and a champion for the prerogative; he was a younger son of Sir Hammond l'Estrange, of Norfolk, who, having conceived hopes of surprising the town of Lynn for his majesty in the year 1644, obtained a commission from the king for that purpose, but being apprehended and tried by a court-martial, for coming into the Parliament's quarters as a spy, he was condemned, and ordered to be executed in Smithfield January 2, 1644-5; but by the intercession of some powerful friends he was reprieved, and kept in Newgate several years. His sufferings made such an impression on his spirit, that on the king's restoration, he was resolved to make reprisals on the whole party. He was master of a fine English style, and of a great deal of keen wit, which he employed, without any regard to truth or candour, in the service of popery and arbitrary power, and in vilifying the best and most undoubted patriots. Never did man fight so to force the Dissenters into the Church, says Coke; and when he had got them there, branded them for trimmers, and would turn them out again. He was a most mercenary writer, and had a pen at the service of those who would pay him best. Forty-one was his retreat against all who durst contend against him and the prerogative. Sir Roger observed no measures with his adversaries in his Weekly Observators, Citt and Bump-

* Detect., p. 500.

kin, Foxes and Firebrands,* and other pamphlets; and when the falseness of his reasoning and insolence of his sarcasm were exposed, like a second Don Quixote, he called aloud to the civil magistrate to come in to his aid. He represented the religion of the Dissenters as a medley of folly and enthusiasm; their principles and tempers as turbulent, seditious, and utterly inconsistent with the peace of the state; their pretences as frivolous, and often hypocritical. He excited the government to use the utmost severities to extirpate them out of the kingdom.† He furnished the clergy with pulpit materials to rail at them, which they improved with equal eagerness and indiscretion; so that popery was forgot, and nothing so common in their mouths as *forty-one.* L'Estrange published some of the incautious expressions of some of the Dissenters in the late times, which he picked out of their writings, to excite the populace against the whole party, as if it had not been easy to make reprisals from the ranting expressions of the Tories of this reign: for these exploits he was maintained by the court, and knighted; and yet, when the tide turned in the reign of King James II., he forgot his raillery against the principles of the Nonconformists, and wrote as zealously for liberty of conscience, on the foot of the dispensing power, as any man in the kingdom.

But in answer to the invectives of this venial tribe, a pamphlet was published with the approbation of several ministers, entitled "The Principles and Practices of several Nonconformists," showing that their religion is no other than what is professed in the Church of England. The authors declare‡ that they heartily own the Protestant Reformation in doctrine, as contained in the articles of the Church of England; that they are willing to embrace.Bishop Usher's model of church government, which King

* Dr. Grey says that Sir Roger l'Estrange was not the author of this work; that the first part was written by Dr. Nalson, and the other parts, if he mistook not, by Mr. Ware, the son of Sir James Ware, the great antiquarian. The most valuable of Sir Roger l'Estrange's publications is reckoned to be his translation of Josephus. His style, which Mr. Neal commends, has been severely censured by other writers. Mr. Gordon says that "his productions are not fit to be read by any who have taste and good-breeding: they are full of technical terms, of phrases picked up in the streets from apprentices and porters, and nothing can be more low and nauseous." Mr. Granger observes, that L'Estrange was one of the great corrupters of our language, by excluding vowels and other letters commonly pronounced, and introducing "pert and affected phrases." He was licenser of the press to Charles and James II., and died 11th of December, 1704, ætat. eighty-eight. Queen Mary, we are told, made this anagram on his name:
Roger l'Estrange,
"Lying Strange Roger."
—*British Biography,* vol. vi., p. 317. *Granger's History of England,* vol. iv., p. 70.—Ed.
† Burnet, vol. ii., p. 252.. Rapin.
‡ To discredit.Mr. Corbet's piece, Dr. Grey refers to Anthony Wood's character of him, as a preacher of sedition, and a vilifier of the king and his party. But with such writers every sentiment that does not breathe the spirit of passive obedience is seditious. Besides, Mr. Corbet's vindication turned on notorious facts.—Ed.

Charles I. admitted; they hold it unlawful, by the Constitution and laws of this kingdom, for subjects to take arms against the king, his office, authority, or person, or those legally commissioned and authorized by him; nor will they endeavour any alteration in Church or State by any other means than by prayer to God, and by petitioning their superiors; they acknowledge the king's supremacy over all persons, &c., within his dominions; they declare that their trine tends to no unquietness or confusion, any more than the doctrine of the Church of England. And they think it not fair dealing in their adversaries to repeat and aggravate all intemperate passages vented in the late times, when impetuous actings hurried men into extremities; and they apprehend it would not tend to the advantage of the conforming clergy if collections should be published of all their imprudences and weaknesses, as has been done on the other side; they abhor seditious conventicles, and affirm that insurrections were never contrived in their meetings, nor in any whereof they are conscious. Experience, say they, hath witnessed our peaceableness, and that disloyalty or sedition is not to be found among us, by the most inquisitive of our adversaries. They desire the Church of England to take notice that they have no mind to promote popish designs; that they are aware of the advantage that papists make of the divisions of Protestants; that the invectives thrown out against them are made up only of big and swelling words, or of the indiscretions of the few, with which they are not chargeable; they do not pretend to be courtiers or philosophers, but they teach their people to fear God and honour the king; to love the brotherhood, to bridle their tongues; to be meek and lowly, and do their own work with quietness.*

Though the persecution continued very fierce, the Nonconformists ventured to assemble in private, and several pamphlets were published about this time [1676] in their defence; as, "The Peaceable Design; or, an Account of the Nonconformist Meetings," by some London ministers, designed, says Dr. Stillingfleet, to be presented to Parliament; "Reasons which prevailed with the Dissenters in Bristol to continue their Meetings, however prosecuted or disturbed;" "Separation no Schism;" "A Rebuke to Informers; with a Plea for the Ministers of the Gospel called Nonconformists, and their Meetings; with Advice to those to whom the Informers apply for Assistance in their Undertaking."

Informers were now become the terror of the Nonconformists, and the reproach of a civilized nation.† They went abroad in disguise, and,

* On the 15th of January, 1675-6, died Dorothy, the wife of Richard Cromwell, in the forty-ninth year of her age, who, it is thought, never saw her husband after he retired into France. She was the daughter of Richard Major, Esq., of Hursly in Hampshire where she was married on the 1st of May, 1649 The character given of her is, "that she was a prudent, godly, practical Christian." So far, it is ob served, this lady has been happy, that, "among the illiberal things that have been levelled against the protectoral house of Cromwell, her character is almost the only one that scandal has left untouched.'
—*Biographia Britan.,* second edition, vol. iv., p. 538.
† Conform. Plea, part iii., p. 8–10.

like wandering strollers, lived upon the plunder of industrious families. They are a select company (says the Conformists' Plea for the Nonconformists), whom the long suffering of God permits for a time ; they are of no good reputation ; they do not so much as know the names or persons in the country whom they molest, but go by report of their under-servants and accomplices. They come from two or three counties off, to set up this new trade.; whether they are papists or nominal Protestants, who can tell ? They never go to their parish churches, nor any other, but lie in wait and ambush for their prey ;.their estate is invisible, their country unknown to many, and their morals are as bad as the very dregs of the age : these are the men who direct and rule many of the magistrates ; who live upon the spoil of better Christians and subjects than themselves, and go away with honest men's goods honestly gotten.* They, are generally poor, says another writer, as are many of the justices, so that they shared the booty belonging to the king as well as the poor among themselves : by which means the king and the poor got but little.†

Their practice was to insinuate themselves into an acquaintance with some under-servants or lodgers in a Nonconformist's family, under the cloak of religion, in order to discover the place of their meeting. They walked the streets on the Lord's Day, to observe which way any suspected persons went. They frequently sat down in coffee-houses and places of public resort, to listen to conversation. They could turn themselves into any shape, and counterfeit any principles, to obtain their ends. When they had discovered a conventicle, they immediately got a warrant from some who were called confiding justices to break open the house. If the minister was in the midst of his sermon or prayer, they commanded him in the king's name to come down from his pulpit ; and if he did not immediately obey, a file of musketeers was usually sent up to pull him down by force, and to take him into custody ; the congregation was broke up, and the people guarded along the street to a magistrate, and from him to a prison, unless they immediately paid their fines ; the goods of the house were rifled, and frequently carried off as a security for the large fine set upon it.

This was a new way of raising contributions, but it seldom or never prospered ; that which was ill gotten was as ill spent, upon lewd women, or in taverns and alehouses, in gaming, or some kind of debauchery. An informer was but one degree above a beggar ; there was a remarkable blast of Providence upon their persons and substance ; most of them died in poverty and extreme misery ; and as they lived in disgrace, they seemed to die by a remarkable hand of God. Stroud and Marshal, with all their plunder, could not keep out of prison ; and when Keting, another informer, was confined for debt, he wrote to Mr. Baxter to endeavour

his deliverance, confessing he believed God had sent that calamity upon him for giving him so much trouble. Another died in the Compter for debt ;.and great numbers, by their vices, came to miserable and untimely ends.

But as some died off others succeeded, who, by the instigation of the court, disturbed all the meetings they could find. The king commanded the judges and justices of London to put the penal laws in strict execution ; and Sir Jos. Sheldon, lord-mayor, and kinsman to the archbishop, did not fail to do his part. . Sir Tho. Davies issued a warrant to distrain on Mr. Baxter for £50 on account of his lecture in Newstreet ; and when he had built a little chapel in Oxenden-street, the doors were shut up after he had preached.in it once. In April this year [1676] he was disturbed by a company of constables and officers, as he was preaching in Swallow-street, who beat drums under the windows, to interrupt the service, because they had not a warrant to break open the house.

The court bishops, as has been observed more than once, pushed on the informers to do all the mischief they could to the Nonconformists : ".The prelates will not suffer them to be quiet in their families,"* says a considerable writer of these times, " though they have given large and ample testimonies that they are willing to live quietly by their church neighbours—" The dissenting Protestants have been reputed the only enemies of the nation, and therefore only persecuted, says a noble writer, while the papists remain undisturbed, being by the court thought loyal, and by our great bishops not dangerous. Mr. Locke, Bishop Burnet, and others have set a mark upon the names of Archbishop Sheldon, Bishop Morley, Gunning, Henchman, Ward, &c., which will not be easily erased ; but I mention no more, because there were others of a better spirit, who resided in their dioceses, and had no concern with the court.

Among these we may reckon Dr. Edward Reynolds, bishop of Norwich, born in Southampton 1599, and educated in Merton College, Oxford ; he was preacher to the society of Lincoln's Inn, and reckoned one of the most eloquent preachers of his age, though he had some hoarseness in his voice.† In the time of the civil wars he took part with the Parliament, and was one of the Assembly of Divines. In the year 1646 he was appointed one of the preachers to the University of Oxford, and afterward a visiter. Upon the reform of the university, he was made dean of Christ Church, and vice-chancellor. After the king's death he lost his deanery for refusing the Engagement, but complied with all the other changes till the king's restoration, when he appeared with the Presbyterians, but was prevailed with to accept a bishopric on the terms of the king's declaration, which never took place. He was a person of singular affability, meekness, and humility, and a frequent preacher.‡ He was a constant

---

* Sewel, p. 493.

† Dr. Grey is angry with Mr. Neal for not quoting the remainder of the paragraph from Sewel ; in which that writer owns that some honest justices discouraged the practices of the informers, and availed themselves of any defect or failure in their evidence to clear those against whom they informed.—ED.

* State Tracts, vol. ii., p. 54, 55 ; vol. iii., p. 42, &c.　　　† Wood's Athen. Oxon., vol. ii., p. 420.

‡ " He was universally allowed," says Mr. Granger, " to be a man of extraordinary parts, and discovers in his writings a richness of fancy as well as a solidity of judgment." He was buried in the new chapel belonging to his palace, which he built at his own expense.—History of England, vol. iii., p. 241.

resident in his diocess, and a good old Puritan, who never concerned himself with the politics of the court. He died at Norwich January 16, 1676, ætatis seventy-six.

[On May the 22d, 1676, died, aged seventy-three, the pious and learned Mr. John Tombes, B.D., ejected from the living of Leominster in Herefordshire. He was born in 1603, at Bewdley in Worcestershire. At fifteen years of age, having made a good proficiency in grammar learning, he was sent to Magdalen Hall, Oxford, where he studied under the celebrated Mr. William Pemble, upon whose decease he was chosen, though but twenty-one years of age, such was the reputation of his parts and learning, to succeed him in the catechetical lecture in that hall. He held this lecture about seven years, and then removed first to Worcester, and then to Leominster; in both places he had the name of a very popular preacher; and of the latter living he was, soon after, possessed; and as the emolument of it was small, Lord-viscount Scudamore, out of respect to Mr. Tombes, made an addition to it. In 1641 he was, through the spirit of the Church party, obliged to leave this town, and fled to Bristol, where General Fiennes gave him the living of All Saints. The city being taken by the king's party, his wife and children being plundered, and a special warrant being out to apprehend him, he escaped with difficulty, and got to London with his family, September 22, 1643. Here he was some time minister of Fenchurch, till his stipend was taken away for not practising the baptism of infants. He was then chosen preacher to the honourable societies at the Temple, on condition that he would not touch on the controversy about it in the pulpit. Here he continued four years, and was then dismissed for having published a treatise on the subject. He was, after this, chosen minister in the town of his nativity, and had also the parsonage of Ross given him, but he gave up his interest in the latter, to accept the mastership of the hospital at Ledbury. When the affections of the people at Bewdley were alienated from him, on account of his sentiments on baptism, he was restored to his living at Leominster. In 1653 he was appointed a trier for candidates for the ministry. After the Restoration he quitted his places, and laid down the ministry, and went to reside at Salisbury; from whence he had not long before married a rich widow, and conformed to the Church as a lay-communicant. He was held in great respect by Lord-chancellor Hyde, Bishop Sanderson, Bishop Barlow, and Dr. Ward, bishop of Salisbury, whom, during his residence in the city, he often visited. Mr. Wood says "that there were few better disputants in his age than he was." Mr. Wall speaks of him as "a man of the best parts in our nation, and perhaps in any." Dr. Calamy represents him as one "whom all the world must own to have been a very considerable man and an excellent scholar." And it perpetuates his memory with honour, that the Lords, in their conference with the Commons, in 1702, on the bill to prevent occasional conformity, supported their argument, that receiving the sacrament in church did not necessarily import an entire conformity, by an appeal to his example: "There was a very learned and famous man," they said, "that lived at Salisbury,

Mr. Tombes, who was a very zealous Conformist in all points but in one, infant baptism." Mr. Tombes was one of the first of his day who attempted a reformation in the Church, and to remove all *human inventions in the worship of God:* with this view he preached a sermon, which he was commanded by the House of Commons to print. So early as the year 1627, being led, in the course of his lectures, to discuss the subject of baptism, he was brought into doubts concerning the authority for that of infants, which for some years he continued to practise only on the ground of the apostle's words, 1 Cor., vii., xiv. But the answer he received to that argument from an ingenious Baptist at Bristol put him to stand as to that text. When he was in London, he consulted some of the learned ministers there on the question, and at a particular conference debated the matters with them; but it broke up without obviating his objections. He afterward laid his reasons for doubting the lawfulness of the common practice in Latin before the Westminster Assembly: after waiting many months, though he had been informed that a committee was to be appointed to consider the point, he could obtain no answer, nor hear that it was so much as admitted to a debate; but his papers were tossed up and down from one to another to expose him. On being dismissed from the Temple, he printed his Apology; of which Mr. Batchiler says, "Having perused this mild Apology, I conceive that the ingenuity, learning, and piety therein contained deserve the press." He repeatedly took up his pen in this controversy, of which he was judged to be a perfect master, and he was often drawn into public disputations on it, particularly with Mr. Baxter, at Bewdley. "The victory, as usual," says Mr. Nelson, "was claimed on both sides: but some of the learned, who were far from approving his cause, yielded the advantage both of learning and argument to Mr. Tombes."[*] He wrote more books on the subject than any one man in England; and, continuing minister of the parish of Bewdley, he gathered a separate church of those of his own persuasion; which, though not large, consisted of some members distinguished for their piety and solid judgment; and three, who were afterward eminent ministers of that persuasion, were trained up in it, viz., Mr. Richard Adams, Mr. John Eccles, and Captain Boylston. It continued till about the time of the king's restoration.—*Crosby's History of the Baptists,* vol. i., p. 278–293. *Palmer's Nonconformists' Memorial,* vol. ii., p 33–37; and *Nelson's Life of Bishop Bull,* p. 249–253.—ED]. (TOULMIN).†

---

[*] Nelson's Life of Bishop Bull, p. 251.

† Mr. Tombes's works are, "Christ's Commination against Scandalizers," in two treatises; "Fermentum Pharisæorum; or, The Leaven of Pharisaical Worship," a sermon on Matt., xv., 9; "Jehovah Jireh," a thanksgiving sermon; 'Anthropolatria;' or, The Sin of glorying in Man;" "Animadversiones quædam in Aphorismos R. Baxteri de justificat;" "True Old Light exalted above pretended New Light," against the Quakers; "Romanism Discussed" (recommended by Baxter); "Serious Consideration of the Oath of Supremacy;" Supplement to ditto; "Septer Sheba," a treatise on swearing; "Saints no Smiters," against fifth-monarchy men; "Theodulia," in defence of hearing ministers in the Church of England; "Emanuel," against the So-

The murmurs of the people against the government increased rather than diminished. When the Parliament met, they addressed the king to enter into an alliance with the Dutch, and other confederates, for preserving the Spanish Netherlands, as the only means to save Great Britain from popery and slavery.* But his majesty declared he would not suffer his prerogative of making war and peace to be invaded, nor be prescribed to as to his alliances. However, he consented to a separate peace with the Dutch, and then prorogued the Parliament to the middle of July, by which time the French had almost completed their conquests of the Spanish Flanders. The chief thing the Parliament could obtain was the repeal of the popish act *de hæretico comburendo*.†

But when the campaign was over, his majesty did one of the most popular actions of his reign, which was marrying the Princess Mary, eldest daughter of the Duke of York, to the Prince of Orange. The king imagined he could oblige the Dutch, by this family alliance, to submit to a disadvantageous peace with the French; but when the prince declared roundly that he would not sacrifice his honour, nor the liberties of Europe, for a wife, his majesty said he was an honest man, and gave him the princess without any conditions, to the great joy of all the true friends of their country, who had now a Protestant heir to the crown in view, though at some distance. The nuptials were solemnized November 4, 1677, and the royal pair soon after embarked privately for Holland.

This year died Archbishop Sheldon, one of

the most inveterate enemies of the Nonconformists, a man of persecuting principles and a tool of the prerogative, who made a jest of religion, any farther than it was a political engine of state.* He was succeeded by Dr. Sancroft, who was deprived for Jacobitism at the Revolution.† Dr. Compton was promoted to the see of London, in the room of Dr. Henchman, a man of weak but arbitrary principles, till it came to his turn to be a sufferer.‡ Many of

* "I scarce believe," says Dr. Grey, "that the moderate, the impartial, the peaceable Mr. Neal, could write down so many untruths, in one paragraph, without blushing." The doctor expresses himself in another place, vol. ii., p. 320, displeased with Mr. Neal for saying that Dr. Sheldon "never gave any great specimens of his piety or learning to the world," vol. iii., p. 388. In reply to this he quotes Bishop Burnet, who allows that Sheldon "was esteemed a learned man before the wars." Here the doctor refers to Bishop Kennet, who says that Sheldon "withdrew from all state affairs some years before his death;" and to Echard, who extols his learning and piety, as well as his munificent benefactions, which we have specified, vol. iii., p. 217, note. Dr. Samuel Parker, who had been his chaplain, says, "He was a man of undoubted piety; but though he was very assiduous at prayers, yet he did not set so great a value upon them as others did, nor regarded so much worship as the use of worship, placing the chief point of religion in the practice of a good life." Mr. Granger represents him as "meriting, by his benevolent heart, public spirit, prudent conduct, and exemplary piety, the highest and most conspicuous station in the Church." These characters of his grace appear to contradict Mr. Neal. On the other hand, he is supported by the testimony of Bishop Burnet, who says, " He seemed not to have a deep sense of religion, if any at all, and spoke of it most commonly as of an engine of government, and a matter of policy:" and the facts adduced above show his intolerant spirit. But all agree in describing him as a man whose generous and munificent deeds displayed a benevolent and liberal mind, and whose pleasantness and affability of manner were truly ingratiating. "His conversation (as Dr. Parker draws his character) was easy; he never sent any man away discontented; among his domestics he was both pleasant and grave, and governed his family with authority and courtesy." His advice to young noblemen and gentlemen, who, by the order of their parents, daily resorted to him, deserves to be mentioned. It was always this: "Let it be your principal care to become honest men, and afterward be as devout and religious as you will. No piety will be of any advantage to yourselves or anybody else, unless you are honest and moral men."—*Granger*, vol. iii., p. 230. *British Biography*, vol. v., p. 25, 26; *note;* and *Burnet*, vol. i., p. 257.—ED.

† "The bare mention of this is sufficient to expose Mr. Neal's sneer upon one of the greatest, the best, and most conscientious prelates."—*Dr. Grey*, vol. iii., p. 376.—ED.

‡ Dr. Grey affects to doubt whether Mr. Neal designed this character for Bishop Henchman or Bishop Compton: though Henchman is the immediate antecedent whose character more properly follows the mention of his death. The doctor appeals from Mr. Neal to Mr. Echard, who commends Bishop Henchman's wisdom and prudence, and his admirable management of the king's escape after the battle of Worcester. Mr. Neal, in speaking of his arbitrary principles, till he was pinched, undoubtedly refers to his conduct when the declaration for liberty of conscience was published. On this occasion he was much alarmed, and strictly enjoined his clergy to preach against popery, though it offended the king. This prelate was lord-almoner, and he was the editor of " Gentleman's Calling," supposed to be

cinians; "Animadversiones in librum G. Bulli, cui titulum fecit, Harmonia apostolica." The following upon Baptism: "An Exercit. about Infant Baptism," presented to the chairman of committee of Assembly of Divines at Westminster; "Examen of Mr. S. Marshal's Sermon;" "Apology" for ditto; "Addition" to ditto, against Bailie; "Antidote against a Passage in Dedication of Baxter's Saint's Rest;" "Præcursor;" "Antipædobaptism;" Ditto, part ii.; Ditto, part iii.; " A Plea for the Antipædobaptists;" "An Answer to the Anabaptists silenced;" " Short Catechism about Baptism;" "Felo de se," against Baxter; "Just Reply to Wills and Blinman."—C.

* Notwithstanding this alarm, on a calculation that was made in the preceding year, the Nonconformists of all sorts, and papists included, were found to be in proportion to the members of the Church of England, as one to twenty; " which was a number," says Bishop Sherlock, " too small to hurt the Constitution."—*His Test Act vindicated*, as quoted by *Dr. Calamy, Own Life*, p. 63, *MS.*—ED.

† This writ was taken away on the principle of the wisdom of prevention, under the apprehension of popery, " to preclude the risk of being burned themselves, not to exempt others from the possibility of being burned." The conduct of administration, in this instance, " was the effect of fear, not of general and enlarged principles."—*Hobhouse's Treatise on Heresy*, p. 29, *note*.

Another modern writer observes, that "though the State, in this instance, showed some moderation, neither then, nor at any subsequent time, has any alteration been made in the constitution of the Church." It still assumes exclusively to itself all truth, and may persecute some sectaries as heretics, and punish them by "excommunication, degradation, and other ecclesiastical censures, not extending to death." It is not clear that ecclesiastical judges may not, even now, doom them to the flames, though the civil power will not execute the sentence.—*High Church Politics*, p. 64.—ED.

the bishops waited on the king this summer for his commands to put the penal laws into execution, which they did with so much diligence, that Mr. Baxter says he was so weary of keeping his doors shut against persons who came to distrain his goods for preaching, that he was forced to leave his house, to sell his goods, and part with his very books.* About twelve years, says he, I have been driven one hundred miles from them, and when I had paid dear for the carriage, after two or three years I was forced to sell them. This was the case of many others, who, being separated from their families and friends, and having no way of subsistence, were forced to sell their books and household furniture, to keep them from starving.

This year [1677] died the Rev. Dr. Tho. Manton, ejected from Covent Garden: he was born in Somersetshire, 1620, educated at Tiverton School, and from thence placed at Wadham College, Oxon. He was ordained by Dr. Hall, bishop of Exeter;† when he was not more than twenty years of age: his first settlement was at Stoke Newington, near London, where he continued seven years, being generally esteemed an excellent preacher, and a learned expositor of Scripture. Upon the death or resignation of Mr. Obadiah Sedgwick, he was presented to the living of Covent Garden by the Duke of Bedford, and preached to a numerous congregation. The doctor was appointed one of the protector's chaplains, and one of the triers of persons' qualifications for the ministry; which service he constantly attended. In the year 1660, he was very forward, in concert with the Presbyterian ministers, to accomplish the king's restoration, and was one of the commissioners at the Savoy Conference; he was then created doctor of divinity, and offered the deanery of Rochester, but declined it. After he was turned out of his living in 1662, he held a private meeting in his own house, but was imprisoned, and met with several disturbances in his ministerial work. He was consulted in all the treaties for a comprehension with the Established Church, and was high in the esteem of the Duke of Bedford, Earl of Manchester, and other noble persons. At length, finding his constitution breaking, he resigned himself to God's wise disposal, and being seized with a kind of lethargy, he died October 18, 1677, in the fifty-seventh year of his age, and was buried in the chancel of the church of Stoke Newington. Dr. Bates, in his funeral sermon, says he was a divine of a rich fancy, a strong memory, and happy elocution, improved by diligent study. He was an excellent Christian, a fervent preacher, and every way a blessing to the Church of God.‡ His practical works were published in five volumes in folio,

written by the author of the "Whole Duty of Man."—*Granger*, vol. iii., p. 233. Bishop Compton's character will appear in the succeeding part of this history.—ED.   * Baxter, part iii., p. 171, 172.

† He never took any other than deacon's orders, and never would submit to any other ordination, for it was his judgment that he was properly ordained to the ministerial office, and that no earthly power had any right to divide and parcel that out at their pleasure.—*Palmer*, vol. i., p. 176.—C.

‡ Calamy, vol. ii., p. 42; and Palmer's Noncon. Mem., vol. i., p. 138.

at several times after his death, and are in great esteem among the Dissenters to this day.*

About the same time died Mr. John Rowe, M.A., born in the year 1626, and educated for some time at Cambridge, but translated to Oxford about the time of the visitation in the year 1648. Here he was admitted M.A. and fellow of Corpus Christi College. He was first lecturer at Witney, in Oxfordshire; afterward preacher at Tiverton, in Devonshire, and one of the commissioners for ejecting ignorant and insufficient ministers in that county. Upon the death of Mr. William Strong, in the year 1654, he was called to succeed him in the Abbey Church of Westminster; at which place, as in all others, his sermons were very much attended to by persons of all persuasions.† On the 14th of March, 1659, he was appointed one of the approvers of ministers by act of Parliament; but on the king's restoration he gave way to the change of the times, and was silenced with his brethren by the Act of Uniformity. He was a divine of great gravity and piety; his sermons were judicious and well studied, fit for the audience of men of the best quality in those times. After the Bartholomew Act, he continued with his people, and preached to them in Bartholomew Close, and elsewhere, as the times would permit, till his death, which happened October 12, 1677, in the fifty-second year of his age. He lies buried in Bunhill Fields, under an altar monument of a brick foundation.‡ The words with which he con-

* Dr. Manton was also in great estimation for his activity and address in the management of public affairs, and was generally in the chair in meetings of the dissenting ministers in the city. Dr. Grey questions the truth of Mr. Neal's assertion that he was ordained at the age of twenty years, especially as he gives no authority for it. "Bishop Hall," he says, "was too canonical a man to admit any person into deacon's orders at that age." If the fact be misstated, he must be destitute of all candour who can impute this to a wilful falsification. Archbishop Usher used to call Dr. Manton a voluminous preacher, meaning that he had the art of reducing the substance of volumes of divinity into a narrow compass. But it was true, in the literal sense, he was voluminous as an author: for his sermons run into several folios, one of which contains one hundred and nineteen sermons on the one hundred and nineteenth Psalm. The task of reading these, when he was a youth, to his aunt, had an unhappy effect on the mind of Lord Bolingbroke. In a letter to Dr. Swift, he writes, "My next shall be as long as one of Dr. Manton's sermons, who taught my youth to yawn, and prepared me to be a High-churchman, that I might never hear him read, nor read him more."—*Granger's History*, vol. iii., p. 304, *note.*—ED. The works of Dr. Manton are at present in very high repute. His five folios are only to be purchased in London at fourteen or fifteen pounds; and several of his minor works have lately been republished. His theology is sound, and the preacher who possesses his works has access to immense treasures.—C.

† Mr. Rowe was a good scholar, and well read in the fathers; and had such a knowledge of Greek, that he began very young to keep a diary in that language, which he continued till his death; but he burned most of it in his last illness.—*Palmer*. His works are very excellent, especially the "Love of Christ in his Incarnation," in thirty sermons, and the "Saint's Triumph."—C.

‡ Calamy, vol. ii., p. 39. Palmer's Noncon. Mem., vol. i., p. 142.

cluded his last sermon were these : "We should not desire to continue longer in this world than to glorify God, to finish our work, and to be ready to say, Farewell, time; welcome, blessed eternity ; even so; come, Lord Jesus !"

CHAPTER X.

FROM THE POPISH PLOT TO THE DEATH OF KING CHARLES II., IN THE YEAR 1684–5.

1678.

THE king having concluded a peace with the Dutch, became mediator between the French and the confederates, at the treaty of Nimeguen ; where the former managed the English court so dexterously, that the emperor and Spaniards were obliged to buy their peace, at the expense of the best part of Flanders.

From this time to the end of the king's reign, we meet with little else but domestic quarrels between the king and his Parliament ; sham plots, and furious sallies of rage and revenge, between the court and country parties. The Nonconformists were very great sufferers by these contests ; the penal laws being in full force, and the execution of them in the hands of their avowed enemies.

No sooner was the nation at peace abroad but a formidable plot broke out at home, to take away the king's life, to subvert the Constitution, to introduce popery, and to extirpate the Protestant religion root and branch. It was called the Popish Plot, from the nature of the design, and the quality of the conspirators, who were no less than Pope Innocent XI., Cardinal Howard, his legate, and the generals of the Jesuits in Spain and at Rome.* When the king was taken off, the Duke of York was to receive the crown as a gift from the pope, and hold it in fee. If there happened any disturbance, the city of London was to be fired, and the infamy of the whole affair to be laid upon the Presbyterians and fanatics, in hopes that the churchmen, in the heat of their fury, would cut them in pieces, which would make way for the more easy subversion of the Protestant religion. Thus an insurrection, and perhaps a second massacre of the Protestants, was intended ; for this purpose they had great numbers of popish officers in pay, and some thousands of men secretly listed to appear as occasion required, as was deposed by the oaths of Bedloe, Tongue, Dr. Oates, and others.

The discovery of this plot spread a prodigious alarm over the nation, and awakened the fears of those who had been lulled into a fatal security. The king's life was the more valuable, as the popish successor was willing to run all risks for the introducing of his religion. The murder of Sir Edmundbury Godfrey† at this juncture,

a zealous and active Protestant justice of peace, increased men's suspicions of a plot, and the depositions upon oath of the above-mentioned witnesses seemed to put it beyond all doubt ; for upon their impeachment, Sir G. Wakeman, the queen's physician, Mr. Ed. Coleman, the Duke of York's secretary, Mr. Richard Langhorne, and eight other Romish priests and Jesuits, were apprehended and secured. When the Parliament met, they voted that there was a damnable and hellish plot contrived and carried on by popish recusants against the life of the king and the Protestant religion. Five popish lords were ordered into custody, viz., Lord Stafford, Powis, Arundel, Petre, and Bellasys. A proclamation was issued against papists, and the king was addressed to remove the Duke of York from his person and councils.

Though the king gave himself no credit to the plot, yet finding it impracticable to stem the tide of the people's zeal, he consented to the execution of the law upon several of the condemned criminals ; Mr. Coleman, and five of the Jesuits, were executed at Tyburn, who protested their innocence to the last ; and a year or two forward, Lord Stafford was beheaded on Tower Hill. But the court party turned the plot into ridicule ; the king told Lord Halifax " that it was not probable that the papists should conspire to kill him, for have I not been kind enough to them ?" says his majesty. " Yes," says his lordship, " you have been too kind, indeed, to them ; but they know you will only trot, and they want a prince that will gallop." The court employed their tool, Sir Roger

most of whom were of eminence and rank.—*Granger's History of England,* vol. iii., p. 400, 8vo.
This shows the interest which the public took in this event. So great was the alarm this plot raised, that posts and chains were put up in all parts of the city, and a considerable number of the trained bands drawn out night after night, well armed, and watching with as much care as if a great insurrection were expected before the morning. The general topics of conversation were designed massacres, to be perpetrated by assassins ready for the purpose, and by recruits from abroad. A sudden darkness at eleven o'clock, on the Sunday after the murder of Sir Edmundbury Godfrey, so that the ministers could not read their notes in the pulpit without candles, was looked upon as awfully ominous. The minds of people were kept in agitation and terror by dismal stories and frequent executions. Young and old quaked with fear. Not a house was unprovided with arms. No one went to rest at night without the apprehension of some tragical event to happen before the morning. This state of alarm and terror lasted not for a few weeks only, but months. The pageantry of mock-processions employed on this occasion heightened the aversion to popery, and inflamed resentment against the conspirators. In one of these, amid a vast crowd of spectators, who filled the air with their acclamations, and expressed great satisfaction in the show, there were carried on men's shoulders, through the principal streets, the effigies of the pope and the representative of the devil behind him, whispering in his ear and caressing him (though he afterward deserted him, before he was committed to the flames), together with the likeness of the dead body of Sir Edmundbury Godfrey, carried before him by a man on horseback, to remind the people of his execrable murder. A great number of dignitaries in their copes, with crosses of monks, friars, Jesuits, and popish bishops with their mitres, trinkets, and appurtenances, formed the rest of the procession.—*Dr. Calamy's Own Life, MSS.,* p. 67, 68.—ED.

---

* Echard, p. 934.
† The death of this gentleman, an able magistrate and of a fair character, was deemed a much stronger evidence of the reality of the plot than the oath of Oates. The foolish circumstance of his name being anagramatized to " I find murdered by rogues," helped to confirm the opinion of his being murdered by papists. His funeral was celebrated with the most solemn pomp. Seventy-two clergymen preceded the corpse, which was followed by a thousand persons,

l'Estrange,* to write a weekly paper against the plot; and the country party encouraged Mr. Car to write a weekly packet of advice from Rome, discovering the frauds and superstitions of that court; for which he was arraigned, convicted, and fined in the Court of King's Bench, and his papers forbid to be printed. An admirable order for a Protestant court of judicature!

But it was impossible to allay the fears of the Parliament, who had a quick sense of the dangers of popery, and therefore passed a bill to disable all persons of that religion from sitting in either house of Parliament, which is still in force, being excepted out of the Act of Toleration.† The act requires all members of Parliament to renounce by oath the doctrine of transubstantiation, and to declare the worship of the Virgin Mary and of the saints, practised in the Church of Rome, to be idolatrous. Bishop Gunning argued against charging the Church of Rome with idolatry; but the House paid him little regard; and when the bill was passed, he took the oath in common with the rest.

The Duke of York got himself excepted out of the bill,‡ but the fears of his accession to the crown were so great, that there was a loud talk of bringing a bill into the House to exclude him from the succession as a papist; upon which the king came to the House November 9, and assured them that he would consent to any bills for securing the Protestant religion, provided they did not impeach the right of succession, nor the descent of the crown in the true line, nor the just rights of any Protestant successor. But this not giving satisfaction, his majesty, towards the end of December, first prorogued, and then dissolved the Parliament, after they had been chosen almost eighteen years.

It may be proper to observe concerning the Popish Plot,§ that though the king's life might not be immediately struck at, yet there was such strong evidence to prove the reality of a plot to subvert the Constitution and introduce popery, that no disinterested person can doubt it. Mr. Rapin, who had carefully considered the evidence, concludes that there was a medi-

---

* This person, of whom we have already spoken, formerly called "Oliver's Fiddler," was now the admired "Buffoon of High Church." He called the shows, mentioned in our last note, "hobby-horsing processions."—*Calamy's MSS.*, p. 67.—Ed.

† Burnet, vol. ii., p. 211.

‡ This point was carried in favour of the duke by no more than two votes. Had it been negatived, he would, in the next place, have been voted away from the king's presence.—*Sir John Reresby's Memoirs*, p. 72.—Ed.

§ It was a happy effect of the discovery of this plot, that while it raised in the whole body of the English Protestants alarming apprehensions of the dangers to which their civil and religious liberties were exposed, it united them against their common enemy. Mutual prejudices were softened: animosities subsided. the Dissenters were regarded as the true friends of their country, and their assemblies began to be more public and numerous. At this time an evening lecture was set up in a large room of a coffee-house in Exchange Alley; it was conducted by Mr. John Shower, Mr. Lambert, Mr. Dorrington, and Mr. Thomas Goodwin; and it was supported and attended by some of the principal merchants, and by several who afterward filled the most eminent posts in the city of London.—*Tong's Life of Shower*, p. 17, 18.—Ed.

tated design, supported by the king and the Duke of York, to render the king absolute, and introduce the popish religion; for this is precisely what was meant by the plot; the design of killing the king was only an appendage to it, and an effect of the zeal of some private persons, who thought the plot would be crowned with the surer success by speedily setting the Duke of York upon the throne. Bishop Burnet adds,* that though the king and he agreed in private conversation that the greatest part of the evidence was a contrivance, yet he confesses it appeared, by Coleman's letters, that the design of converting the nation, and of rooting out the northern heresy, was very near being executed.† To which I beg leave to add, that though the design of killing the king did not take place at this time, his majesty felt the effects of it, in his violent death, four or five years afterward.

This year died Mr. Thomas Vincent, M.A., the ejected minister of Milk-street, born at Hertford May, 1634, and educated in Christ Church, Oxford.‡ He was chaplain to Robert, earl of Leicester, and afterward minister of Milk-street, London, till the Act of Uniformity took place. He was an humble and a zealous preacher, of moderate principles, and an unspotted life. He continued in the city throughout the whole plague, the awfulness of which gave him a peculiar fervency and zeal in his ministerial work. On this occasion he published some very awakening treatises; as, "A Spiritual Antidote for a dying Soul," and "God's terrible Voice in the City."§ He not only preached in public, but visited all the sick who sent for him in their infected houses, being void of all fear of death. He continued in health during the whole of that dreadful calamity, and was afterward useful, as the times would permit, to a numerous congregation, being generally respected by men of all persuasions; but his excessive labours put an end to his life October 15, 1678, in the forty-fifth year of his age.‖

---

* This corresponds with his declarations to Sir John Reresby; whom at one time he told, in the presence of the lord-treasurer, at the Duchess of Portsmouth's lodgings, "he took it to be some artifice, and that he did not believe one word of the whole story." At another time his majesty said to him, "Bedloe was a rogue, and that he was satisfied he had given some false evidence concerning the death of Sir Edmundbury Godfrey."—*Memoirs*, p. 67, 72.

Dr. Grey refers to Echard and Bishop Burnet, as fully discrediting Mr. Neal's account of this plot; and, with this view, gives a long passage from Carte's History of the Duke of Ormond, vol. ii., p. 517. The reader may see the evidence both for and against it fully and fairly stated by Dr. Harris, Life of Charles II., vol. ii., p. 137-157.—Ed.

† Page 198-214.

‡ His father, a pious minister, who died in the vicinity of Durham. was so harassed for his nonconformity, that though he had a large family, not two of his children were born in the same county!—C.

§ Calamy, vol. ii., p. 32. Palmer's Noncon. Mem., vol. i., p. 125.

‖ Mr. Thomas Vincent had the whole New Testament and Psalms by heart. He took this pains, as he often said, "not knowing but they who took from him his pulpit, might in time demand his Bible also."—*Calamy*. Besides his publications enumerated by this writer, Mr. Vincent, on occasion of an eruption of Mount Ætna. published a book entitled "Fire and Brimstone: 1. From heaven in the burning of Sodom

Mr. Theophilus Gale, M.A., and fellow of Magdalen College, Oxford, was ejected from Winchester, where he had been stated preacher for some time ; after which he travelled abroad as tutor to the son of Philip, lord Wharton. Upon his return, he settled with Mr. John Rowe as an assistant, in which station he died. The Oxford historian allows that he was a man of great reading, an exact philologist and philosopher, a learned and industrious divine, as appears by his Court of the Gentiles, and the Vanity of Pagan Philosophy. He kept a little academy for the instruction of youth, and was well versed in the fathers, being, at the same time, a good metaphysician and school divine.* He died of a consumption this year [1678], in the forty-ninth year of his age.†

The king having summoned a new Parliament to meet in March, all parties exerted themselves in the elections ; the Nonconformists appeared generally for those who were for prosecuting the Popish Plot and securing a Protestant succession : these being esteemed patriots and friends of liberty, in opposition to those who made a loud cry for the Church, and favoured the arbitrary measures of the court, and the personal interest of the Duke of York. The elections in many places were the occasion of great heat, but were carried almost everywhere against the court. Mr. Rapin says that the Presbyterians, though long oppressed, were still numerous in corporations. The semi-conformists, as Mr. Echard calls the moderate churchmen, and the Dissenters were on one side, and the High-churchmen and papists on the other. Before the Parliament assembled, the Duke of York was sent out of the way to Flanders, but with this positive assurance, that his majesty would consent to nothing in prejudice of his right of succession. And farther to ingratiate himself with the people, and make a show of moderation, a new privy council was chosen out of the Low Church party ; but this not satisfying as long as the duke's succession was in view, the Commons, soon after the opening the sessions, ordered in a bill to disable the Duke of York from inheriting the imperial crown of England, and carried it through the House with a high hand. Upon which, his majesty came to the House and dissolved them, before they

had sat three months. This threw the nation into new convulsions, and produced a great number of pamphlets against the government, the act for restraining the press being lately expired.

The Popish Plot having fixed a brand of infamy and ingratitude on the whole body of Roman Catholics, the courtiers attempted to relieve them by setting on foot a sham Protestant plot, and fathering it upon the Presbyterians ;* for this purpose, spies and other mercenaries were employed to bring news from all parts of the town, which was then full of cabals. At length a plot was formed by one Dangerfield, a subtle and dangerous papist, but a very villain, who had been lately got out of jail by the assistance of one Mrs. Cellier, a midwife, a lewd woman, who carried him to the Countess of Powis, whose husband was in the Tower for the Popish Plot ; with her he formed his scheme, and having got a list of the names of the chief Protestant nobility and gentry, he wrote treasonable letters to them, to be left at the houses of the Nonconformists and other active Protestants in several parts of England, that search being made upon some other pretences, when the letters were found, they might be apprehended for treason. At the same time, he intruded into the company of some of the most zealous enemies of popery about town, and informed the king and the Duke of York that he had been invited to accept of a commission ; that a new form of government was to be set up ; and that the king and royal family were to be banished. The story was received with pleasure, and Dangerfield had a present, and a pension of £3 a week, to carry on his correspondence. Having got some little acquaintance with Colonel Mansel in Westminster, he made up a bundle of seditious letters, with the assistance of Mrs. Cellier, and having laid them in a dark corner of Mansel's room behind the bed, he sent for officers from the custom-house to search for prohibited goods while he was out of town ; but none were found except the bundle of letters, which, upon examination of the parties concerned before the king and council, were proved to be counterfeit ; upon which the court disowned the plot, and having taken away Dangerfield's pension, sent him to Newgate. Search being made into Mrs. Cellier's house, there was found a little book in a meal-tub, written very fair, and tied up with ribands, which contained the whole scheme of the fiction. It was dictated by Lady Powis, and proved by her maid to be laid there by her order, from whence it obtained the name of the Meal-tub Plot. Dangerfield, who was a notorious liar, finding himself undone if he persisted in what he could not support, made an ample confession, and published a narrative, wherein he declared that he was employed by the popish party ; and chiefly by the popish lords in the Tower, with the Countess of Powis, to invent the Meal-tub Plot, which was to have thrown the Popish Plot wholly upon the Presbyterians. It was printed by order of the House of Commons in the year 1680. Dangerfield being pardoned, went out of the way into Flanders ; but returning to England in King James's reign, he was tried for it, and sentenced to be whipped,

---

and Gomorrah formerly. 2. From earth, in the burning of Mount Ætna lately. 3. From hell, in burning of the wicked eternally," 1670, 8vo.—*Granger's History*, vol. iii., p. 329, *note.*—ED. Mr. Vincent's most popular work, and that by which he is now best known, is his most excellent explanation of the Assembly's Catechism.—C.

* Mr. Gale was a frequent preacher in the University, and a considerable tutor ; Bishop Hopkins was one of his pupils. He left all his real and personal estate for the education and benefit of poor students, and his library to the college in New-England, except the philosophical part, which he reserved for the use of students in England. The world had like to have lost his great and learned work, The Court of the Gentiles, in the fire of London. A friend, to whose care he left his desk while he was travelling, threw it into the cart merely to make the load, when he was removing his own goods.—*Brit. Biog.*, vol. v., p. 182–186.—EN. No theological library of any pretensions can be without this incomparable work of Gale's. He left his valuable theological library to Harvard University.—*Palmer*, vol. i., p. 245.—C.

† Calamy, vol. ii., p. 64. Palmer, vol. i.; p 189.

* Burnet, vol. ii., p. 272. Rapin, vol. ii., p. 741,

at the cart's tail from Newgate to Tyburn; in his return from whence he was murdered by one Frances in the coach. Mrs. Cellier was tried June 11, 1680, before Lord-chief-justice Scroggs, and acquitted for want of evidence. But the discovery, instead of relieving the papists from the charge of the Popish Plot, turned very much to their disadvantage; for when the next Parliament met, the House of Commons resolved that Sir Robert Car be expelled the House, and sent to the Tower, for declaring publicly in the city of Bristol that there was no popish, but a Presbyterian plot.* Sir Robert Yeomans was sent into custody on the same account; and Mr. Richard Thompson, a clergyman, was impeached for decrying the Popish Plot in his sermon, January 30, 1679, and for turning the same upon the Protestants;' for which, and for preaching against the liberty and property of the subject, and the privileges of Parliament, the House declared him a scandal and reproach to his profession.

This year [1679] died the reverend and learned Mr. Matt. Pool, M.A., the ejected minister of St. Michael's Querne; he was born in the city of York, and educated in Emanuel College, Cambridge, a divine of great piety, charity, and literature. He was indefatigable in his labours, and left behind him (says the Oxford historian) the character of a most celebrated critic and casuist. After ten years' close application, he published his Synopsis Criticorum,† in five fo-

* State Tracts, vol. ii., p. 217.
† "The plan of this work," says Mr. Granger, "was judicious, and the execution more free from errors than seems consistent with so great a work, finished in so short a time, by one man." It includes not only an abridgement of the "Critici Sacri," and other expositors, but extracts from a great number of treatises and pamphlets that would have been otherwise lost. It was undertaken by the advice of the learned Bishop Lloyd; it was encouraged and patronised by Tillotson, and the king granted a patent for the privilege of printing it. Mr. Pool formed and completed a scheme for maintaining young men of eminent parts at the University of Cambridge,for the study of divinity; and, by his solicitations, in a short time raised £900 a year for that purpose. The scheme sunk at the Restoration; but to it the world is said, in some measure, to owe Dr. Sherlock, afterward Dean of St. Paul's. While he was drawing up his Synopsis, it was his custom to rise at three or four o'clock, and take a raw egg about eight or nine, and another about twelve; then to continue his studies till the afternoon was far advanced. He spent the evening at some friend's house, particularly Alderman Ashurst's, and would be exceedingly, but innocently, merry: when it was nearly time to go home, he would give the conversation a serious turn, saying, "Let us now call for a reckoning." His "Annotations" were completed by other hands; the fifty-ninth and sixtieth chapters of Isaiah by Mr. Jackson, of Moulsey. Dr. Collinges wrote the notes on the remainder of that prophet, on Jeremiah, Lamentations, the four Evangelists, the Epistles to the Corinthians and Galatians, to Timothy, Titus, and Philemon, and on the Book of Revelations: The annotations on Ezekiel and the minor prophets were drawn up by Mr. Hurst, and on Daniel, by Mr. William Cooper. Mr. Vinke commented on the Acts, Mr. Mayo on the Romans. The notes on the Ephesians, and the Epistles of James, Peter, and Jude, were composed by Mr. Viel; on Philippians and Colossians, by Mr. Thomas Adams; on the Thessalonians, by Mr. Barker; on the Hebrews, by Mr Obad. Hughes. Mr. Howe undertook the three Epistles of John.—*Calamy and Palmer, ut supra.* Gran-

lios. He afterward entered on a commentary upon the whole Bible, but proceeded no farther than the fifty-eighth chapter of Isaiah; however, the design, being valuable, was carried on, and completed by other hands. Mr. Pool published several excellent treatises, as "The Nullity of the Romish Faith," &c., for which he was threatened to be assassinated,* his name being in Dr. Oates's list: he therefore retired to Holland, but died, as it is thought, by poison at Amsterdam, in the month of October, 1679, ætat. fifty-six.

Dr. Thomas Goodwin, born at Rolisby in Norfolk, and educated in Catherine Hall, Cambridge. He was a great admirer of Dr. Preston, and afterward himself a famous preacher in Cambridge. In 1634 he left the university, being dissatisfied with the terms of conformity. In 1639 he went into Holland, and became pastor of an Independent congregation at Arnheim. He returned to London about the beginning of the Long Parliament, and was one of the dissenting brethren in the Assembly of Divines. After the king's death he was made president of Magdalen College, and one of the triers of ministers. He was in high esteem with Oliver Cromwell, and attended him on his deathbed.† In the common register of the university he is said to be,"in scriptis theologicis quam plurimis orbi notus," *i. e.*, well known to the world by many theological writings. After the Restoration he resigned his presidentship, and retired to London, where he continued the exercise of his ministry till his death, which happened February 23, 1679–80, in the eightieth year of his age. He was a good scholar, an eminent divine and textuary. His works are since printed in five folios.‡

ger's History, vol. iii., p. 311; and *Birch's Life of Tillotson*, p. 36.—ED.
* Calamy, vol. ii., p. 14. Palmer's Noncon. Mem., vol. i., p. 133.
† On which occasion he was overheard by Dr. Tillotson to express himself, boldly and enthusiastically, confident of the protector's recovery; and when he found himself mistaken, to exclaim, in a subsequent address to God, "Thou hast deceived us, and we were deceived." He was a man much addicted to retirement and deep contemplation, which dispose the mind to enthusiastical confidence. He and Dr. Owen are called by Wood "the two Atlasses and Patriarchs of Independency." In the fire of London he lost half of his library, to the value of £500, but he was thankful that the loss fell on the books of human learning only, those on divinity being preserved. He is supposed to be the Independent minister and head of a college described by the "Spectator,"No. 494.—*Birch's Life of Tillotson*, Grey, vol. i., p. 185. *Granger*, vol. iii., p. 303.—ED.
‡ Calamy's Account, vol. ii., p. 61. Palmer's Non. Mem., vol. i., p. 236-241. Goodwin's works are exceedingly rare. He was a Calvinist of the Supralapsarian cast, but did not put doctrinal sentiment in place of practical holiness.

I cannot omit to notice that, in the second volume of Dr. Goodwin's works, in his exposition on the Revelations, written in 1639 and printed in 1683, there is a prophetic description of the Oxford Tract Heresy (see 66th and 67th pages). It conveys a remarkable anticipation of the rise, progress, object, and ultimate fall of this popish device, which we now see spreading in the Episcopal Church both in England and America. As very few of the readers of this History can obtain access to Goodwin, I subjoin it.

"Now take the times of popery before the Refor-

The last Parliament being dissolved abruptly, a new one was convened for October 17, 1680, in which the elections went pretty much as in

the last, the cry of the people being, No popery, no pensioners, no arbitrary government. But the king prorogued them from time to time for

mation (that is, before the time the Protestant kingdoms did first begin to cast off the pope), and there were none that were suffered to have such a remiss (no. nor any lesser) kind of owning the Beast, but must all (as they did) receive his mark or his name, and be professed papists, coming to mass, acknowledging the pope, and worshipping his image, or they might not buy and sell, they might not live quietly as others did. Therefore, those that receive the number of his name must be some generation of men risen up since, and that also within those kingdoms (some of them) that have renounced the pope ; for within the popish dominions (unto this day) either the Inquisition suffers none to profess less than the receiving his name at least, or in others, those that are of papists the most moderate, yet receive the name of the Beast at least, and so, more than the number of his name. But this number of his name seems to be a company that proceed not so far as to receive his character, for they do not profess themselves to be papists, and yet are of the number of his name ; that is, do hold and bring in such doctrines and opinions, and such rites in worship, as shall make all men reckon or number them among papists in heart and affection ; and so they are of the number of his name, that is, in account such, they behave themselves to be so as they are, and deserved to be accounted and esteemed papists, and to aim at popery, in the judgment of all orthodox and Reformed Protestants, and that justly ; for although their profession deny it, yet, when their actions, and their *corrupting* of doctrine and worship, shall speak it to all men's minds, they cannot but judge that the pope, and the fear of him, is before their eyes (as David speaks of wicked men), and as those in Titus, that profess they know God, yet in their works deny him, are justly accounted Athe-ists ; so those that shall profess the Reformed religion, yet in all their practices, and *underhand policies*, *depress it, and advance the popish party*, are justly to be accounted papists, and to have received the number of his name.

" The phrase (number of a name) is not only taken for a name consisting of numeral letters, and so, not only for number arithmetical, but the word (number) is in many languages put for the account reckoning or esteem that is commonly had of men ; as in Latin we say, He is one *nullius numeri*, of no number or account. So, then, number of a name is a common esteem or account to be such or such a one ; and so the number of the Beast's name here is the common repute or esteem *to be a papist*, procured through underhand advancing of the popish cause. It being, therefore, spoken in a distinct and lower degree from receiving his name or mark (which note out an open expression), doth yet necessarily import so much inclining and cleaving to him (though secretly) as shall deserve that account and repute to be so numbered, as being, indeed, tacitly and in heart, as truly of his company as those that receive his name. Now if, in opening the meaning of the Holy Ghost in the phrase here, this description shall see to the life to picture out a generation of such kind of popish persons as these in any (even the most famous) of the Reformed churches, 'i. e., *the Church of England*,' certainly there will not want good ground for it ; for though they, with an impudent forehead, renounce the *pope's* character, and the name of *papists*, and will by no means be called *priests of Baal* (though priests they affect to be called), but boast themselves to be of the Reformation, and opposites to the papal faction, yet with as much impudence do they bring in image of popish worship and ceremonies, added to some old limbs, never cast out, other substantial parts, of altars, crucifixes, second service, and the like, so as to make up a full likeness of the public service to that of the

Popish Church ; they bring in the carcass first, which may afterward be inspired with the same opinions. All this, not as popery, or with annexation of popish idolatrous opinions, but upon such grounds only as *Protestants* themselves have continued other ceremonies. And as in worship, so in doctrine, they seek to bring in a *presence* in the sacrament of the Lord's Supper, beyond that which is spiritual, to faith, which yet is not popish transubstantiation ; a power in priests to forgive sins, beyond that which is declarative, yet not that which mass-priests arrogate ; justification by works, yet not so grossly as in the way of popish merit, but as a condition of popish idolatrous opinions, but upon such grounds only as *Protestants* themselves have continued other ceremonies. And as in worship, so in doctrine, they seek to bring in a *presence* in the sacrament of the Lord's Supper, beyond that which is not so grossly as in the way of popish merit, but as a condition of popish merit, but as a condition of popish merit, but as a condition of the Gospel as well as faith ; and many the like to these ; thus truly setting up an image of old popery in a Protestant Reformed way, even as popery is an image of heathenish worship in a Christian way. Say these men what they will, that they hold not of the pope, nor any way intend him, or the introducing of his religion into these churches, yet their *actions* do (and cannot but) make all men number them as such ; and therefore we say, They have gained that esteem at home and abroad in all the churches ; and it is no more than what the Holy Ghost prophesied of, who hath fitted them with a description so characteristical, as nothing is more like them, who are said to receive the *number* of his *name*. And they doing this in a way of apostacy from their former profession and religion in which they were trained up, and in a church so full of light, where God hath more witnesses than in all the rest of the churches, and with an intention and conspiracy in the end to make way for the Beast (this going before, as the twilight doth serve to usher in darkness), therefore the Holy Ghost thought them worthy of this character (in this prophecy), and of a discovery of them unto whom they do belong, especially seeing they would so professedly deny it. And though, happily, but in one of the ten kingdoms (although the *Lutherans* look very like this description also), yet, seeing they were to grow so potent a faction as to have power to hinder the (*buying and selling*) quiet living of others among them who will not receive this worship and doctrine (which is a new refined popery), and with it the number of his name ; that is, those opinions and practices which do deserve that esteem ; and farther, because they were to be the pope's last champions before his fall, when those that are the true saints (of whom the greatest number in the last age before the pope's ruin is in or belonging to that one kingdom) are to encounter and overcome before the ruin of Rome, therefore the Holy Ghost thought not fit to leave such a company out of the Beast's number and followers, and that, also, although they were to continue but a short time ; for the doom of these men we have in another prophecy (as their description also), 2 Tim. iii., from the 1st verse to the 10th, the prophecy there being of a generation of men to arise in the last days (the papists arising is attributed to the *latter days*, in 1 Tim., chap. iv., but the rise of these to the last of the last days), who shall set themselves principally against the power and spirit of true worship, and set up a form or image instead of it, verse 5 ; but their doom is (verse 9), *These shall proceed no farther*, they shall have a stop ; and their folly, and madness, and hypocrisy (to attempt to bring in *popery* with denying it ; and when it is going down, then to build this Babel again) shall appear to all men ; and being discovered, will be their overthrow ; but notwithstanding, they must *proceed farther* than as yet they have done, even to the *killing* of the *witnesses* in that kingdom, or tenth part of the city (as chap. xi. will show, when, in its due order, it shall be opened) ; and because these last champions of the Beast, and healers of the wound given him, should come in the last days of

above a twelvemonth, without permitting them to finish any business. His majesty falling sick in the summer, the Duke of York returned immediately to court without the king's leave,* which alarmed the people; and made them eager for the sitting of the Parliament to regulate the succession.† This gave rise to sundry petitions,‡ signed by a great number of hands both in city and country, which the king received with the utmost displeasure, telling the petitioners that he was sole judge of what was fit to be done : "You would not take it well," says he, "if I should meddle with your affairs, and I desire you will not meddle with mine." After this the king issued out his proclamation, declaring them to be illegal, and forbidding his subjects to promote any subscriptions, or to join in any petitions of this kind, upon peril of the utmost rigour of the law. Warrants were issued against several of the petitioners, and indictments preferred against others. But at the next sessions of the Common Council of London, January 21, the court agreed that no such petition should be presented from them ; and the king returned them thanks for it.§ Upon which, addresses were procured from divers parts of the nation, expressing their detestation and abhorrence of the seditious practice of the late petitioners, and referring the sitting of the Parliament absolutely to the king's sovereign pleasure, from whence they obtained the name of Abhorrers. In these addresses, they offer their lives and fortunes for the preservation of his majesty's person and government, and for the succession of the Duke of York. They renounce the right of the subject's petitioning or intermeddling in affairs of state, and lay their liberties at the feet of the prerogative, promising to stand by it, and to be obedient without reserve to his majesty's commands ; which addresses were printed in the Gazettes, and dispersed over the kingdom. These proceedings threw the people into a ferment : several of the privy council deserted their stations, and desired to be excused their attendance at council ; some in the admiralty resigned, and because they might not petition, an association was formed by sundry persons, and copied af-

all, they were therefore last named, and are said to be last overcome by the witnesses and pourers forth of the vials, as chap. xv., 2."

Who hath ears to hear, let him hear this remarkable prediction.—C.

* If we may credit Sir John Reresby, who says he had the whole story from Feversham, to whose intervention the revocation of the duke was principally owing, the king's illness was pretended, and the duke was sent for with his privity, though not above four persons knew anything of the matter. The Duke of Monmouth, who thought he had the king to himself, knew nothing of it till his highness actually arrived at Windsor : "So close and reserved," says Sir John, "could the king be, when he conceived it to be necessary."—*Memoirs*, p. 97, 98.—ED. † Echard, p. 982, 987.

‡ Dr. Grey, by a quotation from Hornby's "Caveat against the Whigs," brings a charge against these petitions, that the signatures were obtained by bribes and impositions. Such practices, if truly stated in this instance, have not been confined to that occasion or those times; but it is not easy to conceive that a man of integrity, in any party, can have recourse to them. The proposal of adopting them ought to be rejected with contempt and indignation.—ED. § Burnet, vol. ii., p. 276.

ter the example of that in Queen Elizabeth's time, for the defence of his majesty's person and the security of the Protestant religion, and to revenge his majesty's death upon the papists, if he should come to any violent death, a model of which was said to be found among the Earl of Shaftesbury's papers. This was resented very highly at court, as done without the royal authority, and produced the next year another set of ranting addresses from all parts of the kingdom, in which their lives and fortunes were given up to the king, and the associations branded with the names of damnable, cursed, execrable, traitorous, seditious, and a bond of rebellion, which they detest and abhor from their very souls ; in most of which the Nonconformists are marked as enemies of the king and his government, and their conventicles as the encouragement and life of the associations. They promise to stand by the duke's succession, and to choose such members for the next Parliament as shall do the king's business according to his mind. But notwithstanding the utmost efforts of the court, the near approach of a popish successor awakened men's fears, and kept them upon their guard.

The petitioners for the sitting of the Parliament, and their adversaries. the Abhorrers of such petitions, gave rise to the two grand parties which have since divided the nation, under the distinguishing names of Whig and Tory.

The Whigs or Low churchmen were the more zealous Protestants, declared enemies of popery, and willing to remove to a farther distance from their superstitions ; they were firm to the Constitution and liberties of their country ; and for a union, or, at least, a toleration, of dissenting Protestants. The clergy of this persuasion were generally men of larger principles, and therefore were distinguished by the name of Latitudinarian divines; their laity were remarkable for their zeal in promoting the Bill of Exclusion, as the only expedient to secure the Protestant establishment in this kingdom. They were for confining the royal prerogative within the limits of the law, for which reason their adversaries charged them with Republican principles, and gave them the reproachful name of Whigs, or sour milk, a name first given to the most rigid Scots covenanters.

The Tories or High-churchmen stood on the side of the prerogative, and were for advancing the king above law ; they went into all the arbitrary court measures, and adopted into our religion, says Dr. Welwood,* a Mohammedan principle, under the names of passive obedience and nonresistance, which, since the times of that impostor who first broached it, has been the means to enslave a great part of the world. These gentlemen leaned more to a coalition with the papists than with the Presbyterians.† They cried up the name and authority of the Church, were for forcing the Dissenters to conformity, by all kinds of coercive methods ; but, with all their zeal, they were many of them persons of lax and dissolute morals, and would risk the whole Protestant religion rather than go into any measures of exclusion, or limitation of a popish successor. Most of

* Memoirs. p. 125.
† Burnet, Collect. Debates, p. 163.

the clergy, says a member of Parliament, are infected with the Laudean principles of raising money without Parliament; one or two bishops give measures to the rest, and they to their clergy, so that all derive their politics from one or two, and are under the influence of an overawing power. No men did more to enslave the nation, and introduce popery into the establishment, than they: their adversaries, therefore, gave them the name of Tories, a title first given to Irish robbers, who lived upon plunder, and were prepared for any daring or villanous enterprise.

The Nonconformists fell in unanimously with the Whigs or Low-churchmen in all points relating to liberty and the civil constitution, as they must always do if they are consistent with themselves; but these, with their allies, were not a sufficient balance for the Tories, the road to preferment lying through the territories of power; but they were kept in heart with some secret hopes that, by a steady adherence to the Constitution, they should one time or other obtain a legal toleration. But the superior influence of the Tories above the Whigs was the occasion of the severities which befell the Nonconformists in the latter part of this reign.

When Parliament met, October 21, 1680, the Commons were very warm in maintaining the Protestant religion and the privileges of Parliament.* They asserted the rights of the people to petition for the sitting of Parliaments, and voted the Abhorrers betrayers of the liberties of the nation. Among other grievances, they complained that the edge of the penal laws was turned against Protestant Dissenters, while the papists remained in a manner untouched; that the Test Act had little effect, because the papists, either by dispensation obtained from Rome, submitted to those tests, and held their offices themselves; or those put in their places were so favourable to the same interest, that popery itself had rather gained than lost ground by that act. They declared for that very association, to revenge the king's death upon the papists, if his majesty should happen to be assassinated, which the Tories had abhorred; and in the month of November revived the bill to disable the Duke of York from inheriting the imperial crown of these realms. It was introduced by Lord Russel, and passed the Commons by a great majority, but was thrown out of the House of Lords by a majority of thirty voices,† noes 63, yeas 33, the bench of bishops being in the negative, and the king present during the whole debate. It has been said King Charles came into the bill at first, the favourite mistress having prevailed with him to abandon his brother for a large sum of money, and for an

act of Parliament to enable him to dispose of the crown by will, under certain restrictions; but a foreign popish court offering more money, he opposed it to the last.*

The Parliament being inclined to relieve the Nonconformists, appointed a committee November 18, who agreed upon a comprehension with the Dissenters, upon much the same terms with those already mentioned; they were to subscribe the doctrinal articles of the Church; the surplice was to be omitted, except in cathedrals and the king's chapel; the ceremonies to be left indifferent. And as for such Protestants as could not be comprehended within these terms, they were to have a toleration, and freedom from the penal statutes, upon condition of subscribing a declaration of allegiance, &c., and of assembling with open doors. Bishop Burnet says, the bill for a comprehension was offered by the Episcopal party in the House of Commons, but that the friends of the Dissenters did not seem forward to promote it, because, as Mr. Baxter observes, they found the bill would not go; or if it had passed the Commons, it would have been thrown out by the bishops in the House of Lords; the clergy, says Kennet, being no farther in earnest than as they apprehended the knife of the papists at their throats.

When the above-mentioned bill was brought in the House December 21, entitled "An Act for uniting his Majesty's Protestant Subjects," the first gentleman of the court party who spoke against it observed, "that there were a sort of men who would neither be advised nor overruled, but under the pretence of conscience break violently through all laws whatsoever, to the great disturbance both of Church and State; therefore he thought it more convenient to have a law for forcing the Dissenters to yield to the Church, and not to force the Church to yield to them." Another said, "he was afraid, that if once the government should begin to yield to the Dissenters, it would be as in forty-one, nothing would serve but an' utter subversion: the receiving of one thing would give occasion for demanding more; and it would be impossible to give them any satisfaction, without laying all open, and running into confusion."† This was the common language of the Tories. And there have been a loud cry against the Dissenters, for their obstinacy and perverseness, though not a single concession had been offered since the Restoration, to let the world see how far they would yield; or, by receiving a denial, to get an opportunity to reproach them with greater advantage. But in favour of the bill it was urged by others, "that it was intended for the preservation of the Church, and the best bill that could be made in order thereto, all circumstances considered. If we are to deal with a stubborn sort of people, who in many things prefer their humour before reason, or their own safety, or the public good, this is a very good time to see whether they will be drawn by the cords of love or no. The bill will be very agreeable to the Christian charity which our Church professes; and it may be hoped, that in the time of this imminent danger, they will consider their own safety, and the safety of the

* Rapin, vol. ii., p. 714. Echard, p. 995.
† Lord Halifax, a man of the clearest head, finest wit, and fairest eloquence, who was in judgment against the bill, appeared as leader in opposition to it, and made so powerful a defence, that he alone, by the confession of all, influenced the House, and persuaded them to throw out the bill. "One would have thought," says Sir John Reresby, "that so signal a piece of service had been of a degree and nature never to be forgotten." But when the duke afterward came to be king, he removed Lord Halifax from the privy seal to the presidency of the council, purely to make room for another, and in the end quite laid him aside.—*Memoirs*, p. 104, 105.—ED.

* Welwood's Mem., p. 127.   † Echard, p. 999.

Protestant religion, and no longer keep afoot the unhappy divisions among us, on which the papists ground their hopes; but when they see the Church so far condescend as to dispense with the surplice, and those other things they scruple, that they will submit to the rest which are enjoined by law, that so we may unite against the common enemy: But if this bill should not have the desired effect, but, on the contrary, the Dissenters should continue their animosities and disobedience to the Church, I think still the Church will gain very much hereby, and leave the party without excuse." This seems agreeable to reason.

Although the bill for a comprehension was committed, it did not pass the House, being changed for another, entitled "An Act to exempt his Majesty's Protestant Subjects, dissenting from the Church of England, from the Penalties imposed upon the Papists by the Act of 35th Eliz."* By which act Nonconformists were adjudged to perpetual imprisonment, or obliged to abjure, that is, depart the realm never to return. This terrible law had lain dormant almost eighty years, but was now revived, and threatened to be put in execution by the Tories. The repeal passed the House of Commons with a high hand, but went heavily through the House of Lords, the bishops apprehending that the terror of the law might be of some use; but when it should have been offered to the king for the royal assent at the close of the session, it was missing, and never heard of any more, the clerk of the crown having withdrawn it from the table by the king's particular order. The king (says Burnet†) had no mind openly to deny the bill, but less mind to pass it; and therefore this illegal method was taken, which was a high offence in the officer of the House, and would have been severely punished in the next session, if the Parliament had not been abruptly dissolved. Thus the Nonconformists were sawn to pieces between the king, the bishops, and the Parliament; when one party was willing to give them relief, the other always stood in the way. The Parliament was their enemy for about twelve years, and now they are softened, the king and the court bishops are inflexible; and his majesty will rather sacrifice the Constitution to his despotic will, than exempt them from an old law, which subjected them to banishment and death.

However, the morning before the House was prorogued, January 10, two votes were passed of a very extraordinary nature: "1. Resolved *nemine contradicente*, That it is the opinion of this House, that the acts of Parliament made in the reigns of Queen Elizabeth and King James against popish recusants ought not to be extended against Protestant Dissenters. 2. Resolved, That it is the opinion of this House, that the prosecution of Protestant Dissenters upon the penal laws is at this time grievous to the subject, a weakening of the Protestant interest, an encouragement to popery, and dangerous to the peace of the kingdom." Bishop Burnet‡ says these resolutions were thought an invasion of the Legislature, when one house pretended to suspend the execution of the laws, which was to act like dictators in the state.

But, with all due submission, I should think that this cannot be construed a suspension of those laws, and that a House of Commons which is not suffered to sit and repeal laws, or when they have repealed them, have their bills withdrawn illegally by the crown, may have liberty to declare their judgment that the continuance of those laws is burdensome to the state. They must do so, says Mr. Coke,* in order to a repeal. If the bill for the repeal of the old popish act *de hæretico comburendo*, for burning heretics, which the Parliament were afraid might be revived in a popish reign, had been lost in this manner, might not the Parliament have declared the execution of that law a weakening to the Protestant interest, or dangerous to the peace of the kingdom?

While the Parliament was endeavouring to relieve the Dissenters, and charging the miseries of the kingdom upon the papists, many of the bishops and clergy of the Church of England were pleased to see the court inclined to prosecute the Nonconformists. The clergy in general, says Rapin,† were attached to the court; men of doubtful religion were promoted, and there was reason to charge them with leaning to popery. Even some able champions against popery went so far into the court measures as to impute the calamities of the times to the Nonconformists, and to raise the cry of the populace against them. Dr. Edward Stillingfleet, who had written an Irenicum in favour of liberty, and against impositions, in his sermon before the lord-mayor, May 2, this year, entitled "The Mischief of Separation," condemned all the Dissenters as schismatics, and very gravely advised them not to complain of persecution. When the sermon was published, it brought upon the doctor several learned adversaries, as Mr. Baxter, Mr. Alsop, Mr. Howe, Mr. Barrett, and Dr. Owen, from which last divine, who wrote with great temper and seriousness, I will venture to transcribe the following passage, without entering into the argument:‡ "After so many of the Nonconformists have died in common jails," says the doctor, "so many have endured long imprisonments, not a few being at this day in the same durance; so many driven from their habitations into a wandering condition, to preserve for a while the liberty of their persons; so many have been reduced to want and penury, by the taking away their goods, and from some the very instruments of their livelihood; after the prosecution that has been against them in all courts of justice in this nation, on informations, indictments, and suits, to the great charge of all who have been so persecuted, and the ruin of some; after so many ministers and their families have been brought into the utmost outward straits, which nature can subsist under; after all their perpetual fears and dangers wherewith they have been exercised and disquieted, they think it hard to be censured for complaining, by them who are at ease." The doctor endeavoured to support his charge by the suffrage of the French Presbyterians; and Compton, bishop of London, applied to Monsieur le Moyne, and several others,§ for their opinions; as if truth were to be determined by numbers; or as if the English

. * Burnet, vol. ii., p. 300.   † Ibid.
.‡ Ibid., vol. ii., p. 301.

* Page 561.   † Page 711.   ‡ Page 53, 54.
§ Collyer, p. 900.

Presbyterians could pay a vast deference to their judgments, who had so deceived them at the Restoration. The ministers, bred up in French complaisance and under French slavery, after high strains of compliment to the English bishops, declared that they were of opinion their brethren might comply,* and that they were not for pushing things to extremity only for a different form of government, .which the doctor and his friends interpreted as a decision in their favour. But did not the bishops exasperate the spirits of their dissenting brethren by enforcing the sanguinary laws? Were these Protestant methods of conversion, or likely to bring them to temper? The French ministers complained sufficiently of this about five years after, at the revocation of the Edict of Nantz. Bishop Burnet remarks of Dr. Stillingfleet on this occasion,† that he not only retracted his "Irenicum," but went into the humours of the high sort of people beyond what became him, perhaps beyond his own sense of things.

This year [1680] died Mr. Stephen Charnock, B. D., first of Emanuel College, Cambridge, and afterward fellow of New College, Oxford. He was chaplain to Henry Cromwell, lieutenant of Ireland, and was much respected by persons of the best quality in the city of Dublin for his polite behaviour. After the Restoration he returned into England, and became pastor of a separate congregation in London, where he was admired by the more judicious part of his hearers, though not popular, because of his disadvantageous way of reading with a glass ;‡ he was an eminent divine, and had a good judgment, a curious imagination, and a strong manner of reasoning, as appears by his works printed since his death in two volumes folio, which were no other than his common sermons transcribed from his notes ;§ his style is manly and lofty, and his thoughts sublime : his love and charity were very extensive, and there was no

part of learning to which he was a stranger.* He died July 26, 1680, aged fifty-two.

[On December 26, 1680, died at London, where he came to be cut for the stone, with which he was many years afflicted, Mr. John Corbet, ejected from Bramshot in Hants ; a man every way great. He was a native of the city of Gloucester, and a student in Magdalen Hall, Oxon. He began his ministry in the place of his nativity, and lived many years there, and during the civil wars, of which he was a spectator. He wrote the history of the siege of the city, and is thought to have given as good an, insight into the rise and springs of the civil war as can be met with in so narrow a compass. He removed from thence to Chichester, and then to the living from which he was ejected. After this he lived privately in and about London, till King Charles's indulgence in 1671, when part of his flock invited him to return to Chichester, where he continued his ministrations with great assiduity and success. It was during his residence there that Bishop Gunning gave a public challenge to the Presbyterians, Independents, Baptists, and Quakers. (See chapter viii., part iv.) Mr. Corbet accepted it on behalf of the first ; but, after the bishop had fired his own volley of invectives, Mr. Corbet was not permitted to enter into a defence ; nor, though he proposed to do it at any other time and waited on the bishop at his palace, could he afterward obtain a hearing. He was a man of great moderation, a lover of peace, an advocate for catholic communion and union of saints,. and of blameless conversation. He saw some things to approve and some things to dislike in all parties, and valued not the interest of a party or faction. True to his conscience, he had no worldly designs to carry on, but was eminent in self-denial, and managed his ministry with faithfulness and prudence. He was tender of the reputation of his brethren, and rejoiced in the success of their labours as well as of his own. Nor was he apt to speak against those by whom he suffered. He was very free in acknowledging by whom he profited, and preferring others before himself. He was much in the study of his own heart, had the comfort of sensible improvements in faith and holiness, humility and heavenly-mindedness, and died at last in great serenity and peace. He had a considerable hand in compiling Mr. Rushworth's first volume of " Collections," which is reckoned by good judges a masterpiece of the kind. His " Self-employment in Secret," an excellent small piece, recommended lately by Mr. Bulkley in his " Christian Minister," has gone through various editions. Mr. Howe wrote a preface to it. Dr. Wright reprinted it in 1741,. and the Rev. William Unwin, rector of Stock cum Ramsden Belhouse, Essex, published it again in 1773 with the encomiums of a celebrated minister of the Church of England upon it,.

---

* Mr. Neal, it seems, has fallen into a mistake, by supposing that the French Presbyterians favoured English Episcopacy. Their answers were complaisant, but wary. Yet Stillingfleet published their letters as suffrages for Episcopacy, and annexed them to his Treatise on Schism. Mr. Claude, one of those written to, complained of this treatment ; but the letters which contained these complaints were concealed till his death, when his son printed them. In one of them to Bishop Compton, April, 1681, he freely told him that the bishops were blamed for their eagerness to persecute others by penal laws ; for their arbitrary and despotic government ; for their rigid attachment to offensive ceremonies ; for requiring foreign Protestant ministers to be reordained ; and for not admitting any to the ministry without making an oath that Episcopacy is of Divine right, which Mr. Claude called a cruel rack for conscience. He solemnly called on the bishops, in the name of God, to remove these grounds of complaint, to give no cause, no pretext, for separation, to do all in their power to prevent it, and, instead of chafing and irritating people's minds, by all gentle methods to conciliate them. This was excellent advice, but the public were not informed that it had been given by those to whom it was addressed.— *Robinson's Life of Claude*, prefixed to his translation of an *Essay on the Composition of Sermons*, p. 65–67. —Ed.

† Vol. i., p. 276.

‡ In his early ministry he used no notes, and was very popular as a preacher.—C.

§ Calamy, .vol. ii., p. 56. Palmer's Non. Mem., vol. i., p. 159.

* Mr. Johnson, who preached his funeral sermon, says, " he never knew a man in all his life who had attained near to that skill Mr. Charnock had, in the originals of the Old and New Testament, except Mr. Thomas Cawton."—*Granger*, vol. iii., p. 308.—Ed. One of the ablest preachers of the present century in the United States used to advise his students to become masters of Charnock's works, and stated that he had read them with deeper interest than those of any other English divine.—C.

† vol. i., p. 270.

‡ In his early ministry he used no notes, and was very popular as a preacher.—C.

§ Calamy, vol. ii., p. 56. Palmer's Non. Mem., vol. i., p. 159.

One of the ablest preachers of the present century in the United States used to advise his students to become masters of Charnock's works, and stated that he had read them with deeper interest than those of any other English divine.—C.

Engraved by Gardner, from a rare Print.

HANSERD KNOLLYS
M.A.

as "the best manual he knew for a Christian or a minister, furnishing excellent materials for addressing conscience, and directing men to judge of their spiritual state."—*Calamy*, vol. ii., p. 333. *Palmer's Noncon. Mem.*, vol. ii., p. 4. —Ed.]

The king having parted with his last Parliament in displeasure, without being able to obtain any money, resolved once more to try a new one ;* and apprehending that the malecontents were encouraged by the neighbourhood of the city of London, he summoned them to meet at Oxford : the same representatives being rechosen for London, had a paper put into their hands by four merchants, in the name of all the citizens then assembled in the Common Hall, containing a return of their most hearty thanks for their faithful and unwearied endeavours in the last two Parliaments, to search into the depth of the Popish Plot, to preserve the Protestant religion, to promote a union among his majesty's Protestant subjects, to repeal the 35th of Elizabeth, and the Corporation Act, and to promote the Bill of Exclusion, and to request their continuance of the same. The members being afraid of violence, were attended to Oxford with a numerous body of horse, having ribands in their hats with this motto, " No popery—no slavery," the citizens having promised to stand by them with their lives and fortunes. Many other papers of the like nature were presented to the members in the several counties. The king, in his speech at the opening of the session, March 21, reflected severely on the last Parliament, and said, He was resolved to maintain the succession of the crown in the right line, and for quieting people's fears, he was willing to put the administration into the hands of a Protestant regent ; but the Commons rejected the proposal, to the inexpressible joy of the duke's party, and ordered the Bill of Exclusion to be brought in again. In the mean time, a motion was made to consider of the loss of the bill in favour of the Dissenters last Parliament. Sir William Jones said, " The bill was of great moment and service to the country, and might be to their lives, in the time of a popish successor ; but be the bill what it will, the precedent was of the highest consequence ; the king has a negative to all bills, but surely the clerk of the Parliament has not. If this way be found out, that bills shall be thrown by, it may hereafter be said they were forgot and laid by, and so we shall never know whether the king passed them or no : if this be suffered, 'tis in vain to spend time here." In conclusion, this affair was referred to a conference with the House of Lords, which was frustrated by the hasty dissolution of the Parliament.

The next went upon the libel of one Fitz-Harris, an Irish papist, which was a second Meal-tub Plot, promoted in the name of the Nonconformists ;† the libel was to be sent by penny-post letters to the Lords who had protested in favour of the Bill of Exclusion, and to the leading men in the House of Commons, who were immediately to be apprehended and searched. Everard, who was Fitz-Harris's confidant, and betrayed the secret, affirmed that the king himself was privy to it, as Fitz-Harris's

wife averred to a person of worth many years after ; that his majesty had given Fitz-Harris money, and promised him more if it met with success. The libel was to traduce the king and the royal family as papists, and arbitrarily affected from the beginning, and says that King Charles I. had a hand in the Irish rebellion ; that the act forbidding to call the king a papist was only to stop men's mouths, and that it was as much in the power of the people to depose a popish possessor as a popish successor. It was entitled " The True Englishman speaking Plain English ;" and adds, " If James be conscious and guilty, Charles is so too ; believe me, these two brothers in iniquity are in confederacy with the pope and the French to cast off Parliaments, Magna Charta, and the liberty of the subject, as heavy yokes, and to be as arbitrary as the King of France. Let the English move and rise as one man to self-defence ; blow the trumpet, stand on your guard, and withstand them as bears and tigers. Trust to your swords in defence of your lives, liberties, and religion, like the stout earl of old, who told his king if he could not be defended by Magna Charta, he would be relieved by longa spada." He goes on to reproach the king with the breach of his Scots oaths, Breda promises, Protestant profession, liberty of conscience, as designed only to delude Protestants ; and puts him in mind of all his political and moral vices, as intended to debauch the nation, to promote the popish religion and arbitrary government, &c. Thus were the Nonconformists to be exposed again to the resentments of the nation ; but when the sham was discovered to the House of Commons by Sir William Waller, he received the thanks of the House, and Fitz-Harris, though impeached in Parliament, was tried by a jury, and executed with Dr. Plunket, the titular primate of Ireland. The Whigs would have saved Fitz-Harris, though a papist, in hopes of his being an evidence in the Popish Plot ; but the court was resolved to despatch him out of the way, that he might tell no more tales.

His majesty, hearing that the Bill of Exclusion was to be brought into the House again, went suddenly, and not very decently, says Burnet,* to the House of Lords in a sedan, with the crown between his feet, and having put on his robes in haste, called up the Commons, and dissolved his fifth and last Parliament, after they had sat only seven days. As soon as his majesty got out of the House, he posted away in all haste to Windsor, as one that was glad he had got rid of his Parliament, which was the last that he ever convened, though he lived three or four years after. And here was an end of the Constitution and liberties of England for the present ; all that followed, to the king's death, was no more than the convulsions and struggles of a dying man. The king raised what money he wanted without Parliaments ; he took away all the charters of England, and governed absolutely by dint of prerogative. April the 8th, the king published a declaration†

* Echard, p. 1002. Rapin, vol. ii., p. 720.
† Burnet, p. 303, 304.
Vol II.—P p

* Burnet, p. 306.
† It was observed, Dr. Calamy says, that " this declaration was known by M. Barillon, the French ambassador, and by the Duchess of Mazarine, soon-

to all his loving subjects touching the causes and reasons that moved him to dissolve the last two Parliaments, and ordered it to be read in all the churches and chapels throughout England. It contains a recital of his majesty's condescensions for the security of the Protestant religion, as far as was consistent with the succession of the crown in the lineal descent, and a large rehearsal of the unsuitable returns of the Commons. But notwithstanding all this, says his majesty, let not those men who are labouring to poison our people with commonwealth principles persuade any of our subjects that we intend to lay aside the use of Parliaments, for we still declare that no irregularities in Parliaments shall make us out of love with them; and we are resolved, by the blessing of God, to have frequent Parliaments;" although he never called another. Several anonymous remarks were made upon this declaration, to weaken its influence. But the court used all its interest among the people to support its credit: addresses were sent from all parts, thanking his majesty for his declaration, promising to support his person and government with their lives and fortunes. Most of them declared against the Bill of Exclusion, and for the duke's succession,* as has been observed. Some ventured to arraign the late Parliament as guilty of sedition and treason, and to pray his majesty to put in execution the statute of 35 Elizabeth against the Nonconformists. The grand juries, the justices at their sessions, divers boroughs and corporations, the companies in towns, and at last the very apprentices, sent up addresses. Those who presented or procured them were well treated at court, and some of them knighted. Many zealous healths were drank, and in their cups the swaggerings of the old Cavaliers seemed to be revived. One of the most celebrated addresses was from the University of Cambridge, presented by Dr. Gower, master of St. John's, which I shall give the reader as a specimen of the rest. It begins thus: "Sacred sir! We, your majesty's most faithful and obedient subjects, have long, with the greatest and sincerest joy, beheld the generous emulation of our fellow-subjects, contending who should best express their duty to their sovereign at this time, when the seditious endeavours of unreasonable men have made it necessary to assert the ancient loyalty of the English nation. It is at present the great honour of this your university, not only to be steadfast and constant in our duty, but to be eminently so, and to suffer for it as much as the calumnies and reproaches of factious and malicious men can inflict upon us. And that they have not proceeded to sequestration and plunder, as heretofore, next to the overruling providence of Almighty God, is only due to the royal care and prudence of your most sacred majesty, who gave so seasonable a check to their arbitrary and insolent undertakings. We still believe and maintain that our kings derive not their power from the people, but from God;

er than by the king's council, and that it was evidenced to be of French extraction by the Gallicisms in it; and, withal, it had no broad seal to it, and was signed only by a clerk of the council."—*Own Life, MS.*, p. 74.—ED.
  * Burnet, vol. ii., p. 308, 309.

that to him only they are accountable; that it belongs not to subjects either to create or censure, but to honour and obey their sovereign, who comes to be so by a fundamental, hereditary right of succession, which no religion, no law, no fault or forfeiture, can alter or diminish; nor will we abate of our well-instructed zeal for the Church of England as by law established. Thus we have learned our own, and thus we teach others their duty to God and the king." His majesty discovered an unusual satisfaction on this occasion; and, having returned them thanks, was pleased to add, that no other church in the world taught and practised loyalty so conscientiously as they did.

As such abject and servile flattery could not fail of pleasing the king, it must necessarily draw down vengeance on the Nonconformists, who joined in none of their addresses, but were doomed to suffer under a double character, as Whigs and as Dissenters. "This," says Bishop Burnet,* "was set on by the papists, and it was wisely done of them, for they knew how much the Nonconformists were set against them. They made use, also, of the indiscreet zeal of the High Church clergymen to ruin them, which they knew would render the clergy odious, and give the papist great advantage when opportunity offered." The times were boisterous and stormy; sham plots were contrived, and warrants issued against the leaders of the Whig party for seditious language; Shaftesbury, now called the Protestant earl, was sent to the Tower, and Stephen College, the Protestant joiner, was carried to Oxford, and hanged, after the grand jury in London had brought in a bill of indictment against him *ignoramus*. Witnesses were imported from Ireland, and employed to swear away men's lives. "The court intended to set them to swear against all the hot party, which was plainly murder in them who believed them false witnesses," says Burnet,† "and yet made use of them to destroy others." Spies were planted in all coffee-houses to furnish out evidence for the witnesses. Mercenary justices were put into commission all over the kingdom; juries were packed; and, with regard to the Nonconformists, informers of the vilest of the people were countenanced to a shameful degree, insomuch that the jails were quickly filled with prisoners, and large sums of money extorted from the industrious and conscientious, and played into the hands of the most profligate wretches in the nation.

The justices of Middlesex showed great forwardness, and represented to his majesty in December, "that an intimation of his pleasure was necessary at this time to the putting the laws in execution against conventicles, because, when a charge was lately given at the council-board to put the laws in execution against popish recusants, no mention was made of suppressing conventicles." Upon this, his majesty commanded the lord-mayor, aldermen, and justices to use their utmost endeavour to suppress all conventicles and unlawful meetings, upon pretence of religious worship; for it was his express pleasure that the laws be effectually put in execution against them, both in city and country. Accordingly, the justices of peace, at their sessions at Hicks's Hall, January 13, or-

  * Page 306.   † Page 315.

dered, "that whereas the constables and church-wardens, &c., of every parish and precinct within the said county had been enjoined last sessions to make a return the first of this of the names of the preachers in conventicles, and the most considerable frequenters of the same within their several limits; which order not being obeyed, but contemned by some, it was therefore by the justices then assembled desired that the Lord-bishop of London will please to direct those officers which are under his jurisdiction to use their utmost diligence that all such persons may be excommunicated who commit crimes deserving the ecclesiastical censure; and that the said excommunications may be published in the parishes where the persons live, that they may be taken notice of, and be obvious to the penalties that belong to persons excommunicated, viz., not to be admitted for a witness, or returned upon juries, or capable of suing for any debt." They farther ordered, at the same time, "that the statute of the first of Elizabeth and third of King James be put in due execution, for the levying of twelve-pence per Sunday upon such persons who repaired not to Divine service and sermons at their parish or some other public church." All which, says Mr. Echard, made way for all sorts of prosecutions both in city and country, which in many places were carried on with great spite and severity, where there never wanted busy agents and informers, of which a few were sufficient to put the laws in execution; so that the Dissenters this year, and much longer, says he, met with cruel and unchristian usage; which occasioned great complaints among the people, and some severe reflections on the king himself.

It was not in the power of the Church Whigs to relieve the Nonconformists, nor screen them from the edge of the penal laws, which were in the hands of their enemies. All that could be done was to encourage their constancy, and to write some compassionate treatises to move the people in their favour, by showing them, that while they were plundering and destroying their Protestant dissenting neighbours, they were cutting the throat of the Reformed religion, and making way for the triumphs of popery upon its ruins. Among other writings of this sort, the most famous was, "The Conformists' Plea for the Nonconformists," in four parts, by a beneficed minister and a regular son of the Church of England. In which the author undertakes to show, 1. The greatness of their sufferings. 2. The hardships of their case. 3. The reasonableness and equity of their proposals for union. 4. The qualifications and worth of their ministers. 5. Their peaceable behaviour. 6. Their agreement with the Church of England in the articles of her faith. 7. The prejudice to the Church by their exclusion; and then concludes with the infamous lives and lamentable deaths of several of the informers. It was a sensible and moving performance, but had no influence on the Tory justices and tribe of informers. There was no stemming the tide; every one who was not a furious Tory, says Rapin, was reputed a Presbyterian.

Most of the clergy were with the court, and distinguished themselves on the side of persecution. The pulpits everywhere resounded with the doctrines of passive obedience and nonre-

sistance, which were carried to all the heights of King Charles I. No Eastern monarch, according to them, was more absolute than the King of England.[*] They expressed such a zeal for the duke's succession, as if a popish king over a Protestant country had been a special blessing from Heaven. They likewise gave themselves such a loose against Protestant Nonconformists, as if nothing was so formidable as that party. In all their sermons popery was quite forgot, says Burnet, and the force of their zeal was turned almost wholly against Protestant Dissenters. In many country places the parson of the parish, who could bully, and drink, and swear, was put into the commission of the peace, and made a confiding justice, by which means he was both judge and party in his own cause. If any of his sober parishioners did not appear at church, they were sure to be summoned, and instead of the mildness and gentleness of a Christian clergyman, they usually met with haughty and abusive language, and the utmost rigour the law could inflict. There was also a great change made in the commissions throughout England. A set of confiding magistrates was appointed; and none were left on the bench, or in the militia, that did not declare for the arbitrary measures of the court; and such of the clergy as were averse to this fury were declaimed against as betrayers of the Church, and secret favourers of the Dissenters; but the truth is, says the bishop, the number of sober, honest clergymen was not great, for where the carcass is, there will the eagles be gathered together. The scent of preferment will draw aspiring men after it. Upon the whole, the present times were very lowering, and the prospect under a popish successor still more threatening.

It would fill a volume to enter into all the particulars of these unchristian proceedings, which even the black registers of the spiritual courts cannot fully unfold. The Rev. Mr. Edward Bury, assisting at a private fast, on account of the extraordinary drought, was apprehended June 14, and fined £20; and refusing to pay it, because he did not preach, they took away his goods, books, and even the bed he lay upon. The Rev. Mr. Philip Henry was apprehended at the same time, and fined £40, and for nonpayment, they carried away thirty-three loads of corn which lay cut upon the ground, together with hay, coals, and other chattels. The informers took the names of one hundred and fifty more who were at the meeting: they fined the master of the house £20, and £5 more as being constable that year, and exacted 5s. a head from all who were present. Examples of this usage in London, Middlesex, and most of the counties of England, are innumerable.

The Quakers published a narrative of the sufferings of their friends since the Restoration, by which it appeared that great numbers had been fined by the bishops' courts, robbed of their substance, and perished in prison.[†] Many had been so beaten and wounded for attending their meetings, that they died of their wounds. An account was also published of the unjust proceedings of the informers, showing that at their instance many had been plundered without a jurid-

* Rapin. p. 725. Burnet, p. 309
† Sewel, p. 574, 581.

ical process; that seven hundred of them were now in prison in several parts of England, and especially about Bristol; but remonstrances and complaints availed nothing.

In the midst of this furious persecution, the famous Mr. Thomas Gouge, son of Dr. Gouge, of Blackfriars, and the ejected minister of St. Sepulchre's, was taken out of this world : he was born at Bow, near Stratford, 1605, bred at Eton School, and educated in King's College, Cambridge.* He settled at St. Sepulchre's in the year 1638, and for twenty-four years discharged all the parts of a vigilant and faithful pastor. He was a wonder of piety, charity, humility, and moderation, making it his study to keep a conscience void of offence towards God and man. Mr. Baxter says he never heard any man speak to his dishonour, except that he did not conform. He was possessed of a good estate, and devoted the chief of it to charity. He settled schools to the number of three or four hundred, and gave money to teach children to read in the mountainous parts of Wales, where he travelled annually, and preached, till he was forbid by the bishops, and excommunicated, though he still went as a hearer to the parish churches. He printed eight thousand Welsh Bibles,† a thousand of which were given to the poor, and the rest sent to the principal towns of Wales, to be sold at an under rate. He printed five hundred of the " Whole Duty of Man" in Welsh, and gave them away; two hundred and forty New Testaments; and kept almost two thousand Welsh children at school to learn English, Archbishop Tillotson, in his funeral sermon, says that, all things considered, there has not since the primitive times of Christianity been any among the sons of men to whom that glorious character of the Son of God might be better applied, that he went about doing good.‡ He was a divine of a cheerful spirit, and went away quietly in his sleep, October 29, 1681, in the seventy-seventh year of his age.§

* Tillotson's Works, vol. i., p. 265.

† In these charitable works, as we have seen before, he was assisted by his friends. The great business of his life was to do good. He annually travelled over Wales, inspecting the schools and instructing the people both in public and private, till he was between sixty and seventy years of age. He sustained great loss by the fire of London, and after the death of his wife and the settlement of his children, his fortune was reduced to £150 per annum, out of which he constantly expended £100 in works of charity. He had a singular sagacity and prudence in devising the most effectual ways of doing good; and his example gave the first hint to Mr. T. Firmin of that plan of furnishing the poor with employment, which he so extensively and so generously pursued. His funeral sermon was preached by Doctor, afterward Archbishop Tillotson.—Palmer.—ED.

‡ Calamy, vol. ii., p. 8. He used often to say, with pleasure, that he had two livings which he would not exchange for any in England, viz., Christ's Hospital, where he used to catechise the children; and Wales, where he travelled to spread knowledge, piety, and charity.—C.

§ The learned and excellent Dr. William Lloyd, then Bishop of St. Asaph, who endeavoured by argument to remove the scruples of the Dissenters, and to bring them back into the Church by mild and Christian methods, after some private conferences, called on Mr. James Owen to produce his reasons

While the Tories and High Church clergy were ravaging the Dissenters, the court was intent upon subverting the Constitution, and getting the government of the city into their hands. June 24, 1682, there was a contest about the election of sheriffs, which occasioned a considerable tumult. And when the election of a lord-mayor came on at Michaelmas, the citizens were again in an uproar, the lord-mayor or pretending a right to adjourn the court, while the sheriffs, to whom the right belonged, continued the poll till night; when the books were cast up, each party claimed the majority according to their respective books. The contest rose so high, that Sir William Pritchard, lord-mayor, was afterward arrested at the suit of Mr. Papillon and Dubois, and detained prisoner in Skinners' Hall till midnight. But when the affair came to a trial, the election was vacated, Papillon and Dubois were imprisoned, and the leading men of the Whig party, who had distinguished themselves in the contest, were fined in large sums of money, which made way for the loss of the charter.

The court would have persuaded the Common Council to make a voluntary surrender of it to the crown, to put an end to all contests for the future;* but not being able to prevail, they resolved to condemn it by law; accordingly, a quo warranto was issued out of the Court of King's Bench, to see whether its charter had been duly observed, because the Common Council, in one of their addresses, had petitioned the sitting of the Parliament, and had taxed the prorogation as a delay of justice, and because they had laid taxes on their wharfs and markets contrary to law. After trial upon these two points, the chief-justice delivered it as the unanimous opinion of the court, that the liberties and franchises of the city of London had been forfeited, and might be seized into the king's hands, but judgment was not to be entered till the king's pleasure was farther known. In the mean time, the lord-mayor and Common Council, who are the representatives of the city, agreed to submit to the king's mercy, and sent a deputation to Windsor, June 18, 1683, to beg pardon; which the king was pleased to grant on condition that his majesty might have a negative in the choice of all the chief magistrates; that if his majesty disapproved of their choice of a lord-mayor, they should choose another within a week; and that if his majesty disapproved their second choice, he should him-

for preaching without ordination by diocesan bishops, at the public hall of Oswestry, on the 27th of September of the year 1681. The bishop was attended by the learned Mr. Henry Dodwell; Mr. Owen's supporters were, Mr. Philip Henry, Mr. Jonathan Roberts, of Slainvair, in Denbighshire, an excellent scholar and warm disputant. The dispute began at two in the afternoon, and ended between eight and nine. Several points connected with the main question, " concerning the necessity of ordination by diocesan bishops, in uninterrupted succession from the apostles," were debated. The effects of this discussion were various, but no converts were made by it. The bishop procured respect by his exemplary candour; and Mr. Philip Henry, by his prudent and primitive temper, and the mildness of his manner, recommended himself to the high esteem of the prelate and the company.—Mr. James Owen's Life, p. 28–35.—ED.

* Burnet, p. 354–357. Rapin, p. 727.

self nominate a mayor for the year ensuing; and the like as to sheriffs, aldermen, &c.* When this was reported to the Common Council, it was put to the vote, and upon a division, the hundred and four were for accepting the king's regulation, and eighty-six against it; but even these concessions continued no longer than a year. The charter of London being lost, the cities and corporations in general were prevailed with to deliver up their charters, and accept of such new ones as the court would grant, which was the highest degree of perfidy and baseness in those who were intrusted with them, especially when they knew that the design was to pack a Parliament, in order to make way for a popish successor.

Thus the liberties of England were delivered up to the crown; and though the forms of law remained, men's lives and estates were at the mercy of a set of profligate creatures, who would swear anything for hire. Juries, says Burnet,[†] were a shame to the nation and a reproach to religion, for they were packed and prepared to bring in verdicts as they were directed, and not as matters appeared upon the evidence. Zeal against popery was decried as the voice of a faction, who were enemies to the king and his government. All rejoicings on the 5th of November were forbid, and strict orders given to all constables and other officers to keep the peace; but the populace not being so orderly as they should have been, several London apprentices were fined twenty marks for a riot, and set in the pillory. These were the triumphs of a Tory and popish administration.

A little before this died old Mr. Thomas Case, M.A., educated in Christ Church, Oxford, and one of the Assembly of Divines: he was peculiarly zealous in promoting the morning exercises, but was turned out of his living at St. Mary Magdalen, Milk-street, for refusing the Engagement, and imprisoned for Mr. Love's plot; he was afterward rector of St. Giles's, and waited on the king at Breda.[‡] He was one of the commissioners at the Savoy, and silenced with his brethren in 1662. He was an open, plainhearted man, an excellent preacher, of a warm spirit, and a hearty lover of all good men. He died May 30, 1682, aged eighty-four.[§]

Mr. Samuel Clarke, the ejected minister of

* Burnet, vol. ii., p. 403. Gazette, No. —, 1835.
† Page 359.
‡ Calamy, vol. ii., p. 13. Palmer's Non. Mem., vol. i., p. 124.
§ He survived every one of the Dissenters that sat in the Assembly of Divines. Mr. Baxter styles him "a holy, faithful servant of God." It is painful, however, to reflect that a man whose character appears in general to have been venerable and amiable, should be so transported by the heat of the times, as, in a sermon preached before the court-martial in 1614, to say, "Noble sirs, imitate God, and be merciful to none that have sinned of malicious wickedness;" meaning the Royalists, who were frequently styled malignants. This, as Mr. Granger observes, is sanguinary. It may be added, that it conveyed also a false idea of the Divine clemency, which extends its exercise, on repentance, to all characters; to sins of malignity as well as of infirmity.—*Granger's History of England*, vol. iii., p. 317, 318.—ED. Walker reflects severely upon this same sermon, but the cruelties which Mr. Case and his brethren endured from Bishop Wren ought to plead a little in his excuse. Mr. Case took an active part in the attempt to save Charles I. from a trial.—C.

St. Bene't Fink, was an indefatigable student, as appears by his "Martyrology," his "Lives of Eminent Divines," and other historical works: he was a good scholar, and had been a useful preacher in Cheshire and Warwickshire, before he came to London; he was one of the commissioners at the Savoy, and presented the Presbyterian ministers' address of thanks to the king for his declaration concerning ecclesiastical affairs; and though he could not conform as a preacher, he frequently attended the service of the Church as a hearer and communicant. He died December 25, 1682, ætat. eighty.*

While the liberties of England lay bleeding, the fury of the court raged higher than ever against the Nonconformists, as inflexible enemies of their arbitrary measures.[†] Mr. Baxter was surprised in his own house by a company of constables and other peace-officers, who arrested him for coming within five miles of a corporation, and brought warrants to distrain upon him for five sermons, amounting to £195. They took him out of his bed, to which he had been confined for some time, and were carrying him to jail; but Dr. Cox, the physician, meeting him in the way, went and made oath before a justice of peace that he could not be removed to prison without danger of his life, so he was permitted to go home again to bed; but the officers rifled his house, took away such books as he had, and sold even the bed from under him. Dr. Annesley, and several other ministers, had their goods distrained for latent convictions; that is, upon the oaths of persons they never saw, nor received summons to answer for themselves before a justice of peace. This was stabbing men in the dark. Some were imprisoned on the Corporation Act. The Rev. Mr. Vincent was tried and convicted at the Surrey Assizes on the 35th of Queen Elizabeth, already mentioned: he lay in prison

* When Mr. Clarke was ejected, he had been forty years in the ministry, during which time he had been seven or eight years a governor, and two years a president of Sion College. The most valuable of his numerous works are reckoned to be " Lives of the Puritan Divines and other Persons of Note." "The author and the bookseller," says Mr. Granger, " seem to have been thoroughly informed of this secret, that a taking title-page becomes much more taking with an engraved frontispiece before it; and that little pictures in the body of the book are great embellishments to style and matter." He was more a compiler than an author. His name was anagrammatized to *Su*(c)*kall Cream*, alluding to his taking the best parts of those books from which he collected. One is sorry to find in the list of his publications " A Discourse against Toleration.". He enjoyed about nine years the living of Alcester in Warwickshire, where his preaching was very useful, and the town became exemplary for sobriety, which had borne the character of " drunken Alcester." He met death with a lively sense of eternity upon his mind, and a comfortable assurance of his own title to future blessedness.—*Palmer's Noncon. Mem.*, vol. i., p. 88, &c. *Granger's History*, vol. iii., p. 321.—ED. Mr. Clarke was the great-grandfather of Dr. Samuel Clarke, of St. Alban's, the patron of Dr. Doddridge's youthful studies.—ED. Almost all we know of some of the holiest and greatest men of England we owe to the painstaking and laborious efforts of this most industrious man. " Clarke's Martyrology" is deservedly valued, and is now very rare.—C.
† Part iii., p. 191.

many months, but was at last released by the intercession of some great men.. The dissenting laity were harassed everywhere in the spiritual courts, warrants were signed for distresses, in the village of Hackney alone, to the sum of £1400, one of which was £500. The reader will, then, judge what must have been the case of the interest in general.* .

But, in the midst of this oppression and violence, the court found that the spirit of English liberty was not easily to be subdued : there were a set of patriots who stood in their way, and were determined to hazard their lives and fortunes for the Constitution ; these were, therefore, to be removed or cut off, by bringing them within the compass of some pretended plot against the government. Some, who were more zealous than prudent, met together in clubs at the taverns and other places, to talk over the common danger, and what might be done to secure their religion and liberties in case of the king's death ; but there was no formed design in any of them against the king or the present government. The court, however, laid hold of this occasion, and, as Mr. Coke says, set on foot three plots : one, to assassinate the king and duke as they came from Newmarket ; another, to seize the guards ; and a third was called the Blackheath Plot ; in all which, for aught I can find, says he, the fox was the finder. Dr. Welwood adds,† that the shattered remains of English liberty were attacked on every side, and some of the noblest blood in the nation offered up a sacrifice to the manes of popish martyrs. Swearing came into fashion, and an evidence office was set up at Whitehall ; the witnesses were highly encouraged, and, instead of judges and juries that might boggle at half evidence, care was taken to pick out such as should stick at nothing to serve a turn. The plot which the court made use of was called the Ryehouse Plot,‡ from the name of the house where the two royal brothers were to be shot ; it was within two miles of Hodsdon in Hertfordshire, and was first discovered by one Keeling, an Anabaptist ; after him Goodenough, Rumsey, and West made themselves witnesses, and framed a story out of their own heads, of lopping off the two brothers as they came from Newmarket ;. and having heard of conferences between the Duke of Monmouth, Lord Russel, and others, concerning securing the Protestant religion upon the king's decease, they impeached them to the council, upon which

Lord Russel, Algernon Sidney, the Earl of Essex, and Mr. Houblon, were apprehended and sent to the Tower. Warrants were issued out for several others, who, knowing that innocence was no protection, absconded, and went out of the way ; but several were tried, and executed upon the court evidence ; as Mr. Rumbold, the master of the house where the plot was to take place, who declared, at his execution in King James's reign, that he never knew of any design against the king ; as did Captain Walcot and Sir Thomas Armstrong, Rouse, and the rest. Lord Russel was condemned, and beheaded, for being within the hearing of some treasonable words at Mr. Shepherd's, a wine-cooper in Abchurch Lane.* The Earl of Essex's throat was cut in the Tower† during Lord Russel's trial ;‡ and Algernon Sidney was executed for having a seditious libel in his study ;§ of the injustice of which the Parliament at the Revolution was so sensible, that they reversed the judgments. A proclamation was issued out against the Duke of Monmouth, though the king knew where he was ; and after the ferment, brought him to court. Mr. Echard observes, that some have called this the Fanatic, the Protestant, the Whigish, or Presbyterian plot ; others have called it, with more justice, a piece of state policy, and no better than an imposture, for it had no other foundation than

---

* P. 392.

† Dr. Grey censures Mr. Neal's account of the Ryehouse Plot as very faulty, if not false ; "as appears," he says, "from the very best of our historians, and the confession of several that suffered for it." The historians of whom the doctor refers are Echard, Kennet, &c., and principally Bishop Sprat's History of the Ryehouse Plot. As to this work, the most partial to it must own it detracts greatly from its credit ; that it was drawn up to please the court, by one that was wholly in that interest, and, the author, it seems, acknowledges "that King James 11. called for his papers, and having read them, altered divers passages, and caused them to be printed by his own authority."—Calamy's Letter to Archdeacon Echard, p. 55. Dr. Grey ironically calls Mr. Neal's account of the Earl of Essex's death a candid remark ; and then refers to, and quotes largely, Carte's and Echard's representations of that event, to show that the earl was felo de se. This is not the place to discuss the question concerning his lordship's death, whether he committed an act of suicide or was murdered by others. Dr. Harris has fully and impartially stated the arguments on both sides.— History of Charles II., vol. ii., p. 371-376. The same judicious writer has also investigated the evidence concerning the Ryehouse Plot, p. 355-370.—Ed.

‡ Welwood's Memoirs, p. 161.

§ This was an answer to Filmer's book, written to prove the absolute and unlimited power of kings. The leading principle of this MS. was, "that power is delegated from the people to the prince, and that he is accountable to them for the abuse of it." It was urged that he was not proved to have written the piece ; that if he were the author, it contained only his private speculations ; that it could not be admitted as a proof of the plot, for it was written years before, and that, as it was not a finished piece, it could not be known how it would end ; and no general conclusion ought to be drawn from any particular chapter of a work. The book was, however, considered by Jefferies as an overt act, on this principle, Scribere est agere. It is remarkable that, within a few years, the energy and truth of the above principle removed James 11. from the throne, and placed on it the Prince of Orange. So vain is it to fight against just principles !—Ed.

---

* The temper of the court and Church at this time inclined Mr. John Shower to attend the nephew of Sir Samuel Barnardiston on his travels, in compliance with the earnest request of his uncle, in company with several other gentlemen, which we mention here to introduce the following passage. When they were at Geneva, where they continued for some time, they contracted an acquaintance with Turretin, the younger. On their first conversation, they found this learned divine and the rest of the city possessed with very unfavourable sentiments concerning the English Nonconformists. But when Mr. Shower and his companions had stated their case, and the terms required of them, Turretin and the others declared themselves well satisfied with the grounds of their dissent. and treated them, during the remainder of their residence in the city, with a very particular respect.—Tong's Life of Shower, p. 48.—Ed.

† Memoirs, p. 132.

‡ Burnet, vol. ii., p 368-373. . .

the rash and imprudent discourse of some warm Whigs, which, in so critical a conjuncture, was very hazardous ; but no scheme of a plot had been agreed upon, no preparations made, no arms nor horses purchased, nor persons appointed to execute any design against the king or government.* However, the court had their ends in striking terror into the whole party.

Great industry was used by the court to bring the body of Nonconformists into this plot ; it was given out that Dr. Owen, Mr. Mead, and Mr. Griffith were acquainted with it ;† Mr. Mead was summoned before the Council, and gave such satisfactory answers to all questions, that the king himself ordered him to be discharged. The Rev. Mr Carstaires, a Scots divine, was put to the torture of the thummikins in Scotland, to extort a confession, both his thumbs being bruised between two irons till the marrow was almost forced out of the bones : this he bore for an hour and a half without making any confession. Next day they brought him to undergo the torture of the boot, but his arms being swelled with the late torture, and he already in a fever, made a declaration of all that he knew, which amounted to no more than some loose discourse of what might be fit to be done to preserve their liberties and the Protestant religion, if there should be a crisis ;‡ but he vindicated himself and his brethren in England from all assassinating designs,

which, he said, they abhorred. Dr. South was desired to write the history of this plot ; but Dr. Sprat, afterward Bishop of Rochester, performed it, though at the Revolution he disowned it so far as to declare that King James had altered several passages in it before it was published. Bishop Burnet adds, that when the congratulatory addresses for the discovery of this plot had gone all round England, the grand juries made high-presentments against all who were accounted Whigs and Nonconformists. Great pains were taken to find out more witnesses ; pardons and rewards were offered very freely to the guilty, but none came in, which made it evident, says his lordship, that nothing was so well laid, or brought so near execution, as the witnesses had deposed, otherwise the people would have crowded in for pardons. Bishop Kennet says* that the Dissenters bore all the odium, and were not only branded for express rebels and villains, in multitudes of congratulatory and Tory addresses from all parts of the kingdom, but were severally arraigned by the king himself, in a declaration to all his loving subjects, read in all the churches on Sunday, September 9, which was appointed as a day of thanksgiving, and solemnized, after an extraordinary manner, with mighty pomp and magnificence. There was hardly a parish in England that was not at a considerable expense to testify their joy and satisfaction : nay, the papists celebrated in all their chapels in London an extraordinary service on that account ; so that these had their places of public worship, though the Protestant Dissenters were denied them.

The Quakers avowed their innocence of the plot in an address to the king at Windsor,† presented by G. Whitehead, Parker, and two more, wherein they appeal to the Searcher of all hearts, that "their principles do not allow them to take up defensive arms, much less to avenge themselves for the injuries they receive from others. That they continually pray for the king's safety and preservation, and therefore take this occasion humbly to beseech his majesty to compassionate their suffering friends, with whom the jails are so filled that they want air, to the apparent hazard of their lives, and to the endangering an infection in divers places. Besides, many houses, shops, barns, and fields are ransacked, and the goods, corn, and cattle swept away, to the discouraging of trade and husbandry, and impoverishing great numbers of quiet and industrious people ; and this for no other cause but for the exercise of a tender conscience in the worship of Almighty God, who is sovereign Lord and King in men's consciences."

But this address made no impression,‡ all things proceeding triumphantly on the side of the prerogative ;§ the court did what they pleased ; the king assumed the government of the

---

* "Mr. Neal must think his readers," says Dr. Grey, "very easy of belief to swallow down such gross untruths as these, which the smallest dabbler in the history of those times can easily confute." The reader who is not a dabbler in the history of those times is referred to Dr. Harris, as before quoted, for materials on which to form his judgment of the truth of this remark. In the mean time, he may not be displeased with the following plain lines on the death of Sidney :

"Algernon Sidney fills this tomb,
An Atheist for disclaiming Rome ;
A rebel bold for striving still
To keep the laws above the will ;
Crimes damn'd by Church and government,
Alas ! where must his ghost be sent ?
Of heaven it cannot but despair,
If holy pope be turnkey there ;
And hell it ne'er must entertain,
For there is all tyrannic reign.
Where goes it, then ? Where 't ought to go—
Where pope nor devil have to do.",
—Bennet's Memorial, p. 359.—ED.

† Dr. Grey refers to "copies of informations," in the appendix to Sprat's account for a deposition signed by Mr. Carstaires, saying, "The deponent did communicate the design on foot to Dr. Owen, Mr. Griffith, and Mr. Mead, at Stepney, who all concurred in promoting of it, and desired it might take effect." Dr. Grey, by this quotation, means to implicate those gentlemen in the most atrocious part of this plot. But the question returns, What was the design on foot ? what were the nature and extent of it ? Mr. Neal immediately informs us, in his report of the amount of Carstaire's confession, that it did not go to any assassination, but only to preserving their liberties and the Protestant religion. As to Mr Mead, in particular. he went into Holland on this occasion ; and after his return to England, he was summoned to appear before King Charles at the privy council. where he fully vindicated his innocence. and was perfectly discharged.—Pierce's Vindication of the Dissenters, part i., p. 258. Mr. Mead carried with him into Holland the son (the eleventh of thirteen children), whom he placed under an excellent master who afterward rose to the first eminence as a scholar and physician.—Granger's History, vol. iii., p. 333.—ED.

‡ Burnet, vol. ii, p. 426-430.

* Page 402.   † Sewel, p. 585.
‡ The king was touched, for the moment, with the exhibition it gave of the unreasonable and unmerited sufferings of the Quakers and said to one of his courtiers standing by, "What shall we do for this people? the prisons are full of them." The party to whom this query was put, to divert his attention, drew him into conversation upon some other topic, so that little or no relaxation of the oppressive measures resulted from this address, nor during the remainder of the king's reign.—Gough's History of the Quakers, vol. iii., p. 8, 9.—ED.   § Kennet, p. 410.

city of London into his own hands, and appointed a mayor, sheriffs, and aldermen, without the election of the people ; sermons were filled with the principles of absolute obedience and nonresistance, which were carried higher than ever their forefathers had thought of or practised. The University of Oxford passed a decree,* in full convocation, July 21, 1683, against certain pernicious books and damnable doctrines, destructive to the sacred persons of princes, their state and government, and all human society.† It consists of twenty-seven propositions, extracted from the writings of Buchanan, Baxter, Owen, Milton, J. Goodwin, Hobbs, Cartwright, Travers, and others, who had maintained that there was an original contract between king and people ; and that when kings subvert the constitution of their country, and become absolute tyrants, they forfeit their right to the government, and may be resisted : these, and other propositions of a like nature, they declare to be impious, seditious, scandalous, damnable, heretical, blasphemous, and infamous to the Christian religion. They forbid their students to read those writers, and ordered their books to be burned. But how well they practised their own doctrines at the Revolution will be seen in its proper place ; and one of Queen Anne's Parliaments ordered the decree itself to be burned by the hands of the common hangman.‡

* This decree was drawn up by Dr. Jane, dean of Gloucester, and the king's professor of divinity, and subscribed by the whole convocation. It was presented to the king, with great solemnity, on the 24th of July following, and very graciously received. It was ordered, in perpetual memory of it, to be entered in the registry of the convocation, and to be stuck up in the different colleges and halls. Farther to counteract the spread and influence of the propositions against which it was levelled, all readers, tutors, catechists, and others to whom the instruction and care of youth were committed, were commanded to instruct and ground their scholars in "that most necessary doctrine, which, in a manner, is the badge and character of the Church of England, of submitting to every ordinance of man for the Lord's sake, whether it be to the king as supreme, or unto governors, as unto them that are sent by him, for the punishment of evildoers, and for the praise of them that do well ; teaching that this submission is to be clear, absolute, and without any exception of any state or order of men."—High Church Politics, p. 89.
† Another proof of the intolerant spirit which dictated the decrees of the University at this time, offers in its treatment of Dr. Whitby, precentor of the Church of Sarum. This learned writer published in this year, 1683, without his name, his "Protestant Reconciler," humbly pleading for condescension to dissenting brethren, in things indifferent and unnecessary, for the sake of peace ; and showing how unreasonable it is to make such things the necessary conditions of communion. This book gave such high offence, that it was condemned by the university on the above-mentioned day, and burned by the hands of the marshal in the schools', quadrangle. The author was also obliged by Dr. Seth Ward, to whom he was chaplain, to make a public retractation of it on the 9th of the ensuing October. And in the same year, to remove the clamour his piece had raised, he published a second part, "earnestly persuading the dissenting laity to join in full communion with the Church of England, and answering all the objections of the Nonconformists against the lawfulness of the submission to the rites and constitutions of that church."—Birch's Life of Archbishop Tillotson, p. 103-105.—ED.   ‡ Collyer, 902.

Dr. Benjamin Calamy, rector of St. Lawrence Jewry, in one of his printed sermons entitled "A Scrupulous Conscience," invited the Nonconformists to examine what each party had to say for themselves with respect to the ceremonies imposed by the Church, and enforced by the penal laws, calling upon them modestly to propose their doubts, and meekly to hearken to and receive instruction. In compliance with this invitation, Mr. Thomas Delaune, an Anabaptist schoolmaster, and a learned man,* printed a "Plea for the Nonconformists," showing the true state of their case, and justifying their separation. But before it was published, he was apprehended by a messenger from the press, and shut up close prisoner in Newgate, by warrant from the Recorder Jenner, dated November 30, 1683. Mr. Delaune wrote to Dr. Calamy to endeavour his enlargement : "My confinement," says he, "is for accepting your invitation ; I look upon you obliged in honour to procure my sheets, yet unfinished, a public passport,† and to me my liberty : there is nothing in them but a fair examination of those things your sermon invited to, and I cannot find that Christ and his disciples ever forced scrupulous consciences to conformity by such methods as sending them to Newgate ; I beseech you, therefore, in the fear of God, as you will answer it to our great Lord and Master Jesus Christ, that you would endeavour to convince a stranger by something more like reason and divinity than a prison." The doctor at first said he would do him all the kindness that became him.‡

* Mr. Delaune was born at Brini in Ireland, about three miles from Riggsdale. His parents were papists, and very poor, and rented part of the estate of —— Riggs, Esq. This gentleman, observing the early and forward parts of the young Delaune, placed him in a friary at Kilcrash, seven miles from Cork, where he received his education ; when he was about fifteen or sixteen years of age, he removed to Kinsale, and met with Mr. Bampfield, who, discovering his genius and learning, made him clerk of his pilchard fishery there, and was the means of giving his mind a pious and virtuous turn. After some years, during which he enjoyed the high esteem and friendship of Major Riggs and Mr. Bampfield, persecution and troubles induced him to leave Ireland and come over into England, where he married the daughter of Mr. Edward Hutchinson, who had been pastor of a congregation at Ormond, but was also come to England on account of the troubles of the times. After this, Mr. Delaune went to London, kept a grammar-school there, and fell into an intimacy and strict friendship with Mr. Benjamin Keach, and translated the "Philologia Sacra," prefixed to his celebrated work entitled "A Key to open Scripture Metaphors." The narrative published with the subsequent editions of his "Plea for the Nonconformists" fully represents the series of sufferings under which he sunk, and the process of the iniquitous prosecution to which he, his wife and children, became a sacrifice.—C.
† It is to be observed that, notwithstanding all the attempts used to suppress Mr. Delaune's tract, to obstruct its reception, and to prevent its effect on the public mind, by severities against its author, and by committing the piece itself to the flames, there was a great demand for it, and before the year 1733 there had been seventeen impressions of it.—ED.   An American edition of this valuable work, now quite scarce, is a desideratum.—C.
‡ Mr. Neal's account of Dr. Calamy's conduct towards Mr. Delaune is drawn from the injured sufferer's narrative ; and it must be allowed that it reflects on the doctor's character and memory. But though,

But in answer to a second letter, he said he looked upon himself as unconcerned, because he was not mentioned in that sheet he saw with the recorder. Mr. Delaune insisted that his honour was at stake for his deliverance, and prayed him at least to perform the office of a divine, in visiting him in prison, to argue him out of his doubts ; but the doctor, like an ungenerous adversary, deserted him. Mr. Delaune, therefore, was to be convinced by an indictment at law ; for that, on November 30, he did, by force of arms, &c., unlawfully, seditiously, and maliciously write, print, and publish a certain false, seditious, and scandalous libel, of and concerning our lord the king, and the Book of Common Prayer, entitled "A Plea for the Nonconformists." For which offence he was fined one hundred marks, and to be kept prisoner till he paid it ; to find security for his good behaviour for one year, and his books to be burned before the Royal Exchange. The court told him that, in respect of his being a scholar, he should not be pilloried, though he deserved it. Mr. Delaune, not being able to pay his fine, lay in prison fifteen months, and suffered great hardships by extreme poverty, having no subsistence but on charity. He had a wife and two small children with him, who all died in the jail, through the length and closeness of the confinement, and other inconveniences they endured ;* and at length Mr. Delaune himself sunk

by not replying to his book, nor visiting him, he appeared to desert him, yet it appears that the behaviour which Mr. Delaune, in his afflicted situation, felt as a severe neglect, was tempered with more attention to his case and kindness than he seems to have known of. For Dr. Edmund Calamy says, "that his uncle took pains with Jefferies to get him released, but could not prevail, which was no small trouble to him." Dr. Calamy was a man greatly respected ; and, though a true son of the Church, averse to persecution. He was a man of great humanity, courteous and affable in his deportment, and exemplary in his life. His sermons were reckoned to possess great merit. No books in his study appear to have been as much used as Mr. Perkins's works, especially his "Cases of Conscience," which were full of marks and scores. He died when a little turned of forty years of age. The treatment which his neighbour and particular friend, Alderman Cornish, received, greatly affected him, and is thought to have hastened his end.—Dr. Calamy's Own Life, MS., and Biographia Britannica, vol. iii., second edit.—ED.

* The story of Mr. Delaune is very affecting, and cannot but, at this distance of time, move pity and resentment. "The fate of himself and family, perishing in Newgate for want of £70," observes the candid editor of the "Biographia Britannica," second edition, "is not only a disgrace to the general spirit of the times, but casts peculiar dishonour on the Nonconformists of that period. Though there was probably something in his disposition which occasioned his having but few friends, a man of his knowledge, learning, and integrity ought not to have been so fatally neglected. Perhaps the only apology which can be made for the Dissenters of King Charles II.'s reign is, that while so many of their ministers were in a persecuted state, it was impossible for every case of distress to be duly regarded." To this may be added the great number of cases of distress arising from the prosecution and sufferings of the lay Dissenters. Mr. Jeremy White told Mr. John Waldron, of Exeter, that the computation of those who suffered for nonconformity between the Restoration and the Revolution amounted to seventy thousand families ruined, and eight thousand persons destroyed; and the computation was not finished

under his sufferings, and died in Newgate, a martyr to the challenge of this High Church champion. Mr. Francis Bampfield suffered the like, or greater hardships ; he had been educated in Wadham College, Oxford, and was minister of Sherborne, in Dorsetshire.* After the Act of Uniformity, he continued preaching, as he had opportunity, in private, till he was imprisoned for five days and nights, with twenty-five of his hearers, in one room, with only one bed, where they spent their time in religious exercises ; but after some time he was released.† Soon after he was apprehended again, and lay nine years in Dorchester jail, though he was a person of unshaken loyalty to the king, and against the Parliament war ; but this availed nothing to his being a Nonconformist. He afterward retired to London, where, being again apprehended, he was shut up in Newgate, and there died February 16, 1683–4. He was for the seventh-day Sabbath, but a person of unquestionable seriousness and piety.

With him might be mentioned Mr. Ralphson, a learned man, and a fellow-sufferer with Mr. Delaune in Newgate. On the 10th of December, a bill was found against him by the grand jury of London ; on the 13th of the same month he pleaded Not guilty at the Old Bailey. On the 16th of January he was called to the sessions-house, but other trials proving tedious, his did not come on. The next day he was brought to the outer bar ; and after an attendance of divers hours in a place not very agreeable, and in the sharpest winter that had been known, he contracted a violent cold, which issued in a fever, that carried him as well as Mr. Bampfield beyond the reach of tyrants, or the restraint of bail-docks and press-yards, to the mansions of everlasting rest.‡ Mr. Philips, partner with Mr. Bampfield, suffered eleven months' imprison-

when this number was ascertained. The sources of beneficence were also diminished by the effect of the measures pursued on trade; for the customs paid in Bristol only arose, in Charles's persecution, not to £30,000 per annum ; but in King William's reign they advanced to near £100,000.—Waldron's Copy of Neal, penes me.—ED.

† Mr. Bampfield was descended from an ancient and honourable family in Devonshire. The first living he held was more valuable than that of Sherborne, being about £100 per annum ; and having an annuity of £80 per annum settled on him for life, he spent all the income of his place in acts of charity, by employing the poor that could work, relieving the necessities of those who were incapable of any labour, and distributing Bibles and practical books. Soon after his ejectment he was imprisoned for worshipping God in his own family; and it is remarkable that, notwithstanding he was prosecuted with severity, he had been zealous against the Parliament's army and Oliver's usurpation, and always a strenuous advocate for the Royal cause. When he resided in London he formed a church on the principles of the Sabbatarian Baptists at Pinners' Hall, of which principles he was a zealous asserter. He was a celebrated preacher, and a man of serious piety. He bore his long imprisonment with great courage and patience, and gathered a church even in the place of confinement. His fellow-prisoners lamented him, as well as his acquaintance and friends.—Palmer's Noncon. Mem., vol. i., p. 468–472. Crosby's History of the Baptists, vol. i., p. 363–368 ; vol. ii., p. 355–361.—ED. † Calamy, vol. ii., p. 260. ‡ Calamy's Abridg., vol. ii., p. 259–377.

ment in Ilchester jail, in a nasty, stinking hole, to the great hazard of his life. Mr. French, of Town Maulin, was confined six months in Maidstone common jail, in a hard winter, without fire or candle, or any private apartment. Mr. Salkeld, the ejected minister of Worlington in Suffolk, was fined £100, and committed to the common jail of St. Edmundsbury,* for saying popery was coming into the nation apace, and no care taken to prevent it. He lay in prison three years, and was not discharged till the year 1686.

Mr. Richard Stretton suffered six months' imprisonment this year for refusing the Oxford oath, in company with ten ministers more, who were also his fellow-prisoners.† Most of the dissenting ministers were forced to shift their places of abode to avoid discovery, and travel in long nights and cold weather from one village to another, to preach to their people. If at any time they ventured to visit their families in a dark night, they durst not stir abroad, but went away before morning: others their time in woods and solitary places; others, being excommunicated, removed with their effects into other diocesses: great numbers of the common people, taken at private meetings, were convicted as rioters, and fined £10 apiece; and not being able to pay, were obliged to remove into other counties, by which they lost their business, and their families were reduced to want. I forbear to mention the rudeness offered to young women, some of whom were sent to Bridewell, to beat hemp among rogues and thieves: others, that were married and with child, received irreparable damages; even children were terrified with constables and halberdeers breaking open houses, of whom I myself, says Mr. Peirce, being very young, was one example; and the writer of this history could mention others.

In the midst of these violent proceedings, the divines of the Church of England published the "London Cases against the Nonconformists," as if the danger of religion arose from that quarter; they were twenty-three in number, and have since been abridged by Dr. Bennet. These champions of the Church were very secure from being answered, after Mr. Delaune had so lately lost his life for accepting such a challenge.‡ They must, therefore, have the field to themselves, for if their adversaries wrote, they were sure to be rewarded with fines and a prison; but since the return of liberty, they have been answered separately by Mr. Nathaniel Taylor, Mr. James Peirce, and others.

This year [1683] died Dr. John Owen, one of the most learned of the Independent divines;

he was educated in Queen's College, Oxford, but left the university in 1637, being dissatisfied with Laud's innovations.* He was a strict Calvinist, and published his "Display of Arminianism" in 1642, for which the committee of religion presented him to the living of Fordham in Essex. In 1643 he removed to Coggeshall in the same county, where he first declared himself an Independent, and gathered a church according to the discipline of that people. He often preached before the Long Parliament, even about the time the king was beheaded, but always kept his sentiments in reserve upon such a subject. Soon after, Lieutenant-general Cromwell took him into his service as a chaplain in his expedition to Ireland; and when the general marched to Scotland, he obtained an order of Parliament for the doctor to attend him thither. Upon his return, he was preferred to the deanery of Christ Church, and next year to the vice-chancellorship of Oxford, where he presided with great reputation and prudence for five years. He always behaved like a gentleman and scholar, and maintained the dignity of his character. The writer of his life says, that though he was an Independent himself, he gave most of the vacant livings in his disposal among the Presbyterians, and obliged the Episcopal party, by conniving at an assembly of about three hundred of them, almost over against his own doors. The Oxford historian,† after having treated his memory with the most opprobrious language, confesses that he was well skilled in the tongues, in rabbinical learning, and in

* Calamy, vol. ii., p. 58. Palmer's Non. Mem., vol. i., p. 152–158.

† Mr. Wood represents Dr. Owen as a perjured person, a time-server, a hypocrite, whose godliness was gain, and a blasphemer; and, as if this were not sufficient, he has also made him a fop. "All which," observes Mr. Granger, with equal judgment and candour, "means no more than this: that when Dr. Owen entered himself a member of the University of Oxford, he was of the Established Church, and took the usual oaths; that he turned Independent, preached the Engagement, and accepted preferment from Cromwell; that he was a man of good person and behaviour, and liked to go well dressed." "We must be extremely cautious," adds this author, "how we form our judgments of characters at this period; the difference of a few modes or ceremonies in religious worship has been the source of infinite prejudice and misrepresentation. The practice of some of the splenetic writers of this period reminds me of the painter, well known by the appellation of Hellish Brueghel, who so accustomed himself to painting of witches, imps, and devils, that he sometimes made but little difference between his human and infernal figures." To Mr. Neal's delineation of Dr. Owen's character may be added, that he was hospitable in his house, generous in his favours, and charitable to the poor, especially to poor scholars, some of whom he took into his own family, maintained at his own charge, and educated in an academical learning. When he was at Tunbridge, the Duke of York several times sent for him, and conversed with him concerning the Dissenters. On his return to London, King Charles himself sent for him, and discoursed with him two hours; assuring him of his favour and respect, expressing himself a friend to liberty of conscience, and his sense of the wrong done to the Dissenters. At the same time he gave him a thousand guineas to distribute among those who had suffered most.—Granger's History of England, vol. iii., p. 301, 302, note; and Palmer's Noncon. Mem., vol. i., p. 154, 155.—ED.

* It aggravated the iniquity as well as severity of this sentence, that many hundreds of Dr. Salkeld's hearers could testify that what he said was not said as his own language, but that of the Parliament. During his confinement he was helpful to his fellow-prisoners, both as a minister and a cheerful Christian. His table was furnished by his friends at Bury, and his fine afterward remitted by King William. But his estate was much weakened, and his health almost ruined by his imprisonment. After his liberation he continued his ministry at Walsham in the Willows, and died December 20, 1699, aged seventy-seven.—Palmer's Non. Mem., vol. ii., p. 442, 443.—ED.

† Calamy, vol. ii., p. 676.

‡ Peirce, p. 259.

the Jewish rites and customs, and that he was one of the most genteel and fairest writers that appeared against the Church of England. The doctor had a great reputation among foreign Protestants ; and when he was ejected by the Act of Uniformity, was invited to a professorship in the United Provinces. He was once also determined to settle in New-England, but was stopped by express order from the Council. He was pastor of a considerable congregation in London, and died with great calmness and composure of mind, on Bartholomew Day, 1683. His works are very numerous, and still in esteem among the Dissenters, though his style is a little intricate and perplexed.*

[In this year died, aged seventy-two, Dr. Benjamin Whichcote, the friend of Tillotson. He was of an ancient and honourable family in the county of Salop, and was born at Whichcote Hall, in the parish of Stoke, March 11, 1609. He was admitted in Emanuel College, Cambridge, 1626, and graduated bachelor of arts 1629, master of arts 1633, and bachelor in divinity 1640. In the same year that he took his second degree he was elected fellow of the college, and his tutor, Mr. Thomas Hill, leaving the university the year after, Mr. Whichcote took pupils, and became very considerable for his learning and worth, his prudence and temper, his wisdom and moderation, in those times of trial ; nor was he less famous for the number, rank, and character of his pupils, and the care he took of them. Wallis, Smith, Worthington, Cradock, &c., studied under him. In 1626 he set up an afternoon lecture in Trinity Church at Cambridge, which he served twenty years. In 1643 the master and fellows of his college presented him to the living of North Cadbury, in Somersetshire. But he was soon called back to Cambridge, and admitted provost of King's College, March 19, 1644.† In 1649 he was created doctor in divinity. Here he employed his credit, weight, and influence to advance and spread a free and generous way of thinking, and to promote a spirit of sober piety and rational religion. Many, whose talents and learning raised them to great eminence as divines after the Restoration, were formed by him. To his predecessor in the provostship he was generous. His spirit was too noble servilely to follow a party. At the Restoration he was removed from his post, on accepting of which he had resigned the living of Cadbury, and he was elected and licensed to the cure of St. Anne's Blackfriars, November, 1662. This church was burned down in the fire of 1665, and he retired for a while to Milton, a living given to him by his college. He was after this presented, by the crown, to the vicarage of St. Lawrence Jury, which was his last stage. Here he continued, in high and general esteem, preaching twice every week, till his death in 1683. One volume of his sermons, entitled "Select Discourses," was published, after his

* Owen's entire works have been republished in twenty-one volumes, not inclusive of his Notes and Exercitations on the Hebrews ; but such has been the demand for the writings of this divine, that they are again become scarce.—C.

† See before, vol. i., p. 483, text and note, where we have already made respectful mention of Dr. Whichcote.

death, by the Earl of Shaftesbury, author of the "Characteristics," in 1698. Three others by Dr. John Jeffery, archdeacon of Norwich, in 1701 and 1702, and a fourth by Dr. Samuel Clarke. A collection of his "Aphorisms" was printed by Dr. S Salter, in 1753. See the second preface to which, p. 16-27.—Ed.]

This year the king, by the assistance of the Tories and Roman Catholics, completed the ruin of the Constitution, and assumed the whole government into his own hands. The Whigs and Nonconformists were struck with terror by the severe prosecutions of the heads of their party.* Mr. Hampden was fined £40,000, Sir Samuel Barnardiston £10,000, for defaming the evidence in the Ryehouse Plot. Mr. Speke £2000, and Mr. Braddon £1000, for reporting that the Earl of Essex had been murdered in the Tower. Mr. John Duttoncolt £100,000, for scandalum magnatum against the Duke of York, who now ruled all at court. Oates was fined for the same crime £100,000, and never released till after the Revolution. Thirty-two others were fined or pilloried for libelling the king or the Duke of York. In short, the greatest part of the history of this year consists of prosecutions, penalties, and punishments, says Mr. Echard. At the same time, the Earl of Danby and the popish lords were released out of the Tower on bail, the garrison of Tangier was brought over into England, and augmented to a standing army of four or five thousand resolute men, fit for any service the court should employ them in. And the corporations throughout England, having been prevailed with, by promises or threatenings, to surrender their charters,† after the example of London, the whole kingdom was divested of its privileges, and reduced to an absolute monarchy.‡ Whole

* Rapin, p. 733, and note. Echard, p. 1043, 1044.
† Among others, the charter of the city of Chester was surrendered, and a new one joyfully accepted, by which a power was reserved to the crown to put out magistrates and put in at pleasure. This is mentioned to introduce an instance of the conduct of the Dissenters of that day, which reflects honour on their integrity, and shows how far they were from the affectation of power ; as it was also a proof of a disinterested and inviolable attachment to the rights and liberties of their country. About August, 1688, one Mr. Trinder was sent to Chester to new model the corporation according to the power above mentioned. He applied to Mr. Henry, in the king's name, and told him that "his majesty thought the government of the city needed reformation, and if he would say who should be put out, it should be done." Mr. Henry said, "He begged his pardon, but it was none of his business, nor would he in the least intermeddle in a thing of that nature." Trinder, however, got instructions from others. The charter was cancelled, and another of the same import was made out and sent down, nominating to the government all the Dissenters in the city, the seniors to be aldermen, and the juniors common-council-men. When the persons named in it were called together to have notice of it, and to have the time fixed for their being sworn, like true Englishmen, they refused it, and desired that the ancient charter might be re-established, though they knew that none of them would come into power by that, but many of those who were their bitter enemies would be restored. Accordingly, the old charter was renewed in the same state wherein it was made when the Tories surrendered it. — Mr. Thompson's MS. Collections, under the word Chester.—Ed.
‡ Welwood's Memoirs, p. 130.

peals of anathemas were rung out against those patriots who stood in the way against this inundation of power. The Scriptures were wrested to prove the Divine right of tyrants. The absolute government of the Jewish kings was preached up as a pattern for ours.* And Heaven itself was ranked on that side, by some who pretended to expound its will. Instead of dropping a tear over our expiring laws, liberties, and Parliaments, fulsome panegyrics were made upon their murderers, and curses denounced on those who would have saved them from destruction.

In this melancholy situation of public affairs, the prosecution of the Nonconformists was continued, and egged on with an infatuation hardly to be paralleled in any Protestant nation: Dr. Barlow, bishop of Lincoln, published a letter for spiriting up the magistrates against the Dissenters, in concurrence with another drawn up by the justices of peace of Bedford, bearing date January 14, 1684. Many were cited into the spiritual courts, excommunicated, and ruined. Two hundred warrants of distress were issued out upon private persons and families, in the town and neighbourhood of Uxbridge, for frequenting conventicles or not resorting to church.† An order was made by the justices of Exeter, promising a reward of 40s. to any one who should apprehend a Nonconformist minister, which the bishop of the diocess, Dr. Lamplugh, commanded to be published in all the churches, by his clergy, on the following Sunday. The Rev. Dr. Bates, Dr. Annesley, and many of their brethren in the ministry, had their goods seized and confiscated. Mr. —— Mayot, of Oxford, a moderate Conformist, having left Mr. Baxter £600 to distribute among sixty poor ejected ministers, the Lord-keeper North took it from him, as given to a superstitious use; but it lying unappropriated in the Court of Chancery till after the Revolution, it was restored by the commissioners of the great seal under King William. Soon after the justices sent warrants to apprehend Mr. Baxter, as being one in a list of a thousand names who were to be bound to their good behaviour upon latent convictions, that is, without seeing their accusers, or being made acquainted with their charge.‡ Mr. Baxter refusing to open his doors, the officers forced into his house, and finding him locked up in his study, they resolved to starve him from thence by setting six men at the door, to whom he was obliged next day to surrender. They then carried him to the sessions-house two or three times, and bound him in a bond of £400; so that if his friends had not been sureties for him, contrary to his desire, he must have died in prison, as many excellent persons did about this time.

Jefferies, now Lord-chief-justice of England, who was scandalously vicious, and drunk every day, besides a drunkenness of fury in his temper that looked like madness, was prepared for any

dirty work the court should put him upon.* September 23, 1684, Mr. Thomas Rosewel, the dissenting minister at Rotherhithe, was imprisoned in the Gate-house, Westminster, for high treason; and a bill was found against him at the quarter sessions, upon which he was tried November 8, at the King's Bench bar, by a Surrey jury, before Lord-chief-justice Jefferies, and his brethren, viz., Withins, Holloway, and Walcot. He was indicted for the following expressions in his sermon, September 14: That the king could not cure the king's evil, but that priests and prophets by their prayers could heal the griefs of the people; that we had had two wicked kings (meaning the present king and his father), whom we can resemble to no other person but to the most wicked Jeroboam; and that if they (meaning his hearers) would stand to their principles, he did not doubt but they should overcome their enemies (meaning the king), as in former times, with rams' horns, broken platters, and a stone in a sling. The witnesses were three infamous women, who swore to the words without the innuendoes; they were laden with the guilt of many perjuries already, and such of them as could be found afterward were convicted, and the chief of them pilloried before the Exchange. The trial lasted seven hours, and Mr. Rosewel behaved with all the decency and respect to the court that could be expected, and made a defence that was applauded by most of the bearers. He said it was impossible the witnesses should remember, and be able to pronounce so long a period, when they could not so much as tell the text, nor anything else in the sermon, besides the words they had sworn: several who heard the sermon, and wrote it in short-hand, declared they heard no such words. Mr. Rosewel offered his own notes to prove it, but no regard was had to them. The women could not prove, says Burnet, by any one circumstance, that they were at the meeting, or that any person saw them there on that day: the words they swore were so gross, that it was not to be imagined that any man in his wits would express himself so before a wild assembly; yet Jefferies urged the matter with his usual vehemence. He laid it for a foundation, that all preaching at conventicles was treasonable, and that this ought to dispose the jury to believe any evidence upon that head, so the jury brought him in guilty;† upon which,

* Burnet, vol. ii., p. 444, 445.

† As soon as Mr. Rosewel was convicted, Sir John Talbot, who was present at the trial, went to the king, and urged on his majesty, that if such evidence as had appeared against Mr. Rosewel were admitted, no one of his subjects would be safe. Upon this, when Jefferies soon after came into the royal presence, with an air of exultation and triumph, to congratulate his majesty on the conviction of a traitor, the king gave him a cold reception, which damped his ardour in the business. When the court met to hear Mr. Rosewel's counsel, this corrupt judge, who on the trial had intermingled with the examination of the witnesses virulent invectives against him, and with his usual vehemence had endeavoured to prejudice and inflame the jury, now assumed a tone of moderation, and strongly recommended to the king's counsel caution and deliberation, where the life of a man was depending.—See the Trial.—Ed.

N.B. This trial has been reprinted in the Protestant Dissenters' Magazine.

* Mr. Waldron, of Exeter, has written here in his copy of Mr. Neal's work the following note: "The public orator of Cambridge, in a speech to the king at Newmarket, told him that they hoped to see the King of England as absolute as the kings of Israel: as Thomas Quicks, Esq., told me, who stood behind him."—J. W. † Howe's Life, p. 80.

‡ Baxter, part iii., p. 198.

says the bishop,* there was a shameful rejoicing ; and it was now thought all conventicles must be suppressed, when such evidence could be received against such a defence. But when the words came to be examined by men learned in the law, they were found not to be treason by any statute. So Mr. Rosewel moved an arrest of judgment till counsel should be heard ; and though it was doubtful whether the motion was proper on this foundation after the verdict, yet the king was so out of countenance at the accounts he heard of the witnesses, that he gave orders to yield to it ; and in the end he was pardoned.† The court lost a great deal of reputation by this trial ; for besides that Rosewel made a strong defence, he proved that he had always been a loyal man even in Cromwell's days, that he prayed constantly for the king in his family, and that in his sermons he often insisted upon the obligations to loyalty.

Among other sufferers for nonconformity, we must not forget the Rev. Mr. William Jenkyns, M.A., the ejected minister of Christ Church, who died this year in Newgate : he was educated in St. John's College, Cambridge ; and about the year 1641 was chosen minister of this place, and lecturer of Blackfriars, both which pulpits he filled with great acceptance till the destruction of monarchy, after which he was sequestered, for refusing to comply with the orders of Parliament.‡ He was sent to the Tower for Love's plot, but upon his humble petition, and promise of submission to the powers in being, he was pardoned, and his sequestration taken off, but he carefully avoided meddling in politics afterward. He was summoned before the Council January 2, 1661, and reprimanded, because he forgot to pray for the king ;§ and being ejected with his brethren in 1662, he retired into the country ; but upon the indulgence in 1671, he had a new meeting-house erected for him in Jewin-street, where he preached to a crowded audience. He was one of the merchant's lecturers at Pinners' Hall ; and when the indulgence was revoked,

he continued preaching, as he could, till this year ; but September 2, 1684, being at a private fast with some of his brethren, the soldiers broke in and carried Mr. Jenkyns before two aldermen, who treated him very rudely; and, upon his refusing the Oxford oath, committed him to Newgate ; while he was there, he petitioned the king for a release, his physicians declaring that his life was in danger from his close confinement ; but no security would be accepted. So that he soon declined in his health, and died in Newgate in the seventy-third year of his age, January 19, 1684–5, having been a prisoner four months and one week. A little before his death he said, a man might be as effectually murdered in Newgate as at Tyburn. He was buried by his friends in Bunhill Fields with great honour, many eminent persons, and some scores of coaches, attending his funeral.*

This was the usage the Dissenters met with from the Church of England at this time, which has hardly a parallel in the Christian world : remarkable are the words of the Earl of Castlemain ; a Roman Catholic, on this occasion : "'Twas never known," says he, " that Rome persecuted, as the bishops do, those who adhere to the same faith with themselves ; and established an inquisition against the professors of the strictest piety among themselves, and, however the prelates complain of the bloody persecution of Queen Mary, it is manifest that their persecution exceeds it ; for under her there were not more than two or three hundred put to death, whereas, under their persecution, above treble that number have been rifled, destroyed, and ruined in their estates, lives, and liberties, being (as is most remarkable) men, for the most part, of the same spirit with those Protestants who suffered under the prelates in Queen Mary's time."†

This year died Mr. Benjamin Woodbridge, M.A., the ejected minister of Newbury. He was bred up in Magdalen Hall, Oxford ; from thence he went to New-England, and was the first graduate of the college there. On his return to England, he succeeded Dr. Twisse at Newbury, where he had a mighty reputation as a scholar, a preacher, a casuist, and a Christian. He was a great instrument of reducing the whole town to sobriety, and to family, as well as public religion. Upon the Restoration, he was made one of the king's chaplains in ordinary, and preached once before him. He was one of the commissioners at the Savoy, and very desirous of an accommodation with the Church party. He was offered a canonry of Windsor, but refused it, and afterward suffered many ways for his nonconformity, though he was generally respected and beloved by all who were judges of real worth. He had a sound judgment, and was a fine preacher, having a commanding voice and aspect. His temper was cheerful, and his behaviour obliging ; he was exemplary for his moderation, and of considerable learning. When the Five-mile Act took place, he removed from Newbury to a small distance, where he preached as he had

---

* Page 446.

† Calamy, vol. ii., p. 756. Palmer's Non. Mem., vol. ii., p. 512.

‡ Mr. Jenkyns was, by his mother, the grandson of Mr. John Rogers, the protomartyr in the reign of Queen Mary. The order of Parliament to which he refused obedience was one that enjoined a public thanksgiving. The brethren with whom he was keeping a fast when he was apprehended in 1684, were Mr. Reynolds, Mr. Keeling, and Mr. Flavel, who made their escape, which Mr. Jenkyns might have done, had it not been for a piece of vanity in a lady, whose long train hindered his going down stairs ; Mr. Jenkyns, in his great civility, having let her pass before him. At his funeral, which was attended by many eminent persons, and some scores of mourning coaches, his son gave rings with this motto, " William Jenkyns, murdered in Newgate." Upon his death, a nobleman said to the king, " May it please your majesty, Jenkyns has got his liberty." On which he asked, with eagerness, " Ay! who gave it him ?" The nobleman replied, " A greater than your majesty, the King of kings ;" with which the king seemed greatly struck, and remained silent.—*Granger*, vol. iii., p. 317. *Palmer*, vol. i., p. 98–100 ; and *History of the Town of Taunton*, p. 157. *Turner's History of Providence*, chap. cxliii., p. 117.—ED. Mr. Jenkyns's son suffered in the west on account of the Duke of Monmouth. His death was most triumphant.—C. § Kennet's Chron., p. 601.

---

* Mr. Jenkyns's chief work is his exposition of Jude, in two small quartos, one of the best specimens of commentary in the language. It has lately been reprinted.—C. † Peirce, p. 259.

opportunity.* He was liberal to the poor, and in all respects a good and great man. He died at Inglefield, November 1, 1684, in a good old age, after he had been a minister in those parts almost forty years.

The sufferings of the Presbyterians in Scotland run parallel with those of England during the whole course of this reign, but the people were not quite so tame and submissive : the same, or greater acts of severity than those which were made against the Nonconformists in England, were enacted in Scotland. Episcopacy was restored May 8, 1662, and the Covenant declared to be an unlawful oath. All persons in office were to sign a declaration of the unlawfulness of taking up arms against the king, or any commissioned by him, on any pretence whatsoever. The English act against conventicles was copied, and passed almost in the same terms in Scotland. The bishops were some of the worst of men, and hated by the people as they deserved, for their deportment was unbecoming their function, says Bishop Burnet ;‡ some did not live within their diocesses, and those who did seemed to take no care of them : they showed no zeal against vice ; the most eminently vicious in the country were their peculiar confidants : nor had they any concern to keep their clergy to their duty, but were themselves guilty of levity and great sensuality.

The people were generally of the Presbyterian persuasion, and stood firm by each other. In many places they were fierce and untractable, and generally forsook the churches ; the whole country complained of the new Episcopal clergy, as immoray stupid, ignorant, and greedy of gain ; and treated them with an aversion that sometimes proceeded to violence. Many were brought before the Council and ecclesiastical commission for not coming to church ; but the proofs were generally defective, for the people would not give evidence one against another. However, great numbers were cast into prison, and ill used ; some were fined, and the younger sort whipped publicly about the streets ; so that great numbers transported their families to Ulster in Ireland, where they were well received.

The government observed no measures with this people ; they exacted exorbitant fines for their not coming to church, and quartered soldiers upon them till they were ruined. The truth is, says Burnet,§ the whole face of the government looked more like the proceedings of an inquisition than of legal courts. At length, in the year 1666, Sir James Turner being sent into the West to levy fines at discretion, the people rose up in arms, and published a manifesto that they did not take arms against the king, but only that they might be delivered from the tyranny of the bishops, and that Presbytery and the Covenant might be set up, and their old ministers restored. Turner and all his soldiers were made prisoners, but marching out of their own country, they were dispersed by the king's forces, about forty being killed, and one hundred and thirty taken ; many of whom were

hanged before their own doors, and died with great firmness and joy.* Mr. Maccail, their minister, underwent the torture, and died with great constancy ; his last words were, "Farewell sun, moon, and stars ; farewell kindred and friends, world and time, and this weak and frail body ; and welcome eternity, welcome angels and saints, welcome Saviour of the world, and God the judge of all !" which he spoke in such a manner as struck all who heard him. The commander of the king's forces killed some in cold blood, and threatened to spit others and roast them alive.

When the indulgence was published in England the Scots had the benefit of it, but when it was taken away the persecution revived, with the administration of Duke Lauderdale. Conventicles abounded in all parts of the country ; the Presbyterian ministers preached in their own houses to numbers of people that stood without doors to hear them ; and when they were dispersed by the magistrates, they retreated into the fields with their ministers to hear the Word of God ; and, to prevent being disturbed, carried arms sufficient for their defence. Upon which, a very severe act was passed against house conventicles and field conventicles, declaring them treasonable ; and the landlords in whose grounds they were held were to be severely fined, unless they discovered the persons present. But still this did not terrify the people, who met together in defiance of the law.† Writs were issued against many who were called Cameronians, who were outlawed, and therefore left their houses, and travelled about the country, and at length they collected into a body, and declared that the king had forfeited the crown of that kingdom by renouncing the Covenant ; but the Duke of Monmouth, being sent to disperse them, routed them at Bothwell Bridge, killing four hundred, and taking twelve hundred prisoners ; two ministers were hanged, and two hundred banished to the plantations, who were all lost at sea.‡ Cameron, their preacher, fell in battle, but Hackston and Cargill, the two other preachers, died with invincible courage ; as did all the rest, who were offered their lives if they would say, God bless the king ! Hackston had both his hands cut off, which he suffered with a constancy and rapture that were truly amazing. When both his hands were cut off, he asked whether they would cut off his feet too. And notwithstanding all his loss of blood, after he was hanged, and his heart taken out of his body, it was alive upon the hangman's knife.§

At length, says Bishop Burnet,‖ things came to that extremity, that the people saw they must come to church or be undone ; but they came in so awkward a manner, that it was visible they did not come to serve God, but to save their substance, for they were talking or sleeping during the whole service. This introduced a sort of atheism among the younger people. But the inquisition was so terrible, that numbers fled from their native country, and settled in

---

* Calamy, vol. ii., p. 956. Palmer's Non. Mem., vol. i., p. 229.
  † Burnet, vol. i., p. 206–211.
  ‡ Page 317.   § Page 307, 309, 310.

* Burnet, vol. i., p. 348.
  † Burnet, vol. ii., p. 64, 155, 182, 266, 268, 269.
  ‡ Page 223, 224.
  § For a minute account, see Dr. Hetherington's very interesting History of the Church of Scotland, page 262 (Carter's edition).—C.   ‖ P. 341

the plantations. These methods of conversion were subversive of Christianity, and a reproach to a Protestant church and nation ; but oppression. and tyranny had overspread the English dominions ; the hearts of all good men failed them for fear, and for looking after those things that were coming on the land ; the clouds were gathering thick over their heads, and there was no other defence against an inundation of popery and slavery but the thin security of the king's life.

To return to England : when the king had made way for a popish successor, by introducing an arbitrary and tyrannical government, his majesty began to think himself neglected, all the court being made to the rising sun; upon which he was heard to say, in some passion, that if he lived a month longer, he would find a way to make himself easy for the remainder of his life.* This was interpreted as a design to change hands, by sending abroad the Duke of York, and recalling the Duke of Monmouth ; which struck terror into the popish party, and is thought to have hastened his death, for he was seized with a kind of apoplexy February 2, and died on the Friday following, February 6, 1684-5, in the fifty-fourth year of his age, not without violent suspicion of poison, either by snuff or an infusion in broth, as Bishop Burnet and others of undoubted credit have assured us, the body not being suffered to be thoroughly examined.†

King Charles II. was a gentleman of wit and good-nature,‡ till his temper was soured in the latter part of his life by his popish counsellors. His court was a scene of luxury and all kinds of lewdness, and his profuse expenses upon un-

* Welwood's Mem., p. 123, sixth ed.
† Burnet, vol. ii., p. 460.
‡ Charles the Second, "as a gentleman," says Dr. Warner, "was liked by everybody, but beloved by nobody ; and as a prince, though he might be respected for his station, yet his death could not be lamented by a lover of his country upon any other motive but that it introduced a much worse monarch on the throne than he was himself." There was ground, in this view, for the remark of Dr. Gregory Sharpe, "that if the English were in tears when the king died in 1685, it was more to lament the succession than the funeral."—*Ecclesiastical History*, vol. ii., p. 929. *Sharpe's Introduction to Universal History*, p. 256, second ed.

lawful pleasures reduced him to the necessity of becoming a pensioner of France. If he had any religion, it was that of a disguised papist, or, rather, a Deist ; but he was strangely entangled, during his whole life, with the obligations he had been brought under by the Roman Catholics. He aimed at being an absolute monarch, but would be at no farther trouble to accomplish it than to give his corrupt ministry liberty to do what they pleased. The king had a great many vices, says Burnet,* but few virtues to correct them.† Religion was with him no more than an engine of state. He hated the Nonconformists, because they appeared against the prerogative, and received the fire of all the enemies of the Constitution and of the Protestant religion with an unshaken firmness. His majesty's chief concern, at last, was for his brother's succession ; and when he came to die, he spoke not a word of religion, nor showed any remorse for his ill-spent life : he expressed no tenderness for his subjects, nor any concern for his queen, but only recommended his mistresses and their children to his brother's regard.‡ So that no Englishman or friend of his country could weep at his death from any other motive than his keeping out a successor who was worse than himself.

* Vol. ii., p. 165.
To this it may be added, that Charles II. was characterized as having never said a foolish thing nor done a wise one. A late writer of dramatical history, Mr. Thomas Davis, is supposed to have contradicted this by an anecdote he has given : Mrs. Marshall, the first actress on the king's theatre, and a woman of virtue, having been tricked into a sham marriage by a nobleman, King Charles II. obliged him to settle an annual income on her. This indicated equity of mind as well as wisdom.—*Roscius Anglicanus*, p. 19, 24, in the *Literary Museum*, 8vo, printed 1792.—ED.

† Long since Mr. Neal's history was published, it has appeared that there was a design in the reign of Charles II. to place a bishop in Virginia ; and that the letters patent for that purpose were actually made out, and are extant. The design failed, because the whole endowment was fixed on the customs.—*Seck-er's Letter to Mr. Horatio Walpole*, p. 17.—ED.

‡ Charles had fifteen children of whom we have accurate knowledge, but there were probably others who died in infancy. Charles was father to six dukes, who were alive at the same time, and each had a maintenance becoming his dignity.—*Jesse*, vol. iii., p. 382.—C.

ADVERTISEMENT

TO VOL. V. OF DR. TOULMIN'S EDITION.

THIS edition of Mr. Neal's "History of the Puritans," after many interruptions, being at length completed, and the last volume being now presented to
the public, the editor embraces this occasion to make his acknowledgments
to the gentlemen who have assisted and encouraged his design. He feels his
obligations to those who by their names and subscriptions have patronised it;
and he is much indebted to some who, by the communication of books and manuscripts, have aided the execution of it. Situated, as he is, at a great distance
from the metropolis, and the libraries there open to the studious, he sees not
how he could have enjoyed the means of examining Mr. Neal's authorities, in
any extensive degree, and of ascertaining the accuracy of the statements by
an inspection of the writers of the last century, had not his grace the Duke of
Grafton most handsomely offered, and most readily supplied, a great number
of books necessary to that purpose, from his large and valuable libraries.

Some books of great authority were obligingly handed to him by Henry
Waymouth, Esq., of Exeter. His thanks are also due to the Rev. Josiah
Thompson, of Clapham, and to Edmund Calamy, Esq. To the former, for
the free use of his manuscript collections, relative to the history of the dissenting churches; and to the latter, for the opportunity of perusing a manuscript of his worthy and learned ancestor, Dr. Edmund Calamy, entitled "An
Historical Account of my own Life, with some Reflections on the Times I have
lived in." He has been likewise much indebted to a respectable member of the society of Quakers, Mr. Morris Birkbeck, of Wanborough, Surrey,
for his judicious remarks on Mr. Neal, and for furnishing him with Gough's
valuable history of that people.

Taunton, August 11th, 1796.

PART V.

CHAPTER I.

FROM THE DEATH OF KING CHARLES II. TO KING JAMES II.'S DECLARATION FOR LIBERTY OF CONSCIENCE. 1685.

WHEN the news of King Charles's decease was spread over the city, a pensive sadness was visible in most countenances for the fate of the kingdom.* His brother James, who succeeded him, told the privy council at his first meeting them, that "as he would never depart from any branch of the prerogative, so he would not invade any man's property, but would preserve the government as by law established in Church and State;"† which gratified the clergy so much, that the pulpits throughout England resounded with thanksgivings; and a numerous set of addresses flattered his majesty, in the strongest expressions, with assurances of unshaken loyalty and obedience, without limitation or reserve. Among others, was the humble address of the University of Oxford; in which, after expressing their sorrow for the death of the late king, they add,‡ that they can never swerve from the principles of their institution, and their religion by law established,

---

* Bishop Burnet says that the proclamation of the king "was a heavy solemnity; few tears were shed for the former, nor were there any shouts of joy for the present king." It appears that the bishop, who was then abroad, was misinformed in this matter: for Dr. Calamy, who heard the king proclaimed, assures us that his heart ached within him at the acclamations made upon the occasion, which, as far as he could observe, were very general: though he never saw so universal a concern as was visible in all men's countenances at that time; for great numbers had very terrifying apprehensions of what was to be expected. The doctor observes, that it; however, very sensibly discovered the changeableness of this world, that King James should so quietly succeed his brother without anything like a dispute or contest; when, but five years before, a majority of three Houses of Commons were so bent upon excluding him, that nothing could satisfy them if this were not compassed.—*Calamy's Historical Account of his Own Life*, vol. i., p. 95, *MS.*—ED.

† "This speech," Bishop Burnet adds, "was magnified as a security far greater than any that laws could give." The common phrase was, "We have now the word of a king, and a word never yet broken." Of this Dr. Calamy gives a confirmation on the authority of a person of character and worth, who heard Dr. Sharp, afterward Archbishop of York, as he was preaching at St. Lawrence Jewry at the time, when King James gave this assurance, break out into language to this effect: "As to our religion, we have the word of the king, which (with reverence be it spoken) is as sacred as my text." This high flight was much noticed then, and often recollected afterward. The doctor had cause to reflect on it with regret, when he was, for preaching against popery at his own parish church at St. Giles, the first of the clergy that fell under the king's displeasure, and felt the weight and pressure of his arbitrary power.—*Historical Account*, p. 96. *Burnet*, p. 620.—ED.

‡ Gazette. No. 2018.

---

which indispensably binds them to bear faith and true obedience to their sovereign, without any limitation or restriction, and that no consideration whatever should shake their loyalty and allegiance. And the University of Cambridge add, that loyalty [or unlimited obedience] is a duty flowing from the very principle of their religion, by which they have been enabled to breed up as true and steady subjects as the world can show, as well in doctrine as practice, from which they can never depart. The Quakers' address was more simple and honest :* "We are come," say they,† "to testify our sorrow for the death of our good friend Charles, and our joy for thy being made our governor. We are told thou art not of the persuasion of the Church of England no more than we, therefore we hope thou wilt grant us the same liberty which thou allowest thyself; which doing, we wish thee all manner of happiness."‡

The king began his reign with a frank and open profession of his religion ; for, the first Sunday after his accession, he went publicly to mass, and obliged Father Huddleston, who attended his brother in his last hours, to declare to the world that he died a Roman Catholic. His majesty acted the part of an absolute sovereign from the very first; and, though he had declared he would invade no man's property, yet he issued out a proclamation for collecting the duties of tonnage and poundage, &c., which were given to the late king only for life ; and in his letter to the Scots Parliament, which met March 28, he says, "I am resolved to maintain my power in its greatest lustre, that I may be better able to defend your religion against fanatics." Before the king had been two months on

---

* Sewel, p. 594.　　† Echard, p. 1051.

‡ Mr. Neal refers, as one authority for giving this address of the Quakers, to Sewel : but it is not to be found there. A modern historian, who censures it for the "uncouthness and blunt familiarity of expression," calls it "a fictitious address ;" the members of this society, he observes, "were not in the custom of paying complimentary addresses to any man :" if the sufferings of their friends impelled them to apply to their superiors for relief, "their addresses, though expressed in their plain manner, were comprised in respectful terms; void of flattery; but not indecent ; unceremonious, but not uncivil." There is no account of their being in the number of the congratulatory addresses on the accession of James. Their first application to him was to recommend their suffering friends to his clemency. At the death of Charles, notwithstanding that petition upon petition had been presented to him for relief. one thousand five hundred of this society were in prison on various prosecutions. "So that a people paying a strict regard to truth could hardly term him their good friend." The above address was first published by Echard, from whom it should seem Mr. Neal took it, trusting, probably, to the exactness of his reference ; if he did quote Sewel for it. Hume and others have since published it.—*Gough's History of the Quakers*. vol. iii., p. 160, 161.—ED.

his throne, he discovered severe resentments against the enemies of his religion, and of his succession to the crown.* Dr. Oates was brought out out of prison, and tried for perjury in the affair of the Popish Plot, for which he was sentenced to stand in the pillory several times, to be whipped from Aldgate to Newgate, and from thence to Tyburn; which was exercised with a severity unknown to the English nation.† And Dangerfield, who invented the Meal-tub Plot, for which he declared he had received money from the Duke of York, was indicted for a libel, and was fined £500. He was also sentenced to be pilloried, and whipped from Newgate to Tyburn, and in his return home was murdered in the coach by one Frances, a barrister at law, who was afterward hanged for it. The Whigs, who went to court to pay their duty to the king, were received but coldly; some were reproached, and others denied access, especially those who had distinguished themselves for the Bill of Exclusion.‡ In the election of a

* Burnet, vol. iii., p. 29, Edin. edition.

† Oates was whipped a second time, while his back was most miserably swelled with his first whipping, and looked as if it had been flayed. He was a man of undaunted resolution, and endured what would have killed a great many others. He was, in his religious profession, a mere Proteus, but appears to have been uniformly capable of villany. His first education was at Merchant Tailors' School, from whence he removed to Cambridge. When he left that university he gained orders in the Church of England, and after having officiated for a time as curate to his father, he held a vicarage first in Kent and then in Sussex. But previously to this, he was, in his youth, a member of a Baptist church in Virginiastreet, Radcliffe Highway. In 1677 he reconciled himself to the Church of Rome, and is reported to have entered into the society of Jesuits. After having left the whole body of Dissenters for thirty years, he applied to be again admitted into the communion of the Baptists, having first returned to the Church of England, and continued in it about sixteen years. The Baptists, through a prudent jealousy of him, spent almost three years in trial of his sincerity before they received him again: so that he complained it "was keeping him on the rack; it was worse than death, in his circumstances, to be so long delayed." He was restored to their communion in 1698 or 1699, but in less than a year was again excluded as a disorderly person and a hypocrite. He then became a Conformist again. "He was a man of some cunning," says Granger, "more effrontery, and the most consummate falsehood." At one time he was a frequent auditor of Mr. Alsop at Westminster, after the Revolution; and moved for leave to come to the Lord's Table, but was refused on account of his character. Crosby has detailed a long story of a villanous transaction, to ruin a gentleman, to which he was instigated by the spirit of revenge. Dr. Calamy says, "that he was but a very sorry, foul-mouthed wretch, I myself can attest from what I once heard from him, when I was in his company." The Parliament, after the Revolution, left him under a brand, and incapacitated him for being a witness in future. But a pension of £400 a year was given him by King William. "The era of Oates's Plot," remarks Mr. Granger, "was the grand era of Whig and Tory." Whatever infamy rests upon his name, he was, observes Dr. Calamy, the instrument of Providence of good to this nation by awakening it out of sleep, and giving a turn to the national affairs after a lethargy of some years.—*Calamy's Historical Account of his Own Life,* vol. i., p. 98, 99. *Granger's History of England,* vol. iv., p. 201, 349; and *Crosby's History of the Baptists,* vol. iii., p. 166–182.—ED.

‡ Burnet, vol. iii., p. 12, 13, Edin. edition.

new Parliament, all methods of corruption and violence were used to get such members returned as might be supple to the king's arbitrary designs.* When the houses met, May 22, the king repeated what he had declared in council, that he would preserve the government in Church and State as by law established; which, Rapin says, he never intended; for he insinuated in his speech, that he would not depend on the precarious aids of Parliament, nor meet them often, if they did not use him well.† But the Parliament unanimously settled all the revenues of his late majesty upon the king for life, which amounted to more than two millions a year;‡ and presented an address, May 27, to desire him to issue forth his royal proclamation, to cause the penal laws to be put in execution against dissenters from the Church of England. This brought down the storm, and revived the persecution, which had slackened a little upon the late king's death. His majesty was now encouraged to pursue his brother's measures. The Tories, who adhered firmly to the prerogative, were gratified with full license to distress the Dissenters, who were to be sacrificed over again to a bigoted clergy and an incensed king, zealous for their destruction, says Bishop Kennet, in order to unite and increase the strength of popery, which he favoured without reserve. Upon this, all meeting-houses of Protestant Dissenters were shut up, the old trade of informing revived and flourished; the spiritual courts were crowded with business; private conventicles were disturbed in all parts of the city and country. If they surprised the minister, he was pulled out of his pulpit by constables or soldiers, and, together with his people, carried before a confiding justice of peace, who obliged them to pay their fines, or dragged them to prison. If the minister escaped, they ransacked the house from top to bottom; tore down hangings, broke open chambers and closets; entered the rooms of those who were sick; and offered all kinds of rudeness and incivilities to the family, though they met with no manner of opposition or resistance. Shopkeepers were separated from their trades and business, and sometimes wives from their husbands and children; several families were obliged to remove to distant places, to avoid the direful effects of an excommunication from the Commons; and great sums of money were levied as forfeitures, which had been earned by honest labour. Dissenting ministers could neither travel the road, nor appear in public but in disguise; nay, they were afraid to be seen in the houses of their friends, pursuivants from the spiritual courts being always abroad upon the watch.

* Dr. Grey quotes here Echard and Carte, to prove that the new Parliament consisted of as many worthy and great, rich, and wise men as ever sat in the House.—ED. † Gazette, No, 2036.

‡ "The Commons, charmed with these promises, and bigoted as much to their principles of government as the king was to his religion, in about two hours voted him such an immense revenue for life as enabled him to maintain a fleet and army without the aid of Parliament, and, consequently, to subdue those who should dare to oppose his will. In this manner, and without any farther ceremony, did this House of Commons deliver up the liberties of the nation to a popish, arbitrary prince."—*Warner's Ecclesiastical History,* vol. ii., p. 631.—ED.

One of the first who came into trouble was the Rev. Mr. Baxter, who was committed to the King's Bench prison February 28, for some exceptional passages in his paraphrase on the New Testament, reflecting on the order of diocesan bishops, and the lawfulness of resistance in some possible cases. The passages were in his paraphrase on Matt., v., 19. Mark, ix., 39; xi., 31; and xii., 38–40. Luke, x., 2. John, xi., 57; and Acts, xv., 2. They were collected by Sir Roger l'Estrange; and a certain eminent clergyman, reported to be Dr. Sh——ck, put into the hands of his enemies some accusations from Rom., xiii., that might touch his life, but no use was made of them. Mr. Baxter being ill, moved by his counsel for time; but Jefferies said he would not give him a minute's time to save his life. "Yonder stands Oates in the pillory," says he, "and if Mr. Baxter stood on the other side, I would say two of the greatest rogues in England stood there." He was brought to his trial May 30, but the chief-justice would not admit his counsel to plead for their client. When Mr. Baxter offered to speak for himself, Jefferies called him a snivelling, canting Presbyterian, and said, "Richard, Richard, don't thou think we will hear thee poison the court. Richard, thou art an old fellow, and an old knave; thou hast written books enough to load a cart, every one as full of sedition, I might say of treason, as an egg is full of meat; hadst thou been whipped out of thy writing trade forty years ago, it had been happy. Thou pretendest to be a preacher of the Gospel of peace; as thou hast one foot in the grave, 'tis time for thee to begin to think what account thou intendest to give, but leave thee to thyself, and I see thou wilt go on as thou hast begun; but, by the grace of God, I will look after thee. I know thou hast a mighty party, and I see a great many of the brotherhood in corners, waiting to see what will become of their mighty don, and a doctor of the party [Doctor Bates] at your elbow, but, by the grace of Almighty God, I will crush you all." The chief-justice having directed the jury, they found him guilty without going from the bar, and fined him five hundred marks, to lay in prison till he paid it, and be bound to his good behaviour for seven years. Mr. Baxter continued in prison* about

* Dr. Grey has given us, with apparent approbation, what he calls a characteristical epitaph, drawn up for Mr. Baxter by the Rev. Thomas Long, prebendary of Exeter. It shows what different colours a character can receive, according to the dispositions of those who draw the picture; and how obnoxious Mr. Baxter was to some, whose calumnies and censure the reader, perhaps, will think was true praise. It runs thus: "Hic jacet Ricardus Baxter, theologus armatus, Loyolita reformatus, heresiarcha ærianus, schismaticorum antesignanus; cujus pruritus disputandi* peperit, scriptandi cacoëthes nutrivit, prædi-

* "These words," says the author of the article Baxter, in the "Biographia Britannica," "are an allusion to Sir Henry Wotton's monumental inscription in Eton Chapel, 'Hic jacet hujus sententiæ primus author, disputandi pruritus ecclesarum scabies;' i. e., 'Here lies the first author, The itch of disputing is the leprosy of the churches.'" This writer has given the above epitaph in English, thus: "Here lies Richard Baxter, a militant divine, a reformed Jesuit, a brazen heresiarch, and the chief of schismatics, whose itch of disputing begat, whose humour of writing nourished, and whose intemperate zeal in preaching brought to its utmost height, the leprosy of the Church: who dissented from those with whom he most agreed; from himself, as well as all other Nonconformists,

two years, and when the court changed its measures, his fine was remitted, and he was released.

The rebellion of the Duke of Monmouth furnished the court with a plausible handle to carry the prosecution of the Whigs and Dissenters to a farther extremity. There was a considerable number of English fugitives in Holland at this time, some on political accounts, and others on the score of religion. The king, being apprehensive of danger from thence, obliged the Prince of Orange to dismiss the Duke of Monmouth from his court; and to break all those officers who had waited upon him, and who were in his service: this precipitated the counsels of the malecontents, and made them resolve upon a rash and ill-concerted invasion, which proved their ruin. The Earl of Argyle, imagining all the Scots Presbyterians would revolt, sailed to the north of Scotland with a very small force, and was defeated with the effusion of very little blood, before the declaration* which he brought with him could have any effect. After him, the Duke of Monmouth, with the like precipitate rashness, landed June 11, with an inconsiderable force, at Lyme in Dorsetshire; and though he was joined by great numbers in the west country, he was defeated by the king's forces, made prisoner, and executed on Tower Hill; as was the Earl of Argyle at Edinburgh.

Though the body of the Dissenters were not concerned in either of these invasions, they suffered considerably on this occasion; great numbers of their chief merchants and tradesmen in the city being taken up by warrants, and secured in jails, and in the public halls; as were many country Whig gentlemen, in York Castle, Hull, and the prisons in all parts of England; which had this good effect, that it kept them out of harm's way, while many of their friends were ruined by joining the duke;

candi zeius intemperatus maturavit, ecclesiæ scabiem. Qui dissentit ab iis quibuscum consentit maximò: ita sibi, cum aliis nonconformis præteritis, præsentibus et futuris: regum et episcoporum juratus hostis: ipsumq; rebellium solemne fœdus. Qui natus erat per septuaginti annos, et octoginta libros, ad perturbandas regni respublicas, et ad bis perdendam ecclesiam Anglicanam; magnis tamen excidit ausis. Deo gratias." — Grey's Examination, vol. ii., p. 281, note.—ED.

* A full view of the assertions and purport of the Duke of Monmouth's manifesto is given in my History of the Town of Taunton, p. 133-135. It was secretly printed in a private house hired for that purpose at Lambeth by W. C., a man of good sense and spirit, and a stationer in Paternoster Row, who imported the paper. His assistant at the press was apprehended and suffered; he himself escaped into Holland, and absconded into Germany, till he came over with the Prince of Orange, who, when he was settled on the throne, appointed him his stationer. William Disney, Esq., was tried by a special commission upon an indictment of high treason for printing and publishing this declaration, and was convicted, and sentenced to be drawn, hanged, and quartered. — Dr. Grey's Examination, vol. iii., p. 403, 404. —ED.

past, present, and to come; the sworn enemy of kings and bishops, and in himself the very bond of rebels; who was born, through seventy years and eighty books, to disturb the peace of the kingdom, and twice to attempt the ruin of the Church of England; in the endeavour of which mighty mischiefs he fell short. For which thanks be to God."— Biographia Britannica, vol. ii., p. 18, second edition.—ED.

some from a persuasion that the late king was married to his mother, and others in hopes of a deliverance from popery and arbitrary power.

The king, elated with success, resolved to let both Whigs and Dissenters feel the weight of the arm of a conqueror; his army lived upon free quarters in the west, and treated all who were supposed to be disaffected with great rudeness and violence.* Some days after Monmouth's defeat, Colonel Kirk ordered several of the prisoners to be hung up at Taunton, without any trial or form of law, while he and his company was dancing, revelling, and drinking healths at a neighbouring window, with a variety of music, from whence they beheld, with a more than brutish triumph, the dreadful spectacle. The jails being full of prisoners, the king appointed Lord-chief-justice Jefferies to go the western circuit, whose cruel behaviour surpassed all that had been ever heard of in a civilized nation : he was always drunk, either with wine or vengeance. When the juries found persons not guilty, he threatened and confined them till they brought in a verdict to his mind ; as in the case of the old Lady Lisle, who was beheaded for admitting Mr. Hicks, a Nonconformist minister, into her house, though the jury brought her in three times not guilty ; and she solemnly declared that she knew not that he had been in the duke's army. He persuaded many of the prisoners to plead guilty, in hopes of favour, and then taking advantage of their confession, ordered their immediate execution, without giving them a minute's time to say their prayers. Mr. Tutchin, who wrote the "Observator," was sentenced to be imprisoned seven years, and to be whipped once every year through all the towns in Dorsetshire ; upon which, he petitioned the king that he might be hanged.† Bishop Burnet says, that in several places in the west, there were executed near six hundred persons, and that the quarters of two or three hundred were fixed upon gibbets, and hung upon trees all over the country for fifty or sixty miles about, to the terror and even annoyance of travellers. The manner in which he treated the prisoners was barbarous and inhuman ; and his behaviour towards some of the nobility and gentry who were well affected, but appeared to the character of some of the criminals, would have amazed one, says Bishop Burnet, if done by a bashaw in Turkey. The king had advice of his proceedings every day, and spoke of them in a style neither becoming the majesty nor mercy of a great prince.‡ And Jefferies, besides satiating himself with blood, got great sums of money by selling pardons to such as were able to purchase them, from £10 to fourteen thousand guineas apiece.§

After the executions in the west, the king, being in the height of his power, resolved to be revenged of his old enemies the Whigs, by making examples of their chief leaders : Alderman Cornish, who had signalized himself in prosecuting the Popish Plot, and was frequently in company with the late Lord Russel, was taken off the Exchange October 13, and within little more than a week tried, condemned, and executed in Cheapside for high treason, without any tolerable evidence, and his quarters set upon Guildhall. On the same day, Mrs. Gaunt, a Dissenter, who spent a great part of her life in acts of charity, visiting the jails, and looking after the poor of what persuasion soever, having entertained Burton, one of Monmouth's men, in her house, he, by an unheard-of baseness, while she was looking out for an opportunity to send him out of the kingdom, went out and accused her for harbouring him, and by that means saved his own life by taking away hers : she was burned alive at Tyburn, and died with great resolution and devotion.* Mr. Bateman, a surgeon, Mr. Rouse, Mr. Fernerley, Colonel Ayloffe, Mr. Nelthorpe, and others, suffered in like manner. Lord Stamford was admitted to bail, and Lord Delamere was tried by his peers, and acquitted. Many who had corresponded with the Duke of Monmouth absconded, and had proclamations against them, as John Trenchard, Esq., Mr. Speke, and others. But all who suffered in this cause expressed such a zeal for the Protestant religion, which they apprehended in danger, as made great impressions on the spectators. Some say the king was hurried on by Jefferies ; but if his own inclinations had not run strong the same way, and if his priests had not thought it their interest to take off so many active Protestants who opposed their measures, they would not have let that butcher loose, says Burnet, to commit so many barbarous acts of cruelty, as struck a universal horror over the body of the nation. It was a bloody summer, and a dangerous time for honest men to live in.

When the king met his Parliament November 9, he congratulated them on the success of his arms; but told them, that in order to prevent any new disturbances, he was determined to keep the present army together; and "let no man," says his majesty, "take exceptions that some officers are not qualified, for they are most of them known to me for the loyalty of their principles and practices ; and therefore, to deal plainly with you, after having had the benefit of their services in a time of need and danger, I will neither expose them to disgrace, nor myself to the want of them."† Thus we were to have a standing army under popish officers, in defiance of the penal laws and test. The Commons would have given them an act of indemnity for what was past, but the king would not accept it ; and because the House was not disposed to his dispensing power, he prorogued them November 20, when they had sat only eleven days ; and after many successive prorogations in the space of two years, dissolved them ‡

The prosecution of the Dissenters, which was carried on with all imaginable severity this

---

* Burnet, vol. iii., p. 43, Edin. edition.
† Bennet's Memoirs, p. 374, 375, second edit.
‡ Ibid., p. 44, second edit.
§ The reader is referred to the "History of the Town of Taunton" for an ample account of the progress and defeat of the Duke of Monmouth, and a minute detail of the subsequent severities of Kirk and Jefferies, p. 135–170 ; and to "The Bloody Assizes, comprehending a complete History of the Lives, Actions, Trials, Sufferings, dying Speeches, Letters, and Prayers of all those eminent Martyrs who fell in the West of England, from 1678 to 1688, London, 1689." This is a deeply interesting volume, and full of important facts casting light upon this period.—C.

* Burnet, p. 45. † Gazette, 2085.
‡ Burnet, p. 70, 71.

and the last year, forced some of their ministers into the Church; but it had a different and more surprising influence upon others, who had the courage in these difficult times to renounce the Church as a persecuting establishment, and to take their lot among the Nonconformists;[*] as the Rev. Mr. John Spademan, M.A., of Swayton in Lincolnshire; Mr. John Rastrick, vicar of Kirton, near Boston;[†] Mr. Burroughs,. of Frampton; Mr. Scoffin, of Brotherton; Mr. Quip, of Moreton; and à few others, who could be influenced by no other principle but conscience in a cause which had nothing in this world to recommend it but truth, attended with bonds and imprisonment, and the loss of all things.

Great were the oppressions of those who frequented the separate meetings in several counties; the informers broke in upon Sir John Hartoppe, Mr. Fleetwood, and others, at Stoke Newington, to levy distresses per conventicles, to the value of £6000 or £7000: the like at Enfield, Hackney, and all the neighbouring villages near London.[‡] The, justices and confiding clergy were equally diligent in their several parishes. Injunctions were sent out from several of the bishops, under the seal of their offices, requiring all church-wardens to present such as did not repair to church, nor receive the sacrament at Easter; which were read publicly in the churches of Hertfordshire, Essex, &c. And the juries at the assizes gave it as their opinion that the Dissenters should be effectually prosecuted; but the scandalous villanies and perjuries of the informers made wise men abhor the trade; however, so terrible were the times; that many families and ministers removed with their effects to New-England, and other plantations in America; among whom we may reckon the reverend and worthy Mr. Samuel Lee, the ejected minister of Bishopgate, who, in his return to his flock after the Revolution, was made prisoner by the French, and carried to St. Maloes, where he perished in a dungeon, under the hands of those whose tender mercies are cruel.[§] Many ministers were fined and imprisoned, and great numbers of their most substantial hearers cited into the Commons, their names being fixed upon the doors of their parish churches; and if they did not appear, an excommunication and a *capias* followed, unless they found means, by presents of wine, by gold in the fingers of a pair of gloves, or some effectual bribe, to get themselves excused; for which, among others, the name of Dr. Pinfold|| is famous to this day.

The Dissenters continued to take the most

prudent measures to cover their private meetings from their adversaries. They assembled in small numbers; they frequently shifted their places of worship, and met together late in the evenings, or early in the mornings; there were friends without doors, always on the watch to give notice of approaching danger; when the dwellings of Dissenters joined, they made windows or holes in the walls, that the preacher's voice might be heard in two or three houses; they had sometimes private passages from one house to another, and trap doors for the escape of the minister, who went always in disguise, except when he was discharging his office; in country towns and villages, they were admitted through back yards and gardens into the house, to avoid the observation of neighbours and passengers; for the same reason, they never sung psalms, and the minister was placed in such an inward part of the house, that his voice might not be heard in the streets, the doors were always locked, and a sentinel placed near them to give the alarm, that the preacher might escape by some private passage, with as many of the congregation as could avoid the informers. But notwithstanding all their precautions, spies and false brethren crept in among them in disguise, their assemblies were frequently interrupted, and great sums of money raised by fines or compositions, to the discouragement of trade and industry, and enriching the officers of the spiritual courts.

Thus were the Nonconformists ground between the papists on the one hand, and the High Church clergy on the other; while the former made their advantage of the latter, concluding that when the Dissenters were destroyed, or thoroughly exasperated, and the clergy divided among themselves, they should be a match for the hierarchy, and capable of establishing that religion they had been so long aiming to introduce. With this view, swarms of Jesuits and regular priests were sent for from abroad; Jesuits' schools and other seminaries were opened in London and the country; mass-houses were erected in the most considerable towns: four Roman Catholic bishops were consecrated in the royal chapel, and exercised their functions under the character of vicars apostolical; their regular clergy appeared at Whitehall and St. James's in their habits, and were unwearied in their attempts to seduce the common people. The way to preferment was to be a Catholic, or to declare the prerogative, all state affairs being managed by such men. An open correspondence was held with Rome, and many pamphlets were dispersed, to make proselytes to the Romish faith, or, at least, to effect a coalition. Multitudes of the king's subjects frequented the popish chapels; some changed their profession; and all men were forbid to speak disrespectfully of the king's religion.

At length the eyes of many of the clergy began to be opened, and they judged it necessary to preach against the popish doctrines, that they might recover the people, who were deserting in numbers, and rescue the Protestant religion from the danger into which their own follies had brought it. The king being acquainted with this, by the advice of his priests sent circular letters to the bishops, with an order prohibiting the inferior clergy from preaching

---

* Calamy's Abridgment, p. 460, &c.

† Mr. Rastrick published his reasons for this step in a volume entitled " An Account of the Nonconformity of John Rastrick, M.A., some time Vicar of Kirton, Lincolnshire, &c., in a Letter to a Friend," 1705. This friend was Mr. Edmund Calamy. It is an able and satisfactory performance.—C.

‡ Calamy, p. 372, 373; or Palmer's Nonconformists' Memorial, vol. ii., p. 163-168.

§ Palmer's Noncon. Mem., vol. i., p. 95, 96.

|| Dr. Pinfold was a gentleman of the long robe, and was the king's advocate in the prosecution of Bishop Compton. But though he stood at the chancellor's elbow and took notes while the bishop's counsel were pleading, he said nothing by way of reply.—Bishop Compton's Life, p. 37.—Ed.

on the controverted points of religion; which many complained of, though it was no more than King James and Charles I. had done before. However, when their mouths were stopped in the pulpit, some of the most learned and zealous agreed to fight the Catholics with their own weapons, and to publish small pamphlets for the benefit of the vulgar, in defence of the Protestant doctrines. When a popish pamphlet was in the press, they made interest with the workmen, and got the sheets as they were wrought off, so that an answer was ready as soon as the pamphlet was published. There was hardly a week in which some sermon or small treatise against popery was not printed and dispersed among the common people; which, in the compass of a year or two, produced a valuable set of controversial writings against the errors of that church.* The chief writers were, Dr. Tillotson, Stillingfleet, Tenison, Patrick, Wake, Whitby, Sharp, Atterbury, Williams, Aldrich, Burnet, Fowler, &c.,† men of great name and renown, who gained immortal honour, and were afterward advanced to the highest dignities in the Church. Never was a bad cause more weakly managed by the papists, nor a more complete victory obtained by the Protestants.

But the Church party, not content with their triumph, have of late censured the Nonconformists for appearing only as spectators, and not joining them in the combat.‡ But how could the clergy expect this from a set of men whom they had been persecuting for above twenty years, and who had the yoke of oppression still lying on their necks? Had not the Nonconformists been *beforehand with them in their " Morning Exercises against Popery ?"*§ And did not Dr. Owen, Mr. Pool, Baxter, Clarkson, and others, write against the errors of the Church of Rome, throughout the whole reign of King Charles II.? Had not the Nonconformists stood in the gap, and exposed themselves sufficiently to the resentments of the papists, for refusing to come into their measures for a universal toleration, in which they might have been included? Besides, the poor ministers were hardly crept out of corners, their *papers had been rifled, and their books sold or secreted,* to avoid seizure; they had little time to study, and therefore might not be so well prepared for the argument as those who had lived in ease and security. Farther, the Church party was most nearly concerned, the Nonconformists having nothing to lose, whereas all the emoluments of the Church were at stake; and, after all, some of the Dissenters did write;

and, if we may believe Dr. Calamy, Mr. Baxter, and others, their tracts being thought too warm, were refused to be licensed.* Upon the whole, Bishop Burnet wisely observes,† that as the Dissenters would not engage on the side of popery and the prerogative, nor appear for taking off the tests in the present circumstances; so, on the other hand, they were unwilling to provoke the king, who had lately given them hopes of liberty, lest he should make up matters upon any terms with the Church party, at their expense; nor would they provoke the Church party, or by any ill behaviour drive them into a reconciliation with the court; therefore they resolved to let the points of controversy alone, and leave them to the management of the clergy, who had a legal bottom to support them.

The clergy's writing thus warmly against popery broke all measures between the king and the Church of England, and made each party court that body of men for their auxiliaries, whom they had been persecuting and destroying for so many years. His majesty now resolved to introduce a universal toleration in despite of the Church, and at their expense.‡ The cruelty of the Church of England was his common subject of discourse; he reproached them for their violent persecutions of the Dissenters, and said he had intended to set on foot a toleration sooner, but that he was restrained by some of them who had treated with him, and had undertaken to show favour to the papists, provided they might be still suffered to vex the Dis-

---

* A license was refused to a discourse against the whole system of popery, drawn up by the learned Mr. Jonathan Hanmer, who was ejected from Bishops Tawton, in Devon. A discourse against transubstantiation, written by Mr. Henry Pendlebury, ejected from Holcomb Chapel in Lancashire, and afterward published by Archbishop Tillotson, met with the like refusal. An offer that Mr. Baxter should produce a piece against popery every month, if a license might be had, was rejected with scorn. And Mr. Jane, the Bishop of London's chaplain, denied his sanction to a piece he actually drew up on the Church's visibility. But in opposition to what Mr. Neal says above concerning this point, Dr. Grey, it is but justice to observe, gives us letters from Dr. Isham, Dr. Alston, Dr. Batteley, and Dr. Needham, licensers of the press, declaring that they never refused to license a book because written by a Dissenter; and that they did not recollect that any tract of which a Dissenter was the author was brought to them for their sanction. As to Mr. Baxter in particular, Dr. Isham avers that he never obstructed his writing against popery, but licensed one of his books: "and if he had prepared anything against the common enemy," says Dr. Isham, "without striking obliquely at our Church, I would certainly have forwarded them from the press." It is to be added, that one piece from the pen of Mr. Hanmer had the *imprimatur* of Dr. Jane. These authorities appear to contradict each other; but it is, probably, not only a candid, but just method of reconciling them, and preserving our opinion of the veracity of both parties, to suppose that the tracts to which a license was refused were not offered to the gentlemen whose letters Dr. Grey quotes; but to Dr. Jane or other licensers, with whose declaration we are not furnished.—*Bennet's Memorial*, p. 399, 400, second edition. *Baxter's History of his Own Life*, part iii., p. 183, folio. *Palmer's Nonconformists' Memorial*, vol. i., p. 342. Dr. Grey, vol. ii., p. 424–432. The matter was, I understand, discussed by Mr. Tong, in his defence of Mr. Henry's "Notion of Schism."—Ed.   † Page 121, 122.
‡ Burnet, p. 140.

---

* A vast collection of these pieces was published about fifty years ago, in three volumes folio, under the direction of Dr. Gibson, bishop of London. But this contained only a part of the tracts written by the Protestants; and even the catalogues of them drawn up by Dr. Wake, Dr. Gee, and Mr. Francis Peck, were defective in the titles of them.—*Birch's Life of Archbishop Tillotson,* p. 127.—Ed. This collection is very rarely to be met with; and as it may be useful for purposes of reference, I would state that a copy is to be found in the excellent library of the Methodist Book Concern, 192 Mulberry-street, New-York.—C.

† Burnet, vol. iii., p. 79, 80, Edinb. edit.
‡ Calamy, p. 373; and Peirce's Vindication, p. 266.
§ A volume which has never yet been surpassed for point and force of argument.—C.

-senters; and he named the very men, though they thought fit afterward to deny it :' how far the fact is probable must be left with the reader.

It being thought impracticable to obtain a legal toleration in the present circumstances of the nation, his majesty determined to attempt it by the dispensing power; for this purpose, Sir Edward Hales, a popish gentleman of Kent, was brought to trial for breaking through the Test Act, when Sir Edward Herbert, lord-chief-justice, gave judgment in his favour, and declared the powers of the crown to be absolute.* The other judges were closeted, and such displaced as were of a different sentiment; and the king being resolved to have twelve judges of his own opinion,† four had their quietus, and as many new ones were advanced, from whom the king exacted a promise to support the prerogative in all its branches. There was a new call of sergeants, who gave rings with this motto, Deus, rex, lex, "God, the king, and the law;" the king being placed before the law. The privy council was new modelled, and several declared papists admitted into it; two confiding clergy-men were promoted to bishoprics : Parker to Oxford, and Cartwright to Chester. Many pamphlets were written and dispersed in favour of liberty of conscience; and Sir Roger l'Estrange, with other mercenary writers, were employed to maintain that a power in the king to dispense with the laws, is law.‡ But the opinion of private writers not being thought sufficient, it was resolved to have the determination of the judges, who all, except one, gave it as their opinion, 1. That the laws of England were the king's laws. 2. That it is an inseparable branch of the prerogative of the kings of England, as of all other sovereign princes, to dispense with all penal laws in particular cases, and on particular occasions. 3. That of these reasons and necessity the king is sole judge. 4. That this is not a trust now invested in, and granted to, the present king, but the ancient remains of the sovereign power of the kings of England; which was never yet taken from them, nor can be. Thus the laws of England were given up at once into the hands of the king, by a solemn determination of the judges.

This point being secured, his majesty began to caress the Nonconformists. "All on a sudden," says Bishop Burnet,§ "the churchmen were disgraced, and the Dissenters in high favour. Lord-chief-justice Herbert went the western circuit after Jefferies, who was now made lord-chancellor, and all was grace and favour to them : their former sufferings were much reflected upon and pitied; everything was offered that might alleviate them; their ministers were encouraged to set up their conventicles, which had been discontinued, or held very

secretly, for four or five years; intimations were given everywhere that the king would not have them or their meetings disturbed."* A dispensation or license-office was set up, where all who applied might have an indulgence, paying only 50s. for themselves and their families. Many who had been prosecuted for conventicles took out those licenses, which not only stopped all processes that were commenced, but gave them liberty to go publicly to meetings for the future. "Upon this," says the same reverend prelate, "some of the Dissenters grew insolent, but wiser men among them perceived the design of the papists was now to set on the Dissenters against the Church; and therefore, though they returned to their conventicles, yet they had a just jealousy of the ill designs that lay hid under all this sudden and unexpected show of grace and kindness, and they took care not to provoke the Church party." But where then were the understandings of the High Church clergy, during the whole reign of King Charles II., while they were pursuing the Nonconformists and their families to destruction, for a long course of years? Did they not perceive the design of the papists? Or were they not willing rather to court them, at the expense of the whole body of dissenting Protestants? Bishop Laud's scheme of uniting with the papists, and meeting them half way, was never out of their sight; however, when the reader calls to mind the oppression and cruelties that the conscientious Nonconformists underwent from the High Church party for twenty-five years, he will be ready to conclude they deserved no regard, if the Protestant religion itself had not been at stake.

Thus the all-wise providence of God put a period to the prosecution of the Protestant Dissenters from the penal laws, though the laws themselves were not legally repealed or suspended till after the revolution of King William and Queen Mary. It may not, therefore, be improper to give the reader a summary view of their usage in this and the last reign, and of the damages they sustained in their persons, families, and fortunes.

The Quakers, in their petition to King James† the last year, inform his majesty, that of late above one thousand five hundred of their friends were in prison, both men and women; and that now there remain one thousand three hundred and eighty three, of which two hundred are women; many under sentence of premunire; and more than three hundred near it, for refu-

---

* Burnet, p. 73, 74.

† Lord-chief-justice Jones, one of the displaced judges, upon his dismission, observed to the king, "that he was by no means sorry that he was laid aside, old and worn out as he was in his service; but concerned that his majesty should expect such a construction of the law from him as he could not honestly give; and that none but indigent, ignorant, or ambitious men would give their judgment as he expected." To this the king replied, "it was necessary his judges should be all of one mind."—*Memoirs of Sir John Reresby*, p. 233.—ED.

‡ Welwood's Memoirs, p. 194.   § P. 78.

VOL. II.—S s

---

* King James, previously to his adopting these conciliating measures with the Dissenters, such was his art and duplicity, had tried all the methods he could think of to bring the Church into his designs; and twice offered, it was said, to make a sacrifice of all the Dissenters in the kingdom to them, if they would but have complied with them; but, failing in this attempt, he faced about to the Nonconformists. —*Calamy's History of his Own Life*, vol. i., p. 170, MS.—ED.

† It was addressed not to King James only, but to both houses of Parliament. They made also an application to the king alone, recommending to his princely clemency the case of their suffering friends. —*Sewel*, p. 592. This was not so copious a state of their case as the petition to which Mr. Neal refers, and is called by Gough their first address.—Vol. iii., p. 162; and the *Index*, under the word *Address*.—ED.

sing the oath of allegiance because they could not swear.* Above three hundred and fifty have died in prison since the year 1660, near one hundred of which since the year 1680. In London, the jail of Newgate has been crowded within these two years, sometimes with near twenty in a room, whereby several have been suffocated, and others, who have been taken out sick, have died of malignant fevers within a few days; great violences, outrageous distresses, and woful havoc and spoil have been made on people's goods and estates, by a company of idle, extravagant, and merciless informers, by prosecutions on the Conventicle Act and others, as may be seen in the margin.† Also on *qui tam* writs, and on other processes, for £20 a month; and two thirds of their estates seized for the king: some had not a bed left to rest upon; others had no cattle to till the ground, nor corn for seed or bread, nor tools to work with: the said informers and bailiffs in some places breaking into houses, and making great waste and spoil, under pretence of serving the king and the Church. Our religious assemblies have been charged at common law with being riotous routs and disturbances of the peace, whereby great numbers have been confined in prisons, without regard to age or sex; and many in holes and dungeons: the seizures for £20 a month have amounted to several thousand pounds: sometimes they have seized for eleven months at once, and made sale of all goods and chattels both within doors and without, for payment; several who have employed some hundreds of poor families in manufacture, are by those writs and seizures disabled, as well as by long imprisonment; one, in particular, who employed two hundred people in the woollen manufacture. Many informers, and especially impudent women, whose husbands are in prison, swear for their share of the profit of the seizures: the fines upon one justice's warrant have amounted to many hundred pounds; frequently £10 a warrant, and five warrants together for £50 to one man; and for nonpayment, all his goods carried away in about ten cart-loads. They spare neither widows, nor fatherless, nor poor families, nor leave them so much as a bed to lie upon: thus the informers are both witnesses and parties, to the ruin of great numbers

of sober families; and justices of peace have been threatened with the forfeiture of £100 if they do not issue out warrants upon their informations. With this petition, they presented to the king and Parliament a list of their friends in prison in the several counties, amounting to one thousand four hundred and sixty.

But it is impossible to make an exact computation of the number of sufferers, or estimate of the damages his majesty's dissenting subjects of the several denominations sustained by the prosecutions of this and the last reign; how many families were impoverished, and reduced to beggary; how many lives were lost in prisons and noisome jails; how many ministers were divorced from their people, and forced to live as they could, five miles from a corporation; how many industrious and laborious tradesmen were cut off from their trades, and their substance and household goods plundered by soldiers, or divided among idle and infamous informers. The vexatious suits of the Commons, and the expenses of those courts, were immense.

The writer of the preface of Mr. Delaune's "Plea for the Nonconformists," says,* that Delaune was one of near eight thousand Protestant Dissenters who had perished in prison in the reign of King Charles II., and that merely for dissenting from the Church in some points, which they were able to give good reason for; and yet for no other cause, says he, were they stifled, I had almost said, murdered in jails. As for the severe penalties inflicted on them for seditious and riotous assemblies, designed only for the worship of God, he adds, that they suffered in their trades and estates, within the compass of three years, at least £2.000,000; and doubts whether, in all the times since the Reformation, including the reign of Queen Mary, there can be produced anything like such a number of Christians who have suffered death, and such numbers who have lost their substance for religion. Another writer adds,† that Mr. Jeremy White had carefully collected a list of the dissenting sufferers, and of their sufferings; and had the names of sixty thousand persons who had suffered on a religious account, between the restoration of King Charles II. and the revolution of King William, five thousand of whom died in prison. That Mr. White told Lord Dorset that King James had offered him a thousand guineas for the manuscript, but that he refused all invitations and rewards, and concealed the black record, that it might not appear to the disreputation of the Church of England, for which some of the clergy sent him their thanks, and offered him an acknowledgment, which he generously refused. The reader will form his own judgment of the truth of these facts. It is certain that, besides those who suffered in their own country, great numbers retired to the plantations of New-England, Pennsylvania, and other parts of America. Many transported themselves and their effects into Holland,‡ and filled the English churches of

---

* Sewel, p. 588, 593.

† The acts or penal laws on which they suffered were these:
Some few suffered on 27 Henry VIII., cap. xx.
Others on 1 Eliz., cap. ii., for twelve-pence a Sunday.
5 Eliz., cap. xxiii., *de excommu. capiendo.*
23 Eliz., cap. i., for £20 a month.
29 Eliz., cap. vi.; for more speedy and due execution of last statute.
35 Eliz., cap. i., for abjuring the realm on pain of death.
3 King James I., cap. iv., for better discovering and suppressing popish recusants.
13th and 14th of King Charles II., against Quakers, &c., transportation.
17 Charles II., cap. ii., against Nonconformists.
22 King Charles II., cap. i., against seditious conventicles.
N. B. The Quakers were not much affected with the Corporation and Test Acts, because they would not take an oath;
Nor with the Oxford Five-mile Act, which cut the others to pieces.

---

* Preface to Delaune's Plea, p. 5.
† History of the Stuarts, p. 715.
‡ Among these were Mr. Howe, Mr. Shower, Mr. Nat. Taylor, Mr. Papillon, Sir John Thompson (afterward Lord Haversham), Sir John Guise, and Sir Patience Ward. The States of Holland treated the English refugees with particular respect. But as it

Amsterdam, the Hague, Utrecht, Leyden, Rotterdam, and other parts. If we admit the dissenting families of the several denominations in England to be one hundred and fifty, thousand, and that each family suffered no more than the loss of £3 or £4 per annum from the Act of Uniformity, the whole will amount to twelve or fourteen millions; a prodigious sum for those times! But these are only conjectures; the damage to the trade and property of the nation was undoubtedly immense; and the wounds that were made in the estates of private families were deep and large, many of whom, to my certain knowledge, wear the scars of them to this day.

When the Protestant Dissenters rose up into public view as a distinct body, their long sufferings had not very much diminished their numbers; which, though not to be compared with those of the Establishment, or the Tories and Roman Catholics, were yet so considerable as to be capable of turning the scale on either side, according as they should throw in their weight, which might possibly be owing, among others, to the following reasons:

1. To their firmness and constancy in a long course of suffering, which convinced the world that they were not actuated by humour, but conscience.

2. To their doctrine and manner of preaching, which was plain and practical, accompanied with a warm and awakening address to the conscience. Their doctrines were those of the first Reformers, which were grown out of fashion in the Church; and their way of worship was simple and plain, without the ornament of rites and ceremonies.

3. To the severity of their morals, at a time when the nation was sunk into all kinds of vice and luxury, from which they preserved themselves, in a great measure, untainted. Their conversation was sober and virtuous. They observed the Lord's Day with religous strictness, and had a universal reputation for justice and integrity in their dealings.

4. To the careful and strict education of their children, whom they impressed with an early sense of scriptural religion, and educated in their own way, as they had opportunity, under private schoolmasters of their own principles.

5. To a concern for a succession of able and learned ministers; for which purpose they encouraged private academies in several parts of the kingdom; and it is remarkable that many gentlemen and substantial citizens devoted their children to the ministry, at a time when they had nothing in view but worldly discouragements.

6. To the persecuting zeal of the High Church party, attended with an uncommon licentiousness of manners. If their zeal against the Nonconformists had produced a greater sanctity of life and severity of morals among them-

has been pertinently observed, it was a reproach to this nation that, in particular, so excellent a person as Mr. Howe, whose unaffected piety, polite and profound learning, and most sweet, ingenuous, and gentle temper, entitled him to the esteem of the greatest and best men in the land of all persuasions; that such a one at that time could not have a safe and quiet habitation in his native country.—*Tong's Life of Shower*, p. 51.—Ed.

selves, it had been less offensive; but to see men destitute of common virtue signing warrants of distress upon their neighbours, only for worshipping God peaceably, at a separate meeting, when they themselves hardly worshipped God at all, made some apprehend there was nothing at all in religion, and others resolve to take their lot with a more sober people. Finally, To the spirit and principles of Toryism, which began to appear ruinous to the nation. The old English Constitution was in a manner lost, while the Church and prerogative had been trampling on the Dissenters, who had stood firm to it for twenty years, in the midst of reproaches and sufferings. This was the consequence of Tory measures; and popery being now coming in at the gap they had made, the most resolved Protestants saw their error, entertained a favourable opinion of the Dissenters, and many of them joined their congregations.

To return to the history. The Dissenters being now easy, it was resolved to turn the artillery of the prerogative against the Church, and make them feel a little of the smart they had given others; the king and his priests were thoroughly enraged with their opposition to the court, and therefore appointed commissioners throughout England to inquire what money had been raised, or what goods had been seized by distress on Dissenters, on prosecutions for recusancy, and not brought to account in the exchequer. In the Gazette of March 5, 1687, it was advertised that the commissioners appointed to examine into the losses of the Dissenters and recusants, within the several counties of Gloucester, Worcester, and Monmouth, were to hold their sessions for the said counties at the places therein mentioned. Others were appointed for the counties of Middlesex, Essex, &c., to inquire what money or goods had been taken or received for any matters relating to religion since September 29, 1677, in any of the counties for which they were named. They were to return the names of all persons who had seized goods or received money. The parties themselves, if alive, were obliged to appear, and give an account; and if dead, their representatives were to appear before the commissioners for them. This struck terror into the whole tribe of informers, the confiding justices, and others, who expected now to be ruined; but, says Dr. Calamy, the Protestant Dissenters generously refused to appear against their enemies, upon assurances given by leading persons, both clergy and laity, that no such methods should be used for the future. Had this inquiry proceeded, and the Dissenters universally come into it, a black and fraudulent scene would have been opened, which now will be concealed. Bishop Burnet says, "The king ordered them to inquire into all the vexatious suits into which the Dissenters had been brought in the spiritual courts, and into all the compositions they had been forced to make to redeem themselves from farther trouble, which, as was said, would have brought to light a scandalous discovery of all the ill practices of those courts; for the use that many who belonged to those courts had made of the laws with relation to Dissenters was, to draw presents from such as could make them, threatening them with a process in case they failed to do that, and, upon doing it, leaving them at full liberty to neglect the laws as much as they pleased. The commission subsisted till the Revolution, and it was hoped," says his lordship, "that this would have animated the Dissenters to turn upon the clergy with some of that fierceness with which they themselves had been lately treated."*. *But they took no advantage of the disposition of the court,* nor of the opportunity that was put into their hands of making reprisals on their adversaries; which shows the truly generous and Christian spirit of those confessors for religion, and deserved a more grateful acknowledgment.

To humble the clergy yet farther, his majesty, by the advice of Jefferies, erected a new ecclesiastical commission, though the act which took away the High Commission in 1641 had provided that no court of that nature should be erected for the future ; but the king, though a papist, assumed the supremacy, and directed a commission to the Archbishop of Canterbury, Jefferies the chancellor, the Bishops of Durham and Rochester; to the Earl of Sunderland, president of the Council ; Herbert and Wright, lord-chief justices, and Jenner, recorder of London, or any three of them, provided the chancellor was one, " to exercise all manner of jurisdiction and pre-eminence touching any spiritual or ecclesiastical jurisdictions, to visit, reform, redress, and amend all abuses, offences, contempts, and enormities which by the spiritual or ecclesiastical laws might be corrected. They were also to inquire into all the misdemeanors and contempts which might be punished by the censures of the Church, and to call before them all ecclesiastical persons of what degree and dignity soever, and punish the offenders by excommunications, suspensions, deprivations, or other ecclesiastical censures," &c.† This was a terrible rod held out to the clergy, and if the commissioners had had time to proceed in their inquiries according to the mandates sent to the chancellors and archdeacons of the several dioceses, they would have felt more of the effects of that arbitrary power which their indiscreet conduct had brought on the nation ; but Providence was kinder to them than they had been to their brethren ‡ The commission was granted the beginning of April, but was not opened till the beginning of August : the Archbishop of Canterbury was afraid to act in it ;§ Durham was so lifted up, says Burnet, that he said his name would now be recorded in history ; and Sprat, bishop of Rochester, in hopes of farther preferment, swam with the stream.‖ Some

Roman Catholics were in the commission, and, consequently, the enemies of the Protestant religion were to be its judges.

But his majesty, not being willing to rely altogether on the Oxford decree, nor on the fashionable doctrines of passive obedience and nonresistance, which had been preached up for above twenty years as the unalterable doctrines of the Church of England, in order to support his extraordinary proceedings, resolved to augment his standing forces to fifteen thousand men. He was apprehensive of a snake in the grass, or a secret reserve, that might break out when the Church itself came to be pinched ; he therefore ordered his army to encamp on Hounslow Heath, under the command of the Earl of Feversham, to awe the city, and be at hand upon any emergency ; the officers and many of the soldiers were Irish papists, and they had a public chapel in which mass was said every day, so that it was believed the king might introduce what religion he pleased.* It was dangerous to speak or write against his majesty's proceedings ; for when the Rev. Mr. Johnson, a clergyman, ventured to publish a writing, directed to the Protestant officers of the army, to dissuade them from being tools of the court to subvert the Constitution and Protestant religion, diligent search was made for him, and being apprehended, he was sentenced to stand three times in the pillory; to be degraded of his orders, to be whipped from Newgate to Tyburn, and to be fined five hundred marks ; all which was executed with great severity.†

this matter, through his ignorance of the laws, having no objection to the legality of it; with the purpose of doing as much good, and preventing as much evil, as the times would permit. In the execution of it, he pleaded that he had studied to moderate and restrain the violence of others, never giving his consent to any irregular and arbitrary sentence, but declaring against every extravagant decree. His opinions, he said, were always so contrary to the humours of the court, that he often thought himself to be really in as much hazard from the commission itself, by his non-compliance, as any of his brethren could be that were out of it. And at last, rather than concur in the prosecution of such as refused to read the king's declaration, he solemnly took his leave and withdrew from the court.—*Grey's Examination,* vol. iii., p. 405, 406.—ED.

† Mr. Johnson, previously to his sufferings, was degraded in the chapter-house of St. Paul's on the 22d of November, 1686. He bore the whipping on the 1st of December following, with great fortitude. The Revolution restored him to his liberty; the degradation was annulled ; the judgment given against him was declared illegal and cruel; and a pension of £300 a year for his own and son's life was granted to him, with £1000 in money, and a place of £100 a year for his son. His temper, which was haughty, rough, and turbulent, rendered his solicitations for a bishopric, and two addresses of the Lords recommending him to preferment, unsuccessful. He had been chaplain to Lord Russel, and was a man of considerable learning and abilities, of great firmness and fortitude of mind. In 1683–4 he had incurred a heavy sentence in the King's Bench, being fined five hundred marks, and committed to the prison till it was paid, and sureties for his good behaviour for a year were found. This penalty was incurred by the publication of a book entitled "Julian the Apostate," in 1682, intended to expose the doctrines of passive obedience and nonresistance; and to show the great difference between the case of the primitive Chris-

* Burnet, vol. iii., p. 140, 141, Edinb. edit.
† Burnet, p. 82. -   ‡ Welwood, p. 198.
§ It is said that he took exception at the lawfulness of the commission itself. But then, on its being opened, he did not appear and declare against it, as judging it to be against law, contenting himself with not going to it ; and it was not at first apprehended that he made a matter of conscience of it. He was of a timorous nature, and cautious of doing anything that might eventually be prejudicial to his great object, which was to enrich his nephew,—*Burnet,* vol. iii., p. 82, 83. *Grey's Examination,* vol iii., p. 405.—ED.
‖ Though the Bishop of Rochester might, from views to preferment, be induced to act in a commission to which he was, without his knowledge, named, yet he is stated to have acted with integrity in

Affairs in Scotland were in equal forwardness with those of England; the Parliament which met at Edinburgh in May, 1685, while the persecution continued, declared their abhorrence of all principles derogatory to the king's absolute power, and offered their lives and fortunes to defend it against all opposers. They passed an act, making it death to resort to any conventicles in houses or fields; and declared it high treason to give or take the national Covenant, or to write in defence of it. They also obliged the subjects of Scotland to take an oath, when required, to maintain the king's absolute power, on pain of banishment. Popery made very considerable advances in that kingdom, and several persons of character changed their religion with the times.* But the populace were in the other extreme; the Earl of Perth, having set up a private chapel for mass, the mob broke into it with such fury that they defaced and destroyed the whole furniture, for which one of them was apprehended and hanged. When the English court changed measures, the Scots Parliament agreed to a suspension of the penal laws during the king's life; but his majesty insisting upon an entire repeal, which they declined, he dissolved them. The Episcopal clergy were obsequious to the court, and in many places so sunk into sloth and ignorance, that the lower people were quite indifferent in matters of religion; but the Presbyterians, though now freed from the severities they had smarted under so many years, expressed upon all occasions an unconquerable aversion to popery, and by degrees roused the whole nation out of their lethargy.

In Ireland things had still a more favourable aspect for the court: the king had made a greater dependance on the Irish Catholics than upon any other of his subjects. Colonel Talbot, earl of Tyrconnel, was made lord-lieutenant of that country, a vile and profligate officer, who scrupled no kind of barbarity and wickedness to serve his cause; he broke several Protestant officers in the army, and by degrees turned them all out to make room for papists. All officers, both civil and military, were put into the hands of the vilest miscreants; there was not a Protestant sheriff left in that kingdom; the charters were taken away, and new modelled in favour of papists. The corporations were dissolved, and all things managed with an arbitrary hand, so that many, imagining the massacring knife to be at their throats, left the kingdom; some transporting themselves into England, and others into more remote and distant countries. Thus far the prerogative prevailed without any repulse.

tians, who had the laws against them, and ours, who have the laws on our side.—Birch's Life of Archbishop Tillotson, p. 216, &c.—ED.
* Burnet, vol. iii., p. 86, 90.
† So hostile to the cause of liberty were the Irish Catholics, that, not content with oppressing it in their own kingdom, they encouraged the emigration of their own body with a view to check its spread beyond the Atlantic. For they suggested to King James, to grant, in lieu of lands, money to such of their countrymen as were willing to transport themselves into New-England to advance the Catholic faith there, and check the growing independence of that country.—Life of Dr. Increase Mather, p. 43.—ED.

Matters being now ripe for attacking the Church of England in form, it was resolved to begin with making an example of some of their leading divines: Dr. Sharpe, rector of St. Giles's, having disobeyed the king's order of not preaching on the controverted points, and spoken disrespectfully of the king's religion in one of his sermons, the Bishop of London was ordered to suspend him; but the bishop, with all respect and duty to his majesty, sent word that he could not proceed in such a summary way, but that when the cause was heard in the Commons, he would pronounce such sentence, as the canons should warrant; and in the mean time, would desire the doctor to forbear preaching.* The court resenting the bishop's denial, cited him before the ecclesiastical commission August 4, where he was treated by Jefferies in a manner unbecoming his character. The bishop excepted to the authority of the court, as contrary to law, and added, that he had complied in the doctor's case as far as the ecclesiastical laws would permit. However, notwithstanding all that his lordship could say in his defence, he was suspended ab officio,‡ and the Bishops of Durham, Rochester, and Peterborough were appointed commissioners, to exercise jurisdiction during his suspension. But Dr. Sharpe, after having expressed his sorrow, in a petition, for falling under the king's displeasure, was dismissed with a gentle reprimand, and suffered to return to the exercise of his function.

The king's next attempt was upon the universities; he began with Cambridge, and com-

* Burnet, p. 83–85.
† Dr. Compton, the Bishop of London, had, by a conduct worthy of his birth and station in the Church, acquired the love and esteem of all the Protestant churches at home and abroad; and for that reason, was the mark of the envy and hatred of the Romish party at court. He made a distinguishing figure in the following reigns. He was the youngest son of Spencer, earl of Northampton, who was killed in the civil wars. After having studied three years at the university, and made the usual tour of Europe, he became a cornet in the royal regiment of guards; which gave occasion to the following bon-mot: King James, discoursing with him on some tender point, was so little pleased with his answers, that he told him, "He talked more like a colonel than a bishop." To which he replied, "That his majesty did him honour in taking notice of his having formerly drawn his sword in defence of the Constitution; and that he should do the same again, if he lived to see it necessary." Accordingly, he appeared in arms again a little before the Revolution, and at the head of a fine troop of gentlemen and their attendants, carried off the Princess Anne, and marched into Nottingham.— Welwood's Memoirs, p. 175; and Granger's History of England, vol. iv., p. 283, 284.—ED.
‡ Though Bishop Compton was thus deprived of his Episcopal power, he still retained his other capacities, particularly as a governor of Sutton's Hospital, and preserved the intrepidity of his spirit. For when an attempt was made, by the recommendation of the king, to introduce a papist as a pensioner, contrary to the statutes of that institution, the bishop, in conjunction with some other trustees, so firmly opposed the encroachment upon the rights of the foundation, that the court and commissioners saw fit, in the end, to desist from their design.—Life of Bishop Compton, p. 45; where, from p. 22–39, and Biographia Britannica, vol. iv., article Compton, p. 55, 56, second edition, may be seen a full account of his prosecution.—ED.

manded Dr. Peachel, the vice-chancellor, to ad-mit one Albin Francis, a Benedictine monk, to the degree of M.A., without administering to him any oath or oaths whatsoever ; all which, his majesty declared, he would dispense with.* The vice-chancellor, having read the letter to the congregation of regents, it was agreed to petition the king to revoke his mandate ; but, instead of complying with their petition, the king sent for the vice-chancellor before the ecclesiastical commission, by whom he was suspended *ab officio et beneficio*, for disobedience and contempt of the king's commands ; and Dr. Balderston, master of Emanuel College, was chosen vice-chancellor in his room.

Soon after, the king sent a *mandamus* to the vice-president of Magdalen College, Oxford, and to the fellows, to choose Mr. Farmer, a man of ill reputation, their president, in the room of Dr. Clarke, deceased ; but, in defiance of the king's mandate, they chose Dr. Hough, for which they were cited before the ecclesiastical commissioners ; but having proved Farmer to be a man of bad character, the king relinquished him, and ordered them by another mandate, to choose Dr. Parker, bishop of Oxford. The fellows, having agreed to abide by their first choice, refused to elect the bishop, as contrary to their statutes. Upon which the commissioners were sent to visit them, who, after sundry inquiries and examinations, deprived Dr. Hough, and installed the Bishop of Oxford by proxy ; and the fellows, refusing to sign a submission to their new president, twenty-five of them were deprived, and made incapable of any benefice.† Parker died soon after, and one of the popish bishops was by *mandamus* chosen president in his place ; which inflamed the Church party so far, that they sent pressing messages to the Prince of Orange, desiring him to espouse the cause of the Church, and break with the king, if he would not redress their grievances. Thus the very first beginnings of *resistance to King James* came from that very university which, but *four years before, had pronounced this doctrine damnable by a solemn decree ;* and from those very men who were afterward King William's most bitter enemies.‡

The more desperate the war grew between the king and the Church, the more necessary did both parties find it to show kindness to the Dissenters ; for this purpose, his majesty sent agents among them, offering them the royal favour, and all manner of encouragement, if they would concur with him in abrogating the penal laws and test ; he invited some of their ministers to court, and pretended to consult them in the present crisis.§ The clergy, at the same

time, prayed and entreated the Dissenters to appear on their side, and stand by the Establishment, making large promises of favour and brotherly affection, if ever they came into power.

The king, notwithstanding the stubbornness of the clergy, called a council, in which he declared his resolution to issue out a declaration for a general liberty of conscience to all persons, of what persuasion soever ;* "which he was moved to do by having observed, that though a uniformity of worship had been endeavoured to be established within this kingdom, in the successive reigns of four of his predecessors, assisted by their respective Parliaments, yet it had proved altogether, ineffectual. That the restraint upon the consciences of Dissenters had been very prejudicial to the nation, as was sadly experienced by the horrid rebellion in the time of his majesty's father. That the many penal laws made against Dissenters had rather increased than lessened the number of them ; and that nothing could more conduce to the peace and quiet of this kingdom, and the increase of the number as well as the trade of his subjects, than an entire liberty of conscience, it having always been his opinion, as most suitable to the principles of Christianity, that no man should be persecuted for conscience' sake ; for he thought conscience could not be forced, and that it could never be the true interest of a king of England to endeavour to do it."†

This speech meeting with no opposition in the Council, his majesty, on the 4th of April, caused his gracious declaration for liberty of conscience to be published.‡ In the preamble to which, his majesty does not scruple to say, "that he cannot but heartily wish (as it will easily be believed) that all his subjects were members of the Catholic Church, yet it is his opinion that conscience ought not to be forced, for his reasons mentioned in the foregoing speech," which he rehearses at large ; and then adds, "By virtue of his royal prerogative, he thinks fit to issue out his declaration of indulgence, making no doubt of the concurrence of his two houses of Parliament, when he shall grant out licenses directed to the bishops and their officers, to the judges, justices, and all others whom it may concern. The licenses were to this effect : "that the king's pleasure is, that the several persons (named in a schedule annexed) be not prosecuted or molested, 1. For not taking the oaths of allegiance and supremacy : or, 2. Upon the prerogative writ for £20 a month : or, 3. Upon outlawries, or *excom. capiend.* for the said causes : or, 4. For not receiving the sacrament : or, 5. By reason of their conviction for recusancy or exercise of their religion, a command to stay proceedings already begun for any of the causes aforesaid." The price for any one of these licenses was £10 for a single person : but if several joined, the price was £16, and eight persons might join in taking out one license. There were not very many Dissenters that took out these licenses.— *Tong's Life of Mr. Matthew Henry,* p. 45, 46, 12mo. —ED.   * Gazette, No. 2226.

† Under all the pretences of tenderness, liberal policy, and wisdom, which gilded over the king's speech, "it was well understood," observes Sir John Keresby, "that his view was to divide the Protestant churches, *divide et impera ;* that so the papists might with the more ease possess themselves of the highest place."—*Memoirs,* p. 243.—ED.

‡ Gazette, No. 2231.

---

* Burnet, p. 114, 115.

† It will be thought but justice to the memory of Bishop Sprat to state what he himself declared was his conduct on this and the two preceding occasions. It was this : he resolutely persisted in his dissent from every vote that passed against Magdalen College ; he opposed to the utmost the violent persecution upon the University of Cambridge ; and he gave his positive vote for the bishop's acquittal both times, when his suspension came in question.—*Dr. Grey's Examination,* p. 406, 407.—ED.

‡ Burnet, p. 701.

§ Among other measures, which expressed the disposition of the court towards Dissenters, was the power with which some gentlemen were invested to

think it convenient for them to meet. And, first, he declares that he will protect and maintain his archbishops, bishops, and clergy, and all other his subjects of the Church of England, in the free exercise of their religion as by law established, and in the quiet and full enjoyment of their possessions... Secondly, That it is his royal will and pleasure that all penal laws for nonconformity to the religion established, or by reason of the exercise of religion in any manner whatsoever, be immediately suspended. And to the end that, by the liberty hereby granted, the peace and security of the government in the practice thereof may not be endangered, he strictly charges and commands all his subjects, that as he freely gives them leave to meet and serve God after their own way, be it in private houses or places purposely hired and built for that use, so that they take special care that nothing be preached or taught among them which may tend to alienate the hearts of his people from him or his government; and that their meetings or assemblies be peaceably, openly, and publicly held, and all persons freely admitted to them; and that they signify and make known to some one or more of the next justices of peace what place or places they set apart for such uses. And he is desirous to have the benefit of the service of all his subjects, which by the law of nature is inseparably annexed and inherent to his royal person. And that none of his subjects may be for the future under any discouragements or disability, who are otherwise well inclined, and fit to serve him, by reason of some oaths or tests that have usually been administered upon such occasions, he hereby farther declares, that it is his will and pleasure that the oaths of supremacy and allegiance, and the several tests and declarations mentioned in the acts of Parliament made in the 25th and 30th of his brother's reign, shall not hereafter be required to be taken, declared, or subscribed, by any persons whatsoever, who are or shall be employed in any office, or place of trust, either civil or military, under him or in his government. And it is his intention from time to time hereafter to grant his royal dispensation to all his subjects, so to be employed, who shall not take the said oaths, or subscribe or declare the said tests or declarations. And he does hereby give his free and ample pardon to all Nonconformist recusants, and other his subjects, for all crimes and things by them committed, or done contrary to the penal laws formerly made relating to religion, and the profession or exercise thereof. And although the freedom and assurance he has hereby given in relation to liberty and property might be sufficient to remove from the minds of his subjects all fears and jealousies in relation to either, yet he thinks fit to declare, that he will maintain them in all their properties and possessions, as well of church and abbey lands, as in other their estates and properties whatsoever."*

A declaration of the same nature was sent to Scotland, in which the king, "by virtue of his prerogative royal, and absolute authority and power over all his subjects, who are bound to obey him without reserve, repeals all the severe laws made by his grandfather King James I., and takes off all disabilities from his Roman Catholic subjects, which rendered them incapable of employments and benefices. He also slackened the laws against moderate Presbyterians, and promised never to force his subjects by any invincible necessity to change their religion. He also repealed all laws imposing tests on those who held any employments."*

This was strange conduct, says Bishop Burnet, in a Roman Catholic monarch, at a time when his brother of France had just broke the Edict of Nantes, and was dragooning his Protestant subjects out of his kingdom. But the bishop suspects the king's sincerity in his declaration, from his promising to use no invincible necessity to force his subjects to change their religion, as if there was a reserve, and that some degrees of compulsion might be proper one time or other; which seems to have been a parallel case to the doctrine of the Church concerning nonresistance. However, by another proclamation, the king granted full liberty to the Scots Presbyterians to set up conventicles in their own way, which they thankfully accepted; but when his majesty pressed them to dispose their friends to concur with him in taking off the test and penal laws, which they knew was only to serve the papists, they answered only in cold and general terms.

In pursuance of these declarations, the Dissenters of all sorts were not only set at liberty, but admitted to serve in all offices of profit and trust. November 6, the king sent an order to the Lord-mayor of London to dispense with the Quakers taking oaths,† or, at least, not to fine them if they refused to serve, by which means a door was opened to the Roman Catholics, and to all others, to bear offices in the state without a legal qualification. Several addresses were presented to the king upon this occasion from the companies in the city of London, from the corporations in the country, and even from the clergy themselves, thanking his majesty for his

---

sold as slaves." Upon the liberty which the declaration afforded them, Dr. Increase Mather was deputed to take a voyage to England, with addresses of thanks to the king from various towns and churches; though the measure was opposed by the rulers of the province. When he presented them, he was graciously received, and was admitted to different and repeated audiences with the king, who, on receiving the addresses, said, "You shall have Magna Charta for liberty of conscience:" and on its being intimated to him by two of his courtiers, at one of the audiences, that the favour shown to New-England would have a good influence on the body of Dissenters in England, his reply was, "He believed so, and it should be done."—*Life of Dr. Increase Mather*, p. 37, &c.—ED.
* Echard, p. 1083. Burnet, p. 136.
† Sewel informs us, that the king carried his condescension to the Quakers so far, that a countryman of that persuasion coming to him with his hat on his head, the king took off his own hat and held it under his arm: which the other seeing, said, "The king needs not keep off his hat for me." To which his majesty replied, "You do not know the custom here, for that requires that but one hat must be on here."—*Sewel's History*, p. 609.—ED.

---

* The operation of this declaration extended beyond England or Scotland; for it proved beneficial to the people of New-England, whose religious liberties as well as their civil rights were near expiring; and who had been told by some in power, "They must not think to have the privileges of Englishmen follow them to the ends of the earth; and they had no more privileges left them than to be bought and

declaration for liberty of conscience, and his promise to support the Church of England as by law established, assuring him of their endeavours to choose such members for the next Parliament as should give it a more legal sanction.

The several denominations of Dissenters also were no less thankful for their liberty, and addressed his majesty in higher strains than some of their elder and more cautious ministers approved ; Mr. Baxter, Mr. Stretton, and a great many others, refused to join in them ; and Bishop Burnet admits* that few concurred in those addresses,† and that the persons who presented them were, mean and inconsiderable. When there was a general meeting of the ministers to consider of their behaviour in this crisis, and two messengers from court waited to carry back the result of the debate, Mr. Howe delivered his opinion against the dispensing power, and against everything that might contribute assistance to the papists to enable them to subvert the Protestant religion.‡ Another minister stood up, and declared,§ that he apprehended their late sufferings had been occasioned more by their firm adherence to the Constitution than their differing from the Establishment ; and therefore, if the king expected they should give up the Constitution and declare for the dispensing power, he had rather, for his part, lose his liberty, and return to his former bondage.|| In conclusion, Mr. Howe, in his summing up the whole debate, signified to the courtiers that they were, in general, of the same opinion. Mr. Coke adds, that to his knowledge the Dissenters did both dread and detest the dispensing power ; and their steadiness in this crisis was a noble stand by a number of men who subsisted only by the royal favour, which ought not to have been so soon forgotten.

Though the court were a little disappointed

in their expectations from the Dissenters, they put the best face they could on the affair, and received such addresses as were presented with high commendation. The first who went up were the London Anabaptists, who say, that "the sense of this invaluable favour and benefit derived to us from your royal clemency compels us to prostrate ourselves at your majesty's feet with the tender of our most humble thanks for that peace and liberty which both we, and all other Dissenters from the National Church, now enjoy."*

Next came the Presbyterians,† "who acknowledge his majesty's princely compassion in rescuing them from their long sufferings, in restoring to God the empire over conscience, and publishing to the world his royal Christian judgment, that conscience may not be forced ; and his resolution that such force should not be attempted in his reign, which they pray may be long." Then followed the Independents : "Sir, the great calamity we have been a long time under, through the severe execution of the penal laws in matters of religion, has made us deeply sensible of your majesty's princely clemency towards us your dissenting subjects, especially since, in the indulgence vouchsafed, there are no limitations hindering the enjoyment of it, with a good conscience, and that your majesty publisheth to the world that it has been your constant sense and opinion that conscience ought not to be constrained, nor people forced in matters of mere religion."‡ About the same time was published the humble and thankful address of the London Quakers,§ to this purpose : "May it please the king ! Though we are not the first in this way, yet we hope we are not the least sensible of the great favours we are come to present the king our humble, open, and hearty thanks for. We rejoice to

* Page 140.

† Dr. Grey controverts the above assertions of Bishop Burnet : he has given at length eight addresses from different bodies of Dissenters, in different parts of the kingdom, as specimens of the courtly, not to say fulsome and flattering strains, which they on this occasion adopted : and he refers to the Gazettes of the times, as furnishing about seventy other compositions of the same kind ; in which this oppressed body, emancipated from their sufferings, fears, and dangers, poured forth the sentiments of loyalty and gratitude. Mr. Stretton, mentioned above, who had been ejected from Petworth in Sussex, and afterward gathered a congregation in London, which assembled at Haberdasher's Hall, was a minister of great reputation and influence ; an active and a useful character. He made use of the liberty granted by the king's proclamation, but never did nor would join in any address of thanks for it, lest he should seem to give countenance to the king's assuming a power above the law ; and he was instrumental to prevent several addresses.—Henry's Funeral Sermon for Stretton, p. 45. Grey's Examination, vol. iii., p. 410–416.—ED.   ‡ Gazette, No. 2234.

§ This gentleman was Dr. Daniel Williams, who pursued the argument with such clearness and strength, that all present rejected the motion, and the court agents went away disappointed. There was a meeting, at the same time, of a considerable number of the city clergy, waiting the issue of their deliberations, who were greatly animated and encouraged by the bold and patriotic resolution of the dissenting ministers.—Life of Dr. Williams, prefixed to his Practical Discourses, vol. i., p. 10.—ED.

|| Howe's Life, p. 134.

* Gazette, No. 2234. For some very sensible remarks on this address, see Toulmin's History of Protestant Dissenters, p. 291.—C.

† This address had about thirty hands to it : it was presented by Mr. Hurst, Mr. Chester, Mr. Slatter, Mr. Cox, Mr. Roswell, Mr. Turner, Mr. Franklin, Mr. Deal, and Mr. Reynolds. It is preserved at length, with the king's answer, in the "Biographia Britannica," vol. i., article Alsop. It was supposed to have been drawn up by Mr. Alsop, whose feelings and gratitude, on the free pardon which the king had given to his son, convicted of treasonable practices, may be reckoned to have had great influence in dictating and promoting it. After the spirited resolution mentioned above had been carried, some of the ministers were privately closeted with King James, and some few received particular and personal favours : by these fascinating arts they were brought over. And their conduct had its weight in producing similar addresses from the country. Part of the king's answer deserves to be recorded as a monument of his insincerity, and a warning that kings can degrade themselves by recourse to duplicity and falsehood. "Gentlemen," said James, "I protest before God, and I desire you to tell all manner of people, of all persuasions, that I have no other design than I have spoken of. And, gentlemen, I hope to live to see the day when you shall as well have Magna Charta for the liberty of conscience, as you have had for your properties." The ministers went away satisfied with the welcome which they had received from the pleasant countenances of the courtiers, and the courteous words, looks, and behaviour of his majesty.—Palmer's Nonconformists' Memorial, vol. ii., p. 13.—ED.

‡ Gazette, No. 2238.   § Sewel, p. 606.

see the day that a king of England should, from his royal seat, so universally assert this royal principle, that conscience ought not to be restrained, nor people forced for matters of religion."* The several addresses above mentioned express their humble dependance on his majesty's royal promise to secure their rights and properties, and that he will endeavour to engage his two houses of Parliament to concur with him in this good work. Here are no flights of expression, nor promises of obedience without reserve, but purely a sense of gratitude for the restoration of liberty.†

And though it must be allowed that some few Dissenters, from an excess of joy, or, it may be, from a strong resentment against their late persecutors, published some severe pamphlets, and gave too much countenance to the measures of the court, as Mr. Lobb, Alsop, and Penn the Quaker, yet the body of them kept at a distance, and, "as thankful as they were for their liberty," says Lord Halifax, "they were fearful of the issue; neither can any member of consideration among them be charged with hazarding the public safety by falling in with the measures of the court, of which they had as great a dread as their neighbours."‡ And the Lords, in a conference with the House of

---

* There are, it has been justly observed to the editor, some errors in the above extract, viz., the word *royal* instead of *glorious*, before *principle*; and the omission of *mere* before *religion.*—Ed.

† Though Mr. Neal's character of the addresses which he quotes be admitted as just, it will not apply to all which the Dissenters presented on this occasion: "Some of them," Dr. Calamy observes, "ran high." But for the strong language in which they were expressed, or for the numbers to which they amounted, an apology may be drawn from the excess of joy with which the royal indulgence, though an insidious measure, naturally inspired those who, for many years, had groaned under the rod of persecution. It should also be considered, that but very few, comparatively, think deeply or look far. Present, pleasing appearances mislead and captivate the generality. There is also a propensity in mankind to follow those who take the lead, and a readiness to credit and flatter royalty and greatness. The Dissenters, however, not without reason, incurred censure for "a vast crowd of congratulatory addresses, complimenting the king in the highest manner, and protesting what mighty returns of loyalty they would make;" and were called "the pope's journeymen to carry on his work." But these censures came with an ill grace, as Dr. Calamy remarks, "from the Church party, who had set them the pattern;" who in a most luxuriant manner had thanked King Charles for dissolving one of the best Parliaments; who were mighty forward in the surrender of charters; and who, in their fulsome addresses, made no other claim to their liberties and civil rights than as concessions from the crown, telling the king, "every one of his commands was stamped with God's authority." The University of Oxford, in particular, promised King James to obey him without limitations or restrictions. —*Dr. Grey*, and *Calamy's Life of Howe*, p. 137, 138. —Ed.

‡ "The churchmen, on their side," says Dr. Warner, "did all that lay in their power to establish a union, as the only possible means of their joint security. They published pamphlets from time to time, acknowledging their error in driving the Presbyterians to extremities; confessing that they were not enough upon their guard against the artifices of the court, and promising a very different behaviour on the re-establishment of their affairs. It must be owned that this conduct was dexterous, and sensible,

---

Commons upon the Occasional Bill, in the first year of Queen Anne, say, "that in the last and greatest danger the Church was exposed to, the Dissenters joined with her, with all imaginable zeal and sincerity, against the papists, their common enemies, showing no prejudice to the Church, but the utmost respect to the bishops when sent to the Tower."

But as the king and ministry carried all before them, the Church party were in despair, and almost at their wits' end; they saw themselves on the brink of ruin, imagining that they should be turned out of their freeholds for not reading the king's declaration, and that the Nonconformists would be admitted into their pulpits; as Dr. Sherlock, master of the Temple, acknowledged in conversation to Mr. Howe;* and that, as the papists had already invaded the universities, they would in a little time overset the whole hierarchy. In this distress, they turned their eyes all around them for relief: they applied to the Dissenters, giving them the strongest assurances of a comprehension and toleration in better times, if they would but assist in delivering them out of their present troubles. Bishop Burnet says that the clergy here in England wrote to the Prince of Orange, and desired him to send over some of the dissenting preachers, whom the violence of the former times had driven into Holland, and to prevail effectually with them to oppose any false brethren whom the court might have gained over; and that they sent over very solemn assurances, which passed through his own hands, that in case they stood firm now to the common interest, they would in a better time come into a comprehension of such as could be brought into conjunction with the Church, and to a toleration of the rest. Agreeably to these assurances, when the Rev. Mr. Howe, Mr. Mead, and other refugee ministers, waited on the Prince

and just. It must be said, however," observes this author, "that they had not attained this wisdom till it was almost too late; at least, not during the space of twenty years, and till by their absurd principles of passive obedience, taught in their pulpits, and acts of Parliament, they had enabled the king to become arbitrary and tyrannical. It is no less true, that an accusation lies against them of having forgotten this promise after the Revolution, as they did at the restoration of Charles II."—*Eccles. Hist.*, vol. ii., p. 639, 640.—Ed.

* "Who knows," said Dr. Sherlock, "but Mr. Howe may be offered to be master of the Temple?" Mr. Howe replied, "that he should not balk an opportunity of more public service, if offered on terms he had no just reason to except against." But then he added, "that he would not meddle with the emolument, otherwise than as a hand to convey it to the legal proprietor." Upon this, the doctor, not a little transported with joy, rose up from his seat and embraced him, saying, "that he had always taken him for that ingenuous, honest man that he now found him to be." Mr. Howe afterward told this passage to a dignitary of the Church, to whom the doctor was well known; signifying how little he was prepared to reply to a supposition that had not so much as once entered into his thoughts before. The gentleman answered, "Sir, you say you had not once thought of the case, or so much as supposed anything like it; but you must give me leave to tell you, if you had studied the case seven years together, you could not have said anything more to the purpose, or more to the doctor's satisfaction."—*Calamy's Life of Howe*, p. 141, 142.—Ed.

of Orange, to return him thanks for the protection of the country, and to take their leave, his highness made them some presents to pay their debts and defray their charges home ; and having wished them a good voyage, he advised them to be very cautious in their addresses, and not to suffer themselves to be drawn into the measures of the court so far as to open a door for the introducing of popery, by desiring the taking off the penal laws and test, as was intended.* He requested them, also, to use their influence with their brethren to lay them under the same restraints. His highness sent orders likewise to Monsieur Dykvelt, his resident, to press the Dissenters to stand off from the court; and to assure them of a full toleration and comprehension, if possible, when the crown should devolve on the Princess of Orange. Agents were sent among the Dissenters to soften their resentments against the Church, and to assure them that for the future they would treat them as brethren, as will be seen in the next chapter.

The Dissenters had it now in their power to distress the Church party, and, it may be, to have made reprisals, if they would have given way to the revenge, and fallen heartily in with the king's measures. They were strongly solicited on both sides ; the king preferred them to places of profit and trust, and gave them all manner of countenance and encouragement ; and the churchmen loaded them with promises and assurances what great things they would do for them, as soon as it should be in their power. But, alas ! no sooner was the danger over than the majority of them forgot their vows in distress ; for when the *Convocation* met the first time after the Revolution, *they would not hear of a comprehension*, nor so much as acknowledge the *foreign churches* for *their brethren*, seeming rather inclined to return to their old methods of persecution. So little dependance ought to be placed on High Church promises !

But in their present circumstances it was necessary to flatter the Nonconformists, and weaken the king's hands, by dissuading the Dissenters from placing any confidence in their new friends : for this purpose, a pamphlet, written by the Marquis of Halifax, and published by advice of some of the most eminent dignitaries of the Church, was dispersed, entitled " A Letter to a Dissenter upon occasion of his Majesty's late gracious Declaration of Indulgence." It begins with saying, " that churchmen are not surprised nor provoked at the Dissenters accepting the offers of ease from the late hardships they lay under ; but desired them to consider, 1. The cause they had to suspect their new friends ; and, 2. Their duty in Christianity, and prudence not to hazard the public safety by a desire of ease or revenge.

"With regard to the first, the Church of Rome," says the author, "does not only dislike your liberty, but, by its principles, cannot allow it : they are not able to make good their vows ; nay, it would be a habit of sin that requires absolution ; you are therefore hugged now, only that you may be the better squeezed another time. To come so quick from one extreme to another is such an unnatural motion, that you ought to be on your guard : the other day you

were sons of Belial, now you are angels of light. Popery is now the only friend of liberty, and the known enemy of persecution. We have been under shameful mistakes if this can be either true or lasting."

The letter goes on to insinuate, "that some ministers had been bribed into the measures of the court ; that they were under engagements, and empowered to give rewards to others, where they could not persuade. Now if these or others should preach up anger and vengeance against the Church of England, ought they not rather to be suspected of corruption, than to act according to judgment ? If they who thank the king for his declaration should be engaged to justify it in point of law, I am persuaded it is more than the addressers are capable of doing. There is a great difference between enjoying quietly the advantage of an act irregularly done by others, and becoming advocates for it ; but frailties are to be excused. Take warning by the mistake of the Church of England, when, after the Restoration, they preserved so long the bitter taste of your rough usage to them, that it made them forget their interest, and sacrifice it to their revenge. If you had now to do with rigid prelates, the argument might be fair on your side ; but since the common danger has so laid open the mistake, that all former haughtiness towards the Dissenters is forever extinguished, and the spirit of persecution is turned into a spirit of peace, charity, and condescension, will you not be moved by such an example ? If it be said the Church is only humble when it is out of power, the answer is, that is uncharitable, and an unseasonable triumph ; besides, it is not so in fact, for if she would comply with the court, she could turn all the thunder upon yourselves, and blow you off the stage with a breath ; but she will not be rescued by such unjustifiable means. You have formerly very justly blamed the Church of England for going too far in her compliance with the court ; conclude, therefore, that you must break off your friendship, or set no bounds to it. The Church is now convinced of its error, in being too severe to you ; the next Parliament will be gentle to you ; the next heir is bred in a country famous for indulgence ; there is a general agreement of thinking men, that we must no more cut ourselves off from foreign Protestants, but enlarge our foundations ; so that all things conspire to give you ease and satisfaction, if you do not too much anticipate it. To conclude, the short question is, Whether or no you will join with those who must in the end run the same fate with you ? If the Protestants of all sorts have been to blame in their behaviour to each other, they are upon equal terms, and for that very reason ought now to be reconciled." How just soever the reasoning of this letter may be, either the author did not know the spirit of the Church party (as they were called), or he must blush when he compared it with the facts that followed the Revolution. Twenty thousand copies were dispersed about the city and country, and had the desired effect, the honest, well-meaning Dissenters making no advantage of the favourable juncture ; they entered into no alliance with the papists, nor complied with the court measures, any farther than to accept their own liberty, which they had a natural right to,

* Calamy's Life of Howe, p. 132.

and of which they ought never to have been deprived.

The war between the king and the Church being now declared, each party prepared for their defence; the points in debate were, a general toleration, and the dispensing power; the latter of which the High Church party had connived at during the late reign ; but when the edge of it was turned against themselves (the king having used it to break down the fences of the Church, by abrogating the penal laws and tests, and making an inroad upon the two universities), they exclaimed against it as subversive of the whole Constitution ; and, forgetting their late addresses, contested this branch of the prerogative. The king had secured the opinion of the judges in favour of it ; but this not giving satisfaction, he determined to obtain a parliamentary sanction. For this purpose, he published the following order in the Gazette : "That whereas his majesty was resolved to use his utmost endeavours that his declaration of indulgence might pass into a law, he therefore thought fit to review the lists of deputy-lieutenants, and justices of peace in the several counties, that those may be continued who would be ready to contribute what in them lies towards the accomplishment of so good and necessary a work,' and such others added to them, from whom his majesty may reasonably expect the like concurrence and assistance." Pursuant to this resolution, the king's first Parliament was dissolved, and agents were employed to dispose the people to the choice of such new members as might facilitate the court measures. The king himself went a progress round the country* to ingratiate himself with the people ; and it can hardly be expressed, says Echard, with what joyful acclamations his majesty was received; and what loyal acknowledgments were paid him in all places ; but in the affair of the tests, says Burnet,[†] there was a visible coldness among the nobility and gentry, though the king behaved in a most obliging manner.

When the king returned from his progress, he began to change the magistracy in the several corporations in England, according to the powers reserved to the crown in the new charters ; he turned out several of the aldermen of

---

* When he came to Chester (it being intimated that it would be expected, and the churchmen having led the way, and divers of the Lancashire ministers coming thither on purpose to attend the king), Mr. Matthew Henry, and Mr. Harvey, minister of another dissenting congregation in that city, with the heads of their societies, joined in an address of thanks to him, not for assuming a dispensing power, but for their ease, quiet, and liberty, under his protection. They presented it to him at the bishop's palace in the abbey court ; and he told them he wished they had a Magna Charta for their liberty. They did not promise to assist in taking away the tests, but only to live quiet and peaceable lives. This, however, was severely censured by some of their brethren. But the expressions of thankfulness for their liberty were very different from the high flights and promises of Sir Richard Lieving, the recorder of Chester at that time ; who, in a speech to King James, on his entering into the city, told him " that the corporation was his majesty's creature, and depended on the will of its creator ; and that the sole intimation of his majesty's pleasure should have with them the force of a fundamental law."—*Mr. Thompson's MS. Collections*, under the word " *Chester*."—ED. † Page 143.

---

the city of London, and placed new ones in their room. He caused the lists of lord-lieutenants and deputy-lieutenants to be reviewed, and such as would not promise to employ their interests in the repeal of the penal laws were discarded. Many Protestant Dissenters were put into commission on this occasion, in hopes that they would procure such members for the next Parliament as should give them a legal right to what they now enjoyed only by the royal favour ; but when the king pressed it upon the Lord-mayor of London, and the new aldermen, who were chiefly Dissenters, they made no reply.

The reason of the Dissenters' backwardness in an affair that so nearly concerned them, and in which they have *since* expressed so strong a desire, was their concern for the *Protestant religion, and their aversion to popery.* The king was not only a Roman Catholic, but a bigot ; and it was evident that the plucking up the fences at this time must have made a breach at which popery would enter.* If the king had been a Protestant, the case had been different, because papists could not take the oaths of allegiance and supremacy to a prince who stood excommunicated by the Church of Rome; but now there would be no obstacle, or, if there was, the king would dispense with the law in their favour : the Dissenters, therefore, were afraid that if they should give in to his majesty's measures, though they might secure their liberty for the present, it would stand on a precarious foundation ; for if popery came in triumphant, it would not only swallow up the Church of England, but the whole Protestant interest. They chose, therefore, to trust their liberty to the mercy of their Protestant brethren, rather than receive a legal security for it under a popish government.

According to this resolution, Bishop Burnet observes,[†] that Sir John Shorter, the new lord-mayor, and a Protestant Dissenter, thought fit to qualify himself for this office according to law, though the test was suspended, and the king had signified to the mayor that he was at liberty, and might use what form of worship he thought best in Guildhall, which was designed as an experiment to engage the Presbyterians to make the first change from the established worship, concluding, that if a Presbyterian mayor did this one year, it would be easy for a popish mayor to do it the next ; but his lordship referred the case to those clergymen who had the government of the diocess of London during the bishop's suspension, who assured his lordship it was contrary to law ; so that though the lord-mayor sometimes to the meetings of Dissenters, he went frequently to church, and behaved with more decency, says his lordship, than could have been expected. This disobliged the king to a very high degree, insomuch that he said the Dissenters were an ill-natured sort of people, that could not be gained.

This opposition to the king heightened his resentments, and pushed him on to rash and

---

* Nothing can surpass the prudence and fidelity of the Nonconformists at this juncture: They preserved their integrity alike inviolably, whether the court frowned or smiled upon them.—C.

† Burnet, p. 145.

violent measures : if he had proceeded by slow degrees, and secured one conquest before he had attempted another, he might have succeeded, but he gave himself up to the fury of his priests, who advised him to make haste with what he intended. This was discovered by a letter from the Jesuits from Liege to those of Friburgh, which says, the king wished they could furnish him with more priests to assist him in the conversion of the nation, which his majesty was resolved to bring about, or die a martyr in the attempt.' He said he must make haste, that he might accomplish it in his lifetime ;* and when one of them was lamenting that his next heir was a heretic, he answered, God will provide an heir; which argued either a strong faith, or a formed design of imposing one on the nation. Father Petre was the king's chief minister, and one of his majesty's privy council, a bold and forward man, who stuck at nothing to ruin the Church. The king designed him for the Archbishopric of York, now vacant, and for a cardinal's cap,† if he could prevail with the pope; for this purpose, the Earl of Castlemain was sent ambassador to Rome ; and a nuncio was sent from thence into England, to whom his majesty paid all possible respect, and gave an audience at Windsor, though it was contrary to law, all commerce with the court of Rome having been declared high treason by the statute of King Henry VIII. ; but the king said he was above law; and because the Duke of Somerset would not officiate in his place at the ceremony, he was dismissed from all his employments. ·

It was strange infatuation in King James to put a slight on the ancient nobility, and turn most of his servants out of their places because they were Protestants ; this weakened his interest, and threw a vast weight into the opposite scale. Indeed, it was impossible to disguise his majesty's design of introducing popery ;‡ and therefore Parker, bishop of Oxford, was employed to justify it, who published a book entitled " Reasons for abrogating the Test imposed on all Members of Parliament ;" which must refer to the renouncing transubstantiation, and the idolatry of the Church of Rome, because the members of Parliament had no other qualification imposed upon them besides the oaths of allegiance and supremacy. The bishop said much to excuse the doctrine of transubstantiation, and to free the Church of Rome from the charge of idolatry. His reasons were licensed by the Earl of Sunderland, and the stationer was commanded not to print any answer to them ; but Dr. Burnet, then in Holland, gave them a very smart and satirical reply, which quite ruined the bishop's reputation.

But his majesty's chief dependance was upon the army, which he was casting into a popish mould ; Protestant officers were cashiered ; Portsmouth and Hull, the two principal seaports of England, were in popish hands ; and the majority of the garrisons were of the same religion. Ireland was an inexhaustible seminary, from whence England was to be supplied with a Catholic army ; an Irish Roman Catholic, says Welwood, was a most welcome guest at Whitehall ; and they came over in shoals.

Over and above complete regiments of papists, there was scarce a troop or company in the army wherein some of that religion were not inserted, by express orders from court. Upon the whole, the affairs of the nation were drawing to a crisis ; and it was believed that what the king could not accomplish by the gentler methods of interest and persuasion, he would establish by his sovereign power. The army at Hounslow was to awe the city and Parliament ; and if they proved refractory, an Irish massacre, or some other desperate attempt, might possibly decide the fate of the nation.

About this time died the Rev. David Clarkson, B.D., born at Bradford in Yorkshire, February, 1621-22, and fellow of Clarehall, Cambridge, where he was tutor to Dr. Tillotson, afterward Archbishop of Canterbury. Dr. Bates, in his funeral sermon, gives him the character of a man of sincere godliness and true holiness : humility and modesty were his distinctive characters ; and his learning was superior to most of his time, as appears by his " Treatise of Liturgies," his "Primitive Episcopacy," his "Practical Divinity of Papists destructive to Men's Souls," and his volume of Sermons, printed after his death. He was some time minister of Mortlake in Surrey, but after his ejectment he gave himself up to reading and meditation, shifting from one place of obscurity to another, till the times suffered him to appear openly ; he was then chosen successor to the Rev. Dr. John Owen,* in the pastoral office to his congregation. Mr. Baxter says he was a divine of solid judgment, of healing, moderate principles, of great acquaintance with the fathers, of great ministerial abilities, and of a godly, upright life. Great was his solemnity and reverence in prayer ; and the method of his sermons was clear, deep, and instructive. His death was unexpected, though ; as he declared, it was no surprise to him, for he was entirely resigned to the will of God, and desired not to outlive his usefulness. This good man, says Dr. Bates, like holy Simeon, had Christ in his arms, and departed in peace, to see the salvation of God above, in the sixty-sixth year of his age.

Dr. Thomas Jacomb was born in Leicestershire, and educated first in Magdalen Hall, Oxon, and after in Emanuel College, Cambridge, from whence he removed to Trinity College, of which he was fellow. He came to London in 1647, and was soon after minister of Ludgate parish, where he continued till he was turned out in 1662. He met with some trouble after his

* This is an inaccuracy: he was chosen co-pastor with Dr. Owen, July, 1682, a year before the doctor's death. To the above account of Mr. Clarkson it is not improper to add, that his excellent pupil, Bishop Tillotson, always preserved that respect for him which he had contracted while he was under his tuition. His book on Diocesan Episcopacy shows him, says Mr. Granger, to have been a man of great reading in Church history. In his conversation, a comely gravity, mixed with innocent pleasantness, were attractive of respect and love. He was of a calm temper, not ruffled with passions, but gentle, and kind, and good ; his breast was the temple of peace. — Palmer's Nonconformists' Memorial, vol. ii., p. 451. Birch's Life of Tillotson, p. 4 ; and Granger's History of England, vol. iii., p. 310, 8vo. — Ed. Mr. Clarkson's folio volume of Sermons is highly valued, and also his treatise styled "No Evidence for Diocesan Episcopacy in Primitive Times."—C.

* Burnet, p. 135.   † Ibid., p. 168.
‡ Ibid., p. 178.

ejectment, but being received into the family of the countess dowager of Exeter, daughter of the Earl of Bridgewater, he was covered from his enemies. This honourable and virtuous lady was a comfort and support to the Nonconformist ministers throughout the reign of King Charles II. Her respects to the doctor were peculiar, and her favours extraordinary, for which he made the best returns be was able. The doctor was a learned man, an able divine, a serious, affectionate preacher, of unspotted morals, and a Nonconformist upon moderate principles. He died of a cancerous humour, that put him to the most acute pain, which he bore with invincible patience and resignation till the 27th of March, 1687, when he died in the Countess of Exeter's house, in the sixty-sixth year of his age.*

Mr. John Collins was educated at Cambridge, New-England, and returned from thence in the times of the civil war, became a celebrated preacher in London, having a sweet voice, and a most affectionate manner in the pulpit. He was chaplain to General Monk when he marched out of Scotland into England, but was not an incumbent anywhere when the Act of Uniformity took place. Being of the Independent denomination, he succeeded Mr. Mallory as pastor of a very considerable congregation of that persuasion, and was one of the Merchant lecturers at Pinners' Hall. He was a man mighty in the Scriptures; of an excellent natural temper; very charitable to all good men, without regard to parties; and died universally lamented,† December 3, 1687.

[It seems to have escaped Mr. Neal's attention to notice, at this period, two eminent persons, who died in the year 1686, Pearson, bishop of Chester, and Fell, bishop of Oxford.

Dr. John Pearson, born in 1612, was successively master of Jesus and Trinity Colleges, in Cambridge; and also Margaret-professor of divinity in that university. He had the living of St. Clement's, Eastcheap, and was consecrated Bishop of Chester February 9, 1672. He was a great divine, a profound and various scholar,

* It is a proof what different colouring a character derives from the dispositions and prejudices of those whose pen draws it, that Dr. Sherlock, who seems to have received some provocation from Dr. Jacomb, represents him "as the prettiest, nonsensical, trifling goose-cap that ever set pen to paper." This description is contradicted by the nature of his library, if the choice of books indicate the turn of the mind He left an incomparable collection of the most valuable books in all kinds of learning, and in various languages, which sold for £1300.—*Granger's History of England*, vol. iii., p. 307.—ED. Dr. Bates preached his funeral sermon from John, xii., 26. This discourse has long been regarded as one of the finest in our language. It is full of beauty, and possesses great force of illustration.—C.

† When, during his illness, Mr. Mead affectionately prayed for his recovery at the Pinners' Hall lecture, scarcely a dry eye was to be seen through the numerous auditory. Mr. Collins printed one sermon in the Morning Exercises, vol. iii., with the signature N. N., on this question, "How the religious of a nation are the strength of it!"—*Mather's History of New-England*, book iv., p. 200: where may be seen a Latin epitaph for him.—ED. There is also a good sermon of his, in the London Collection of Farewell Sermons, on Jude, 3; "Contend earnestly for the faith." His father was deacon of the Church at Cambridge, Massachusetts.—C.

eminently read in ecclesiastical history and antiquity, and an exact chronologist. He united with his learning clearness of judgment and strength of reason. As a preacher, he was rather instructive than pathetic. The character of the clergyman was adorned by an excellent temper, distinguished humility, primitive piety, and spotless manners: as a bishop, he was deemed too remiss and easy in his Episcopal function. "He was," says Bishop Burnet, "a striking instance of what a great man could fall to: for his memory went from him so entirely, that he became a child some years before he died." His late preferment to the Episcopacy, and the great decay of his faculties, which it is to be supposed came on gradually, may account for his remissness in that station. His works were few, but of great reputation. The chief were, "A Vindication of St. Ignatius's Epistles," in Latin; and "An Exposition of the Apostle's Creed," esteemed one of the most finished pieces in theology in our language. The substance of it was originally delivered in sermons to his parishioners. This work has gone through twelve or thirteen editions. "It is itself," says Mr. Granger, "a body of divinity, but not a body without a spirit. The style of it is just; the periods are for the most part well turned; the method is very exact; and it is, in general, free from those errors which are too often found in theological systems."—*Burnet's History*, vol. iii., 12mo, p. 109, 110. *Granger's History of England*, vol. iii., p. 251, 8vo; and *Richardson's Godwin de Præsulibus*, p. 779.

Dr. John Fell was the son of Dr. Samuel Fell, some time the dean of Christ Church, Oxford: he received his classical education in the free-school at Thame in Oxfordshire: at eleven years of age he was made student at Christ Church, in 1636, and in 1643 graduated master of arts. About this time he took arms, within the garrison of Oxford, in the king's cause, and was made an ensign. In 1648, when he was in holy orders, he was displaced by the Parliamentary visiters; from that year to the Restoration, he spent his time in retirement and study, observing the devotions of the Church of England with other oppressed Royalists. After the Restoration he was installed canon, and then dean of Christ Church, November 30, 1660, being then doctor in divinity, and one of the king's chaplains in ordinary. In the years 1667, 1668, and 1669, he was vice-chancellor of the university; and February 6, 1675, he was consecrated Bishop of Oxford. Soon after his preferment he rebuilt the palace of Cusedon, belonging to the see. He was a munificent benefactor to his college, and raised its reputation by his discipline. He settled on it no less than ten exhibitions; and the best rectories belonging to it were his purchase. He expended great sums in embellishing and adorning the University of Oxford. Learning was greatly indebted to his patronage and munificence. He liberally improved the press of the university; and the books that came from the Sheldonian theatre perpetuate, in this respect, his praise. For many years he annually published a book, generally a classic author, to which he wrote a preface and notes, and presented it to the students of his house as a new-year's gift: among these was an edition of the Greek Testament, in 12mo, 1675, which Dr. Harwood pronounces to be "a very valuable and excellent edition, that does honour to the bishop, because it is, upon the whole, a correct book, and exhibits the various readings very faithfully." His edition of the works of Cyprian affords also a conspicuous proof of his industry and learning. But he did not lay out his fortune in public acts of splendid munificence only: the private charities of life partook of his beneficence.. To the widow he was a husband, to the orphan a father, and to poor children a tender parent, furnishing them with instruction, and placing them out in life. "He was in all respects a most exemplary man, though," says Bishop Burnet, "a little too much heated in the matter of our disputes with the Dissenters. But, as he was among the first of our clergy that apprehended the design of bringing in popery, so he was one of the most zealous against it." It is a deduction from the merit of his character as the patron of learning, that he was not well affected to the Royal Society; and it is to be regretted that he was not friendly to that excellent man, Archbishop Tillotson; which was probably owing to a sense of his own sufferings before the Restoration, for he was not superior to a party spirit.—*Wood's Athenæ Oxon.*, vol. ii., p. 602, 605. *Richardson, de Præsulibus.* p. 548. *Burnet's History*, vol. iii., p. 100. *Granger's History of England*, vol. iii., p. 252. *British Biogr.*, vol. v., p. 11; and *Birch's Life of Tillotson*, p. 100.]

CHAPTER II.

FROM KING JAMES'S DECLARATION FOR LIBERTY OF CONSCIENCE TO THE ACT OF TOLERATION IN THE REIGN OF KING WILLIAM AND QUEEN MARY. 1668.

THOUGH the projects of the Roman Catholics were ripe for execution, there was one circumstance which spread a black cloud over all their attempts, which was the near prospect of a Protestant successor to the crown: this was the only hope of the Protestant cause, and the terror of the papists. To remove this impediment, his majesty first attempted to convert his eldest daughter Mary, princess of Orange, to the Roman Catholic religion, or, at least, to consent to the making way for it, by taking off the penal laws. To accomplish this, his majesty wrote an obliging letter to his daughter, reciting the motives of his own conversion; which were, the "great devotion of the Church of Rome; the adorning their churches; their acts of charity, which were greater than the Protestants could boast of; the numbers who retired from the world, and devoted themselves to a religious life.* He was convinced that Christ had left an infallibility in the Church, which the apostles acknowledged to be in St. Peter.—Acts, xv. It was the authority of the Church," says he, "that declared the Scriptures to be canonical; and certainly they who declared them could only interpret them; and wherever this infallibility was, there must be a clear succession. Which could be now here but in the Church of Rome, the Church of England not pretending

to infallibility, though she acted as if she did, by persecuting those who differed from her, as well Protestant Dissenters as papists; but he could see no reason why Dissenters might not separate from the Church of England, as well as the Church of England had done from that of Rome."

The princess answered the king's letter with great respect; "she affirmed the right of private judgment, according to the apostle's rule, of proving all things, and holding fast that which is good. She saw clearly from the Scriptures that she must not believe by the faith of another, but according as things appeared to herself. She confessed, if there was an infallibility in the Church, all other controversies must fall before it, but that it was not yet agreed where it was lodged, whether in a pope, or a general council, or both; and she desired to know in whom the infallibility rested when there were two or three popes at a time, acting one against another; for certainly the succession must then be disordered. She maintained the lawfulness and necessity of reading the Holy Scriptures; for, though faith was above reason, it proposed nothing contradictory to it. St. Paul ordered his epistles to be read in all the churches; and he says in one place, 'I write as to wise men, judge ye what I say:' and if they might judge an apostle, much more any other teacher. She excused the Church of England's persecuting the Dissenters in the best manner she could; and said the Reformers had brought things to as great perfection as those corrupt ages were capable of; and she did not see how the Church was to blame, because the laws were made by the State, and for civil crimes, and that the grounds of the Dissenters leaving the Church were different from those for which they had separated from the Church of Rome."* It was impossible for the princess to clear up this objection. But Bishop Burnet* adds, very justly, that the severities of the Church against the Dissenters were urged with a very ill grace, by one of the Church of Rome, that has delighted herself so often by being, as it were, bathed with the blood of those they call heretics. Upon the whole, it appeared that her highness was immovably fixed in her religion, and that there was not the least prospect of her departing from it.

At the same time his majesty attempted the Prince of Orange, for which purpose he employed one Mr. James Steward, a Scotch lawyer, who wrote several letters upon this argument to pensionary Fagel, in whom the prince placed an entire confidence.† The pensionary neglected his letters for some time; but at length, it being industriously reported that the silence of the prince was a tacit consent, pensionary laid all his letters before his highness, who commissioned the pensionary to draw up such an answer as might discover his true intentions and sense of things.

The answer was dated from the Hague, November 4, 1687, and begins with assurances of the prince and princess's duty to the king; and, since Mr. Steward had given him to understand that his letters were written with the king's knowledge and allowance,‡ the pensionary as-

---

sures him, in the name of their highnesses, that it was their opinion that "no Christian ought to be persecuted for his conscience, or be ill used because he differs from the established religion : and therefore they agreed that the papists in Scotland and Ireland should have the free exercise of their religion in private as they had in Holland ; and as to Protestant Dissenters, they heartily approved of their having an entire liberty of their religion, without any trouble or hinderance ; and their highnesses were ready to concur in the settling it, and giving their guarantee to protect and defend it. If his majesty desired their concurrence in repealing the penal laws, they were ready to give it, provided the laws by which Roman Catholics were excluded from sitting in both houses of Parliament, and from all employments, ecclesiastical, civil, and military, remained in force ; and likewise those other laws which secure the Protestant religion against all attempts of the Roman Catholics ; but they could not consent to the repeal of those laws which tended only to secure the Protestant religion, such as the tests, because they imported no more than a deprivation from public employments, which could do them no great harm. If the number of the papists were inconsiderable, it was not reasonable to insist upon it ; and if those few that pretend to public employments would do their party so much injury as not to be content with the repeal of the penal laws, unless they could get into offices of trust, their ambition only was to be blamed."* This letter was carried by Mr. Steward to the king, and read in the cabinet council, but it had no effect ; only the king ordered Mr. Steward to write back that he would have all or nothing. However, the Church party were satisfied with the prince's resolution to maintain the tests ; the Protestant Dissenters were pleased with their highnesses' declaration for the repeal of the penal laws so far as concerned themselves, and they placed an entire confidence in their word. The lay-papists and seculars pressed the king to accept of the repeal of so much of the penal laws as was offered, and blamed the ambition of the Jesuits and courtiers, who, rather than abate anything, would leave them exposed to the severity of the law when a freedom was offered. At length the pensionary's letter was printed by allowance of the prince, and dispersed over England, which provoked the king to use such a degree, that he spoke indecently of his highness to all the foreign ministers, and resolved to show him the severest marks of his displeasure.

The first project of gaining the prince having failed, his majesty went upon another, which, had it succeeded, must effectually have defeated the Protestant succession ; and that was, providing the nation with an heir of his own body by the present queen, though for many years she had been reckoned incapable of having children. This was first whispered among the courtiers, but was soon after confirmed by a proclamation in the Gazette of January 2 and 26, 1687–88, in words to this effect: "That it had pleased Almighty God to give his majesty apparent hopes, and good assurance, of having issue by his royal consort the queen, who,

through God's great goodness, was now with child ;"* wherefore his majesty appoints, that on the 15th of January, in the cities of London and Westminster ; and on the 29th in all other places of England ; and on the 29th of January and 19th of February in all places in Scotland, public thanksgiving and solemn prayer be offered up to God on this occasion ; and a form of prayer was drawn up accordingly by the Bishops of Durham, Rochester, and Peterborough ; in which were these expressions : " Blessed be that good Providence that has vouchsafed us fresh hopes of royal issue by our gracious Queen Mary ; strengthen her, we beseech thee, and perfect what thou hast begun: Command thy holy angels to watch over her continually, and defend her from all dangers and evil accidents ; that what she hath conceived may be happily brought forth, to the joy of our sovereign lord the king, the farther establishment of his crown, the happiness and welfare of the whole kingdom, and the glory of thy great name," &c.† This struck all the Protestant part of the nation with consternation, except a few ranting Tories, whose religion was at the service of the king, whensoever he should call for it. The conception was looked upon by the Jesuits as miraculous, and as the effect of a vow the queen had made to the Lady of Loret-to ; they prophesied it would certainly be a prince ; while the Protestants sighed in secret, and suspected a fraud ; the grounds of which suspicion the historians of these times have related at large.

The king, imboldened with the prospect of a popish successor, instead of venturing first upon a Parliament, published another declaration for liberty of conscience, April 27, in higher strains, and more advantageous to the papists, than the former ; the substance of it was as follows :

"JAMES REX.

" Our conduct has been such in all times as ought to have persuaded the world that we are firm and constant to our resolutions ; yet, that easy people may not be abused by the malice of crafty, wicked men, we think fit to declare that our intentions are not changed since the 4th of April, 1687, when we issued our declaration for liberty of conscience in the following terms."‡ [Here the declaration is recited at large, and then it follows.] "Ever since we granted the indulgence, we have made it our care to see it preserved without distinction, as we are encouraged to do daily by multitudes of addresses, and many other assurances we receive from our subjects of all persuasions, as testimonies of their satisfaction and duty ; the effects of which we doubt not but the next Parliament will show, and that it will not be in vain that we have resolved to use our utmost endeavours to establish liberty of conscience on such just and equal foundations as will render it unalterable, and secure to all people the free exercise of their religion forever, by which future ages may reap the benefit of what is so undoubtedly for the general good of the whole kingdom. It is such a security we desire, without the burden and constraint of oaths and tests, which have, unhappily, been made by some govern-

* Burnet, p. 167.

* Gazette, Nos. 2306 and 2316.
† Calamy's Abridgment, p. 382.
‡ Gazette, No. 2342.

ments, but could never support any. Nor could men be advanced by such means to offices and employments, which ought to be the reward of services, fidelity, and merit. We must conclude, that not only good Christians will join in this, but whoever is concerned for the wealth and power of the nation. It would, perhaps, prejudice some of our neighbours, who might lose part of those vast advantages they now enjoy, if liberty of conscience were settled in these kingdoms, which are above all others most capable of improvements, and of commanding the trade of the world. In pursuance of this great work, we have been forced to make many changes, both of civil and military officers, throughout our dominions, not thinking any ought to be employed in our service who will not contribute towards the establishing the peace and greatness of their country, which we most earnestly desire, as unbiased men may see by the whole conduct of our government, and by the condition of our fleet and of our armies, which, with good management, shall constantly be the same, and greater, if the safety or honour of the nation require it. We recommend these considerations to all our subjects, and that they will reflect on their ease and happiness, now that above three years it has pleased God to permit us to reign over these kingdoms, we have not appeared to be that prince our enemies would make the world afraid of ; our chief aim having been, not to be the oppressor, but father of our people ; of which we can give no better evidence, than by conjuring them to lay aside private animosities, as well as groundless jealousies, and to choose such members of Parliament as may do their parts to finish what we have begun, for the advantage of the monarchy over which Almighty God has placed us, being resolved to call a Parliament that shall meet in November next at farthest."

This declaration was published in the usual manner, and ordered to be read in time of Divine service in all churches and chapels in and about London, May 20th and 27th ; and in all the rest of England and Wales on the 3d and 10th of June following, upon penalty of being prosecuted in the ecclesiastical commission.* For this purpose, the bishops were required to cause it to be distributed throughout their respective dioceses : some of them, says Burnet, carried their compliance to a shameful pitch, offering up their allegiance to the king without limitation or reserve. Dr. Crew, bishop of Durham, Barlow of Lincoln,† Cartwright

of Chester, Wood of Litchfield and Coventry, Watson of St. David's, Sprat of Rochester, and Parker of Oxford, went all the lengths of the court, and promoted addresses of thanks to his majesty in the most exalted language, for the promise he had made in his late declaration, to maintain the Church of England as by law established ;* though nothing was more evident than his design to subvert it. An address came from the clergy of Chester, justifying the declaration, as issuing from the prerogative of the king's supremacy, and insisting that the clergy were obliged by what is called statute law, the rubric of their liberty, to publish what was required by the king or their bishop, and therefore they were troubled to hear of the disobedience of some of that bench, who, though they tenderly promised the Dissenters something, yet refused to do their part about the declaration, lest they should be parties to it ; which reason we, with due modesty, esteem insufficient. Herbert Croft, bishop of Hereford, published his reasons for reading the declaration, from that passage of Scripture, "Submit yourselves to every ordinance of man for the Lord's sake, whether it be to the king as supreme," &c. "Now the king commanding it to be read, without requiring our assent, consent, or allowance; I cannot see," says the bishop, "how it can be refused. If it be said this is to admit of a dispensing power, yet it is not contrary to the Word of God. If the king should aver his dispensing power to be inherent in the crown, and will use it as he pleases, I should beseech him not to exert it in so high a manner ; but after this, what have bishops to do but submit, since here is no doctrine affirmed, but only a declaration of matter of fact !"

However, the majority of the clergy were of different sentiments ; eighteen bishops, and the chief of their clergy, refused to publish the declaration, so that it was read, says Burnet,† only in seven churches in London, and in about two hundred all over England.‡ The commissioners for ecclesiastical affairs sent out citations by the king's order§, requiring the chancellors and archdeacons to send in lists of all who had obeyed, and of those who had not obeyed, the order of council ; together with the places where it had been neglected.|| Most of the bishops disobeyed, and generously undertook to stand in the gap, and screen the inferior clergy from prosecution : seven of them met at Lambeth, and after consultation signed an address, in behalf of themselves and several of

* Gazette, No. 2344.

† Dr. Grey thinks that Bishop Barlow could not be so forward a promoter of such addresses, because that, in a letter to one of his clergy, dated May 29th, he informed him that the clergy in London generally refused to read the declaration : and added, " As to myself, I shall neither persuade nor dissuade you, but leave it to your prudence and conscience whether you will or not read it.' But only this I shall advise, that if, after serious consideration, you find that you cannot read it but reluctante vel dubitante conscientia, in that case to read it with your sin, and put you to blame for doing it." Notwithstanding Bishop Barlow wrote so candidly on the matter, in this instance, he sent up a letter of thanks to King James for his first declaration, published reasons for reading the second, and asserted and vindicated, in an elaborate tract, the regal power of dispensing with penal laws. This bishop was not a consistent character ; he was timid and complying, accommo

dating himself to the times, and ready to side with the strongest. At one time he was a seeming friend to the papists, then a distinguished writer against popery. Now an enemy to the Duke of York ; then ever expressing his submission to King James ; and afterward taking the oaths to his successors.—Biographia Britannica, vol. i., article Barlow. Godwin de Præsulibus, p. 305.—Ed.

* Gazette, No. 2374.   † Page 178.

‡ Some who read it on the first Sunday, changed their minds before the second. Others declared, in their sermons, that, though they obeyed the order, they did not approve the declaration. And one, more pleasantly than gravely, told his people, that though he was obliged to read it, they were not obliged to hear it ; and stopped till they all went out, and then read it to the walls.—Burnet's History, vol. iii., p. 178.—Ed.

§ Burnet, p. 184. || Gazette, No. 2364.

their absent brethren, setting forth, "that they were not averse to the publishing his majesty's declaration for want of duty to his majesty, or due tenderness towards Dissenters, in relation to whom (say they) we are willing to come to such a temper as shall be thought fit, when the matter comes to be considered and settled in Parliament; but the declaration, being founded on such a dispensing power as may at present set aside all laws ecclesiastical and civil, appears to us illegal, and did so to the Parliament in 1672; and it is a point of such great consequence, that we cannot make ourselves party to it, so far as the reading of it in the church in time of Divine service will amount to, and distributing it all over the kingdom."[*] Signed by Sancroft, archbishop of Canterbury,[†] Lloyd, bishop of St. Asaph, Kenn of Bath and Wells, Turner of Ely, Lake of Chichester, White of Peterborough, and Trelawny of Bristol.

The king was startled at the address, and answered, in a very angry tone, "I have heard of this before, but did not believe it; I did not expect this from the Church of England, especially from some of you. If I change my mind, you shall hear from me; if not, I expect my commands shall be obeyed."[‡] And added, that they should be made to feel what it was to disobey him. The six bishops who brought the address replied, "The will of God be done."

Let the reader now judge whether the slavish doctrine of nonresistance and unlimited obedience, which the High Church party had been preaching up for above twenty years as the doctrine of the Church of England, had not brought the nation to the very verge of ruin. A doctrine destructive of all law, and of the safety of society, and which has been fatal to many crowned heads. If the king had not relied on the flattering addresses of these men, under which it seems there was a reserve, he would have stopped short, and taken other measures; but he did not perceive the mine till it was

* Burnet, p. 176. Welwood's Memoirs, p. 184, sixth edition.

† Archbishop Sancroft, in this instance, acted contrary to what had been his conduct and avowed principle in the former reign. For when, in 1681, Charles II. published his declaration to satisfy his people about dissolving his Parliament, Sancroft moved that an order should be added to it, requiring the clergy to publish it in all the churches in England. This was looked on, says Burnet, as a most pernicious precedent, by which the clergy were made the heralds to publish the king's declarations, that might, in some instances, come to be not only indecent, but mischievous. But this, whatever was now his judgment, had been his decided opinion. For, on the present occasion, Dr. Cartwright, the bishop of Chester, who had been one of the prebendaries of Durham, it appears, from a paper among the MSS. of Mr. Talents, of Shrewsbury, which fell into the hands of Mr. Archer, of Tunbridge, could produce, and did show to the king, a revised copy of the liturgy in 1661, given by Bishop Cosins to the library at Durham; in which Sancroft had added to the rubric, where it was said, "Nothing is to be read in churches but by the bishop's order or the king's order." Yet, when King James commanded a declaration in favour of the Dissenters to be read, this archbishop was among the first to oppose it, in contradiction to the clause which he had dictated, and the example he had given.—Calamy's History of his Own Life, vol. i., p. 173, 176.—ED.

1 Burnet, p. 177.

VOL. II.—U u

sprung, and blew up his whole government at once. This was the crisis upon which the fate of the nation depended.

While the king was deliberating what to do with the bishops, he was for some time in great perplexity; several of the popish nobility pressed him to retreat; but at length, at the instigation of Father Petre, Mr. Lob, and some others, he ordered the bishops to be prosecuted; and they, refusing to enter into bonds for their appearance at the King's Bench bar, on account of their peerage, were sent to the Tower by water;[*] June 8, but were discharged within a week, upon entering into bonds for small sums to answer to the information that day fortnight. On the 29th of June they were brought to the King's Bench bar in Westminster Hall, attended by several of the nobility, and a vast crowd of common people, and, after a long trial of ten hours, were acquitted;[†] upon which there was a general joy, and such loud acclamations as resounded not only in the city, but even in the army at Hounslow.[‡]

The bishop's address was printed by authority, with a satirical paraphrase, setting forth,

* The bishops, as they took boat, looked all very cheerfully; and the people flocked round them in great numbers, to condole with them, and ask their blessing. When they were confined, ten Nonconformist ministers visited them; which the king took very heinously, and sent for four of them, and reprimanded them. Their answer was, "that they could not but adhere to the bishops, as men constant and firm to the Protestant faith." Even the soldiers that kept guard would frequently drink health to the bishops; and when an order was sent to the captain of the guard to see it was done no more, the reply was, "that the soldiers were doing it at the very instant, and would, during the imprisonment of the bishops, drink no other health." So that, in an early stage of this prosecution, one of the privy council owned, "that had the king known how far the thing would have gone, he had never enjoined the reading of the declaration in the churches."—Reresby's Memoirs, p. 261, 262.—ED.

† "There were," Dr. Welwood observes, "two remarkable things in this trial. King James saw the illegality of his new-assumed prerogative exposed on one of the most solemn causes, in Westminster Hall, before one of the greatest auditories, by the counsel of the bishops; who boldly and learnedly argued against the dispensing power, and proved it, by invincible arguments, to be an open violation of the laws and Constitution of the kingdom." Another remarkable circumstance was, "that they who had contributed to enslave their country by false notions of law, now changed their opinion; and others who, through two successive Parliaments, had, at the expense of their own sufferings, stood up for the liberty of their country, did now endeavour to stretch the prerogative beyond its just limits, as they had before opposed it. So hard is it for mankind to be, at all times, and upon all turns, constant to themselves."—Welwood's Memoirs, p. 185, 186.—ED.

‡ The bishops were complimented on their victory, in the highest manner, by all orders of men. They were ranked with the primitive confessors, and loaded with praises: they were compared to the seven golden candlesticks, and to the seven stars in Christ's right hand. Their pictures were publicly sold in all printsellers' shops, and bought up in vast numbers, as guardians of the laws, liberties, and religion of their country. Their conduct affected King James more than any other opposition he met with.—Dr. Grey's Examination, vol. iii., p. 420, 421. And on the day after the trial, he was observed to labour under a very great disturbance of mind.—Sir John Reresby's Memoirs, p. 264.—ED.

that though the bishops had, without any bowels of tenderness, exercised many inhuman cruelties upon the Dissenters, they promise now to
come to a temper, but it is only such a one as
they themselves should settle in convocation ;
and though they had all along vigorously endeavoured to advance above all law that arbitrary power upon which they suppose his majesty's declaration was founded, when it could
be strained to the oppression of Dissenters, yet
now they oppose it, and are desirous in this
juncture (as in the year 1672) that the laws for
persecution should retain their force, and the
dispensing power not to be countenanced, though
designed for a general good.

But this was too late ; the controversy between the court and the Church was now no
longer to be decided by the pen ; and it was apparent, beyond contradiction, that the hearts of
the people were alienated from the king ; even
the Dissenters (says Echard) showed an unusual readiness to join the Church against their
common enemy ; and whatever might be in the
hearts of some, the Church party continued to
discover an equal willingness to coalesce with
the Dissenters. When Dr. Lloyd, bishop of St.
Asaph, passed through Oswestry, in Shropshire,
he sent for Mr. James Owen, the dissenting
minister, and ventured to acquaint him with the
secret of the Prince of Orange's invitation by
some great persons, in which he had joined ;
and added, he hoped the Protestant Dissenters
would concur in promoting the common interest, for you and we are brethren (says he) ; we
have, indeed, been angry brethren, but we have
seen our folly, and are resolved, if ever we have
it in our power, to show that we will treat you
as brethren.

Even Archbishop Sancroft,* in the circular
letter which he sent to the clergy of his province,
exhorted them to cultivate a good correspondence with the Dissenters.† The eleventh article of his letter,‡ dated July 16, has these words :
"That they (viz., the clergy) should walk in
wisdom towards them who are not of our communion ; and if there be in their parishes any
such, that they neglect not frequently to converse with them in the spirit of meekness, seeking by all good ways and means to gain and
win them over to our communion ; more especially that they have a tender regard to our
brethren the Protestant Dissenters ; that upon
occasion offered they visit them at their houses,
and receive them kindly at their own, and treat
them fairly wherever they meet them, persua-

ding them (if it may be) to a full compliance
with our church ; or, at least, that whereunto
we have already attained, we may all walk by
the same rule, and mind the same things ; and
in order thereunto, that they take opportunities
of assuring and convincing them that the bishops
of this church are really and sincerely irreconcilable enemies to the errors, superstitions, idolatries, and tyrannies of the Church of Rome ;
and that the very unkind jealousies which some
have had of us to the contrary were altogether
groundless. And in the last place, that they
warmly and affectionately join us in daily fervent prayer to the God of peace for a universal
blessed union of all Reformed churches at home
and abroad against our common enemy." Such
was the language of the Church in distress !*

It was often said, that if ever God should deliver them out of their present distress, they
would keep up their domestic quarrels no more ;†
which were so visibly and yet artfully managed
by our adversaries, as to make us devour one
another. Again, "I do assure you, and I am
certain I have the best grounds in the world for
my assurance," says one, "that the bishops,
when the happy opportunity shall offer itself,
will let the Protestant Dissenters find that they
will be better than their word given in their famous petition."‡ Remarkable are the words
of another reverend divine on the same occasion : "The bishops have under their hands
declared their dispositions to come to a temper
in matters of conformity, and there seems to be
no doubt of their sincerity. If ever God brings
us into a settled state out of the storms into
which our passions and folly, as well as the
treachery of others, have led us, it cannot be
imagined that the bishops will go off from those
moderate resolutions which they have now declared ; and they continuing firm, the weak and
indiscreet passions of any of the inferior clergy
must needs vanish. And I will boldly say, that
if the Church of England, after she has got out
of this storm, will return to hearken to the peevishness of some sour men, she will be abandoned both of God and man, and will set heaven
and earth against her. The nation sees too
clearly how dear the dispute about conformity
has cost us, to stand upon such punctilios ; and
those in whom our deliverance is wrapped up
judge too right, that ever they will be priest-
ridden in this point. And if any argument was
wanting to conclude the certainty of this point,
the wise and generous behaviour of the main
body of the Dissenters in this present juncture
has given them so just a title to our friendship,
that we must resolve to set all the world against

* Sancroft seems to have been a man of integrity.
At the Revolution he refused to take the oaths to
the new government, for which, of course, he was
suspended and deprived ; he died in retirement, November 24, 1693.—*Walton's Lives*, p. 392.—C.
† Calamy's Abridgment, vol. i., p. 385.
‡ One of the articles of this letter enjoined the clergy, four times at least in the year, to teach the people, in their sermons, "that the king's power being
in his dominions highest under God, all priests should,
upon all occasions, persuade the people to loyalty
and obedience to his majesty, in all things lawful, and
to patient submission in the rest, promoting, as far as
in them lies, the public peace and quiet of the world."
This was a renewal of certain orders, issued out to
the several bishops of their provinces, with the king's
consent, by the Archbishops of Canterbury and York,
August 4th, 1622, and repeated in the reign of Charles
II.—*High Church Politics*, p. 84.—Ed.

* It was rather a novel sight for bishops to call the
Nonconformists brethren, and to ask favours of
those whom they had been trampling under their feet.
What a change, however, will not adversity effect !
a dying profligate, with his crimes staring in his
face, commonly promises amendment should he be
restored to health ; but as his resolution is built upon
fear, it vanishes when that subsides, and he returns
to his former evil courses. The Church of England
was then in an eclipse, a very proper time to reflect
upon her past crimes, but her humility was the offspring of necessity, and therefore forgotten when she
assumed the reins. Is it possible in all this not to
discover the vilest hypocrisy ?—*Wilson's Dissenting
Churches*, vol. iv., p. 528.—C. † Burnet, p. 142.
‡ Calamy's Abridgment, vol. i., p. 336.

us if we can ever forget it; and if we do not make them all the returns of ease and favour when it is in our power to do it."*

The reader has now seen the various and strong assurances of favour, given by the Church party in distress, to the Nonconformists, all which, in a few months, entirely evaporated. Nevertheless, I am fully of opinion that the Low Church clergy meant honestly, and designed to be as good as their word; for which purpose, a scheme was proposed to review and amend the liturgy by corrections and additions, and leaving some few ceremonies indifferent; but there was another party which lay behind the curtain, and meant no more by their protestations and promises than to deliver themselves out of trouble; who, as they renounced the doctrine of nonresistance only to serve their turn, when that was effected they seemed willing to forget what they had done, and were desirous of becoming as cruel persecutors as ever; they were enemies to revolution principles; and when the Prince of Orange had rescued them, they would have sent him back from whence he came; these men were afterward distinguished by the names of Nonjurors, Jacobites, and High-fliers, whose numbers were greater than the Low Church clergy imagined. They prevailed in convocation, intimidated the friends of liberty and moderation, and put an effectual stop to all farther attempts of a general comprehension.†

While the bishops were in the Tower, and the Princess Anne at Bath, the queen was declared to be delivered of a prince on Sunday, June 10, between the hours of nine and ten in the morning. This mysterious birth was conducted with great artifice or great imprudence; no care had been taken to satisfy the Protestant part of the nation that the queen was with child, though it was ridiculed in pamphlets dispersed about Whitehall. None of the Protestant ladies were admitted to be with her, when she changed her linen; nor to see the milk in her breasts, nor to feel the child move within her; but all about her were Italian women. The place where her majesty was to lie in was unknown till a few days before her delivery; and it was oddly circumstanced as to time, most of the Protestant ladies being out of the way, and preparing for church; the Dutch ambassador, then in town, was not called to be a witness, on behalf of the Princess of Orange, the presumptive heir; all being finished in about two hours. The birth was attended with great rejoicings of the popish party; a day of public thanksgiving was appointed, on which occasion a form of thanksgiving was prepared by the Bishop of Rochester, and a new set of congratulations sent up from all parts of the kingdom.

Bishop Burnet, Mr. Echard, and others, have examined into the legitimacy of this birth with all possible exactness, but they have left the matter under great uncertainties. Some have pronounced it suppositious, and no better than the last desperate effort of the popish party to perpetuate their religion. Others, who credited the birth, have assigned very plausible reasons to suspect that the present pretender was not the queen's child, but another's clandestinely substituted. Bishop Burnet is of opinion that

the proofs of its legitimacy were defective. However, all the hopes of a Protestant successor seemed now at an end, and the joys of the papists consummated, the English reformation was expiring, and nothing short of a total subversion of the civil and ecclesiastical establishment to be expected.

The Princess of Orange being thus cut off from the succession, his highness gave greater attention to the advices he received from England of the queen's having miscarried some months before, and that therefore the present child must be suppositious. The Church party, being driven to distress from their favourite doctrine of nonresistance, fled with others, to the Prince of Orange as their last refuge, and prayed him to come over to their rescue; with this view, Admiral Russel, and several eminent persons, repaired to the Hague, on various plausible pretences, but in reality to invite the prince, and concert measures with him for his expedition to England; who received them favourably, and discovered a good disposition to espouse their cause, considering that his own right to the crown was now lost, and that if popery was established in England, Holland, and the rest of the Reformed interests, must be exposed to the utmost hazard. Little persuasion was wanting to prevail with the States-General to assist the English Protestants; but all the difficulty was to keep it secret while they were preparing for so difficult an undertaking. The States made use of the differences about the election of an Archbishop of Cologne as a reason to form an army for the security of their own borders; and the prince, who had the administration in his hands, set himself under this cover to prepare all necessaries for his intended embarcation, while Mr. Zuylestein brought him from time to time the strongest assurances of the disposition of the body of the English Protestants to appear for him at his landing, which fully fixed him in his purpose.

But the French ambassador at the Hague kept a watchful eye upon the prince's motions, and gave timely notice of the extraordinary preparations for war that were making in Holland, to his master Louis XIV., from whom King James had the first intelligence. Mr. Skelton, the English envoy at Paris, also wrote five or six letters to court on the same head but King James gave little heed to his advices, because the Prince of Orange carried it in a most courteous and respectful manner, complimenting his majesty on the birth of the Prince of Wales, and causing his name to be added to the rest of the princes of the royal family to be prayed for in his chapel. However, the French king continued to acquaint the court of England with the intended invasion, and offered to send over fifteen thousand men, or as many more as should be wanted, to his assistance; but the Earl of Sunderland, who had lately complimented the king with his religion, prevailed with his majesty not to transport an army of French papists into his dominions, lest it should confirm the suspicions of the Protestants, that he designed the overthrow of their religion and liberties.*

The king, being at length convinced of the Prince of Orange's design, ordered the fleet to

---

* Calamy's Abridgment, vol. i., p. 426.
† Calamy's Abridgment, p. 384, note.

* Burnet, p. 217.

be fitted out, and the army to be augmented; and despatched orders to Tyrconnel to send hither several regiments from Ireland, which put the people under terrible apprehensions of an Irish massacre.

September 21, his majesty issued out his proclamation for the meeting of a new Parliament, " intimating his royal purpose to endeavour a legal establishment of a universal toleration, and inviolably to preserve the Church of England in possession of the several acts of uniformity, as far as they were consistent with such a toleration.* And farther to quiet the minds of his Protestant subjects, he was content that the Roman Catholics should remain incapable of being members of the House of Commons, that so the Legislature might continue in the hands of the Protestants." September 23, the king was farther assured, by letters from the Marquis of Abbeville at the Hague, that pensionary Fagel had owned the design of the Prince of Orange to invade England.† Upon which, the king turned pale and speechless for a while, and like a distracted man looked round every way for relief, but was resolute in nothing. He postponed the meeting of the Parliament, and, by advice of his council, applied to the bishops then in town for advice what was necessary to be done to make the Church easy. The bishops moved him to annul the ecclesiastical commission, and the dispensing power; to recall all licenses and faculties for papists to keep schools; to prohibit the four pretended vicars apostolical invading the ecclesiastical jurisdiction; to fill the vacant bishoprics; to restore the charters, and to call a free and regular Parliament, by which the Church of England might be secured according to the Act of Uniformity; and provision made for a due liberty of conscience. Pursuant to this advice, the king and court began to tread backward, concluding, that if they could satisfy the bishops and recover the affection of the Church, all would do well. The Bishop of London's suspension was taken off, the ecclesiastical commission dissolved, the city charter and the fellows of Magdalen College were restored, and other illegal practices renounced;‡ but upon the news of the Prince of Orange's fleet being dispersed by a storm, and that they would hardly be able to put to sea again till next spring, his majesty withdrew his hand from any farther redress of grievances.

But the prince having repaired the damages of the storm, sailed a second time, November 1, and after a remarkable passage, in which the wind chopped about almost miraculously, in his favour,§ landed at Torbay, November 5, with about fourteen thousand men, without meeting

the king's fleet, which was at sea in order to intercept them. The prince brought over with him a declaration, dated October 10, divided into twenty-six articles, but reducible to three principal heads: 1. An enumeration of the public grievances, with regard to religion and civil government. 2. The fruitless attempts which had been made to redress those grievances: under which mention is made of the suspicious birth of the pretended Prince of Wales. 3. A protestation that the present expedition was intended for no other purpose than to procure a free and lawful Parliament; to which the prince would refer the redress of all the grievances complained of; and for the obtaining such a Parliament, his highness declares he had been most earnestly solicited by a great many lords, both spiritual* and temporal, and by many gentlemen, and other subjects of all ranks, to come over to England; and to encourage the Protestant Dissenters, his highness adds, that he would recommend to the Parliament the making such new laws as might establish a good agreement between the Church of England and all Protestant Nonconformists, and in the mean time would suffer such as would live peaceably to enjoy all due freedom in their consciences.

The king, who had relied too much on the clergy's professions of unlimited obedience, being surprised at the expressions in the prince's declaration that he had been invited by the lords spiritual, sent for the bishops then in town, and insisted not only upon their disowning the fact, but upon their signing a paper, expressing their abhorrence of the intended invasion; but they excused themselves only with a general profession of their allegiance and duty. The Church party, says Burnet,† now showed their approbation of the prince's expedition in such terms that many were surprised at it, both then and since that time; they spoke

" Heaven's favourite, for whom the skies do fight,
And all the winds conspire to guide thee right."
—*Burnet's History*, vol. iii., p. 252, Edin. edit., 12mo.
—ED.

* Dr. Grey, though he cannot deny that the Prince of Orange averred, in his declaration, that he was invited over by lords spiritual, yet is not inclined to admit the fact. He quotes, with a view to invalidate it, some letters from Sir Jonathan Trelawny, bishop of Winchester, written to Mr. Echard in the years 1716 and 1718-19, in which this concurrence of the bishops, and of themselves, in the invitation to the Prince of Orange, is absolutely denied. To these assertions is added a memorandum, made by Sir Jonathan Trelawny, of a conversation which he had with Mr. Francis Robarts, son to the Earl of Radnor, shortly after the king's coronation, on this point; who said that he had asked Commissary William Harbord, that came over with the prince, whether it was true that the bishops had taken a part in that invitation. To which Harbord answered, with a curse, " No, they were not so honest. But I caused it to be put in to raise a jealousy and hatred on both sides, that King James believing it, might never forgive them; and they, fearing he did believe it, might be provoked, for their own safety, to wish and help on his ruin." Against these authorities, it is to be observed that Bishop Burnet asserts, that the Earl of Danby drew in the Bishop of London to join in the design of bringing over the Prince of Orange; and that Trelawny, besides going into it, engaged also his brother, the Bishop of Bristol, into it.—*Grey's Examination*, vol. iii., p. 422; and *Burnet*, vol. iii., p. 214, 215,—ED.   † Burnet, p. 243, 244.

* Gazette, No. 2344.   † Ibid., No. 2386.
‡ Ibid., Nos. 2388, 2391.
§ Bishop Burnet, who minutely describes the circumstances of the Prince of Orange's landing, says, that though he was never inclined to superstition, but rather to be philosophical on all occasions, yet the strange ordering of the winds and seasons to change, just as their affairs required it, made a deep impression on himself, and on all who observed it. The famous verses of Claudian seemed to be more applicable to the prince than to him on whom they were made:

" O nimium dilecte Deo, cui militat æther,
Et conjurati veniunt ad classica venti."

openly in favour of it; they expressed their grief to see the wind so cross, and wished for a Protestant wind that might bring the prince over. His majesty, therefore, finding himself deceived in the Church party, and that he had no other reliance but his army, used all imaginable diligence to strengthen it. In obedience to the orders already given, two thousand five hundred men [chiefly papists] were landed at Chester from Ireland. Commissions were given out for raising ten new regiments of horse and foot. Three thousand Scots were ordered from that country. All the militia were commanded to be in readiness to march on the first summons; and a proclamation was issued out, requiring all horses and cattle to be removed twenty miles from those parts of the seacoast where it was apprehended the prince would land; but so great was the people's disaffection, that they paid little regard to his majesty's orders.

Soon after his highness's landing, the body of the nation discovered their inclinations so evidently, that the king lost both head and heart at once. The city of London was in confusion; reports were spread that the Irish would cut the throats of the Protestants throughout the nation in one and the same night, which awakened the people's fears, and kept them all night on their guard. When this fright was allayed, the mob rose and pulled down the mass-houses, and burned the materials in the streets: Father Petre, with the swarms of priests and Jesuits who had flocked about the court, disappeared, and retired into foreign parts; and several of the king's arbitrary ministers, who had brought him under these difficulties, forsook him and absconded. Jefferies was taken in Wapping in a sailor's habit, and would have been torn in pieces by the mob if he had not been conducted by a strong guard to the Tower, where he died before he came to his trial. The unhappy king, being left in a manner alone, retired with a small retinue to his army at Salisbury.

The Prince of Orange, having refreshed his forces, marched from Torbay to Exeter, where the nobility and gentry signed an association to support and assist his highness in pursuing the ends of his declaration, and that if any attempt was made on his person, it should be revenged on all by whom or from whom it should be made. Great numbers of common people came in to the prince at Exeter; and as soon as he marched forward towards London, Prince George of Denmark, the Dukes of Ormond, Grafton, Lord Wharton, Churchill, and others of the first distinction, deserted the army at Salisbury, and joined the prince, with a great many Protestant officers and soldiers: so that his majesty perceived that even the army, which was his last refuge, was not to be relied on; and to complete his unhappiness, Princess Anne, his younger daughter, withdrew privately from court, with the Bishop of London, who put on his buff coat and sword, and commanded a little army for her highness's defence.

Dr. Finch, son to the Earl of Winchelsea, and warden of All Souls College in Oxford, was sent to the prince from some of the heads of colleges to invite him to Oxford, and to assure him they were ready to declare for him, and that their plate should be at his service. The prince intended to have accepted their invitation, but all things being in a ferment at London, he was advised to make all the haste thither that he could.* So he sent to Oxford to excuse his visit, and to offer them the association, which was signed by almost all the heads and the chief men of the university; even by those who, being disappointed in the preferments they aspired to, became afterward his most implacable enemies.† Archbishop Sancroft also sent his compliments to the prince, and, with seven or eight other bishops, signed the association, having changed the word revenge into that of punishment. This was a sudden turn, says the bishop, from those principles which they had carried a few years before. The Dissenters went cheerfully into all the prince's measures, and were ready to sign the "association;" there were few or no Jacobites or Nonjurors among them; and throughout the whole course of King William's reign, they were among his most loyal and zealous subjects.

In this critical juncture, the queen and the young Prince of Wales were sent to France, December 9, the king himself following the latter end of the month, having first caused the writs for calling a new Parliament to be burned, and the great seal to be thrown into the Thames.‡ After his majesty's first attempt to leave the kingdom he was seized at Feversham,§ and prevailed with to return back to London; but when the prince resolved to come to Whitehall, and sent his majesty a message that he thought it not consistent with the peace of the city, and of the kingdom, for both of them to be there together, his majesty retired a second time to Rochester with the prince's consent, and after a week's stay in that place went away privately in a vessel to France, leaving a paper behind him, in which he declared, that though he was going to seek foreign assistance, he would not make use of it to overthrow the established religion or the laws of his country.

Thus ended the short and unhappy reign of James II., and with him the male line of the royal house of Stuarts, a race of princes raised up by Providence to be the scourge of these nations, for they were all chargeable with tyranny and oppression, favourers of popery and invaders of the legal Constitution of their country in Church and State. They enfeebled the nation by encouraging licentiousness of manners, and sunk a bold and brave people into contempt among foreign powers.‖

---

* Burnet, p. 257, 258.　　　† Echard, 1138.
‡ Burnet, p. 260, 263.
§ He was seized by Mr. Hunt, at that time a custom-house officer, who died so lately as the 24th of July, 1752, at Feversham. He boarded the ship in which the king was, by virtue of his office; and taking his majesty for a suspicious person, brought him ashore without knowing his quality; but was greatly terrified when he found it was the king.—*Gentleman's Magazine* for July, 1752, p. 337.—ED.
‖ It is a very common thing for writers of a certain stamp to run down the period of the Commonwealth as an age of enthusiasm and hypocrisy. Those who speak in this manner, however, would do well to bear in mind the latter times of the Stuarts; and consider if they can be at all equalled for deep-rooted hypocrisy, for the most unblushing licentiousness of manners, for the most deliberate cru-

Nothing could have been more fortunate for the Prince of Orange than the king's flight from Rochester to France, which furnished a plausible occasion for the Convention Parliament to pass a vote that the king had abdicated the crown, and that the throne was vacant; though it would have looked more like a voluntary desertion, if his majesty had gone off the first time from Feversham, and had not declared in the paper he left behind him that he was going to seek for foreign assistance; it is certain the king was frightened away by his priests, who possessed him with an apprehension that he was already a prisoner; and by his queen, who prevailed with him to consult his own and family's safety, by leaving the kingdom for the present. Thus a great and powerful monarch was in a few weeks reduced to a condition little better than that of a wandering pilgrim.*

The Prince of Orange arrived at St. James's December 18, and on the 21st following, the Bishop of London, with several of the clergy, and some dissenting ministers, waited upon his highness to congratulate him on the happy success of his glorious expedition; when his lordship acquainted his highness, in the name of the clergy, that there were some of their dissenting brethren present who were herein entirely of the same sentiments with themselves.† But on the 2d of January about ninety of the Nonconformist ministers attended the prince at St. James's in a distinct body, being introduced by the Earl of Devonshire, and the Lords Wharton and Wiltshire; when the Rev. Mr. Howe, in the name of the rest, assured his highness "of their grateful sense of his hazardous and heroical expedition, which the favour of Heaven had made so surprisingly prosperous. That they esteemed it a common felicity that the worthy patriots of the nobility and gentry of this kingdom had unanimously concurred with his highness's designs, by whose most prudent advice the administration of public affairs was devolved, in this difficult conjuncture, into hands which the nation and the world knew to be apt for the greatest undertakings, and so suitable to the present exigency of our case. They promised their utmost endeavours, in their several stations, to promote the excellent and most desirable ends for which his highness had declared. They added their continual fervent prayers to the Almighty for the preservation of his highness's person, and the success of his future endeavours for the defence and propagation of the Protestant interest throughout the Christian world; that they should all most willingly have chosen that time for the season of paying their duty to his highness, when the lord-bishop and the clergy of London attended his highness for the same purpose (which some of them did, and which his lordship was pleased condescendingly to make mention of to his highness), had their notice of that intended applica-

tion been so early as to make their more general attendance possible at that time. Therefore, though they did now appear in a distinct company, it was not on a distinct account, but on that only which was common to them, and to all Protestants; and though there were some of their brethren of eminent note whom age or present infirmities hindered from coming with them, yet they concurred in the same grateful sense of their common deliverance."* His highness received them very favourably, and returned them the following answer: "My great end was the preservation of the Protestant religion; and, with the Almighty's assistance and permission, so to defend and support the same, as may give it strength and reputation throughout the world, sufficient to preserve it from the insults and oppression of its most implacable enemies; and that more immediately in these kingdoms of England, Scotland, and Ireland; and I will use my utmost endeavours so to settle and cement all different persuasions of Protestants in such a bond of love and community, as may contribute to the lasting security and enjoyment of spirituals and temporals to all sincere professors of that holy religion."

In order to settle the government, the prince published an order, desiring all persons who had served as knights, citizens, or burgesses, in any of the Parliaments in the reign of King Charles II., to meet him at St. James's on Wednesday, the 26th of December, at ten in the morning; and that the lord-mayor and court of aldermen of the city of London would be present, and fifty of the Common Council.† This assembly desired the prince to take upon himself the administration of the government for the present; and a Convention Parliament was chosen with all expedition, in which various methods were proposed of settling the government: some were for compromising matters with King James, and others for a regency; but after long and warm debates, the throne was declared vacant, King James having abdicated the government, and broken the original contract with his people. When the question was put whether to fill the throne with a king or to appoint a regent, it was carried for the former only by two voices, fifty-one being for a king, and forty-nine for a regent, among which latter were twelve or thirteen bishops, two only, viz., the Bishops of London and Bristol, being for a king; the reason of which was, their reluctance to contradict the doctrine they had been so long preaching, viz., that the regal power was *jure divino*, and his majesty's character indelible. They had, indeed, concurred in inviting the Prince of Orange to come to the relief of their religion; but, the storm being appeased, they thought it not incumbent on them wholly to depart from their old principles, and therefore voted for a regency; but, the question being carried (says Bishop Burnet), nature was so strong in them, that it was too hard for their doctrine.‡ And a declaration being prepared for asserting and vindicating the ancient rights and liberties of the subject, the crown was offered to the Prince and Princess of Orange, the latter of whom arrived from Holland the day before; and, both having declared their acceptance, were proclaim-

elties committed under a pretence of religion, and for a barefaced invasion of the civil and religious liberties of Englishmen. A careful examination of this period must excite in every one who makes any pretensions to Christianity or a love of freedom, sentiments of rooted disgust at a political hierarchy usurping the name of a church, and at a race of kings who should have been banished at a much earlier period.—*Wilson,* vol. iv., p. 529.—C.

* Burnet, p. 274.　　　† Calamy, p. 387.

* Howe's Life, p. 142.　　† Gazette, No. 2414.
‡ Burnet, p. 282.

ed King and Queen of England, &c., February 13, 1688–89, and crowned at Westminster April 11 following, amid the joyful acclamations of all the friends of the Protestant religion and liberties of their country.*

Thus a wonderful revolution was effected with little or no effusion of blood; and it is surprising to reflect on the remarkable appearances of Divine Providence in the rise, progress, and consummation of this important event; how the court of England and the Roman Catholic powers were all infatuated or asleep while the design was forming; and when it was carrying into execution, how the winds were subservient, and the hearts of the people united till it was brought to maturity: and it will amaze all posterity to read the inconsistent and dishonourable part which the High Church clergy and their friends acted on this occasion; for, after they had preached their hereditary prince into a belief of their unlimited loyalty, and assured him in numberless addresses that their lives and fortunes were absolutely at his service; and after the University of Oxford, by a solemn decree, had declared all manner of resistance damnable and infamous to the Christian religion, they appeared among the first who resisted him; and, by opening a reserve which lay hid under their unbounded professions of duty and allegiance, let him fall into that pit out of which he could never escape. As soon as the *jure divino* king invaded the *properties of the universities*, and threatened to take down the *fences of their ecclesiastical preferments*, they invited the Prince of Orange with an armed force to their rescue; they signed an association to support and assist him; they offered him their plate, and declared for him in a body, even while their sovereign was on the throne. Nevertheless, the moment they thought their power and preferments secure, they would have retracted, and made up matters again with King James; they opposed the motion in the Convention Parliament for declaring the throne vacant; and when the government came to be settled upon King William and Queen Mary, great numbers of them would not submit, and those who did, acted a treacherous and dishonourable part to their great deliverer, throughout the course of his reign. What inconsistencies are these! What oaths and declarations can hold men who burst such bands, and cut such sacred cords asunder! The like must be observed as to their

* The Scotch also, in 1689, sent up commissioners to their majesties at Whitehall, to make a tender of their crown. On being introduced, they presented, according to the powers on which they acted, an address from the estates, the instrument of government, a recital of grievances, and a request that the convention might be converted into a Parliament. The king having promised to concur with them in all just measures for the interest of the kingdom, the coronation oath was tendered to their majesties. His conduct on this occasion deserves particular notice: it was cautious and liberal. The oath contained a clause by which they should engage to root out heresy: the king demurred on this, and declared he would not oblige himself to act as a persecutor. The commissioners replying that such was not the meaning or import of the oath, he desired them and others present to bear witness to the exception he made.— *Burnet's History*, vol. iv.; p. 34, 12mo; and *Lindsey's Historical View of the State of Unitarianism*, p. 303, note.—ED.

vows and promises to the Nonconformists, all which were forgot or broken as soon as the Church was delivered. The Dissenters acted a more consistent part; for, not being entangled with the same fetters, they went heartily into the revolution, and were among King William's best and steadiest friends, when others forsook and opposed him.*

No sooner were King William and Queen Mary settled on the throne, than the dissenting ministers in and about the city of London waited on their majesties with an address of congratulation, when Dr. Bates, at their head, made the two following speeches: —

" To the King.

"May it please your majesty,

"The series of successful events which have attended your glorious enterprise for the saving of these kingdoms from so imminent and destructive evils has been so eminent and extraordinary; that it may force an acknowledgment of the Divine Providence from those who deny it, and cause admiration in all who believe and reverence it. The beauty and speed of this happy work are the bright signatures of His hand, who creates deliverance for his people: the less of human power, the more of Divine wisdom and goodness has been conspicuous in it. If the deliverance had been obtained by fierce and bloody battles, victory itself had been dejected and sad, and our joy had been mixed with afflicting bitterness; but as the sun, ascending the horizon, dispels without noise the darkness of the night, so your serene presence has, without tumults and disorders, chased away the darkness that invaded us. In the sense of this astonishing deliverance, we desire with all possible ardency of affection to magnify the glorious name of God, the author of it, by whose entire efficacy the means have been successful; and we cannot without a warm rapture of thankfulness recount our obligations to your majesty, the happy instrument of it. Your illustrious greatness of mind, in an undertaking of such vast expense, your heroic zeal in exposing your most precious life in such an adventurous expedition, your wise conduct and unshaken respedition in prosecuting your great ends, are above the loftiest flights of language, exceed all praise. We owe to your majesty the two greatest and most valuable blessings that we can enjoy, the preservation of the true religion, our most sacred treasure; and the recovery of the falling state, and the establishing it upon just foundations. According to our duty, we promise unfeigned fidelity and true allegiance to your majesty's person and government. We are encouraged by your gracious promise, upon our first address, humbly to desire and hope that your majesty will be pleased, by your wisdom and authority, to establish a firm union of your Protestant subjects in matters of religion, by making the rule of Christianity to be the rule of conformity. Our blessed union, in the purity and peace of the Gospel, will make this church a fair and lovely type of heaven, and terrible to our

* A very edifying study is afforded here to those who love to dilate upon Puritan and Nonconformist hypocrisy! Truly might Hume say that the precious spark of liberty was fanned and kept alive by the Puritans.—C.

antichristian enemies : this will make England the steady centre from whence a powerful influence will be derived for the support of Reformed Christianity abroad. This will bring immortal honour to your name, above the trophies and triumphs of the most renowned conquerors. We do assure your majesty that we shall cordially embrace the terms of union which the ruling wisdom of our Saviour has prescribed in his Word. We shall not trespass farther on your royal patience, but shall offer up our fervent prayers to the King of kings, that he will please to direct your majesty by his unerring wisdom, and always incline your heart to his glory, and encompass your sacred person with his favour as with a shield, and make your government a universal blessing to these kingdoms."

To which his majesty was graciously pleased to make the following answer :

" I take kindly your good wishes ; and whatever is in my power shall be employed for obtaining such a union among you. I do assure you of my protection and kindness."

" To the Queen.

"May it please your majesty,

"Your happy arrival into your native country, and accession to the crown, has diffused a universal joy through this kingdom. It is an auspicious sign of public felicity, when supreme virtue and supreme dignity meet in the same person. Your inviolable firmness in the profession of the truth, and exemplary piety, are the most radiant jewels in your crown. The lustre of your conversation, unstained in the midst of tempting vanities, and adorned with every grace, recommends religion as the most honourable and amiable quality, even to those who are averse from hearing sermons, and apt to despise serious instructions and excitations to be religious. We humbly desire that your majesty would be pleased, by your wisdom and goodness, to compose the differences between your Protestant subjects in things of less moment concerning religion. We hope those reverend persons who conspire with us in the main end, the glory of God and the public good, will consent to the terms of union wherein all the Reformed churches agree. We shall sincerely address our requests to God, that he will please to pour down in a rich abundance his blessings upon your majesty's person and government, and preserve you to his heavenly kingdom."

Her majesty was graciously pleased to answer,

" I will use all endeavours for the obtaining a union that is necessary for the edifying of the Church.* I desire your prayers."

---

* This was in the spirit of a noble answer which her majesty made to Dr. Increase Mather, who was introduced to her to solicit a new charter for New-England. He represented that her subjects in that country were generally Nonconformists, but carried it with all due respect to others ; and added, that this nation had cause to bless God for the indulgence it now enjoyed under the king and her majesty. The queen answered, "It is what I am for. It is not in the power of men to believe what they please ; and therefore, I think, they should not be forced in matters of religion contrary to their persuasions and their consciences. I wish all good men were of one mind ; however, in the mean time, I would have them live

Though the joy that accompanied the revolution had a considerable influence on the choice of representatives in Parliament, yet there being no court to make interest among the people, it appeared that the late king had a party in both houses sufficient to perplex the government, who first proposed the choice of a new Parliament, in order to throw the nation into a ferment ;* but this being overruled, a bill was brought in, and passed, January 23, to turn the present Convention into a Parliament, it being wisely concluded, that those who had set the king on the throne, would be most zealous to maintain him there ; but when the House was called over, and the members required to take the oaths, eight bishops absented, viz., Dr. Sancroft, archbishop of Canterbury, Turner of Ely, Lake of Chichester, Kenn of Bath and Wells, White of Peterborough, Thomas of Worcester, Lloyd of Norwich, and Frampton of Gloucester ; however, that they might recommend themselves by a show of moderation, before they withdrew they moved the House of Lords for a bill of toleration, and another of comprehension, which were drawn up accordingly by the Earl of Nottingham, and were much the same with those prepared for the House of Commons in King Charles II.'s time, during the debates about the Bill of Exclusion.

The clergy in general took the oaths, but it became visible that many among them took them only as oaths of submission to usurpers, with this reserve, that it was still lawful to assist King James if he should attempt to recover the crown, and that he was still their king *de jure*, though the Prince of Orange was king *de facto*, contrary to the plain meaning of the words ; but the clergy broke through all these fetters, says the bishop,† to the reproach of their profession ; and the prevarication of so many in so sacred a matter, contributed not a little to the atheism of the age. Indeed, they had embarked so far in their doctrines of absolute submission and the Divine right of monarchy, that they knew not how to disengage themselves with honour or conscience. Many suffered the time limited for taking the oaths to elapse, and yet officiated afterward contrary to law. They threatened the Church with a new separation, which terrified the moderate clergy, and put a stop to all amendments of the liturgy for the ease of Dissenters, lest the Nonjurors should gain over great numbers of the laity, by pretending to abide by the old liturgy, in opposition to the reformed one. Thus the Nonconformists were sold to the Jacobites ; for the timidity of their real friends ; for the High Church party discovered an irreconcilable enmity to an accommodation, and seemed only to wish for an occasion to renew old severities. Those who had moved for a comprehension, and brought the bill into the House of Lords, acted a very disingenuous part, says Burnet ;‡ for while they studied to recommend themselves, by seeming to countenance the bill, they set on their friends to oppose it, representing the favourers of it as enemies to the Church.§

peaceably, and love one another."—*Increase Mather's. Life*, p. 49.—ED.

* Burnet, vol. iv., p. 7, 8, Edin. ed., 12mo.

† Ibid., vol. iii., p. 303.   ‡ Ibid.

§ No one can study the merits of this history with-

When the king came to the House, March 16, he made the following speech :*

" My Lords and Gentlemen,

" Now I have occasion of coming hither to pass these bills, I shall put you in mind of one thing which will conduce much to our settlement, as a settlement will to the disappointment of our enemies. I am, with all the expedition I can, filling up the vacancies that are in the offices and places of trust by this late revolution. I hope you are sensible there is a necessity of some law to settle the oaths to be taken by all persons to be admitted to such places. I recommend it to your care to make a speedy provision for it ; and as I doubt not but you will sufficiently provide against papists, so I hope you will leave room for the admission of all Protestants that are willing and able to serve. This conjunction in my service will tend to the better uniting you among yourselves, and the strengthening you against your common enemies." It appears, by this, that King William was for taking off the test, and abrogating the penal laws, as far as related to dissenting Protestants, though the Parliament were of another mind.

When a bill was brought into the House of Lords for abrogating the oaths of allegiance and supremacy, and framing other oaths in their stead, a committee was appointed to insert a clause to take away the necessity of receiving the sacrament in order to make a man capable of enjoying any office, employment, or place of trust ; but when the clause was reported to the House, it was rejected by a considerable majority, the Earls of Stamford and Chesterfield, the Lords Lovelace, Delamere, North and Grey, Wharton, and Vaughan, entering their protests.†

After this another clause was offered, by which it was provided that such should be sufficiently qualified for any office who, within a year before or after their admission, did receive the sacrament, either according to the usage of the Church of England, or in any other Protestant congregation, and could produce a certificate under the hands of the minister, and two other creditable persons, members of such a congregation. The question being put whether this clause should be a part of the bill, it

passed in the negative, the Lords Oxford, Lovelace, Wharton, Mordaunt, Montague, and Paget entering their protests.*

It was proposed farther, in a committee of the House of Lords, to dispense with kneeling at the sacrament ; but when the question was put whether to agree with the committee in leaving out the clause, the votes were equal, and so, according to the usage of the House, it passed in the negative.† The like fate attended the motion about the cross in baptism, and explaining the words assent and consent in subscription. Thus the several attempts for alterations in the church-service, at a time when the Legislature was in a temper for accommodating lesser differences, were frustrated by a rising party of Jacobites and Tories, who threatened the new government with a revolt unless they were humoured ; and, for fear of them, all promises of accommodation with the Dissenters were of no avail.

Soon after a bill for toleration‡ of Protestant Dissenters was brought into the House, and had an easy passage ; though some proposed that the act should be only temporary, as a necessary restraint, that the Dissenters might so demean themselves as to merit the continuance of it, when the term of years first granted should expire ; but this was rejected. Bishop Burnett says that his zeal for this act lost him his credit with the Church party, by which it appears they did not much like it. It is entitled " An Act for exempting their Majesties' Protestant Subjects dissenting from the Church of England from the Penalties therein mentioned." But the Corporation and Test Acts were

* One reason on which the Lords protested was, " that mysteries of religion and Divine worship are of Divine original, and of a nature so wholly distinct from the secular affairs of public society, that they cannot be applied to those ends ; and therefore the Church, by the law of the Gospel, as well as common prudence, ought to take care not to offend either tender consciences within itself, or give offence to those without, by mixing their sacred mysteries with secular interests."—A Complete Collection of Protests, p. 64, 65.— ED. -† Burnet, p. 155.
‡ " The Act of Toleration," remarks a late writer, " was another interference of the State to check the power of ecclesiastics, but without altering the constitution of the Church. Laymen had before declared what should be deemed heresy in the spiritual courts ; they now exempted some descriptions of Dissenters wholly from their jurisdiction, while all others, and oppugners of the Trinity by name, were expressly reserved for the persecuting spirit of the Church to operate upon." How truly then might Mr. Locke, writing to Limborch (Locke's Works, vol. iv., p. 406), soon after the passing of this act, say, " Tolerantiam apud nos jam tandem lege stabilitatem, te anto hæc audiisse, nullus dubito. Non ea forsan latitudine quâ tu et tui similes veri, et sine ambitione vel invidiâ, Christiani optarent. Sed aliquid est prodire tenus. His initiis jacta spero sunt libertatis et pacis fundamenta, quibus stabilienda olim erat Christi ecclesia."—High Church Politics, p. 66. In English thus : " I doubt not before this you have heard that toleration is at last established here by law. Not, indeed, with that latitude that you, and other Christians like you, unambitious and unprejudiced, and lovers of truth, might wish. But it is a great point to proceed so far. In these beginnings, I hope, are laid those foundations of liberty and peace, on which the Church of Christ will be finally established."—Toulmin's History of Protestant Dissenters, p. 25.—C. § History, p. 14.

out carefully perusing the admirable works of Bishop Burnet. His History of the Reformation and of his own Times are indispensable to a full and adequate perception of the dangers, cruelties, and difficulties of this period. The History of the Reformation is reprinted by the Appletons at a very cheap price, and should be widely circulated.—C.
* Gazette, No. 2436.
† The protests of the dissentient peers were grounded on the following reasons : " That a hearty union among Protestants is a greater security to the Church and State than any test that could be invented ; that this obligation to receive the sacrament is a test on Protestants rather than on papists ; that so long as it continued, there could not be that hearty and thorough union among Protestants as has always been wished, and is at this time indispensably necessary ; and, lastly, that a greater caution ought not to be required from such as were admitted into offices than from the members of the two houses of Parliament, who were not obliged to receive the sacrament to enable them to sit in either house."—A Complete Collection of Protests, p. 62, 63 ; and Birch's Life of Tillotson, p. 170, 171.—ED.

not inserted in this act, and therefore remain in full force: there is an exception, likewise, of such as deny the doctrine of the Trinity; and Quakers are excused taking the oaths to the government, upon their making a solemn declaration therein mentioned. This act excuses all Protestant Dissenters from the penalties of the laws therein mentioned for not coming to church, provided they take the oaths, and subscribe the declarations therein mentioned. And dissenting ministers are tolerated on the like conditions, and on their subscribing the doctrinal articles of the Church of England. But this being the basis and boundary of their present liberty, I have inserted the act in the Appendix, No: XIII.

While the bill for a toleration was depending, a motion was made in the House of Lords for a comprehension, which was received, and some progress made towards effecting it; but a proviso being offered, and pressed with great earnestness by some temporal lords, that, in imitation of the acts passed in the reigns of King Henry VIII. and Edward VI., a number of persons, both of clergy and laity, might be empowered to prepare materials for such a reformation of the Church as might be fit to offer the king and Parliament, it was warmly debated, and at length rejected by a small majority. Bishop Burnet* was against the proviso, for fear of offending the clergy, who would look upon it as taking the reformation out of their hands; but adds, " I was convinced soon after that I had taken wrong measures, and that the method proposed by the Lords was the only one like to prove effectual." Dr. Tillotson, being of the same mind with Burnet, advised the king to refer the affair to a synod of divines, whose determinations he apprehended would stop the mouths of papists, who reproached our reformation as built chiefly on parliamentary authority, and would be better received by the body of the clergy.†

Accordingly, it was agreed in council that a select number of learned divines should be appointed by the royal mandate, to meet and consult about the most proper methods of healing the wounds of the Church; that their determinations should be laid before the Convocation, and from thence receive the sanction of Parliament. Agreeably to this resolution, the king issued out a commission to thirty divines, of which ten were bishops, whose names were,

Dr. Lamplugh, Archbishop of York.
Compton, Bishop of London.
Mew, Bishop of Winchester.
Lloyd, Bishop of St. Asaph.
Sprat, Bishop of Rochester.
Smith, Bishop of Carlisle.
Sir Jonathan Trelawney, Bishop of Exeter.
Dr. Burnet, Bishop of Sarum.
Humphreys, Bishop of Bangor.
Stratford, Bishop of Chester.

To these were added the following divines:

Dr. Stillingfleet,	Dr. Alston,	Dr. Beaumont,
Tillotson,	Scot,	Goodman,
Sharp,	Grove,	Battely,
Aldridge,	Patrick,	Tennison,
Hall,	Maggot,	Fowler,
Montague,	Kidder,	Williams.
Beveridge.	Jane,	

* Burnet, vol. iv., p. 14.
† Birch's Life of Tillotson, p. 179.

Their commission was as follows:—
" Whereas the particular forms of Divine worship, and the rites and ceremonies appointed to be used therein, being things in their own nature indifferent and alterable, and so acknowledged, it is but reasonable that, upon weighty and important considerations, according to the various exigencies of times and occasions, such changes and alterations should be made therein as to those that are in place and authority should from time to time seem either necessary or expedient.

" And whereas the Book of Canons is fit to be reviewed, and made more suitable to the state of the Church; and whereas there are defects and abuses in the ecclesiastical courts and jurisdictions; and particularly, there is not sufficient provision made for the removing of scandalous ministers, and for the reforming of manners, either in ministers or people; and whereas it is most fit that there should be a strict method prescribed for the examination of such persons as desire to be admitted into holy orders, both as to their learning and manners:

" We, therefore, out of our pious and princely care for the good order, edification, and unity of the Church of England, committed to our charge and care, and for the reconciling as much as is possible of all differences among our good subjects, and to take away all occasion of the like for the future, have thought fit to authorize you, &c., or any nine of you, whereof three to be bishops, to meet from time to time as often as shall be needful, and to prepare such alterations of the liturgy and canons, and such proposals for the reformation of the ecclesiastical courts, and to consider of such other matters, as in your judgments may most conduce to the ends above mentioned."*

The committee having assembled in the Jerusalem Chamber, a dispute arose about the legality of their commission; Sprat, bishop of Rochester, one of King James's ecclesiastical commissioners, being of the number, they pretended to fear a premunire, though there was not so much as a shadow for such a pretence, the king's supremacy, if it means anything, empowering him to appoint proper persons to prepare matters for the Legislature: however, upon this debate, Mew, bishop of Winchester, Sprat of Rochester, with Dr. Jane and Dr. Aldridge, withdrew.† Some of them declared plainly they

* Life of Archbishop Tennison, p. 10, &c.
† ALDRIDGE AND JANE.—These men were of much note in their day, and are deserving of some notice here. Dr. Henry Aldridge, born in Westminster in 1647, was a pupil under the famous Dr. Busby, and was elected a student of Christ Church, Oxford, 1662. In due time he took orders, and became an eminent tutor. In 1681 be was installed canon of Christ Church, and became its dean in 1689. He presided over this college with great zeal for its interest, and being a single man, displayed much munificence in its patronage. That beautiful piece of architecture called Peckwater Quadrangle was designed by him, He annually published as a new-year's gift to his students a piece of some ancient Greek author. He wrote a system of logic, which passed through many editions; and, with Bishop Sprat, he revised Clarendon's History of " The Rebellion." He had a great share in the popish controversies in the reign of James II. In 1702 he was chosen prolocutor of the Convocation. He died at Christ Church 14th December, 1710, in the sixty-third year of his age. He

were against all alterations whatsoever; they thought too much would be done for the Dissenters in granting them an act of toleration, and they would do nothing to make conformity easier. They said, farther, that altering the customs and constitutions of the Church, to gratify a peevish and obstinate party, was likely to have no other effect than to make them more insolent.* But was it ever tried? Did the Convocation or Parliament make a single abatement from the year 1662 to this time? If the experiment had been tried, and proved ineffectual, the blame might have been cast upon the Dissenters; but to call them peevish and obstinate, without offering them any, even the smallest concessions, deserves no better a name than unjust calumny. Was there no obstinacy and peevishness on the side of the Church in retreating from so many promises without a single offer? But it was said, farther, that the Church, by proposing these alterations, seemed to confess that she had hitherto been in the wrong, and that the attempt would divide them among themselves, and lessen people's esteem for the liturgy, if it appeared that it wanted correction. Such were the reasonings of those high divines, if they deserve the name, some of whom but a few months before had made the warmest pretences to a spirit of moderation!

It was alleged on the other side, that if a few corrections or explanations were allowed, there was reason to hope it would bring over many of the people, if not the teachers themselves; at least, if the prejudices of the present Dissenters were too strong, it might have a good effect on the next generation; nor could it be any reproach to the Church, since the offers were made only in regard to their weakness. Ritual matters were of an indifferent nature, and became necessary in virtue only of the authority that enjoined them, therefore it was an unreasonable stiffness to deny any abatements, in order to heal the Church's divsions. Great changes had been made by the Church of Rome in

is described as a universal scholar, and to have had a fine taste in architecture. His modesty and humility were evident and acknowledged.—*British Biography*, book viii, p. 42, *note.*

Dr. William Jane was the son of Joseph Jane, of Liskeard, Cornwall, author of "Ikon Iclastos," in answer to Milton. He was member for Liskeard in the Long Parliament, and was a great sufferer for his adherence to the house of Stuart. Dr. Jane was born 1644, educated at Westminster, and elected student at Christ Church, 1660. He became lecturer of Carfax Church, Oxford, chaplain to Bishop Compton, and prebendary of Paul's Cathedral. In 1678 he was installed canon of Christ Church. In 1679 he proceeded doctor of divinity. In 1681 he was appointed regius professor of divinity. In 1685 he was made Dean of Gloucester, and held it with the precentorship of the church at Exeter. He lived some time after Queen Anne's accession to the throne, but received no preferment, and died 1707. He published a treatise entitled "The present Separation self-condemned, and proved to be Schism." He was also considered to have the chief hand in penning the decree and judgment of the University of Oxford against certain seditious books and damnable doctrines passed in the Convocation July, 1683, presented to and approved by Charles II., but burned by the hangman in pursuance to an order of the House of Lords in 1720!—See *Birch's Life of Tillotson,* p. 188; and *British Biography*, vol. ix., p. 32, *note.*—C.
* Burnet, vol. iv. p. 44.

her rituals; and among ourselves since the Reformation, in the reigns of King Edward VI., Queen Elizabeth, King James, and King Charles II., and it seemed necessary at this time to make the terms of communion as large as might be, that so a greater number might be brought over, since, by the Act of Toleration, they might dissent with safety.

But while these matters were debating, the Jacobite party took hold of the occasion to inflame men's minds against the government. It was pretended the Church was to be pulled down, and Presbytery established: the universities took fire, and declared against alterations, and against all who promoted them, as men who intended to undermine the hierarchy. Severe reflections were cast on the king himself, as not being in the interest of the Episcopacy, for the cry of the Church's danger was raised by the enemies of the government, as that under which they thought they might safely shelter their evil designs. Great interest was made in the choice of Convocation men, to whom the determinations of the committee were to be referred, so that it was quickly visible that the laudable designs of the king and the ecclesiastical commissioners would prove abortive.

However, the committee continued their work till they had finished it; they had before them all the exceptions that either the Puritans before the war, or the Nonconformists since the Restoration, had made to the church-service.* They had also many propositions and advices that had been suggested at several times, by many of our bishops and divines, upon these heads; matters were well considered, and freely and calmly debated, and all was digested into an entire correction of everything that seemed liable to any just exception. Dr. Nichols says, they began with reviewing the liturgy, and first in examining the calendar; they ordered, in the room of the Apocryphal lessons, certain chapters of canonical Scripture to be read, that were more to the people's advantage; Athanasius's creed being disliked, by reason of the damnatory clauses, it was left to the ministers choice to use it, or change it for the Apostles' Creed.† New Collects were drawn up, more agreeable to the Epistles and Gospels, for the whole course of the year, with that elegance and brightness of expression, says the doctor, and such a flame of devotion, that nothing could more affect and excite the hearts of the hearers, and raise up their minds towards God: they were first prepared by Dr. Patrick; Dr. Burnet added to them farther force and spirit; Dr. Stillingfleet afterward examined them with great judgment, carefully weighing every word in them; and Dr. Tillotson had the last hand, giving them some free and masterly strokes of his sweet and flowing eloquence. Dr. Kidder made a new version of the Psalms, more agreeable to the original. Dr. Tennison made a collection of the words and expressions throughout the liturgy which had been excepted against, and proposed others in their room that were clear and plain, and less liable to exception—singing in cathedrals was to be laid aside—the Apocryphal lessons were to be omitted, together with the legendary saints' days—the cross in baptism to be left to the choice of the parent—and kneel-

* Burnet, p. 44. † Apparatus, p. 95, 96.

ing at the sacrament to be indifferent—the intention of Lent fasts was declared to consist only in extraordinary acts of devotion, not in distinction of meats—the word priest was to be changed for minister—the use of the surplice is left to the discretion of the bishop, who may dispense with it, or appoint another to read the service—godfathers and godmothers in baptism may be omitted if desired, and children presented in their parents' names—reordination of those who had been ordained by presbyters was to be only conditional ; but these, with some other useful alterations in the litany, communion-service, and canons, will not be known till the papers themselves are made public. However, these concessions and amendments would, in all probability, have brought in three parts in four of the Dissenters.*

, While these things were debating in Parliament, and among the commissioners, an address was presented, April 19, praying that, according to the ancient custom and usage of the kingdom in time of Parliament, his majesty would issue out his writ for calling a convocation of the clergy to be advised with in ecclesiastical matters, assuring his majesty that it was their intention forthwith to proceed to the consideration of giving ease to the Protestant Dissenters ; but when they met, it quickly appeared that the High Church party were superior to the moderate, by their choosing Dr. Jane,† who drew up the Oxford decree, prolocutor, in preference to Dr. Tillotson.‡ His

majesty sent a letter, or message, by the Earl of Nottingham, assuring them of his constant favour and protection, and that he had summoned them, not only because it was usual upon holding Parliaments, but out of a pious zeal to do everything that might tend to the best establishment of the Church of England, and desiring them to consider of such things as by his order should be laid before them, with a due and impartial zeal for the peace and good of the Church. But there was no room for his majesty's interposition, the Lower House of Convocation quickly coming to a resolution not to enter into any debates with relation to alterations ; and it was not without difficulty carried to make a decent address to the king, thanking him for his promise of protection. And the address which the bishops sent down, acknowledging the protection which the Protestant religion in general, and the Church of England in particular, had received from his majesty, the Lower House would not agree to it, because it imported their owning some common union with the foreign churches.* They would thank his majesty for his care to establish the Church of England, whereby the interest of the Protestant churches abroad would be better secured, but would not insert the words "this and all other Protestant churches," as the bishop had desired.

The Bishop of London, in his answer to the prolocutor's speech, told them that they ought to endeavour a temper of things not essential to religion ; and that it was their duty to show the same indulgence and charity to the Dissenters under King William which some of the bishops and clergy had promised in their addresses to King James.† But all these promises, says Bishop Burnet, were entirely forgotten. It was in vain, therefore, to refer the amendments of the ecclesiastical commissioners to a number of men who had resolved to admit of no alterations ; and it is thought that if the Act of Toleration had been left to their decision, it would have miscarried.‡ The king, observing such a want of temper, broke up the sessions ; and seeing they were in no disposi-

---

* Calamy's Abridgment, vol. i, p. 452, 464. See, also, Birch's Life of Tillotson, p. 182, 196. There is little reason to doubt this statement, and the careful observer of English dissent must be convinced of the truth of Mr. Neal's remark.—C.

† The election of Dr. Jane to be prolocutor, as it showed the sentiments and spirit of a great majority, so it was the principal occasion that nothing succeeded. For as soon as he got into the chair, he addressed the Lower House in a speech, which, besides extolling the Church of England above all other Christian communities, he concluded with these words : " Nolumus leges Angliæ mutare ;" i. e., " We will not change the laws of England ;" and, in the progress of the session, he opposed everything that was intended or proposed by the royal commission.—Bishop Compton's Life, p. 52 ; and Life of Dr. Prideaux, p. 54. The conclusion of the prolocutor's speech, it is excellently observed in a late valuable publication, was " to be admired from the mouth of an old English baron ; consistent, perhaps, with the declaration of a conclave, if matters of faith and worship were in agitation there ; but ill suited, to the greatest degree, on such an occasion, to the character of a Protestant divine."—Hints, &c., by a Layman, p. 27, fourth edition.—ED.

‡ It is disgraceful to human nature, and painful to the generous mind, that the most liberal and excellent designs are defeated by revenge and disappointed ambition. This was the case in the affair before us. The election of Dr. Jane was effected by the intrigues of two noble lords, who, being disappointed in their expectations of advancement to some of the higher employments, after the Revolution, on account of their relation to the queen, out of resentment contrived to have Dr. Jane called to the chair, that they might baffle what was intended by the Convocation, and so embarrass government. He was also, on the like principles, a man fit for their purpose ; for having been refused the see of Exeter, before promised to Bishop Trelawney, which he asked when he was sent from the University of Oxford to make an offer of their plate to the Prince of

Orange, he was so disgusted, that he became a professed enemy to King William.—Life of Dr. Prideaux, p. 54, 55.—ED.

* This was the first foundation of the differences in the Convocation, which have ever since been kept up, to the grief of pious minds, and to the disgrace of the clergy. For the inferior clergy not agreeing to this address, another address was drawn up and presented to the king by the Bishop of London, six of his brethren, and several doctors in divinity, who were solemnly introduced to his majesty, sitting on his throne in the Banqueting House, by the lordchamberlain.—Bishop Compton's Life, p. 54, 55.—ED.

† Bishop Compton closed his speech, which breathed a different spirit from that of Dr. Jane, with these words of Joseph's to his brethren, " Ne multi animi in consiliis vestris ;" thereby exhorting them to unanimity and concord.—Bishop Compton's Life, p. 53.—ED.

‡ It marks the mischief and the evil of the spirit of opposition, that among the other instances in which the design of holding this convocation miscarried, was the failure of an attempt to restore family devotion ; for a book, containing directions and forms for family worship, was provided to be authorized by this convocation. It was left in the hands of Dr. Williams, bishop of Chichester, but has been since lost.—Dr. Prideaux's Life, p. 61, 65.—ED.

tion to do good, they were kept from doing mis-chief by prorogations for a course of ten years. This was the last fruitless attempt* for a comprehension of Dissenters within the Establishment; and such was the ungrateful return that these stubborn churchmen made to those who had assisted them in their distress! For it ought to stand upon record, that the Church of England had been *twice rescued from the most imminent danger* by men for whose satisfaction they would not move a pin nor *abate a ceremony*; first in the year 1660, when the Presbyterians restored the king and Constitution without making any terms for themselves; and now again at the Revolution, when the Church fled for succour to a Presbyterian prince, and was delivered by an army of fourteen thousand Hollanders, of the *same principles with the English Dissenters;* and how uncivilly those troops were afterward used, is too ungrateful a piece of history to remember.

But besides the strong disposition of the High Church clergy and their friends to return to their allegiance to King James, there was another incident that sharpened their resentments against the king and the Dissenters, which was his majesty's consenting to the abolition of Episcopacy in Scotland, which could not be prevented without putting all his affairs into the utmost confusion; the bias of that people was strong to presbytery, and the more so, because the Episcopal party went almost universally into King James's interests, so that the

---

* I am tempted to give here the reflections of an admirable piece, which report ascribes to a *noble* pen. "The prolocutor's veto has hitherto proved triumphant; and we have too much reason to apprehend that, on one pretence or other, these laws, binding the consciences of men, will become, in effect, as unalterable as those of the Medes and Persians ever were; though probably, in these days, few will venture to hold a doctrine so thoroughly repugnant to all religious liberty. Such, however, was the fate of this attempt to render the service of the Established Church as pure as possible, and to clear away those parts which, from that day to the present, continue to offend so many respectable and conscientious persons. Considering the character and abilities of those who undertook the task, it can never be sufficiently lamented that their endeavours proved so unsuccessful." For Archbishop Wake, speaking of them before the Lords, while he was Bishop of Lincoln, thus expresses himself: "They were a set of men, than which this church was never, at any one time, blessed with either wiser or better, since it was a church; and a design that, I am persuaded, would have been for the interest and peace of our Church and State, had it been accomplished." And when we find among them names whose memory we revere, Compton, Lloyd, Burnet, among the bishops, with Tillotson, Stillingfleet, Patrick, Sharpe, Kidder, &c., among the others, it is clear that posterity has confirmed the testimony of this learned and sagacious prelate, and regrets the more the loss of their beneficent intentions.—*Hints, &c., by a Layman,* p. 27–29. To the names mentioned by this writer we would particularly add Dr. Humphrey Prideaux, as he was not only a great friend to the scheme then on foot for a comprehension with the Dissenters, but published a piece in favour of that design, under the title of "A Letter to a Friend relating to the present Convocation at Westminster," which was highly applauded by moderate and candid men, and of which several thousands were sold within a fortnight after its publication.—*British Biography,* vol. vii., p. 224, 225.—ED.

Presbyterians were the only friends the king had in that kingdom.* There was a convention called in Scotland like that in England, who on the 11th of April, the day on which King William and Queen Mary were crowned in England, passed judgment of forfeiture on King James, and voted the crown of Scotland to King William and Queen Mary. They drew up a claim of rights, by one article of which it was declared, that the reformation in Scotland having begun by a party among the clergy, prelacy in the Church was a great and insupportable grievance to the kingdom. The bishops and their adherents having left the convention, because not summoned by writ from King James, the Presbyterians had a majority of voices; whereupon the abolishing Episcopacy in Scotland was made a necessary article of the new settlement. The Episcopal party sent the Dean of Glasgow to King William to know his intentions concerning them, who answered he would do all he could to preserve them consistent with a full toleration to the Presbyterians, provided they concurred in the new establishment; but if they opposed it, he should not enter into a war for their sakes. The bishops, instead of submitting to the Revolution, resolved unanimously to adhere firmly to King James, and declared in a body with so much zeal against the new settlement, that it was not possible for the king to support them. The clergy sent for King James into Scotland, and the Earl of Dundee collected some thousands of Highlanders to make a stand; but General Mackay, who was sent with a body of forces to disperse them, routed them at a place called Killicranky, and killed the Earl of Dundee upon the spot. So that Episcopacy in Scotland fell a sacrifice to the interest of King James.†

But though it was impossible to stop the torrent of the Scots people's zeal for Presbytery, and though the king had only Presbyterians on his side in that kingdom, yet the suffering it to take place increased the disaffection of the English clergy. Reports of the king's dislike of the hierarchy were spread with great industry; the leading men of both universities were possessed with it, says Burnet,‡ though the king had joined in communion with the Church, and taken the sacrament according to law; but it was given out that men zealous for the Church were neglected, and that those who were indifferent to the ceremonies were promoted. His majesty promised the Scots clergy to moderate matters in their favour, and Lord Melvil, secretary of state, engaged very solemnly for the same purpose; but when the Presbyterians threatened to desert the court if they were deserted by them, Melvil thought it the king's interest to secure them in all events, which could not be done but by abandoning the ministers of the Episcopal persuasion. Such, therefore, as refused to read the proclamation of King William and Queen Mary by the prefixed day were deprived of their livings; which being published up and down England, and much aggravated, raised the aversion of the friends of the Church

---

* Burnet, vol. iv., p. 32.

† Mr. Mann, in his judicious lectures on Church History, observes, that the abolition of Episcopacy in Scotland was called for by the whole nation, p. 415. —C.

‡ Burnet, p. 40

against the Presbyterians so high, says Bishop Burnet,[*] that they began to repent their having granted a toleration to a party who, where they prevailed, showed so much fury against those of the Episcopal persuasion. It ought, however, to be remembered, that this was a government case; that the fate of the Revolution in that kingdom depended upon it; and that the bishops and Episcopal clergy, almost to a man, were determined Jacobites, and refused to take the oaths to King William and Queen Mary. Besides, what reason had the Scots Presbyterians to trust the Episcopal clergy, when it was in their power to do themselves justice? Had they not deceived them out of their discipline in 1662, and persecuted them cruelly ever since! Whoever peruses the dreadful sufferings of the Kirk in the reign of Charles II., will judge how far they had reason to replace them in the saddle, and deliver the reins into their hands.

But the disaffection of the High Church clergy stopped not short of the king himself, who was made uneasy by their malignant spirit, and restless endeavours to clog the wheels of his government;[†] insomuch that his majesty sometimes declared, with more than ordinary vehemence, that he would not stay in England and hold an empty name; that it was not easy to determine which was best, a commonwealth or kingly government; but he was sure the worst of all governments was a king without treasure, and without power. He once resolved to return to Holland, and leave the government in the queen's hands, imagining they would treat her better;[‡] and he communicated his design to the Marquis of Carmarthen, the Earl of Shrewsbury, and others, who besought him, with tears, to change his resolution, and at last prevailed: but had his majesty declared this from the throne, the nation was in a temper to have done him justice on the incendiaries; for notwithstanding their clamours, they knew their desperate situation if the king should desert them, having renounced their allegiance to King James, and gone such lengths as he could never forgive. But King William, having a generous mind, imagined they might be gained by gentleness and kindness, and therefore took up with a motley ministry, which distressed him to the last. Thus the Tories and High Church clergy enjoyed the advantages of this glorious revolution, while they acted a most ungrateful part towards their deliverer, and a most unkind and ungenerous one to their dissenting brethren.§

Nor have these gentlemen ceased to discover their enmity to the Dissenters since that time, as often as the power has been in their hands. It was impossible to injure them while King William lived, but no sooner was Queen Anne advanced to the throne, than they endeavoured to cramp the toleration by the bill against occasional conformity, which was brought into the House one session after another, till at length it obtained the royal assent in the latter end of the year 1711, under the specious title of "An Act to preserve the Protestant Religion, and to confirm the Toleration, and farther to secure the Protestant Succession." It makes some few concessions in support of the toleration, but then it enacts, "that if any persons in office, who by the laws are obliged to qualify themselves by receiving the sacrament or test, shall ever resort to a conventicle or meeting of Dissenters for religious worship during the time of their continuance in such office, they shall forfeit twenty pounds for every such offence, and be disqualified for any office for the future, till they have made oath that they have entirely conformed to the Church, and not been at any conventicle for the space of a whole year." So that no person in the least office in the customs, excise, or Common Council, &c., could ever enter the doors of a meeting-house. But the reader may peruse the act at large in the Appendix, No. xiv.

In the last year of Queen Anne the toleration was farther straitened by an act to prevent the growth of schism; for with these gentlemen all Dissenters are schismatics: and in order to prevent their increase, the education of their children was taken out of the hands of their friends, and intrusted only with such who were full and entire Conformists.

And if any schoolmaster or tutor should be willingly present at any conventicle of Dissenters for religious worship, he shall suffer three months' imprisonment, and be disqualified, as above, from teaching school for the future. The act was to take place August 1, 1714, the very day the queen died; but his late majesty King George I. being fully satisfied that these hardships were brought upon the Dissenters for their steady adherence to the Protestant succession in his illustrious house, against a Tory and Jacobite ministry, who were paving the way for a popish pretender, procured the repeal of them in the fifth year of his reign. The last-mentioned act, with the repeal, is inserted in the Appendix, Nos. xv. and xvi., together with a clause which forbids the mayor, or other magistrate, to go into any meeting for religious worship with the ensigns of his office.

Many of the ejected ministers of 1662, and

* Burnet, p. 42.   † Ibid., p. 49.
‡ Ibid., p. 55, 56.
§ After having effected a glorious revolution, and delivered the country from a most intolerable yoke and grievous slavery, both civil and religious, William was called to a better world. Smollet, the historian, caricatures him in a few words: "William was a fatalist in religion, indefatigable in war, enterprising in politics, dead to all the warm and generous emotions of the human heart, a cold relation, an indifferent husband, a disagreeable man, an ungracious prince, and an imperious sovereign." Another writer of as nice taste, just discrimination, and accurate judgment as Dr. Smollet, has given a very different account, with this in his favour—that he personally knew him: he thus speaks: "William had a mind vast and comprehensive, his imagination

fruitful and sprightly, his memory large and tenacious; his thoughts were wise and secret, his words few but comprehensive, his actions many and brave; he was religious without superstition, just without rigour, merciful without partiality, and, I may add (though I am sorry to say it), meritorious without thanks. It is no wonder that such a prince lived beloved, and died lamented by all good men; for he honoured God, and God honoured him." His love to his queen and other relatives is described in striking contrast with the picture drawn by the infidel historian above quoted.—Hume and Smollet, vol. ix., p. 443. Fleming on Death of William, p. 164–5. Burnet's Own Times, vol. iii., p. 417–25.—C.

others, survived the Revolution, and made a considerable figure in the reigns of King William and Queen Mary. As,

Rev. William Bates, D.D.
" Obad. Grew, D.D.
" Sam. Annesly, D.D.
" John Collings, D.D.
" Richard Baxter.
" Vincent Alsop, M.A.
" John Howe, M.A.
" Tho. Doolittle, M.A.
" Phil. and Matt. Henry, M.A.
" John Flavel.
" Matthew Barker, M.A.
" George Cockayne.
" John Faldo.
" W. Lorimer, M.A.
" Tho. Gilbert, B.D.
" Jos. Hill, B.D.
" Robert Bragge.

Rev. Matth. Mead.
" Jas. Forbes, M.A.
" Tho. Cole, M.A.
" Geo. Griffith, M.A.
" Nath. Mather.
" Edward Veal.
" John Quick.
" Nath. Vincent, M.A.
" Rd. Stretton, M.A.
" Richard Kentish.
" H. Newcome, M.A.
" Matt. Sylvester.
" Christ. Nesse, M.A.
" John Humphrys, M.A.
" Richard Mayo.
" Matth. Clarke, Sen.
" Isaac Chauncey, M.D.

Rev. Sam. Slater, M.A.
" Daniel Williams, D.D.
" John Spademan, M.A.
" Robert Billlo.
" Rich. Steele, M.A.

Rev. Nath. Taylor.
" R. Flemming, M.A.
" Daniel Burgess.
" James Owen; &c.

These, and others who deserve an honourable mention, were learned and useful men, and most of them popular preachers, serviceable to the societies for reformation of manners, and eminent confessors in the cause of liberty and scriptural religion ; but their deaths not happening within the compass of this work, I must leave them to be remembered by the historians of after times.*

* Notices of many of these excellent ministers will be found in the Appendix, derived from a variety of sources.—C.

END OF MR. NEAL'S HISTORY.

S U P P L E M E N T,

CONTAINING

A SKETCH OF THE HISTORY OF THE BAPTISTS AND QUAKERS.

CHAPTER I.

SOME ACCOUNT OF THE BAPTISTS, OR ANTIPÆDO-BAPTISTS, FROM THE DAYS OF WICKLIFFE TO THE REIGN OF JAMES I., A.D. 1370–1600.

ALTHOUGH the Baptist profession does not assume a visible appearance in England, by the formation of churches in a state of separation from their brethren of the Pædobaptist persuasion, earlier than the reign of James I., it is beyond all reasonable doubt that individuals were to be found maintaining those principles in every subsequent age from the days of Wickliffe, that morning star of the Reformation.

It is perhaps impossible for us, after a lapse of four or five centuries, to decide the question whether the great English Reformer did or did not oppose the baptism of infants. It is a fact, however, which admits of no dispute, that he maintained and propagated those principles which, when carried out into their legitimate consequences, are wholly subversive of the practice in question. And if Wickliffe himself did not pursue the consequence of his own doctrines so far, yet many of his followers did, and were made Baptists by it.*

One of the maxims held by this Reformer

* Respecting Wickliffe's sentiments on this subject, many writers have positively asserted that he opposed this practice. Dr. Hurd, in his *History of all Religions*, says, "It is pretty clear, from the writings of many learned men, that Dr. John Wickliffe, the first English Reformer, either considered infant baptism unlawful, or, at best, not necessary." The author of a *History of Religion*, published in London in 1764, in four volumes octavo, says, "It is clear from many authors that Wickliffe rejected infant baptism, and that on this doctrine his followers agreed with the modern Baptists:" Thomas Walden and Joseph Vicecomes, who had access to his writings, have charged him with denying Pædobaptism, and they brought their charge at a time when it might have been easily contradicted if it had not been true. The first of these charges him with holding the following opinions about baptism : "That baptism doth not confer, but only signifies grace which was given before; that those are fools and presumptuous who baptize infants not to be saved as die without baptism; and asserted that the baptism of the Spirit." A council was held at Blackfriars June 11, 1382, to condemn Wickliffe and his sect, at which time, while his enemies were in convocation, that terrible earthquake happened which is mentioned in the Chronicles of St. Alban's, and of which Wickliffe also takes notice in his writings. This greatly alarmed his persecutors, but did not prevent their framing many articles of accusation. The eleventh article was, *that the children of believers might be saved without baptism.*—Walden, tom. ii., 93, 108. *Danvers's Treatise*, p. ii., p. 287. *Ivimey*, vol. i., p. 72.—C.

VOL. II.—Y y

was, "that wise men leave that as impertinent which is not plainly expressed in Scripture ;"* in other words, that nothing should be practised in the Church of God, as a branch of worship, which is neither expressly commanded nor plainly exemplified in the New Testament. It is upon this principle that the Baptists make their stand." They examine the sacred writings, and there find, that in their Lord's commission, baptism stands connected with the preaching of the everlasting Gospel ; that the apostles, who well understood their Master's will, administered it to none but those who professed to repent and believe the Gospel ; and that thus it was the first disciples "put on Christ," or were initiated into his visible kingdom ; for such as gladly received the Word were baptized and added to the churches.

All our historians agree in affirming that the doctrines of Wickliffe spread very extensively throughout the country ; insomuch that, according to Knighton, a contemporary historian, "more than half the people of England embraced them and became his followers." Soon after his death, they began to form distinct societies in various places. Rapin tells us that, "in the year 1389, the Wickliffites, or Lollards, as they were commonly named, began to separate from the Church of Rome, and appoint priests from among themselves to perform Divine service after their own way. Though some were from time to time persecuted by the bishops, yet their persecutions were not rigorous. Their aim seemed to be only to hinder them from pleading prescription. Besides, a petition presented to the king by a former Parliament, to revoke the power granted to the bishops to imprison heretics, restrained the most forward."†

During the usurpation of Henry IV., A.D. 1400, the clergy, who had been instrumental to his elevation, obtained from him a law for the burning of heretics, which they were not long in carrying into operation. One of the first victims to their sanguinary edict was William Sawtre, said to have held the principles of the Baptists, and who was burned in London in the year 1400. He had been some time minister of the parish of St. Margaret, in the town of Lynn ; but, adopting the tenets of the Lollards, he was convicted of heresy by the Bishop of Norwich, and though by temporizing he for a while averted the dreadful sentence, yet he ultimately fell a martyr to the cause of truth. If we may credit the testimony of those who lived near the time when this took place, the diocess of

* Fuller's Church History, p. 133.
† Rapin's Hist. of England, vol. i., p. 480.

Norwich, in which Sawtre resided, abounded with persons of similar sentiments; but the cruel and ignominous death of this good man struck terror into the followers of Wickliffe, and made them more cautious how they exposed themselves to a similar fate by divulging their opinions. Yet Fuller relates that, such was the craft and diligence of the clergy, they found out means to discover many of them, and by *ex officio* informations which they now obtained, they persecuted them with great cruelty, so that the prisons were filled with them : many were induced to recant, and such as refused were treated without mercy.*

That the denial of the right of infants to baptism was a principle generally maintained among the Lollards or followers of Wickliffe, is abundantly confirmed by the historians of those times. Thomas Walden, who wrote against Wickliffe, terms this reformer " one of the seven heads that rose up out of the bottomless pit for *denying infant baptism,* that *heresie of the Lollards,* of whom he was so great a ringleader." Walsingham, another writer, says, " It was in the year 1381 that that damnable heretic, John Wickliffe, received the cursed opinions of Be- rengarius," one of which unquestionably was the denial of infant baptism. The Dutch Martyrology also gives an account of one Sir L. Clifford, who had formerly been a Lollard, but had left them, and who informed the Archbishop of Canterbury that the Lollards would not baptize their new-born children. The fact is, therefore, put beyond dispute, that the principles of the Antipædobaptists were prevalent during the whole of the fifteenth century, though we are unable to trace them as imbodied in the formation of distinct churches under that denomination.

In the history of the Welsh Baptists compiled by Mr. Joshua Thomas, of Leominster, we have some interesting information respecting a Mr. Walter Brute, who is said to have been a gentleman of rank, learning, and parts, in the diocess of Hereford, about the end of the fourteenth century. This person, though reckoned a layman by the popish clergy, was indefatigable in propagating the truth himself, " teaching openly and privately, as well the nobles as the commons." In this good work he was assisted by two of his intimate friends, viz., Mr. William Swinderby and Mr. Stephen Ball, who were both of them preachers of note, and all maintaining the doctrines of Wickliffe. Fox, the martyrologist, has given a particular account of Mr. Brute, and of his religious sentiments, extracted from the register of the Bishop of Hereford. One of his tenets was, that *faith ought to precede baptism,* and that baptism was not essential to salvation. A commission was granted by Richard II. about the year 1392, addressed to the nobility and gentry of the county of Hereford, and to the mayor of the city, authorizing them to prosecute Brute on a charge of preaching heresy in the diocess and places adjacent, and also with keeping conventicles. In consequence of this, Mr. Brute retired into privacy, and Swinderby and his friends fled into Wales, to be out of the county and diocess of Hereford. Amid the mountains and valleys of the principality they continued for some time,

instructing all that came unto them. They seem, however, ultimately to have been appre.. hended and brought to trial, and Fox mentions that Swinderby, the friend of Walter Brute, was burned alive for his profession in Smithfield, A.D. 1401 ; what became of the latter he does not particularly say, but from what he relates of his bold and spirited defence upon his trial, it is probable that he shared the same fate.*

Dr. Wall, the learned author of the " History of Infant Baptism," seems desirous of persuading his readers that there were no Baptists in England when Henry VIII. ascended the throne at the commencement of the sixteenth century, A.D. 1511. But, upon that supposition, it is. not easy to account for the sanguinary statutes which in the early part of this reign were put forth against the Anabaptists. In the year 1535, ten persons avowing these sentiments are mentioned in the registers of the metropolis as having been put to death in different parts of the country, while an equal number saved themselves by recantation. In the following year the Convocation sat, and after some matters re-. lating to the king's divorce had been debated, the lower house presented to the upper a catalogue of religious tenets which then prevailed in the realm, amounting to sixty-seven articles, and they are such as respected the Lollards, the new Reformers, and the Anabaptists. The latter are most particularly pointed at ; the indispensable necessity of baptism for attaining eternal life is most peremptorily insisted on ;. that " infants must needs be christened, because they are born in original sin, which sin must needs be remitted, and which can only be done by the sacrament of baptism, whereby they receive the Holy Ghost, which exerciseth his grace and efficacy in them, and cleanseth and purgeth those from sin by his most secret virtue and operation. *Item.* That children or men once baptized, can, nor ought ever to be bap- *tized again.' Item.* That they ought to repute and take all the Anabaptists, and every other man's opinions agreeable to the said Anabaptists, for detestable heresies, and utterly to be condemned." On the 16th November, 1538, a proclamation was issued condemning all the books of the Anabaptists, and ordering those to be punished who vended them ; and in the fol-. lowing month a circular letter was addressed to all the justices of peace throughout England, solemnly warning them to take care that all the injunctions, laws, and proclamations against the Anabaptists and others, be duly executed. In the same year an act of grace was passed, from the provisions of which all Anabaptists. were excepted.† If the country did not abound with Baptists at this time, why were those se- vere measures enforced against them ?

We learn from " Fuller's Church History," that " at the period when Henry VIII. was married to Anne of Cleves, the Dutch flocked into England in great numbers, and soon after began to broach their strange opinions, being branded with the general name of Anabaptists." He adds, that " these Anabaptists, in the main, are

* Fuller's Church History, p. 164.

* The reader should look on to a passage on page 364 in relation to the church at Chesterton, alluded to by Robinson, and which existed in 1457.—C. ·
† Burnet's History of the Reformation, vol. iii., book iii.

but Donatists new dipped. And this year their name first appears in our English Chronicles, where I read that four Anabaptists, three men and one woman, all Dutch, bare fagots at Paul's Cross; and, three days after, a man and a woman of their sect were burned in Smithfield."* ; : When the historian says that it was in the year 1538 that the names of these sectaries first appeared in an English Chronicle, there is considerable obscurity attached to his meaning. To suppose him to assert that the Anabaptists do not appear in the annals of England before that year, is to accuse him of contradicting his own writings, and violating the truth of history. Bishop Burnet says that "in May, 1535, nineteen Hollanders were accused of holding heretical opinions, among which was a denial that the sacraments had any effect on those that received them: fourteen of them remained obstinate, and were burned by pairs in several places."† This denial of the efficacy of the sacraments evidently points to the Baptists, who strenuously opposed the administration of that ordinance to infants on the ground of its saving efficacy. In the same year, as has been already stated, the registers of London mention certain Dutch Baptists, ten of whom were put to death; and in the articles of religion set forth by the king and Convocation, A.D. 1536, the sect of the Anabaptists is specified and condemned. In fact, it is easy to trace the Baptists in England at least a hundred years prior to the time mentioned by Fuller. His words must, therefore, be restricted to the punishments first inflicted in England upon the Mennonites, or Dutch Baptists, who had emigrated to this country.

In the year 1539, the thirtieth of the reign of Henry VIII., we find certain legal enactments promulgated, one of which was, "that those who are in any error, as Sacramentaries, Anabaptists, or any others that sell books having such opinions in them, being once known, both the books and such persons shall be detected, and disclosed immediately to the king's majesty, or one of his privy council, to the intent to have it punished without favour, *even with the extremity of the law*."‡ From this it appears that the Baptists not only existed in England, but that they were in the habit of availing themselves of the art of printing, which had not long been discovered, for the defence of their peculiar and discriminating tenets; and to such an extent, too, as to alarm the clergy, and induce them to call upon the Legislature for measures of severity, in order to restrain their circulation. In the same year, it appears, from the Dutch Martyrology, that sixteen men and fifteen women were banished the country for opposing infant baptism. They retired to Delft, in Holland, where they were pursued and prosecuted before the magistrates as Anabaptists, and put to death for their supposed errors, the men being beheaded and the women drowned. Such were the sanguinary proceedings against the Baptists in the reign of Henry VIII., a monarch who professedly espoused the cause of reformation. Edward VI. ascended the throne in 1547; and, though only nine years of age, he was evi-

dently a great blessing to the country. He encouraged the reading of the Scriptures in his own language, received home again such as had been banished during the former reign, and restrained persecution in all its direful forms to the utmost of his power. Fox tells us that "during the whole time of the six years' reign of this young prince, much tranquillity, and, as it were, a breathing-time, was granted to the whole Church of England; so that, the rage of persecution ceasing, and the sword taken out of the adversaries' hand, there was now no danger to the godly, unless it were only by wealth and prosperity, which many times bringeth more damage in corrupting men's minds than any time of persecution or affliction. In short, during all this time, neither in Smithfield nor in any other quarter of this realm was any heard to suffer for any matter of religion, either papist or Protestant, two only excepted; one an English woman, called Joan of Kent; and the other, a Dutchman, named George."* Bishop Burnet informs us that at this time there were many Anabaptists in several parts of England. These persons laid it down as a foundation principle, that the Scripture was to be the only rule of Christians. They denied that the baptism of infants could be fairly deduced from Scripture: "they held that to be no baptism, and so were rebaptized.", On the 12th of April, 1549, there was a complaint brought to the council that, with the strangers that were lately come into England, some of that persuasion had come over, who were disseminating their errors, and making proselytes. A commission was accordingly ordered for the Archbishop of Canterbury, the Bishops of Ely, Worcester, Westminster, Lincoln, and Rochester, &c., &c., to examine and search after all Anabaptists, heretics, or contemners of the Common Prayer; to endeavour to reclaim them, or, if obstinate, to excommunicate and imprison them, and deliver them over to the secular power, to be farther proceeded against. Some tradesmen in London were brought before the commissioners, and were persuaded to abjure their former opinions, one of which was, "that the baptism of infants was not profitable."

One of those who thus abjured was commanded to carry a fagot on the following Sunday at St. Paul's, where a sermon was to be preached setting forth his heresy. But Joan Boucher, commonly called Joan of Kent, was extremely obstinate. "The excuse for thirsting after this woman's blood," says one of our older historians, "which Cranmer and the other bishops evinced, was, that she was an Anabaptist, and that the Anabaptists in Germany had turned all religion into allegories, and denied the principles of the Christian faith; that they had also broke out into rebellion, and driven the bishops out of Munster, where they set up John of Leyden, one of their teachers, for king, and called the city New Jerusalem." But Joan Boucher was not charged with rebellion, nor yet with a breach of peace. And Bishop Burnet himself acknowledges that there were Anabaptists of gentle and moderate principles and manners, whose only crime was that they thought baptism ought not to be given to infants, but to grown persons alone. If the bishops did not

* Fuller's Church History, book iv. Stowe's Chronicle, p. 576.

† History of the Reformation, vol. i., book iii., p. 195. ‡ Fox's Martyrs, vol. ii., p. 440.

* Acts and Monuments, p. 685.

distinguish this moderate sort of Baptists from the madmen of Munster, there is reason to judge the death of Joan Boucher to be no better than murder. She was, indeed, charged with maintaining, besides adult baptism, "that Christ was not truly incarnate of the Virgin, whose flesh being sinful, he could not partake of it, but the Word, by the consent of the inward man in the Virgin, took flesh of her :" a scholastic distinction, incapable of doing much mischief, and far from deserving so severe a punishment. "The principles of orthodoxy surely ought not to destroy the principles of humanity! It is not in a man's power to believe all that another may tell him; but is he, therefore, to be burned for not effecting an impossibility? Had the apostles promulgated any such doctrine among either Jews or Gentiles, when Christ sent them to preach the Gospel to *all nations*, and baptize those that believed, not even the power of miracles would have been sufficient to establish a religion thus founded on cruelty and injustice."*

The bishops named in the commission for searching after the Baptists were Cranmer, Ridley, Goodrich, Heath, Scory, and Holbeach, two of whom were, in the following reign, themselves burned for heresy. When this poor woman had been convicted, and condemned as an obstinate heretic, she was given over to the secular power, and Cranmer was employed to persuade the king to sign the warrant for her execution. But the young monarch was so struck with the cruelty and unreasonableness of the sentence passed upon her, that when he was requested to sign the warrant for her execution, he could not, for some time, be prevailed on, to do it. Cranmer argued from the law of Moses, according to which blasphemers were to be stoned : he said he made a great difference between other points of divinity and those which were levelled against the Apostles' Creed ; that there were impieties against God which a prince, being his deputy, ought to punish, just as the king's deputies were obliged to punish offences against the king's person ! These, certainly, were very futile pleas, and Bishop Burnet says they rather silenced than satisfied the young king, who still thought it a hard thing, as, in truth it was, to proceed so severely in such cases. Accordingly, he set his hand to the warrant with tears in his eyes, telling Cranmer that if he did wrong, as it was done in submission to his authority, *he* (the archbishop) should answer for it to God! This struck the prelate with much horror, so that he was very unwilling to have the sentence carried into effect. Every effort was now made to induce the woman to recant : both Cranmer and Ridley took her in custody to their own houses, to try if they could prevail upon her to do so ; but, remaining inflexible, she was executed May 2, 1550, Bishop Scory preaching at her burning.†

It would seem, at first sight, a little remarkable that so much pains should have been taken with Joan Boucher to make her retract her opinions ; but our surprise will cease when we attend to the account which Strype gives of her in his "Annals of the Reformation:" "She was,"

says he, "a great disperser of Tyndal's New Testament, translated by him into English, and printed at Cologne ; and was, moreover, a great reader of Scriptures herself ; which book also she dispersed in the court, and so became known to certain women of quality, and was particularly acquainted with Mrs. Anne Askew. She used, for greater secrecy, to tie the books with strings under her apparel, and so pass with them into court."* From this it would appear that she was a person of no ordinary rank in life, but one whose sentiments on religious subjects were entitled to respect ; and that, having tasted of the good Word of God herself, and knowing its ineffable value to the souls of her fellow-creatures, she was not afraid of hazarding her own personal safety, in those perilous times, to put others in possession of the oracles of eternal truth.

There is a remarkable circumstance connected with the burning of this *illustrious* female related by Fox, which is worth inserting in these pages. I extract it from Crosby's History, vol. i., p. 59, who tells us that he has taken it from "Peirce's Answer to Nichols." "When the Protestant bishops," says Fox, "had resolved to put [this woman] to death, a friend of Mr. John Rogers,† the divinity reader in St. Paul's Church, came to him, earnestly entreating him to use his interest with the archbishop that the poor woman's life might be spared, and other means used to prevent the spreading of her opinions which might be done in time ; urging, too, that though while she lived she infected few with her opinions, yet she might bring many to think well of them by suffering for them. He therefore pleaded that it was much better she should be kept in some prison, where she had no opportunity of propagating her notions among weak people, and thus she would be precluded from injuring others, while she might live to change her own mind. Rogers, on the other hand, pleaded that she ought to be put to death ; then, said his friend, if you are resolved to put an end to both her life and her opinions, choose some other kind of death more consonant to the gentleness and mercy prescribed in the Gospel, there being no need that such tormenting deaths should be resorted to in imitation of the papists. Rogers answered, that *burning alive was not a cruel death*, but easy enough ! On hearing these words, which expressed so little regard to the poor creature's sufferings, his friend replied with great vehemence, at the same time striking Rogers's hand, which before he had held fast, "Well, perhaps it may so happen that you yourselves will one day have your hands full of *this mild burning !*" And so it came to pass, for Rogers was the first man who was burned in Queen Mary's reign !".

The pious Bishop Latimer lived during the reign of Edward VI., and has borne a very honourable testimony to the Baptists of his day. In his Lent sermons preached before the king, he says, "The Anabaptists that were burned [during the reign of Henry VIII.] in divers towns in England, as I heard of credible men, for I saw them not myself, went to their death intrepidly, as ye will say, without any fear of the world, but cheerfully."

* Oldmixon's History of England, p. 187.

† Burnet's Hist. Reformation, vol. ii., part ii., p. 110.

* Eccles. Mem., vol. ii., p. 214.

† Supposed by Mr. Peirce to be *Fox himself !*

That the Baptists were very numerous at this period is unquestionable; and that many of those who were led to the stake in the reign of Queen Mary were of that persuasion, is equally clear ; though historians have not been very careful in recording their opinions on that point. Indeed, there is no want of proof concerning the hatred in which they were held by the ruling party, one instance of which may be mentioned. In the year 1550, after much cavilling in the state, an act of grace was passed, extending the king's general pardon to all persons, those confined in the Tower for crimes against the state, and also all *Anabaptists*, being excepted! In the same year, Ridley, who had recently been raised to the bishopric of London, held a visitation of his diocess ; and among other articles enjoined on his clergy, this was one : " to see whether any Anabaptists or others held private conventicles, with different opinions and forms from those established by law." This excellent young prince, who was of the most promising expectations, and, in the judgment of many impartial persons, the very phœnix of his time, was removed by death in the seventeenth year of his age, and the seventh of his reign ; by some, suspected to be owing to poison. Dr. Leighton, speaking of his premature death, says, " This king, a gracious plant, whereof the soil was not worthy, like another Josiah, setting himself with all his might to promote the Reformation, abhorred and forbid that any mass should be permitted to his sister. Farther, he was desirous not to leave a hoof of the Romish beast in his kingdom, as he was taught by some of the sincerer sort. But, as he wanted instruments to effect this good, so he was mightily opposed in all his good designs by the prelatists, which caused him, in his godly jealousy, in the very anguish of his soul, to pour out his soul in tears."[*]

Of the short and sanguinary reign of Queen Mary, Mr. Neal has furnished a faithful compendium, vol. i., p. 57–70, and we have little to add to his narrative. In the first year of her reign, a person of the name of Woodman was cited before the Bishop of Winchester to answer to certain allegations touching his orthodoxy. " Hold him a book," said the bishop : " if he refuse to swear, he is an Anabaptist, and shall be excommunicated." This criterion for ascertaining whether or not the poor man was or was not infected with heresy, is no farther entitled to notice than as it proves two things : namely, the existence of Baptists at that time in the country, and the severity of the penal laws against them. On another occasion, when Mr. Philpot was under examination by the lords of the council (November 5, 1555), it was remarked by one of his judges, that " all heretics boast of the Spirit of God, and every one would have a church of his own, as Joan of Kent and the Anabaptists !" A pretty plain indication that the Baptists of that day were not only contending for the Divine authority of their institution, but also for the necessity of their separating themselves unto the law of the Lord, and maintaining the importance of their own principles. It is painful to dwell upon the merciless

proceedings of this reign, and we shall dismiss it with a few additional remarks. In the beginning of June, 1558, a proclamation was issued, of which the following is a copy :

"BY THE KING AND QUEEN.

" Whereas divers books, filled with heresy, sedition, and treason, have of late, and be daily brought into this realm, out of foreign countries, and places beyond the seas ; and some also *covertly printed within this realm*, and cast abroad in sundry parts thereof, whereby not only God is dishonoured, but also encouragement given to disobey lawful princes and governors : the king and queen's majesties, for redress hereof, do, by their own proclamation, declare and publish to all their subjects that whosoever shall, after the proclaiming hereof, be found to have any of the said wicked and seditious books, or, finding them, do not forthwith burn the same, shall, in that case, be reported and taken for *a rebel*, and shall, without delay, *be executed* for that offence, *according to martial law*."

A week after the publishing of this proclamation, a meeting of Protestants was detected at Islington, and twenty-two individuals, men and women, were seized and taken before Sir Roger Cholmley, who turned them over to the Bishop of London, who, in the cruelty of his tender mercies, turned thirteen of them over to the executioners, seven of them to be burned in Smithfield, and six at Brentford !*

Among those who were committed to the flames in Smithfield, on this occasion, was Mr. Roger Holland, a gentleman descended from a very respectable family in Lancashire, where several of his predecessors are to be found enrolled in the list of sheriffs for the county. At a hearing before Bishop Bonner, Lord Strange, son of the Earl of Derby, Sir Thomas Gerrard, Mr. Eccleston, of Eccleston, with many other gentlemen of the county, appeared to speak on his behalf. In his youthful days, Mr. Holland had been not only a bigoted papist, but also a very dissipated and profligate young man. He was, however, converted from the error of his ways by the pious instructions of a servant-maid in the family in which he resided. She put into his hands some books, both in defence of the truth of the Gospel and against the errors of popery. These means were, through the blessing of Heaven, so efficacious, that he became the member of a Congregational church in London, married the female to whom he was under such lasting obligations, and sealed the profession of the Gospel with his blood : his wife also suffered great affliction for maintaining the same truths. Two others of the Islington congregation were taken by Bonner, stripped naked, and flogged in his garden at Fulham, in a most unmanly posture, to such a degree, that a bundle of rods was worn out in scourging them ! But on the character of this queen, and the general complexion of her reign, let it suffice in this place to give an extract from an oration, composed by the learned John Hailes, Esq.,[†] and delivered to Queen Elizabeth soon after her accession to the throne.

---

* For Dr. Toulmin's reflections on the state of the Baptists during the reign of Edward VI., see vol. i., p. 57, of this work.

, * Oldmixon's England, vol. i., p. 284, *folio*.
† Mr. Hailes, the writer of this oration, was bred at Oxford, and deservedly held in high reputation for

" It was not enough for these unnatural English tormentors," says Mr. Hailes,· "these tyrants and false Christians, to be lords of the goods, possessions, and bodies of their brethren and countrymen ; but, being very antichrists and enemies of the cross of Christ, they would be gods also, and reign in the consciences and souls of men. · Every man, woman, and child must deny Christ in word openly, abhor Christ in their deeds, slander him with word and deed, worship and honour false gods as they would have them, and as themselves did, and so give body and soul to the devil, their master: or secretly flee, or, after inward· torments, be burned openly. O cruelty, cruelty ! far exceeding all the cruelties committed by those famous ancient tyrants, Herod, Caligula, Nero, Domitian, &c., &c., whose names, for their cruel persecution of the people of God, have been, and ever will be, held in perpetual hatred. If any man would undertake to set forth particularly all the acts that have been done these full five years by this unnatural woman (rather say, this monster covered with the shape of a woman), as it is necessary for the glory of God, and the profit of the Church, and of this realm, that it should be done, he will find it subject sufficient for a perfect and a great history, and not to be contained in an oration to be uttered at one time by the voice of man: But, to comprehend the sum of all their wickedness in few words, behold, whatever malice in mischief, covetousness in spoil, cruelty in punishing, tyranny in destruction, could do—that, all this poor English nation, these full five years, either suffered already, or should have suffered, had not the great mercy of God prevented it."*

Queen Elizabeth ascended the throne in the year 1558 ; and, though a decided enemy to popery, or, more properly speaking, to the authority of the pope, yet such was her blind and bigoted determination to enforce a uniformity of worship among all her subjects, that the Baptists were called to no small share of suffering, for conscience' sake, during the whole of her reign., The complexion of her reign, however, was very different from that of her sister. The fires of Smithfield were not lighted up in such profusion ; but the same sanguinary laws remained in force ;· and all who disclaimed human authority in the kingdom of Christ—who maintained the Word of God to be the only rule of faith and duty, were either compelled to temporize and conceal their convictions, or were subject to great pains and penalties. The queen, says Sir Francis Walsingham, when sketching the features of her government, " laid down two maxims of state ; one was, not to force consciences ; the other was, not to let factious practices go unpunished because they were covered by pretexts of conscience." The strictures which Mr. Neal has passed on these maxims of government, vol. i., p. 74–77, are so exceedingly pertinent, that it is needless here to enlarge upon them. Bishop Burnet tells us that she did not at first revive those severe laws which were passed in her father's time, by which the refusal of the oath of supremacy

was made *treason*, but left her subjects to the freedom of their thoughts, and only made it penal to extol a foreign jurisdiction. She also laid aside the title "supreme head" of the Church, and those who refused the oath were only disabled, from holding benefices during their refusal. But after the twentieth year of her reign, the political posture of affairs compelled her, we are told, to adopt a different line of conduct. " Then, pecuniary punishments were inflicted on such as withdrew from the Church ; and, in conclusion, she was forced to make laws of greater rigour. As for the Puritans, as long as they only inveighed against some abuses, such as pluralities, nonresidents, or the like, it was not their zeal against those, but their violence that was condemned. *When they refused to comply with some ceremonies,* and *questioned the superiority of the bishops, and de-*clared for a democracy in the Church, they were connived at with great gentleness ; but they set up a new model of church discipline, *without waiting for the civil magistrate,* and entered into combination ; then it appeared that it was faction, and not zeal, that animated them. Upon that, the queen found it necessary to restrain them more than she had done formerly." Such is Bishop Burnet's apology for the intolerant proceedings of this reign.

The share which the Baptists had in these severities will appear from the mention of a few instances. Dr. Wall relates, that about the sixteenth year of Queen Elizabeth, a congregation of Dutch Antipædobaptists was discovered without Aldgate, in London, of whom twenty-seven were taken and imprisoned ;· and the following month one man and ten women of them were condemned.* Another writer informs us that it was at Easter, 1575, that this took place, and that four of them recanted at Paul's Cross, on the 25th May, and that the rest were banished the kingdom.† The following is the form of their abjuration :

" Whereas we, being seduced by the devil, the spirit of error, and by false teachers, have fallen into these most damnable and detestable heresies, that Christ took not flesh of the substance of the Virgin Mary ; that the infants of the faithful ought not to be baptized ; and that a Christian man may not be a magistrate, or bear the sword and office of authority ; and that it is not lawful for a Christian man to take an oath : now, by the grace of God, and by the assistance of good and learned ministers of Christ's Church, I understand the same to be most damnable and detestable heresies ; and do ask God, before his Church, mercy for my said former errors, and do forsake, recant, and renounce them ; and I abjure them from the bottom of my heart, protesting I certainly believe the contrary. And, farther, I confess that the whole doctrine established and published in the Church of England, and also that which is received in the Dutch church in London, is found true and according to God's Word : whereunto in all things I submit myself, and will be most gladly a member of the said Dutch church ; from henceforth utterly abandoning and forsaking *all and every Anabaptistical error.*"‡

<hr>

his learning. He was highly esteemed by the lordkeeper, Sir Nicholas Bacon, and by Lord Burleigh, two of the greatest men of that age. ·
* Oldmixon, p. 293.

* History of Infant Baptism, book ii., p. 212.
† D'Assigny's Mystery of Anabaptism, p. 368.
‡ Crosby, vol. i., p. 68.

This abjuration oath, which was administer-ed by Dr. Delaune, then minister of the Dutch church, Austin Friars, sufficiently indicates the arbitrary and intolerant spirit of the age. Fuller, the historian, mentions the same facts, with some additional circumstances. "Now began the Anabaptists," says he, "wonderfully to increase in the land; and as we are sorry that any countrymen should be seduced with that opinion, so we are glad that the English, as yet, were free from that infection." He then goes on to relate the apprehension of the twenty-seven Baptists at Aldgate, and adds, that two of them were so obstinate, that orders were issued for their being committed to the flames in Smithfield. This induced the celebrated John Fox, the martyrologist, to interpose in their behalf, supplicating her majesty to reprieve them. The letter was written in Latin, but Mr. Crosby has furnished us with the following translation of it:

"Most serene and happy princess—most illustrious queen, the honour of our country, and ornament of the age. As nothing has been farther from my thoughts and expectations than ever to disturb your most excellent majesty by my troublesome interruption, so it grieves me very much that I must break that silence which has hitherto been the result of my mind. But so it now happens, by I know not what infelicity, that the present time obliges me, contrary to my hope and opinion, to that which of all things in the world I least desired; and, though hitherto I have been troublesome to nobody, I am now, contrary to my inclination, constrained to be importunate, even with my princess: not in any matter or course of my own, but through the calamity brought upon others. And by how much the more sharp and lamentable that is, by so much the more I am spurred on to deprecate it.

"I understand there are some here in England, though not English, but come hither from Holland, I suppose both men and women, who, having been tried according to law, publicly declared their repentance, and are happily reclaimed. Many others are condemned to exile—a light sentence, in my opinion. But I hear there are one or two of these who are appointed to the most severe of punishments, namely, burning, unless your clemency prevent it. Now in this one affair I consider there are two things to be considered : the one is, the wickedness of their errors ; the other, the severity of their punishment. As to their errors, indeed, no man of sense can deny that they are most absurd ; and I wonder that such monstrous opinions could come into the mind of any Christian ; but such is the state of human weakness, if we are left never so little a while destitute of the Divine light, whither is it that we do not fall ? And we have great reason to give God thanks on this account, that I hear not of any Englishman that is inclined to this madness. As to these fanatical sects, therefore, it is certain they are by no means to be countenanced in a commonwealth, but, in my opinion, ought to be suppressed by proper correction. But to *roast alive* the bodies of poor wretches, that offend rather through blindness of judgment than perverseness of will, *in fire and flames* raging *with pitch and brimstone*, is a hard-hearted thing, and more

agreeable to the practice of the Romanists than to the custom of the Gospellers : yea, it is evidently of the same kind as if it had flowed from the Romish priests, from the first author of such cruelty, Innocent III. Oh, that none had ever brought such a Phalarian bull into the meek Church of Christ ! I do not speak these things because I am pleased with their wickedness, or favour the errors of any men ; but seeing I am myself a man, I must therefore favour the life of man—not that he should err, but that he should repent. Nay, my pity extends not only to the life of man, but even to the beasts.

"For it is, perhaps, folly in me ; but I speak the truth, that I can hardly pass by a slaughter-house where cattle are killing, but my mind revolts with a secret sense of their pains. And truly I greatly admire the clemency of God in this, who had such regard to the mean brute creatures, formerly prepared for sacrifices, that they must not be committed to the flames before their blood had been poured out at the foot of the altar. Whence we may gather, that in afflicting punishments, however just, we must not be over rigorous, but temper the sharpness of rigour with clemency. Wherefore, if I may be so bold with the majesty of so great a princess, I humbly beg of your royal highness, for the sake of Christ, who was consecrated to suffer for the lives of many, this favour at my request, which even the Divine clemency would engage you to, that if it may be, and what cannot your authority do in such cases ? these miserable wretches may be spared ; at least, that a stop may be put to the horror, by changing their punishment into some other kind. There are excommunications and close imprisonment ; there are bonds ; there is perpetual banishment, burning of the hand, and whipping, or even slavery itself. This one thing I most earnestly beg, that the piles and flames in Smithfield, so long ago extinguished by your happy government, may not now be again revived. That if I may not obtain this, I pray with the greatest earnestness that, out of your great pity, you would grant us a month or two, in which we may try whether the Lord will give them grace to turn from their dangerous errors ; lest, with the destruction of their bodies, their souls be in danger of eternal ruin."[*]

So far the venerable John Fox : but what a train of reflection does this letter give rise to, were this the place to indulge in it ! One natural inference is, that, in his judgment, the power of the civil magistrates may very properly be exercised in coercing opinions in matters of religion, and in punishing those who dare to think differently from the national standard, provided the punishment be not excessive ! These " fanatical sects are by no means to be countenanced in a commonwealth—but *ought to be suppressed with proper correction ;*" " there are excommunications and close imprisonment ;" " exile is a light sentence" in his opinion ; " there are bonds, perpetual banishment, burning of the hand, and whipping, or even slavery itself." To any of these the venerable martyrologist could give his consent ; but the *roasting alive* of human beings is a " hard-hearted thing," from which his compassionate heart revolted. Her majesty's heart, however, it appears, was not

* The original of this letter is given in the Appendix to this volume, No. III.

quite so soft; for though she had a high respect for the writer, and constantly called him her "Father Fox," she was not his dutiful daughter, but met his request with a flat denial, "unless, after a month's reprieve and conference with divines, they would recant their errors." "She declared their impieties to be damnable, and that she was necessitated to this severity, because, having formerly punished some *traitors*, were she now to spare these *blasphemers*, the world would condemn her as being more earnest in asserting her own safety than the honour of her God." All the difference, then, between her majesty and the learned martyrologist, in this instance, merely regarded the *quantum* of punishment to be inflited, for on the principle they were fully agreed ! And certainly, where the point in dispute was so *trivial*, it was very proper that the queen should follow her own judgment. Accordingly, the writ *De heretico comburendo*, that is, for burning heretics, which for seventeen years had only hung up *in terrorem*, was now taken down and put in execution, and the two Anabaptists, John Wielmaker and Henry Torwoort, were committed to the flames in Smithfield, July 22, 1575.

I have dwelt the more largely upon this affair, because it presents us with a fair specimen of the state of the public mind in regard to toleration during the boasted reign of Queen Elizabeth. And now, before we dismiss the matter wholly, let us pause and examine a little coolly "these monstrous opinions," which Fox wonders should ever enter the mind of any Christian ; "this madness," which "endangered the eternal ruin of their souls," according to his notion of the matter, and which her majesty considered to be "damnable impieties," implying *blasphemy* against God; not to be expiated but by the extremest tortures.

The first article in this dreadful catalogue of crimes respected the human nature of the Son of God ; a speculation indulged by Joan of Kent, and many other truly pious persons in that day. They had read, in the writings of the holy Evangelist, that Christ's human nature was *miraculously* formed in the womb of a virgin, by the power of the Most High coming upon her ; that the body of the Saviour was not produced according to the ordinary laws of generation ; and that, consequently, "that *holy thing* which was born of her" was not subject to the original taint which descended from Adam to his posterity. Even admitting that it was improper to indulge speculation on this sublime mystery, which we ought to receive as it is delivered to us, without curiously prying into things quite beyond our reach, it is not easy to find the monstrous impiety, the damnable heresy, in it which should entitle its abetters to such condign punishment. For aught we can see, it was a harmless speculation, which noway affected either the faith or the obedience of the Gospel. And as to the other articles of their impeachment, it would be trifling with the reader's time here to enlarge upon them. That infants *ought not* to be baptized, must be allowed by all who admit that either precept or example is necessary to authorize us in whatever we practice as a branch of worship The unlawfulness of taking an oath, and of Christians filling the offices of civil magistracy, though to me they both appear unfound-

ed objections, originating in a misapplication of certain texts of Scripture, were nevertheless opinions that had been current among the Waldenses, Albigenses, and Wickliffites, and, indeed, have been prevalent in every age of the Church since the days of the apostles. Now, to say nothing of the infernal cruelty of roasting alive these individuals, there is something monstrously wicked even in compelling them to abjure these harmless opinions as "most damnable and detestable heresies ;" to abjure them, "from the bottom of their heart, protesting that *they certainly believed the contrary."* Alas, humanity sickens at such an outrage on the prerogative of the Most High and the rights of mankind !

From this period to the end of Queen Elizabeth's reign, the whole body of the Puritans appear to have been treated with great severity, of which the Baptists certainly came in for their due share. Many of them quitted the kingdom, and those who remained in it were perpetually harassed and tormented by fine and imprisonment. In the county of Norfolk (Mr. Neal says Suffolk, see vol. i., p. 153), an application was made to the justices of peace in behalf of some of the Brownists who had been long and illegally imprisoned by the Bishop of Norwich, entreating that their worships would be pleased to move that prelate in their favour. His lordship was so displeased with them for their interference in what he considered to be his own prerogative, that he drew up twelve articles of impeachment against the justices themselves, and caused them to be summoned before the queen and council to answer for their conduct. The particulars are given by Mr. Neal, vol. i., p. 153; and we only refer to it here for the purpose of remarking, that in the supplication to the justices, the terms *Anabaptists* and *Brownists* are used as synonymous, and also that they were allowed no quarter in that district.

In the year 1589, when the reign of this queen drew towards a close, a treatise appeared against the Puritans from the pen of a clergyman of the name of Some, in which he undertook to show the coincidence that existed between the Anabaptists and some of the leading men among the former. The sentiments which he charged the Baptists of that day with holding are, that the ministers of the Gospel ought to be maintained by the voluntary contributions of the people ; that the civil magistrate has no right to make and impose laws on the consciences of men ; that the people ought to have the right of choosing their own ministers ; that the High Commission Court was an antichristian usurpation ; that such as are qualified to preach ought not to be hindered by the civil magistrate from doing so ; that no forms of prayer should be imposed upon the Church ; that the baptisms administered in the Church of Rome were invalid ; and that a true constitution and discipline are essential to a true church. Such were the *heterodox* principles maintained by the Anabaptists of Queen Elizabeth's times, according to the testimony of this learned doctor ; principles well supported by the Word of God, and which, therefore, every intelligent and consistent Baptist of the present day is proud to avow. The doctor touches, also, on their opinions of baptizing none but professed believers ; that they hold the worship of God as conducted in the Church of England to be 'in many respects defective; and brings up the rear of their crimes by adding, that they count it blasphemy for any man to arrogate to himself the title of Doctor in Divinity, or, as he explains it, to be called Rabbi; that is, lord and master of other men's faith! He acknowledges that there were several Anabaptistical conventicles, both in the metropolis and other parts of the kingdom, in his day; a fact which we shall find abundantly confirmed in the following chapter.

<hr>

CHAPTER II.

HISTORY OF THE BAPTISTS DURING THE REIGNS OF JAMES I. AND CHARLES I., A.D. 1602–1650.

HITHERTO we have been engaged rather in tracing out obscure notices of the Antipædobaptists, as of individuals scattered throughout the country, maintaining their discriminating sentiment, yet mingling with their pædobaptist brethren in church communion, than as forming a distinct body or denomination contending for the Divine authority of the baptismal institute, and its indispensable obligation as a term of communion; but we shall presently find them separating themselves to the law of their Lord, avowing their convictions and advocating their principles through the medium of the press.

In the year 1608 there was a small piece published by Enoch Clapham, representing, in a way of dialogue, the opinions of the different sects of Protestants at that period. He speaks of some of them as leaving the kingdom to form churches among people of another language; and others, who remained in England, he censures for withdrawing from the national worship, and assembling in woods, stables, and barns for religious service. He particularly distinguishes from Puritans and Brownists, on the one hand, and from Arians and Socinians, on the other, those who, by way of reproach, were called Anabaptists,* and who separated

* In the dialogue of Enoch Clapham, above mentioned, the Anabaptist is asked what religion he is of; and is made to answer, "Of the true religion, commonly termed Anabaptism, from our baptizing." When he is interrogated concerning the church or congregation he was connected with in Holland, he answers, "There be *certain English people of us that came out from the Brownists.*"* When the Arian says, "I am of the mind that there is no true baptism upon earth," he replies, "I pray thee say not so; the congregation I am of can and doth administer true baptism." When an inquirer after truth offers, on his proving what he has said, to leave his old religion, the Anabaptist answers, "You should not, if God will give you grace to leave it; for it is a particular favour to leave Sodom and Egypt, spiritually so called." When the same person offers to unite with them, the Anabaptist replies, "The dew of heaven come upon you: to-morrow I will bring you into our sacred congregation, that so you may come to be informed of the faith, and after that be purely baptized." This representation of the Baptists in the year 1608, though furnished by one who wrote against them, deserves regard, especially as he assures his readers that the characters which he has drawn of each sect had not been done without several years' experience and

* The reader will find some reference to the Baptist division of the Brownists in Holland in Mr. Young's interesting volume, the " Chronicles of the Pilgrims."—C.

VOL. II.—Z z

both from the Church and other Dissenters. Whatever may be thought concerning the truth and justness of their views on the question relative to baptism, their great seriousness of spirit and diligence in inquiry must be praised by all candid persons. They arose out of those who, being tired with the yoke of superstitious ceremonies, the traditions of men, and corrupt mixtures in the worship of God, resolved, by the grace of God, not to receive or practise any piece of positive worship which had not precept or example in his Word. On this principle they pursued their researches, which they accompanied with fasting and prayer. When, after long search and many debates, it appeared to them that infant baptism was a mere innovation, and even a profanation of a Divine ordinance, they were not brought to lay it aside without many fears and tremblings, lest they should be mistaken, considering how many learned and godly men were of an opposite persuasion; and gladly would they have had the concurrence of their brethren with them. But since there was no hope of this, they concluded that a Christian's faith must not stand in the wisdom of man, and that every one must give account of himself to God; so they resolved to practise according to their own convictions. They were persuaded that believers were the only proper subjects of baptism, and that immersion, or dipping the whole body into water, was the appointed rite. But as this was not practised in England, they were at a loss for an administrator to begin the practice. After often meeting together to pray and confer about this matter, they agreed to send over into Holland Mr. Richard Blount, who understood the Dutch language, to a Baptist church there: he was kindly received by the society and their pastor, and upon his return he baptized Mr. Samuel Blacklock, a minister; these two baptized the rest of the company, to the number of fifty-three. Some few others of this persuasion were among the original planters of New-England. They who continued in England, published, in the year 1615, a small treatise to justify their separation from the Church of England, and to prove that every man has a right to judge for himself in matters of religion; and that to persecute any one on this account is illegal, antichristian, and contrary to the laws of God, as well as several declarations of his majesty.

The title of this pamphlet is as follows: "Persecution for Religion judged and condemned, in a Discourse between a Christian and Antichristian: proving, by the Law of God, and by King James's many Declarations, that no Man ought to be persecuted for his Religion, so they testify his Allegiance by the Oath appointed by Law." The style of this work is easy, correct, and, considering the age when it was composed, very perspicuous, the reasoning strong and conclusive, and the dialogue well maintained. It presents a favourable specimen of the principles and abilities of the authors. They inveigh against the pride, luxury, and oppression of the bishops; declare their respect for magistrates; protest against the political errors of the papists; condemn those who, through fear, comply with any external worship contrary to their own conscience of them.—*Ivimey's English Baptists*, vol. i., p. 122.

science ; and refer, for evidence of their senti-ments, to the confession of faith published in 1611.

But the principal glory of this piece is the manly and explicit avowal which the authors make of the true principles of Christian liberty, at a time when they were either unknown, or opposed, by almost every other party. They preserve a just distinction between civil and religious concerns ; and while they fully allow the magistrate his proper authority in the former, they boldly maintain every man's right to judge and act for himself in the latter. In a dedication to all that truly wish Jerusalem's prosperity and Babylon's destruction, they declare, " We do unfeignedly acknowledge the authority of earthly magistrates, God's blessed ordinance, and that all earthly rule and command appertain unto them : let them command what they will, we must obey, either to do or to suffer. But all men must let God alone with his right, who is to be Lord and Lawgiver of the soul ; and not command obedience for God when he commandeth none." " If I take," says Christian, in another place, " any authority from the king's majesty, let me be judged worthy of my desert ; but, if I defend the authority of Christ Jesus over men's souls, which appertaineth to no mortal man whatsoever, then know you, that whosoever would rob him of that honour which is not of this world, he will tread them under foot. Earthly authority belongs to earthly kings ; but spiritual authority belongeth to that spiritual King who is King of kings."* When we consider the state of the times, this intrepid and dignified language must excite our just admiration.

In the year 1618, another vindication of their principles came from the press, entitled " A plain and well-grounded Treatise concerning Baptism." It was a translation from a Dutch piece, and is thought to be the first that was published in English against the baptism of infants. But the vindication of their principles procured them no security against the power of persecution. They were inveighed against from the pulpits, and harassed in the spiritual courts. Their goods were seized, and their persons confined by long and lingering imprisonments, under which many of them died, leaving widows and children. This drew from them, in 1620, during the sitting of Parliament, an humble supplication to King James, representing their miseries, avowing their loyal and blameless behaviour, and remonstrating against the cruel proceedings under which they suffered, as unbecoming the charity and goodness of the Christian religion, tempting men to hypocrisy, and exhibiting the marks of antichrist, and humbly beseeching his majesty, the nobles, and Parliament to consider their case, and, according to the direction of God's Word, to let the wheat and tares grow together till the harvest. Notwithstanding the odium cast upon them, and the severities used against them, they maintained their separate meetings, had many disciples, and supported an exemplary purity of character.†

Mr. Neal states that, in the year 1644, there were forty-seven congregations of this denomi-

nation in the country, and seven in London. It cannot be doubted that they gradually rose into such a number. Mr. Crosby says that the Baptists, who had hitherto been intermixed with other Nonconformists, began to form themselves into separate societies in 1633. The first instance of this secession was that of part of the Independent congregation, then under the ministry of Mr. John Lathrop, which had been gathered in 1616, and of which Mr. Henry Jacob was the first pastor. The minister of these Separatists was Mr. John Spilsbury ; their number is uncertain, because, after specifying the number of about twenty men and women, it is added—with divers others. In the year 1638, Mr. William Kiffin, Mr. Thomas Wilson, and others, adopted the same opinions concerning baptism ; and having been, at their own request, dismissed from the Independent church, joined the new congregation. Mr. Neal is mistaken when he represents this separation as taking place under Mr. Jessey, who did not settle with it as a pastor till about midsummer, 1637 ; and did not change his sentiments on the questions concerning baptism till the summer of 1645, when he was baptized by Mr. Knowles. The division of the people into two congregations, one continuing with him, and the other joining themselves to Mr. Praise-God Barebones, on the 18th of May, 1640, arose not from any difference of sentiment about baptism, but from their becoming so numerous that they could not meet together in one place without being discovered.*

In 1639 another congregation of Baptists was formed, which met in Crutched Friars, the chief promoters of which were Mr. Green, Mr. Paul Hobson, and Captain Spencer. A pamphlet appeared at this time, under the title of " New Preachers, New," designed to hold up to scorn and contempt the leading members of this church. Among other foolish things, it is remarked that " Green the felt-maker (that is a hatter), Spencer the horse-rubber, Quartermine the brewer's clerk, and some few others, were mighty sticklers in this new kind of talking trade, which many ignorant coxcombs call preaching." Green appears to have been a very zealous man, and to have excited no inconsiderable attention by his preaching. In the pamphlet above mentioned, some account is given of " a tumult raised in Fleet-street, by the disorderly preachment, pratings, and prattlings of Mr. Barebones the leather-seller, and Mr. Green the felt-maker, on Sunday last, the 19th of December (1641). Barebones is called a reverend unlearned leather-seller, memorable for his fiery zeal, and both he and his friend Green were apprehended while " preaching or prating among a hundred persons" on that day. The following extract from this pamphlet is too good to be lost :

" After my commendations, Mr. Rawbones (Barebones I should have said), in acknowledgment of your too much troubling yourself and molesting others, I have made bold to relate your last Sunday's afternoon work, lest in time your meritorious painstaking should be forgotten (for the which, you and your associate, Mr. Green, do well deserve to have your heads in the custody of young Gregory, to make buttons for

---

* Persecution judged and condemned, passim.
† See Crosby's History of the English Baptists, vol. i., p. 88–139.

* Jessey's Life, p. 7, 11, 83.

hempen loops!);, you two, haying the Spirit so full, that you must either rent or burst, did on the Sabbath aforesaid, at your house near Fetter Lane, and in Fleet-street, at the sign of the Lock and Key,-there and then did you and your consort,.by turns, unlock most delicate strange doctrine, where was _about thousands of people_, of which number the most ignorant applauded your preaching, and those that understood anything derided your ignorant prating/ But, after four hours' long and tedious tattling; the house where you were was beleaguered with multitudes that thought it fit to rouse you out of your blind devotion, so that your walls were battered, your windows all fractions, torn into tattling shivers ; and worse the hurly-burly might have been, but that sundry constables came in, with strong guards of men to keep the peace, in which conflict your sign was beaten down and unhinged, to make room for the owner to supply the place : all which shows had never been, had Mr. Green and Mr. Barebones been content, as they should have done, to have gone to their own parish churches.". The same writer, addressing Green, asks, "Do not these things come from proud spirits, that. Mr. Spencer, a horse-keeper, and you, a hat-maker, will take upon you to be ambassadors of God, to teach your teachers, and take upon you to be ministers of the Gospel in these days of light ?' Consider, I pray you, that our Lord would not have had the ass, Matt., xxi., 3' if he had not stood in need of him.' Now the truth is, the Church hath no need of such as you, an unlearned, self-conceited hat-maker. It is true that, in the beginning of Queen Elizabeth's reign, the papist priests and friars being dismissed, there was a scarcity for the present of learned men, and so some tradesmen were permitted to leave their trades, and betake themselves to the ministry ; but it was necessity that did then constrain them so to do ; but, thanks be to God, we have now no such necessity, and therefore this practice of you and your comrades casts an ill aspersion upon our good God, that doth furnish our church plentifully with learned men ; and it doth also scandalize our church, as if we stood in need of such as you to preach the Gospel.' This you call preaching, or prophesying ; and thus, as one of them told the lords of Parliament, that they were all preachers, for so they practise and exercise themselves as young players do in private, till they be by their brethren judged fit for the pulpit, and then they go, and, like mountebanks, play their part. Mr. Green, Mr. Green, leave off these ways : bring home such as you have caused to stray. It is such as you that vent their venom against our godly preachers, and the Divine forms of prayer, yea, against all set forms of prayers ; all is from antichrist, but that which you preach is most divine : _that_ comes from the Spirit, the other is an old dead sacrifice, composed (I should have said, killed) so long ago that it now stinks. It is so that, in the year 1549, it was compiled by Dr. Cranmer, Dr. Goodricke, Dr. Skip, Dr. Thirlby, Dr. Day, Dr. Holbecke, Dr. Ridley, Dr. Cox, Dr. Taylor, Dr. Harris, Dr. Redman, and Mr. Robinson, archdeacon of Leicester ; but what are all these? they are not to be compared to John Green, a hat-maker, for he thinketh what he blustereth forth upon the sudden is far better than that which these did maturely and deliberately compose !"

This extract is interesting on various accounts : the pamphlet from-which it is taken is evidently the production of one of those _clerical_ bigots of the Establishment, of whom abundance are to be found in every age since national establishments of Christianity were introduced ; a privileged order of men, who, having found out the means of making their profession of religion subservient to their worldly interest, take it mightily amiss that any persons should presume to disturb them in their slumbers, or caution their fellow-creatures against being deceived by them. Hence all their _cant and whining about_ "learned and godly ministers,"! as _though anybody complained of either their learning or their godliness ;*_ or as though their having been _licensed_ by their fellow-creatures to officiate in parish churches were a substantial reason why another, who obtains his livelihood by honest industry, should not raise his voice in defence of the despised truth of the Gospel, hold forth the Word of Life, and contend for the laws and institutions of Christ, against all who would corrupt them by human traditions. It is interesting, too, as furnishing a pretty correct idea of the manner in which the earliest Baptist churches in England conducted their public worship. Taking the New Testament for their guide, they seem evidently to have discarded "the one-man system," as it has been significantly termed, and which obtains so universally in our day. We may also learn from it the opposition which the Baptists of that day had to sustain in yielding obedience to the will of their God and Saviour.

But there are accounts of some societies existing in the country long before these congregations in London were formed. There is great reason to believe that the Baptist society at Shrewsbury has subsisted, through all the revolutions of time to this day, from the year 1627.‡ The congregation at Bickenhall, now at Hatch, six miles from Taunton, in Somerset, had, according to the opinion of its oldest members, about twenty years ago, subsisted near two hundred years ; and they had a clear tradition of its assemblies having been held so early as 1630, in the woods and other places of concealment, on account of the severity of the times.§ Even in 1457 there was a congregation of this sort at Chesterton, near Cambridge : six of them were accused of heresy, and condemned to abjure and do penance, half naked, with a fagot to their backs and a taper in their hands, in the public market-places of Ely and Cambridge.‖

But, notwithstanding this early appearance of the sect, it laboured under such difficulties, from the odium with which it was regarded by the people, and from the severities practised against it by the ruling powers, that its progress was for many years impeded. From what Bishop Jewel says, in the "Defence of his Apolo-

* This is keenly expressed, but in bad taste.—C.
† The results of the "any-man system" in the Scotch Baptist churches are not very much in favour of its adoption.—C.
‡ A Letter from the Rev. Josiah Thompson to the Editor.
§ MS. Collections concerning the History of Protestant Dissenters, communicated by Mr. Thompson.
‖ Robinson's Claude, vol. ii. Dissertation on Preaching, p. 54.

gy," written about the seventh year of Queen Elizabeth, it appears that it was then almost totally suppressed in these kingdoms ; for, while he speaks of them as finding harbour in Austria, Silesia, and Moravia, he adds, "they have no acquaintance with us in England, or any other place where the Gospel of Christ is clearly preached." This is to be concluded, also, from a passage in Dr. Featley, who says, "This fire in the reigns of Queen Elizabeth, King James, and our gracious sovereign, till now, was covered in England under the ashes ; or, if it broke out at any time, by the care of the ecclesiastical or civil magistrate it was soon put out."

But in the times of the civil war, so difficult or so impossible is it to extirpate opinions, this sect revived, held its weekly assemblies for religious worship, and printed various pieces in defence of their sentiments and practice : the number of converts to it rapidly increased, and it boasted in that prophecy, "that many shall run to and fro, and knowledge shall be increased."*†

Among the publications in their own vindication was a piece in 1641, by Edward Barber, entitled "A Treatise of Baptism, or Dipping ; wherein is clearly showed that our Lord Christ ordained Dipping, and that sprinkling of Children is not according to Christ's Institution ; and also the Invalidity of those Arguments that are commonly brought to justify that Practice." In the same year appeared a quarto pamphlet of six pages, relating chiefly, if not wholly, to the Baptists. It is entitled "The Brownists' Synagogue ; or, a late Discovery of their Conventicles, Assemblies, and Places of Meeting, where they preach, and the Manner of their praying and preaching, with a Relation of the Names, Places, and Doctrines of those which do commonly preach ; the chief of which are these : Green, the Felt-maker ; Marler, the Button-maker ; Spencer, the Coachman ; Rogers, the Glover ; *which Sect is much increased of late within this City.*" In this squib, Messrs. Green and Spencer, who were over the Baptist church in Crutched Friars, are termed "the two arch Separatists, demi-gods, who are here, and there, and everywhere." In the conclusion of the piece, the writer gives the following account of their meeting : "In the house where they meet, one is appointed to keep the door, and to give notice if there should be any insurrection, that warning may be given them. They do not flock together, but come two or three in a company, and all being gathered together, the man appointed to teach stands in the midst of the room, and his audience gather about him. He then prays for the space of about half an hour, and part of his prayer is, that those who come thither to scoff and laugh, God would be pleased to turn their hearts. His sermon is about the space of an hour, and then another stands up to make the text more plain ; and at the latter end he entreats them all to go home severally, lest

at their next meeting they should be interrupted by those who are of the opinion of the wicked. They seem very steadfast in their opinions, and say, 'rather than turn, they will burn.'"

In the next year came out another treatise, written by A. R., called "The Vanity of Children's Baptism." Mr. Francis Cornwell, M.A., published, in 1643, a small tract, dedicated to the House of Commons, with this title : "The Vindication of the Royal Commission of Jesus." It was given to divers members at the door of the House, which caused it to make a great noise and be much circulated. Its design was to show that the practice of christening children opposes the commission granted by our Lord and Saviour ; that it was a Romish or antichristian custom, and was established by Pope Innocent III., who made a decree that the baptism of the infants of believers should succeed circumcision. This piece gave great offence. Dr. Featley made several remarks upon it ; and a piece called "A Declaration against Anabaptists" was published in answer to it.* As they were frequently inveighed against, not only on account of their peculiar sentiments concerning the subjects and mode of baptism, but were also loaded with all the opprobrium which fell on the opinions deemed heretical, and were often reproached, both from the pulpit and the press, with being Pelagians, Socinians, Arminians, Soul-Sleepers, and the like, they published, in 1643, a "Confession of their Faith," mentioned and quoted by Mr. Neal, to vindicate themselves from these reflections, and to show their general agreement with other Protestants in all points except that of baptism. It was the first that was ever published by the English Baptists, and extends to fifty-two articles, which we shall give in the Appendix, No. xi. It passed through several editions in 1644 and 1646, one of which was licensed by authority, dedicated to the high court of Parliament, and put into the hands of several members. Their greatest adversaries, and among them Dr. Featley and Mr. Marshall, one of the Assembly of Divines, acknowledged that it was an orthodox confession.†

This confession must be understood as expressing the sentiments of those Baptists only who joined in it, and not as applying to all who differed from other Christians on the questions concerning baptism ; for, from the beginning of the Reformation, there was a difference between the Baptists themselves on doctrinal points ; and they divided, particularly, into two parties ; one embracing the Calvinistic scheme of doctrines, and from the particular point therein, viz., personal election, called Particular Baptists ; the others, professing the Arminian or remonstrant tenets, from their leading principle, viz., universal redemption, were styled General Baptists.

It is remarkable that some eminent men, who did not join their communion, were strongly in favour of their sentiments. The Right Honourable Lord Robert Brook‡ published about this time *A Treatise on Episcopacy,* in which he says, "I must confess that I begin to think there may

---

* Crosby, vol. i., p. 160, 161. Wall's History of Infant Baptism, vol. ii., p. 212–214.

† More to this effect may be found in "Featley's Dipper Dipped," in Baxter, and in Lightfoot's Diary, &c. The person against whom Lightfoot published a pamphlet, entitled "Hornets' Nests," under the name of his brother Peter, was a Baptist.—C.

* Crosby, vol. i., p. 151, 152, and 345.
† Ibid., vol. i., p. 170, 171.
‡ The friend of Lord Say and Seal, from whose title and his own our Saybrook in Connecticut received its name.—C.

be perhaps something more of God in these sects, which they call new schisms, than appears at first glimpse: I will not, I cannot, take upon me to defend that which men *generally call* *Anabaptism*; yet I conceive that sect is twofold: some of them hold free-will, community of goods, deny magistracy, and refuse to baptize their children; these truly are such heretics, or atheists, that I question whether any divine should honour them so much as to dispute with them. There is another sort of them who only deny baptism to their children till they come to years of discretion, and then they baptize them." He censured the applying to this people the opprobrious name of schismatics, and gave it as his judgment, that it was very easy for those who held that we should go no farther than the Scriptures for doctrine or discipline, to err on this point, since the Scriptures seem not to have clearly determined it. He went even so far as to call in question the accuracy and conclusiveness of the argument urged against them from circumcision, which he looked upon as a fine rational argument to illustrate a point well proved before, but he doubted whether it was proof enough for that which some would prove by it; because, besides the difference in the ordinances, the persons to be circumcised were stated by a positive law so expressly as to leave no room for scruple: " but it was otherwise with baptism, where all the designation of persons fit to be partakers, for aught I know," said his lordship, "is only such as believe; for this is the qualification which, with exactest search, I find the Scriptures require in persons to be baptized; and this it seems to require in all such persons. Now, how infants can properly be said to believe, I am not yet fully resolved." Having mentioned this nobleman, we cannot deny ourselves the pleasure of here introducing some remarks on his character from the writings of one of his contemporaries, namely, the great Milton, who, in his " Speech for the Liberty of unlicensed Printing," addressed to the Parliament of England [1645,] thus proceeds :

" What would be the best advised, then, if it be found so hurtful, and so unequal to suppress opinions for their newness or their unsuitableness to a customary acceptance, will not be my task to say. I shall only repeat what I have learned from one of your own honourable members, a right noble and pious lord, who, had he not sacrificed his life and fortunes to the Church and commonwealth, we had not now missed and bewailed a worthy and undoubted patron of this argument. Ye know him, I am sure; yet I, for honour's sake, and may it be eternal to him, shall name him, the LORD BROOK. He, writing of Episcopacy, and by the way treating of sects and schisms, left ye his vote, or, rather, now the last words of his dying charge, which I know will ever be of dear and honoured regard with you, so full of meekness and breathing charity, that next to *his* last testament who bequeathed love and peace to his disciples, I cannot call to mind where I have read or heard words more mild and peaceful. He there exhorts us to bear with patience and humility those, however they be miscalled, that desire to live purely, in such a use of God's ordinances as the best guidance of their consciences gives them, and to tolerate

them, though in some disconformity to ourselves. The book itself will tell us more at large, being published to the world, and dedicated to the Parliament by him, who, both for his life and for his death, deserves that what advice he left be not laid by without perusal."* Such praise from such a writer as Milton, who would not be proud of ? Granger informs us that Lord Brook, who was a zealous patriot and an avowed advocate for liberty, on account of the arbitrary measures of Charles I., had determined to seek freedom in America, and had agreed with Lord Say to transport themselves to New-England,† but upon the meeting of the Long Parliament, and the sudden change of public affairs, they were prevented from taking the voyage. He was afterward commander of the Parliament army, and lost his life at Litchfield in storming a close, to which Lord Chesterfield had retired with a body of the king's troops. He received a musket-shot in the eye, of which he instantly expired, in the year 1643.

A divine also, of great fame in that age, Mr. Daniel Rogers, candidly declared, in a book on the Sacrament, that he was unconvinced by any determination of Scripture for infant baptism. The learned and eminent Dr. Jeremiah Taylor, bishop of Down and Connor, published, in 1647, his treatise on "The Liberty of Prophesying ;"‡ in which he stated the opinion of the Antipædobaptists with such advantages of style and elaborate chain of argument, that he was thought to have said more for the Baptists than they were able to offer for themselves. The design of this excellent prelate, in exhibiting the weight of the arguments they could allege, and the great probability of truth on their side, was to abate the fury of their adversaries, and to show that they were, if in an error, still entitled to candour and indulgence.§

But neither their own vindications, nor the pleas of so generous an advocate, could screen them from that spirit of intolerance which actuated the predominant parties of those times. One of the seventeen canons which were passed by the Convocation of 1640, viz., the fifth canon, particularly decreed that another canon, which was directed against the papists, should be in full force against all Anabaptists.‖ In the following years they were inveighed against from the press and the pulpit. Dr. Featley owned that, in writing against them, he could hardly dip his pen in anything but gall. The severe ordinances of the day were aimed at them as well as the other sectaries. Edwards, in his "Gangræna," proposed a public disputation with them, and that, on their being found in an error, the Parliament would forbid all dipping, and take some severe course with all dippers, as the Senate of Zurich did. In this he referred to an edict published at Zurich in 1530, which made

---

* Milton's Prose Works, by Burnet, vol. i., p. 320.
† He obtained a patent for Saybrook in Connecticut.—C.
‡ This part of his treatise was reprinted in a detached form, under the title of "The Baptists justified, by Jeremy Taylor," 12mo, edited by the late learned Rev. Wm. Anderson, tutor in the Baptist College at Bristol, and to whom the editor is indebted as a faithful teacher at Dunstable, where Mr. A. was settled many years.—C.
§ Crosby, vol. i., p. 165–169.
‖ Mr. Neal, vol. i., p. 344.

it death for any to baptize by immersion.* On this law some, called Anabaptists, were tied back to back, and thrown into the sea : others were burned alive, and many starved to death in prison.† But this was not the wish of Edwards alone. There was a general cry against toleration, especially of these people. In the petition of the lord-mayor, court of aldermen, and Common Council, in 1646, that a speedy course might be taken to suppress all private and separate congregations, the Anabaptists were by name specified.‡

Sentiments against the rights of conscience, advanced by writers of reputation, and sanctioned by public acts, must be supposed to be productive of sufferings to individuals. It is proper to enter into the detail of these, as Mr. Neal has been thought to pass them over too generally, or to have represented them too partially.

Among others who felt the rage of bigotry was Mr. Vavasor Powell. This eminent Cambro-Briton was a native of Radnorshire, born in the year 1617, and descended from some of the best families in that county, as well as in those of Montgomery and Salop. Having received a liberal education in his native place, he was entered of Jesus College, Oxford, where he made great proficiency in the learned languages. On leaving college he took orders in the Establishment Church about the year 1640, and at first officiated in Wales, as curate to his uncle, Erasmus Powell. He had not been long, however, in that situation when he joined the Puritans, from a conviction that their principles and proceedings were more consonant to the Scriptures than those on which the National Establishment is founded. In the earlier part of his life he was remarkably thoughtless and vain ; a ringleader among the votaries of folly and dissipation, insomuch that he was called by his schoolfellows *dux omnium malorum,* "a ringleader in all manner of wickedness ;" we must, however, except the vice of drunkenness, of which he had so strong an abhorrence, that he used to speak of it as an *unnatural* vice, from which even the beasts were free, and he wondered how any rational being could possibly be addicted to a practice that was so entirely destitute at once of true pleasure, profit, and honour.

Having given up his connexion with the Established Church, and cast his lot among the Puritans, he began to preach among his countrymen, in the character of an itinerant evangelist, and his zeal and fortitude were soon called into exercise by the rage of bigotry, and the severe persecution to which he was exposed. He was often attacked and assaulted by violent men, and repeatedly exposed to the danger of his life by those who laid in wait, or bound themselves by oath, to kill him, or made an attempt on it. In 1640, he, and fifty or sixty of his hearers, when he was preaching in a house in Bracknockshire, were seized, about ten o'clock at night, by fifteen or sixteen men, under the pretence of a warrant from Justice Williams, and secured in a church. The next morning they were conducted to the justice's house, who committed them to the hands of the constable. On the following day they were examined before that justice and two or three more, and six

or seven clergymen ; but, after much conference and many threats, were at that time dismissed. After this, Mr. Powell, preaching at Launger in Radnorshire, in the field, because the house was not large enough to hold the auditory, was seized and committed by the high sheriff, Mr. Hugh Lloyd. The constables, sixteen or seventeen, who were charged with the execution of the *mittimus,* except one, refused it. This man, taking Mr. Powell to his own house, and permitting him to lodge there that night, because the prison was at a great distance, was so affected with his devotions in the family, that he would proceed no farther, but absconded himself, leaving Mr. Powell in his house ; who, to prevent damage to the man, bound himself with two sufficient sureties to appear at the next assizes at Radnorshire. Accordingly, he delivered himself up at that season, and three bills of indictment were preferred against him. But, after the traverse, he was acquitted, and invited to dine with the judges, who, desiring him to give thanks, one of them said, " It was the best grace he had ever heard in his life." But the high sheriff was so offended at the lenity shown to him, and the impressions made by his conduct and preaching, that on the commencement of the war he persecuted him out of the county.*

The public have lately been favoured with a copious memoir of Vavasor Powell, in the " Welsh Nonconformists' Memorial," compiled by the late Rev. Dr. Richards, of Lynn, in Norfolk,† and edited by John Evans, LL.D. Dr. Richards has bestowed much industry in tracing out the history of this eminent Nonconformist, and rescuing his character from many false and malignant aspersions cast upon it by his adversaries. He seems to think that he embraced the sentiments of the Baptists, and was himself baptized towards the end of the year 1655, which must have been a dozen years after he had quitted the Church of England. In proof of this, he quotes a letter from Mr. Secretary Thurloe to Henry Cromwell, dated January 1, 1656, and preserved in Thurloe's State Papers, vol. iv., p. 373. " Among other things," says Thurloe, " which are daily sent abroad for inflaming the people, your lordship will receive herewith a paper newly exhibited to the world, by Vavasor Powell, who is lately religious, and *several others of his party ;* whereupon I will make no observations, though many others do," &c.

It appears that, previous to his embracing the sentiments of the Baptists, Mr. Powell was in high estimation with the Presbyterian party. The situation of Wales in regard to religion was reported to the Parliament as being most deplorable. The people were so destitute of means of religious information, that they had neither Bibles nor catechisms. Their clergy were both ignorant and indolent, so that they had scarcely a sermon from one quarter of a year to another, nor was there any suitable provision made for the maintenance of such as were capable of instructing them. The Parliament took their case into consideration, and passed an

* Gangræna, part iii., p. 177.
† Crosby, vol. i., p. 183.   ‡ Ibid., p. 184.

* Crosby, vol. i., p. 217-219. Vavasor Powell's Life, p. 125-127.
† This gentleman left his valuable library to Brown University, R. I. It was very rich in its collections on Puritanism and Dissent.—C.

act, February 22, 1649, " for the better propagating and preaching of the Gospel in Wales," and commissioners were appointed for carrying it into effect. Mr. Vavasor Powell was at the head of these commissioners, and exerted himself most indefatigably in this office, the beneficial effects of which soon became apparent. Whitelocke, speaking of the year 1652, says, " By this time there were a hundred and fifty good preachers in the thirteen Welsh counties, most of whom preached three or four times a week: they were placed in every market town; and in most great towns two schoolmasters, able, learned, and university men,"* &c.

Soon after the passing of this act, Mr. Powell, who had for several years taken up his residence in the neighbourhood of London, returned to Wales, where he continued some years diligently exerting himself in promoting the objects of it, and especially in preaching the Gospel throughout the country. There was scarcely a neighbourhood, a parish, or a village in the country which was not visited by him, and that did not hear from his mouth the cheering invitations of the Gospel. Even to this day places are pointed out, in the most obscure and unfrequented parts of the principality, where Vavasor Powell is said to have preached to numerous congregations. In these excursions he was often accompanied by other ministers of the same active turn and fervent spirit with himself; and their labours were eminently successful. Even as early as the year 1654, the Christians in Wales connected with Vavasor Powell were calculated to amount to no less than twenty thousand.†

It is said that Mr. Powell was much in favour with the protector, Cromwell, at one period of his life; but when the latter had assumed the supreme power, he openly opposed his elevation, and thereby lost his favour.‡ From that moment he appears to have been continually the object of mistrust, and, consequently, became closely watched. All his movements were scrutinized narrowly, and as everything is yellow to the jaundiced eye, the basest motives were imputed to every part of his conduct. One while Powell was said to be preparing for war, busily engaged in enlisting troops; at another he was actually up in arms at the head of a troop of horse, ready to fight it out! Even his labours in preaching the Gospel, and the great concourse of people that attended him, were looked upon with an evil eye, and generally represented in a very unfavourable and suspicious light; and he often felt the effects of them in the persecutions which he was called to endure. But though these suspicions and evil surmises must have proved very painful to him, and detrimental to his labours in the propagation of the Gospel, yet it does not appear that they damped his courage, or cooled his zeal, or slackened his diligence in the prosecution of his important undertaking. He steadily persevered in the work of the Lord, till the new order of things under Charles II. deprived him of his liberty, and compelled him to desist.

Vavasor Powell was among the first victims to the tyrannical measures of Charles II. No sooner was the restoration resolved on, than the busy agents of government marked him out for their prey. They had even formed their plan and executed it before the king's arrival; such was their breathless haste to ruin this worthy man. On the 28th of April, 1660, he was seized in his own house by a party of soldiers, and conducted to the county jail; from thence he was removed to Shrewsbury, where he remained a prisoner nine weeks, but was then discharged. Returning into Montgomeryshire, he began to preach as usual, when the sheriff of the county lodged a complaint against him with Mr. Secretary Morrice, charging him with sedition, rebellion, and treason; and before any return could be received from the government, the sheriff issued a warrant to apprehend him, which was accordingly done, having enjoyed his liberty only twenty-four days. Soon after, he was removed by a warrant from the secretary of state, to London, and committed to the Fleet prison, where he lay two years, so closely confined, that he was not allowed to go out of his chamber door, which, added to the offensive effluvia of a dunghill that lay before his window, so much impaired his health that he never perfectly recovered it. During this period he wrote " A brief Narrative of the former Propagation and late Restoration of the Gospel in Wales," of which a second edition was published in 1662. In this piece he challenged his adversaries to substantiate the least of their calumnious charges against him. But in vain did he justify his character; innocence could procure him no redress. Having lain in the Fleet nearly two years, he was removed at an hour's notice, on the 30th of September, 1662, to South Sea Castle, near Portsmouth, 'where he remained a close prisoner for five years longer. On the fall of Lord Clarendon, Mr. Powell sued for a habeas corpus, and soon after, by an order from the king in council, obtained his liberty.

But scarcely had ten months elapsed before Mr. Powell was again apprehended, as he was passing from Bristol to Monmouthshire, over the hills of Glamorgan, in his way to his own residence, and committed to prison. He had preached at different stations, as he came along, to large congregations; and the people eagerly flocked to hear him from all parts. He had preached at Newport, in Monmouthshire, and from thence proceeded to Merthyr Tidvil, in Glamorganshire, a place now become famous for its iron-works, the most celebrated and extensive in Britain, as well as for the number of its inhabitants, having in a few years, from an inconsiderable village, become the most populous place in all the principality of Wales. When Mr. Powell arrived at Merthyr, he found assembled in and about the churchyard a large congregation, waiting to hear the Word of God. He discoursed to them from Jer., xvii., 7, 8. For this act of mercy the clergyman of the parish deposed against him, in consequence of which he was seized and lodged in his majesty's jail of Cardiff; from thence he was, some time afterward, cited before six deputy-lieutenants at Cowbridge, where he underwent a long examination, after which he was remanded to

---

* Whitelocke's Memorials, p. 518.

† See Thurloe's State Papers, vol. iii.

‡ Mr. Powell and Christopher Feake openly denounced Oliver Cromwell, in their sermons two days after his installation as lord-protector.—*Godwin's History Commonwealth,* vol. iv., p. 59.—C.

prison and recommitted. His friends in London now interested themselves in his behalf, and procured a writ of habeas corpus to remove him to the Court of Common Pleas; which was for some time resisted, but at length they succeeded, and on the 16th of October, 1669, he arrived in London, where, after an examination, he was committed once more to the Fleet. Here he remained till discharged by death, on the 27th of October, 1670, in the fifty-third year of his age, *eleven years of which he had passed in prison!* He was a person of the strictest integrity, the most fervent piety, and the most intrepid courage. He bore his illness with great fortitude and resignation to the will of God, and, in the highest paroxysms of his disorder, could with difficulty be restrained from breaking out into acts of devotion, and expressing his sentiments of zeal and piety. His remains were interred in Bunhill Fields, whither they were followed by an innumerable crowd of the Dissenters, who attended him to his grave. The inscription on his tombstone, which was drawn up by his friend Edward Bradshaw, describes him as "a successful teacher of the past, a sincere witness of the present, and a useful example of the future age; who, in the defection of many, found mercy to be faithful: for which, being called to many prisons, he was tried and would not accept deliverance, expecting a better resurrection."* But to return.

In 1641, Mr. Edward Barber, minister to a small congregation of Baptists in London, was kept eleven months in prison for denying the baptism of infants, and that to pay tithes to the clergy was a Divine ordinance under the Gospel.

In 1643, some pious persons at Coventry,† who had embraced the opinion of Antipædobaptism, invited Mr. Benjamin Cox, an aged minister of good reputation for learning and piety, the son of a bishop, and some time minister at Bedford, to come to them and assist them in forming themselves into a distinct church. Several Presbyterian ministers, among whom was Mr. Baxter, had taken refuge in that city; who, being alarmed at the spread of baptistical sentiments, Mr. Baxter challenged Mr. Cox to dispute with him about the points in difference between them. This was done *vivâ voce* and by writing; but it was broken off by the interference of the committee; who required Mr. Cox to depart from the city, and to promise not to return to it. As he refused this, he was immediately committed to prison, and remained there for some time; till, in consequence of Mr. Pinson's application to Mr. Baxter, his release was procured.‡

Another sufferer on this side was Mr. Henry Denne, who had been ordained by the Bishop of St. David's, and held the living of Pyrton, in Hertfordshire, for ten years. In 1644 he was apprehended in Cambridgeshire by the committee of that county, and sent to jail, for preach-

ing against infant baptism, and baptizing those who had received no other. After he had been confined some time, his case, through the intercession of some friends, was referred to a committee of Parliament, and he was sent up to London, and detained in the Lord Petre's house, in Aldergate-street, till the committee had heard his cause and released him. In June, 1646, he was apprehended a second time at Spalding, in Lincolnshire. He was seized on a Lord's Day, and kept in custody, to prevent his preaching. Upon hearing the charge against him, which was for baptizing, as but one witness appeared to support it, and according to the maxim of law, *Nemo tenetur seipsum accusare,* he refused to be his own accuser. The ceremony had been performed in the night, which indicates the severity of the times against such as held his principles and acted upon them : just as the primitive Christians, under persecution, held their assemblies at that season.*

About the same time, Mr. Coppe, a minister in Warwickshire, and preacher to the garrison in Compton House in the said county, for rebaptizing was committed to Coventry jail. On publishing the ordinance of Parliament, in 1645, against unordained ministers, the lord-mayor sent his officers, on a Sunday, to the Baptist meeting in Coleman-street, London, on an information that laymen preached there. The officers found the religious exercises conducted by Mr. Lamb, the elder of the church, and a young man who was a teacher among them. Some of the congregation, incensed at the disturbance given to their worship, used rough language to them; but Mr. Lamb behaved respectfully, requested leave to finish the religious service, and engaged to appear before the lord-mayor at six o'clock. The officers acquiesced, and withdrew; and at the time appointed Mr. Lamb and his assistant met at his lordship's house. He was interrogated on what authority he presumed to preach, and was told that he had transgressed the ordinance of Parliament. Mr. Lamb replied, "No; for that he was called and appointed to the office by as reformed a church as any in the world," alluding to the words of the ordinance. But he acknowledged that he rejected the baptism of infants as invalid. After the examination, they were bound over to answer before the committee of the Parliament, who, after hearing them, committed both to jail, where they lay till the intercession of friends procured their liberty.†

In the same year, Mr. Paul Hobson, a Baptist minister, was taken into custody by the governor of Newport Pagnel for preaching against infant baptism; and reflecting on the order against the preaching of laymen. After a short confinement, he was sent prisoner to London. He was soon cited before the committee ; and, having several friends of rank and influence, he was immediately discharged, and preached publicly at a meeting-house in Moorfields.‡

The case of Mr. Hanserd Knollys runs into more particulars. He was a man of piety and learning, and had received ordination from the Bishop of Peterborough, but was afterward a

---

* Richards's Cambro-British Biography, p. 141–186. Dr. Toulmin, in a note respecting Vavasor Powell, says, "His sentiments were those of a Sabbatarian Baptist;" but Dr. Richards assures us there is no foundation for considering him a Sabbatarian. Very few men of that age did more for the advancement of true godliness than Mr. Powell.—C.

† The Baptist church at Coventry has continued to this day.—See *Ormes's Life of Baxter.*—C.

‡ Crosby, p. 220, 221; and Baxter's Life, p. 46.

* Crosby, vol. i., p. 221–224, where are the examinations taken on the occasion.

† Crosby, vol. i., p. 225, 226.

‡ Edwards's Grangræna, vol. i., p. 34, 37.

zealous opposer of Episcopacy and the liturgy. Preaching one Lord's Day, at the earnest and repeated request of the church-wardens, when they wanted a minister, in Bow Church, Cheapside, he was led by his subject to speak against the practice of infant baptism. This gave great offence to some of the auditory ; a complaint was lodged against him with the Parliament ; and, by a warrant from the Committee for Plundered Ministers, he was apprehended by the keeper of Ely House, and kept several days in prison, bail being refused. At length he was brought to a hearing before the committee, when about thirty of the Assembly of Divines were present. The answers which he gave on his examination, about his authority to preach, the occasion of his appearing in the pulpit at Bow Church, and the doctrine he had there advanced being satisfactory, he was discharged without blame or paying fees ; and the jailer was sharply reproved for refusing bail, and threatened to be turned out of his post.

Soon after this, Mr. Knollys went into Suffolk, and preached in several places, as opportunity offered, at the request of friends. But as he was accounted an Antinomian and Anabaptist, his supposed errors were deemed as criminal as sedition and faction, and the virulence of the mob was instigated against him by the high-constable. At one time he was stoned out of the pulpit ; at another time the doors of the church were shut against him and his hearers. Upon this, he preached in the churchyard, which was considered as a crime too great to be connived at or excused. At length he was taken into custody, and was first prosecuted at a petty sessions in the county, and then sent up a prisoner to London, with articles of complaint against him to the Parliament. On his examination, he proved, by witnesses of reputation, that he had neither sowed sedition nor raised a tumult, and that all the disorders which had happened were owing to the violence and malignity of his opposers, who had acted contrary both to law and common civility. He produced copies of the sermons he had preached, and afterward printed them. His answers were so satisfactory, that on the report made by the committee to the House, he was not only discharged, but a vote passed that he might have liberty to preach in any part of Suffolk, when the minister of the place did not himself preach there. But, besides the trouble which this business occasioned to him, it devolved on him an expense of £60.

Mr. Knollys, finding how much offence was taken at his preaching in the church, and to what troubles it exposed him, set up a separate meeting in Great St. Helen's, London, where the people flocked to hear him, and he had generally a thousand auditors. Great umbrage was taken at this ; the landlord was prevailed upon to warn him out of the place, and Mr. Knollys was summoned before a committee of divines, who used to sit in the room called the Queen's Court, Westminster, to answer for his conduct in this matter. The chairman asked why he presumed to preach without holy orders. To which he replied, he was in holy orders. The chairman, on this, was informed that he had renounced Episcopal ordination : this Mr. Knollys confessed, but pleaded that he was now ordained,

Vol. II —A a a

in a church of God, according to the order of the Gospel, and then explained the manner of ordination among the Baptists. At last he was commanded to preach no more ; but he told them that he would preach the Gospel, both publicly and from house to house, saying, " It was more equal to obey Christ who commanded him, than those who forbade him ;" and so went away. A letter, which Mr. Knollys wrote to Mr. Dutton, of Norwich, in which were some reflections on the persecuting measures of those times, and which, coming into the hands of the Suffolk committee, was sent up to London, and presently is supposed to have inflamed the proceedings against him.* As it is short, I will give a copy of it below.† It was too common a practice then to seize and publish the letters of those who were called sectaries.

The unsettled state of the times in which Mr. Knollys's lot was cast occasioned a great variation in his circumstances, and obliged him often to change his place of abode. Sometimes he was possessed of several hundred pounds, the fruits of his industry in teaching youth ; at others, he had neither home to dwell in, nor food to eat, nor money to purchase it ! And frequently was he burried from place to place, by the evil of the times, and the malice of his persecutors. When the rage of his adversaries would no longer permit him to remain in Lincolnshire, he removed to London. Here he opened a school upon Tower Hill, and took a few young men under his care, to finish their education and fit them for the work of the ministry. He was also chosen master of the Free School in St. Mary Axe ; but the oppressive hand of power compelled him to abandon this employment, and seek an asylum across the Atlantic. There he continued about five years, preaching the Gospel and building up the churches that had lately been gathered in that wilderness. In 1641 he returned to his native country, at the pressing solicitation of his aged father. At this time Mr. Knollys was reduced to great straits in his worldly circumstances, but his friends were numerous, and often interposed with seasonable relief. The

* Crosby, vol. i., p. 226-230 ; and a very short and partial account in Edwards's Gangræna, vol. i., p. 39.

† " Beloved Brother,
" I salute you in the Lord. Your letter I received the last day of the week ; and upon the first day I did salute the brethren in your name, who resalute you, and pray for you. The city Presbyterians have sent a letter to the synod, dated from Sion College, against any toleration ; and they are fasting and praying at Sion College this day, about farther contrivings against God's poor innocent ones ; but God will doubtless answer them according to the idol of their own hearts. To-morrow there is a fast kept by both houses, and the synod at Westminster. They say it is to seek God about the establishing of worship according to their covenant. They have first vowed, now they make inquiry. God will certainly ' take the crafty in their own snare, and make the wisdom of the wise foolishness ;' for ' He chooseth the foolish things of this world to confound the wise, and weak things to confound the mighty.' My wife and family remember their love to you. Salute the brethren that are with you. Farewell.
" Your brother in the faith and fellowship of the Gospel,
' Hanserd Knollys.
" London, the 13th day of the 11th month, }
called January, 1645." }

words of the apostle were, indeed, literally fulfilled in the experience of this good man, that
"we have here no continuing city?" We can
trace him from this country to America, and
then back again; from England into Wales;
from London to Holland, and from thence into
Germany; then back to Rotterdam, and from
the latter place to London once more. These
wanderings about, too, were not the effects of
choice, but of necessity. They tended, however, greatly to the exercise of his graces, and furnished him with numerous instances of the prov-
idential mercies of God towards him.   '
   Shortly after the Restoration, in 1660, Mr.
Knollys, with many other innocent persons,
was dragged from his own dwelling-house and
committed to Newgate, where he was kept in
close custody for eighteen weeks, until released
by an act of grace, on the king's coronation.
At that time four hundred persons were confined
in the same prison for refusing to take the oaths
of allegiance and supremacy. A royal proclamation was issued at this time, prohibiting Anabaptists and other sectaries from worshipping
God in public, except at their parish church.
This cruel edict was the signal for persecution,
and the forerunner of those sanguinary laws
which disgraced the reigns of the Stuarts; and
to these must be attributed the frequent removals to which Mr. Knollys was compelled to have
recourse. During his absence in Holland and
Germany, his property was confiscated to the
crown, and when the law did not sanction the
act, a party of soldiers was despatched to take
forcible possession of his property. When the
Conventicle Act passed in 1760, Mr. Knollys
was apprehended at a place of worship in
George-yard, and committed to prison. But
here he obtained favour of his jailer, who allowed him to preach to the prisoners twice a
week during his confinement.
   Mr. Knollys lived to the advanced age of
ninety-three, and quitted the world in a transport of joy, 19th of September, 1691. He was
buried in Bunhill Fields.*
   Mr. John Sims, who preached at Southampton, was a sufferer among the Baptists during
this period (1646). He was prevailed on, in a
journey to Taunton, to preach in the parish
church of Middlesey. On this he was seized by
virtue of the act against unordained ministers,
and several letters, which he was to deliver to
some pious friends, were taken from him.
These, with the examination, were sent to London, by way of complaint against him, and printed. The charges specified in the examination
were for preaching and denying infant baptism.
He admitted the latter, and pleaded against the
former, that "as Peter was called, so was he."†
   The next name on the list of sufferers is Mr.
Andrew Wyke. On his examination he refused
to answer to the questions concerning the doctrines he held, or his authority for preaching;
alleging that, as a freeman of England, he was
not bound to answer to any interrogatories,
either to accuse himself or others; but if they
had aught against him, they should lay their

charge, and produce their proofs. This conduct was looked upon as great obstinacy, and
expressive of high contempt of authority; and
he was therefore sent to jail, 3d of June, 1646.
The duration of his imprisonment is not known;
but while he was under confinement, a pamphlet,
drawn up by himself or some friend, entitled
"The Innocent in Prison complaining," being
a narrative of the proceedings against him, was
published, in which the committee and some
members of it did not escape severe reflection.*
   The last person whom I shall mention as
suffering in this period is Mr. Samuel Oates,
whose name is brought forward by Mr. Neal in
a manner that has provoked, not wholly without reason, the severe censure of Mr. Crosby;
for it leaves the reader to confound this Oates
with Titus Oates,† so noted in our historians,
with a brand of infamy upon him, and uninform-
ed of the issue of the proceedings against him
on the heavy charge of murder.
   This Mr. Samuel Oates was a popular preacher and great disputant. On a journey into Essex in 1646, he preached in several parts of
that country, and baptized by immersion a great
number of people, especially about Bocking,
Braintree, and Tarling. Among the hundreds
he baptized, one died within a few weeks after,
and her death was imputed to her being dipped
in cold water. The magistrate was prevailed
upon to apprehend Mr. Oates on this charge,
and to send him to prison, and to put him in
irons as a murderer, in order to his trial at the
ensuing assizes. The name of the woman was
Ann Martin, and the report spread against Mr.
Oates was, that in the administration of baptism, "he held her so long in the water, that
she fell presently sick; that her belly swelled
with the abundance of water she took in; that
within a fortnight or three weeks she died, and
on her deathbed expressed this dipping to be the
cause of her death." He was arraigned for his
life at Chelmsford assizes; but on the trial
several credible witnesses, among them the
mother of the deceased, deposed on oath, that
"Ann Martin was in better health for several
days after her baptism than she had been for
some time before, and that she was seen to
walk abroad afterward very comfortably." So
that, notwithstanding all the design and malignity which discovered themselves in the trial,
he was brought in Not guilty. But this verdict
was not sufficient to disarm the rage of the populace against him; for a little time after, some
who were known to have been baptized going,
occasionally, to Wethersfield in Essex, on alarm
being given that Mr. Oates and his companions
were come, the mob arose and seized upon
these innocent persons, dragged them to a
pump, and treated them like the worst of villains; though Oates, against whom they were
chiefly enraged, was not of the party. Not
long after this, the mob, without any provocation, but because he dared to come to the place,
drew him out of a house at Dunmow, and threw
him into a river, boasting that they had thoroughly dipped him.‡

---

* Crosby's Baptists, vol. iii., p. 93; and vol. iv., p.
295. Brooks's Puritans, vol. iii., p. 491.
   † Crosby, vol. i., p. 232, 233; and Edwards's Gangræna, vol. ii., p. 50, &c., where four of the letters
are printed.

* Edwards, vol. ii., p. 169. Crosby, vol. i., p. 235.
   † I believe he was the father of Titus.—C.
   ‡ Edwards's Gangræna, vol. i., p. 121; and Crosby, vol. i., p. 236–238, and p. 240. In the preceding
detail, the disturbance iven to an assembly at Dead-

The preceding facts show that obloquy attached itself to the principles of the Baptists, and that they were marked out as objects for the virulence of the populace and the animadversion of the magistrate. Next to the Quakers, observes a late historian, " they were perhaps the most hated and persecuted sect."* But it should be owned, in mitigation of the conduct of their persecutors, that at least in some instances they inflamed the spirits of men against them, as Mr. Neal suggests, by their own imprudence and the impetuosity of their zeal. Much enthusiasm appears to have animated the profession of their opinions ; and it was the fashion of the times for every party to advance its peculiar sentiments in coarse and irritating language ; each assumed this licentiousness of speech, but none took it patiently from others. The Baptists incurred censure, and excited jealousy and resentment, by disturbing congregations and dispersing challenges to dispute with any minister or ministers on the questions relative to baptism. This was much according to the practice of the times.† Mr. Baxter, we have seen, challenged Mr. Cox; and Dr. Gunning, afterward regius professor of divinity at Cambridge, and Bishop of Ely, in the year 1656, went into the congregation of Mr. Biddle, and began a dispute with him. But while the members of the dominant parties did this uncensured, it was considered, and treated, as insolence in the minority to advance their opinions, even in their own assemblies only. When the public peace is broken, men are justly amenable to the civil magistrate ; but for the breach of the peace merely, and not for the sentiments they may at the time avow. Violence, penalties, and imprisonment on account of religious tenets are in no view justifiable. Against error they are needless ; for that, not being founded in reason and proof, will of itself die away : against truth they are ineffectual ; for that will finally prevail, by its own weight and evidence, above all opposition. Every person against whom they are directed feels them to be in his own case iniquitous and cruel.

The only good effect which persecution hath ever produced has been, opening the eyes of men to see the iniquity of it, and raising in their hearts an abhorrence of it. The severities of which the Baptists were the marked objects led them to be advocates for liberty and toleration. So

man's Place, January 18, 1640, mentioned by Fuller, is omitted ; because he is mistaken in calling it an Anabaptistical congregation ; and the matter has been stated before by Mr. Neal, vol. i., p. 361. But it may be added to what is there said, either in the text or the notes, concerning this congregation and its ministers, that Mr. Hubbard, or Herbert, its first pastor, was a learned man, and had received Episcopal ordination ; that in his time, the church accompanied him to Ireland, where he died ; that it then returned to England ; that Mr. Stephen Moore, its minister in 1640, who had been a deacon of it, was possessed of an estate, a man of good reputation, and endowed with a considerable share of ministerial abilities ; and that it was severely persecuted by the clergy and the bishops' courts.—*Crosby*, vol. i. ; p. 163-165.

   * Gough's History of the Quakers, vol. i., p. 52, note.

   † These disturbances often occurred by the officers of the army, and many of the officers were Baptists.—*C.*

far back as the year 1615, Mr. Helwise and his church, at London, published a treatise, entitled ‘‘ Persecution for Religion Judged and Condemned,’’ the dedication to which was subscribed thus : " By Christ's unworthy witnesses, his majesty's faithful subjects, commonly, but falsely, called Anabaptists." In this piece they asserted " that every man hath a right to judge for himself in matters of religion, and that to persecute any one on that account is illegal and antichristian."*

In a book called " The Bloody Tenet," printed in 1644, and in another entitled " The Compassionate Samaritan," they advanced this principle, " That it is the will and command of God that since the coming of his Son, a permission of the most paganish, Jewish, Turkish, or antichristian consciences and worships, be granted to all men in all nations ; that the doctrine of persecution in case of conscience maintained by Calvin, Beza, Cotton, and the ministers of New-England, is guilty of all the blood of the souls crying for vengeance under the altar." They besought the Parliament " to allow public protection to private as well as public congregations ; to review and repeal the laws against the Separatists ; to permit a freedom of the press to any man who writes nothing scandalous or dangerous to the state ; to prove themselves loving fathers to all good men, and so to invite equal assistance and affection from all." These opinions were in those times censured as most damnable doctrines, and the Parliament was invoked, by the pen of Dr. Featley, utterly to exterminate and banish out of the kingdom the Baptists, because they avowed and published them.† But the good sense and liberality of more modern times will not only admit these principles as maxims of good policy and sound Christianity, but respect the despised people who brought them forward and stated them, at a period when they were scarcely received by any others, and were held by the generality as most highly obnoxious : when even the great and good Mr. Baxter could declare, " I abhor unlimited liberty, or toleration of all."‡

It remains to take notice of some of the more distinguished preachers among this denomination of Christians, who died in the period of which we are speaking.

Mr. Thomas Helwise, according to the order of time, seems to deserve the first mention ; a man of good natural parts, and not without some acquired ones, though he had not the advantage of a learned education. He was a member of the ancient church of the Separatists in the beginning of Queen Elizabeth's reign, and accompanied them when they transported themselves out of England into Holland to escape persecution. He was of great service to them, and esteemed a man of eminent faith, charity, and spiritual gifts. When Mr. Smith, whose history we have given before,§ raised the controversy about infant baptism, Mr. Helwise became a convert to his sentiments, received baptism from him, and was one of the first in the constitution of his church, of which, after his death, he had the pastoral care. He and his

   * Crosby, vol. i., p. 272.

   † Robinson's Translation of Claude, vol. i., p. 250, note.   ‡ Plain Scripture Proof, p. 246.

   § See Young's Chronicles of the Pilgrims.—*C.*

people, soon after Smith's decease, published a
confession of their faith, entitled "The Confession of Faith, published in certain Conclusions,
by the Remainder of Mr. Smith's Company."*
At the end of it there was an appendix, giving
some account of Mr. Smith's last sickness and
death. Three years after, Mr. Robinson, the
pastor of the English congregation of Brownists
at Leyden, published remarks upon it. About
the same time Mr. Helwise began to reflect
upon his own conduct, that of the other
English Dissenters, in leaving their friends and
country to avoid persecution : whether it did not
proceed from fear and cowardice ; and whether
they ought not to return to bear their testimony
to the truth, and to countenance and encourage
their suffering brethren. The result was, that
he and his church quickly left Amsterdam, and
removed to London, where they continued to
preserve their church state, and to hold their
assemblies for worship, as the times would permit. He wrote a piece in justification of this
conduct, entitled "A short Declaration," wherein he stated in what cases it was lawful to fly
in times of persecution ; to which Mr. Robinson
replied. The conduct of Mr. Helwise and his
friends displeased the Nonconformists in exile,
who censured it as vainglorious, and imputed it
to natural confidence under the appearance of
religious fortitude. It is not known when Mr.
Helwise died, but, from the publications of the
day, it appears that he went on with great courage and resolution ; and the church, under all
the severities they experienced from the civil
powers, increased in numbers.†
   Mr. John Morton, another of Mr. Smith's disciples, appears to have been a man of note and
reputation, of considerable learning and abilities.
He was conversant with the Oriental languages
and the writings of the fathers, and was a zealous remonstrant. After his return from Holland he settled in the country. These circumstances are inferred from a manuscript written
by J. Morton, supposed to be the same person,
which was found at the beginning of the civil
wars, on demolishing an old wall near Colchester. It was printed by the General Baptists,
and passed through several impressions. Its
title was "Truth's Champion." It discussed
the questions concerning baptism, and the points
disputed between the Arminians and Calvinists.
The piece was written in a good style, and the
argument managed with much art and skill; and,
not without reason, held in considerable estimation by the remonstrants.‡
   A more particular and full account of some,
whose names have been brought forward in the
preceding narrative, will fall under the following periods of this history, the learning and
abilities of whom, it will appear, did credit to
the sect to which they belonged. Mr. Neal has
asserted that "its advocates were for the most
part of the meanest of the people ; their preachers were generally illiterate, and went about the
countries making proselytes of all that would
submit to their immersion, without a due regard
to their acquaintance with the principles of religion or their moral character." It is to be regretted that our respectable author, by this gen-

eral representation, without producing any authority, or alleging attested facts to justify it, hath
laid himself open to severe animadversion. Mr.
Crosby exclaims, "What a malicious slander is
this cast upon a whole body of Christians, consisting of fifty-four congregations, according to
his own acknowledgments!"* It may be supposed that Mr. Neal has here paid too great a
deference to such writers as the author of the
"Gangræna ;" and, on the other hand, Mr.
Crosby may have been too partial to his own
sect, and not allowed for the operation of a precipitate and injudicious zeal, by which a new
and persecuted sect is generally actuated ; he
may have forgotten that a great number of its
preachers would of course be unlearned and
ignorant men, when the liberty of prophesying,
as any individual was authorized and qualified
by the gift or influence of the Holy Spirit, was
a received principle ; for such gift would, where
it was supposed to exist and display itself, supersede acquired abilities and human literature.

CHAPTER III.

THE protectorate of Cromwell, though restricted to the short space of ten years, was a
most eventful period in the annals of ecclesiastical history. Both in our own country and
upon the Continent of Europe, it will ever be
memorable for the collision of parties, and the
extraordinary incidents to which it gave birth.
The sanguinary measures carried on by the instigation of Louis XIV., against the Waldenses
in the valleys of Piedmont ; the dispersion of
the Protestant churches in that long and highly
favoured country, and the deep interest which
Cromwell, as the head of the English government, aided by the pen of his Latin secretary,
our immortal Milton, took in the melancholy
fate of the meek confessors of Savoy, are events
with which few of the Dissenters of the present
day are unacquainted. But Mr. Neal has already entered pretty fully into the general history of this period, and traced the contest between the Episcopalians, the Presbyterians, and
the Independents, which we shall not resume.
Our object is merely to supply a little additional information respecting a class of professors
whom he appears to have overlooked or neglected as unworthy of his notice ; and to do this, it
may not be amiss to look back a little, and
glance at the aspect which the laws of the country bear towards the Baptists in particular.
   The great increase of the Baptists seems to
have provoked the Presbyterians, who were
now the ruling party, to a very high degree ;
and the same spirit of intolerance which the
Episcopalians had manifested towards the Puritans was now exhibited by them against all Dissenters from what they, who could now prove
the Divine right of Presbytery, were pleased to
decree. The whole of their conduct, in respect
of those who differed from them, shows what
Milton said to be true, that "New Presbyter is
but Old Priest writ large."†

---

* See Crosby, vol. ii. Appendix, No. i.
† Ibid., vol. i., p. 269-275.
‡ See Crosby, vol. i., p. 276-278.

* Vol. i., Preface, p. 5.
† Milton writes, "Under the Gospel, the first of

Their spirit of intolerance may be learned from the history of those times, and especially from some acts of the government. On May 26, 1645, the lord-mayor, Court of Aldermen, and Common Council, presented a petition to Parliament, commonly called "The City Remonstrance," in which they desired "that some strict and speedy course might be taken for the suppressing all private and separate congregations; that all Anabaptists, Brownists, heretics, schismatics, blasphemers, and all other sectaries who conformed not to the public discipline established or to be established by Parliament, might be fully declared against, and some effectual course settled for proceeding against such persons; and that no person disaffected to Presbyterial government, set forth or to be set forth by Parliament, might be employed in any place of public trust."*

This remonstrance was supported by the whole Scotch nation, who acted in concert with their English brethren, as appears by a letter of thanks to the lord-mayor, and Common Council, from the General Assembly, dated June 10, 1646, within a month after the delivery of the remonstrance. The letter commends their courageous appearance against sects and sectaries; their firm adherence to the Covenant, and their maintaining the Presbyterian government to be the government of Jesus Christ. It beseeches them to go on boldly in the work they had begun, till the three kingdoms were united in one faith and worship. At the same time they directed letters to the Parliament, beseeching them also, in the bowels of Jesus Christ, to give to Him the glory due to his name, by an immediate establishment of all his ordinances in their full integrity and power, according to the Covenant. Nor did they forget to encourage the Assembly at Westminster to proceed in their zeal against sectaries, and to stand boldly for the sceptre of Jesus Christ against the encroachments of earthly powers.

The arguments which this grave assembly used to withhold from others the blessing of Christian liberty, came with a bad grace from men who had as earnestly pleaded for the privilege while they were smarting under the lash of the prelates. "To comply with this request [of granting toleration], would open a gap for all sects to challenge such a liberty as their due : this liberty is denied by the churches in New-England, and we have as great right to deny it as they. This desired forbearance will make a perpetual division in the Church, and be a perpetual drawing away from the churches under the rule. Upon the same pretence, those who scruple infant baptism may withdraw from their churches, and so separate into another congregation; and so in that some practice may be scrupled, and they separate again. Are these divisions and subdivisions as lawful as they are infinite? Or must we give that respect to the errors of men's consciences, so as to satisfy their scruples by allowance of this liberty to them? Scruple of conscience is no cause of separation, nor doth it take off causeless separation from being schism, which may arise from errors of conscience as well as carnal and corrupt reason : therefore we conceive the causes of separation must be shown to be such, *ex natura rei*, as will bear it out; and, therefore, we say that granting the liberty desired will give a countenance to schism."

Many instances of this spirit might be adduced, but we shall only notice the following. A work was published by the Assembly in 1650, entitled "A Vindication of the Presbyterial Government and Ministry ; with an Exhortation to all Ministers, Elders, and People within the Province of London, &c. Published by the Ministers and Elders met together in a Provincial Assembly. George Walker, Moderator ; Arthur Jackson and Edmund Calamy, Assessors ; Roger Drake and Elidad Blackwell, Scribes."

This work contains the following expressions : "Whatsoever doctrine is contrary to godliness, and opens a door to libertinism and profaneness, you must reject it as soul poison : such is the doctrine of a universal toleration in religion." The ministers in the different parts of the country seem to have been of the same mind. Those in Lancashire published a paper in 1648, called "The Harmonious Consent of the Lancashire Ministers with their Brethren in London ;" in which they say, "A toleration would be putting a sword into a madman's hand ; a cup of poison into the hand of a child ; a letting loose of madmen with firebrands in their hands, and appointing a city of refuge to men's consciences for the devil to fly to ; a laying a stumbling-block before the blind ; a proclaiming liberty to the wolves to come into Christ's fold to prey upon the lambs : neither would it be to provide for tender consciences, but to take away all conscience."*

We turn away with disgust from these intolerant sentiments, and rejoice that the attempt has been made, and that none of the predicted effects have ensued.

It was very common at this time for the enemies of the Baptists to represent the practice of immersion as indecent and dangerous, and to argue that it could not be according to Divine authority, because a breach of the sixth commandment, "Thou shalt not kill :" and the Divine declaration, "I will have mercy, and not

the sacraments, commonly so called, is baptism, wherein the bodies of believers who engage themselves to newness of life are immersed in running water,* to signify their regeneration by the Holy Spirit, and their union with Christ in his death, burial, and resurrection." From this statement he argues, "Hence it follows that infants are not to be baptized, inasmuch as they are incompetent to receive instruction, or to believe, or enter into a covenant, or answer for themselves, or even to bear the Word. For how infants, who understand not the Word, be purified thereby any more than adults can receive edification by hearing an unknown language? For it is not that outward baptism, which purifies only the filth of the flesh, which saves us, but the answer of a good conscience, as Peter testifies, of which infants are incapable. Besides, baptism is not merely a covenant containing a stipulation on one side, with a corresponding engagement on the other, which, in the case of an infant, is impossible ; but it is a vow, and as such, can neither be pronounced by infants nor required of them. It is remarkable to what fertile arguments those divines have recourse who maintain the contrary opinion."—*Ivimey's Milton*, p. 261.—C.

* There were at that time no baptisteries ; the Baptists used the rivers as their fonts.—C.

* Crosby, vol. i.. p. 148.

* Crosby, vol. i., p. 190.

sacrifice." Who would have thought that Mr. Richard Baxter could have expressed himself in language like the following? "My sixth argument shall be against the usual manner of their baptizing, as it is by dipping over head in a river, or other cold water. That which is a plain breach of the sixth commandment, 'Thou shalt not kill,' is no ordinance of God, but a most heinous sin. But the ordinary practice of baptizing over head and in cold water, as necessary, is a plain breach of the sixth commandment, therefore it is no ordinance of God, but a heinous sin. And, as Mr. Cradock shows in his book of Gospel Liberty, the magistrate ought to restrain it, to save the lives of his subjects. That this is flat murder, and no better, being ordinarily and generally used, is undeniable to any understanding man; and I know not what trick a covetous landlord can find out to get his tenants to die apace, that he may have new fines and heriots, likelier than to encourage such preachers, that he may get them all to turn Anabaptists. I wish that this device be not it, which countenanceth these men; and covetous physicians, methinks, should not be much against them. Catarrhs and obstructions, which are the too great fountains of most mortal diseases in man's body, could scarce have a more notable means to produce them where they are not, or to increase them where they are. Apoplexies, lethargies, palsies, and all other comatous diseases, would be promoted by it. So would cephalalgies, hemicranies, phthises, debility of the stomach, crudities, and almost all fevers, dysenteries, diarrhœas, colics, iliac passions, convulsions, spasms, tremours, and so on. All hepatic, splenetic, and pulmonic persons, and hypochondriacs, would soon have enough of it. In a word, it is good for nothing but to despatch men out of the world that are burdensome, and to ranken churchyards. I conclude, if murder be a sin, then dipping ordinarily over head in England is a sin; and if those who would make it men's religion to murder themselves, and urge it upon their consciences as their duty, are not to be suffered in a commonwealth, any more than highway murderers; then judge how these Anabaptists, that teach the necessity of such dipping, are to be suffered. My seventh argument is also against another wickedness in their manner of baptizing, which is their dipping persons naked, which is very usual with many of them, or next to naked, as is usual with the modestest that I have heard of. If the minister must go into the water with the party, it will certainly tend to his death, though they may escape that go in but once. Would not vain young men come to a baptizing to see the nakedness of maids, and make a mere jest and sport of it?"*

It is with pleasure we give a place to the reflections of the late venerable Abraham Booth on these remarks, which certainly merited severe animadversion, especially as they were published at a time when, as the sequel will show, they were calculated to produce some serious consequences towards those who were in the practice of baptizing by immersion. "Were this representation just," says Mr. Booth, "we should have no reason to wonder if his following words expressed a fact : 'I am

still more confirmed that a visible judgment of God doth still follow anabaptizing wherever it comes.' It was not without reason, I presume, that Mr. Baxter made the following acknowledgment : 'I confess my style is naturally keen.' I am a little suspicious, also, that Dr. Owen had some cause to speak of his writings as follows : 'I verily believe that if a man who had nothing else to do, should gather into a heap all the expressions which in his late books, confessions, and apologies, have a lovely aspect towards himself, as to ability, diligence, sincerity, on the one hand ; with all those which are full of reproach and contempt towards others, on the other ; the view of them could not but a little startle a man of so great modesty, and of such eminency in the mortification of pride, as Mr. Baxter is.' Hence we learn that the Baptists are not the only persons who have felt the weight of Mr. Baxter's hand ; so that if a recollection of others having suffered under his keen resentment can afford relief, the poor Baptists may take some comfort ; and it is an old saying,

Solamen miseris socios habuisse doloris.

"Before I dismiss this extraordinary language of Mr. Baxter," adds Mr. Booth, "it is proper to be observed, that the charge of shocking indecency, which he lays with so much confidence against the Baptists of those times, was not suffered by them to pass without animadversion. No, he was challenged to make it good : it was denied, it was confuted by them. With a view to which, Dr. Wall says, 'The English Antipædobaptists need not have made so great an outcry against Mr. Baxter for his saying, that they baptized naked ; for if they had, it had been no more than the primitive Christians did.' But surely they had reason to complain of misrepresentation ; such misrepresentation as tended to bring the greatest odium upon their sentiments and practice. Besides, however ancient the practice charged upon them was, its antiquity could not have justified their conduct, except it had been derived from Divine command or apostolical example ι neither of which appears."†

It is a little extraordinary that in the next year, 1647, considerable favour was manifested towards the Baptists. Perhaps it arose from the policy of Cromwell, wishing to check the overgrown power of the Presbyterians, or from some of his officers and other persons of considerable influence embracing their sentiments, and using their interest in their behalf.

In a declaration of the Lords and Commons, published March 4, 1647, it is said, "The name of Anabaptism hath, indeed, contracted much odium by reason of the extravagant opinions of some of that name in Germany, tending to the disturbance of the government and the peace of all states, which opinions and practices we abhor and detest. But their opinion against the baptism of infants, it is only a difference about a circumstance of time in the administration of an ordinance, wherein in former ages, as well as in this, learned men have differed both in opinion and practice. And though we could wish that all men would satisfy themselves, and join with us in our judgment and pratice in this point, yet herein we hold it fit that men

---

* Baxter's Plain Scripture Proof, p. 134–137.

* Pædobap. Exam., vol. i., p. 263–265.

should be convinced by the Word of God, with great gentleness and reason, and not beaten out of it by force and violence."*

This declaration discovered much of a truly Christian spirit; and happy would it have been if all governments had always acted on such principles. But it is lamentable to observe, that the very next year, a more severe law was passed than any that had been made in England since the Reformation. It bore date May 2, 1648, and was entitled "An Ordinance of the Lords and Commons assembled in Parliament for the Punishment of Blasphemies and Heresies." One article was, "Whosoever shall say that the baptism of infants is unlawful, or that such baptism is void, and that such persons ought to be baptized again, and in pursuance thereof shall baptize any person formerly baptized; or shall say the church government by Presbytery is antichristian or unlawful, shall, upon conviction by the oath of two witnesses, or by his own confession, be ordered to renounce his said error in the public congregation of the parish where the offence was committed; and in case of refusal, he shall be committed to prison till he find sureties that he shall not publish or maintain the said error any more."†

It is likely that the death of the king in this year, and the confusion which resulted from it, might prevent this cruel and shameful ordinance from being carried into effect, as we do not hear that any were prosecuted upon it.

The government was now altered, and instead of being in the Parliament, was vested in a single person. This was the General Oliver Cromwell, whose title was to be His Highness, Lord-protector of the Commonwealth of England, Scotland, and Ireland, and of the dominions thereunto belonging.

The Baptists in the army seem to have been apprehensive that he entertained designs against them, as appears from the following letter, which we insert, not because we approve of its spirit, but because it may cast some light upon the history of the times. It was probably written by some of his officers, who were envious at his exaltation, and offended that he had deserted his Republican sentiments. It is entitled "A short Discovery of his Highness the Lord-protector's Intentions touching the Anabaptists in the Army, and all such as are against his reforming Things in the Church; which was first communicated by a Scotch Lord who is called Twidle, but is now come to the Ear of the Anabaptists: upon which there are propounded thirty-five Queries for his Highness to answer to his Conscience. By a Well-wisher to the Anabaptists' Prosperity, and all the rest of the Separatists in England."‡

* Crosby, vol. i., p. 196.   † Ibid., vol. i., p. 203.
‡   "To His Highness the Lord-protector.

"My Lord,
"There is some intelligence abroad, which I desire to communicate in a private way, lest I become a prey to the malice or envy of the roaring lion. But to the matter intended, and that is this: It seems your highness, being discoursing with a Scotch lord, who is called the Lord Twidle, you were pleased to say that there was something amiss in the Church and State, which you would reform as soon as may be. Of those that were amiss in the State, some were done and the rest were doing; and as for those things that were amiss in the Church, you hoped to

rectify them by degrees, as convenient opportunity presented itself; but before you could do this work, the Anabaptists must be taken out of the army; and this you could not do with sharp corrosive medicines, but it must be done by degrees. From which there are two things observable: 1. The work. 2. The way you intend to do this work.

"First, to the work; and that is church-work. It seems you intend to follow the steps of them that are gone before, which could not be content to meddle with state affairs, and to make laws and statutes, and impose them upon the people as rules of Divine worship. And this is the work you intend to be at, under pretence of correcting error, and so to destroy truth.

"But who could have thought, when you made your last speech to Parliament, when your tongue was so sweetly tipped for the liberty of conscience, reproving the Parliament for having a finger on their brother's conscience; who could have imagined that then heard you, that you would have been so soon at the same trade, unless he had supposed a fountain could have sent forth sweet water and bitter? But,

"Secondly, the way you intend to take to bring about this design is twofold: 1, To purge the army of the Anabaptists. 2. To do it by degrees. But, Oliver, is this thy design? And is this the way to be rid of the Anabaptists? And is this the reason, because they hinder the things amiss in the Church? I confess they have been enemies to the Presbyterian church government; and so were you at Dunbar in Scotland; or, at least, you seemed to be so by your words and actions; for you spake as pure Independency as any of us all then; and made this an argument why we should fight stoutly, because we had the prayers of the Independents and baptized churches. So highly did you seem to love the Anabaptists then, that you did not only invite them into the army, but entertain them in your family; but it seems the case is altered. But, I pray, do not deceive yourself, nor let the priests deceive you; for the Anabaptists are men that will not be shuffled out of their birthrights, as free-born people of England. And have they not filled your towns, your cities, your provinces, your islands, your castles, your navies, your tents, your armies (except that which went to the West Indies, which prospers so well), your court? your very council is not free; only we have left your temples for yourself to worship in. So that I believe it will be a hard thing to root them out; although you tell the Scotch lord you will do it by degrees, as he reports.

"May it please your highness seriously to consider what hath been said, and answer these ensuing queries to your own conscience:

"1. Whether your highness had come to the height of honour and greatness you are now come to, if the Anabaptists, so called, had been so much your enemies as they were your friends?

"2. Whether the Anabaptists were ever unfaithful, either to the commonwealth in general, or to your highness in particular? And if not, then what is the reason of your intended dismission?

"3. Whether the Anabaptists be not as honest now as in the year 1650, and 51, and 52, &c.? And if so, why not as useful now as then?

"4. Whether the Anabaptists are not to be commended for their integrity, which had rather keep faith and a good conscience, although it may lose them their employments, than to keep their employments with the loss of both?

"5. Whether the Anabaptists may not as justly endeavour to eat out the bowels of your government, as your highness may endeavour to eat them out of their employments?

"6. Whether the Anabaptists did not come more justly into their employments in the army than your highness came into the seat of government?

"7. Whether, if the Anabaptists had the power in

tists were in the king's army, yet there seem to have been some of that persuasion among the troops of the Parliament; and it has been as signed as a reason for disbanding one entire

their hands, and were as able to cast you out as you were them, and they did intend it to you as you do to them; whether, I say, your highness would not call them all knaves?

" 8. Whether this be fair dealing in the sight of God and man, to pretend a great deal of love to the Anabaptists, as to Major Pack and Mr. Kiffin, and a hundred more that I could name, when at the same time you intend evil against them?

" 9. Whether the Anabaptist will not be in a better condition in the day of Christ that keeps his covenant with God and men, than your highness will be if you break with both?

" 10. Whether a hundred of the old Anabaptists, such as marched under your command in 48, 49, 50, &c., be not as good as two hundred of your new courtiers, if you were in such a condition as you were at Dunbar in Scotland?

" 11. Whether the cause of the army's defeat in Hispaniola was because there were so many Anabaptists in it? And if so, if that be the only reason why they are so much out of date?

" 12. Whether your highness hath not changed your former intention, to have an equal respect to the godly, though different in judgment? And if so, whether it be not from the better to the worse?

" 13. Whether your highness's conscience was not more at peace, and your mind more set upon things above, when you loved the Anabaptists, than it is now, when you hate their principles, or their service, or both?

" 14. Whether your highness's court is not a greater charge to this nation than the Anabaptists in the army? And if so, whether this be the ease which you promised the people?

" 15. Whether there be any disproportion between the state of things now and the state of things in the days of old? And if there be, show us where it lieth, how, and when?

" 16. Whether the moneys laid out in the making of the new rivers and ponds at Hampton Court might not have been better bestowed in paying the public faith, or the Anabaptists' arrears before their dismission?

" 17. Whether it is not convenient for the Anabaptists to provide for their own safety, seeing from you they can expect none?

" 18. Whether it will be any more treason to fight for our liberties and civil properties in these days, if they be denied us, than it was to fight for them in the days of the king?

" 19. Whether the instrument of government be as the laws of the Medes and Persians, that alter not? If so, how is it that Mr. John Biddle is now a prisoner?

" 20. Whether your highness may not as well violate the whole instrument of government as the 37th and 38th articles? If so, what security have the people for their liberty?

" 21. Whether our liberty doth not wholly depend upon your will, and the will of a future protector, seeing the instrument of government is so little useful? If so, whether our condition be not as bad as ever?

" 22. Whether you may not as justly suffer all to be put in prison that differ from the Church of England, as to suffer Mr. Biddle to be imprisoned?

" 23. Whether it will not be more abominable to the Anabaptists, or Independents, or Mr. Biddle, or any other professing faith in God by Jesus Christ, and are not disturbers of the civil peace, nor turn their liberty into licentiousness, to suffer for their consciences under your government, that promised liberty to such, than it was to have suffered under the king, that promised them none?

" 24. Whether your highness will not appear to be a dreadful apostate and fearful dissembler, if you suffer persecution to fall upon the Anabaptists, or Independents, or them of Mr. Biddle's judgment, seeing you promised equal liberty to all?

" 25. Whether this will not prove your highness's ruin, if you join with such a wicked principle to persecute for conscience, or to turn men out of the army for being Anabaptists, or for any such thing as differs from the Church of England, seeing God hath confounded all such as have done so?

" 26. Whether the old Parliament was not turned out for leaving undone that which they ought to have done? And if so, whether those things have been done since?

" 27. Whether the little Parliament was not turned out for doing that which the other left undone, or taking away of tithes and other grievances? And if so, then,

" 28. Whether you did not intend your own ends more than you did the nation's good, in breaking the first Parliament, and calling the second, and dissolving them again?

" 29. Whether the instrument of government was not preparing eight or nine days before the breaking up of the little Parliament? And if so, whether you did not intend their dissolving?

" 30. Whether you did not tell a shameful untruth, to the last Parliament, saying that you did not know of their dissolving, that is to say, the little Parliament, till they came to deliver up their power to you?

" 31. Whether your highness did not put a slur upon the Lord Lambert, when he should have gone lord-deputy to Ireland, in telling the Parliament it savoured too much of a monarchy, and so sent Fleetwood with a lower title?

" 32. Whether your highness do not intend to put another slur upon the Lord Lambert, in sending for the lord-deputy to come into England, to make him generalissimo of the armies in England, Scotland, and Ireland?

" 33. Whether it is not convenient for the Lord Lambert to consider of those actions, and to have an eye to your proceedings, lest by degrees you eat him out of all, as you intend to do the Anabaptists?

" 34. Whether the excessive pride of your family do not call for a speedy judgment from heaven, seeing pride never goeth without a fall?

" 35. Whether the six coach-horses did not give your highness a fair warning of some worse thing to follow, if you repent not, seeing God often forewarns before he strikes home?

" THE CONCLUSION.

" My Lord,

" My humble request is, that you will seriously consider of these few lines: although you may dislike the way by which they are communicated, yet let the matter sink deep into your heart; for these things should have met you in another manner, had not your highness cast off all such friendly communication by word of mouth, and the persons too, if they did but tell you plainly their minds. And take heed of casting away old friends for new acquaintance, as Rehoboam did, who forsook the counsel of his good old friends, and consulted with his young courtiers; which caused the ten tribes to revolt from him.*. And it is a deadly sign of a speedy ruin, when a prince or a state casts off the interests of the people of God; as you may see how Joash forsook the people and the house of God, and then his house fell before a few of the Assyrians, and at last his own servants conspired against him, and slew him.

" And therefore, O Cromwell! leave off thy wicked design of casting off the interest of the people of God; and let my counsel be acceptable to thee; and break off thy sins by righteousness, and thy iniquity by showing mercy to the poor, and it may be a lengthening out of thy tranquillity.' For it is not strength united with policy, but righteousness accompanied with strength, that must keep alive your interest with God and the people. And when both these die, that

*1 Kings, xii., 8.

regiment in the army of the Earl of Essex, that the colonel himself countenanced the Separatists, particularly the Anabaptists. Although their numbers increased considerably from about the year 1649, to such a degree, indeed, as that the principal officers in different regiments both of horse and foot became Baptists, particularly in Cromwell's own regiment of horse, and in that of the Duke of Albemarle's regiment of foot, yet it is said, on good information, that previous to this there were not to be found, at any time, twenty persons of this denomination *vested with command* of any kind in the whole army. Until the year 1648, two only of this profession, Mr. Lawrence, and Mr. John Fiennes, a son of Lord Say, were members of the House of Commons; and in that year, before the death of the king, they withdrew from the Parliament because they disapproved of its proceedings, and lived in retirement for about six years, when Mr. Lawrence was again called into public employment. In 1650, Captain Mildmay, Captain Pack, and Sir John Harman, who were all Baptists, were preferred to commands at sea.*† Major-general Harrison, whom Baxter pronounces "a man of excellent parts for affection and oratory, though not well seen in the principles of his religion,"‡ was the only Baptist among the king's judges; and, indeed, it appears that he himself was not, actually baptized till 1657, which was several years after that tragical event had taken place.◊ The following extract of a letter from Captain Richard Deane to Dr. Barlow, bishop of Lincoln, furnishes considerable information concerning the state of the Baptists at this period, and their conduct in the affairs of the state:

"My Lord,

"The ground of my humbly tendering these ensuing pages to your lordship is your declared condescension to peruse any small treatise that should be presented to you concerning the proper subject and administration of baptism. That they may in your lordship's charity, so far as their conversation suits with their doctrine, be admitted among the number of sincere Christians, I intend to bring to your remembrance some of their leaders, and the occasions which prepared the way for the increase of their numbers.

"About thirty-eight years since, in the heat of our late troubles, Episcopacy being laid aside, and Presbytery only as it were by way of experiment for a season attempted, but never in a national way prosecuted with effect, every man was at liberty to pursue the persuasions of his own mind as to entering into church-fellowship in distinct congregations, and therein to Join with such as he conceived came nearest to

is to say, righteousness and sincerity, then adieu to thy greatness here, and thy eternal happiness hereafter.

"From him who wishes your happiness so long as you do well.—*Printed for the information of all such as prize the liberty of their consciences, for which so much blood has been spilt.*"*

* Crosby's History of the Baptists, vol. ii., p. 2–5.
† See Pepy's Diary for proof of the existence of Baptist influence in the English navy at this period. —C. ‡ Baxter's Life, part i., p. 57.
◊ The reader is referred to Harrison's life in Noble's Regicides, Burnet, and Godwin.—C.

* Crosby, vol. iii., p. 231–242.

the primitive pattern in worship and discipline. About that time and a little after there were many ministers, some who had been before ordained, and others who had been admitted to parochial and other public charges: among whom of my acquaintance were Mr. Tombes, some time preacher at the temple; Mr. Christopher Blackwood in Kent, Mr. Benjamin Cox at Bedford, Mr. Edward Harrison, Mr. Daniel Dyke, and some others in or near Hertfordshire; Mr. Hansard Knollys, and many others who did openly profess, and several of them write and publish their opinions concerning the proper subject and manner of baptism. Some of them voluntarily left their parochial charges and benefices, as not approving the baptizing of infants, and collected distinct congregations of such as agreed with them in this doctrine of baptism; which, by a succession of ordained ministers in the places of such as are dead, remain to this day.

"In the year 1649 the Baptists greatly increased in the country, and their opinions did likewise spread themselves into some of the regiments of horse and foot in the army; and that in 1650 and afterward, some professing this opinion were called from their private employments, and preferred to commands at sea: among others, Captain Mildmay to command the admiral flag-ship, under the late Duke of Albemarle, when he was one of the generals at sea; Captain Pack, to command the flag-ship under Sir George Ascue, rear-admiral; Sir John Harman, to command the admiral flag-ship under his royal highness the Duke of York.

"But, notwithstanding some of this sect had that countenance given them as I have mentioned, by such as had the principal management of affairs, yet this sect in general, as they have published in their apologies, were the least of any sort of people concerned in any vicissitudes of government that happened among us. My station within the afore-mentioned ten years gave me opportunity to know most persons and actions of note, in reference as well to civil as martial affairs, and particularly those of this sect. And although in and after the year 1649 their numbers did increase, insomuch that the principal officers in divers regiments of horse and foot became Anabaptists, particularly in Oliver Cromwell's own regiment of horse when he was captain-general of all the Parliament's forces, and in the Duke of Albemarle's own regiment of foot when he was general of all the English forces in Scotland; yet, by the best information I could have, there were not, at any time before the year 1649, twenty Anabaptists in any sort of command in the whole army; and until after the year 1648, there were no more than two, viz., Mr. Lawrence, and Mr. John Fiennes, one of the Lord Say's sons, who made profession of this opinion, chosen into the Commons' House of Parliament, and both these did in that year and in the lifetime of Charles I., as I have been credibly informed, voluntarily depart from that Parliament, as not approving their proceedings against the person of the king, and sat no more in it, but lived privately until about six years afterward. A new form of government being then formed, and in appearance settled, Mr. Lawrence was again called into public employment.

"I confess to your lordship, I never heard of any Anabaptists in the king's army during the contest between his majesty and the Parliament; and perhaps, because there were some in the Parliament's army and none in the king's army, some persons have from thence taken occasion to affirm that the opinion of Anabaptism in the Church is opposite to monarchy in the State. It is true, as before is mentioned, that this opinion was no general bar to the continuance of such as did embrace it in public employments, though I have cause to believe that one special reason of disbanding one entire regiment in the Earl of Essex's army was, because the colonel entertained and gave countenance to Separatists and some Anabaptists. And that which occasioned Oliver Cromwell, after he usurped the government of lord-protector, to discharge at once all the principal officers of his own regiment upon other pretences was, for that they were all Anabaptists."[*]

It belongs to this period, also, to introduce some account of another distinguished military officer, who ranks among the denomination of Baptists. I refer to Colonel Hutchinson, who was governor of Nottingham Castle during the time of the civil wars. He was one of the king's judges; and, whether in the senate or the field, uniformly distinguished himself as a person of great courage, judgment, piety, and liberality. An interesting narrative of his life and times, drawn up by his amiable and accomplished wife, has been recently issued from the press, in which the following account is given of the manner in which he was led to embrace the sentiments of the Baptists: the circumstances are related with the characteristic simplicity and good sense which pervade the whole work.

"At Nottingham they had gotten a very able minister into the great church, but a bitter Presbyterian. Him and his brethren my Lady Fairfax caressed with so much kindness, that they grew impudent to preach up their faction openly in the pulpit, and to revile the others, and at length they would not suffer any of the army chaplains to preach in the town. They then, coming to the governor and complaining of their unkind usage, he invited them to come: and preach in his house, which, when it was known they did, there was a great concourse of people came thither to them; and the Presbyterians, when they heard it, were madded with rage, not only against them, but against the governor, who accidentally gave them another occasion about the same time. When formerly the Presbyterian ministers forced him, for quietness' sake, to go, and break up a private meeting in the cannoniers' chamber, there were found some notes concerning Pædobaptism, which, being brought into the governor's lodgings, his wife having then more leisure to read than he, having perused and compared them with the Scriptures, found not what to say against the truths they asserted concerning the misapplication of that ordinance to infants; but, being then young and modest, she thought it a kind of virtue to submit to the judgment and practice of most

churches, rather than defend a singular opinion of her own, she not being then enlightened in that great mistake of the national churches. But in this year, she happening to be with child, communicated her doubts to her husband, and desired him to endeavour her satisfaction; and while he did, he himself became as unsatisfied, or, rather, satisfied, against it. First, therefore, he diligently searched the Scriptures alone, and could find in them no ground at all for this practice. Then he bought and read all the treatises on both sides, which at that time came thick from the presses, and still was cleared in the error of the Pædobaptists. After this, his wife being brought to bed, that he might, if possible, give the religious party no offence, he invited all the ministers to dinner, and propounded his doubt and the ground thereof to them. None of them could defend their practice with any satisfactory reason, but the tradition of the Church from the primitive times, and their main buckler of federal holiness, which Tombes and Denne had excellently overthrown. He and his wife then professing themselves unsatisfied in the practice, desired their opinions what they ought to do. Most answered, to conform to the general practice of other Christians, how dark soever it were to themselves; but Mr. Foxcraft, one of the assembly, said, that except they were convinced of the warrant of that practice from the Word, they sinned in doing it: whereupon that infant was not baptized. And now the governor and his wife, notwithstanding that they forsook not their assemblies, nor retracted the benevolences and civilities from them, yet they were reviled by them, called fanatics and Anabaptists, and often glanced at in their public sermons. Not only the ministers, but all their zealous sectaries, conceived implacable malice against them on that account, which was carried on with a spirit of envy and persecution to the last; though he, on his side, might well have said to them, as his Master to the old Pharisees, 'Many good works have I done among you; for which of these do ye hate me?' Yet the generality even of that people had a secret conviction upon them that he had been faithful to them, and deserved their love; and, in spite of their own bitter zeal, they could not but have a reverent esteem for him whom they often railed at for not thinking and speaking according to their opinions."[*]

Having introduced this excellent man to the reader's notice, it possibly may not be altogether unacceptable to him to be furnished with a few more particulars of his personal history, and that of his amiable consort.

He was descended of an ancient and honourable family, and born at Nottingham, in the month of September, 1616. He was the eldest surviving son of Sir Thomas Hutchinson and Lady Margaret, his first wife, a daughter of Sir John Biron, of Newsted,[†] in the same county. As soon as his age permitted, he was placed under the tuition of Mr. Theobalds, then master of the free school at Nottingham; and shortly afterward he was sent to the free school at Lincoln, which was conducted by a Mr. Clarke. This person, though pious, was remarkable for

* Crosby, vol. ii., Preface, p. 2–5.
† Clarendon speaks in high terms of a young Anabaptist, without naming him, who, in time of Cromwell, brought an application on their part to Charles II., then on the Continent.—C.

* Ed. 2, p. 271, 272.
† Ancestor of the poet. Newsted Abbey was then the seat of the family.—C.

his pedantry; which so disgusted young Hutchinson, that he could never profit under his instructions. While at this seminary, he was taught the military exercise by an old soldier, who was kept by the master to give his pupils some notion of the art of war. He was again sent to the free school at Nottingham, in which he made very great proficiency; and from this place went to the University of Cambridge, and there was made a fellow-commoner of Peter House. The tutor of his college was Mr. Norwich, a person of great learning, and of an amiable disposition. Under this perceptor he made rapid progress in his studies, received great applause for several public exercises, and obtained a degree as a testimony of his merits. After remaining at college five years, he returned to his father's house at Nottingham. He was now about twenty years old, having hitherto resisted the temptations of youth, and been noted for the sobriety and consistency of his deportment. His father had been for some time married to a second wife, and was surrounded by a youthful and increasing progeny. This circumstance was not altogether agreeable to young Hutchinson, who, however, wishing to avoid any complaints that he might make if he continued at home, adopted the resolution of visiting London. There he entered Lincoln's Inn; but soon found the study of the law so irksome and unpleasant, that he very shortly abandoned it. Soon afterward, in 1638, he entered into the marriage relation with Miss Lucy Apsley, second daughter of Sir Alleh Apsley, lieutenant of the Tower. She was a young lady of great beauty, parts, and acquirements, and wrote the memoirs of her husband, which have been lately published by a descendant of the family. During two years' leisure that Mr. Hutchinson now enjoyed, he directed his attention to several branches of divinity. In October, 1641, he retired to his seat at Owthorpe, in Nottinghamshire. About this time was perpetrated the Irish massacre, which filled the nation with horror, and preceded those civil commotions and distresses with which Britain was about to be chastised. This massacre, and the conversation which it everywhere occasioned, led Mr. Hutchinson to employ his thoughts on the political state of the country; and the result of this inquiry was a persuasion that the cause of the Parliamentarians was supported by justice. He, with some others, was requested by nearly all the freeholders and middle classes in his native county to present a petition to the king, then at York, to return to Parliament. Soon afterward he took up arms, though not till necessity compelled him; for a warrant was issued for his apprehension, and he, with his wife, was obliged to quit home. He accepted the commission of lieutenant-colonel among the forces appointed by the Parliament to be raised. He was then engaged, in conjunction with many Parliamentarians, in the defence of Nottingham; and when the troops there quartered were called out to the relief of General Essex, he was appointed, by the committee of that town, to the government of its castle.

In 1643 his father died, having left his personal estate, and all his property that was unsettled at Mr. Hutchinson's marriage, to his second wife and children. The enemies of Colonel Hutchinson then seized, by violence, the rents of his tenants, which he was about to receive; and his estate being sought for by several, promise of it was obtained from the king. In this extremity, though he had supported the garrison chiefly at his own expense, and thus lessened his pecuniary resources; and though he was repeatedly tempted with the most flattering promises to desert his party, he remained inflexibly firm. He adopted the most salutary measures for the protection of the castle and town; but his efforts were frequently rendered abortive by the treachery of some under his command. By them a party of the Royalists were one night admitted into the town, but were soon expelled by the prudence and intrepidity of the governor. A few of the committee, wishing to ruin their commander, that they might obtain authority themselves, endeavoured to excite a spirit of discontent among the soldiers and townsmen, and had the effrontery to lay a statement of their pretended grievances before a committee of both nations. The result of this contest was a perfect justification of Colonel Hutchinson, and the disgrace of his infamous calumniators. His office had been previously ratified by Parliament, who had also intrusted him with the government of the town, and presented him with thanks for his services. While he held these commissions he often distinguished himself for his bravery. At the siege of Shelford, in which was a garrison under the command of Colonel Philip Stanhope, eldest son to the Earl of Chesterfield, he exposed himself to the greatest dangers, and was the first that scaled the walls. He was also at the siege of Newark, which surrendered to him and his men.

Having been chosen a member of Parliament in the place of his father, he came to London to discharge the duties of his new office. The Parliament were at that time divided by the factions and animosities of the Independents and the Presbyterians. Colonel Hutchinson was soon marked as a strenuous Independent; and, in the controversy between the army and the Presbyterians, he ranked himself with the army. Returning, at the settlement of Parliament, to his garrison at Nottingham, he found it consisted only of the castle, and that all his regiment, except two companies, had been disbanded. This being the case, he resigned his commission, and went, with his family, to live at Owthorpe. His house was almost in ruins, but he then had not money sufficient to repair it. He was, however, earnestly entreated to resume his commission, but in vain; for his health was now rather delicate, and he wished to enjoy a little peace and retirement.

Being again summoned to Parliament, he was nominated one of the commissioners for the trial of King Charles I. To this nomination he at first felt considerable reluctance to accede. But being convinced, after mature deliberation, and fervent prayer for direction, that the measure was fully justifiable, he no longer hesitated. Whatever were the motives which induced that assembly to judge and condemn their sovereign, or whatever opinion may be formed of their proceedings, the conduct of Colonel H. in that affair was certainly dictated by conscientious principles.

After the dissolution of Parliament, he returned to Owthorpe, and devoted his time to the education of his children (who had, besides, the ablest masters); to the suppression of disorders in his neighbourhood; and to the administration of justice. He was elected a member of the Parliament summoned April 25, 1660, but was soon suspended, on account of the part he took in the transactions relative to Charles I.; and his punishment was a sentence of dismissal from the present house of Parliament, and of incapacity to sustain any public office, civil or military, forever. This sentence must be allowed not to have been very severe; but he was not permitted to live unmolested. He was accused, without the least shadow of proof, of treasonable designs and practices. His house was pillaged of all his armour, to the value of £100; and some pictures that had once belonged to the late king, and which he had purchased in London during the interregnum, to the amount of £1000 or £1500, were wrested from him by an order from the secretary of state. By a warrant from the same secretary, he was seized one Sunday evening, while expounding to his family a portion of the Epistle to the Romans. After undergoing very severe treatment, he was dismissed; but in a short time again apprehended, thrust into a filthy prison, where he fell sick, and commanded by the king to be carried to London in custody. Having with much pain arrived there, he was committed to the Tower, and bore several petty examinations. Sir John Robinson, then keeper, as worthless character, was as cruel and hardened as a torturer in the Inquisition, and employed every method he could devise of insulting and injuring Colonel H.

Under all these multiplied calamities, Colonel Hutchinson was patient and submissive. An order at length came for his removal to Sandown Castle, in Kent, whither he was still pursued by the malice and cruelty of his adversaries. He was confined to a dreary, damp room, that was exposed to the piercing air of the sea, and against the bottom of which the waves dashed in angry murmurs. In this miserable condition, his wife, who had attended him in all his sufferings, brought some books for his entertainment; but he declared, that if he were to remain in prison all his life, he would read nothing but the Bible. This book, indeed, afforded him divine consolation, so that he said to his disconsolate partner, what reason she had to rejoice that God supported him under his trials, and did not suffer his patience or spirits to fail. He was even thankful for his afflictions, considering them as tokens of his heavenly Father's love, who chastises all his children. Symptoms of disease now began to appear, and he very rapidly grew weaker. In his sickness he was wonderfully cheered by the comforts of religion; and to a person who asked him how he did, he replied, "Incomparably well, and full of faith." He continued in this happy frame, giving serious advice to those that were around him, and pouring out his desires in ejaculatory prayers. When he was questioned as to the ground of his hope, he said, "There's none but Christ, none but Christ, in whom I have unspeakable joy, more than I can express;" and on the Sabbath-day, September 11, 1664, his spirit winged her flight to the regions of everlasting repose. Of

the political conduct of Colonel Hutchinson various sentiments are entertained, but none question his integrity or piety.

CHAPTER IV

HISTORY OF THE BAPTISTS FROM THE RESTORATION OF KING CHARLES II. TO THE BANISHMENT OF THE EARL OF CLARENDON, A.D. 1660–1670.

WHATEVER concern the Baptists may be supposed to have had in national affairs, while the unhappy contest was pending between Charles I. and his army, it is sufficiently apparent, from what has been seen in the foregoing chapter, that it soon ceased after Cromwell assumed the reins of government, who, when he thought himself well settled, and perceived that it would please the dominant party, began to undermine the sectarians, and, in particular, to suppress the Baptists. Mr. Baxter charges them with growing insolent both in England and Ireland after Cromwell's death, and the succession of his son Richard was set aside; and that, joining their brethren in the army, they were everywhere put in power. He complains of some personal insults and ungenerous treatment which he received from some who resided near to him, irritated by their remembrance of the opposition he had made to their sentiments, and who; though not many more than twenty, "talked,'" as he expresses it, "as if they had been lords of the world."* This spirit of resentment and triumph was soon humbled by the disappointment of hope, and a subsequent series of sufferings.

This appears, in the first instance, from a petition presented to King Charles II., signed by thirty-five, on behalf of many others in Lincolnshire. It stated, that not only their meetings for religious worship were interrupted by the magistrates, and bonds for good behaviour were imposed upon them, for the violation of which, on account of renewing their assemblies, they were prosecuted as peace-breakers; but that they were abused in the streets, and their own houses could not afford them protection; for, if they were heard praying to God in their families, they were insulted by sounding of horns, heating against their doors, and threats that they should be hanged. If they appealed to the magistrates, the rage of their adversaries received a sanction from the odious terms with which those who sat on the bench of justice reviled them. Many of them were indicted at the sessions for not attending on the preaching of the Episcopal clergy, and alarmed with a design of levying from every one of them a penalty of £20 a month.

The petition was graciously received by the king, who promised that he would take particular care that none should trouble them, on account of their conscience, in things pertaining to religion; and immediately directed a member of Parliament to go to the lord-chancellor and secretary, that the proper measures for this end might be taken.

In the same year, another petition and representation of their sufferings was presented by some Baptists, inhabitants of Kent, and prison-

* His own Life, part ii., p. 206.

ers in the jail at Maidstone. In this paper they appealed to their "Confession of Faith," as truly representing their principles concerning magistracy and government; and deplored the danger which threatened their lives, and the ruin which hung over their wives and little ones, by the violence exercised against them; for, besides being made prisoners, the houses of some had, without any authority from the executive power, been broken open in the dead of night; and from others their goods and cattle had been taken away and detained.

Great, also, were the sufferings of those who resided in Gloucestershire. The most eminent Cavaliers rode about armed with swords and pistols, ransacking their houses, and abusing their families in a violent manner. At the house of Mr. Helme, at Winchcombe, the bed whereon his children laid was not spared; and their outrageous conduct so frightened his wife as to throw her into an illness which threatened her life. Mr. Warren, who possessed the parsonage of Rencome, was, with his wife and family, penned up into an upper room of his house, and so harassed night and day by the violence of the assailants and the noise of hautboys, that he died in the place. Mr. Fletcher, who had been put into a vacant place by authority, was so beat and inhumanly treated by a Cavalier of his parish, that he and his family fled for their lives. One pious minister was assaulted as he was entering his pulpit. Another was violently pulled out of his house; his wife, children, and goods were thrown into the street; none of the parish were allowed to give them entertainment, and he himself was haled to jail.*

It is less surprising that these people were insulted by the ignorant populace, and were abused by the petty officers of power, when even the Legislature marked them as the objects of suspicion, hatred, and severity; for the Parliament assembled upon the Restoration, when it passed an act for confirming all ministers in the possession of their benefices, how heterodox soever they had been, provided they would conform for the future, excepted such as had been of the Baptist persuasion.†

So far from being encouraged to conform, or being permitted in peace and security to dissent, they were pursued with cruelty. Divers of them were cast into Reading prison for conscientiously scrupling to take some oaths administered to them. At Newport in Wales, at the end of sermon, two were set upon by soldiers with swords and staves.‡ At London, Dr. John Griffith was committed to Newgate, where he lay seventeen months, for no other crime but preaching to a congregation of Protestants. In Lincolnshire, Mr. Thomas Grantham§ and some others were taken from their meeting at Boston by some soldiers, and after having been lodged all night in a public inn, had their rest disturbed, and their minds grieved, by the incessant curses and oaths of their guards; they were, on the next morning, conveyed to the common jail,

and detained there, without so much as the least pretence of any crime laid to their charge, till the assizes, when they were dismissed. At Dover, the magistrates were severe against them, taking them from their meeting-houses, and committing them to prison. After fourand-twenty days they were admitted to bail, and appearing at the assizes, were forbidden to assemble any more in their own place of worship, but were allowed the use of one of the churches. This privilege, which they enjoyed about the space of five months, was afterward denied to them. Upon meeting again in their own place, their worship was disturbed, and twenty-four of them, under different commitments, sent to prison; at the Quarter Sessions, a bill of indictment was found against them; some traversed it, others submitted to the court, and the rest were remitted to prison again.*

A circumstance which much aggravated the proceedings against these people was, that they were not apprehended by the peace-officers only, but by rude, youthful, and mercenary soldiers, who seized them, to the terror of women and children, with muskets and drawn swords, did violence to their persons, and spoiled their goods.†

In June, 1661, one of these military banditti went to a meeting-house in Whitechapel, and laid hands on more than twenty; one of whom refusing to go with them unless they produced their warrant, they not only pulled him along by force, and beat him about the head with their hangers, but lifting him up several times between three or four, let him fall with violence, and drove his breast and stomach against the rails with such force, that his health was greatly injured by the blows and falls. When a suit was commenced against the actors of this tragedy, the persons at whose complaint the soldiers were arrested were themselves arrested, and sent to Newgate, where they lay about ten or twelve days before they could be bailed, and were held bound from sessions to sessions; for a long time, before they could be discharged.

The persons assembling in the same meeting-house were assaulted by a like body of soldiers, October the 20th, 1661, and one of them, the minister objecting to the authority under which they professed to act, was by a mittimus pretending and asserting great matters, cast into Newgate, where he lay thirty weeks, without anything laid to his charge, and then they released him.

On the 3d of November, in the same year, a similar outrage was committed, in the same place, with as little show or face of law. The preacher and three more were seized, and thrown into New Prison, from which, in time of sessions, one was removed to Newgate, under pretence of being brought to his trial; which, however, he could never procure, though he called for it in the face of the court, nor was his name returned in the calendar. Yet be was kept in jail twelve weeks, till fetched out by a person in authority. He suffered in all eighteen, and the other persons twenty-eight, weeks' imprisonment.‡

In the following year, their religious assemblies, in different parts of the town, met with

---

* Crosby, vol. ii., p. 1–30.
† Wall's History of Infant Baptism, vol. ii., p. 215.
‡ Crosby, vol. ii., p. 94, 97.
§ The author of "Primitive Christianity," in folio, a very able performance. Mr. Grantham was a General Baptist,—C.

* Crosby, vol. ii., p. 149, 153, 154, 155.
† Ibid., p. 161.   ‡ Ibid., p. 162–165.

the like violent interruptions from the soldiery, breaking in with their swords and muskets, and acting under the authority of Sir John Robinson, lieutenant of the Tower, as in the former cases. In one instance a child in the cradle was awaked out of its sleep by their violence, and so terrified, that it fell sick, and died in three days. In other instances, the forms and furniture of their places of worship were broken and destroyed. Robinson, being told by them that they had broken the pulpit in Brick Lane, replied, " It was well done," and gave them a piece of gold as a reward for their good service. In all cases, the persons of those assembled were exposed to their indiscriminating rage ; neither sex, nor childhood, nor old age, nor women with child, were spared. At one place the mob was let in to act with soldiers, at the direction of Robinson. Many of the conscientious sufferers, by illegal commitments, were cast into prison. Even the walls of the prison did not afford them a secure retreat. In the prison itself they were exposed to outrage and fury. When they have been engaged together in religious conversation and acts of devotion, the felons of the jail, the thieves and housebreakers, the pickpockets and highwaymen have been let into their rooms, have threatened them, violently assaulted, and beaten them.*

But in the country were usually the greatest injustice and cruelty practised. The gentlemen in the commission of the peace, near Aylesbury in Buckinghamshire, distinguished themselves by their virulence in prosecuting the Nonconformists, and particularly the Baptists. They filled not the county jail only with prisoners of this description, but hired large houses in Aylesbury, and converted them into prisons ; and not contented with the severities in daily exercise, such as confiscation of goods and imprisonment, they attempted to revive the old practice of punishing heretics with banishment and death. They grounded their proceedings on the oppressive act of the 35th of Elizabeth for the punishment of persons obstinately refusing to come to church ;† which went to banish them, if, after three months' imprisonment, they refused conformity ; and if they did not leave the kingdom within a limited time, or should return, to inflict death without benefit of clergy. In 1664, some of these justices proceeded on this act against ten men and two women, all Baptists, who had been apprehended at their meeting in or near Aylesbury : on these persons, because they refused to conform, and to abjure the realm, sentence of death was passed, and immediately their goods also were seized. The other Dissenters, who constituted the majority of inhabitants in the town, alarmed at these proceedings, and anticipating their own doom, shut up their shops : this stop to commerce struck the whole town with horror and surprise. A son of one of the condemned persons immediately took horse for London, and was introduced, by Mr. William Kiffin, a gentleman of note among the Baptists,‡ and of interest at court, to Chancellor Hyde, who was easily engaged to lay the

case before the king. His majesty expressed great surprise that any of his subjects should be put to death for their religion, and inquired whether any law in force justified such proceedings. Being satisfied on this point, he promised his pardon. But, lest any precipitancy in executing the sentence should supersede the benefit of his grace, while the pardon was passing through the usual forms, the king, on a renewed application, granted an immediate reprieve. The condemned persons, however, were continued close prisoners till the next assizes, and then the judge brought down his majesty's pardon, and they were all set at liberty.* This would undoubtedly check the disposition of the justices to a similar process. But the virtuous sufferers, besides their other calamities, owed their safety to favour instead of law ; and appeared under the ignominious character of pardoned criminals, when they ought to have enjoyed the security and reputation of peaceable and innocent subjects.

The rage of the people, sanctioned by the conduct of the magistrates and the clergy towards the Baptists, rose to such a height as to deny them the benefit of the common burying places. Nay, there wanted not instances of their being taken out of their graves. The inhabitants of Croft in Lincolnshire in this manner the corpse of Mr. Robert Shalder, in the year 1666. He had suffered much by imprisonment, and died soon after his release. He was buried among his ancestors ; and on the same day his grave was opened, and his body taken out, dragged on a sledge to his own gate, and left there.

In the year 1670, the Baptists of Lewes, and other places in the county of Sussex, suffered in their property by the proceedings of Sir Thomas Nutt and other justices, on the Conventicle Act. They were convicted without being admitted to plead in their own defence. They were fined in an arbitrary manner ; and those fines were recovered in a way exceedingly oppressive and injurious, by distress and sale of goods. Where the fines amounted, as levied on various persons, to £5, there were enacted, by distraints, £29 17s. In some instances, four cheeses were seized to recover 10s., five pair of shoes for 5s., a cow for £2 15s., and a horse for 5s. Cattle worth £27 were sold for £14 5s. as a distress for £11 10s. One person, for a meeting held in his house, was fined £20, for which were taken from him six cows, two young bullocks, and a horse, his whole stock. On entering an appeal, they were returned to him ; but, being cast at the sessions, he was fined £60, which was at last remitted to £23. For nonpayment of this sum he was committed to the jailer's hands, though the vicar of the parish, touched with remorse for his share in the prosecution, offered his bond to pay the whole fine within a quarter of a year.†

It was remarked by one who had been bound over to several assizes and sessions for having religious assemblies held at his house, that the justices, who in criminal matters were often silent, and generally cool and disposed to lenity, when any person or accusation came before them concerning Dissenters, were very forward speakers, and zealously aggravated the charge.

---

* Crosby, vol. ii., p. 172–179.
† See Neal, vol. i., p. 198, of this edition.
‡ The autobiography of this excellent man was published by the late Rev. W. Orme, the biographer of Richard Baxter.—C.

* Crosby, vol. ii., p. 180–185.   † Ibid., p. 244–258.

But nothing more strongly marked the malignant temper of the times against the Baptists than the publication of a pamphlet, in the year 1673, avowedly designed to raise an abhorrence of the sect, and to stand " as an eternal memorial of their cruelty and hatred to all orthodox ministers." It was entitled "Mr. Baxter baptized in Blood." The story it exhibited was, that Mr. Josiah Baxter, a godly minister of New-England, for no other reason than because he had worsted the 'Baptists in a'disputation,' had been\murdered in his own house, amid "the howlings, groans, and screechings of his dear relations, lying bound by him;" and it represented this murder as committed with circumstances of peculiar atrocity and cruelty ; he being first stripped and severely whipped, and then unbowelled and flayed alive. To give it the air of authenticity, the pamphlet was pretended to be published by the mournful brother of the said minister, an inhabitant of Fenchurch-street, London; and it was actually licensed by Dr. Samuel Parker. This vile tale had its origin in invention and malice alone ; for the king's privy council examined the case, and detected the forgery. It appeared, on the oaths of the officers in Fenchurch-street, that no such person as Benjamin Baxter, the pretended publisher, had, in their memory, lived there ; and on the affidavits of a master of a vessel, and of a merchant who sailed from Boston about twenty days after this murder was said to be committed, it also appeared that no such fact had taken place, nor had there been such a person as Mr. Josiah Baxter. The whole story was pronounced by an order of council "altogether false and fictitious ;" and Dr. Parker* confessed his mistake and credulity in licensing the pamphlet, and acknowledged, by a testimonial under his hand, his conviction that the whole was " both false and groundless." Mr. Andrew Marvel, not without intimating a suspicion that Dr. Parker was concerned in the fabrication, says, that " from beginning to end there never was a completer falsehood invented."† It grieves and shocks a good mind to think that, in any age or party, men can be found to invent and countenance such groundless and malevolent forgeries.

Besides this general survey of the persecutions to which the Baptists were exposed throughout the kingdom, it may be proper briefly to notice two or three particular cases. One is that of Mr. John James, the minister of a congregation of Baptists, who observed the seventh day as a Sabbath, and assembled in Bulstake Alley. Towards the end of the year 1661, they were interrupted in their worship by a justice and headborough, as Mr. James was preaching, whom they commanded in the king's name to be silent and come down, having spoken treason against the king. As Mr. James proceeded in his discourse without noticing his summons, it was repeated with a threat of pulling him down. On this the disturbance grew so great, that Mr. James was obliged to stop ; but still refusing to leave the pulpit, he was pulled down, and haled away ; and the hearers were carried, by sevens, before the justices sitting at the Half-moon tavern, and those

who refused the oath of allegiance were committed to prison. Mr. James was examined in the meeting-house ; insult and threats accompanied the interrogatories, and he was committed on the charge of speaking treasonable words against his majesty. On this charge, he was tried, condemned, and executed. Previously to the execution, his wife delivered to the king a petition, stating his innocence, and the character of the witnesses against him, signifying who she was, which the king received with a taunt : "Oh ! Mr. James ! he is a sweet gentleman ;" and when she attempted to follow for some farther answer, the door was shut against her. On the next morning she renewed her attendance and suit ; and his majesty replied, "that he was a rogue, and should be hanged." A lord in waiting asked who was meant : the king answered, "Oh, John James, that rogue; he shall be hanged ; yea, he shall be hanged."* The celebrated Mr. Benjamin Keach had also no small share in the sufferings of the times. He was seized when preaching, and committed to jail; sometimes bound, sometimes released upon bail, and sometimes his life was threatened. Troopers, who were sent down into Buckinghamshire to suppress the meetings of Dissenters, entered into an assembly, where he was conducting the worship, with great violence, and swearing that they would kill the preacher. He was accordingly seized, and four of them declared their resolution to trample him to death with their horses. They bound him, laid him on the ground, and were going to spur all their horses at once upon him, when their officer, seeing their design, rode up towards them and prevented its execution. Mr. Keach was taken up, tied behind one of the troopers, across his horse, and carried to jail, where he suffered some time great hardships before he was released.

In the year 1644, Mr. Keach printed, at the request of friends, without his name, and with a recommendatory preface by another hand, a little piece entitled "The Child's Instructer ; or, a New and Easy Primer." In this book were advanced several principles contrary to the doctrines and ceremonies of the Church of England ; viz., That infants ought not to be baptized ; that laymen having abilities may preach the Gospel ; that Christ should reign personally upon the earth in the latter day, &c. Soon after this tract was printed, and Mr. Keach had received some copies of it, his house was searched for it ; all the copies of it they found were seized, and he was bound over to the assizes in a recognisance of £100, and two sureties with him in £50 each. On October 8, Mr. Keach was brought to the bar of Aylesbury, where the assizes were held, before Lord-chief-justice Hyde. The judge not only interrogated him whether he were the author of the Primer, but, by unjust reflections and angry insults, endeavoured to incense the jury against him, and to render him odious. Mr. Keach was refused a copy of his indictment till he had pleaded to it. In the course of the trial, abuse and contempt were cast upon him from the bench. The jury were intimidated when they hesitated on their verdict. Mr. Keach was

---

* See his character finely drawn in Edinburgh Review, " Andrew Marvel."—C.

† Crosby, vol. ii., p. 278–294.

* Crosby, vol. ii., p. 165–171.

convicted; and the sentence passed was, that he should be committed to jail for a fortnight, stand in the pillory for two hours on the following Saturday at Aylesbury, with a paper on his head with this inscription: "For writing, printing, and publishing a schismatical book, entitled 'The Child's Instructer; or, a New and Easy Primer;'" that the same punishment, under like circumstances, should be inflicted on him on the next Thursday, at Winslow; that there his book should be openly burned before his face, in disgrace of him and his doctrine; that he should be fined £20, and that he should remain in jail until he found sureties for his good behaviour and appearance at the next assizes; then to renounce his doctrines, and make such public submission as should be enjoined him. No pardon could be obtained, nor the least relaxation of the sentence, which the sheriff took care should be punctually executed.*

The spirit of persecution thus raged against this people; but not without a mixture of events which were adapted seriously to affect the minds of their persecutors, and to alarm them to reflection. On the day of the king's proclamation at Waltham, near Theobalds, there was a man who, at the bonfire in the evening, expressed a rage against the Dissenters, and the Baptists in particular, by violence of language and oaths; and as he threw fagots into the fire, cried, " Here is a Roundhead; here is an Anabaptist!" he was struck with death that night, and never saw the morning. A minister at one place inveighing in his sermon against this fact, fell into a swoon, and was speechless for two hours, so that it was apprehended that he would never recover out of the fit. At Brockington, in Gloucestershire, a young woman, who had bitterly reviled them, giving a sudden shriek as the preacher was discoursing on Jude, 14, 15, dropped down in the religious assembly, and never recovered. The sufferings and character of the Dissenters were made a jest upon the stage at Oxford. In a play acted there by the scholars, one personated the old Puritan, who broke a vein and vomited so much blood, that his immediate death was apprehended, and he lay some time dangerously ill. Two of the actors, and a woman that joined them in this dramatic exhibition, were cut off by death.† Some remarkable calamities befell those who were instruments in the prosecution of Mr. John James.‡ One of the actors in the rude and unnatural treatment of Mr. Shalder's corpse, after it was interred, died suddenly; and another languished for some time, terrified with the remembrance of the insults he had offered to the dead.§ A woman named Anne Clemens at Chipping Norton, distinguished by her rage and malice against the Dissenters, fell into such circumstances of poverty as to be obliged to sell her land, and mortgage her house for near its worth. Not one of her children, who resided in the neighbourhood, was in a comfortable condition; and she herself was so reduced as to beg alms of those she had hated and persecuted. Her affliction was heightened by a diseased appetite, which called for as much as would satisfy two or three persons; and by a disposition to breed vermin, so that, though her clothes were

not only washed, but ovened, she could not be kept clean. Richard Allein, an active informer, and violent in his conduct towards the Dissent-ers, fell into afflictions that shortened his days. His eldest son was killed at London; and about the same time, another was accused and convicted for robbing on the highway, and by great friends and fees escaped with his life. An officer in the county troops of Oxford, with an income of £70 per annum, before he could accomplish his design of suppressing the Dissenters, sunk in his own estate, died greatly in debt, and his son's children became common beggars. One Werg, a forward and active constable, did not long survive the expiration of his office, and imputed his death to watching one cold night to take the Dissenters at their meeting. Five persons, who received pensions as spies and informers, were observed not to prosper afterward, and every one of them shortly died. An Irish peer, and three Irish justices of title and rank, bitter persecutors, it was remarked, while they were directing their whole power to the ruin of the Dissenters, were themselves ruined, their estates were sold, and their families became extinct. Whereas Sir Littleton Obaldiston, a justice of peace, who had been heard to rail at the Dissenters, and acted with others in committing them to prison, afterward laid aside his enmity, was instrumental in releasing several, and conducted himself in a friendly manner; and it was noticed that his estate continued to his posterity. And it was remarked that —— Howard, Esq., a justice and officer in Oxfordshire, who had from an enemy become a friend to the Dissenters, though he adhered to the established worship, was the only one of those who had molested and harassed them that was living on the 30th of December, 1707, being then an old man, full of days, wealth, and honour.*

It becomes us, I am sensible, to be very cautious how we construe the events which are common to all men. " There is usually," says an excellent writer, " much rashness and presumption in pronouncing that the calamities of sinners are particular judgments of God; yet if, from sacred and profane, from ancient and modern historians, a collection were made of all the persecuting tyrants who delighted in tormenting their fellow-creatures; and who died not the common death of all men, nor were visited after the visitation of all men such whose plagues were horrible and strange, even a skeptic would be moved at the evidence, and would be apt to suspect that it was θειον τι, that the hand of God was in it."†

But the history which we are detailing presents objects to our consideration more pleasing than the sufferings of the persecuted, or calamities that befell persecutors. It records the virtues which the persecuted displayed, and the consolations in which, under their heavy trials, they rejoiced. We see the power of faith and piety, when we hear the Baptists confined in Reading jail declaring, " Our Lord and King, whom we serve, hath brought us under his own pavilion; and his banner over us hath been and still is love, and hath been teaching of us these

_____

* Crosby, vol. ii., p. 185–209.   † Ibid., p. 30–34.
‡ Ibid., p. 172.   § Ibid., p. 241.

† Crosby, vol. ii., p. 259–263.
† Jortin's Remarks on Ecclesiastical History, vol. iii., p. 247, 1754.

HISTORY OF THE BAPTISTS. 385

'lessons following: 1st. In the loss of all outward things, having Christ, we enjoy all things, and are satisfied in the Lord : we shall take the spoiling of our goods with far more comfort than the enemy will do in the spending of them, for that word, Job, xx., 22, 23, is very much on our hearts concerning him. 2dly. We hope we have learned, in whatsoever condition we are, to be therewith contented ; and are persuaded in our hearts this is given us in answer of many prayers breathed forth unto the Lord on our behalfs. 3dly. That whereas formerly we could hardly part with anything for the Lord, we are now made willing by him to part with all things for him, and to say with good old Eli, ' It is the Lord, let him do what he pleaseth ;' and that in Job is set before us for our example, upon whom the ends of the world are come : ' The Lord giveth, and the Lord taketh away ; blessed be the name of the Lord. In all this Job sinned not.' &c... 4thly. We have, since our confinement, tasted a greater sweetness in the promises of the Lord than formerly ; and particularly these places following, we have sweet experience of, and we can truly say by experience, ' That faithful is he that hath thus promised, for he hath also done it : it is the Lord's doing, and it is marvellous in our eyes.'—Phil., iv., 19. 1 Pet., v., 7. Deut. xxxiii, 25. We are also brought by the power of his grace to a more watchful frame over our hearts, thoughts, and actions, by these trials than formerly. One thing had almost slipped our memory, the knowledge of which will, we hope, rejoice our hearts : that our relations, that are precious to the Lord and to us, bear this our suffering with incomparable patience, rather singing for joy than weeping for grief. Also our societies, from whence we were taken, are exceeding cheerful, and a very lively spirit of faith and prayer is among them ; and their meetings rather increase than otherwise. Sure, ' That the Lord is near, his wondrous works declare ; for the singing of birds is come, and the turtle is heard in our land.' And now, brethren, forasmuch as the mercies expected and prayed for by us are to be enjoyed in the way of righteousness, it greatly concerns us that we cry mightily to the Lord, as did his servant of old, Isa., lxii., 1. Then shall we have that new name which God will give us, which is expressed in the last verse of that chapter. Now the God of all peace fill you with peace and joy in believing ; so pray your brethren through grace."*

In the spirit of these pious sufferers, one whose property was seized told those who took distress, " he never sold anything to so great advantage, for this would bring him a hundredfold." And another, on goods from his shop to the value of 50s. being seized for a fine of 30s., assured them " that he parted as willingly with them as with any goods he ever sold."†

When Mr. John James was brought to the bar to receive sentence, he was asked what he had to say for himself why sentence of death should not be passed upon him. In a manner very expressive of pious submission and fortitude, he answered, " That he had not much to say, only two or three Scriptures he would leave with them." The first Scripture was Jer., xxvi., 14, 15 : " As for me, do as seemeth good unto

you. But know ye for certain, that if ye put me to death, ye shall surely bring innocent blood upon yourselves, and upon this city, and upon the inhabitants thereof." The second Scripture was Psalm cxvi., 15 : " Precious in the sight of the Lord is the death of his saints." He also reminded them of that good word of the Lord, " He that toucheth the Lord's people, toucheth the apple of his eye."

The deportment of Mr. Keach when he stood in the pillory at Aylesbury was singularly serious, devout, and undaunted. To his friends who accompanied him, expressing their sense of his sufferings, he said, with a cheerful countenance, " The cross is the way to the crown." When his head and hands were fixed, he addressed the spectators to this effect : " Good people, I am not ashamed to stand here this day, with this paper on my head. My Lord, Jesus was not ashamed to suffer on the cross for me, and it is for his cause that I am made a gazing-stock. Take notice, it is not for any wickedness that I stand here ; but for writing and publishing his truths, which the Spirit of the Lord hath revealed in the Holy Scriptures. It is no new thing for the servants of the Lord to suffer and to be made a gazing-stock ; and you that are acquainted with the Scriptures know that the way to the crown is by the cross. The apostle saith, ' that through many tribulations, we must enter into the kingdom of heaven ;' and Christ saith, ' He that is ashamed of me and my words, in an adulterous and sinful generation, of him shall the Son of Man be ashamed before the Father, and before the holy angels.' " After frequent interruptions from the jailer and standing some time silent, disengaging one of his hands, he pulled his Bible out of his pocket, and held it up to the people, saying, " Take notice that the things which I have written and published, and for which I stand here this day a spectacle to men and angels, are all contained in this book, as I could prove out of the same, if I had opportunity." The jailer took it from him, and fastened up his hand again ; but it was almost impossible to keep him from speaking, saying, " It seems I cannot be suffered to speak to the cause for which I stand here ; neither could I be suffered the other day (viz., on his trial) ; but it will plead its own innocency, when the strongest of its opposers shall be ashamed. I do not speak this out of prejudice to any person, but do sincerely desire that the Lord would convert them, and convince them of their errors, that their souls may be saved in the day of the Lord Jesus. Good people, the concernment of souls is very great ; so great, that Christ died for them. And truly, a concernment for souls was that which moved me to write and publish those things for which I now suffer, and for which I could suffer far greater things than these. It concerns you, therefore, to be very careful, otherwise it will be very sad with you at the revelation of the Lord Jesus from heaven, for we must all appear before his tribunal." Here he was interrupted, but after some time he again ventured to break silence. " I hope," said he, " the Lord's people will not be discouraged at my sufferings. Oh ! did you but experience the great love of God, and the excellences that are in him, it would make you willing to go through any sufferings

* Crosby, vol. ii., p. 93–95.　† Ibid., p. 249.
Vol. II.—C c c

for his sake. And I do account this the greatest honour that ever the Lord was pleased to confer upon me." He was not suffered to speak much more after this, and the officers were commanded to keep the spectators at a greater distance from him. He found an opportunity, however, to say at one time, "This is one yoke of Christ, which I can experience is easy to me, and a burden which he doth make light;" and to utter also this sentence, "Blessed are they that are persecuted for righteousness' sake, for theirs is the kingdom of heaven." When the time for his standing was expired, and his head and hands were at liberty, he blessed God, with a loud voice, for his great goodness unto him.*

Such sentiments, such a spirit expressed in the moment of suffering, it may be supposed, would disarm the rage of some, and possess the minds of many in favour of the pious sufferer. But the Baptists did not leave their principles to the recommendation and support which the conduct and temper of those who, in the: profession of them, endured cruel trials, might afford. They adopted every method of softening prejudice and conciliating regard, by addresses from the press, and applications to the throne. With this view, they published, in 1660, a "Brief Confession or Declaration," to inform all men of their innocent belief and practice. It was owned and approved by more than twenty thousand. This was presented to his majesty, and met with his approbation. It was reprinted at London in 1691.† Petitions also, as we have noticed, were in this year delivered to the king, representing their pacific principles, and imploring his protection.‡ Three persons of this denomination, about this time published a declaration after their sentiments concerning opposing magistracy, in which they advanced principles to which the most zealous advocates for passive obedience and nonresistance could not object: professing that, in such instances wherein they could not in conscience obey, they ought "not to resist them, but patiently suffer whatever they should inflict for non-obedience to their requirements."§ The persons who signed this declaration apologize for their paucity, and seemed not pleased with their brethren, because they were not of their judgment on this point. But their difference in opinion from other Baptists shows that a uniformity of sentiment concerning the extent of the magistrate's authority, and the right of resistance, had no necessary and direct connexion with an agreement on the questions concerning baptism. In the year 1661, the hardships under which many of this profession groaned again excited them to seek mercy from the higher powers. A petition was presented to the king, on behalf of themselves and others, from some confined in the prison at Dover, and another to the Duke of York; describing their great sufferings, protesting that innocence was found in them, and that against the king and his government they had done no harm, soliciting with much importunity to be set at liberty, and that they might not be interrupted in their worship of the God of heaven as they were

taught it in his Word, which they prized above all the world; and urging that it might be considered "how disagreeable it is with Christianity to bring tribulation upon any for conscience' sake, seeing all things in worship must be done in faith and love."*

But the application for redress of their grievances, which particularly deserves notice, was an address to the king, Parliament, and people, in a treatise entitled "Sion's Groans for her Distressed; or, Sober Endeavours to prevent Innocent Blood," &c. This was not a petition only for toleration for themselves, but an able and spirited defence of the rights of conscience. Its design was to prove how contrary to the Gospel "of the Lord Jesus, and to good reason, it is for any magistrate, by outward force, to impose anything in the worship of God on the consciences of those whom they govern; but that liberty ought to be given to all such as disturb not the civil peace, though of different persuasions in religious matters." The question is handled on liberal principles, also with copiousness and strength. The spirit and the reasoning do honour to the people from whom it came; especially when it is recollected that the assembly at Westminster, and the ministers of London and other parts, had from the pulpit and the press opposed the principles of toleration.

It is argued that the power of directing conscience by outward force doth not attach itself to the office of magistracy itself, because then all magistrates in all nations have the same power; the Mohammedan to enforce the reception of the Koran, the Spaniard to enjoy popery, and every succeeding magistrate to sanction his own religion, to the overthrow of what his predecessor established: because the apostles, who command obedience to magistrates, in matters of religion refused obedience; because all the Scriptures of the New Testament enjoining obedience to magistrates, being written when the emperors were idolaters, such injunctions cannot be understood as applying to religion: because, if the commands of the magistrate in religious matters were obligatory, there could be no persecutions, and the way to heaven, so far from being strait and narrow, any might be a disciple of Christ without taking up the cross. And the conduct of Gallio, who declined interfering in a matter relative to God's law, and restrained the exercise of his authority to civil injuries only, is with great propriety appealed to, as a worthy example for the imitation of magistrates.

That the Christian magistrate, as such, has no power over conscience, nor authority to impose anything in religion by outward force, is argued from the conduct of Christ Jesus, who never compelled men by force to receive his doctrine; from the conduct of the apostles, and the elders of the primitive Church, who disclaimed any such power.—1 Cor., i., 24. Matt., xx., 25. 1 Pet., v., 2, 3. "Why, therefore," say the authors of this piece, "the Christian religion should be built and supported by violence, when the foundation was laid, and the work carried on during all the apostles' days, and some hundred years after, by a quite contrary means, is a question should be resolved by

* Crosby, vol. ii., p. 204–208.
† Ibid., vol. ii., p. 18; and Appendix, No. iv.
‡ Ibid., p. 19–26.
§ Ibid., vol. ii., p. 19. Appendix, No. v.

* Crosby, vol. ii., p. 155–160.

those whose strongest arguments for the support of their religion is, Take him, jailer; or such is the difference between the way which the apostles and primitive saints took in carrying on the work of the Gospel, and approving themselves to be the ministers of God, and the way now used by the national clergy, than which nothing is more unlike." In the prosecution of their argument, they reason forcibly from the parable of the tares and wheat, as forbidding any outward force or violence to be used upon false worshippers and heretics as such. "Hath the magistrate (it is asked) power to remove those out of the world that God would have permitted to live?" The fallibility of the magistrate furnishes another argument against the exercise of his power in religion; a fallibility which woful experience hath taught the world in all ages; the magistrate of one country establishing the principles and practices which that of another country condemns and persecutes; nay, the same magistrate, at different periods, reversing his own decrees; and now rejecting what he had just before defended by his pen or supported by his laws: as was the case of Henry VIII. To this fallibility he is equally liable, whether he confide in his own wisdom, or rely on the authority of popes, synods, or general councils. This point is illustrated by various examples. As to national conventions and synods, so far are they from any show of infallibility, it is justly observed, "that the same complexion and temper the nation is of, wherein they are called, you shall be sure to find them of; because they have their dependancy on the authority that calls them together." Among other arguments, it is stated that, for the magistrate to inflict temporal punishments upon any for not conforming to those decrees which enjoin any spiritual worship or service, is a breach of the royal law, "Whatsoever ye would that men should do to you, do ye even so to them." This is a rule which all sorts of men, while under persecution, are ready to receive and plead. Nor would they who are forward to persecute be very zealous in their proceedings, if they were sure that those whom they persecute should have power on their sides to "mete the same measure unto them." It is well observed, that such proceedings may sometimes prove inconsistent with the very being of nations. "For, suppose any nation were wholly heathen idolaters, and the Word of God coming in among them should convert the chief magistrate, and one twentieth part of the nation more; must he then with that twentieth part destroy all the other nineteen, if they will not be converted, but continue in their heathenish idolatry? It cannot possibly be supposed to be warrantable. And the reason holds good, likewise, against the rooting up and destroying heretics out of the world."

These just sentiments are followed by a full answer to the argument in favour of the magistrate's power in religious matters, drawn from the example of the kings of Israel and Judah. In reply to this, it is observed, that the power of kings to punish idolaters and blasphemers was given them by God, and written in plain precepts in the Mosaical law: but hath the Lord Jesus invested magistrates with such power? if he have, where is it written? The

Jews, all the time they kept to the law of God, had a standing oracle among them, the Urim and Thummim, and the counsels of extraordinary prophets to assist them to judge righteous judgments. Besides, the Gospel is a dispensation far different from the law in all its ordinances and administrations, under which the Lord Jesus is the only lawgiver.

Such is the strain of this piece: the importance of the subject, the force of the argument, and the liberality of the spirit, entitle it to particular notice; and will, it is presumed, make this review of it acceptable.* The authors of it, whose names are subscribed to the prefatory epistle, were, Thomas Monck, Joseph Wright, George Hammon, William Jeffery, Francis Stanley, William Reynolds, and Francis Smith. While they earnestly recommend their treatise to deliberate and serious perusal, our design, they say, "in what we beg may be perused, is general good; in setting at liberty that which God made free, even the conscience."

The only particulars I can find concerning these able advocates for liberty are, that Mr. Wright, born in 1623, was a physician: he was educated at the university, and was a man of great learning and piety; a serious and diligent preacher, and greatly promoted the cause of the Baptists. He was confined twenty years in the jail at Maidstone; in this town he died, aged eighty, in 1703.† Mr. George Hammon, eminent for the ardour and freedom with which he vindicated what he judged to be truth on all occasions, and very much persecuted on that account, was pastor of a congregation at Biddendon in Kent, and died at Haseldens-wood, in the parish of Cranbrook.‡ Mr. William Jeffery, born in 1616, of pious parents, in the parish of Penshurst, lived at Bradbourn, in Sevenoaks, Kent, where he and his brother were the great supporters, if not the founders, of a meeting. By his diligence, and that of several others, more than twenty congregations were formed in that county, on the principles laid down in Heb., vi., 1, 2,§ without entering on speculative and controverted points. As he was vigorous, unwearied, and successful in his labours, so with great patience and pleasure he suffered much for his principles; these he also often defended in public disputations. He was much valued for his steady piety and universal virtue, and died in a good old age.|| His son succeeded him in his church. Mr. Francis Stanley was a man noted for his zeal and piety, and was imprisoned for preaching, in the jail of Northampton. He bore his sufferings like a Christian, and died about the year 1696. He was a native of Northamptonshire, and was buried at East Haddon, in that county.¶ Of the other persons Mr. Crosby gives no particular account. In the same year in which appeared the piece on Toleration, there were published a small piece entitled "A Complaint of the Oppressed against the Oppressors; or, the unjust and arbitrary Proceedings of some Soldiers and Justi-

* Mr. Crosby has preserved it entire in his History, vol. ii., p. 100–114.
† Crosby, vol. iii., p. 116.   ‡ Ibid., p. 103.
§ Among us called "Six Principle Baptists." A few of these churches only remain, and are chiefly to be found in Rhode Island.—C.
|| Crosby, p. 97, 98.   ¶ Ibid., vol. iii., p. 127.

ces against some sober, godly Persons, in and near London, who now lie in stinking Jails, for the Testimony of a good Conscience ; with some Reasons why they cannot swear Allegiance to obtain their Liberty ;" and a tract entitled "A Plea for Toleration of Opinions and Persuasions in Matters of Religion differing from the Church of England : humbly presented to the King's most excellent Majesty : by Mr. John Sturgeon, a Baptist." The former was written by Dr. John Griffith, a worthy man, who suffered a long imprisonment in Newgate for nonconformity. Each piece was an affecting remonstrance on the unjust proceedings by which many pious and innocent persons, of unblemished characters, in London, and in almost all the counties of England, were suffering ; being taken out of their beds at midnight by soldiers, acting without warrant, and with drawn swords, to the great terror of their wives and children ; and being thrust into prisons, in such crowds that the jailers complained they had too many guests; and detained there to the ruin of their families.*

Mr. James Atkins, one of those who were harassed by the magistrates of Dover, on his own behalf, and in the cause of his fellow-sufferers, addressed a letter to the mayor and justices of that town, under the name of "A Poor Subject ;" acknowledging a submission to the civil magistrate, except in what concerned the worship of God, and entreating in the bowels of love a consideration of the evil of restraining their liberty.†

In the year 1662, there came from the press a small pamphlet, entitled "Behold, a Cry ; or, a true Relation of the inhuman and violent Outrages of divers Soldiers, Constables, and others, practised upon many of the Lord's People, commonly, though falsely, called Anabaptists, at their several Meetings in and about London."

An incident which took place in Lincolnshire in 1670, called forth a vindication of their principles from this denomination in a different form from the preceding publications. Mr. Robert Wright, who had been a preacher among them, but was, on account of his irregular life and conversation, excluded their society, having spent his estate, applied to Dr. William Fuller, the bishop of that diocess, for orders and a benefice ; promising to renounce his sentiments concerning baptism, and to preach against the Baptists. The bishop accepted his offer ; he was admitted in the ministry of the Church of England, and preached in support of the baptism of infants, in opposition to that of believers, with great ardour and confidence. This excited great attention ; the minds of many were much impressed by it, and it was supposed that most, if not all the ministers of the Baptist churches, would be easily confuted. They, in their own vindication, at the assizes, posted up, in different parts of the city of Lincoln, four papers, addressed to the citizens and inhabitants, inviting Mr. Wright to a friendly conference, and offering to maintain the doctrine and baptism of repentance to be from heaven, and the sprinkling and crossing of infants to be man's tradition. They were dated the 11th day of the first month (vulg.), March, 1670. Two of them were taken down

in the morning; and were, it was supposed, carried to the bishop and the judge. The other two were permitted to remain till the afternoon, and were read by many, till they were removed by the clergy, who threatened the writers of them should answer for it before the council-table. But though the bishop, it was well known, was not a little moved by these proceedings of the Baptists, no other step was taken on the occasion than sending to them an angry paper, drawn up by Mr. William Silverton, the bishop's chaplain, who called them erroneous, antic Baptists. To this paper Mr. Grantham replied, promising Mr. Silverton either to hear and discuss his arguments in a free audience, if he would fix a convenient time and place for the purpose ; or to reply to him, if he would defend his sentiments from the press. Here the matter ended, as Mr. Silverton saw fit to be silent.*

The only publication which remains to be noticed in this period was, "A Narrative of the late Proceedings of some Justices and others, pretending to put in execution the late Act against Conventicles ; against several peaceable People in and about the Town of Lewes in Sussex, only for their being quietly met to worship God : together with a brief Account of the like Proceedings against some at Brighthelmstone, and others at Chillington, in the same County." This professed to be a faithful narrative, published with a view to encourage others to suffer the spoiling of their goods by the example of many who endured it with patience and joyfulness ; and with the hope that by it the harsh proceedings against a peaceable people might come to the knowledge of some in authority, who, out of pity to the distressed, and justice to their righteous cause, would redress their grievances.† Such narratives were, indeed, well adapted to each purpose, and were an affecting appeal to the sense of humanity and equity.

CHAPTER V.

A CONTROVERSY arose among the Baptists, about this time, respecting the laying on of hands, which created not a little altercation and trouble. Hitherto, it appears that this rite was practised by them as an apostolical ordinance, and was accompanied with prayer over the newly-baptized. A treatise, entitled "A Search after Schism," was published in opposition to it. This was answered by Dr. John Griffith, in a piece called "The Searchers after Schism searched," and it drew from Mr. Grantham his "Sigh for Peace ; or, the Cause of Division discovered." The appearance of this piece occasioned a meeting between Mr. Grantham and Mr. Ives, when the subject was debated with temper and good humour ; and Mr. Ives is reported, on finding himself gravelled, to have broken up the meeting in a friendly and peaceable manner. About three years after, Mr. Danvers published a treatise against laying on of hands, which was answered by Mr. Benjamin Keach, and also by Mr. Grantham, who annexed to his answer "A Treatise of the Successors of the Apostles."

* Crosby, vol. ii., p. 144-148 ; and vol. iii., p. 120.
† Ibid., vol. ii., p. 151, 152.

* Crosby, vol. ii., p. 241-244. † Ibid., p. 245, 246.

In 1674 the Baptists were engaged in a controversy with the Quakers, which created a noise, and was conducted, as is usual, by mutual criminations. Mr. Thomas Hicks, a minister of the former, published several pamphlets in succession, under the title of "A Dialogue between a Christian and a Quaker." The title these pieces bore was certainly invidious, and held up the Quakers as not deserving to be ranked among Christians. It was also complained of, that the design of them was not so much to investigate truth as to represent the Quaker a deformed, ridiculous, and erroneous being. The great Penn, on this occasion, became the advocate of the people to whom he had joined himself, in two books; the first entitled "Reason against Railing;" and the other, "The Counterfeit Christian detected." But as Mr. Hicks had reflected upon some particular members by name, an appeal was made to the Baptists in and about London for justice against him. A meeting was accordingly appointed to hear the charges against him; but they are censured for fixing the time when the complainants, Penn and Whitehead, were absent from the city, at a distance too remote to be apprized of the intended meeting. It was urged in defence of the Baptists, that they were informed that Penn was not far from London several days after the notice of the meeting was sent, and even at his own house, at no great distance from the town, the very day preceding; and that they had invited others of the society, particularly John Osgoods, to be present, who declined it. The meeting took place, and Mr. Hicks was examined by his own friends only on the charges brought against him by the Quakers; and he endeavoured to establish the representations he had made of their principles and doctrines by quotations from their own writers. These were pronounced, by nineteen of his own denomination, to be truly recited, and the church to which he belonged, in public print, cleared him from the charge which the Quakers alleged against him. This decision was deemed partial. On the face of it, though the business was said to be conducted with great fairness, it was open to objection. The Baptists refused to defer the meeting, though solicited. No Quaker was present to be heard on the grounds of the charges; and, though the passages might be quoted with verbal exactness, which Mr. Hicks brought as his authorities, yet they were detached from their connexion, and a meaning affixed to them which probably the writers, if they had been there to explain themselves, would not have admitted as their sense. New complaints were brought forward against the Baptists, and justice again demanded. A meeting for a rehearing was obtained; but Mr. Hicks would not attend it, but sent some others with Mr. Ives; "who," says Crosby, "so managed the Quakers, that they were obliged to break up without any farther proceedings in the matter." "By clamours and rudeness," says Gough, "they diverted the complainants from prosecuting the charge against Hicks, and carried their point so far as to prevent its being heard, though frequent attempts were made to read it."

The Baptists published an account of these meetings, under the title of "A Contest for Christianity." Mr. Tho. Welwood, in behalf of

his friends, appealed to the public, first in a single sheet, entitled "A fresh Pursuit;" and then, in reply to the "Contest," which was written by Mr. Thomas Plant, in a piece entitled "Forgery no Christianity." The issue of this controversy is represented, on the one hand, to be, that the Quakers were so chafed in these disputes, that they did not only brand the Baptists with infamy, but denounced curses and judgments upon them. On the other side it is said, "that the aim of this unprovoked assault upon the principles and reputation of this society was remarkably frustrated; and these dialogues, with their ungenerous and unequitable method of defending them and their author, promoted what they were designed to prevent; for not a few of their members, offended at their proceedings, deserted their meetings and society, went over to the injured party, and joined them in religious fellowship."[*]

In the year 1677, the Baptists published "A Confession of their Faith, set forth by the Elders and Brethren of many Congregations of Christians, baptized upon Profession of their Faith, in London and the Country." Their avowed design in this publication was, not only to give an account of themselves on the points wherein they differed from other Christians, but also to instruct and establish others in the great principles in which there was a mutual agreement between them. They aimed to express themselves, on the former heads, with a modesty and humility that would render the freedom with which they declared themselves inoffensive to those whose sentiments were different from their own. The general plan of their confession was after the order and method observed in that of the Assembly of Westminster, and afterward adopted by the Congregational churches; and in the margin they affixed such texts as, in their opinion, confirmed each article. Two things they earnestly desired: that full credit might be given to their declaration of contention being most remote from their design in all that they did in this matter; and that all into whose hands this piece might come "would follow that never-enough-commended example of the noble Bereans, who searched the Scriptures daily, that they might find out whether the things preached to them were so or not." This Confession of Faith was reprinted in the year 1689, and was approved and recommended by the ministers and messengers of above a hundred congregations, met in London from the third to the eleventh day of the seventh month. It was signed by thirty-seven persons, in the name and behalf of the whole assembly. It has continued to be generally received by those congregations that hold the doctrine of personal election, and the certainty of the saints' final perseverance.[†] In 1790 it was reprinted by Dr. John Rippon, with a list of the thirty-seven ministers who recommended it; and to this edition were added the places where they all laboured. In 1791, there appeared a new edition of the translation of it in Welsh,[‡] revised by the Rev. Joshua

---

[*] Crosby's History of the English Baptists, vol. ii., p. 294–310. Gough's History of the Quakers, vol. ii., p. 368–371.

[†] Crosby, vol. ii., p. 317; vol. iii., p. 258; and Appendix, No. ii.

[‡] Rippon's Baptist Annual Register, p. 124, 191.

Thomas, of Leominster. The first edition, besides an introductory advertisement to the judicious "and impartial reader," was accompanied by an Appendix—a judicious, candid, and conciliating piece, in which they discuss the arguments alleged against their distinguishing sentiment and practice, and give the reasons, with brevity and plainness, why, they could not acquiesce in them.*

This denomination now greatly increased. Their arguments weighed with many ; their exemplary lives spoke in their favour ; but the number of their converts excited against them a spirit of jealousy and resentment, and they were the objects of clamour and defamation. Many books were published, misrepresenting them, and their chiefs were reproached as Jesuits and heretics. This induced them to publish many confessions of faith ; some in vindication of particular churches, others of particular persons. In 1678 one was agreed to, and signed by fifty ministers and messengers in the several counties of Bucks, Hertford, Bedford, and Oxford, in behalf of themselves and many others, containing fifty articles. It was soon published, under the title of "An Orthodox Creed ; or, a Protestant Confession of Faith ; being an Essay to unite and confirm all true Protestants in the fundamental Articles of the Christian Religion, against the Errors and Heresies of the Church of Rome."† As the Baptists consisted of two parties, distinguished by the names General and Particular, when one published a declaration of their principles, the other soon after did the same.‡

In this period may be placed several who made a distinguished figure as ministers among the Baptists, the time of whose deaths is not ascertained.

The first was Mr. William Dell, A.M., famous in the time of the civil wars : he received his education at the University of Cambridge, and held the living of Yeldon, in the county of Bedford, worth about £200 a year. About the year 1645 he became chaplain to the army, constantly attending Sir Thomas Fairfax, and preaching at the headquarters. In 1649, when several were turned out of the universities for refusing to take the oaths to the government, he was made master of Caius College at Cambridge, which preferment he held, with his living at Yeldon, till he was ejected by the Act of Uniformity. Party prejudice fixed on his memory the charge of glaring contradictions and inconsistencies of conduct, from which more candid posterity has vindicated him. The fact was, that he was at first satisfied with Episcopacy and the ceremonies ; but when the change in the state brought on a reformation in religion, he was one of the first and most zealous to promote it, and would have carried it farther than was agreeable to the principles and views of many others. He was obnoxious to the rigid Presbyterians, whose attempts to monopolize all power, in civil and ecclesiastical affairs, he opposed. A sermon at Marston occasioned him much trouble, and another on a fast-day, before the House of Commons, led him into a controversy with Mr. C. Love, who opposed him in the afternoon of the

same day : they thus were made the heads and champions of the two contending parties of the nation. Mr. Love justified the punishing of heretics and schismatics, and vindicated the authority of the civil magistrate in imposing articles of faith and a form of worship ; in a word, pleaded for persecution. Mr. Dell was the advocate of liberty : he preached against making a whole kingdom a church ; he thought that no power belonged to the clergy but what is spiritual ; he protested against blending the civil and the ecclesiastical power together, as the constant method of setting up a spiritual tyranny ; he pleaded that all persons ought to have liberty to worship God in the manner they think most agreeable to his Word ; and argued, that the imposition of uniformity and all compulsion in matters of religion were antichristian. These principles created him enemies, who blackened his character by odious names. But, though he was tinctured with the enthusiasm of the times, he was a man of substantial learning, of real piety, and a noble defender of the rights of conscience. Besides several sermons and a tract written in this cause, he was the author of a tract in quarto, 1648, entitled "The Doctrine of Baptism reduced from its Ancient and Modern Corruptions."*

Another person of note was Mr. Francis Cornwell, M.A., who was some time student of Emanuel College, Cambridge, and commenced master of arts in that university. When he left it, he was preferred to a living in the Established Church ; and, at the beginning of the civil wars, was minister at Orpington, in Kent. In the reign of Charles I. he was imprisoned for nonconformity, refusing to wear the surplice, to kneel at the sacrament, and to use the sign of the cross in baptism. His companion in Maidstone jail was Mr. Wilson, of Otham, near that town. Among the visiters who came to see them was a woman, who had some doubts in her mind whether the baptism of infants could be proved from Scripture. Mr. Cornwell endeavoured, by the best scriptural arguments he could produce, to resolve her doubts, but found he could not do it so well to her or his own satisfaction as he could wish. When this visitant had left him, he conversed on the subject with his fellow-prisoner, Mr. Wilson ; who assured him he never thought that infant baptism could be proved from Scripture, but had its authority from human tradition, being handed down from primitive times as a practice generally received from the Church. Mr. Cornwell, taking the Scriptures to be the only rule of faith, and considering that on this principle alone all the Protestant churches vindicated their separation from the Church of Rome against all her impositions, founded on pretended primitive antiquity, was induced to make a more diligent search. The result was, that infant baptism did not appear to him to derive its authority from the Scriptures, but to have had its dependance, in all ages, on the decrees, canons, and councils of the Church. Entering into these views of the subject, he relinquished the doctrine of infants' baptism, and adopted the opinion of those who think that believers only, making profession of their faith and repentance, are the proper sub-

---

* See it at length in Crosby, vol. ii., p. 317–344.
† Crosby, vol. iii., Appendix, No. i.
‡ Ibid., vol. ii., p. 344, 345.

* Crosby, vol. i., p. 323–333. Palmer's Nonconformists' Memorial, vol. i., p. 201, and p. 225, note.

jects of this institution.* . In 1643 he publicly avowed this principle, and wrote in defence of it a tract entitled " The Vindication of the Royal Commission of Jesus." After the publication of this book, he went on to preach and propagate his opinion. In 1644, in a visitation sermon preached at Cranbrook in Kent; from Mark, vii., 7, before the ministers of those parts, he took the liberty of freely declaring his sentiments, and asserted that Pædobaptism was an antichristian innovation, a human tradition, and a practice for which there was neither precept, nor example, nor true deduction from the Word of God. This, as might be expected, much startled the clergy who were present, but greatly offended several of them. The matter was debated between them, and the argument in support of Antipædobaptism was strongly pushed by Mr. William Jeffrey, of Sevenoaks, who had baptized Mr. Cornwell, and to whom he had referred them, till Mr. Christopher Blackwood, one of the ministers, desired them to desist at that time, for he had taken down the sermon in shorthand, and would return an answer in print, which he hoped might be to the satisfaction of them all.† His advice was adopted; it was agreed to postpone, for the present, the discussion of the question, to re-examine the point, and to bring their collections together at the next meeting, which was to be within a fortnight. In the mean time, Mr. Blackwood studied the question with great diligence and close attention. The impression made on his mind was very different from what was anticipated. He began to suspect that infant baptism was no more than a human tradition, and was attended with evil consequences; and when they met he brought in his arguments against it. As no one produced any defence, one, properly observing that they sought for truth, and not victory, proposed that Mr. Blackwood's papers should be left with them for examination; to this motion he acceded; but when, after waiting a long time, no answer was given to his arguments, he sent for his papers, and published them with corrections and enlargements. Thus the controversy was revived in the county of Kent, and the sentiments of the Baptists gained ground. Mr. Cornwell soon after this withdrew from the National Church, for he disapproved both of national and parochial churches, and taught that a church was to consist of such only as professed repentance from dead works, and faith in the Lord Jesus Christ, and were baptized according to his commands, after the pattern of the first churches in Judea. He quickly gathered a church in Kent, formed on this plan, of which he was pastor to the day of his death, and was succeeded in that place and office by his son. It reflects honour on Mr. Cornwell's name and memory, that he was a zealous opposer of persecution and an imposed uniformity. He wrote against the ordinance of Parliament made to silence all lay-preachers, that is, such as had not received Episcopal or Presbyterian ordination, or who should preach anything contrary to the articles of faith and directory for public worship set forth by the Assembly. The piece

which he published on this occasion was entitled " Two Queries worthy of Consideration."

Q. 1. Whether that ministry that preacheth freely the Gospel faith, that 'the Lord Jesus is the Christ, as the Apostle Peter did, be not truly orthodox?

Q. 2. Whether it be agreeable to the Word of God, contained in the sacred Scriptures, to silence or inhibit any ministers of Jesus Christ for preaching this Gospel freely?

He affirmed the former, and maintained it by several arguments; the latter he denied, and intimated, that they who were guilty of such practices acted like the Jews of old, who cast the blind man out of the temple for confessing that Jesus was the Christ.*

In close connexion with Mr. Cornwell's history stands, as we have seen, that of Mr. Blackwood, who, in consequence of his visitation sermon, become a proselyte to believers' baptism, and, with Mr. Richard Kingsnorth, who likewise was convinced by it, gathered a church at Staplehurst in Kent; but his sentiments being Calvinistic, and contrary to those of the society, he afterward left it under the pastoral care of Mr. Kingsnorth, who held universal redemption and final perseverance.† Mr. Blackwood was possessed, at the beginning of the civil wars, of a parochial church in the county of Kent; from whence it is probable that he was educated at one of the universities. After he changed his sentiments on the questions concerning baptism, he did not continue long in the Established Church; for he was as zealous against national churches as against infant baptism. He was an advocate for liberty of conscience, and opposed the establishment of Presbyterianism. In the first piece he published, he joined together infant baptism and compulsion of conscience, and called them " the last two and strongest garrisons of antichrist." He was reckoned among " those worthy guides, well qualified in all respects for the ministry," who voluntarily left their benefices in the Establishment, by one who lived in those times. He appears, in 1653, to have gone into Ireland with the army under the command of General Fleetwood and Lieutenant Ludlow. He lived till after the Restoration, and signed the apology of the Baptists in 1660, declaring against Venner's insurrection.

Another, who was reckoned among the worthies of this denomination at this period, was Mr. Benjamin Cox, who made no mean figure in his time. He was the son of a bishop,‡ was a man of great learning, and a graduate in one of the universities. He was for some time a minister in the Established Church, had a parochial charge in the county of Devon, and was very zealous for the superstitious ceremonies that prevailed in Bishop Laud's time. But when the affairs of state led men to think more freely in matters of religion, Mr. Cox was among the first in promoting a reformation, and had before him flattering prospects of eminence and preferment in this kingdom, when he rejected the baptism of infants, as it appeared to him not

---

*, Mr. Thompson's Collections, MSS., under the words *Staplehurst* and *Smarden*.

† Mr. Thompson's Collections, MSS.

* Crosby, vol. i., p. 334–349; and vol. iii., p. 6–9.

† Thompson's Collections, MSS.

‡ It seems more probable that he was the grandson of one, as Dr. Richard Cox, bishop of Ely, who filled that see twenty years, died in 1580.—*Richardson de Præsulibus.*

founded in the Scriptures ; but this obstructed his advancement in the Established Church, and prejudiced against him the divines who were at the head of ecclesiastical affairs. He preserved, however, the character of a man of abilities and great learning. After Episcopacy and the Common Prayer were laid aside, he was for some time minister at Bedford. In 1645 he came to London, and was one of the principal managers on the part of the Baptists in a public dispute concerning infant baptism at Aldermanbury Church, to which a stop was afterward put by the government. In the year 1646, when seven churches in London, called-Anabaptists, published a confession of their faith, and presented it to Parliament, his name, in behalf of one of those congregations, was subscribed to it. Though, when the act of Uniformity, in 1662, took place, he at first conformed, yet his conscience soon after upbraiding him for that step, he obeyed its dictates by throwing up his living, and died a Nonconformist and a Baptist, in a very advanced age ; for Mr. Baxter, with whom he had a dispute by word of mouth and by writing, called him, at the beginning of the civil wars, an ancient minister. He suffered imprisonment for his opinions concerning baptism in the city of Coventry.*

Here is a proper place for observing, that at the Restoration, several parishes were found to have Baptist ministers fixed in them. The cause of this was, that in the year 1653, when a certain number of men called triers were authorized to examine and approve candidates for the ministry, Mr. Tombs, notwithstanding his difference in opinion from the rest, such was the estimation in which his character was held, was appointed to be one of them. Among other good effects that followed upon this, one was, that the commissioners agreed to own Baptists their brethren ; and that if any such applied to them for probation, and appeared in other respects duly qualified, they should not be rejected for holding their sentiments.†

The history of the Baptists from the accession of James II. to the Revolution is confined to some brief accounts of the sufferings and characters of several ministers who were in estimation among them, and died in this period. But we should first mention one whose name should have been introduced in the preceding reign : Mr. Abraham Chear, a native of Plymouth, who, though he did not enjoy a liberal education, knew the Scriptures from his childhood, and delighted in searching them. About 1648 he was baptized, and joined the Baptist church in that town, and was soon after invited to be their pastor, for which character he was fitted by peculiar gifts and graces. In 1661 he suffered three months' imprisonment in Exeter jail, on the Conventicle Act. In 1662 he was again cast into that prison ; after his release he was imprisoned at the Guildhall in Plymouth; then, after a month's detention, he was confined, under military guard, in the Isle of Plymouth, where, after full five years' imprisonment in different jails, and enduring many inhumanities from merciless jailers, he yielded up his spirit without pang or considerable groan, the 5th of March, 1668. At his death the

* Crosby, vol. i., p. 353, 354. † Ibid., p. 289.

church consisted of one hundred and fifty members. After this the persecution broke out with greater fury, and it suffered much till King James's declaration for liberty of conscience revived their drooping spirits, and were almost twenty years destitute of a pastor. Mr. Chear was a laborious and successful preacher. In his cofinement he wrote several religious tracts, and letters to his friends full of Christian exhortations to constancy and steadfastness. One of these, an acknowledgment of some provisions sent to him and his fellow-prisoners, most expressive of cheerfulness in their sufferings and gratitude to their benefactors, is preserved by Crosby. During his illness, almost to his last moment, he continued glorifying God, and exhorting all who visited him to perseverance in those perilous times ; speaking with earnest concern about the guilt contracted in these nations by persecuting God's faithful servants ; and with great joy and assurance concerning the delight which God takes in his suffering saints, and the ample recompense he will hereafter render for their present sorrows ; particularly on the Lord's Day preceding his dissolution. About three hours before it, a friend, perceiving him under great pressures, said softly to him, "They looked unto the Lord, and were lightened : a right look will bring down relief under all difficulties." "Yea," he replied, with great strength and earnestness, "and their faces were not ashamed."*

In the reign of James II. died, at Kelby in Leicestershire, where he was a minister of a Baptist congregation, Mr. Richard Farmer, the friend of Mr. Clarke and Mr. Shuttleworth, eminent ejected ministers in that county. He was a hard student and an affecting preacher, and frequently officiated among the Independents. He had a small estate to live upon, in which he suffered greatly for his religious principles, as distress was made by virtue of a justice's warrant upon his goods ; and they took from him, in one year, to the value of £110.†

Another, who suffered much in this period for his nonconformity, and was several times prisoner at York, at Leeds, and at Chester, was Mr. Thomas Hardcastle, ejected from Bramham, in the county of York. He was born at Barwick-upon-Holm, and received his education under Mr. Jackson, of that town, a learned divine. He had not been long in the ministry when the Act of Uniformity passed : he preached afterward at Shadwell Chapel and other places. He was a man of pregnant parts, eminent learning and piety, of great moderation and catholicism, though of a bold spirit, which feared no danger. In 1671 he was, on the death of Mr. Ewins,‡ invited to be pastor of a congrega-

* Thompson's Collections, MSS., and Crosby's History of the English Baptists, vol. iii., p. 11-24.
† Ibid., p. 118, 119.
‡ Mr. Ewins was ejected from a living in Bristol : though he was no scholar, and had been a mechanic, he was esteemed as a judicious, methodical preacher ; was remarkable for his meekness, patience, and charity : in his ministerial duties he was popular, laborious, and successful, ready to preach on those days when not otherwise employed ; grave and serious everywhere, and full of good discourse. He was so scrupulous about maintenance, that he would accept no tithes nor salary, but only free gifts. The Bishop of Bristol invited him to conform, but he could

tion of Baptists, who had separated from the Establishment early in 1640, though they continued their attendance at sermon, but not at the prayers, in the parish church on the morning of by no means be satisfied to comply. When, in 1651, he was invited by the Separatists at Bristol to become their minister, he was a Pædobaptist. About 1654 he embraced the opinions of the Baptists, and was baptized in London. In 1660 the members of his society were turned out of the churches, and in 1662 he was ordained their pastor. He went through a variety of persecutions, and was often in prison, once for a whole year, when he preached twice a day. There he contracted a lethargic distemper, of which he died, aged about sixty, in April, 1670, greatly lamented. He was buried in St. James's churchyard, April 29, and a vast concourse of people attended his funeral. He was sometimes abused in the streets, but would not attempt to retaliate; for he said, " Vengeance is God's ; my duty is patience."—*Palmer's Nonconformists' Memorial*, vol. ii., p. 351 ; and *Thompson's Collections*, MSS.

The following letter, addressed to Mr. Ewins by the mayor, aldermen, and steward of Bristol, inviting him to Bristol from his parish at Lanvaughas, clearly proves his high reputation as a preacher: the church of which he became pastor still exists, and is known as the Broadmead Church :

" Good Sir—In pursuance of an act of Parliament for the better maintenance of ministers to preach the Gospel, we, the commissioners by the said act appointed, being met together to consider and advise of able and godly men to preach the Gospel in Bristol, having much assurance of your faithfulness and sufficiency for that work, do desire you, sir, that you will please to come unto us, and perform the work and service of a faithful dispenser of the Word of the Gospel in this city ; and forasmuch as there is a power given us by the said act to make provision for a competent number of good ministers, we doubt not but we shall provide a sufficient and comfortable maintenance for you. We shall expect to hear from you, and remain, sir, your loving friends, &c.

" *Bristol, the* 14*th of July*, 1651."

Thus Mr. Ewins was settled over the church, and by the mayor appointed city lecturer. He was to preach at St. Nicholas's " every third day" (Tuesday). On Lord's Day morning he preached to his own people at Christ Church ; and in the afternoon, at the desire of the corporation, at the church of St. Maryleport. In summer he frequently preached at St. Thomas's and St, Philip's, they being spacious, and capable of accommodating a large number of hearers. On a Friday he preached alternately at St. Philip's and St. Michael's almshouses, besides attending the conference meetings of his own church on Thursdays. A sermon which was preached by him on the narrative of Blind Bartimeus was the means of the conversion of many; and in those " halcyon days of prosperity, liberty, and peace," it pleased the Lord to favour his church with a large increase of light and purity. Mr. Ewins was remarkable for meekness, patience, and charity ; and so scrupulous about maintenance, that he would accept neither tithes nor salary, but only free gifts. This noble feeling cannot be too highly commended. It was a source of satisfaction to an inspired apostle. Not that he thought it *wrong* to receive remuneration : on the contrary, he pleaded for it not as a favour, but as a *right*. But he gloried in being able to decline receiving that to which he and all faithful ministers are entitled. It is much to be deplored that, in the present degenerate state of the Church, " free gifts" would not always be adequate ; and yet they should be; and in proportion as we appreciate the Gospel, and the value of the soul, they will be. A penurious church cannot expect a blessing from a bountiful Lord.—*The Rise and Progress of Dissent in Bristol, chiefly in relation to Broadmead Church, by J. G. Fuller*, 1840, p. 31, 32.—C.

VOL. II.—D D D .

the Lord's Day, spending the afternoon and evening in religious exercises among themselves. Mr. Cann, the author of the marginal references to the Bible, preached adult baptism to them, and settled them in church order, without making baptism a term of communion. On Mr. Hardcastle's settlement with them, they took four rooms on the Lamb pavement, Broadmead, and made them into one of sixteen yards long and fifteen broad. At Bristol he was sent to the House of Correction ; he died suddenly, 20th of August, 1678, universally lamented. He published one practical treatise.[*] He was succeeded by another ejected minister.

Mr. George Fownes, who settled with this society September 16, 1679, found the number of members, which amounted, when Mr. Hardcastle became their pastor, to a hundred, increased to one hundred and sixty-six, of which thirty-one were Pædobaptists. Mr. Fownes was born in Shropshire, and received his classical education at Shrewsbury, where his grandson, the ingenious and learned Mr. Joseph Fownes, was for many years a dissenting minister. His father dying, he was sent to Cambridge. He was an able preacher, and a man of great learning, and was conversant in law, physic, and other branches of science. He voluntarily quitted the parish church before the Restoration, though he continued preaching in different places till he fixed at Bristol. About the time of what was called the Presbyterian Plot, he was taken in the pulpit, and committed to Newgate ; but, by virtue of a flaw in the *mittimus*, he was in six weeks removed by a habeas corpus to the King's Bench, and acquitted. He was afterward apprehended on the highway in Kingswood, on suspicion of only coming from a meeting, and committed to Gloucester jail, for refusing the corporation oath, and riding within five miles of a corporation : witnesses were suborned to swear a riot against him, though no other rioter was named in the bill ; he pleaded his own cause very pleasantly, telling them " that he and his horse could not be guilty of a riot without company ;" and the jury brought in their verdict, Not guilty : yet he was returned back to prison ; and refusing to give a bond for good behaviour, of which he knew preaching would be interpreted to be a forfeiture, he was detained there for two years and a half, till God released him by death in December, 1685. He was afflicted with the stone, and a physician declared " that his confinement was his death ; and that it was no less murder than if they had run him through the first day he came in, and more cruel."[†]

Another eminent minister and writer among the Baptists at this time was Mr. Henry d'Anvers, a worthy man, of unspotted life and conversation, a joint elder of a Baptist congregation at Aldgate, London, and author of " A Treatise of Baptism," which drew him into a controversy with Mr. Wills, Mr. Blinman, and Mr. Baxter, in whose writings, if we may credit a letter published by Mr. d'Anvers, and sent

---

[*] Thompson's Collections, MSS. Crosby, vol. iii., p. 27, 28 ; and Palmer's Nonconformists' Memorial, vol. ii., p.

[†] Palmer's Nonconformists' Memorial, vol. i., p. 243, &c. Crosby, vol. iii., p. 28, 29; and Thompson's Collections, MSS.

to him by a person of quality, of known worth, ability, and moderation, "there were more heat, passion, and personal reflections, than of reason or a sober inquisition of truth." Mr. d'Anvers was descended from honourable parents, his father being a gentleman who had an estate of £400 a year; he himself was governor of Stafford, and a justice of peace, some time before Oliver's usurpation, and well beloved by the people. He was noted for one who would take no bribes. At Stafford he first embraced the opinions of the Baptists.*

In 1687, May 14th, died Mr. Thomas Wilcox, minister of a congregation, which met, previous to the plague, at his own house in Cannon-street, but afterward at the Three Cranes in the Borough, Southwark; and author of a popular little piece, which has been frequently reprinted, entitled "A Drop of Honey from the Rock Christ." He was born at Linden, in the county of Rutland, August, 1622; was several times confined in Newgate for nonconformity, and suffered very much. He was a moderate man, and of catholic principles, well beloved by all denominations, and frequently preached among the Presbyterians and Independents.

October 3, 1687, died, aged fifty-three, Mr. John Gosnold, who had been a scholar at the Charter House, and a student at Pembroke Hall, Cambridge, a man of great learning and piety, a pious, practical preacher, of singular modesty and moderation; intimately acquainted with Tillotson, whose weekly lecture he used to attend, and was much esteemed and valued by other men of note and dignity in the Established Church, who kept up a correspondence with him. He was educated for the pulpit in the Establishment, but, by the Act of Uniformity, made incapable of any settlement in it. He was chaplain to Lord Grey. Having joined the Baptists, he was chosen pastor of a congregation at Barbican, in London, and was one of the ministers who subscribed the apology presented to Charles II. on occasion of Venner's conspiracy. Though he was always peaceably-minded, he was often forced to conceal himself. His flock held him in great respect, and his preaching was so popular as to draw after him people of all denominations. His audience was usually computed to be near three thousand; and among them very often six, or seven clergymen in their gowns, who sat in a convenient place, under a large gallery, where they were seen by few. The number of his auditors, and the figure which some of them made, occasioned, after the fire of London, an application from the officers of the parish of Cripplegate to request a collection for the poor, who abounded in that parish. The request was complied with, upward of £50 was raised, and the church voluntarily continued the collection for above twenty years. His publications were, a small treatise entitled "The Doctrine of Baptism;" and another concerning "The Laying on of Hands." He was buried in Bunhill Fields, with this simple inscription:

"Here lieth the body of Mr. John Gosnold, a faithful minister of the Gospel, who departed this life October the 3d, 1678, and in the fifty-third year of his age."

(I am sure the reader will be pleased to possess an additional record to the memory of men of whom the world was not worthy; I therefore subjoin a valuable article from Dr. Toulmin's very respectable work entitled "The History of the Protestant Dissenters," London, 1814.

Dr. Toulmin remarks that there were many individuals particularly esteemed, and regarded as men of talents and influence, and says, "Among these was Mr. William Kiffin, who began his ministry with the Independents, but afterward taking a part in the conferences that were held in the congregation of Mr. Henry Jessey, when the majority of them adopted the sentiments of the Baptists, Mr. Kiffin at that time changed his opinion, and joined himself to the church of Mr. John Spilsbury. A difference arose between them about permitting an individual to preach to them who had not been initiated into the Christian Church by immersion, as if the conscientious omission, on one side, of a rite considered as an institution of Christ by the other party, could vitiate the functions of the minister, or as if a mutual indulgence to the dictates of conscience could be a criminal connivance at error. On this point these good men parted, but to their credit they kept up a friendly correspondence. Mr. Kiffin became the pastor of a Baptist congregation in Devonshire Square, London. After the Restoration he had great influence at court, both with the king and Chancellor Hyde; and possessing opulence, is reported to have supplied his majesty, on pressing emergencies, with a present of ten thousand pounds. He improved his interest with the king to obtain an order for the examination, in council, of a scurrilous and malignant pamphlet, meant to defame the Baptists, entitled 'Baxter baptized in Blood.' Another effect of his influence was the pardon of twelve Baptists, who were condemned to death at Aylesbury for refusing to conform to the Established Church, under a clause in the Conventicle Act of the 35th of Queen Elizabeth; by the justices of the county at a quarter sessions: a proceeding which surprised the king, who could scarcely believe that any law to justify putting his subjects to death for religion only could be in force.* Mr. Kiffin himself had, in the time of the Commonwealth, been prosecuted under the ordinance of Parliament, enacted with a designed reference to Mr. Riddle, for punishing blasphemies and heresies. On the 12th of July, 1655, he was summoned before the lord-mayor, and charged with a breach of this ordinance, by preaching that, 'the baptism of infants was unlawful.' That magistrate being busy, the execution of the penalty incurred was referred to the following Monday.† The influence which he had at court, instead of abashing malignity, provoked it, and increased the number of his enemies, and they formed a design upon his life, which coming to his knowledge by a letter that was intercepted, he was so happy as to escape. He and Mr. Knollys advocated the principles of the Baptists against Dr. Grew and Dr. Bryan, in a disputation held at Coventry; in which both sides claimed the victory, but which was conducted with good temper and great moderation,

---

* Crosby, vol. iii., p. 90. This individual is severely treated in Wall's History of Baptism.—C.

* Crosby, vol. ii., p. 181, and vol. iii., p. 5.
† Ibid., vol. i., p. 215.

and closed without any diminution of friendly regards. Mr. Kiffin lived to be very old, and preached to the last. He was a man of considerable parts, had learning, and was an acute disputant. It is a sign of his weight, and of the estimation in which he was held by the religious and political communities, that he was one of the five Baptists who were made aldermen by King James II. when. he deprived the city of London of its charter.*

"Another individual who obtained distinction among the Baptists of that day, and was the author of a treatise in 4to on the subject of baptism, was Mr. Thomas Patient, who began his ministry among the Independents in New-England; but, by his own reflections in reading the Scriptures, was led to conclude that infant baptism had no foundation in them. This change of sentiments provoked the resentment of his brethren, and exposed him to much suffering, and which induced him to emigrate to England, where he became co-pastor with Mr. William Kiffin. He accompanied General Fleetwood to Ireland, and settled there; and after Dr. Winter was removed by the general, usually preached in the cathedral. The interest of the Baptists was much advanced by his labours in that kingdom, and he is thought to have formed the Baptist church at Cloughkeating, which, in the year 1740, consisted of between two or three hundred members united in one communion, though some were of the *general* and others of the *particular* persuasion. This church was implicated in the prosecutions which followed the suppression of Monmouth's insurrection, and the minister and all the members were tried for their lives. The foreman of the Jury swore, before he went into the court, that he would not leave it till he had brought them all in guilty :: a rash and profane way of prejudging a cause. As soon as he entered the court he died, and the rest of the jury acquitted them.†

"There did not arise among this denomination of Christians a more remarkable character, in many respects, than Mr. John Bunyan, who was born of honest but poor parents, at Elstow in Bedfordshire, in 1628. His father was a tinker: his education consisted only in being taught to read and write; and after he was grown up, he followed his father's occupation. In 1645 he served as a soldier in the Parliament's army at the siege of Leicester. In his youth he was very vicious, and greatly corrupted the manners of his young companions. He became at length a thoughtful and pious man. Different incidents seem to have awakened the principle of conscience in his breast, and to have led him into deep, serious, and penitent reflections. The reproof of a woman, a notoriously wicked character, addressed to him with sharpness, when he was cursing and swearing in a vehement manner, and reproaching him as able to spoil all the youth in the town, filled him with shame, and determined him to refrain from that profane practice. An accidental conversation with a poor man on religion induced him to apply himself to reading the Scriptures; which was followed by such a reformation, both in his words and life, that the change in his manners filled his neighbours with astonishment, and converted their former censures of his conduct into

commendation and praise. A casual conference also with four poor women, into whose company he fell at Bedford, on the subject of the new birth, left very serious impressions on his mind. He himself, it appears, ascribed his conversion principally, or in the first instance, to a sudden voice from Heaven, saying, 'Wilt thou leave thy sins, and go to heaven; or have thy sins, and go to hell?' and accosting him when he was at play with his companions. This excited such an astonishment, that he immediately left his sport, and looking up to heaven, whence the voice seemed to come, he thought he saw the Lord Jesus looking down upon him and threatening him with some grievous punishment for his irreligious practices. This supposed phenomenon indicated a state of mind previously much agitated and affected with conscious guilt, aided by the force and vivacity of an imagination strongly tinctured with enthusiasm, of the influence of which his history affords various instances; for on other and future occasions he conceived that he saw visions and heard voices from heaven. The turn of his thoughts, and the natural power of fancy, presenting images suitable to his remorse and fears, were as really the means which a gracious Providence employed to bring him to repentance, and the effect was the same, as if a real supernatural impression had been made on his ear, or a miraculous scene had been presented to his eye. He became a man of sincere piety and blameless morals; though the latter did not screen him from malicious and groundless calumnies, and the former was unhappily accompanied with great bigotry and a censorious spirit. When he married, he was extremely poor, not having so much furniture as even a dish or a spoon, and all the portion his wife brought him consisted in two books, 'The Plain Man's Pathway to Heaven,' and 'The Practice of Piety.' After his conversion he was baptized by Mr. Gifford, the minister of the Baptist church in Bedford, and admitted a member of it about the year 1655.* His talents, and gifts, and religious

* "Long before the year 1650, there were in this town and neighbourhood pious persons, who felt a detestation of Episcopal superstition and tyranny, and united in searching after Nonconformists, called in that day *Puritans*. The chief among these were the Rev. Mr. Man, Mr. John Grew, Mr. John Eston, and Mr. Anthony Harrington. They neither were nor desired to be formed into a church; but were zealous to edify each other, and to promote the Gospel by their liberality and friendship, always keeping a door open; and a table furnished, for those ministers and Christians who evinced a zeal for the purity and practice of religion. About the year 1650 came among them Mr. John Gifford, a native of Kent, who had been a great Royalist and a major in the king's army, but had recently been under deep religious impressions, and had commenced preacher. His labours in that character were acceptable, and successful in awakening in the minds of some a religious concern, and in engaging these friends of piety to form themselves into a church, of which he was chosen the pastor or elder.

"The principles on which they entered into fellowship one with another, and on which they received new members into their Christian association, were *faith in Christ* and *holiness of life*, without respect to this or that circumstance of opinion in outward or circumstantial points. By these means faith and holiness were encouraged, love and amity were maintained, disputing and occasional janglings were avoid-

* Crosby, vol. iii., p. 3, 4, 5. † Ibid., vol. iii., p. 43.

gions spirit attracted the attention of this congregation, among whom he for some time gave
a word of exhortation, or led their worship, till
they called him to the character of a public minister, and set him apart to that office by fasting
and prayer. He was a popular preacher, and
generally spoke with much fluency and with
great effect. A Cambridge scholar, who afterward became a very eminent minister in the
county, is particularly mentioned as an instance
of the power and success of his preaching. Mr.
Bunyan was to appear on a week day in the
pulpit of a church in a country village in the
county, and a great number of people was collected together to hear him. The Cambridge
student riding by at the time inquired, What
meant the concourse of people? He was told
that one Bunyan, a *tinker*, was to preach there ;
in a sportive mood he committed his horse to
the care of a boy, saying 'he was resolved to
hear the *tinker prate*,' and went into the church.
His attention was fixed; he was affected and
impressed ; he came out serious and thoughtful, and much changed, and would, when he
could gratify his taste, hear none but the *tinker*
for a long time.* *The learned Dr. Owen, the
vice-chancellor of the University of Oxford, countenanced his ministerial 'labours, and attended his
sermons.* The intolerance of the government,
in a few years, put a stop to this course of services. On the 12th of November, 1660, he was
requested to preach at Gansel, near Harlington,
in Bedfordshire ; and there he was apprehended
by virtue of a warrant granted by Francis Win-
gate, Esq., a justice of peace, before whom he
was taken, and then committed to Bedford jail.
After an imprisonment of seven weeks he was
tried on an indictment at Bedford quarter sessions, charged with ' having *devilishly* and *perniciously* abstained from coming to church to
hear Divine service ; and with being a common
upholder of several unlawful meetings and conventicles, to the great *disturbance* and *distraction*
of the good subjects of this kingdom, contrary
to the laws of our sovereign lord the king.' All,
it has been justly observed, that John Bunyan
had been guilty of, though it was alleged to be
thus ' *devilish* and *pernicious*, and so wickedly
calculated to *disturb* and *distract* the good people of England,' was merely worshipping God
according to the dictates of his own conscience,
and endeavouring to propagate his own religious
opinions. But even the facts stated in this ridiculous indictment were not proved, no witnesses were produced against him; but some
words which came from him in the course of a
conversation with the justices, were taken for
a conviction and recorded : he was sent back
to prison, under this sentence, to lie there for
three months ; and if he did not then engage to
hear Divine service, and attend in the church,
and desist from preaching, to be banished the
realm ; and in case of not leaving the realm
on an appointed day, or of returning to it with-

out a special license from the king, to be hanged.*

" His wife, to whom, at the time of his commitment, he had been married almost two
years,† on the following assizes addressed herself to the judges ; but the justices had prejudiced them to the utmost they could against
him. Sir Matthew Hale, who was one of them,
and appeared to know nothing of his history, indeed, had the matter come judicially before him,
seemed desirous to afford him relief, and advised his wife to procure a writ of error : but
Bunyan and his friends were either too poor, or
too little acquainted with such matters, to take
the necessary steps to obtain his enlargement.
The sentence of banishment was never executed against him ; but he was detained in prison
from sessions to sessions, from assizes to assizes, without being brought before the judges,
and obtaining permission to plead his cause, till
his imprisonment lasted twelve years. He endured the evils of this long confinement with perfect resignation and patience ; learned to make
long tagged thread-laces, and supported himself
by it ; and wrote many of his tracts, though his
library is said to have consisted only of his Bible and the Book of Martyrs. His enlargement
at last is ascribed to the compassion and interest of the worthy prelate Dr. Barlow, bishop of
Lincoln, and to the interference of Dr. Owen.‡
There was an existing law, which invested a
bishop with the power to release a prisoner, situated as was Mr. Bunyan, if any two persons
would join in a cautionary bond that he should
conform in half a year. Dr. Owen readily consented, on being requested, to give his bond.
The bishop, on application being made to him,
declined availing himself of his Episcopal prerogative ; but as the law provided that, in case
of a bishop's refusal, application should be made
to the lord-chancellor to issue out an order to
take the cautionary bond and release the prisoner, the bishop proposed this mode of proceeding as more safe for himself at that critical time,
as he had many enemies, and promised a compliance with the order of the chancellor. This
measure, though it was not so direct as the other, and was more expensive, was adopted, and
Mr. Bunyan was released. In the last year of
his imprisonment, 1671, on the death of Mr.
Gifford, he had been unanimously chosen to succeed him in the pastoral office.

" After his enlargement, he employed himself
in preaching and writing, and made journeys
into various parts of the kingdom to visit pious
persons of his own religious views, which visi-
tations fixed on him the title of ' Bishop Bunyan.' When James II. published his declaration for the liberty of conscience in 1687, though
he saw it proceeded not from kindness to Protestant Dissenters, and his piercing judgment anticipated the black cloud of slavery which the
sunshine of transient liberty was intended to introduce, yet he thought it right to improve the
present day ; and by the contributions of his
followers built a public meeting-house at Bedford, in which he constantly preached to large
congregations. It was his constant practice

---

ed, and many that were weak in the faith were confirmed in the principles of eternal life."* In consistency with the large basis on which this church was
constituted, its next minister, Mr. Bunyan, was an
advocate for the mixed communion of Christians
who differed in opinion on the questions relative to
baptism.   * Crosby, vol. iii.; p. 65.

* Thomson's Collections, vol. i., Bedford MSS.

* Biographia Britannica, by Kippis and others, vol.
iii., article *Bunyan*, page 12, note 1.
    † She was his second wife.
    ‡ British Biography, vol. vi., p. 106.

also, after his liberty, to visit London once a year, where he preached in several places, particularly in Southwark, to numerous auditors, with great acceptance. At last he fell, not a victim to the malignant spirit of persecution, but a sacrifice in the event, to the pacific kindness of his own heart. A young gentleman having fallen under the resentment of his father, requested Mr. Bunyan's reconciliatory offices to make up the breach. He undertook, and happily effected this benevolent office. On his return to London, from the journey which it occasioned, he was overtaken with excessive rains, and contracted a cold from being very wet, which brought on a violent fever, that in ten days put a period to his life, at the house of Mr. Straddocks, a grocer, on Snow Hill, on the 12th of August, in the 60th year of his age. According to the description of his person, and the delineation of his character, drawn by the continuator of his life, ' he appeared in countenance to be of a stern and rough temper, but was in his conversation mild and affable; not given to loquacity or much discourse in company, unless some urgent occasion required it; *observing neber to boast of himself or his parts, but rather seemed low in his own eyes, and submitted himself to the judgment of others ;* abhorring lying and swearing, being just, in all that lay in his power, to his word, not seeming to revenge injuries, loving to reconcile differences, and making friendship with all ; he had an excellent discernment of persons, being of good judgment and quick wit. As for his person, he was tall of stature, strong-boned, though not corpulent, somewhat of a ruddy face, with sharp and sparkling eyes, wearing his hair on his upper lip after the old British fashion ; his hair reddish, but in his latter days time had sprinkled it with gray ; his nose well-set, but not declining or bending, and his mouth moderately large, his forehead something high, and his habit always plain and modest.'*

" 'When he arrived at the 60th year of his age, he had written books,' it has been observed, ' equal to the number of his years.' His works, which had been long printed in detached pieces on tobacco paper, were collected together and reprinted in 1736 and 1737, in two volumes folio ; and have since been reprinted in a fairer edition, particularly in one impression with a recommendation from the pen of Mr. George Whitfield. The Pilgrim's Progress had, in the year 1784, passed through upward of fifty editions.

" Bunyan, 'who had been mentioned,' says Mr. Granger, ' among the least and lowest of our writers, deserves a much higher rank than is commonly imagined. His master-piece is his " Pilgrim's Progress,"† one of the most pop-

ular, and, I may add, one of the most ingenious books in the English language.* It gives us a clear and distinct idea of Calvinistical divinity. The allegory is admirably carried on, and the characters are justly drawn and uniformly supported. The author's original and poetic genius shines through the coarseness and vulgarity of his language, and intimates that if he had been a master of numbers, he might have composed a poem worthy of Spenser himself. As this opinion may be deemed paradoxical, I shall venture to name two persons of eminence of the same sentiments ; one, the late Mr. Merrick, of Reading, who has been heard to say in conversation, " that his invention was like that of Homer ;" the other, Dr. Roberts, fellow of Eton College.'†

"The mixture of the dramatic and narrative, enlivening the style, Lord Kaimes remarks, has rendered the 'Pilgrim's Progress' and ' Robinson Cruso' great favourites of the vulgar, and has been the cause of their having been translated into several European languages. Bunyan had such an extraordinary knack in amusing and parabolical compositions under the form of visions, that some thought there were communications made to him in *dreams,* and that he first really dreamed over the matter contained in his writings of this kind. This notion was not a little propagated by his picture prefixed to some of his treatises, in which he is represented in a sleeping posture. An anonymous author in 1729, speaking of the ' Pilgrim's Progress,' remarked that ' it had infinitely outdone The Tale of a Tub, which perhaps had not made one convert to infidelity; whereas the Pilgrim's Progress had converted many sinners to Christ.'‡

" Dr. Kippis, with great deference to the opinions of such judges as Mr. Merrick and Dr. Roberts, doubts whether Bunyan could ever have been capable of rising to a production worthy a Spenser. The poverty, not with regard to numbers only, but to fancy, visible in the specimens of his versification, justifies an apprehension that, with the best advantages of education, he would scarcely have attained to complete poetical composition. ' He had the invention, but not the other natural qualifications which are necessary to constitute a great poet. If his genius had intended him to be anything more than a poet in prose, it would probably, like Shakspeare's, have broken through every difficulty of birth and station.'

" It may be added, that a learned bishop,§ whose practical writings glow with a devotional spirit, and whose commentaries are still in high estimation, published also an allegorical work, entitled ' The Pilgrim,' but not with a success or reputation that could in any degree rival Bunyan's performance. The writer of this

---

* Biographia Britannica, ut ante, note Z.

† I have much pleasure in speaking favourably of Cheever's admirable Lectures upon the Pilgrim's Progress, published in New-York by Wiley and Putnam ; and the reader who is curious to know more about the life of Bunyan will be greatly interested by consulting his autobiography, published by Dodd of New-York, and the Life of Bunyan, by the Rev. Robert Philip, of London ; this last very interesting volume is published by Messrs. Appleton and Co. The beautiful edition of this immortal work published by Martin is familiar to the reader, and the literary man need hardly be told of Southey's memoir,

which, however, is written in a spirit far from doing full justice to the Nonconformist. Bunyan's Holy War is an admirable work, and ought to be better known than it is. Gould, Kendall, and Lincoln, of Boston, have issued a cheap and neat edition, edited by President Malcom of Kentucky.—C.

* This observation, Mr. Granger observes in the margin, is not to be extended to the second part.

† Granger's History of England, vol. iii., p. 348, 8vo ed., 1779.

‡ The above remarks are taken from Mr. Oldy's MSS. See Biographia Britannica, ut ante, p. 13, note L.   § Bishop Patrick.

recollects that at a classical lesson, when he was at St. Paul's school, Mr. Allen, the learned editor of Demosthenes, passed high encomiums on the latter work, as greatly superior in point of invention to the former, which has now sunk into oblivion.

"This article, it may be apprehended, has been carried to a length beyond the proportion of room it should occupy in a work not professedly biographical; but the singularity of the character will be admitted as an apology.*

"In the list of those who sustained great trials in a conscientious adherence to their religious profession, was Mr. Henry Forty, in his early years a member of Mr. Jessey's congregation, and afterward pastor of the church at Abingdon. His own parents, as well as many other persons, received a pious determination of mind from his preaching. He lay twelve years, for the testimony of a good conscience, in prison at Exeter, and died in the 67th year of his age, in 1692, with the character of a man of great piety and unblamable manners. Mr. Benjamin Keach preached his funeral sermon.

"The short history of the next person, Mr. Isaac Lamb, was marked with many peculiar circumstances. He was a native of Colchester, where he was born in 1650, and for some time attended his father in Cromwell's army. From his youth he discovered an affectionate attachment to piety, and took great delight in the perusal of the Scriptures. His progress in that study surpassed what could be expected from his years. The gravity of his aspect and the seriousness of his deportment gave him so manly and dignified an appearance, that at the age of 16 he was made chaplain of the Constant Warwick, a man-of-war in Oliver's navy. He often preached before Admiral Blake, and once in the presence of him, Admiral Penn, and another naval officer of the same rank. He delivered serious, interesting thoughts in an agreeable manner. At one time six of the ship's crew were baptized by him in an arm of the sea. After having been on different occasions, not fewer than twenty times, on the French and Spanish shores, and at other places, he returned from Holland in 1660 in the same fleet which brought over Charles II. His principles of nonconformity soon exposed him to privations and sufferings. He was offered a benefice of £100 per annum, which, as he could not, consistently with his sentiments, sprinkle the children of the parish, he declined to accept. It was proposed to him to do this part of his parochial duty by another; but it was repugnant to his sense of religious simplicity and integrity to engage a substitute to perform a service, which in his view was a misapplication of a Christian institution. He therefore refused the living. It heightened the merit of this sacrifice to the delicacy of principle, that he lost by his refusal £200 due on the living, and ready to be paid to the next incumbent. Being fixed by this determination among the Dissenters, he became pastor of a congregation in East Smithfield. It greatly increased under his popular strain of preaching, and removed to a new building, erected for its accommodation, in Virginia-street,

Ratcliffe Highway, where the auditory was numereus, and the communicants amounted, at times, to three hundred. Their worship was often disturbed by officers and soldiers in King Charles's reign. Once an officer with his military subalterns came and commanded him to be silent. He answered in the words of the apostle, 'Whether it be right in the sight of God to hearken unto you more than unto God, judge ye.' Upon which the officer with his soldiers went off. At another time, Sir William Smith, Mr. Bury, Mr. Brown, and four other justices, came in their coaches with a mob, to break the windows and to tear up the pews and pulpit of the meeting-house, as they had before done at the meeting-house of Mr. Hercules Collins, in the neighbourhood. But Mr. Lamb, having previously received notice of their intention, had, by the advice of a friend, removed all the furniture of the place, except a few loose forms, so that they were disappointed in their purpose; on which one of the justices said that his name ought to have been Fox, and not Lamb. He died on the 20th of August, 1691. He was a man of sweet temper and exemplary conversation, and great usefulness marked his course.*

"One of the most distinguished characters among the Baptists of the time was Mr. Thomas Grantham, descended from a reduced branch of an ancient family of rank and opulence in Lincolnshire. He was born in the year 1634, in the village of Halton, near Spilsby ; and the house in which he drew his first breath is still shown to those who venerate his memory. As his parents were in low circumstances, he was brought up a tailor, but he afterward directed his attention to agriculture, and occupied a farm. From an early period of his life his mind received a serious and religious tincture, and he was baptized, on the profession of his faith in the Gospel, about the age of nineteen, and joined the church at Boston. In the year 1656, when he was twenty-two years of age, he was chosen pastor of a church in the South Marsh parts of the county, consisting then only of four persons. He had for several years associated with them, and been active in assisting their religious improvement by procuring ministers to preach to them publicly, or exercising his own gifts for prayer and instruction among them privately. This small society was a branch of a church which arose in 1644, formed at first on the principle of rejecting in the administration of baptism, while they retained the practice of sprinkling, the cross and sponsors. Some of them afterward, as they pursued their religious inquiries, saw reasons to adopt the practice of immersion on a profession of faith. This change in the sentiments of some did not meet with the concurrence of all : disagreements arose, which terminated in a disunion in 1651. The few who embraced the principles of the Baptists, after Mr. Grantham's connexion with them as a pastor, soon increased in numbers. His zeal and energy animated the rest. As they had an accession of new members, there arose among them several who became acceptable and useful ministers. They drew the attention of their neighbours on themselves, and were exposed to the malignity of enemies. Mr. Grantham and several others were summoned before the ma-

---

* Biographia Britannica ; Granger's History of England; British Biography, as before, and Crosby, vol. iii., p. 63-75.

* Crosby, vol. iii., p. 100-103.

gistrates, who, as the accusations alleged against them had no foundation but in lies and forged stories, soon perceived their innocence, and they were set at liberty, and went on cheerfully; though often insulted by the mob and opposed by the clergy. Even during the protectorate or interregnum, their preachers were interrupted in their discourses, and sometimes dragged out of doors, and pelted and stoned with barbarous violence. All this abuse they bore with patience and meekness. Their meetings were held first, at Halton and other places, in private houses; at length they obtained a grant of Northolem Chapel, near Croft, and not far from Waynfleet. Here they remained some years, and had many accessions of members to their communion. Among others, Mr. John Watts, a person of eminence and reputation in those parts, who had been educated for the ministry at the university, but not being able, from a principle of conscience, to conform to the rites and practices of the National Church, he had obtained no dignity or preferment. He became, after he had joined himself to Mr. Grantham and his friends, the worthy pastor of a Baptist church gathered by his ministry, and which held their assemblies for Divine worship in his own house.

"Mr. Grantham is supposed to have drawn up the 'Narrative and Complaint,' stating the sufferings of the Baptists, which accompanied the 'Brief Confession of Faith' and 'Petition,' presented to the king, Charles II., on the 26th of July, 1660.* About 1662 he was apprehended, carried before a magistrate, and bound over to the assizes, to be holden for the county of Lincoln. At the same time many of the Baptists were harassed with prosecutions for absence from the Established Church, and with the exaction of penalties of £20 per month. The consequence of the proceedings against Mr. Grantham was an imprisonment for fifteen months. Obloquy and insult were added to the evils of confinement. Several clergymen who visited him upbraided him with being a Jesuit, and a rumour was spread that he was a papist. To confute this calumny, and counteract the impressions which it made, he published a controversy which he maintained with a Roman Catholic, and entitled it 'The Baptist against the Papist.' By this prudent conduct he silenced the report. During his imprisonment he published a treatise entitled 'The Prisoner against the Prelate; or, a Dialogue between the Common Jail of Lincoln and the Cathedral;' and another work under the title of 'Christianismus Primitivus.' In these publications, as the designed brevity of 'The Brief Confession' had occasioned some ambiguity, he treated the subject more explicitly and fully. When we consider the prevailing sentiments of that age concerning the doctrine of the Trinity, it is a singular circumstance that the first article in this Confession expresses the doctrine of the Unity of God with a scriptural simplicity, that is, in obvious contrast to the received standards, the Catechism of the Westminster Assembly, and the Thirty-nine Articles of the Church of England. This may justly excite our surprise, while

* Universal Theological Magazine, vol. iii., p. 8. N.B. The brief Confession is given by Crosby, vol. ii., Appendix, No. iv.; and in the preceding Miscellany, p. 9, 10; and No. xiv., p. 57-59.

it recommends itself to our approbation. It runs thus: 'We believe, and are very confident, that there is but ONE God, the Father, of whom are all things from everlasting to everlasting, glorious and unwordable in all his attributes.'— 1 Cor., viii., 6. Isa., xl., 28. At the assizes, in the spring of 1663, no one appearing, and no crime being alleged against them, Mr. Grantham, and his virtuous fellow-sufferers who had been committed with him, were discharged, and returned to the churches to which they belonged, who received them with no small joy.

"Mr. Grantham suffered a second imprisonment under the operation of the Conventicle Act, which was first passed for seven years, in 1663, and was revived at the expiration of that term, with additional clauses of heightened severity in 1670: under the authority of this act soldiers were empowered to disarm those that dissented from the National Establishment. Though no arms were found in the possession of the Baptists, yet their houses were rifled, their goods carried off, and they themselves forced away from their wives and families, without knowing whither they were to be driven, or whether they should be prosecuted by law, or fall a sacrifice to military force. They were dragged from town to town, and compelled to run like lackeys by the sides of the soldiers' horses. Mr. Grantham, Mr. John Gree, and Mr. John Green, with several others, were thus the victims of armed insolence and violence. Mr. Grantham and his friends were lodged, tied up during the whole night, at an inn, in a room not fit for entertainment: their situation drove sleep from their eyes; nor would the soldiers take any rest, but sat up near them, and with rioting and revellings, oaths and curses, annoyed and shocked these pious prisoners. On the morning they were conducted to Louth, put into the House of Correction, and afterward brought before the committee. At this tribunal, instead of well-supported charges against them, insidious questions were put, to draw from them some ground of accusation, and they were asked to pledge themselves on oath to conformity. Though the times afforded many examples of those who had been terrified into a dereliction of their principles, these good men, and the Baptists in general, remained firm and unshaken in their religious profession. Mr. Grantham and his two fellow-sufferers were by strict command sent to jail, where they lay for half a year. During their imprisonment the assizes came on, but their enemies prevented their cause from being heard. They were afterward, at the Quarter Sessions, brought before the justices; but the bench refused to enter into the case, or proceed against them. Upon this, the sheriff pleaded that, as he had produced them in open court, he was free from his charge; and so they were set at liberty, but without any compensation for their unjust imprisonment and attendant sufferings.

"Mr. Grantham, soon after his liberation, was harassed under a different and unsanctioned mode of persecuting malignity. He was prosecuted on action of £100, for with force of arms beating and uncivilly treating the wife of a certain person, merely on the ground of his having baptized her. But to the shame of his prosecutors, the cause which threatened his ruin was thrown out of court at the next assizes as a malicious prosecution.

'.." 'The malice and violence of their enemies against Mr. Grantham and his adherents often carried them to the greatest and most shocking lengths. Defamation and lying accusations were among their most common weapons : the worst of men appearing as *informers*, the worst of *magistrates* abetting and encouraging them, and the worst of priests, who first began to blow the fire, now seeing how it spread, clapping their hands, and hallooing them on to this evil work.'* In vindication of themselves and their principles against this malicious treatment, Mr. Grantham drew up a small piece, which was never published, entitled 'The Baptist's Complaint against the persecuting Priest,' &c. This tract was a remonstrance against the persecuting spirit, to which this denomination of Christians, notwithstanding their friendly deportment, and faithful endeavours to maintain peace and brotherly concord, had been exposed for more than thirty years, which stirred up persons in authority to harass them by imprisonment and seizure of their goods ; and which expressed itself in irreligious abuse and invectives even from the pulpit, where they were stigmatized as 'heretics' and 'damned fanatics.' This malicious treatment was provoked only by their 'dissent from the Church of England in some practices, which, the most learned confessed, had neither *precept* nor *precedent* in the Word.' It was more criminal in the clergy to manifest this conduct towards Baptists, because they had never withheld from them their dues, but had paid them their demands as punctually as any others, and, as they alleged, probably from better principles. 'For we consider,' they pleaded, 'that when we either hire or purchase land, the *tenth* is excepted, and is therefore not ours. But yet it is also to be considered, that tithes were not given to maintain men in drunkenness, lording over, persecuting, and ruining such as fear God, merely because they dissent from them in the things aforesaid ; yet thus goes the business in these days, by which unreasonable practices they outdo the false prophets who were of old, for they prepared war against those that did not put into their mouths, but these devour those that labour to maintain them.' A concluding sentiment in this 'Complaint' deserves, for its justness and force, to be repeated. 'We believe,' observes Mr. Grantham, in the name of his fellow-sufferers, 'and are sure, that to persecute is no mark of the true Church, but to suffer persecution is so ; and that religion is not worth professing in time of peace, which is not worth owning in the time of the greatest trouble.'†

"Mr. Grantham, after this recent discharge from jail, again suffered imprisonment several times, and continued to be very sorely harassed and oppressed during the remainder of that infamous reign. About the end of it, or soon after James II. succeeded to the throne, he removed from Lincolnshire and settled in the city of Norwich. This change of his residence did not abate or diminish his activity and labours. He was still firm to the cause for which he had so long and severely suffered, and was unwea-

ried in his exertions to promote it. He soon raised and formed a church in that city, on the principles of the General Baptists, which met at the *White Friars' yard*, and which still exists.* He directed his attention, with similar success, to the populous town of Yarmouth. In the year 1688, or 1689, he visited, with the same laudable views, the town of Lynn Regis, at the other extremity of the county. He first preached in the town-hall to a numerous and attentive auditory. The prospect was so favourable, that it encouraged a friend, Mr. James Marham, at whose house he was entertained, to procure and fit up a convenient place of worship ; a church was gathered, and Mr. Marham was the first pastor of it. Though the place was duly registered according to the directions and authority of the Act of Toleration, which passed just as the building was completed, yet the minister and hearers were harassed by a prosecution, on the Conventicle Act, in 1691.† The Revolution and the Act of Toleration, though, great blessings to the nation, did not immediately effect a change in the views and temper of the mass of the people. It required time for the violence of a persecuting spirit to subside, and for just sentiments on religious liberty to take possession of the public mind, and spread their influence to any considerable extent. The malignity of old prejudices, against the Baptists in particular, was softened, in many places at least, very slowly and partially. Mr. Grantham continued to feel its effects till the time of his death. The envenomed tongue of scandal, in particular, employed itself in vile calumnies and charges of gross immoralities. Among those who traduced his character were Mr. Toathby, who had been a magistrate, and took his rank in society as a gentleman and a clergyman, and Mr. John Willet, the rector of Tattershall in Lincolnshire. The latter had the effrontery and baseness to declare, in writing under his own signature, 'that he saw Mr. Grantham stand in the pillory two hours, at Louth, for stealing sheep and hurdles, and that he saw him hold up his hand at the bar.' This falsehood was circulated both at Norwich and Yarmouth, and

* A grandson of Mr. Grantham, Grantham Killingworth, Esq., who died about the year 1779, left a considerable part of his property for the support of the minister at the White Friars' yard. He was a leading character among the Baptists, and the author of various theological tracts, written with ability and judgment. He was particularly on the alert to seize the opportunities afforded by any controversy of his times, to graft on it arguments in defence of his own views on the nature and subjects of baptism. When the "Sermons against Popery" were preached at Salters' Hall, he published a tract, entitled "A Supplement to the Sermons lately preached at Salters' Hall against Popery, with a view to show that, on the Reasonings of the Preachers, *Infant Sprinkling* was another *great Corruption* of the Christian Religion." This pamphlet came to a fifth edition, in which other points, viz., Mr. Emlyn's Previous Question, &c., were discussed. On occasion of the controversy with the author of "Christianity not founded on Argument," Mr. Killingworth published "Remarks on the several Answers to it," in which his aim was to turn the reasonings of the authors, who were Pædobaptists, against themselves — See *Bulkley's Notes on the Bible*, vol. iii., *Life*, p. 15, 16, *note*.

* Universal Theological Magazine, ut ante, p. 63.
† Crosby, vol. iii., p. 84-88.

† Universal Theological Magazine, ut ante, p. 111, 112.

Mr. Grantham was induced to refer the matter to Thomas Blofield, Esq., mayor of Norwich. The accuser, on being brought before this magistrate, confessed the absolute falsehood of the charge which he had promulgated and signed; and with cryings, and tears, and wringing of his hands, over and over implored Mr. Grantham's forgiveness. The mayor, on Mr. Grantham's readily forgiving him, commanded, with expressions of his strong abhorrence of the rector's conduct, a record of the confession to be made out by the clerk, and to be signed and sealed by the calumniating clergyman,[*] who, after this was done, as he had no money, would have been committed to prison for charges, had not Mr. Grantham, on the true Christian principle of rendering good for evil, given the officer of the court ten shillings to set his enemy at liberty.

"Mr. Grantham died on the 17th of January, 1692, at the age of 58. Indecencies were threatened to his corpse, but they were happily prevented. Soon after his decease, a paper was published and signed by eight friends, containing his dying words, addressed to them within two minutes of his death, mostly in the language of Scripture, expressive of his sense of his approaching end, of the testimony of his conscience as to the integrity of his conduct, and of the disinterested purity of his motives in preaching the Gospel; of his affection to his friends, leaving with them his last counsels in a strain of apostolic admonitions, casting his eyes back on his sufferings in being made a scoff and a gazing-stock to many people, cordially forgiving his enemies, and soliciting the prayers of his friends for their forgiveness; taking a final leave of them with affection, devotion, and sacred hope, 'Friends,' he began, 'I am in a very weak condition, and as this is the Sabbath with me, it will be the everlasting Sabbath; for now I am going off the stage of this World.' He concluded thus: 'To be short, I must leave you. Do not grieve or mourn for me; though I die, yet I shall rise to glory, where I desire we may all meet and see one another's face at the last day, knowing one another, and rejoicing in glory; for I have conquered the infernal enemy by this faith, and have made the way plain and easy to me. And now I commit you to the grace of our Lord Jesus Christ; and the love of God, and the communion of the Holy Ghost, be with you all. Amen.'[†]

"Mr. Grantham, besides the treatises already mentioned, wrote 'The Pædobaptists' Apology for the Baptized Churches.' The design of the tract was to show, by quotations from the writings of Pædobaptists, that the practice of the Baptists, as to the mode and subject of baptism, was most ancient and apostolical, and that infant baptism was a novelty. The deductions from these premises were, that the sufferings inflicted on the Baptists were no less a glory to them than a shame to their persecutors.[‡]

"Report has represented Mr. Grantham as acquainted with eight or nine languages. This is most probably an exaggerated account of his

attainments. His grandson, Mr. Grantham Killingworth, it appears, spoke of him as able to write the Latin with considerable ease and correctness. His writings afford proofs of his having acquired some proficiency in the learned languages: his polemical publications were thought to do credit to his abilities, and to his acuteness in the art of reasoning; though he himself, in the preface to 'A Defence of the Christian Religion against human Invention and pretended Revelations,' dated from the Castle of Lincoln, 10th January, 1663, apologized for the defects which might be discovered in his language and method, by pleading that 'he got his bread by the labour of his hands, and had never saluted the schools to gain a knowledge of their arts.' That he possessed no small share of literary attainments, of address, and of weight of character, is reasonably inferred from his being frequently delegated to take an active and leading part in the concerns of the Baptists of that day, even in their applications to the throne, when there was not a want of men of real learning, who had been educated at the university.

"Mr. James Marham, whose name occurs in the preceding memoir, merits more particular notice, as a conspicuous and distinguished person among the Baptists in Lincolnshire and Norfolk. The time and place of his nativity are not ascertained. He seems to have commenced his appearance on the stage of public life at Holbeach in Lincolnshire, in 1681 or 1682. He was the first of that class of Dissenters in that place; and soon after his settlement in it, assemblies for religious worship were held in his house; the original preachers were Mr. Samuel Philips and Mr. William Rix; the first was pastor of the church in Deadman's-Lane in Wisbeach. In the reign of King James he was settled in Wapool-bell, a town in Norfolk, where the people, having never heard of the name of Baptists, called him 'an outlandish professor.' Here he laid the foundation of a church of the Baptist denomination, which now exists, and from which originated another church formed in Wisbeach. On the death of his wife, Mr. Marham removed to Lynn; in this town, also, though on his settlement in it there was not another Baptist there, he hired and furnished a place for religious worship, and engaged the services of Mr. Grantham and Mr. Long, a messenger from the Baptist churches in London, whom he entertained at his own house and table without any pecuniary compensation for some months; and by these means raised a church, of which he afterward became himself the pastor.

"The conspicuous activity and zeal of this excellent man exposed him to various sufferings. About three years before the death of Charles II. he was harassed by prosecutions from court to court, and carried from one justice to another, for four weeks; and though by his vigorous interference he procured the liberation of his ministers, Mr. Rix and Mr. Phillips, he himself suffered imprisonment, and a fine of several score pounds was levied on him, for having disturbed and broken the uniformity of his religious profession of the town. After this his goods were distrained. When he had lived three weeks at Wapool-bell, he was commanded by the officers of the town to frequent the parish church, or to appear before the justice and parson of the parish, Mr. Harbe. He complied with the latter requisition, and underwent an examination of four hours in the presence of several gentlemen. This did not terminate to the satisfaction of the clerical examiner, and a time for another investigation was fixed ; but on the proclamation for liberty of conscience, this inquiry was declined. At Lynn, new troubles awaited him. In July, 1691, he, with others, as before noticed, were prosecuted on the Conventicle Act, though the place of meeting had been registered according to the act of Parliament, and their goods were seized by a levy granted against him. He petitioned the judge, Sir E—— N——, at Norwich in September following, and was forced to prefer the same complaint to some of the great council at the sessions of Parliament. After Parliament had risen, he was prosecuted on the same grounds, and involved in troubles that threatened his ruin. In the following October, the informers against him, affecting great remorse, obtained from him a discharge from their false information, by entering into bonds of an amicable tenour ; but they were base and daring enough after this actually to seize his goods on the former levy. On this he was advised to sue the bonds, and the Baptists at London were solicited to unite in his support with all possible liberality and energy. It is to be regretted that no documents offer themselves to throw light on the termination of this vexatious suit; and farther to elucidate the history and character of this virtuous sufferer, to whose piety, zeal, and benevolence this imperfect detail affords pleasing and affecting testimonies.[*]

"Another character among the Baptists of those times, distinguished by some peculiar circumstances, was Mr. Edward Morecock, a man of eminence, of great zeal and firmness, and much courted on King James's accession. He was born in January, 1626, and died in August, 1693. He was originally in the naval service, and in the protectorate was captain of a man-of-war, when he was shot in an engagement through the body with a musket-ball. He made a handsome provision for a family of nearly twenty children, by his skill in fishing up shipwrecks ; especially by his recovering, after the Dutch war in 1672, ships sunk in the River Medway, which had come so close to Chatham as to throw many of their shot into the town, one of which was found in Captain Morecock's garden. After this he engaged in the pastoral care of a church in that place, and so entirely devoted himself to its duties, that he declined very advantageous offers made to him if he would undertake to recover wrecks at sea. His unblamable manners and obliging deportment gained him the esteem and affection of the gentlemen in the neighbourhood, insomuch that when any warrant was issued for seizing his person—as he was harassed by frequent warrants against his body and goods towards the end of King Charles the II.'s reign—one of the justices would privately send his servant to apprize him of it before the officers could execute it. On receiving the intelligence, he usually

retired to the house of one of his daughters in Essex. He was, however, fined with monthly penalties for non-attendance at the parish church, till he was exchequered to the amount of £800. His house was often plundered, and his goods were seized and carried off. To secure himself from these ruinous depredations, on the ground of his nonconformity, he made his fortune over to an intimate friend, who, acting on the principles of justice and honour, restored it when the danger was past. One Hinton, an informer against him, often threatened that he would have him cast into prison, and possess himself of his furniture, which he promised to give to a lewd woman who attended him. But Mr. Morecock, through a good Providence, always escaped imprisonment, while many of his brethren suffered by it. On visiting some of them, once in Rochester jail, he saw this Hinton confined in it, upon which he accosted him, 'I see, friend, you have got hither before me.' This man afterward died miserably, the flesh rotting from his bones. Lord Roper, a Roman Catholic, on the accession of James II., offered Mr. Morecock any post that he would accept ; but he absolutely refused any commission under that king, assigning to his friends as a reason for his refusal, ' that the favours offered by him to Dissenters were designed only to draw them into a snare ;' a reason which did credit to his sagacity, judgment, and disinterested principles. His firmness of conduct was at one time the occasion of a design against his life. Two witnesses were suborned to swear that he had been an officer in Monmouth's army ; but, by unexceptionable evidence, he proved that he was in another place at the time that he was charged with being in the army.[*]

Mr. John Miller, a native of Hinton Marton, in the county of Dorset, descended from parents who were in affluent circumstances, a man of great piety, worth, and usefulness, deserves to be mentioned with respect. He was educated by a Presbyterian minister, but a studious and diligent inquiry in after life led him to embrace the opinions of the Baptists, and he was pastor of a congregation of this denomination at Minchinton, in the county in which he drew his first breath. He died on the 15th of May, 1694. His active labours as a preacher were not limited to his own congregation ; he travelled from place to place, disseminating the principles of religion, and planting several churches in agreement with his ideas of Christian truth. His nonconformity and opinions exposed him to severe sufferings : he lay ten years in prison, and very narrowly escaped a præmunire. In the year preceding the death of Charles II., he was harassed by vexatious proceedings, and greatly injured in his property by extortions. A distress was first taken on his goods on the Three Week Act; then he was apprehended and cast into prison at Dorchester ; at the summer assizes he was indicted for eleven months nonconforming, and a neighbouring justice, to supply the deficiency of evidence against him, swore to the indictment ; and though he pleaded that he had, contrary to the laws of England, suffered already in two courts for that offence, he was fined £220. At Michaelmas, possession was taken of his assets by the baliffs under the

* Crosby, vol. iii., p. 109-112.

* "A brief Relation of the remarkable Services and Troubles that went before the present Trouble of our Brother James Marham," quoted in Universal Theol. Mag., ut ante, p. 112, &c., note.

warrant of the under-sheriff, who seized and wasted between 400 and £500, and his eldest son was obliged to flee, in consequence of a warrant granted against him for taking an account of the goods that were sold. He petitioned the king for redress, not to procure the restoration of his goods, but only to secure the corn that was left from farther depredation ; he obtained, however, no other relief than what was implied in this imperious and insultory language, 'I have nothing to say to you : you must go home and conform.' The virtuous sufferer went home, but not to sacrifice principle by conformity ; he sold his estate, retired to a solitary place, rented a small farm, and spent his remaining days in quiet. There was one occurrence in the life of Mr. Miller, which indicates that though he was the mark of persecuting malignity, his talents and character commanded respect ; and, in such times, it was peculiarly honourable to the clergymen who were parties in it. This was a disputation, after liberty of conscience was granted, held with Dr. Beach and four other ministers of the Established Church, the time and place having been first published in three market-towns. The subjects of disputation were the consonance of their baptism, church, and ministry, with the Scriptures, and the charges of schism against Mr. Miller and his adherents. The questions concerning baptism came first under discussion. The clerical gentlemen were so impressed with Mr. Miller's arguments, that no reply was made, except that Dr. Beach ingenuously confessed that the point was difficult, and they waved entering into the other questions. On withdrawing to another house, they sent for their opponent, received him with politeness and respect, apologized for having troubled him, and assured him that they would never dispute the point with the Baptists again ; and thus they separated with expressions of good-will and friendship.*

"With the preceding names of those who, by their abilities, zeal, and characters, did credit to the denomination of Dissenters of which we are speaking, may be enrolled Mr. George Hammon, pastor of a congregation at Biddenden, in the county of Kent, the author of several publications suitable to the theological controversies and religious taste of the age. He was active in vindicating what appeared the truth to his own mind on all occasions, eminent for his ministerial exertions, and marked by the persecutions which he suffered. He died at Hasleden's Wood, in the parish of Cranbrook. In connexion with him may be mentioned Mr. Richard Hobbs, pastor of a congregation at Dover, distinguished by his piety and worth, and by his sufferings for religion. His seriousness and piety spoke so strongly in his favour, that when he was a prisoner in Dover, he was now and then allowed to go from his prison. In his confinement he addressed a letter to Dr. Hind, proposing for solution, in a modest and candid manner, two queries grounded on the Scriptures. One was, whether the baptism practised in the Church was not at variance with the directions of the Scriptures, in the administration, subject, and administration ? The other was, whether the Church, by *forcing* all into it as communicants, however sinful and impious,

did not pervert the Gospel, overthrow the way of the new covenant, and give ground for pious and conscientious men to question the Divine authority of its worship ? Dr. Hind, instead of replying to these queries, instigated the magistrates to deprive him of the indulgence which he had received, and to enjoin an unrelaxed confinement. 'These proceedings,' Mr. Hobbs observed, 'bore a great likeness to those beyond the seas, at Rome, where, if any do but question the truth of their worship, it is a hundred to one if they have not the Inquisition for their pains. Doubtless such kind of proceedings do sound more like the pope's anathemas, than in the least savour of a Protestant spirit.'*

" It is a just tribute of respect to integrity and fortitude to mention the names of others who were great sufferers for nonconformity. Mr. Tidmarsh, a Baptist minister at Oxford, a man greatly esteemed ; Mr. John Amory, a man of good literary attainments, of Wrington, in Somersetshire ; Mr. Thomas Burgess, pastor of a church at Taunton ; Mr. James Hirid, of Langport, and minister of Kinsbury ; Mr. William Richards, who preached at Draycott ; Mr. Peter Coles, of Downton, near Sarum ; Mr. Walter Penn, pastor of a church in Sarum ; Mr. John Kingman, of Burford, near that city ; Mr. John Sanger, a schoolmaster and minister at Downton ; Mr. Roger Applin, of Ellerton, and pastor of a congregation at Whitechurch ; Mr. John Tredwell, a serious and useful preacher, and a man of unblemished manners ; Mr. Francis Stanley, of Northamptonshire, noted for his piety and zeal ; Mr. John Grauden, of Cocket, near Towcester ; Mr. John Staunton, of Blissworth ; Mr. Stephen Curtis, a native of Harringworth, in Northamptonshire, and a very useful minister in that place ; Mr. Joseph Slater, Mr. William Stanger, and Mr. Robert Bringhurst, who fled from the country to escape imprisonment ; Mr. Benjamin Morley, of Ramsthorp ; Mr. John Reas, of East Haddon ; Mr. William Smith, Mr. William Blisse, of Welston ; Mr. John Gilby, of Long Bugby, in Northampshire, suffered imprisonment, and were despoiled of their goods by distresses, or almost ruined by heavy fines and charges. Mr. James Wilmot, a minister at Hooknorton, Oxfordshire, besides being confined twice in the prison of Oxford, and sustaining losses by distresses and fines, when he was released from the jail in Whitney, was excommunicated, and was obliged to abscond, in order to escape the writs which were issued out against him. In some instances the sufferings of these conscientious professors were aggravated by the fraudulent practices of their persecutors, who seized their goods under false warrants. This act was practised, in November, 1682, against Mr. Samuel Taverner, who was born at Romford, in Essex, in July, 1621. He was originally an officer in the army ; afterward governor of Deal Castle. He embraced the principles of the Baptists, on being led to entertain their views by his conversation with Dr. Prescot, pastor of the church at Dover, and was baptized at Sandwich, 13th of April, 1663. He was ordained elder of the church at Dover on the 13th of October, 1681. He suffered much for adherence to his religious profession, and died on the 4th of August, 1696, in the 75th year of his

* Crosby, vol. iii., p. 121-124.

* Crosby, vol. iii., p. 103, 104.

age, having obtained celebrity for piety and usefulness. The severity of the jailer, at times, denied the imprisoned the consolation of any act of social devotion among themselves; at Oxford they were not permitted to pray together, and even the usual expression of piety at their meals was interrupted by the entrance of the jailer in a rage, and by his taunting inquiry, 'What, are you preaching over your meal?'

"The history of these pious sufferers affords examples of the death of persecutors, which were so circumstanced as to mark a great depravity of character, and the base principles by which the men were actuated, though it belong not to men, who are incompetent judges of the ways of Providence, decidedly to pronounce them Divine judgments. Mr. Richard Farmer, minister at Kibley, in Leicestershire, a hard student, and a very affecting preacher, by a warrant to seize his goods, lost in one year £120. One of the informers against him, who boasted on a Christmas, at Trinity Market, of his proceedings against him, and declared exultingly that before Candlemas he should by informations make a good portion for his daughter, was thrown from his horse as he was riding home over a boggy place, where there was a little brook, and drowned in a quantity of water not deep enough

to cover his body. Another informer, soon after he had sworn against Mr. Farmer, died of a swollen tongue, without being suspected of having taken a false oath.*

"If the characters which have passed under our review be not transmitted down to our times as having enlarged the bounds of science, nor of criticism or philosophy, yet by their religious integrity, and by their zeal and fortitude, they gained the respect of the sect to which they conscientiously adhered, and the interests of which they were active in promoting. In the history of that sect, though it be a circumscribed theatre of fame, they have a claim to honourable mention. The hardships, losses, and sufferings which they experienced in the cause that they espoused, hold forth instructive warnings to future times of the malignity of an intolerant and persecuting spirit among Protestants; and show us with what a slow progress, and partial operation of better principles, that spirit had declined among the mass of those who were dissidents from the Church of Rome, though a hundred and fifty years had elapsed since the separation of England from that ecclesiastical tyranny."—C.)

* Crosby, vol. iii., p. 112, 118, 124–128.

CHAPTER I.

FROM THE PROTECTORSHIP OF CROMWELL TO THE
DECLARATION OF INDULGENCE, 1674.

MR. NEAL has allowed a few pages only to the History of the Quakers, and they are chiefly spent on the wild extravagances and sufferings of James Naylor. But the lot of this people, while other sectarists breathed a freer air under the protectorship of Cromwell, was peculiarly hard and afflictive. The change of government, on his taking the reins, produced no revolution in their favour, but their sufferings continued to increase with the increase of their numbers. The subordinate magistrates were continued in office; and the ecclesiastics, their former persecutors, retained power, to be troublesome to them. The protector has been represented as the friend of religious liberty; and so, in some instances, he certainly showed himself; but the Quakers derived little benefit from his liberal views and regard to the rights of conscience; for, though he himself did not openly disturb them on account of their religious opinions and practices, yet those who acted under his authority grievously persecuted them, and he gave little or no check to their intolerance, although he had the power, and was repeatedly and earnestly solicited to do it. The dominant parties had imbibed a spirit of hatred and animosity against this people; and the protector, it is supposed, might be fearful of disobliging them, by animadverting on their oppressive measures; or he might consider the Quakers as too contemptible or too pacific a body to fear any danger from, even under the greatest provocations.*

To give some colour of law to the severities practised against them, pretexts were drawn from supposed violations of the regulations of civil policy. "A Christian exhortation to an assembly, after the priest had done and the worship was over, was denominated interrupting public worship, and disturbing the priest in his office: an honest testimony against sin in the streets or markets was styled a breach of the peace: and their appearing before the magistrates covered, a contempt of authority: hence proceeded fines, imprisonments, and spoiling of goods. Nay, so hot for persecution were some magistrates, that, by an unparalleled misconstruction of the law against vagrants, they tortured with cruel whippings the bodies of both men and women of good estate and reputation, merely because they went under the denomination of Quakers."†

In 1656, Henry Clifton, only riding through Upwell, in Cambridgeshire, after having been carried before two justices, was sent to prison, where he lay a considerable time in the dungeon among condemned felons. Richard Hubberthorn and Richard Weaver, travelling from home to pay a friendly visit to Ann Blakely, who was, for her open testimony against the sins of the times, imprisoned at Cambridge, were also committed to prison. Thomas Curtis, a woollen-draper of Reading, going to Plymouth on business, and from thence to West Alvington, accompanied by John Martindale, were both cast, as vagrants, into Exeter jail; and at the ensuing assizes brought before the judge, where nothing was laid to their charge. But, for not taking off their hats, they were fined £40 each for contempt, and, for nonpayment, detained above a year in prison. During this term, Martindale, having obtained leave of the jailer to visit a friend at Ilchester, went to a meeting at Colyton; where he, Humphrey Sprague, and Thomas Dyer, lodging at a friend's house, were apprehended by a warrant, and carried before the justices at the quarter sessions at Honiton; and, though one of them was but two, and another but five miles from home, were sentenced, as vagrants, to be whipped in the market-place, and sent with a pass from tithing to tithing; which was accordingly done. George Whitehead, a virtuous and learned young man of a reputable family in Westmoreland, preaching at Nayland in Suffolk, April, 1657, was sentenced by two justices to be openly whipped as a vagrant, till his body was bloody. The constable to whom the warrant was given employed a foolish fellow, void of discretion and feeling, to execute it, who laid on his stripes with unmerciful violence, whereby Whitehead's back and breasts were grievously cut, his skin torn, and his blood shed in abundance. But the insensible fool went on, unrestrained by the cry of the spectators, who, affected with the cruelty, called out to him to stop. Humphrey Smith and Samuel Curtis, riding together near Axminster, George Bewley, John Ellis, and Humphrey Sprague, after a meeting in Bridport, were whipped as vagabonds, and sent away with passes. Joan Edmunds, wife of Edward Edmunds, of Totness, about ten miles from home, being stopped by a drunken fellow, who took away her horse, on complaining to a justice, was sent to Exeter jail because she had no pass: her horse was ordered to be sold, and part of the money applied to defray the charge of carrying her to prison. Her habitation lying in the direct road, she was taken six miles. about, to prevent this injustice being exposed among her neighbours, who well knew she was no vagrant.*

Another pretext on which many of these people suffered, under the form of law, very illegal severities, was that of breaking the Sabbath. Their religious zeal, in frequenting their assemblies for public worship, obliged them to travel to the places where they were held, sometimes at a considerable distance from their habitations. This was called a breach of the

* Gough's Hist. of the Quakers, vol. i., p. 132, 198.
† Ibid., p. 139, 140.

* Gough's History, vol. i., p. 225-232.

Sabbath; and it was punished by impounding their horses, by distress of goods, by fines, by imprisonment, by whipping, and by sitting in the stocks.*

If magistrates could be guilty of such unrighteous severities, it is not surprising that the licentious rabble should attack this people with violence and abuse. In numerous instances, and in various places, the houses in which they held their assemblies for religious worship were riotously assaulted. Their services were interrupted by hallooing, singing, and railing; the windows were broken by stones and bullets; their persons were buffeted and stoned, their faces and clothes daubed with filth and excrements; some were knocked down, and others had their teeth beaten out; nor did the tenderness of sex protect the women. The rabble were too often led and encouraged by clergymen.

"Many of these abuses," observes the historian, "being committed on the first day of the week, the day they called their Sabbath, with impunity, under a government and by a people who pretended to make it a point to observe it with all the pharisaical strictness, and in many cases beyond the strictness, which the Mosaical law appointed for observing the seventh day, furnish an occasion to reflect upon the irrational inconsistency of superstition in every shape, by which I understand an over-zealous attachment to some circumstantials of religion, while the essential part, viz., the inwardly sanctifying power thereof, whereby we are taught to honour God, and love and do good to mankind, is overlooked. These men, it is probable, would have thought it a heinous crime to have been employed on that day in any honest labour, though in itself lawful, and in some sort necessary, and yet showed no reluctance or compunction in committing unlawful actions, as opposite to good government as religion, in assaulting persons, and destroying the property of inoffensive, unresisting neighbours and fellow-citizens with violence and outrage, whose only crime was the applying the day to the best purpose, the assembling to worship their Maker in that way they were persuaded in their consciences was most acceptable to him."†

So general was the persecution under which this people suffered, that scarcely one of them, whose travels and services to the society are preserved on record, escaped personal abuse or cruel imprisonment, in any quarter of the nation.

George Fox, in 1653, was summoned before the magistrates at Carlisle, and committed to prison till the assizes, as a blasphemer, and heretic, and a seducer. He had exasperated them by his plain-dealing, in endeavouring to show them that, although they, being Presbyterians and Independents, were high in the profession of religion, they were without the possession of what they professed. The ground of his being summoned was his having exhorted the people to truth and honesty, at the market-cross on a market-day, and having preached to them on the Sunday after the service was concluded; on which he had been assaulted by rude people in the church, and rescued by the governor. Du-

ring his confinement, the general wish was "that he might be hanged;" and the high-sheriff declared, with rancour, that he would guard him to execution himself. At the assizes, it was found that the charge of blasphemy could not be made good, and it was concluded not to bring him to trial, and he was left with the magistrates of the town. By their order he was put among the felons and murderers, in a dungeon, noisome and filthy to the last degree, where men and women were kept together, one of whom was almost eaten up with lice; and the deputy of the jailer would often fall on him, and the friends who visited him, with a cudgel: while the prisoners, vile as they were, behaved affectionately to him, received his admonitions with deference, and some embraced his doctrine. At length, the Parliament, having instituted an inquiry concerning his situation, and the governor having remonstrated on it, he was released. In 1654, at Whetstone in Leicestershire, he was brought before Colonel Hacker, who gave him liberty to go home, if he would stay there, and not go abroad to meetings. To this Fox replied, "If he should agree thereto, it would imply that he was guilty of something, for which his home was made his prison; and if he went to meeting, they would consider that as a breach of their order: therefore he plainly told them he should go to meeting, and could not answer their requirings." Upon this he was next day carried prisoner, by Captain Drury, to London. When Cromwell was informed of his arrival, he sent to him this message: "That the protector required of George Fox that he should promise not to take up the sword or any other weapon, against him or the government as it then was; that he should write it in what words he saw proper, and set his hand to it." Fox returned an answer to this effect, and was afterward introduced to Cromwell, and they had much discourse about religion, in which the protector carried himself with great moderation; and Fox had his liberty given him.*

In 1656, Fox, accompanied by William Salt, of London, and Edward Pyott, of Bristol, travelled through Devonshire into Cornwall, to market Jew, where he wrote a paper, containing an exhortation to fear God, and learn of Christ the light; which fell into the hands of Major Ceely, a justice of St. Ives, who committed Fox and his companions to Launceston jail, on the charge of spreading papers to the disturbance of the public peace, and having no pass, though persons unknown, for travelling up and down, and refusing to take the oath of abjuration, and to give sureties for their good behaviour. After nine weeks' confinement they were brought to their trial, before Judge Glyn, at the assizes: here they demanded justice for their false imprisonment; and Major Ceely, not adhering to the charges in the mittimus, brought up new accusations of a treasonable proposal, and an assault; and they were indicted for coming, by force and arms, into a court, into which they were conducted as prisoners. But on no ground could any illegal criminality be proved against them. The judge ordered them to be taken away, and, in their absence, fined them twenty marks apiece for coming into court with their

---

* Gough's History, vol. i., p. 271, 272, note.
† Ibid., p. 267-271, and the note.

* Gough's History, vol. i., p. 132-136, 155, 156.

hats on, and commanded that they should be detained in prison till their fines were paid. Seeing no prospect of an immediate release from such a commitment, they discontinued the weekly payment of seven shillings apiece for themselves, and as much for their horses, which the jailer had extorted. Upon this, they were turned into a dismal and most noisome dungeon, called Doomsdale, where the excrements of former prisoners had been accumulating for many years. They were not allowed beds or straw to lie on ; and the filthiness of the place not allowing them room to sit down, they were obliged to stand all night. Neither were they permitted to cleanse it, or to have any victuals but what they received with difficulty through the grate. This cruel treatment continued till the sessions at Bodmin, when, on a representation of their case to the justices, an order was obtained for opening the door of Doomsdale, and for permission to clean it, and to buy their provisions in the town. About the end of thirty weeks they were discharged by an order from Major-general Desborrow, in consequence of applications made in their favour to Cromwell. During this imprisonment one of Fox's friends offered himself to the protector to lie in prison, body for body, in his stead : to which proposal Cromwell answered, he could not grant it; being contrary to law; and turning to some of his council standing by him, asked, "Which of you would do as much for me, if I were in the same condition !"* The next places at which we find Fox are Cardiff, Swansea, and Brecknock. He visited these towns in 1657 ; settled a meeting at Swansea ; and at the latter place met with rude treatment, and was exposed to danger from the populace, raised and stimulated to riot and tumult by the magistrates.†

Another sufferer among the Quakers was Miles Halhead, one of their first zealous preachers, who, at Skipton and Doncaster, was sorely beaten and bruised by the populace, and left for dead. Thomas Briggs, in Lancaster, Robert Widders and William Dewsbury, in Cumberland, were also severely abused in like manner.‡ John Cam and John Audland were assaulted at Bristol, to the great risk of their lives, by hundreds of the rabble, instigated by Farmer, a clergyman. William Caton and John Stubbs, besides being haled before the magistrates at Dover, were at Maidstone sent to the House of Correction, stripped, and their necks and arms put into the stocks, and so cruelly whipped with cords as to draw tears from the spectators. After this, under the plea that "he that would not work should not eat," they were kept several days without victuals, only on the allowance of a little water once a day ; and soon after were sent out of town, by different ways, with a pass, as vagabonds.§

At Wymondham in Norfolk, Richard Hubberthorn was committed to bridewell for addressing the congregation after sermon in the parish church : and on the next day removed to a very incommodious prison, being a poor hole in a cross wall of Norwich Castle, where he was detained till the sessions. The justices then, waiving the original ground of the commitment, charged

him with contempt of authority for appearing before them with his hat on, and under this pretence recommitted him to prison, where he lay a long time.*

The sufferings in which the members of this society were involved by the sentence of magistrates were in many instances heightened by the severity and injustice of the jailers : James Lancaster, George Whitehead, and Christopher Atkinson, for not complying with the jailer's extravagant demands, were obliged to lie in their clothes on the floor, in the prison of Norwich, for eight weeks, in the cold winter of 1654.† At St. Edmundsbury, 1655, the same Whitehead, John Harwood, George Rose, George Fox the younger, and Henry Marshall, because they refused to gratify the avaricious demands of the jailer for lodgings, and required a free prison, were turned down to the common ward among the felons, in a low dungeon, with a damp earthen floor, where they lay upon rye-straw. In this situation they were exposed to abuse from the prisoners, who frequently took away their food and other necessaries, alleging the jailer's permission : one desperate fellow frequently kicked and smote, and in a drunken fit threatened to kill them, saying, "If he killed them, he should not be hanged for it." After they had been in prison thirty weeks, arrears of dues of fourteen pence a week were demanded from each of them ; and on their remonstrating against it, the turnkey was ordered to take away their clothes and boxes, which was done, with a threat to take their coats from off their backs ; and, for the space of twenty-four weeks, they were obliged to lie upon part of their body-clothes on straw. Some necessaries of linen brought to them by a friend were seized, and the provisions sent to them were examined. Their friends were not admitted in ; and, if they attempted to speak to them at the window or door of the jail, water was frequently thrown on them to drive them away. At length, in consequence of an application to the protector, an inquiry into the treatment they had received was instituted, and the jailer was restrained from exercising or permitting the cruel abuse they had hitherto suffered. After an imprisonment of from twelve to fifteen months, through repeated applications to Cromwell, seconded by the private solicitations of Mrs. Mary Sanders, a waiting gentlewoman in his family, an order for their release was obtained, directed to Sir Francis Russel, a man of moderation, and averse from persecution, who immediately caused them to be set at full liberty.‡ But the case of James Parnal, a native of Retford in Nottinghamshire, who was educated in the schools of literature, in the sixteenth year of his age joined the Quakers, and, though a youth, was a pathetic preacher and able disputant, and discovered the wisdom and understanding of age and experience, afforded most affecting instances of the severities a cruel jailer could inflict. His constitution was tender, and after ten or eleven months sunk under the multiplied hardships of his imprisonment, about the age of nineteen, the consideration of his youth exciting no commiseration.§

Besides the personal injuries these virtuous people suffered, they were exposed to great dep-

* Gough's History, vol. i., p. 210–217.
† Ibid., p. 289.   ‡ Ibid., p. 137.
§ Ibid., p. 162, 166, 167.

* Gough's History, vol. i., p. 169.   † Ibid., p. 170.
‡ Ibid., p. 176–180.   § Ibid., p. 180–188.

redations in their property, by unreasonable fines and exorbitant distraints, especially on account of tithes, into the details of which we have not room to descend. Suffice it to say, that in 1659, where £53 13s. 6d. only could be demanded, £138 were exacted.*

To sum up this view of their sufferings, it may be observed, that when a printed account of them was presented to the Parliament which the protector convened, it appeared that one hundred and forty of them were then in prison ; and of one thousand nine hundred who had suffered in the preceding six years, twenty-one had died in prison, generally by hardship or by violent abuses.†

It is to be remarked, that they supported themselves under severe persecution with meekness, patience, and fortitude, " as lambs dumb before their shearers ;" and there were not wanting instance of their being so borne up by inward consolal and peace, by faith and hope in their afflictions, as frequently to sing praises to God, to the astonishment of the spectators and of their fellow-prisoners.

While they were exposed to hatred, contempt, and abuse from without, brotherly kindness and unfeigned charity increased, and connected them among themselves. While each seemed regardless of his own liberty, they were zealous advocates for that of their brethren, and almost incessant in their representations to those in authority of the sufferings of their friends ; going so far in their charity as to offer themselves freely, person for person, to lie in prison, instead of such as they apprehended were in danger of perishing through the length or extremity of their confinement.‡

This mutual and generous attachment was amiable ; their moral conduct was regular ; and their conscientious regard to fidelity in their commerce begat confidence. They were careful to manufacture or choose such goods as were substantial, and would answer the expectations of the purchasers ; moderate in their profits ; sparing in their commendations ; punctual in their payments ; they asked no more for their ware than the precise sum they were determined to accept ; and they took no advantage of ignorance. So that, under all their sufferings, they prospered, and verified the proverb, that " Honesty is the best policy."§

It was also a distinguishing trait in the character of this people, that they attached themselves to none of the political parties of the day, nor entered into their ambitious views. It was with them a principle of religion to have no intermeddling with secular factions, and to demean themselves quietly and peaceably under the existing government. When the nation was in great commotion and fluctuation on the death of Cromwell, George Fox addressed an exhortation to his friends " to live in love and peace with all men, to keep clear of all the commotions of the world, and not to intermeddle with the powers of the earth, but to let their conversation be in heaven." He remarked, that " all who pretend to fight for Christ are deceived, for his kingdom is not of this world, and therefore his servants do not fight." When Sir George Booth rose in arms in favour of the exiled mon-

arch, the committee of safety invited the Quakers to take up arms, offering considerable posts and commands to some of them. But they es. teemed war and violence to be inconsistent with pure Christianity, and were not to be corrupted by the prospects of preferment and honours.*

Unassisted by any alliance with the state, nay, treated with severity by all the contending powers in their turn, and everywhere pursued with contempt and cruel abuse, they increased, and spread themselves over the kingdom. In the year 1652, meetings of them were settled in many of the central and northern parts of the nation. Their preachers were zealous and active ; not intimidated by sufferings, nor wearied by journeys and labours. Francis Howgill and Edward Boroughs, with Anthony Pearson, travelled to London ; John Cam and John Audland to Bristol ; Richard Hubberthorn and George Whitehead to Norwich, and others to other parts. And we find George Fox disseminating their principles, and meeting the severest sufferings in the remotest parts of the kingdom. The evils which this people endured with singular meekness and patience had great effect in awakening attention to their preaching, and softening the minds of numbers to the reception of their doctrine. It was justly remarked by Hugh Peters to Oliver Cromwell, " that he could not give Fox a better opportunity of spreading his principles in Cornwall than by imprisoning him. there."†

The instances of the persecution and sufferings they endured, which we have selected, for we do not pretend to give their history in a minute detail, reflect disgrace on the magistracy of the age, and are a reproach to the administration of justice. But the Mayor of Oxford, in the year 1654, deserves to be mentioned as an example of a more equitable and humane disposition. Elizabeth Heavens and Elizabeth Fletcher, two north-country women, were apprehended and sent to Bocardo, a prison usually appropriated to the reception of felons and murderers, for having exhorted the people, after service, in one of the churches. The mayor being sent for to meet the justices, by whose order they had been committed, to examine the Quakers, he replied to the message, " Let them who committed them deal with them according to law ; for my part, I have nothing against them : if they wanted food, money, or clothes, I would willingly supply them." The justices, however, met, attended by Dr. Owen the vice-chancellor, who was the principal in examining them ; and the sentence passed on them was, that they should be whipped out of the city. This sentence, according to the constitution of the town, was not valid without the signature and seal of the mayor, which, as he judged it unmerited and unjust, he refused to affix to it. But, by the order of the vice-chancellor and his coadjutors, it was severely executed without being legalized by his sanction, though the conviction of their innocence affected even the heart of the executioner to that degree that he performed his office with manifest reluctance.‡

_____

* Gough's History, p. 284.   † Ibid., p. 274.
‡ Ibid., p. 140, 175, 176.   § Ibid., p. 141.

* Gough's History, p. 273, 274, 277.
† Ibid., p. 217.
‡ These women had, a few days before, for exhorting the inhabitants and students to repentance, been pumped on by the scholars of St. John's Col-

Another more remarkable and more public instance of protection and justice, which this people were so happy as once to receive in those times, reflects honour on the name of General Monk. On a complaint against some of his soldiers for disturbing their meetings, he issued out this order:

"St. James's, March 9, 1659.

"I do require all officers and soldiers to forbear to disturb the peaceable meetings of the Quakers, they doing nothing prejudicial to the Parliament or commonwealth of England.

"GEORGE MONK."*

I am sensible that wild flights of rudeness and enthusiasm, that violations of decency, decorum, and order, are imputed to the Quakers at this period. Mosheim stigmatizes them as "pernicious fanatics," and speaks, as it were with approbation, of their being "severely chastised for their extravagance and folly." But granting the justness of these imputations, which I conceive, however, are by no means to be admitted in all instances and to their full extent, and will scarcely apply to those cases of suffering which we have stated, every equitable and humane mind will feel indignant at seeing folly illegally chastised, and enthusiastic extravagances restrained by acts of cruelty. Extravagance and folly rank almost with wisdom and virtue, when compared with the injustice and inhumanity of the magistrates from whom the Quakers suffered persecution.

The society of those called Quakers considered the restoration of Charles II. as a signal instance of the interposition of Providence to restore peace and order to a distracted nation; and soon after he was placed on the throne, Mr. Richard Hubberthorn obtained access to the king, and stated the excessive sufferings which his friends had sustained, and under which they were still smarting. The king entered into free conversation with him on the principles of the Quakers, and promised them his protection, saying, "Of this you may be assured, that you shall none of you suffer for your opinions or religion so long as you live peaceably, and you have the word of a king for it; and I have also given forth a declaration to the same purpose, that none shall wrong or abuse you."†

This assurance raised in their minds the encouraging expectation of not being molested in their religious worship and profession. Better times than they had hitherto experienced appeared to be opening upon them. Their meetings were large and quiet. Numbers, drawn by curiosity, or better motives, flocked to them, and embraced their sentiments; but this calm was of no long duration; and they soon found that the word of a king could be a delusive ground of dependance. Venner's insurrection brought on them new and severe persecution; though they were, by the dying testimony of lege till they were almost suffocated: they were then tied arm to arm, and dragged up and down the college, and through a pool of water; and Elizabeth Fletcher, a young woman, was thrown over a grave, whereby she received a contusion on her side, from which she never recovered, but soon after died. Yet it does not appear that the magistrates animadverted on this inhuman outrage.—*Gough's History,* vol. i., p. 147–149.   * Gough's History, vol. i., p. 279.
, † Ibid., p. 440.
ᴋ.. VOL. II.—F F F

the sufferers at their execution, exculpated from all knowledge of the design. Their meetings were broken up by soldiers. Their persons were abused by the populace. Their houses were ransacked. They were forced from their employments, and cast into jails among felons, who rifled them of their money and clothes. And even the sick were dragged out of their beds to prisons; one of whom, Mr. Patchen, a man of considerable estate, being in a fever, died there.*

. This persecution was not confined to the city of London, but spread with similar violence over all or most parts of the nation. They were, without conviction, without crimination, without any legal cause, violently haled to prison, and crowded together in close, damp, or unwholesome rooms, in such numbers as almost to the danger of suffocation. In Bristol, near one hundred and ninety were imprisoned: in Lancaster were two hundred and seventy prisoners: in Westmoreland, one hundred and sixteen: in the West Riding of Yorkshire were not fewer than two hundred and twenty-nine; and the number in the North Riding amounted to a hundred and twenty-six. And the treatment which they received in prison was generally as cruel as the commitment was unjust.†

When the members of this society had cleared themselves from the imputation of being parties in Venner's insurrection, they were proceeded against on new grounds; and old laws, made in the reigns of Henry VIII. and Queen Elizabeth, were revived and made rules for proceeding against them; namely, the laws against the subtraction of tithes, and neglecting to resort to the parish church, or some other, on every Sunday or holyday. They were also prosecuted on an act made in the beginning of Queen Elizabeth's reign, for administering the oath of supremacy, and on one of the third of James, enjoining the oath of allegiance. When there remained no shadow of reason to detain those whom they had imprisoned on account of the rising of the fifth-monarchy men, it was a usual method with the magistrates to tender them the oath of allegiance, which they knew they would not take, that their refusal might be a pretext for still holding them in confinement; though their demeanour was peaceable and unresisting, and, by the most explicit declarations, they solemnly expressed and pledged their allegiance.‡ By the misapplication of the law of James, many of them suffered the loss of personal liberty, and of all their substance, and were exposed to very hard and illicit treatment. The case of Thomas Goodyear and Benjamin Staples, at the Quarter Sessions at Oxford, is a striking instance of this. Thomas Goodyear, after receiving the sentence of præmunire, was brought into court, like a common malefactor, with bolts on his legs, and on asking "whether the jailer had orders to fetter him," he was answered, "The jailer may do as he will with you, for you are out of the king's protection." This man, encouraged by the example of his superior, when he brought them back to prison, told the other prisoners, "that if they wanted clothes, they might take theirs off their backs, for they can have no law against you." But one of the prisoners humane-

* Gough's History, p. 441, 445. .
† Ibid., p. 446–451.   ‡ Ibid., p. 457–466..

ly answered, he would rather go naked than strip, honest men of their clothes, who were stripped of all they had besides.[*]

It is but candid, however, to remark that though the justices and inferior magistrates from their bitterness against the Nonconformists, were disposed, in some cases, to put the 35th of Elizabeth in full force, yet the instances of enforcing this law, through the intervention of higher authority, were not many, nor equally encouraged with other modes of prosecution; as the full enforcing thereof must have terminated in public executions.[†]

But notwithstanding this instance of moderation, violent prejudices against the Quakers were so universal, that they were left unmolested in few or no parts of the kingdom. In 1662, Mr. George Fox represented to the king that, since his restoration, three thousand and sixty-eight of their friends had been imprisoned. A narrative signed by twelve witnesses attested that four thousand two hundred of those called Quakers, both men and women, were in prison. No age or sex found commiseration. Men of seventy, or more years old, were subjected to all the rigours of a jail. In London and its suburbs, five hundred were, at this time, confined; suffering every severity, their trades ruined, and their families exposed to ruin. The treatment of this people, even in this city, resembled the French dragoonings of the Huguenots, rather than the condition of those who were entitled to the privileges of a constitution limited to legal rule. They were beaten with cudgels, cut with swords, and dragged into the streets; there they lay in the kennels, senseless and helpless, besmeared with their blood; and the passengers and spectators, moved by the sight of their condition, would sometimes cry out shame upon the perpetrators, that such a resemblance of massacre should be committed in the streets of London. Some, for these expressions of compassion, had their share of the like treatment. The soldiers being asked why they could be so cruel to their neighbours, one of them answered, "Nay, we are more merciful than we ought to be, for we have orders to kill; and that his musket was double-charged, as most of those of the party were to his knowledge." Through this treatment, some who were haled out of the meeting at Bull-and-Mouth, 31st of August, 1662, were so disabled as to keep their beds for some time: one was so wounded in the head that his brains were visible, and one died of the bruises and wounds he received. The coroner's jury, which was impanelled to view the body, broke up without giving a verdict; alleging as their reason, that if they pronounced it wilful murder, and the perpetrator could not be found, the city would be liable to a fine. The king, when an account of these barbarous transactions was presented to him by one of the society, said; "I assure you it was not by my advice that any of your friends should be slain; you must tell the magistrates of the city of it, and prosecute the law against them." The mayor was, by letter, duly apprized of these proceedings, but offered no redress. The letter, accompanied by a narrative, was printed and published; for which the author was committed to

Newgate by Sir Richard Brown, the mayor, on the charge of dispersing scandalous papers.[*]

After the murder we have mentioned, the meetings in the city were generally undisturbed for six weeks; then similar practices of injustice and cruelty were renewed, under the sanction of the magistrates, and continued nearly to the end of the year 1662. By this time no less than twenty persons had died prisoners in Newgate, and seven more by sickness contracted there soon after their discharge.[†]

The king's declaration of indulgence retarded, in 1663, the furious career of the persecuting magistrates; and few instances of sufferings in the metropolis occur in this year compared with the preceding. Yet the Quakers did not remain quite unmolested; for Sir John Robinson, who preceded Sir R. Brown in the mayoralty, ordered a guard to be placed at the entrance of the Bull-and-Mouth meeting-house, to prevent any persons from entering into it. The meetings, on this, were held in the streets; but those who preached or prayed were generally haled away to prison, and blows were unmercifully dealt on the heads both of men and women who did not disperse at the command of the mayor and his officers. In this year there was also a severe persecution of this people at Colchester in Essex. Their meetings were interrupted by acts of violence; and many were disabled and bruised, and the lives of others were brought into great danger by blows with clubs, carbines, and swords. One of them, when a trooper was beating him with a sword, and the blade fell out of the hilt, took and gave it to him, saying, "I will give it thee up again; I desire the Lord may not lay this day's work to thy charge."[‡]

The operation of the Conventicle Act, passed in 1664, though levelled at every body of Dissenters, fell with peculiar weight on the Quakers; numbers of them, and of them only, were condemned to transportation upon this act; and the proceedings against them were conducted with peculiar and hostile precipitancy. For, "as the penalty for the first offence was imprisonment for a term not exceeding three months, and for the second not exceeding six, at the arbitrary discretion of two justices," it was usual for these justices to commit them for a few days for the first and second offences, not out of tenderness, but in order to subject them more speedily to the penalty of transportation for the third offence; for, from their long-approved constancy, they promised themselves an assurance of finding them again at their religious assemblies as soon as at liberty.[§] The privileges of the subject were held at this time by so precarious a tenure, that the history of this society furnishes instances of the judges refusing to accept the verdict of the grand jury when they have returned the bill *ignoramus;* and of his sending them out again with menaces and fresh instructions.[||] The evidence produced against them, on their trial, was sometimes so insufficient, that the jury remonstrated against it, and entreated not to be troubled any more with such evidence. When

* Gough's History, vol. i., p. 531, 533.
† Ibid., p. 537.

* Gough, vol. i., p. 538-546.
† Ibid., vol. ii., p. 1, 2.   ‡ Ibid., vol. ii., p. 21-24.
§ Ibid., vol. ii., p. 112, 116.
|| Ibid., vol. ii., p. 117, 118.

neither persuasions nor menaces could induce a jury to alter their verdict to the dictates of the court, some of them were bound in £100 each to appear at the King's Bench bar the first day of the following term.*

The awful visitation of Providence, by a destructive pestilence in 1665, had no effect in softening the enmity of their persecutors. Persecution continued, and the meetings were disturbed as before. Many who were cast into the filthy holes of Newgate were released by this disease, which had infected the jails, from a life worse than death. "But," says my author, "what must fix an indelible stamp of utter insensibility to every motive of humanity, of civility, or common decency, on the characters of the magistrates, to the disgrace of the government, and of that church with which they were so zealous to enforce conformity, was, that during the very height of the contagion, they continued to crowd the infected prisons with fresh prisoners."†

In 1668 the Quakers were not, in comparison with former years, much disturbed by the civil power; their sufferings were mostly by excommunications, imprisonments, and distraints, for their conscientious scruples against paying ecclesiastical demands, several of which, however, were unreasonably severe.

The third act against conventicles, which was carried into a law in 1670, opened new scenes of persecution, in which the Quakers had their peculiar share. Many were cruelly spoiled of their property; people of considerable substance were reduced to extreme poverty; and the sick had their beds taken from under them, and were reduced to lie on the floor. When the sufferers, according to the privilege allowed by the act, appealed against the heavy fines and the exorbitant distraints, they generally obtained little by the appeal but additional loss. The influence of the convicting justice, the partiality of the bench, corrupt juries, or a neglect in putting into due execution the decrees of the Quarter Sessions, to which they appealed, left them unredressed. A misconstruction of the word conventicles, which the act limited to meetings for religious worship contrary to the liturgy of the Church of England, often exposed them to illegal fines; for, if they met merely to provide for their poor, or visited a sick friend, or attended the funerals of the deceased, there were not wanting informers hardy enough to swear such meetings conventicles, nor justices prejudiced against them to issue their warrants to levy the fines accordingly; of which Mr. Gough gives various instances.* The penalty on the preacher being £20 for the first offence, and £40 for the second, the desire of gain often tempted the unprincipled informer to swear against a preacher when there was not a word spoken in the meeting. At other times, a word spoken, though not on subjects of religion, was termed preaching; and an answer to an impertinent question, extorted from some one or other present, bore the same construction. The magistrates were as ready to fine as the informer to swear; and, by this iniquitous combination, the innocent were robbed under the cover of an act of Parliament.§ It is a pleasure to find, and truth re-

quries one to add, that some justices, apprized of the villany of the informers, had too much honour to encourage their vicious disposition to plunder without mercy, and to swear without scruple. The Lord-mayor of London, in particular, sitting in a court of aldermen, in the year 1670, when an informer made his appearance with such a number of informations as would have wronged the accused of £1500, with abhorrence broke up the court.* This year affords another peculiar instance of the illegal proceedings by which this society were harassed; which, notwithstanding the king's repeated professions of favour towards them, originated with the court. On the 29th of July, an order was issued by the king and council for demolishing the meeting-house at Horsley Down, Southwark. It was grounded on a pretence that the persons who assembled in it behaved in a riotous and tumultuous manner, than which charge nothing could be more rupugnant to their avowed principles, and uniform manners. The pulling down of the building was, by express command, committed to Christopher Wren, Esq., the surveyor-general of his majesty's works. After this order was affixed to the meeting-house, the members of the society continued their assemblies in it till it was demolished; they then met upon the rubbish. By this they exposed themselves to repeated outrages and cruel abuses from the military, into whose hands was put the despotic treatment of this assembly, and who, at one assault, sorely bruised and wounded twenty, at a second thirty, and at a third more than fifty persons. When the soldiers were reprehended for their cruelty, some of them answered, "If you knew what orders we have, you would say we dealt mercifully with you." Others being asked, How can you deal thus with a people that have love and goodwill to all men, and make no resistance or opposition? replied, "We had rather, and it would be better for us, if they did resist and oppose." This was looked upon by the sufferers as if they sought occasion to imbrue their hands more deeply in blood, and take the lives and estates of honest people for their prey. At length these military violations of the peace of the city roused the civil officers to interpose their authority; but it was too weak to protect this unarmed body against the number of armed men let loose upon them. These proceedings of the soldiers having been represented to the king and council, a temporary cessation of these cruelties was procured, but they were not wholly discontinued. A building at Ratcliffe, belonging to this society, was subjected to the like violence with that of Horsley Down, and on the 2d of September, without any legal process, was demolished. On that day and the night following, twelve cart-loads of doors, windows, and floors, with other materials, were carried away. Some of the materials were sold on the spot for money and strong drink. Thus, grievous sufferings, exorbitant spoil, and illegal depredation, were the lot of an inoffensive and peaceable class of subjects. These evils were inflicted by those whose duty it was to protect the rights and property of the people, even by the officers under government.†

* Gough, vol. ii., p. 128, 129.   † Ibid., p. 139, 140.
‡ Ibid., p. 305–316.   § Ibid., p. 316–318.

* Gough's History, vol. ii., p. 316–318.
† Ibid., vol. ii., p. 341–352.

While these calamities awaited the general body of this people on account of their conscientious profession, it is to be supposed that the more active and distinguished members of the society were peculiar marks for prejudice and malignity. Of this the history of the Quakers furnishes many examples, which we must not pass over unnoticed, though our limits will not allow us to go into a minute detail of each case.

George Fox, eminent for his activity and zeal in disseminating his principles, was among the first who, after the restoration of Charles II., and for some years, felt the rage of bigotry. In 1660 he was apprehended by a warrant from Mr. Henry Porter, the mayor of Lancaster, at the house of Margaret Fell at Swaithmore, and carried to Ulverston, where he was guarded for the night by fifteen or sixteen men, some of whom kept sentry at the chimney, for fear he should escape by that passage ; " so darkened," observes the historian, " were they by superstitious imaginations." Next morning he was escorted, with abusive and contumelious treatment, to Lancaster, and brought before the mayor, who committed him to prison, refused bail, and denied him a copy of the mittimus. Two friends having, however, been permitted to read it, he published an immediate reply to the charges which they reported to him it contained. Application was made to the king for a habeas corpus to remove him to London, and was obtained. In consequence of this writ, though his persecutors, for two months, obstructed the operation of it, he presented himself in the Court of King's Bench ; the justices, being dispassionate and favourable, caused the sheriff's return of the habeas corpus to be laid before the king, who, when Fox had suffered for more than twenty weeks an unjust and severe imprisonment, gave directions for his release. His enemies, on his obtaining his liberty, were filled with vexation and fear, as they were conscious of the illegality of their proceedings ; and now was advised, by some in authority, to make the mayor and the rest examples ; but he meekly replied, " I shall leave them to the Lord ; if He forgive them, I shall trouble myself no farther about them."*

On occasion of rumours of a conspiracy set on foot in the north among the Republicans and Separatists, warrants were again issued out, in 1663, to apprehend George Fox ; as he was on his tour through the northern counties, he was not met with ; but at length, finding that they continued their pursuit, he resolved to stand his ground, and was apprehended ; when no evidence could be produced to justify committing him on the pretended plot, the justices contented themselves with his engaging to appear at the sessions : he appeared at it, but finding no grounds to effect their purpose, either upon the plot or the act against meetings, they committed him, for refusing the oath of allegiance, to a very incommodious room in Lancaster Castle, where he was kept close prisoner till after the spring assizes, 1665 ; after that he was removed to Scarborough Castle, where he was detained upward of a year longer ; when, finding means to have his case laid before the king, he soon after obtained his release, having suffered an arbitrary and very rigorous imprisonment of more than

* Gough's History, vol. i., p. 432–439.

three years.* At Lancaster, he was locked up in a smoky tower, sometimes so filled with smoke that a burning candle was scarcely visible,† and so open as to admit the rain in upon his bed. The room allotted to him in Scarborough Castle was little better, if not worse; and when, at his own expense, he had made it tolerable, he was removed into another room, without chimney or fireplace, and so open to the seaside, that the rain, violently driven by the wind, poured into the room. A sentinel was placed at his door; few or none of his friends were permitted to visit him, or even to bring him food ; but numbers of others were admitted in to gaze upon him or dispute with him.‡ His removal from one prison to another, when he was in a very weak condition, was attended with a treatment in many respects uncivil and rude. To the rigour and hardships of his imprisonment were added, to terrify him, the frequent menaces of his keepers. The deputy-governor once told him, " that the king, knowing that he had a great interest in the people, had sent him thither, that if there should be any stirring in the nation, they should hang him over the wall." He replied to this menace, " If that was what they desired, and it was permitted them, he was ready, for he never feared death or sufferings in his life ; but was known to be an innocent, peaceable man, free from stirrings and plottings, and one that sought the good of all men." His patience surmounted the hardships to which he was exposed ; and his innocence pleading in his favour, his keepers at length relaxed their severity, and treated him with favour and respect. When, on obtaining his release, Mr. Fox offered an acknowledgment for his late civility and kindness to the governor of Scarborough Castle, he refused it ; adding, " whatever good he could do him or his friends, he would do it, and never do them any hurt." His consequent conduct made good this promise, for it was ever favourable to the Quakers.§

Mrs. Margaret Fell, who had been a widow about two years, in 1660 was, in a degree, involved in the severe proceedings against Fox ; for, that they might lay hold of him, they forcibly entered and searched her house ; of this she complained in an appeal to the public, as an injury offered to herself, and a violation of the liberty of the subject.|| In the year 1663, this lady, the widow of a judge and a woman of estate, was cited before the justices, and questioned about keeping meetings at her house, and the oath of allegiance was tendered to her ; on which she expostulated with them, that as " they knew she could not swear; why should they send for her from her own house and her lawful affairs to insnare her ?" adding, " What have I done ?" This remonstrance, for the instant, impressed their minds, and they declared they would not urge the oath, if she would not keep meetings at her house.¶ To this proposal she magnanimously replied, " she would not

* Gough's History, vol. ii., p. 25–29.
† Ibid., p. 29. ‡ Ibid., p. 152, 153.
§ Ibid., p. 150–156. || Ibid., vol. i., p. 435, 436.
¶ Mr. Gough properly remarks on this proposal, that it was a plain confession, that the tender of the oath was a mere pretext to be vexatious to the subject, an arbitrary measure assumed for the mere purpose of persecution

deny her faith and principles for anything they could do, against her, and while it should please the Lord to let her have a house, she would endeavour to worship Him in it." On this the oath was tendered, and on her refusal, she was committed to Lancaster Castle, a prison then crowded with numbers of the same profession, and the state of which heightened the evil of confinement. Here she was detained till next year.*

When, in the month of August, she was, at the assizes, brought to her trial on the same account, she persevered in refusing the oath, and answered the judge with good sense and pious intrepidity. Her counsel was admitted to plead an arrest of judgment, after the jury gave a verdict against her, and found several errors in the indictment, but they were not admitted by the judge, and sentence of præmunire was passed upon her. She remained in prison twenty months before she could obtain liberty to go to her own house, which she procured for a little time, and returned to prison again, where she continued about four years, till released by an order of the king and council.†

Another of the society of Quakers, whose sufferings are recorded in a distinct narrative, was their noted preacher, Mr. Francis Howgill. This respectable man, as he was in the market-place at Kendal on his lawful business, was summoned before the magistrates then sitting in a tavern, who tendered him the oath of allegiance, and, on his conscientious refusal of it, committed him to prison till the next month. At the spring assizes of 1663, the oath was again administered unto him, and on his refusal, an indictment was drawn up against him, which he traversed. A bond for his good behaviour till his trial came on being required of him, he suffered himself to be recommitted to prison rather than give it, as he apprehended it would be a tacit acknowledgment of past ill-behaviour, and his attendance at meetings in the mean time, which a sense of duty would not suffer him to neglect, would be interpreted as a breach of engagement.‡ As he was going to the prison he turned to the people, and uttered this devout wish, "The fear of God be among you all." And the people generally appeared very affectionate to him, and pitied his hard circumstances;§ while the justices of Westmoreland endeavoured to prepossess the judge and court against him by invidious reflections on him and the society, and by the weight of their united influence and enmity.

At the summer assizes he was again brought to the bar. Modesty, equanimity, good sense, sober reasoning, and deep impressions of religion, marked his conduct at both assizes, and appear to have softened the sternness of his judges. The sentence, which confiscated his lands to the king during his life, and his goods and chattels forever, and consigned him to prison for the rest of his days, was, however, passed upon him; though the judge, it was observed, pronounced it with a faint and low voice, as if he was sensible that this man was greatly wronged, and that himself did not entirely approve of the sentence he was passing.‖ "In mistaken

zeal for religion," our historian remarks, "the plainest rules of morality are violated, and in forcing uniformity in unessential points, the substantial parts, mercy, justice, and truth, are obliterated."

The case of Hannah Trigg, on account of the singular severity of it, deserves particular mention. She was one of twelve Quakers who received sentence of transportation, being tried and convicted on a bill of indictment preferred against them for the third offence. The circumstance which particularly marked the tyranny and illegality of the treatment of this young woman was, that she was not sixteen years of age, and the certificate of her birth was arbitrarily rejected by the justices. After sentence she sickened in Newgate, and died there. The unfeeling inhumanity, which was insatiate with her life, was extended to her corpse. Her relations were deprived of the consolation of interring her as they desired, but she was carried to the burying-place of the felons; and when the bearers came to the ground, finding no grave made, they left the corpse unburied, saying they would make a grave next morning. The girl's mother attending the funeral, had the grief and anguish to behold this treatment of her daughter's remains in silent sorrow, without the power of remedy.*

The sufferings, also, of Joseph Fuce, a man of patient and meek spirit, and very laborious as a preacher, when died in the White Lion prison in Southwark in 1665, should not pass unnoticed. In 1660, being at a meeting at Deal, he, with twenty-three others, was seized by several armed men, and being committed to Sandown Castle, they were kept there several nights and days, their friends not being allowed to bring them either food to eat or straw to lie on. He and another were afterward removed to Dover Castle, with five other of their friends, were locked up in one room, from which they were permitted no egress, not even for the necessities of nature, nor were their friends allowed any access to them; and the servant of the marshal, for showing them some little favour, was dismissed from his place. Joseph Fuce remonstrating, when an opportunity offered, on the cruel usage they received, was answered with a volley of oaths and execrations. His pious ears being wounded with this profaneness, he bore his testimony against it by a serious reproof. The marshal at this, exasperated to rage, caused him to be dragged headlong down several stone steps into a dungeon, overrun with filth and vermin, into which no light or air could enter but by some holes cut in the door. He was kept there two days and two nights, without fire, candle, straw, or anything to lie on but an old blanket. When he had obtained some straw, for want of air, through the damp and stench of his dismal lodging, he fell sick; and after nine days' confinement, as he seemed at the point of death, the fear of being questioned for murdering him moved the marshal to remove him, and to permit him to return to his fellow-prisoners, with whom he continued several months till released by the king's proclamation.†

Neither the calamities to which the society of Quakers were exposed, nor the sufferings which with peculiar severity were felt by some

---

* Gough, vol. ii., p. 29, &c.   † Ibid., p. 92–96.
‡ Ibid., p. 31, 32.   § Ibid., p. 100.
‖ Ibid., p. 108.

* Gough, vol. ii., p. 127.   † Ibid., p. 143–145.

of its most eminent and worthy members, could damp the ardour of their zeal in defending their cause and disseminating their principles, but served to call forth their vigorous exertions. Margaret Fell, on the apprehension of George Fox, published a brief narrative of that violent proceeding, and took a journey to London to lay the case before the king, requesting his favourable interposition, "to cause him to be removed to London, and hear his cause himself:" in which suit she was heard.* When, in consequence of the insurrection of the fifth-monarchy men, many of the Quakers, without crimination, without conviction, were violently haled to prison, in addition to the endeavours used for their relief, by publishing and presenting to the king a declaration from that people against all sedition, plotters, fighters, &c.; the same lady several times waited personally upon the king to solicit his indulgence and protection for them; at her first admission she signified to him, "they were an innocent, peaceable people, who did no injury; and administered no occasion of offence, except in keeping up their religious meetings, for no other purpose than worshipping God in that way they were persuaded was most acceptable to him, and edifying one another in his fear; which being to them a conscientious matter of duty to God, they could not violate it, in compliance with the ordinances or laws of man, whatever they suffered." In consequence of her applications and the declaration above mentioned, the king sent out a proclamation, "forbidding soldiers to search any house without a constable." At length he was prevailed upon to issue out a declaration, ordering "the Quakers to be set at liberty without paying the fees."† Burrough, Hubberthorn, and Whitehead, among others, were active advocates for their suffering brethren. They attended Parliament to solicit against the bill brought in in 1661 passing into an act. Burrough presented to the king and council in the same year a paper entitled "A Just and Right Plea," representing their sentiments respecting oaths, and their established religious principle, "to enter into no plots, combinations, or rebellion against government; nor to seek deliverance from injustice or oppression by any such means." In this he was seconded by Hubberthorn and Whitehead, who with ability and spirit entered into a vindication of the religious meetings of their society.‡ Two letters, about this time, were addressed to the king, remonstrating on the countenance given to profane shows and sports, and the encouragement afforded to prosecutors, and boldly reproving his majesty for his personal conduct. The one was written by George Fox the elder, so called for distinction, as the elder brother of the society; the other was drawn up by George Fox the younger. They afford a specimen, as the historian observes, "of the honest plaindealing of men who, with Elihu, knew not to flatter, lest, in so doing, their Maker should take them away." When the last of the two letters was delivered to the king, he seemed considerably affected with the contents. His brother, the Duke of York, whose temper was more gloomy, reserved, and vindictive, being greatly exasperated with the writer, advised the king to punish him; but,

with much propriety, he replied, "It were better for us to mend our lives."‡* These epistles of the Foxes, however, left no permanent impression on the royal mind. In the year 1662, the universal rage against the peaceable society of the Quakers left them unmolested in few or no parts of the nation. On this, George Fox again addressed the king on behalf of the suffering Friends, and stated that since his restoration three thousand and sixty-eight had been imprisoned, and a narrative signed by twelve witnesses was printed, which represented that the number of men and women then in prison amounted to upward of four thousand and two hundred. Humanity revolts at the circumstances of cruelty with which the members of this society were treated at this time; when their meetings were broken up by men with clubs, they themselves were thrown into the water, and trampled under foot till the blood gushed out.† Among other endeavours that George Fox used to remove suspicion and soften enmity, was a paper which he wrote in 1663, as a testimony against all plots and conspiracies whatever; to admonish his friends to circumspection in their words and actions, and not to meddle in their civil commotions : copies of which he dispersed through the northern counties, and sent one to the king and council.‡ Others of this society, besides George Fox, took up their pens in the cause of their innocent and oppressed brethren. When the Conventicle Act was passed in 1664, George Whitehead published a piece to expose the severity of the persecutors, to exculpate his friends from the charge of obstinacy, to strengthen their steadfastness, and to remonstrate on the unequal and arbitrary manner in which the judges enforced the act. Another remonstrance was also published about the same time, by Josiah Coale, against persecution, addressed to the king and both houses of Parliament.§ In the year 1666 the cause of the Quakers began to derive great support and credit from the abilities and virtues of the celebrated William Penn, who in that year joined their society, and became one of its most eminent advocates and ornaments. His pen was soon employed in its defence. His first piece was entitled "The Sandy Foundation shaken." This gave great offence to some powerful ecclesiastics, and it was answered by an accustomed mode of reply, namely, an order for imprisoning him. He was closely confined seven months in the Tower, and denied the visits of his friends. This precluded him from his ministerial labours; but, several treatises were the fruits of his solitude, particularly one of great note, entitled "No Cross, no Crown;" in which, Dr. Henry More observed, "Mr. Penn has treated the subject of a future life and the immortality of the soul with a force and spirit equal to most writers."‖ The first of the above pieces was occasioned by a particular circumstance, which called on the Quakers to vindicate themselves in a public disputation. Mr. Thomas Vincent, a Presbyterian minister of eminent piety, and who distinguished himself by his ministerial labours in the time of the plague, but whose zeal in this in-

* Gough, vol. i., p. 435–437.   † Ibid., p. 455, 456.
‡ Ibid., p. 500, 505.

* Gough, vol. i., p. 510, 513.   † Ibid., p. 538.
‡ Ibid., vol. ii., p. 25.   § Ibid., p. 115.
‖ British Biography, vol. vii., p. 139.

stance misled him, had, on two of his hearers going to the Quakers' meetings, indulged himself in invectives from the pulpit against that people, and in a license of expression beyond the bounds of Christian moderation and common decency. . This reaching the ears of some of those at whom they were cast, they demanded of him a public meeting to vindicate themselves from his severe reflections, or to give him an opportunity to support them by proof, to which, after some demur, Mr. Vincent agreed. Before the hour appointed the house was filled with his own hearers and partisans ; and he was accompanied by three other Presbyterian ministers as his assistants, Mr. Thomas Dawson, Mr. Thomas Doolittle, and Mr. William Maddocks. George Whitehead and William Penn, on the side of their friends, attended to his charges against the Quakers. Instead of bringing them forward, Mr. Vincent opened the conference with this question, "Whether they owned one Godhead in three distinct and separate persons ?" He framed on this, according to the mode of argumentation then in use, a syllogism. George Whitehead rejected his terms as unscriptural, and not deducible from the text he quoted, and desired him to explain them so that they might be understood ; observing, "that God did not use to wrap his truths in heathenish metaphysics, but deliver them in plain language." But Mr. Vincent and his coadjutors would neither keep to Scripture terms nor allow them in their antagonists. After many insults offered to the Quakers, and opprobrious names cast upon them, the meeting was broken up by a prayer from Mr. Vincent, in which these people were accused as blasphemers. Some people staying after he and their brethren withdrew, the Quakers found an opportunity of exculpating themselves from the invectives of their adversaries. Another debate was desired, but evaded. On this, Penn appealed to the public.*

It falls within the period of which we are writing to notice the remarks on the third Conventicle Act, which George Fox, being in London at the time, published in 1670, in order, if possible, to move the government to moderation. Apprehending an impending storm, he wrote also, at the same time, an epistle to his friends, to exhort them to faithfulness and steadfastness in their testimony to the truth, and to Christian patience, in bearing the sufferings which might be permitted to try their faith.†

Under a successive train of severe trials, this people maintained patience, resignation, and a blameless demeanour ; and, with the powers of the world against them, their numbers were continually increasing. In the year 1666 they were become a large body. This gave them courage and resolution to erect in that year a new meeting-house in Whitehart Court, Gracechurch-street, which, from its central situation, became afterward the place for their yearly meetings.‡

The affairs of this society began now to range into a regular and systematic form. George Fox, as soon as he was released from his long confinement, proceeded as usual in his labours ; and when he was so weak, and stiff, and benumbed in his joints, by a cruel imprisonment

for the greatest part of three years, that it was with difficulty he could mount his horse or alight, he went from Yorkshire to London. . He saw it necessary to increase the number of meetings of discipline, as the exigencies and the numbers of the society were increased. In 1660 a general meeting for church affairs had been held at Skipton, in Yorkshire. . The business of it was confined to the taking an account of their sufferings, and to collections for the relief of the poor. Quarterly meetings were afterward established in London, which, in addition to the former subjects of attention, had the charge of the reputation of the society, to watch over the members, and admonish and exhort such as might appear disorderly and uncircumspect in their conversation, not agreeable to the strictness of their religious profession ; besides the women's meetings, which had chiefly the care of poor widows and orphans. During George Fox's stay in London, there were established, at his recommendation, five monthly meetings of men and women in that city, to transact the business which had before employed the quarterly meetings; and a general meeting once in three months, as hitherto, for mutual counsel, advice, and deliberation in relation to the common affairs and care of the whole body in the city. . He afterward procured his plan of monthly meetings to be adopted through all the counties, in Scotland, Ireland, Holland, and the Continent of America. The business of the monthly meetings was, at his advice and admonition, after this, extended to the taking cognizance of the orderly proceedings towards marriage, to see "that the parties who proposed marriage were clear from other engagements, that their relations were satisfied, that widows had made provision for their first husbands' children before they married again, and to institute whatever other inquiries were necessary for keeping all things clean and pure, in good order and righteousness, to the glory of God."

Some time after monthly and quarterly meetings were established, viz., in the year 1669, it was found expedient, and agreed upon, to hold a general meeting in London, representative of the whole body in England, and all other parts where any of the society were settled ; which has, from that time, been held annually, and is called "The Yearly Meeting in London." It is formed of deputies from each quarterly meeting in England, and from the half years' meetings in Ireland, without restraining from an attendance any member in unity with the society. Such places in Europe and America as are too remote conveniently to send representatives keep up a correspondence with this meeting by epistles. A committee of correspondence in London and several counties and other places, to be consulted in the intervals between the yearly meetings, upon any emergency, was also established. The members appointed correspondents in London, to meet the sixth day in every week, to consult upon such matters as may be laid before them, particularly any suffering cases of friends, from whence it is called "The Meeting for Sufferings," and is a meeting of record.

From the meetings of discipline no members of the society are excluded. A regular record of all their proceedings is kept by a clerk, who,

* Gough, vol. ii., p. 226–228. † Ibid., p. 318.
‡ Ibid., p. 157.

at 'the desire of the meeting, voluntarily undertakes the office. The business of these meetings is preceded by a solemn meeting of worship. An inquiry whether meetings for discipline and worship are duly attended, the preservation of love and unity, the religious education of youth, are some of the leading objects of these associations. Inquiries are also made whether a faithful and Christian testimony is borne against the receiving or paying tithes, priests' demands, or those called church-rates. Whether friends are careful to avoid all vain sports, places of diversion, gaming, and all unnecessary frequenting of ale-houses or taverns, excess in drinking, and intemperance of every kind? Whether friends are just in their dealings, and punctual in fulfilling their engagements, and are advised carefully to inspect the state of their affairs once in the year? Whether early care be taken to advise and deal with such as appear inclinable to marry contrary to the rules of the society; and whether any remove from or into monthly or two weekly meetings without certificates? And whether two or more faithful friends are deputed in each particular meeting to have the oversight thereof; and care be taken, when anything appears amiss, that the rules of their discipline be put in practice?

This sketch of the discipline and ecclesiastical government of this society cannot fail to give us a favourable idea of the spirit and principles which actuate it. It is recommended by the method and regularity which mark it; and it is a great excellence of it, that it is directed to the encouragement and promotion of good morals, of a peaceable, upright, and blameless conduct in social life. For a more full and accurate view of its nature and design, the reader may be referred to a long and judicious disquisition on it in Mr. Gough's History;* which when he has perused, he will determine for himself whether it may not be justly extolled, as "bearing marks of a peculiar wisdom in the contrivance and goodness of heart in the ends in view, realized in the beneficial effects it then had, and hath since continued to produce."

The Quakers, besides supporting a series of sufferings with patience and fortitude, disseminating their principles through England, Wales, and Scotland with unabating zeal, and forming their society upon a regular plan of government, traversed the Atlantic Ocean, carried their sentiments into America, and established themselves in the Western Continent. The undertaking was arduous; new calamities and persecutions awaited them in new countries.† Their pious efforts, however, were eventually successful in the transatlantic regions. The brevity we must observe does not allow us to go here into particulars. But two instances of their zeal, at this period, to propagate their doctrine in the foreign parts of Europe, were of so singular a nature as to call for particular notice.

About the year 1661, two women, Catharine Evans and Sarah Cheevers, moved with a religious concern to diffuse their principles, took their passage in a ship bound from London to Leghorn: after various trials and storms, they arrived at that city; and, during their stay in

it, they dispersed books, explaining the doctrines of the society, and discoursed with people of all ranks, numbers, of whom curiosity daily drew after them; and here they met with no molestation. They sailed from thence in a Dutch ship bound to Alexandria, the master of which put into Malta. Going on shore the day after their arrival, they were met by an English consul, who invited them to his house, where they continued about three months. They were visited by many, whom they found it their concern to call to repentance, and were repeatedly summoned before the inquisitors, whose interrogatories they answered in such a manner as not to give them the advantage they sought, nor to resign their own principles by the least compliance with the superstitious and showy religion of the country. The consul, at last, overcome by flattery, menaces, and bribery, gave up his guests to the inquisitors, who would not venture to take them without his consent or acquiescence. Having undergone an examination, which they supported with simplicity and firmness, they were imprisoned in a close, dark room, with only two little holes for light and air, and so extremely hot in that warm climate, that it seemed as if the intention of the inquisitors was to stifle them to death. This imprisonment lasted three or four years. They were continually beset and perplexed with the impertinences of monks and friars, to cajole or terrify them into their superstitions. But neither flattery nor menaces could pervert these innocent women from their profession. Upon this, they were put into a room so exceedingly hot, close, and suffocating, that they were often forced to rise out of their bed, to lie down at the chink of the door for air to draw breath; their faces were excessively stung by gnats; and such was the effect of the heat of the room and the climate, their skin was parched, their hair fell off, and they frequently fainted away. They were tempted at times to wish for death, to end their sorrows. Catharine Evans fell into a fit of sickness, and the physician said, "they must have air, or else they would die." On this, the door was ordered to be set open six hours in the day. Soon after they were separated, in hope that an impression might be made on their minds if they were separately attacked; but each was immovable. They not only resisted every attempt to draw them off from their religious profession to the superstitions of popery, but, as the house of inquisition was rebuilding, or repairing in some parts, for the space of a year and half, they embraced the opportunities which offered to incite the people to repentance, both the workmen who were obliging to them, and the citizens of better quality who came to view the building. The apartment of Catharine being near the street, she frequently accosted with admonitions those that passed by, many of whom would stay to hear as long as they durst, and were much affected. After enduring the severities of an imprisonment in the inquisition upward of three years, and several unsuccessful attempts to procure their release, George Fox engaged the friendly and humane interposition of Lord d'Aubigny with the magistrates, whose mediation was effectual; and being liberated, they returned to England. On their passage home, a pas-

* Gough, vol. ii., p. 161-198.
† Ibid., vol. ii., chap. ix.

senger who was a knight of Malta, and the in-quisitor's brother, interested himself with the captain to secure them every accommodation the ship could afford. The merchants at Leghorn, where the vessel stopped, treated them with great kindness, and supplied them with wine and other articles for their refreshment. At Tangier, the governor courteously received them, and would have given them money, which they declined accepting, though they gratefully acknowledged his kindness. They freely addressed their admonitions to him, and exhortations to amendment of life to the people who flocked to the house where they lodged. Previously to their discharge from Alexandria, their tried integrity and blameless manners had made impressions in their favour, both on the magistrates and the inquisitor, the latter of whom relaxed in his severity, and granted them the use of pen, ink, and paper, to write to their friends.*

The sufferings of these women, in the singular enterprise to which their apprehensions of duty animated them, fell short of those which befell two men in a similar undertaking, namely, John Philly and William Moore. These persons, being in Germany with other friends in the beginning of 1662, felt a concern to proceed into Hungary, and to visit the Hortesche brethren, who were a kind of Baptist that lived in a community, hundreds of them together in a family, having their goods and possessions in common; they also refused to swear or fight. This was a design attended with peculiar difficulties and perils, as it would lead them, on a long journey, through a tract of country unknown to them, and among people differing from them in language, in sentiments, and in manners. But such were their views of the obligations lying upon them, they were not intimidated by the prospect of difficulties, and actually made a prosperous journey to the nearest body of that people, residing at Cushart, near Presburg, where they were pretty hospitably entertained, and dispersed some religious books, which they had taken for that purpose. From hence they set off for Pattock, a city three hundred miles farther on in Upper Hungary, and accompanied each other to Comora in Schut, an island in the Danube, encompassed with dangers on all hands: on the one side, of being killed by the Turks, or of being put to death at Newhausel, according to the practice of that garrison towards those who were found there, it being tributary to the Turks, without permission. At Comora, first, Moore was apprehended, searched and stripped, and carried to the guards with his hands and feet shackled, and an insinuation was thrown out that he should be roasted on a spit. Philly was afterward apprehended at his lodgings. They were committed to separate prisons; Moore to the Stock-house, and Philly to a room appropriated to the inhuman purpose of putting prisoners to the rack. On the next day they were brought before the inquisitor to be examined, by whom, among other questions, they were asked, If they did not know that Catholics had laws to burn and torment heretics, and such as carried such books as they had with them? To which Moore warily replied, "I should not have expected such dealings among good Christians." They

were for eight days repeatedly brought to, examination, and insnaring questions put to them, as, What they thought of the sacrament? to which Moore replied, "The flesh profiteth little; it is the spirit that quickeneth." This inquisitor was so strangely unacquainted with the Scriptures, that, in his surprise, he applied to a priest present, "Sir father, how is that?" who, recollecting himself, said, "He did remember such an expression." The inquisitor next asked him if he would turn Catholic; to which he made this rational reply: "If I should do so for fear of favour of you, the Lord not requiring it of me, I should not have peace in my conscience, and the displeasure of the Lord would be more intolerable than yours;" adding, "that compulsion might make hypocrites; but not change the heart."

After this they were put to the torture; first, their thumbs were screwed to extort the confession of some crime, and then they were racked, with such violence in the case of Moore, that his chin was close to his breast, and his mouth so closed that he was almost choked. They were then threatened with death. Philly, by calling out to the governor, as he was passing in his coach, obtained some redress of their calamities; and they were allowed to earn a trifle, to buy bread, by working at the wheel-barrow, though often their wages were kept back. After sixteen weeks they were conveyed in chains, by a wagon, under a guard, to General Nadash, the emperor's lord-chamberlain. They were examined before him and several lords of the kingdom, some of whom seemed affected with their answers, and none objected thereto. They were sentenced, however, to be burned, if they would not embrace the popish religion; and a priest was sent to convert them. These endeavours proving ineffectual, they were removed to a place within about five German miles of Vienna, where, falling into the hands of priests, their perils became aggravated: they were again searched, their books and papers taken away, insnaring questions were put to them, and they were threatened with the execution of various tortures, and of the sentence of death. But the frauds and menaces of their persecutors were frustrated by the steadfastness of these confessors. Manacles were then put on their wrists, so small, as, when locked by main force, put them to extreme pain. They were thrust into a narrow hole with some Turks, that were prisoners, where they had scarcely room to sit down. At length they found a friend in the person who was invested with the chief civil authority in the place, whose dispositions to protect them and afford them relief were much strengthened by the influence of one Adam Bien, his barber, a religious man, who had been educated among the Hortesche brethren. The priests were restrained from keeping them any longer in their hole of a prison, and using them with the cruelty they had done before. Those who had distinguished themselves by promoting malicious insults, endeavoured to ingratiate themselves; and after the prospects of obtaining their liberty had been repeatedly clouded over by the sickness of the governor, or by the attention he had been induced to give to insinuations against them, and by some renewed suf-

* Gough, vol. ii., p. 51–63.

ferings from the priests and soldiers; by Adam Bien's steadfast friendship, and persevering solicitations in their favour, they were released, September, 1663.*

Whatever opinion may be entertained of the prudence of these and other pious persons belonging to the society of Quakers, in exposing themselves to such perils, without possessing ordinary or supernatural means of succeeding in their well-meant efforts, the patience, firmness, and fortitude which they displayed under the most trying circumstances, must be allowed singular merit and praise. Patience and meekness, indeed, were general characteristics of this people. They met and supported the exertions of malicious violence and wanton despotism with resigned acquiescence, and in humble dependance upon Divine protection and support, without fainting in their minds.

They were also distinguished, from the beginning, by their charitable regard towards each other. There were some among them who were not only examples of steadfastness, but, by their exhortations, in word and writing, encouraged their brethren to perseverance. In the time of the plague they were exemplary for the care and tenderness with which they relieved the affliction of the widows and orphans of their friends without that calamity carried off. They held occasional meetings in the city to provide for the necessities of the poor; and when the number of objects proved too many for the men to assist by these meetings, they called upon the most grave and tender-hearted of their female friends to aid them in the offices of humanity, who for this purpose met once a week. Not the resident inhabitants only were exercised in this care; but several, as George Whitehead, Alexander Parker, Josiah Coale, and others, came out of the country to London, as with their lives in their hands, supported by the sentiments of faith and resignation, to suffer with their friends there, whatever might be permitted to befall them, to strengthen and encourage them to keep up their meetings, to edify them with their gifts, and to visit and comfort the sick and imprisoned. And through all they were mercifully preserved from the infection, and from imprisonment in this season of danger.†

The benevolence of their minds was not confined to the acts of fraternal regards to one another, in the season of calamity and persecution, but took a wider scope. Their attention to their poor, that there should be no beggar among them, nor any sent to the parish for relief; and to afford their children instruction, and put them out apprentices to suitable trades, hath deservedly attracted notice, and commanded general approbation. They have, moreover, cheerfully paid their quota to the poor of their respective parishes, and proper objects of any denomination have been relieved by their private donations.‡ It frequently happened that justices and military officers, on coming to break up their general meeting at Skipton, when they saw their accounts of their collections and disbursements, and the care taken that one county should help another, as circumstances might require, have been obliged to commend their care,

and have left them undisturbed in the exercise of the laudable object of their meeting. The poor of other societies, frequently gathered in crowds upon these occasions, partook of their liberality; for it was their custom, after the meeting was over, to send to the bakers for bread, and distribute a loaf to each, how many soever they were.*

Our sketch of the history of this society will not be complete if we do not notice some who were eminent ministers in it, and died at this period.

The first to be mentioned is Richard Hubberthorn, the son of a reputable yeoman in the north of Lancashire, who, after two months' imprisonment, through the effect of the throng of prisoners and the vitiated air on his tender constitution, died in Newgate on the 17th of June, 1662. He was from his youth inclined to piety, sobriety, and virtue. When he arrived to years of maturity, he obtained a post in the Parliament's army, and preached occasionally to the soldiers. When he joined the society of the Quakers, he quitted, agreeably to their principle of peace, his military employment. He was one of the first ministers of this society. His stature was low, his constitution infirm, and his voice weak; but he was powerful, able, and successful as a minister. In the exercise of this office he travelled, in different parts of the nation, for the space of nine years. He knew his season, when to speak and when to be silent; when he spoke, he delivered himself with plainness and pertinency to the subject before him. He was a man of much meekness, humility, patience, and brotherly kindness; and of distinguished equanimity, neither easily depressed in adversity, nor elated in prosperity. His life was spent in acts of righteousness and the pursuit of peace, of which his latter end exhibited the happy effects, the peaceful tenour of his conscience stripping death of all its terrors, and, in the full assurance of faith, he looked forward to the near approach of future happiness.

About the same time, and in the same prison, died, in the twenty-eighth year of his age, having been ten years a zealous and powerful preacher, Mr. Edward Burrough. He was born in or near Underbarrow, a village in the barony of Kendal, in Westmoreland, of parents in repute for their honest and virtuous conduct, and of competent substance. His puerile years exhibited proofs of manly sense and religious thoughtfulness. He was fond of the conversation of such as were in esteem for piety, and placed his satisfaction in perusing the Scriptures, in which he was well versed. He was educated in the Episcopal way of worship; but, about the age of twelve years, began to frequent the meetings of the Prerbyterians, till he was seventeen. He then became possessed with serious apprehensions of great deficiency in the knowledge of God and internal purity of heart, and felt considerable uneasiness and fear; and, dissatisfied with the doctrine he heard, as resulting, in his view, from mere speculation and the experience of others, and not the fruit of their own experience, he withdrew from the teachers of it. On George Fox's coming into the parts where he resided, he went to hear him preach, and afterward entered into reasoning with him upon religious subjects. The con-

* Gough, vol. ii., p. 63–83.   † Ibid., p. 149, 150.
‡ Ibid., p. 189.

* Gough, vol. i., p. 432.

sequence was, that he joined the society of the Quakers, in which he became a most servicea-ble member and eminent minister. On forming this connexion his relations discarded him, his father expelled him from his house, and he felt himself exposed to many hardships, all which evils he bore with exemplary patience. His la-borious exertions, both by word and writing, were indefatigable, and his religious exercises as a preacher were the whole business of his life; he allowed himself few hours of repose, and did not appropriate one week at a time, for many years, to himself or his private concerns. He travelled through England, Scotland, Ireland, and Flanders; but the principal field of his min-isterial labours was London. As he was preach-ing at the meeting at Bull-and-Mouth, he was violently taken down by the soldiers, and carried before Alderman Brown, who committed him to Newgate. Some weeks after, he was brought to trial at the Old Bailey, fined by the court twenty marks, and condemned to lie in prison till he paid the fine, which amounted to perpet-ual imprisonment, as the principles of the Qua-kers led them to consider a voluntary and ac-tive compliance with the penalty as a tacit con-fession of guilt. A special order from the king was sent to the sheriffs for his release, and that of some other prisoners, but the magistrates of the city found means to prevent the execution of it. He met his dissolution, brought on by disease and imprisonment, with the consolatory review of a life spent in the service of his Crea-tor. "I have had the testimony of the Lord's love unto me," said he, "from my youth; and my heart, O Lord, hath been given up to do thy will. I have preached the Gospel freely in this city, and have often given up my life for thy Gospel's sake; and now, O Lord, my life open my heart, and see if it be not right before thee." As his dissolution drew nigh, he said, "Though this body of clay must turn to dust, yet I have a testimony that I have served God faithfully in my generation; and that spirit that hath lived, and acted, and ruled in me, shall yet break forth in thousands."

Another zealous preacher among this people was William Ames, who travelled in the work of the ministry not in England only, but much in Holland and Germany, where several were convinced by him, especially in the palatinate. These palatines, removing soon after to Penn-sylvania, escaped the general devastation of their country by the French, which happened soon after. Ames was, at first, after his mind took a serious turn, a teacher among the Bap-tists; he was also a military officer in Crom-well's army in Ireland, in which post, being strict and regular in his own conduct, he exerted himself to introduce and preserve the like regu-larity among the soldiers under his command by a strict discipline. Francis Howgill and Ed-ward Burrough coming into Ireland, he went to hear them, and embraced their doctrine. He and several others were afterward taken, by two musketeers, out of a private house in Lon-don, forced to St. Paul's churchyard, where they were derided and abused by the soldiers, and afterward taken before Alderman Brown, who committed them to hard labour in Bridewell. Here they were so severely treated, that Ames grew dangerously ill; and being an inhabitant

of Amsterdam, he was discharged for fear of his dying in prison. He returned, upon his release, to this city, and supported himself by wool-combing, but so injured in his health that he never recovered, but died within the current year, 1662.*

Near the close of the year 1662, John Aud-land, a native of Camsgill, in Westmoreland, was taken off by a consumption in an early stage of life. When a child, he discovered a quick understanding and retentive memory. As he approached a state of maturity, he applied the attention of his mind to religious thought and to reading the Scriptures, and became an eminent teacher among the Independents, of whom he had a very numerous auditory. He was one of the principal preachers at Firbank Chapel, at the time when George Fox had a memorable meeting there, and became a con-vert to his doctrine, which he afterward zeal-ously and ably exerted himself to disseminate, travelling through sundry parts of the nation with this view; foregoing the comforts of do-mestic life, and separating himself, with her con-sent, from his wife, who entered into his views, a virtuous and well-accomplished young wom-an, of a good family, to whom he was married about the twentieth year of his age. He was one of the earliest preachers of this persuasion who visited the city of Bristol and the western counties. The number of his hearers increased to such a degree in that place, that, for want of a house large enough, the meetings were fre-quently held in an orchard. He was a parta-ker with his brethren in repeated imprisonments and abuses of his person. His sufferings and exertions were beyond his strength, and brought on a cough, which appeared consumptive, and finally terminated in a slow fever, that put a pe-riod to his life at the age of thirty-four years. He was not only preserved in peaceful serenity of mind at this solemn season, but at times filled even with joy at the prospect of his approaching felicity; from the impression whereof his soul, under extreme bodily weakness, was raised up in praise to the Almighty, and in prayer for the prosperity of his friends in righteousness.†

In 1667, after about fifteen years spent in act-ing and suffering for those doctrines he had re-ceived for truth, died Richard Farnsworth, ex-horting his friends with affecting energy and strength of spirit, as if he were in full health, and giving evidence of his full assurance of faith. He was one of the first who embraced the principles of George Fox, soon after his re-lease from his imprisonment at Derby, while the name of Quaker was but just known. He join-ed him in society and ministerial labours, and many were converted by him. For not pulling off his hat to a justice of peace in the streets of Banbury, in 1656, he was, after the justice had struck it off in passion, sent for and committed to prison. Next day, when passion subsided, his release was offered him on paying the jailer's fees, and promising to leave the town that night. He would promise nothing, knowing that he had been illegally committed. The oath of abjura-tion was then tendered to him, and on his refu-sing it, he was recommitted to prison, where he lay about six months.‡

---

* Gough, vol. ii., p. 2–15. † Ibid., p. 83–88.
‡ Ibid., p. 222, 223.

In the latter part of the year 1668 and the beginning of the next, this society was deprived of three eminent and serviceable members: Thomas Loe, Josiah Coale, and Francis Howgill.

Thomas Loe was a man of fine natural temper, easy, affable, and pleasing in conversation, benevolent and sympathizing in his disposition. He travelled on foot through the greatest part of the nation, and visited Ireland several times. His gifts were attractive, and he had generally crowded audiences. He was several times imprisoned for his testimony, and his natural strength was impaired by his travels and labours. His convert, William Penn, visited him in his last sickness, whom he addressed thus: "Bear thy cross and stand faithful to God, then He will give thee an everlasting crown of glory that shall not be taken from thee. There is no other way which shall prosper than that which the holy men of old walked in. God hath brought immortality to light, and life immortal is felt. His love overcomes my heart. Glory be to His name for evermore." He accosted others with similar sentiments; and his parting breath expressed a song of praise to that almighty Being whose goodness preserved him through life, and deserted him not in his end.*

Josiah Coale was born at Winterborne, Gloucestershire, near Bristol, and received his impressions in favour of the Quakers' doctrine under the preaching of John Audland, about the year 1655. He proved an able and zealous minister: his testimony was sharp and piercing against the workers of iniquity, while it flowed in a stream of life and encouraging consolation to the pious and virtuous. In 1656, after having been first grievously abused by the populace, and dragged bareheaded under the spouts in a time of rain, he was imprisoned in Newgate, at Bristol. In the same year, he was, with three other friends, severely abused and beaten by the mob, and then committed to prison by the mayor, at Melcomb Regis. In 1658, a sense of duty determined him to pay a religious visit to the English colonies in America. As no master of a ship would take him to New-England, for fear of the penalties enacted in that state against such as should bring in any Quakers, he got a passage, in company with Thomas Thirston, to Virginia; from whence they made their way on foot through a wilderness of several hundred miles, till then deemed impassable for any but the Indians. By these people, of the Susquehanna tribe, they were treated with remarkable attention and hospitality, entertained with lodging and provisions, and furnished with guides to the Dutch plantations. Their journey was, however, attended with great hardships and dangers. They met with very different treatment from the lofty professors of New-England, whose tempers were imbittered, whose natural tenderness and compassion were eradicated, by false principles of religion. Here Coale was violently haled out and sent to prison, and some time after banished to Maryland. He travelled through this state and Barbadoes; and, in Europe, through most parts of England, in Holland, and the Low Countries; going through many perils, imprisonments, and persecutions, valiant in what he regarded as the

cause of truth, undaunted in danger, and borne above the fear of man by the supports of a peaceful conscience. He not only in his travels bore his own charges abroad, but was an exemplary pattern of liberality at home, and freely spent his estate in the service to which he devoted himself. His natural temper was cheerful, religion tempered it with seriousness; his unaffected affability was mixed with a circumspect and exemplary deportment; his whole conversation illustrated the purity of his religion, and was an ornament to his profession. After ministerial services of twelve years, he fell into a decline, and departed in the arms of his friends, as one falling into a deep sleep, full of consolation, exhorting others to "be faithful to God, and have a single eye to his glory," expressing his own confidence that "the majesty of God was with him, and his crown of life upon him," at the age of thirty-five years and two months.*

The last person to be noticed is Francis Howgill, a principal as well as early promulgator of the doctrine of the Quakers, and a valuable member of their community. He was a native of Westmoreland, and received his education, for the priest's office in the Church, at the university; but, being scrupulous of complying with the ceremonies, he withdrew from the National Church, and joined the Independents, and was an eminent preacher among them, laborious and zealous as a minister, and esteemed for his virtue and exemplary conversation. In 1652 he became a proselyte to the doctrines of George Fox, on hearing him at Firbank Chapel. He was, soon after this, sent, with James Naylor, to the jail at Appleby. In 1654, he and Edward Burrough, in company with Anthony Pearson, travelled to London, and were the first of this society who held meetings in that city, and by whose preaching many there were brought over to the same profession. While he was there, he went to court to intercede with Oliver Cromwell, that a stop might be put to the persecution of the members of his society, and he wrote also to the protector, on the same subject, in a plain and bold strain, but without any good effects. It does not appear that they met with any personal molestations in the metropolis; and when they had gathered and settled meetings there, they went to Bristol. Multitudes flocked to hear them, and many embraced their doctrine. The clergy were alarmed, and they were summoned before the magistrates, and were commanded to leave the city immediately. To this order they answered, "We came not in the will of man, nor stand in the will of man, but when He shall move us to depart who moved us to come hither, we shall obey; we are free-born Englishmen, and have served the commonwealth faithfully, being free in the sight of God from the transgression of any law: to your commandments we cannot be obedient; but if by violence you put us out of the city, and have power to do it, we cannot resist." Having said this, they went out of the court, but tarried in the city, preaching as before, for some time.† In 1663, Francis Howgill was summoned before the justices, as he was in the market-place at Kendal on his business; and, for refusing the

---

* Gough, vol. ii., p. 229-231; and vol. i., p. 318, 31C.

* Gough, vol. ii., p. 231-236.
† Ibid., vol. i., p. 112, 126, 144, &c.

oath of allegiance, was committed to prison till the summer assizes, at which the oath was again tendered to him, and upon refusal an indictment was drawn up against him, which he traversed: But as he would not enter into bond for his good behaviour, which he considered as a tacit acquiescence in the charge of ill behaviour, and a bar to attendance on meetings, he was recommitted to prison. At the spring assizes he was brought to his trial, when, under a rigorous sentence of præmunire, he was sent back to the prison, where he remained, till released by death, for nearly five years, deprived of every comfort and convenience his persecutors could take from him. He died, after a sickness of nine days, the 20th of January, 1668-9. During his confinement he evidenced the peaceful and even tenour of his soul by his patience, and preserved to the last an amiable equanimity, which had characterized him through life, the serenity of his conscience bearing him superior to his sufferings and to the fear of death. He wrote a copious treatise against oaths, wherein he maintained the unlawfulness of swearing under the Gospel. His virtues, innocence, and integrity of life were conspicuous. He was generally respected by those who knew him; his sufferings were commiserated, and the unmerited enmity and cruelty of his persecutors condemned. Several of the principal inhabitants of Appleby, and particularly the mayor, visited him in his sickness; and some of them praying that God might speak peace to his soul, he answered, "He hath done it." He also expressed himself thus: "That he was content, and ready to die; praising the Almighty for the many sweet enjoyments and refreshing seasons he had been favoured with on his prison bed, wherein he lay, freely forgiving all who had a hand in his restraint." A few hours before he departed, he said, "I have sought the way of the Lord from a child, and lived innocently as among men; and if any inquire concerning my latter end, let them know that I die in the faith in which I lived and suffered for." After these words, he uttered some others in prayer to God, and so finished his life in perfect peace, in the fiftieth year of his age.

Mr. Gough has preserved a letter of useful instructions, addressed to his daughter, which he left behind him. His will, made some time before his decease, bequeathed out of his real estate, his personal having been forfeited to the king, a legacy to his poor friends in those parts where he lived, and a token of his affectionate remembrance to several of his brethren and fellow-labourers in the ministry.*

———————

CHAPTER II.

FROM THE DECLARATION OF INDULGENCE TO THE REVOLUTION. A.D. 1674-1688.

When the king published his declaration of indulgence, the Quakers, who did not rank with any political party merely to enjoy the ease and liberty to which peaceable and virtuous subjects have a right, accepted the protection it afforded. But those who were at liberty, from that spirit of sympathy and brotherly concern

* Gough, vol. ii., p. 31, 96-108, and 236-241.

which pervades the society, could not enjoy their own exemption from penal statutes without exerting themselves for the relief of their brethren who had been, for several years, kept immured in uncomfortable prisons. George Whitehead, Thomas Moor, and Thomas Green, invited by the present disposition of government, waited on the king and council to solicit the discharge of their friends, who, convicted on transportation, or on præmunire, or for fines, confiscations, or fees, were still in prison; and they were so successful as to obtain the king's letters patent, under the great seal, for their pardon and discharge. In the accomplishing of this business, a difficulty arose from the amount of the fees to be paid in the sundry offices through which the letters patent would pass, as upward of four hundred persons would be included in them.* But when the lord-keeper, Sir Orlando Bridgeman, generously and voluntarily remitted his fees, they applied to the king to moderate the rest, who accordingly issued his order, "that the pardon, though comprehending a great number of persons, do yet pass as one pardon, and pay but as one."

Their success gave them an opportunity to show the universality of their charity to other Dissenters, many of whom were confined in prison, and whose solicitors, observing the happy issue of the Quakers' suit, applied to Whitehead for his advice and assistance, to have the names of their own friends inserted in the same instrument. In consequence of his advice, they petitioned the king, and obtained his warrant for that purpose. "This I was glad of," says Whitehead, "that they partook of the benefit through our industry. And, indeed, I was never spared to do give any of them my advice for their help, when any of them in straits have applied for it; our being of different judgments and societies did not abate my sympathy or charity, even towards them who, in some cases, had been our opposers." The Quakers were thus freed, for a time, from the severities of persecution. The public testimony which they continued, in the severest times, to bear to the principles they received as truth, and the firmness with which they held their meetings at the appointed times and places, or, when kept out of their places of worship by force, assembled in the streets, baffled the scheme of establishing uniformity, countenanced and assisted by the temporizing conduct of other Dissenters; and abated the heat of persecution, and blunted the edge of the sword before it reached the other sects; the more ingenuous of whom, therefore, esteemed their intrepidity, regarded them with gratitude as the bulwark that kept off the force of the stroke from themselves, and prayed that they might be preserved steadfast, and enabled to break the strength of the enemy. Some of the Baptists especially expressed a high opinion both of the people and their principles, which sustained them in undergoing sufferings that others thought of with terror.†

When the revocation of the indulgence, and the displeasure of the court against the Dissenters, let loose the whole tribe of informers, and

* The patent, when made out, contained eleven skins of vellum.

† Gough's History of the Quakers, vol. ii., p. 364-368.

gave fresh spirit to persecuting magistrates, prosecutions, in every mode of distress, were renewed against this people, at the capricious will of every justice. Severe proceedings against them were grounded on the statute of præmunire of James I. for refusing to swear; on the obsolete statute of £20 per month for absence from the parish church, which penalty, or two thirds of a person's estate, were seized by exchequer process ; and for tithes, to excommunication and procuring writs *de excommunicatio capiendo* to be issued, to throw them into prison. They became a prey to idle and profligate informers, encouraged and instigated by their superiors ; and, instead of obtaining durable and effectual relief, their sufferings became heavier and more aggravated during the remainder of this reign to the end of it.*

In 1675, William Hall, of Congleton, being fined £20 for a meeting at his house, had his house broken open, and two cartloads of goods, to the worth of £40, besides a mare, were carried away. About the same time cattle and goods to the value of £100 were taken from sundry persons in and about Nantwich ; and from one person the bed on which he lay, and even the dunghill in his yard.†

In the next year, prosecutions on the Conventicle Act subsided in London, but the rigorous enforcing of the ecclesiastical laws was rarely or never suspended. The number plundered, excommunicated, imprisoned, and of those who died in prison, was too large to be recited.‡ But while the penal laws were suffered to lie dormant in London, they were enforced with rigorous severity in other parts of the nation. In one instance, a poor man, with a wife and five children, had little to pay the fine for being at a meeting but his bed, which the compassion of the officers would not permit them to seize ; but the obdurate magistrate commanded them to take it. The wife, endeavouring afterward to maintain her children by baking a little bread, and selling it in the market, it was seized at one time to the value of nineteen pence, and at another to the value of fourteen pence. From another person, for a fine of £7, goods to the worth of near £18 were taken.§ The distresses made this year in Nottinghamshire, upon the members of this society, for their religious assemblies only, amounted to £712 and upward. In the city of Hereford, as prosecutions on the law were ineffectual to suppress their meetings, lawless violence and gross abuse were offered by the populace ; the windows of their meeting-houses were broken by stones, and sometimes the roof was untiled ; their assemblies were interrupted by the sound of the horn, shouting, and casting stones and filth, and their persons assaulted. The mob, instead of being restrained and punished for these outrages, were, if not stimulated to them, abetted and encouraged in them by the magistrates and clergy. Appeals to the Quarter Sessions for redress against exorbitant exactions were unsuccessful, as the juries were overawed, or their verdicts for the appellants rejected.‖

In the year 1677, the officers, encouraged by the magistrate, who acted the part of an inform-

er, took away from six friends in Cheshire, for one meeting, £200. In Gloucestershire, a justice of the peace, besides indicting at the sessions twenty-seven for absence from the national worship, who had suffered deeply before on the Conventicle Act, and levying heavy fines, unmercifully beat some with his own hands, plucked two out of the meeting by the hair of their heads, and drew his knife, if he had not been prevented by his servants, to wound others. At Plymouth, their meetings were forcibly interrupted and dispersed : their property suffered by fines and distresses, and their persons were abused by the rabble, and by the officers and soldiers of the garrison, who, among other insults, threw squibs of fire and hot burning coals upon them. In many other parts they were treated with no less severity. The parish officers were sometimes instigated by menacing letters, or impelled to act against their inclinations by the clergy exciting the justices to punish by fines and imprisonment, for neglect of duty, such whose moderation and humanity rendered them reluctant to prosecute or plunder their conscientious neighbours.*

Through the succeeding years they continued to be harassed with prosecutions on all the variety of penal laws, which were rigorously enforced on great numbers of this society, who suffered all the hardships imposed on them by unreasonable men with pious fortitude and resignation. In 1682, the persecution of this people broke out, and was carried on with uncommon outrage and cruelty at Bristol. The damage done to their meeting-houses was computed at £150. A rabble of rude boys was encouraged to insult and abuse the female part of the assembly, even women of repute and consideration, and to tear their dresses. The signal for this attack was, "Have a care of your hoods and scarfs." Many of them were thrown into prison, where their health was endangered for want of room, many beds being crowded into one small apartment ; and some were obliged to lie on the ground, in a filthy place which had been a dog-kennel. The remonstrances of the prisoners to the magistrates on the straitness and noisomeness of their prison, and the certificates of physicians on the subject, were treated with equal disregard. "As their constancy in the great duty of assembling to worship God, while at liberty, was invincible, so a prison could not confine the freedom of their spirits, or the impulse of their consciences : they continued the practice of this duty in their imprisonment." This drew on them gross abuse, even from the sheriff, who fell furiously on several, threw one headlong down to the great hazard of his life, and commanded another to be ironed and put down into the condemned felons' place. Many suffered, as in former years and other places, by heavy fines and grievous distraints : goods to the value of £155 being seized to discharge a fine of £79. When most or all of the men were imprisoned, the women kept up their religious meeting, till they also were cast into jail. When their parents were in confinement, the children, after their example, regularly held their meetings, behaving on those occasions with much gravity and composure, and undergoing many abuses with patience. Their age exempted

* Gough, vol. ii., p. 392–397. † Ibid., p. 406.
‡ Ibid., p. 414. § Ibid., p. 416, 417.
‖ Ibid., p. 420–424.

* Gough, vol. ii., p. 426–429, 438.

them from the lash of the law, but their minority could not screen them from furious assaults; some were put in the stocks, others were unmercifully beaten with twisted whalebone sticks. Persecution was not at this period peculiar to Bristol, but carried on, in most parts, with great animosity; and many families were ruined in their circumstances. In 1683, about eighty persons were at one time committed to Chester Castle, where they could find neither rooms nor lodgings for such a number, so that they were obliged for two nights, some of them to walk about, others to lie on tables and benches, and some on flags spread on the floor: At length thirty of them were put into a filthy dungeon, out of which the felons were then removed. In Somersetshire, informers were encouraged against them, and protected in perjury; their meeting-houses were defaced, and they were, in great numbers, imprisoned, fined, distrained, and excommunicated. When shut out of their meeting-houses for divers years, in and about the city of London, they assembled in the streets in all weather: this they did in the year 1683, for three months together, when the River Thames was so frozen that horses, coaches, and carts could pass to and fro upon it, and a street be erected and stand over it.* There was computed to be upward of seven hundred members of this society in the different prisons of England this year. Sir Christopher Musgrave, though a zealous churchman, expressed his utter dislike of the severe usage of this people, saying, "The prisons were filled with them, that many of them had been excommunicated and imprisoned for small matters, and that it was a shame and scandal for their church to use the Quakers so hardly on very trivial occasions."† Severe prosecutions, similar acts of injustice, oppression, violence, and cruelty, against this society, marked the year 1684, which were the disgrace of the preceding years.‡

Among those who suffered from bigotry, armed with power, the name of George Fox takes the lead. After his return from America in 1673, as he was on his road to visit his mother on her deathbed, Fox and Thomas Lower, who was his wife's son-in-law, were seized as they were in conversation in a friend's parlour at Tredington in Worcestershire, and sent to the county jail. They applied, by letter, to the lord-lieutenant and deputy-lieutenant of the county, for the interposition of their authority for their release: stating their case, the illegality of their commitment, and Fox's solicitude for liberty to pay the last debt of affection and duty to his dying parent. But the application was ineffectual. Lower, by the interposition of his brother, who was the king's physician, might have obtained his liberty, as a letter to Lord Windsor for his release was procured; but, bearing too great a respect to his father-in-law to leave him in prison alone, he suppressed the letter, and voluntarily continued his companion there. At the Quarter Sessions they were produced in court, when, on the examination, it appearing that they had been causelessly imprisoned, and had a right to an immediate release, the oaths of allegiance and supremacy were tendered to Fox, and on his refusing to

take them, he was remanded. But Lower, on account of his powerful connexions, was discharged. Soon after, Fox was removed by a habeas corpus to the King's Bench bar at Westminster. The judges, influenced by the reports and representation which Parker, the justice who first apprehended him, had dispersed, remanded him to Worcester jail; only indulging him with liberty to go down his own way, and at his leisure, provided he would not fail to be there by the following assizes, in April, 1674. He accordingly appeared, when the judge, Turner, who had before passed sentence of præmunire against him at Lancaster, referred the matter back again to the sessions. He was then charged with holding a meeting at Tredington from all parts of the nation, to the terrifying of the king's subjects. Though Fox vindicated himself from this misrepresentation, yet, as he again refused the oaths, an indictment was drawn up and delivered to the jury, who, under the instruction of the chairman, found the bill against him. This he determined to traverse; and, on refusing to give bail, or any other security for his appearance but his promise, he was sent back to prison. By the interposition of some moderate justices, however, in about two hours after he had liberty given him to go at large till the next Quarter Sessions. In the mean time he attended the yearly meeting in London, and delivered before some of the justices of the King's Bench a declaration of his fidelity to the king, and denial of the pope's supremacy and power; but, as his case was under cognizance of the Quarter Sessions at Worcester, the judges were unwilling to meddle with it, not being regularly before them. At the next sessions he appeared to traverse the indictment; but when he proceeded to show the errors which were sufficient to quash it, the oath was again required of him, and upon his refusal to take it, the jury found him guilty. An admonition of the consequence of a præmunire being given him in court, this was, after he was sent out of court, clandestinely recorded in his absence, for the sentence thereof; and, under it he was remanded to prison. Here he was seized with a great sickness, which reduced him to extreme weakness, and made his recovery doubtful. His wife came from the north to attend him, and solicit his discharge: after continuing with him three or four months, and her endeavours to procure his release proving unsuccessful, she went to London, and solicited the king in person, who would have released him by a pardon; but Fox declined obtaining his liberty in this mode, as he conceived that it would be a tacit acknowledgment of guilt; and he declared, "he had rather lie in prison all his days, than come out in any way dishonourable to the truth he made profession of." He preferred having the validity of his indictment tried before the judges, and with this view procured a habeas corpus to remove him to the King's Bench bar. On his appearing before four judges, his counsellor, Mr. Thomas Corbet, advanced a new plea in his favour, and gained himself great credit by ably urging "that by law they could not imprison a man upon præmunire." The judges required time to consult their books and statutes on this plea, and postponed the hearing until next day.

* Gough, vol. ii., p. 522–525, 528–532, 547, 548.
† Ibid., p. 536, 508.   ‡ Ibid., vol. iii., p. 24–30.

They then proceeded, though they found the advocate's opinion well founded, to examine the indictment, in which the errors were so many and so gross, that they were unanimous in judgment "that the indictment was quashed and void, and that George Fox ought to be set at liberty." Thus he honourably obtained his discharge, after an unjust imprisonment of a year and almost two months. Some of his enemies, insinuating " he was a dangerous man to be at liberty," moved the judges that the oaths might be tendered to him; but Sir Matthew Hale would not consent to it, saying, " he had, indeed, heard some such reports of George Fox, but he had also heard more good reports of him."*

He appears to have been unmolested after, till the year 1681, when he and his wife were sued in small tithes in the Exchequer, although they had in their answer to the plaintiff's bill proved that no such tithe had been demanded or paid off her estate during forty-three years she had lived there: yet, because they could not answer upon oath, they were run up to a writ of rebellion, and an order of court was issued to take them both into custody. Fox, understanding this, laid the case before the barons of the Exchequer. On the hearing of the cause, a sequestration was earnestly pleaded for, on the ground of his being a public man, as if that affected the merits and justice of the cause; and was obtained, though at first two of the barons declared that he was not liable to tithes; but one of them was afterward brought over to decide with the adverse barons: the sequestration was, however, limited to the sum proved due, to the great disappointment of the prosecutor's aim, who wanted it without limitation, that they might be their own carvers in making distraint. In the course of this trial was produced an engagement, under the hand and seal of George Fox, that he would never meddle with his wife's estate: this raised the admiration of the judges, as an instance of self-denial rarely to be met with in these ages.†

In 1680, George Whitehead and Thomas Burr, as they were on a journey from different quarters to pay a religious visit to their friends, happened to meet at Norwich. As the former was preaching on the succeeding first day of the week, a rude company, chiefly of informers, rushed into the meeting with tumult and violence, and pulled him down; to the requisition to show some legal authority for their proceedings, they returned abusive language, only with an insinuation to the people " that he might be a Jesuit." The sheriff, coming afterward, took them prisoners, and carried them before the recorder, Francis Bacon, Esq., who was a justice. He examined them of their names, habitations, and trades; " if they were in orders, or had orders from Rome." A fine of £20 each was demanded of them; on refusing to pay this, the oath of allegiance was proposed. While the examination was going on, the informer, with the sanction of the justice, went to seize their horses, but was disappointed in his attempt, as they had been removed without the knowledge of the prisoners. The recorder poured out his bitter invectives, and threatened to have them hanged if they did not abjure the realm, and if

the king would, by his orders, enforce the execution of a statute made in the reign of Queen Elizabeth. They were then committed to jail till the ensuing sessions. Then, after the recorder had, by taunting reflections and partial proceedings, expressed his aversion to them, they were discharged by the court from the charges exhibited in the mittimuses; but as they refused again the oath, which he insisted upon administering to them, they were recommitted to prison till the following sessions. In the mean time he was deprived of his office; in consequence of which change and the interposition of friends, they were, at the sessions, cleared by proclamation, and discharged from their imprisonment, after a confinement of sixteen weeks. It showed the prejudice and enmity of this man, that he first insinuated that they were probably papists; and when they procured certificates to the contrary, he would not permit them to be read in the court.*

In the next and succeeding year, George Whitehead was fined three or four times; and the loss he sustained by distraints, and by the expenses of inefficacious appeals, besides the damage done to his house and goods, amounted to £61 7s. The evil of those seizures was aggravated by a particular instance of injustice in the distrainers, who would not suffer an inventory to be taken, or the goods, chiefly in grocery ware, to be weighed or appraised. On one occasion, two friends, for persuading the constables to moderation, and to suffer an inventory to be taken, were apprehended and prosecuted for a riot, on the evidence of one constable; for which they were fined, committed to Newgate, and confined there ten weeks.†

The fines levied on this people, on the statute of £20 for absence from the national worship, amounted, in the year 1683, to the enormous sum of £16,400, for which several were distrained; but how much of these fines was actually levied is not certainly known.

In this year, the case of Richard Vickris deserves particular notice. He was the son of Mr. Robert Vickris, a merchant and alderman of Bristol; he embraced the sentiments of the Quakers in his youth; but, to divert him from joining them, his father sent him abroad to travel in France. Here he was a witness to the superstitions of the ceremonious religion of that country, which created a disgust, and confirmed him in the adoption of one that rejected ceremony and vain show. His father's views were disappointed, and on his return home he openly professed himself a Quaker, at the risk of a variety of sufferings and hardships. In 1680 he was imprisoned upon an excommunication; he was afterward, for attending meetings, subject to frequent fines and distraints, and at last he was proceeded against on the statute of the 35th of Elizabeth. At the sessions before Easter, in 1683, he was indicted on that statute; demurring to the jurisdiction of the court, and refusing to plead, he was committed to prison. At a following sessions he was admitted to bail, and at the midsummer sessions procured a habeas corpus. His trial was hastily brought on in August, though he solicited time to prepare his defence. He found means, however, to retain counsel, who ably pleaded his cause, as

* Gough, vol. ii. p. 377–391.   † Ibid., p. 514, 515.   * Gough, vol. ii., p. 501–505.   † Ibid., p. 520, 521

signed a variety of errors in his indictment, and showed that the witnesses had not established the charge against him. The court overruled every plea, and the jury (selected from men of mean occupation) found their verdict guilty; and sentence was passed on him to conform, or abjure the realm in three months; or suffer death as a felon, without benefit of clergy. He lay in prison under this sentence till the next year, when, the time for his abjuring the realm being expired, he was liable to the execution of it, to which his enemies seemed determined to proceed. That they might give some colour to their design, they blackened and calumniated his character, representing him as a person disaffected to government, and endeavouring, before they took away his life, to despoil him of his good name. His wife, in her distress, determined on a personal application to government; with this view, she took a journey to London, and, by the assistance of her friends, got admission to the Duke of York, who bore the chief sway at court, and laid her husband's hard case before him. When he had heard it, he replied, "that neither his royal brother nor himself desired that any of his subjects should suffer for the exercise of their consciences who were of peaceable behaviour under his government." Accordingly, effectual directions for his discharge were given. He was removed by habeas corpus from Newgate in Bristol to London, and brought to the King's Bench bar: there, upon the errors in the indictment assigned by Counsellor Pollexfen, he was legally discharged by Sir George Jefferies. His father survived his return only three days, by whose will he succeeded to his estate and seat at Chew Magna, in which he fixed his residence, and lived in honour, conspicuous for his virtue and benevolence, and an ornament to his place and station.*

The Quakers, under the severe sufferings to which their body in general, and some individual members of their society in particular, were exposed, were not wanting in lawful and commendable measures to procure an exemption from these grievous evils. In the year 1674, application was made to the judges, before they went their several circuits, for their compassionate attention to the hard cases of several of the sufferers, and to interpose their authority to secure them relief, in the following address:

"*To the king's justices appointed for the several circuits throughout England.*

"Many of our friends, called Quakers, being continued prisoners, many prosecuted to great spoil by informers, and on *qui-tam* writs, and by presentments and indictments for £20 *per mensem*, in divers counties throughout England, only on the account of religion and tender conscience towards Almighty God, we esteem it our duty to remind you of their suffering condition, as we have done from time to time, humbly entreating you in the circuits to inquire into the several causes of their commitments, and other sufferings which they lie under, and to extend what favour you can for their ease and relief, praying the Almighty to preserve and direct you."†

But little redress could be obtained. In 1677, an account being taken, at the yearly meeting,

of sufferings by confiscation to two thirds of the estates of those who had been prosecuted on the 23d of Elizabeth, a specification of this grievance was drawn up and laid before the Parliament then sitting, with a petition for relief, but without effect.* Towards the close of this year, George Fox, having returned from Holland, and visited the meetings of his friends in various parts of England, on coming to London found them engaged in fresh solicitations for relief from prosecutions on the laws made against popish recusants only; and he joined them in these applications; but a sudden prorogation of Parliament put a stop to their proceedings. When it met again, he, William Penn, George Whitehead, and others, renewed their suit, and they conceived some hopes of relief, as many of the members, convinced that they suffered grievously and unjustly, and were much misrepresented by their adversaries, manifested a tender and compassionate regard towards them. But the attention of Parliament was soon called off by the discovery of what was called the Popish Plot; an advantage was taken of the alarm this occasioned to increase the rigorous persecution of a people of opposite principles and conduct, under the pretext of the necessity, at this season of danger, to exert additional vigilance in guarding against seditious assemblies; and some members, whose residence, occupation, and manner of life were well known, were imprisoned under a pretended suspicion of being papists or concealed Jesuits.† Penn had several years before this been happily successful in solicitations for friends suffering by heavy fines and imprisonments in Ireland: for, at a half-yearly meeting held at his house in 1670, an account of their sufferings was drawn up in an address to the lord-lieutenant, which was presented to him, and an order of council obtained for the release of those who were imprisoned.‡ In Scotland, the persecuted members of this society met with an advocate in Barclay, and owed some relief to his powerful exertions. In 1676, the magistrates of Aberdeen made a handle of the declaration issued by the council at Edinburgh, re-enforcing former acts of Parliament against conventicles, to oppress the Quakers, many of whom were seized, committed to prison, detained near three months without being called before the commissioners, and, notwithstanding the able defence they set up, were fined in different sums, but in general to a heavy amount, and remanded to prison till the fines were paid. Robert Barclay, being then in London, gained admittance to the king, delivered to him a narrative of the severe and irregular proceedings of the magistrates, and interceded with him to recommend their case to the favourable notice of the council of Scotland. On this, the king ordered the Earl of Lauderdale to recommend the narrative to their consideration. The matter was referred to the former commissioners, in conjunction with three others; but their liberty was not obtained till the fines were discharged by exorbitant and oppressive distraints!§ When, in 1680, the Quakers were maliciously represented as concerned in the Popish Plot, George Fox published a declaration, addressed to the Parliament, in defence of him-

---

* Gor.gh, vol. ii., p. 539-544. † Ibid., p. 394.

* Gough, vol. ii., p. 425. † Ibid., p. 433-435.
‡ Ibid., p. 479. § Ibid., p. 460-470.

self and friends, to remove such suspicions, professing it to be their "principle and testimony to deny and renounce all plots and plotters against the king or any of his subjects; that, in tenderness of conscience, they could not swear or fight, but that they would use every endeavour in their power to save the king and his subjects, by discovering all plots and plotters that should come to their knowledge; and praying not to be put on doing those things which they had suffered so much and so long for not doing."* When, in the same year, a bill was brought into Parliament to exempt his majesty's Protestant subjects, dissenting from the Church of England, from the penalties of the act of the 35th of Elizabeth, the Quakers, with a laudable attention to their own ease, and from a generous sympathy with their friends under persecution, improved the favourable opportunity for promoting liberty of conscience. Divers of them attended the committee, when the bill was committed, early and late, in order to solicit the insertion of such clauses as might give ease to the tender consciences of their friends, whose religious dissent was scrupulous in some matters beyond other Dissenters; and they obtained a clause to be inserted for accepting a declaration of fidelity instead of the oath of allegiance. Although this design failed, by the bill being lost, yet a foundation was laid for reviving and completing it in the succeeding reign of King William III. But in the following year an event took place which must be considered as giving a turn to the fortunes of this society, and advancing them, in the event, to a peculiar degree of respectability and influence. Sir William Penn had, at the time of his death, a considerable debt due to him from the crown, either for arrears or advances made to government in the sundry expeditions in which he was engaged, while he was employed as an admiral, both under Oliver Cromwell and King Charles II, To discharge this debt, the king, by letters patent bearing date the 4th of March, 1680–1, granted to his son William Penn, and his heirs, that province lying on the west of the river of Delaware, in North America, formerly belonging to the Dutch, and then called the New Netherlands. This grant, by which Penn and his heirs were made governors and absolute proprietors of that tract of land, was owing to the influence of the Duke of York, with whom Admiral Penn was a peculiar favourite. In the summer of 1682 Penn took possession of this province, and he formed a government in it on the most liberal principles with respect to the rights of conscience. The leading article of his new constitution was this: "That all persons living in this province, who confess and acknowledge the one almighty and eternal God to be the creator, upholder, and ruler of the world, and that hold themselves obliged in conscience to live peaceably and justly in civil society, shall in nowise be molested or prejudiced for their religious persuasion or practice in matters of faith and worship; nor shall they be compelled at any time to frequent or maintain any religious worship, place, or ministry whatsoever." This settlement, in the first instance, afforded an asylum to many of his friends, who were glad to remove to a government formed on principles

* Gough, vol. ii., p. 506.

of humanity, and with a religious regard to justice and equity.* When the system of legislation was matured and completed, it excited the admiration of the universe. This oppressed society, in a few years, had the happiness and honour of seeing its tenets fixed on the other side of the Atlantic in security and peace, and itself extending through a wide territory, which enlarged the domains of their native country, and made a principal figure in the New World. The wisdom and virtues of the founder of this government, the excellent principles on which it was formed, and the prosperity to which it rose, reflected credit on the Quakers, and gave them weight in the political scale. Civil society has felt its obligations to them; and from this time their religious profession became more and more secure and respectable. The prognostications of William Penn, it hath been observed, have been remarkably verified. "If friends here keep to God, and in the justice, mercy, equity, and fear of the Lord, their enemies will be their footstool."

During the preceding period, from the declaration of indulgence to the end of Charles II.'s reign, this society lost several active and eminent members by death.

Among these was William Baily, who died 1675, at sea, in his voyage from the West Indies. He had preached among the Baptists at Pool in Dorsetshire, when, convinced by the ministry of George Fox, he embraced the principles of the Quakers in 1655, among whom he became a bold and zealous preacher, not in England only, but while he followed a seafaring life in distant countries, being concerned to propagate righteousness whenever an opportunity presented itself, and he displayed a like fortitude in suffering for his testimony; for he was frequently imprisoned in different jails, both during the time of the commonwealth and after the Restoration. He also suffered much corporeal abuse by blows, by being thrown down and dragged along the ground by the hair of his head, trampled upon by a corpulent man, and his mouth and jaws attempted to be rent asunder. On a voyage from Barbadoes, he was visited with a disease which terminated his life and sufferings. Among other sensible observations, expressive of the serenity of his mind, and of devout confidence and hope, addressing himself to the master of the vessel, he said, "Shall I lay down my head in peace upon the waters?† Well, God is the God of the whole universe; and though my body sink, I shall live atop of the waters." He afterward added, "The creating word of the Lord endures forever."‡

* Gough's History of the Quakers, vol. ii., p. 515, and vol. iii., p. 131–147.
† Gough, vol. ii., p. 407–411.
‡ This William Baily married Mary Fisher, a woman of singular ardour and resolution in the propagation of her religious principles; for, besides going to Boston in America, and meeting severe sufferings there, she engaged, after her return to England, in a more arduous undertaking. This was to pay a visit to Sultan Mohammed IV., encamped with his army near Adrianople. She proceeded on her way as far as Smyrna, when the English consul stopped her, and sent her back to Venice. Not disheartened from the prosecution of her design, she made her way by land, and escaped any manner of abuse, through a long journey of five or six hundred miles. She went

In 1679 died, at Goodnestone Court in Kent, in the sixty-third year of his age, Isaac Pennington, of Chalfont in Buckinghamshire, an honourable, useful, and virtuous member of this society. He was heir to a fair inheritance, being the eldest son of Alderman Pennington, of London, a noted member of the Long Parliament, and nominated, though he never sat, one of the king's judges. His education had all the advantages the schools and universities of his own country could afford him; his rank in life threw him into the company of some of the most learned and considerable men of the age; his understanding was by nature good; his judgment and apprehension quick; his disposition was mild and affable; and his conversation cheerful, but guarded, equally divested of moroseness and levity. From his childhood he was religiously inclined, and conversant with the Scriptures; the wonder of his acquaintance, from his awful frame of mind and retired life. When he first met with the writings of the Quakers, he threw them aside with disdain; and when he fell into conversation with some of them, though they engaged his affectionate regard, yet he could not but view them in a contemptuous light, as a poor and weak generation. But afterward, being invited to a meeting in Bedfordshire where George Fox preached, his prejudices gave way; he joined the society, against all the influence of connexions and worldly prospects, and became a very eminent and serviceable member in it. He diligently visited and administered to the afflicted in body and mind. He opened his heart and house to the reception of friends. His preaching was very successful in proselyting many and conforming many. He was an excellent pattern of piety, virtue, and the strictest morality. He was a most affectionate husband, a careful and tender father, a mild and gentle master, a sincere and faithful friend, compassionate and liberal to the poor; affable to all, ready to do good to all men, and careful to injure none. But neither rank of life, benevolence of disposition, inculpable innocence of demeanour, nor the universal esteem of his character, could secure him from the sufferings attendant upon his religious profession. His imprisonments were many, and some of them long and severe. These he bore with great firmness and serenity, and the sharp and painful distemper which put an end to his life gave no shock to his internal peace.[*]

In the next year, 1680, died, leaving behind him deep impressions of grateful respect and

to the camp alone, and obtained an audience of the sultan, who received her with great courtesy, and heard her with much seriousness and gravity, invited her to stay in the country, and offered her a guard to Constantinople. This she declined, but reached that city in safety without the least injury or insult, and afterward arrived in England. The conduct of the Mohammedans towards her, as Gough remarks, was a striking contrast to that of the professors of New England. "We cannot but regret," he properly adds, "that the best religion the world was ever blessed with, and in its own purity so far surpassing in excellence, should, on comparison with human infidelity, be so tarnished through the degeneracy of its professors, who, under the name of Christians, in morality, generosity, and humanity, fall far short of those who name not the name of Christ."—*Gough*, vol. i., p. 423.   * Ibid., vol. ii., p. 430–447.

honourable esteem, in the hearts of many, Giles Barnadiston, of Clare in Suffolk, aged fifty-six. He was born in 1624, of a respectable and opulent family, and being designed for the pulpit in the Establishment, he received a liberal education both in seminaries of literature and in university, where he spent six years. But when he was called on to accept an offer of preferment in the Church, and to take orders, from a consciousness of wanting the internal purity and spiritual wisdom essential to a minister of the Gospel, he resolutely declined the proposal. Though in this instance he was governed by a just and serious view of things, he had not firmness to resist the allurements of pleasure and sensual gratifications. On the breaking out of the civil war, he obtained a colonel's commission in the army; but he soon grew weary of a military life, accompanied with violence and bloodshed, laid down his commission, and retired to Wormingford Lodge in Essex, commenced a stricter life than before, and became thoughtful about the way of salvation. In this state of mind he felt an inclination to acquaint himself with the principles of the Quakers, and in 1661 invited some of them to his house; the consequence of his conversation with George Fox the younger, and George Weatherly, who paid him a visit, was his joining himself with this society; and he willingly took part in the storm of persecution to which this people were exposed, and constantly attended their religious meetings in the hottest time of it. In 1669 he removed to Clare, the place of his nativity, and in the same year he made his appearance in the ministry, in which he acquitted himself with faithfulness, fervency, wisdom, and success. He had but a tender constitution; yet, animated by a devotedness to the glory of God, and by a generous concern to promote the well-being of mankind, he took many journeys, and travelled into Holland, as well as divers parts of England, to make known to others what he judged to be the truth. He died on his return from London to Chelmsford, after a short illness, in which he expressed his resignation, "that the Lord was his portion, and that he was freely given up to die, which was gain to him."[*]

In 1681 died, at Stafford, where he had resided several years, and left a good report among the inhabitants of the town, Thomas Taylor, aged sixty-five years, an ancient and faithful minister of this society. He was born at or near Shipton in Yorkshire, about the year 1616, and received a liberal education at the University of Oxford. He was first a lecturer in this county, and then obtained a living in Westmoreland, which he held till the year 1652, when he voluntarily relinquished it. His audience was principally composed of Puritans, among whom he ranked, for he declined the use of ceremonies, and would neither baptize children at the font, nor sign them with the sign of the cross. On having an interview with George Fox at Swarthmore, he embraced his doctrine, and joined him as a companion in his travels and ministerial labours. He resigned his living on a conviction of the unlawfulness of preaching for hire. He travelled through many parts of England, disseminating the doctrine of the Quakers, which he maintained at Oxford against the learned Dr.

     * Gough, vol. ii., p. 549–553.

Owen, at that time vice-chancellor of the university, with great advantage in the opinion of the academies. But his travels were interrupted by a succession of imprisonments, one of which lasted for ten years, till Charles II. issued his letters patent for the general discharge of the Quakers from prison in 1672. Supported by consciousness of a good cause, and patient acquiescence in the Divine disposals, he held his integrity to the last.*

In 1684 died William Bennet, of Woodbridge in Suffolk, a man of a religious turn of mind from his infancy, which, as he grew up, led him to associate with the strictest professors. His first connexions were among the Independents; he then joined the Quakers, and continued a steady, serviceable, and honourable member of their society till his death. He travelled in the exercise of his ministry, edifying his friends and making converts, through many parts of England, adorning his character by the innocence and integrity of his life, so as to gain universal esteem, and to extort from his adversaries an acknowledgment of his personal merit. Yet his sufferings were remarkable; he appears to have spent, at least in the latter part of his life, nearly as much, if not more time in prison, than in the enjoyment of his liberty; till, growing weaker and weaker by close and continued confinement, he fell a sacrifice to the sentence of partial magistrates and the forced construction of unequal laws.

This year died also, in Carlisle jail, Thomas Stordy, descended from a family of repute in Cumberland, and born to the inheritance of a handsome estate. About middle age he became seriously thoughtful in the pursuit of pure religion. He first joined the Independents, among whom his talents in exhortations and religious exercises were highly esteemed. After some time he left them, and connected himself with the Quakers; in this society he spent the remainder of his life, respected in his neighbourhood as a man of circumspect, sober, and temperate demeanour, upright in his dealings, obliging in his disposition, hospitable in his house, and liberally charitable to the poor around him. But this honest, respectable citizen was harassed by prosecution upon prosecution, and penalty upon penalty; he was detained a close prisoner at Carlisle, under a præmunire, till released by the king's declaration in 1672. He was fined for a meeting, under a similar restraint several miles from it. On the statute of the 23d of Elizabeth he was cast into jail, and confined there several years, till his death. Not long before his decease, being visited by some of his friends, he encouraged them to faithfulness in these words: "If you continue faithful unto the Lord while you live in this world, he will reward you, as he now rewards me, with his sweet peace." He was so confident in his opinion concerning tithes, that he not only refused to pay, but to receive them; for, inheriting from his ancestors an impropriation of £10 per annum, he quitted all claim to it for himself, his heirs, and assigns forever, and, by a legal instrument, released the owners of the lands from whence the tithes accrued.†

Another eminent minister and member of this society, who finished a useful life this year, was

William Gibson, of London. He was born at Caton, in Lancashire, in 1629, and in the civil wars enlisted as a soldier. Being in the garrison at Carlisle, he went to a Quakers' meeting, with three of his comrades, to insult and abuse the preacher; arriving at the place before his companions, after the minister had begun, he was so impressed and affected, that, instead of executing his purpose, he stepped up near to the preacher to defend him from insult, if it should be offered. From that time he frequented the meetings of the society, soon quitted his military employment, and after three years became a preacher. In 1662 he married, and settled near Warrington, and his ministry, while resident in that country, was very successful; and on his removal, he left a good report, and impressions of affectionate respect to his memory. He afterward fixed in London, where his service was conspicuous against hypocrisy, formality, and libertinism, and his circumspect conversation was a credit to his ministry. He suffered persecution in the loss of substance by various distraints, in divers imprisonments, and in personal abuses. In Shropshire, the jailer would not permit his food to be taken to him, but obliged him to draw it up by a rope, and also threw him down a pair of stone stairs, whereby his body was greatly bruised, and beat him to that degree that he was ill near six months. He was engaged in some controversies concerning tithes; was the author of several treatises serviceable at the time, and employed a part of his time in his imprisonment in writing epistles to his friends for their edification in righteousness. He died, recommending union, and exhorting to faithfulness and confidence in the Lord, at the age of fifty-five, and his funeral was attended to Bunhill Fields by many hundreds of friends and others.*.

While the society derived honour, at this period, from the virtues of character, and fortitude under sufferings, of distinguished members, it was greatly indebted to the able writings of Penn and Barclay. The former, the year before the king's declaration, 1671, employed the time of his confinement in prison in writing "The great Cause of Liberty of Conscience briefly debated and defended," and several other pieces. In 1675, on account of the divisions and animosities prevailing in the nation, he published a treatise, entitled "England's Present Interest considered," to show the consistency of a general liberty of conscience with the peace of the kingdom; and the remedies which he proposes to be adopted for allaying the heat of contrary interests were "an inviolable and impartial maintenance of English rights; our superiors governing themselves upon a balance, as near as may be, towards the several religious interests; and a sincere promotion of general and practical religion." Solid reasoning and a multitude of authorities are employed to support these propositions, which form the groundwork of a treatise: "a work," says Gough, "wherein the liberal charity of real Christianity, and the candid spirit of genuine patriotism, are eminently conspicuous." The preface, addressed to the higher powers, exhibits a pathetic representation of the severities of the times: when "to see the imprisoned was crime enough for a jail;

Footnotes:

* Gough, vol. ii., p. 554–557.   † Ibid., p. 34–37.   *. Gough, vol. iii., p. 154–157.

to visit the sick, to make a conventicle: when whole barns of corn were seized, thrashed, and carried away; parents left without their children, children without their parents, and both without subsistence. But that which aggravates the cruelty," he adds, " is, the widow's mite hath not escaped their hands; they have made her cow the forfeiture of her conscience, not leaving her a bed to lie on, nor a blanket to cover her; and what is yet more barbarous, and helps to make up this tragedy, the poor orphan's milk, boiling over the fire, hath been flung to the dogs, and the skillet made part of the prize; so that, had not nature in neighbours been stronger than cruelty in such informers, to open her bowels for their relief and subsistence, they must have utterly perished." In the same year in which this piece appeared, Penn likewise wrote a treatise on oaths, to show the reason for not swearing at all.*

A work of extensive and permanent celebrity came this year from the pen of Robert Barclay, entitled " An Apology for the true Christian Divinity, being an Explanation and Vindication of the Principles and Doctrines of the People called Quakers." It was prefaced with an address to King Charles II., remarkable for its plaindealing and honest simplicity, and as important, curious, and extraordinary as any part of the work. It has been admired both by our own countrymen and strangers. The work itself has been universally allowed to surpass everything of its kind, and to set the principles of the Quakers in the fairest light possible. The author sent two copies of it to each of the public ministers then at the famous Congress of Nimeguen, where it was received with all imaginable favour and respect, and the knowledge, charity, and disinterested probity of its author justly applauded. It was printed in Latin at Amsterdam, 1676, and was quickly translated into High Dutch, Low Dutch, French, and Spanish. As it attracted great notice, so it drew out various answers, abroad and at home; some from the pens of men who had before gained a considerable reputation in the learned world. These replies contributed to spread and advance the fame of Barclay's work; and it is remarkable, that while these have been little regarded and sunk into oblivion, this treatise maintains its celebrity. Though it had not the desired effect of stopping the persecution against the people in whose cause it was written, " yet it answered (as it is observed) a more important end, by showing that the pretences upon which they were persecuted were false and ill-grounded; and that those who on one side represented them as concealed papists, and such as on the other hand denied their being Christians, were equally in the wrong, and equally misled by their prejudices." The work did, in this view, great service to those of the author's persuasion; while Quakerism, which before had been looked on as a heap of extravagancies and visions, assumed in this treatise a systematic form, was reduced to fixed principles, and recommended itself to the judicious and enlightened mind. " It was an essay," says Gough, " to strip Quakerism of the disguise in which enmity or ignorance had dressed it up, and to represent it to the world in its genuine shape and complexion. A work

* Gough, vol. ii., p. 397–400.

which, with unprejudiced readers, answered the end of its publication, and gained the author the approbation of the ingenuous in general."* It is some proof of the high estimation in which it hath been held, that Mr. Baskerville printed a very elegant edition of it. A Scots poet, writing of the two famous Barclays, William and John, hath concluded with these verses upon Robert:

" But, lo! a third appears, with serious air;
His prince's darling, and his country's care.
See his religion, which so late before
Was like a jumbled mass of dross and ore,
Refined by him, and burnish'd o'er with art,
Awakes the spirits, and attracts the heart."†

In 1676 Barclay published a work entitled " The Anarchy of the Ranters and other Libertines, the Hierarchy of the Romanists and other pretended Churches, equally refused and refuted." This is pronounced to be a learned and excellent treatise, containing as much sound reasoning as any book of its size in ours, or perhaps in any modern language. The design of it was to vindicate the discipline established among the Quakers against those who accused them of confusion and disorder on one hand, or calumniated them with tyranny and imposition on the other. The causes and consequences of superstition on one hand, and of fanaticism on the other, we are told, are laid open in this very curious and instructive work with much solidity and perspicuity.‡ It drew upon its author, at the time of its appearance, much reproach and invective from certain Separatists, who had risen up several years.

The leaders of these Separatists were John Wilkinson and John Story, two ministers in the north, who took disgust at the discipline of the society, as an imposition on Gospel liberty, and setting up some men in the Church to usurp authority over their brethren: " pleading that nothing ought to be given forth in the Church of Christ but by way of advice or recommendation; and that every man ought to be left at his liberty to act according to the light of his own conscience, without censure or being accountable to any man, but to God, the sole proper judge of conscience. They particularly objected to women's meetings, as usurping authority in the Church, contrary to the Apostle Paul's prohibition. They gained over adherents from the weaker and looser members of the society; and caused a rent and division in the quarterly meeting of Westmoreland, to which they belonged. After several publications on this subject, pro and con, especially by William Rogers, a merchant at Bristol, in favour of the Separatists, and in reply by Thomas Elwood; and after the matter had been referred to different meetings, and their objections been heard, they found

* Gough, vol. ii., p. 401–406. Biographia Britan., vol. ii., second edit., art. Barclay. Dictionnaire des Hérésies, vol. ii., p. 460. Mosheim, however, has not treated this work with candour or justice, but endeavours to depreciate it, and asperses the author, charging him with duplicity, and with giving a fallacious account of the principles of this society, by which he has exposed himself to the just animadversions of the historian of this society—*Mosheim's Eccles. History*, vol. v., p. 36, *note* (b), second edit., and Gough, *ut suprà*.

† Biograph. Brit., vol. ii., p. 602 of the second ed.
‡ Ibid., p. 592, 593. Gough, vol. iii., p. 15.

themselves too loosely compacted to adhere long together; some, judging their separation to be causeless, reunited themselves to the body of the society, and the rest soon fell to pieces and dwindled away.*

When James II. came to the throne, the Quakers drew up a petition, as we have seen, stating their grievous sufferings by no less than ten penal laws; but it is not certain whether they had an opportunity of presenting it, for their proceedings were interrupted by the landing of the Duke of Monmouth, which for a time engaged all the attention of the court and the nation. But in March, 1685-6, they made an application to the throne, soliciting the liberation of their imprisoned friends, and they obtained a warrant for their release, directed to Sir Robert Sawyer, attorney-general. He was then at his seat in Hampshire; that this business might be expedited, therefore, George Whitehead and John Edge, accompanied by Rowland Vaughan, waited on him there, and were received and entertained with great civility, till liberates could be made out for the prisoners in the city; after his return to London, by the exertion of the said friends, the discharge of the prisoners in different parts of the kingdom was obtained.†

The attention which the king gave their grievances, in this and other instances, encouraged them to present a complaint and petition against the informers and their iniquitous practices. This was followed by a request to the king to examine into the truth of the allegations, by giving the petitioners an opportunity to prove them to the informers' faces. The request was granted, and a commission was issued to Richard Graham and Philip Burton, Esqrs., who summoned the informers, sufferers, and witnesses to appear before them at Clifford's Inn, the 4th of June, 1686. Fifty-four cases were selected from which to establish their charges. When all the parties came to Clifford's Inn, the informers seeing the numerous company that appeared against them, expressed their malice in this ribaldry: "Here come all the devils in hell;" and observing George Whitehead, they cried, "And there comes the old devil of all." The first charge, proved in thirty-four cases, was, that "they had sworn falsely in fact:" then were laid before the commissioners sundry cases, wherein the doors of houses and shops were broken open with violence, by constables and informers, to make severe and exorbitant distraints, by which household and shop goods were carried away by cart-loads. The commissioners grew weary before they had gone through one fourth of the cases, and adjourned for ten days. At the second meeting, the lawyer whom the informers had employed to plead their cause was quickly silenced by the number of facts and the evidence produced, and before half the cases prepared for cognizance were examined, the commissioners thought they had sufficient grounds for a report to the king. A report was accordingly drawn up, to which George Whitehead, on a sight of it, objected as very deficient and improper; being rather a proposal to limit prosecutions to the less ruinous penal laws, than a plain statement of facts, and of the various perjuries, and of the illegal and

injurious acts of the informers. The reason of this was, that they had received a message from a great person or persons in the Church, soliciting them to do or report nothing that might invalidate the power of the informers. But, on Whitehead's pleading for justice to be done in regard to matters of fact, the report was amended; and framed more to the purpose. The king, on receiving it, referred it to the lord-chancellor, in order to correct the irregular proceedings of some justices and the informers. He signified, also, his pleasure to the subordinate magistrates and justices, that they should put a stop to the depredations of these men; instead, therefore, of being encouraged, they were discountenanced. The court withdrawing its protection, other Dissenters prosecuted them; and the scenes of their iniquity being laid open, some fled the country, and the rest were reduced to beggary.*

The Quakers, who had suffered more severely than any other sect, that they might not seem less sensible of the relief they had received, when addresses were presented to the king for his declaration for liberty of conscience, also waited on him with an address of thanks; first, from those of their society who resided in or about London, and then in the name and on behalf of the community at large. And while the other Dissenters were censured in this business, as countenancing the king's dispensing power, the Quakers were guarded in this respect; for they expressed their hope "that the good effects of the declaration of indulgence on the trade, peace, and prosperity of the kingdom, would produce such a concurrence from the Parliament as would secure it to their posterity;" modestly hinting, it hath been observed, their sentiments of what they apprehended yet wanting to be done to complete the favour.†

When the bishops were committed prisoners to the Tower, and it was understood that they reflected on the Quakers as belying them, and reporting that they had been the cause of the death of some of them, Robert Barclay paid the bishops a visit, and laid before them undeniable proofs that some, by order of bishops, had been detained in prison until death, though they had been apprized of their danger by physicians who were not Quakers; but he added, "that since, through the change of circumstances, they themselves were now under oppression, it was by no means the intention of the people called Quakers to publish such incidents, or to give the king or their adversaries any advantage against them thereby." They were accordingly very careful to refrain from every measure, in word or deed, that might in any respect aggravate the case of the prisoners, esteeming it no time to aggravate old animosities, when the common enemy was seeking an advantage.‡

When persecution subsided, and liberty of conscience was enjoyed without molestation, the Quakers thought it a convenient season to apply for relief in a point where they were still exposed to considerable trouble and detriment, and at their yearly meeting in London, in the summer of 1688, they drew up an address to the king, soliciting him to interpose for their

---

* Gough, vol. iii., p. 9-24.   † Ibid., p. 164-169.

* Gough, vol. ii., p. 172-176.
† Ibid., p. 189-195.   ‡ Ibid., vol. iii., p. 198, 199.

relief from sufferings for tithes, and in the case of oaths. The address was presented and well received, but before the time for holding a Parliament arrived, the king found it out of his power to redress their grievances or support himself on the throne. The legal confirmation and enlargement of their liberty were reserved for the next reign.*

During the short reign of James II., the society of Quakers lost several respectable members; the most eminent of whom was Colonel David Barclay, the father of the apologist, of an ancient and honourable family in Scotland, a man universally esteemed and beloved. He adopted the principles of the Quakers in 1666, and is said to have been brought over to them by Mr. Swinton, a man of learning, very taking in his behaviour, naturally eloquent, and in great credit among them.† The acquisition of so considerable and respectable a person as Colonel Barclay was of no small use to this persuasion. He was a man venerable in his appearance, just in all his actions, had showed his courage in the wars in Germany, and his fortitude in bearing all the hard usage he met with in Scotland, with cheerfulness as well as patience; for he very soon found himself exposed to persecutions and sufferings on the score of his religion. He spent, however, the last twenty years of his life in the profession with great comfort to himself, being all along blessed with sound health and a vigorous constitution; and he met death, in the seventy-sixth year of his age, September, 1686, at his seat at Ury in Scotland, with resignation and patience under great pain, and with the feelings of a lively hope. His last expressions were uttered in prayer: "Praises to the Lord! Let now thy servant depart in peace. Into thy hands, O Father, I commit my soul, spirit, and body. Thy will, O Lord, be done on earth, as it is in heaven." And soon after he breathed his last; and though he gave express directions, agreeably to his principles, that none but persons of his own persuasion should be invited to his funeral, yet, the time being known, many gentlemen, and those, too, of great distinction, attended him to the grave, out of regard to his humanity, beneficence, and public spirit, virtues

which endeared him to the good men of all parties.*

On the 17th of July, 1688, died at Warwick, in a good age, William Dewsbury, who was early distinguished among the foremost members of this society by the depth of his religious experience, the eminence of his labours in the ministry, and the severity of his sufferings. He was first bred to the keeping of sheep, and then was put apprentice to a clothier. In early life he was religiously inclined, and associated with the Independents and Baptists. In the civil wars he entered into the Parliament army, but, as he grew more seriously attentive to religious considerations, the recollection of the words of Christ, "Put up thy sword into the scabbard; if my kingdom were of this world, then would my servants fight," affected his mind with a lively conviction of the inconsistency of war with the peaceable Gospel of Christ. Under this conviction he left the army and resumed his trade. When George Fox was at Wakefield, he joined him in fellowship and in the ministry. He travelled much in different parts of England to promote righteousness, and to propagate what was, in his view, Divine truth; for which, like his brethren, he met with much personal abuse, and was frequently thrown into prison at various places, at York, Northampton, Exeter, London, and Warwick. In this last place he was detained till the general release by King James. At length his health and strength were so impaired by the many violent abuses and long imprisonments he had endured, that he was obliged to rest frequently in walking from his house to the meeting-place in the same town. A distemper contracted in prison terminated his life. He was seized with a sharp fit of it when in London to attend the yearly meting, so that he was obliged to return home by short journeys, but survived his departure from the city only seventeen days. To some friends who came to visit him, he said, just before he expired, "Friends, be faithful, and trust in the Lord your God; for this I can say, I never played the coward, but as joyfully entered prisons as palaces. And in the prison-house I sang praises to my God, and esteemed the bolts and locks put upon me as jewels, and in the name of the eternal God I always got the victory; for they could not keep me any longer than the time determined of Him." Continuing his discourse, he said, "My departure draws nigh; blessed be God, I have nothing to do but to die, and put off this corruptible and mortal tabernacle, this body of flesh that hath so many infirmities; but the life that dwells in it ascends out of the reach of death, hell, and the grave; and immortality and eternal life is my crown forever and ever." He concluded in prayer to the Lord for all his people everywhere, especially for the friends then assembled in London, reaping the present reward of his fidelity, patience, and sincerity, in the peaceful tenour of his mind, and looking death in the face, not only without terror, but with a holy triumph over its power.†

The history of this society has, with an impartial and commendable disregard to the distinction of sex, made honourable mention of

---

* Gough, vol. iii., p. 199–202.

† This Mr. Swinton was attainted after the restoration of Charles II. for having joined Cromwell, and was sent down into Scotland to be tried; it was universally believed that his death was inevitable; but when he was brought before the Parliament at Edinburgh, 1661, to show cause why he should not receive sentence, having become a Quaker, when he might have set up two pleas, strong in point of law, he answered, consonantly to his religious principles, "that he was, at the time his political crimes were imputed to him, in the gall of bitterness and bond of iniquity, but that, God having since called him to the light, he saw and acknowledged his past errors, and did not refuse to pay the forfeit for them, even though in their judgment his life should extend to his life." His speech was, though modest, so majestic, and though expressive of the most perfect patience, so pathetic, that, notwithstanding he had neither interest nor wealth to plead for him, yet the impression made by his discourse on that illustrious assembly was such, that they recommended him to the king as a proper object of mercy, when they were very severe against others.—*Biog. Brit.*, vol. ii., p. 590; and *Burnet's History*, vol. i., p. 182.

---

* Gough, vol. iii., p. 181–183; and Biog. Brit., vol. ii., p. 590, 591, second edition.

† Gough, vol. iii., p. 223–228.

those women to whose piety and zeal it was indebted. One of these, at this period, was Rebecca Travis, born 1609, who had received a religious education, and was a zealous professor among the Baptists: In the year 1654, prompted by curiosity, but possessed with strong prejudices against the Quakers, as a people in the north remarkable for simplicity and rusticity of behaviour, a worship strangely different from all others, and a strenuous opposition to all public teachers, she attended a public disputation between James Naylor, then in London, and the Baptists, in which it appeared to her he had the advantage, by close and powerful replies, over his learned antagonists. This excited her desire to hear him in the exercise of his ministry ; she had soon an opportunity of gratifying her wishes ; and the result was, that from that time she attended the meetings of this people, and after some time laboured herself in the ministry among them, in London and its neighbourhood. The impressions made on her mind by the preaching of Naylor, and her observation of his circumspect conduct, engaged her affectionate esteem for him, and she cheerfully administered every charitable service in her power to his relief under his grievous sufferings ; though she was a woman of too much discretion and stability in religion to carry her regard beyond its proper limits, or to such extravagant lengths as those weak people who contributed to his downfall. She had the character of a discreet and virtuous woman, much employed in acts of charity and beneficence; of sympathetic tenderness towards the afflicted, and therefore one of the first of those faithful women to whom the care of the poor, the sick, and the imprisoned members of the community was assigned ; this care, in conjunction with others, she religiously discharged. After a long life of virtuous and charitable deeds, she died in much peace, on the 15th of July, 1688, in the eightieth year of her age.*

Another of these women, who was esteemed an ornament to her profession, and who undauntedly suffered when it fell to her lot, was Ann Downer, first married to Benjamin Greenwell, a grocer in Bishopsgate-street, and then to the celebrated George Whitehead. She was one of the first who received the doctrine of the Quakers, when its ministers came to London, and at length became a preacher of it. In 1656 she was sent for to attend George Fox and his fellow-prisoners at Launceston, and travelled thither on foot, two hundred miles : on her journey she was instrumental to bring many over to the doctrine she published, some of whom were persons of account in the world. In 1658 she travelled in the southern counties and the Isle of Wight. She was remarkably conspicuous in her day for her singular piety, benevolence, and charity, spending much of her time in visiting the poor, the imprisoned, the sick, the fatherless, and widows in their affliction ; and in her exertions to do good had few equals. She died on the 27th of August, 1686, aged sixty-three, expressing to her friends who visited her the sentiments of resignation and lively hope, and leaving impressions of affectionate regard to her memory in the hearts of many whom she had helped by her charitable services.†

REFLECTIONS

ON THE

REVOLUTION AND THE ACT OF TOLERATION.

THE Revolution is the grand event, in which the affecting and interesting scenes and transactions of the preceding periods, from the Reformation to the accession of William III., happily and gloriously close. Here the struggles of the several parties have their termination ; and though the Episcopal form of church government obtains at last an establishment and permanent pre-eminence, yet that superiority is made easy to the other parties by the security to their respective religious professions, and by the equality among themselves which they enjoy by the Act of Toleration. Here the reader pauses with pleasure and hope ; humanity rejoices that there is a period to the animosities and calamities that had torn and afflicted this country nearly a century and a half, and the prospect of better times opens before the wearied mind. The history through which he has been led, by its various details, giveth him a strong impression of the importance and happiness of the era to which he is at length arrived. Here despotism hath drawn its last breath ; here religious liberty commenceth its reign : royal prerogative bows and yields to the voice of the people ; and conscience feels itself, though not entirely emancipated, yet walking at large and breathing the open air.

Our author's narrative affords convincing and satisfactory proofs of the importance and felicity of the new state of things to which it brings us. But yet some considerations, arising from facts not mentioned by him, may be properly presented to the reader, to heighten his sense of the deliverance effected by the Revolution. Two singular doctrines had been industriously disseminated : viz., "That there was no such thing as passive obedience for the cause of religion"; and that kings are so far infallible, as that what religion they establish is the true worship of God in their dominion." To insinuate more universally and effectually these sentiments, they were inserted and enlarged upon in the common almanacs.‡ No doubt can remain concerning the design of James II. from a review of the measures he actually executed ; and yet it is useful and interesting to bring forward the secret councils from whence those measures

* Gough, vol. iii., p. 219–223.   † Ib., p. 183–195.
‡ Crosby's History of the Baptists, vol. iii., p. 88.

flowed, and to exhibit the systematical plan, for which, if they were not parts of it, and first attempts at the execution of it, they were evidently calculated to prepare the way.

Some time before the abdication of James, a "Memorial" was presented to him, drawn up by a Jesuit, and exhibiting the methods he should pursue, not only to root out the Protestant religion, but to prevent even the possibility of its revival. The great outlines of the scheme were, "that a council of reformation should be established, which, avoiding the name, as odious and offensive at the beginning, should pursue some good and sound manner of inquisition; nay, should order, in divers points, according to the diligent and exact proceedings of the Court of Inquisition in Spain, that the authority of the Church should take place of the king's authority, and the civil powers be subjected to the ecclesiastical; that the state of the Catholic religion, and the succession of the crown, should be so linked together, that one might depend on and be the assurance of the other; that new ways of choosing Parliaments should be followed, particularly one very extraordinary, viz., that the bishop of the diocess should judge concerning the knights of the shire, and, as they were thought fit to serve in Parliament by such bishops or not, so they were to confirm the election or have a negative voice in it. The Catholic prince, whom God should send, is represented as being well able to procure such a Parliament as he would have. Many new laws were to be made, that should quite alter the whole constitution; but it was to be made treason forever for any man to propose anything for change of the Catholic Roman faith when it was once settled. As to those in low circumstances, effectual care was to be taken to keep them low. New methods were to be observed for letting of lands, disposing of children, and ordering of servants." The "Memorial" complains, "that in Queen Mary's time, when so many were imprisoned, so many stripped of their estates, and so many burned, there was a want of zeal, to the grief and discouragement of many; that some things were then tolerated upon constraint, and fear of farther inconveniences; and it is added, that matters are not to be patched up any more by such gentle and backward proceedings. For it is laid down as a first principle, that as soon as a good Catholic prince should be established upon the throne of these nations, he must make account that the security of himself, his crown, and successor dependeth principally on the assurance and good establishment of the Catholic religion within his kingdom." The proposals in this piece were brought forward, not merely as measures which the writer desired to see executed, but such as he apprehended, nay, was confident, the temper and circumstances of the nation would soon afford an opportunity to accomplish. Several things are reckoned up, which gave great force to the Roman Catholics in England. It is said that England would more easily receive popery than any other Protestant country; nay, that difficulties which arose in some Catholic countries would not be found here. "All now," says the author, "is zeal and integrity in our new clergy (Almighty God be thanked for it!), and no less in our laity, and Catholic gentlemen in

England, that have borne the brunt of persecution."

These specimens of the designs formed are proofs to what extent the scheme of combining the re-establishment of popery with arbitrary power was to be carried; and show what vast consequences were involved in the success of the spirited opposition that led James to abdicate the throne.

Important, valuable, and happy as was the state of things introduced by this event, especially as it affected religious liberty, the operation of it was partial and limited: when even a bill of rights, after the settlement of King William on the throne, defined our constitution, and fixed the privileges of the subject, the rights of conscience were not ascertained, nor declared by that noble deed. The Act of Toleration, moved by Lord Nottingham in the House of Peers, and seconded by some bishops, though more out of fear than inclination,* exempted from the penal statutes then in existence Protestant dissentients only, and not all of them, for the Socinians are expressly excepted, nor did secure any from the influence of the Corporation and Test Acts. It left the English Catholics under severe disabilities; it left many penal statutes unrepealed. The same reign which gave us the blessing of the Toleration Act was marked by an act of another complexion; for the prince to whom we owe the former was prevailed on to pass another statute, adjudging heavy penalties, fines, and imprisonments to those who should write or speak against the doctrine of the Trinity. There are claims of power over conscience not yet abolished: there are rights of conscience not yet fully recovered and secured. The very term toleration shows that religious freedom is not yet enjoyed in perfection; it indicates that the liberty which we possess is a matter of sufferance, lenity, and indulgence, rather than the grant of justice and right. It seemeth to admit and imply a power to restrain conscience and to dictate to faith, but the exercise of which is generously waived. The time is, even now, at this distance from the Revolution, yet to come when the enjoyment of religious liberty shall no longer be considered as a favour; the time is yet to come when Christians, of all religious forms and creeds, shall be on the equal footing of brethren, and of children in the house of the same heavenly Parent; the time is yet to come when acts of toleration shall everywhere give place to bills of right.

But, though much is yet wanting to complete and perfect the blessings of the Revolution, yet we cannot but review the Act of Toleration as a great point gained, as a noble effort towards the full emancipation of conscience. The preceding periods had been only those of oppression and thraldom. The exertions of any to procure release from severe laws were rather attempts to gain the power of tyrannizing over conscience into their own hands, that they themselves might be free, and all other parties remain slaves, than liberal endeavours to ascertain and secure to every one security and peace in following the judgment of his own mind. The preceding ages exhibit a series of severe statutes following each other; from passing the act for burning of heretics in the reign of Henry IV., to the enacting

* Sir John Reresby's Memoirs, p. 323.

of that of uniformity, and of the Oxford conventicle acts, in the reign of Charles II. At the commencement of the Reformation, we have seen, that on the one hand, they who could not admit, from religious reverence to the pope's authority, the supremacy of the king, and, on the other, they who discarded any of the six articles which he formed into a standard of faith, were alike doomed to the sentence of death. In the reign of Edward VI., the pious and amiable Hooper, for refusing to wear a particular dress, was imprisoned.; and Joan Boucher, who religiously read and dispersed the New Testament, was burned at the stake. Intolerant statutes marked the government of Queen Elizabeth. Persecution, in various forms, by laws and by prerogative, stigmatized the successive reigns of the Stuarts. In the interval, during the suspension of their power, a severe ordinance against heresy was passed; the livings of the Episcopal clergy were sequestered; those ministers suffered under severe oppressions, and Presbyterianism was found to be not more friendly to the rights of conscience, or averse from intolerance, than had been the fallen hierarchy. Among two despised sects, hated and persecuted by all parties, the Baptists and Quakers, among almost them only, the principles of liberty had found able and generous advocates; their writings placed the rights of conscience on a broad and liberal bottom. But they could support them by the pen only; they were never in power, and, consequently, had never, in this country,* an opportunity to carry their principles into practice, and to show that they could rule according to the maxims for which, when oppressed, they could forcibly plead.

This having been the state of things, the Act of Toleration, the consequence of the Revolution, was a great acquisition. It was the first legal sanction given to the claims of conscience; it was the first charter of religious freedom; it was a valuable, important, and permanent security to the dissenting subject. It opened to him the temple of peace, and afforded the long-wished-for asylum. To adopt the language of high authority: "The Toleration Act rendered that which was illegal before, now legal; the dissenting way of worship is permitted and allowed by that act; it is not only exempted from punishment, but rendered innocent and lawful; it is established; it is put under the protection, and not merely the connivance, of the law."† It hath been followed with a universal good effect and happy influence; it hath been the basis of the religious liberty enjoyed ever since that period; and with respect to the state of freedom and religious inquiry in these kingdoms, it was, as it were, a new creation. Before that period, darkness, in a manner, hung over the spacious field of knowledge and Divine truth, and the path to it was guarded by a flaming sword. That act said, "Let there be light, and light there was." "The bounds of free inquiry

were enlarged; the volume in which are the words of eternal life was laid open to examination." And the state of knowledge and liberty has been, ever since, progressive and improving.

To this general view of the effects of the Revolution, it is proper to add, "that it drew considerable consequences after it all over Europe. It kept the Reformed interests from sinking, secured the liberty of the British and the Netherlands, and disappointed the French of that universal monarchy which they had been eagerly expecting, and had great hopes of reaching. And among other happy fruits of it, it was not the least considerable that it was the means of saving the poor Vaudois of Piedmont from utter ruin, and of their re-establishment in their own country. These people were the remains of the primitive Christians, who were never tainted with the papal corruptions and impurities. In the year 1686, the Duke of Savoy, at the instigation of Louis XIV., because they would not forsake their religion, drove them from their houses and possessions, forced them out of the valleys, and obliged them to take shelter among the Switzers and others that would afford them an asylum. But in September, 1689, eight or nine hundred of them assembled together in the woods of Nion, not far from Geneva, crossed the Lake Leman in the night, and entered Savoy under the conduct of their minister, M. Arnold. They marched through that country, fourteen or fifteen days' journey, in which march they were obliged to climb up high mountains, force divers strait passes, well guarded by soldiers, with swords in their hands, till at length they reached their valleys, of which they took possession, and in which, under the singular protection of Providence, they maintained themselves, successfully encountering their enemies who at any time assaulted them."*

Here seems to be a proper place, before the history of this period is closed, to notice a noble and generous exertion of a few Dissenters, which has with great good effect been resumed and perpetuated to the present times. It was the founding of a school in Gravel Lane, Southwark, for the instruction of children in reading,

---

* It is said in *this* country; for when the forming the government of Pennsylvania and Rhode Island in America rested, the latter with the Baptists, and the former with the Quakers, to their honour it should be said, that their conduct was consistent with the arguments they had advanced, and liberty of conscience, on an extensive and liberal scale, was a leading feature of each constitution.   † Lord Mansfield.

* Calamy's History of his Own Times, MS. Dr. Calamy was told, several remarkable particulars concerning this march by Mr. Arnold, who came afterward to England to solicit the assistance of King William. One was, that when they were come pretty near to their valleys, they were in such straits for provisions, that they were in great fear of starving. But there came a sudden thaw, which in a night's time melted the snow, and in the morning they discovered a considerable quantity of wheat standing in the earth, ready for the sickle, which had been left there from the preceding summer, and had been covered all winter by the snow; the sudden fall prevented the proprietors from reaping it at the proper season. These destitute people beheld it with admiration and thankfulness, reaped it with joy, and were supported by it after their return into their valleys, where, without such a supply, they might have perished. Another resource, especially together their ministers and schoolmasters, was derived from the overplus of the collections made for them in England during the protectorship of Cromwell, which had been lodged by them, when their wants had been effectually relieved, in the hands of the magistrates of Geneva, on condition of receiving such an allowance from year to year as was agreed on.—*Calamy, ut suprà.*

writing, and arithmetic, and the girls in sewing and knitting, and furnishing them with books for their instruction in these arts, and with Testaments, catechisms, and Bibles. One Poulton had opened a school in these parts, and given public notice that he would teach the children of the poor gratis. To counteract his designs, and to afford the poor an easy opportunity of having their children educated in Protestant principles, three worthy gentlemen, Mr. Arthur Shallet, Mr. Samuel Warburton, and Mr. Ferdinando Holland, members of Mr. Nathaniel Vincent's church, instituted this seminary, which has continued ever since, maintained by voluntary subscriptions, annual collections, and legacies. The number of scholars at first was forty; afterward it increased to fifty; then to one hundred and forty; and has since been two hundred. It was the first institution of the kind wherein the Protestant Dissenters were concerned; and into it objects are received without distinction of party. Such an institution has the merit of being a rational, fair, and benevolent mode of opposing superstition and bigotry, abridging no one's security and rights, and leaving the event to the operation of knowledge and understanding; and it reflects honour on the spirit and resolution of its first founders, who set it on foot in the reign of the tyrannical and bigoted prince, James II., when the Dissenters had scarcely emerged out of a state of persecution.

It will not, it is presumed, be thought beneath the importance and dignity of general history to mention here two small publications which the press produced at this period, especially as the history through which the reader has been led records the virtuous and manly struggles made to secure the liberty of writing and publishing on the subject of religion, according to the views any might entertain, and exhibits memoirs of the progress of theological inquiries. The importance of publications is also to be estimated, not by the number of pages, but by the nature of the subject, the ability with which they are executed, and the effect they produced, or the impression they were calculated to leave, on the public mind.

One of the pieces, both anonymous, to which we refer, was entitled "A brief History of the Unitarians, called also Socinians: in four Letters to a Friend." The publisher to whom they were written having left them some time with a gentleman, a person of excellent learning and worth, they were returned to him with a letter, expressing great approbation of them, which was printed with each edition. The first of these letters represented the Unitarian doctrine concerning the unity of God, the humanity of Christ and the Holy Spirit, as the power and inspiration of God; aimed to confirm and prove it by a series of scriptural arguments, and closed with a concise history of it. The design of the three following letters was to reply to the arguments of the orthodox; and, that the answer might be full and satisfactory, they were occupied in the illustration of all the texts usually alleged as proofs of the Trinitarian doctrine. The passages out of the Old Testament are first explained, then those out of the Gospels and Acts; and, lastly, those out of the Epistles and the Revelations. This mode of discussing a question, which depends purely on Divine revelation, will be admitted to be proper and fair. It showed that the author was not afraid to lodge his appeal with the Scriptures, and it was adapted to lead the reader into an investigation of their meaning according to the rules of sober criticism and just explanation. It went, particularly, to obviate a reflection cast upon the Unitarians, as exalting their reasonings above the plain and express revelation of the Scriptures. The first edition of this tract was in 12mo, in 1687. It was afterward reprinted in a collection of Unitarian Tracts, in quarto, 1691.

The other tract published at this period, which I have mentioned as worthy of particular notice, was entitled "A Rational Catechism." It was distinguished not only by the good sense, and the vein of close but familiar reasoning which ran through it, but by the peculiar method in which it was drawn up. Catechisms, in general, have consisted principally, if not solely, of speculative points, drawn from the theological systems of the day, and of the country where they are published. These are conveyed in an authoritative manner, as absolutely necessary to salvation; and are to be committed to memory, without any attempt to prove them by reasoning level to the capacity of the learner. The author of this tract, conceiving that neglecting to examine into the bottom of things was the cause of that variety of opinions whence arose rash judgments, animosities, hatreds, and persecution, began his piece with the first principles discernible in human nature; and, avoiding all sentiments controverted among Christians, confined himself to such truths only as all agree in, and which lead directly unto practice, professing not to advance everything that he might think useful, but only what he judged most useful. The dialogue into which form the work is thrown divides itself into three parts: the principles of natural religion; those of Christianity, or the great advantages derived from the Gospel; and the rules of conduct which it supplies. The instructions and conclusions which the catechumen is led, in a great degree, to draw for himself, and by his own reflections, arise in a chain of reasoning from this principle, "that every man seeks happiness;" which happiness must be, principally, mental and spiritual. The means of attaining to it in the knowledge of God and the practice of his will are hence gradually developed. This piece is ascribed to Mr. Popple. It was first printed, by license, in 1688; another edition of it appeared 1690, 12mo; and it was reprinted at Amsterdam in 1712.*

* Preface to the work. Hollis's Memoirs, p. 263; and a Critical Review of it in the Bibliothèque Universelle Historique, tom. ix., p. 95, &c.

APPENDIX.

No. I

A declaration of certain principal articles of religion, set out by order of both archbishops, metropolitans, and the rest of the bishops, for the unity of doctrine to be taught and holden of all parsons, vicars, and curates: as well in testification of their common consent in the said doctrine, to the stopping of the mouths of them that go about to slander the ministers of the Church for diversity of judgment, and as necessary for the instruction of their people, to be read by the said parsons, vicars, and curates, at their possession taking, or first entry into their cures; and also after that yearly, at two several times; that is to say, the Sunday next following Easter Day, and St. Michael the Archangel, or on some other Sunday within one month after those feasts, immediately after the Gospel.

FORASMUCH as it appertaineth to all Christian men, but especially to the ministers and pastors of the Church, being teachers and instructers of others, to be ready to give a reason of their faith when they shall be thereunto required; I, for my part, now appointed your parson, vicar, or curate, having before mine eyes the fear of God, and the testimony of my conscience, do acknowledge for myself, and require you to assent to the same:

1. "That there is but one living and true God, of infinite power, wisdom, and goodness; the maker and preserver of all things; and that in unity of this Godhead there be three persons of one substance, of equal power and eternity, the Father, the Son, and the Holy Ghost.

2. "I believe, also, whatsoever is contained in the holy canonical Scriptures, in the which Scriptures are contained all things necessary to salvation; by the which, also, all errors and heresies may sufficiently be reproved and convicted, and all doctrines and articles necessary to salvation are established. I do also most firmly believe and confess all the articles contained in the three creeds; the Nicene Creed, Athanasius's Creed, and our common creed, called the Apostles' Creed; for these do briefly contain the principal articles of our faith, which are at large set forth in the Holy Scriptures.

3. "I do acknowledge, also, that church to be the spouse of Christ wherein the Word of God is truly taught, the sacraments orderly ministered according to Christ's institution, and the authority of the keys duly used; and that every such particular church hath authority to institute, to change, and clean to put away, ceremonies, and other ecclesiastical rights, as they be superfluous or abused; and to constitute others, making more to seemliness, to order, or edification.

4. "Moreover, I confess that it is not lawful for any man to take upon him any office or ministry, either ecclesiastical or secular, but such only as are lawfully thereunto called by the high authorities, according to the ordinances of the realm.

5. "Furthermore, I do acknowledge the queen's majesty's prerogative and superiority of government of all estates, and in all causes, as well ecclesiastical as temporal, within this realm, and other her dominions and countries, to be agreeable to God's Word, and of right to appertain to her highness, in such sort as in the late act of Parliament expressed, and since then by her majesty's injunctions declared and expounded.

6. "Moreover, touching the Bishop of Rome, I do acknowledge and confess that, by the Scriptures and the Word of God, he hath no more authority than other bishops have in their provinces and dioceses, and therefore the power which he now challengeth, that is, to be the supreme head of the universal Church of Christ, and so to be above all emperors, kings, and princes, is a usurped power, contrary to the Scriptures and Word of God, and contrary to the example of the primitive Church; and therefore is, for most just causes, taken away and abolished in this realm.

7. "Furthermore, I do grant and confess that the book of Common Prayer and administration of the holy sacraments set forth by the authority of Parliament is agreeable to the Scriptures; and that it is catholic and apostolic, and most for the advancing of God's glory, and the edifying of God's people: both for that it is in a tongue that may be understood of the people, and also for the doctrine and form of administration contained in the same.

8. "And although in the administration of baptism there is neither exorcism, oil, salt, spittle, nor hallowing of the water now used; and for that they were of late years abused and esteemed necessary, whereas they pertain not to the substance and necessity of the sacrament, and therefore be reasonably abolished; yet is the sacrament full and perfectly administered, to all intents and purposes, agreeable to the institution of our Saviour Christ.

9. "Moreover, I do not only acknowledge that private masses were never used among the fathers of the primitve Church, I mean, public minisrtation and receiving of the sacrament by the priest alone, without a just number of communicants, according to Christ's saying, 'Take ye, and eat ye,' &c., but also that the doctrine that maintaineth the mass to be a propitiatory sacrifice for the quick and the dead, and a mean to deliver souls out of purgatory, is neither agreeable to Christ's ordinance, nor grounded upon doctrine apostolic, but contrariwise most ungodly, and most injurious to the precious redemption of our Saviour Christ, and his only sufficient sacrifice, offered once forever upon the altar of the cross.

10. " I am of that mind, also, that the holy communion or sacrament of the body and blood of Christ, for the due obedience to Christ's institution, and to express the virtue of the same, ought to be ministered unto the people under both kinds ; and that it is avouched by certain fathers of the Church to be a plain sacrilege to rob them of the mystical cup for whom Christ has shed his most precious blood, seeing he himself hath said, ' Drink ye all of this ;' considering, also, that in the time of the ancient doctors of the Church, as Cyprian, Jerome, Augustine, Gelasius, and others, six hundred years after Christ, and more, both the parts of the sacrament were ministered to the people.

Last of all, " As I do utterly disallow the extolling of images, relics, and feigned miracles ; and also all kind of expressing God invisible, in the form of an old man, or the Holy Ghost in the form of a dove ; and all other vain worshipping of God, devised by men's fantasy, besides or contrary to the Scriptures ; as wandering on pilgrimages, setting up of candles, praying upon beads, and such like superstition ; which kind of works have no promise of reward in Scripture, but contrariwise, threatenings and maledictions ; so I do exhort all met to the obedience of God's law, and to the works of faith, as charity, mercy, piety, alms, devout and fervent prayer, with the affection of the heart, and not with the mouth only ; godly abstinence and fasting, chastity, obedience to the rulers and superior powers, with such like works, and godliness of life commanded by God in his Word ; which, as St. Paul saith, ' hath the promise both of this life, and of the life to come ;' and are works acceptable only in God's sight.

" These things above rehearsed, though they be appointed by common order, yet do I, without all compulsion, with freedom of mind and conscience, from the bottom of my heart, and upon most sure persuasion, acknowledge to be true, and agreeable to God's Word. And therefore I exhort you all to whom I have care, heartily and obediently to embrace and receive the same ; that we all joining together in unity of spirit, faith, and charity, may also at length be joined together in the kingdom of God, and that through the merits and death of our Saviour Jesus Christ ; to whom, with the Father and the Holy Ghost, be all glory and empire, now and forever. Amen."

No. II.

A copy of the Letter sent to the Bishops and Pastors of England, who have renounced the Roman Antichrist, and profess the Lord Jesus Christ in sincerity.

The superintendent ministers, and commissioners of charges within the realm of Scotland, to their brethren the bishops and pastors of England, who have renounced the Roman Antichrist, and do profess with them the Lord Jesus in sincerity, desire the perpetual increase of the Holy Spirit.

By word and writ, it is come to our knowledge, reverend pastors, that divers of our dearest brethren, among whom are some of the best learned within that realm, are deprived from ecclesiastical function, and forbidden to preach, and so by you, that they are straight to promote the kingdom of Jesus Christ, because their consciences will not suffer to take upon them (at

the commandment of authority) such garments, as idolaters, in time of blindness, have used in their idolatry, which bruit cannot but be most dolorous to our hearts, mindful of that sentence of the apostle, saying, " If ye bite and devour one another, take heed, lest ye be consumed one of another." We purpose not at this present to enter into the ground of that question which we hear, of either part, to be agitate with greater vehemency than well liketh us ; to wit, whether that such apparel is to be accounted among things that are simply indifferent or not ; but in the bowels of the Lord Jesus we crave that Christian charity may so prevail in you, we say, the pastors and leaders of the flock within that realm.

That ye do not to others that which ye would not others should do to you. Ye cannot be ignorant how tender a thing the conscience of man is. All that have knowledge are not alike persuaded ; your consciences reclaim not at wearing of such garments, but many thousands, both godly and learned, are otherwise persuaded, whose consciences are continually stricken with these sentences : "What hath Christ Jesus to do with Belial ?" " What fellowship is there betwixt darkness and light ?" If surplice, corner cap, and tippet have been badges of idolaters in the very act of their idolatry, what have the preachers of Christian liberty, and the open rebukers of all superstition, to do with the dregs of the Romish beast ? Our brethren, that of conscience refuse that unprofitable apparel, do neither damn yours, nor molest you that use such vain trifles : if ye shall do the like to them, we doubt not but therein ye shall please God, and comfort the hearts of many which are wounded with extremity, which is used against those godly, and our beloved brethren. Colour of rhetoric or manly persuasion will we use none, but charitably we desire you to call that sentence of pity to mind : " Feed the flock of God which is committed to your charge, caring for them, not by constraint, but willingly ; not as though ye were lords over God's heritage, but that ye may be examples to the flock." And farther, also, we desire you to meditate that sentence of the apostle, saying, " Give none offence, neither to the Jews nor to the Grecians, nor to the Church of God." In what condition of time ye and we both travel in the promoting of Christ's kingdom, we suppose you not to be ignorant ; and therefore we are more bold to exhort you to walk more circumspectly, than that for such vanities the godly should be troubled. For all things that may seem lawful, edify not. If the commandment of authority urge the consciences of your and our brethren more than they can, bear, we unfeignedly crave of you that ye remember that ye are called the light of the world and the earth.

All civil authority hath not the light of God always shining before their eyes in their statutes and commandments ; but their affections oft-time savour too much of the earth, and of worldly wisdom.

And therefore we think that ye should boldly oppose yourselves to all power that will or dare extol itself, not only against God, but also against all such as do burden the consciences of the faithful farther than God hath burdened them by his own Word. But herein we confess our offence, in that we have entered farther in reasoning than we purposed and promised at the beginning; and therefore we shortly return to our former humble supplication, which is, that our brethren who among you refuse the Romish rags, may find of you, the prelates, such favours as our Head and Master commands every one of his members to show one to another, which we look to receive of your gentleness, not only for that ye fear to offend God's majesty, in troubling of your brethren for such vain trifles; but also because ye will not refuse the humble requests of us your brethren and fellow-preachers of Jesus Christ, in whom, albeit, there appear no great worldly pomp, yet we suppose ye will not so far despise us, but that ye will esteem us to be of the number of those that fight against the Roman antichrist, and travail that the kingdom of Christ Jesus universally may be maintained and advanced. The days are evil; iniquity abounds; Christian charity, alas! is waxen cold; and therefore we ought the more diligently to watch; for the hour is uncertain when the Lord Jesus shall appear, before whom we your brethren, and ye, may give an account of our administration.

And thus, in conclusion, we once again crave favour to our brethren, which granted, ye in the Lord shall command us in things of double more importance. The Lord Jesus rule your hearts in his true fear to the end, and give unto us victory over that conjured enemy of all true religion; to wit, over that Roman antichrist, whose wounded head Satan, by all means, labours to cure again, but to destruction shall he and his maintainers go, by the power of the Lord Jesus: to whose mighty power and protection we heartily commit you.

Subscribed by the hands of superintendents, one part of ministers, and scribed in our general assemblies, and fourth session thereof, at Edinburgh, the 28th day of December, 1566.

Your loving brethren and fellow-preachers in Christ Jesus,

Jo. Craig,	Rob. Pont,
Da. Lyndesay,	Jo. Wiram,
Guil. Gislisomus,	Jaco. Mailvil,
Jo. Spottiswood,	Jo. Erskin,
Jo. Row,	Nic. Spital.

No. III.

John Fox's Letter to Queen Elizabeth, to dissuade her from burning two Dutch Anabaptists for heresy in Smithfield. 1575.

SERENISSIMA beatissima princeps, regina 'illustrissima, patriæ decus, sæculi ornamentum! Ut nihil ab animo meo omnique expectatione abfuit longius quam ut majestatis tuæ amplissimam excellentiam molesta interpellatione obturbarem; ita vehementer dolet silentium hoc, quo hactenus constanter sum usus, non eadem constantia perpetuo tueri ita ut volebam licuisse. Ita nunc præter spem ac opinionem meam nescio qua infelicitate evenit, ut quod omnium volebam minime, id contra me maxime faciat hoc tempore. Qui cum ita vixerim hucusque, ut molestus fuerim nemini, invitus nunc cogor contra naturam principi etiam ipsi esse importunus, non re ulla aut causa mea, sed aliena inductus calamitate. Quæ quo acerbior sit et luctuosior,

hoc acriores mihi addit ad deprecandum stimulos. Nonnullos intelligo in Anglia hic esse non Anglos, sed adventitios, Belgas quidem opinor, partim viros, partim feminas, nuper ob improbata dogmata in judicium advocatos. Quorum aliquot feliciter reducti publica luerunt pœnitentia; complures in exilium sunt condemnati, idque rectissime meo judicio factum esse arbitror. Jam ex hoc numero unum esse aut alterum audio, de quibus ultimum exustionis supplicium (nisi succurrat tua pietas) brevi est statuendum. Qua una in re duo contineri perspicio, quorum alterum ad errorum pravitatem, alterum ad supplicii acerbitatem attinet. Ac erroribus quidem ipsis nihil possit absurdius esse, sanus nemo est qui dubitat, mirorque tam fæda opinionum portenta in quosquam potuisse Christianos cadere. Sed ita habet humanæ infirmitatis conditio, si divina paululum luce destituti nobis relinquimur, quo non ruimus præcipites? Atque hoc nomine Christo gratias quam maximas habeo, quòd Anglorum hodie neminem huic insaniæ video. Quod igitur ad phanaticas istas sectas attinet, eas certe in republica nullo modo fovendas esse, sed idonea comprimendas correctione censeo. Verum enim vero ignibus ac flammis pice ac sulphure æstuantibus viva miserorum corpora torrefacere, judicii magis cœcitate quam impetu voluntatis erantium, durum istud ac Romani magis exempli esse quam evangelicæ consuetudinis videtur, ac plane ejusmodi, ut nisi a Romanis pontificibus, authore Innocentio tertio, primum profluxisset, nunquam istum Perilli taurum quisquam in mitem Christi ecclesiam importavisset. Non quod maleficiis delecter, aut erroribus cujusquam faveam, dicta hæc esse velim; vitæ hominum, ipse homo cum sim, faveo; ideoque faveo, non ut erret, sed ut resipiscat: ac neque hominum solum, utinam et pecudibus ipsis opitulari possem. Ita enim sum (stulte fortassis hæc de meipso, at vere dico), macellum ipsum, ubi mactantur etiam pecudes, vix prætereo, quin tacito quodam doloris sensu mens refugiat. Atque equidem in eo Dei ipsius valde admiror, venerorque toto pectore clementiam, qui in jumentis illis brutis et abjectis, quæ sacrificiis olim parabantur, id prosperexerat, ne prius ignibus mandarentur quam sanguis eorum ad basim altaris effunderetur. Unde disceremus, in exigendis suppliciis, quamvis justis, non quid omnino rigori liceat, sed ut clementia simul adhibita rigoris temperet asperitatem.

Quamobrem si tantum mihi apud principis tanti majestatem audere liceret supplex pro Christo rogarem clementissimam hanc regiæ sublimitatis excellentiam, præ authoritate hac *mea (lege tua)* qua ad vitam multorum *consecrandam pellere (l. conservandam pollere)* te divina voluit clementia, ut vita si fieri possit (quid enim non posset iis in rebus authoritas tua!), miserorum parcatur, saltem ut horrori obsistatur, atque in aliud quodcunque commutetur supplicii genus. Sunt ejectiones, inclusiones retrusæ, sunt vincula, sunt perpetua exilia, sunt stigmata et πλήγματα aut etiam patibula; id unum valde deprecor, ne piras ac flammas Smithfieldianas jam diu faustissimis tuis auspiciis huc usque sopitas, sinas nunc recandescere. Quod si ne id quidem obtineri possit, id saltem omnibus supplicandi modis efflagito, τοῦτο τὸ πελαργικὸν pectoris tui implorans, ut mensem tamen unum aut alterum nobis concedas, quo interim experiamur, an a periculosis erroribus dederit dominus ut resanescant, ne cum corp rum jactura, animæ pariter cum corporibus de æterno periclitentur exitio.*

No. IV.

A Directory of Church Government, anciently contended for, and, as far as the times would suffer, practised by the first Nonconformists in the days of Queen Elizabeth, found in the study of the most accomplished divine, Mr. Thomas Cartwright, after his decease.

The sacred Discipline of the Church described in the Word of God.

THE discipline of Christ's Church, that is necessary for all times, is delivered by Christ, and set down in the Holy Scriptures; therefore the true and lawful discipline is to be fetched from thence, and from thence alone; and that which resteth upon any other foundation ought to be estemed unlawful and counterfeit.

Of all particular churches, there is one and the same right, order, and form : therefore, also, no one may challenge to itself any power over others, nor any right which doth not alike agree to others.

The ministers of public charges, in every particular church, ought to be called and appointed to their charges by a lawful ecclesiastical calling, such as hereafter is set down.

All these, for the divers regard of their several kinds, are of equal power among themselves.

No man can be lawfully called to public charge in any church but he that is fit to discharge the same. And none is to be accounted fit but he that is endued with the common gifts of all the godly, that is, with faith, and a blameless life; and farther, also, with those that are proper to that ministry wherein he is to be used, and necessary for the executing of the same; whereupon, for trial of those gifts, some convenient way and examination are to be used.

The party to be called must first be elected; then he is to be ordained to that charge whereunto he is chosen by the prayers of that church whereunto he is to be admitted, the mutual duties of him and of the church being before laid open.

The ministers of the church are, first, they that are ministers of the Word: In their examination, it is specially to be taken heed unto that they be apt to teach, and tried men, not utterly unlearned, nor newly planted and converted to the faith.

Now these ministers of the Word are, first, pastors which do administer the Word and sacraments; then, teachers, which are occupied in wholesome doctrine.

Besides, there are also elders, which watch over the life and behaviour of every man; and deacons, which have care over the poor.

Farther, in every particular church there ought to be a presbytery, which is a consistory, and, as it were, a senate of elders. Under the name of elders here are contained, they who in the Church minister doctrine, and they who are properly called elders.

By the common counsel of the eldership all

things are directed that belong to the state of their church. First, such as belong to the guidance of the whole body of it in the holy and common assembly, gathered together in the name of the Lord, that all things may be done in them duly, orderly, and to edification. 2. Then, also, such as pertain to particular persons. First, to all the members of that church, that the good may enjoy all the privileges that belong unto them; that the wicked may be corrected with ecclesiastical censures, according to the quality of the fault, private and public, by admonishing and by removing either from the Lord's Supper by suspension (as it is commonly called), or out of the church by excommunication. The which belong specially to the ministers of public charge in the church to their calling, either to be begun or ended, and ended either by relieving or punishing them, and that for a time by suspension, or altogether by deposition.

For directing of the eldership, let the pastors be set over it; or if there be more pastors than one in the same church, let the pastors do it in their turns.

But yet, in all the greater affairs of the church, as in excommunicating of any, and in choosing and deposing of church ministers, nothing may be concluded without the knowledge and consent of the church.

Particular churches ought to yield mutual help one to another; for which cause they are to communicate among themselves.

The end of this communicating together is, that all things in them may be so directed, both in regard of doctrine, and also of discipline, as by the Word of God they ought to be.

Therefore the things that belong hereunto are determined by the common opinion of those who meet so to communicate together, and whatsoever is to be amended, furthered, or procured in any of those several churches that belong to that assembly. Wherein, albeit, no particular church hath power over another, yet every particular church of the same resort, meeting, and counsel, ought to obey the opinion of more churches with whom they communicate.

For holding of these meetings and assemblies, there are to be chosen, by every church belonging to that assembly, principal men from among the elders, who are to have their instructions from them, and so to be sent to the assembly. There must also be a care had that the things they shall return to have been godly agreed on by the meetings be diligently observed by the churches.

Farther, in such assemblies there is also to be chosen one that may be set over the assemblies, who may moderate and direct them. His duty is to see that the assemblies be held godly, quietly, and comely : therefore it belongeth unto him to begin and end the conference with prayer; to know every man's instructions; to propound in order the things that are to be handled; to gather their opinions, and to propound what is the opinion of the greater part. It is also the part of the rest of the assembly to speak their opinions of the things propounded godly and quietly. :

The Synodical Discipline gathered out of the Synods and use of the Churches which have restored it according to the Word of God, and out

---

of elders here are contained, they who in the Church minister döctrine, and they who are properly called elders.

By the common counsel of the eldership all

* Fuller's Church History of Britain, p. 104, 105.

also the part of the rest of the assembly to speak their opinions of the things propounded godly and quietly.

The Synodical Discipline gathered out of the Synods and use of the Churches which have restored it according to the Word of God, and out

Engraved by Gimber from an Original.

EDMUND CALAMY, B.D.

of sundry Books that are written of the same, and referred under certain Heads.

Of the Necessity of a Calling.

Let no man thrust himself into the executing of any part of public charge in the administration of the Word, sacraments, discipline, or care over the poor. Neither let any such sue or seek for any public charge of the church; but let every one tarry until he be lawfully called.

The Manner of entering and determining of a Calling, and against a Ministry of no certain Place, and the Desertion of a Church.

Let none be called but unto some certain charge ordained of God, and to the exercising of the same in some particular congregation; and he that is so called, let him be so bound to that —— church, that he may not after be of any other, or depart from it without the consent thereof. Let none be called but they that have first subscribed the confession of doctrine and of discipline, whereof let them be admonished to have copies with themselves.

In the examination of ministers, the testimony of the place from whence they come is to be demanded, whereby it may be understood what life and conversation he hath been of, and whether he hath been addicted to any heresy, or to the reading of any heretical books, or to curious and strange questions, and idle speculations; or, rather, whether he be accounted sound and consenting in all things to the doctrine received in the church. Whereunto if he agree, he is also to expound some part of the Holy Scriptures twice or oftener, as it shall seem meet to the examiners, and that before the conference, and that church which is interested. Let him also be demanded of the principal heads of divinity; and whether he will diligently execute and discharge his ministry; and in the execution thereof propound unto himself, not his own desires and commodities, but the glory of God and edification of the church. Lastly, whether he will be studious and careful to maintain and preserve wholesome doctrine and ecclesiastical discipline. Thus, let the minister be examined, not only by one eldership, but also by some greater meeting and assembly.

Of Election.

Before the election of a minister, and the deliberation of the conference concerning the same, let there be a day of fast kept in the church interested.

Of the Place of exercising this Calling.

Albeit it be lawful for a minister, upon just occasion, to preach in another church than that whereof he is minister, yet none may exercise any ordinary ministry elsewhere but for a certain time, upon great occasion, and by the consent of his church and conference.

Of the Office of the Ministers of the Word; and, first, of the Order of Liturgy or Common Prayer.

Let the minister that is to preach name a psalm, or a part of a psalm, beginning with the first, and so proceeding, that may be sung by the church, noting to them the end of their singing, to wit, the glory of God and their own edification. After the psalm, let a short admonition to the people follow, of preparing them-

selves to pray duly unto God: then let there be made a prayer containing a general confession, first of the guilt of sin, both original and actual, and of the punishment which is due by the law for them both: then, also, of the promise of the Gospel, and, in respect of it, supplication of pardon for the said guilt and punishment, and petition of grace promised, as for the duties of the whole life, so especially for the godly expounding and receiving of the Word. Let this petition be concluded with the Lord's Prayer. After the sermon, let prayer be made again; first, for grace to profit by the doctrine delivered, then for all men, but chiefly for the universal Church, and for all estates and degrees of the people; which is likewise to be ended with the Lord's Prayer and the singing of a psalm, as before. Last of all, let the congregation be dismissed with some convenient form of blessing taken out of the Scripture; such as is Numb., vi., 24; 2 Cor., xiii., 14.

Of Preaching.

Let him that shall preach choose some part of the canonical Scripture to expound, and not of the Apocrypha. Farther, in his ordinary ministry, let him not take postils, as they are called, but some whole book of the Holy Scripture, especially of the New Testament, to expound in order: in choice whereof regard is to be had both of the minister's ability, and of the edification of the church.

He that preacheth must perform two things: the first, that his speech be uncorrupt; which is to be considered both in regard of the doctrine, that it be holy, sound, wholesome, and profitable to edification; not devilish, heretical, leavened, corrupt, fabulous, curious, or contentious; and also in respect of the manner of it, that it be proper to the place which is handled, that is, which either is contained plainly in the very words; or if it be gathered by consequent, that the same be fit and clear, and such as may rise upon the property of the Word, grace of speech, and suit of the matter; and not be allegorical, strange, wrested, or far-fetched. Now let that which is such, and chiefly which is fittest for the times and occasions of the church, be delivered. Farther, let the explication, confirmation, enlargement, and application, and the whole treatise and handling of it, be in the vulgar tongue; and let the whole confirmation and proof be made by arguments, testimonies, and examples taken only out of the Holy Scriptures, applied fitly, and according to the natural meaning of the places that are alleged.

The second thing to be performed by him that preacheth is a reverend gravity; this is considered first in the style, phrase, and manner of speech, that it be spiritual, pure, proper, simple, and applied to the capacity of the people; nor such as human wisdom teacheth, nor savouring of new-fangledness, nor either so affectate as it may serve for pomp and ostentation, or so careless and base as becometh not ministers of the Word of God. Secondly, it is also to be regarded as well in ordering the voice, in which a care must be had that (avoiding the keeping always of one tone) it may be equal, and both rise and fall by degrees: as also in ordering the gesture, wherein (the body being upright) the guiding and ordering the whole body is to follow the voice, there being avoided in it all unseemly gestures of the head or other parts, and often turning of the body to divers sides. Finally, let the gesture be grave, modest, and seemly, not utterly none, nor too much, neither like the gestures of players or fencers.

These things are to be performed by him that preacheth ; whereby, when need requireth, they may be examined who are trained and exercised, to be made fit to preach : let there be, if it may be, every Sabbath-day, two sermons, and let them that preach always endeavour to keep themselves within one hour, especially on the week-days. The use of preaching at burials is to be left as it may be done conveniently, because there is danger that they may nourish the superstition of some, or be abused to pomp and vanity.

Of the Catechism.

Let the catechism be taught in every church. Let there be two sorts : one more large, applied to the delivering of the sum of religion by a suit and order of certain places of the Scriptures, according to which some point of the holy doctrine may be expounded every week ; another of the same sort, but shorter, fit for the examination of the rude and ignorant before they be admitted to the Lord's Supper.

Of the other Parts of Liturgy or Divine Service.

All the rest of the liturgy or Divine service consisteth in the administration of the sacraments, and, by the custom of the Church, in the blessing of marriage : the most commodious form thereof is that which is used by the churches that have reformed their —— discipline according to the Word of God.

Of Sacraments.

Let only a minister of the Word, that is, a preacher, minister the sacraments, and that after the preaching of the Word, and not in any other place than in the public assemblies of the Church.

Of Baptism.

Women only may not offer unto baptism those that are to be baptized, but the father, if it may be, or, in his name, some other. They which present unto baptism ought to be persuaded not to give those that are baptized the names of God, or of Christ, or of angels, or of holy offices, as of Baptist, Evangelist, &c., nor such as savour of paganism or popery ; but chiefly such whereof there are examples in the Holy Scriptures, in the names of those who are reported in them to have been godly and virtuous.

Of the Communion,

Let the time of celebrating the Communion be made known eight days before, that the congregation may prepare themselves, and that the elders may do their duty in going to and visiting whom they ought.

Of signifying their Names that are to communicate.

Let them which before have not been received to the Lord's Table, when they first desire to come to it, give their names to the minister seven days before the Communion, that care of inquiring of them may be committed to the el-

ders ; that if there be any cause of hinderance, there may be stay made betimes ; but if there be no such thing, let them proceed (where need may be) to the examining of their faith, before the Communion. Let this whole treatise of discipline be read in the consistory ; and let the ministers, elders, and deacons be censured one after another, yet so that the minister concerning doctrine be censured of ministers only.

Let them only be admitted to the Communion that have made confession of their faith, and submitted themselves to the discipline : unless they shall bring letters testimonial of good credit from some other place, or shall approve themselves by some other sufficient testimony.

Children are not to be admitted to the Communion before they be of the age of fourteen years, except the consistory shall otherwise determine.

On the Sabbath-day next before the Communion, let mention be made in the sermon of the examination whereunto the apostle exhorteth, and of the peace that is by faith ; in the day of the Communion, let there be speech of the doctrine of the sacraments, and especially of the Lord's Supper.

Of Fasting.

Let the day of fasting be published by the pastor according to the advice of the consistory, either for supplication, for turning away of calamities present, or for petition of some special grace. Let the sermons upon the same day, before and after noon (as on the Lord's Day), be such as may be fit for the present occasion.

Of Holydays.

Holydays are conveniently to be abolished.

Of Marriage.

Let espousing go before marriage. Let the words of espousing be of the present time, and without condition, and before sufficient witnesses on both sides. It is to be wished that the minister, or any elder, be present at the espousals, who, having called upon God, may admonish both parties of their duties. First, may have care of avoiding the degrees forbidden both by the law of God and man ; and then they may demand of them whether they be free from any bond of marriage : which, if they profess and be strangers, he may also require sufficient testimony. Farther, also, they are to be demanded whether they have been married before, and of the death of the party with whom they were married, which, if they acknowledge and be strangers, he may demand convenient testimony of the death of the other party. Finally, let them be asked if they be under the government of any ; whether they whom it concerneth have consented.

The espousals being done in due order, let them not be dissolved, though both parties should consent. Let the marriage be solemnized within two months after. Before the marriage let the promise be published three several Sabbath-days ; but first, let the parties espoused, with their parents or governors, desire the publishing thereof, of the minister and two elders at the least, that they may be demanded of those things that are needful ; and let them require to see the instrument of the covenant of the marriage; or, at least, sufficient testimony of the espousals. Marriage may be solemnized and blessed upon any ordinary day of public prayer, saving upon a day of fast.

Of Schools.

Let children be instructed in schools, both in other learning, and especially in the catechism, that they may repeat it by heart, and understand it : when they are so instructed, let them be brought to the Lord's Supper, after they have been examined by the minister and allowed by him.

Of Students of Divinity, and their Exercises.

In every church where it may conveniently be done, care is to be had that some poor scholars, studious of divinity, being fit for theological exercises, and especially for expounding of Holy Scripture, may, by the liberality of the godly rich, be taught and trained up to preach.

Let that exposition, as often as it shall be convenient to be had, be in the presence at least of one minister, by whose presence they may be kept in order, and in the same sort (as touching the manner of preaching) that public sermons are made: which being ended, let the other students (he being put apart that was speaker) note wherein he hath failed in any of those things that are to be performed by him that preacheth publicly, as is set down before ; of whose opinion let the minister that is present, and is moderator of their exercise, judge and admonish the speaker as he shall think meet.

Of Elders.

Let the elders know every particular house and person of the church, that they may inform the minister of the condition of every one, and the deacons of the sick and poor, that they may take care to provide for them : they are not to be perpetual, neither yet easily to be changed.

Of Consistories.

In the consistory the most voices are to be yielded unto. In it only ecclesiastical things are to be handled. Of them, first, they are to be dealt with such as belong to the common direction of the public assembly, in the order of liturgy, or Divine service, sermon, prayers, sacraments, marriages, and burials. Then with such also as pertain to the oversight of every one, and their particular deeds. Farther, they are to cause such things as shall be thought meet to be registered and written in a book. They are also to cause to be written in another book the names of them that are baptized, with the names of their parents and sureties : likewise of the communicants. Farther, also, are to be noted their names that are married, that die, and to whom letters testimonial are given.

Of the Censures.

None is to be complained of unto the consistory, unless first the matter being uttered with silencing the parties' names, if it seem meet so to be done by the judgment of the consistory.

In private and less faults, the precept of Christ, Matt., xviii., is to be kept.

Greater and public offences are to be handled by the consistory. Farther, public offences are to be esteemed, first, such as are done openly before all, or whomsoever, the whole church knowing of it. Secondly, such as be done in a public place, albeit few know it. Thirdly, that are made such by pertinacity and contempt. Fourthly, that for the heinousness of the offence are to be punished with some grievous civil punishment.

They that are to be excommunicated; being in public charge in the church, are to be deposed also from their charges. They also are to be discharged that are unfit for the ministry, by reason of their ignorance, or of some incurable disease, or by any other such cause are disabled to perform their ministry; but in the room of such as are disabled by means of sickness or age, let another be placed without the reproach of him that is discharged ; and farther, so as the reverence of the ministry may remain unto him, and he may be provided for, liberally and in good order.

When there is question concerning a heretic complained of to the consistory, straight let two or three neighbour ministers be called, men godly and learned, and free from that suspicion, by whose opinion he may be suspended till such time as the conference may take knowledge of his cause.

The obstinate, after admonition by the consistory, though the fault have not been so great, are to be suspended from the Communion ; and if they continue in their obstinacy, this shall be the order to proceed to their excommunication. Three several Sabbath-days after the sermon, publicly let be declared the offence committed by the offender. The first Sabbath let not the offender's name be published : the second, let it be declared, and withal a certain day of the week named to be kept for that cause in fasting and prayer : the third, let warning be given of his excommunicating to follow the next Sabbath after, except there may be showed some sufficient cause to the contrary : so, upon the fourth Sabbath-day, let the sentence of excommunication be pronounced against him, that his spirit may be saved in the day of the Lord.

He that hath committed great offences, opprobrious to the church, and to be grievously punished by the magistrate's authority, albeit he profess his repentance in words, yet for the trial thereof, and to take away the offence, let him for a time be kept from the Communion ; which, how often and how long it is to be done, let the consistory, according to their discretion, determine ; after which, if the party repent, he is brotherly to be received again, but not until he have openly professed his repentance before the church, by consent whereof he should have been excommunicated.

If the ministers of any public charge of the church commit any such thing, they are to be deposed from their charge.

Of the Assemblies of the Church.

Particular churches are to communicate one with another, by common meetings and resorts : in them only ecclesiastical matters are to be handled, and of those, only such as pertain to the churches of that resort ; concerning other churches, unless they be desired, they are to determine nothing farther than to refer such matters to their next common and great meeting.

Let the order of proceeding in them be this : first, let the survey be taken of those that are present, and the names of those that are absent, and should be there, be noted, that they may give a reason at their next meeting of their absence, or be censured by the judgment of the assembly. Next, let the acts of the last assembly of that kind be read, that if any of the same remain unfinished, they may be despatched: then, let those things be dealt in that are properly belonging to the present assembly, where first the instructions sent from the churches are to be delivered by every one in order, as they sit together; with their letters of credence. Secondly, let the state of the churches of that resort be considered; to wit, how they are instructed and guided; whether the holy doctrine and discipline be taught and exercised in them; and whether the ministers of public charges do their duty, and such like. Furthermore, they shall determine of those things that do appertain to the common state of all the churches of that resort, or unto any of the same; which way may be sufficient for the oversight of the churches. Lastly, if it seem meet, the delegates present may be censured.

They that are to meet in such assemblies are to be chosen by the consent of the churches of that assembly and conference to whom it may appertain.

Let such only be chosen that exercise public function in the church of ministry or eldership, and which have subscribed to the doctrine and discipline, and have promised to behave themselves according to the Word of God; notwithstanding, it may be lawful also to be present for other elders and other ministers; and likewise (if the assembly think it meet) for deacons, and for students in divinity, especially those that exercise themselves in expounding the Holy Scriptures in the conferences, and be asked their opinion; which in students is to this end, that their judgment, in handling matters ecclesiastical, may be both tried and sharpened. But they only are to give voice which are chosen by the churches, and have brought their instructions signed from them.

If there fall out any very weighty matter to be consulted of, let notice of it be given to the moderator of the assembly next going before, or to the minister of that church where the next meeting is to be: the same is to send word of it in due time to the minister of every church of that assembly, that they may communicate it aforehand with those to whom it appertaineth, that the delegates resorting to the next meeting may understand and report their judgments.

In appointing of the place for the assembly, regard must be had of the convenient distance, and other commodities; that no part may justly complain that they are burdensome above others.

In every such ecclesiastical assembly it is meet there be a moderator: he is to have charge of the assembly, to see if kept in good order. He is always, if it may be conveniently, to be changed. The choice is to be in this manner: The moderator of the former assembly of that kind, or, in his absence, the minister of the church where they meet, having first prayed fitly to that purpose, is to move the assembly to choose a moderator. He being chosen is to provide that the things done in the assembly may be written, that the delegates of every church may write them out, and communicate

them with the conferences from whence they came.

The moderator is also, by the order and judgment of the assembly, to give answer, either by speech or by letters, to such as desire any answer; and to execute censures, if any be to be executed. Farther, he is to procure all things to be done in it godlily and quietly; exhorting to meekness, moderation of spirit, and forbearing one of another where need shall be, and referring it to the assembly to take order for such as are obstinate and contentious. Lastly, he is to remember them of the next meeting following, with thanks for their pains, and exhortation to proceed cheerfully in their callings; and so courteously to dismiss the assembly. Before such time none may depart without leave of the assembly.

Those assemblies, according to their kinds, have great authority if they be greater, and less if they be less. Therefore, unless it be a plain act, and manifest unto all, if any think himself injured by the less meeting, he may appeal still unto a greater, till he come to a general council, so that he ascend orderly from the less to the next greater. But it is to be understood that the sentence of the assemblies be holden firm until it be otherwise judged by an assembly of greater authority.

Assemblies or Meetings are either Conferences or Synods.

Conferences are the meetings of the elders of a few churches, as, for example, of twelve. There are to meet in a conference, chosen of the eldership of every particular church, one minister and one elder. The conferences are to be kept once in six weeks.

They are specially to look into the state of the churches of that resort and conference, examining particularly these several points: Whether all things be done in them according to the holy doctrine and discipline of the Gospel; to wit, whether any questions be moved concerning any point of doctrine? Whether the ecclesiastical discipline be duly observed? Whether any minister be wanting in any of those churches, that a sufficient one in due time may be procured? Whether the other ministers of public charge in the church be appointed in every congregation? Whether care be had of schools, and for the poor? Finally, they are to be demanded wherein any of them needeth the advice of the conference for the advancement of the Gospel among them.

Before the end of the meeting, if it shall be so thought good by them, let one of the ministers assembled in conference, either chosen by voice, or taking it by turn, preach publicly. Of his speech, let the rest judge among themselves, the elders being put apart, admonish him brotherly, if there be any cause, examining all things according to those rules that are before declared in the chapter concerning the things that are to be performed by those that preach.

Of Synods.

A synod is the meeting of chosen men of many conferences: in them let the whole treatise of discipline be read: in them, also, other things first being finished, as was said before, let all those that are present be censured, if it may be done conveniently, and let them also have a communion in and with the church where they were called. ·····

There are two sorts of synods: the first is particular, which comprehendeth both the provincial and national synod. A provincial synod is the meeting of the chosen men of every conference within the province. A province containeth four and twenty conferences.

A fit way to call a provincial council may be this: the care thereof, except themselves will determine of it, may be committed to the particular eldership of some conference within the province; which, by advice of the same conference, may appoint the place and time for the meeting of the provincial synod.

To that church or eldership are to be sent the matters that seemed, to the particular conferences, more difficult for them to take order in, and such as belong to the churches of the whole province; which is to be done diligently and in good time, that the same may, in due season, give notice of the place and time of the synod, and of the matters to be debated therein, that they which shall be sent may come the better prepared, and judge of them according to the advice of the conferences.

Two ministers, and as many elders, are to be sent from every conference unto the provincial synod. The same is to be held every half year, or oftener, till the discipline be settled. It is to be held three months before every national synod, that they may prepare and make ready those things that pertain to the national. The acts of the provincial synod are to be sent unto the national, by the eldership of that church in which it was holden; and every minister is to be furnished with a copy of them, and with the reasons of the same. A national synod, or convocation, is a meeting of the chosen men of every province within the dominion of the same nation and civil government. The way to call it, unless it shall determine otherwise, may be the same with the provincial, that is, by the eldership of some particular church, which shall appoint the time and place of the next national convocation; but not otherwise than by the advice of their provincial synod.

Out of every provincial synod there are to be chosen three ministers, and as many elders, to be sent to the national. They are to handle the things pertaining to the churches of the whole nation or kingdom, as the doctrine, discipline, ceremonies, things not decided by inferior meetings, appeals, and such like. By the order of the same, one is to be appointed which may gather into one book the notes of every particular church.

Thus much for particular meetings; the universal followeth, which is called a general or œcumenical council, which is a meeting of the chosen men of every national synod. The acts of all such councils are to be registered and reported in a book.

The discipline, entitled "The Discipline of the Church," described in the Word of God, as far as we can judge, is taken and drawn from the most pure fountain of the Word of God, and containeth in it the discipline of the Church that is necessary, essential, and common to all ages of the Church.

The synodical also adjoined, as it resteth upon the same foundations, is likewise necessary and perpetual; but as far as it is not expressly confirmed by authority of the Holy Scripture, but is applied to the use and times of the Church as their divers states may require, according to the analogy and general rules of the same Scripture, is to be judged profitable for the churches that receive it, but may be changed in such things as belong not to the essence of the discipline upon a like godly reason, as the divers estates of the Church may require.

The Form of the Subscription.

The brethren of the conference of N., whose names are here underwritten, have subscribed this discipline after this manner: This discipline we allow as a godly discipline, and agreeable to the Word of God; yet so as we may be satisfied in the things hereunto noted, and desire the same so acknowledged by us, to be furthered by all lawful means, that by public authority of the magistrate and of our church it may be established.

Which thing, if it may be obtained of her rign·· excellent majesty, and other the magistrates or this kingdom, we promise that we will do nothing against it, whereby the public peace of the Church may be troubled. In the mean time, we promise to observe it, as far as may be lawful for us so to do, by the public laws of this kingdom, and by the peace of our church.

No. V.

A Letter of the Puritan Ministers imprisoned to her Majesty, in Vindication of their Innocence, dated April, 1592.

"May it please your excellent majesty,

"THERE is nothing, right gracious sovereign, next to the saving mercy of Almighty God, that can be more comfortable than your highness's favour, as to all other your faithful and dutiful subjects, so to us your majesty's most humble suppliants, who are by our calling ministers of God's holy Word, and by our present condition now, and of long time, prisoners in divers prisons in and about the city of London, for which cause our most humble suit is, that it may please your most excellent majesty graciously to understand our necessary answer to such grievous charges as we hear to be informed against us, which, if they were true, might be just cause of withdrawing forever from us your highness's gracious protection and favour, which, above all other earthly things, we most desire to enjoy. The reason of our trouble is a suspicion that we should be guilty of many heinous crimes; but these supposed crimes we have not been charged with in any due and ordinary course of proceeding, by open accusation, and witnesses. But being called up to London by authority of some of your majesty's commissioners in causes ecclesiastical, we have been required by them to take an oath of inquisition or office, as it is called, for not taking whereof we were first committed to prison, and since have continued there a long time, notwithstanding that all of us, save one, have been deprived of our livings and degraded of our ministry.

"Wherefore, for that the oath is the next and immediate cause of our trouble, we have made our answer first to that, and then alter also to the crimes that are suggested, and secretly informed against us.

The Oath.

" As for the oath, the reason why we took it not is because it is without limitation of any certain matter, infinite and general, to answer whatsoever shall be demanded of us. Of this kind of oath we find neither rule nor example in the Word of God; but contrariwise, both precepts and precedents of all lawful oaths reported in the same tend to this, that an oath ought to be taken with judgment, and so as he that sweareth may see the bounds of his oath, and to what condition it does bind him, &c. But this oath is to inquire of our private speeches and conferences with our dearest and nearest friends, yea, of the very secret thoughts and intents of our hearts, that so may we furnish both matter of accusation and evidence of proof against ourselves, which was not used to be done in causes of heresy or high treason ; for these are the words of the statutes of your most noble father, Henry VIII. :* ' For that the most expert and best learned cannot escape the danger of such captious interrogatories (as the law calleth them) which are accustomed to be administered by the ordinaries of this realm ; as also that it standeth not with the right order of justice, or good equity; that any person should be convicted, or put to the loss of life, good name, or goods, unless it be by due accusation and witness, or by presentment, verdict, confession, or process of outlawry ; and farther, for the avoiding untrue accusations and presentments which might be maliciously conspired, and kept secret and unrevealed, till time might be espied to have men thereof by malice convicted,' it was ordained that none should be put to answer but upon accusation and presentments taken in open and manifest courts, by the oath of twelve men.†

Schism.

" As to the charge of schism, and that we so far condemned the state of the Church, that we hold it not for any true, visible Church of God, as it is established by public authority within the land, and therefore refuse to have any part or communion with it in public prayers, or in the ministry of the Word and sacraments : if this were true, we were of all men living the most unthankful, first to Almighty God, and next to your excellent majesty, by whose blessed means we are partakers of that happy liberty of the profession of the Gospel, and of the true service of God, that by your highness's gracious government we do enjoy. We acknowledge unfeignedly, as in the sight of God, that this our church, as it is by your highness's laws and authority established among us, having that faith professed and taught publicly in it that was agreed of in the Convocation of 1562, and such form of public prayers and administration of the sacraments as, in the first year of your most gracious reign was established (notwithstanding anything that may need to be revised and further reformed), is a true visible Church of Christ, from the holy communion whereof, by way of schism, it is not lawful to depart.

" Our whole life may show the evident proof

* An. 25 Hen. VIII., cap. xiv.
† Ibid., cap. xv., § 3.

hereof ; for always before the time of our trouble we have lived in the daily communion of it, not only as private men, but at the time of our restraint (as many years before) preached and exercised our ministry in the same ; and at this present most earnestly beseech all in authority that is set over us, especially your excellent majesty, that we may so proceed to serve God and your highness all the days of our life.

Rebellion.

" Another crime suggested against us is, that we should practice or purpose rebelliously to procure such farther reformation of our church as we desire by violent and undutiful means. Whereunto our answer is, that we think it not lawful to make a schism in the Church for anything that we esteem needful to be reformed in it, so do we, in all simplicity and sincerity of heart, declare, in the presence of Almighty God, to whom all secrets are known, and of your excellent majesty, to whom the sword is given of God for just vengeance and punishment of transgressors, that for procuring reformation of anything that we desire to be redressed in the state of our church, we judge it most unlawful and damnable by the Word of God to rebel, and by force of arms or any violent means to seek redress thereof ; and moreover, that we never intended to use or procure any other means for the furtherance of such reformation than only prayer to Almighty God, and most humble suit to your excellent majesty, and others in authority, with such like dutiful and peaceful means as might give information of this our suit, and of the reasons moving us thereunto.

Supremacy.

" The third crime misinformed against us is, that we impeach your majesty's supremacy. For answer whereunto we unfeignedly protest (God being witness that we speak the truth herein from our hearts) that we acknowledge your highness's sovereignty and supreme power, next and immediately under God, over all persons, and in all causes, as well ecclesiastical as civil, in as large and ample manner as it is agnized by the High Court of Parliament in the statute of recognition, as is set down in the oath of supremacy enacted by the same ; and as it is farther declared in your majesty's injunctions, and also in the articles of religion agreed in the Convocation, and in sundry books of learned men of our nation, published and allowed by public authority. We add yet hereunto, that we acknowledge the same as fully as ever it was in old time acknowledged by the prophets to belong to the virtuous kings of Judah ; and as all the Reformed churches in Christendom acknowledge the same to their sovereign princes, in the confessions of their faith exhibited unto them, as they are set down in a book named the Harmony of Confessions, and the observations annexed thereunto.

" And besides the protestation, we appeal to the former whole course of our lives, wherein it cannot be showed that we ever made question of it ; and more particularly by our public doctrine, declaring the same ; and by our taking the oath of supremacy as occasion hath required.

Excommunication.

" It hath been odiously devised against us,

concerning the persons subject to excommunication, and the power thereof, how far it extendeth ; touching the former, we judge not otherwise herein than all the Reformed churches that are this day in the Christian world, nor than our own English Church, both always heretofore hath judged, and doth still at this present, as may appear by the articles of religion agreed by the Convocation, and by a book of homilies allowed by the same, and also by sundry other books of greatest credit and authority in our church ; which is, that the Word of God, the sacraments, and the power of binding and loosing, are all ordinances of Almighty God, graciously ordained for the comfort and salvation of the whole Church ; and that therefore no part or member of it is to be denied the comfortable, wholesome aid and benefit thereof, for the furtherance of their faith, and (as need may require) of their repentance, &c.

" For the other part, how far this censure extendeth, we profess that it depriveth a man only of their comforts, as of being partaker of the Lord's Table, and being present at the public prayers of the Church, or such like, without taking away either liberty, goods, lands, government private or public whatsoever, or any other civil or earthly commodity of this life. Wherefore, from our hearts we detest and abhor that intolerable presumption of the Bishop of Rome, taking upon him, in such cases, to depose sovereign princes from their highest seats of supreme government, and discharging their subjects from that dutiful obedience that, by the laws of God, they ought to perform.

Conferences.

" Concerning our conferences, we have been charged to have given orders, and made ministers, and to have administered the censures of the Church, and, finally, to have exercised all ecclesiastical jurisdiction. To which suggestion we answer, that indeed of long time we have used, as other ministers have done (as we think in most parts of the land), to meet sometimes and confer together ; which being granted to all good and dutiful subjects upon occasion to resort and meet together, we esteem it is lawful for us to do so.

" For besides the common affairs of all men, which may give them just cause to meet with their acquaintance and friends, mutually to communicate for their comfort and help one with another, men professing learning have more necessary and special use of such conferences, for their furtherance in such knowledge as they profess. But such as are professed ministers of the Word have sundry great and necessary causes so to do more than others, because of the manifold knowledge both of divinity, and also of divers tongues and sciences, that are of great use for the better enabling them for their ministry ; in which respect the conferences of the ministers were allowed by many bishops within their dioceses, and to our knowledge never disallowed or forbidden by any. Some late years, also, have given us more special cause of conferring together, where Jesuits, Seminarists, and other heretics sought to seduce many ; and wherein, also, some schismatics condemned the whole state of our church, as no part of the true visible Church of Christ, and

therefore refused to have any part or communion with it : upon which occasion, it is needful for us to advise of the best way and means we could to keep the people that we had charge to instruct from such damnable errors.

" Farther also particularly, because some reckoned us to have part with their schism, and reported us to agree in nothing, but to differ one from another in the reformation we desire ; we have special cause to confer together, that we might set down some things touching such matters, which at all times, whensoever we should be demanded, might be our true and just defence, both to clear us from partaking with the schism, and to witness for us that we agreed in the reformation we desire.

" But as touching the thing surmised of our meetings, that we exercise in them all ecclesiastical jurisdiction, in making ministers, in censuring and excommunicating, in ordaining constitutions and orders upon such censures to bind any, we protest before God and the holy angels that we never exercised any part of such jurisdiction, nor had any purpose agreed among us to exercise the same, before we should by public law for authorized thereunto.

" Farther, also, touching such our meetings, we affirm that they were only of ministers (saving in some parts where a schoolmaster, two or three, desirous to train themselves to the ministry, joined with us); and the same, but of six or seven, or like small number in a conference, without all deed of appearance that might be offensive to any.

Singularity.

" Which, though it be not subject to any punishment of law, yet is suggested against us by such as favour not our most humble desire of a farther reformation, to disgrace us, and make us odious with others, and chiefly with your excellent majesty ; whereunto our answer is, that the discipline of the primitive Church is ancient, and so acknowledged by the Book of Common Prayer, in these words, ' that there was a godly discipline in the primitive Church ; instead whereof, until the said discipline may be restored again (which thing is much to be wished), it is thought convenient to use such a form of commination as is prescribed.'

" Farther, also, if it please your majesty with favour to understand it from us, we are ready to show, that in such points of ecclesiastical discipline of our church, which we desire most humbly may be reformed, we hold no singular or private opinion, but the truth of the Word of God, acknowledged to be such by all the best churches and writers of ancient time, and of this present age.

" Thus have we declared, right gracious sovereign, truly and sincerely, as we will answer it before God, and to your majesty upon our allegiance, what judgment we are of concerning the matters informed against us ; and farther testify, that no minister within this land desiring a farther reformation, with whom we have had any private acquaintance or conference of these matters (whosoever may be otherwise informed), is of any other mind or opinion in these cases that have been named ; by which declaration, if (according to our earnest prayers to Almighty God) your majesty shall clearly discern us to stand free from all such matters as we are charged with, our most humble suit is, that your majesty's gracious favour (which is more dear and precious to us than our lives) may be extended to us, and that by means thereof we may enjoy the comfortable liberty of our persons and ministry, as we did before our troubles; which, if by your highness's special mercy and goodness we may obtain, we promise and vow to Almighty God, and your excellent majesty, to behave ourselves in so peaceable and dutiful sort in every respect, as may give no just cause of your highness's offence, but according to our callings, both in doctrine and example as heretofore, so always hereafter, to teach due obedience to your majesty among other parts of holy doctrine; and to pray for your majesty's long and blessed reign over us," &c.*

No. VI.

Articles of Religion agreed upon by the Archbishops and Bishops, and the rest of the Clergy of Ireland, in the Convocation holden at Dublin, in the year of our Lord 1615, for the avoiding of Diversities of Opinions, and the establishing of Consent touching true Religion.

N.B. In these articles are comprehended, almost word for word, the nine articles agreed on at Lambeth, the 20th of November, 1595. This mark * points at each of them, and their number.

Of the Holy Scriptures and the Three Creeds.

1. THE ground of our religion, and the rule of faith, and all saving truth, is the Word of God, contained in the Holy Scripture.
2. By the name of Holy Scripture we understand all the canonical books of the Old and New Testament, viz.,

Of the Old Testament.

The five books of Moses,	Job,
Joshua,	Psalms,
Judges,	Proverbs,
Ruth,	Ecclesiastes,
The first and second of Sam-	The Song of Solomon,
uel,	Isaiah,
The first and second of Kings,	Jeremiah, his prophecy and
The first and second of	Lamentation,
Chronicles,	Ezekiel,
Ezra,	Daniel,
Nehemiah,	The twelve less prophets.
Esther;	

Of the New Testament.

The Gospels according to	The First and Second Epis-
Matthew,	tle to the Thessalonians,
Mark,	The First and Second Epis-
Luke,	tle to Timothy,
John,	Titus,
The Acts of the Apostles,	Philemon,
The Epistle of St. Paul to	Hebrews,
the Romans,	The Epistle of St. James,
The First and Second Epis-	The two Epistles of St. Pe-
tle to the Corinthians.	ter,
Galatians,	The three Epistles of St.
Ephesians,	John,
Philippians,	St. Jude,
Colossians,	The Revelation of St. John.

All which we acknowledge to be given by the inspiration of God, and in that regard to be of most certain credit and highest authority.
3. The other books, commonly called Apocryphal, did not proceed from such inspiration, and therefore are not of sufficient authority to establish any point of doctrine; but the Church doth read them as books containing many worthy things for example of life and instruction of manners.

* Strype's Ann., vol. ult., p. 85, &c.

Such are these following.

The third book of Esdras,	Baruch, with the Epistle of
The fourth book of Esdras,	Jeremiah,
The book of Tobias,	The Song of the Three Chil-
The book of Judith,	dren,
Additions to the book of Es-	Susannah,
ther,	Bel and the Dragon,
The book of Wisdom,	The Prayer of Manasses,
The book of Jesus the Son	The first book of Maccabees,
of Sirach, called Ecclesi-	The second book of Macca-
asticus,	bees.

4. The Scriptures ought to be translated out of the original tongues into all languages, for the common use of all men. Neither is any person to be discouraged from reading the Bible in such language as he doth understand, but seriously exhorted to read the same with great humility and reverence, as a special means to bring him to the true knowledge of God, and of his own duty.

5. Although there be some hard things in the Scriptures (especially such as have proper relation to the times in which they were first uttered, and prophecies of things which were afterward to be fulfilled), yet all things necessary to be known unto everlasting salvation are clearly delivered therein; and nothing of that kind is spoken under dark mysteries in one place, which is not in other places spoken more familiarly and plainly to the capacity both of learned and unlearned.

6. The Holy Scriptures contain all things necessary to salvation, and are able to instruct sufficiently in all points of faith that we are bound to believe, and all duties that we are bound to practise.

7. All and every the articles contained in the Nicene Creed, the creed of Athanasius, and that which is commonly called the Apostles' Creed, ought firmly to be received and believed, for they may be proved by most certain warrant of Holy Scripture.

Of Faith in the Holy Trinity.

8. There is but one living and true God, everlasting. Without body, parts, or passions, of infinite power, wisdom, and goodness; the maker and preserver of all things, both visible and invisible. And in unity of this Godhead there be three persons of one and the same substance, power, and eternity, the Father, the Son, and the Holy Ghost.

9. The essence of the Father doth not beget the essence of the Son; but the person of the Father begetteth the person of the Son, by communicating his whole essence to the person begotten from eternity.

10. The Holy Ghost, proceeding from the Father and the Son, is of one substance, majesty, and glory with the Father and the Son, very and eternal God.

Of God's eternal Decree and Predestination.

11. God from all eternity did, by his unchangeable counsel, ordain whatsoever in time should come to pass; yet so as thereby no violence is offered to the wills of the reasonable creatures, and neither the liberty nor the contingency of the second cause is taken away, but established rather.

* 12. "By the same eternal counsel God hath predestinated some unto life, and reprobated some unto death; of both which there is a certain number, known only to

God, which can neither be increased nor diminished."

13. Predestination to life is the everlasting purpose of God, whereby, before the foundations of the world were laid, he hath constantly-decreed in his secret counsel to deliver from curse and damnation those whom he hath chosen in Christ out of mankind, and to bring them by Christ unto everlasting salvation, as vessels made to honour.

* II. 14. "The cause moving God to predestinate unto life is not the foreseeing of faith, or of perseverance, or of goods works, or of anything which is in the person predestinated, but only the good pleasure of God himself."

For all things being ordained for the manifestation of his glory, and his glory being to appear both in the works of his mercy and of his justice, it seemed good to his heavenly wisdom to choose out a certain number, towards whom he would extend his undeserved mercy, leaving the rest to be spectacles of his justice.

15. Such as are predestinated unto life be called according unto God's purpose (his Spirit working in due season), and through grace they obey the calling; they be justified freely; they be made sons of God by adoption; they be made like the image of his only-begotten Son Jesus Christ; they walk religiously in good works, and at length, by God's mercy, they attain to everlasting felicity.

* IV. "But such as are not predestinated to salvation shall finally be condemned for their sins."

16. The godly consideration of predestination, and our election in Christ, is full of sweet, pleasant, and unspeakable comfort to godly persons, and such as feel in themselves the working of the Spirit of Christ, mortifying the works of the flesh, and their earthly members, and drawing up their minds to high and heavenly things, as well because it doth greatly confirm and establish their faith of eternal salvation to be enjoyed through Christ, as because it doth fervently kindle their love towards God; and on the contrary side, for curious and carnal persons lacking the Spirit of Christ, to have continually before their eyes the sentence of God's predestination, is very dangerous.

17. We must receive God's promises in such wise, as they be generally set forth unto us in Holy Scripture; and in our doings, that will of God is to be followed which we have expressly declared unto us in the Word of God.

Of the Creation and Government of all Things.

18. In the beginning of time, when no creature had any being, God by his word alone, in the space of six days, created all things; and afterward by his Providence doth continue, propagate, and order them according to his own will.

19. The principal creatures are angels and men.

20. Of angels, some continued in that holy state wherein they were created, and are by God's grace forever established therein; others fell from the same, and are reserved in chains of darkness unto the judgment of the great day.

21. Man being at the beginning created according to the image of God (which consisted especially in the wisdom of his mind and the true holiness of his free-will), had the covenant of the law ingrafted in his heart, whereby God did promise unto him everlasting life, upon condition that he performed entire and perfect obedience unto his commandments, according to that measure of strength wherewith he was endued in his creation, and threatened death unto him if he did not perform the same.

Of the Fall of Man, Original Sin, and the State of Man before Justification.

22. By one man sin entered into the world, and death by sin, and so death went over all men, forasmuch as all have sinned.

23. Original sin standeth not in the imitation of Adam (as the Pelagians dream), but is the fault and corruption of the nature of every person that naturally is engendered and propagated from Adam, whereby it cometh to pass that man is deprived of original righteousness, and by nature is bent unto sin; and, therefore, in every person born into the world, it deserveth God's wrath and damnation.

24. This corruption of nature doth remain even in those that are regenerated, whereby the flesh always lusteth against the Spirit, and cannot be made subject to the law of God. And howsoever, for Christ's sake, there be no condemnation to such as are regenerate and do believe, yet doth the apostle acknowledge that in itself this concupiscence hath the nature of sin.

* IX. 25. "The condition of man after the fall of Adam is such, that he cannot turn and prepare himself, by his own natural strength and good works, to faith, and calling upon God."

Wherefore we have no power to do good works, pleasing and acceptable unto God, without the grace of God preventing us, that we may have a good-will, and working with us, when we have that good-will.

26. Works done before the grace of Christ and the inspiration of his Spirit are not pleasing unto God, forasmuch as they spring not of faith in Jesus Christ, neither do they make men meet to receive grace (or, as the school authors say, to deserve grace of congruity); yea, rather, for that they are not done in such sort that God hath willed and commanded them to be done, we doubt not but they are sinful.

27. All sins are not equal, but some far more heinous than others; yet the very least is of its own nature mortal, and without God's mercy maketh the offender liable unto everlasting damnation.

28. God is not the author of sin: howbeit he doth not only permit, but also by his providence govern and order the same, guiding it in such sort by his infinite wisdom as it turneth to the manifestation of his own glory, and to the good of his elect.

Of Christ, the Mediator of the Second Covenant.

29. The Son, which is the Word of the Father, begotten from everlasting of the Father, the true and eternal God, of one substance with the Father, took man's nature in the womb of the blessed Virgin, of her substance; so that two whole and perfect natures, that is to say, the Godhead and manhood, were inseparably joined in one person, making one Christ, very God and very man.

30. Christ, in the truth of our nature, was made like unto us in all things, sin only excepted, from which he was clearly void, both in his life and in his nature. He came as a lamb without spot to take away the sins of the world, by the sacrifice of himself once made, and sin (as St. John saith) was not in him. He fulfilled the law for us perfectly; for our sakes he endured most grievous torments immediately in his soul, and most painful sufferings in his body. He was crucified, and died to reconcile his Father unto us; and to be a sacrifice not only for original guilt, but also for all our transgressions. He was buried, and descended into hell, and the third day rose from the dead, and took again his body, with flesh, bones, and all things appertaining to the perfection of man's nature, wherewith he ascended into heaven, and there sitteth at the right hand of his Father, until he return to judge all men at the last day.

Of the communicating of the Grace of Christ.

31. They are to be condemned that presume to say that every man shall be saved by the law or sect which he professeth, so that he be diligent to frame his life according to that law, and the light of nature; for Holy Scripture doth set out unto us only the hame of Jesus Christ whereby men must be saved.

32. * VIII. "None can come unto Christ unless it be given unto him, and unless he draw him. And all men are not so drawn by the Father, that they may come unto the Son [* VII.]; neither is there such a sufficient measure of grace vouchsafed unto every man, whereby he is enabled to come unto everlasting life."

33. All God's elect are in their time inseparably united unto Christ, by the effectual and vital influence of the Holy Ghost, derived from him, as from the head, unto every true member of his mystical body. And being thus made one with Christ, they are truly regenerated, and made partakers of him and all his benefits.

Of Justification and Faith.

34. We are accounted righteous before God only for the merit of our Lord and Saviour Jesus Christ, applied by faith, and not for our own works or merits. And this righteousness, which we so receive of God's mercy and Christ's merits, embraced by faith, is taken, accepted, and allowed of God for our perfect and full justification.

35. Although this justification be free unto us, yet it cometh not so freely unto us that there is no ransom paid therefore at all. God shewed his mercy in delivering us from our former captivity, without requiring any ransom to be paid, or amends to be made, on our parts, which thing by us had been impossible to be done. And whereas all the world was not able of themselves to pay any part towards their ransom, it pleased our heavenly Father, of his infinite mercy, without any desert of ours, to provide for us the most precious merits of his own Son, whereby our ransom might be fully paid, the law fulfilled, and his justice fully satisfied; so that Christ is now the righteousness of all them that truly believe in him : he for them paid their ransom by his death; he for them fulfilled the law in his life; that now in him, and by him, every true Christian man may be called a ful

filler of the law; forasmuch as that which our infirmity was not able to effect, Christ's justice hath performed; and thus the justice and mercy of God do embrace each other, the grace of God not shutting out the justice of God in the matter of our justification, but only shutting out the justice of man (that is to say, the justice of our own works) from being any cause of deserving our justification.

36. When we say that we are justified by faith only, we do not mean that the said justifying faith is alone in man without true repentance, hope, charity, and the fear of God (for such a faith is dead, and cannot justify); neither do we mean that this our act to believe in Christ, or this our faith in Christ, which is within us, doth of itself justify us, or deserve our justification unto us (for that were to account ourselves to be justified by the virtue or dignity of something that is within ourselves); but the true understanding and meaning thereof is, that although we hear God's Word, and believe it; although we have faith, hope, charity, repentance, and the fear of God within us, and add never so many good works thereunto, yet we must renounce the merit of all our said virtues, of faith, hope, charity, and all our other virtues and good deeds, which we either have done, shall do, or can do, as things that be far too weak, and imperfect, and insufficient to deserve remission of our sins, and our justification; and therefore we must trust only in God's mercy, and the merits of his most dearly-beloved Son, our only Redeemer, Saviour, and Justifier, Jesus Christ. Nevertheless, because faith doth directly send us to Christ for our justification, and that by faith, given us of God, we embrace the promise of God's mercy and the remission of our sins (which thing none other of our virtues or works properly doth), therefore the Scripture useth to say, that faith without works, and the ancient fathers of the Church to the same purpose, that only faith doth justify us.

37. By justifying faith we understand, not only the common belief of the articles of the Christian religion, and a persuasion of the truth of God's Word in general, but also a particular application of the gracious promises of the Gospel to the comfort of our own souls, whereby we lay hold on Christ with all his benefits, having an earnest trust and confidence in God, that he will be merciful unto us for his only Son's sake.

* VI. "So that a true believer may be certain, by the assurance of faith, of the forgiveness of his sins, and of his everlasting salvation by Christ."

38. * V. "A true, lively, justifying faith, and the sanctifying Spirit of God, is not extinguished, nor vanisheth away in the regencrate, either finally or totally."

Of Sanctification and Good Works.

39. All that are justified are likewise sanctified, their faith being always accompanied with true repentance and good works.

40. Repentance is a gift of God, whereby a godly sorrow is wrought in the heart of the faithful for offending God, their merciful Father, by their former transgressions, together with a constant resolution for the time to come to cleave unto God, and to lead a new life.

41. Albeit that good works, which are the

fruits of faith, and follow after justification, cannot make satisfaction for our sins, and endure the severity of God's judgment ; yet are they pleasing to God, and accepted of him in Christ, and do spring from a true and lively faith, which by them is to be discerned as a tree by the fruit.

42. The works which God would have his people to walk in are such as he hath commanded in his Holy Scripture, and not such works as men have devised out of their own brain, of a blind zeal and devotion, without the warrant of the Word of God.

43. The regenerate cannot fulfil the law of God perfectly in this life, for in many things we offend all ; and if we say we have no sin, we deceive ourselves, and the truth is not in us.

44. Not every heinous sin willingly committed after baptism is sin against the Holy Ghost and unpardonable ; and, therefore, to such as fall into sin after baptism, place for repentance is not to be denied.

45. Voluntary works, besides over and above God's commandments, which they call works of supererogation, cannot be taught without arrogancy and impiety ; for by them men do declare that they not only render unto God as much as they are bound to do, but that they do more for his sake than of bounden duty is required.

Of the Service of God.

46. Our duty towards God is to believe in him, to fear him, and to love him with all our heart, with all our mind, and with all our soul, and with all our strength : to worship him, and to give him thanks; to put our whole trust in him, to call upon him, to honour his holy name and his Word, and to serve him truly all the days of our life.

47. In all our necessities we ought to have recourse unto God by prayer, assuring ourselves that whatsoever we ask of the Father in the name of his Son (our only mediator and intercessor) Christ Jesus, and according to his will, he will undoubtedly grant it.

48. We ought to prepare our hearts before we pray, and understand the things that we ask when we pray, that both our hearts and voices may together sound in the ears of God's majesty.

49. When Almighty God smiteth us with affliction, or some great calamity hangeth over us, or any other weighty cause so requireth, it is our duty to humble ourselves in fasting, to bewail our sins with a sorrowful heart, and to addict ourselves to earnest prayer, that it might please God to turn his wrath from us, or supply us with such graces as we greatly stand in need of.

50. Fasting is a withholding of meat, drink, and all natural food, with other outward delights, from the body, for the determined time of fasting. "As for those abstinences which are appointed by public order of our state for eating of fish, and forbearing of flesh at certain times and days appointed, they are noways meant to be religious fasts, nor intended for the maintenance of any superstition in the choice of meats, but are grounded merely upon politic considerations, for provision of things tending to the better preservation of the commonwealth."

51. We must not fast with this persuasion of mind, that our fasting can bring us to heaven, or ascribe outward holiness to the work wrought ; for God alloweth not our fast for the work's sake (which of itself is a thing merely indifferent), but chiefly respecteth the heart, how it is affected therein ; it is therefore requisite that first, before all things, we cleanse our hearts from sin, and then direct our fast to such ends as God will allow to be good ; that the flesh may thereby be chastened, the spirit may be more fervent in prayer, and that our fasting may be a testimony of our humble submission to God's majesty when we acknowledge our sins unto him, and are inwardly touched with sorrowfulness of heart, bewailing the same in the affliction of our bodies.

52. All worship devised by man's fantasy, besides or contrary to the Scriptures (as wandering on pilgrimages, setting up of candles, stations, and jubilees, pharisaical sects, and feigned religions, praying upon beads, and such like superstition), hath not only no promise of reward in Scripture, but contrariwise, threatenings and maledictions.

53. All manner of expressing God the Father, the Son, and the Holy Ghost in an outward form, is utterly unlawful ; as also all other images devised or made by man to the use of religion.

54. All religious worship ought to be given to God alone, from whom all goodness, health, and grace ought to be both asked and looked for, as from the very author and giver of the same, and from none other.

55. The name of God is to be used with all reverence and holy respect, and therefore all vain and rash swearing is utterly to be condemned ; yet notwithstanding, upon lawful occasions, an oath may be given and taken, according to the Word of God, justice, judgment, and truth.

56. The first day of the week, which is the Lord's Day, is wholly to be dedicated to the service of God; and therefore we are bound therein to rest from our common and daily business, and to bestow that leisure upon holy exercises, both public and private.

Of the Civil Magistrate.

57. The king's majesty under God hath the sovereign and chief power, within his realms and dominions, over all manner of persons, of what estate, either ecclesiastical or civil, soever they be, so as no other foreign power hath or ought to have any superiority over them.

58. We do profess that the supreme government of all estates within the said realms and dominions, in all causes, as well ecclesiastical as temporal, doth of right appertain to the king's highness. Neither do we give unto him hereby the administration of the Word and sacraments, or the power of the keys, but that prerogative only which we see to have been always given unto all godly princes in Holy Scripture by God himself; that is, that he should contain all estates and degrees committed to his charge by God, whether they be ecclesiastical or civil, within their duty, and restrain the stubborn and evildoers with the power of the civil sword.

59. The pope, neither of himself, nor by any authority of the Church or See of Rome, nor by any other means with any other, hath any power or authority to depose the king, or dispose of

any of his kingdoms or dominions, or to authorize any other prince to invade or annoy him or his countries, or to discharge any of his subjects of their allegiance and obedience to his majesty, or to give license or leave to any of them to bear arms, raise tumult, or to offer any violence or hurt to his royal person, state, or government, or to any of his subjects within his majesty's dominions.

60. That princes which be excommunicated or deprived by the pope may be deposed or murdered by their subjects, or any other whatsoever, is impious doctrine.

61. The laws of the realm may punish Christian men with death for heinous and grievous offences.

62. It is lawful for Christian men, at the command of the magistrate, to bear arms, and to serve in just wars.

Of our Duty towards our Neighbours.

63. Our duty towards our neighbours is to love them as ourselves, and to do to all men as we would they should do to us : to honour and obey our superiors, to preserve the safety of men's persons, as also their chastity, goods, and good names ; to bear no malice nor hatred in our hearts ; to keep our bodies in temperance; soberness, and chastity ; to be true and just in all our doings ; not to covet other men's goods, but labour truly to get our own living, and to do our duty in that estate of life unto which it pleaseth God to call us.

64. For the preservation of the chastity of men's persons, wedlock is commanded unto all persons that stand in need thereof. Neither is there any prohibition by the Word of God, but that the ministers of the Church may enter into the state of matrimony, they being nowhere commanded by God's law either to vow the state of single life, or to abstain from marriage ; therefore it is lawful also for them, as well as for all other Christian men, to marry at their own discretion, as they shall judge the same to serve better to godliness.

65. The riches and goods of Christians are not common, as touching the right, title, and possession of the same, as certain Anabaptists falsely affirm ; notwithstanding, every man ought, of such things as he possesseth, liberally to give alms to the poor, according to his ability.

66. Faith given is to be kept, even with heretics and infidels.

67. The popish doctrine of equivocation and mental reservation is most ungodly, and tendeth plainly to the subversion of all human society.

Of the Church and outward Ministry of the Gospel.

68. There is but one Catholic Church (out of which there is no salvation), containing the universal company of all the saints that ever were, are, or shall be gathered together in one body, under one head, Christ Jesus ; part whereof is already in heaven triumphant, part as yet militant here upon earth. And because this Church consisteth of all those, and those alone, which are elected by God unto salvation, and regenerated by the power of his Spirit, the number of whom is known only unto God himself, therefore it is called the catholic or universal, and the invisible Church.

69. But particular and visible churches (consisting of those who make profession of the faith of Christ, and live under the outward means of salvation) be many in number ; wherein, the more or less sincerely, according to Christ's institution, the Word of God is taught, the sacraments are administered, and the authority of the keys used is, the more or less pure are such churches to be accounted.

70. Although in the visible Church the evil be ever mingled with the good ; and sometimes the evil have chief authority in the ministration of the Word and sacraments, yet, forasmuch as they do not the same in their own name, but in Christ's, and minister by his own commission and authority, we may use their ministry both in hearing the Word, and in receiving the sacraments. Neither is the effect of Christ's ordinance taken away by their wickedness, nor the grace of God's gifts diminished from such as by faith do rightly receive the sacraments ministered unto them, which are effectual, because of Christ's institution and promise, although they be ministered by evil men. Nevertheless, it appertaineth to the discipline of the Church that inquiry be made of evil ministers, and that they be accused by those that have knowledge of their offences, and finally, being found guilty by just judgment, be deposed.

71. It is not lawful for any man to take upon him the office of public preaching, or ministering the sacraments of the Church, unless he be first lawfully called, and sent to execute the same. And those we ought to judge lawfully called and sent which be chosen and called to this work by men who have public authority given them in the Church to call and send ministers into the Lord's vineyard.

72. To have public prayer in the Church, or to administer the sacraments in a tongue not understood of the people, is a thing plainly repugnant to the Word of God and the custom of the primitive Church.

73. That person which by public denunciation of the Church, is rightly cut off from the unity of the Church, and excommunicate, ought to be taken of the whole multitude of the faithful as a heathen and publican, until, by repentance, he be openly reconciled and received into the Church by the judgment of such as have authority in that behalf.

74. God hath given power to his ministers not simply to forgive sins (which prerogative he hath reserved only to himself), but in his name to declare and pronounce unto such as truly repent, and unfeignedly believe his holy Gospel, the absolution and forgiveness of sins. Neither is it God's pleasure that his people should be tied to make a particular confession of all their known sins unto any mortal man ; howsoever, any person grieved in his conscience upon any special cause, may well resort unto any godly and learned minister, to receive advice and comfort at his hands.

Of the Authority of the Church, General Councils, and Bishop of Rome.

75. It is not lawful for the Church to ordain anything that is contrary to God's Word ; neither may it so expound one place of Scripture that it be repugnant to another. Wherefore, although the Church be a witness, and a keeper

of holy writ, yet, as it ought not to decree anything against the same, so besides the same ought it not to enforce anything to be believed upon necessity of salvation.

76. General councils may not be gathered together without the commandment and will of princes; and when they be gathered together (forasmuch as they be an assembly of men not always governed with the Spirit and Word of God), they may err, and sometimes have erred, even in things pertaining to the rule of piety; wherefore things ordained by them as necessary to salvation have neither strength nor authority, unless it may be showed that they be taken out of the Holy Scriptures.

77. Every particular church hath authority to institute, to change, and clean to put away, ceremonies and other ecclesiastical rites, as they be superfluous, or be abused, and to constitute other, making more to seemliness, to order, or edification.

78. As the churches of Jerusalem, Alexandria, and Antioch have erred, so also the Church of Rome hath erred, not only in those things which concern matters of practice and point of ceremonies, but also in matters of faith.

79. The power which the Bishop of Rome now challengeth, to be the supreme head of the universal Church of Christ, and to be above all emperors, kings, and princes, is a usurped power, contrary to the Scriptures and Word of God, and contrary to the example of the primitive Church, and therefore is, for most just-causes, taken away and abolished within the king's majesty's realms and dominions.

80. The Bishop of Rome is so far from being the supreme head of the universal Church of Christ, that his works and doctrine do plainly discover him to be that man of sin foretold in the Holy Scriptures, "whom the Lord shall consume with the spirit of his mouth, and abolish with the brightness of his coming."

Of the State of the Old and New Testament.

81. In the Old Testament the commandments of the law were more largely, and the promises of Christ more sparingly and darkly, propounded; shadowed with a multitude of types and figures, and so much more generally and obscurely delivered, as the manifesting of them was farther off.

82. The Old Testament is not contrary to the New; for both in the Old and New Testament everlasting life is offered to mankind by Christ, who is the only mediator between God and man, being both God and man; wherefore they are not to be heard which feign that the old fathers did look only for transitory promises, for they looked for all the benefits of God the Father, through the merits of his Son Jesus Christ, as we now do; only they believed in Christ which should come, we in Christ already come.

83. The New Testament is full of grace and truth, bringing joyful tidings unto mankind, that whatsoever formerly was promised of Christ is now accomplished; and so, instead of the ancient types and ceremonies, exhibiteth the things themselves, with a large and clear declaration of all the benefits of the Gospel. Neither is the ministry thereof restrained any longer to one circumcised nation, but is indifferently propound-

ed unto all people, whether they be Jews or Gentiles: so that there is now no nation which can truly complain that they be shut forth from the communion of saints, and the liberties of the people of God.

84. Although the law given from God by Moses, as touching ceremonies and rites, be abolished, and the civil precepts thereof be not of necessity to be received in any commonwealth, yet notwithstanding, no Christian man whatsoever is freed from the obedience of the commandments which are called moral.

Of the Sacraments of the New Testament.

85. The sacraments ordained by Christ are not only badges or tokens of Christian men's profession, but rather certain sure witnesses, and effectual or powerful signs, of grace and God's good-will towards us, by which he doth work invisibly in us, and not only quicken, but also strengthen and confirm, our faith in him.

86. There be two sacraments ordained of Christ our Lord in the Gospel, that is to say, baptism and the Lord's Supper.

87. Those five which by the Church of Rome are called sacraments, to wit, confirmation, penance, orders, matrimony, and extreme unction, are not to be accounted sacraments of the Gospel, being such as have partly grown from corrupt imitation of the apostles, partly are states of life allowed in the Scriptures, but yet have not like nature of sacraments with baptism and the Lord's Supper, for that they have not any visible sign or ceremony ordained of God, together with a promise of saving grace annexed thereunto.

88. The sacraments were not ordained of Christ to be gazed upon or to be carried about, but that we should duly use them. And in such only as worthily receive the same, they have a wholesome effect and operation; but they that receive them unworthily, thereby draw judgment upon themselves.

Of Baptism.

89. Baptism is not only an outward sign of our profession, and a note of difference, whereby Christians are discerned from such as are no Christians; but much more, a sacrament of our admission into the Church, sealing unto us our new birth (and, consequently, our justification, adoption, and sanctification) by the communion which we have with Jesus Christ.

90. The baptism of infants is to be retained in the Church, as agreeable to the Word of God.

91. In the administration of baptism, exorcism, oil, salt, spittle, and superstitious hallowing of the water, are for just causes abolished; and without them the sacrament is fully and perfectly administered to all intents and purposes, agreeably to the institution of our Saviour Christ.

Of the Lord's Supper.

92. The Lord's Supper is not only a sign of the mutual love which Christians ought to hear one towards another, but much more, a sacrament of our preservation in the Church, sealing unto us our spiritual nourishment, and continual growth in Christ.

93. The change of the substance of bread and wine into the substance of the body and blood of Christ, commonly called transubstantiation,

APPENDIX.

cannot be proved by holy writ, but is repugnant to plain testimonies of the Scripture, overthroweth the nature of a sacrament, and hath given occasion to most gross idolatry and manifold superstitions.

94. In the outward part of the Holy Communion, the body and blood of Christ is in a most lively manner represented, being no otherwise present with the visible elements than things signified and sealed are present with the signs and seals ; that is to say, symbolically and relatively. But in the inward and spiritual part, the same body and blood is really and substantially presented unto all those who have grace to receive the Son of God, even to all those that believe in his name. And unto such as in this manner do worthily and with faith repair unto the Lord's Table, the body and blood of Christ is not only signified and offered, but also truly exhibited and communicated.

95. The body of Christ is given, taken, and eaten, in the Lord's Supper, only after a heavenly and spiritual manner ; and the mean whereby the body of Christ is thus received and eaten is faith.

96. The wicked, and such as want a lively faith, although they do carnally and visibly, as St. Augustine speaketh, press with their teeth the sacrament of the body and blood of Christ, yet in nowise are they made partakers of Christ, but rather to their condemnation do eat and drink the sign or sacrament of so great a thing.

97. Both the parts of the Lord's sacrament, according to Christ's institution and the practice of the ancient Church, ought to be ministered unto all God's people ; and it is plain sacrilege to rob them of the mystical cup, for whom Christ hath shed his most precious blood.

98. The sacrament of the Lord's Supper was not by Christ's ordinance reserved, carried about, lifted up, or worshipped.

99. The sacrifice of the mass, wherein the priest is said to offer up Christ for obtaining the remission of pain or guilt for the quick and the dead, is neither agreeable to Christ's ordinance,

nor grounded upon doctrine apostolic ; but contrariwise, most ungodly, and most injurious to that all-sufficient sacrifice of our Saviour Christ, offered once forever upon the cross, which is the only propitiation and satisfaction for all our sins.

100. Private mass, that is, the receiving the Eucharist by the priest alone, without a competent number of communicants, is contrary to the institution of Christ.

Of the State of the Souls of Men after they be departed out of this Life, together with the general Resurrection and the last Judgment.

101. After this life is ended, the souls of God's children are presently received into heaven, there to enjoy unspeakable comforts ; the souls of the wicked are cast into hell, there to endure endless torments.

102. The doctrine of the Church of Rome, concerning *limbus patrum, limbus puerorum*, purgatory, prayer for the dead, pardons, adoration of images and relics, and also invocation of saints, is vainly invented, without all warrant of Holy Scripture, yea, and is contrary to the same.

103. At the end of this world the Lord Jesus shall come in the clouds with the glory of his Father, at which time, by the almighty power of God, the living shall be changed, and the dead shall be raised, and all shall appear both in body and soul before his judgment-seat, to receive according to that which they have done in their bodies, whether good or evil.

104. When the last judgment is finished, Christ shall deliver up the kingdom to his Father, and God shall be all in all.

The Decree of the Synod.

If any minister, of what degree or quality soever he be, shall publicly teach any doctrine contrary to these articles agreed upon, if, after due admonition, he do not conform himself, and cease to disturb the peace of the Church, let him be silenced, and deprived of all spiritual promotions he doth enjoy.

No. VII.

ARTICLES OF THE CHURCH OF ENGLAND, *Revised and altered by the Assembly of Divines, at Westminster, in the year 1643, with Scripture References.*

THE ARTICLES OF THE CHURCH OF ENGLAND.

ARTICLE I.

Of Faith in the Holy Trinity.

THERE is but one(1) living and true God,(2) everlasting;(3) without body, parts,(4) or passions ;(5) of infinite power,(6) wisdom,(7) and goodness ;(8) the maker and preserver of all things, both visible and invisible.(9) And in unity of this Godhead there be three persons, of one substance, power, and eternity, the Father, the Son, and the Holy Ghost.(10)

ARTICLE I.

Of Faith in the Holy Trinity.

THERE is but one living and true God, everlasting, without body, parts, or passions ; of infinite power, wisdom, and goodness ; the maker and preserver of all things both visible and invisible. And in unity of this Godhead there be three persons, of one substance, power, and eternity, the Father, the Son, and the Holy Ghost.

ARTICLE II.

Of the Word, or Son of God, which was made very Man.

The Son, which is the Word of the Father, begotten from everlasting of the Father,(11) the very(12) and eternal God,(13) of one substance with the Father,(14) took man's nature in the womb of the blessed Virgin, of her substance ;(15) so that two whole and perfect natures, that is to say, the Godhead and the manhood, were joined together in one person, never to be divided, whereof is one Christ, very God and very man,(16) who for our sakes truly suffer-

ARTICLE II.

Of the Word, or Son of God, which was made very Man.

The Son, which is the Word of the Father, begotten from everlasting of the Father, the very and eternal God, of one substance with the Father, took man's nature in the womb of the blessed Virgin, of her substance ; so that two whole and perfect natures, that is to say, the Godhead and manhood, were joined together in one person, never to be divided, whereof is one Christ, very God and very man, who truly suffered, was crucified, dead, and buried, to reconcile

(1) Isa., xlvi., 9. 1 Cor., viii., 4, 6.—(2) Jer., x., 10. 1 Thes., i., 9.—(3) Psal. xc., 2. Rom., xvi., 26—(4) Deut., iv., 15, 16. John, iv., 24, with Luke, xxiv., 39.—(5) Acts, xiv., 15. James, i., 17.—(6) Jer., xxxii., 17, 27. Mark, x., 27.—(7) Psal. cxlvii., 5. Rom., xi., 33.—(8) Psal. cxix., 68, with Matt., xix., 17.—(9) Neh., ix., 6. Col., i., 16, 17.—(10) Matt., iii., 16, 17 ; xxviii., 19. 1 John, iv., 7.—2 Cor., xiii., 14—(11) Prov., vii., 22-31. John, i., 12, 14.—(12) 1 John, v., 20. Rom., ix., 5.—(13) John, xvii., 5. Heb., i., 8, with Psal. xlv., 6.—(14) John, x., 30. Heb., i., 3.—(15) John, i., 14. Isa., vii., 14. Luke, i., 35. Gal., iv., 4.—(16) Isa., vii., 14, with Matt., i., 23. Rom., i., 3, 4. Heb., xiii., 8.

Articles revised.

ed most grievous torments in his soul from God,(1) was crucified, dead, and buried,(2) to reconcile his Father to us,(3) and to be a sacrifice, not only for original guilt, but also for actual sins of men.(4)

ARTICLE III.

As Christ died for us, and was buried, so it is to be believed that he continued in the state of the dead and under the power and dominion of death,(5) from the time of his death and burial until his resurrection ;(6) which hath been otherwise expressed thus : he went down into hell.

ARTICLE IV.

Of the Resurrection of Christ.

Christ did truly rise again from death,(7) and took again his body, with flesh, bones, and all things appertaining to the perfection of man's nature,(8) wherewith he ascended into heaven, and there sitteth,(9) until he return to judge(10) all men(11) at the general resurrection of the body at the last day.(12)

ARTICLE V.

Of the Holy Ghost.

The Holy Ghost is very and eternal God, of one substance,(13) majesty,(14) and glory with the Father and the Son,(15) proceeding from the Father and the Son.(16)

ARTICLE VI.

Of the Sufficiency of the Holy Scriptures for Salvation.

Holy Scripture(17) containeth all things necessary to salvation ;(18) so that whatsoever is not read therein, nor may be proved thereby, is not to be believed as an article of faith, or necessary to salvation.(19)

By the name of Holy Scripture we understand all the canonical Books of the Ol and New Testament which follow :

Of the Old Testament.

Genesis, Exodus, &c.

Of the New Testament.

The Gospel of St. Matthew, &c.

All which books, as they are commonly received, we do receive, and acknowledge them to be given by the inspiration of God ; and in that regard, to be of most certain credit, and highest authority.

ARTICLE VII.

Of the Old Testament.

The Old Testament is not contrary to the New, in the doctrine contained in them ;(20) for both in the Old and New Testament everlasting life is offered to mankind by Christ,(21) who is the only mediator between God and man,(22) being both God and man.(23) Wherefore they are not to be heard which feign that the old fathers did look only for temporary promises.(24)

Although the law given from God by Moses, as touching ceremonies and rites, do not bind Christians ;(25) nor the civil precepts given by Moses, such as were peculiarly fitted to the commonwealth of the Jews, are of necessity to be received in any commonwealth ;(26) yet notwithstanding, no Christian man whatsoever is free from the obedience of the commandments which are called moral.(27) By the moral law, we understand all the Ten Commandments taken in their full extent.

Articles of the Church of England.

his Father to us, and to be a sacrifice, not only for original guilt, but also for all actual sins of men.

ARTICLE III.

Of the going down of Christ into Hell.

As Christ died for us, and was buried, so also is it to be believed that he went down into hell.

ARTICLE IV.

Of the Resurrection of Christ

Christ did truly rise again from death, and took again his body, with flesh, bones, and all things appertaining to the perfection of man's nature, wherewith he ascended into heaven, and there sitteth. until he return to judge all men at the last day.

ARTICLE V.

Of the Holy Ghost.

The Holy Ghost, proceeding from the Father and the Son. is of one substance, majesty, and glory with the Father and the Son, very and eternal God.

ARTICLE VI.

Of the Sufficiency of the Holy Scriptures for Salvation

Holy Scripture containeth all things necessary to salvation ; so that whatsoever is not read therein, nor may be proved thereby, is not to be required of any man that it should be believed as an article of the faith, or be thought requisite or necessary to salvation. In the name of the Holy Scripture, we do understand those canonical books of the Old and New Testament, of whose authority was never any doubt in the Church.

Of the Names and Number of the Canonical Books.

Genesis, Exodus, Leviticus, Numbers, &c.

And the other books, as Hierome saith, the Church doth read for example of life and instruction of manners, but yet doth it not apply them to establish any doctrine : such are these following :

Third of Esdras, Book of Tobias, Fourth of Esdras, Judith, &c.

All the books of the New Testament, as they are commonly received, we do receive, and account them for canonical.

ARTICLE VII.

Of the Old Testament.

The Old Testament is not contrary to the New ; for both in the Old and new Testament everlasting life is offered to mankind by Christ, who is the only mediator between God and man, being both God and man. Wherefore they are not to be heard which feign that the old fathers did look only for transitory promises. Although the law given from God by Moses, as touching ceremonies and rites, do not bind Christian men ; nor the civil precepts thereof ought of necessity to be received in any commonwealth ; yet notwithstanding, no Christian man whatsoever is free from the obedience of the commandments which are called moral.

ARTICLE VIII.

Of the Three Creeds.

The three creeds, Nice Creed, Athanasius's Creed, and that which is commonly called the Apostles' Creed, ought thoroughly to be received and believed, for they may be proved by most certain warrants of holy writ.

(1) Isa., liii., 10, 11. Mark, xiv., 33, 34.—(2) 1 Peter, ii., 24. Phil., ii., 1. 1 Cor., xv., 3, 4.—(3) Ezek., xvi., 63 Rom., iii., 25. 2 Cor., v., 12.—(4) Isa., liii., 10. Eph., v., 2. 1 John, i., 7. Heb., ix., 26.—(5) Psal. xvi., 10, with Acts, ii., 24–27, 31.—(6) Rom., vi., 9. Matt., xii., 40.—(7) 1 Cor., xv., 4. Rom., viii., 34. Psal. xvi., 10, with Acts, ii., 31. Luke, xxiv., 34.—(8) Luke, xxiv., 39, with John, xx., 25.—(9) Psal. lxviii., 18, with Eph., iv., 8. Psal. cx., 1, with Acts, ii., 34, 35. Mark, xix., 10. Rom., viii., 34.—(10) Acts, iii., 21. Psal. cx., 1, with 1 Cor., xv., 25, 26. Acts, i., 11.—(11) 2 Cor., v., 20. Acts, xvii., 31.—(12) Exod., iii., 6, with Luke, xx., 37, 38. Acts, xxiv., 14, 15. 1 Cor., xv., 12, to the end. John, v., 28, 29.—(13) 2 Sam., xxiii., 2, 3. Isa., vi., 5, 8, with Acts, xxviii., 25, and v., 3, 4. 1 Cor., iii., 16, and vi., 19.—(14) Job, xxvi., 13, 14. 2 Cor., iii., 17.—(15) 1 Cor., xii., 11. Eph., i., 17, and 1 Cor., ii., 8, with 1 Pet., iv., 14.—(16) John, xv., 26, and Matt., x., 20, and 1 Cor., ii., 11, 12. with Gal., iv., 6, and Rom., viii., 9, and Phil., i., 9. John, xiv., 16. Isa., xi., 2. Gal., i., 2. 2 Chron., xv., 1.—(17) Rom., i, 2. 2 Tim., iii., 15. 2 Pet., i., 20, 21.—(18) Psal. xix., 7. 2 Tim., iii., 15–17. James, i., 21, 25. Acts, xx., 32.—(19) Prov., xxx., 5, 6. Isa., viii., 20. Acts, xxvi., 22, with ver. 20, 27. Gal., i., 8, 9. John, v., 39.—(20) Acts, xxvi., 21, 23. 2 Pet., iii., 2. Luke, xxiv., 44. Rom., iii., 31. Gal., iii., 21, 23, 24.—(21) Gen., iii., 15; xxii., 18, with Gal., iii., 8, 14. 1 Cor., x., 2, 4. Luke, i., 69, 70. Acts, iii., 24.—(22) Dan., ix., 17. Rom., viii., 3. John, it., 1. Heb., vii., 25. 1 Tim., ii., 5. John, xiv., 6.—(23) Gal., iv., 4, 5. Acts, xx., 28. Phil., ii., 7, 8.—(24) Acts, xxvi., 6, 7. Rom., iv., 11. Gal., iii., 8. Heb., xi., 10, 16, 35.—(25) Gal., iv., 10, 16, 17. Col., ii., 14, 16, 17. Heb., ix., 9, 10.—(26) Acts, xxv., 9, 10, 25, with Deut., xvii., 8–13. Rom., xiii., 1, 5. Tit., iii., 1. 1 Pet., ii., 13, 14.—(27) Matt., v., 17, to the end. Rom., xiii., 8–10. Eph., vi., 1–3. James, ii., 8–12. Rom., vii., 25; iii., 31. Matt., vii., 12.

Articles revised.

ARTICLE IX.

Of Original or Birth Sin.

Original sin(1) standeth not in the following of Adam, as the Pelagians do vainly talk,(2) but, together with his first sin imputed, it is the fault and corruption of the nature of every man that naturally is propagated from Adam ;(3) whereby man is wholly deprived of original righteousness,(4) and is of his own nature inclined to evil.(5) So that the lust of the flesh, called in Greek φρόνημα σαρκὸς, which some do expound the wisdom, some sensuality, some the affection, some the desire of the flesh; is not subject to the law of God ;(6) and, therefore, in every person born into this world, it deserveth God's wrath and damnation.(7) And this infection of nature doth remain, yea, in them that are regenerate,(8) whereby the flesh lusteth always contrary to the Spirit.(9) And although there is no condemnation for them that are regenerate, and do believe,(10) yet the apostle doth confess that concupiscence and lust is truly and properly sin.(11)

ARTICLE X.

Of Free-Will.

The condition of man after the fall of Adam is such, that he cannot turn or prepare himself, by his own natural strength and good works, to faith and calling upon God ;(12) wherefore we have no power to do good works pleasing and acceptable to God,(13) without the grace of God by Christ, both preventing us, that we may have a good will, and working so effectually in us, as that it determineth our will to do that which is good,(14) and also working with us when we have that will unto good.(15)

ARTICLE XI.

Of the Justification of Man before God.

We are justified, that is, we are accounted righteous before God, and have remission of sins,(16) not for our own works or deservings,(17) but freely by his grace,(18) only for our Lord and Saviour Jesus Christ's sake,(19) his whole obedience and satisfaction being by God imputed unto us,(20) and Christ, with his righteousness, being apprehended and rested on by faith only.(21) The doctrine of justification by faith only is a wholesome doctrine, and very full of comfort ;(22) notwithstanding, God doth not forgive them that are impenitent, and go on still in their trespasses.(23)

ARTICLE XII.

Of Good Works.

Good works, which are the fruits of faith,(24) and follow after justification,(25) cannot put away our sins,(26) and endure the severity of God's judgment ;(27) yet are they, notwithstanding their imperfections, in the sight of God pleasing and acceptable unto him in and for Christ,(28) and do spring out necessarily of a true and lively faith,(29) insomuch that by them a lively faith may be evidently known as a tree discerned by the fruits.(30)

ARTICLE XIII.

Of Works before Justification.

Works done before justification by Christ, and regeneration by his Spirit, are not pleasing unto God,(31) forasmuch as they spring not of faith in Jesus Christ ;(32) neither do they make men meet to receive grace, or (as the school authors say) deserve grace of congruity ; yea, rather, for that they are not done as God hath willed and commanded them to be done, they are sinful.(33)

ARTICLE XIV.

Of Works of Supererogation.

Voluntary works, besides over and above God's commandments, which they call works of supererogation; cannot be taught(34) without arrogancy and impiety ;(35) for by them we do declare that they do not only render unto God as

---

Articles of the Church of England.

ARTICLE IX.

Of Original or Birth Sin.

Original sin standeth not in the following of Adam, as the Pelagians do vainly talk, but it is the fault and corruption of the nature of every man that naturally is engendered of the offspring of Adam, whereby man is very far gone from original righteousness, and is of his own nature inclined to evil, so that the flesh lusteth always contrary to the Spirit, and therefore in every person born into this world, it deserveth God's wrath and damnation. And this infection of nature doth remain, yea, in them that are regenerated, whereby the lust of the flesh, called in Greek φρόνημα σαρκὸς, which some do expound the wisdom, some sensuality, some the affection, some the desire of the flesh, is not subject to the law of God. And although there is no condemnation for them that believe and are baptized, yet the apostle doth confess that concupiscence and lust hath of itself the nature of sin.

ARTICLE X.

Of Free-Will.

The condition of man after the fall of Adam is such that he cannot turn and prepare himself by his own natural strength and good works to faith and calling upon God. Wherefore we have no power to do good works pleasant and acceptable to God, without the grace of God by Christ preventing us, that we may have a good will, and working with us when we have that good will.

ARTICLE XI.

Of the Justification of Man.

We are accounted righteous before God only for the merit of our Lord and Saviour Jesus Christ, by faith, and not for our own works or deservings. Wherefore, that we are justified by faith only, is a most wholesome doctrine, and very full of comfort, as more largely expressed in the homily of justification.

ARTICLE XII.

Of Good Works.

Albeit that good works, which are the fruits of faith, and follow after justification, cannot put away our sins, and endure the severity of God's judgment, yet are they pleasing and acceptable to God in Christ, and do spring out necessarily of a true and lively faith, insomuch that by them a lively faith may be as evidently known as a tree discerned by the fruit.

ARTICLE XIII.

Of Works before Justification.

Works done before the grace of Christ and the inspiration of his Spirit are not pleasant to God, forasmuch as they spring not of faith in Jesus Christ; neither do they make men meet to receive grace, or (as the school authors say) deserve grace of congruity ; yea, rather, for that they are not done as God hath willed and commanded them to be done, we doubt not but they have the nature of sin.

ARTICLE XIV.

Of Works of Supererogation.

Voluntary works, besides over and above God's commandments, which they call works of supererogation, cannot be taught without arrogancy and impiety ; for by them men do declare that they do not only render unto God as much

---

(1) Psal. li., 5. John, iii., 5, 6.—(2) Job, xiv., 4 ; xv., 14. Rom., vi., 6. John, iii., 3, 5, 7.—(3) Rom., v., 12-19. Gen., ii., 17, with 1 Cor., xv., 22.—(4) Col., ii., 13. Rom., vii., 18. Eccl., vii., 29.—(5) Gen., vi., 5 ; viii., 21. Jer., xvii., 9. Rom., vii., 8. James, i., 14.—(6) Rom., viii., 7. 1 Cor., ii., 14. Col., i., 21.—(7) Eph., ii., 3. Rom., viii., 6, 7.—(8) Prov., xx., 9. Rom., vii., 17, 20, 23, 25.—(9) Gal., v., 17.—(10) Rom., viii., 1, 13. John, iii., 13.—(11) Rom., viii., 17, 20.—(12) Eph., ii., 1, 5. 1 Cor., ii., 14. Eph., ii., 8-10. John, vi., 44, 65.—(13) Rom., viii., 8. Heb., xi., 6.—(14) Ezek., xi., 19, 20 ; xxxvi., 26, 27. Jer., xxxi., 32, 33, with Heb., x., 11. Phil., ii., 12, 13. John, vi., 45. Eph., i., 19, 20. 1 Cor., iv., 7.—(15) Heb., xiii., 21. Phil., viii., 1, 6. Heb., xii., 22. 1 Pet., v., 10. 1 Thes., v., 23, 24. 1 Kings, viii., 57, 58.—(16) Rom., iv., 5-7. Psal. xxxii., 1, 2.—(17) Rom., iii., 20. Gal., ii., 16 ; iii., 10, 11. Phil., iii., 9.—(18) Rom., iii., 24. Tit., iii., 7.—(19) Rom. iii., 24, 25 ; v., 1. 2 Cor., v., 18, 19.—(20) Rom., v., 9, 17-19 ; iii., 25, 26 ; iv., 6, 24. 2 Cor., v., 21.—(21) Rom., iii., 22, 25, 26, 28. Gal., ii., 16. Isa., xxviii., 16, with Rom., ix., 33, and 1 Pet., ii., 6. Phil., iii., 9.—(22) 2 Tim., i., 13. Rom., v., 1, 2, 8, 11 ; xv., 13. 1 Pet., i., 8.—(23) Psal. lxviii., 20, 21. Exod., xxxiv., 6, 7. Luke, xliii., 3, 5.—(24) Gal., v., 22. James, ii., 17, 18, 22.—(25) Tit., ii., 14 ; iii., 7, 8. Eph., i., 8, 9, 18.—(26) Rom., iii., 20, 21 ; iv., 4-9. Dan., ix., 18, 19.—(27) Neh., xiii., 22. Psal. cxliii., 2. Job, ix., 14, 15, 19, 20. Exod., xxviii., 38. Rev., viii., 3, 4.—(28) 1 Peter, ii., 5. Heb., xi., 20, 21. Col., i., 10. Phil., iv., 18.—(29) James, ii., 16. 1 John, i., 4.—(30) James, ii., 18, 19. John, xv., 4, 5. 1 John, ii., 3, 5. Matt., xii., 33.—(31) Tit., i., 15, 16. Matt., vii., 18. Rom., viii., 8.—(32) Heb., xi., 6. Rom., xiv., 23.—(33) 2 Tim., i., 9. John, i., 13. Rom., viii., 7, 8. Hag., ii., 14. Isa., lviii., 1-5 ; lxvi., 2. 2.—(34) Matt., v., 48. Mark, xii., 30, 31. Phil., iv., 8, 9.—(35) Job, ix., 2, 3, 20, 21. Psal. cxliii., 2. Prov., xx., 9. Phil., iii., 8-15.

Articles revised.	*Articles of the Church of England.*
much as they are bound to do, but that they do more' for his sake than of bounden duty is required ; whereas Christ saith plainly; " When ye have done all those things that are commanded you,'say,'We are unprofitable servants,,we have done that which was' our duty to do.''(1) /	as they are bound to do, but that they do more for his sake than of bounden duty is required; whereas Christ plainly, " When ye have done all that are commanded to you, say, We are unprofitable servants."

<table>
<tr><td>. ARTICLE XV;.
. Of Christ alone without Sin.</td><td>ARTICLE XV.
. Of Christ alone without Sin. .</td></tr>
<tr><td>Christ, in the truth of our nature, was made like unto us all things, sin only excepted,(2). from which he ;was early void both in his flesh and in his spirit ; he came to the Lamb without spot,(3). who, by sacrifice of him-self(4) once made,(5) should take away the sins' of the world ;(6) and sin (as St. John saith) was not in him.(7) But all we the rest, although baptized 'and regenerate, yet offend in many things ; and " if we say we have no sin, we deceive ourselves, and the truth.is not in us.''(8)</td><td>Christ, in the truth of our nature, was made like unto us; in all things, siu only except, from which' he was clearly void; both in his flesh and in his spirit. He came to be a Lamb without spot, who, by sacrifice of himself once made, should take away the sins of the' world ; and sin (as St. John saith) was not in him. But·all the rest (although baptized, and born again in Christ) yet offend in many things ; and " if we say we have no sin, we deceive ourselves and,the truth is not in us."</td></tr>
</table>

CHARLES HERLE, *Prolocutor.*
HENRY ROBOROUGH, *Scribe.*
ADONIRAM BYFIELD, *Scribe.*

N.B. The Assembly proceeded no farther in the revisal.`

No. VIII.

THE DIRECTORY FOR THE PUBLIC WORSHIP OF GOD,.

Agreed upon by the Assembly of Divines at. West-minster ; examined and approved, Anno' 1654, by the General Assembly of the Church of Scot-land, and ratified by Act of Parliament the same Year.

THE PREFACE.

IN the beginning of the blessed Reformation, our wise and 'pious ancestors took care to set forth an order for redress of many things, which they then by the Word discovered to be vain, erroneous, superstitious, and idolatrous, in the public worship of God. 'This occasioned many godly and learned men to rejoice much in the Book of Common Prayer at that time set forth ; because the mass, and the rest of the Latin service, being removed, the public worship was celebrated in our own tongue ; many of the common people also received benefit by hearing the Scriptures read in their own language, which formerly were unto them as a book that is seal-ed.

'Howbeit, long and sad experience hath.made it.manifest that the liturgy used in the Church of England (notwithstanding all the pains and religious' intentions of the compilers' of it) hath pi oved an offence, not only to many of the god-ly 'at home, but also to the Reformed churches abroad.' For, not to speak of urging the read-ing of all the. prayers, which very greatly in-creased the burden of·it, .the many unprofitable and burdensome ceremonies contained in it have occasioned much mischief, as well by dis-quieting the consciences of many godly ·minis-ters and people, who could not yield unto them, as by depriving them of the ordinances of God, which they might not enjoy without conforming or subscribing to those ceremonies, sundry good Christians have been; by. means thereof, kept from the Lord's Table,' and. divers able and faithful ministers debarred from the exercise of their ministry (to the endangering of many thou-sand souls, in a time of such scarcity of faithful pastors), and spoiled of their livelihood, to the undoing of them and their families. Prelates and

their faction have laboured to raise the estima-tion of it to such a height, as if there were no oth-er worship or way of worship of God among us. but only the Service; Book ; to the great hinder-ance of the preaching of the Word, and (in some places; especially of late) to the justling of it out,. as·unnecessary, or, at best, as 'far inferior to the reading of common prayer, which was made no better than an idol by many ignorant and super-stitious people, who, pleasing themselves in.their presence at that service,.and their. lip-labour in hearing a part of it, have thereby hardened them-selves, in their ignorance and carelessness of saving knowledge and true piety.

In the mean time, papists boasted .that the. book was a compliance with them in a great part of their service ; and so were not a little confirmed in their superstition and idolatry, ex-pecting rather our return to them, than endeav-ouring the reformation of themselves : in which expectation they were of late very much en-couraged, when, upon the pretended warranta-bleness of imposing the former ceremonies, new ones were daily obtruded upon the Church.

Add hereunto (which was not foreseen, but since hath come to pass), that the liturgy hath been a great means, as on the one hand to make: and increase an "idle and unedifying ministry, which contented itself with set forms made to their hands by others, without putting forth themselves to exercise the gift of prayer, with which our Lord Jesus Christ ·pleaseth. to fur-nish all his servants whom he calls to that of-fice : so, on the other side, it hath been (and ever would be, if continued) a matter of endless. strife and contention in the Church, and a snare both to many godly and faithful ministers, who have been persecuted and silenced upon that oc-casion, and to others of hopeful parts, many of. which have been, and more still would ,be, di-verted from all thoughts of the ministry to other studies ; especially in these later times, wherein God vouchsafed to his people more and better. means for the discovery of error and supersti-tion, and for attaining of knowledge in the mys-· teries of godliness, and gifts in preaching and prayer.·

Upon these, and many the like weighty con-. siderations, in reference to the whole book .in. general, and because of divers particulars con-tained in it ; not from any love to novelty, or· intention to disparage our 'first Reformers (of whom we are persuaded that, were they now

(1) Luke, xvii.; 10, with ver. 7-9.—(2) Isa., liii., 3-5. Heb., ii., 17, with v., 15.—(3) Luke, i., 35, with Acts, iii., 14. John, xiv., 30. 2 Cor., v., 21. Heb., vii., 26.—(4) 1 Pet., i., 19.—(5) Eph., y., 2,—(6) Heb , ix., 26, 28 ; x., 11, 12.—(7) John, i., 29.—(8) 1 John, iii., 5. James, iii., 2.
1 John, i., 8, 10.

alive, they would join with us in this work, and whom we acknowledge as excellent instruments, raised by God, to begin the purging and building of his house, and desire that they may be had of us and posterity in everlasting remembrance, with thankfulness and honour), but that we may, in some measure, answer the gracious providence of God, which at this time calleth upon us for farther reformation, and may satisfy our own consciences, and answer the expectation of other Reformed churches, and the desires of many of the godly among ourselves, and, withal, give some public testimony of our endeavours for uniformity in Divine worship, which we have promised in our solemn League and Covenant: we have, after earnest and frequent calling upon the name of God, and after much consultation, not with flesh and blood, but with his holy Word, resolved to lay aside the former liturgy, with the many rites and ceremonies formerly used in the worship of God, and have agreed upon this following Directory for all the parts of public worship, at ordinary and extraordinary times.

Wherein our care hath been to hold forth such things as are of Divine institution in every ordinance; and other things we have endeavoured to set forth according to the rules of Christian prudence, agreeably to the general rules of the Word of God : our meaning therein being only, that the general heads, the sense and scope of the prayers, and other parts of public worship, being known to all, there may be a consent of all the churches in those things that contain the substance of the service and worship of God ; and the ministers may be hereby directed, in their administrations, to keep like soundness in doctrine and prayer ; and may, if need be, have some help and furniture ; and yet so, as they become not hereby slothful and negligent, in stirring up the gifts of Christ in them ; but that each one, by meditation, by taking heed to himself, and the flock of God committed to him, and by wise observing the ways of Divine Providence, may be careful to furnish his heart and tongue with farther or other materials of prayer and of exhortation as shall be needful upon all occasions.

Of the assembling of the Congregation, and their Behaviour in the Public Worship of God.

When the congregation is to meet for public worship, the people (having before prepared their hearts thereunto) ought all to come, and join therein; not absenting themselves from the public ordinances through negligence, or upon pretence of private meetings.

Let all enter the assembly, not irreverently, but in a grave and seemly manner, taking their seats or places without adoration, or bowing themselves towards one place or other.

The congregation being assembled, the minister, after solemn calling on them to the worshipping of the great name of God, is to begin with prayer.

" In all reverence and humility acknowledging the incomprehensible greatness and majesty of the Lord (in whose presence they do then in a special manner appear), and their own vileness and unworthiness to approach so near him, with their utter inability of themselves to so great a work ; and humbly beseeching him for

pardon, assistance, and acceptance in the whole service then to be performed ; and for a blessing on that particular portion of his Word then to be read ; and all in the name and mediation of the Lord Jesus Christ."

The public worship being begun, the people are wholly to attend upon it, forbearing to read anything except what the ministers is then reading or citing ; and abstaining much more from all private whisperings, conferences, salutations, or doing reverence to any persons present or coming in ; as also from all gazing, sleeping, or other indecent behaviour, which may disturb the minister or people, or hinder themselves and others in the service of God.

If any, through necessity, be hindered from being present at the beginning, they ought not, when they come into the congregation, to betake themselves to their private devotions, but reverently to compose themselves to join with the assembly in that ordinance of God which is then in hand.

Of Public Reading of the Holy Scriptures.

Reading of the Word in the congregation, being part of the public worship of God (wherein we acknowledge our dependance upon him, and subjection to him), and one means sanctified by him for the edifying of his people, is to be performed by the pastors and teachers.

Howbeit, such as intend the ministry may occasionally both read the Word, and exercise their gift in preaching in the congregation, if allowed by the presbytery thereunto.

All the canonical books of the Old and New Testament (but none of those which are commonly called Apocrypha) shall be publicly read in the vulgar tongue, out of the best allowed translation, distinctly, that all may hear and understand.

How large a portion shall be read at once is left to the wisdom of the minister ; but it is convenient that ordinarily one chapter of each Testament be read at every meeting ; and sometimes more, where the chapters be short, or the coherence of matter requireth it.

It is requisite that all the canonical books be read over in order, that the people may be better acquainted with the whole body of the Scriptures; and, ordinarily, where the reading in either Testament endeth on one Lord's Day, it is to begin the next.

We commend, also, the more frequent reading of such Scriptures as he that readeth shall think best for edification of his hearers, as the book of Psalms, and such like.

When the minister who readeth shall judge it necessary to expound any part of what is read, let it not be done until the whole chapter or psalm be ended ; and regard is always to be had unto the time, that neither preaching, nor other ordinances, be straitened or rendered tedious ; which rule is to be observed in all other public performances.

Besides public reading of the Holy Scriptures, every person that can read is to be exhorted to read the Scriptures privately (and all others that cannot read, if not disabled by age or otherwise, are likewise to be exhorted to learn to read), and to have a Bible.

Of Public Prayer before the Sermon.

After reading of the Word (and singing of the

psalm), the minister who is to preach is to endeavour to get his own and his hearers' hearts to be rightly affected with their sins, that they may all mourn in sense thereof before the Lord, and hunger and thirst after the grace of God in Jesus Christ, by proceeding to a more full confession of sin, with shame and holy confusion of face, and to call upon the Lord to this effect:

"To acknowledge our great sinfulness; first, by reason of original sin, which (besides the guilt that makes us liable to everlasting damnation) is the seed of all other sins, hath depraved and poisoned all the faculties and powers of soul and body, doth defile our best actions, and (were it not restrained, or our hearts renewed by grace) would break forth into innumerable transgressions, and greatest rebellions against the Lord, that ever were committed by the vilest of the sons of men. And, next, by reason of actual sins, our own sins, the sins of magistrates, of ministers, and of the whole nation, unto which we are many ways accessory; which sins of ours receive many fearful aggravations, we having broken all the commandments of the holy, just, and good law of God, doing that which is forbidden, and leaving undone what is enjoined; and that not only out of ignorance and infirmity, but also more presumptuously, against the light of our minds, checks of our consciences, and motions of his own Holy Spirit, to the contrary, so that we have no cloak for our sins; yea, not only despising the riches of God's goodness, forbearance, and long-suffering, but standing out against many invitations and offers of grace in the Gospel; not endeavouring, as we ought, to receive Christ into our hearts by faith, or to walk worthy of him in our lives.

"To bewail our blindness of mind, hardness of heart, unbelief, impenitency, security, lukewarmness, barrenness; our not endeavouring after mortification and newness of life, nor after the exercise of godliness in the power thereof; and that the best of us have not so steadfastly walked with God, kept our garments so unspotted, nor been so zealous of his glory, and the good of others, as we ought; and to mourn over such other sins as the congregation is particularly guilty of, notwithstanding the manifold and great mercies of our God, the love of Christ, the light of the Gospel, and reformation of religion, our own purposes, promises, vows, solemn covenant, and other special obligations, to the contrary.

"To acknowledge and confess that, as we are convinced of our guilt, so, out of a deep sense thereof, we judge ourselves unworthy of the smallest benefits, most worthy of God's fiercest wrath, and of all the curses of the law, and heaviest judgments inflicted upon the most rebellious sinners; and that he might most justly take his kingdom and Gospel from us, plague us with all sorts of spiritual and temporal judgments in this life, and after cast us into utter darkness, in the lake that burneth with fire and brimstone, where is weeping and gnashing of teeth for evermore.

"Notwithstanding all which, to draw near to the throne of grace, encouraging ourselves with hope of a gracious answer of our prayers, in the riches and all-sufficiency of that one only oblation, the satisfaction and intercession of the Lord Jesus Christ, at the right hand of his Father, and our Father; and in confidence of the exceeding great and precious promises of mercy and grace in the new covenant, through the same Mediator thereof, to deprecate the heavy wrath and curse of God, which we are not able to avoid or bear; and humbly and earnestly to supplicate for mercy, in the free and full remission of all our sins; and that only for the bitter sufferings and precious merits of our only Saviour Jesus Christ.

"That the Lord would vouchsafe to shed abroad his love in our hearts by the Holy Ghost; seal unto us, by the same Spirit of adoption, the full assurance of our pardon and reconciliation; comfort all that mourn in Zion, speak peace to the wounded and troubled spirit, and bind up the broken-hearted; and as for secure and presumptuous sinners, that he would open their eyes, convince their consciences, and turn, them from darkness unto light, and from the power of Satan unto God, that they also may receive forgiveness of sin, and an inheritance among them that are sanctified by faith in Christ Jesus.

"With remission of sins through the blood of Christ, to pray for sanctification by his Spirit; the mortification of sin dwelling in, and many times tyrannizing over us; the quickening of our dead spirits with the life of God in Christ; grace to fit and enable us for all duties of conversation and calling towards God and men; strength against temptations, the sanctified use of blessings and crosses, and perseverance in faith and obedience unto the end.

"To pray for the propagation of the Gospel and kingdom of Christ to all nations, for the conversion of the Jews, the fulness of the Gentiles, the fall of antichrist, and the hastening of the second coming of our Lord; for the deliverance of the distressed churches abroad from the tyranny of the antichristian faction, and from the cruel oppressions and blasphemies of the Turk; for the blessing of God upon all the Reformed churches, especially upon the churches and kingdoms of Scotland, England, and Ireland, now more strictly and religiously united in the solemn national League and Covenant; and for our plantations in the most remote parts of the world; more particularly for that church and kingdom whereof we are members, that therein God would establish peace and truth, the purity of all his ordinances, and the power of godliness; prevent and remove heresy, schism, profaneness, superstition, security, and unfruitfulness, under the means of grace; heal our rents and divisions, and preserve us from breach of our solemn covenant.

"To pray for all in authority, especially for the king's majesty, that God may make him rich in blessings, both in his person and government; establish his throne in religion and righteousness, save him from evil counsel, and make him a blessed and glorious instrument for the conservation and propagation of the Gospel, for the encouragement and protection of them that do well, the terror of all that do evil, and the great good of the whole Church, and of all his kingdoms; for the conversion of the queen, the religious education of the prince, and the rest of the royal seed; for the comforting the afflicted Queen of Bohemia, sister to our sovereign; and for the restitution and establishment of the illustrious Prince Charles, elector palatine of the Rhine, to all his dominions and dignities; for a blessing on our High Court of Parliament {when sitting in any of these kingdoms respectively), the nobility, the subordinate judges and magistrates, the gentry, and all the commonalty; for all pastors and teachers, that God would fill them with his Spirit, make them exemplarily holy, sober, just, peaceable, and gracious in their lives; sound, faithful, and powerful in their ministry; and follow all their labours with abundance of success and blessing; and give unto all his people pastors according to their own heart; for the universities, and all schools and religious seminaries of Church and commonwealth, that they may flourish more and more in learning and piety; for the particular city or congregation, that God would pour out a blessing upon the ministry of the Word, sacraments, and discipline, upon the civil government, and all the several families and persons therein; for mercy to the afflicted under any inward or outward distress; for seasonable weather and fruitful seasons, as the time may require; for averting the judgments that we either feel, or fear, or are liable unto, as famine, pestilence, the sword, and such like.

"And, with confidence of his mercy to his whole Church, and the acceptance of our persons, through the merits and mediation of our high-priest the Lord Jesus, to profess that it is the desire of our souls to have fellowship with God, in the reverend and conscionable use of his holy ordinances; and to that purpose, to pray earnestly for his grace and effectual assistance to the sanctification of his holy Sabbath, the Lord's Day, in all the duties thereof, public and private, both to ourselves, and to all other congregations of his people, according to the riches and excellence of the Gospel, this day celebrated and enjoyed.

"And, because we have been unprofitable hearers in times past, and how cannot of ourselves receive, as we should, the deep things of God, the mysteries of Jesus Christ, which require a spiritual discerning, to pray that the Lord, who teacheth to profit, would graciously please to pour out the Spirit of grace, together with the outward means thereof, causing us to attain such a measure of the excellence of the knowledge of Jesus Christ our Lord, and in him, of the things which belong to our peace, that we may account all things but as dross in comparison of him; and that we, tasting the first-fruits of the glory that is to be revealed, may long for a more full and perfect communion with him, that where he is we may be also, and enjoy the fulness of those joys and pleasures which are at his right hand for evermore.

"More particularly, that God would in special manner furnish his servant (now called to dispense the bread of life unto his household) with wisdom, fidelity, zeal, and utterance, that he may divide the Word of God aright, to every one his portion, in evidence and demonstration of the Spirit and power; and that the Lord would circumcise the ears and hearts of the hearers, to hear, love, and receive with meekness the ingrafted Word, which is able to save their souls; make them as good ground to receive in the good seed of the Word, and strengthen them against the temptations of Satan, the cares of the world, the hardness of

their own hearts, and whatsoever else may hinder their profitable and saving hearing; that so Christ may be so formed in them, and live in them, that all their thoughts may be brought into captivity to the obedience of Christ, and their hearts established in every good word and work forever."

We judge this to be a convenient order in the ordinary public prayers; yet so as the minister may defer (as in prudence he shall think meet) some part of these petitions till after his sermon, or offer up to God some of the thanksgivings hereafter appointed, in his prayer before his sermon.

Of the Preaching of the Word.

Preaching of the Word being the power of God unto salvation, and one of the greatest and most excellent works belonging to the ministry of the Gospel, should be so performed that the workman need not be ashamed, but may save himself, and those that hear him.

It is presupposed (according to the rules for ordination) that the minister of Christ is in some good measure gifted for so weighty a service by his skill in the original languages, and in such arts and sciences as are handmaids unto divinity; by his knowledge in the whole body of theology, but most of all in the Holy Scriptures; having his senses and heart exercised in them above the common sort of believers; and by the illumination of God's Spirit, and other gifts of edification, which (together with reading and studying of the Word) he ought still to seek by prayer and an humble heart, resolving to admit and receive any truth not yet attained, whenever God shall make it known unto him. All which he is to make use of, and improve in his private preparations, before he deliver in public what he hath provided.

Ordinarily, the subject of his sermon is to be some text of Scripture, holding forth some principle or head of religion, or suitable to some special occasion emergent; or he may go on in some chapter, psalm, or book of the Holy Scripture, as he shall see fit.

Let the introduction to his text be brief and perspicuous, drawn from the text itself, or context, or some parallel place, or general sentence of Scripture.

If the text be long (as in histories and parables it sometimes must be), let him give a brief sum of it; if short, a paraphrase thereof, if need be: in both, looking diligently to the scope of the text, and pointing at the chief heads and grounds of doctrine which he is to raise from it.

In analyzing and dividing his text, he is to regard more the order of matter than of words; and neither to burden the memory of the hearers in the beginning with too many members of division, nor to trouble their minds with obscure terms of art.

In raising doctrines from the text, his care ought to be, first, that the matter be the truth of God; secondly, that it be a truth contained in or grounded on that text, that the hearers may discern how God teacheth it from thence; thirdly, that he chiefly insist upon those doctrines which are principally intended, and make most for the edification of the hearers.

The doctrine is to be expressed in plain terms; or, if anything in it need explication, it is to be opened, and the consequence also from the text cleared. The parallel places of Scripture, confirming the doctrine, are rather to be plain and pertinent than many, and (if need be) somewhat insisted upon, and applied to the purpose in hand.

The arguments and reasons are to be solid, and, as much as may be, convincing. The illustrations, of what kind soever, ought to be full of light, and such as may convey the truth into the hearer's heart with spiritual delight.

If any doubt obvious from Scripture, reason, or prejudice of the hearers seem to arise, it is very requisite to remove it by reconciling the seeming differences, answering the reasons, and discovering and taking away the causes of prejudice and mistake; otherwise it is not fit to detain the hearers with propounding or answering with vain or wicked cavils, which, as they are endless, so the propounding and answering of them doth more hinder than promote edification.

He is not to rest in general doctrine, although never so much cleared and confirmed, but to bring it home to special use by application to his hearers; which, albeit it prove a work of great difficulty to himself, requiring much prudence, zeal, and meditation, and to the natural and corrupt man will be very unpleasant, yet he is to endeavour to perform it in such a manner that his auditors may feel the Word of God to be quick and powerful, and a discerner of the thoughts and intents of the heart; and that, if any believer or ignorant person be present, he may have the secrets of his heart made manifest, and give glory to God.

In the use of instruction or information in the knowledge of some truth, which is a consequence from his doctrine, he may (when convenient) confirm it by a few firm arguments from the text in hand, and other places of Scripture, or from the nature of that commonplace in divinity whereof that truth is a branch.

In confutation of false doctrines, he is neither to raise an old heresy from the grave, nor to mention a blasphemous opinion unnecessarily; but if the people be in danger of an error, he is to confute it soundly, and endeavour to satisfy their judgments and consciences against all objections.

In exhorting to duties, he is, as he seeth cause, to teach also the means that help to the performance of them.

In dehortation, reprehension, and public admonition (which require special-wisdom), let him, as there shall be cause, not only discover the nature and greatness of the sin, with the misery attending it, but also show the danger his hearers are in to be overtaken and surprised by it, together with the remedies and best way to avoid it.

In applying comfort, whether general against all temptations, or particular against some special troubles or terrors, he is carefully to answer such objections as a troubled heart and afflicted spirit may suggest to the contrary.

It is also sometimes requisite to give some notes of trial (which is very profitable, especially when performed by able and experienced ministers, with circumspection and prudence, and the signs clearly grounded on the Holy Scripture), whereby the hearers may be able to examine themselves whether they have attained those graces and performed those duties to which he exhorteth, or be guilty of the sin reprehended and in danger of the judgments threatened, or are such to whom the consolations propounded do belong; that accordingly they may be quickened and excited to duty, humbled for their wants and sins, affected with their danger; and strengthened with comfort, as their condition upon examination shall require.

And as he needeth not always to prosecute every doctrine which lies in his text, so is he wisely to make choice of such uses as, by his residence and conversing with his flock, he findeth most needful and seasonable; and among these, such as may most draw their souls to Christ, the fountain of light, holiness, and comfort.

This method is not prescribed as necessary for every man or upon every text, but only recommended as being found by experience to be very much blessed of God, and very helpful for the people's understandings and memories.

But the servant of Christ, whatever his method be, is to perform his whole ministry,

1. Painfully, not doing the work of the Lord negligently.

2. Plainly, that the meanest may understand, delivering the truth, not in the enticing words of man's wisdom, but in demonstration of the Spirit and of power, lest the cross of Christ should be made of none effect; abstaining also from an unprofitable use of unknown tongues, strange phrases, and cadences of sounds and words, sparingly citing sentences of ecclesiastical or other human writers, ancient or modern, be they never so elegant.

3. Faithfully, looking at the honour of Christ, the conversion, edification, and salvation of the people, not at his own gain or glory, keeping nothing back which may promote those holy ends, giving to every one his own portion, and bearing indifferent respect unto all, without neglecting the meanest, or sparing the greatest in their sins.

4. Wisely framing all doctrines, exhortations, and especially his reproofs, in such a manner as may be most likely to prevail, showing all due respect to each man's person and place, and not mixing his own passion or bitterness.

5. Gravely, as becometh the Word of God, shunning all such gesture, voice, and expressions as may occasion the corruptions of men to despise him and his ministry.

6. With loving affection, that the people may see all coming from his godly zeal and hearty desire to do them good.

7. As taught of God, and persuaded in his own heart that all that he teacheth is the truth of Christ, and walking before his flock as an example to them in it; earnestly, both in private and public, recommending his labours to the blessing of God, and watchfully looking to himself and the flock whereof the Lord hath made him overseer; so shall the doctrine of truth be preserved uncorrupt, many souls converted and built up, and himself receive manifold comforts of his labours even in this life, and afterward the crown of glory laid up for him in the world to come.

Where there are more ministers in a congregation than one, and they of different gifts, each may more especially apply himself to doctrine or exhortation, according to the gift wherein he most excelleth, and as they shall agree between themselves.

Of Prayer after Sermon.

The sermon being ended, the minister is "to give thanks for the great love of God in sending his Son Jesus Christ unto us; for the communication of his Holy Spirit; for the light and liberty of the glorious Gospel, and the rich and heavenly blessings revealed therein—as, namely, election, vocation, adoption, justification, sanctification, and hope of glory; for the admirable goodness of God in freeing the land from antichristian darkness and tyranny, and for all other national deliverances; for the reformation of religion, for the Covenant, and for many temporal blessings.

"To pray for the continuance of the Gospel, and all ordinances thereof, in their purity, power, and liberty; to turn the chief and most useful heads of the sermon into some few petitions; and to pray that it may abide in the heart, and bring forth fruit.

"To pray for preparation for death and judgment, and a watching for the coming of our Lord Jesus Christ; to entreat of God the forgiveness of the iniquities of our holy things, and the acceptation of our spiritual sacrifice, through the merit and mediation of our great High-Priest and Saviour the Lord Jesus Christ." —

And because the prayer which Christ taught his disciples is not only a pattern of prayer, but itself a most comprehensive prayer, we recommend it also to be used in the prayers of the Church.

And whereas, at the administration of the sacraments, the holding public fasts, and days of thanksgiving, and other special occasions, which may afford matter of special petitions and thanksgivings, it is requisite to express somewhat in our public prayers (as at this time it is our duty to pray for a blessing upon the Assembly of Divines, the armies by sea and land, for the defence of the king, Parliament, and kingdom), every minister is herein to apply himself in his prayer, before or after sermon, to those occasions; but for the manner he is left to his liberty, as God shall direct and enable him, in piety and wisdom to discharge his duty.

The prayer ended, let a psalm be sung, if with convenience it may be done; after which (unless some other ordinance of Christ, that concerneth the congregation at that time, be to follow), let the minister dismiss the congregation with a solemn blessing.

THE ADMINISTRATION OF THE SACRAMENTS.

AND, FIRST, OF BAPTISM.

Baptism, as it is not unnecessarily to be delayed, so it is not to be administered in any case by any private person, but by a minister of Christ, called to be the steward of the mysteries of God.

Nor is it to be administered in private places or privately, but in the place of public worship, and in the face of the congregation, where the people may most conveniently see and hear, and, not in the places where fonts, in the time

of popery, were unfitly and superstitiously placed.

The child to be baptized, after notice given to the minister the day before, is to be presented by the father, or (in case of his necessary absence) by some Christian friend in his place, in professing his earnest desire that the child may be baptized.

Before baptism, the minister is to use some words of instruction, touching the institution, nature, use, and ends of this sacrament, showing,

"That it is instituted by our Lord Jesus Christ; that it is a seal of the covenant of grace, of our ingrafting into Christ, and of our union with him, of remission of sins, regeneration, adoption, and life eternal. That the water in baptism representeth and signifieth both the blood of Christ, which taketh away all guilt of sin, original and actual; and the sanctifying virtue of the Spirit of Christ against the dominion of sin, and the corruption of our sinful nature; that baptizing, or sprinkling and washing with water, signifieth the cleansing from sin by the blood and for the merit of Christ, together with the mortification of sin, and rising from sin to newness of life by virtue of the death and resurrection of Christ; that the promise is made to believers and their seed; and that the seed and posterity of the faithful, born within the Church, have by their birth interest in the covenant, and right to the seal of it, and to the outward privileges of the Church under the Gospel, no less than the children of Abraham in the time of the Old Testament; the covenant of grace, for substance, being the same, and the grace of God and the consolation of believers more plentiful than before; that the Son of God admitted little children into his presence, embracing and blessing them, saying, 'For of such is the kingdom of God;' that children, by baptism, are solemnly received into the bosom of the visible Church, distinguished from the world and them that are without, and united with believers; and that all who are baptized in the name of Christ do renounce, and by their baptism are bound to fight against, the devil, the world, and the flesh; that they are Christians, and federally holy before baptism, and therefore are baptized; that the inward grace and virtue of baptism is not tied to that very moment of time wherein it is administered, and that the fruit and power thereof reacheth to the whole course of our life; and that outward baptism is not so necessary, that through the want thereof the infant is in danger of damnation, or the parents guilty, if they do not contemn or neglect the ordinance of Christ, when and where it may be had."

In these, or the like instructions, the minister is to use his own liberty and godly wisdom, as the ignorance or errors in the doctrine of baptism, and the edification of the people shall require.

He is also to admonish all that are present

"To look back to their baptism; to repent of their sins against their covenant with God; to stir up their faith; to improve and make the right use of their baptism, and of the covenant sealed thereby between God and their souls."

He is to exhort the parent

"To consider the great mercy of God to him and his child; to bring up the child in the knowledge of the grounds of the Christian religion, and in the nurture and admonition of the Lord; and to let him know the danger of God's wrath to himself and child if he be negligent, requiring his solemn promise for the performance of his duty."

This being done, prayer is also to be joined with the word of instruction for sanctifying the water to this spiritual use, and the minister is to pray to this or the like effect:

" That the Lord, who hath not left us as strangers without the covenant of promise, but called us to the privileges of his ordinances, would graciously vouchsafe to sanctify and bless his own ordinance of baptism at this time; that he would join the inward baptism of his Spirit with the outward baptism of water; make this baptism to the infant a seal of adoption, remission of sin, regeneration, and eternal life, and all other promises of the covenant of grace; that the child may be planted into the likeness of the death and resurrection of Christ; and that the body of sin being destroyed in him, he may serve God in newness of life all his days."

Then the minister is to demand the name of the child, which being told him, he is to say (calling the child by his name), *I baptize thee in the name of the Father, and of the Son, and of the Holy Ghost:*

As he pronounceth these words, he is to baptize the child with water; which, for the manner of doing it, is not only lawful, but sufficient, and most expedient to be, by pouring or sprinkling of the water on the face of the child, without adding any other ceremony.

This done, he is to give thanks, and to pray to this or the like purpose:

"Acknowledging with all thankfulnes that the Lord is true and faithful in keeping covenant and mercy; that he is good and gracious, not only in that he numbereth us among his saints, but is pleased also to bestow upon our children this singular token and badge of his love in Christ; that in his truth and special providence he daily bringeth some into the bosom of his Church, to be partakers of his inestimable benefits, purchased by the blood of his dear Son for the continuance and increase of his Church.

" And praying that the Lord would still continue and daily confirm more and more this his unspeakable favour; that he would receive the infant now baptized, and solemnly entered into the household of faith, into his fatherly tuition and defence, and remember him with the favour that he showeth to his people; that if he shall betaken out of this life in his infancy, the Lord, who is rich in mercy, would be pleased to receive him up into glory; and if he live, and attain the years of discretion, that the Lord would so teach him by his Word and Spirit, and make his baptism effectual to him, and so uphold him by his divine power and grace, that by faith he may prevail against the devil, the world, and the flesh, till in the end he obtain a full and final victory, and so he kept by the power of God through faith unto salvation, through Jesus Christ our Lord."

Of the Celebration of the Communion, or Sacrament of the Lord's Supper.

The Communion, or Supper of the Lord, is frequently to be celebrated; but how often, may be considered and determined by the ministers and other church governors of each congregation, as they shall find it most convenient for the comfort and edification of the people committed to their charge: and, when it shall be administered, we judge it convenient to be done after the morning sermon.

The ignorant and the scandalous are not fit to receive this sacrament of the Lord's Supper.

Where this sacrament cannot with convenience be frequently administered, it is requisite that public warning be given the Sabbath-day before the administration thereof; and that either then, or on some day of that week, something concerning that ordinance, and the due preparation thereunto, and participation thereof be taught, that by the diligent use of all means sanctified of God to that end, both in public and private, all may come better prepared to that heavenly feast.

When the day is come for administration, the minister having ended his sermon and prayer, shall make a short exhortation,

"Expressing the inestimable benefit we have by this sacrament, together with the ends and use thereof; setting forth the great necessity of having our comforts and strength renewed thereby in this our pilgrimage and warfare; how necessary it is that we come unto it with knowledge, faith, repentance, love, and with hungering and thirsting souls after Christ and his benefits; how great the danger to eat and drink unworthily.

"Next, he is, in the name of Christ on the one part, to warn all such as are ignorant, scandalous, profane, or that live in any sin or offence against their knowledge or conscience, that they presume not to come to that holy table, showing them that he that eateth and drinketh unworthily, eateth and drinketh judgment unto himself; and on the other part, he is in especial manner to invite and encourage all that labour under the sense of the burden of their sins, and fear of wrath, and desire to reach out unto a greater progress in grace than yet they can attain unto, to come to the Lord's Table, assuring them, in the same name, of ease, refreshing, and strength to their weak and wearied souls."

After this exhortation, warning, and invitation, the table being before decently covered, and so conveniently placed that the communicants may orderly sit about it or at it, the minister is to begin the action with sanctifying and blessing the elements of bread and wine set before him (the bread in comely and convenient vessels, so prepared, that, being broken by him, and given, it may be distributed among the communicants, the wine also in large cups); having first, in a few words, showed that those elements, otherwise common, are now set apart and sanctified to this holy use by the word of institution and prayer.

Let the words of institution be read out of the Evangelists, or out of the First Epistle of the Apostle Paul to the Corinthians, chap. xi., verse 23: "I have received of the Lord," &c., to the twenty-seventh verse, which the minister may, when he seeth requisite, explain and apply.

Let the prayer, thanksgiving, or blessing of the bread and wine be to this effect:

" With humble and hearty acknowledgment of the greatness of our misery, from which neither man nor angel was able to deliver us, and of our great unworthiness of the least of all God's mercies ; to give thanks to God for all his benefits, and especially for that great benefit of our redemption, the love of God the Father, the sufferings and merits of the Lord Jesus Christ the Son of God, by which we are delivered ; and for all means of grace, the Word, and sacraments ; and for this sacrament in particular, by which Christ, and all his benefits, are applied and sealed up unto us, which, notwithstanding the denial of them unto others, are in great mercy continued unto us, after so much and long abuse of them all.

" To profess that there is no other name under heaven by which we can be saved but the name of Jesus Christ, by whom alone we receive liberty and life, have access to the throne of grace, are admitted to eat and drink at his own table, and are sealed up by his Spirit to an assurance of happiness and everlasting life.

" Earnestly to pray to God, the Father of all mercies and God of all consolation, to vouchsafe his gracious presence, and the effectual working of his Spirit in us, and so to sanctify these elements, both of bread and wine, and to bless his own ordinance, that we may receive by faith the body and blood of Jesus Christ crucified for us, and so to feed upon him that he may be one with us and we with him ; that he may live with us, and we in him and to him who hath loved us, and given himself for us."

All which he is to endeavour to perform with suitable affections, answerable to such a holy action, and to stir up the like in the people.

The elements being now sanctified by the Word and prayer, the minister, being at the table, is to take the bread in his hand, and say, in these expressions (or other the like, used by Christ or his apostle upon this occasion),

" According to the holy institution, command, and example of our blessed Saviour Jesus Christ, I take this bread, and having given thanks, I break it, and give it unto you [there the minister, who is also himself to communicate, is to break the bread and give it to the communicants] : ' Take ye, eat ye ; this is the body of Christ which is broken for you ; do this in remembrance of him.' "

In like manner the minister is to take the cup, and say, in these expressions (or other the like, used by Christ or the apostle upon the same occasion),

" According to the institution, command, and example of our Lord Jesus Christ, I take this cup, and give it unto you [here he giveth to the communicants] : ' This cup is the New Testament in the blood of Christ, which is shed for the remission of the sins of many ; drink ye all of it.' "

After all have communicated, the minister may, in a few words, put them in mind

" Of the grace of God in Jesus Christ held forth in this sacrament, and exhort them to walk worthy of it."

The minister is to give solemn thanks to God

" For his rich mercy and invaluable goodness vouchsafed to them in that sacrament, and to entreat for pardon for the defects of the whole service, and for the gracious assistance of his good Spirit, whereby they may be enabled to walk in the strength of that grace, as becometh those who have received so great pledges of salvation."

The collection for the poor is so to be ordered that no part of the public worship be thereby hindered.

Of the Sanctification of the Lord's Day.

The Lord's Day ought to be so remembered beforehand as that all worldly business of our ordinary callings may be so ordered, and so timely and seasonably laid aside, as they may not be impediments to the due sanctifying of the day when it comes.

The whole day is to be celebrated as holy to the Lord, both in public and private, as being the Christian Sabbath ; to which end it is requisite that there be a holy cessation, or resting all the day, from all unnecessary labours ; and an abstaining, not only from all sports and pastimes, but also from all worldly words and thoughts.

That the diet on that day be so ordered as that neither servants be unnecessarily detained from the public worship of God, nor any other persons hindered from the sanctifying that day.

That there be private preparation of every person and family, by prayer for themselves, and for God's assistance of the minister, and for a blessing upon his ministry ; and by such other holy exercises as may farther dispose them to a more comfortable communion with God in his public ordinances.

That all the people meet so timely for public worship that the whole congregation may be present at the beginning, and with one heart solemnly join together in all parts of the public worship, and not depart till after the blessing.

That what time is vacant between or after the solemn meetings of the congregation in public be spent in reading, meditation, repetition of sermons (especially by calling their families to an account of what they have heard), and catechising of them, holy conferences, prayer for a blessing upon the public ordinances, singing of psalms, visiting the sick, relieving the poor, and such like duties of piety, charity, and mercy, accounting the Sabbath a delight.

The Solemnization of Marriage.

Although marriage be no sacrament, nor peculiar to the Church of God, but common to mankind, and of public interest in every commonwealth, yet, because such as marry are to marry in the Lord, and have special need of instruction, direction, and exhortation from the Word of God at their entering into such a new condition, and of the blessing of God upon them therein, we judge it expedient that marriage be solemnized by a lawful minister of the Word, that he may accordingly counsel them, and pray for a blessing upon them.

Marriage is to be between one man and one woman only, and they such as are not within the degrees of consanguinity or affinity prohibited by the Word of God ; and the parties are to be of years of discretion, fit to make their own choice, or upon good grounds to give their mutual consent.

Before the solemnizing of marriage between any persons, their purpose of marriage shall be published by the minister, three several Sabbath-days, in the congregation, at the place or places of their most usual and constant abode respectively. And of this publication, the minister who is to join them in marriage shall have sufficient testimony, before he proceed to solemnize the marriage.

Before that publication of such their purpose (if the parties be under age), the consent of the parents, or others under whose power they are (in case the parents be dead), is to be made known to the church officers of that congregation, to be recorded.

The like is to be observed in the proceedings of all others, although of age, whose parents are living, for their first marriage. And in after marriages of either of those parties, they shall be exhorted not to contract marriage without first acquainting their parents with it (if with conveniency it may be done), endeavouring to obtain their consent.

Parents ought not to force their children to marry without their free consent, nor deny their own consent without just cause.

After the purpose or contract of marriage hath been thus published, the marriage is not to be long deferred. Therefore, the minister having had convenient warning, and nothing being objected to hinder it, is publicly to solemnize it in the place appointed by authority for public worship, before a competent number of credible witnesses, at some convenient hour of the day, at any time of the year, except on a day of public humiliation. And we advise that it be not on the Lord's Day.

And because all relations are sanctified by the Word and prayer, the minister is to pray for a blessing upon them to this effect:

"Acknowledging our sins, whereby we have made ourselves less than the least of all the mercies of God, and provoked him to imbitter all our comforts; earnestly, in the name of Christ, to entreat the Lord (whose presence and favour is the happiness of every condition, and sweetens every relation) to be their portion and to own and accept them in Christ, who are now to be joined in the honourable estate of marriage, the covenant of their God; and that, as he hath brought them together by his providence, he would sanctify them by his Spirit, giving them a new frame of heart, fit for their new estate; enriching them with all graces, whereby they may perform the duties, enjoy the comforts, undergo the cares, and resist the temptations which accompany that condition, as becometh Christians."

The prayer being ended, it is convenient that the minister do briefly declare unto them out of the Scripture,

"The institution, use, and ends of marriage, with the conjugal duties which, in all faithfulness, they are to perform each to other; exhorting them to study the holy Word of God, that they may learn to live by faith, and to be content in the midst of all matrimonial cares and troubles, sanctifying God's name, in a thankful, sober, and holy use of all conjugal comforts; praying much with and for one another; watching over and provoking each other to love and good works; and to live together as the heirs of the grace of life."

After solemn charging of the persons to be married before the great God, who searcheth all hearts, and to whom they must give a strict

Vol. II.—N N N.

account at the last day, that if either of them know any cause, by precontract or otherwise, why they may not lawfully proceed to marriage, that they now discover it: the minister (if no impediment be acknowledged) shall cause first the man to take the woman by the right hand, saying these words:

"I, N., do take thee, N., to be my married wife, and do, in the presence of God, and before this congregation, promise and covenant to be a loving and faithful husband unto thee, until God shall separate us by death."

Then the woman shall take the man by his right hand, and say these words:

"I, N., do take thee, N., to be my married husband; and I do, in the presence of God, and before this congregation, promise and covenant to be a loving, faithful, and obedient wife unto thee, until God shall separate us by death."

Then, without any farther ceremony, the minister shall, in the face of the congregation, pronounce them to be husband and wife, according to God's ordinance; and so conclude the action with prayer to this effect:

"That the Lord would be pleased to accompany his own ordinance with his blessing, beseeching him to enrich the persons now married; as with other pledges of his love, so particularly with the comforts and fruits of marriage, to the praise of his abundant mercy, in and through Christ Jesus."

A register is to be carefully kept, wherein the names of the parties so married, with the time of their marriage, are forthwith to be fairly recorded in a book provided for that purpose, for the perusal of all whom it may concern.

Concerning Visitation of the Sick.

It is the duty of the minister, not only to teach the people committed to his charge in public, but privately and particularly to admonish, exhort, reprove, and comfort them, upon all seasonable occasions, so far as his time, strength, and personal safety will permit.

He is to admonish them, in time of health, to prepare for death; and for that purpose, they are often to confer with their minister about the estate of their souls; and in times of sickness, to desire his advice and help, timely and seasonably, before their strength and understanding fail them.

Times of sickness and affliction are special opportunities put into his hand by God to minister a word in season to weary souls, because then the consciences of men are or should be more awakened to bethink themselves of their spiritual estates for eternity; and Satan also takes advantage then to load them more with sore and heavy temptations: therefore, the minister being sent for, and repairing to the sick, is to apply himself, with all tenderness and love, to administer some spiritual good to his soul to this effect.

He may, from the consideration of the present sickness, instruct him out of Scripture, that diseases come not by chance, or by distempers of body only, but by the wise and orderly guidance of the good hand of God, to every particular person smitten by them. And that, whether it be laid upon him out of displeasure for sin, for his correction and amendment, or for trial and exercise of his graces, or for other special and excellent ends, all his sufferings shall turn to his profit, and work together for his good, if he sincerely labour to, make a sanctified use of God's visitation, neither despising his chastening, nor waxing weary of his correction.

If he suspect him of ignorance, he shall examine him in the principles of religion, especially touching repentance and faith ; and as he seeth cause, instruct him in the nature, use, excellence, and necessity of those graces ; as also touching the covenant of grace, and Christ the Son of God, the mediator of it, and concerning remission of sins by faith in him.

He shall exhort the sick person to examine himself, to search and try his former ways, and his estate towards God.

And if the sick person shall declare any scruple, doubt, or temptation that is upon him, instructions and resolutions shall be given to satisfy and settle him.

If. it appear that he hath not a due sense of his sins, endeavours ought to be used to convince him of his sins, of the guilt and desert of them ; of the filth and pollution which the soul contracts by. them ; and of the curse of law, and wrath of God, due to them ; that he may be truly affected with and humble for them ; and, withal, to make known the danger of deferring repentance. and of neglecting salvation at any time offered ; to awaken his conscience, and rouse him up out of a stupid and secure condition, to apprehend the justice and. wrath of God, before whom none can stand but he that, being lost to himself, layeth hold upon Christ by faith.

If he have endeavoured to walk in the ways of holiness, and to serve God in uprightness, although not without many failings and infirmities ; or if his spirit be broken with the sense of sin, or cast down through want of the sense of God's favour, then it will be fit to raise him up, by setting before him the freeness and fulness of God's grace; the sufficiency of righteousness. in Christ, the gracious offers in the Gospel, that all who repent and believe with all their heart in God's mercy through Christ, renouncing their own righteousness, shall have life and salvation in him : it may also be useful to show him that death hath in it no spiritual evil to be feared by those that are in Christ, because sin, the sting of death, is taken away by Christ, who hath delivered all that are his from the bondage of the fear of death, triumphed over the grave, given us victory, is, himself entered into glory, to prepare a place for his people : so that neither life nor death shall be able to separate them from God's love in Christ, in whom such are sure, though now they must be laid in the dust, to obtain a joyful and glorious resurrection to eternal life.

Advice also may be given, as to beware of an ill-grounded persuasion on mercy, or on the goodness of his condition for heaven, so to disclaim all merit in himself, and to cast himself wholly upon God for mercy, in the sole merits and mediation of Jesus Christ, who hath engaged himself never to cast off them who in truth and sincerity come unto him. Care, also must be taken that the sick person be not cast down into despair, by such a severe representation of the wrath of God due to him for his sins, as is not mollified by a seasonable propounding

of Christ and his merit, for a door of hope to every penitent believer.

When the sick person is best composed, may he least disturbed, and other necessary offices about him least hindered, the minister, if desired, shall pray with him, and for him, to this effect :

"Confessing and bewailing of sin, original and actual, the miserable condition of all by nature, as being children of wrath, and under the curse ; acknowledging that all diseases, sicknesses, death, and hell itself, are the proper issues and effects thereof; imploring God's mercy for the sick person through the blood of Christ ; beseeching that God would open his eyes, discover unto him his sins, cause him to see himself lost in himself, make known to him the cause why God smiteth him, reveal Jesus Christ to his soul for righteousness and life, give unto him his Holy Spirit to create and strengthen faith, to lay hold upon Christ, to work in him comfortable evidences of his love, to arm him against temptations, to take off his heart from the world, to sanctify his present visitation, to furnish him with patience and strength to bear it, and to give him perseverance in faith to the end.

"That if God shall please to add to his days, he would vouchsafe to bless and sanctify all means of his recovery, to remove the disease, renew his strength, and enable him to walk worthy of God, by a faithful remembrance and diligent observing of such vows and promises of holiness and obedience as men are apt to make in times of sickness, that he may glorify God in the remaining part of his life.

"And if God have determined to finish his days by the present visitation, he may find such evidence of the pardon of all his sins, of his interest in Christ, and eternal life by Christ, as may cause his inward man to be renewed, while his outward man decayeth ; that he may behold death without fear, cast himself wholly upon Christ without doubting, desire to be dissolved and be with Christ, and so receive the end of his faith, the salvation of his soul, through the only merits and intercession of the Lord Jesus Christ, our alone Saviour, and all-sufficient Redeemer."

The minister shall admonish him also (as there shall be cause) to set his house in order, thereby to prevent inconveniences; to take care for the payment of his debts, and to make restitution or satisfaction where he hath done any wrong, to be reconciled to those with whom he hath been at variance, and fully to forgive all men their trespasses against him, as he expects forgiveness at the hand of God.

Lastly, the minister may improve the present occasion to exhort those about the sick person to consider their own mortality, to return to the Lord and make peace with him ; in health to prepare for sickness, death, and judgment ; and all the days of their appointed time so to wait until their change come, that when Christ, who is our life, shall appear, they may appear with him in glory.

Concerning Burial of the Dead.

When any person departeth this life, let the dead body, upon the day of burial, be decently attended from the house to the place appointed for public burial, and there immediately interred, without any ceremony.

And because the customs of kneeling down, and praying by or towards the dead corpse, and other such usages, in the place where it lies, before it be carried to burial, are superstitious; and for that praying, reading, and singing, both in going to, and at the grave, have been grossly abused, are no way beneficial to the dead, and have proved many ways hurtful to the living, therefore let all such things be laid aside.

Howbeit, we judge it very convenient that the Christian friends which accompany the dead body to the place appointed for public burial, do apply themselves to meditations and conferences suitable to the occasion; and that the minister, as upon other occasions, so at this time, if he be present, may put them in remembrance of their duty.

That this shall not extend to deny any civil respects or deferences at the burial suitable to the rank and condition of the party deceased while he was living.

Concerning Public Solemn Fasting.

When some great and notable judgments are either inflicted upon a people, or apparently imminent, or by some extraordinary provocations notoriously deserved; as, also, when some special blessing is to be sought and obtained, public solemn fasting (which is to continue the whole day) is a duty that God expecteth from that nation or people.

A religious fast requires total abstinence, not only from all food (unless bodily weakness do manifestly disable from holding out till the fast be ended, in which case somewhat may be taken, yet very sparingly, to support nature; when ready to faint), but also from all worldly labour, discourses, and thoughts, and from all bodily delights (although at other times lawful), rich apparel, ornaments, and such like, during the fast; and much more from whatever is, in the nature or use, scandalous and offensive, as gaudish attire, lascivious habits and gestures, and other vanities of either sex; which we recommend to all ministers, in their places, diligently and zealously to reprove, as at other times, so especially at a fast, without respect of persons; as there shall be occasion.

Before the public meeting, each family and person apart are privately to use all religious care to prepare their hearts to such solemn work, and to be early at the congregation.

So large a portion of the day as conveniently may be is to be spent in public reading and preaching of the Word, with singing of psalms, fit to quicken affections suitable to such a duty, but especially in prayer, to this or the like effect:

"Giving glory to the great majesty of God, the creator, preserver, and supreme ruler of all the world, the better to affect us thereby with a holy reverence and awe of him; acknowledging his manifold, great, and tender mercies, especially to the Church and nation, the more effectually to soften and abase our hearts before him; humbly confessing of sins of all sorts, with their several aggravations; justifying God's righteous judgments, as being far less than our sins do deserve; yet humbly and earnestly imploring his mercy and grace for ourselves, the Church, and nation, for our king, and all in authority, and for all others for whom we are bound

to pray (according as the present exigence requireth), with more special importunity and enlargement than at other times; applying by faith the promises and goodness of God for pardon, help, and deliverance from the evils felt, feared, or deserved; and for obtaining the blessings which we need and expect, together with a giving up of ourselves wholly and forever unto the Lord."

In all these, the ministers, who are the mouths of the people unto God, ought so to speak from their hearts, upon serious and thorough premeditation of them, that both themselves and the people may be much affected, and even melted thereby; especially with sorrow for their sins, that it may be indeed a day of deep humiliation and afflicting of the soul.

Special choice is to be made of such Scriptures to be read, and of such texts for preaching, as may best work the hearts of the hearers to the special business of the day, and most dispose them to humiliation and repentance; insisting most on those particulars which each minister's observation and experience tell him are most conducing to the edification and reformation of that congregation to which he preacheth.

Before the close of the public duties, the minister is, in his own and the people's names, to engage his and their hearts to be the Lord's, with professed purpose and resolution to reform whatever is amiss among them, and more particularly such sins as they have been more remarkably guilty of; and to draw nearer unto God; and to walk more closely and faithfully with him in new obedience, than ever before.

He is, also to admonish the people, with all importunity, that the work of that day doth not end with the public duties of it, but that they are so to improve the remainder of the day, and of their whole life, in re-enforcing upon themselves and their families in private, all those godly affections and resolutions which they professed in public, as that they may be settled in their hearts forever, and themselves may more sensibly find that God hath smelt a sweet savour in Christ from their performances, and is pacified towards them, by answers of grace, in pardoning of sin, in removing of judgments, in averting or preventing of plagues, and in conferring of blessings, suitable to the conditions and prayers of his people by Jesus Christ.

Besides solemn and general fasts enjoined by authority, we judge that at other times congregations may keep days of fasting, as Divine Providence shall administer unto them special occasions. And also, that families may do the same, so it be not on days wherein the congregation to which they do belong is to meet for fasting or other public duties of worship.

Concerning the Observation of Days of Public Thanksgiving.

When any such day is to be kept, let notice be given of it, and of the occasion thereof, some convenient time before, that the people may the better prepare themselves thereunto.

The day being come, and the congregation (after private preparations) being assembled, the minister is to begin with a word of exhortation, to stir up the people to the duty for which they are met, and with a short prayer for God's assistance and blessing (as at other conventions for public worship), according to the particular occasion of their meeting.

Let him then make some pithy narration of the deliverance obtained, or mercy received, or of whatever hath occasioned that assembling of the congregation, that all may better understand it, or be minded of it, and more affected with it.

And because singing of psalms is of all other the most proper ordinance for expressing of joy and thanksgiving, let some pertinent psalm or psalms be sung for that purpose, before or after the reading of some portion of the Word, suitable to the present business.

Then let the minister who is to preach proceed to farther exhortation and prayer before his sermon, with special reference to the present work; after which, let him preach upon some text of Scripture pertinent to the occasion.

The sermon ended, let him not only pray, as at other time after preaching is directed, with remembrance of the necessities of the Church, king, and state (if before the sermon they were omitted), but enlarge himself in due and solemn thanksgiving for former mercies and deliverances, but more especially for that which at the present calls them together to give thanks: with humble petition for the continuance and renewing of God's wonted mercies, as need shall be, and for sanctifying grace to make a right use thereof. And so, having sung another psalm suitable to the mercy, let him dismiss the congregation with a blessing, that they have some convenient time for their repast and refreshment.

But the minister (before their dismission) is solemnly to admonish them to beware of all excess and riot, tending to gluttony or drunkenness, and much more of these sins themselves, in their eating and refreshing; and to take care that their mirth and rejoicing be not carnal, but spiritual, which may make God's praise to be glorious, and themselves humble and sober; and that both their feeding and rejoicing may render them more cheerful and enlarged, farther to celebrate his praises in the midst of the congregation, when they return unto it, in the remaining part of that day.

When the congregation shall be again assembled, the like course in praying, reading, preaching, singing of psalms, and offering up of more praise and thanksgiving, that is before directed for the morning, is to be renewed and continued, so far as the time will give leave.

At one or both of the public meetings that day, a collection is to be made for the poor (and in the like manner upon the day of public humiliation), that their loins may bless us, and rejoice the more with us. And the people are to be exhorted, at the end of the latter meeting, to spend the residue of that day in holy duties, and testifications of Christian love and charity one towards another, and of rejoicing more and more in the Lord, as becometh those who make the joy of the Lord their strength.

Of Singing of Psalms.

It is the duty of Christians to praise God publicly, by singing of psalms together in the congregation; and also privately in the family.

In singing of psalms, the voice is to be tuna-

bly and gravely ordered; but the chief must be to sing with understanding, and with grace in the heart, making melody unto the Lord.

That the whole congregation may join herein, every one that can read is to have a psalm-book; and all others, not disabled by age or otherwise, are to be exhorted to learn to read. But for the present, where many in the congregation cannot read, it is convenient that the minister, or some other fit person appointed by him, and the other ruling officers, do read the psalm line by line, before the singing thereof.

An Appendix, touching Days and Places of Public Worship.

There is no day commanded in Scripture to be kept holy under the Gospel but the Lord's Day, which is the Christian Sabbath.

Festival days, vulgarly called holydays, having no warrant in the Word of God, are not to be continued.

Nevertheless, it is lawful and necessary, upon special emergent occasions, to separate a day or days for public fasting or thanksgiving, as the several eminent and extraordinary dispensations of God's providence shall administer cause and opportunity to his people.

As no place is capable of any holiness, under pretence of whatsoever dedication or consecration, so neither is it subject to such pollution by any superstition formerly used, and now laid aside, as may render it unlawful or inconvenient for Christians to meet together therein for the public worship of God; and therefore we hold it requisite that the places of public assembling for worship among us should be continued and employed to that use.

No. IX.

THE FORM OF PRESBYTERIAL CHURCH GOVERNMENT

Agreed upon by the Assembly of Divines at Westminster; examined and approved, Anno 1645, by the General Assembly of the Church of Scotland, &c.

THE PREFACE.

JESUS CHRIST, upon whose shoulders the government is, whose name is called Wonderful, Counsellor, the mighty God, the everlasting Father, the Prince of Peace,* of the increase of whose government and peace there shall be no end, who sits upon the throne of David, and upon his kingdom, to order it, and to establish it with judgment and justice, from henceforth even forever, having all power given unto him even in heaven and in earth by the Father, who

---

* Isa., ix., 6, 7.

raised him from the dead, and set him at his own right hand, far above all principalities, and power, and might, and dominion, and every name that is named, not only in this world, but also in that which is to come, and put all things under his feet, and gave him to be the head over all things to the Church, which is his body; the fulness of him that filleth all in all: he being ascended up far above all heavens, that he might fill all things, received gifts for his Church, and gave offices necessary for the edification of his Church, and perfecting of his saints. -

Of the Church.

There is one general Church visible held forth in the New Testament, 1 Cor., xii., 12, 13, 28, together with the rest of the chapter.

The ministry, oracles, and ordinances of the New Testament, given by Jesus Christ to the general Church visible, for the gathering and perfecting of it in this life, until his second coming, 1 Cor., xii., 28 ; Eph., iv., 4, 5, compared with ver. 10-16 of the same chapter.

Particular visible churches, members of the general Church, are also held forth in the New Testament, Gal., i., 21, 22 ; Rev., i., 4, 20, and Rev., ii., 1. Particular churches, in the primitive times, were made up of visible saints, viz., of such as, being of age, professed faith in Christ, and obedience unto Christ, according to the rules of faith and life taught by Christ and his apostles ; and of their children, Acts, ii., 38, 41 ; and ver. last, compared with v. 14 ; 1 Cor., i., 2, compared with 2 Cor., ix., 13 ; Acts, ii., 39 ; 1 Cor., vii., 14 ; Rom., ix., 16, and so forward ; Mark, x., 14, compared with Matt., xix., 13, 14 ; Luke, xviii., 15, 16.*

Of the Officers of the Church.

The officers which Christ hath appointed for the edification of his Church, and the perfecting of the saints, are,

Some extraordinary, as apostles, evangelists, and prophets, which are ceased.

Others ordinary and perpetual, as pastors, teachers, and other church governors and deacons.

Pastors.

The pastor is an ordinary and perpetual officer in the Church : Jer., iii., 15-17 ; prophesying of the time of the Gospel : 1 Pet., v., 2-4 ; Eph., iv., 11-13.

First, it belongs to his office

To pray for and with his flock, as the mouth of the people unto God, Acts, vi., 2-4 ; Acts, xx., 36 ; where preaching and prayer are joined as several parts of the same office, James, v., 15. The office of the elder, that is, the pastor, is to pray for the sick, even in private, to which a blessing is especially promised : much more, therefore, ought he to perform this in the public execution of his office, as a part thereof, 1 Cor., xiv., 15, 16.

To read the Scripture publicly ; for the proof of which,

1. That the priests and Levites in the Jewish Church were trusted with the public reading of the Word, as is proved Deut., xxxi., 9-11 ; Neh., viii., 1, 2, 13.

---

* Matt., xxviii., 19-20. Eph., i., 20-22, compared with iv., 8-11, and Psalm lxviii., 18.

---

2. That the ministers of the Gospel have as ample a charge and commission to dispense the Word, as well as other ordinances, as the priests and Levites had under the law, proved Isa., lxvi., 21, and Matt., xxiii., 34, where our Saviour entitleth the officers of the New Testament, whom He will send forth, by the same names as the teachers of the Old.

Which propositions prove, that therefore (the duty being of a moral nature) it followeth, by just consequence, that the public reading of the Scriptures belongeth to the pastor's office.

To feed the flock, by preaching of the Word, according to which he is to teach, convince, reprove, exhort, and comfort.—1 Tim., iii., 2. 2 Tim., iii., 16, 17. Tit., i., 9.

To catechise, which is a plain laying down the first principles of the oracles of God, Heb., v., 12 : or of the doctrine of Christ, and is a part of preaching.

To dispense other Divine mysteries, 1 Cor., iv., 1, 2.

To administer the sacraments, Matt., xxviii., 19, 20. Mark, xvi., 15, 16. 1 Cor., xi., 23-25, compared with x., 16.

To bless the people from God, Numb., vi., 23-26, compared with Rev., xiv., 5 (where the same blessings, and persons from whom they come, are expressly mentioned) ; Isa., lxvi., 21, where, under the names of priests and Levites to be continued under the Gospel, are meant evangelical pastors, who, therefore, are by office to bless the people, Deut., x., 8. 2 Cor., xiii., 14. Eph., i., 2.

To take care of the poor, Acts, xi., 30 ; iv., 34-37 ; vi., 2-4. 1 Cor., xvi., 1-4. Gal., ii., 9, 10.

And he hath also a ruling power over the flock as a pastor, I Tim., v., 17. Acts, xx., 17, 28. 1 Thess., v., 12. Heb., xiii., 7, 17.

Teacher or Doctor.

The Scripture doth hold out the name and title of teacher as well as of pastor, 1 Cor., xii., 28. Eph., iv., 11.

Who is also a minister of the Word as well as the pastor, and hath power of administration of the sacraments.

The Lord having given different gifts, and divers exercises according to these gifts, in the ministry of the Word, Rom., xii., 6-8 ; 1 Cor., xii., 1, 4-7, though these different gifts may meet in, and accordingly be exercised by, one and the same minister, 1 Cor., xiv., 3 ; 2 Tim., iv., 2 ; Tit., i., 9 ; yet, where be several ministers in the same congregation, they may be designed to several employments, according to the different gifts in which each of them doth most excel, Rom., xii., 6-8 ; 1 Pet., iv., 10, 11. And he that doth more excel in exposition of Scriptures, in teaching sound doctrine, and in convincing gainsayers, than he doth in application, and is accordingly employed therein, may be called a teacher or doctor (the places alleged by the notation of the Word do prove the proposition) ; nevertheless, where is but one minister in a particular congregation, he is to perform, so far as he is able, the whole work of the ministry, as appeareth in 2 Tim., vi. 2 ; Tit., i. 9, before alleged, 1 Tim., vi., 2.

A teacher or doctor is of most excellent use in schools and universities : as of old in the schools of the prophets, and at Jerusalem, where Gamaliel and others taught as doctors.

Other Church Governors.

As there were in the Jewish Church elders of the people joined with the priests and Levites in the government of the Church (as appeareth in 1 Chron., xix., 8–10), so Christ, who hath instituted a government and governors ecclesiastical in the Church, hath furnished some in his Church, besides the ministers of the Word, with gifts for government, and with commission to execute the same when called thereunto, who are to join with the minister in the government of the Church, Rom., xii., 7, 8 ; 1 Cor., xii., 28 ; which officers Reformed churches commonly call elders.

Deacons.

The Scripture doth hold out deacons as distinct officers in the Church.—Phil., i., 1. 1 Tim., iii., 8.

Whose office is perpetual.—1 Tim., iii., 8, to verse 15. Acts, vi., 1–4. To whose office it belongs not to preach the Word or administer the sacraments, but to take special care in distributing to the necessities of the poor.—Acts, vi., 1–4, and the verses following.

Of Particular Congregations.

It is lawful and expedient that there be fixed congregations, that is, a certain company of Christians to meet in one assembly ordinarily for public worship. When believers multiply to such a number that they cannot conveniently meet in one place, it is lawful and expedient that they should be divided into distinct and fixed congregations, for the better administration of such ordinances as belong unto them, and the discharge of mutual duties.—1 Cor., xiv., 26 : " Let all things be done unto edifying ;" and 33 and 40.

The ordinary way of dividing Christians into distinct congregations, and most expedient for edification, is by the respective bounds of their dwellings.

1st. Because they who dwell together, being bound to all kind of moral duties one to another, have the better opportunity thereby to discharge them ; which moral tie is perpetual, for Christ came not to destroy the law, but to fulfil it.—Deut., xv., 7, 11. Matt., xxii., 39 ; v., 17.

2dly. The communion of saints must be so ordered as may stand with the most convenient use of the ordinances, and discharge of moral duties, without respect of persons.—1 Cor., xiv., 26 : " Let all things be done unto edifying." Heb., x., 24, 25. James, ii., 1, 2.

3dly. The pastor and people must so nearly cohabit together as that they may mutually perform their duties each to other with most conveniency.

In this company some must be set apart to bear office.

Of the Officers of a Particular Congregation.

For officers in a single congregation, there ought to be one, at the least, both to labour in the Word and doctrine, and to rule.—Prov., xxix., 18. 1 Tim., v., 17. Heb., xiii., 7.

It is also requisite that there should be others to join in government.—1 Cor., xii., 28.

And likewise it is requisite that there should

be others to take special care for the relief of the poor.—Acts, vi., 2, 3.

The number of each of which is to be proportioned according to the condition of the congregation.

These officers are to meet together at convenient and set times, for the well ordering the affairs of that congregation, each according to his office.

It is most expedient that, in these meetings, one whose office is to labour in the Word and doctrine, do moderate in their proceedings.—1 Tim., v., 17.

Of the Ordinances in a Particular Congregation.

The ordinances in a single congregation are, prayer, thanksgiving, and singing of psalms (1 Tim., ii., 1 ; 1 Cor., xiv., 15, 16), the Word read (although there follow no immediate explication of what is read), the Word expounded and applied, catechising, the sacraments administered, collection made for the poor, dismissing the people with a blessing.

Of Church Government, and the several sorts of Assemblies for the same.

Christ hath instituted a government, and governors ecclesiastical in the Church : to that purpose the apostles did immediately receive the keys from the hand of Jesus Christ, and did use and exercise them in all the churches of the world, upon all occasions.

And Christ hath since continually furnished some in his Church with gifts of government, and with commission to execute the same, when called thereunto.

It is lawful and agreeable to the Word of God that the Church be governed by several sorts of assemblies, which are congregational, classical, and synodical.

Of the Power in Common of all these Assemblies.

It is lawful and agreeable to the Word of God that the several assemblies before mentioned have power to convene, and call before them, any person within their several bounds whom the ecclesiastical business which is before them doth concern ; proved by Matt., xviii.

They have the power to hear and determine such causes and differences as do orderly come before them.

It is lawful and agreeable to the Word of God that all the said assemblies have some power to dispense church censures.

Of Congregational Assemblies, that is, the Meeting of the ruling Officers of a particular Congregation for the Government thereof.

The ruling officers of a particular congregation have power, authoritatively, to call before them any member of the congregation, as they shall see just occasion.

To inquire into the knowledge and spiritual estate of the several members of the congregation.

To admonish and rebuke.

Which three branches are proved by Heb., xiii., 17 ; 1 Thess., v., 12, 13 ; Ezek., xxxiv., 4.

Authoritative suspension from the Lord's Table of a person not yet cast out of the Church, is agreeable to the Scripture :

1st. Because the ordinance itself must not be profaned.

2dly. Because we are charged to withdraw from those that walk disorderly.

3dly. Because of the great sin and danger, both to him that comes unworthily, and also to the whole Church.—Matt., vii., 6. 2 Thess., iii., 6, 14, 15. 1 Cor., xi., 27, to the end of the chapter, compared with Jude, 23. 1 Tim., v., 22. And there was power and authority, under the Old Testament, to keep unclean persons from holy things.—Levit., xiii., 5. Numb., ix., 7. 2 Chron., xxiii., 19.

The like power and authority, by way of analogy, continues under the New Testament.

The ruling-officers of a particular congregation have power authoritatively to suspend from the Lord's Table a person not yet cast-out of the Church.

1st. Because those who have authority to judge of and admit such as are fit to receive the sacrament, have authority to keep back such as shall be found unworthy.

2dly. Because it is an ecclesiastical business of ordinary practice belonging to that congregation.

When congregations are divided and fixed, they need all mutual help one from another, both in regard to their intrinsic weaknesses and mutual dependance, as also in regard of enemies from without.

Of Classical Assemblies.

The Scripture doth hold out a presbytery in the Church, both in the First Epistle to Timothy, iv., 14, and in Acts, xv., 2, 4, 6.

A presbytery consisteth of ministers of the Word, and such other public officers as are agreeable to, and warranted by, the Word of God, to be church governors, to join with the ministers in the government of the Church; as appeareth Rom., xii., 7, 8; 1 Cor., xii., 28.

The Scripture doth hold forth that many particular congregations may be under one presbyterial government.

This proposition is proved by instances:

I. First. Of the Church of Jerusalem, which consisted of more congregations than one, and all these congregations were under one presbyterial government.

This appeareth thus:

1. First. The Church of Jerusalem consisted of more congregations than one, as is manifest,

1st. By the multitude of believers mentioned in divers places: both before the dispersion of the believers there by the persecution (mentioned in the Acts of the Apostles, chap. viii.; in the beginning thereof, witness chap. i., verse 11; ii., 41, 46, 47; iv., 4; v., 14, and vi. of the same book of the Acts, verses 1 and 7), and also after the dispersion, ix., 31; xii., 24.; and xxi., 20, of the same book.

2dly. By the many apostles and other preachers in the Church of Jerusalem; and if there were but one congregation there, then each apostle preached but seldom; which will not consist with chap. vi., verse 2, of the same book of the Acts of the Apostles.

3dly. The diversity of languages among the believers, mentioned both in the second and sixth chapters of the Acts, doth argue more congregations than one in that church.

2. Secondly. All those congregations were under one presbyterial government; because,

1st. They were one church, Acts, viii., 1; ii., 47, compared with v., 11; xii., 5; and xv., 4, of the same book.

2dly. The elders of the Church are mentioned, Acts, xi., 30; xv., 4, 6, 22; and xxi., 17, 18, of the same book.

3dly. The apostles did the ordinary acts of presbyters, as presbyters in that kirk; which proveth a presbyterial church before the dispersion.—Acts, vi.

4thly. The several congregations in Jerusalem being one church, the elders of that church are mentioned as meeting together for acts of government, Acts, xi., 30; xv., 4, 6, 22; and xxi., 17, 18, and so forward; which proves that those several congregations were under one presbyterial government.

And whether these congregations were fixed or not fixed, in regard of officers or members, it is all one, as to the truth of the proposition.

Nor doth there appear any material difference betwixt the several congregations in Jerusalem, and the many congregations now in the ordinary condition of the Church, as to the point of fixedness required of officers or members.

3. Thirdly. Therefore the Scripture doth hold forth that many congregations may be under one presbyterial government.

II. Secondly. By the instance of the Church of Ephesus; for,

1. That there were more congregations than one in the Church of Ephesus, appears by Acts, xx., 31, where is mention of Paul's continuance at Ephesus in preaching for the space of three years; and Acts, xix., 18-20, where the special effect of the Word is mentioned; and verses 10 and 17 of the same chapter, where is a distinction of Jews and Greeks; and 1 Cor., xvi., 8, 9, where is a reason of Paul's stay at Ephesus until Pentecost; and verse 19, where is mention of a particular church in the house of Aquila and Priscilla, then at Ephesus; as appears Acts, xviii., 19, 24, 26. All which laid together, doth prove that the multitude of believers did make more congregations than one in the Church of Ephesus.

2. That there were many elders over these many congregations, as one flock, appeareth Acts, xx., 17, 25, 28, 30, 36, 37.

3. That these many congregations were one church, and that they were under one presbyterial government, appeareth Rev., ii., the first six verses, joined with Acts, xx., 17, 18.

Of Synodical Assemblies.

The Scripture doth hold out another sort of assemblies, for the government of the Church, besides classical and congregational, all which we call synodical, Acts, xv. Pastors and teachers, and other church-governors (as also other fit persons, when it shall be deemed expedient), are members of those assemblies which we call synodical, where they have a lawful calling thereunto.

Synodical assemblies may lawfully be of several sorts, as provincial, national, and œcumenical.

It is lawful and agreeable to the Word of God that there be a subordination of congregational, classical, provincial, and national assemblies, for the government of the Church.

Under the head of ordination of ministers is to be considered, either the doctrine of ordination, or the power of it.

Touching the Doctrine of Ordination.

No man ought to take upon him the office of a minister of the Word without a lawful calling.—John, iii., 27. Rom., x., 14, 15. Jer., xiv., 14. Heb., v., 4.

Ordination is always to be continued in the Church.—Tit., i., 5. 1 Tim., v., 21, 22.

Ordination is the solemn setting apart of a person to some public church office.—Numb., viii., 10, 11, 14, 19, 22. Acts, vi., 3, 5, 6.

Every minister of the Word is to be ordained by imposition of hands and prayer, with fasting, by those preaching presbyters to whom it doth belong.—1 Tim., v., 12. Acts, iv., 23, and xiii., 3.

It is agreeable to the Word of God, and very expedient, that such as are to be ordained ministers be designed to some particular church, or other ministerial charge.—Acts, xiv., 23. Tit., i., 5. Acts, xx., 17, 28.

He that is to be ordained minister must be duly qualified, both for life and ministerial abilities, according to the rules of the apostle.—1 Tim., iii., 2–6. Tit., i., 5–9.

He is to be examined and approved by those by whom he is to be ordained.—1 Tim., iii., 7, 10, and v., 22.

No man is to be ordained a minister for a particular congregation if they of that congregation can show just cause of exception against him.—1 Tim., iii., 2. Tit., i., 7.

Touching the Power of Ordination.

Ordination is the act of a presbytery, 1 Tim., iv., 14. The power of ordering the whole work of ordination is in the whole presbytery, which, when it is over more congregations than one, whether those congregations be fixed or not fixed in regard of officers or members, it is indifferent as to the point of ordination.—1 Tim., iv., 14.

It is very requisite that no single congregation, that can conveniently associate, do assume to itself all and sole power in ordination.

1. Because there is no example in Scripture that any single congregation, which might conveniently associate, did assume to itself all and sole power in ordination ; neither is there any rule which may warrant such a practice.

2. Because there is in Scripture example of an ordination in a presbytery over divers congregations : as in the Church of Jerusalem, where were many congregations, these many congregations were under one presbytery, and this presbytery did ordain.

The preaching presbyters orderly associated, either in cities or neighbouring villages, are those to whom the imposition of hands doth appertain for those congregations within their bounds respectively.

1. No man ought to take upon him the office of a minister of the Word without a lawful calling.—John, iii., 27. Rom., x., 14, 15. Jer., xiv., 14. Heb., v., 4.

2. Ordination is always to be continued in the Church.—Tit., i., 5. 1 Tim., v., 21, 22.

3. Ordination is the solemn setting apart of a person to some public church office.—Numb., viii., 10, 11, 14, 19, 22. Acts, vi., 3, 5, 6.

4. Every minister of the Word is to be ordained by imposition of hands and prayer, with fasting, by those preaching presbyters to whom it doth belong.—1 Tim., v., 22. Acts, xiv., 23, xiii., 3.

5. The power of ordering the whole work of ordination is in the whole presbytery, which, when it is over more congregations than one, whether those congregations be fixed or not fixed in regard of officers or members, it is indifferent as to the point of ordination.—1 Tim., iv., 14.

6. It is agreeable to the Word, and very expedient, that such as are to be ordained ministers be designed to some particular church, or other ministerial charge.—Acts, xiv., 23. Tit., i., 5. Acts, xx., 17, 28.

7. He that is to be ordained minister must be duly qualified, both for life and ministerial abilities, according to the rules of the apostle.—1 Tim., iii., 2–6. Tit., i., 5–9.

8. He is to be examined and approved of by those by whom he is to be ordained.—1 Tim., iii., 7, 10 ; v., 22.

9. No man is to be ordained a minister for a particular congregation if they of that congregation can show just cause of exception against him.—1 Tim., iii., 2. Tit., i., 7.

10. Preaching presbyters orderly associated, either in cities or neighbouring villages, are those to whom the imposition of hands do appertain for those congregations within their bounds respectively.—1 Tim., iv., 14.

11. In extraordinary cases, something extraordinary may be done, until a settled order may be had, yet keeping, as near as possible may be, to the rule.—2 Chron., xxix., 34–36 ; xxx., 2–5.

12. There is at this time (as we humbly conceive) an extraordinary occasion for a way of ordination for the present supply of ministers.

The Directory for the Ordination of Ministers.

It being manifest, by the Word of God, that no man ought to take upon him the office of a minister of the Gospel until he be lawfully called and ordained thereunto ; and that the work of ordination is to be performed with all due care, wisdom, gravity, and solemnity, we humbly tender these directions as requisite to be observed.

1. He that is to be ordained, being either nominated by the people, or otherwise commended to the presbytery for any place, must address himself to the presbytery, and bring with him a testimonial of his taking the Covenant of the three kingdoms ; of his diligence and proficiency in his studies ; what degrees he hath taken in the university, and what hath been the time of his abode there ; and, withal, of his age, which is to be twenty-four years ; but especially of his life and conversation.

2. Which being considered by the presbytery, they are to proceed to inquire touching the grace of God in him, and whether he be of such holiness of life as is requisite in a minister of the Gospel ; and to examine him touching his

learning and sufficiency, and touching the evidences of his calling to the Holy ministry, and, in particular, his fair and direct calling to that place.

THE RULES FOR EXAMINATION ARE THESE.

1. That the party examined be dealt, withal, in a brotherly way, with mildness of spirit, and with special respect to the gravity, modesty, and quality of every one.

2. He shall be examined touching his skill in the original tongues, and his trial to be made by reading the Hebrew and Greek Testaments, and rendering some portion of some into Latin; and if he be defective in them, inquiry shall be made more strictly after his other learning, and whether he hath skill in logic and philosophy.

3. What authors in divinity he hath read, and is best acquainted with. And trial shall be made in his knowledge of the grounds of religion, and of his ability to defend the orthodox doctrine contained in them against all unsound and erroneous opinions, especially those of the present age ; of his skill in the sense and meaning of such places of Scripture as shall be proposed unto him in cases of conscience, and in the chronology of the Scripture, and the ecclesiastical history.

4. If he hath not before preached in public, with approbation of such as are able to judge, he shall, at a competent time assigned him, expound before the presbytery such a place of Scripture as shall be given him.

5. He shall also, within a competent time, frame a discourse in Latin upon such a commonplace or controversy in divinity as shall be assigned him, and exhibit to the presbytery such theses as express the sum thereof, and maintain a dispute upon them.

6. He shall preach before the people, the presbytery, or some of the ministry of the Word appointed by them, being present.

7. The proportion of his gifts, in relation to the place unto which he is called, shall be considered.

8. Besides the trial of his gifts in preaching, he shall undergo an examination in the premises two several days, and more, if the presbytery shall judge it necessary.

9. And as for him that hath formerly been ordained a minister, and is to be removed to another charge, he shall bring a testimonial of his ordination, and of his abilities and conversation, whereupon his fitness for that place shall be tried by his preaching there (if it shall be judged necessary) by a farther examination of him.

3. In which he being approved, he is to be sent to the church where he is to serve, there to preach three several days, and to converse with the people, that they may have trial of his gifts for their edification, and may have time and occasion to inquire into, and the better to know his life and conversation.

4. In the last of these three days appointed for the trial of his gifts in preaching, there shall be sent from the presbytery to the congregation a public intimation in writing, which shall be publicly read before the people, and after affixed to the church door, to signify that such a day, a competent number of the members of that con-

gregation, nominated by themselves, shall appear before the presbytery, to give their consent and approbation to such a man to be their minister; or otherwise to put in, with all Christian discretion and meekness, what exceptions they have against him ; and if, upon the day appointed, there be no just exception against him, but the people give their consent, then the presbytery shall proceed to ordination.

5. Upon the day appointed for ordination, which is to be performed in that church where he that is to be ordained is to serve, a solemn fast shall be kept by the congregation, that they may the more earnestly join in prayer for a blessing upon the ordinance of Christ, and the labours of his servant for their good. The presbytery shall come to the place, or at least three or four ministers of the Word shall be sent thither from the presbytery ; of which one, appointed by the presbytery, shall preach to the people concerning the office and duty of ministers of Christ, and how the people ought to receive them for their work's sake.

6. After the sermon, the minister who hath preached shall, in the face of the congregation, demand of him who is now to be ordained concerning his faith in Christ Jesus, and his persuasion of the truth of the Reformed religion according to the Scripture ; his sincere intentions and ends in desiring to enter into this calling ; his diligence in prayer, reading, meditation, preaching, ministering the sacraments, discipline, and doing all ministerial duties towards his charge ; his zeal and faithfulness in maintaining the truth of the Gospel, and unity of the Church against error and schism ; his care that himself and his family may be unblameable, and examples to the flock ; his willingness and humility, in meekness of spirit, to submit unto the admonitions of his brethren and discipline of the Church ; and his resolution to continue in his duty against all trouble and persecution.

7. In all which having declared himself, professed his willingness, and promised his endeavours, by the help of God, the minister likewise shall demand of the people concerning their willingness to receive and acknowledge him as the minister of Christ ; and to obey, and submit unto him, as having rule over them in the Lord ; and to maintain, encourage, and assist him in all parts of his office.

8. Which being mutually promised by the people, the presbytery, or the ministers sent from them for ordination, shall solemnly set him apart to the office and work of the ministry, by laying their hands on him, which is to be accompanied with a short prayer or blessing, to this effect :

"Thankfully acknowledging the great mercy of God in sending Jesus Christ for the redemption of his people ; and for his ascension to the right hand of God the Father, and thence pouring out his Spirit, and giving gifts to men, apostles, evangelists, prophets, pastors, and teachers, for the gathering and building up of his Church ; and for fitting and inclining this man to this great work ;* to entreat him to fit him with his Holy Spirit to give him (who in his name we thus set apart to this holy service) to fulfil the work of his ministry in all things, that

---

* Here let them impose hands on his head.

he may both save himself, and his people committed to his charge." .

9. This, or the like form of prayer and blessing being ended, let the minister who preached briefly exhort him to consider of the greatness of his office and work, the danger of negligence both to himself and his people, the blessing which will accompany his faithfulness in this life, and that to come; and, withal, exhort the people to carry themselves to him, as to their minister in the Lord, according to their solemn promise made before; and so by prayer commending both him and his flock to the grace of God, after singing of a psalm, let the assembly be dismissed with a blessing.

10. If a minister be designed to a congregation who hath been formerly ordained presbyter, according to the form or ordination which hath been in the Church of England, which we hold for substance to be valid, and not to be disclaimed by any who have received it, then, there being a cautious proceeding in matters of examination, let him be admitted without any new ordination.

11. And in case any person already ordained minister in Scotland, or in any other Reformed church, be designed to another congregation in England, he is to bring from that church to the presbytery here, within which that congregation is, a sufficient testimonial of his ordination, of his life and conversation while he lived with them, and of the causes of his removal; and to undergo such a trial of his fitness and sufficiency, and to have the same course held with him in other particulars, as is set down in the rule immediately going before, touching examination and admission.

12. That records be carefully kept in the several presbyteries of the names of the persons ordained, with their testimonials, the time and place of their ordination, of the presbyters who did impose hands upon them, and of the charge to which they are appointed.

13. That no money or gift of what kind soever shall be received from the person to be ordained, or from any on his behalf, for ordination, or aught else belonging to it, by any of the presbytery, or any appertaining to any of them, upon what pretence soever.

Thus far of Ordinary Rules, and Course of Ordination in the Ordinary Way; that which concerns the Extraordinary Way, requisite to be now practised, followeth.

1. In these present exigencies, while we cannot have any presbyteries formed up to their whole power and work, and that many ministers are to be ordained for the service of the armies and navy, and to many congregations where there is no minister at all; and, where (by reason of the public troubles) the people cannot either themselves inquire, and find out one who may be a faithful minister for them, or have any such safety sent unto them for such a solemn trial as was before mentioned in the ordinary rules, especially when there can be no presbytery near unto them to whom they may address themselves, or which may come or send to them a fit man to be ordained in that congregation, and for that people; and yet, notwithstanding, it is requisite that ministers be ordained for them by some who, being set apart

themselves for the work of the ministry, have power to join in the setting apart others who are found fit and worthy. In those cases, until, by God's blessing, the aforesaid difficulties may be in some good measure removed, let some godly minister in or about the city of London be designed by public authority, who, being associated, may ordain ministers for the city and the vicinity, keeping as near to the ordinary rules forementioned as possibly they may; and let this association be for no other intent or purpose but only for the work of ordination.

2. Let the like association be made by the same authority in great towns, and the neighbouring parishes in the several counties, which are at the present quiet and undisturbed, to do the like for the parts adjacent,

3. Let such as are chosen, or appointed for the service of the armies or navy, be ordained as aforesaid, by the associated ministers of London, or some others in the country.

4. Let them do the like when any man shall duly and lawfully be recommended to them for the ministry of any congregation, who cannot enjoy liberty to have a trial of his parts and abilities, and desire the help of such ministers so associated for the better furnishing of them with such a person as by them shall be judged fit for the service of that church and people.

THE CONTENTS OF THE FORM OF PRESBYTERIAL CHURCH GOVERNMENT.

The preface.	Of congregational assemblies.
Of the Church.	that is, the meeting of the
Of the officers of the Church.	ruling officers of a partic-
Pastors.	ular congregation for the
Teacher or doctor.	government thereof.
Other church governors.	Of classical assemblies.
Deacons.	Of synodical assemblies.
Of particular congregations.	Of ordination of ministers.
Of the officers of a partic-	Touching the doctrine of or-
ular congregation.	dination.
Of the ordinances in a par-	Touching the power of ordi-
ticular congregation.	nation.
Of church government, and	Concerning the doctrinal part
the several sorts of assem-	of the ordination of minis-
blies for the same.	ters.
Of the power in common of	The directory for the ordina-
all these assemblies.	tion of ministers.

No. X.

The Assembly's Declaration of the Falsehood and Forgery of a lying, scandalous Pamphlet, put forth under the Name of their Reverend Brother, Master Alexander Henderson, after his Death.

THE General Assembly of this kirk having seen a printed paper, entitled "The Declaration of Mr. Alexander Henderson,' principal Minister of the Word of God at Edinburgh, and Chief-commissioner for the Kirk of Scotland to the Parliament and Synod of England, made upon his Deathbed;" and taking into their serious consideration how many gross lies and impudent calumnies are therein contained; out of the tender respect which they do bear to his name (which ought to be very precious to them and all posterity, for his faithful service in the great work of reformation in these kingdoms, wherein the Lord was pleased to make him eminently instrumental); and lest, through the malice of some, and ignorance of others, the said pamphlet should gain belief among the weaker sort, they have thought fit to make known and declare, concerning the same, as followeth : .

That after due search and trial, they do find that their worthy brother, Master Alexander Henderson, did, from the time of his coming from London to Newcastle, till the last moment of his departure out of this life, upon all occasions manifest the constancy of his judgment touching the work of reformation in these kingdoms, namely, in all his discourses and conferences with his majesty, and with his brethren who were employed with him in the same trust at Newcastle; in his letters to the commissioners at London, and particularly in his last discourse to his majesty, at his departing from Newcastle, being very weak, and greatly decayed in his natural strength. When he was come from Newcastle by sea to this kingdom, he was in such a weak, worn, and failed condition, as it was evident to all who saw him that he was not able to frame any such declaration: for he was so spent, that he died within eight days after his arrival; and all that he was able to speak in that time did clearly show his judgment of, and affection to, the work of reformation and cause of God, to be every way the same then that it was in the beginning and progress thereof; as divers reverend brethren who visited him have declared to this assembly, and particularly two brethren who constantly attended him from the time he came home till his breath expired. A farther testimony may be brought from a short confession of faith under his hand, found among his papers, which is expressed as his last words, wherein, among others mercies, he declareth himself most of all obliged to the care and goodness of God, for calling him to believe the promises of the Gospel; and for exalting him to be a preacher of them to others; and to be a willing, though a weak instrument, in this great and wonderful work of reformation, which he earnestly beseeched the Lord to bring to a happy conclusion. Other reasons may be added from the levity of the style, and manifest absurdities contained in that paper. Upon consideration of all which, this assembly doth condemn the said pamphlet as forged, scandalous, and false, and farther declare the author and contriver of the same to be void of charity and a good conscience, and a gross liar and calumniator, led by the spirit of the accuser of the brethren.

August 7, 1648. Ante meridiem. Sess. 31.

No. XI.

A Confession of Faith of Seven Congregations or Churches of Christ in London, which are commonly, but unjustly, called Anabaptists; published for the Vindication of the Truth and Information of the Ignorant: likewise for the taking off those Aspersions which are frequently, both in Pulpit and Print, unjustly cast upon them.
Printed at London, Anno 1646.

I. THE Lord our God is but one God, whose subsistence is in himself; whose essence cannot be comprehended by any but himself; who only hath immortality, dwelling in the light which no man can approach unto; who is in himself most holy, every way infinite, in greatness, wisdom, power, love; merciful and gracious, long-suffering, and abundant in goodness

and truth: who giveth being, moving, and preservation to all creatures.*

II. In this divine and infinite Being there is the Father, the Word, and the Holy Spirit; each having the whole Divine essence, yet the essence undivided; all infinite without any beginning, therefore but one God, who is not to be divided in nature and being, but distinguished by several peculiar relative properties.†

III. God hath decreed in himself, before the world was, concerning all things, whether necessary, accidental, or voluntary, with all the circumstances of them, to work, dispose, and bring about all things according to the counsel of his own will, to his glory (yet without being the author of sin, or having fellowship with any therein): in which appears his wisdom in disposing all things, unchangeableness, power, and faithfulness in accomplishing his decree; and God hath, before the foundation of the world, foreordained some men to eternal life, through Jesus Christ, to the praise and glory of his grace: leaving the rest in their sin, to their just condemnation, to the praise of his justice.‡

IV. In the beginning God made all things very good; created man after his own image, filled with all meet perfection of nature, and free from all sin; but long he abode not in this honour, Satan using the subtlety of the serpent to seduce first Eve, then by her seducing Adam, who, without any compulsion, in eating the forbidden fruit, transgressed the command of God, and fell, whereby death came upon all his posterity: who now are conceived in sin, and by nature the children of wrath, the servants of sin, the subjects of death, and other miseries in this world, and forever, unless the Lord Jesus Christ set them free.§

V. God, in his infinite power and wisdom, doth dispose all things to the end for which they were created; that neither good nor evil befalls any by chance, or without his providence; and that whatsoever befalls the elect is by his appointment, for his glory, and their good.||

VI. All the elect, being loved of God with an everlasting love, are redeemed, quickened, and saved, not by themselves, nor their own works, lest any man should boast, but only and wholly by God, of his free grace and mercy, through Jesus Christ, who is made unto us by God, wisdom, righteousness, sanctification, and redemption, and all in all, that he that rejoiceth might rejoice through the Lord.¶

* 1 Cor., viii., 6. Isa., xliv., 6; and xlvi., 9. Exod., iii., 14. 1 Tim., vi., 16. Isa., xliii., 15. Psalm cxlvii.; Job, xxxii., 3. Job, xxxvi., 5. Jer., x., 12. Exod., xxxiv., 6, 7. Acts, xvii., 28. Rom., xi., 36.
† 1 Cor., i., 3. John, i., 1; and xv., 26. Exod., iii., 14. 1 Cor., viii., 6.
‡ Isa., xlvi., 10. Eph., i., 11. Rom., xi., 33. Psalm xxviii., 15; cxv., 3; cxxxv., 6; and cxliv. 1 Sam., x., 9, 26. Prov., xvi., 4, 33; and xxi., 6. Exod., xxi., 13. Isa., xlv., 7. Matt., vi., 28, 30. Col., i., 16, 17. Numb., xxiii., 19, 20. Rom., iii., 4. Jer., x., 10; xiv., 22. Eph., i., 4. Jude, 4, 6.
§ Gen., i., 1; and iii., 1, 4, 5. Col., i., 16. Isa., xlv., 12. 1 Cor., xv., 45, 46. Eccles., vii., 29. 2 Cor., xi., 3. 1 Tim., ii., 14. Gal., iii., 22. Rom., v., 12; vi., 22; and xviii., 19. Eph., ii., 3.
|| Isa., xlvi., 11. Isa., xlvi., 10, 11. Eccles., iii., 14. Mark, x., 29, 30. Exod., xxi., 13. Prov., xvi., 33. Rom., viii., 28.
¶ Jer., xxiii., 6; and xxxi., 2. Eph., i., 3, 7; and

VII. And this is life eternal, that we might know him the only true God, and Jesus Christ whom he hath sent. And on the contrary, the Lord will render vengeance, in flaming fire, to them that know not God, and obey not the Gospel of Jesus Christ.*

VIII. The rule of this knowledge, faith, and obedience concerning the worship of God, in which is contained the whole duty of man, is (not men's laws, or unwritten traditions, but) only the Word of God contained in the Holy Scriptures; in which is plainly recorded whatsoever is needful for us to know, believe, and practise; which are the only rules of holiness and obedience for all saints, at all times, in all places, to be observed.†

IX. The Lord Jesus Christ, of whom Moses and the prophets wrote, the apostles preached, he is the Son of God, the brightness of his glory, &c., by whom he made the world; who upholdeth and governeth all things that he hath made; who also, when the fulness of time was come, was made of a woman, of the tribe of Judah, of the seed of Abraham and David; to wit, of the Virgin Mary, the Holy Spirit coming down upon her, the power of the Most High overshadowing her; and he was also tempted as we are, yet without sin.‡

X. Jesus Christ is made the mediator of the new and everlasting covenant of grace between God and man, ever to be perfectly and fully the prophet, priest, and king of the Church of God for evermore.§

XI. Unto this office he was appointed by God from everlasting; and in respect of his manhood, from the womb called, separated, and anointed most fully and abundantly, with all gifts necessary, God having without measure poured out his Spirit upon him.‖

XII. Concerning his mediatorship, the Scripture holds forth Christ's call to his office; for none takes this honour upon him but he that is called of God, as was Aaron, it being an action of God, whereby a special promise being made, he ordains his Son to this office; which promise is, that Christ should be made a sacrifice for sin; that he should see his seed, and prolong his days, and the pleasure of the Lord shall prosper in his hand; all of mere free and absolute grace towards God's elect, and without any condition foreseen in them to procure it.¶

XIII. This office to be mediator, that is, to be prophet, priest, and king of the Church of God, is so proper to Christ, that neither in whole, nor any part thereof, it can be transferred from him to any other.*

XIV. This office to which Christ is called is threefold—a prophet, priest, and king: this number and order of offices is necessary, for, in respect of our ignorance, we stand in need of his prophetical office; and in respect of our great alienation from God, we need his priestly office to reconcile us; and in respect of our averseness and utter inability to return to God, we need his kingly office, to convince, subdue, draw, uphold, and preserve us to his heavenly kingdom.†

XV. Concerning the prophecy of Christ, it is that whereby he hath revealed the will of God, whatsoever is needful for his servants to know and obey; and therefore he is called not only a prophet and doctor, and the apostle of our profession, and the angel of the covenant, but also the very wisdom of God, in whom are hid all the treasures of wisdom and knowledge, who forever continueth revealing the same truth of the Gospel to his people.‡

XVI. That he might be a prophet every way complete, it was necessary he should be God, and also that he should be man: for unless he had been God, he could never have perfectly understood the will of God; and unless he had been man, he could not suitably have unfolded it in his own person to men.§

That Jesus Christ is God, is wonderfully clearly expressed in the Scriptures. He is called the mighty God, Isa., ix., 6. That Word was God, John., i., 1. Christ, who is God over all, Rom., ix., 5. God manifested in the flesh, 1 Tim., iii., 16. The same is very God, John, v., 20. He is the first, Rev., i., 8. He gives being to all things, and without him was nothing made, John., i., 2. He forgiveth sins, Matt., ix., 6. He is before Abraham, John., viii., 58. He was, and is, and ever will be the same, Heb., xiii., 8. He is always with his to the end of the world, Matt., xxviii., 20. Which could not be, if he were not God. And to the Son he saith, Thy throne, O God, is forever and ever, Heb., i., 8. John., i., 18.

Also, Christ is not only perfectly God, but perfect man, made of a woman, Gal., iv., 4. Made of the seed of David, Rom., i., 3. Coming out of the loins of David, Acts., ii., 30. Of Jesse and Judah, Acts., xiii., 23. In that the children were partakers of flesh and blood, he himself likewise took part with them, Heb., ii., 14. He took not on him the nature of angels, but the seed of Abraham, ver. 16. So that we are bone of his bone, and flesh of his flesh, Eph., v., 30. So that he that sanctifieth, and they that are sanctified, are all of one, Heb., ii., 11. See Acts., iii., 22. Deut., xviii., 15. Heb., i., 1.

XVII. Concerning his priesthood, Christ, having sanctified himself, hath appeared once to put away sin by that one offering of himself a sacri-

ii., 8, 9. 1 Thess., v., 9. Acts, xiii., 38. 2 Cor., v., 21. Jer., xi., 23, 24. 1 Cor., i., 30, 31.

* John, vi., 36; and xvii., 3. Heb., v., 9. 1 Thess., i., 8.

† Col., ii., 23. Matt., xv., 9, 6. John, v., 39. 2 Tim., iii., 15–17. Isa., viii., 20. Gal., i., 8, 9. Acts, iii., 22, 23.

‡ Gen., iii., 15; xxii., 18; and xlix., 9, 10. Dan., vii., 13; and ix., 24, &c. Prov., viii., 23. John, i., -3. Heb., i., 8; ii., 16; iv., 15; and vii., 14. Gal., iv., 4. Rev., v., 1. Rom., i., 3; and ix., 10. Matt., i., 16. Luke., iii., 23, 26. Isa., liii., 3–5.

§ 1 Tim., ii., 5. Heb., ix., 15. John., xiv., 6. Isa., ix., 6, 7.

‖ Prov., viii., 23. Isa., xi., 2–5; xliii., 6; xlix., 15; and lxi., 1, 2. Luke, iv., 17, 22. John, i., 14, 26; and iii., 34.

¶ Heb., v., 4–6. Isa., liii., 10, 11. John, iii., 16. Rom., viii., 32

* 1 Tim., ii., 5. Heb., vii., 24. Dan., vii., 14. Acts., iv., 12. Luke, i., 33. John, xiv., 6.

† Deut., viii., 15. Acts, iii., 22, 23; and xxvi., 18, Heb., iii., 3; and iv., 14, 15. Psalm ii., 6. 2 Cor., v., 20. Col., i., 21. John, xvi., 8. Psalm cx., 3. Cant. i., 3. John, vi., 44. Phil., iv., 13. 2 Tim., iv., 18.

‡ John, i., 18; xii., 49, 50; and xvii., 8. Matt., xxiii., 10. Deut., xviii., 15. Heb., iii., 1. Gal., iii., 1. 1 Cor., i., 24. Col., ii., 3. Mal., iii., 2.

§ John, i., 18. Acts, iii., 22. Deut., xviii., 15. Heb., i., 1.

fice for sin, by which he hath fully finished and suffered all things. God required for the salvation of his elect, and removed all rites and shadows, &c., and is now entered within the veil into the holy of holies, which is the presence of God. Also, he makes his people a spiritual house, a holy priesthood, to offer up spiritual sacrifice acceptable to God through him. Neither doth the Father accept, nor Christ offer to the Father, any other worship or worshippers.*

XVIII. This priesthood was not legal or temporary, but according to the order of Melchisedeck, and is stable and perfect, not for a time, but forever, which is suitable to Jesus Christ, as to him that ever liveth. Christ was the priest, sacrifice, and altar; he was a priest according to both natures; he was a sacrifice according to his human nature; whence in Scripture it is attributed to his body, to his blood; yet the effectualness of this sacrifice did depend upon his Divine nature; therefore it is called the blood of God. He was the altar according to his Divine nature, it belonging to the altar to sanctify that which is offered upon it, and so it ought to be of greater dignity than the sacrifice itself.†

XIX. Concerning his kingly office, Christ being risen from the dead, and ascended into heaven; and having all power in heaven and earth, he doth spiritually govern his Church, and doth exercise his power over all, angels and men, good and bad, to the preservation and salvation of the elect, and to the overruling and destruction of his enemies. By this kingly power he applieth the benefits, virtue, and fruits of his prophecy and priesthood to his elect, subduing their sins, preserving and strengthening them in all their conflicts against Satan, the world, and the flesh, keeping their hearts in faith and filial fear by his Spirit; by this his mighty power he ruleth the vessels of wrath, using, limiting, and restraining them, as it seems good to his infinite wisdom.‡

XX. This his kingly power shall be more fully manifested when he shall come in glory to reign among his saints, when he shall put down all rule and authority under his feet, that the glory of the Father may be perfectly manifested in his Son, and the glory of the Father and the Son in all his members.§

XXI. Jesus Christ by his death did purchase salvation for the elect that God gave unto him; these only have interest in him, and fellowship with him, for whom he makes intercession to his Father in their behalf, and to them alone doth God by his Spirit apply this redemption; as also the free gift of eternal life is given to them, and none else.‖

XXII. Faith is the gift of God, wrought in the hearts of the elect by the Spirit of God; by which faith they come to know and believe the truth of the Scriptures, and the excellence of them above all other writings, and all things in the world, as they hold forth the glory of God in his attributes, the excellence of Christ in his nature and offices, and of the power and fulness of the Spirit in his workings and operations; and so are enabled to cast their souls upon this truth thus believed.*

XXIII. All those that have this precious faith wrought in them by the Spirit can never finally nor totally fall away, seeing the gifts of God are without repentance; so that he still begets and nourisheth in them faith, repentance, love, joy, hope, and all the graces of the Spirit, unto immortality; and though many storms and floods arise, and beat against them, yet they shall never be able to take them off that foundation and rock, which by faith they are fastened upon; notwithstanding, through unbelief, and the temptations of Satan, the sensible sight of this light and love be clouded and overwhelmed for a time; yet God is still the same, and they shall be sure to be kept by the power of God unto salvation, where they shall enjoy their purchased possession, they being engraved upon the palms of his hands, and their names having been written in the Book of Life from all eternity.†

XXIV. Faith is ordinarily begotten by the preaching of the Gospel, or Word of Christ, without respect to any power or agency in the creature; but it being wholly passive, and dead in trespasses and sins, doth believe and is converted by no less power than that which raised Christ from the dead.‡

XXV. The preaching of the Gospel to the conversion of sinners is absolutely free; no way requiring, as absolutely necessary, any qualifications, preparations, or terrors of the law, or preceding ministry of the law, but only and alone the naked soul, a sinner, and ungodly, to receive Christ crucified, dead, and buried, and risen again; who is made a prince and saviour for such sinners as through the Gospel shall be brought to believe on him.§

XXVI. The same power that converts to faith in Christ carrieth on the soul through all duties, temptations, conflicts, sufferings; and whatsoever a believer is, he is by grace, and is carried on in all obedience and temptations by the same.‖

XXVII. All believers are by Christ united to God; by which union God is one with them, and they are one with him; and that all believers are the sons of God, and joint heirs with

---

* John, xvii., 19. Heb., v., 7-10, 12. Rom., v., 19. Eph., v., 2. Col., i., 20. Eph., ii., 14, &c Rom., viii., 34. Heb., viii, 1; and ix., 24. 1 Pet., ii., 5. John. iv., 23, 24.

† Heb., v., 6; vii., 16, &c.; ix., 13, 14; x., 10; and xiii., 10, 12, 15. 1 Pet., i., 18, 19. Col., i., 20, 22. Acts, xx., 28. Matt., xxiii., 17. John, xvii., 19.

‡ 1 Cor., xv., 4. 1 Pet., iii., 21, 22. Matt., xxviii., 18, 19. Luke. xxiv., 51. Acts, i., 1; and v., 30, 31. John, v., 26, 27; xix., 36; and xvi., 15. Rom., i., 21; v., 6-8; xiv., 9, 17; and xvii., 18. Gal., v., 22, 23. Mark, i., 27. Heb., i., 14. Job, ii., 8; and xvii., 18. Eph., iv., 17, 18. 2 Pet., ii.

§ 1 Cor., xv., 24, 28. Heb., ix., 28. 1 Thess., iv., 15-17. 2 Thess., i., 9, 10. John, xii., 21, 26.

‖ Eph., i., 14. Heb., v., 19 and vii., 25. Matt.,

i., 21. John, xvii., 6. 1 Corinthians, ii., 12. Rom., viii., 29, 30. 1 John, v., 12. John, xv., 13; and iii., 16.

* Eph., ii., 8. John, ix., 10; vi., 29, 63; and xvii., 17. Phil., i., 29. Gal., v. Heb., iv., 11, 12.

† Matt., vii., 24, 25. John, xiii., 10; and x., 28, 29. 1 Pet., i., 4-6. Isa., xlix., 13-16.

‡ Rom., x., 17. 1 Cor., i., 28. Rom., i., 16; iii., 12; and ix., 16. Ezek., xvi., 16. Eph., i., 19. Col., ii., 12.

§ John, i., 12; and iii., 14, 15. Isa., lv., 1. John, vii., 37. 1 Tim., i., 15. Rom., iv., 5; and v., 8. Acts, v., 30, 31; and ii., 36. 1 Cor., i., 22, 24.

‖ 1 Pet., i., 5. 1 Cor., xv., 10. 2 Cor., xii., 9. Phil., ii., 12, 13. John, xv., 5. Gal., ii., 19, 20.

Christ, to whom belong all the promises of this life, and that which is to come.*

XXVIII. Those that have union with Christ are justified from all their sins by the blood of Christ, which justification is a gracious and full acquittance of a guilty sinner from all sin, by God, through the satisfaction that Christ hath made by his death for all their sins, and this applied (in the manifestation of it) through faith.†

XXIX. All believers are a holy and sanctified people, and that sanctification is a spiritual grace of the new covenant, and an effect of the love of God manifested in the soul, whereby the believer presseth after a heavenly and evangelical obedience to all the commands which Christ, as head and king in his new covenant, hath prescribed to them.‡

XXX. All believers, through the knowledge of that justification of life given by the Father, and brought forth by the blood of Christ, have, as their great privilege of that new covenant, peace with God, and reconciliation, whereby they that were afar off are made nigh by that blood, and have peace passing all understanding; yea, joy in God through our Lord Jesus Christ, by whom we have received the atonement.§

XXXI All believers, in the time of this life, are in a continual warfare and combat against sin, self, the world, and the devil ; and are liable to all manner of afflictions, tribulations, and persecutions, being predestinated and appointed thereunto ; and whatsoever the saints possess or enjoy of God spiritually, is by faith ; and outward and temporal things are lawfully enjoyed by a civil right by them who have no faith.‖

XXXII. The only strength by which the saints are enabled to encounter with all opposition and trials is only by Jesus Christ, who is the captain of their salvation, being made perfect through sufferings ; who hath engaged his faithfulness and strength to assist them in all their afflictions, and to uphold them in all their temptations, and to preserve them by his power to his everlasting kingdom.¶

XXXIII. Jesus Christ hath here on earth a spiritual kingdom, which is his Church, whom he hath purchased and redeemed to himself as a peculiar inheritance ; which Church is a company of visible saints, called and separated from the world by the Word and Spirit of God, to the visible profession of the faith of the Gospel, being baptized into that faith, and joined to the Lord, and each to other, by mutual agreement in the practical enjoyment of the ordinances commanded by Christ, their head and king.**

XXXIV. To this Church he hath made his

promises, and giveth the signs of his covenant, presence, acceptation, love, blessing, and protection. Here are the fountains and springs of his heavenly graces flowing forth to refresh and strengthen them.*

XXXV. And all his servants of all estates are to acknowledge him to be their prophet, priest, and king ; and called thither to be enrolled among his household servants, to present their bodies and souls, and to bring their gifts God hath given them, to be under his heavenly conduct and government, to lead their lives, in this walled sheepfold and watered garden, to have communion here with his saints, that they may be assured that they are made meet to be partakers of their inheritance in the kingdom of God ; and to supply each other's wants, inward and outward (and although each person hath a property in his own estate, yet they are to supply each other's wants, according as their necessities shall require, that the name of Jesus Christ may not be blasphemed through the necessity of any in the Church) ; and also being come, they are here by himself to be bestowed in their several order, due place, peculiar use, being fitly compact and knit together, according to the effectual working of every part, to the edifying of itself in love.†

XXXVI. Being thus joined, every church hath power given them from Christ, for their well-being, to choose among themselves meet persons for elders and deacons, being qualified according to the Word, as those which Christ hath appointed in his Testament for the feeding, governing, serving, and building up of his Church ; and that none have any power to impose on them either these or any other.‡

XXXVII. That the ministers lawfully called, as aforesaid, ought to continue in their calling and place, according to God's ordinance, and carefully to feed the flock of God committed to them, not for filthy lucre, but of a ready mind.§

XXXVIII. The ministers of Christ ought to have whatsoever they shall need, supplied freely by the Church, that, according to Christ's ordinances, they that preach the Gospel should live of the Gospel by the law of Christ.‖

XXXIX. Baptism is an ordinance of the New Testament, given by Christ, to be dispensed upon persons professing faith, or that are made disciples ; who, upon profession of faith, ought to be baptized, and after to partake of the Lord's Supper.¶

XL. That the way and manner of the dispensing this ordinance is dipping or plunging the body under water ; it being a sign, must answer the things signified, which is, that interest

* 1 Thess., i., 1.   John, xvii., 21 ; and, fx., 17. Heb., ii., 11.   1 John, iv., 16.   Gal., ii., 19, 20.
† 1 John, i., 7.   Heb., x., 14 ; and ix., 26.   2 Cor., v., 19.   Rom., iii., 23, 25, 30 ; and v., 1.   Acts, xiii., 38, 39.
‡ 1 Cor., xii.   1 Pet., ii., 9.   Eph., i., 4.   1 John, iv., 16.   Matt., xxviii., 20.
§ 2 Cor., v., 19.   Rom., v., 9, 10.   Isa., xx. ; and liv., 10.   Eph., ii., 13, 14 ; and iv., 7.   Rom., v., 10, 11.
‖ Rom., vii., 23, 24 ; and viii., 29.   Eph., vi., 10, 11, &c.   Heb., ii., 9, 10.   2 Tim., iii., 13.   1 Thess., iii., 3.   Gal., ii., 19, 20.   2 Cor., v., 7.   Deut., ii., 5.
¶ John, xv., 5 ; and xvi., 33.   Phil., iv., 11.   Heb., ii., 9, 10.   2 Tim., iv., 18.
** Matt., xi., 11 ; xviii., 19, 20.   2 Thess., i., 1.   1 Cor., i., 2.   Eph., i., 1.   Rom., i., 7.   Acts, xix., 8, 9 ; and xxvi., 18.   2 Cor., vi., 17.   Rev., x., iii., 4.   Acts, ii., 37, 42 ; ix., 26 ; and x., 37.   Rom., x., 10.   1 Pet., ii., 5.

* Matt., xxviii., 18, &c.   1 Cor., iii., 21 ; and xi., 24.   2 Cor., vi., 18.   Rom., ix., 4, 5.   Psalm cxxxiii.,.   Rom., iii., 7, 10.   Ezek., xlvii., 2.
† Acts, ii., 41, 44, 45, 47.   Isa., iv., 3.   1 Cor., xii., 6, 7, &c.   Ezek., xx., 37, 40.   Cant., iv. 12.   Eph., ii., 19.   Rom., xii., 4–6.   Col., i., 12 ; and ii., 5, 6, 19.   Acts, iv., 34, 35 ; v., 4 ; and xx., 32.   Luke, xiv., 26.   1 Tim., vi., 1.   Eph., iv., 16.
‡ Acts, i., 23, 26 ; vi., 3 ; and xv., 22, 25.   Rom., xii., 7, 8.   1 Tim., iii., 2, 6, 7.   1 Cor., xii., 8, 28.   Heb., xiii., 7, 17.   1 Pet., v., 1–3 ; and iv., 15.
§ Heb., v., 4.   John, x., 3, 4.   Acts, xx., 28, 29.   Rom., xii., 7, 8.   Heb., xiii., 7, 17.   1 Pet., v., 1–3.
‖ 1 Cor., ix., chap.   Gal., vi., 8.   Phil., iv., 15, 16.   2 Cor., x., 4.   1 Tim., i., 2.   Psalm cx., 3.
¶ Matt., xxviii., 18, 19.   John, iv., 1.   Mark, xvi., 15, 16.   Acts, ii., 37, 38 · and viii., 36, 37, &c.

the saints have in the death, burial, and resur- rection of Christ; and that, as certainly as the body is buried under water, and risen again, so certainly shall the bodies of the saints be raised by the power of Christ, in the day of the resur- rection, to reign with Christ.*

The word *baptizo* signifies to dip or plunge (yet so as convenient garments be both upon the administrator and subject with all modesty).

XLI. The person designed by Christ to dis- pense baptism, the Scripture holds forth to be a disciple; it being nowhere tied to a particular church officer, or person extraordinarily sent, the commission enjoining the administration being given to them as considered disciples, be- ing men able to preach the Gospel.†

XLII. Christ hath likewise given power to his Church to receive in and cast out any mem- ber that deserves it; and this power is given to every congregation, and not to one particular person, either member or officer, but in relation to the whole body, in reference to their faith and fellowship.‡

XLIII. And every particular member of each church, how excellent, great, or learned soever, is subject to this censure and judgment; and that the Church ought not, without great care and tenderness, and due advice, but by the rule of faith, to proceed against her members.§

XLIV. Christ, for the keeping of this Church in holy and orderly communion, placeth some special men over the Church, who, by their of- fice, are to govern, oversee, visit, watch; so, likewise, for the better keeping thereof, in all places by the members, he hath given authori- ty, and laid duty upon all to watch over one another.‖

XLV. Also, such, to whom God hath given gifts in the Church may and ought to prophesy, according to the proportion of faith, and so to teach publicly the Word of God, for the edifica- tion, exhortation, and comfort of the Church.¶

XLVI. Thus, being rightly gathered, and con- tinuing in the obedience of the Gospel of Christ, none are to separate for faults and corruptions (for as long as the Church consists of men sub- ject to failings, there will be difference in the true constituted Church), until they have in due order, and tenderness sought redress thereof.**

XLVII. And although the particular congre- gations be distinct, and several bodies, every one as a compact and knit city within itself, yet are they all to walk by one rule of truth: so also they (by all means convenient) are to have the counsel and help one of another, if necessi-

* Matt., iii., 6, 16. Mark, xv., 9, reads [into Jor- dan] in Greek. John, iii., 23. Acts, viii., 38. Rev., i., 5; and vii., 14. Heb., x., 22. Rom., vi., 3–6. 1 Cor., xv., 28, 29.
† Isa., viii., 16. Eph., ii., 7. Matt., xxviii., 19. John, iv., 2. Acts, xx., 7; and xi., 10. 1 Cor., xi., 2; and x., 16, 17. Rom., xvi., 2. Matt., xviii., 17.
‡ Rom., xvi., 2. Matt., xviii., 17. 1 Cor., v., 4, 11, 13; xii., 6; and ii., 3. 2 Cor., xi., 6, 7.
§ Matt., xviii., 16; and xvii., 18. Acts, xi., 2, 3. 1 Tim., v., 19, &c. Col., iv., 17. Acts, xiv., 1–3.
‖ Acts, xx., 27, 28. Heb., xiii., 17, 24. Matt., xxiv., 45. 1 Thess., v., 2, 14. Jude 3, 20. Heb., x., 34, 35; and xii., 15.
¶ 1 Cor., xiv., 3, &c. Rom., xii., 6. 1 Pet., iv., 10, 11. 1 Cor., xii., 7. 1 Thess., v., 19, &c.
** Rev., ii. and iii. Acts, xv., 12. 1 Cor., i., 10. Heb., x., 25. Jude, 19. Rev., ii., 20, 21, 27. Acts, xv., 1, 2. Rom., xiv., 1; and xv., 1–3.

ty require it, as members of one body, in the common faith, under Christ, their head.*

XLVIII. A civil magistracy is an ordinance of God, set up by him for the punishment of evildoers, and for the praise of them that do well; and that in all lawful things commanded by them, subjection ought to be given by us in the Lord, hot only for wrath, but for conscience' sake; and that we are to make supplications and prayers for kings, and all that are in author- ity, that under them we may live a quiet and peaceable life, in all godliness and honesty.† The supreme magistracy of this kingdom we acknowledge to be the king and Parliament (now established), freely chosen by the kingdom, and that we are to maintain and defend all civil laws and civil officers made by them, which are for the good of the commonwealth. And we acknowledge with thankfulness, that God hath made this present king and Parliament honour- able in throwing down the prelatical hierarchy, because of their tyranny and oppression over us, under which this kingdom long groaned, for which we are ever engaged to bless God, and honour them for the same. And concerning the worship of God: there is but one lawgiver, which is able to save and destroy, James, iv., 12, which is Jesus Christ, who hath given laws and rules sufficient in his word for his worship; and for any to make more, were to charge Christ with want of wisdom, or faithfulness, or both, in not making laws enough, or not good enough for his house: surely it is our wisdom, duty, and privilege, to observe Christ's laws only, Psalm ii., 6, 9, 10, 12. So it is the magistrates' duty to tender the liberty of men's consciences, Eccles., viii., 8 (which is the tenderest thing to all conscientious men, and most dear unto them, and without which all other liberties will not be worth the naming, much less enjoying), and to protect all under them from all wrong, injury, oppression, and molestation: so it is our duty not to be wanting in anything which is for their honour and comfort, and whatsoever is for the well-being of the commonwealth wherein we live, it is our duty to do; and we believe it to be our express duty, especially in matters of religion, to be fully persuaded in our minds of the lawfulness of what we do, as knowing what- soever is not of faith is sin. And as we cannot do anything contrary to our understandings and consciences, so neither can we forbear the do- ing of that which our understandings and con- sciences bind us to do. And if the magistrates should require us to do otherwise, we are to yield our persons in a passive way to their pow- er, as the saints of old have done, James, v., 4. And thrice happy shall he be that shall lose his life for witnessing (though but for the least tit- tle) of the truth of the Lord Jesus Christ, 1 Pet., v.; Gal., v.

XLIX. But in case we find not the magis- trate to favour us herein, yet we dare not sus- pend our practice, because we believe we ought to go in obedience to Christ, in professing the faith which was once delivered to the saints,

* 1 Cor., iv., 17; xiv., 33, 36; and xvi., 1. Psalm cxxii., 3. Eph., ii., 12, 19. Rev., xxi. 1 Tim., iii., 15; vi., 13, 14. 1 Cor., iv., 17. Acts, xv., 2, 3. Cant., viii., 8, 9. 2 Cor., viii., 1, 4; and xiii., 14.
† Rom., xiii., 1, 2, &c. 1 Pet., ii., 13, 14. 1 Tim., ii., 1–3.

which faith is declared in tne Holy Scriptures, and this our confession of faith a part of them, and that we are to witness to the truth of the Old and New Testament unto the death, if necessity require, in the midst of all trials and afflictions, as his saints of old have done;·not accounting our goods, lands, wives, children, fathers, mothers, brethren, sisters, yea, and our own lives, dear to us, so we may finish our course with joy; remembering, always, that we ought to obey God rather than men, who will, when we have finished our course, and kept the faith, give us the crown of righteousness; to whom we must give an account of all our actions, no man being able to discharge us of the same.*

L. It is lawful for a Christian to be a magistrate or civil officer; and since it is lawful to take an oath, so it be in truth, and in judgment, and in righteousness, for confirmation of truth, and ending of all strife; and that by rash and vain oaths the Lord is provoked, and this land mourns.†

LI. We are to give unto all men whatsoever is their due, as their place, age, estate, requires; and that we defraud no man of anything, but to do unto all men as we would they should do unto us.‡

LII. There shall be a resurrection of the dead, both of the just and unjust, and every one shall give an account of himself to God, that every one may receive the things done in his body, according to that he hath done, whether it be good or bad.§

THE CONCLUSION.

Thus we desire to give unto Christ that which is his; and unto all lawful authority that which is their due; and to owe nothing to any man but love; to live quietly and peaceably, as it becometh saints, endeavouring in all things to keep a good conscience, and to do unto every man (of what judgment soever) as we would they should do unto us, that as our practice is, so it may prove us to be a conscionable, quiet, and harmless people (no ways dangerous or troublesome to human society), and to labour and work with our hands, that we may not be chargeable to any, but to give to him that needeth, both friends and enemies, accounting it more excellent to give than to receive. Also, we confess that we know but in part, and that we are ignorant of many things which we desire and seek to know; and if any shall do us that friendly part, to show us from the Word of God that we see not, we shall have cause to be thankful to God and them; but if any man shall impose upon us anything that we see not to be commanded by our Lord Jesus Christ, we should in his strength rather embrace all reproaches

* Acts, ii., 40, 41; iv., 19; v., 28, 29; and xx., 23. 1 Thess., iii., 3. Phil., i., 28, 29. Dan., iii., 16, 17; and vi., 7, 10, 22, 23. 1 Tim., vi., 13, 14. Rom., xii., 1, 8. 1 Cor., xiv., 37. Rev., ii., 20. 2 Tim., iv., 6–8. Rom., xiv., 10, 12. 2 Cor., v., 10. Psal. xlix., 7; and l., 22.
† Acts, viii., 38; and x., 1, 2, 35. Rom., xvi., 23. Deut., v., 13. Rom., i., 9. 2 Cor., x., 11. Jer., iv., 2. Heb., vi., 16.
‡ 1 Thess., iv., 6. Rom., xiii., 5–7. Matt., xxii., 21. Titus, iii. 1 Pet., ii., 15, 17; and v., 5. Eph., v., 21, 23; and vi., 1, 9. Titus, iii., 1–3.
§ Acts, xxiv., 15. 1 Cor., v., 10. Rom., xiv., 12.

and tortures of men, to be stripped of all outward comforts, and, if it were possible, to die a thousand deaths, rather than to do anything against the least tittle of the truth of God, or against the light of our own consciences. And if any shall call what we have said heresy, then do we with the apostle acknowledge, that after the way they call heresy, worship we the God of our fathers, disclaiming all heresies, rightly so called, because they are against Christ, and to be steadfast and immovable, always abounding in obedience to Christ, as knowing our labour shall not be in vain in the Lord.*

Arise, O God, plead thine own cause; remember how the foolish man blasphemeth thee daily. Oh, let not the oppressed returned ashamed, but let the poor and needy praise thy name.

Come, Lord Jesus, come quickly

No. XII.

A CONCISE VIEW OF THE CHIEF PRINCIPLES OF THE CHRISTIAN RELIGION, AS PROFESSED BY THE PEOPLE CALLED QUAKERS. BY ROBERT BARCLAY.

THE FIRST PROPOSITION.

Concerning the true Foundation of Knowledge.

SEEING the height of all happiness is placed in the true knowledge of God (this is life eternal, to know thee the only true God, and Jesus Christ whom thou hath sent),† the true and right understanding of this foundation and ground of knowledge is that which is most necessary to be known and believed in the first place.

THE SECOND PROPOSITION.

Concerning immediate Revelation.

Seeing no man knoweth the Father but the Son, and he to whom the Son revealeth him;‡ and seeing the revelation of the Son is in and by the Spirit; therefore the testimony of the Spirit is that alone by which the true knowledge of God hath been, is, and can be, only revealed; who as, by the moving of his own Spirit, he converted the chaos of this world into that wonderful order wherein it was in the beginning, and created man a living soul, to rule and govern it, so by the revelation of the same Spirit he hath manifested himself all along unto the sons of men, both patriarchs, prophets, and apostles; which revelations of God by the Spirit, whether by outward voices and appearances, dreams, or inward objective manifestations in the heart, were of old the formal object of their faith, and remain yet so to be; since the object of the saint's faith is the same in all ages, though set forth under divers administrations. Moreover, these Divine inward revelations, which we make absolutely necessary for the building up of true faith, neither do nor can contradict the outward testimony of the Scriptures, or right and sound reason. Yet from hence it will not follow that these Divine revelations are to be subjected to the examination either of the outward testimony of the Scriptures, or of the natural reason of man, as to a more noble or certain rule or touchstone; for this Divine revelation and inward illumination is that which is evident and clear of itself, forcing, by its own evidence and clearness, the well-disposed understanding to assent,

* Psalm lxxiv., 21, 22.
† John, xvii., 3.
‡ Matt., xi., 27.

irresistibly moving the same thereunto; even as the common principles of natural truths move and incline the mind to a natural assent; as that the whole is greater than its parts; that two contradictory sayings cannot be both true, nor both false; which is also manifest according to our adversaries' principle, who (supposing the possibility of inward Divine revelations) will nevertheless confess, with us, that neither Scripture nor sound reason will contradict it; and yet it will not follow, according to them, that the Scripture or sound reason should be subjected to the examination of the Divine revelations in the heart.

THE THIRD PROPOSITION.

Concerning the Scriptures.

From these revelations of the Spirit of God to the saints have proceeded the Scriptures of truth, which contain, 1. A faithful historical account of the actings of God's people in divers ages, with many singular and remarkable providences attending them. 2. A prophetical account of several things, whereof some are already past, and some yet to come. 3. A full and ample account of all the chief principles of the doctrine of Christ, held forth in divers precious declarations, exhortations, and sentences, which, by the moving of God's Spirit, were at several times, and upon sundry occasions, spoken and written unto some churches and their pastors; nevertheless, because they are only a declaration of the Fountain, and not the Fountain itself, therefore they are not to be esteemed the principal ground of all truth and knowledge, nor yet the adequate primary rule of faith and manners. Nevertheless, as that which giveth a true and faithful testimony of the first foundation, they are and may be esteemed a secondary rule, subordinate to the Spirit, from which they have all their excellence and certainty: for as by the inward testimony of the Spirit we do alone truly know them, so they testify that the Spirit is that guide by which the saints are led into all truth;* therefore, according to the Scriptures, the Spirit is the first and principal leader. And seeing we do therefore receive and believe the Scriptures, because they proceeded from the Spirit; therefore, also, the Spirit is more originally and principally the rule, according to that received maxim in the schools, " Propter quod unumquodque est tale, illud ipsum est magis tale." Englished thus: That for which a thing is such, that thing itself is more such.

THE FOURTH PROPOSITION.

Concerning the Condition of Man in the Fall.

All Adam's posterity (or mankind),† both Jews and Gentiles, as to the first Adam or earthly man, is fallen, degenerated, and dead, deprived of the sensation or feeling of this inward testimony or seed of God; and is subject unto the power, nature, and seed of the serpent, which he sows in men's hearts, while they abide in this natural and corrupted state; from whence it comes, that not their words and deeds only, but all their imaginations, are evil perpetually in the sight of God, as proceeding from

this depraved and wicked seed. Man, therefore, as he is in this state, can know nothing aright; yea, his thoughts and conceptions concerning God and things spiritual, until he be disjoined from this evil seed, and united to the Divine light, are unprofitable both to himself and others. Hence are rejected the Socinian and Pelagian errors, in exalting a natural light; as also those of the papists, and most Protestants, who affirm that man, without the true grace of God, may be a true minister of the Gospel. Nevertheless, this seed is not imputed to infants until, by transgression, they actually join themselves therewith: for "they are by nature the children of wrath, who walk according to the power of the prince of the air."*

THE FIFTH AND SIXTH PROPOSITIONS.

Concerning the Universal Redemption by Christ, and also the Saving and Spiritual Light, wherewith every Man is enlightened.

THE FIFTH PROPOSITION.

God, out of his infinite love, who delighteth not in the death of a sinner, but that all should live and be saved, hath so loved the world, that he hath given his only Son a light, that whosoever believeth in him should be saved; who enlighteneth every man that cometh into the world, and maketh manifest all things that are reprovable, and teacheth all temperance, righteousness, and godliness:† and this light enlighteneth the hearts of all in a day,‡ in order to salvation, if not resisted. Nor is it less universal than the seed of sin, being the purchase of his death, who "tasted death for every man :" "for as in Adam all die, even so in Christ shall all be made alive."§

THE SIXTH PROPOSITION.

According to which principle, or hypothesis, all the objections against the universality of Christ's death are easily solved; neither is it needful to recur to the ministry of angels, and those other miraculous means, which, they say, God makes use of to manifest the doctrine and history of Christ's passion unto such who (living in those places of the world where the outward preaching of the Gospel is unknown) have well improved the first and common grace: for hence it well follows, that as some of the old philosophers might have been saved, so also may now some (who by Providence are cast into those remote parts of the world, where the knowledge of the history is wanting) be made partakers of the Divine mercy, if they receive and resist not that grace, a manifestation whereof is given to every man to profit withal.‖ This certain doctrine, then, being received, to wit, that there is an evangelical and saving light and grace in all, the universality of the love and mercy of God towards mankind, both in the death of his beloved Son, the Lord Jesus Christ, and in the manifestation of the light in the heart, is established and confirmed against all the objections of such as deny it. Therefore Christ

---

* John, xvi., 13.   Rom., viii., 14.
† Rom., v., 12, 15.
Vol. II.—P p p

* Eph., ii., 1.
† Ezek., xviii., 23.   Isa., xlix., 6.   John, iii., 16; and i., 9.   Titus, ii., 11.   Eph., v., 13.   Heb., ii., 9.
‡ *Pro tempore*, for a time.   § 1 Cor., xv., 22.
‖ 1 Cor., xii., 7.

"hath tasted death for every man;"*. not only for all kinds of men, as some vainly talk, but for every one, of all kinds; the benefit of whose offering is not only extended to such who have the distinct outward knowledge of his death and sufferings, as the same is declared in the Scriptures, but even unto those who are necessarily excluded from the benefit of this knowledge by some inevitable accident; which knowledge we willingly confess to be very profitable and comfortable, but not absolutely needful unto such, from whom God himself hath withheld it; yet they may be made partakers of the mystery of his death, though ignorant of the history, if they suffer his seed and light, enlightening their hearts, to take place, in which light, communion with the Father and Son is enjoyed, so as of wicked men to become holy, and lovers of that power, by whose inward and secret touches they feel themselves turned from the evil to the good, and learn to do to others as they would be done by; in which Christ himself affirms all to be included. As they, then, have falsely and erroneously taught, who have denied Christ to have died for all men; so neither have they sufficiently taught the truth, who, affirming him to have died for all, have added the absolute necessity of the outward knowledge thereof, in order to the obtaining its saving effect: among whom the remonstrants of Holland have been chiefly wanting, and many other asserters of universal redemption, in that they have not placed the extent of this salvation in that Divine and evangelical principle of light and life wherewith Christ hath enlightened every man that comes into the world; which is excellently and evidently held forth in these Scriptures: Gen., vi., 3. Deut., xxx., 14. John, i., 7-9. Rom., x., 8. Tit., ii., 11.

THE SEVENTH PROPOSITION.

Concerning Justification.

As many as resist not this light, but receive the same, in them is produced a holy, pure, and spiritual birth; bringing forth holiness, righteousness, purity, and all those other blessed fruits which are acceptable to God, by which holy birth (to wit, Jesus Christ formed within us, and working his works within us), as we are sanctified, so are we justified in the sight of God, according to the apostle's words: "But ye are washed, but ye are sanctified, but ye are justified, in the name of the Lord Jesus, and by the Spirit of our God."† Therefore, it is not by our works wrought in our will, nor yet by good works, considered as of themselves, but by Christ, who is both the gift and the giver, and the cause producing the effects in us: who, as he hath reconciled us while we were enemies, doth also in his wisdom save us, and justify us after this manner; as saith the same apostle elsewhere, "According to his mercy he saved us, by the washing of regeneration, and the renewing of the Holy Ghost."‡

THE EIGHTH PROPOSITION.

Concerning Perfection.

In whom this holy and pure birth is fully brought forth, the body of death and sin comes

to be crucified and removed, and their hearts united and subjected to the truth, so as not to obey any suggestion or temptation of the evil one, but to be free from actual sinning and transgressing the law of God, and in that respect perfect.* Yet doth this perfection still admit of a growth; and there remaineth a possibility of sinning, where the mind doth not most diligently and watchfully attend unto the Lord.

THE NINTH PROPOSITION.

Concerning Perseverance, and the Possibility of falling from Grace.

Although this gift and inward grace of God be sufficient to work out salvation, yet in those in whom it is resisted, it both may and doth become their condemnation. Moreover, in whom it hath wrought in part, to purify and sanctify them, in order to their farther perfection, by disobedience such may fall from it, and turn it to wantonness, making shipwreck of faith; and after having tasted of the heavenly gift, and been made partakers of the Holy Ghost, again fall away.† Yet such an increase and stability in the truth may in this life be attained, from which there cannot be a total apostacy.

THE TENTH PROPOSITION.

Concerning the Ministry.

As by this gift, or light of God, all true knowledge in things spiritual is received and revealed; so by the same, as it is manifested and received in the heart, by the strength and power thereof, every true minister of the Gospel is ordained, prepared, and supplied in the work of the ministry; and by the leading, moving, and drawing hereof, ought every evangelist and Christian pastor to be led and ordered in his labour and work of the Gospel, both as to the place where, as to the persons to whom, and as to the times when, he is to minister. Moreover, those who have this authority may and ought to preach the Gospel, though without human commission or literature, as, on the other hand, those who want the authority of this Divine gift, however learned or authorized by the commissions of men and churches, are to be esteemed but as deceivers, and not true ministers of the Gospel. Also, who have received this holy and unspotted gift, as they have freely received, so are they freely to give,‡ without hire or bargaining, far less to use it as a trade to get money by it: yet if God hath called any from their employments or trades, by which they acquire their livelihood, it may be lawful for such, according to the liberty which they feel given them in the Lord, to receive such temporals as, what, may be needful to them for meat and clothing, as are freely given them by those to whom they have communicated spirituals.

THE ELEVENTH PROPOSITION.

Concerning Worship.

All true and acceptable worship to God is offered in the inward and immediate moving and drawing of his own Spirit, which is neither limited to places, times, nor persons: for though

---

* Heb., ii., 9. † 1 Cor., vi., 11. ‡ Tit., iii., 5.

‹ Rom., vi., 2, 14, 18, and viii., 13. 1 John, iii., 6. † 1 Tim., i., 6. Heb., vi., 4–6. ‡ Matt., x., 8.

we he to worship him always, in that we are to fear before him, yet, as to the outward signification thereof in prayers, praises, and preachings; we ought not to do it where and when we will, but where and when we are moved thereunto by the secret inspirations of his Spirit in our hearts; which God heareth and accepteth of, and is never wanting to move us thereunto when need is, of which he himself is the alone proper judge. All other worship, then, both praises, prayers, and preachings, which man sets about in his own will, and at his own appointment, which he can both begin and end at his pleasure, do or leave undone as himself sees meet; whether they be a prescribed form, as a liturgy, or prayers conceived extemporarily, by the natural strength and faculty of the mind, they are all but superstitious, will-worship, and abominable idolatry in the sight of God;* which are to be denied, rejected, and separated from, in this day of his spiritual arising: however it might have pleased him, who winked at the times of ignorance, with respect to the simplicity and integrity of some, and of his own innocent seed, which lay, as it were, buried in the hearts of men, under the mass of superstition; to blow upon the dead and dry bones, and to raise some breathings, and answer them, and that until the day should more clearly dawn and break forth.

THE TWELFTH PROPOSITION.

Concerning Baptism.

As there is one Lord and one faith, so there is one baptism; which is not putting away the filth of the flesh, but the answer of a good conscience before God, by the resurrection of Jesus Christ.† And this baptism is a pure and spiritual thing, to wit, the baptism of the Spirit and fire, by which we are buried with him, that, being washed and purged from our sins, we may walk in newness of life;‡ of which the baptism of John was a figure, which was commanded for a time, and not to continue forever. As to the baptism of infants, it is a mere human tradition, for which neither precept nor practice is to be found in all the Scripture.

THE THIRTEENTH PROPOSITION.

Concerning the Communion, or Participation of the Body and Blood of Christ.

The communion of the body and blood of Christ is inward and spiritual,§ which is the participation of his flesh and blood,|| by which the inward man is daily nourished in the hearts of those in whom Christ dwells; of which things the breaking of bread by Christ with his disciples was a figure, which they even used in the Church for a time, who had received the substance, for the cause of the weak; even as abstaining from things strangled, and from blood, the washing one another's feet, and the anointing of the sick with oil;¶ all which are commanded with no less authority and solemnity

* Ezek., xiii. Mark, x., 20. Acts, ii., 4, and xviii., 5. John, iii., 6, and iv., 21. Jude, 19. Acts, xvii., 23.
† Eph., iv., 5. 1 Pet., iii., 21. Rom., vi., 4. Gal., iii., 27. Col., ii., 12. John, iii., 30. ‡ 1 Cor., i., 17.
§ 1 Cor., x., 16, 17.
|| John, vi., 32, 33, 35. 1 Cor. v., 8.
¶ Acts, xv., 20. John, xiii., 14. James, v., 14.

than the former; yet seeing they are but the shadows of better things, they cease in such as have obtained the substance.

THE FOURTEENTH PROPOSITION

Concerning the Power of the Civil Magistrate in Matters purely Religious, and pertaining to the Conscience.

Since God hath assumed to himself the power and dominion of the conscience, who alone can rightly instruct and govern it, therefore it is not lawful for any whatsoever, by virtue of any authority or principality they bear in the government of this world, to force the consciences of others;* and therefore all killing, banishing, fining, imprisoning, and other such things which men are afflicted with, for the alone exercise of their conscience or difference in worship or opinion, proceedeth from the spirit of Cain the murderer, and is contrary to the truth: provided, always, that no man, under the pretence of conscience, prejudice his neighbour in his life or estate, or do anything destructive to, or inconsistent with, human society; in which case the law is for the transgressor, and justice to be administered upon all, without respect of persons.

THE FIFTEENTH PROPOSITION.

Concerning the Salutations and Recreations, &c.

Seeing the chief end of all religion is to redeem man from the spirit and vain conversation of this world, and to lead into inward communion with God,† before whom, if we fear always, we are accounted happy, therefore all the vain customs and habits thereof, both in word and deed, are to be rejected and forsaken by those who come to this fear; such as the taking off the hat to a man, the bowings and cringings of the body, and such other salutations of that kind, with all the foolish and superstitious formalities attending them; all which man has invented in his degenerate state, to feed his pride in the vain pomp and glory of this world; as also the unprofitable plays, frivolous recreations, sportings and gamings; which are invented to pass away the precious time, and divert the mind from the witness of God in the heart, and from the living sense of his fear, and from that evangelical spirit wherewith Christians ought to be leavened, and which leads into sobriety, gravity, and godly fear; in which, as we abide, the blessing of the Lord is felt to attend us in those actions in which we are necessarily engaged, in order to the taking care for the sustenance of the outward man.

No. XIII.

The Toleration Act, entitled "An Act for exempting their Majesties' Protestant Subjects dissenting from the Church of England from the Penalties of certain Laws."

FORASMUCH as some ease to scrupulous consciences, in the exercise of religion, may be an effectual means to unite their majesties' Protestant subjects in interest and affection:‡

* Luke, ix., 55, 56. Matt., vii., 12, 29. Titus, iii., 10.
† Eph., v., 11. 1 Pet., i., 14. John, v., 44. Jer. x., 3. Acts, x., 26. Matt., xv., 13. Col., ii., 8.
‡ 1 William and Mary, cap. xviii.

I. Be it enacted by the king and queen's most excellent majesties, and with the advice and consent of the lords spiritual and temporal, and commons in this present Parliament assembled, and by the authority of the same, that neither the statute made in the twenty-third year of the reign of the late Queen Elizabeth,* entitled "An Act to retain the Queen's Majesty's Subjects in their due Obedience ;" nor that statute made in the twenty-ninth year of the said queen,† entitled "An Act for the more speedy and due Execution of certain Branches of the Statute made in the twenty-third year of the Queen's Majesty's Reign," viz., the aforesaid acts ; nor that branch or clause of a statute made in the first year of the reign of the said queen, entitled "An Act for the Uniformity of Common Prayer and Service in the Church and Administration of the Sacraments,"‡ whereby all persons, having no lawful or reasonable excuse to be absent, are required to resort to their parish church or chapel, or some usual place where the Common Prayer shall be used, upon pain of punishment by the censures of the Church ; and also upon pain that every person so offending shall forfeit for every such offence twelve-pence ; nor that statute made in the third year of the late King James the First,§ entitled "An Act for the better discovering and repressing Popish Recusants ;" nor that after statute made in the same year,|| entitled "An Act to prevent and avoid Dangers which may grow by Popish Recusants ;" nor any other law or statute of this realm made against papists or popish recusants, except the statute made in the twenty-fifth year of King Charles II.,¶ entitled "An Act for preventing Dangers which may happen from Popish Recusants ;" and except, also, the statute made in the thirtieth year of the reign of the said King Charles II.,** entitled "An Act for the more effectual preserving the King's Person and Government, by disabling Papists from sitting in either House of Parliament," shall be construed to extend to any person or persons dissenting from the Church of England, that shall take the oaths mentioned in a statute made this present Parliament, entitled "An Act for removing and preventing all Questions and Disputes concerning the assembling and sitting of the present Parliament," shall make and subscribe the declaration mentioned in a statute made in the thirtieth year of the reign of King Charles II.,†† entitled "An act to prevent Papists from sitting in either House of Parliament." Which oaths and declaration the justices of peace, at the general sessions of the peace to be held for the county or place where such person shall live, are hereby required to tender and administer to such persons as shall offer themselves to take, make, and subscribe the same, and thereof to keep a register. And likewise none of the persons aforesaid shall give or pay, as any fee or reward, to any officer or officers belonging to the court aforesaid, above the sum of sixpence, nor that more than once, of his or their entry of his taking the said oaths, and making and subscribing the said declaration ; nor above the farther sum of sixpence for any certificate of the same, to be made out and signed by the officer or officers of the said court.

II. And be it farther enacted by the authority aforesaid, that all and every person and persons already convicted, or prosecuted in order to conviction, of recusancy, by indictment, information, action of debt, or otherwise grounded upon the aforesaid statutes, or any of them, that shall take the said oaths mentioned in the said statutes made this present Parliament, and make and subscribe the declaration aforesaid, in the Court of Exchequer, or Assize, or General or Quarter Sessions, to be held for the county where such person lives, and to be thence respectively certified into the exchequer, shall be thenceforth exempted and discharged from all the penalties, seizures, forfeitures, judgments, and executions incurred by force of any of the aforesaid statutes, without any composition, fee, or farther charge whatsoever.

III. And be it farther enacted by the authority aforesaid, that all and every person and persons that shall, as aforesaid, take the said oaths, and make and subscribe the declaration aforesaid, shall not be liable to any pains, penalties, or forfeitures mentioned in an act made in the thirty-fifth year of the reign of the late Queen Elizabeth,* entitled "An Act to retain the Queen's Majesty's Subjects in their due Obedience." Nor in an act made in the twenty-second year of the reign of the late King Charles II.,† entitled "An Act to prevent and suppress Seditious Conventicles." Nor shall any of the said persons be prosecuted in any ecclesiastical court for or by reason of their nonconforming to the Church of England.

IV. Provided, always, and be it enacted by the authority aforesaid, that if any assembly of persons dissenting from the Church of England shall be held in any place for religious worship, with the doors locked, barred, or bolted, during any time of such meeting together, all and every person or persons that shall come to and be at such meeting shall not receive any benefit from this law, but be liable to all the pains and penalties of all the aforesaid laws recited in this act, for such their meeting, notwithstanding his taking the oaths, and his making and subscribing the declaration aforesaid.

V. Provided, always, that nothing herein contained shall be construed to exempt any of the persons aforesaid from paying of tithes, or other parochial duties, or any other duties, to the church or minister ; nor from any prosecution in any ecclesiastical court, or elsewhere, for the same.

VI. And be it farther enacted by the authority aforesaid, that if any person dissenting from the Church of England, as aforesaid, shall hereafter be chosen, or otherwise appointed to bear the office of high-constable, or petit-constable, churchwarden, overseer of the poor, or any other parochial or ward office, and such person shall scruple to take upon him any of the said offices, in regard of the oaths, or any other matter or thing required by the law to be taken or done in respect of such office, every such person shall and may execute such office or employment by a sufficient deputy, by him to be provided, that shall comply with the laws on this behalf ; provided, always,

---

* 23 Eliz., cap. i.　　† 29 Eliz., cap. vi.
‡ Ibid., cap. ii.　　§ 3 Jac. I., cap. iv.
|| Ibid., cap. v.　　¶ 25 Car. II., cap. ii.
** 30 Car. II., stat. 2, cap. i.
†† Ibid., stat. 2, chap. i.

* 25 Eliz., cap. i.　　† 22 Car. II., cap. i.

the said deputy be allowed and approved by such person or persons, in such manner as such officer or officers respectively should by law have been allowed and approved.

VII. And be it farther enacted by the authority aforesaid, that no person dissenting from the Church of England in holy orders, or pretended holy orders, or pretending to holy orders, nor any preacher or teacher of any congregation of dissenting Protestants, that shall make and subscribe the declaration aforesaid,* and take the said oaths, at the General or Quarter Sessions of the peace to be held for the county, town, parts, or division where such person lives, which court is hereby empowered to administer the same; and shall also declare his approbation of, and subscribe the articles of religion mentioned in the statute made in the thirteenth year of the reign of the late Queen Elizabeth,† except the 34th, 35th, and 36th, and these words of the 20th article, viz., "the Church hath power to decree rites or ceremonies, and authority in controversies of faith;" nor yet shall be liable to any of the pains or penalties mentioned in an act made in the seventeenth year of the reign of King Charles II.,‡ entitled "An Act for restraining Nonconformists from inhabiting in Corporations;" nor the penalties mentioned in the aforesaid act made in the twenty-second year of his said late majesty's reign, for or by reason of such persons preaching at any meeting for the exercise of religion. Nor to the penalties of £100 mentioned in an act made in the thirteenth and fourteenth of King Charles II.,§ entitled "An Act for the Uniformity of Public Prayers, and administering of Sacraments, and other Rites and Ceremonies; and for establishing the Form of making, ordaining, and consecrating of Bishops, Priests, and Deacons in the Church of England," for officiating in any congregation for the exercise of religion permitted and allowed by this act.

VIII. Provided, always, that the making and subscribing the said declaration, and the taking the said oaths, and making the declaration of approbation and subscription to said articles, in manner as aforesaid, by every respective person or persons hereinbefore mentioned, at such General or Quarter Sessions of the peace as aforesaid, shall be then and there entered of record in the said court, for which sixpence shall be paid to the clerk of the peace, and no more; provided that such person shall not at any time preach in any place but with the doors not locked, barred, or bolted, as aforesaid.

IX. And whereas some dissenting Protestants scruple the baptizing of infants, be it enacted by the authority aforesaid, that every person in pretended holy orders, or pretending to holy orders, or preacher, or teacher, that shall subscribe the aforesaid articles of religion, except as before excepted; and also except part of the 27th article teaching infant baptism, and shall take the oaths, and make and subscribe the declaration aforesaid, in manner aforesaid; every such person shall enjoy all the privileges, benefits, and advantages which any other dissenting minister, as aforesaid, might have or enjoy by virtue of this act.

X. And be it farther enacted by the authority

aforesaid, that every teacher or preacher in holy orders, or pretended holy orders, that is, a minister, preacher, or teacher of a congregation, that shall take the oaths herein required, and make and subscribe the declaration aforesaid, and also subscribe such of the aforesaid articles of the Church of England as are required by this act in manner aforesaid, shall be thenceforth exempted from serving upon any jury, or from being chosen or appointed to bear the office of churchwarden, overseer of the poor, or any other parochial or ward office, or other office in any hundred, or any shire, city, town, parish, division, or wapentake.

XI. And be it farther enacted by the authority aforesaid, that any justice of the peace may at any time, hereafter require any person that goes to any meeting for exercise of religion, to make and subscribe the declaration aforesaid, and also to take the said oaths, or declaration of fidelity hereinafter mentioned; in case such person scruple the taking of an oath; and upon the refusal thereof, such justice of the peace is hereby required to commit such person to prison, without bail or mainprize, and to certify his name of such person to the next General or Quarter Sessions of the peace to be held for that county, city, town, part, or division where such person then resides; and if such person so committed shall, upon a second tender at the General or Quarter Sessions, refuse to make and subscribe the declaration aforesaid, such person refusing shall be then and there recorded, and shall be taken thenceforth to all intents and purposes for a popish recusant convict, and suffer accordingly, and incur all the penalties and forfeitures of the aforesaid laws.

XII. And whereas there are certain other persons, dissenters from the Church of England, who scruple the taking of any oath, be it enacted by the authority aforesaid, that every such person shall make and subscribe the aforesaid declaration, and also this declaration of fidelity following :*

I, A. B., do sincerely promise, and solemnly declare before God, and the world, that I will be true and faithful to King William and Queen Mary. And I solemnly profess and declare that I do from my heart abhor, detest, and renounce, as impious and heretical, that damnable doctrine and position, that princes excommunicated, or deprived by the pope, or any authority of the See of Rome, may be deposed or murdered by their subjects, or any other whatsoever. And I do declare that no foreign prince, person, prelate, state, or potentate hath, or ought to have, any power, jurisdiction, superiority, pre-eminence, or authority, ecclesiastical or spiritual, within this realm.

And shall subscribe a profession of their Christian belief in these words :

I, A. B., profess faith in God the Father, and in Jesus Christ his eternal Son, the true God, and in the Holy Spirit, one God blessed for evermore; and do acknowledge the Holy Scriptures of the Old and New Testament to be given by Divine inspiration.

Which declaration and subscription shall be made and entered on record at the General Quarter Sessions of the peace for the county, city, or place where every such person shall then re-

---

* 17 Car. II., cap. ii., 13 and 14.   Car. II., cap. iv.
† 13 Eliz., cap. xii.   ‡ 17 Car. II., cap. ii.
§ 13 and 14 Car. II., cap. iv.

8 Geo. I., cap. vi.

side.· And every such person that shall make acted by the authority aforesaid, that neither· and subscribe the two declarations and profes- this act, nor any clause, article, or thing herein sion aforesaid, being thereunto required, shall contained, shall extend, or be construed to ex- be exempted from all the pains and penalties tend, to give any ease, benefit, or advantage to of all and every the aforementioned statutes any papist or popish recusant whatsoever, or made against popish recusants or Protestant any person that shall deny, in his preaching or Nonconformists, and also from the penalties of writing, the doctrine of the blessed Trinity, as it an act made in the fifth year of the reign of the is declared in the aforesaid articles of religion. late Queen Elizabeth,* entitled "An Act for the · XVII. Provided, always, and be it enacted by assurance of the Queen's Royal Power over all the authority aforesaid, that if any person or Estates and Subjects within her Dominions," persons, at any time or times after the 10th day for or by reason of such persons not taking or of June, do, and shall willingly and of purpose, refusing to take the oath mentioned in the said maliciously, or contemptuously, come into any act ; and also from the penalties of an act made cathedral or parish church, chapel, or other in the thirteenth and fourteenth years of the congregation permitted by this act, and disquiet reign of King Charles II.,† entitled "An Act or disturb the same, or misuse any preacher or for preventing Mischiefs that may arise by cer- teacher, such person or persons, upon proof there- tain Persons called Quakers refusing to take of before any justice of the peace, by two or lawful Oaths," and enjoy all other the benefits, more sufficient witnesses, shall find two sureties privileges, and advantages, under the like limita- to be bound by recognisance in the penal sum of tions, provisoes, and conditions, which any oth- £50, and in default of such sureties shall be com- er Dissenters should or ought to enjoy by virtue mitted to prison, there to remain till the next of this act. General or Quarter Sessions; and upon convic-

XIII. Provided, always, and be it enacted by tion of the said offence at the said General, or the authority aforesaid, that in case any person Quarter Sessions, shall suffer the pain and pen- shall refuse to take the said oaths when ten- alty of £20, to the use of the king's and queen's dered to them, which every justice of the peace majesties, their heirs and successors.* is hereby empowered to do, such person shall XVIII. Provided, always, that no congrega- not be admitted to make and subscribe the two tion or assembly for religious worship shall be declarations aforesaid, though required there- permitted or allowed by this act until the place unto, either before any justice of the peace, or at of such meeting shall be certified to the bishop the General or Quarter Sessions, before or after of the diocess, or to the archdeacon of that arch- any conviction of popish recusancy as aforesaid, deaconry, or to the justices of the peace at the unless such person can, within thirty-one days General or Quarter Sessions of the peace for the after such tender of the declaration to him, pro- county, city, or place in which such meeting duce two sufficient Protestant witnesses to tes- shall be held, and registered in the said bishop's tify upon oath that they believe him to be a or archdeacon's court respectively, or recorded Protestant Dissenter, or a certificate under the at the said General or Quarter Sessions, the reg- hands of four Protestants who are conformable ister or clerk of the peace whereof respectively to the Church of England, or have taken the is hereby required to register the same, and to oaths and subscribed the declaration above na- give certificate thereof to such person as shall med, and shall produce a certificate under the demand the same, for which there shall be no hands and seals of six or more sufficient men of greater fee or reward taken than the sum of the congregation to which he belongs, owning sixpence. him for one of them.

XIV. Provided, also, and be it enacted by the authority aforesaid, that until such certificate, as No. XIV. under the hands of six of his congregation, as

aforesaid, be produced, and two Protestant wit- *The occasional Conformity Act, entitled "An Act nesses come to attest his being a Protestant for Preserving the Protestant Religion, by bet-* Dissenter, or a certificate under the hands of *ter securing the Church of England, as by law* four Protestants, as aforesaid, be produced, the *established; and for confirming the Toleration* justice of peace shall, and hereby is required to *granted to Protestant Dissenters by an Act, en-* take a recognisance, with two sureties, in the *titled 'An Act for exempting their Majesties'* penal sum of £50, to be levied on his goods and *Protestant Subjects, dissenting from the Church* chattels, lands and tenements, to the use of the *of England, from the Penalties of certain* king's and queen's majesties, their heirs and *Laws,'" and for supplying the Defects thereof;* successors, for his producing the same; and if *and for the farther securing the Protestant Suc-* he cannot give such security, to commit him to *cession, by requiring the Practisers of the Law* prison, there to remain until he has produced *in North Britain to take the Oaths and subscribe* such certificate, or two witnesses as aforesaid. *the Declaration therein mentioned.†*

XV. Provided, always, and it is the true in- WHEREAS, an act was made in the thirteenth · tent and meaning of this act, that all the laws year of the reign of the late King Charles II., made and provided for the frequenting of Divine entitled "An Act for the well-governing and service, on the Lord's Day, commonly called regulating of Corporations;" and another act Sunday, shall be still in force, and executed was made in the five and-twentieth year of the against all persons that offend against the said reign of the late King Charles II , entitled laws, except such persons come to some con- "An Act for the preventing Dangers which may gregation, or assembly of religious worship, al- happen from Popish Recusants," both which acts lowed or permitted by this act. were made for the security of the Church of

XVI. Provided, always, and be it farther en- England, as by law established : Now, for the

* 5 Eliz., cap. i.   † 13 and 14 Car. II., cap. i.

* See Geo. I., stat. ii., cap v., sec. iv.
† 10th of Queen Anne.

better securing the said church, and quieting the minds of her majesty's Protestant subjects dissenting from the Church of England, and rendering them secure in the exercise of their religious worship; as also for the farther strengthening the provision already made for the security of the succession to the crown in the house of Hanover; be it enacted by the queen's most excellent majesty, by and with the advice and consent of the lords spiritual and temporal, and commons in Parliament assembled, and by the authority of the same, that if any person or persons, after the five-and-twentieth day of March, which shall be in the year of our Lord one thousand seven hundred and twelve, either peers or commoners, who have or shall have any office or offices, civil or military, or receive any pay, salary, fee, or wages, by reason of any patent or grant from or under her majesty, or any of her majesty's predecessors, or of her heirs or successors, or shall have any command or place of trust from or under her majesty, her heirs or successors, or from any of her majesty's predecessors, or by her or their authority, or by authority derived from her or them, within that part of Great Britain called England, the dominion of Wales, or town of Berwick-upon-Tweed, or in the navy, or in the several islands of Jersey or Guernsey, or shall be admitted into any service or employment in the mean order or family of her majesty, her heirs or successors; or if any mayor, alderman, recorder, bailiff, town-clerk, common-councilman, or other person bearing any office of magistracy, or place of trust, or other employment relating to or concerning the government of any of the respective cities, corporations, boroughs, cinque-ports, and their members, or other port towns within that part of Great Britain called England, the dominion of Wales, town of Berwick, or either of the isles aforesaid, who by the said recited acts, or either of them, were or are obliged to receive the sacrament of the Lord's Supper, according to the rites and usage of the Church of England, as aforesaid, shall, at any time after their admission into their respective offices or employments, or after having such patent or grant, command or place of trust, as aforesaid, during his or their continuance in such office or offices, employment or employments, or having such patent or grant, command or place of trust, or any profit or advantage from the same, knowingly or willingly resort to, or be present at, any conventicle, assembly, or meeting, within England, Wales, Berwick-upon-Tweed, or the isles aforesaid, for the exercise of religion in other manner than according to the liturgy and practice of the Church of England, in any place within that part of Great Britain called England, dominion of Wales, and town of Berwick-upon-Tweed, or the isles aforesaid, at which conventicle, assembly, or meeting, there shall be ten persons or more assembled together, over and besides those of the same household, if it be in any house where there is a family inhabiting, or if it be in a house or place where there is no family inhabiting, then where any such ten persons are so assembled, as aforesaid ; or shall knowingly and willingly be present at any such meeting, in such house or place as aforesaid; although the liturgy be there used, where her majesty, whom God long preserve, and the

Princess Sophia, or such others as shall from time to time be lawfully appointed to be prayed for, shall not there be. prayed for in express words according to the liturgy of the Church of England, except where such particular offices of the liturgy are used, wherein there are no express directions to pray for her majesty and the royal family, shall forfeit £40, to be recovered by him or them that shall sue for the same, by any action of debt, bill, plaint, or information, in any of her majesty's courts at Westminster, wherein no essoin, protection, or wager of law shall be allowed, or any more than one imparlance.

And be it farther enacted, that every person convicted in any action to be brought, as aforesaid, or upon any information, presentment, or indictment in any of her majesty's courts at Westminster, or at the assizes, shall be disabled from thenceforth to hold such office or offices, employment or employments, or to receive any profit or advantage by reason of them, or of any grant as aforesaid, and shall be adjudged incapable to bear any office or employment whatsoever within that part, of Great Britain called England, the dominion of Wales, or the town of Berwick-upon-Tweed, or the isles of Jersey or Guernsey.

Provided, always, and be it farther enacted by the authority aforesaid, that if any person or persons who shall have been convicted as aforesaid, and thereby made incapable to hold any office or employment, or to receive any profit or advantage by reason of them, or of any grant as aforesaid, shall, after such conviction, conform to the Church of England, for the space of one year, without having been present at any conventicle, assembly, or meeting as aforesaid, and receive the sacrament of the Lord's Supper, according to the right usage of the Church of England, at least three times in the year, every such person or persons shall be capable of the grant of any of the offices or employments aforesaid.

Provided, also, and be it farther enacted, that every such person so convicted, and afterward conforming in manner as aforesaid, shall, at the next term after his admission into any such office or employment, make oath in writing, in some one of her majesty's courts at Westminster, in public and open court, or at the next Quarter Sessions for that county or place where he shall reside, between the hours of nine and twelve in the forenoon, that he hath conformed to the Church of England for the space of one year before such his admission, without having been present at any conventicle, assembly, or meeting as aforesaid, and that he hath received the sacrament of the Lord's Supper at least three times in the year ; which oath shall be there enrolled and kept upon record.

Provided that no person shall suffer any punishment for any offence committed against this act, unless oath be made of such offence before some judge or justice of the peace (who is hereby empowered and required to take the said oath) within ten days after the said offence committed, and unless the said offender be prosecuted for the same within three months after the said offence committed ; nor shall any person be convicted for any such offence, unless upon the oaths of two credible witnesses at the least.

Provided, always, that this act, or anything therein contained, or any offence against the same, shall not extend or be judged to take away or make ·void any office of inheritance, nevertheless, so as such person having or enjoying any such office of inheritance do or shall substitute and appoint his sufficient deputy (which such officer is hereby empowered from time to time to make or change, any former law or usage to the contrary notwithstanding) to exercise the said office, until such time as the person haying such office shall conform as aforesaid.

And it is hereby farther enacted and declared by the authority aforesaid, that the toleration granted to Protestant Dissenters, by the act made in the first year of the reign of King William and Queen Mary, entitled "An Act for exempting their Majesties' Protestant Subjects, dissenting from the Church of England, from the Penalties of certain Laws," shall be, and is hereby ratified and confirmed, and that the same act shall at all times be inviolably observed, for the exempting of such Protestant Dissenters, as are thereby intended from the pains and penalties therein mentioned.

And for rendering the said last-mentioned act more effectual, according to the true intent and meaning thereof, be it farther enacted and declared by the authority aforesaid, that if any person dissenting from the Church of England (not in holy orders, or pretended holy orders, or pretending to holy orders, nor any preacher or teacher of any congregation), who should have been entitled to the benefit of the said last-mentioned act, if such person had duly taken, made, and subscribed the oaths and declaration, or otherwise qualified him or herself, as required by the said act, and now is or shall be prosecuted upon or by virtue of any of the penal statutes from which Protestant Dissenters are exempted by the said act, shall, at any time during such prosecution, take, make, and subscribe the said oaths and declaration, or, being of the people called Quakers, shall make and subscribe the aforesaid declaration, and also the declaration of fidelity, and subscribe the profession of their Christian belief according to the said act, or before any two of her majesty's justices of the peace (who are hereby required to take and return the same to the next Quarter Sessions of the peace, to be there recorded), such person shall be and is hereby entitled to the benefit of the said act, as fully and effectually as if such person had duly qualified himself within the time prescribed by the said act, and shall be thenceforth exempted and discharged from all the penalties and forfeitures incurred by force of any of the aforesaid penal statutes.

And whereas it is or may be doubted whether a preacher or teacher of any congregation of dissenting Protestants, duly in all respects qualified according to the said act, be allowed, by virtue of the said act, to officiate in any congregation, in any county other than that in which he so qualified himself, although in a congregation or place of meeting duly certified and registered as is required by the said act; be it declared and enacted by the authority aforesaid, that any such preacher or teacher, so duly qualified according to the said act, shall be and is hereby allowed to officiate in any congregation,

although the same be not in the county where in he was so qualified; provided that the said congregation or place of meeting hath been, before such officiating, duly certified and registered or recorded according to the said act; and such preacher or teacher shall, if required, produce a certificate of his having so qualified himself under the hand of the clerk of the peace for the county or place where he so qualified himself, which certificate such clerk of the peace is hereby required to make; and shall also, before any justice of the peace of such county or place where he shall so officiate, make and subscribe such declaration, and take such oaths as are mentioned in the act, if thereunto required.

And be it farther enacted by the authority aforesaid, that on or before the fifteenth day of June next, all advocates, writers to the signet, notaries public, and other members of the college of justice, within that part of her majesty's kingdom of Great Britain called Scotland, shall be and are hereby obliged to take and subscribe the oath appointed by the act of the sixth year of her majesty's reign, entitled "An Act for the better security of her Majesty's Person and Government," before the lords of session of the aforesaid part of her majesty's kingdom, except such of the said persons who have already taken, the same ; and if any of the persons aforesaid do, or shall neglect or refuse to take and subscribe the said oath as aforesaid, such person shall be ipso facto adjudged incapable, and disabled in law to have, enjoy, or exercise in any manner his said employment or practice.

And be it farther enacted by the authority aforesaid, that in all time coming, no person or persons shall be admitted to the employment of advocate, writer to the signet, notary public, or any other office belonging to the said college of justice, until he or they have taken and subscribed the aforesaid oath, in manner as is above directed.

No. XV.

The Schism Act, entitled "An Act to prevent the Growth of Schism, and for the farther security of the Churches of England and Ireland, as by Law established."[*]

WHEREAS, by an act of Parliament made in the thirteenth and fourteenth years of his late majesty King Charles II., entitled "An Act for the Uniformity of Public Prayers, and Administration of Sacraments, and other Rites and Ceremonies ;' and for establishing the Form of making, ordaining, and consecrating Bishops, Priests, and Deacons in the Church of England," it is, among other things, enacted, that every schoolmaster keeping any public or private school, and every person instructing or teaching any youth in any house or private family, as a tutor or schoolmaster, should subscribe, before his or their respective archbishop, bishop, or ordinary of the diocess, a declaration or, acknowledgment, in which, among other things, was contained as follows, viz.; "I, A. B., do declare that I will conform to the liturgy of the Church of England, as it is now by law established ;" and if any schoolmaster or other person, instructing or teaching youth in any private house or family, as a tutor or schoolmaster, should instruct or teach any youth as a tutor or schoolmaster before license obtained from his respective archbishop, bishop, or ordinary of the diocess, according to the laws and statutes of this realm, for which he should pay twelve-pence only, and before such subscription and acknowledgment made as aforesaid, then every such schoolmaster and other, instructing and teaching as aforesaid, should, for the first offence, suffer three months' imprisonment, without bail or mainprize ; and for every second and other such offence, should suffer three months' imprisonment, without bail or mainprize, and also forfeit to his majesty the sum of five pounds. And, whereas, notwithstanding the said act, sundry papists, and other persons dissenting from the Church of England, have taken upon them to instruct and teach youth, as tutors or schoolmasters, and have for such purpose openly set up schools and seminaries, whereby, if due and speedy remedy be not had, great danger might ensue to this church and state : for the making the said recited act more effectual, and preventing the danger aforesaid, be it enacted by the queen's most excellent majesty, by and with the advice and consent of the lords spiritual and temporal, and commons in this present Parliament assembled, and by the authority of the same, that every person or persons who shall, from and after the first day of August next ensuing, keep any public or private school or seminary, or teach and instruct any youth, as tutor or schoolmaster, within that part of Great Britain called England, the dominion of Wales, or town of Berwick-upon-Tweed, before such person or persons shall have subscribed so much of the said declaration and acknowledgment as is before recited, and shall have had and obtained a license from the respective archbishop, bishop, or ordinary of the place, under his seal of office (for which the party shall pay one shilling, and no more, over and above the duties payable to her majesty for the same), and shall be thereof lawfully convicted, upon an information, presentment, or indictment, in any of her majesty's courts of record at Westminster, or at the assizes, or before justices of Oyer and Terminer, shall and may be committed to the common jail of such county, riding, city, or town corporate as aforesaid, there to remain, without bail or mainprize, for the space of three months, to commence from the time that such person or persons shall be received into the said jail.

Provided, always, and be it hereby enacted, that no license shall be granted by an archbishop, bishop, or ordinary, unless the person or persons who shall sue for the same shall produce a certificate of his or their having received the sacrament according to the usage of the Church of England, in some parish church, within the space of one year next before the grant of such license, under the hand of the minister and one of the church-wardens of the said parish, nor until such person or persons shall have taken and subscribed the oaths of allegiance and supremacy, and abjuration, as appointed by law, and shall have made and subscribed the declaration against transubstantiation, contained in the act made in the twenty-fifth year of the reign of King Charles II., entitled "An Act for preventing Dangers which may happen from Popish

Recusants," before the said archbishop, bishop, or ordinary ; which said oaths and declarations the said archbishop, bishop, or ordinary is hereby empowered and required to administer and receive ; and such archbishops, bishops, after ordinaries are required to file such certificates, and keep an exact register of the same, and of the taking and subscribing such oath and declarations.

And be it farther enacted by the authority aforesaid, that any person who shall have obtained a license, and subscribed the declarations, and taken and subscribed the oaths as above mentioned, and shall at any time after, during the time of his or their keeping any public or private school or seminary, or instructing any youth as tutor or schoolmaster, knowingly or willingly resort to or be present at any conventicle, assembly, or meeting, within England, Wales, or town of Berwick-upon-Tweed, for the exercise of religion in any other manner than according to the liturgy and practice of the Church of England, or shall knowingly and willingly be present at any meeting or assembly for the exercise of religion, although the liturgy be there used, where her majesty (whom God long preserve), and the Elector of Brunswick, or such others as shall from time to time be lawfully appointed to be prayed for, shall not there be prayed for in express words, according to the liturgy of the Church of England, except where such particular offices of the liturgy are used wherein there are no express directions to pray for her majesty and the royal family, shall be liable to the penalties in this act; and from thenceforth be incapable of keeping any public or private school or seminary, or instructing any youth as tutor or schoolmaster.

And be it farther enacted by the authority aforesaid, that if any person licensed as aforesaid shall teach any catechism than the catechism set forth in the Book of Common Prayer, the license of such person shall from thenceforth be void, and such person shall be liable to the penalties of this act.

And be it farther enacted by the authority aforesaid, that it shall and may be lawful to and for the bishop of the diocess, or other proper ordinary, to recite any person or persons whatsoever, keeping school or seminary, or teaching without license as aforesaid, and to proceed against and punish such person or persons by ecclesiastical censure, subject to such appeals as in cases of ordinary jurisdiction : this act or any other law to the contrary notwithstanding.

Provided, always, that no person offending against this act shall be punished twice for the same offence.

Provided, also, that where any person shall be prosecuted without fraud or covin in any of the courts aforesaid for any offence contrary to this act, the same person shall not afterward be prosecuted for the same offence in any of the said courts while such former prosecution shall be pending and carried on without any wilful delay ; and in case of any such after-prosecution, the person so doubly prosecuted may allege, plead, or show forth in his defence against the same, such former prosecution, pending, or judgment, or sentence thereupon given, the said pleader first making oath before the judge or judges of the court where such after-prosecution shall be pending, and which said oath he or they are hereby empowered and required to administer, that the said prior prosecution was not commenced or carried on by his means, or with his consent or procurement, or by any fraud or collusion of any other person, to his knowledge or belief.

Provided, always, that this act, or anything therein contained, shall not extend, nor be construed to extend, to any tutor teaching or instructing youth in any college or hall within either of the universities of that part of Great Britain called England, nor to any tutor who shall be employed by any nobleman or noblewoman to teach his or her own children, grandchildren, or great-grandchildren only, in his or her family; provided such tutor so teaching any nobleman or noblewoman's family do in every respect qualify himself according to this act, except only in that of taking a license from the bishop.

Provided, also, that the penalties in this act shall not extend to any foreigner or alien of the foreign Reformed churches allowed or to be allowed by the queen's majesty, her heirs or successors, in England, for instructing or teaching any child or children, or any such foreigner or alien only, as a tutor or schoolmaster.

Provided, always, and be it farther enacted by the authority aforesaid, that if any person who shall have been convicted as aforesaid, and thereby made incapable to teach or instruct any youth as aforesaid, shall, after such conviction, conform to the Church of England for the space of one year, without having been present at any conventicle, assembly, or meeting as aforesaid, and receive the sacrament of the Lord's Supper, according to the rites and usage of the Church of England, at least three times in that year, every such person or persons shall be again capable of having and using a license to teach school, or to instruct youth as a tutor or schoolmaster, he or they also performing all that is made requisite thereunto by this act.

Provided, also, and be it farther enacted, that every such person so convicted, and afterward conforming in manner as aforesaid, shall, at the next term after his being admitted to, or taking upon him, to teach or instruct youth as aforesaid, make oath in writing, in some one of her majesty's courts at Westminster, in public and open court, or at the next Quarter Sessions for that county or place where he shall reside, between the hours of nine and twelve in the forenoon, that he hath conformed to the Church of England for the space of one year before such his admission, without having been present at any conventicle, assembly, or meeting as aforesaid, and that he hath received the sacrament of the Lord's Supper at least three times in the year, which oath shall be there enrolled, and kept upon record.

Provided, always, that this act shall not extend, or be construed to extend, to any person who, as a tutor or schoolmaster, shall instruct youth in reading, writing, arithmetic, or any part of mathematical learning only, so far as such mathematical learning relates to navigation, or any mechanical art only, and so as such reading, writing, arithmetic, or mathematical learning shall be taught in the English tongue only.

And whereas, by act of Parliament made in Ireland, in the seventeenth and eighteenth years of his said late majesty King Charles II., entitled "An Act for the Uniformity of Public Prayers, and Administration of the Sacraments, and other Rites and Ceremonies; and for establishing the Form of making, ordaining, and consecrating of Bishops, Priests, and Deacons in the Church of Ireland," it is enacted, concerning schoolmasters, and other persons in, structing youth in private families in Ireland, as in and by the above-recited act is enacted concerning schoolmasters and others instructing youth in private families in that part of Great Britain called England; and whereas it is reasonable, that where the law is the same, the remedy and means for enforcing the execution of the law should be the same, be it therefore enacted, by the authority aforesaid, that all and every the remedies, provisions, and clauses in and by this act given, made, and enacted, shall extend, and be deemed, construed, and adjudged to extend, to Ireland, in as full and effectual manner as if Ireland had been expressly named and mentioned in all and every the clauses in this act.

No. XVI.

The Repeal, entitled "An Act for strengthening the Protestant Interest in these Kingdoms." [*]

WHEREAS an act of Parliament was made in the tenth year of the reign of the late Queen Anne,[†] entitled "An Act for preserving the Protestant Religion by better securing the Church of England as by Law established, and for confirming the Toleration granted to Protestant Dissenters, by an Act entitled 'An Act for exempting their Majesties' Protestant Subjects dissenting from the Church of England from the Penalties of certain Laws;' and for supplying the Defects thereof, and for the farther securing the Protestant Succession, by requiring the Practisers of the Law in North Britain to take the Oaths and subscribe the Declaration therein mentioned;" and whereas part of the said act, as also another act hereinafter mentioned, have been found to be inconvenient, be it therefore enacted by the king's most excellent majesty, by and with the advice of lords spiritual and temporal, and commons in Parliament assembled, and by the authority of the same, that the said recited act, passed in the tenth year of the late Queen Anne,[‡] from the beginning thereof to these words, "And it is hereby farther enacted and declared, by the authority aforesaid, that the toleration granted to Protestant Dissenters;" and also one act made in the twelfth year of the reign of the late Queen Anne, entitled "An Act to prevent the Growth of Schism, and for the farther security of the Churches of England and Ireland as by Law established," shall be and are hereby repealed, annulled, and made void.

Provided, always, and be it enacted by the authority aforesaid, that if any mayor, bailiff, or other magistrate, in that part of Great Britain called England, the dominion of Wales, or town of Berwick-upon-Tweed, or the isles of Guernsey or Jersey, shall knowingly or willing-

* 5th of King Geo. I., cap. iv.   † 10 Annæ, cap. ii.
‡ 10 Annæ, cap. ii. ; and 12 Annæ, stat. ii., cap. vii.

ly resort to, or be present at, any public meeting for religious worship, other than the Church of England as by law established, in the gown, or other peculiar habit, or attended with the ensign or ensigns of or belonging to such his office, that every such mayor, bailiff, or other magistrate, being thereof convicted by due course of law, shall be disabled to hold such office or offices; employment or employments, and shall be adjudged incapable to bear any public office or employment whatsoever within that part of Great Britain called England, the dominion of Wales, and town of Berwick-upon-Tweed, or isles of Jersey and Guernsey.

No. XVII.

Notice of James Naylor.

NAYLOR was one of the first persons who invented and published the doctrines, and adopted the manners of the Quakers, and as a preacher of Quakerism was scarcely inferior in celebrity to George Fox himself; continually travelling through the kingdom, and everywhere haranguing, not only in private rooms, where *Friends* usually met, but in streets and fields, wherever he could find an audience inclined to hear him. He was born at Ardisloe, near Wakefield, in Yorkshire, and was bred up as a husbandman, and possessed some property ; there he lived twenty two or twenty-three years. *according to the world*, as he expressed it ; then he married and removed into the parish of Wakefield, where he continued till the civil wars began, in which he was a soldier in the Parliament's army, serving under several commanders, particularly under Lord Fairfax, and was at last quartermaster in Major-general Lambert's troop, in which service he continued till disabled by sickness in Scotland, after which he retired to his own home, having been a soldier eight or nine years, from which service arrears were due to him at the time of his punishment. Some five or six years after this, being at plough, and meditating on the things of God, suddenly, says he, " I heard a voice saying unto me, ' Get thee out from thy kindred and from thy father's house.' And shortly after, going a gate-ward with a friend from my own house, having on an old suit, without any money ; having neither taken leave of wife or children, not thinking then of any journey, (as) I was commanded to go into the west (Westmoreland), not knowing whither I should go, nor what I was to do there; but when I had been there a little while, I had given me what I was to declare ; and ever since I have remained, not knowing to-day what I was to do to-morrow." It was in 1652 that he was first noticed in Westmoreland as a preacher among the Quakers, and there, after a very curious examination before the magistrates, he was imprisoned at Appleby for the apparent blasphemy of his doctrines, and for the contumacy of his behaviour in not pulling off his hat, &c. In 1655 he went to London, soon after which it must have been that he made a progress into the west of England, intending to go into Cornwall. By this time he had by his preaching attached to himself a considerable number of followers, men and women, who attended him with the most enthusiastic devotion,

considering him as the very Word of God, and calling him, as mentioned above, by the most blasphemous appellations. These enthusiastic tokens of devotion overthrew his reason, and he became (as he afterward confessed) actually crazed. His friend and editor thus expresses his situation : " He came to be clouded in his understanding, bewildered, and at a loss in his judgment. Thus, poor man ! he stood not in his dominion," &c. ; and afterward he mentions his recovery : nevertheless, his conduct and his language during his whole life gave manifest tokens of insanity. At the time of which we are now speaking, instead of rebuking the madness of his followers, he suffered them to go on with their blasphemous conduct. After some stay in London, where he was imprisoned, he went to Bristol, and from thence to Exeter. At Exeter he was brought before Major Saunders, and dismissed with leave to prosecute his journey ; but, after having gone twenty miles, he was brought back, fined 20 marks for not taking off his hat, and committed to the common jail as a vagrant, whence he and his company being delivered by an order from the council, they set out on their return to Bristol. During their progress through Somersetshire, their fanaticism reached its utmost height of absurdity and impiety ; for as he rode into Wells, Glastonbury, and other towns, his company spread their garments before him, handkerchiefs, aprons, scarves, and the like, and even gloves, singing " Holy, holy, holy," &c. October 24th, 1656, they came through Bedminster : Naylor rode on horseback, and there were six more in his company, one of whom, a young man, bareheaded, led his horse by the bridle, and another uncovered before him, through the dirty way in which carts and horses, and none else, usually go, and with them two men on horseback, with each of them a woman behind him, and one woman walking on the better way or path. In this posture did they march ; and in such a case, that one George Wetherley, noting their condition, asked them to come into the better road, adding that God expected no such extremity ; but they continued on their way, not answering in any other notes but what were musical, singing ' Holy, holy, holy, Lord God of Sabbaoth,' &c.

" Thus continued they till by their wandering they came to the almshouse within the suburbs of Bristol, where one of the women alighted, and she, with the other of her own sex, lovingly marched on either side of Naylor's horse. This Wetherley saith he supposes they could not be less deep in the muddy way than to the knees (and at this very time it happened to rain so violently that the water ran in streams from their cloathes), and he saith they sang, but sometimes with such a buzzing, melodious noyse, that he could not understand what it was. This the said Wetherley gave in upon oath. Thus did they reach Ratcliffe Gate, with Timothy Wedlock, of Devon, bareheaded, and Martha Symonds, with the bridle on one side, and Hannah Stranger on the other side of the horse. This Martha Symonds is the wife of Thomas Symonds, of London, bookbinder (and sister to Giles Calvert, the bookseller, living at the Black Spread-Eagle at the west end of Paul's, publisher of most of the fanatic books of that day), and Hannah Stranger is the wife of John Stranger (alias Stånger), of London, combmaker, who sang ' *Holy, holy, holy Lord God of Israel*.' Thus did he ride to the High Crosse in Bristol, and after that to the White Hart in Broad-street, which the magistrates hearing, they were apprehended and committed to prison by Joseph Jackson, the mayor; being searched, letters and other papers, twenty-one in all, were found upon them, some extracts from which are here subjoined, for the purpose of showing the great ignorance (rather than impiety), as well as the inconceivable nonsense of the early Quakers."

A Letter from Hannah Stranger to James Naylor, of Exeter.

" James Naylor, in the pure feare and power of God my soule salutes thee, thou everlasting son of righteousnesse and prince of peace. Oh! how my soule travelleth to see this day, which Abraham did and was glad, and shall all that are of faithfull Abraham. Oh! suffer me to speake what the Lord hath moved. There is one temptation neere, the like unto the first; and is like the wisdome of God, but it is not, and therefore it must be destroyed: oh, it defileth and hateth the innocent; I beseech thee wait: my soule travelleth to see a pure image brought forth," &c.: the remainder being of the same kind.

" From London, 16th day of the 7th month."

Another letter she begins thus :

" Oh thou fairest of ten thousand, thou only-begotten son of God, how my heart panteth after thee," &c.

Her husband, John Stranger, adds this postscript :

" Remember my dear love to thy master ; thy name is no more to be called James, but Jesus."

The magistrates of Bristol, on Saturday, October 25th, examined the whole company, and the several examinations are printed in the pamphlet marked E, from which the following passages are extracted :

Being asked whether his name was James Naylor, he replied, " The men of this world call me James Naylor."

Q. " Art not thou the man that rid on horseback into Bristoll?" &c.

A. " I rid into a town, but what its name was I know not; and by the Spirit a woman was commanded to hold my horse's bridle ; and some there were that cast down cloathes, and sang praises to the Lord, such songs as the Lord put into their hearts, and it's like it might be the song of *t* Holy, holy, holy,' " &c.

Q. " Whether or no didst thou reprove those women ?"

A. " Nay ; but I bad them take heed that they sang nothing but what they were moved to of the Lord."

Q. " Dost thou own this letter which Hannah Stranger sent unto thee ?"

A. " Yea, I do own that letter."

Q. " Art thou, according to that letter, the fairest of ten thousand ?"

A. " As to the visible, I deny such attribute to be due unto me ; but if as to that which the Father has begotten in me, I shall own it."

Q. " Have any called thee by the name of Jesus ?"

A. " Not as unto the visible, but as Jesus, the Christ that is in me."

Q. " Whether art thou more sent than others ?"

A. " As to that, I have nothing at present given me of my Father to answer."

Q. " Art thou the everlasting Son of God ?"

A. " Where God is manifest in the flesh, there is the everlasting Son, and I do witness God in the flesh. I am the Son, and the Son of God is but one."

Q. " Art thou the Prince of Peace ?"

A. " The Prince of everlasting Peace is begotten in me."

Q. " Art thou the everlasting Son of God, the King of Righteousness ?"

A. " I am, and the everlasting righteousness is wrought in me : if ye were acquainted with the Father, ye would also be acquainted with me."

Q. " Did any kisse thy feet ?"

A. " It might be they did ; but I minded them not."

Q. " How dost thou provide for a livelyhood ?"

A. " As I do the lillies, without care, being maintained by my Father."

Q. " What businesse hadst thou at Bristoll, or that way ?"

A. " I was guided and directed by my Father."

Q. " What wentest thou for to Exeter ?"

A. " I was to Lawson (perhaps Launceston) to see the brethren."

Q. " What estate hast thou ?"

A. " I take no care for that."

Q. " Doth God, in an extraordinary manner, sustain thee without any corporeal food ?"

A. " *Man doth not live*, &c. : the same life is mine that is in the Father, but not in the same measure."

Q. " How art thou clothed ?"

A. " I know not."

Q. " Dost thou live without bread ?"

A. " As long as my heavenly Father will. I have tasted of that bread, of which he that eateth shall never die."

Q. " How long hast thou lived without any corporeal sustenance ?"

A. " Some fifteen or sixteen days, sustained without any other food except the Word of God."

Q. " Thou hast a wife at this time ?"

A. " A woman I have, whom by the world is called my wife ; and some children I have, which according to the flesh are mine," &c., &c.

Martha Symonds being examined, saith " she knew James Naylor formerly ; for he is no more James Naylor, but refined to a more excellent substance."

Q. " What made thee lead his horse ?" &c.

A. " I was forced thereto by the power of the Lord."

Q. " He is styled in Hannah Stranger's letter the fairest of ten thousand, &c. : dost thou so esteem him ?"

A. " That James Naylor of whom thou speakest is buried in me, and he hath promised to come again."

Q. " Hast thou a husband ?"

A. " I have a man, which thou callest my husband."

Q. " What made thee to leave him, and to follow James Naylor in such a manner?"

A. " It is our life to praise the Lord ; and the Lord my strength, who filleth heaven and earth, is manifest in James Naylor."

Q. " Oughtest thou to worship James Naylor, as thou didst, upon thy knees ?"

A. " Yea, I ought so to do."

Q. " Why oughtest thou so to do ?"

A. " He is the Son of Righteousness ; and the new man within him is the everlasting Son of Righteousness ; and James Naylor will be Jesus when the new life is born in him," &c., &c.

The examinations of Hannah Stranger and her husband, and of Timothy Wedlock, contain matter of the same kind. The extravagance of Dorcas Erbury goes beyond them all. She says that James Naylor raised her from the dead.

Q. " In what manner?"

A. " He laid his hand on my head after I had been dead two daies, and said, ' Dorcas, arise !' and I arose, and live, as thou seest."

Q. " Jesus Christ doth sit at the right hand of the Father, where the world shall be judged by him ?"

A. " He whom thou callest Naylor shall sit at the right hand of the Father, and shall judge the world with equity."

The author of " Rabshakeh's Outrage," &c., wishes it to be believed that the seven persons who attended Naylor into Bristol were not Quakers, giving as a reason because there were then many more than 700 Quakers in and about Bristol, not one of whom attended him, and these seven were publicly disowned. On the other hand, it does not appear that they were inhabitants of Bristol, and therefore they could not belong to the congregation at Bristol, but they might have belonged to some other congregation : their language and manners were those of the Quakers, and the two who were dismissed, Samuel Cater and Robert Crab, went to the Quakers' meeting the same day. The writer would have done well if he had mentioned how, and when, and where they were disowned by the Quakers ; but if they were disowned at all, it was not until after their mad behaviour at Bristol. As for Naylor himself, there is abundant evidence that he was a Quaker before and after his folly, and a principal one ; he is considered as such in all the contemporary books that I have seen, and was usually called so ; his editor, George Wetherley, in 1716, himself a Quaker, and well acquainted with him, speaks of him as such, and generally with great approbation ; and Naylor himself calls George Fox his dear brother George ; and if Naylor was a Quaker, the probability is that his followers were of the same description.

The examination taken before the magistrates of Bristol were attested by the mayor, sealed with the city seal, and sent by letter to Mr. Robert Aldworth, their goodly town-clerk and burgess of Parliament, and upon this report the House sent a messenger for Naylor, who, with four of his company, were sent off November 10th. With them the Common Council sent Mr. Philip Dorney, their clerk, and Mr. William Grigge, a member of the Common Council, a tanner, living in St. James's parish, near the Quakers' Meeting-house, in Broadmead.

The author of " Rabshakeh's Outrage," &c., says that Mr. Grigge would not set out on his journey until he had five pounds paid to him towards his expenses, and in all respects he expresses a very contemptuous opinion of him. These are his words : " Without reflecting on the magistrates of Bristol their wisdom, let me say it, it was not their master-piece to send such a busie, pragmatical person as thou art to London, there to make a speech to a committee of Parliament, which had in it neither head nor tail, nor good sense nor reason, but for the greatest part composed of fawning, falsehood, and pitiful, lame compliments, crying ' Sir, Gentlemen, and Your Honours,' but speaking of nothing of weight or importance relating to the matter then in debate. Reader, thou must know that this envious person is a great speech-maker in the Common Council of Bristol ; and if he had so high an esteem of that which he made in the Painted Chamber as to judge it polite and learned enough to merit the public views, thou mayest thence easily judge what sad oratory do serve the turn within the walls of that council."

The House of Commons appointed a committee to examine the whole affair, which sat in the Painted Chamber, and of which " godly Mr. Bamfield, of Exeter, was chairman." Here James Naylor and his company were charged with blasphemy in assuming, first, the gesture, words, honour, worship, and miracles of our blessed Saviour ; and, secondly, the names and incommunicable attributes and titles of our Lord. The committee re-examined all the prisoners, at which the answers given and the facts proved seem to have been nearly the same as at Bristol ; with this additional information, on the oath of Thomas Perkins and Thomas Cole : Thomas Perkins informeth, that " after Naylor's imprisonment at Bristol, Dorcas Erbury fell down at his feet and kissed them ; and the same evening one Alice Brooks fell on her knees before the said Naylor, and Naylor put his hands upon her head, and said, ' Stand fast,' &c. And Thomas Cole informeth, that on the 25th of October, Martha and Hannah Stranger, being called out of Naylor's room into their own lodging, they one after another kneeled before Naylor and laid their heads on his knees, and he laid his hands on their heads, making a groaning noise within himself, and before they rose from their knees, he crossed his hands over their heads." And it appeared to the committee, by the information of John Baynam, deputy to the sergeant of the House, to whose custody Naylor and his company were committed, " that, the usual posture of James Naylor is sitting in a chair, and his company, both men and women, do sometimes kneel ; and when they were weary of kneeling, they sat upon the ground before him, singing these and divers other words to the like purpose, ' Holy, holy,' &c., and thus they do usually all the day long ;" but the informer never heard Naylor sing as aforesaid. And he saith " there is great resort to the said Naylor by divers persons, who most of them kneel before him in the manner aforesaid." (However, the note says that this they did, whether James Naylor was absent or present.) " And Martha Symonds, in the posture aforesaid, sung, ' This is the joyful day ; behold, the King of Righteousness is come ;' " and farther the informer saith, "that he never knew the said Naylor show any dislike, either by reproof or otherwise, of that honour or worship which John Stranger and his wife, Martha Symonds, Dorcas Erbury, and the rest, gave him as aforesaid." And a member of the House being lately at the place where Naylor is now a prisoner, informs the committee " that he saw Naylor and his company in the posture aforesaid, and heard John Stranger and one of the women sing ' Holy, holy, holy Lord God, and holy, holy to thee, thee, Lord God ;' and while John Stranger sang these words, he did sometimes look upward and sometimes upon James Naylor." Another member informs us, as upon his own view, to the same purpose. And at Naylor's last examination before the committee, being Wednesday, December 3, one William Piggot did inform " that Naylor, sitting in a chair where he is now a prisoner, one Sarah Blackberry came to him and took him by the hand, and said, ' Rise up, my love, my dove, my fair one, and come away ; why sittest thou among the pots?' and presently put her mouth upon his hand, and sunk down upon the ground before him." Being asked what he had finally to offer in his own vindication, he said, " I do abhor that any of that honour that is done to God should be given to me, as I am a creature. But it pleased the Lord to set me up as a sign of the coming of the righteous one ; and what hath been done in my passing through the towns, I was commanded by the power of the Lord to suffer such things to be done to the outward man as a sign: I abhor my honour as a creature."

The trial lasted several days, and the committee agreed that all the charges were proved. Their report, consisting of fifteen sheets of paper, was received and read in the House December 5th, and debated thirteen separate days, when at last they convicted him of horrid blasphemy, and nem. con. voted him to be a grand impostor, and deceiver of the people. December 16, it was proposed that the punishment of James Naylor should be death, and the question being put, " the noes went forth 96, the yeas 82, so it passed in the negative." On the next day (Wednesday, the 17th) the House agreed to the following sentence :

" Resolved, That James Naylor be set on the pillory, with his head in the pillory, in the Palace-yard, Westminster, during the space of two hours, on Thursday next, and shall be whipped by the hangman through the streets from Westminster to the Old Exchange, London, and there likewise be set on the pillory, with his head in the pillory, for the space of two hours, between the hours of eleven and one, on Saturday next, in each place wearing a paper containing an inscription of his crimes ; and that, at the Old Exchange, his tongue be bored through with a hot iron, and that he be there also stigmatized in the forehead with the letter B, and that he be afterward sent to Bristol, and be conveyed into and through the said city on horseback, bare-ridged, with his face backward, and there also publicly whipped the next market-day after he comes thither ; and that from thence he be committed to prison in Bridewell, London, and there restrained from the society of all people, and there to labour hard, till he shall be released by

Parliament ; and during that time be debarred the use of the pen, ink, and paper, and shall have no relief but what he earns by his daily labours."

This inhuman sentence was fully executed on the unhappy maniac. Thursday, December 18, he stood in the pillory in Palace-yard, and was from thence whipped to the Old Exchange, receiving 310 lashes, one on crossing each gutter. On this same day several petitions were presented to Parliament, containing complaints against the growth and exorbitance of the people called Quakers : one from Devonshire and Exeter ; one from the ministers in Northumberland, Durham, and Newcastle ; one from the justices of the peace, gentry, ministers of the Gospel, &c., in Cheshire ; another from the mayor, aldermen, and ministers of Chester ; another from divers well-affected persons, gentlemen, ministers, &c., in Cornwall ; and another humble remonstrance and petition from the mayor, aldermen, and common council, ministers of the Gospel, and other chief inhabitants of Bristol, in which they complain that "they have lyen long under much reproach and ignominy, occasioned by the increase of a generation of seduced and seducing Quakers, who were at first supported and upheld by some soldiers (Captain Beal and Captain Watson), then in chief command, in the absence of the governor of the garrison." They complain of the frequent disturbance which they gave to the public worship, and of their confused and tumultuous meetings, and of their profaning the Sabbath by multitudes of their proselytes flocking from all parts of the country round about us on that day. They particularly complain of Naylor, a ringleader and head of that faction ; they complain that they have not power to restrain these enormities, and pray the Parliament " to restrain the insolencies of this people, that so the reproach, not only of this city, but of the whole nation and government, may be rowled away." All these petitions were referred to a committee to consider of them, and to collect the heads of all the Quakers for suppressing the mischiefs and inconveniences complained of.

Saturday, December 20, James Naylor was to have suffered the remaining part of his sentence, but on the morning of that same day a petition was presented to the House, signed by Joshua Sprigge, formerly an eminent Independent preacher, author of a book quoted above, T. Z. and Jer. White [Cromwell's chaplain], C. H., representing the wretched condition of the prisoner, and the danger to his life if he should receive the remainder of his punishment, and praying in the name of many honourable persons, both citizens and others, wholly unconnected with him, for a week's respite, which was granted. Meanwhile many well-affected and respectable persons, of whom Colonel Scrope, some time governor of the castle and fort of Bristol, was the first, name shocked at the inhumanity of the sentence, petitioned Parliament for a remission of the remaining part of it. Many of the members were against admitting the petition ; but being put to the vote, it was admitted. The petition was presented on Tuesday, December 23, at the bar of the House, by Mr. Joshua Sprigge above mentioned, accompanied by about one hundred eminent persons in behalf of the whole. Mr. Sprigge made a sho.t speech on presenting it, but it was unsuccessful. The petitioners then applied to his highness the Protector, still without effect. On Wednesday, December 24, five Presbyterian or Independent ministers, Caryl, Manton, Nye, Griffith, and Reynolds, went to James Naylor in Newgate, and it was said that they did so by order of the Parliament; but Naylor persisting in his ordinary discourse and usual answers, they left him wroth.

On Saturday, December 27, he suffered the remaining part of his punishment. "About 11 o'clock he was carried in a coach from Newgate to the Black Boy, near the Royal Exchange, in which house he continued till the clock had struck 12 at noon, when, by divers on foot, with halberds, he was guarded to the pillory, where, when he came, they presently put his head into the same, and having pinned it down, came up Martha Symonds, and with her two others, who were said to be Hannah Stranger and Dorcas Erbury; the first seated herself just behind on the right, and the two latter before him, and Robert Rich likewise accompanied him with comfortable words, kissing and stroking on his face. He having stood till two, the executioner took him out, and having bound his arms with cords to the pillory, and he having put forth his tongue, which he freely did, the executioner, with a red-hot iron about the bigness of a quill, bored the same, and by order from the sheriff held it in a small place, to the end that the beholders might see and bear witness that the sentence was thoroughly executed; then having taken it out, and pulled the cap off that covered his face, he put a handkerchief over his eyes, and putting his left hand to the back part of his head, and taking the red-hot iron letter in his other hand, put it to his forehead till it smoked : all of which time James never so much as winced, but bore it with astonishing and heart-melting patience. Being unbound, he took the executioner in his arms, embracing and hugging him ; after which, Robert Rich, through his ardent love, licked the wound on his forehead. And James was conveyed to the Black Boy, and from thence to Newgate."

This Robert Rich had been a merchant in London, an enthusiastic follower of Naylor, a perfect maniac, but religious and harmless. After James Naylor had been on the pillory some time, "he took a paper out of his pocket, and placed it over his head, whereon was written, ' It is written, Luke, xxiii., 38, This is the King of the Jews.' But presently an officer stepped up and pulled it down, and turned Robert Rich and the two women off the pillory ; but after a while they lifted up Robert Rich again on the pillory, where he stayed till James Naylor had undergone his sufferings for that time, and held him by the hand while he was burning, and afterward licked and sucked the fire out of his tongue, and led him by the hand from off the pillory. This also was very remarkable, that notwithstanding there might be many thousands of people, yet they were very quiet, few being heard to revile him, or seen to throw any one thing at him. And when he was a burning, all the people before him, and behind him, and on both sides of him, with one consent stood bareheaded.

"Afterward he was sent by the sheriffs of London to Bristol, and the sheriffs of Bristol had warrant under the speaker's hand to see the sentence executed as far as they were concerned therein. January 16, 1656–7, he arrived at Lawford's Gate, where he slept. January 17, this day James Naylor took horse at Lawford's Gate, and rode on a horse bareridged, with his face to the tail, through the city without Redcliff Gate, and there alighted, and was brought to the middle of Thomas-street, and there stripped and tied to the horse, to be whipped from thence back again to the middle of Broad-street."

Before his whipping the following order was sent to the keeper of Newgate : "Mr. Roch.: Cause Naylor to ride in at Lawford's Gate, from thence along Wine-street to the Tolsey, thence down High-street over the bridge, and so out at Redcliff Gate. There let him alight, and bring him into Thomas-street, and cause him to be stripped, and there made fast to the carthorse, and in the market first whipped ; from thence to the foot of the bridge, there whipped ; thence to the end of the bridge, there whipped ; thence to the middle of High-street, there whipped; thence to the Tolsey, there whipped ; thence to the middle of Broad-street, there whipped, and then taña (turn) into the Tailors' Hall : there release him from the carthorse, and let him put on his clothes; and carry him thence to Newgate by Tower Lane, the back way."

And whereas, of custom, the bellman goes before and makes proclamation of the offence of the offender, yet here the keeper commanded the bellman to the contrary (as was said), and suffered one Jones (a coppersmith and ugly Quaker) to hold back the beadle's arm when striking, so that in all the way the bell rang but six times—a trait of mercy in the midst of such brutality which ought to be recorded to the credit of the magistracy of Bristol.

All the while he passed along, his dear and worthy friend, Robert Rich, the maniac above mentioned, rode bareheaded before him, having a mermaid's head (such was the length of his hair), singing "Holy, holy," &c. After this the sheriffs of Bristol sent him up to the governors of Bridewell, London. who had before received orders from the speaker as to that part of the sentence wherein they were concerned, where he continued till the wise providence of God released him. After his discharge from Bridewell he returned to this city, and in a meeting with some of his friends he made a public recantation of his errors in so affecting a manner that they were convinced of the sincerity of his repentance. He lived some time afterward in this city in a serious and becoming manner, and died on a journey from hence to Wakefield, in Yorkshire, where he was born in 1616.—*Sayer's History of Bristol, in* 4to, 1828, vol. ii., chap. xxix.—C.

No. XVIII.

The closing chapter of Godwin's History of the Commonwealth.

Government of Cromwell considered.—Character of the Nation over which he presided.—Majority of the Nation hostile.—The People in gen-

eral favourable to the ancient Line of their Kings.—Spirit of Liberty that had sprung up. —Sentiments extensively prevailing in behalf of a Government according to Law.—Religious Character of the Nation.—The People divided into the Humorous and the Demure.— The Noble and Rich unfriendly to Cromwell.—Religious and Moral Character of the Protector.— He aims at the Reformation of the Law.—His Clemency and humane Disposition.—His Patronage of Letters and Learned Men.—A free Parliament would have restored the Stuarts.— Arbitrary Imprisonments resorted to by Cromwell.—Unpalatable Measures to which he had recourse.—Some of them unavoidable.—Others of a doubtful Character.—Dissatisfaction they produced.—High Reputation of his Lawyers.— Violent Character of his Administration.—Its apparent Versatility.—Sequel of his Government, if he had lived longer, considered.

HAVING traced the reign of Cromwell from its rise to its termination, it now becomes one of the duties of history to look back on the sum of the path through which we have travelled. The first characteristic of this period of history, from the day on which the Independents and army rose upon the Parliament, is, that the affairs of the nation were directed by a small portion of themselves, seizing on the supreme authority by force, and retaining it by superior talents and intellect.

The government of a nation, particularly in such circumstances, is a complicated science, with difficulty mastered in theory, and with difficulty reduced to practice. It is comparatively easy for the philosopher in his closet to invent imaginary schemes of policy, and to show how mankind, if they were without passions and without prejudices, might best be united in the form of a political community. But, unfortunately, men in all ages are the creatures of passions, perpetually prompting them to defy the rein, and break loose from the dictates of sobriety and speculation. Thus far as to the general nature of man. And, besides these generalities, in each particular age men have aspirations and prejudices, sometimes of one sort, and sometimes of another, rendering them very unlike the pieces on a chessboard, which the skilful practitioner moves this way and that, without its being necessary to take into his estimate the materials of which they are made, and adapting his proceedings to their internal modifications.

Neither the Republicans, who governed England for four or five years from the death of Charles the First, nor Cromwell, who displaced them, were fated to lie on a bed of roses, or to wander upon a soft and level carpet of verdure. Let us apply this to the history of Cromwell.

The people of England, whom we may call his subjects, were divided into different bodies and factions of men, none of them disposed passively to be guided by his wishes or his will. The first consideration that occurs under this head is that of the government under which England had been placed for ages previously to the civil war. The thing most obvious to the grossest capacity, and which, therefore, had a mighty influence with a great portion of the community, was, that we had had at the head

of our government an individual with the appellation of king. From the days of William the Conqueror at least, this office had continued in an hereditary line, with such deviations as circumstances seemed to dictate, but never with a total disregard of this ground of succession.

Charles the Second was the eldest son of his father, the lineal descendant of the Edwards and Henries, who figure so greatly in our history, and the legal successor of Elizabeth, whose memory was dear, and worthily dear, to the people of this country. A prince, laying indisputable claim, so far as this circumstance is of force, to the crown of a country, is an intelligible object, to which persons of the plainest understanding may attach and devote themselves. A great part of the people of England had rallied round the standard of his father, and been loyal to his cause; a very small portion had, even in thought, thrown off the claim of him and his son to the throne. It was impossible, therefore, that this circumstance, the existence of the lawful prince in exile, the multitudes of men that superstitiously loved him,* and the great numbers who, without personal partiality, had yet the feeling that the throne of England was his proper place, and that England would never be as it should be without him,† should not materially modify the purposes and authority of Cromwell.

The next circumstance to which it was necessary for Cromwell, whether he would or not, to attend, was the spirit of liberty which was abroad in the land.

The men who understood this best, and loved it with the purest affection, were the Republicans. And these men, alike from their talents, their station in society, and their ascendency in the army, were at all times formidable to the protector.

But there were various men and bodies of men, who, without so illuminated an understanding, had still a strong partiality to the doctrines of liberty. These were the men who claimed a government according to law; and they had always formed a considerable portion of the people of England. And this, in however confined a point of view, in a certain sense is liberty. The vilest of all slaveries is subjection to the arbitrary will of a master; to live, as is said to be the case in some Oriental sovereignties, where the supreme magistrate can at his pleasure take from you your property, and subject you to corporal punishment or death. To live under the empire of law has two advantages; though, alas! these advantages are often visionary. If the law be ever so iniquitous, you seem to know what you have to look to, and can shape your conduct accordingly. Unfortunately, however, where the law has interpreters, professional men whose business it is to quibble on words and explain away equity, this benefit is very equivocal. Secondly, we are told that justice is blind, and the law speaks the same language indifferently to all. But this is by no means universally the case. The rich man, and the man of powerful connexions, will often be successful in the courts, where the poor and the friendless man has a small chance. These, however, are exceptions. In the majority of cases law is, a rule serving to protect the plain man in his honest undertakings and pursuits.

The English people are habitually a calculating and reasoning race. They find themselves more at home and more satisfied with a logical process than most other nations. Hence the subtleties of law have been extensively cultivated among us. And we feel ourselves better contented with the issue of our controversy, be it what it will, when all is done by the application of a rule, than when the whole is disposed of by barefaced power, and the sudden impulse of an arbitrary will.

A third thing of material importance to Cromwell was the religious state of the community. In this respect the English nation was much divided. Many still adhered to the discipline and forms of the old Episcopal Church as patronised by Elizabeth; the bulk of the nation seems to have been wedded to the exclusive doctrines of Presbyterianism; and a party by no means contemptible for either numbers or importance, were the strenuous advocates of independence and toleration. Cromwell courted the Presbyterians, but secretly, and in his heart, was the friend of the Independents.

The latter of these parties, with all their numerous divisions, demanded the greatest degree of attention, on account of the fervour of their religious enthusiasm. A large portion of the Independents, and the whole body of the Anabaptists, were strenuous Republicans, and more directly and openly thwarted Cromwell in his favourite projects than any other set of men in the nation.

Nothing can be of greater importance in a state than the religious dispositions of its members. It not unusually happens that, when all other things give way, these will prove invincible to all the arts and the force that can be brought against them. The influence of the priesthood, the inspirations of fanaticism, and the salvation of souls, will often present an impenetrable barrier to all the designs of the politician. And the influence of religious considerations was never so powerful as in the times of the English Commonwealth.

The enemies of the protector may be divided into two classes, the grave and the humorous. The people of England, with the exception of the Royalists, were for the most part sedate, atrabilarious, and demure. The adherents of the house of Stuart ran into the opposite extreme of licentiousness and buffoonery. They assailed Cromwell with all the weapons of ridicule, scurrility, and contempt. This, however, scarcely rendered them less formidable on occasions of moment. They hated him more sincerely than they pretended to despise him, and were perpetually ready with plots, conspiracies, and the dagger, to bring his power to a sudden termination.

The ancient nobility and the great land proprietors of England are also well entitled to consideration. A small number in these classes were friendly to the present system, but the great mass of them were by no means so. This was an unnatural situation in the state, and could only be found to prevail in unquiet times. The friends of constitutional liberty in the early periods of the civil war, and the com-

monwealthsmen afterward, bore down by their energies what are commonly found to be the most influential, but the least enterprising part of the community. These, for the greater part, took refuge in a sullen and temporizing neutrality. The Earl of Northumberland may serve as a specimen of this class. It was reasonable to expect that Cromwell would bear this description of men much in his mind; and we find, in fact, that he did so.

Such were the elements of the nation Cromwell took upon himself to rule; and materials more intractable to command could scarcely be found in any climate or age. The Lord Protector of England had no friends, except the few that he made so by his personal qualities, and his immediate powers of conciliation. The Royalists, and the votaries of liberty in general, the Episcopalians, the Presbyterians, and the Independents, the fanatics of all descriptions, and a great part of the army, were his inveterate foes. He stood alone, with little else to depend upon but the energies of his mind, and the awe which his character impressed on unwilling subjects. And all this happened, not so much from any ill qualities that could be ascribed to him, but as the natural result of his ambition. His enemies for the most part confessed his talents and the elevation of his soul, his high courage, his eminent sagacity, the vastness of his comprehension and his spirit, his intellectual intrepidity of purpose, the inexhaustible resources of his mind, his good-nature, his generosity, and the clemency and humanity that governed his decisions. His fault was ambition. The pride of the English nation could not endure that a man who but the other day had been one of the ranks, and whom they would scarcely allow to be a gentleman, should now claim to be lord of all. Divided they were among themselves into a thousand factions; but they all agreed in this, to condemn the protector.

It is only by dint of bringing these circumstances together that we are enabled to form a judgment of the administration of Cromwell. His was strictly a government of expedients; and he could only pursue the object he had most at heart by means of a thousand deviations and in the most circuitous manner.

The object uppermost in the mind of the protector, as has repeatedly been said, was the true interest and happiness of the people over whom he presided. He believed of himself that he had only accepted the rule for the purpose of securing their welfare. He was most anxious for the moral and religious improvement of his subjects, and aimed at the merit of being the father of his people.

The character of Cromwell has been little understood. No wonder. The man who has many enemies will be sure to be greatly misrepresented. And no man had ever so many enemies in the compass of one island composed of forty little counties, as Cromwell had. The Restoration speedily followed upon his decease. And it behooved the adherents of the house of Stuart to blacken by all imaginable means the memory of the protector, that they might thus spread a sort of borrowed lustre, the result of the darker shades of the picture, upon Charles the Second.

Cromwell was a man most sincere in his religion, and singularly devoted to the cause of good morals. It is thus that Milton speaks of him: "If thou," says he, "the patron of our liberty, and its tutelar divinity : it he, of whom we have held that no mortal was ever more just, more saintlike and unspotted, should undermine our freedom, which he had so lately built up, this would prove not only deadly and destructive to his own fame, but to the entire and universal cause of religion and virtue."

The beginning of Cromwell's public life was answerable to this character. He says of himself, "I raised such men as had the fear of God before them, and made conscience of what they did ; and from that day forward they never were beaten, but beat the enemy continually." Milton expands this circumstance in his beautiful language. "He was a soldier thoroughly accomplished in the art of self-knowledge, and his first successes were against the internal enemies of human virtue; vain hopes, fears, aspirings, and ambition. His first triumphs were over himself; and he was thus enabled, from the day that he beheld an enemy in the field, to exhibit the endowments of a veteran. Such was the temper and discipline of his mind, that all the good and the valiant were irresistibly drawn to his camp, not merely as the best school of martial science, but also of piety and religion ; and those who joined it were necessarily rendered such by his example. In his empire over the minds of his followers he was surpassed neither by Epaminondas, nor Cyrus, nor any of the most vaunted generals of antiquity. Thus he formed to himself an army of men, who were no sooner under his command, than they became the patterns of order, obedient to his slightest suggestions, popular and beloved by their fellow-citizens, and to the enemy not more terrible in the field than welcome in their quarters. In the towns and villages where they sojourned, in no way offensive or rapacious, abstaining from violence, wine, intemperance, and impiety, so that suddenly the inhabitants, rejoicing in their disappointment, regarded them not as enemies, but as guests and protectors, a terror to the disorderly, a safeguard to the good, and by precept and example the teachers of all piety and virtue." Milton concludes, "As long as you, Cromwell, are preserved to us, he must want reliance on the providence of God who fears for the prosperity and happiness of the English nation, you being so evidently the object of Divine favour and protection."

Remarkably coincident with the above picture is what is related of him in 1654 on the authority of George Fox, the founder of the Quakers. Fox, being brought into his presence, "expatiated with that zest and unction upon true religion, and a holy and disinterested zeal for its cause, with which he was so remarkably endowed ; and the protector, who had been accustomed deeply to interest himself in such discourses, was caught by his eloquence. He pressed his hand, and said, Come again to my house ; if thou and I were together but one hour in every day, we should be nearer to each other."

In perfect correspondence with this is the declaration made by Cromwell respecting the Protestants of Piedmont, that "the calamities of these poor people lay as near, or rather nearer to his heart, than if it had concerned the dearest relations he had in the world."

One of the measures of Cromwell, which may be cited as an example of his anxiety for the moral and religious improvement of his countrymen, is his ordinance for ejecting scandalous and insufficient ministers among those who received stipends from the public. This, like almost all his measures, was made a subject of misrepresentation. Let us call to mind the judgment of Baxter on the subject. "The commissioners under this act saved many a congregation from ignorant, ungodly, drunken teachers, that sort of men who intend no more in the ministry than to say a sermon, as readers say their common prayers, and so patch a few good words together to talk the people asleep on Sunday, and all the rest of the week go with them to the ale-house, and harden them in sin ; and that sort of ministers who either preach against a holy life, or preach as men that were never acquainted with it : these they usually rejected, and in their stead admitted any, that were able, serious preachers, and lived a godly life, of what tolerable opinion soever they were. So that, though many of them were somewhat partial to the Independents, Separatists, Fifth-monarchy Men, and Anabaptists, and against the Prelatists and Arminians, yet so great was the benefit, above the hurt that they brought to the Church, that many thousands of souls blessed God for the faithful ministers whom they let in, and grieved when the Prelatists afterward [in August, 1662] cast them out again."

In the instructions and orders given to the major-generals in 1655, particular attention was bestowed on the question of the public morals. They were required " in their carriage and conversation to promote godliness and virtue, and to endeavour, with the justices of peace, clergy, and proper officers, to put down drunkenness, blasphemy, and licentiousness ; to inform themselves of idle and loose persons, who had no visible means of livelihood, that they might be compelled to work, or sent out of the commonwealth ; to take bonds of such masters of families as had been in arms against the Parliament for the good and orderly behaviour of their servants ; and to put down in London and Westminster all gaming-houses and houses of ill fame."*

In Cromwell's speech respecting the omissions and imperfections of the petition and advice, he notices that they had said nothing respecting the reformation of manners. He recommends that particular attention should be paid as to the education of gentlemen's sons. He complains that in many cases our children are sent into France, and return with all the licentiousness of that nation ; no care being taken to educate them before they go, nor to keep them in good order when they come home. He urges the necessity of something effectual being done on the subject of public morality, without sparing any condition of men, and the youth of the nation, though they be noblemen's sons. Let them be who they will that are debauched, he adds, it is for the glory of God that nothing of outward consideration should save them from just punishment and reformation; and truly there was nothing for which he would more bless God, than to see something done, and that heartily, not only in reference to the persons mentioned, but to all the nation, that there might be a general stop put to the current of vice and wickedness.*

The reformation of the law was the perpetual subject of Cromwell's solicitude. He says in the speech just quoted, " If any man should ask me how this is to be done, I confess I am not fully prepared to enter into particulars. But I think, at least, the delays of suits, the costliness of suits, the excessiveness of fees, and those things they call demurrers, loudly demand the interference of the Legislature."†

In a conversation recorded by Ludlow, Cromwell affirmed to him, that the main operation of the law, as at present constituted, was to maintain the lawyers, and assist the rich in oppressing the poor. He added, that Cooke, then justice in Ireland, by proceeding in a summary and expeditious way, determined more causes in a week than Westminster Hall in a year. Ireland, said Cromwell, is a clean paper in that particular, and capable of being governed by such laws as shall be found most agreeable to justice; and these may be so impartially administered there, as to afford a good precedent to England itself, where, when we shall once perceive that property may be preserved at so easy and cheap a rate, we shall certainly never allow ourselves to be cheated and abused as we have been.

The clemency which Cromwell practised on so many occasions is closely allied to those moral and religious habits which he so remarkably cultivated. Even with regard to his campaign in Ireland, which was stained with sanguinary proceedings the most alien to his nature, he says, in his despatches, This bitterness, I am persuaded, will hereafter prevent much effusion of blood ; and adds, These are the satisfactory grounds to such actions, which otherwise cannot but work remorse and regret. He would have saved the life of Love, the minister, had it not been that he was necessarily absent from the capital ; and he told Manton that Hewit, who was executed three months before the death of the protector, should not have died, but for his invincible persistence in disingenuity and prevarication. He never allowed sentence of death to pass upon any Republican but Sindercombe, the assassin; and the short imprisonments that he imposed upon the majority of those, both Republicans and Royalists, who were accused of treason against him, and their early dismission, have had the effect with his enemies of inducing them to allege that he got up imaginary plots, to make it appear that his government was in greater danger than that to which it was actually exposed.

The clemency of Cromwell was doubly meritorious, inasmuch as he was so extensively hated. The consciousness of the ill-will of others is the most irresistible spur to blood-guiltiness and cruelty. It was this that made such monsters of Tiberius, and Caligula, and Nero. But, the soul of Cromwell was so well balanced, that

nothing could move it from its centre; and the knowledge that the eyes of nine tenths of those he governed were animated with hostility against him, could not for a moment destroy the serene and exemplary composure of his mind.

Another feature of the character of Cromwell proper to be recorded in this place, is his anxiety for the prosperous condition of letters and learning. We have seen in the eighth chapter of this book how firm was the stand he made against the mistaken fanatics who aimed at the destruction of the universities, and to what eminence science and polite literature consequently rose under him in those seminaries. He also founded a college at Durham for the convenience of students in the north, with a provost, four professors, and a certain number of fellows and tutors.* He settled a pension on Usher.† He applied to Cudworth to recommend to him proper persons to be employed in political and civil affairs.‡ He made a proposal to Dr. Meric Casaubon to write a history of the civil war.§ He issued his orders that the paper employed by Dr. Bryan Walton in printing his Polyglot Bible should be allowed to be imported duty free.‖ We have already spoken of the pensions and appointments bestowed by him on Milton, Marvel, Hartlip, and Biddle.

Reviewing all these qualities and dispositions in the Lord Protector of England, we should be almost disposed to place him in the number of the few excellent princes that have swayed a sceptre, were it not for the gross and unauthorized manner in which he climbed to this eminence, by forcibly dispersing the remains of the Long Parliament, that Parliament by which he had originally been intrusted with the command, and then promulgating a constitution, called the Government of the Commonwealth, which originated singly in the council of military officers. To this we must add, that he became the chief magistrate solely through his apostacy, and by basely deceiving and deserting the illustrious band of patriots with whom he had till that time been associated in the cause of liberty.

With the admirable dispositions above enumerated, Cromwell committed the grossest faults, left behind him a memory which few were disposed to cherish ; and all his projects, and his plans for a permanent settlement of the people of England under a system of rational liberty, and a dynasty of kings sprung from his own issue, were buried in the same grave with their author.

How happened this ? It was not for the want of talents and the most liberal intentions. But he was not free. He governed a people that was hostile to him. His reign, therefore, was a reign of experiments. He perpetually

* Peck's Memoirs of Cromwell, Appendix, No. 20.
† Bernard, chaplain to Usher, in a Life of him published during the protectorate, p. 103, 104, af. firms this, and says the money passed regularly through his hands. Parr, another of his chaplains, in a Life published under James the Second, denies it. Such is the voice of fame.
‡ Life of Cudworth, prefixed to Intellectual System, p. 8, 9.
§ Athenæ Oxonienses, vol. ii., p. 485, 486.
‖ This fact is mentioned in Walton's original Preface to his publication in 1657, but was suppressed afterward. The advantage was first given by the Council of State in 1652.

* Monarchy Asserted, p. 105, 106. † Ibid., p. 105.

did the thing he desired not to do, and was driven from one inconsistent and undesirable mode of proceeding, to another, as the necessity of the situation in which he was placed impelled him.

The nucleus of all the difficulties which Cromwell's administration had to struggle with is comprehended in the assertion of Whitlocke, confirmed by every page of this history, that the calling a "truly free Parliament was the ready way for the king's restoration." This consideration heightened the prejudices of all against him, and gave new vigour to the hatred of the Royalist, the man of rank, the Episcopalian, the fanatic, and the leveller.

The Commonwealthsmen had distinctly seen this, and for that reason had set themselves by every method they could devise to protract the dissolution of the Long Parliament, and, when that event should occur, to provide that the present sitting members should be authorized to take their places in the new Parliament without a fresh election. Cromwell, during the last period of the Long Parliament, did not see this, or pretended not to see it, and made this policy his ground of accusation against the Republicans, as if it had been dictated by no other motive than a grovelling ambition, and that they could not bear, having tasted the sweets of power, to resign it even for a moment, and place themselves on the same level as their fellow-citizens. But he had no sooner, by the strong hand of power, thrust them from their places, and made a clear space for any practicable system of representative government, than he was compelled to feel, and by his actions to confess, the truth of the maxim which had regulated their conduct.

The worst and most unjustifiable things that Cromwell did in his protectorate probably were the frequent imprisonments without reason assigned, that he authorized from political motives. When Harrison and others were repeatedly put in durance for a week or a month, and then dismissed without anything farther being done respecting them, it seems not unjust to conclude that this proceeding was by no means necessary, and that it afforded proof of some deficiency in Cromwell for holding the reins of a civil government. In enumerating the good qualities of the protector, we spoke of the short imprisonments he inflicted upon both Republicans and Royalists, as instances of his clemency. But they may also be considered in another point of view. They are the indications and the sallies of an arbitrary temper. Cromwell was drunk with the philtre of his power. The impulses of his mind were quick and impatient; and he decided to cut the Gordian knot of difficulties, being destitute of the moderation required to unloose it. The protector did not check himself in proceedings of this kind, when the question was of individuals against whom there existed a presumptive case. But it may be doubted whether he ever suffered an undue precipitation to interfere, in the cardinal questions upon which the safety of the state was suspended.

A great part of his proceedings, as has appeared in the progress of our narrative, even when they bore most the hue of an arbitrary character, were such as it was impossible for

him to omit, without striking a blow at the very root of the political power which now guided the helm of the state. The dissolution of the two Parliaments of 1654 and 1656 has appeared to be of this sort. His conduct in the lawsuit of Cony, and respecting the resignation of three of his judges, Rolle, Newdigate, and Thorpe, could not have been other than it was, without an immediate dissolution of the government.

Sometimes, however, his measures bore an arbitrary stamp, at the contemplation of which a cool judgment and an impartial mind feels itself called on to pause. The extraordinary proviso in the government of the Commonwealth, that the protector and council should have power to raise money for the public defence, and to promulgate laws and ordinances which should be of force till the Parliament might otherwise direct, was, perhaps, under all the circumstances of the then state of England, unavoidable. But the institution of the major-generals, and decimation of the income of the Royalists, were proceedings that we shall find it more difficult fully to vindicate. The capricious exclusion of one hundred of the representatives of the people at the meeting of the Parliament of 1656 was, perhaps, the most violent and astounding of all the acts of Cromwell. It may be that each of these acts was necessary to prevent the immediate dissolution of the government; and a necessity of this kind is the strongest of all arguments; but such a necessity the contemplative politician and the historian can scarcely at any time fully perceive; and the measures must, therefore, always remain impressed with at least a very equivocal character.

But all the actions of Cromwell of which we have here spoken, as they had the appearance of being dictated by the bare will of the chief magistrate, had a powerful tendency to increase the number of his disapprovers and enemies. The Royalists and the Republicans would probably never have been contented, and would have condemned whatever he did. But there was another set of political critics who had a very considerable influence in fixing finally the character of the protectorate. These were the persons calling themselves friends of liberty, whose favourite theme and object was a government according to law.

The period of the protectorate was eminently a period of accomplished lawyers. There have seldom existed in any epoch of English history men more profound in this science than St. John, and Glyn, and Maynard, and Hale: to whom we may add Whitlocke, Widdrington, and Rolle. The judges of Charles the Second sink into utter contempt in the comparison. Clarendon has sufficiently described those of the period that preceded, where he says, "The damage and mischief cannot be expressed that the crown and state sustained by the deserved reproach and infamy that attended the judges, who were made use of in the affair of ship-money and other the like acts of power."

It must be confessed, however, that the government of Cromwell was in a very imperfect degree a government according to law. A settlement was the thing wanted. The state had been wrenched from its basis. The institution of a king and a House of Lords had been abolished by the laws of February, 1649. It may, perhaps, be admitted by the man who looks down upon all ages and nations from the unclouded regions of philosophy, that as good a constitution may be found as the constitution of the government of England, as it previously existed in its elements, and as it has been practised since the year 1688. But a beneficent and sound constitution was the present desideratum, a constitution in which the spirit of liberty should be combined with the venerableness of order; and especially (which is implied in the very name constitution) a system in which sobriety and consistency should be principal features, a system in which every man should know what to look to and to expect, in which the rights of all should be distinctly recognised, and where they should be never, or in as few and slight instances as possible, impeached and violated. But the administration of Cromwell was a government of experiments. He began with the daring blow of dispersing the remains of the Long Parliament, the only legitimate authority at that time existing in England. The power of the state by that act devolved into the hands of his council of officers. They nominated an assembly of one hundred and forty-four persons, arbitrarily styled representatives for the different counties of England, for Ireland, Scotland, and Wales, but really chosen by the council of officers only. This assembly is known in history by the name of Barebone's Parliament. It was, after a sitting of somewhat more than five months, brought to an irregular termination. The council of officers then resumed the power of the state, and, four days after, produced an instrument, entitled the Government of the Commonwealth, by which Cromwell, having waived the title of king, was constituted Lord Protector of England, a Parliament regularly chosen was directed to meet in the autumn of that year, and afterward once in every three years, and in the mean time Cromwell and his council were authorized to raise money, and to make such laws and ordinances as the public welfare might require. The Parliament sat at the appointed time, and after a session somewhat shorter than that of Barebone, during which it ran in almost all things counter to the purposes of the protector, was suddenly dissolved without completing any one measure for the maturing which Parliaments in this country have usually been summoned. A second Parliament was assembled after an interval of twenty months; and the first occurrence that signalized their meeting was Cromwell's exclusion of one hundred of its members by his sole authority. This Parliament, however, though with diminished numbers, entered on the most important functions, gave to the protector a species of legal authority, and decreed the existence of all future Parliaments in the form of two houses. Meanwhile, the experiment of a second house of the Legislature seemed to turn out unfortunately, and led to another example of an abrupt dissolution, a proceeding which, especially in critical times, must in a considerable degree tend to weaken the whole fabric of the government.

The result of all this was most unfortunate for the friends of a Republican government, and for those who desired the establishment of mon-

archy in a new race of kings, and most favourable for the adherents of the house of Stuart. The obvious inference to draw from these perpetual vicissitudes was, England will never be well, nor her government fixed on a secure basis, till the restoration of the exiled family. Sober and moderate men of various classes in the community became daily more favourable to, or more fixed in the opinion, that the old constitution of government by king, lords, and commons, as it had prevailed ever since the days of Edward the First, must be set up again.

What would have been the result, if Cromwell's life had been prolonged to the established period of human existence, or ten years longer than it was, it may be allowed, and, indeed, it is almost unavoidable, that we should inquire. His character perpetually rose in the estimation of his subjects. He appeared to them every day more like a king, and less like the plain and unambitious descendant of the Cromwells of Hinchinbrook and Ramsey. His abilities were every hour more evident and confessed. At first he showed like a presumptuous demagogue, like the man in the Bible, who began to build, but was not able to finish. He was, such was the judgment that in the beginning was passed upon him by many, a bold, bad man, a common disturber and incendiary, well qualified to throw everything into confusion, and to leave no memory but that of calamity and desolation behind him. His capacity for government became daily more unquestionable. He looked into everything; he provided for everything; he stood, himself unmoved, yet causing every threatening and tempestuous phenomenon by which he was assailed to fly before him. Distinguished as were his talents for governing from the hour he assumed the sceptre, they daily became more consummate. He felt his situation, and his ideas accommodated themselves to whatever it required. He dwelt at home;* he scarcely at any time dismissed the character and the views that befitted the first magistrate of a great country. Fluctuating and uncertain as his government had been hitherto, he deeply felt the necessity of its being rendered unalterable and unchanged. This had been especially his view in calling the Parliament of 1656. Ill satisfied as he was with the tenure of his government as it originated with the council of officers, he determined to obtain for it a legislative sanction. It was with this purpose that he was induced to concur in the otherwise unpalatable provisions, that no member of the House of Commons should henceforth be moved from his seat but by the will of the House itself, that no law should be promulgated but by parliamentary authority, and that another house of legislature should be constituted to stand between the chief executive magistrate and the representatives of the people. It was with the same purpose that he desired the title of king. He, no doubt, was profoundly convinced of the truth of what he had said to Desborough and Fleetwood, that the diadem was but a feather in a man's cap, to please children of whatever stature and age. But he, at the same time, felt the truth of what was alleged by the lawyers, that the name and the powers of a king are in-

---

Tecum habita.—Persius.

extricably bound up in our laws. And he saw that the assumption of the crown was the only sure method for obtaining that favourite purpose of his thoughts, the entailing the chief magistracy in the line of his descendants.

The system of Cromwell's government was more consistent and of greater steadiness, as it related to other countries, than his own. He gave prosperity to Scotland; he gave tranquillity to Ireland. He was, perhaps, himself superior to the contagion of prejudices. But he saw that government could not be carried on among the people with whom he had to do but with a certain accommodation to prejudices. His authority, as it regarded foreign countries, had always been great; but it had lately been greater than ever. The homage that had been paid him by the court of France was truly surprising; and he had, in the course of the last campaign, disarmed the hostility of Spain, and rendered the threatened invasion impossible. The government of England had never been so completely freed from the fear of all enemies, both from within and within, as at the period of the death of Cromwell. In a word, we are almost compelled to conclude that, if he had lived ten years longer, the system of his rule would continually have grown more firm and substantial, and the purposes and ideas to the accomplishment of which he had devoted all the powers of his soul would not have been antiquated and annihilated almost as soon as they were deprived of his energies to maintain them.

It was not difficult for a sagacious mind, rising above the atmosphere of prejudice, to foresee, from the death of Cromwell, that the restoration of Charles the Second was inevitable. The details of what occurred in the interval may at some time be given; but whether by the writer of these volumes under the title of a History of the Restoration, is altogether uncertain.—C.

No. XIX.

CHARACTERISTICS OF THE NONCONFORMISTS OF THE SEVENTEENTH AND NINETEENTH CENTURIES.

(From the London Congregational Magazine for February, 1844.)

As it is now very frequently asserted that the Nonconformists of England have changed their opinions on Christian doctrine and ecclesiastical polity, it may be interesting and seasonable to take a rapid historical survey of the characteristics, both of their ministers and people, two centuries ago and in the present age; which may assist the reader to ascertain what amount of truth there is in that assertion, and how far it reflects on the piety and intelligence of those to whom it applies.

The existence of Nonconformity in this country must be dated from the commencement of the reign of Queen Elizabeth, whose taste and temper led her to procure the first Act of Uniformity. That legislative measure, which not only prescribed a uniformity of Common Prayer and service in the Church and administration of the sacraments, but also empowered the queen "to ordain and publish such farther ceremonies and rites as may be for the advancement of God's glory, and edifying of his Church, and

the reverence of Christ's holy mysteries and sacraments," passed through Parliament in the month of April, 1559, and received the royal assent without any sanction from the convocation of the clergy—a circumstance which led Heath, the Archbishop of York, to observe, " that not only the orthodox, but even the Arian emperors ordered that points of faith should be examined by councils; and Gallio by the light of nature knew that a civil judge ought not to meddle with matters of religion."[*] Fond of pompous ceremonies, and most tenacious of royal prerogatives, Elizabeth was little disposed to consult the feelings of those who desired to see the work of reformation from popery carried forward, and who longed to witness the ecclesiastical polity of the country in better agreement with the genius and pattern of the New Testament. Her haughty temper led her to maintain with unyielding firmness the supremacy her father had usurped, and throughout her long reign, to punish the unhappy Nonconformist, whether papist or Puritan, who dared to question it, with a severity that will ever be a reproach on her character and government. Her Stuart successors inherited all her Tudor notions, and resisted with equal dislike, though not with equal success, the many attempts that were made for civil and ecclesiastical reformation.

A combination of disastrous measures, throughout the reigns of James I. and Charles I., at length brought on a civil war, which terminated in the overthrow of the prelacy, and the decapitation of the king. That impolitic and unconstitutional measure was, however, followed by a degree of religious liberty before unknown; and while we must deplore many events that transpired during those twenty years of civil conflict and constrained legislation, yet it must be regarded by all impartial persons as a period eminently favourable to religious freedom, biblical learning, and true piety. The Puritan ministers who had outlived the cruelties of the preceding reigns now taught from the pulpit, the press, and the professor's chair, those opinions which they had derived from primitive Christianity as exhibited in the Word of God.

While, however, there prevailed among them a very general agreement respecting Christian doctrines, as was demonstrated by their unanimity on the doctrinal articles of the confession of divines at Westminster, yet there existed considerable diversity of opinion upon all the questions of church polity and discipline. Their grand object, however, was to diffuse among the people a knowledge of the truth as it is in Jesus; and it is probable that religion never was in a more prosperous state in this country than during the period of their unrestricted ministrations. The restoration of the Stuart family to the British throne was quickly followed by the second Act of Uniformity, which ejected from their livings more than two thousand ministers, who, on various considerations, chose rather to expose themselves and their families to all the inconveniences of poverty and persecution, than to sacrifice their consciences on the altar of a state religion. These venerable men were the fathers of nonconformity in the

* Neal's Puritans, chap. iv.

seventeenth century, and it is the characteristics of them and their people that we propose to compare with those of the Nonconformists of the present age.

In proceeding to portray the Nonconformist ministers of the seventeenth century, we may observe, that time has not destroyed the efforts of art to preserve, for the gratification of their posterity, the venerated features of those extraordinary men. We gaze upon their portraits, and imagine that we behold in the countenances of the Puritans and the confessors of Bartholomew's Day the traces of inflexible firmness protracted labour, and unusual suffering; while in the pictures of the later Nonconformists we discover the fine intelligence, the philosophic wisdom, the poignant wit, and the courtly bearing, which were developed by their controversies, and demanded by their associations. But it is not with their appearance, but with their characters that we have to do; and we shall attempt to describe them.

1. *As Divines.*—Besides the advantages which they derived from having prosecuted their studies either in the British or Continental universities, at a period when the spirit of the Reformation had just unsealed the fountains of learning, and had cast therein the salt of godliness, by which they were sweetened and sanctified; besides these advantages, the peculiar circumstances of their times were highly favourable to their eminence in theological learning. While civil war desolated the provinces, and a deadly pestilence wasted the population of our cities, and persecution forbade their approach to any market town, they were necessarily shut up to the seclusion of their studies for years together. The activity of minds like theirs could only find relief in the exercises of extraordinary devotion, and in interesting efforts of intellectual labour. To solve the problems of Christian casuistry, to sound the depths of theological truth, to develop the secrets of Christian experience, to illustrate the duties of a life of godliness, were the business of their days and nights through many dreary years. Often, no doubt, they looked forth from their secluded homes upon the giddy multitudes who were living in pleasure, and were dead while they lived, with tender compassion, and longed for permission to beseech them in Christ's stead to be reconciled to God. But an all-wise, though to them inscrutable Providence, had determined that their profound views of Divine truth, their rich experience of the power and grace of Christ, and their elevated maxims of practical godliness, should not all evaporate in the routine labours of the ministry, but should be condensed like some precious essence, and preserved in their works to refresh and gladden succeeding generations. In those works our fathers have bequeathed to us a rich inheritance. In the expository labours of Ainsworth and Hildersham, of Cradock and Greenhill, of Caryl and Borroughs, of Gouge and Owen, of Henry and Poole, what stores have we of sound criticism, and faithful interpretation of the sacred text! While the writings of Bates and Howe, Owen and Baxter, Manton and Flavel, Charnock and Goodwin, with a multitude of their coadjutors, have supplied the text-books of most who, in succeeding times, have wished to combine harmonious views of evangelical truth with

an experience of its power in consoling the heart and sanctifying the life. Most blessed men! Your watchings and prayers have not been in vain. Multitudes, since you entered into the joy of your Lord, have learned from your labours the truth as it is in Jesus; and while the works of licentious poets and scoffing philosophers are accumulating for them, from age to age, a fearful amount of retribution, it is well for you that the fruits of your assiduous studies, painful-sufferings, and persevering prayers continue to multiply from age to age, and will at length be seen in an innumerable company turned by your toils to righteousness, among whom you shall shine forth as stars forever and ever.

2. *As Preachers.*—On this part of their character there exists a great diversity of evidence. Were you to consult the sermons of Dr. South, you would find that he described their preaching "as crude incoherences, nauseous tautologies, and saucy familiarities with God." He will tell you that " Latin was with them a mortal crime; and Greek, instead of being owned for the language of the Holy Ghost, was looked upon as a sin against it; so that, in a word, they had all the confusion of Babel among them, without the diversity of tongues." But this was Dr. South. Happily, we possess testimony of a very different class. In "The Directory for the Public Worship of God," &c., put forth by the Assembly of Divines, there is a section on preaching the Word, from which we shall see that a very different method was recommended by the preachers at Westminster.

" It is presupposed (according to the rules for ordination) that the minister of Christ is in some good measure gifted for so weighty a service, by his skill in the original languages, and in such arts and sciences as are handmaids unto divinity, by his knowledge in the whole body of theology, but most of all in the Holy Scriptures; having his senses and heart exercised in them above the common sort of believers; and by the illumination of God's Spirit, and other gifts of edification, which (together with reading and studying of the Word) he ought still to seek by prayer, and an humble heart, resolving to admit and receive any truth not yet attained, whenever God shall make it known unto him. All which he is to make use of, and improve, in his private preparations, before he deliver in public what he hath provided."

" He is not to rest in general doctrine, although never so much cleared and confirmed, but to bring it home to special use, by application to his hearers; which, albeit it prove a work of great difficulty to himself, requiring much prudence, zeal, and meditation, and to the natural and corrupt man will be very unpleasant; yet he is to endeavour to perform it in such a manner that his auditors may feel the Word of God to be quick and powerful, and a discerner of the thoughts and intents of the heart; and that if any unbeliever or ignorant person be present, he may have the secrets of his heart made manifest, and give glory to God."

" But the servant of Christ, whatever his method be, is to perform his whole ministry,

"1. Painfully, not doing the work of the Lord negligently.

"2. Plainly, that the meanest may understand, delivering the truth, not in the enticing word's of man's wisdom, but in demonstration of the Spirit and of power, lest the cross of Christ should be made of none effect ; abstaining, also, from an unprofitable use of unknown tongues, strange phrases, and cadences of sounds and words, sparingly citing sentences of ecclesiastical or other human writers, ancient or modern, be they never so elegant.

"3. Faithfully, looking at the honour of Christ, the conversion, edification, and salvation of the people, not at his own gain or glory, keeping nothing back which may promote those holy ends, giving to every one his own portion, and bearing indifferent respect unto all, without neglecting the meanest, or sparing the greatest in their sins.

"4. Wisely, framing all his doctrines, exhortations, and especially his reproofs, in such a manner as may be most likely to prevail, snowing all due respect to each man's person and place, and not mixing his own passion or bitterness.

"5. Gravely, as becometh the Word of God, shunning all such gesture, voice, and expressions as may occasion the corruptions of men to despise him and his ministry."

"6. With loving affection, that the people may see all coming from his godly zeal and hearty desire to do them good. And,

"7. As taught of God, and persuaded in his own heart, that all that he teaches is the truth of Christ, and walking before his flock as an example to them in it ; earnestly, both in private and public, recommending his labours to the blessing of God, and watchfully looking to himself and the flock, whereof the Lord hath made him overseer ; so shall the doctrine of truth be preserved uncorrupt, many souls converted and built up, and himself receive manifold comforts of his labours even in this life, and afterward the crown of glory laid up for him in the world to come."

Daniel De Foe himself, one of the ablest and most captivating writers of which our country can boast, has said of them, " They preached sound doctrine without jingle or trifling ; they studied what they delivered ; they *preached* their sermons rather than read them in the pulpit ; they spoke from the heart to the heart ; nothing like our cold ; declaiming way, entertained now as a mode, and read with a flourish, under the ridiculous notion of being methodical; but what they conceived by the assistance of the great Inspirer of his servants, the Holy Spirit, they delivered with a becoming gravity, a decent fervour, an affectionate zeal, and a ministerial authority, suited to the dignity of the office and majesty of the work ; and, as a testimony of this, their practical works left behind them are a living specimen of what they performed among us. Such are the large volumes of divinity remaining of Dr. Goodwin, Dr. Manton, Dr. Owen, Dr. Bates, Mr. Charnock, Mr. Poole, Mr. Clarkson, Mr. Baxter, Mr. Flavel, Mr. Howe, and others too numerous to mention."*

How perseveringly they preached under all the discouragements of their position, ought not to be overlooked : they endured extraordinary fatigue, and exposed themselves to no common danger, that they might preach Christ to their

* Present State of Parties; p. 289, 290.

neglected countrymen ; and in many a barn or in many a wood, have they at the midnight hour addressed a hungry multitude on the truths of the Gospel. The city of London, too, when suffering under the successive calamities of plague and fire, witnessed their compassionate zeal for perishing souls. At the height of the pestilence, ten thousand persons died in a single week ; and under that appalling scourge, the Episcopal clergy yielded to the almost universal panic, and fled from their pulpits, and abandoned their poor parishioners to their fate. But the Nonconformist ministers, though proscribed, resolved to visit the sick, relieve the poor, and to preach in the forsaken pulpits ere the people died. And when the devouring fire had reduced the city to a smouldering heap, and most of the churches were involved in the common ruin, regardless of the threatening penalties, they obtained places in which to preach to the inquiring multitudes, who, aroused by successive calamities, were constrained to ask, 'What must we do to be saved ?'*

3. *As Nonconformists.*—While a happy uniformity of sentiment respecting the great verities of the Gospel prevailed among them, there was no little diversity of opinion upon subjects connected with church government. The great majority of them were Presbyterians, who earnestly wished to see established by law a system of church polity analogous to that of Scotland or

* " The silenced ministers had till this time preached very privately, and but to a few. But when the plague grew hot, and the ministers in the city churches fled and left their flocks in the time of their extremity, several of the Nonconformists, pitying the distressed and dying people, that had none to call the impenitent to repentance, nor to help them to prepare for another world, nor to comfort them in their terrors, when about ten thousand died in a week, were convinced that no obedience to the laws of any mortal man whosoever could justify their neglecting men's souls and bodies in such extremities ; and, therefore, they wished to stay with the people, enter the forsaken pulpits, though prohibited, and give them what assistance they could under such an awakening providence, and also visit the sick and get what relief they could for the poor, especially such as were shut up.

" The persons that set upon this work were Mr. Thomas Vincent, Mr. Chester, Mr. Janeway, Mr. Turner, Mr. Grimes, Mr. Franklyn, and some others. Those often heard them one day who were sick the next, and quickly died. The face of death did so awake preachers and hearers, that the former exceeded themselves in lively, fervent preaching, and the latter heard with a peculiar ardour and attention ; and, through the blessing of God, many were converted from their carelessness, impenitence, and youthful lusts and vanities, and religion took that hold on the people's hearts as could never afterward be loosed.

" This unhappy fire (of London) made the way of the Nonconformists yet the plainer to them ; for the churches being burned, and the parish ministers gone, for want of places and maintenance, the people's necessities became unquestionable ; for they had no places now to worship God in, save a few churches that were left standing, which would not hold any considerable part of them ; wherefore the Nonconformists opened public meeting-houses, and were very full. And as circumstances then stood, to have forbid the people to hear them had been, in effect, to forbid them all public worship of God, and require them to live like atheists:"—*Calamy's Abridgment of Baxter's Life and Times*, vol. i., p. 130, 135.

Geneva. Some of them were the friends of a modified Episcopacy, and would have cheerfully sat down under a system such as Archbishop Usher had proposed; while others were Erastians, who would not have quarrelled with any ecclesiastical polity that would not impose its usages upon their conscientious observance. The most active, though certainly not the largest body, were the Independents, or, as they preferred to be called, the Congregational brethren, and who principally maintained those opinions which prevailed among ourselves. With this class we may include the Baptist brethren, and many others, who were then contemptuously called Sectaries, and some of whom unquestionably held mystical and eccentric opinions, but who had learned at least one lesson, at that time known only to a few—how to distinguish between spiritual and civil power, and to define, with something like correctness, the appropriate sphere of each. Between these advocates of opposing systems of church order there were no affinities but such as their love of the Gospel, and their unaffected integrity and honour supplied. What the heat of Christian love could not accomplish, the fire of persecution effected, and these various bodies were fused into one mass by that law which made them Nonconformists. It is, perhaps, desirable to recite the leading requirements of the Act of Uniformity, in order to ascertain what great principles were actually avowed by their resignation of their ecclesiastical benefices, and to what extent we are entitled to name the illustrious *two thousand* as our fathers in Nonconformity.

That act required: 1. That they should virtually renounce their ordination by presbyters, and submit to be episcopally ordained. 2. That they should declare their unfeigned assent and consent to all and every thing in the Book of Common Prayer, and administration of the sacraments, and other rites and ceremonies of the Church; and they were required to subscribe, *ex animo*, these words: " That the Book of Common Prayer, and of ordaining bishops, priests, and deacons, containeth in it nothing contrary to the Word of God; and that it may be lawfully used; and that they themselves would use the Form in the said books prescribed, in public prayer, and administration of the sacraments, and no other." 3. That they should take oath of canonical obedience, and swear subjection to their ordinary, according to the canons of the Church. 4. That they should abjure the solemn League and Covenant, and declare it an unlawful oath, and not obligatory on those who took it; and lastly, 5. That they should declare that it is not lawful, upon any pretence whatever, to take up arms against the king.

Now it must be conceded, respecting a law of such ample and varied enactments, and for the calm consideration of which no adequate time was allowed, that it is not possible accurately to determine in what degree the whole body of Nonconformists were affected by its requirements. Some might object to all, while others might only object to one or two of its impositions. As Mr. Richard Baxter, however, may be considered as the leader and representative of the moderate and more numerous portion of the ejected ministers, we may fairly gather from his book, "The English Nonconformity

VOL. II.—S s s

truly Stated and Argued," what were the great points of objection with him and his brethren. We learn on his authority that they were then decidedly opposed to arbitrary power, and would not swear that it is always unlawful to take up arms against the king. They were fully convinced of the validity of ordination by presbyters, and would not renounce their own ministerial character, nor virtually disown the ordination of their brethren of the Reformed churches in general. They were familiar with the exercise of free prayer, and were reluctant to have that gift superseded by an unvarying formulary. They had specific objection to the Book of Common Prayer, especially to the services of baptism and the burial of the dead, and also to the Athanasian Creed. They saw that extensive church reform was necessary, and, therefore could not abandon the solemn League and Covenant. But the greatest principle they asserted by their noble sacrifice was the supreme authority of conscience in matters of religion, and the lawfulness of refusing obedience in matters of faith and practice to the impositions of the civil power. They generally believed in the lawfulness of a state religion, and, consequently, were not dissenters from the principle of an establishment, but objected to certain things imposed and practised by it. This led many of the most eminent of the ejected ministers to attend the public services of the Church of England, and frequently to commune at her altars.[*]

* The Rev. John Humfrey, an ejected minister, writing to Ralph Thoresby, of Leeds, on the subject of occasional conformity, says :

" I will tell you first my own judgment and practice, which is perhaps singular. There is our stated communion and our occasional communion. Our moderate Nonconformist Presbyterians are for their stated communion with the congregations where they are pastors or members, but they will join in their parish churches for occasional communion, or else they think themselves guilty of schism. Thus Dr. Bates does some time in the year receive the sacrament in his parish, and Mr. Baxter did often in the parish I am. But as for myself, I declare my stated communion to be with the parish (where we have a very ingenious, diligent, and exemplary doctor for our minister), and my occasional communion with the Nonconformist meetings, where I go sometimes ; and sometimes I am called to preach. In short, I am a Nonconformist minister, but a conformist parishioner." This is confirmed by the testimony of Dr. John Sharp, archbishop of York, who, writing to Thoresby on the same subject, says, " Mr. Humfrey, I am sure, will vindicate your practice of communicating with us in the holy sacrament, because it is what himself doth, both as to prayers and sacraments, and so did Mr. Baxter ; for so long as he lived in my parish (St. Giles's in the Fields, 1677), he seldom failed, when he was well, of coming to our prayers and sermons twice every Lord's day ; and receiving the communion with us, kneeling at the rails, once or twice every year ; this I speak of my own knowledge."—*Letters addressed to R. Thoresby*, vol. i., p. 274, 321.

Mr. Baxter's own words may be quoted to complete the evidence. " I constantly join with the church in common prayer; I communicate in the Lord's Supper with the Church of England; I exhort the people to communion, and I go into the church from my own house in the people's view, that I may persuade them by my example as well as my doctrine."

Dr. John Owen was of another mind, and published " An answer unto Two Questions, with Twelve Arguments against any conformity to worship not of

Dr. John Owen, however, and the Congregational brethren in general, questioned the lawfulness of these acts of occasional conformity, and did not hesitate to gather separate churches of believers wherever they were prepared to do so.

4. *As Philanthropists.*—It has sometimes been insinuated that the Nonconformist ministers of the seventeenth century were deficient in that expansive zeal and benevolence which the love of Christ in the heart invariably inspires. A candid view of their position, and that of our country too at that period, would at once dispel this notion, and show that, according to their opportunities, they were as vigorous and devoted as any of their descendants. The commercial enterprise and the colonial empire of England were then in their infancy. The few settlements we then possessed in the West Indies and North America were not contiguous to any great heathen nation. The claims of the North American Indians, however, were not overlooked by the Puritan ministers, when they had influence over the minds and purses of their countrymen. During the Commonwealth they formed a society for the promotion of the Gospel ; and Eliot, the apostle of the Indians, was one of their first and most successful missionaries. After the ejectment, many of these confessors thought of the claims of the heathen. Baxter, writing to Eliot, says, " Though our sins have separated us from the people of our love and care, and deprived us of all public liberty of the Gospel of our Lord, I greatly rejoice in the liberty, help, and success which Christ has so long vouchsafed you in his work. There is no man on earth whose work I think more honourable and comfortable than yours ; to propagate the Gospel and kingdom of Christ into those dark parts of the world is better work than our devouring and hating one another. There are many here who would be ambitious of being your fellow-labourers, but that they are informed you have access to no greater number of Indians that you yourself and your present assistants are able to teach. There are many here, I conjecture, who would be glad to go anywhere—to Persians, Tartarians, Indians, or any unbelieving nation, to propagate the Gospel."* In zeal, also, for the extension of the Gospel at home, they were fully equal to them that have succeeded them, not excepting the leaders of Methodism themselves. Time would fail to tell of their lengthened itinerancies, and of the perseverance with which they taught the people at the hazard of their liberty, if not their lives.

Nor were they less willing to exert themselves in more tranquil times. When the neglected condition of Wales was made known, an association was formed on the most catholic principles, in 1674, to establish schools, and to circulate the Scriptures and other religious books in that principality. The names of Bates and

Baxter, of Gouge and Firmin, are associated with those of Tillotson, Outram, Partrick, and Stillingfleet, to accomplish this benevolent object.

It is an ancient proverb, founded upon obvious laws, " like priest, like people," and it was, therefore, humanly impossible that such as adhered to their persecuted ministers should fail to imbibe something of their zeal for doctrinal and practical religion. The families of the Nonconformists of the seventeenth century were trained up to write and repeat the sermons they heard, to attend lengthened fasts and family devotions, and to understand most of the theological questions of their times. The strictness of their manners accord with the sternness of their principles, and thus their rigid observance of the Sabbath, and their entire withdrawal from frivolous amusements, exposed them to the ridicule and contempt of worldly minds. Their liberality was proved by the contributions which were made for the relief of the persecuted Piedmontese, and for the support of Christian missions to the Indians of New-England.*

After the Nonconformist ministers had made their costly sacrifices, it was expected that persecution and reproach would break their spirits, destroy their influence, and extinguish their race. By far the greater part of the twenty-six years that elapsed between the return of the Stuarts and the Revolution were years of unpitying severity and cruel wrong, both to them and to their people. Mr. J. White collected a list of the names of sixty thousand Nonconformists who suffered in various ways for their principles from the Restoration to the Revolution. Nearly eight thousand perished in noxious dungeons during Charles II.'s reign, besides those who died in bitter exile from their native land.

It is computed that within three years property to the amount of two millions of money was extorted from these faithful confessors, by all the forms of legal robbery and oppression ; and happy would they have been could they have purchased at such a price the liberty of worshipping God, according to the dictates of their own minds.

Persecution, however, rarely accomplishes its object, for it mostly exerts a conservative influence in favour of the system intended to be repressed. Such was the effect of high-church malignity in the present instance. The people pitied the suffering Nonconformists, admired their holy, self-denying lives, and were thankful for their constant devotedness to genuine Protestantism ; so that they, at length, formed the strength of that party who narrowly watched the popish tendencies and priestly intrigues of the restored Stuarts, and had their full share in consummating that work of England's freedom at the glorious Revolution, which they or their fathers commenced in what Clarendon calls " the great rebellion."

But it is now time that we should speak of the Nonconformists of our own age. As those of the seventeenth century, were di-

Divine institution."—(Works, xxi., 519, 536.) At a somewhat later period of the history of nonconformity, the Rev. John Howe vindicated occasional conformity from the attacks of Daniel Defoe. That powerful writer replied to Mr. Howe, which brought the Rev. James Owen, of Shrewsbury, into the field, and several other writers *pro et contra* on the same subject.   * Orme's Life of R. Baxter, p. 166.

* " The protector," says Whitlock, " appointed a solemn day of humiliation to be kept, and a large contribution to be gathered throughout the nation." The sum raised was £38,000, besides £2000 which Oliver himself contributed. The New-England mission had property to the amount of £700 per annum.

vided into several classes, so their descendants continue to retain their denominational distinctions. There exists at present, however, a far greater uniformity of sentiment on questions of church polity than obtained among the fathers of nonconformity.

The Baptist and Congregational denominations maintain nearly the same principles of ecclesiastical government; and many of the English Presbyterian body, who have unhappily departed from orthodox opinions, are much more like Independents than the Kirk of Scotland in their affairs. The evangelical Nonconformists alone have now a much larger body of ministers than were ejected on Bartholomew's day; while the principles of virtual nonconformity have been spread and acted upon by a large and influential body, once in close relationship with the Church of England, but now declaring its separate and independent church existence.; while the numerous offshoots of Wesleyan Methodism have become still more decidedly dissenting in their principles and practices. Thus, within a century and a half, there have grown up separate communities of evangelical nonconforming Christians, who, in the aggregate number of their congregations, it is probable, are fully equal to that of the Episcopal Church itself, and are constantly extending their influence throughout the land. Our remarks, however, must be restricted to those who avow this nonconformity, and will apply to modern dissenting ministers and churches, excepting that inconsiderable portion of the whole body who profess Unitarian opinions.

The theological sentiments of the living, working portion of modern Nonconformists, are decidedly influenced by the doctrinal views which were maintained by their Puritan forefathers. The fall and ruin of man; the deity and incarnation of the Son of God; the priestly office and atoning sacrifice of the Saviour; justification by faith, and salvation by free and sovereign grace; the work, power, and grace of the Holy Spirit; the regeneration of the human heart, and the vital, experimental nature of true godliness—these, and their associated and subordinate truths, continue not only to be the creed, but the consolation of the churches. In these principles the candidates for the pastoral office in the various dissenting colleges are trained; and their acceptance among the churches greatly depends on the prominence they give to those great doctrines of the Reformation. In the public worship of modern Nonconformists, hymns are sung in accordance with those of the first Christians, " Carmenque Christo quasi Deo dicere;" and their free prayers are characterized by frequent invocations on the name of the Lord Jesus. Within a few years new editions of the voluminous works of Owen, Baxter, Howe, Bates, Charnock, Flavel, Heywood, and other Bartholomew confessors, have been published; while the smaller treatises of these illustrious men, and of their contemporaries, are continually issuing from the press in every variety of form, to meet the increasing demand for their doctrinal, experimental, and practical writings. These, with similar facts, are sufficient to put to shame the oft-repeated and designing slander that our churches are corrupted by the Socinian heresy.

Their opinions on Church polity, as we have said, are far more settled and uniform than were those of the early Nonconformists. It is now almost universally agreed among at least the older nonconforming bodies, "that the power of the Christian Church is purely spiritual, and should in no way be corrupted with temporal or civil power." "That Christ is the only head of the Church, and the officers of each church under him are ordained to administer his laws impartially to all; and that their only appeal in all questions touching their religious faith and practice is to the Holy Scriptures;"* that the ministers of religion should be supported, not by the imposts of civil governments, but by the free-will offerings of the people who enjoy their services; that, consequently, national establishments of Christianity are calculated to deteriorate and impede the religion they propose to extend.

It is for the maintenance of these opinions that we are reproached with having fallen from the sentiments of our forefathers, and adopted "the various novelties and fancies which arose about the time of the French Revolution." It was, indeed, about that time that there appeared from the pen of the venerable William Graham, of Newcastle, "A Review of Ecclesiastical Establishments in Europe," fraught with these sentiments; deduced, however, not from the writings of French encyclopædists, but from the pages of inspired Scripture.

But the illustrious John Locke recognised the truth and justice of these opinions, when he prepared the draught of a Constitution for the State of South Carolina in 1682; and where he learned them may be fairly gathered from the testimony of a late distinguished statesman and philosopher, Sir James Mackintosh : " Educated, then, among the English dissenters, during the short period of their political ascendency, Mr. Locke early imbibed that deep piety and ardent love of liberty which actuated that body of men ; and he probably imbibed, also, in their schools the disposition to metaphysical inquiries, which has everywhere accompanied the Calvinistic theology. Sects founded on the right of private judgment, naturally tend to purify themselves from intolerance, and in time learn to respect in others the freedom of thought, to the exercise of which they owe their own existence. By the Independent divines who were his instructers, our philosopher was taught those principles of religious liberty which they were the first to disclose to the world." Let those who doubt the existence of these opinions in the time of the Commonwealth, read Milton's treatise " On the Means to Remove Hirelings out of the Church," and they will find it contains a noble argument for the full application of the voluntary principle. But admit these to be novel opinions, are they, therefore, necessarily erroneous? The progress of our views on ecclesiastical freedom is not equal to the advance which our countrymen have made towards political and commercial liberty. The expulsion of the Stuarts, the accession of William and Mary, the Bill of Rights, the Act of Settlement, and the long series of concessions to popular claims which have followed those

* Declaration of Faith and Order, &c., of Congregational Churches.

great events, have necessarily resulted from great principles, which, by the good providence of God, were imbodied in the constitutional maxims and ancient usages of our Saxon ancestors. The germes of our liberties were there, though it required the experience and the sufferings of ages to develop and mature them. So we believe our church principles were prescribed and practised by the apostles of Jesus, though it has required the labours and sufferings of sixteen centuries to demonstrate the wisdom and the rectitude of acting upon them.

It is also alleged that modern Nonconformists have deteriorated in domestic and personal religion. In comparing their habits with those of their ancestors, there are shades of difference to be seen sufficient to justify this remark, and yet the present generation may not have retrograded. The fact is, that various causes combined to produce a frightful declension in the seriousness of the Nonconformists a century ago. Job Orton, in one of his letters, says, "It grieves me to hear of a growing spirit of levity and dissipation among the people, which is very unfavourable to the interest of religion and a comfort of ministers, and which every good minister should exert all his powers to restrain; though, unhappily, some of our divines have set themselves to plead for such a compliance with fashionable amusements, as tends to the utter ruin of our interest, and, I fear, will be greatly injurious to the best interests of particular persons. Strange that all our learned and wise fathers should be so wretchedly mistaken, in labouring to keep their people from ' the course of this world,' and the love of pleasure and dissipation. But we foolishly throw off our fathers' real excellences with their old fashions and peculiar sentiments, and have not either judgment to see the difference between them, or not resolution enough to withstand the customs and fashions of the age."

The blessed revival of religion, which commenced with the labours of the Methodists, and which the writings of Watts and Doddridge so greatly promoted, quickened the languid piety of the old Independent and Baptist churches; and thus, at the present time, they are found in a greatly revived state as compared with that of the eve of Methodism, although they may not be equal to the spirituality and devotedness of their eminent forefathers.

Beneficence towards mankind will supply a test of our piety towards God; and the Nonconformists of the present day have been among the earliest and most steady advocates of all those noble efforts by which the sufferings of humanity are ameliorated, and the ignorance of mankind dispelled. For the abolition of the slave-trade and slavery in the West, and for the suppression of infanticide, sutteeism, and other cruelties of the Hindoos in the East, they have pleaded in common with spiritual Christians of other communities with successful importunity. When the education of the people had been entirely neglected, and the Sunday School system, projected by a benevolent Episcopalian, languished in the hands of worthless hirelings, the Nonconformist churches supplied that voluntary agency which rescued the project from extinction, and carried its blessings through every district of the nation. In the associations

for the diffusion of Bibles and other religious books, modern Nonconformists have felt themselves happy to unite with great and good men of other communions, and have borne their full share in the labours of the study and the platform, in pecuniary contributions, and personal agency for the translation and circulation of the Holy Scriptures and religious tracts at home and abroad. The duty of missions to the heathen has been extensively recognised by the Nonconformist churches during the last half century, and the claims of our countrymen in neglected districts, at home and in the British colonies, have not been overlooked.

These diversified schemes of Christian philanthropy could not be permanently sustained but by a large substratum of real religion. Excitement may do much for a temporary object, but a work that is to be continued through long years of patient and apparently unproductive labour can alone be upheld by principles that rule the conscience and regulate the life. Still we have need to be on our guard as to the outdoor habits which religion has assumed. It was the devotional retirement of our forefathers that gave firmness to their convictions, and nerved their souls to deeds of moral heroism. In the light of the eternal throne they beheld the utter vanity of all earthly things, and saw that to "win Christ, and to be found in him," would far transcend the concentrated honours and enjoyments of time.

Let us emulate their deep piety, and seek that the hidden life of God in our souls may be invigorated by fervent, persevering prayer. Let the devotional writings of our eminently holy ancestors be the chosen companions of our closet hours, and then the sacred Scriptures be consulted as the only "oracle" to which we can implicitly give heed. Then we shall be fitted for the work to which the providence of God may call us, and act as becometh those "on whom the ends of the world are come."—C.

No. XX.

A Brief Sketch of the Efforts made by the Nonconformists to Educate their rising Ministry: taken from the History of the Protestant Dissenters.

AMONG those who engaged in the education of youth, and presided over seminaries with reputation and success, were Mr. Woodhouse, Mr. Warren, Mr. Morton, Mr. Frankland, Mr. Doolittle, Mr. Shuttlewood, and Mr. Veal.

No. 1. Mr. Woodhouse's Academy.

Mr. Woodhouse, though not ejected, not being fixed at that time in any place as a minister, was silenced by the Act of Uniformity while he resided in Nottinghamshire. He afterward married a lady of good fortune, the daughter of Major Hubbard, of Leicestershire; yet he did not consider himself as excused from active and useful exertions; but opened a seminary in the manor-house of Sheriffhales, near Shiffnal, in Shropshire, which flourished in King Charles II.'s reign, and obtained celebrity. The mixture of sweetness with authority in the government of his academy gave him a beneficial influence over his pupils, whose studies he directed with singular ability, diligence, and fidelity; youth from the most considerable families in those parts were placed under his care. At one time his students amounted to between forty and fifty. Many, who afterward made an eminent figure in the world as gentlemen and magistrates, as well as excellent divines, were educated by him. He piously managed his house as a nursery for heaven, as well as a school for learning; and on those who were intended for the pulpit, he frequently inculcated a faithful, diligent aim to promote the salvation of souls as a matter of the highest account. A list of some who received from him the principles of learning and religion, especially of those who were assistants and immediate successors to the ejected ministers, and who sustained the character themselves with exemplary assiduity in its duties, does honour to his memory.* When circumstances led him to break up his seminary, his mind, which revolted at the thought of a useless life, was greatly dejected; and it was his frequent lamentation, "Now every field is unpleasant, for I fear I shall live to no purpose." But Providence soon opened to him a new sphere of service, for he was invited to be pastor of a congregation at Little St. Helen's, Bishopsgate-street, London, where he discharged the duties of his ministry with affection, zeal, and usefulness, till within a few days of his death, which took place in 1700. Dr. J. C. Woodhouse, the present dean of Litchfield, the author of a translation and exposition of the Book of the Revelation, a valuable work, written in the spirit of true criticism, is his great-grandson. The late excellent Christian, and candid biblical critic, Mr. John Simpson, of Bath, was descended from this worthy man, and by marriage became more closely connected with the family of Woodhouse.

The students in the seminary at Sheriffhales were conducted through a course of lectures on logic, anatomy, and mathematics, beginning usually with the first, and sometimes with one or the other of these branches of knowledge. These were followed by lectures in physics, ethics, and rhetoric. They were heard successively in Greek and Hebrew at other times of the day or week. A law lecture was read one day in the week to those who had entered at the Inns of Court, or were designed for the law: and they who were intended for the pulpit were conducted through a course of theological reading. All the students were obliged to read, in Natural Theology, Grotius's "De Veritate Christianæ Religionis," construing and giving the sense of it as one of their Latin authors: to this succeeded the reading of Wilkins's "Principles of Natural Religion," Fleming's "Confirming Work," Baxter's "Reasons of the Christian Religion," Bates "On the Existence of God, Immortality of the Soul, and Divinity of the Christian Religion," and Stillingfleet's "Origines Sacræ," with parts of Bochart. In Logic they began with Burgedicius, which was gone through a second time with Heereboord's Commentary; Sanderson, Wallis, Ramus, and his commentator Dowman, were recommended to their private perusal. The mathematical au-

* See Palmer's Nonconformist's Memorial, vol. ii, p. 297, 298; and Thompson's Account of Dissenting Academies, MS., p. 1, 2.

thors through which they were conducted were principally Galtruchius, Leybourn, Moxon, Gunter, Gassendi, and Euclid's Elements, which were read late. In Geography, Echard, and in History, Puffendorf, furnished the textbooks. In Natural Philosophy, the authors read and explained were Heereboord, Magirus, Des Cartes's "Principia," Rhegius, Rohault, and De Stair, for both old and new physics. In Anatomy, with Gibson was joined the perusal of Blancardi "Anatomia Reformata," and Bartholine. The writers adopted to guide them in their ethical studies were Eustachius, Whitby, More, and Heereboord's "Colleg. Ethic;" and in Metaphysics, Froamenius, Facchæus, and Baronius; to whom were added Blank's "Theses," and Davenant or Ward's "Determinationes." In Rhetoric they were assisted by Radau, Quinctilian, and Vossius. In Law they read "Doctor and Student," Littleton's "Tenures," or Coke on Littleton. In Theology, the authors read and explained were, the Westminster Assembly's "Confession of Faith" and "Larger Catechism," Corbet's "Humble Endeavour," Russonius's "Compendium of Turretin." These were followed by Calvin's "Institutes," Pareus on Ursin, Baxter's "End of Controversy," and "Methodus Theologiæ," Williams's "Gospel Truth," Le Blane's "Theses," and Dixon's "Therapeutica Sacra."

In all lectures the authors were strictly explained, and commonly committed to memory, at least as to the sense of them. On one day, an account of the lecture of the preceding day was required before a new lecture was read; and on Saturday a review of the lectures of the five days before was delivered. When an author had been about half gone through, they went that part over again, and so the second part passed under a second perusal, so that every one author was read three times; and after this they exercised one another by questions and problems on the most difficult points that occurred.

Practical exercises accompanied the course of lectures, and the students were employed at times in surveying land, composing almanacs, making sundials of different constructions, and dissecting animals. On one day of the week, Latin, Greek, and Hebrew nouns and verbs were publicly declined in the lecture-room; disputations, after a logical form, were holden on Friday afternoon; they were accustomed to English composition under the form of letters and speeches, and the students designed for the ministry, according to their seniority, were practised in analyzing some verses of a psalm or chapter, drawing up skeletons or heads of sermons, and short schemes of prayer and devotional specimens, according to Bishop Wilkin's method, and were called on to pray in the family on the evening of the Lord's Day, and to set psalms to two or three tunes. On the Saturday evening, a didactical or polemical lecture on divinity, either on Wollebius's "Compendium Theologiæ," or on Ames's "Medulla Theologiæ," was read by the tutor to the senior class, and the class was required to give the literal sense of the author. On the Lord's Day morning, at the time of family prayer, another lecture on divinity took place, when the junior class gave an account of some portion of Vincent's "Exposition of the Assembly's Shorter Catechism," representing the sense of the author, on which the tutor enlarged as the occasion dictated and the subject required. Once a year there was a repetition of all the grammars, especially of the Oxford Latin Grammar, by all the students. The Hebrew was taught by Bythner's "Grammar" and "Lyra," as well adapted to each other.*

No. 2. *Mr. Warren's Academy.*

Mr. Matthew Warren, of Oxford University, the younger son of Mr. John Warren, a gentleman of good fortune, at Otterford, in Devon, being ejected from the chapelry of Downhead, in Somersetshire, soon engaged, at the importunity of some friends, in the honourable literary employment of educating youth for the Christian ministry; and, after meeting with many difficulties and molestations in the reigns of Charles II. and James II., he was for many years at the head of a flourishing academy at Taunton, in Somersetshire. He was generally acknowledged to be well qualified for his office as tutor by a good share of useful learning, and by humility, modesty, and good-humour, which were distinguishing traits in his character peculiarly adapted to the various temper and genius of young persons, and to conciliate the affections of his pupils. Convinced of the great importance, and even necessity, for the conduct of future life, of furnishing the youthful minds with principles of morality, he directed his particular attention to the improvement of his pupils' understandings in that part of learning. In reading lectures he had the happy art of explaining things even to the lowest capacities. He had been himself educated in the old logic and philosophy, and was little acquainted with the improvements of the new; yet it was expressive of liberality of mind and good sense that he encouraged his pupils in freedom of inquiry, and in the study of those authors who were better suited to gratify the love of knowledge and truth, even though they differed from the writers on whom he had formed his own

* From MS. papers with which John Woodhouse Crompton, Esq., of Birmingham, favoured the author. Among them is a certificate of the ordination of Mr. William Woodhouse, of Rearsby, in the county of Leicester, 21st of August, 1702. This gentleman was the son of the tutor. It is a document which shows the practice of the day, and the idea then entertained of the nature and efficiency of the service. It runs thus :- "Forasmuch as Mr. William Woodhouse, of Rearsby, in the county of Leicester, has desired to enter orderly, according to the rules of the Gospel, into the sacred office of the ministry, and has requested us, whose names are underwritten, solemnly to invest him with the ministerial authority; and knowing him to be sound and orthodox in his judgment, of a pious and unblameable life, and sufficient ministerial abilities (no exception being made against his ordination and admission), we have approved him, and proceeded solemnly to set him apart to the office of a presbyter, and all the parts and duties belonging to it, with fasting, prayer, and imposition of hands, and do, so far as concerns us, empower him to perform all the offices and duties of a minister of Jesus Christ. In witness whereof we have hereunto set our hands, this twenty-first day of August, Anno Dom. 1702.

" JOHN DOUGHTY, Minister of the Gospel.
MICHAEL MATTHEWS, Minister of the Gospel.
SAMUEL LAWRENCE, Minister of the Gospel."

sentiments. While Bergedicius or Derodon, and in Ethics Eustachius, were used as text-books in the lecture-room, Locke, Le Clerc, and Cumberland were guides to just thinking, close reasoning, and enlightened views in their closets. Mr. Warren was never confident or imposing ; never vehement or rigid in his own opinion, but open to argument, and disposed to prefer the judgment of others to his own. He was reckoned among the moderate divines of the day : ever studious of the things that make for peace, and promote Christian harmony and love. He encouraged the free and critical study of the Scriptures. Many young gentlemen who afterward filled civil stations with respectability and worth, and others who appeared in the ministry with credit and usefulness, were educated under him. The name of Mr. Grove, a genius, character, and talents were formed in his seminary, is alone sufficient to do honour to its president.* Mr. Warren died in 1706.

No. 3, *Mr. Charles Morton's Academy.*

Mr. Charles Morton, ejected from the rectory of Blisland, in Cornwall, of Wadham College, Oxford, was descended from an ancient family at Morton, in Nottinghamshire, the seat of J. Morton, secretary to King Edward III. He was a general scholar, but was particularly eminent for his knowledge of the mathematics, on which account he was greatly valued by Dr. Wilkins, the warden of the college of which he was a fellow. After his ejectment he removed to a small tenement, his own property, in the parish of St. Ives, where he resided till the fire of London, in which he sustained great loss. He was solicited by several friends to undertake the instruction of youth in academical learning, for which he had extraordinary qualifications. With this view he settled at Newington Green. He had a peculiar talent of winning youth to the love of virtue and learning by the pleasantness of his conversation, and by a familiar way of making difficult subjects easily intelligible. He drew up systems of the several arts and sciences for the use of his pupils, which he explained in his lectures, and which the students copied. One, entitled *Eutaxia*, exhibited the principles of policy exactly correspondent to the English Constitution, asserting at once the rights and honour of the crown and the liberties of the subject. It traced the original of all government to the institution of God ; enforced from the subject love to the person of the king, obedience to the laws, and a dutiful submission to legal taxes for the support of the crown and the laws. It confirmed the ordinary method of succession ; and, in case of total subversion or failure, gave a right to the *ordines regni* to restore the Constitution by the extraordinary call of some person to the throne. It is pronounced by one who had seen it to have been so complete, ingenious, and judicious a system as to be equal, if not superior, to any printed composition of the kind. He also drew up a Compendium of Logic, which was the text-book in Harvard College after he became president of that American seminary, till it was superseded by one on a more improved plan by

* Palmer's Nonconformist's Memorial, vol. ii., p. 358; Grove's Works, preface, vol. i., p. 14 ; and Sprint's Funeral Sermon for Warren, p. 45, 46, 50.

Mr. Brattle, minister of the church in Cambridge. A copy of each, as rare specimens of American literature, are preserved in the cabinet of the Historical Society. A great many young ministers were educated by him, as well as other good scholars, and numbers of each class were afterward very useful in Church and state; and the seminary was marked by a universal sentiment of respect for the great and excellent men of the episcopal order, and an emulation of their virtues. Mr. Morton himself was a pious, learned, and ingenious man; of a sweet natural temper and a generous public spirit; an indefatigable friend, beloved and valued by all that knew him. After having appeared in the character of a tutor with reputation for twenty years, he was so harassed with processes in the ecclesiastical court that he found himself constrained to relinquish it; and, being under great apprehensions for the interests of the nation, he emigrated to New-England in 1685, and was chosen pastor of a church in Charlestown, over against Boston, and vice-president of Harvard College. Mr. Morton died, April, 1697; in the eightieth year of his age. In the Philosophical Transactions of the Royal Society there is a treatise of his, entitled "A Discourse on Improving the County of Cornwall," the seventh chapter of which is on sea sand for manure. He published several small treatises, as he was an enemy to large volumes, and often said, Μεγα βιϐλιον μεγα κακον, "a great book is a great evil." Dr. Calamy has preserved, besides his vindication of himself and brethren from the charge of perjury, on account of teaching university learning, "Advice to Candidates for the Ministry under the present discouraging Circumstances." It was drawn up in the reign of Charles II., but deserves the frequent perusal and serious attention of those who bear that character in the present day. Both these pieces afford proofs of the talents and excellent spirit of the author. It is to be regretted that only few names of his students are come down to us.*

No. 4. *Mr. Richard Frankland's Academy.*

Mr. Richard Frankland, who was ejected from a lectureship at Bishop's-Aukland, in the county of Durham, was born in 1630, at Rathmill, in the parish of Gigleswick, in Craven; a division of the West Riding of Yorkshire, and received his classical learning at a famous school there. In 1647 he was entered a student in Christ College, Cambridge, of which Dr. Samuel Bolton was master; where he made a good proficiency in human and sacred literature, and imbibed a deep sense of religion. There he took the degree of master of arts, and on his removal from college, after a short residence at Hexham on an invitation thither, he successively preached at Haughton-le-Spring, Lancaster, and Bishop's-Aukland. The living of Aukland-St. Andrews, which was a valuable one, was presented to him by Sir Arthur Haslerig. It is a testimony that he was well known, and

that his learning and character were esteemed, that when the protector Cromwell had erected a college for academical learning at Durham, in 1657, Mr. Frankland was fixed upon to be a tutor in it. By the destruction of the institution at the Restoration he lost the office, and the Act of Uniformity, with which he refused to comply, though solicited to it by Bishop Cosins with a promise of preferment, excluded him from his living, and he retired to his own estate at Rathmill. Here the persuasions of friends prevailed with him to open a private academy, and so much was he encouraged in this liberal employment of his talents, that in the space of twenty-nine years there hundred young gentlemen had received their education under him. In the mean time he repeatedly changed the place of his abode, but still carried on his academy wherever he went. In 1674 he removed to Natland, near Kendal, in Westmoreland, on an invitation to become the minister of a church there. By the harassing operation of the Five-mile Act he was obliged to leave that place, and removed, in succession, to Dawsonfold in the same county, to Harthurrow in Lancashire, to Calton in Craven, in Yorkshire, to Attercliffe, near Sheffield, and again to Rathmill. He had the reputation of being an acute mathematician, an eminent divine, sagacious in the detection of error, and able in the defence of truth, and a solid interpreter of Scripture; a zeal to promote the Gospel in all places, united with great moderation, humility of mind, and affability of deportment, liberality to the poor, and an amiable attention to all relative duties, formed in his character leading features. He was generally beloved, and very useful; yet his patience and fortitude were tried by many and various troubles, and even after the Revolution to his death in 1698, when he was sixty-eight years of age, there was scarcely a year passed in which he did not meet with some disturbance. Dr. Latham has given us a list of his pupils.*

No. 5. *Mr. Doolittle's Academy.*

Mr. Doolittle, A.M., of Pembroke Hall, Cambridge, was a native of Kidderminster, and ejected from the rectory of St. Alphage, London Wall. He first opened a boarding school in Moorfields, which was much encouraged and patronised; he had twenty-eight pupils when that malignant fever called the plague broke out; on this he removed to Woodford Bridge, on Epping Forest. Upon a license granted by King Charles II. in 1672, he returned to the vicinity of the city, opened the pastor of a large congregation in Monkwell-street,† and set up a seminary on a more extensive plan, at Islington, to educate young men for the ministry, in which

* Calamy's Account, p. 284-288; Continuation, vol. i., p. 453. Palmer's Nonconformist's Memorial, vol. i., p. 488-491.

† This was the first meeting-house built after the fire of London, 1662. In the vestry is preserved, framed and glazed, the royal license which Mr. Doolittle took out on the Declaration of Indulgence granted to the Nonconformists in 1672, signed by his majesty's command. Arlington. It is thought to be the only memorial of the kind existing in the city — See Wilson's Dissenting Churches, vol. iii., p. 186, 187, where the author has given an exact copy of it for the satisfaction of the curious.

* Palmer's Nonconformist's Memorial, vol. i., p. 273, 274; Calamy's Account, p. 144; Continuation, vol. i., p. 176-211; Dr. Eliot's American Biographical Dictionary, article Morton; Sam. Palmer's Defence of the Education in Dissenting Academies, p. 10; and Vindication of the Dissenters, in Answer to Mr. Wesley's Defence, &c., 4to, 1705, p. 52-54.

he had the assistance of Mr. Thomas Vincent, M.A., of Christ Church, Oxford, ejected from St. Mary Magdalen, Milk-street, London, a gentleman well qualified for the office. When the Oxford Act passed he removed to Wimbledon, and his lectures were privately attended by several of his pupils, who accommodated themselves with lodgings in the neighbourhood. Among the names of those who studied under him are some who afterward made a figure, and soared above the lessons they had received in the academy. Mr. Doolittle, though a very worthy and diligent divine, was not very eminent for compass of knowledge or depth of thought.*

' No. 6. *Mr. John Shuttlewood's Academy.*

Mr. John Shuttlewood, A.B., of Christ College, Cambridge, born at Wymeswold, Leicestershire, January 3, 1631, was ejected from Raunston and Hoose, in the same county. He was a considerable sufferer for his nonconformity; for not only was he deprived of his living, but was harassed with various prosecutions, which obliged him to frequent removals, sometimes taking his abode in Leicestershire, and sometimes residing in Northamptonshire; yet he could not secure his person from imprisonment, nor evade the seizure of his goods. His health was much affected and injured by his ministerial labours in incommodious places and at unseasonable hours, and by the evils of persecution in those rigorous and cruel times. His troubles, however, did not prevent his keeping a seminary at Sulby, near Welford, Northamptonshire, and at Little Creaton, where he lived, and died in the year of the Revolution. It appears, from a memorandum in his pocket almanac, "that six students were added to his seminary in one year." It seems to have had a good degree of reputation, and to have been sometimes flourishing. The list of students which time has transmitted down to us reflects credit on his academy, if not by the number of names, yet by eminence of character to which they rose. Mr. Shuttlewood was a man of ability and learning; an acceptable and useful preacher; much esteemed, not only in the places of his residence, but through the neighbouring country. Of this the concise but impressive inscription on his tombstone was an honourable testimony, recording that he was " multum dilectus, multum deflendus," much beloved, much lamented.† He was the father of the dissenting cause in that part of Northamptonshire in which he fixed his residence.

No. 7. *Mr. Samuel Cradock's Academy.*

Among others who, when they were silenced by the Act of Uniformity, employed their talents and learning for the instruction of youth, was Mr. Samuel Cradock, B.D., fellow of Emanuel College, Cambridge, ejected from the rectory of North Cadbury, Somersetshire. The sacrifice he made of this valuable living to the principle of conscience was compensated to him

by the will of a gentleman to whom he was next heir, Mr. Walter Cradock, of Wickham Brook, in Suffolk, who bequeathed his estate to him. He used to acknowledge, with great thankfulness, this allotment of Providence in his favour, and on the occasion took for his motto, " Nec ingratus nec inutilis videar vixisse." He went some years after and resided in the mansion of his deceased friend, but not to indulge in useless inactivity. For some years he usually preached twice every Lord's Day, gratuitously, to the neighbourhood, and commenced an instructer of youth in academical learning. In the number of those who studied under him were some who were afterward distinguished by their stations in life and by worth of character. His lectures were grounded on systems of logic, natural and moral philosophy, and metaphysics, composed by himself and extracted out of a variety of authors. His pupils were obliged to copy them out for their own use : they considered this a great drudgery ; but Dr. Calamy, who was one of them, was inclined to think that the benefits attending this task overbalanced the inconveniences and labour of it. Mr. Cradock treated his pupils in a gentlemanlike manner, lived upon his own estate, kept a good house, and was much respected by all the gentlemen around the country. This was the natural consequence of a mind truly catholic, that regarded with esteem every man for his goodness, and secured the esteem of all who were truly good : a return for affable and courteous manners. His deportment was condescending, and his temper forgiving. " We had," says Dr. Calamy, " our innocent diversions, and used to ride and visit any acquaintance we had at Bury, Sudbury, Newmarket, Cambridge, and other places in the neighbourhood ; but I never knew anything like debauchery among Mr. Cradock's domestics." His publications remain as proofs of his solid judgment, digested thought, clear method, and unaffected style as a writer, while they breathe the spirit of serious and manly piety. His commentaries are still esteemed as valuable, and his treatise entitled " Knowledge and Practice" has been recommended as the best book of the kind for young ministers.*

Among others who, after they were expelled from the pulpit, assisted the studies of young men, was Mr. Edward Veal, of Christ Church, Oxford, and afterward of Trinity College, Dublin, who at first exercised his ministry in Dublin and its vicinity, and when he was deprived of his fellowship for nonconformity, became chaplain to Sir William Waller, in Middlesex, and on the death of his patron settled as a minister with a congregation at Wapping, and remained in this connexion to a good old age. The infirmities of declining life obliged him to relinquish his pulpit and academy some years before his death, June 6, 1708, æt. 76. Mr. Nathaniel Taylor, an eminent and popular preacher, a pastor of the congregation at Salter's Hall, called by Dr. Doddridge, on account of his vast wit and strength of expression, the dissenting *South*, who died suddenly in April,

* Palmer's Nonconformist's Memorial, vol. i., p. 80–88. Matth. Henry's Life, p. 77. Emlyn's Works, vol. i.
† Palmer's Nonconformist's Memorial, vol. ii., p. 123–128 ; and Thompson's MS. Collections, vol. ii., article Creaton.

* Palmer's Nonconformist's Memorial, vol. ii., p. 353, 354 ; Dr. Calamy's History of His Own Life and Times, MS. ; and Doddridge's Preaching Lectures, p. 82, 12mo, 1804.

1702, is the only one of those who studied un-der Mr. Veal, whose name has been delivered down to us.

Others deserve to be mentioned with respect as assisting the studies of youth, especially of those who were designed for the ministry, though the records of the times supply but very few particulars relative to their mode of instruction, and those who enjoyed the benefit of it. Among these was

The excellent Mr. Philip Henry, who, after he was ejected from Worthenbury, and removed to Broad Oak, till his death in 1696, frequently received into his house young gentlemen who had in other seminaries finished a course of university learning, and were desirous of the benefit of his instructions and counsels, and who assisted in the education of his own children. One of the first who joined his family, in 1668, was Mr. William Turner, of Edmund's Hall, in Oxford, and afterward for many years vicar of Walburton, in Sussex; a serious, laborious, and useful preacher, author of an elaborate "History of all Religions," in 1695, and of "A History of Remarkable Providences, &c.," the plan of which was suggested by Mr. Matthew Pool. Another, who had been a commoner in Edmund's Hall, and then pursued his studies under Mr. Henry's roof, was his kinsman, Mr. Robert Bozier, a young man of pregnant parts, great application, and exemplary piety, who died of a fever, in the twenty-third year of his age, September 13, 1680, at Mr. Doolittle's, Islington, into whose seminary he had entered himself a few weeks before with Mr. Matthew Henry. Mr. Samuel Lawrence, of Nantwich, who spent some time in Mr. Morton's academy at Newington Green; Mr. John Wilson, of Warwick, pupil, also, of Mr. Thomas Rowe; and Dr. Benion, of Shrewsbury, who studied likewise at Glasgow, placed themselves under the direction of Mr. Henry. The great thing which he used to press upon those who were candidates for the ministry was, to study the Scriptures and make them familiar. *Bonus textuarius est bonus theologus* was his favourite maxim. He would say to them, "You come to me as Naaman did to Elisha, expecting that I should do this or that for you, and, alas! I can but say as he did, *Go, wash in Jordan;* go study the Scriptures. I profess to teach no other learning but Scripture learning." With this view, it was his custom to recommend to them the study of the Hebrew, and the use of an interleaved Bible, into which to transcribe the expositions and observations which might occur in reading, and which often surpass those that are to be met with in professed commentators.*

Dr. Theophilus Gale, the learned author of "The Court of the Gentiles" (who died in 1678, and expressed his liberal zeal for the encouragement of learning by leaving all his real and personal estate for the education of poor scholars, and by the bequest of the philosophical part of his well-chosen library to students at home, and all the rest of it to Harvard College, New-England), opened an academy about the year 1666, at Newington Green, for the direction of which he was eminently qualified by his

deep and universal learning. Mr. John Ashwood, a pious and excellent man, whose life was written by Mr. Thomas Reynolds, and Mr. Thomas Rowe, and Mr. Benoni Rowe, to whose names celebrity is attached, studied under him.

Dr. Henry Langley, a judicious and solid divine, fellow of Pembroke College, Oxford, afterward appointed master by ordinance of Parliament, in 1647, and in the next year made canon of Christ Church, when, at the Restoration, he was deprived of both these preferments by the visiters, retired to Tubney, near Abingdon, and instructed young men in academical learning. He died September 10, 1779. Mr. James Waters, of Uxbridge, whose daughter married Mr. Mason, the author of the treatise on "Self-Knowledge," commenced his studies under Dr. Langley.*

Mr. John Malden, ejected from Newport, in Shropshire, a man of great learning, an excellent Hebrecian, and a solid preacher, as well as exemplary for piety and deep humility, afterward kept a private academy near Whitchurch, in the same county, and had under his care many young men of great promise, among others Mr. Samuel Lawrence, after he left Mr. Henry, at the time of his death, on May 23, 1681, æt. 60.†

Dr. Obadiah Grew, ejected from St. Michael's, Coventry, after the grant of public liberty, added to his ministerial labours the tuition of some young men for the ministry; an employment for which he was as eminently qualified by solid learning, sedateness of temper, and courteous manners, as by regular piety and great candour. His death terminated his useful exertions October 22, 1689. Mr. Samuel Pomfret, a pious and popular preacher in London, who formed a church of his own gathering about the end of the seventeenth century, and which consisted of more than 800 communicants, some years before his death, on the 11th January, 1721-22, commenced his academical studies under Dr. Grew.

Mr. Thomas Shewell, M.A., a native of Coventry, educated in the University of Cambridge, and ejected by the Act of Uniformity from the vicarage of Lenham, in Kent, succeeded Dr. Grew in his two characters of pastor and tutor, and conducted his academy till his death, January 19, 1693.‡

Dr. Joshua Oldfield, who had been a student in Christ's College, Cambridge, on settling at Coventry as successor to Mr. Shewell, followed the steps of his predecessors in teaching academical learning, and pursued this literary employment here for a considerable time with great reputation, till his removal to London in 1700, where he resumed it in conjunction with other learned divines, though during his residence at Coventry he met with much opposition from the spiritual courts. He was assisted in his labours as a tutor by his co-pastor Mr. Tong §

Mr. Henry Newcome, of Manchester, who had been forced to remove to Ellenbrook by the Oxford Act, when he had liberty to license a place of worship in 1672, united with the character of the pastor that of the teacher of aca-

---

* Theological and Biblical Magazine, vol. vii., p. 347. Philip Henry's Life, p. 128, 1699. Vol. II.—T T T

* Theological and Biblical Magazine, *ut ante*, p. 349.   † Ibid., p. 311.
‡ Ibid., p. 312.   § Ibid., p. 312, 313.

demical literature, for which he was well qualified by his great proficiency in philosophy and theology, and by his ease and freedom in communicating from his stores of acquired knowledge. After his death in 1695, Mr. John Chorlton, a native of Salford, near Manchester, a student under Mr. Frankland, and first assistant and then successor to Mr. Newcome in his pastoral office, also engaged in the liberal employment of educating candidates for the ministry.*

Mr. James Coningham, M.A., educated in the University of Edinburgh, taught academical learning first at Penrith in Cumberland, where he began his ministry, and on removing to Manchester in 1700, to be co-pastor with Mr. Chorlton, united with him in his literary labours of tuition. He had to contend with persons inimical to the Dissenters after Mr. Chorlton's death in 1705, and was prosecuted by government for keeping an academy. This seminary appears to have been broken up on Mr. Coningham's removal to London to succeed Mr. Stretton, in 1712.†

Mr. Ralph Button, B.D., canon of Christ Church, Oxford, and orator of the University, who lost both his preferments at the Restoration, though he had celebrated that event in a Hebrew and Latin poem, should be mentioned as one of those who devoted their time and talents, when laid aside from their labours as ministers, to the laudable employment of training up youth in science and literature. After he was expelled from his posts in the university, he removed with his family to Brentford, where he was induced by the persuasions of two gentlemen, who were knights, privately to instruct their sons, for which he was cast into jail and suffered an imprisonment of six months. On the indulgence he removed to Islington, and opened a private academy. Mr. Baxter adds, to an encomium on his moral and religious character, that he was an excellent scholar. In the early part of his life he had been an eminent tutor in Exeter College, to a vacant fellowship in which he had been previously chosen by the recommendation of Dr. Prideaux, its rector, in 1633. In 1642 he removed to London, on the breaking out of the civil wars, and had been elected professor of geometry in Gresham College. These situations had prepared him for private tuition, and were proofs of his literary qualifications. He died in 1680. Among his pupils were Mr. Samuel Pomfret, who finished his studies under him ; Mr. King, of Wellingborough ; and Sir Joseph Jekyll, the son of a clergyman, afterward, as Mr. Whiston delineates his character with force and conciseness, " the most excellent and upright Master of the Rolls." He was distinguished by his disinterested and steady attachment to the cause of civil and religious liberty; and by the patronage he afforded to sacred literature and its friends. Instances of this were a pension of £50 per annum to Mr. Whiston, and an annual salary to Mr. Chubb, whom, before he fell into a skeptical state of mind, Mr. Whiston had introduced to him. To Sir Joseph Jekyll were dedicated, by their respective authors, Bishop Butler's Sermons, preached in the Rolls

Chapel, and Mr. Lowman's " Paraphrase and Notes on the Revelation."

Mr. William Wickens, stated by Calamy to have been ejected from St. Andrew Hubbard, Little East-cheap, London, though at the Restoration it should seem he was not in possession of that living, but preacher at the Poultry Compter, is in the list of those who presided over private academies at Newington Green, where he preached to a small congregation till within two years of his death, September 22, 1699, æt. 85. It may be concluded that he was eminently qualified to assist theological studies, from his familiar acquaintance with the Old and New Testaments in the original languages, so that in his closet he seldom had recourse to any translation. His favourite study, next to the Holy Scriptures, was Oriental learning, especially the Jewish laws and customs, in the knowledge of which he had few equals.*

Mr. Stephen Lobb, son of Richard Lobb, Esq., high-sheriff of Cornwall, and member of Parliament for St. Michael, in that county, in 1659 (who was the pastor of an Independent congregation in Fetter, London, and made a conspicuous figure among the Dissenters during the reign of James II., and had a great share in the controversy with Dr. Williams), is not to be forgotten in the enumeration of those who directed the studies of candidates for the ministry. He is said to have enjoyed every advantage of not only a pious, but liberal education, first commenced in a dissenting academy, and then completed in Holland ; to have possessed a discerning, penetrating spirit, a firm and sound judgment, and great strength of mind ; and to have united with these natural abilities a close application to study, and was a great master of the art of reasoning. These qualifications will justify us in forming a high estimate of his fitness for the province of a tutor. He died in the vigour of life, June 3, 1699. Mr. Francis Glascock (a gentleman, it is apprehended, of Scotch extraction, and educated in one of the universities of North Britain) ought to be mentioned in connexion with the two preceding names. He was predecessor to Dr. Jabez Earle as pastor of a congregation which assembled, first in Drury-lane, and then in Hanover-street, Longacre. He died in 1706, and a few months before his death had been chosen, though a Presbyterian, a Tuesday's lecturer at Pinner's Hall, where he delivered, as well as in his own pulpit, many elaborate discourses, which discovered not less ability than they expressed zeal in defence of what he judged to be the great doctrines of the Gospel, more especially the deity of Jesus Christ. On the occasion of the excellent Mr. Morton's being induced, by the rigour of the times, to seek a sphere of usefulness and a peaceable asylum in America, Mr. Glascock, Mr. Lobb, and Mr. Wickens undertook to give private lectures to the students deprived of his assistance by his emigration, and disposed to form themselves into a class, and to others who, through the severity of the times, were deprived of more public means of improvement. Among these, while others of Mr. Morton's pupils went to Geneva, was Mr. John Beaumont, a native of London,

---

* Theological and Biblical Magazine, ut ante, p. 348, 349.   † Ibid., p. 348, 349.

* Theological and Biblical Magazine, ut ante, p. 374.

who received his classical education in St. Paul's School under the learned Dr. Thomas Gale, with whom his great love of learning made him a favourite. Mr. Beaumont, when he entered on the office of the minister, besides preaching with great acceptance at Fareham, in Hampshire, and other places, was successful in raising and forming three congregations, one at Swallowfield in Berkshire, a second at Peckham, and a third at Battersea in Surrey, and assisted in gathering another at Chertsea in the same county, and was afterward thirty-two years pastor of a congregation at Deptford in Kent, where he died in 1730. Dr. Gale, when he was fit for the university, urged him, and held out offers to induce him, to enter in one of the colleges at Cambridge, which he declined from conscientious scruples on conformity. He was ordained, after the Presbyterian model, July 1, 1689, with Mr. Hughes, of Canterbury, by Dr. Annesley, Mr. John Reynolds, Mr, Robert Franklin, and Mr. John Quick. His first settlement as a pastor was at Battersea, where he spent five years. His character as a Christian was distinguished by a holy, blameless, and inoffensive conversation, and by great patience and resignation under uncommon afflictions, and, as a divine, by his zeal in asserting the doctrines that are called orthodox.*

Mr. Benjamin Robinson, who succeeded Mr. Woodhouse in the pastoral connexion in Little St. Helen's, and was for twenty years a minister of eminence in London, dying April 30, 1724, in the early days of his ministry was engaged in the education of youth. The foundation of his qualifications for this province was laid by a considerable progress in the Latin, Greek, and Hebrew languages, under Mr. Ogden, a polite scholar, and master of a school in Derby, of which town Mr. Robinson was a native; from whose care he was removed to pursue academical studies under Mr. Woodhouse. At Findern, near Derby, where he was solemnly ordained to the work of the ministry in October, 1688, he first opened a grammar-school in 1693. In this situation he was highly esteemed by many worthy clergymen and others on account of his learning and good sense; his unaffected piety, and obliging deportment, and had offers of preferment in the national Church ; yet these circumstances, so honourable to his character and so propitious to his pursuits, did not screen him from a citation into the Bishop of Litchfield and Coventry's court. But his acquaintance with and personal application to Dr. Lloyd, the bishop, and who afterward kept up an epistolary correspondence with him, soon relieved him from the trouble of this litigious process. Within a few years he removed to Hungerford in Berkshire, where, at the earnest request of his brethren in those parts, he opened an academy. This measure awakened enmity against him, and a complaint was lodged against him with the eminent prelate Bishop Burnet, who sent for him as he passed through Hungerford on the progress of a visitation, to whom he gave such satisfaction, both as to his undertaking and his nonconformity, as paved the

* Theological and Biblical Magazine, ut ante, p, 374–376; Wilson's History of Dissenting Churches, vol. iii, p. 436, 437–445 ; and Dr. A. Taylor's Funeral Sermon for Mr. Beaumont, p. 43–46.

way for a kind intimacy ever after. He is said to have been distinguished by a regard to the strict and genuine sense of Scripture according to the best rules of interpretation. Many were educated under him for the ministry, and some younger ministers, settled in his neighbourhood, derived great benefit from the light he cast on subjects in private conferences, and at quarterly meetings held in Newbury, at which it was customary to handle on some theological subject, in which mode of discussion Mr. Robinson excelled. He appears to have been assisted in his academical department, for a year or two, by Mr. Edward Godwin,* who had studied under the learned Mr. Samuel Jones, at Tewkesbury, and settled as a minister in Hungerford, and became, in 1722, co-pastor with Mr. Robinson at Little St. Helen's. To Mr. Godwin's judgment Dr. Doddridge was indebted for several important alterations and improvements in the manuscript of his " Family Expositor," and by his friendly and assiduous services that excellent work was carried through the press. Mr. Robinson's seminary was broken up by his removal to London.

Another gentleman usefully engaged at this period in plans of education was Mr. Henry Hickman, B.D., whom the Act of Uniformity deprived of a fellowship in Magdalen College, Oxford, on which he went over to Holland. On his return, he fixed his residence in a retired situation near Stourbridge, in Worcestershire, his native county. Here he opened a private seminary to read lectures in logic and philosophy. He had the character of being a man of excellent and general learning, a celebrated preacher, and an acute disputant. The titles of his publications afford a presumption of his talents as a scholar and a disputant. He was, in the latter part of his life, minister of an English church at Leyden, and died at Utrecht, in a very advanced age, in 1691 or 2. The names of two of his disciples are transmitted down to these times. One was Mr. John Ball, many years the revered minister of a congregation at Honiton, in Devon, where he died May 6, 1745, in the ninety-first year of his age ; he had exercised his ministry in this town above half a century, and preached but a few days before his death with great fluency and vivacity. He was the son of a learned and excellent minister, Mr. Nathaniel Ball, ejected from Royston, in Herts. He spent some time under Mr. John Short, also the son of a minister, ejected from Lyme Regis, in Dorsetshire, a man of learning, and who educated young men for the ministry at Lyme and Culliton. Mr. Ball likewise studied at Utrecht, with a closeness of application that brought on a severe illness and a weakness of several years. He spoke the Latin tongue with great fluency, could read any book in Greek with the same ease as in English, and generally carried the Hebrew Psalter into the pulpit to expound from it. He could repeat the Psalms by heart, and seldom passed a day without hearing or reading six or eight chapters in the Bible. It was his usual custom to pray six times a day; a learned person, not particularly favourable to

* Wilson's History of Dissenting Churches, vol. i., p. 382. Dr. Cumming's Funeral Sermon for Mr. Robinson, p. 55, 56, 57.

him, owned that "he prayed like an apostle." His great affability and good temper endeared him to persons of all parties, and for his general knowledge of the world and facetious conversation, his company was esteemed and courted. He was liberal to the poor. In his pastoral duties he was peculiarly diligent and active in catechising, and had at one time above two hundred catechumens. A person, remarkable for his bias to Deism, said of him, "that man is what a minister should be." Mr. Ball's name will occur in a subsequent period of this history. In the persecuting times of Charles II. and James II., Mr. Ball was connived at in the education of a select number of gentlemen's sons, whose fathers did not accord with him in sentiments ; for he was greatly beloved by persons of rank and influence, as well as of different parties, in the neighbourhood.*

Another minister who studied a short time under Mr. Hickman, and but a short time, on account of the infirmities of his declining years, was Mr. Thomas Cotton, M.A., born at or near Workly, in Yorkshire. His father was a considerable iron-master in that county, and noted for his great hospitality and kindness to the ejected ministers ; one of whom, Mr. Spawford, ejected from Silkestone, he received into his family as tutor to his son till his death. Mr. Cotton removed from Mr. Hickman's academy to Mr. Frankland's, in Westmoreland, and finished his academical course of studies at Edinburgh about the year 1677. After this he was engaged to be chaplain to Lady Sarah Houghton, daughter of the Earl of Chesterfield, for about a year, when a severe illness obliged him to leave that situation. When he had recovered his health, he preached in his father's house till persecution obliged him to desist. By the advice of his friends, on this account, he accepted an invitation to go abroad as governor to a young gentleman, with whom he spent three years in travelling through several parts of Europe. When they were at Paris, where during their stay they attended public worship in the English ambassador's chapel, and were greatly pleased with the useful and serious preaching of Dr., afterward archbishop, Wake, they received continual melancholy accounts of the deplorable state of the Protestants in the southern parts of France, and they were afterward witnesses to many very afflicting instances of persecution. Assemblies of several thousands were broken up with floods of tears ; the nearest relations were rent from one another ; numberless families were utterly and barbarously destroyed ; ministers were silenced, banished, or stripped of all they had ; some were made slaves, and some put to the most cruel deaths. The reports of the persecution all over France, which on leaving Paris they received at Lyons, were so distressing and lamentable that they resolved to turn their course to a Protestant country, and they were quickened in the execution of their purpose by the bitter reflections against the Protestants and the new insults and threatenings produced by the intelligence which reached Lyons at that time of Monmouth's rout in England. They

went next to Geneva, where their sympathy was exercised and their minds were afflicted by frequent reports of the sufferings of the Vaudois, and the barbarities practised on them. Mr. Cotton, on his return to England, continued in the capacity of a tutor for some months, as his health was much impaired. His income in that connexion was very considerable. His prospects, if he had inclined to any civil employment, were flattering, and, as he was determined for the ministry, he had the offer of a good living with the recommendation of the former incumbent, as well as the friendship of the patron, and the overture of maintaining a reader to perform such offices as he should appoint. But he chose to take his lot with the Protestant Dissenters. He was first the pastor of a small congregation in Hoxton, with whom he remained under very little encouragement, for five or six years. He then spent two or three years at Ware in Hertfordshire. He removed thence to settle with a congregation in St. Giles's in the Fields, near Great Russel-street, Bloomsbury. He was very useful and laborious, and when his health permitted, besides preaching, he expounded in the forenoon and catechised in the afternoon. He also supplied as chaplain to the two ladies Russell; the widows of Lord Robert and Lord James, which engaged much time and attendance. He was a man of good, useful learning, without show ; of great piety and seriousness, without austerity and moroseness ; and of great regularity in his whole behaviour, without being troublesome to any body. His deportment showed the Christian, the minister, and the gentleman. He was a solid preacher, and had a very happy talent of suiting his discourses to particular persons and occasions. "From him I learned," said his nephew, Dr. Wright, "in a manner that I have reason to be thankful for, that *application* is the very *life of preaching*." The scenes of dragooning and persecution of which he had been a witness made him an enemy to subscriptions to human articles of faith, and gave him a lively conviction of the necessity of maintaining the great Protestant principle—the right of private judgment. Mr. Cotton died in 1730.*

---

* Waldron's Funeral Sermon for Mr. Ball, p. 22, 23; and Palmer's Nonconformist's Memorial, vol. 1., p. 191.

* In the "Memoirs" of his travels, written for his own use, he related many affecting scenes of this kind of which he was a spectator, at Ludun, Poictou, and Saumure. At Poictou, in particular, he was exceedingly moved with the vast numbers at their last public worship, and the great difficulty with which all broke out into a flood of tears. The last religious assembly on a lecture-day at Saumure, Mr. Cotton could never recollect without lively emotions : the congregation all in tears, the singing of the last psalm, the pronouncing of the blessing, and afterward all the people passing before their ministers to receive their benedictions, were circumstances he wanted words to describe. The ministers and professors were banished, and he attended them to the vessel in which they sailed. The affecting sight of the vast assemblage which formed the church at Charenton, and of such numbers devoted to banishment, slavery, and the most barbarous deaths, was a spectacle that overpowered the mind. The stay at Saumure had been very pleasant, and tho agreeable acquaintance they had formed in that town invited their continuance in it, till it became a scene of great danger and affliction ; especially after an or

These historical gleanings concerning the academical institutions of the first Nonconformists; few and imperfect as they may be deemed, are sufficient to expose the iniquity and folly of the times. The necessity of such institutions arose from the spirit of intolerance which had excluded from the Church and from the universities so many men of learning and talents. The vexatious and continued persecutions which pursued them into the retirements of science and literature, showed a virulence and malignity of temper. It was great injustice to debar men from the honourable and pacific employment of their acquirements, genius, and intellect; an employment highly useful to the community, and in many instances necessary to the support of themselves and their families, as well as affording a solace when si-

der was issued to require all strangers, particularly the English, to accompany and assist the severe proceedings against the Protestants. When the governor received authoritative directions to see their church demolished, the tearing down of that temple was extremely distressing; the very graves were opened, and the utmost ravages committed. The destruction of it was attended with a remarkable occurrence, which Mr. Cotton recorded as an instance of the contradictory interpretations which the same act of Providence may receive, according to the different principles of those who pass their opinion on it. A person who was ambitious to have his daughter pull down the first stone of the church, had her taken from him a few days after by death. The parent, and others of his persuasion, looked upon her death as a speedy call to heaven, in reward of so meritorious an act; the persecuted Protestants regarded it as a just and very affecting judgment. On his journey from Poictou, Mr. Cotton was deeply impressed by the agitations of mind and the expressions of an old gentleman who came into an inn nearly at the same instant with him, who stood leaning on his staff, and shaking his head and weeping, cried out, *"Unhappy France! If I and mine were but now entering into some country of refuge and safety, where we might have liberty to worship God according to our consciences, I should think myself the happiest man in the world, though I had only this staff in my hand."* This person was found to be the eldest son of a very considerable family, and possessed of a large estate.—*Dr. Wright's Sermon on the Death of the Rev. Thomas Cotton,* p. 34–36, notes.

lenced as ministers. It heightened this injustice, done not to them only, but to the whole body of Dissenters, that the law made the universities the property of one persuasion, and rendered private academies necessary for the youth who were excluded by the Act of Uniformity from being candidates for the degrees and preferments of those seminaries, and from the advantages of being students in them, but on the condition of conformity. This conduct was, in reality, repugnant to the spirit and design of the Act of Toleration. The Dissenters were allowed by that act the just liberty of worshipping God according to their own consciences, and, in the first instance, the benefit of a ministry of their own choosing; but these severities, by which the education of their youth was obstructed, if not absolutely prevented, went to preclude them from the enjoyment of a succession of ministers of learning and ability. With great inconsistency, the end was granted, but the means of attaining the end were denied to them.

"As in all cases, so in this, the measures dictated by a spirit of persecution were not only unjust, but impolitic. The evil and mischief was not confined to the Dissenters, it affected the interests of the nation, on which it had an unfavourable aspect by obliging the more opulent, at a great expense, and at the risk of imbibing sentiments not congenial to the English manners and Constitution, to send their youth abroad for education. It affected the interests of literature. Where a competition of religious parties exists, there is a rivalship in the means of giving support to and reflecting honour on each. "While the Protestant religion was publicly professed in France, learning flourished there. After the revocation of the edict of Nantes, literature declined. The priests having none to expose their ignorance, grew lazy and sensual. Where a strict uniformity has been required, and no Dissenters tolerated, it has been observed learning is at a low ebb, as in Italy and Spain."*—C.

* Moderation a Virtue. By James Owen. Part ii., p. 99.

No. XXI.

*An Historical and Critical Account of Hugh Pe-
ters, after the manner of Mr. Bayle.* London :
Printed for J. Noon, Cheapside, and A. Mil-
lar, in the Strand. 1751.

HUGH PETERS,* born in the year 1599, was
the son of considerable parents, of Foy in Cornwall. His father was a merchant ; his mother
of the ancient family of the Treffys,† of Place,
in that town. He was sent to Cambridge at
fourteen years of age, where, being placed in
Trinity College, he took the degree of Bachelor
of Arts in 1616, and of Master in 1622. He
was licensed by Dr. Mountain, bishop of London, and preached at Sepulchre's with great
success.‡ Meeting with some trouble on the
account of his nonconformity,§ he went to Hol-

---

* Chiefly extracted from "A Dying Father's last
Legacy to an only Child; or, Mr. Hugh Peters's Advice to his Daughter," London, 1660, 12mo.

† Thus the name is spelled in *Peters's Last Legacy*;
but the same family was lately, if it is not now in
being, in the same house, whose name is always, I
think, spelled Treffry. However, from hence it is
very apparent that Peters's parentage by the mother
was very considerable ; for the antiquity of the family is known to most, nor does it yield in gentility to
any of the Cornish ; which is no mean character in
the eyes of those who value themselves on birth and
descent.

‡ His account of his coming to Sepulchre's, and
the success that he met with, will let us see something of the man.* "To Sepulchre's I was brought
by a very strange providence ; for preaching before
at another place, and a young man receiving some
good, would not be satisfied but I must preach at
Sepulchre's once monthly for the good of his friends.
In which he got his end (if I might not show vanity),
and he allowed thirty pounds per annum to that lecture : but his person unknown to me. He was a
chandler, and died a good man, and member of Parliament. At this lecture the resort grew so great,
that it contracted envy and anger ; though I believe
above a hundred every week were persuaded from
sin to Christ : there were six or seven thousand bearers, and the circumstances fit for such good work."
Great success this ! and what few preachers are
blessed with. But some, I know, would attribute this
to enthusiasm, which is very contagious, and produces
surprising, though not lasting effects. However this
be, it is no wonder envy and anger were contracted
by it ; for church governors are wont to dislike popular preachers, especially when they set themselves
to teach in a manner different from them. I will
only remark farther, that Peters was as great a con-
verter as our modern Methodists.

§ Never was there anything in the world more inconsistent with Christianity or good policy than persecution for conscience' sake. Yet such was the
madness of the prelates during the reigns of the Stuarts, as to harass and distress men most cruelly,
merely on account of nonconformity to ecclesiastical
ceremonies. Laud was an arch-tyrant this way, as
is known to all acquainted with our histories ; nor
were Wren and others much inferior to him. The
very spirit of tyranny actuated their breasts, and
made them feared and loathed while living, caused
them to be abhorred since dead, and will render them
infamous throughout all generations. I can add nothing to what Locke and Bayle have said on the
reasonableness and equity of toleration ; to them I
will refer those who have any doubts about it. Only
as to the popular objections of its being inconsistent
with the good of the state, and the wars and tumults
occasioned by it, I will beg leave to observe, that it is
evident to a demonstration that those communities
are more happy in which the greatest number of sects

---

* Peters's Legacy, p. 101.

---

land, where he was five or six years,* from
whence he removed to New-England, and, after
residing there seven years, was sent into England by that colony to mediate for ease in customs and excise. The civil war being then on
foot, he went into Ireland, and upon his return
was entertained by the Earl of Warwick, Sir
Thomas Fairfax, and Oliver Cromwell, afterward protector.† He was much valued by the
abound. Holland, the free cities of Germany, and
England since the Revolution, prove the truth of
my assertion. And I will venture, without pretending to the spirit of prophecy, to affirm, that whenever
the sects in England shall cease learning and liberty
will be no more among us. So that, instead of suppressing, we ought to wish their increase ; for they
are curbs to the state clergy, excite a spirit of emulation, and occasion a decency and regularity of behaviour among them, which they would probably use
otherwise strangers to.

And for civil wars about religion ; they are so far
from arising from toleration, that, for the most part,
they are the effect of the prince's imprudence..." He
must needs," says an indisputable judge, "have un-
seasonably favoured one sect at the expense of another ; he must either have too much promoted, or too
much discouraged the public exercise of certain forms
of worship ; he must have added weight to party
quarrels, which are only transient sparks of fire when
the sovereign does not interfere, but become confla-
grations when he foments them. To maintain the
civil government with vigour, to grant every man a
liberty of conscience, to act always like a king, and
never put on the priest, is the sure means of preserving a state from those storms and hurricanes which
the dogmatical spirit of divines is continually labouring to conjure up."* Had Charles the First had the
wisdom and prudence of this great writer, he never
had plunged his kingdoms into the miseries of a civil
war, nor, by hearkening to his chaplains, refused
terms which would have prevented his unhappy catastrophe

* It seems that he behaved himself so well during
his stay in Holland as to procure great interest and
reputation in that country ; for being afterward in
Ireland, and seeing the great distress of the poor
Protestants that had been plundered by the Irish
rebels, he went into Holland, and procured about
thirty thousand pounds to be sent from thence into
Ireland for their relief.—*Ludlow's Memoirs*, vol. iii.,
p. 75.

† Mr. Whitlock shall be my voucher for this.†
Mr. Peters, says he, gave a large relation to the Commons of all the business of Lyme, where he was with
the Earl of Warwick. Again,‡ Mr. Peters, who
brought up letters from Sir Thomas Fairfax, was
called into the House, and made a large relation of
the particular passages in the taking of Bridgewater.
And§ Mr. Peters was called into the House and gave
them a particular account of the siege of Bristol ; and
he pressed the desire of Sir Thomas Fairfax to have
recruits sent him. Letters‖ brought by Mr. Peters
from Lieutenant-general Cromwell, concerning the
taking Winchester Castle ; after which he was called
in and gave a particular relation of it. He¶ came
from the army to the House, and made them a narration of the storming and taking of Dartmouth, and
of the valour, unity, and affection of the army, and
presented several letters, papers, crucifixes, and other
popish things taken in the town. It is plain, from
these quotations, that Peters must have been in favour with the generals, and that he must have made
some considerable figure in the transactions of those
times. It is not improbable that the distinction with
which he was treated, by them attached him so
firmly to their interest, that in the end it cost him
his life.

* Anti-Machiavel Eng., Trav., p. 328, edit. 1741.
† Whitlock's Memorials, p. 92, Lond., 1732, folio.
‡ Ibid., p. 163.   § Ibid., p. 171
‖ Ibid., p. 175.   ¶ Ibid., p. 189.

Parliament, and improved his interest with them in the behalf of the unfortunate.* He was very zealous and active in their cause, and had presents made him, and an estate given him by them.† He assisted Mr. Chaloner in his last moments, as he afterward did Sir John Hotham.‡

* "At his trial he averred he had a certificate under the Marchioness of Worcester's hand, beginning with these words: I do here testify, that in all the sufferings of my husband, Mr. Peters was my great friend. And, added he, I have here a seal (and then produced it) that the Earl of Norwich gave me to keep for his sake for saving his life, which I will keep as long as I live."* And how great the opinion was of his interests with the persons in power, we find from the following words in a letter addressed to Secretary Nicholas, March 8, 1648: Mr. Peters, presenting yesterday Hamilton's petition to the speaker, made many believe he at last would escape.† Indeed, here he was unsuccessful; but his good-nature and readiness to oblige were manifested, and, one would have thought, should have merited some return to him when in distress

† We find in Whitlock, that he had £100 given him when he brought the news of taking Bridgewater; £50 when he brought letters from Cromwell concerning the taking Winchester Castle; that there was an order for £100 a year for him and his heirs; and another ordonnance for £200 a year.‡ To all which we may add the estate the Parliament gave him, mentioned in the body of the article (if it was distinct from the 100 and £200 per annum mentioned by Whitlock), which was part of the Lord Craven's; and the bishop's books (Laud's, I suppose), valued, as he tells us, at £140; and likewise the pay of a preacher as he could get it.§ These were handsome rewards, and show the Parliament to have been no bad masters. But, notwithstanding, "he says he lived in debt, because what he had others shared in."‖ From hence generosity or prodigality of temper may be inferred; but as it may as well be attributed to the former as to the latter, I know not why we should not consider him rather as laudable than culpable. Indeed, the clergy have been branded for their covetousness; though certain it is, there have been some among them who have performed as many generous, good-natured actions, as any of their ill-willers.

‡ Mr. Chaloner was executed¶ for what was called Waller's Plot, an account of which is to be found in the historians of those times. He owned he died justly, and deserved his punishment. In compliance with Peters's request, he explained the part he had in it, and being desired by him, Peters prayed with him.** The business of Sir John Hotham is well known. Peters attended him on the scaffold,†† and received public thanks on it from him. I will transcribe part of his speech, and likewise of Peters's by his command, that the reader may judge something of his temper and behaviour. "I hope," said Sir John. "God Almighty will forgive me, the Parliament and the court-martial, and all inen' that have had anything to do with my death. And, gentlemen, I thank this worthy gentleman‡‡ for putting me in mind of it." Then Mr. Peters spoke again [he had before mentioned the desire of Sir John not to have many questions put to him, he having fully discovered his mind to him and other ministers, but that he might have liberty to speak only what he thought fit con-

* Exact and Impartial Account of the Trial of the Regicides. Lond., 4to, 1660, p. 173.
† Ormond's Papers, published by Carte, vol. i., p. 233, Lond., 1739.
‡ See note †, 2d col. of previous page.
§ Peters's Legacy, p. 102, 104, 115.
‖ Ibid., p. 103.
** Rushw. Hist. Collect., part iii.; vol. ii., p. 327, 328, Lond., 1692, fol.
†† January 2, 1644.
‡‡ He was hereunto moved by Mr. Peters, says Rushworth.

He could fight as well as pray,* though perhaps in his capacity as a preacher he was most serving himself], "and told the audience that he had something farther to commend unto them from Sir John Hotham, which was, that he had lived in abundance of plenty, his estate large, about £2000 a year at first, and that he had gained much to it; that in the beginning of his days he was a soldier in the Low Countries, and was at the battle of Prague; that at his first going out for a soldier, his father spoke to him to this effect: Son! when the crown of England lies at stake, you will have fighting enough. That he had run through great hazards and undertakings; and now coming to this end, desired they would take notice in him of the vanity of all things here below, as wit, parts, prowess, strength, friends, honour, or what else.

"Then, Mr. Peters having prayed, and after him Sir John, they sung the 38th Psalm; and Sir John, kneeling behind the block, spent above a quarter of an hour in private prayer; after which, lying down, the executioner at one blow did his office."*

We see nothing here but great civility in Peters, and the due discharge of his office. Here is nothing troublesome or impertinent, but as one would wish to have it in like circumstances. Let the reader compare the following account of Sir John's behaviour with Rushworth's, and judge of the truth of the narration, and the justness of the epithet bestowed on Peters.

"The poor man (Sir John Hotham) appeared so dispirited that he spoke but few words after he came upon the scaffold, and suffered his ungodly confessor, Peters, to tell the people that he had revealed himself to him, and confessed his offences against the Parliament; and so he committed his head to the block."†

Peters, we see, said nothing like his having confessed his offences against the Parliament. This, therefore, is mere invention, like too many other things to be found in this celebrated history; the charge of interpolations, and additions against which I am sorry, for the noble writer's sake, to find affirmed to be groundless, by so worthy a man, and so good a judge, as Mr. Birch.‡ As to the epithet ungodly conferred on Peters, the considerate reader will judge of it as it deserves.

* Let us hear Whitlock. "Mr. Peters, at the beginning of the troubles in Ireland, led a brigade against the rebels, and came off with honour and victory."§ So that we see he knew how to use both swords, and could slay and kill, as well as feed the sheep, which, in the opinion of Baronius, Christ gave Peter authority to exercise equally as occasion might require.‖ But to be serious. This leading a brigade against the Irish rebels ought not to be imputed to Peters as a crime, it being equally as justifiable as Archbishop Williams's arming in the civil wars in England, or Dr. Walker's defending Londonderry, and fighting at the battle of the Boyn (in which he gloriously lost his life) in Ireland; more especially as the Irish, against whom Peters fought, were a bloodthirsty crew, who had committed¶ acts of wickedness hardly to be paralleled even in the annals of Rome papal. Against such villains, therefore, it was meritorious to engage, and Peters was undeniably praiseworthy; for there are times and seasons when the gown must give place to arms, even at those times when our laws, liberties, and religion are endangered by ambitious, bloody, and superstitious men. And were the clergy in all countries as much concerned for these blessings as they ought, they would deserve the reverence of all orders of men.

* Rushworth, p. 803, 804.
† Clarendon's History of the Grand Rebellion, vol. ii., part ii., p. 622, Oxford, 1707.
‡ Life of Hampden, among the Lives of Illustrious Men, n. 78.
§ Whitlock, p. 426.
‖ Bedel's Life, p. 6, 8vo, London, 1685.
¶ See a brevviate of some of the cruelties, murders, &c., committed by the Irish papal rebels upon the Protestants, October, 23, 1641, in Rushworth, part iii., vol. 1, p. 405.

viceable to the cause.* He was thought to be deeply concerned in the king's death, and his name has been treated with much severity by reason of it.† He was appointed one of the tri-

* Whitlock tells us,* that when Sir Thomas Fairfax moved for storming Bridgwater anew, and it was assented to, the Lord's Day before, Mr. Peters, in his sermon, encouraged the soldiers to the work. And at Milford Haven the country did unanimously take the Engagement, and Mr. Peters opened the matter to them, and did much encourage them to take it.† He preached also in the market-place at Torrington, and convinced many of their errors in adhering to the king's party.‡ A man of this temper, it is easily seen, must be of great service to any party, and seems to deserve the rewards he received; for in factions it is the bold and daring man, the man that will spare no pains, that is to be valued and encouraged, and not the meek, the modest, and moderate one. A man of wisdom would not have taken these employments upon him, nor would a minister, one should think, who was animated by the meek and merciful spirit of the Gospel, have set himself from the pulpit to encourage the soldiers to storm a town in which his brethren and countrymen were besieged. If storming was thought necessary by the generals, they themselves should have encouraged the soldiers thereunto; but Peters, as a minister of the Gospel, should have excited them rather to spare the effusion of human blood as much as possible, and to have compassion on the innocent. Peters, however, was not singular in his conduct. The immortal Chillingworth, led away with party spirit, and forgetting that he was a minister of the Prince of Peace, attended the king's army before Gloucester; and "observing that they wanted materials to carry on the siege, suggested the making of some engines after the manner of the *Roman testudines cum pluteis.*§ Indeed, the divines of both sides too much addicted themselves to their respective parties, and were too unmindful of the duties of their function.

† Every one knows he suffered for this after the restoration. He had judgment passed on him as a traitor, and as such was executed,‖ and his head afterward set on a pole on London Bridge.

Burnet¶ tells us, "that he had been outrageous in pressing the king's death, with the cruelty and rudeness of an inquisitor."; Dr. Barwick says, "he was upon no slight grounds accused to have been one of the king's murtherers, though it could not be sufficiently proved against him."**

And we find in a satirical piece, styled *Epulæ Thyestæ,* printed 1649, the following lines:

"There's Peters the denyer (nay, 'tis said
He that (disguised) cut off his Master's head);
That godly pigeon of apostacy
Does buzz about his Anti-Monarchy,
His scaffold doctrines."

One Mr. Starkey, at his trial,†† swore that "he styled the king tyrant and fool, asserted that he was not fit to be a king, and that the office was dangerous, chargeable, and useless."

It was likewise sworn on his trial, that in a sermon a few days before the king's trial, he addressed himself to the members of the two Houses, in these terms:‡‡ "My lords, and you, noble gentlemen, it is you we chiefly look for justice from. Do not prefer the great Barabbas, murtherer, tyrant, and traylor, before these poor hearts (pointing to the red coats) and the army, who are our saviours."

In another sermon before Cromwell and Bradshaw, he said, "Here is a great discourse and talk in the world; what, will ye cut off the head of a

* Whitlock. p. 162. † Ibid., p. 447. ‡ Ibid., p. 194.
§ Maizeaux's Life of Chillingworth, p. 280, Lond., 1725, 8vo; and Rushworth, part iii., vol. ii., p. 290.
‖ October 16, 1660.
¶ History of his own Times, Dutch edit., in 12mo, vol. i., p. 264.
** Barwick's Life, Eng. trans., p. 296, London, 1724.
†† Trial of the Regicides, v. 159. ‡‡ Ibid., p. 166.

ers for the ministry,* and a commissioner for

Protestant prince? Turn to your Bibles, and ye shall find it there, 'Whosoever sheds man's blood, by man shall his blood be shed.' I see neither King Charles, Prince Charles, Prince Rupert, nor Prince Maurice, nor any of that rabble excepted out of it."* These, and many other things of the like nature, were sworn against him at his trial, and notwithstanding his denial of the most part of them, caused his condemnation. So that there seems pretty clear proof of his guilt, and sufficient reason for his censure.

Let us now hear Peters speak for himself: "I had access to the king, he used me civilly; I, in requital, offered my poor thoughts three times for his safety; I never had band in contriving or acting his death, as I am scandalized, but the contrary, to my mean power."† Which, if true, no wonder he should think the Act of Indemnity would have included him, as well as others, as he declares he did, of which we shall speak more hereafter.

That he was useful and serviceable to the king during his confinement, there is undeniable proof. Whitlock writes, "that upon a conference between the king and Mr. Hugh Peters, and the king desiring one of his own chaplains might be permitted to come to him, for his satisfaction in some scruples of conscience, Dr. Juxon, bishop of London, was ordered to go to his majesty."‡ "And Sir John Denham being intrusted by the queen to deliver a message to his majesty, who at that time was in the hands of the army, by Hugh Peters's assistance, he got admittance to the king."§

These were considerable services, and could hardly have been expected from a man who was outrageous in pressing the king's death with the cruelty and rudeness of an inquisitor.

And as to what was said of his being supposed to be the king's executioner, one, who was his servant, deposed on his trial that he kept his chamber, being sick on the day the king suffered; and no stress was laid by the king's council on the suspicions uttered against him on this head. So that, in all reason, Dr. Barwick should have forborne saying, "That he was upon no slight grounds accused to have been one of the king's murtherers."

Certain it is, he too much fell in with the times, and, like a true court chaplain, applauded and justified what his masters did, or intended to do; though he himself might be far enough from urging them beforehand to do it. He would, perhaps, have been pleased if the king and army had come to an agreement; but as that did not happen, he stuck close to his party, and would not leave defending their most iniquitous behaviour.

Which conduct is not peculiar to Peters. Charles the First, at this day, is spoken of as the best, not only of men, but of kings; and the Parliament is said to have acted right in opposing his tyranny, and likewise in bringing him to the block, by the stanch party men of each side respectively. No wickedness is owned, no errors are acknowledged on the one part, nor is there any such thing to be granted as wisdom or honesty on the other. These are the men that often turn the world upside down, and spirit up mobs, tumults, and seditions, till at length they become quite contemptible, and perhaps undergo the fate allotted to folly and villany.

* These were men appointed by Cromwell to try the abilities of all entrants into the ministry, and likewise the capacity of such others as were presented, or invited to new places. Butler, according to his manner, has represented their business in a ludicrous light, in the following lines:

"Whose business is, by cunning slight,
To cast a figure for men's light;
To find in lines of beard and face
The physiognomy of grace;

* Trial of the Regicides, p. 168.
† Peters's Legacy, p. 102. ‡ Whitlock, p. 370.
§ Denham's Epist. Dedicat. to Charles II., of his Poems, 2d edit., 1671.

amending the laws, though poorly qualified for it.* He is accused of great vices, but whether

> And if by the sound and twang of nose,
> If all be sound within disclose ;
> Free from a crack or flaw of sinning,
> As men try pipkins by the ringing."
> *Hudib.*, canto iii.

However, jesting apart, it must be owned the thing in itself was good enough; but instead of examining those who came before them in languages, divinity, and more especially morality, things of the highest importance, one should think, they used to ask them whether they had ever any experience of a work of grace on their hearts;* and according as they could answer hereunto, were they received or rejected. How much more intelligible would it have been to have inquired whether they were "blameless, husbands of one wife, vigilant, sober, of good behaviour, given to hospitality, apt to teach, not given to wine, no strikers, not greedy of filthy lucre, patient, not brawlers, not covetous?" Whether they ruled well their own houses, and had a good report of them which were without?"† I say, how much more intelligible and important would these questions have been, yea, how much easier and more certainly determined, than that above mentioned? But it is a very long time ago that these were the qualifications required and expected from clergymen; for ages past, subscription to doubtful articles of faith, declarations very ambiguous, or most difficult to be made by understanding minds, or the shibboleth of the prevailing party in the Church, have been the things required and insisted on. Whence it has come to pass that so many of our divines, as they are styled, understand so little of the Scriptures, and that they know and practise so little of pure, genuine Christianity. I would not be thought to reflect on any particular persons; but hope those in whose hands the government of the Church is lodged will consider whether they are not much too careless in their examinations of young men for ordinations ? Whether very many of them are not unqualified to teach and instruct, through neglect of having carefully studied the Word of God ? And whether their conversation be not such as is unsuitable to the character conferred on them ? It is with uneasiness one is obliged to hint at these things ; but surely it is more than time that they were reformed, and St. Paul's rules were put in practice.

A wise, virtuous, prudent clergy, is the glory and happiness of a community, and there cannot be too much care taken to procure it.‡ But if triers neglect the means of doing this, and admit all who are presented to a curacy to orders, if so be they will make use of the terms in vogue, whether they understand them or no, they deserve censure, and are answerable for all the sad consequences which flow from ignorance, folly, and vice:

* He as good as owns this in the following passage : " When I was a trier of others, I went to hear and gain experience, rather than to judge; when I was called about mending laws, I rather was there to pray than to mend laws ; but in all these I confess I might as well have been spared."§ This is modest and very ingenuous ; but such a confession as few of our gentlemen concerned in such matters would choose to make. They frequently boast of the great share they have in business, though many of them may well be spared. Let us confirm the truth of Peters's confession by Whitlock : "I was often advised with by some of this committee, and none of them was more active in this business than Mr. Hugh Peters the minister, who understood little of the law, but was very opinionative, and would frequently mention some proceedings of law in Holland, wherein he was altogether mistaken."|| The ignorance and inability of the man with regard to

justly or not is a question*. He was executed these matters, we see, are as plainly described here as in his own words; though how to reconcile his own opinionativeness and activity in it with his going to the committee rather to pray than to mend laws, I confess I know not. Perhaps he had forgotten the part he had acted. This* "committee were to take into consideration what inconveniences were in the law, how the mischiefs that grow from delays, the chargeableness and irregularities in the proceedings of the law may be prevented, and the speediest way to prevent the same." In this committee with Peters were Mr. Fountain, Mr. Rushworth, and Sir Anthony Ashley Cooper, afterward Earl of Shaftesbury and lord-high-chancellor, besides many others of rank and figure. No great matters followed from this committee, by reason of the hurry of the times and the opposition which the lawyers made to it. But the Parliament had a little before† passed an " act that all the books on the law should be put into English, and that all writs, process, and returns thereof, and all patents, commissions, indictments, judgments, records, and all rules and proceedings in courts of justice, shall be in the English tongue only." This act or ordinance (to speak in the language of the times of which I am writing) does great honour to the Parliament, and is an argument of their good sense and concern for the welfare of the people. It is amazing so good a law should not have been continued by proper authority after the Restoration ! But it was a sufficient reason then to disuse a thing, though ever so good in itself, that it had been enacted by an usurped power. Of such fatal consequences are prejudices ! But thanks be unto God ! we have seen the time when this most excellent ordinance has been again revived, and received the sanction of the whole Legislature. How much were it to be wished that a committee of wise and prudent persons were once more employed to revise, amend, and abridge our laws ! that we might know ourselves how to act, and not be necessitated to make use of those who (we are sensible) live on our spoils. This would add greatly to the glory of our most excellent prince, and would be the best employment of that peace which his wisdom has procured for us. But much is it to be feared that our adversaries will be too hard for us, and that we shall be obliged, for a time at least, to submit to their yoke. But whenever the spirit of true patriotism shall generally possess the breasts of our senators, I doubt not but that they will apply themselves to our deliverance in good earnest and bring it to perfection (as it was long ago done in Denmark, and very lately in Prussia), inasmuch as the happiness of the community absolutely depends thereon.

* I will transcribe Dr. Barwick at large.‡ "The wild prophecies uttered by his (Hugh Peters's) impure mouth were still received by the people with the same veneration as if they had been oracles, though he was known to be infamous for more than one kind of wickedness ; a fact which Milton himself did not dare to deny, when he purposely wrote his Apology; for this very end, to defend even by name (as far as was possible) the very blackest of the conspirators, and Hugh Peters among the chief of them, who were by name accused of manifest impieties by their adversaries." Burnet§ says likewise, " He was a very vicious man." And Langbaine|| hints something of an " affair that he had with a butcher's wife of Sepulchre's." Peters himself was not insensible of his ill character among the opposite party, nor of the particular vice laid to his charge by Langbaine ; but he terms it reproach, and attributes it to his zeal in the cause. " By my zeal it seems I have exposed myself to all manner of reproach ; but wish you to know that (besides your mother) I have had no fellowship that way with any woman since I knew her, having a godly wife before also, I bless God."¶

---

* Howe's Life, by Calamy, p. 21, London, 1724, 8vo.
† 1 Tim., iii., 2–7.
‡ See Hutchinson's Introduction to Moral Philosophy, b. iii., ch. viii., sect. 1. § Peters's Legacy, p. 109.
|| Whitlock, p. 521.

* This committee was appointed Jan. 20, 1651.
† Oct. 25, 1650, Whitlock, p. 475.
‡ Barwick's Life, p. 155, 156. § Hist , vol. i., p. 264.
|| Dramatic Poets, p. 339. ¶ Legacy, p. 106.

shortly after the Restoration, though doubtless he had as much reason to think he should have

A man is not allowed to be a witness in his own cause; nor should, I think, his adversaries' testimony be deemed full proof. One loaden with such an accusation as Peters was, and suffering as a traytor, when the party spirit ran high, and revenge actuated the breasts of those who bore rule; for such a one to be traduced and blackened beyond his deserts, is no wonder. It is indeed hard to prove a negative; and the concurring testimony of writers to Peters's bad character makes one with difficulty suspend assent unto it. But if the following considerations be weighed, I shall not, perhaps, be blamed for saying it was a question whether he was accused justly or not.

1. The accusations against him came from known enemies, those who hated the cause he was engaged in, and looked on it as detestable. It may easily, therefore, be supposed that they were willing to blacken the actors in it, or, at least, that they were susceptible of ill impressions concerning them; and ready to believe any evil thing they heard of them. This will, if attended to, lessen the weight of their evidence considerably, and dispose us to think that they may have misrepresented the characters of their opponents. Barwick, at first sight, appears an angry, partial writer; Burnet's characters were never thought too soft; they were both enemies to the Republican party, though not equally furious and violent. Add to this, that neither of them, as far as appears, knew anything of Peters themselves; and therefore what they write must be considered only as common fame, than which nothing is more uncertain.

2. The times in which Peters was on the stage were far enough from favouring vice (public vice, for it is of this Peters is accused) in the ministerial character. He must be a novice in the history of those times who knows not what a precise, demure kind of men the preachers among the Parliamentarians were. They were careful not only of their actions, but likewise of their words and looks, and allowed not themselves in the innocent gayeties and pleasures of life. I do not take on me to say they were as good as they pretended to be; for aught I know, they might be, yea, perhaps were proud, conceited, censorious, uncharitable, avaricious. But then drunkenness, whoredom, adultery, and swearing were things quite out of vogue among them, nor was it suffered in them. So that how vicious soever their inclinations might be, they were obliged to conceal them, and keep them from the eye of the public. It was this sobriety of behaviour, this strictness of conversation, joined with their popular talents in the pulpit, that created them so much respect, and caused such a regard to be paid unto their advice and direction. The people in a manner adored them, and were under their government almost absolutely. So that the leading men in the House of Commons, and those who, after the king's death, were in the administration of affairs, were obliged to court them, and profess to admire them. Hence it was that men of such sense as Pym, Hampden, Holles, Whitlock, Selden, St. John, Cromwell, &c., sat so many hours hearing their long-winded, weak prayers and preachments; that men of the greatest note took it as an honour to sit with the Assembly of Divines, and treated them with so much deference and regard. For it was necessary to gain the preachers in order to maintain their credit with the people; now certainly, if Peters had been a man so vicious as he is represented, he could have had no influence over the people, nor would he have been treated by the then great men in the manner he was; for they must have parted with him even for their own sakes, unless they would have been looked on as enemies to godliness. But Peters was caressed by the great; his prophecies were received as oracles by the people, and he was of great service to Cromwell; and therefore he could not surely (at least publicly) be known to be infamous for more than one kind of

escaped as many others * The charge against wickedness, as Barwick asserts. In short, hypocrisy was the characteristic of Peters's age; and

" Hypocritic zeal
Allows no sins, but those it can conceal."—*Dryden.*

3. Peters's patrons seem to render the account of his wickedness very improbable. We have seen that he was entertained by the Earl of Warwick, sir Thomas Fairfax, and Oliver Cromwell, and that he was much caressed and rewarded by the Parliament. How improbable, then, is it that Peters should be infamous for wickedness! His patrons were never accused of personal vices; they were men who made high pretensions to religion; and the cause they fought for, they talked of (if they did not think it to he) as the cause of God. Now, with what face could they have done this, if their chaplain, confidant, and tool had been known to have been a very vicious man? Or how could they have talked against scandalous ministers, who employed one most scandalous? In short, how could they reward Peters publicly, when they always professed great zeal for godliness, and were for promoting it to the highest pitch? Men of their wisdom can hardly be thought to have acted so inconsistent a part; nor is there anything in their whole conduct which would lead one to think they could be guilty of it. From all these considerations, therefore, I think it reasonable to make it a question whether Peters was charged justly with great vices.

* "I thought the Act of Indemnity would have included me; but the hard character upon me excluded me."* And no wonder he should think so, if it was true "that he never had his hand in any man's blood, but saved many in life and estate."† All that was laid to Peters's charge was words; but words, it must be owned, unfit to be uttered? yet, if we consider how many greater offenders than Peters escaped capital punishment, we may possibly think he had hard measure. Harry Martyn, John Goodwin, and John Milton, spoke of Charles the First most reproachfully, and the two latter vindicated his murther in their public writings. As early as 1643, we find Martyn speaking out plainly, "That it was better the king and his children were destroyed, than many;" which words were then looked on as so high and dangerous, that he was committed by the House to the Tower; though shortly after released and readmitted to his place in Parliament.‡ He continued still virulent against the king, was one of his judges, and acted as much as possible against him. Goodwin justified the seclusion of the members, which was the prelude to Charles's tragedy; vindicated his murther, and went into all the measures of his masters; and being a man of ready wit and great learning, was of good service to them. And as for Milton, there is no one but knows that he wrote most sharply against King Charles, and set forth his actions in a terribly black light. To take no notice of his writings against Salmasius and More, what could be more cruel against Charles than his Iconoclastes! How bitter are his observations, how cutting his remarks on his conduct! How horribly provoking to point out Sir Philip Sidney's Arcadia as the book from whence the " prayer in the time of captivity," delivered to Dr. Juxon, immediately before his death, was chiefly taken?§ One should have thought this an indignity never to have been forgotten nor forgiven, especially as it was offered by one who was secretary to Cromwell, and who had spent the best part of his life in the service of the anti-royalists. But yet Milton was preserved as to life and fortune (happy for the polite arts he was preserved), and lived in great esteem among men of worth all his days. Goodwin had the same good fortune; and Martyn escaped the fate of many of his fellow-judges; though

* Peters's Legacy, p. 105.
† Ibid., p. 104. See note *, col. i., p. 501.
‡ Whitlock, p. 71.
§ Vid. Bayle's Dict., article Milton. Milton's works, or Toland's Amyntor.

him was for compassing and imagining the death of the king, by conspiring with Oliver Cromwell on his trial he behaved no way abjectly or meanly. All this had the appearance of clemency. and Peters might reasonably have expected to share in it. But poor wretch! he had nothing to recommend him as these had, and, therefore, though more innocent, fell without pity. Martyn, as it was reported, escaped merely by his vices;* Goodwin having been a zealous Arminian, and a sower of division among the sectaries, on these accounts had friends; but what Milton's merit with the courtiers was, Burnet says not. Though, if I am not mistaken, it was with his having saved Sir William Davenant's life formerly, which was the occasion of the favour shown to him. Merit or interest, in the eyes of the then courtiers, these had; but Peters, though he had saved many a life and estate, was forgotten by those whom in their distress he had served, and given up to the hangman. But the sentence passed on him, and much more the execution of it, will seem very rigorous if we consider that it was only for words, for words uttered in a time of confusion, uproar, and war. I am not lawyer enough to determine whether, by any statute then in force, words were treason. Lord Strafford,† in his defence at the bar of the House of Lords, says expressly, "No statute makes words treason." But allowing they were, such a law must be deemed to have been hard, and unfit for execution, especially as the words were spoken in times of civil commotion; for in such seasons men say and do, in a manner, what they list, the laws are disregarded, and rank and character unminded, contempt is poured on princes, and the nobles are had in derision. These are the natural consequences of wars and tumults; and wise men foresee and expect them. But were all concerned in them to be punished, whole cities would be turned into shambles. To overlook and forgive what has been said on such occasions, is a part of wisdom and prudence, and what has been almost always practised. Never were there greater liberties taken with princes, never more dangerous doctrines inculcated by preachers, than in France during part of the reigns of the 3d and 4th Henry. "The College of Sorbonne, by common consent, concluded that the French were discharged from the oath of allegiance to Henry the Third, and that they might arm themselves in opposition to him." In consequence of which, the people vented their rage against him in satyrs, lampoons, libels, infamous reports and calumnies, of which the most moderate were tyrant and apostate. And the curates refused absolution to such as owned they could not renounce him.‡ And the same Sorbonists decreed all those who favoured the party of Henry the Fourth, to be in a mortal sin, and liable to damnation; and such as resisted him, champions of the faith, and to be rewarded with a crown of martyrdom.§ These decrees produced terrible effects; and yet, when Henry the Fourth had fully established on the throne, I do not remember that he called any of these doctors to an account, or that one of them was executed. That wise prince undoubtedly considered the times, and viewed these wretches with pity and contempt for being the tools of cunning, artful men, who veiled their ambitious designs under the cloak of religion:

So that, really considering what had passed abroad, and what passed under his own observation, Peters had reason to think that the Act of indemnity would have included him. But setting aside all this, I believe all impartial judges will think he had hard measure dealt him, when they consider that those who preached up doctrines in the pulpit as bad as Peters's, and those likewise who, though guardians of our laws and liberties, and sworn to maintain them,

* Burnet, vol. i., p. 265.
† Trial, p. 561, fol., London, 1680.
‡ Maimbourgh's History of the League, translated by Dryden, Oct. 1684, Lond., p. 433 and 437.
§ Ibid., p. 805.

at several times and places, and procuring the soldiers to demand justice, by preaching divers sermons to persuade them to take off the king, comparing him to Barabbas, &c. : to which he pleaded in his own defence, that the war began before he came into England; that, since his arrival, he had endeavoured to promote sound religion, the reformation of learning and the law, and employment of the poor; that, for the better effecting these things, he had espoused the interest of the Parliament, in which he had acted without malice, avarice, or ambition; and that whatever prejudices or passions might possess the minds of men, yet there was a God who knew these things to be true.

At the place of execution, when Chief-justice Coke was cut down and embowelled, Hugh Peters was then ordered to be brought that he might see it; and the executioner came to him, rubbing his bloody hands, and asked him how he liked that work. He told him he was not at all terrified; and that he might do his worst. And when he was upon the ladder, he said to the sheriff, " Sir, you have butchered one of the servants of God before my eyes, and have forced me to see it, in order to terrify and discourage me, but God has permitted it for my support and encouragement."

One of the prodigies of those times attended Peters going to the gibbet,* which, as it may delivered opinions destructive of them, even from the bench : I say, whoever considers the comparatively mild treatment these men have met with, will be apt to judge the punishment of Peters very severe. What was the crime of Peters? Was it not the justifying and magnifying the king's death? And is this worse than the doctrine of Montague, Sibthorp, and Manwaring, which set the king above all laws, and gave him a power to do as he list? is this worse than the opinion of the judges in Charles the First and James the Second's time, whereby it was given for law, that the king might take from his subjects without consent of Parliament, and dispense with the laws enacted by it? Far from it; for the depriving the people of their rights and liberties, or the arguing for the expediency and justice of so doing, is a crime of a higher nature than the murthering or magnifying the murther of the wisest and best prince under heaven. The loss of a good prince is greatly to be lamented, but it is a loss which may be repaired; whereas the loss of a people's liberties is seldom or ever to be recovered; and, consequently, the foe to the latter is much more detestable than the foe to the former. But what was the punishment of the justifiers and magnifiers of the destruction of the rights and liberties of the people? Reprimands at the bar of one or other of the houses, fines, or imprisonment; not a man of them graced the gallows, though none, perhaps, would better have become it. Peters, therefore, suffered more than others, though he had done less to deserve it than others, which we may well suppose, was contrary to his expectation.

" Among the innumerable libels which they (the fanatics) published for two years together, those were most pregnant with sedition which they published concerning prodigies. Among these, all the prodigies in Livy were seen every day : two suns; ships sailing in the air; a bloody rainbow; it rained stones; a lamb with two heads : cathedral churches everywhere set on fire by lightning; an ox that spoke; a hen turned into a cock; a mule brought forth; five beautiful young men stood by the regicides while they suffered; a very bright star shone round their quarters that were stuck upon the city gates. A certain person rejoicing at the execution of Harrison the regicide, was struck with a sudden palsy; another inveighing against Peters as he went to the

afford some diversion to the reader, I shall give an account of. . . . . He was weak, ignorant, and zealous, and, consequently, a proper tool for ambitious, artful men to make use of.* All preachers ought to be gibbet; was torn and almost killed by his own favourite dog;-with an infinite number of such prodigious lies."* What ridiculous tales are here! How worthy to be preserved in a work called a history! The fanatics, if they reported these things, undoubtedly reported lies; though many of them, in great simplicity of heart, believed them. However, it is no great wisdom to relate idle stories to disgrace the understanding or impeach the honesty of parties; for weak, credulous, superstitious men, are to be found on all sides. The reader, as he has a right, is welcome to laugh at these stories; and to contribute to his mirth, I will add the following "relation of a child born in London with a double or divided tongue, which, the third day after it was born, cried A king, a king, and bid them bring it to the king. The mother of the child saith it told her of all that happened in England since, and much more which she dare not utter. A gentleman in the company took the child in his arms, and gave it money, and asked what it would do with it. To which it answered aloud, that it would give it to the king." This story matches pretty well the others, and, I believe, will be thought equally as ridiculous, and yet the relator of it (no less a man than Bishop Bramhall) says he cannot esteem it less than a miracle.† But let us away with these trifles; they are fit for nothing but ridicule, and can serve no purpose, unless it be to show the weakness of the human understanding, or the wickedness of the human heart; though these are many times, by other things, but too apparent.

.* Peters's weakness, ignorance, and zeal appear from his own confession, as well as the testimony of Whitlock, before quoted. Now such a man as this was thoroughly qualified to be a tool, and could hardly fail of being employed for that purpose. Fools are the instruments of knaves; or, to speak softer, men of small understandings are under the direction and influence of those who possess great abilities. Let a man be ever so wise and ambitious, he never would gain the point he aims at, were all men possessed of equal talents with himself; for they would see his aims, and would refuse to be made use of as tools to accomplish them. They would look through his specious pretences, they would separate appearances from realities, and frustrate his selfish intentions; so that his skill would stand him in little stead.

But as the bulk of men are formed, nothing in the world is easier than to impose on them. They see not beyond the present moment, and take all for gospel that is told them. And of these, there are none who become so easily the dupes of crafty, ambitious men, as those who have attained just knowledge enough to be proud and vain; it is but to flatter them, and you become their master, and lead them what lengths you please; and if they happen to have active spirits, you may make them accomplish your designs even without their being sensible of it. Those who have great things to execute know this, and therefore are careful to have as many of these instruments as possible to manage the multitude when there is occasion; for which end they carefully observe their foibles, and seemingly fall in with their notions, and thereby secure them. Hence it has come to pass, that real great men have paid very uncommon respect to those they despised; they knew they might be of use, and therefore were worth gaining. Peters must necessarily have appeared in a contemptible light to Cromwell; but as his ignorance and zeal qualified him for business, which wiser and more moderate men would have declined, he was thought worthy of being caressed, and had that respect paid him which

warned by his fate against going out of their province,* and meddling with things which no was necessary to keep him tight to the cause. And, generally speaking, they have been men of Peters's size of understanding who have been subservient to the interests of aspiring statesmen, and the implements of those in power. Were not Shaa* and Pinker weak men, in assisting the then Duke of Gloucester, protector, afterward Richard the Third, to fix the crown on his own head? Armed with impudence, Shaa at Paul's Cross declared the children of Edward the Fourth bastards; and Pinker, at St. Mary's Hospital, sounded forth the praise of the protector; both so full, adds the historian, of tedious flattery, as no man's ear could abide them. What was John Padilla's† priest, who did not fail every Sunday to recommend him, and the sedition of which he was the great promoter, with a pater-noster and an ave Maria? Indeed, ill usage from the rebels caused him to change his note soon after, and to advise his people to cry out, Long live the king, and let Padilla perish!

To come nearer home. Was not Sacheveral a weak, ignorant man, to be made the tool of a party? Would any but such a one have exposed himself by a nonsensical sermon, set the nation in a flame, and brought himself into trouble? But he was in the hands of intriguing politicians, who spurred him on, and made him the instrument of raising a cry of an imaginary danger, which served many purposes to themselves, though detrimental to the nation. And what character have our Jacobite clergymen universally deserved? If we will not be uncharitable, we must impute their behaviour to ignorance, and the influence they have been under; for men of sense, and penetration could have set themselves to infuse notions into their flocks, which have no other tendency than to enslave body and soul. And men uninfluenced would not run the risk of the gallows for the sake of nonsense and absurdity, as Jacobitism really is. But they have been the dupes of wicked, artful, and ambitious men, who have blinded their understandings, and by flatteries and caresses gained their affections, and consequently the poor wretches are the objects of pity.

So that Peters, we see, was as his brethren have been and are. His faults arose chiefly from his weakness, and his being in the hands of those who knew how to make use of him. Had he contented himself with obscurity, he had avoided danger; which, indeed, is the chief security for the virtue, ease, and welfare of men, in such a noisy, contentious world as this.

.* The business of the clergy is that of instructing the people in piety and virtue. If ever they meddle with civil matters, it ought to be only with an intent to promote peace and happiness, by exhorting princes to rule with equity and moderation, and the subjects to obey with willingness and pleasure. This, I say, is what alone concerns them, and if they confine themselves within these bounds, they merit praise. But if, instead hereof, they mix with civil factions, and endeavour to promote hatred, strife, and contention; if they aspire to bear rule and attempt to embroil matters, in order to render themselves of some importance, they then become not only really contemptible, but likewise criminal.

"The clergy," as the Marquis of Ormonde justly observes, "have not been happy to themselves or others when they have aspired to a rule so contrary to their function." Nature never seems to have intended the clergy, any more than the Gospel, for state affairs. For men brought up in colleges, and little versed in the world, as they generally are, make wretched work when they come to intermeddle with secular matters. To govern well requires great knowledge of human nature, the particular interests, dispositions, and tempers of the people one has to do

* Parker's Hist. of his own Time, p. 23, translated by Newlin, London, 1727, 8vo.
† Ormonde's Papers, by Carte, vol. ii., p. 208.

* Speed's History, p. 902. fol., London, 1632.
† Bayle's Dict., article Padilla (John de).
‡ Ormonde's Papers, vol. ii., p. 457.

way belong to them. But ᴛ a they are cautioned in vain.* pe h ps

with, the law of nations,' and more especially the laws of the country. ˅ Great skill and address likewise are required to manage the different and contradictory tempers of men, and make them conspire to promote the public happiness; as likewise great practice in business, in order to despatch it with speed and safety. And therefore it is evident, that the clergy, from the nature of their education, as well as their profession, cannot be qualified for it. They should therefore, seriously weigh their incapacity for civil affairs, and how inconsistent they are with the business to which they have solemnly engaged to devote themselves: They should consider how contemptible and ridiculous they render themselves in the eyes of all wise and good men when they engage in parties, and most hateful when they stir up wars and tumults. They should have the dignity of their character before their eyes, and scorn to disgrace it by letting themselves out to ambitious, self-interested men.· These things they should do; and a very small degree of knowledge and reflection will enable them to keep themselves from this, which is one of the greatest blemishes which can be found in their character.

·If this is not sufficient, let them call to their minds Peters, who, after having been sought to, and caressed by the most eminent personages, was obliged to skulk about privately; was seized by the officers of public justice; laden with infamy and reproach, and embowelled by the hangman. He that hath ears to hear, let him hear.

* No men in the world seem less willing to hearken to advice than the clergy; puffed up with conceit of their own knowledge and abilities, and being used to dictate uncontrolled from the pulpit, they with contempt hearken to instruction, and are uninfluenced by persuasion; for which reason, I say, perhaps they are cautioned in vain; Peters's fate will not deter them, but engage in factions they still will. After the restoration, the pulpits sounded loud with the doctrines of passive obedience and non-resistance; the Whigs and Presbyterians were represented as villains; the power of the Church was magnified, and the regal power was represented, as sacred as that of God himself. Then Sam. Parker and his fellows arose, full of rage and venom, who treated all who opposed them with ill manners and severity. Then were Englishmen pronounced slaves, in effect, by Hicks, in his Jovian; and then was the infamous Oxford Decree framed, which was doomed to the flames by the sentence of the most august assembly in the world, anno 1710.

The bishops stood firm by the Duke of York; and the whole clergy in a manner damned the Bill of Exclusion. In short, such was their behaviour, that they fell under great contempt, and were treated with much severity. Under James the Second they acted the same part, and would undoubtedly have continued his fast friends, had he not given liberty to the Dissenters, and touched them in their most tender part, even that of their revenue, by thrusting in popish persons into their colleges. This alarmed them; they suddenly tacked about, wished heartily for the coming of the Prince of Orange, and prayed for his success; he came and delivered them, out of the hands of their enemies; but they could not be quiet and thankful; numbers of them refused to own his government; many of them joined in measures to restore the tyrant James, and a great part did all that in them lay to blacken and distress their deliverer. Lesly, Sacheveral, &c., worked hard to inculcate on men's minds the danger of the Church, the designs of the Dissenters, the villany of the ministry. during the first and glorious part of Queen Anne's reign, in which they were but too successful. When the Protestant succession took place, it was railed at, and even cursed by these men, and many of them attempted to set up an abjured pretender. Their attempts, however, were vain; though

Postscript.—Since transcribing these papers for the press, a very learned gentleman* has been so kind as to impart to me an account of Peters's writings (his Last Legacy excepted, from which a good deal has been inserted in this work), which I doubt not will be highly acceptable to the curious; t as likewise a letter from

for these their endeavours, Parson Paul made his exit at the gallows, and the celebrated Atterbury died in exile.˙ What has been, and is the temper since, every one knows; the Oxford affair is too fresh in memory to let us remain ignorant of the disposition of many of the clergy; they are of Peters's busy, meddling disposition; though I hope they will not merit his fate. ⸳

Far be it from me to point these reflections at the: whole body of the clergy; numbers of them have been, and are men of great worth, who not only dignify their office, but add lustre to the human nature. He must have lost all sense of excellence who is not struck with the generosity of Tillotson, the integrity of Clarke, the Christian sentiments of Hoadley, the worth of Butler (on whose late advancement I beg leave to congratulate the public), and the piety, human, , and patriotism of Herring.'

·. These and many others have been ornaments of the body to which they belong, and have never stud ied to embroil us, or promote a party spirit among us.' Rectitude and benevolence, piety and self-government, have been their themes; these with uncommon abilities they have taught; and those who tread in their steps cannot fail of being honoured now and forever! But those who make it their business to poison the minds of the people with factious and seditious discourses; those who censure their governors for actions of which they are frequently no competent judges, and traduce and vilify everything, right or wrong; those who Join with the sworn foes of the best of princes, and strive to promote an interest incompatible with the public good, are the men who deserve titles which I do not care to give'; and they may be certain,.that though, through the lenity of the present government, they may escape unpunished, yet contempt will be their portion from all inen of sense; for when men pervert so excellent an office as that of the ministry to the purposes of ambition and the lust of power, hardly any censure too severe can be cast on them.

* The Reverend Mr. Birch, F.R.S.

t In April, 1646, he preached a sermon before both houses of Parliament, the lord-mayor and aldermen of London, and the Assembly of Divines, which was printed in quarto. In this sermon he expresses his desire that "some shorter way might be found to further justice; and that two or three friend-makers might be set up in every parish, without whose labour and leave none should implead another." He proposed likewise that the Charter House should be converted into a hospital for lame soldiers.

In the same year, 1646, he published at London, in quarto, a pamphlet of fifteen pages, entitled "Peters's last Report of the English Wars, occasioned by the Importunity of a Friend pressing an Answer to some Queries;"

I. Why he was silent at the surrender of Oxford?

II. What he observed at Worcester, it being the last town in the king's hand?

III. What were best to be done with the army?'

IV. If he had any expedient for the present difference?

V. What his thoughts were in relation to foreign states?

VI. How these late mercies and conquests might be preserved and improved?

VII. Why his name appears in so many books, not without blots, and he never wipe them off?

In this pamphlet he observes, p. 14, that he had lived about six years near that famous Scotsman, Mr John Forbes: "With whom," says he. "I travelled into Germany, and enjoyed him in much love

APPENDIX.

Colonel Lockhart to Secretary Thurloe, concerning Peters, which, as very characteristical of the man, and containing some curious particulars relating to him, I cannot forbear giving at length.*—C.

and sweetness constantly; from whom I never had but encouragement, though we differed in the way of our churches. Learned Amesius breathed his last breath into my bosom, who left his professorship in Friezland to live with me, because of my church's independency, at Rotterdam; he was my colleague and chosen brother to the Church, where I was an unworthy pastor."

In 1647, he published at London, in quarto, a pamphlet of fourteen pages, entitled "A Word for the Army, and two Words to the Kingdom, to clear the one and cure the other, forced in much Plainness and Brevity, from their faithful Servant, Hugh Peters."

It appears by a pamphlet, printed in 1651, written by R. V., of Gray's Inn, and entitled "A Plea for the Common Laws of England," that it was written in answer to Mr. Peters's "Good Work for a good Magistrate, or a short Cut to great Quiet;" in which Mr. Peters had proposed the extirpation of the whole system of our laws, and particularly recommended that the old records in the Tower should be burned, as the monuments of tyranny.

. Colonel Lockhart to Secretary Thurloe.
. . From Dunkirk, July 8-18, 1658.

"May it please your lordship,

"I could not suffer our worthy friend, Mr. Peters, to come away from Dunkirk without a testimony of the great benefits we have all received from him in this place, where he hath laid himself forth in great charity and goodness in sermons, prayers, and exhortations, in visiting and relieving the sick and wounded; and in all these, profitably applying the singular talent God hath bestowed upon him to the chief ends proper for our auditory; for he hath not only showed the soldiers their duty to God, and pressed it home upon them, I hope to good advantage, but hath like-

wise acquainted them with their obligations of obedience to his highness's government, and affection to his person. He hath laboured among us here with much good-will, and seems to enlarge his heart towards us, and care of us for many other things, the effects whereof I design to leave upon that Providence which has brought us hither. It were superfluous to tell your lordship the story of our present condition, either as to the civil government, works, or soldiery; he who hath studied all these more than any I know here, can certainly give the best account of them. Wherefore I commit the whole to his information, and beg your lordship's casting a favourable eye upon such propositions as he will offer to your lordship for the good of this garrison.

"I am, may it please your lordship,
"Your most humble, faithful,
"And obedient servant,
"WILL. LOCKHART."

[This part is all written with Lockhart's own hand.]

"Mr. Peters hath taken leave at least three or four times, but still something falls out which hinders his return to England. He hath been twice at Bergh, and hath spoken with the cardinal* three or four times; I kept myself by, and had a care that he did not importune him with too long speeches. He returns loaded with an account of all things here, and hath undertaken every man's business. I must give him that testimony, that he gave us three or four very honest sermons; and if it were possible to get him to mind preaching, and to forbear the troubling himself with other things, he would certainly prove a very fit minister for soldiers. I hope be cometh well satisfied from this place. He hath often insinuated to me his desire to stay here if he had a call. Some of the officers also have been with me to that purpose; but I have shifted him so handsomely, as I hope he will not be displeased; for I have told him that the greatest service he can do us is to go to England, and carry on his propositions, and to own us in all our other interests, which he hath undertaken with much zeal."

---

* Thurloe's State Papers, vol. vii., p. 249.

* Mazarine.

No. XXII.

[The following Discourse was preached by Mr. Mayhew, minister of the West Church in Boston. It comprises a lucid and well-timed illustration of several important topics connected with the history of the Puritans, which recent arrogant assumptions on the part of the Oxonian ecclesiastics, and their like-minded American consociates, render necessary again to be examined and accurately understood. Therefore, as the oracular opinions and decision of the Puritans, both Anglo-American and British, the sermon is here annexed in *perpetuam rei memoriam !*]

Unlimited Submission and Nonresistance to the Higher Powers; with some Reflections on the Resistance made to King Charles I., and on the Anniversary of his Death: in which the mysterious Doctrine of that Prince's Saintship and Martyrdom is unriddled. A Sermon preached in the West Meeting-house, in Boston, on the Lord's Day after the thirtieth of January, 1750. By Jonathan Mayhew.

He that ruleth over men must be just, ruling in the fear of God.—DAVID.

I have said, ye are gods, but ye shall die like men, and fall like one of the princes.—DAVID.

Fear God, honour the king.—PAUL.

Quid memorem infandas cædes ! Quid facta tyranni
Effera ? Dii capiti ipsius generique reservent.
Necuon Threicius longa cum veste sacerdos,
Obloquitor.—ROM. VAT. PRIN.

PREFACE.

" ALL Scripture is profitable for doctrine, for reproof, for correction, for instruction in righteousness." Why, then, should not those parts of Scripture which relate to civil government be examined and explained as well as others ? Obedience to the civil magistrate is a Christian duty, and why should not the nature, grounds, and extent of it be considered in a Christian assembly ? Besides, if it be said that it is out of character for a Christian minister to meddle with such a subject, this censure will fall upon the holy apostles. They write upon it in their epistles to Christian churches; and surely it cannot be deemed either criminal or impertinent to attempt an explanation of their doctrine.

It was the near approach of the thirtieth of January that turned my thoughts to this subject. On that day the slavish doctrine of passive obedience and nonresistance is often warmly asserted, and dissenters from the Established Church represented, not only as schismatics, with more of triumph than of truth, and of choler than Christianity, but, also, as persons of seditious, traitorous, and rebellious principles. God be thanked, one may speak freely both of government and religion ; and avow that he is engaged on the side of liberty, the Bible, and common sense, in opposition to tyranny, priestcraft, and nonsense, without being in danger either of the Bastile or the Inquisition ; though there will always be some interested politicians, contracted bigots, and hypocritical zealots for a party to take offence at such freedoms. Their censure is praise ; their praise is infamy. A spirit of domination is always to be guarded against both in Church and State, even in times of the greatest security. Those nations who are now groaning under

the iron sceptre of tyranny, were once free. So they might probably have remained by a seasonable caution against despotic measures. Civil tyranny is usually small in its beginning, like " the drop of a bucket," till at length, like a mighty torrent, or the raging waves of the sea, it bears down all before it, and deluges whole countries and empires. Thus it is as to ecclesiastical tyranny also—*the most cruel, intolerable, and impious of any.* From small beginnings " it exalts itself above all that is called God, and that is worshipped." People have no security against being unmercifully priest-ridden but by keeping all imperious bishops and other clergymen, who love to " lord it over God's heritage," from getting their foot into the stirrup at all. Let them be once fairly mounted, and their " beasts, the laity," may prance and flounce about to no purpose, and they will, at length, be so jaded and hacked by these reverend jockeys, that they will not even have spirit enough to complain that their backs are galled ; or, like Balaam's ass, to " rebuke the madness of the prophet."

" The mystery of iniquity began to work" even in the days of some of the apostles. But the kingdom of antichrist was then in one respect like the kingdom of heaven, however different in all others. It was " as a grain of mustard-seed." This grain was sown in Italy, also, though it were " the least of all seeds," it soon became a mighty tree. It has long since overspread and darkened the greatest part of Christendom, so that we may apply to it what is said of the tree which Nebuchadnezzar saw in his vision, " The height thereof reached unto heaven, and the sight thereof to the end of all the earth, and the beasts of the field have shadow under it." Tyranny brings ignorance and brutality along with it ; it degrades men from their just rank into the class of brutes ; it damps their spirits ; it suppresses arts ; it extinguishes every spark of noble ardour and generosity in the breasts of those who are enslaved by it ; it makes naturally strong and great minds feeble and little, and triumphs over the ruins of virtue and humanity. This is true of tyranny in every shape : there can be nothing great and good where its influence reaches. For which reason it becomes every friend to truth and human kind, every lover of God and the Christian religion, to bear a part in opposing this hateful monster. It was a desire to contribute a mite towards carrying on a war against this common enemy that produced the following discourse, and if it serve, in any measure, to keep up a spirit of civil and religious liberty among us, my end is answered. There are virtuous and candid men in all sects ; all such are to be esteemed : there are also vicious men and bigots in all sects ; and all such ought to be despised.

JONATHAN MAYHEW.

UNLIMITED SUBMISSION AND NONRESISTANCE
TO THE HIGHER POWERS.

ROMANS, xiii., 1-7: Let every soul be subject unto the higher powers. For there is no power but of God ; the powers that be are ordained of God. Whosoever, therefore, resisteth the power, resisteth the ordinance of God ; and they that resist shall receive to themselves damnation. For rulers are not a terror to good works, but to the evil. Wilt thou then not be afraid of the power ? Do that which is good, and thou shalt have praise of the same. For he is the minister of God to thee for good. But if thou do that which is evil, be afraid; for he beareth not the sword in vain; for he is the minister of God, a revenger to execute wrath upon him that doeth evil. Wherefore ye must needs be subject, not only for wrath, but also for conscience' sake. For this cause pay you tribute also: for they are God's ministers, attending continually upon this very thing. Render, therefore, to all their dues: tribute to whom tribute is due; custom, to whom custom; fear, to whom fear; honour, to whom honour.

Civil government may properly fall under a moral and religious consideration, at least so far as it relates to the general nature and end of magistracy, and to the grounds and extent of that submission which persons of a private character ought to yield to those who are vested with authority. This must be allowed by all who acknowledge the divine original of Christianity. For although there be a very plain and important sense in which Christ's "kingdom is not of this world," his inspired apostles have nevertheless laid down some general principles concerning the office of civil rulers and the duty of subjects, together with the reason and obligation of that duty. Hence it follows, that it is proper for all who acknowledge the authority of Jesus Christ, and the inspiration of his apostles, to endeavour to understand what is the doctrine which they have delivered concerning this matter. It is the duty of Christian magistrates to inform themselves what it is which their religion teaches concerning the nature and design of their office, and it is equally the duty of all Christian people to inform themselves what it is which their religion teaches concerning that subjection which they owe to the high powers.

This passage of Paul's is the most full and express of any in the New Testament, relating to rulers and subjects; therefore I thought it proper to ground upon it what I had to propose to you with reference to the authority of the civil magistrate, and the subjection which is due to him.

There were some persons among the Christians of the apostolic age, and particularly those at Rome, to whom Paul is here writing, who seditiously disclaimed all subjection to civil authority; refusing to pay taxes, and the duties laid upon their traffic and merchandise; and who scrupled not to speak of their rulers without any due regard to their office and character. Some of these turbulent Christians were converts from Judaism, and others from Paganism. The Jews in general, long before this time, had taken up a strange conceit, that being the peculiar people of God, they were therefore exempted from the jurisdiction of any heathen princes or governors. Upon this ground it was that some of them, during the public ministry of our blessed Saviour, came to him with that question, "Is it lawful to give tribute unto Cæsar or not?" This notion many of them retained after they were proselyted to the Christian faith. As to the Gentile converts, some of them grossly mistook the nature of that liberty which the Gospel promised, and thought that, by virtue of their subjection to Christ, the only king and head of his Church, they were wholly freed from subjection to any other prince; as though Christ's kingdom "had been of this world," in such a sense as to interfere with the civil powers of the earth, and to deliver their subjects from that allegiance and duty which they before owed to them. Of these visionary Chris-

tians in general, who disowned subjection to the civil powers in being, where they respectively lived, there is mention made in several places in the New Testament. The apostle Peter, in particular, characterizes them in this manner: "Them that despise government, presumptuous are they, self-willed; they are not afraid to speak evil of dignities." Now, with reference to these doting Christians, the apostle speaks in the passage before us.

The apostle begins thus: "Let every soul be subject unto the higher powers; for there is no power but of God: the powers that be are ordained of God."* As if he had said, "Whereas, some professed Christians vainly imagine that they are wholly excused from all manner of duty and subjection to civil authority, refusing to honour their rulers and to pay taxes—which opinion is not only unreasonable in itself, but also tends to fix a lasting reproach upon the Christian name and profession—I now, as an apostle, and ambassador of Christ, exhort every one of you to pay all dutiful submission to those who are vested with any civil office; for there is, properly speaking, no authority but what is derived from God, as it is only by his permission and providence that any possess it. I may add, that all civil magistrates, as such, although they may be heathens, are appointed and ordained of God; for it is certainly God's will that so useful an institution as that of magistracy should take place in the world for the good of civil society." The apostle proceeds: "Whosoever, therefore, resisteth the power, resisteth the ordinance of God; and they that resist shall receive to themselves damnation." "Think not, therefore, that ye are guiltless of any crime or sin against God when ye factiously disobey and resist the civil authority. For magistracy and government being the ordinance and appointment of God, it follows, that to resist magistrates in the execu-

* Every soul. This is an Hebraism, which signifies every man; so that the apostle does not exempt the clergy, such as were endowed with the gift of prophecy, or any other miraculous powers which subsisted in the Church at that day; and, by his using the Hebrew idiom, it seems that he had the Jewish converts principally in his eye.

The higher powers: more literally, the overruling powers, which term extends to all civil rulers in common.

By power, the apostle intends not lawless strength and brutal force, without regulation or proper direction, but just authority, for so the word here used properly signifies. There may be power where there is no authority. No man has any authority to do what is wrong and injurious, though he may have power to do it.

The powers that be: Those persons who are, in fact, vested with authority; those who are in possession. Who those are, the apostle leaves Christians to determine for themselves; but, whoever they are, they are to be obeyed.

Ordained of God: As it is not without God's providence and permission that any are clothed with authority; and as it is agreeable to the positive will and purpose of God that there should be some persons vested with authority for the good of society. Not that any rulers have their commission immediately from God, the supreme Lord of the Universe. If any assert that kings or any other rulers are ordained of God in the latter sense, it is incumbent upon them to show the commission which they speak of, under the broad seal of heaven, and when they do this they will no doubt be believed.

tion of their offices is really to resist the will and ordinance of God himself; and they who thus resist will accordingly be punished by God for this sin in common with others." The apostle goes on : " For rulers are not a terror to good works, but to the evil. Wilt thou, then, not be afraid of the power? Do that which is good, and thou shalt have praise of the same : for he is the minister of God to thee for good."* "That you may see the truth and justness of what I assert, that magistracy is the ordinance of God, and that you sin against him in opposing it, consider that even pagan rulers are not, by the nature and design of their office, enemies and a terror to the good and virtuous actions of men, but only to the injurious and mischievous to society. Will ye not, then, reverence and honour magistracy when ye see the good end and intention of it ? How can ye be so unreasonable ? Only mind to do your duty as members of society, and this will gain you the applause and favour of all good rulers. For while you do thus, they are by their office, as ministers of God, obliged to encourage and protect you ; it is for this very purpose that they are clothed with power." The apostle subjoins : " But if thou do that which is evil, be afraid, for he beareth not the sword in vain. For he is the minister of God, a revenger, to execute wrath upon him that doeth evil."† "But, upon the other hand, if ye refuse to do your duty as members of society ; if ye refuse to bear your part in the support of government; if ye are disorderly, and do things which merit. civil chastisement, then, indeed, ye have reason to be afraid : for it is not in vain that rulers are vested with the power of inflicting punishment. They are, by their office, not only the ministers

* For rulers are not a terror to good works, but to the evil. It cannot be supposed that the apostle designs here, or in any of the succeeding verses, to give the true character of Nero, or any other civil powers then in being, as if they were, in fact, such persons as he describes, a terror to evil works only, and not to the good ; for such a character did not belong to them, and the apostle was no sycophant or parasite of power, whatever some of his pretended successors have been. He only tells what rulers would be, provided they acted up to their character and office.

† It is manifest that when the apostle speaks of it, as the office of civil rulers to encourage what is good, and to punish what is evil, he speaks only of civil good and evil. They are to consult the good of society as such, not to dictate in religious concerns ; not to make laws for the government of men's consciences, and to inflict civil penalties for religious crimes. It is sufficient to overthrow the doctrine of the authority of the civil magistrate in affairs of a spiritual nature (so far as it is built upon anything which is here said by St. Paul, or upon anything else in the New Testament) only to observe, that all the magistrates then in the world were heathen, implacable enemies to Christianity ; so that to give them authority in religious matters would have been, in effect, to give them authority to extirpate the Christian religion, and to establish the idolatries and superstitions of paganism. And can any one reasonably suppose that the apostle had any intention to extend the authority of rulers beyond concerns merely civil and political, to the overthrowing of that religion which he himself was so zealous in propagating ? But it is natural for those whose religion cannot be supported upon the footing of reason and argument to have recourse to power and force, which will serve a bad cause as well as a good one, and, indeed, much better.

of God for good to those that do well, but also his ministers to revenge, to discountenance, and punish those that are unruly and injurious to their neighbours." The apostle proceeds : " Wherefore ye must needs be subject, not only for wrath, but also for conscience'- sake." " Since, therefore, magistracy is the ordinance of God, and since rulers are, by their office, benefactors to society, by discouraging what is bad and encouraging what is good, and so preserving peace and order among men, it is evident that ye ought to pay a willing subjection to them ;·not to obey merely for fear of exposing yourselves to their wrath and displeasure, but also in point of reason, duty, and conscience. Ye are under an indispensable obligation, as Christians, to honour their office, and to submit to them in the execution of it." The apostle goes on : " For for this cause pay you tribute also : for they are God's ministers, attending continually upon this very thing." "And here is a plain reason, also, why ye should pay tribute to them ; for they are God's ministers, exalted above the common level of mankind, not that they may indulge themselves in softness and luxury, and be entitled to the servile homage of their fellowmen, but that they may execute an office no less laborious than honourable, and attend continually upon the public welfare. This being their business and duty, it is but reasonable that they should be requited for their care and diligence in performing it, and enabled, by taxes levied upon the subject, effectually to prosecute the great end of their institution—the good of society." The apostle sums up all in the following words : " Render, therefore, to all their dues : tribute, to whom tribute is due ; custom, to whom custom ; fear, to whom fear ; honour, to whom honour."* ˉ " Let it not therefore be said of any of you hereafter, that you contemn government, to the reproach of yourselves and of the Christian religion. Neither your being Jews by nation, nor your becoming the subjects of Christ's kingdom, gives you any dispensation for making disturbances in the government under which you live. Approve yourselves, therefore, as peaceable and dutiful subjects. Be ready to pay to your rulers all that they may, in respect of their office, justly demand of you. Render tribute and custom to those of your governors to whom tribute and custom belong ; and cheerfully honour and reverence all who are vested with civil authority according to their deserts."

The apostle's doctrine, in the passage thus explained, concerning the office of civil rulers and the duty of subjects, may be summed up in the following observations :

That the end of magistracy is the good of civil society, as such.

That civil rulers, as such, are the ordinance and ministers of God ; it being by his permission and providence that any bear rule, and agreeable to his will that there should be some

. * Grotius observes, that the Greek words here used answer to the tributum and vectigal of the Romans ; the former was the money paid for the soil and poll, the latter the duties laid upon some sorts of merchandise. What the apostle here says deserves to be seriously considered by all Christians concerned in that common practice of carrying on an illicit trade and running of goods.

persons vested with authority in society for the well-being of it.

That which is here said concerning civil rulers extends to all of them in common. It relates, indifferently, to monarchical, republican, and aristocratical government, and to all other forms which truly answer the sole end of government, the happiness of society; and to all the different degrees of authority in any particular state; to inferior officers no less than to the supreme.

That disobedience to civil rulers, in the due exercise of their authority, is not merely political sin, but heinous offence against God and religion.,

That the true ground and reason* of our obligation to be subject to the higher powers is the usefulness of magistracy, when properly exercised, to human society, and its subserviency to the general welfare.

That obedience to civil rulers is here equally required under all forms of government which answer the sole end of all government, the good of society; and to every degree of authority in any state, whether supreme or subordinate.

Whence it follows, that if unlimited obedience and nonresistance be here required as a duty under any one form of government, it is also required as a duty under all other forms; and as a duty to subordinate rulers as well as to the supreme; and that those civil rulers to whom the apostle enjoins subjection are the persons in possession; the powers that be; those who are actually vested with authority.†

* Some suppose the apostle in this passage enforces the duty of submission with two arguments quite distinct from each other; one taken from this consideration, that rulers are the ordinance and the ministers of God (ver. 1, 2, and 4), and the other from the benefits that accrue to society from civil government (ver. 3, 4, and 6). And, indeed, these may be distinct motives and arguments for submission, as they may be separately viewed and contemplated; but when we consider that rulers are not the ordinance and the ministers of God but only so far forth as they perform God's will, by acting up to their office and character, and so, by being benefactors to society, this makes these arguments coincide and run up into one at last; at least, so far that the former of them cannot hold good for submission where the latter fails. Put the supposition, that any man, bearing the title of a magistrate, should exercise his power in such a manner as to have no claim to obedience by virtue of that argument which is founded upon the usefulness of magistracy, and you equally take off the force of the other argument also, which is founded upon his being the ordinance and the minister of God; for he is no longer God's ordinance and minister than he acts up to his office and character by exercising his power for the good of society: this is, in brief, the reason why it is said above, in the *singular* number, *the true ground and reason*, &c. The use and propriety of this remark may be more apparent in the progress of the argument concerning resistance.

† This must be understood with this proviso, that they do not grossly abuse their power and trust, but exercise it for the good of those that are governed. Who these persons were, whether Nero, &c., or not, the apostle does not say, but leaves it to be determined by those to whom he writes. God does not interpose in a miraculous way to point out the persons who shall bear rule, and to whom subjection is due. And as to the unalienable, indefeasible right of primogeniture, the Scriptures are entirely silent, or, rather, plainly contradict it, Saul being the first king among the Israelites, and appointed to the royal

There is one very important and interesting point which remains to be inquired into, namely, the *extent* of that subjection to the higher powers which is here enjoined as a duty upon all Christians. Some have thought it warrantable and glorious to disobey the civil powers in certain circumstances; and in cases, of very great and general oppression, when humble remonstrances fail of having any effect, and, when the public welfare cannot be otherwise provided for and secured, to rise unanimously, even against the sovereign himself, in order to redress their grievances; to vindicate their natural and legal rights; to break the yoke of tyranny, and free themselves and posterity from inglorious servitude and ruin. It is upon this principle that many royal oppressors have been driven from their thrones into banishment, and many slain by the hands of their subjects. It was upon this principle that Tarquin was expelled from Rome, and Julius Cæsar, the conqueror of the world, and the tyrant of his country, cut off in the senate-house. It was upon this principle that Charles I. was beheaded before his own banqueting-house. It was upon this principle that James II. was made to fly that country, which he aimed at enslaving. Upon this principle was that revolution brought about which has been so fruitful of happy consequences to Britain. But, in opposition to this principle, it has often been asserted that the Scripture in general, and the passage under consideration in particular, makes all resistance to princes a crime in any case whatever. If they turn tyrants, and become the common oppressors of those whose welfare they ought to regard with a paternal affection, we must not pretend to right ourselves unless it be by prayers, and tears, and humble entreaties: and if these methods fail of procuring redress, we must not have recourse to any other, but suffer ourselves to be robbed and butchered at the pleasure of the Lord's anointed, lest we should incur the sin of rebellion and the punishment of damnation. For he has God's authority and commission to bear him out in the worst of crimes, so far that, he may not be withstood or controlled. Now, whether we are obliged to yield such an absolute submission to our prince, or whether disobedience and resistance may not be justifiable in some cases, notwithstanding anything in the passage before us, is an inquiry in which we are all concerned.

Now there is no necessity to suppose that absolute, unlimited obedience, whether active or passive, is here enjoined, because the precept is delivered in absolute terms, without any exception or intimation expressly mentioned. We are enjoined to be "*subject to the higher powers*," and to be "*subject for conscience' sake*;" and because these expressions are absolute and unlimited, or, more properly, general, some have inferred that the subjection required in them must be absolute and unlimited also; at least, so far as to make passive obedience and non-dignity during his own father's lifetime; and he was succeeded, or, rather, superseded by David, the *last* born among many brethren. Now, if God has not invariably determined this matter, it must, of course, be determined by men; and if it be determined by men, it must be determined either in the way of *force* or of *compact*, and which of these is the most equitable can be no question.

resistance a duty in all cases whatever, if not active obedience likewise ; though there is here no distinction between active and passive obedience ; and if, either of them be required in an unlimited sense, the other must be required in the same sense also, because the expressions are equally absolute with respect to both. But that unlimited obedience of any sort cannot be argued merely from the indefinite expressions in which obedience is enjoined, appears hence, that expressions of the same nature frequently occur in Scripture, upon which it is confessed that no such absolute and unlimited sense ought to be put. For example : " *Love not the world, neither the things that are in the world ;*" " *Lay not up for yourselves treasures on earth ;*" " *Take, therefore, no thought for the morrow,*" are precepts expressed in at least equally absolute and unlimited terms ; but they are to be understood with certain restrictions and limitations, some degree of love to the world, and the things of it, being allowable. Nor, indeed, do the right reverend fathers in God, and other dignified clergymen of the Established Church, seem to be altogether averse to admitting of restrictions in the latter case, how warm soever any of them may be against restrictions and limitations in the case of submission to authority, whether civil or ecclesiastical. Patience and submission under private injuries are enjoined in much more peremptory and absolute terms than any that are used with regard to submission to the injustice and oppression of civil rulers. Thus : " *I say unto you, that you resist not evil ; but whosoever shall smite thee on the right cheek, turn to him the other also.* And *if any man will sue thee at the law, and take away thy coat, let him have thy cloak also. And whosoever shall compel thee to go a mile with him, go with him twain.*" Any man may be defied to produce such strong expressions in favour of a passive and tame submission to unjust, tyrannical rulers, as are here used to enforce submission to private injuries. But how few are there that understand those expressions literally ; and the reason why they do not is because, with submission to the FRIENDS, common sense shows that they were not intended to be so understood.'

Some Scripture precepts which are more directly to the point in hand. Children are commanded to obey their parents, and servants their masters, in as absolute and unlimited terms as subjects are here commanded to obey their civil rulers.' Thus this same apostle : " *Children, obey your parents in the Lord, for this is right. Honour thy father and mother, which is the first commandment with promise. Servants, be obedient to them that are your masters, according to the flesh, with fear and trembling, with singleness of your heart as unto Christ.*" Thus, also, wives are commanded to be obedient to their husbands : " *Wives, submit yourselves unto your own husbands as unto the Lord ; for the husband is the head of the wife, even as* CHRIST IS THE HEAD OF THE CHURCH. *Therefore, as the Church is subject unto Christ, so let the wives be to their own husbands* IN EVERYTHING." In all these cases submission is required in terms as absolute and universal as are ever used with respect to rulers and subjects ; but who supposes that the apostle ever intended to teach that children,

servants, and wives, in all cases whatever, should obey their parents, masters, and husbands, respectively, never making any opposition to their will, even although they should require them to break the commandments of God, or should causelessly make an attempt upon their lives ? No one puts such a sense upon these expressions, however absolute and unlimited. Why, then, should it be supposed that the apostle designed to teach universal obedience, whether active or passive, to the higher powers, merely because his precepts are delivered in absolute and unlimited terms ? If it be said that resistance and disobedience to the higher powers are here said positively to be a sin, so also is the disobedience of children to parents, servants to masters, and wives to husbands, in other places of Scripture. But the question still remains, Whether in all these cases there be not some exceptions ? In the three latter it is allowed there are. Hence it follows, that barely the use of absolute expressions is no proof that obedience to civil rulers is in all cases a duty, or that resistance in all cases is a sin.

There is, indeed, one passage in the New Testament where it may seem, at first view, that an unlimited submission to civil rulers is enjoined : " *Submit yourself to every ordinance of man for the Lord's sake.*" To *every ordinance of man*. However, this expression is no stronger than that before taken notice of with relation to the duty of wives, " *So let the wives be subject to their own husbands* IN EVERYTHING." But the true solution of this difficulty is this : by "*every ordinance of man*"* is not meant every command of the civil magistrate without exception, but every order of magistrates appointed by man, whether superior or inferior ; for so the apostle explains himself in the very next words : " *Whether it be to the king as supreme, or to governors, as unto them that are sent,*" &c. (1 Pet. ii., 13, 14). But although the apostle has not subjoined any such explanation, the reason of the thing itself would have obliged us to limit the expression, " *every ordinance of man,*" to such human ordinances and commands as are not inconsistent with the ordinances and commands of God, the supreme lawgiver, or with any other higher and antecedent obligations.

It is to be observed, also, that as the duty of universal obedience and nonresistance to the higher powers cannot be argued from the absolute, unlimited expressions which the apostle here uses, so neither can it be argued from the scope and drift of his reasoning, considered with relation to the persons he was here opposing. As was observed already, there were some professed Christians in the apostolic age who disclaimed all magistracy and civil authority in general, " *despising government and speaking evil of dignities ;*" some under a notion that Jews ought not to be under the jurisdiction of Gentile rulers, and others, that they were set free from the temporal powers by Christ. Now it is with persons of this licentious opinion and character that the apostle is concerned, and all that was directly to his point was to show that

---

* Literally, *every human institution or appointment.* By which manner of expression the apostle plainly intimates that rulers derive their authority *immediately*, not from *God*, but from *men*

they were bound to submit to magistracy in general. This is a circumstance very material to be taken notice of, in order to ascertain the sense of the apostle; for this is sufficient to account for all that he says concerning the duty of subjection, and the sin of resistance, to the higher powers, without having recourse to the doctrine of unlimited submission and passive obedience in all cases whatever. Were it known that those, in opposition to whom the apostle wrote, allowed of civil authority in general, and only asserted that there were *some cases* in which obedience and nonresistance were not a duty, there would then, indeed, be reason for interpreting this passage as containing the doctrine of unlimited obedience and nonresistance, as it must in this case be supposed to have been levelled against those who denied that doctrine. But since it is certain that there were persons who vainly imagined that civil government in general was not to be regarded by them, it is most reasonable to, suppose that the apostle designed his discourse only against them. Agreeably to this supposition, we find that he argues the usefulness of civil magistracy in general; its agreeableness to the will and purpose of God, who is over all; and so deduces thence the obligation of submission to it. But it will not follow that because civil government is a good institution, and necessary to the peace and happiness of human society, therefore there are no supposable cases in which resistance to it can be innocent; so that the duty of unlimited obedience, whether active or passive, can be argued neither from the manner of expression here used, nor from the general scope and design of the passage. If we attend to the nature of the argument with which the apostle here enforces the duty of submission to the higher powers, we shall find that it concludes, not in favour of submission to all who bear the title of rulers in common, but only to those who actually perform the duty of rulers by exercising a reasonable and just authority for the good of human society. Now the question before us turns very much upon the truth or falsehood of this position. It is obvious that the civil rulers whom the apostle here speaks of, and obedience to whom he presses upon Christians as a duty, are good rulers,* such as are, in the exercise of their office and power, benefactors to society. Such they are described to be throughout this passage. Thus it is said that they are not "*a terror to good works, but to the evil*;" that they are God's "*ministers for good; revengers to execute wrath upon him that doeth evil;*" and that "*they attend continually upon this very thing.*" Peter gives the same account of rulers: they are "*for a praise to them that do well, and the punishment of evil doers.*" This character and description of rulers agree only to such as are rulers in fact, as well as in name; to such as govern well and act agreeably to their office. The apostle's argument for submission to rulers is wholly built and grounded upon a presumption that they do, in fact, answer this character; and

* By good rulers are not intended such as are good in a *moral* or *religious*, but only in a *political* sense; those who perform their duty so far as their office extends, and so far as civil society is concerned in their actions.

is of no force at all upon the supposition of the contrary. If "*rulers are a terror to good works, and not to the evil;*" if they are not "*ministers for good to society,*" but for evil and distress, by violence and oppression; if they "*execute wrath upon*" sober, peaceable persons, who do their duty as members of society, and suffer rich and honourable knaves to escape with impunity; if, instead of "*attending continually upon*" the good work of advancing the public welfare, they attend only upon the gratification of their own inst, and pride, and ambition, to the destruction of the public welfare; if this be the case, the apostle's argument for submission does not reach them. They are not the same, but different persons from those whom he characterizes, and who must be obeyed according to his reasoning. Let me illustrate the apostle's argument by the following similitude. Suppose, then, it was allowed that the clergy are a useful order of men; that they ought to be "*esteemed very highly in love for their works' sake;*" and to be decently supported by those whom they serve, "*the labourer being worthy of his reward.*" Suppose, farther, that a number of reverend and right reverend drones, who work not; who preach perhaps but once a year, and then not the Gospel of Jesus Christ, but the divine right of tithes: the dignity of their office as ambassadors of Christ; the equity of fine cures and a plurality of benefices; the excellency of the devotions in that Prayer Book which some of them hire chaplains to use for them; or some favourite point of Church tyr- anny and antichristian usurpation; suppose such men as these, spending their lives in effeminacy, luxury, and idleness, or when they are not idle, doing that which is worse than idleness; suppose such men, merely by the merit of ordination and consecration, and a peculiar, odd habit, should claim great respect and reverence from those whom they civilly called the "*beasts of the laity,*" and should demand thousands per annum for that good service which they never perform, and for which, if they had peformed it, this would be much more than a *quantum meruit*; suppose this should be the case, would not everybody be astonished at such insolence, injustice, and impiety? Ought not such men to be told plainly that they could not reasonably expect the esteem and reward due to the ministers of the Gospel unless they did the duties of their office? Should they not be told that their title and habit claimed no regard, reverence, or pay, separate from the care, and work, and various duties of their function? and that while they neglected the latter, the former served only to render them the more ridiculous and contemptible? The application of this similitude to the case in hand is very easy. If those who bear the title of civil rulers do not perform the duty of civil rulers, but act directly counter to the sole end and design of their office; if they injure and oppress their subjects, instead of defending their rights and doing them good, they have not the least pretence to be honoured, obeyed, and rewarded, according to the apostle's argument; for his reasoning, in order to show the duty of subjection to the higher powers, is built wholly upon the supposition that they do in fact perform the duty of rulers.

-. It has been said that the apostle nere uses another argument for submission to the higher powers, besides that which is taken from the usefulness of their office to civil society, when properly discharged and executed.; that their power is from God; that they are ordained of God; and that they are God's-ministers; and that this argument for submission to them will hold good, although they do not exercise their power for the benefit, but for the ruin and destruction of human society. But rulers have not authority from God to do mischief. They are not God's ordinance, or God's ministers, in any other sense than as it is by his permission and providence that they are exalted to bear rule; and as magistracy duly exercised, and authority rightly applied, in the enacting and executing good laws attempered and accommodated to the common welfare of the subjects, must be supposed to be agreeable to the will of the beneficent author and supreme Lord of the universe, whose "*kingdom ruleth over all,*" and whose "*tender mercies are over all his works,*" it is blasphemy to call tyrants and oppressors God's ministers. They are more properly "*the messengers of* Satan *to buffet us.*" No rulers are God's ministers but such as are "*just, ruling in the fear of God.*" When once magistrates act contrary to their office and the end of their institution; when they rob and ruin the public, instead of being guardians of its peace and welfare, they immediately cease to be the "*ordinance* and *ministers of God,*" and no more deserve that glorious character than common pirates and highwaymen. So that whenever that argument for submission fails, which is grounded upon the usefulness of magistracy to civil society, as it always does when magistrates do hurt to society instead of good, the other argument, which is taken from their being the ordinance of God, must necessarily fail also—no person of a civil character being God's minister in the sense of the apostle, any farther than he performs God's will by exercising a just and reasonable authority, and ruling for the good of the subject.

: Let us now trace the apostle's reasoning in favour of submission to the higher powers, and it will appear how good and conclusive it is for submission to those rulers who exercise their power in a proper manner; and how weak, and trifling, and unconnected it is, if it be supposed to be meant by the apostle to show the obligation and duty of obedience to tyrannical, oppressive rulers, in common with others of a different character.

The apostle enters upon his subject thus: "*Let every soul be subject unto the higher powers; for there is no power but of God: the powers that be are ordained of God.*" Here he urges the duty of obedience, because civil rulers, as they are supposed to fulfil the pleasure of God, are the ordinance of God. But how is this an argument for obedience to such rulers as do not perform the pleasure of God, by doing good; but the pleasure of the devil, by doing evil; and such as are not, therefore, God's ministers, but the devil's! "*Whosoever, therefore, resisteth the power, resisteth the ordinance of God; and they that resist, shall receive to themselves damnation.*" Here the apostle argues, that those who resist a reasonable and just authority, which is agreea-

ble to the will of God, do really resist the will of God himself, and will therefore be punished by him. But how. does this prove that those who resist a lawless, unreasonable power, which is contrary. to the will of God, do therein resist the will and ordinance of God? Is resisting those who resist God's will the same thing with resisting God? . Or shall those who do so, "*receive to themselves damnation!* · *For rulers are not a terror to good works; but to the evil. Wilt thou then, not be afraid of the power? Do that which is good, and thou shalt have praise of the same; for he is the minister of God to thee for good.*" Here the apostle argues more explicitly than he had before done for revering and submitting to magistracy, from this consideration, that such as really perform the duty of magistrates, would be enemies. only to the evil actions of men, and would befriend and encourage the good; and so be a common blessing to society. But how is this an argument that we must honour and submit to such magistrates as are not enemies to the evil actions of men, but to the good; and such as are not a common blessing, but a common curse, to society! "*But if thou do that which is evil, be afraid; for he is the minister of God, a revenger, to execute wrath upon him that doeth evil.*" Here the apostle argues from the nature and end of magistracy, that such as did evil, and such only, had reason to be afraid of the higher powers; it being part of their office to punish evildoers, no less than to defend and encourage such as do well. But if magistrates are unrighteous; if they are respecters of persons; if they are partial in their administration of justice; then those who do well have as much reason to be afraid as those that do evil. There can be no safety for the good, nor any peculiar ground of terror to the unruly and injurious. So that in this case, the main end of civil government will be frustrated. What reason is there for submitting to that government which does by no means answer the design of government! "*Wherefore ye must needs be subject not only for wrath, but also for conscience' sake.*" Here the apostle argues the duty of a cheerful and conscientious submission to civil government, from the nature and end of magistracy, as he had before laid it down; as the design of it was to punish evildoers, and to support and encourage such as do well; and as it must, if so exercised, be agreeable to the will of God. But how does what he here says prove the duty of a cheerful and conscientious subjection to those who forfeit the character of rulers? to those who encourage the bad, and discourage the good? The argument here used no more proves it to be a sin to resist such rulers, than it does to "*resist the devil*, that he may *flee from us.*" For one is as truly the minister of God as the other. "*For after this cause pay you tribute also; for they are God's ministers, attending continually upon this very thing.*" . Here the apostle argues the duty of paying taxes, from this consideration, that those who perform the duty of rulers are continually attending upon the public welfare. But how does this argument conclude for paying taxes to such princes as are continually endeavouring to ruin the public? and especially when such payment would facilitate and promote this wicked design! "*Ren-*

der, therefore, to al. their dues: tribute, to whom tribute is due; custom, to whom custom; fear, to whom fear; honour, to whom honour." Here the apostle sums up what he had been saying concerning the duty of subjects to rulers. His argument stands thus: "Since magistrates who execute their office well are common benefactors to society, and may, in that respect, be properly styled the ministers and ordinance of God; and since they are constantly employed in the service of the public, it becomes you to pay them tribute and custom; and to reverence, honour, and submit to them in the execution of their respective offices." This is apparently good reasoning. But does this argument conclude for the duty of paying tribute, custom, reverence, honour, and obedience to those persons, although they bear the title of rulers, who use all their power to hurt and injure the public? such as are not God's ministers, but Satan's? such as do not take care of, and attend upon the public interest, but their own, to the ruin of the public? that is, in short, to such as have no natural and just claim at all to tribute, custom, reverence, honour, and obedience? It is to be hoped that those who have any regard to the apostle's character as an inspired writer, or even as a man of common understanding, will not present him as reasoning in such a loose, incoherent manner, and drawing conclusions which have not the least relation to his premises. For what can be more absurd than an argument thus framed? "Rulers are, by their office, bound to consult the public welfare and the good of society: therefore you are bound to pay them tribute, to honour and submit to them, even when they destroy the public welfare, and are a common pest to society, by acting in direct contradiction to the nature and end of their office."

Thus, upon a careful review of the apostle's reasoning in this passage, it appears that his arguments to enforce submission are of such a nature as to conclude only in favour of submission to such rulers as he himself describes: those who rule for the good of society, which is the only end of their institution. Common tyrants and public oppressors are not entitled to obedience from their subjects by virtue of any thing here laid down by the inspired apostle.

The apostle's argument is so far from proving it to be the duty of people to obey and submit to such rulers as act in contradiction to the public good,* and to the design of their office, that it proves the direct contrary. For if the end of all civil government be the good of society; if this be the thing that is aimed at in constituting civil rulers; and if the motive and argument for submission to government be taken from the apparent usefulness of civil authority, it follows, that when no such good end can be answered by submission; there remains no argument or motive to enforce it; if, instead of this good end's being brought about by submission, a contrary end is brought about, and the ruin and misery of society effected by it;

here is a plain and positive reason against submission in all such cases; should they ever happen. Therefore, in such cases, a regard to the public welfare ought to make us withhold from our rulers that obedience and subjection which it would otherwise be our duty to render to them. If it be our duty, for example, to obey the king merely for this reason, that he rules for the public welfare, which is the only argument the apostle makes use of, it follows, by parity of reason, that when he turns tyrant and makes his subjects his prey to devour and to destroy, instead of his charge to defend and cherish, we are bound to throw off our allegiance to him, and to resist. Not to discontinue our allegiance in this case, would be to join with the sovereign in promoting the slavery and misery of that society, the welfare of which we ourselves, as well as our sovereign, are indispensably obliged to secure and promote. It is true, the apostle puts no case of such a tyrannical prince; but by his grounding his argument for submission wholly upon the good of civil society, it is plain he implicitly authorizes, and even requires us to make resistance whenever this shall be necessary to the public safety and happiness. Let me use this easy and familiar similitude to illustrate the point in hand: Suppose God requires a family of children to obey their father and not to resist him, and enforces his command with this argument: that the superintendence, and care, and authority of a just and kind parent will contribute to the happiness of the whole family, so that they ought to obey him for their own sakes more than for his. Suppose that this parent at length becomes distracted, and attempts, in his mad fits, to cut his children's throats. Now, in this case, is not the reason before assigned why these children should obey their parent while he continued of a sound mind, their common good, a reason equally conclusive for disobeying and resisting him, since he is become delirious, and attempts their ruin? It makes no alteration in the argument, whether this parent, properly speaking, loses his reason, or, while he retains his understanding, does that which is as fatal in its consequences as any thing he could do, were he really deprived of it.

But it ought to be remembered, that if the duty of universal obedience and nonresistance to our king or prince can be argued from this passage, the same unlimited submission under a republican, or any other form of government, and even to all the subordinate powers in any particular state, can be proved by it as well, in which is more than those who allege it for the mentioned purpose would be willing should be inferred from it. So that this passage does not answer their purpose, but really overthrows and confutes it. This matter deserves to be more particularly considered. The advocates for unlimited submission and passive obedience always speak with reference to kingly or monarchical government, as distinguished from all other forms; and with reference to submitting to the will of the king, in distinction from all subordinate officers acting beyond their commission, and the authority which they have received from the crown. It is not pretended that any person besides kings have a divine right to do what they please; so that no one may

<hr>

* This does not intend their acting so in *a few particular instances*, which the best of rulers may do through mistake. but their acting so *habitually*, and in a manner which plainly shows that they aim at making themselves great by the ruin of their subjects.

resist them without incurring the guilt of fac- tiousness and rebellion. If any other supreme powers oppress the people, it is generally allowed that the people may get redress by resistance if other methods prove ineffectual ; and if any officers in a kingly government go beyond the limits of that power which they have derived from the crown, the supposed original source of all power and authority in the state, and attempt illegally to take away the property and lives of their fellow-subjects, they may be forcibly resisted. But as to the sovereign himself, they say he may not be resisted in any case, nor any of his officers, while they confine themselves within the bounds which he has prescribed to them. This is a true sketch of the principles of those who defend the doctrine of passive obedience and non-resistance. *Now there is nothing in Scripture which supports this scheme of political principles.* As to the passage under consideration, the apostle here speaks of civil rulers in general ; of all persons in common, vested with authority for the good of society, without any particular reference to one form of government more than to another ; or to the supreme power in any particular state more than to subordinate powers. The apostle does not concern himself with the different forms of government.* This he supposes left entirely to human prudence and discretion. Now the consequence of this is, that unlimited and passive obedience is no more enjoined in this passage under monarchical government, or to the supreme power in any state, than under all other species of government which answer the end of government ; or to all the subordinate degrees of civil authority, from the highest to the lowest. Those, therefore, who would from this passage infer the guilt of resisting kings in all cases whatever, though acting ever so contrary to the design of their office, if they will be consistent, must go much farther, and infer from it the guilt of resistance under all other forms of government ; and of resisting any petty officer in the state, though acting beyond his commission in the most arbitrary, illegal manner possible. The

* The essence of government (I mean good government, and this is the only government which the apostle treats of in this passage) consists in the making and executing of good laws—laws attempered to the common felicity of the governed. If this be in fact done, it is evidently in itself a thing of no consequence at all what the particular form of government is ; whether the legislative and executive power be lodged in one and the same person, or in different persons ; whether in one person, whom we call an absolute monarch ; whether in a few, so as to constitute an aristocracy ; whether in many, so as to constitute a republic ; or whether in three co-ordinate branches, in such manner as to make the government partake something of each of these forms, and to be at the same time essentially different from them all. If the end be attained, it is enough. But no form of government seems to be so unlikely to accomplish this end as absolute monarchy ; nor is there any one that has so little pretence to a divine original, unless it be in this sense, that God first introduced it into, and thereby overturned the commonwealth of Israel as a curse upon that people for their folly and wickedness, particularly in desiring such a government.—1 Samuel. viii. Just so God before sent quails among them as a plague and a curse, and not as a blessing.—Numbers, xi.

argument holds equally strong in both cases. All civil rulers, as such, are the ordinance and ministers of God ; and they are all, by the nature of their office, and in their respective spheres and stations, bound to consult the public welfare. With the same reason, therefore, that any deny unlimited and passive obedience to be here enjoined under a republic or aristocracy, or any other established form of civil government, or to subordinate powers acting in an illegal and oppressive manner, with the same reason others may deny that such obedience is enjoined to a king or monarch, or any civil power whatever. For the apostle says nothing that is peculiar to kings ; what he says extends equally to all other persons whatever vested with any civil office. They are all in exactly the same sense the "*ordinance of God*," and the "*ministers of God ;*" and obedience is equally enjoined to be paid to them all. For, as the apostle expresses it, "*there is no power but of God*." And we are required to "*render to all their dues*," and not more than their dues. What these dues are, and to whom they are to be rendered, the apostle saith not, but leaves to the reason and consciences of men to determine.

Thus it appears that the common argument grounded upon this passage in favour of universal and passive obedience, really overthrows itself by proving too much, if it proves anything at all—that no civil officer, in any case whatever, is to be resisted, though acting in express contradiction to the design of his office, which no man in his senses ever did or can assert.

If we calmly consider the nature of the thing itself, nothing can well be imagined more directly contrary to common sense than, to suppose that millions of people should be subjected to the arbitrary, precarious pleasure of one single man, who has naturally no superiority over them in point of authority, so that their estates and everything that is valuable in life, and even their lives also, shall be absolutely at his disposal, if he happens to be wanton and capricious enough to demand them. What unprejudiced man can think that God made ALL to be thus subservient to the lawless pleasure and phrensy of one, so that it shall always be a sin to resist him ! Nothing but the most plain and express revelation from heaven could make a sober, impartial man believe such a monstrous, unaccountable doctrine ; and, indeed, the thing itself appears so shocking, so out of all proportion, that it may be questioned whether all the miracles that ever were wrought could make it credible that this doctrine really came from God. *There is not the least syllable in Scripture which gives any countenance to it.* The hereditary, indefeasible, divine right of kings, and the doctrine of nonresistance, which is built upon the supposition of such a right, are altogether as fabulous and chimerical as transubstantiation, or any of the most absurd reveries of ancient or modern visionaries. These notions are fetched neither from Divine revelation nor human reason ; and if they are derived from neither of those sources, it is no matter whence they come or whither they go ; only it is a pity that such doctrines should be propagated in society to raise factions and rebellions as they have been, both in the last and in the present reign.

But then, if unlimited submission and passive obedience to the higher powers in all possible cases be not a duty, it will be asked, "How far are we obliged to submit? If we may innocently disobey and resist in some cases, why not in all? Where shall we stop? What is the measure of our duty? This doctrine tends to the total dissolution of civil government, and to introduce such scenes of wild anarchy and confusion, as are more fatal to society than the worst of tyranny."

After this manner some men object, and, indeed, this is the most plausible thing that can be said in favour of such an absolute submission as they plead for. But there is very little strength or solidity in it; for similar difficulties may be raised with respect to almost every duty of natural and revealed religion. To instance only in two, both of which are near akin, and exactly parallel to the case before us. It is unquestionably the duty of children to submit to their parents, and of servants to their masters. But no one asserts that it is their duty to obey and submit to them in all supposable cases, or universally a sin to resist them. Now does this tend to subvert the just authority of parents and masters? or to introduce confusion and anarchy into private families? How, then, does the same principle tend to unhinge the government of that larger family, the body politic? We know, in general, that children and servants are obliged to obey their parents and masters respectively. We know also, with equal certainty, that they are not obliged to submit to them in all things, without exception; but in some cases reasonably, and therefore innocently, may resist them. These principles are acknowledged upon all hands, whatever difficulty there may be in fixing the exact limits of submission. Now there is at least as much difficulty in stating the measure of duty in these two cases as in the case of rulers and subjects. So that this is really no reasonable objection against resistance to the higher powers, for it will hold equally against resistance in the other cases mentioned. It is indeed true, that turbulent, vicious-minded men may take occasion from this principle, that their rulers in some cases may be lawfully resisted to raise factions and disturbances in the state, and to make resistance where resistance is needless, and therefore sinful. But is it not equally true that children and servants of turbulent, vicious minds, may take occasion from this principle that parents and masters may in some cases be lawfully resisted, to resist when resistance is unnecessary, and therefore criminal? Is the principle in either case false in itself, merely because it may be abused, and applied to legitimate disobedience and resistance in those instances to which it ought not to be applied? According to this way of arguing there will be no true principles in the world, for there are none but what may be wrested and perverted to serve bad purposes, either through the weakness or wickedness of men.*

* We may safely assert these two things in general without undermining government : one is, that no civil rulers are to be obeyed when they enjoin things that are inconsistent with the commands of God. All such disobedience is lawful and glorious, particularly if persons refuse to comply with any le-

A people really oppressed to a great degree by their sovereign, cannot be insensible when gal establishment of religion, because it is a gross perversion and corruption as to doctrine, worship, and discipline, of a pure and divine religion brought from heaven to earth by the Son of God, the only King and Head of the Christian Church, and propagated through the world by his inspired apostles. All commands running counter to the declared will of the Supreme Legislator of heaven and earth are null and void. Therefore, disobedience to them is a duty, not a crime. Another thing that may be asserted with equal truth and safety is this, that no government is to be submitted to at the expense of that which is the sole end of all government—the common good and safety of society. Because, to submit in this case, would evidently be to set up the means as more valuable, and above the end, than which there cannot be a greater solecism and contradiction. The only reason of the institution of civil government, and the only rational ground of submission to it, is the common safety and utility. If, therefore, in any case the common safety and utility would not be promoted by submission to government, but the contrary, there is no ground or motive for obedience and submission.

Whoever considers the nature of civil government, must indeed be sensible that a great degree of implicit confidence must unavoidably be placed in those that bear rule; this is implied in the very notion of authority's being originally a trust committed by the people to those who are vested with it, as all just and righteous authority is: all besides is mere lawless force and usurpation. Neither God nor nature has given any man a right of dominion over any society, independently of that society's approbation and consent to be governed by him. Now as all men are fallible, it cannot be supposed that the public affairs of any state should be always administered in the best manner possible, even by persons of the greatest wisdom and integrity. Nor is it sufficient to legitimate disobedience to the higher powers that they are not so administered, or that in some instances they are very ill managed; for, upon this principle, it is scarcely supposable that any government at all could be supported or subsist. Such a principle manifestly tends to the dissolution of all government, and to throw all things into confusion and anarchy. But it is equally evident that those in authority may abuse their trust and power to such a degree that neither the law of reason nor of religion requires our obedience or submission should be paid to them; but, on the contrary, that they should be totally discarded, and the authority which they were before vested with transferred to others, who may exercise it more to those good purposes for which it is given. Nor is this principle that resistance to the higher powers, in some extraordinary cases, is justifiable, so liable to abuse as many persons seem to apprehend it; for, although there will be always some petulent, querulous men in every state—men of factious, turbulent, and carping dispositions—glad to lay hold of any trifle to justify and legitimate their caballing against their rulers, and other seditious practices, yet there are, comparatively speaking, but few men of this contemptible character. Mankind, in general, have a disposition to be as submissive and passive, and tame under government, as they ought to be. Witness the greatest part of the known world who are now groaning, but not murmuring, under the heavy yoke of tyranny! While those who govern do it with any tolerable degree of moderation and justice, and in any good measure act up to their office and character by being public benefactors, the people will generally be easy and peaceable, and be rather inclined to flatter and adore than to insult and resist them. Nor was there ever any general complaint against any administration which lasted long but what there was good reason for. Till people find themselves greatly abused and oppressed by their governors, they are not apt to complain; and

they are so oppressed. Such a people, if I may allude to the ancient fable, like the hesperian fruit, have a dragon for their protector and guardian; nor would they have any reason to mourn, if some Hercules should appear to despatch him. For a nation thus abused to arise unanimously and to resist their prince, even to the dethroning of him, is not criminal, but a reasonable way of vindicating their liberties and just rights. It is making use of the only means which God has put into their power for mutual and self-defence, and it would be highly criminal in them not to make use of those means. It would be stupid tameness and unaccountable folly for whole nations to suffer *one* unreasonable, ambitious, and cruel man to wanton and riot in their misery; and, in such a case, it would be more rational to suppose that they who did not resist, than that they who did, would *receive to themselves damnation.*

KING CHARLES'S SAINTSHIP AND MARTYRDOM.

This naturally brings us to make some reflections upon the resistance which was made about a century since to that unhappy prince, Charles I., and upon the anniversary of his death. This is a point which I should not have concerned myself about were it not that some men continue to speak of it with a great deal of warmth and zeal; and in such a manner as to undermine all the principles of liberty, civil or religious; and to introduce the most abject slavery both in Church and State; so that it is become a matter of universal concern. What I have to offer upon this subject will be comprised in a short answer to the following queries:

For what reason the resistance to King Charles I. was made? By whom it was made? Whether that resistance was rebellion* or not? How the anniversary of King Charles's death came at first to be solemnized as a day of fasting and humiliation? And why those of the Episcopal clergy who are very high in the principles of ecclesiastical authority continue to speak of that unhappy man as a great saint and a martyr?

For what reason, then, was the resistance to King Charles made? The general answer to this inquiry is this, that it was on account of the tyranny and oppression of his reign. Not whenever they do find themselves thus abused and oppressed, they must be stupid not to complain. To say that subjects in general are not proper judges when their governors oppress them and play the tyrant, and when they defend their rights, administer justice impartially, and promote the public welfare, is as great treason as ever man uttered: it is treason, not against one single man, but the state—against the whole body politic; it is treason against mankind; it is treason against common sense; it is treason against God. This impious principle lays the foundation for justifying all the tyranny and oppression of which any prince ever was guilty. The people know for what end they set up and maintain their governors, and they are the proper judges when they execute their trust as they ought to do it; when their prince exercises an equitable and paternal authority over them; when from a prince and common father he exalts himself into a tyrant; when from subjects and children, he degrades them into the class of slaves; plunders them, makes them his prey, and unnaturally sports himself with their lives and fortunes.

..* I speak of rebellion, treason, saintship, martyrdom, &c., in the scriptural and theological sense.

VOL. II.—Y y

a great while after his accession to the throne, he married a French papist, and with her seemed to have wedded the politics, if not the religion of France. For afterward, during a reign, or, rather, a tyranny, of many years, he governed in a perfectly wild and arbitrary manner, paying no regard to the Constitution and the laws of the kingdom, by which the power of the crown was limited, or to the solemn oath which he had taken at his coronation. It would be endless, as well as needless, to give a particular account of all the illegal and despotic measures which he took in his administration; partly from his own natural lust of power, and partly from the influence of wicked counsellors and ministers. He committed many illustrious members of both houses of Parliament to the Tower for opposing his arbitrary schemes. He levied many taxes upon the people without consent of Parliament, and then imprisoned great numbers of the principal merchants and gentry for not paying them. He erected, or at least revived, several new and arbitrary courts, in which the most unheard-of barbarities were committed with his knowledge and approbation. *He supported that more than fiend, Archbishop Laud, and the clergy of his stamp, in all their church tyranny and hellish cruelties.* He authorized a book in favour of sports upon the Lord's Day, and several clergymen were persecuted by him and his inquisitor prelate, Laud, for not reading it to the people after Divine service. When the Parliament complained to him of the arbitrary proceedings of his corrupt ministers, he told that august body, in a rough, domineering manner, that he wondered any one should be so foolish and insolent as to think that he would part with the meanest of his servants upon their account. He refused to call any Parliament at all for the space of twelve years, during all which time he governed in an absolute, lawless, and despotic manner. He took all opportunities to encourage the papists, and to promote them to the highest offices of honour and trust. He abetted the horrid massacre in Ireland, in which two hundred thousand Protestants were butchered by the Roman Catholics. He sent a large sum of money, which he had raised by his arbitrary taxes, into Germany, to raise foreign troops, in order to force more arbitrary taxes upon his subjects. He not only by a long series of actions, but also in plain terms, asserted an absolute, uncontrollable power; saying in one of his speeches to Parliament, that, as it was blasphemy to dispute what God might do, so it was sedition in subjects to dispute what the king might do. Towards the end of his tyranny, he went to the House of Commons with an armed force,* and demanded five of its principal members to be delivered up to him. All this was a prelude to that unnatural war which he soon after levied against his own dutiful subjects, whom he was bound by all the laws of honour, humanity, piety, and of interest also, to defend and cherish with a paternal affection. I have only time to hint all these facts, and many more of the same tenour

* Historians are not agreed what number of soldiers attended him in this monstrous invasion of the privileges of Parliament. Some say 300, some 400. The author of "The History of the Kings of Scotland" says 500.

may be proved by good authorities. So that the figurative language which John uses, concerning the just and beneficent deeds of our blessed Saviour, may be applied to the unrighteous and execrable deeds of this prince, " *There are also many other things which King Charles did, the which, if they should be written every one, I suppose that even the world itself could not contain the books that should be written.*" Now it was on account of King Charles's thus assuming a power above the laws, in direct contradiction to his coronation oath, and governing the greatest part of his time in the most arbitrary, oppressive manner, that the resistance was made to him which at length issued in the loss of his crown, and of that head which was unworthy to wear it.

But by whom was that resistance made? Not by a private junto, not by a small seditious party, not by a few desperadoes, who, to mend their fortunes, would embroil the state; but by the Lords and Commons of England. They almost unanimously opposed the king's measures for overturning the Constitution, and changing that free government into a wretched, absolute monarchy. It was they, when the king was about levying forces against his subjects, in order to make himself absolute, who commissioned officers and raised an army to defend themselves and the public; and it was they that maintained the war against him till he was made a prisoner. This is indisputable. Though, properly speaking, it was not the Parliament, but the army, who put him to death afterward. And it ought to be freely acknowledged, that most of their proceedings, in order to get the matter effected, and particularly the court by which the king was at last tried and condemned, was little better than a mere mockery of justice.

The next question which naturally arises is this : Was the resistance which was made to the king by the Parliament properly rebellion, or not? The answer to which is plain, it was not. It was a most righteous and glorious stand, made in defence of the natural and legal rights of the people, against the natural and illegal encroachments of arbitrary power. Nor was it a rash and sudden opposition. The nation had been patient under the oppressions of the crown, even to long suffering, for a course of many years, until there was no rational hope of redress in any other way. Resistance was absolutely necessary in order to preserve the nation from slavery, misery, and ruin. And who were so proper to make this resistance as the houses of Lords and Commons ; the whole representative body of the people ; guardians of the public welfare ; and each of which, in point of legislation, was vested with an equal, co-ordinate power, with that of the crown !* Here

were two branches of the Legislature against one; two of which had law, equity, and the Constitution on their side, against one which was impiously attempting to overturn law, and equity, and the Constitution ; and to exercise a wanton, licentious sovereignty over the properties, consciences, and lives of all the people ; such a sovereignty as some inconsiderately ascribe to the Supreme Governor of the world. I say *inconsiderately*, because God himself does not govern in an absolutely arbitrary and despotic manner. The power of the Almighty King—I speak it with caution and reverence—the power of this Almighty King is limited by the eternal laws of truth, wisdom, and equity ; and the everlasting tables of right reason, tables that cannot be repealed, or thrown down and broken like those of Moses. But King Charles sat himself up above all these, as much as he did above the written laws of the realm ; and made mere humour and caprice, which are no rule at all, the only rule and measure of his administration. Is it not perfectly ridiculous to call resistance to such a tyrant by the name of rebellion ? the grand rebellion ? Even that Parliament which brought Charles II. to the throne, and which run loyally mad, severely reproved one of their own members for condemning the proceedings of that Parliament which first took up arms against the former king. Upon the same principles that the proceedings of that Parliament may be censured as wicked and rebellious, the proceedings of those who since opposed James II., and brought the Prince of Orange to the throne, may also be censured as wicked and rebellious. The cases are parallel.

by the voluntary consent of the people. And agreeably thereto the prerogative and rights of the crown are stated, defined, and limited by law, as truly and strictly as the rights of any inferior officer in the state, or of any private subject, and it is only in this respect that it can be said that "the king can do wrong." Being restrained by the law, while he confines himself within those just limits which the law prescribes to him as the measure of his authority, he cannot injure and oppress the subject. The king, in his coronation oath, swears to exercise only such a power as the Constitution gives him ; and the subject, in the oath of allegiance, swears only to obey him in the exercise of such a power. The king is as much bound by his oath not to infringe the legal rights of the people, as the people are bound to yield subjection to him. Whence it follows, that as soon as the prince sets himself up above law, he loses the king in the tyrant : he does to all intents and purposes unking himself, by acting out of, and beyond that sphere which the Constitution allows him to move in. In such cases, he has no more right to be obeyed than any inferior officer who acts beyond his commission. The subjects' obligation to allegiance then ceases of course ; and to resist him is no more rebellion than to resist any foreign invader. There is an essential difference between government and tyranny ; at least under such a constitution as the English. The former consists in ruling according to law and equity, the latter in ruling contrary to law and equity. So there is an essential difference between resisting a tyrant and rebellion ; the former is a just and reasonable self-defence ; the latter consists in resisting a prince whose administration is just and legal ; and this is what demonstrates it a crime. Now it is evident that King Charles's government was illegal, and very oppressive through the greatest part of his reign. Therefore, to resist him was no more rebellion than to oppose any foreign invader, or any other domestic oppressor.

---

* The English Constitution is originally and essentially free. The character which Julius Cæsar and Tacitus both give of the ancient Britons is this ! That they were extremely jealous of their liberties, as well as a people of a martial spirit. Nor have there been wanting frequent instances and proofs of the same glorious spirit, in both respects, remaining in their posterity ever since ; in the struggles they have made for liberty, both against foreign and domestic tyrants. Their kings hold their title to the throne solely by grant of Parliament, in other words,

If it be said that, although the Parliament which first opposed King Charles's measures, and at length took up arms against him, were not guilty of rebellion, yet certainly those persons were who condemned and put him to death; even this is not true, for he had unkinged himself long before, and had forfeited his title to the allegiance of the people. So that those who put him to death at most were only guilty of murder, which, indeed, is bad enough, if they were really guilty of that, *which is disputable.* Cromwell, and those who were principally concerned in the nominal king's death, might possibly have been wicked and designing men. Nor shall I say anything in vindication of the reigning hypocrisy of those times, or of Cromwell's administration during the interregnum, for it is truth, and not a party that I am defending. But still it may be said that Cromwell and his adherents were not guilty of rebellion, because he whom they beheaded was not, properly speaking, their king, but a lawless tyrant. Much less are the whole body of the nation at that time to be charged with rebellion on that account, for it was not the national act; it was not done by a free Parliament. Much less still is the nation at present to be charged with the great sin of rebellion for what their ancestors did, or rather did not, a century ago.

But how came the anniversary of King Charles's death to be solemnized as a day of fasting and humiliation? The true answer to which inquiry is this: this fast was instituted by way of compliment to Charles II. upon the Restoration. All were desirous of making their court to him—of ingratiating themselves, and of making him forget what had been done in opposition to his father, so as not to revenge it. To effect this, they ran into the most extravagant professions of affection and loyalty to him, insomuch that he himself said, " *It is a mad and hair-brained loyalty which they profess.*" Among other strange things which his first Parliament did, they ordered the thirtieth day of January, the day on which his father was beheaded, to be kept as a day of solemn humiliation-to deprecate the judgments of Heaven for the rebellion which the nation had been guilty of, which was not a national thing, and which was not rebellion in them that did it. Thus they soothed and flattered their new king at the expense of their liberties, and were ready to yield up freely to Charles II. all that enormous power which they had justly resisted Charles I. for usurping to himself.

The last query mentioned was this, Why those of the Episcopal clergy who are very high in the principles of ecclesiastical authority continue to speak of that unhappy prince as a great saint and a martyr? This they constantly do, especially upon the *thirtieth* of *January,* a day appropriated to the extolling of him, and to the reproaching of those who are not of the Established Church. " *Out of the same mouth* on this day *proceedeth blessing and cursing, therewith bless they their God, even* Charles, *and therewith curse they*" the Dissenters; and their "*tongue can no man tame; it is an unruly evil, full of deadly poison.*" King Charles, upon this solemnity, is frequently compared to our Lord Jesus Christ, both in respect of the holiness of his life, and the greatness and injustice of his

sufferings; and it is a wonder that they do not add something concerning the merits of his death also. But *blessed saint* and *royal martyr* are as humble titles as any that are thought worthy of him.

Now this may well appear to be a very strange phenomenon; for King Charles was really a man black with guilt and " *laden with iniquity,*" as appears by his crimes before mentioned. He lived a tyrant, and it was the oppression and violence of his reign that brought him to his untimely and violent end at last. Now, what of saintship or martyrdom is there in all this? What of saintship is there in encouraging people to profane the Lord's Day? What of saintship in falsehood and perjury? What of saintship in repeated robberies and depredations? What of saintship in throwing real saints and glorious patriots into jails? What of saintship in overturning an excellent civil constitution, and proudly grasping at illegal and monstrous power? What of saintship in the murder of thousands of innocent people, and involving a nation in all the calamities of a civil war? What of martyrdom is there in a man's bringing an immature and violent death upon himself, by " *being wicked overmuch?*" Is there any such thing as *grace without goodness?* As being a follower of Christ, without following him? As being his disciple, without learning of him to be just and beneficent? Or, as *saintship without sanctity?** If not, it will be hard to prove this man a saint! Verily, one would be apt to suspect that that church must be but poorly stocked with saints and martyrs which is forced to adopt such enormous sinners into her calendar in order to swell the number.

But, to unravel this mystery of nonsense as well as of iniquity, which has already worked for a long time among us, or, at least, to give the most probable solution of it, it should be remembered that King Charles, this burlesque upon saintship and martyrdom, though so great an oppressor, was a true friend to "the *Church;*" so true a friend to her, that he was very well affected towards the Roman Catholics, and would not, probably, have been very unwilling to unite Lambeth and Rome: this appears by his marrying a true daughter of the true "*mother of harlots,*" which he did with a dispensation from the pope, that supreme Lord, to whom, when he wrote, he gave the title of Most Holy Father. His queen was extremely bigoted to all the follies and superstitions, and to the hierarchy of Rome, and had a prodigious ascendency over him all his life. It was partly owing to this that he abetted the massacre of the Protestants in Ireland; that he assisted in extirpating the French Protestants at Rochelle;

---

* Is it any wonder that even persons who do not walk after their own lusts should scoff at such saints as this, both in the first and in the last days? But perhaps it will be said that these things are mysteries, which, although very true in themselves, *lay understandings* cannot comprehend; or, indeed, any other persons among us besides those who, being inwardly moved by the Holy Ghost, have taken a trip across the Atlantic to obtain Episcopal ordination and the indelible character. However, if these consecrated gentlemen do not quite despair of us, it is hoped that, in the abundance of their charity, they will endeavour to elucidate these dark points.

that he all along encouraged papists, and popishly affected clergymen, in preference to all other persons; and that he upheld that monster of wickedness, Archbishop Laud, and the prelates of his stamp, in all their church tyranny and diabolical cruelties. In return for his kindness and indulgence in those respects, they caused many of the pulpits throughout the nation to ring with the divinely, absolute, and indefeasible right of kings; with the praises of Charles and his reign, and with the damnable sin of resisting the Lord's Anointed, let him do what he would. So that not Christ, but Charles, was commonly preached to the people. *There seems to have been an impious bargain struck up between the sceptre and the surplice for enslaving both the bodies and souls of men. The king appeared to be willing that the clergy should do what they would—set up a monstrous hierarchy like that of Rome—a monstrous inquisition like that of Spain or Portugal, or anything else to which their own pride and the devil's malice could prompt them, provided always that the clergy would be tools to the crown; that they would make the people believe that kings had God's authority for breaking God's law; that they had a commission from Heaven to seize the estates of their subjects at pleasure; and that it was a damnable sin to resist them, even when they did such things as deserved more than damnation.* This is the true key for explaining the mysterious doctrine of King Charles's saintship and martyrdom. He was a saint, not because he was in his life a good man, but a good churchman; not because he was a lover of holiness, but the hierarchy; not because he was a friend to Christ, but the craft. He was a martyr in his death, not because he bravely suffered death in the cause of truth and righteousness, but because he died an enemy to liberty and the rights of conscience; and not because he died an enemy to sin, but Dissenters. For these reasons, all bigoted clergymen and friends to church power paint this man as a saint in life, though he was such a mighty, such a royal sinner; and as a martyr in his death, though he fell a sacrifice only to his own ambition, avarice, and unbounded lust of power. From prostituting their praise upon King Charles, and offering him that incense which is not his due, it is natural for them to make a transition to the Dissenters, as they commonly do, and to load them with that reproach which they do not deserve, they being generally professed enemies both to civil and ecclesiastical tyranny. We are commonly charged, upon the thirtieth of January, with the guilt of putting the king to death, under a notion that it was our ancestors that did it; and so we are represented in the blackest colours, not only as schismatics, but also as traitors and rebels! Those lofty gentlemen usually rail upon this head in such a manner as plainly shows that they are either grossly ignorant of the history of those times of which they speak, or, what is worse, that they are guilty of the most

shameful prevarication, slander, and falsehood! But every petty priest, with a roll and a gown, thinks he must do something in imitation of his betters in law, and show himself a true son of the Church; and thus, through a foolish ambition to appear considerable, they only render themselves contemptible.

But suppose our forefathers did kill their mock saint and martyr a century ago, what is that to us now! If I mistake not, those gentlemen generally preach down the doctrine of the imputation of Adam's sin to his posterity as absurd and unreasonable, notwithstanding they have solemnly subscribed it in their own articles of religion. Therefore, one would hardly expect that they would lay the guilt of the king's death upon us, although our forefathers had been the only authors of it. But this conduct is much more surprising, when it does not appear that our ancestors had any more hand in it than their own. However, bigotry is sufficient to account for this and many other phenomena which cannot be accounted for in any other way.

Although the observation of this anniversary seems to have been superstitious in its original, and although it is often abused to very bad purposes by the established clergy, as they serve themselves of it to perpetuate strife, a party spirit, and divisions in the Christian Church; yet it is to be hoped that one good end will be answered by it quite contrary to their intention; it is to be hoped that it will prove a standing memento that Britons will not be slaves, and a warning to all corrupt counsellors and ministers not to go too far in advising arbitrary, despotic measures.

To conclude: let us all learn to be free and to be loyal. Let us not profess ourselves vassals to the lawless pleasure of any man on earth, but let us remember, at the same time, government is sacred, and not to be trifled with. It is our happiness to live under the government of Prince George II., who is satisfied with ruling, according to law, as every other good prince will. It becomes us, therefore, to be contented and dutiful subjects. Let us prize our freedom, but not " *use our liberty for a cloak of maliciousness.*" There are men who strike at liberty under the term licentiousness; there are others who aim at popularity under the disguise of patriotism. There is at present among us more danger of the latter than of the former, for which reason I exhort you to pay all due regard to the government over us, and to " *lead a quiet and peaceful life.*" And while I am speaking of loyalty to our earthly prince, be loyal also to the Supreme Ruler of the universe, " *by whom kings reign, and princes decree justice.*" To which king eternal, immortal, invisible, the only wise God, be all honour and praise, dominion, and thanksgiving, through Jesus Christ our Lord. Amen.

INDEX.

The letters *n*. and *ns*. stand for note and notes.

Burroughs, Mr. J., i., xxii., n.
Burroughs, Mr. Jerem., retires to Holland, i. 341. His
declaration in the name of the Independents, ii., 17. His
death and character, 40.
Burrough, Edward, his death, ii., 418.
Burton, Mr., his sufferings, i., 317, 327.
Bury, Mr. Edward, his sufferings, ii., 299.
Bushnell, Mr., ejected, ii., 148. His narrative, and the
commissioners answer, 148.
Butler, Major, his report of Cromwell's last prayer, ii.,
181.
Button, Mr., some account of him, ii., 72.
Byfield, Mr., burned, i., 35.
Byfield, Rev., his death and character, i., 273.

C.

Cabal, their character, ii., 269. Their projects to make
the King absolute, 271. Are attacked by Parliament, 280.
Calvus lost from the English, i., 70.
Calamy, Mr., a passage in his sermon about Christmas,
i., 500. Sent to Newgate, ii., 250. His death and charac-
ter, 258, n.
See "Calendar" and "Catherine" under K.
Calvin's judgment of the English liturgy, i., 67. Of the
English ceremonies, 68.
Calvinism discountenanced at court, i., 272.
Cambridge address, ii., 298. Privileges invaded, 325.
Cameronians in Scotland, ii., 310.
Campion-the Jesuit, &c., executed, i., 151.
Canne, Mr. and editions of his Bible, i., 244, 361, and n.
Canons, act for revising them; never done, i. 34. Another act for it; which also comes to nothing, 50. New
ones, 173. Abstract of those of 1603, 238. Conclusion
and ratification of them, 240. Bishops obliged to relax
their rigour for a time, 241. Book of canons for Scotland,
322. Canons of 1640, 345. Unacceptable to the clergy,
347. Execution of them suspended, 347. Speeches in Parliament against them; and Resolutions of Parliament
thereupon, 352. Objections of the Commons against them,
354. They are justified by Laud, 355.
Canterbury cathedral, its decorations, i., 304. Furniture
of its altar consecrated, 315.
Capel, Mr. Richard, his death and character, ii., 168.
Careless, Mr., an eminent martyr, his disputes in prison,
and confession of faith, i., 65.
Carew, Mr., his sufferings, i., 167.
Caroline, Princess of Wales, her interview with Mr.
Neal, i., xix.
Carter, Rev. J., his death and character, i., 320.
Cartwright, Mr., his sentiments of the ecclesiastical supremacy, i., 74. He opposes the hierarchy of the church;
his positions, 114. He writes to the secretary, 115. He is
expelled the University, and retires beyond sea, 115. Being returned, he draws up the Puritans' second admonition to the Parliament, 121. His famous dispute with
Whitgift, and his standard of discipline and church government, 123. His hard usage, 125. His second reply to
Whitgift, 125. A proclamation against him, 129. He as-
sists in framing a discipline for Guernsey and Jersey, 136.
Is chosen preacher to the English factory at Antwerp,
144. Returns to England, and settles at Warwick, 176.
Forbid by the Archbishop to answer the Rhemist Testament, 178. Examination of him and his brethren before
the high-commissioners; and articles exhibited against
him, which he refuses to answer on oath, 194. He is released, and restored to his hospital at Warwick, but his
brethren continue in suspension, 195. He defends himself
and his brethren from being concerned with Hacket, 196.
His death and character, 234. His confutation of the Rhe-
mish Testament, and other works, 234.
Caryl, Joseph, his death and exposition on Job, ii., 275, n.
Carstairs, Mr., tortured, ii., 303.
Case, Thomas, his death, ii., 301, and n.
Cases of Conscience, by Perkins, mentioned, ii., 305, n.
Castlemain, Earl of, his censure of the Church's perse-
cuting the dissenters, ii., 309.
Catechisms, Assembly's larger and shorter, approved
and allowed by the Parliament, ii., 42.
Cathedral worship disliked by the Puritans, i., 107.
Request against them, 181. Decorations of them, 303.
Hacket's defence of them, 381. Burgess's speech against
them, 381. Memorandum for reforming them, 384. Their
state at the beginning of the civil war, 382. Ordinance
for seizing their revenues, ii., 20. Vacancies filled, ii., 207.
Cavaliers, refer to Royalists.
Cawdrey, Mr., his sufferings, i., 185. His farther sufferings, and appeal to the court of exchequer, 195.
Cawton, Thomas, Charles's letter to him, ii., 195. His
death, 199, and n.
Censures of the Church, Puritans' opinion concerning
them, i., 249.
Ceremonies of the Church, debates in convocation about
them, i., 88. A considerable number of the clergy that
were for amending them, 88. Several of them scrupled

by the Puritans, 93. Objected against by the Puritans,
232, 240. Defended by Bishop Moreton, &c., 247. See
Rites.
Chadderton, Rev. Dr., his death and character, i., 349.
Chambers, Dr. Humphrey, his death, ii., 246.
Chancellors, patents, and censures, canons about them,
i., 347.
Chandler, Dr., i., xxiii., n.
Charles I. when Prince of Wales, his oath to observe
the articles of the Spanish match. i., 273. His journey to
Madrid and letter to the pope, 274. His accession and
character, 278. His marriage, and character of his queen,
279. Character of his ministers, 279. His speech to his
first Parliament, 281. His answer to the Commons' petition, 281. He favours the Papists, 282. Contributes to
the loss of Rochelle, 282. Dissolves the Parliament, 283.
Raises money by arbitrary methods, 283-286. His coronation, 283. His second Parliament, 284. Dissolved, 284.
His proclamation for putting an end to the disputes of the
Calvinists and Arminians, 285. Enters into a war with
France, 287. His third Parliament, and speech to them,
287. Passes the petition of right, 287. Prorogues the Parliament, and answers their remonstrance, 288. His declaration before the thirty-nine articles, 291. His arbitrary
proceedings, 293, 297. Speech at dissolving his third Parliament, 295. Reasons for dissolving them, 295. His
proclamations against prescribing a time for calling parliaments, 295. His instructions about lectures, 298. His
progress into Scotland, 309. His usage of the Scots Parliament, 309. Revives the Book of Sports, 312. Forbids
the Puritans to transport themselves, 330. His reasons for
compiling the Scots liturgy, 334. He threatens the Scots,
337. Resolves on a war with the Scots, 339. Marches
against them, but agrees to a pacification, 341. His instructions to his high-commissioner, 342. Refuses to confirm the Scots acts of Parliament, 342. Calls an English
Parliament, but dissolves them in anger, 343, 344. Continues to raise money by the prerogative, 345. Marches a
second time against the Scots, but is unsuccessful, 348.
Opens the Long-parliament, 351. His speech in favour
of the hierarchy, 369. Favours the papists, 373. His answer to the remonstrance of the Commons against them,
373, 374. His design of bringing the army to London, 375.
His ministers terrified, 376. Passes the act for continuing
the Parliament, 377. His conduct at passing the bills for
the abolition of the high-commission and star-chamber,
387. Resolves on a progress to Scotland, 390. His concessions there, 390. He repents of them, 390. His imprudent conduct, 398. His letter in favour of the hierarchy,
399. Fills up the vacant bishoprics, 399. The grand remonstrance of the Commons presented to him, 399. His
answer to their petition, and to-the remonstrance, 401.
Goes to the house to seize five of the members, 406.
Leaves Whitehall, 407. Passes the act to take away the
votes of the bishops, 408. Resolutions of his cabinet council at Windsor, 409. Refuses the Scots mediation, 412.
His high language to his Parliament, 413. Denied entrance into Hull, and his proceedings in the north, 413.
Orders the courts of justice to follow him, 413. His answer to the Parliament's memorial, 414. And to their
proposals, 415. His preparation for war, 416. His proposals for borrowing money, 417. Applies to the papists,
419. His letter to the council of Scotland, 421. Sets up
the standard at Nottingham, 423. Of his clergy, 427. Of
his army, 428. His proclamation for the better government of it, 428. His evil counsellors, 429. Pursues his
march to London after the battle of Edge-hill, 441. Takes
Reading and Brentford, 441. Retreats again, 441. Motives of his march, 442. His letter to the Duke of Hamilton, 442. Encouraging prospect of his affairs, 443. His
truce with the Irish rebels, 443. Parliament's propositions
to him at the treaty of Oxford, 444. His own proposals,
445. His answer to the Parliament commissioners, 446.
Which breaks off the treaty, 446. His proclamations
against the city of London, 448. Success of his affairs,
448. Makes reprisals on the Parliamentarians in relation
to the clergy, 453. Dissolves their monthly fast, and appoints another, 455. Prohibits the assembly of divines,
459. Forbids the taking of the covenant, 469. Brings
over forces from Ireland, 469. Ill consequences of it to
his affairs, 470. His protestation, 470. His reply to the
assembly's letter to foreign Protestants, 472. Remarks
upon it, 473. He holds a Parliament at Oxford, which
comes to nothing, 477. His letter to the queen, 477. Character of his army, 479. Bad state of his affairs, 479. He
forbids the use of the directory, 497. Some arbitrary
clauses in his speeches and proclamations, 503. His conduct in the treaty of Uxbridge, 527. More letters of his to
the queen, 527, 532; ii., 22. His instructions to the commissioners on the head of religion, 529. His concessions,
531. His letter to the Duke of Ormond, 532. Queen's as-
cendant over him, 533. His warrant to the Earl of Glamorgan about the Irish papists, 533. Progress of his forces, and his defeat in the battle of Naseby, ii., 6. He fo-

THE END.

CONTENTS

OF

THE SECOND VOLUME.

E R R A T A.

THE editor regrets that his absence from the city when the first number of this work was passing through the press occasioned the omission of a few lines in the original notes of Toulmin. They are restored by this errata ; and the editor takes this opportunity to state, that the mistake is wholly his own, and not to be ascribed to the publishers.

P. 53.—" Mr. Neal, in his review of the transactions of this year, has also omitted to inform his readers that the doctrines established by the Reformers by no means met with an implicit reception from all. The doctrine of the Trinity was denied by many, and Unitarian sentiments were so plainly avowed, and spread so fast, that the leading churchmen were alarmed at it, and feared their general prevailing. Mr. Strype's words are, ‘Arianism now showed itself so openly, and was in such danger of spreading farther, that it was thought necessary to suppress it, by using more rugged methods than seemed agreeable to the merciful principles of the profession of the Gospel.’ "—Lindsey's Historical View of the State of the Unitarian Doctrine and Worship, p. 84.—ED.

P. 63.—" The title of this piece plainly indicates that no calm investigation of truth, or candid retracting of intemperate language and spirit, is to be expected in it. Mr. Lindsey has given it at length in his ‘ History of Unitarian Worship,’ with pertinent, judicious, and valuable remarks, to which with pleasure we refer the reader, p. 84 to 194."—ED.

P. 65.—" Mr. Neal's language and sentiments are

not here the most correct. Disputes, arising from differences of opinion on points of speculation, may be proofs of the frailty of our nature ; as they show that all cannot attain to precise ideas, a clear discernment, and comprehensive views on subjects that are attended with many difficulties. But how do they indicate the corruption of human nature? That betrays their intemperate spirit and language with which they are managed, and should be imputed, not to human nature, but to the want of self-government in those individuals who thus offend. It is not proper indiscriminately to condemn disputes, because such censures operate as discouragements and bars to the investigation of the truth."—ED.

P. 138.—" It should be added, that one ground of the odium which fell on those who were called Anabaptists, was their deviation from the established creed, in their ideas concerning the person of Christ and the doctrine of the Trinity, which shows at how early a period of the Reformation Unitarian sentiments arose among the more thoughtful and inquisitive, but the hand of power was lifted up to suppress their growth and spread."—ED.

Lightning Source UK Ltd.
Milton Keynes UK
UKHW020617110119
335177UK00005B/230/P